A NEW LAND LAW
SECOND EDITION 2003

Peter Sparkes' path-breaking text on land law has been rewritten almost sentence by sentence partly to incorporate the seismic changes introduced by the Land Registration Act 2002, along with commonholds, the explosion of human rights jurisprudence, and the unremitting advance of judicial exposition. Partly also, to accommodate the author's developing thinking on the structural aspects of the subject, jolted by the new clearer structure for land registration with its much greater clarity of function behind the means of protecting third party interests.

The book opens with a series of shorter chapters each exploring a fundamental building block—registration, houses, flats and commonholds, land, ownership and its transactional powers, social controls balanced by human rights to property, fragmentation by time (the doctrine of estates), divisions of ownership and proprietary rights. In terms of substantive chapters the book opens with discussion of the new transfer system—paper-based transfer alongside the evolution towards electronic conveyancing—and the consequent changes to the proof of registered titles and to the registration curtain. The new approach to adverse possession against registered titles has called for extended discussion, as has the authoritative elucidation of the concept of adverse possession in *Pye*, enlightenment provided, as is so typical of our judicial system, just as the concept itself has become practically redundant. In terms of proprietary interests the fundamentals are seen as rights to transfer, beneficial interests under trusts which are overreachable, burdens which are endurable, leases, money charges such as mortgages which are redeemable, and the obligations enforceable within the neighbour principle—easements covenants and positive covenants being treated as a semi-coherent whole. An attempt has been made to assist students by moving some of the more arcane learning later into the book or into separate chapters where these matters might be more readily ignored by a candidate concerned primarily to prepare for an examination.

The premise of the first edition was that changes to the land registration scheme made in 1997 and the steady march towards a universal register meant that it was opportune to abandon the unregistered/registered dichotomy in favour of a division between registered and registrable land, and that this in turn required an integrated treatment highlighting how the registered system was intended to dovetail with the unregistered. So this edition continues to see one set of principles with two mechanistic implementations, an approach which has on balance, adverse possession apart, been vindicated by the Land Registration Act 2002.

FROM THE REVIEWS OF THE FIRST EDITION

A NEW LAND LAW

SECOND EDITION

PETER SPARKES, LLB,
Professor of Law,
The University of Southampton

·HART·
PUBLISHING

OXFORD AND PORTLAND, OREGON
2003

Published in North America (US and Canada) by
Hart Publishing
c/o International Specialized Book Services
5804 NE Hassalo Street
Portland, Oregon
97213-3644
USA

Hart Publishing is a specialist legal publisher based in Oxford, England.
To order further copies of this book or to request a list of other publications
please write to:

Hart Publishing, Salter's Boatyard, Folly Bridge,
Abingdon Road, Oxford OX1 4LB
Telephone: +44 (0)1865 245533 or Fax: +44 (0)1865 794882
e-mail: mail@hartpub.co.uk
WEBSITE: http//:www.hartpub.co.uk

British Library Cataloguing in Publication Data
Data Available
ISBN 1–84113–380–9 (paperback)

Typeset by Hope Services (Abingdon) Ltd.
Printed and bound in Great Britain on acid-free paper by
Biddles Ltd, _www.biddles.co.uk_

CONTENTS

CHAPTER 24: TRANSFER RIGHTS

PREFACE TO THE SECOND EDITION

What Paul Sinclair liked when he first encountered the Provençal utopia of Eden Olympia was that

> "There's no ground already staked out, no title deeds going back to bloody Magna Carta. You feel anything could happen."[1]

I hope to have captured some of that spirit in the *New Land Law*. Most students today know little of *1066 and All That*[2] and view even 1925 as a form of prehistory. So my aim is to rid land law of its feudal roots and its history and to modernise the badly dated statutory language—eschewing Latin,[3] terms lacking gender neutrality, and most of the baffling "ees" and "ors" of conventional land law. In Cornwall "a man who has lost his language has also lost his land", but not I hope, his land law.

This new edition comes after only four years but it is not a case of "the paper never refusing the ink". A sentence by sentence rewriting has been required to accommodate the seismic changes of the Land Registration Act 2002,[4] not to mention common-holds, the explosion of human rights jurisprudence and the remorseless grind of the case law up to the end of 2002. I have taken the opportunity thus presented to reflect the development of my thinking on the structural aspects of the subject, jolted by the new functional structure for protecting third party interests against registered land. Hence the completely new shape to this edition.

A series of shorter opening chapters each explores one fundamental building block —registration, land, fragmentation by time (the doctrine of estates), ownership and its transactional powers, titles to houses flats and commonholds, social controls balanced by the human rights to property, and finally proprietary rights.

The premise of the first edition was that the changes to the land registration scheme made in 1997 meant it was opportune to abandon the unregistered-registered dichotomy in favour of a division between registered and registrable land, and that this in turn required an integrated treatment highlighting how the substantive principles of the two systems dovetail.[5] We are now four years closer to a universal register. The linkage of the substantive principles of the two systems has been greatly strengthened as from the October 2003 implementation date of the Land Registration Act 2002 even as the mechanics are diverging ever more widely. Electronic conveyancing has important consequences for the proof of title and the registration curtain.

---

[1] JG Ballard, *Super Cannes* (Flamingo, 2001), 79.
[2] WC Sellar & RJ Yeatman (Methuen).
[3] *Fryer* v. *Pearson* [2000] Times April 4th.
[4] The implementation date is October 13th 2003.
[5] *City of London BS* v. *Flegg* [1988] AC 54, 84G, Lord Oliver.

Adverse possession against registered titles will be reduced to a shell giving the register a much greater degree of finality. I only hope that my doubts prove to be misplaced. Extended treatment has also been required of the authoritative elucidation of the concept of adverse possession in *Pye*,[6] enlightenment provided by the courts so typically just as the concept itself has become practically redundant. The chapters on adverse possession and the registration curtain appeared at the end of the first edition for no better reason than I came to write them last and they now move forward to a proper and prominent position. The mystery of the new system of alteration of the register is how it links to the old case law on rectification, a topic on which I have provided some educated guesses.

The new machinery enacted for trusts of land in 1996 implied the need for wider changes than most teachers of land law were prepared to countenance when this book first appeared in 1999, but the task of consolidation of all aspects of trusts is now completed, with beneficial co-ownership now fully integrated into the main treatment. Ownership rights remain separated from occupation rights. A warm welcome is given to the closer alignment of notice through occupation and the new form of the occupation-based overriding interest.[7] An attempt has been made to assist students by moving some of the more arcane learning into a separate chapter on management trusts where examination candidates may be able to ignore this material more readily.

The Land Registration Act 2002 has greatly improved the law of burdens. Priority is simpler—and fits better into my four headings—protected interests, value, diligence and honesty. Burdens are classified in a new way to draw out the parallels between the two systems, the fundamentals being rights to transfer, beneficial interests under trusts that are not overreached, leases, money charges such as mortgages which are redeemable, and the obligations enforceable within the neighbour principle—easements covenants and positive covenants being treated as one semi-coherent whole. This mess should be slightly less confusing in this form.

The chapters on leases have been rewritten to link better to the structure of *A New Landlord and Tenant*,[8] where security of tenure and enfranchisement schemes are considered in detail. Mortgages are integrated with other money charges but kept separate from the domestic borrower protection—carved out of the existing administrative controls, statutory protection against repossession, and the case-law developments in the field of undue influence. *Etridge* seems a mere footnote in a sea of change.[9] Emphasis is placed on the crucial importance of physical division of land, and the integrated treatment of the obligations enforceable between neighbours is continued even if the law has to be forced into shape. Surely there is an urgent case for reform here? Sadly there is no longer space for any serious consideration of planning law or compulsory purchase.

Readers can be left to judge the opinion of one Regius professor that land law is complex but not in the end very difficult.[10] My own view is that the subject is running out of control—changing too fast to too little purpose—but that may simply be the

---

[6] *JA Pye (Oxford)* v. *Lambert* [2002] UKHL 30, [2002] 3 All ER 865.
[7] LRA 2002 sch 3 para 2.
[8] Hart, 2001.
[9] *Royal Bank of Scotland* v. *Etridge (No 2)* [2001] UKHL 44, [2002] 2 AC 773.
[10] PBH Birks "Before We Begin: Five Keys to Land Law" ch 18 in Bright & Dewar, 457.

advance of middle age. One could scarcely imagine a monarch of the twenty-first century devoting time to the exposition of land law to his nobles, as Edward IV is said to have done, but still teaching and writing in the subject remains a noble occupation. This book continues to be dedicated to Helen. Whilst engaged in my calling over the past four years my debt to her has increased very considerably.

New Forest
February 2003

ABBREVIATIONS

[ ]	Paragraph number
AEA	Administration of Estates Act
Applic	Application
BS	Building Society
C	Contract
CCR	County Court Rules
CD	Consulation Document
Chold and L Ref A	Commonhold and Leasehold Reform Act
CLR	Chief Land Registrar
COA	Charging Orders Act
Corp	Corporation
CP	Consultation Paper
CPR	Civil Procedure Rules
Div Ct	Divisional Court
DLRR	Draft Land Registration Rules
E	Estate(s)
EN	Explanatory Note
EuCtJ	European Court of Justice
FLA	Family Law Act
HA	Housing Act
HRA	Human Rights Act
H Ass	Housing Association
IA	Insolvency Act
Law Com CP	Law Commission Consultation Paper
Law Com	Law Commission (Report)
LCA	Land Charges Act
LP (MP) A	Law of Property (Miscellaneous Provisions) Act
LPA	Law of Property Act
LR	Land Registry
LRA	Land Registration Act
L Ref A	Leasehold Reform Act
LRR	Land Registration Rules
LTA	Landlord and Tenant Act
L Tr	Land Tribunal
MBS	Mutual Building Society
MCA	Matrimonial Causes Act
MHA	Matrimonial Homes Act
O	Order

PAA	Powers of Attorney Act
PBS	Permanent Building Society
PCA	Planning and Compensation Act
prs	Personal representatives
Reg	Regulations
RSC	Rules of the Supreme Court
S	Settlement(s)
SCS	Standard Conditions of Sale (3rd ed)
SLA	Settled Land Act
SS	Secretary of State
T	Trust(s)
TA	Trustee Act
TCPA	Town and Country Planning Act
TLATA	Trusts of Land and Appointment of Trustees Act
WP	Law Commission Working Paper

BOOKS FREQUENTLY REFERRED TO

Places of publication are in England unless otherwise stated

Birks' *English Private Law*	PBH Birks *English Private Law* (Oxford UP, 2002)
Blackstone's *Commentaries*	Sir W Blackstone *Commentaries on the Laws of England* (Oxford, 1st ed, 1766); page references are to RM Kerr (Murray, 3rd ed, 1862)
Bright & Dewar	S Bright & J Dewar *Land Law – Themes and Perspectives* (Oxford, 1998)
Cheshire & Burn	GC Cheshire and EB Burn *The Modern Law of Real Property* (Butterworths, 16th ed, 2000)
Chappelle *Land Law*	D Chappelle *Land Law* (Longman, 5th ed, 2001)
Coke on *Littleton*	Sir E Coke *Commentaries on Littleton's Tenures* (1st ed, 1628); paras are common to all editions
Dixon's *Principles*	Martin Dixon *Principles of Land Law* (Cavendish, 3rd ed, 2000)
Encyclopædia FP	Lord Millett *Encyclopædia of Forms and Precedents* (Butterworths, 5th ed, 1993 and reissues)
Goo's *Sourcebook*	SH Goo *Sourcebook on Land Law* (Cavendish, 3rd ed, 2002)
Gravells, *LL – Text and Materials*	NP Gravells *Land Law – Text and Materials* (Sweet & Maxwell, 2nd ed, 1999)
Grays' *Elements* (3rd ed)	K Gray & SF Gray *Elements of Land Law* (Butterworths, 3rd ed, 2000)
Hayton's *Registered Land*	DJ Hayton *Registered Land* (Sweet & Maxwell, 3rd ed, 1981)
Holdsworth's *History*	WS Holdsworth *History of English Law* (15 vols, Stevens), page references are to (Methuen, 3rd ed)
Hopkins *Informal Acquisition*	N Hopkins *Informal Acquisition of Rights in Land* (Sweet & Maxwell, 2000)
Jackson & Wilde	P Jackson & DC Wilde *Property Law – Current Issues and Debates* (Dartmouth Ashgate, 1999)
Litteton's *Tenures*	Litteton's *Tenures* (1st ed, c 1481); references are to paras common to all editions
Maitland's *Equity*	FW Maitland *Equity* (Cambridge UP, 2nd ed by J Brunyate, 1936)
Maudsley & Burn *LL – Cases and Materials*	Maudsley & Burn *Land Law – Cases and Materials* (Butterworths, 7th ed by EH Burn, 1998)
Megarry & Wade	Sir RE Megarry & Sir HWR Wade & C Harpum, *The Law of Real Property* (Stevens, 6th ed by C Harpum, 2000)

Panesar's *General Principles*	S Panesar *General Principles of Property Law* (Longman, 2001)
Ruoff & Roper	TBF Ruoff and RB Roper *The Law of Registered Conveyancing* (Sweet & Maxwell, 6th ed looseleaf, 1996)
Smith's *Property Law*	RJ Smith *Property Law* (Longman, 4th ed, 2002)
P Sparkes *NLL*	P Sparkes *A New Land Law* (Hart, 1st ed, 1999)
P Sparkes *NLT*	P Sparkes *A New Landlord and Tenant* (Hart, 2001)
Thompson *Modern LL*	MP Thompson *Modern Land Law* (Oxford, 2001)
Wolstenholme & Cherry	Wolstenholme & Cherry's *Conveyancing Statutes* (Stevens, 12th ed by BL Cherry, DH Parry & JRP Maxwell, 1932); (Oyez,13th ed by JT Farrand, 1972)

CASES

CASES

LAW COMMISSION PAPERS

LEGISLATION

STATUTORY INSTRUMENTS

DRAFT LAND REGISTRATION RULES 2003

WEBSITES

Acts	www.legislation.hmso.org.uk
Council of Mortgage Lenders	www.cml.org.uk
Electronic conveyancing	www.e-conveyancing.gov.uk
Financial Services Agency	www.fsa.gov.uk
HL cases and bills	www.parliament.uk
Human rights cases	http://hudoc.echr.coe.int/hudoc
Land Registry	www.landregistry.gov.uk
Law Commission	www.lawcom.gov.uk
Lord Chancellor's Department	www.lcd.gov.uk
tScheme	www.tscheme.org.uk

1

REGISTRATION

The idea. Universal registration. Estates. An individual register. Central concepts. Sources of substantive law. Registration legislation. Dovetailing of substantive law.

A. THE IDEA OF A REGISTER

[1.01] Grey squirrels are leaner and fitter and better able to adapt to changes than red squirrels. If we appropriate a metaphor from the law of restitution[1] and apply it to land, we can observe the same process of natural selection. Registration[2] is the intruding grey squirrel which has largely seen off the unregistered red squirrel, with its echoes of a cosy Edwardian England now being lost for ever. This image is so apt because once a colony of red squirrels is destroyed it never recovers,[3] just as there is no going back once land reaches the register.[4] However much we may pine for romantic losers, history remembers only winners. It is conventional to contrast "registered land" with "unregistered land", or new with old, but all land now has to be registered after it is dealt with, and it would be more accurate to talk of land being either registered or registrable. This book integrates the treatment of both systems and highlights their essential similarities.[5]

Land was made to be registered. In order to keep track of its population, a state registers births, marriages and deaths, or lists its electors, and in order to tax car owners it sets up a vehicle licensing centre. Conveyancing[6] demands a register of land ownership. This was obvious to Oliver Cromwell even though his reform proposal failed,[7] as did 26 Bills introduced between 1535 and 1832,[8] and a mid Victorian registration

---

[1] PBH Birks, *Restitution, The Future* (Federation Press, Sydney, 1992) ch 2, 26.

[2] The classic practitioners' work is Ruoff & Roper, *Registered Conveyancing* (6th ed, 1996). Also: Cheshire & Burn (16th ed), 100–110; Dixon's *Principles* (3rd ed) ch 2; G Ferris "Structural Differences between Registered and Unregistered Land Law – A Flickering Awareness" in Jackson and Wilde, ch 7; Goo's *Sourcebook* (3rd ed) ch 8; Gravell's *LL – Text* (2nd ed) ch 3; Grays' *Elements* (3rd ed), 191–219; Maudsley & Burn *LL – Cases* (7th ed) ch 2; Megarry & Wade (6th ed) ch 6; Smith's *Property* Law (4th ed) chs 10–11; Thompson's *Modern LL* ch 5.

[3] The reappearance of red squirrels at Fazakerley near Liverpool is the first recolonisation on record: S Barnes *Times*, November 15th 2000.

[4] Unless the land escheats, see below **[3.43ff]**.

[5] Cheshire's *Modern Real Property* (1st ed, 1925) contained one brief mention of the LRA 1925 (at 8), even though there were already 1/4 million titles in London.

[6] The word refers to the process of transferring land from one person to another; see below **[9]**.

[7] WS Holdsworth (1926) 42 *LQR* 158, 165–168.

[8] HW Wilkinson (1972) 36 *Conv (NS)* 390.

Act.[9] More successful was the Land Transfer Act 1875 which set up the framework for the present Land Registry, which flourished once compulsion was introduced in central London.[10] The Land Registration Act 1925 built on this scheme with unqualified success,[11] to such an extent that 80 years on it is finally set fair to become the universal form of land holding. The attractions are now increased by a modern legislative framework, the Land Registration Act 2002. In retrospect they are irresistibly obvious.[12] What took so long?

B. TOWARDS A UNIVERSAL REGISTER

1. Introduction of compulsion

[1.02] Walk down any street in England or Wales[13] and you will pass buildings of two kinds, some with registered titles while others continue to be unregistered. They will look identical to a casual passer-by, and the ownership and enjoyment of the land is unaffected by the form of the title. The difference between the two systems is mechanical, how title is proved and how the land is sold. Which predominates will depend on the part of the country that you choose for your walk. Central London became a compulsory area between 1899 and 1902,[14] so it is a fair bet that most buildings will have been sold at some time in the last 95 years, and that most inner London titles will by now have been registered. The Home Counties succumbed next. An apocryphal story relates how an eminent conveyancer was taken to the top of a hill in the Home Counties and asked how he liked the view. "Take me down", he pleaded, "the sight of all this registered land makes me feel sick."[15] Supposing that your doctor diagnosed this malady, where should you choose to live? Nowhere in England and Wales would be entirely safe, but since the rural outposts of Leominster, Sherborne and Oswestry were among the last strongholds to fall in 1990, the Welsh borders would be likely to give the best chance of an unregistered neighbour. But you would be better advised to seek a cure: universal registration is coming, and soon, and it will be good for you.

The 1875 scheme foundered because registration was voluntary.[16] Compulsion was essential. It began under the Land Transfer Act 1897 in the (then) County of London. Approximately 10% of the population lived in areas of compulsory registration at the end of 1925 but a ten year moratorium was imposed on the designation of new compulsory areas. After that time, compulsion could be introduced to the area of a local

---

[9] Land Registry Act 1862. New registrations were barred by Land Transfer Act 1875 s 125, sale since then will have caused a conversion to the modern register (LRA 1925 s 137(2)), and the register is now shut (LRA 2002 s 122).

[10] Land Transfer Act 1897.

[11] AW Withers (1946) 62 *LQR* 167.

[12] A Pottage, "Evidencing Ownership" ch 5 in Bright & Dewar, 142.

[13] See the LR Welsh language website.

[14] Land Transfer Act 1897 s 20; LRA 1925 s 120; S Anderson, "The 1925 Property Legislation: Setting Contexts" ch 4 in Bright & Dewar, 119; JS Anderson *Lawyers and the Making of English Land Law 1832–1940* (Clarendon, 1992), 302.

[15] JE Adams [1985] *LSG* 2399 (the title of the article is "Stop the RoT"); query the attribution to Underhill who favoured more radical reform in 1925; PH Kenny [2002] *Conv* 3 (nostalgia understandable).

[16] Land Transfer Act 1875.

authority by an order in council made after a local referendum, a power of veto exploited by the solicitors' profession for many years.[17] By 1939 only inner London, Eastbourne, Hastings, Middlesex[18] and Croydon were within the net. Extension to Surrey in 1952 was disputed, but the proponents of registration won the vote, and this proved a decisive turning point. Starting in the 1960s and gathering pace during the 1980s, government policy was to extend compulsory registration to the entire country as quickly as possible. This led to the last rural districts becoming registrable on December 1st 1990.[19] Since that date all land in England and Wales has been either registered or registrable.

2. Completion of the register

[1.03] That is far from representing the completion of the register because, as must be explained, registration is only compulsory following a dealing with the property. New triggers were introduced in 1997 in order to try to speed up the completion of the register.[20]

When compulsion was introduced in 1898 there were just over five thousand titles.[21] Growth thereafter was rapid, as shown by the following rounded figures:[22]

Year	Population in compulsory areas (%)	Registered titles (millions)
1925	10%	0.25
1951	15%	1
1961	20%	1.7
1971	45%	3.5
1981	75%	7
1991	100%	14
1996	100%	16
2001	100%	19

Figure 1-1 Spread of compulsion and registered titles

---

[17] LRA 1925 s 120, suspended in 1966 and finally repealed in 1997.

[18] There was an earlier system of deeds registration which also applied in Yorkshire. Middlesex (1709–1938), East Riding of Yorkshire (1708–1974), North Riding except York (1736–1970), West Riding (1704–1970); Statute 2 & 3 Ann c 4; Middlesex Registry Act 1708; Middlesex Deeds Act 1940. Deeds affecting unregistered land were deposited as they were made, but there was no attempt to collate the information contained in them. The registries are now shut and the records transferred to the modern register: LPA 1969 s 16; SI 1974/221; J Howell [1999] *CLJ* 366.

[19] Registration of Title Order 1989, SI 1989/1347.

[20] See below [9.24].

[21] S Anderson, *Lawyers and the Making of English Land Law 1832–1940* (Clarendon, 1992) appendix, table 2.

[22] *Completing the Land Register* (LR, 1992), 9; LR *Annual Reports;* LR *Quinquennial Review* (LCD, June 2001), [5.1].

C. REGISTRATION OF ESTATES

[1.04] The name of the "Land Registration Act 2002" suggests that there is a system of registration of *land*, and indeed it is convenient to follow the statute in referring to registered land even if this is strictly speaking a shorthand.[23] Were land registered directly, a single register would record details of each particular physical piece of land. It would be very difficult to decide how to deal with land which was subject to a lease: should the landlord or the tenant be registered?[24] The whole problem is avoided because, in fact, it is title to an *estate in land* which is registered,[25] and it would be more accurate to speak of registration of estates or of title.[26] This subtlety calls for explanation.[27]

Essentially an estate in land is a right to ownership of land for a particular duration of time. Several estates can co-exist in the same physical piece of land, and this implies that there may be also several registers. Registration applies to each estate independently of any others in the same physical land, so one estate may be registered while others remain unregistered.

Modern English law admits only two forms of ownership right.[28] The freehold estate represents ownership of the land in perpetuity, that is for ever. A leasehold estate is the ownership right created by a lease, that is it gives ownership of the land for a fixed period of years. Leases are registrable if there is more than seven years of the term outstanding at the time of registration.[29] So if a landlord grants a lease to a tenant for 99 years, two registers run side by side in the same land. The process of division can be continued by creating a sub-lease, a sub-under-lease, and so on without limit. Hence any physical piece of land could be represented by any number of titles, any number of which may be registered.

D. AN INDIVIDUAL REGISTER

1. The global register and individual registers

[1.05] Our legislation uses the word "register" with some abandon, and occasionally the lack of precision may matter.[30] Often the reference is to the global register of 19 million plus separate titles, but more often what is intended is the record of one particular title, called an "individual register".[31]

Individual registers are identified by a unique title number,[32] and each is subdivided

---

[23] As is made clear in LRA 2002 s 132.
[24] If land is held for *A for life, remainder to B in fee simple* who should be registered, A or B or both?
[25] LRA 2002 s 2. This describes registrable estate which when registered become registered estates.
[26] Title means the right to an estate in land, and also the means of proving the right to it.
[27] See below **[3.03]**.
[28] LPA 1925 s 1(1); see below **[3.06]**.
[29] For more detail see below **[25.35]**.
[30] On LRA 1925 see: Hayton's *Registered Land*, 29–30; *Strand Securities* v. *Caswell* [1965] Ch 958, CA; *AJ Dunning & Sons (Shopfitters)* v. *Sykes & Sons (Poole)* [1987] Ch 287, CA.
[31] DLRR 2003 r 3.
[32] DLRR 2003 r 4(1).

into three parts – the property, proprietorship, and charges registers – the contents of which are now described.

2.   A specimen register

[1.06] Somewhat simplified, a register of the title of an individual piece of land might look like this.[33]

| LAND REGISTRY | TITLE NUMBER WX87654 |

A. PROPERTY REGISTER

COUNTY: WESSEX   DISTRICT: UPPER WESSEX

The freehold land shown and edged with red on the plan of the above Title filed at the registry registered on 10th January 1990 known as no 10 Egdon Heath Road, Casterbridge together with the rights granted by a conveyance of 5th May 1890 referred to in Entry no 1 of the Charges Register.

B. PROPRIETORSHIP REGISTER

TITLE ABSOLUTE

Proprietor: Thomas Hardy of 10 Egdon Heath Road, Casterbridge.

C. CHARGES REGISTER

1. 10th January 1990. A conveyance of the land in this title dated 5th May 1899 by Diggory Venn to Gabriel Oak contains restrictive covenants.
2. 10th January 1990. Charge dated 2nd January 1990 to secure the money therein mentioned.
3. Proprietor: Woodlands Building Society registered on 10th January 1990.

Figure 1-2 An individual register

Registration collects together all details relevant to the ownership of the land, found in unregistered land from the title deeds and land charges register,[34] and presents them in a coherent up to date form. Information provided includes the identity of the current owner, the nature of his ownership right, and details of the rights now affecting the land; it presents a snapshot of the current state of the title. A register is not designed to say how things came about, so that the history of the title becomes irrelevant.[35] The registry has already done all the hard work by reading through the unregistered title deeds and selecting those parts which continue to affect the land. The result should be as easy to read as a newspaper, *The Independent* if not perhaps

---

[33] *Encyclopaedia FP* (5th ed, 1999 reissue) vol 25(1), [3001–3012].
[34] See below **[3.01ff]**.
[35] But see: LRA 2002 s 69; DLRR 2003 rr 144–145; below **[8.16]**.

The Sun, though a lay reader might want to check some of the legal jargon to ensure, for example, that a charge is the same as a mortgage.[36]

3. The property register

[1.07] The property register[37] defines which estate is registered, using the words "freehold" or "leasehold". In the latter case there will be a brief description of the main terms of the lease – the parties, its date and the length of the lease.[38]

A second aspect of the property register is its description of the land. Registration scores with its superior method of describing the physical extent of the land owned. While land remains unregistered, a "parcels clause" has to be inserted in the conveyance each time the land is sold, but this can only refer back to the description of the land transferred by older title deeds. If title is registered, an up to date description and plan is provided. The function of the property register is to describe the physical extent of the land sold, though descriptions of urban land are brief and often consist of no more than the postal address, supplemented by a title plan drawn from the large scale Ordnance Survey plan. Unregistered titles frequently use plans which are out of date or inaccurate, so that the accuracy of the filed plan is an undoubted advantage, even if the scale of the plan is too small to fix precise boundaries.[39]

Benefitting rights are also contained in the property register. These plusses add some extra advantageous feature, such as the benefit of a right of way to gain access to the land,[40] and since these can only be enjoyed with some physical land they must not be registered separately, but only as an appurtenance on the property register of that benefitted land.[41]

4. The proprietorship register

[1.08] The owner of a registered estate is named in the proprietorship register and described as the "registered proprietor".[42] Ownership coincides with proprietorship when the person recorded on the register is entitled to the land for his own benefit. On the specimen register, reproduced above, Thomas Hardy appears to be a beneficial owner because there is no restriction on the register. Other proprietors may be trustees or personal representatives, named on the register but holding the land for beneficiaries who are not named on the register.[43] The person on the register is always presumed to have full powers of ownership unless a limitation exists (for example the inability of a single trustee to sell the land) and it is demonstrated to the outside world by entry of a restriction on the register.[44] Much of the early part of this book will

---

[36] See below **[28.04]**.
[37] DLRR 2003 r 5(1).
[38] DLRR 2003 r 6.
[39] In urban areas the usual scale is 1/1250.
[40] See below **[34.01ff]**.
[41] LRA 2002 s 59; DLRR 2003 r 5(1)(b).
[42] An address for service is required and the registered number for a company since 1996 or a limited liability partnership since 2002: DLRR 2003 r 8.
[43] See below **[14.24]**.
[44] See below **[13.30–13.38]**.

concern trusts. Proprietorship is perfectly adequate as a basis of registration of title because the register is a conveyancing register designed to identify the person entitled to sell the land. Were it intended to be a register to determine (say) liability to council tax it would have to take a quite different form, because then one would need to know the beneficial entitlement.

Other matters included are a pending bankruptcy notice, positive covenants affecting the land and any modification of the covenants for title. The price paid for the land is also recorded.[45]

5. The charges register – burdens

[1.09] The charges register lists the burdens or adverse interests affecting the land, such as mortgages or restrictive covenants, those disadvantageous features of the land being the minuses.[46] Complexity in the ownership of land makes it likely that any particular parcel of land will be subject to a number of adverse interests. Our specimen title[47] included reference to restrictive covenants (entry 1) which restrict the use of the land and to a mortgage (or charge) in favour of a building society to secure repayment of the money borrowed to pay for the purchase of the land (entries 2 & 3). When the registrar collects together the adverse interests he provides a list in order of entitlement to claim the land, an advantage wholly lacking from the unregistered system.

E. FOUR CENTRAL CONCEPTS

1. Substantive registration

[1.10] A separate register is created for each registrable estate in the land,[48] the process described in this book as substantive registration. It applies to the freehold estate and long legal leasehold estates, as well as to legal charges[49] and one or two more abstruse rights.[50] Substantive registration carries a registry guarantee.[51]

2. Protection of burdens

[1.11] Many interest exist as adverse rights against a registered title. A notice needs to be entered against the title affected. The right is not guaranteed,[52] the effect being merely to bring the claim to a burden to the attention of a purchaser of the land, so that buyers will be bound by whatever right exists. The process of making an entry in the register to protect an interest to the title is described in this book as protection of the interest.[53]

---

[45] DLRR 2003 r 8.
[46] Hayton's *Registered Land*, 31.
[47] See above at [1.06].
[48] LRA 2002 s 2. When registered, it becomes a registered estate.
[49] The process here is slightly different in that registration occurs against an estate that is registered.
[50] See below [20.04].
[51] See below [20.04].
[52] Unless it happens to be a long lease the benefit of which is substantively registered.
[53] See below at [20.02ff].

3. Protection by occupation

[1.12] If a right is not protected by notice it will nevertheless bind a purchaser if the person entitled to the right is in actual occupation of the land. His rights are said to override the register,[54] or, in the much more convenient older terminology, the right protected by the occupation is an overriding interest.[55]

4. Overriding interests

[1.13] The register is not comprehensive because a number of matters are allowed to override the register (again, in older terminology, overriding interests[56]). Examples are short leases, many easements, and local land charges.[57]

F. SOURCES OF SUBSTANTIVE LAND LAW

[1.14] Laborious research[58] has greatly enlightened us about the mysterious and secretive processes by which a whole century of reform activity suddenly culminated just after the First World War in the emergence of a property law fit for the twentieth century, a land law fit for heroes.[59]

1. Older principles surviving the 1925 reforms

[1.15] Elements of the substantive law predating the 1925 property legislation include:

common law cases which laid down the doctrine of estates;
equitable case law development of the trust, the borrower's equity of redemption in mortgaged property and much else; and
statutes unconsolidated in 1925, especially[60] *Quia Emptores 1290*.[61]

2. The 1925 property legislation as a source of substantive law

[1.16] Modern land law remains firmly rooted in the 1925 property legislation, six great statutes,[62] each of which came into force on January 1st 1926.[63] It is a lasting

---

[54] LRA 2002 sch 3 para 2.

[55] LRA 1925 s 70(1)(g); many of the leading cases of the 1980s and 1990s concern this paragraph; see below **[15.32ff]**.

[56] LRA 1925 s 70.

[57] LRA 2002 schs 1, 3; see below **[20.25ff]**.

[58] A Offer (1977) 40 *MLR* 505; S Anderson, *Lawyers and the Making of English Land Law 1832–1940* (Clarendon, 1992); A Offer, *Property & Politics 1870–1914: Landownership, Law, Ideology & Urban Development in England* (Cambridge UP, 1981); S Anderson (1984) 37 *CLP* 63; JH Johnson (1926) 42 *LQR* 67; S Anderson "The 1925 Property Legislation: Setting Contexts" ch 2 in Bright & Dewar.

[59] JS Anderson *Lawyers and the Making of English Land Law 1832–1940* (Clarendon, 1992) ch 8.

[60] Others are: Prescription Act 1832 (acquisition of rights of way and other easements by long use); Fines and Recoveries Act 1833 (barring entails); and the perpetually renewable leases provisions of LPA 1922.

[61] Which prescribes a substitutional effect for a sale, see below **[3.23]**.

[62] In order of enactment: Settled Land Act 1925, Trustee Act 1925, Law of Property Act 1925, Land Registration Act 1925, Land Charges Act 1925 and Administration of Estates Act 1925.

[63] So: "before 1926", "after 1925".

monument to Lord Birkenhead LC and a team of draftsmen led by Sir Benjamin Cherry.[64] Although many details have been changed, the basic principles laid down have proved to have enduring value. In particular the Law of Property Act 1925 remains the main source of modern land law The Jackson Pollock like mess that was land law was shaken up, systematised and made coherent. A number of different types of legislation need to be distinguished[65]:

1. anachronisms removed in 1925 especially the Statute of Uses 1535;[66]
2. pre-1926 case law principles codified or amended in 1925;
3. pre-1926 statutes consolidated unamended in 1925;
4. pre-1926 statutes amended in 1922[67] and then consolidated as amended;[68]
5. further amendments in 1924 and some afterthoughts.[69]
6. errors of consolidation leading to inadvertent changes to the law[70] caused by shoddy carpentry when the statute law as it had been amended in 1922 was divided into the six Acts of 1925.[71]

It is very rarely necessary to go back to the old law since "the docked tail must not be allowed to wag the dog".[72]

3. Post-1925 reform

[1.17] Large parts of the legislation have been amended. The Land Charges Act was rewritten in 1972, the Settled Land Act 1925 has been reduced to a small walk on part,[73] and the Trustee Act 1925 and Administration of Estates Act 1925 have each suffered major reform, though despite these various indignities the general framework laid down in 1925 has survived. This even more true of the Law of Property Act 1925 which remains the cornerstone of modern land law despite its archaic language and the subsequent reshaping of important parts.[74] If one had to pick just two vitally important amendments they would be the Law of Property (Miscellaneous Provisions) Act 1989, a rewrite of the formality requirements for deeds and contracts, and the Trusts of Land and Appointment of Trustees Act 1996 which has replaced trusts for sale with trusts of land and prohibited new strict settlements. Numerous

---

[64] P Sparkes *NLL* (1st ed), 21.

[65] P Sparkes [1988] *Stat LR* 146; RE Megarry (1958) 74 *LQR* 487, (1959) 75 *LQR* 307, (1960) 70 *LQR* 197.

[66] Listed by Cheshire & Burn (15th ed), 88–89 (dropped from 16th ed).

[67] Eg the Partition Acts: *Re Mayo* [1943] Ch 302, 304, Simonds J; R Cocks [1982] *Conv* 415, [1984] *Conv* 198; *City of London BS* v. *Flegg* [1988] AC 54, 77D, Lord Oliver.

[68] *Grey* v. *Inland Revenue Commissioners* [1960] AC 1, HL; *Re King* [1963] Ch 459, 490–491; *Midland Bank Trust Co* v. *Green* [1981] AC 513, 532.

[69] LP (Amendment) Acts 1924, 1926 and 1929.

[70] There is one very important illustration where the intended protection for occupiers of unregistered land was removed by inadvertence in 1925; see below **[21.40]**.

[71] This was not done by people of the same calibre as the 1922 draftsman Sir Benjamin Cherry: S Anderson, *Lawyers and the Making of English Land Law 1832–1940* (Clarendon, 1992), 310–311.

[72] *Maunsell* v. *Olins* [1975] AC 373, 392, Lord Simon; *Farrell* v. *Alexander* [1977] AC 59, 72, Lord Wilberforce; *Pepper* v. *Hart* [1993] AC 593, HL.

[73] See below **[14.10ff]**.

[74] PH Kenny [1999] *Conv* 281.

smaller reforms have chipped away at details so that the statute book is in a sorry state, and it essential to use an up to date version of the statutes.[75]

Many property lawyers adopt the conservative principle that:

> *"The rules of law relating to property are simple and may be easily learnt if they are not altered."*[76]

Students will disagree. Since the Law Commission was formed in 1965 to promote the reform of the law[77] a prime objective has been to bring order to the jumbled mass of property law. Even ignoring the work on land registration, considered next, a truly impressive collective cv has been built up by successive property Commissioners – Julian Farrand, Trevor Aldridge, Charles Harpum and Stuart Bridge – as shown by the table of reports affecting land law at the start of this book.[78]

G. REGISTRATION LEGISLATION

1. Land Registration Act 2002

[1.18] The register and land registry set up by the Land Transfer Act 1875 were continued by the Land Registration Act 1925 and are carried forward once more by the Land Registration Act 2002.[79] The implementation date announced for the new Act[80] is October 13th 2003.[81] On that date the Land Registration Act 1925[82] will be repealed, little lamented,[83] along with all the other legislation affecting the registration system.[84] A major headline change is the preparations made for electronic conveyancing,[85] the reason the Act secured such speedy implementation because the Government needed some way of giving effect to its manifesto commitment to improve house buying. The legislation passed with little technical debate so little illumination comes from *Hansard* on technical issues.[86] Another major change is the

---

[75] The fullest is published by Butterworths but students seeking an unannotated version for use in examinations will prefer the edition by Blackstones or Sweet & Maxwell.

[76] *Cadell* v. *Palmer* (1833) 1 Cl & F 372, 406, 6 ER 956.

[77] Law Commissions Act 1965 s 1; TC Aldridge "The Role of the Law Commission" ch 2 in Jackson & Wilde; C Harpum "The Law Commission and the Reform of Land Law" ch 6 in Bright & Dewar.

[78] See above, at cvii.

[79] S 1(1) in each case.

[80] Robert Abbey & Mark Richards, *Blackstone's Guide to the Land Registration Act 2002* (OUP, 2002); E Cooke [2002] *Conv* 11; PH Kenny [2001] *Conv* 216; PH Kenny [2002] *Conv* 3; B Bogusz (2002) 65 *MLR* 536.

[81] By order under LRA 2002 s 136.

[82] This was a consolidation of the Land Transfer Act 1875 and changes made by LPA 1922 ss 164–187, sch 16; LP (Amendment) A 1924 s 8, sch 8; LRA 1925 s 147, sch; *Chowood* v. *Lyall (No 2)* [1930] 2 Ch 156, 165, Lord Hanworth MR. However, very few cases were decided before 1925 and it is common to see the LRA 1925 as a legislative curtain.

[83] *Central London Commercial Estates* v. *Kato Kagaku* [1998] 4 All ER 948, 953, Sedley J.

[84] LRA 2002 sch 13 repeals: LRA 1925, LRA 1936, LR & LC A 1971, LRA 1986 ss 1–4, LRA 1988, LRA 1997 ss 1–3, 5(4)–(5), sch 1 paras 1–6.

[85] LRA 2002 ss 91–95; see below **[7.09ff]**.

[86] Lords: July 3rd 2001 (second reading); July 17th and 19th 2001 (Committee stage); October 3rd 2001 (Report); November 8th 201 (third reading); Commons: December 3rd 2001 (second reading); December 11th and 13th 2001 (Standing committee D); February 11th 2002 (Report stage); Lords consideration of Commons amendments: February 26th 2002.

protection of registered proprietors against the effect of adverse possession,[87] which can be seen as effecting a fundamental change summed up in the jingle "registration of title becomes title by registration".[88] More recherché is the bizarre scheme for registration of Crown land.[89] All these are essentially mechanical changes.

However, the new legislation goes far beyond that, the culmination[90] of a the largest reform project undertaken by the Law Commission effecting a useful spring cleaning and re-jigging. Settled principles of land registration are mainly retained, though with a host of minor changes of detail, and the whole superstructure has then been completely rewritten. The practical effect for most day to day transactions will be minimal[91] as may be expected of a system that is working well, but it is by no means a normal consolidation since the most basic principles are restated in a new form. This form of legislation is not calculated to make it easy since it can rarely be said that the law is the same or that it has been amended, but usually only that it has been replicated. Professor Kenny has well likened it to a kaleidoscope in which a twirl of the same basic elements causes a completely new picture to emerge.[92] Great caution is needed in using pre-2003 case law.

2. Rules

[1.19] The legislative revamp will be completed by the Land Registration Rules 2003. A more logical division has been attempted between primary and secondary legisla-tion,[93] rules being designed to implement practical procedures and forms to imple-ment policies set out in the Act. The 1925 rules were to have the same force as if enacted by Parliament, an unusual provision which produced odd results[94] which is now dropped.

H. DOVETAILING OF SUBSTANTIVE LAW

[1.20] The preface to the first edition of this text[95] set out the author's basic philosophy in these words:

"The traditional division between registered and unregistered land ceases to be tenable when all land has to be registered after any dealing. Unregistered land is an exotic facing extinc-tion. It is time to see how, as Lord Oliver observed in *City of London BS* v. *Flegg*,[96] the two systems are designed to dovetail together. . . . [W]hen the central concepts of land law are

---

[87] LRA 2002 ss 96–98; see below **[11.28ff]**.

[88] Law Com 254 (1998), [2.6].

[89] LRA 2002 ss 79–85; see below **[3.36]**.

[90] For earlier stages of the review see P Sparkes *NLL* (1st ed), 33–34.

[91] PH Kenny [2002] *Conv* 523, 524.

[92] PH Kenny [2002] *Conv* 431.

[93] LRA 2002 ss 126–128, sch 10; Law Com 271 (2001) part XVII, EN [548–553], EN [759–778]; this book relies on the DLRR 2003 as published on the LR legislation website; DLRR CD (2002).

[94] LRA 1925 s 144(2); *Re Dance's Way, West Town, Hayling Island* [1962] Ch 490, 499, 508; *Celsteel* v. *Alton House Holdings* [1985] 1 WLR 204, 221D–E, Scott J.

[95] P Sparkes *NLL* (1st ed), xiii.

[96] [1986] AC 54, 84G.

introduced . . . registered and unregistered land are treated in parallel at all stages, two conveyancing mechanisms working towards common ends."

Dovetailing should apply to all substantive principles which are not driven by the different mechanics of the two systems.

The existence of the register necessarily implies changes to the mechanics of conveying land. Since the register records proprietorship of the land, legal ownership can only pass when a transfer is sent for registration whereas legal ownership of unregistered land passes immediately on the execution of a conveyance. Equally fundamental are the differences in the method of protecting burdens enforceable against land, since the charges register of a registered title provides a convenient collection point for a record of all rights affecting the land but this is quite lacking with an unregistered title. Hence the need for a register of land charges, that is burdens attaching to an unregistered title and registered against the name of the estate owner. Methods of creation and protection of interests necessarily differ.

In general substantive law should not diverge. Case law developments have forced some fissures, most notably in the general protection of occupiers in registered conveyancing and much patchier operation of this protection before first registration. In other cases in which the systems have diverged it has usually been because the courts have misunderstood the registered scheme and has worked to the disadvantage of that system.[97] In one important particular – adverse possession – the two systems have been moved further apart by the Land Registration Act 2002 but, that egregious blunder apart, the new legislation demonstrates the underlying linkage of the two systems much more closely than before, particularly the alignment of the quality of occupation necessary to give notice and to give overriding status,[98] and in the classification of protectible interests in which the restriction/notice divide now follows the divide between overreachable and endurable burdens in the substantive law,[99] so that on balance the dovetailing is now much closer than before.

---

[97] See below [15.43].
[98] See below [15.42].
[99] See below [20.13].

2

LAND

Property. Formality. Reality. Why land law? Land and not-land borderline. Fixtures. Things found. Flora and fauna.

A. PROPERTY

1. Things of value

[2.01] Property consists of those possessions which are of value.[1] Among these things is land, a major subset of property, defined most obviously by its characteristic of being immoveable. Land is distinct in this way from the other forms of property, called in this book not-land, which consists of things that are either moveable or intangible (abstract) in nature. Chattels is the term used to describe moveable things like cars, furniture and jewellery, which can, it is no surprise to find, be transferred by physical delivery. They are choses in possession. Intangibles such as shares and copyrights have no real existence except as rights which can be enforced in the courts, so they are choses (or things) in action.

2. Classification

[2.02] How should one arrange the things described above into legal subjects? Logic cannot help, since the question whether to study property law or land law is one of utility. Are the rules governing land sufficiently different from the general rules of property to require separate treatment? Readers will deduce from the title to this book the author's conclusion that land has a distinctiveness and separateness which requires distinct and separate treatment. Also it is a question of weight since the rules of property law are just too great to be treated comfortably as a single whole. Our subject is land law. And our way of visualising property is as follows:

---

[1] *Collins English Dictionary* (5th ed, 2000), 1238; this is the second sense given in the *OED*.

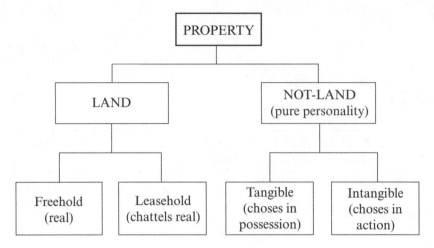

Figure 2-1 A Map of Property Law

3. The value of land

[2.03] In any society, some things are coveted above all others. Property law reflects the perceptions of wealth of its members, but the reflection occurs only through a time warp mirror since society changes more quickly than property law can adapt. Those who could afford to litigate in the medieval courts could think only of land – the source of status, income, and power, and the only worthwhile investment. When the Conqueror sent out his men to survey his kingdom at the time of Domesday (1086) he did not need to compile a *Who's Who?* of powerful men but merely a list of land-owners. Property was coincident with power. Development of the common law by litigation over the next three or four centuries necessarily skewed the law towards an endless refinement of the rules regulating the ownership of land, the most prized asset.

Primeval instincts still guide modern aspirations. Land remains an overriding concern. Houses in the UK are worth a total of £2,100,000,000,000, a staggering figure which may triple by 2020.[2] The figure does not include farmland, offices, business parks, and any Government property or Crown estates. The "property as porn" pages at the beginning of *Country Life*[3] show the same lust for ownership as the medieval baron, even if the primary lure has become capital investment and use value of land rather than power.

4. Value in other assets

[2.04] Personal possessions were once so few that medieval law recognised a funda-mental chasm between land on the one hand and all other possessions, which, for want of a convenient technical term, are described in this book as "not land".[4] The

[2] Centre for Economics and Business Research Report, *Guardian* April 22nd 2002.
[3] Kit Hesketh-Harvey, *Just a Minute* (BBC, Radio 4), August 2002.
[4] Or in conventional terminology "pure personalty".

main constituent of that category is physical moveable things, called chattels by the medieval lawyers[5] after the beasts which then formed the predominant form of medieval wealth, though quite why they are named after cows rather than pigs and sheep remains obscure. The medieval law of chattels was almost empty of content since "money was scarce and luxurious refinements unknown."[6] Society now attaches greater relative value to possessions, which has led to a corresponding refinement of legal principle and an expansion of the interests permitted to exist in goods.[7] Some physical things now rival land as receptacles of wealth, in the past a Leonardo, now a Monet or Picasso, and for the future a pile of bricks or half a pickled sheep. A legal classification based on value would not distinguish cars and houses, since a Ferrari costs far more than a back-to-back in a former mining village.

When the *Sunday Times* compiles a list of the 100 Richest they include the subject's central London pad and the country estate since a wealthy person is likely to own a large house, along with the collection of Porsches and the collection of modern art. But land and moveables are no longer the sources of mega wealth. Leisure and excess are the fruits of owning a software house or media, a stake in an oil corporation or a back catalogue of hit songs – shares and copyrights rather than swathes of the rural shires. These things are intangibles. The question "animal, vegetable or mineral" can only be answered "abstract", having no existence except by suing to enforce them.[8] This general shift[9] from land to intangibles suggests that social evolution has overtaken the conditions in which our property categories were formed. But among average men and women there remains a logic in keeping land on its pedestal since buying a house remains the biggest commitment most people will ever make.

B. FORMALITY

1. Informal not-land

[2.05] Personal property *can* be passed by document, but it would be an eccentric way to give a watch or a newspaper. These tangible things are generally transferred by delivery. (Intangible property such as shares and copyrights is documentary; lacking any physical existence these things require a document to give them some visible reality.) Goods are more common. If I walk up to a news stand, ask for a newspaper, and hand over the money, when I pick up the paper it is mine. Having read it, suppose I offer you my newspaper. "Have you finished with it?" you will ask, to confirm your permission to take it permanently. An affirmative answer, and it is yours. Physical delivery with an intention to give makes the gift. Contracts and trusts of goods can also be created orally. Imagine, if you can, a world in which a document was required for every transfer of every physical object. The world would collapse under paper. This leaves not-land (personal property) with a simple system of law.

---

[5] Or in law French choses in possession – moveable things.
[6] Blackstone's *Commentaries* book II, ch XXIV, 391.
[7] A Clarke [1997] *CLP* 119.
[8] In law French choses in action.
[9] Panesar's *General Principles*, 92–95.

2.   Documentary land

[2.06] Formality requirements were introduced in 1677[10] to prevent fraudulent claims, and it was natural to limit these to dealings with land, the major repository of wealth. This is no longer so and if a legislator could cast off this history and begin afresh, there would be no logic in restricting documentary formalities to land. As it is the classifier reaches for the cleaver when he considers the formality required for sale or gift. Legal title to land can only be passed by deed, a specially formal type of document,[11] but contracts[12] and equitable interests[13] generally require some form of signed writing.

3.   Informality

[2.07] Requirements of formality can work injustice. It is wise to write down arrangements made in relation to property but sometimes very unfair to refuse to recognise an arrangement where this has been forgotten. The test for the enforcement of informal arrangements is whether it is unconscionable for a property owner who has promised a particular right to deny it later on the basis that it has not been formalised. Unconscionability is based on the existence of a common intention between the parties and detrimental reliance on the promised right by the person claiming the informal right. An oral contract to buy a house is not enforceable, but the owner cannot deny its existence if the buyer has sold his own house, paid the price, and moved in. In the context of a claim to a share of a home, this is a claim to an interest under a constructive trust,[14] whereas in other contexts it is a claim to an equity created by proprietary estoppel.[15]

C.   REAL NATURE

1.   Recoverability in early law

[2.08] In Latin a thing is a *res* and the law treats it as real if the law allows the recovery of the thing itself. English law affords a near perfect correlation between reality and land.[16] Its two categories are land and not-land,[17] the former including both freehold and leasehold land. In simple terms, land can be recovered itself whereas damages are payable for the loss of personal property.

Unfortunately, the term *real property* does not correspond to the property that is real, purely and simply because terminology was fixed in a distant past before the

---

[10] Successively: Statute of Frauds 1677 ss 1–9; Real Property Act 1845 s 3; LPA 1925 ss 52–55.
[11] See below **[7]**.
[12] See below **[22]**.
[13] See below **[16.12]**.
[14] See below **[17]**.
[15] See below **[23]**.
[16] P Birks "Before We Begin: Five Keys to Land Law" ch 18 in Bright & Dewar, 471; Cheshire & Burn (16th ed), 36–37; Panesar's *General Principles*, 43–60; W Swadling "Property" ch 4 in Birks' *English Private Law*, [4.45–4.50].
[17] Traditionally pure personalty.

modern law of recoverability was settled. Real property consists of freehold land and interests such as a mortgage secured on freehold land. *Personal property* includes tangible moveable property (chattels) and intangibles (such as debts) but also (the cause of the mismatch) leasehold land. This is anomalous since a leasehold house is immovable, like a freehold house, and unlike a cow.[18] *Chattel real* is the term coined to reflect this dichotomy.[19]

2. Leasehold land

[2.09] When Bracton borrowed his classification (c 1250)[20] from Roman law,[21] leases were purely personal contracts between landlord and tenant, whose only remedy for eviction was damages. Two and a half centuries later leasehold estates were fully established to the extent that a dispossessed tenant was allowed to recover the land itself for the remainder of the lease. Simpson[22] attributes this change to a mistake which occurred in 1499, but the new law was no longer contentious in 1525. Common law classification was already set in concrete and thenceforth leasehold land occupied this curious middle ground as a chattel real – classified as personal property but with specific recovery allowed.

3. Modern law of recoverability

[2.10] Procedurally the real actions were hopeless as a means of pursuing land that had been stolen. For example the right to trial by battle was exercised in one isolated case as late as 1819.[23] Long before that, the superior procedures had led to the victory of the personal actions used today for the recovery of land. Successive improvements in procedure[24] saw the introduction of possessory assizes in 1166,[25] writs of entry, and (much later) ejectment as an off-shoot of trespass.[26] Forms of action were finally abolished as part of the judicature reform in 1875, leaving a single action for the recovery of land available equally to the freeholder or leaseholder,[27] derived from the personal action in trespass but giving a judgment for possession of the land itself.

[18] The word "chattel" is related to "cattle".

[19] AWB Simpson, *A History of the Land Law* (Oxford, 2nd ed, 1986) chs II, VII; FW Maitland, *Forms of Action at Common Law* (Cambridge, 1936); JH Baker, *An Introduction to English Legal History* (Butterworths, 3rd ed, 1990) ch 4; SFC Milsom, *Historical Foundations of the Common Law* (Butterworths, 3rd ed, 1981) ch 2.

[20] SE Thorne, *Bracton's On the Laws and Customs of England* (Selden Society, 1968) fo 59, vol 3, 13.

[21] Bracton, like Roman law, concentrated on the process by which a case was brought to court whereas it is more sensible to focus on the form of judgment, which in England is real against land: T Cyprian Williams (1888) 4 *LQR* 394.

[22] *A History of the Land Law* (Oxford, 2nd ed, 1986), 144; Holdsworth's *History* vol 3, 214; Fitzherbert, *Natura Brevium*, 220; Megarry & Wade (6th ed), 1442–1443.

[23] *Ashford* v. *Thornton* (1818) 1 B & Ald 405, 106 ER 149. Battle was abolished by the Real Property Limitation Act 1833 s 36.

[24] Megarry & Wade (6th ed), appendix.

[25] DW Sutherland, *The Assize of Novel Disseisin* (Oxford, 1973), 7.

[26] Developed for leaseholders but adapted by means of a fictional lease for use by freeholders. In *Doe d X* v. *Y*, Doe was a fictional character, d a fictional demise (= lease), leaving a genuine action between X the claimant of freehold land and Y whom it is sought to evict. Fictitious elements were removed by the Common Law Procedure Act 1852 s 168.

[27] Rules of the Court issued under the Supreme Court of Judicature Act 1873.

Holders of personal property are now in an improved position. Damages remain the basic remedy for loss of goods – usually equal to the value of the thing lost. Further, a modern statute confers a discretion for a court to order specific restitution, a discretion generally exercised where the goods are of particular value.[28] Nevertheless, a functional analysis of modern property law would need to distinguish between land (where recovery is as of right) and not-land (where damages remain usual).

4. Intestate succession before 1926

[2.11] The law of succession had a Dadaist absurdity before 1926, since a death intestate[29] caused real and personal property to devolve separately. A house built on land that was split between a freehold and a leasehold title,[30] would be split legally on a death between two different owners. The freehold part was real property which passed to the heir,[31] usually the eldest son,[32] determined according to the archaic principle of male[33] primogeniture. The leasehold part of the house was personal property which was divided between the next of kin, that is it was shared equally between all relatives of equal rank (for example, all children).

5. Limited assimilation

[2.12] On January 1st 1926 the law of intestate succession was assimilated. Death is no longer an occasion on which one needs to divide an estate into real and personal parts.[34] An intestate's estate passes in its entirely – freehold and leasehold land and everything else – to personal representatives to be divided between the next of kin.[35] Land never passes to the heir of the deceased,[36] male primogeniture is abolished, and the law secures equal division between children. The Law of Property Act 1922 aimed "to assimilate and amend the law of Real and Personal Estate"[37] and "to amend the law . . . of intestacy",[38] but the ambition of the legislators was limited to that very modest form of assimilation.

There is a pernicious belief that the 1925 legislation created a unified system of property law of universal application. That law would apply equally to a house and a car, to a leasehold greengrocer's and its stock of decaying oranges, to a mortgage and

---

[28] Torts (Interference with Goods) Act 1977.

[29] Ie where a person dies without an effective will.

[30] An example suggested by Sir Arthur Underhill's own house: *A Concise Explanation of Lord Birkenhead's Act* (Butterworths, 1922), 46.

[31] Subject to any special custom such as gavelkind which divided land between all sons equally in Kent and Portland. Local customs were abolished in 1925.

[32] Dower was used to provide a home and maintenance to the surviving spouse. Remnants of the concept remain in the title of a Dowager Duchess (the present Duke's mother) and in dower houses.

[33] Some 42% of heirs were female: E Spring [1995] *CLJ* 171; but only 4% actually inherited because of tails male designed to prevent female succession.

[34] Real property only remains relevant if an eccentric testator leaves *my real property to X and my personal property to Y.*

[35] See below [14.23].

[36] Entails are the solitary exception, see below [18.04].

[37] This ensured common devolution of legal titles: AEA 1925 part I ss 1–3.

[38] This is concerned with a common scheme of beneficial entitlement: AEA 1925 ss 45–46 as amended.

the money lent. Not! The misconception is fuelled by an early passage in Cheshire's text which, when referring to real and personal property, said that the 1925 legislation:[39]

> "put the two forms of property as nearly as possible upon the same footing. . . . [T]he law of personal property, which thus became the dominating system, was itself amended in several particulars."[40]

Cheshire meant only that the law of real property (freehold land) was made to correspond to the law of chattels real (leasehold land),[41] by reforms which were so technical that explanation could not be attempted without a long historical pre-amble.[42] Full assimilation had been proposed, but much more cautious proposals emanating from Haldane, Wolstenholme and Cherry[43] were enacted. Outside the law of succession, the effect was a failure of assimilation.

6. Real property as a synonym for land

[2.13] America took English law from Blackstone and so still thinks of land as real estate. That is the old world. "Real property" also appears in the titles of the two longest established texts on the legislation, Cheshire's *The Modern Law of Real Property* and Megarry and Wade's *The Law of Real Property*, but despite their archaic titles these two great books do, of course, cover leaseholds. Modern texts such as Gray's *Elements* use some variant of the phrase *Land Law* to describe their field, and indeed that is the proper subject for study.

D. LAND OR PROPERTY?

[2.14] We are left with two possible subjects – property law or land law, the choice a matter of utility based on function and weight. Enquiry into the characteristics of land should make it possible to determine whether land should be split from not-land, two Kingdoms as different as are plants and animals. Do we need a register of titles to land or a register of things of value?

1. For property law

[2.15] Areas in which there is a single law of property include:

(1) succession;

---

[39] Cheshire refers specifically to part I of the LPA 1922, reforms now scattered throughout the 1925 consolidation.

[40] (15th ed), 6; (1st ed, 1926), 7.

[41] G Cheshire, *Modern Law of Real Property* (2nd ed, 1927), 65 ("solution adopted"); F Birkenhead, *Frederick Edwin, Earl of Birkenhead*, (Thornton Butterworth, 1935), 206.

[42] Cheshire & Burn, (15th ed, 1995), 88; Cheshire lists seven anachronisms repealed: *Shelley's case* (1581) 1 Co Rep 88b, 76 ER 199; contingent remainder rules; *Whitby* v. *Mitchell* (1890) 44 Ch D 85; old canons of descent; *Dumpor's case* (1603) 4 Co Rep 119b, 76 ER 1110; the rule that husband and wife were sometimes one person; and special occupancy.

[43] S Anderson, *Lawyers and the Making of English Land Law* (Clarendon, 1992), 254–257; A Offer (1977) 40 *MLR* 505.

(2) bankruptcy; and

(3) fundamental rights to property and a fair trial.

2. For land law

[2.17] A rather longer and more impressive list can be compiled of areas in which land law has so many distinctive characteristics that they compel separate treatment, such as:

formality;
recoverability;
rights of beneficiaries under trusts;
registration;
estate ownership theory;
adverse possession;
land use controls;
relations between neighbours; and
mortgages.

In short, the proper study for mankind is land.

E. THE LAND-NOT-LAND BORDERLINE

1. Extended definition of land

[2.17] Land has a wide legislative definition[44] to include interests in land.[45] This avoids much repetition. Since a deed is needed to pass legal title to land,[46] a deed is also required for legal creation of interests in land such as a lease, a mortgage or an easement. Electricity cables can be placed in tunnels as well through buildings.[47] It is not necessary to legislate for each case separately.

2. Cases where it uncertain whether a chattel has become land

[2.18] Land is immoveable whereas not-land is moveable or abstract, so that the question of allocating a particular asset to the appropriate category is almost always simplicity itself. Blurring is possible in marginal cases where, for example, a slate is fixed to a roof or a ring is dropped into a pond. The first is handled by the law of fixtures and the second by the land of finding and it is to these two matters that we now turn.

---

[44] LPA 1925 s 205(1)(ix); LRA 1925 s 3(viii); *UCB Group* v. *Hedworth* [2002] EWCA Civ 708, [2002] 46 EG 200; but LRA 2002 s 132 does not align properly since "land" is limited to physical things and "registered land" is limited to estates substantively registered. A lease granted by a registered proprietor for 4 years is land under LPA 1925 but not under LRA 2002.

[45] Goo's *Sourcebook* (3rd ed) 29–40; Gravells *LL – Text* (1999), 1–3; Grays' *Elements* (3rd ed), 1–62; K Gray [1991] *CLJ* 252, 305.

[46] LPA 1925 s 52.

[47] Electricity Act 1989 sch 4 para 6; *British Waterways Board* v. *London Power Networks* [2002] EWHC 2417, [2003] 1 All ER 187.

F. FIXTURES

1. Introduction

[2.19] A person expects the house he buys to include the garage, and shrubs in the garden, and the flagstones on the terrace,[48] but he does not want the seller's cat nor expect his car. Items that are freely movable are obviously distinct from things (called fixtures) that are attached to the land. Lay expectations may not match legal categories,[49] since, for example bayonet cap lamp bulbs are readily movable and can be taken by a seller, though most buyers expect them to be left.[50]

2. Physical parts of the land

[2.20] Things which form part of the land itself are owned with it.[51] *Elitestone* v. *Morris*[52] concerned one of the plots on Holtsfield, a 14 acre site on the Gower Peninsula containing 27 chalets and a community of almost 80 people. Morris paid an annual licence fee and was undoubtedly a tenant of the *land* comprised in his plot. Rent Act 1977 security of tenure attached if his lease also included the *chalet*.[53] This had been built in 1945 without any physical connection to the land, since it rested under its own weight on a separate base.[54] Old cases permitting the removal of wooden buildings resting on their own weight were doubted.[55] Morris' chalet was unlike a Portakabin or mobile home, because it was so constructed that it could only be enjoyed in situ and removal would involve its total destruction. So, it had become a part of the land, was included in the lease, and Morris did enjoy security of tenure.

A building starts off as a pile of breeze blocks, bricks, and tiles, which are brought on to the building site as chattels. Incorporation into the building causes them to lose their character as individual bricks, and become incorporated in the wall as a part of the land. So do the component parts of a dry stone wall on a moor land farm.[56] A conservatory physically incorporated into a house is a part of the structure and cannot be removed when the house is sold.[57] So too are doors, central heating boilers and radiators.[58]

---

[48] *Taylor* v. *Hamer* [2002] EWCA Civ 1130, [2002] 33 EG 96 (CS).

[49] Cheshire & Burn (16th ed), 151–157; Grays' *Elements* (3rd ed), 41–55;
Maudsley & Burn *LL – Cases* (7th ed), 90–95; Megarry & Wade (6th ed), [14.311–14.326]; Smith's *Property Law* (4th ed), 83–90.

[50] *British Economical Lamp Co* v. *Empire, Mile End*, (1913) 29 TLR 386.

[51] [1997] 1 WLR 687, 691G, Lord Lloyd.

[52] [1997] 1 WLR 687, HL; HW Wilkinson [1997] *NLJ* 1031; S Bridge [1997] *CLJ* 498; H Conway [1998] *Conv* 418.

[53] This implied that the rent would be regulated; the site owner had increased the annual licence fee from £85 to £1000.

[54] At 694E–F, Lord Clyde.

[55] At 692B–C, Lord Lloyd, 697G–698G, Lord Clyde; *Reid* v. *Smith* (1905) 3 CLR 656.

[56] *Holland* v. *Hodgson* (1872) LR 7 CP 328, 335, Blackburn J.

[57] *Buckland* v. *Butterfield* (1820) 2 Brod & Bing 54, 129 ER 878; *Montague* v. *Long* (1972) 24 P & CR 240 (bridge).

[58] *Boswell* v. *Crucible Steel Co* [1925] 1 KB 119, 123, Atkin LJ (plate glass windows not fixture); *Holiday Fellowship* v. *Hereford* [1959] 1 WLR 211; *Elitestone* [1997] 1 WLR 687, 690G, Lord Lloyd.

The principle of *Elitestone* does not make a houseboat into "land", as shown in *Chelsea Yacht and Boat Club* v. *Pope*.[59] A landing craft, used on D day, was converted and moored at Chelsea in such a way that it was afloat for six hours and aground for the next six. Occupation was held under a document which described the parties as landlord and tenant and which was in a form appropriate to a letting, but the degree of physical annexation to the land was slight. Hoses brought in water, gas, electricity, telephone and vacuum drainage, and the "boat" was also attached to pontoons, to rings in embankment and to an anchor in the river bed anchor, but all could be undone and were not apt to make the boat part of the land.[60] Without annexation, the purpose of fixing the thing was irrelevant. A boat used as a home is not of the same genus as "real property" – that is land, and the boat remained a mere chattel.

3. Heirlooms

[2.21] Some moveable chattels are so much a part of the land that they pass with it. On death they pass with the land, which is why they are called heirlooms.[61] In the past these chattels were often settled on trusts so as to pass to the successive life tenants of the land, and the Settled Land Act 1925 contained special powers to deal with them.[62] Examples are house keys,[63] title deeds, patents creating a peerage, an ancient tenure horn, and the Crown jewels.[64]

4. Fixtures

[2.22] Fixtures are objects which are physically removable without overwhelming damage to the fabric of the land, but they become part of the land by being affixed to it.[65] Identification becomes an issue when ownership of the land is divided between competing claimants, for example on sale, death of a landowner, a lender's sale, or under a lease. Whether an item remains a chattel is determined objectively from two factors:[66]

(1) the degree of annexation; and
(2) the object of annexation.

(1) Degree of annexation

[2.23] Objects firmly annexed to land are more likely to be fixtures than those lying on top of the land. The amount of damage required to remove an item tends to show the

[59] [2000] 1 WLR 1941, CA; D Gibbs [2001] *CLJ* 200; MP Thompson [2001] *Conv* 417; HW Wilkinson [2001] *NLJ* 419; *R(JR) Prankerd* v. *Carrick DC* [1999] QB 1119, Lightman J.
[60] *Cory* v. *Bristow* [1877] 2 AC 262, HL; *Forrest* v. *Greenwich Overseers* (1858) 8 E & B 890, 120 ER 332; *Westminster CC* v. *Woodbury* [1991] 2 EGLR 173, CA; *Stubbs* v. *Hartnell* (1977) 74 P & CR D36 (poll tax).
[61] Loom = tool or utensil; NM Dawson (2000) 51 *NILQ* 1.
[62] SLA 1925 s 67; *Re Beresford-Hope* [1917] 1 Ch 287, Eve J.
[63] *Moody* v. *Steggles* (1879) 12, Ch D 261.
[64] *Hill* v. *Hill* [1897] 1 QB 483, 494–496, Chitty LJ. Before 1926 some items (such as the best bed) could pass by special custom. Hence Shakespeare's gift of the second best bed to his wife.
[65] *Bradshaw* v. *Davey* [1952] 1 All ER 350 (rateable value includes fixtures).
[66] *Leigh* v. *Taylor* [1902] AC 157, 161, Halsbury LC (fact); *Berkley* v. *Poulett* [1977] 1 EGLR 86, 88K, Scarman LJ (fact); *Reynolds* v. *Ashby* [1904] AC 466 (law).

degree to which annexation has occurred.[67] If total destruction is involved, this must signal that the item forms an integral part of the land. But even looms nailed to the floor and easily removable are still fixtures.[68]

"Mere juxtaposition" does not usually make an object a fixture. Something lying on land under its own weight is not a fixture,[69] even if it is a printing machine weighing several tons,[70] a greenhouse[71] or free standing statue.[72] *Elitestone* v. *Morris*[73] shows that a chalet resting on land may form a part of it. So physical annexation is not decisive either way, but merely raises a presumption for or against the thing being a fixture, rebuttable either way. A simple act like nailing machines to wooden plugs in the floor to keep them steady during use[74] has shifted the presumption towards them being fixtures.

(2) Object of annexation

[2.24] Modern law treats this as the primary rule. A chattel is not a fixture if the object of attaching it was to improve its convenience of use as a chattel.[75] *Leigh* v. *Taylor*[76] involved a valuable tapestry displayed by its owner in the drawing room of Luton Hoo, which she occupied as tenant for life. Strips of wood were nailed to the walls, canvas stretched between them, and the tapestry was fastened to the canvas with tacks. The tapestry had not become a fixture. The court found it unnecessary to investigate the length of the screws![77] Other examples are oak panelling and a chimney piece,[78] picture frames screwed into recesses in the dining room panelling and a half-ton statue of a Greek athlete,[79] and cinema seats.[80] On the other hand, objects forming part of the overall architectural composition of the house are fixtures.[81]

No one can make a thing real or personal merely by wishing it so.[82] Sufficient fixing makes it a part of the land irrespective of intention. Contracts to retain ownership of fixtures are invalid. *Melluish* v. *BMS (No 3)*[83] concerned central heating equipment

---

[67] *Spyer* v. *Phillipson* [1931] 2 Ch 183, 209, 210, Romer LJ.

[68] *Holland* v. *Hodgson* (1872) LR 7 CP 328; *Boyd* v. *Sharrock* (1867) LR 5 Eq 72.

[69] *Bain* v. *Brand* (1876) 1 App Cas 762, HL; *Deen* v. *Andrews* [1986] 1 EGLR 262, 264G, Hirst J.

[70] *Hulme* v. *Brigham* [1943] KB 152. Movable parts follow the character of the machine: *Mather* v. *Fraser* (1856) 2 K & J 536, 69 ER 895.

[71] *HE Dibble* v. *Moore* [1970] 2 QB 181.

[72] *Berkley* v. *Poulett* [1977] 1 EGLR 86, CA.

[73] [1997] 1 WLR 687, HL; *Hamp* v. *Bygrave* [1983] 1 EGLR 174, 177A; *R(JR) Westminster CC* v. *SS for Environment T&R* [2001] EWHC 270, [2002] 1 P & CR 8, Jackson J.

[74] *Holland* v. *Hodgson* (1872) LR 7 CP 328. Blackburn J gives (at 335) the example of a ship's anchor which is obviously not a part of the sea bed.

[75] [1997] 1 WLR 687, 692C–693H, Lord Lloyd.

[76] [1902] AC 157, HL. In any event a tenant for life could remove objects of ornament; see below **[2.26]**.

[77] *Re De Falbe* (the same case in the CA), [1901] 1 Ch 523, 531, Rigby LJ.

[78] *Spyer* v. *Phillippon* [1931] 2 Ch 183.

[79] *Berkely* v. *Poulett* [1977] 1 EGLR 86, CA.

[80] *Vaudeville Electric Cinema* v. *Muriset* [1923] 2 Ch 74; *Lyon & Co* v. *London City & Midland Bank* [1903] 2 KB 135.

[81] *D'Eyncourt* v. *Gregory* (1866) LR 3 Eq 382 (Baroque fittings at Harlaxton, Lincolnshire); but see *Re De Falbe* [1901] 1 Ch 523, 531, 532.

[82] *Dixon* v. *Fisher* (1843) 5 D 775, 793, Lord Cockburn; *Elitestone* [1997] 1 WLR 687, 698H, Lord Clyde.

[83] [1996] AC 454, HL; *Aircool Installations* v. *British Telecommunications* [1995] CLYB 821; *Stokes* v. *Costain Property Investments* [1983] 1 WLR 907, Harman J. Tax rules have been tightened.

supplied to a local authority for installation in 180 of its houses, on terms which provided for ownership to be retained by the hiring company. Also in issue were plant for swimming pools, alarm systems for sheltered housing, lifts for car parks and cremators. The equipment belonged to the local authority for the duration of the time that it was annexed to the authority's land, that the only relevant intention was that deduced from the degree and purpose of annexation.[84]

5. Importance of deciding whether item is a fixture

[2.25] Disputes most often arise on *sale*. Fixtures pass on a conveyance or transfer,[85] and in equity under a contract, so the buyer is entitled to all fixtures attached to the land at the time of the contract for sale.[86] Conversely he is entitled to receive the land clear of rubbish.[87] Borderline questions often arise. Light fittings are fixtures, but not the bulbs.[88] A carpet may not be a fixture even if nailed down,[89] though the old reasoning that they are removed so often for cleaning may have been superseded in some households.[90] Doors and windows are clearly fixtures.[91] Greenhouses may count as fixtures if they are attached to a mortared foundation and walls,[92] but most are now free-standing.[93] Wooden or iron fences are fixtures, but not movable hurdles.[94] Problem cases are best avoided by agreement between buyer and seller about what is to be included. Particulars prepared by the seller's estate agent raise an estoppel[95] and a specific list is provided on a property information sheet compiled by the seller[96] It is permissible to exclude from the price on which stamp duty is paid fittings such as curtains and carpets which do not form part of the land.

A *mortgage* of land involves a division of ownership between the borrower and the lender who has rights in the property mortgaged until repayment of the loan. Fixtures form part of the mortgage security, and the borrower is not entitled to remove them.[97] The defendant in *Botham* v. *TSB Bank*[98] bought a flat in London as a shell for £130,000 and proceeded to furnish it lavishly at a total cost of £60,000. After repossession, the Court of Appeal allowed the lenders to keep the bathroom and kitchen

---

[84] At 473B, Lord Browne-Wilkinson; *Elitestone* [1997] 1 WLR 687, 690E, Lord Lloyd.

[85] LPA 1925 s 62.

[86] *Phillips* v. *Lamdin* [1949] 2 KB 33, 41 (Adam front door).

[87] *Hynes* v. *Vaughan* (1985) 50 P & CR 444; HW Wilkinson [1986] *Conv* 73.

[88] *Sewell* v. *Angerstein* (1868) 18 LT 300 (gasoliers); *British Economical Lamp Co* v. *Empire, Mile End* (1913) 29 TLR 386.

[89] *Hellawell* v. *Eastwood* (1851) 6 Exch 295, 155 ER 554.

[90] *Boyd* v. *Shorrock* (1867) LR 5 Eq 72.

[91] *Cooke's case* (1582) Moore KB 177, 72 ER 515; *Climie* v. *Wood* (1869) LR 4 Exch 328.

[92] *Jenkins* v. *Gething* (1862) 2 John & H 520, 70 ER 1165.

[93] *Deen* v. *Andrews* [1986] 1 EGLR 262; *HE Dibble* v. *Moore* [1970] 2 QB 181; PV Baker (1970) 86 *LQR* 19.

[94] *Re Maberley ex p Belcher* (1835) 4 Deac & Ch 703.

[95] *Hamp* v. *Bygrave* [1983] 1 EGLR 174, 177, Boreham J.

[96] JE Adams (1986) 136 *NLJ* 652.

[97] *Vaudeville Electric Cinema* v. *Muriset* [1923] 2 Ch 74; *Longbottom* v. *Berry* (1869) LR 5 QB 137. A secured lender prevails over a finance company with a hire purchase agreement: *Hobson* v. *Gorringe* [1897] 1 Ch 182; *Holland* v. *Hodgson* (1872) LR 7 CP 328; HN Bennett & CJ Davies (1994) 110 *LQR* 448.

[98] (1997) 73 P & CR D1, CA; *Smith* v. *Bridgend BC* [2001] UKHL 58, [2002] 1 AC 336 (floating charge included equitable title to coal washing plant).

units and recessed ceiling lights. Botham retained ownership of light fittings, carpets, curtains and blinds, gas fires and kitchen white goods.

Fixtures must be differentiated from moveable chattels on the *death* of a landowner who makes a will containing separate gifts of his land[99] and chattels.[100]

Between *landlord and tenant*, the tenant is entitled to fixtures during the term, but at the end of the lease they pass to the landlord.[101] Similar issues arise between a life tenant under a settlement and those entitled in remainder.[102] However, the law is heavily modified because limited owners may remove many fixtures at the end of the lease.

6.   Removable fixtures

[2.26] Three classes of fixture can be removed by tenants or beneficiaries, that is ornamental and domestic fixtures, trade fixtures, and agricultural fixtures. However, ownership of the chattel only passes to the tenant at the time of removal and until then it is part of the landlord's holding.[103]

Ornamental and domestic fixtures obviously belong to the tenant, whose short term interest in the land means that he does not decorate for the benefit of the landlord. Panelling was once an essential attribute of a fashionable house, but few tenants now install or remove panelling,[104] or move with chimney glasses, stoves, grates, and ranges. Items of decoration may not be fixtures at all, but if they are ones which the tenant for life could remove.[105]

Trade fixtures are those which the tenant himself has fixed to the premises for the purposes of his trade.[106] This ancient exception to encourage trade[107] was formalised by *Poole's case*,[108] which allowed a soap boiler to remove his vats and coppers. Examples from Her Majesty's Theatre, Haymarket, included seats bolted to the ground, brackets for wall lights, and electric transformers.[109] The same applies to fittings of a pub[110] and petrol pumps,[111] but not plant for the manufacture of sulphuric acid.[112]

---

[99] *Bain* v. *Brand* (1876) 1 App Cas 762, 767, Cairns LC.

[100] *Elwes* v. *Maw* (1802) 3 East 38, 102 ER 510 (first head); *Re Whaley* [1908] 1 Ch 615; *Re Lord Chesterfield's SEs* [1911] 1 Ch 237 (Grinling Gibbons carvings); *Leigh* v. *Taylor* [1902] AC 157, HL.

[101] *Never-Stop Rly (Wembley)* v. *British Empire Exhibition (1924)* [1926] Ch 857; *Webb* v. *Frank Bevis* [1940] 1 All ER 247, CA; *Elitestone* v. *Morris* [1997] 1 WLR 687, 694H–696C, Lord Clyde; P Sparkes *NLT*, 696–700.

[102] *Elwes* v. *Maw* (second and third heads); *Berkley* v. *Poulett* [1977] 1 EGLR 86, 88, Scarman LJ.

[103] *Melluish* v. *BMS (No 3)* [1996] AC 454, HL. Removal is not permitted after the tenant's lease has been terminated by a forfeiture by peaceable re-entry in a pizza bar: *Re Palmeiro* [1999] 3 EGLR 27, Ch D.

[104] *Spyer* v. *Phillipson* [1931] 2 Ch 183.

[105] *Re de Falbe* [1901] 1 Ch 523, CA; *Spyer* v. *Phillipson* [1931] 2 Ch 183, 205, Lord Hanworth MR (very substantial fixing).

[106] *New Zealand Government Property Corp* v. *HM & S* [1982] QB 1145, 1157A–B, Lord Denning MR.

[107] *Penton* v. *Robart* (1801) 2 East 88, 90, 102 ER 302, Kenyon CJ (glass houses).

[108] (1703) 1 Salk 368, 91 ER 320; *Mansfield* v. *Blackburne* (1840) 6 Bing NC 426, 133 ER 165.

[109] [1982] QB 1145, 1157A–B.

[110] *Elliott* v. *Bishop* (1845) 10 Exch 496, 156 ER 534.

[111] *Smith* v. *City Petroleum Co* [1940] 1 All ER 260.

[112] *Pole-Carew* v. *Western Counties & General Manure Co* [1920] 2 Ch 97.

Agricultural fixtures were not regarded as trade fixtures.[113] Statutory regimes have achieved justice for agricultural tenants[114] who attach fixtures to the holding or erect buildings.[115] Items which are not removable are replacements of landlord's fixtures and those the tenant has contracted to provide. A notice procedure applies when a tenancy ends, giving the landlord a right to require the tenant to leave a fixture, by offering its fair value in compensation.[116]

7. Exercise of right to remove

[2.27] A contractual right to remove chattels gives an equitable right of entry which binds a buyer,[117] except one without notice. Removal is bound to cause some damage, but there must be no material damage to freehold.[118] Any damage caused either by installation *or* by removal must be remedied.[119] Removal rights continue throughout the lease, during renewals,[120] and perhaps for a short period afterwards.[121] However, on a surrender it is wise to preserve the right of removal expressly.

G. THINGS FOUND

1. Treasure

[2.28] From Edward the Confessor's time, treasure from the earth has belonged automatically to the Crown.[122] Today, most finds are made by metal detectors. Finds of treasure must be reported[123] and handed over, though compensation is paid to the finder.[124] The old law of treasure trove was inadequate to safeguard antiquities[125] but the more expansive protection has been provided by the Treasure Act 1996[126] has led

---

[113] *Elwes* v. *Maw* (1802) 3 East 38, 102 ER 510 (animal house, carpenter's sheds, fuel shed, wagon-house, fold yard).

[114] Not tenants for life.

[115] Agricultural Tenancies Act 1995 s 8 (post-1995 tenancies); Agricultural Holdings Act 1986 s 10 (earlier tenancies). It extends to fixtures by predecessor tenants. The old Acts were subject to contracting out: *Premier Dairies* v. *Garlick* [1920] 2 Ch 17. Under the 1995 Act, this requires advance agreement and compensation will be payable.

[116] Agricultural Holdings Act 1986 s 10(4).

[117] *Re Morrison Jones & Taylor* [1914] 1 Ch 50, 58; *Poster* v. *Slough Estates* [1968] 1 WLR 1515, 1520G, 1521C; AG Guest & J Lever (1963) 27 *Conv (NS)* 30; *Bland* v. *Ingram's Estates Ltd (No 2)* [2001] EWCA Civ 1088, [2002] 1 All ER 264, [75–78] (Uddin knew of claim to relief from forfeiture by previous tenant and right to remove chattels).

[118] *Buckland* v. *Butterfield* (1820) 2 Brod & B 54, 129 ER 878 (conservatory); *Gibson* v. *Hammersmith & City Ry Co* (1863) 2 Drew & Sm 603, 62 ER 748, Kindersley V-C.

[119] *Mancetter Developments* v. *Garmenson* [1986] QB 1212, CA.

[120] *New Zealand Government Property Corp* v. *HM & S* [1981] 1 WLR 870, CA; (1982) 98 *LQR* 342; HW Wilkinson (1982) 132 *NLJ* 786; G Kodilinye [1987] *Conv* 253.

[121] *Penton* v. *Robart* (1801) 2 East 88, 102 ER 302; *Weeton* v. *Woodcock* (1840) 7 M & W 14, 151 ER 659 (rights lost on forfeiture).

[122] Or the Duchies of Cornwall or Lancaster; rights can now be franchised out: Treasure Act 1996 s 4.

[123] Within 14 days; coroners continue to resolve the status of finds: Treasure Act 1996 ss 7–9; Coroners Act 1988 s 30.

[124] Treasure Act 1996 ss 10–11; J Marston & L Ross [1998] *Conv* 252 (Code of Practice); Megarry & Wade (6th ed), [3.052].

[125] NE Palmer (1981) 44 *MLR* 178.

[126] Treasure Act 1996 ss 1–2; PH Kenny [1996] *Conv* 321; in force September 24th 1997, SI 1997/1977.

to a ten-fold increase in the reports of findings of archaeological artefacts. So successful has it been that the acquisition funds of museums are exhausted. Finds needing to be reported fall into five classes: (1) Objects 300 years old with at least 10% content of the precious metals gold and silver.[127] (2) Coins 300 years old found in a group of 10 or more irrespective of the metallic composition.[128] Under the old law, a hoard of Roman coins found with a metal detector at Coleby in Lincolnshire did not qualify as treasure trove because they were made of an alloy with a tiny percentage of silver.[129] These would now be treasure. (3) Prehistoric metal objects other than coins if they are of base metal but found in a group of more than one or if they are partly of gold or silver;[130] (4) Other objects 200 years old within classes designated as being of outstanding historical, archaeological or cultural importance.[131] (5) Treasure trove as anciently defined and so restricted to objects made from the two precious metals, gold and silver: treasure was "trove" if it was hidden (as an individual object or as a hoard) in a house or the earth or any private place, with an unknown owner,[132] and with the intention of recovery. This definition excludes things lost or abandoned.[133]

2. Finders

[2.29] "Finders Keepers" is a good starting point.[134] Discovery of an item and taking possession of it gives title against subsequent recipients. In *Amory* v. *Delamirie*[135] a chimney sweep had sufficient property in a jewel found in a chimney to sue a goldsmith with whom it had been lodged for valuation and who had decided to keep it. However, the finder's title is subordinate to the true owners,[136] unless he has abandoned ownership of the thing,[137] for example by throwing coins into a river. A finder must behave honestly by taking reasonable steps to trace the owner.[138] Employees usually have an obligation to hand over the things they find while working to their employers.[139]

The finder's title may be subordinate to that of the owner of the land on which the object is found. Here the critical issue is whether the thing is found "on" or "in" the land.[140]

---

[127] S 3(3).

[128] *Att-Gen for the Duchy of Lancaster* v. *GE Overton (Farms)* [1982] Ch 277; AA Preece [1981] *Conv* 385.

[129] CS Emsden (1926) 42 *LQR* 368; N Cookson [1991] *NLJ* 1255.

[130] SI 2002/2666.

[131] Treasure Act 1996 s 2(1); classes can also be excluded: s 1(2), 2(2).

[132] *Att-Gen* v. *Moore* [1893] 1 Ch 676, 683.

[133] Eg the Sutton Hoo treasure.

[134] Grays' *Elements* (3rd ed), 22–30; Smith's *Property Law* (4th ed), 56–63.

[135] (1722) 1 Str 505, 93 ER 664.

[136] *Amory* v. *Delamirie* (1772) 1 Str 505, 93 ER 664; *Waverley BC* v. *Fletcher* [1996] QB 334, 339G, Auld LJ.

[137] *Moorhouse* v. *Angus & Robertson* [1981] 1 NSWLR 700 (manuscript); R Hudson (1984) 100 *LQR* 110.

[138] *Parker* v. *British Airways Board* [1982] QB 1004, 1017, Donaldson LJ.

[139] *South Staffordshire Water Co* v. *Sharman* [1896] 2 QB 44, CA; *London Corp* v. *Appleyard* [1963] 2 All ER 834, McNair J; *Parker* [1982] QB 1004, 1013, 1017.

[140] *Parker* v. *British Airways Board* [1982] QB 1004, Donaldson LJ; *Waverley BC* v. *Fletcher* [1996] QB 334, 346B–C, Auld LJ.

(1) Things found on land

[2.30] An item which is lost usually rests on the surface of the land where it is dropped.[141] In *Bridges* v. *Hawkesworth*,[142] a bundle of banknotes was found by a customer in the public part of a shop, presumably having been dropped by a previous customer. Ownership belonged to the finder rather than the owner of the shop in which they were found, since they were not within the protection of the shop. *Parker* v. *British Airways Board*[143] concerned a gold bracelet found in an international departure lounge at Heathrow, operated by the Board as tenants. Parker, who found it, was entitled rather than the operators of the terminal building.

A landowner who asserts control of things found on land prevails over the finder. In *Parker* v. *British Airways Board* the Board did not assert control of the public areas of the terminal buildings at Heathrow Airport.[144] In *Bridges* v. *Hawkesworth* the shop owner did not control the part of the shop open to public access. Opinions differ about whether control would have existed if an item had been dropped behind the counter in the part of the shop to which only the shopkeeper had access.[145] Something more than occupation of the land is needed to manifest the necessary intention.[146] An object found by a person while trespassing belongs to the owner of the land on which he is trespassing, at least if an attempt is made to control trespass.[147]

(2) Things in (or attached to) land

[2.31] *Waverley BC* v. *Fletcher*[148] concerned a medieval gold brooch (perhaps the hat pin of Henry VIII himself) worth £35,000 found buried nine inches beneath a municipal park at Farnham. Mr Fletcher found it with his metal detector, but he was compelled to hand it over to the council, which owned the park where it was found.[149] Once a thing that had been lost was lodged *in* the land, removal necessarily involved interference with the land. Similarly in *Elwes* v. *Brigg Gas Co* a prehistoric boat discovered during work on the construction of a gasholder was held to belong to the freeholder as part of the soil.[150] Two rings found by workmen cleaning a pond on the orders of the landowner in *South Staffordshire Water Co* v. *Shearman*[151] were just on the "in" side of the line, and so belonged to the owner of the pond.[152] A landowner necessarily intends to exercise control over embedded items.[153]

---

[141] AL Goodhart (1927) 3 *CLJ* 195.

[142] (1851) 21 LJQB 75; *Parker* [1982] QB 1004, 1011–1012, Donaldson LJ; *South Staffs* [1896] 2 QB 44, 46–47, Lord Russell CJ; *Waverley BC* v. *Fletcher* [1996] QB 334, 341–342, Auld LJ.

[143] [1982] QB 1004, CA; A Tettenborn [1982] *CLJ* 242; D Hoath [1990] *Conv* 348.

[144] [1982] QB 1004, 1018–1019, Donaldson LJ.

[145] *Parker* [1982] QB 1004, 1014A, 1020F–H, 1021E.

[146] *South Staffs* [1896] 2 QB 44, 46–47, Lord Russell CJ; *Parker* [1982] 1 QB 1004, 1014B.

[147] *Hibbert* v. *McKiernan* [1948] 1 All ER 860 (picking up golf balls was theft); OR Marshall (1949) 2 *CLP* 68, 80–85.

[148] [1995] QB 334, CA; J Stevens [1996] *Conv* 216; C MacMillan (1995) 58 *MLR* 101.

[149] Permitted recreations did not include interference with the soil.

[150] (1886) 33 Ch D 562, Chitty J; *Fletcher* [1996] QB 334, 340C–341B, Auld LJ.

[151] [1896] 2 QB 44; [1996] QB 334, 341C, Auld LJ.

[152] *Att-Gen for the Duchy of Lancaster* v. *GE Overton (Farms)* [1982] Ch 277 (coins belonged to the owner of the farm in preference to the metal detector who found them).

[153] *Waverley BC* v. *Fletcher* [1996] QB 334, 341C–346A, Auld LJ; AL Goodhart (1929) 3 *CLJ* 195,

It is true that in *Hannah* v. *Peel*[154] a soldier who found a brooch in a crevice in the bedroom of a requisitioned house was entitled to keep it against the owner of the house who had never occupied it. The Crown was the occupier of land under requisition.[155]

(3) Which landowner?

[2.32] In reported disputes between tenant and freeholder, the freeholder has generally won, on the terms of the specific leases, taking for example a prehistoric boat[156] and a wall safe containing £5,728 in notes.[157]

(4) Things hidden

[2.33] The general principle arose for decision in unusual circumstances in *Moffatt* v. *Kazana*.[158] Three years after Kazana had bought a bungalow, some bricks were dislodged from the kitchen chimney, and the biscuit tin discovered was found to contain pound notes. The seller had died, but the evidence was that the seller had placed the biscuit tin there, for when his son-in-law had wanted to borrow, the seller had disappeared through a trap door into the loft and reappeared with money. It was held that the money belonged to the seller's estate. The true owner was able to assert title to chattels against the owner of the land on which they were lodged.

H. FLORA AND FAUNA

1. Plants

[2.34] Land includes trees, shrubs, hedges, plants and flowers, whether cultivated or wild.[159] Uprooting an entire plant will be protected by the law of theft,[160] though not wild mushrooms, flowers, fruit or foliage cut for non-commercial purposes.[161]

2. Animals

[2.35] Tame animals can be owned in the same way as any other item of personal property. For a car read a cat.[162] When a pet animal strays onto neighbouring land[163]

206–207; *City of London Corp* v. *Appleyard* [1963] 1 WLR 982, 987, McNair J; *Parker* v. *British Airways Board* [1982] QB 1004, 1010, Donaldson LJ.

[154] [1945] KB 509; DEW (1945) 9 *CLJ* 247.
[155] [1982] QB 1004, 1011B, Donaldson LJ.
[156] *Elwes* v. *Brigg Gas Co* (1886) 33, Ch D 562.
[157] *City of London Corp* v. *Appleyard* [1963] 1 WLR 982, McNair J; (1964) 80 *LQR* 151.
[158] [1969] 2 QB 152; *Re Cohen* [1953] Ch 88, Vaisey J (£6,000 found hidden in radio; passed to estate of deceased person who had hidden it); *Parker* [1982] QB 1004, 1011A, 1016H, Donaldson LJ.
[159] *Stukely* v. *Butler* (1615) Hob 168, 170, 80 ER 316; *Lilford's case* (1614) 11 Co Rep 46b, 77 ER 1206; *Monsanto* v. *Tilly* [2000] Env LR 313, 322, Stuart-Smith LJ.
[160] Wildlife and Countryside Act 1981 s 13(1), s 2(3); Criminal Damage Act 1971 s 10(1)(b).
[161] Theft Act 1968 s 4(3). Many wild species are now protected.
[162] *McQuaker* v. *Goddard* [1940] 1 KB 687, 696 (camel domestic); *Behrens* v. *Betram Mills Circus* [1957] 2 QB 1 (elephant wild); see Megarry & Wade (6th ed), [3.054].
[163] *Kearry* v. *Pattinson* [1939] 1 KB 471, CA (bees swarming).

it does not become the property of the landowner, and he cannot kill it,[164] though he might have an action in tort. Wild animals are different. Until captured or killed, no one owns them,[165] and they are free to fly or move to the neighbouring land. There is however a qualified property in wild animals on one's land, which gives the right to hunt them, the right to protect them against pollution,[166] and to prevent poaching.[167]

---

[164] *Hamps* v. *Darby* [1948] 2 KB 311, 318–322, Evershed LJ (doves away from the dovecote).
[165] *Case of Swans* (1592) 7 Co Rep 15b, 17b, 77 ER 435; *Kenny* v. *Pattinson* [1939] 1 KB 471; *Sutton* v. *Moody* (1679) 1 Ld Raym 250, 91 ER 1063; *Gott* v. *Measures* [1948] 1 KB 234, Div Ct. It is not theft to kill them: Theft Act 1968 s 4(4). There is no duty to control the burrowing of wild rabbits: *Hall* v. *Dart Valley Light Rly* [1998] CLYB 3933.
[166] *Nicholls* v. *Ely Beet Sugar Factory* [1936] Ch 343, CA.
[167] *Blades* v. *Higgs* (1865) 11 HLC 621, 11 ER 1474.

3

ESTATES

Slicing by time. Estates. The fee simple absolute in possession. Division by time in equity. Words of limitation. Transfer. Freedom of sale. Rentcharge conveyances. Undocumented shifting. The Crown. registration of Crown estate. Escheat to the Crown.

A. LOAVES AND FISHES

[3.01] What to do if you want to buy some bread? Naturally, you find a baker's and ask for what you want. If it is an unsliced loaf, then, after it has been paid for, the baker simply hands over the bread. It may have a piece of paper with which to handle it, but that is just for the sake of hygiene. An unfastidious buyer could pick up the loaf, put it in his bag, and walk out of the shop. How different things are with a sliced loaf. While unwrapped it would be impossible to handle, for it would fall open into its constituent slices. Wrapping is essential to make it saleable.

Consider how things were with land. Suppose that Fish has left his house to each of his children successively for life: it is to pass from A to B to C to D. How could you go about buying it? The only way would be collect together all of the different slices of benefit – to buy from A and from B, not forgetting C and D and, most importantly, not forgetting whoever is entitled in remainder after all the life interests have expired. Let us call our buyer Shark, a person quite unconnected with the Fishes. If he buys from A he will acquire an interest limited to the life of A:

to Shark for the life of A.

This interest *pur autre vie* (for the life of another) is not really a commerciable interest. It is difficult to value because it relies on the contingency of a life outside the family. What is needed is a wrapper, some means of allowing Shark to snap up outright ownership of the land while, at the same time, allowing Fish to splinter the ownership of his house between all the little Fishes. How to do this without making land unsaleable? Lord Birkenhead's legislation ensures that a person buying land gets a complete loaf – the land for ever – and is not concerned about whether there are slices within. What keeps it all together is the estate in fee simple absolute in possession or, more simply, the freehold estate in land. Reform of the doctrine of estates for unregistered land paved the way for the success of registration of title.

B. TIME

1. A fourth dimension

[3.02] If the physical extent of land can be visualised in three dimensions, there is also a fourth dimension of time.[1] The endurability of land has played strongly with those patriarchs who have exhibited a strong desire to found a dynasty by directing how their land is to pass after their death.[2] Land can be fragmented between future generations, a process less common today but which has played a key role in the development of the common law.

2. Estate ownership

[3.03] Section 1 makes no radical change to the conceptual structure of ownership which continues to be based on the medieval conceptions. An abstract entity called an estate is interposed between the physical land and the person who owns it.[3] An *estate* is simply a right to hold land for a particular duration of the time,[4] that is according to Pollock and Maitland's description it is "projected on the plane of time". Different durations or quantities define different estates.[5] As the Crown argued in *Walsingham's case*:[6]

> "[L]and itself is one thing and the estate in the land is another thing, for an estate in the land is a time in the land, or land for a time, and there are diversities of estates which are no more than diversities of time, for he who has a fee simple in the land has a time in the land without end, he who has land in tail has a time in the land for as long as he has issues of his body, and he who has an estate in land for life has no time in it longer than his own life, and so of which who has an estate in land for the life of another or for years."

If A holds land subject to a legal lease to B for 99 years, a civilian legal system has to identify A as owner and treat B as having a burden enforceable against A's ownership. A common lawyer can accommodate several ownership rights in the same land, giving to the freeholder and each leaseholder his own estate in the land. What Pollock & Maitland described as a "wonderful calculus of estates"[7] is a system of mathematical precision with which property concepts can be manipulated to secure precise results. Our mathematical language is now over-refined for the work left for it post-1925.

---

[1] *Newlon HT* v. *Alsulaimen* [1999] 1 AC 313, 317C, Lord Hoffmann; Grays' *Elements* (3rd ed), 62–77.

[2] PBH Birks "Before We Begin: Five Keys to Land Law" ch 18 in Bright & Dewar, 462.

[3] This is an off-shoot of the now defunct feudal system; see below [3.32].

[4] S Bright "Of Estates and Interests: A Tale of Ownership and Property Rights" ch 21 in Bright & Dewar; Chapelle's *LL* (5th ed) chs 1, 5, 6; Cheshire & Burn (16th ed), 25–37; Dixon's *Principles* (3rd ed) ch 1; Goo's *Sourcebook* (3rd ed) ch 1; Grays' *Elements* (3rd ed) ch 4; Maudsley & Burn *LL – Cases* (7th ed), 3–25; Megarry & Wade (6th ed), [4.030–4.038]; W Swadling "Property" ch 4 in Birks' *English Private Law*, [4.53–4.82]; Thompson's *Modern LL* ch 2.

[5] F Pollock & FW Maitland, *History of English Law* (Cambridge, 2nd ed, 1898) vol 2, 10.

[6] (1573) 2 Plowd 547, 555, 75 ER 805; *Fraser* v. *Canterbury Diocesan Board of Finance* [2001] Ch 669, [42], Mummery LJ.

[7] Pollock & Maitland as above, vol 2, 11; B Rudden [1980] *Conv* 325.

3. Fragmentation of ownership

[3.04] This book takes the view, espoused by Honoré that the theory of ownership through the vehicle of an estate gives no reason to abandon the terminology of ownership.[8]

4. New and old worlds

[3.05] A radical restructuring estates was made by the Law of Property Act 1925. If section 1 is in some senses parochial,[9] there is another level at which it is truly fundamental, the cause of a major rupture within the common law world.[10] Australia, Canada and the USA form an Old World where it remains possible to divide legal ownership between successive generations. The Brave New World consists of England and Wales.[11]

C. MODERN ESTATES

1. Legal estates

[3.06] A reduction in the number of legal estates permitted was made by the very first and central provision of the Law of Property Act 1925.[12] The reform had been proposed in the middle of the nineteenth century.[13] As from January 1st, 1926:

> "the only estates in land which are capable of subsisting or of being conveyed or created at law are –
> (a) an estate in fee simple absolute in possession;
> (b) a term of years absolute."

Section 1 identifies the main commercial interests in land, those which are bought and sold. Of these the indivisible freehold estate defined in paragraph (a) is the more fundamental ownership right. An estate in fee simple absolute in possession equal to absolute ownership when it is unencumbered by adverse interests.[14] Paragraph (b) describes the leasehold estate,[15] used for the ownership of flats, as well as rented accommodation, many offices and much farmland.

---

[8] AM Honoré "Ownership" ch 5 in AG Guest *Oxford Essays in Jurisprudence* (OUP, 1961), 144; see below **[4]**.

[9] B Rudden (1982) 2 *OJLS* 238, 239.

[10] Civil law applies on most of the continent of Europe. EU law does not impact on property law: Treaty of Rome article 295, ex article 222.

[11] P Sparkes *NLL* (1st ed) ch 2.

[12] S 1(1), re-enacting LPA 1922 s 1.

[13] WS Holdsworth (1926) 42 *LQR* 158, 173.

[14] AM Honoré "Ownership" ch 5 in AG Guest *Oxford Essays in Jurisprudence* (OUP, 1961), 124; see below **[4.03]**.

[15] See below **[25]**.

2. Registered estates requiring substantive registration

[3.07] Reform of the system of estates was stimulated by the needs of land registration. Clearly a register would be of limited value if the interest shown on it is liable to terminate at some uncertain time, particularly if the register gives no warning of this fact. Registered freehold estates must be perpetual so that it is safe to rely on the official record. If, say, A is entitled for life to be followed by B, who should be registered? Registration of A would make it impossible to buy the land on the strength of the register, because you might buy an interest limited to A's life. If B was entered, it would mean that the registered proprietor was not necessarily entitled to sell the land with the right to immediate possession.[16] Early registration schemes did not work precisely because they operated against a backcloth of family ownership.[17] Far better was the Birkenhead solution. Land is vested in some person who holds a perpetual freehold estate, and registration occurs in that name.

What estates may be registered mirror the legal estates for unregistered land, that is:

the freehold estate; and
long leasehold estates – legal leases created by deed with more than seven years unexpired when registration is required.

Short leases are excluded from the register because it is not sensible to go through expensive registration routines for transitory interests and these are either noted against the register or allowed to override it.[18]

The freehold is clearly the more fundamental ownership right. A registered estate will not end suddenly when the present proprietor dies or when he marries or reaches 30 years of age. There should be no hidden surprises. Very exceptionally,[19] an unregistered estate may terminate, and if so a registered estate will also terminate. The two systems mesh and mirror each other. Section 1 created an estate which was suitable for entry on a register, and also lessened the need for registration since in some senses a fee simple absolute in possession is "registration without a register."[20] On first registration, the existing estate is vested in the proprietor and continues unaffected by its reincarnation.[21]

3. Commonhold estates

[3.08] The Commonhold and Leasehold Reform Act 2002 has created a new way of holding land, the commonhold, which can be expected to predominate in new blocks of flats. Commonholds can only be created if title is registered. Each flat will consti-

---

[16] Land Registry Act 1862 s 4 required all legal owners to consent to registration; Land Transfer Act 1875 s 5 only allowed registration of a person with the fee simple but SLA 1882 made it probable that there would be some registrable person.

[17] S Anderson, "The 1925 Property Legislation: Setting Contexts" ch 4 in Bright & Dewar, 117.

[18] LRA 2002 ss 3, 4, 27, sch 2. This is a reduction by from the previous period of 21 years: LRA 1925 s 2; see below **[25.43]**.

[19] See below **[3.30]**.

[20] S Anderson, *Lawyers and the Making of English Land Law 1832–1940* (Clarendon Press, 1992), 250, quoting Brickdale.

[21] See below **[11.06]**.

tute one commonhold unit, in which the owner will hold a form of freehold estate, and also a share of the common parts of the block and its grounds. Although the ownership interests in individual flats will end, for example if the block burns down, nevertheless, despite this potential for termination, the commonhold estate in each flat will be legal.[22]

D. THE FEE SIMPLE ABSOLUTE IN POSSESSION

[3.09] Like a diamond, a freehold estate[23] is for ever. If "for ever" is a difficult concept to grasp in an ever changing world such as the coastline of the Cote d'Azur[24] it is simplicity itself in land law. In chronological order, the component parts of the definition of the estate are the right in possession to a fee simple which is absolute.[25] "In fee simple absolute in possession" is synonymous with "in perpetuity" or "for ever". It has been possible to create such an interest in land for many centuries, but section 1(1) of the Law of Property Act 1925 prohibits any legal division of the freehold and so ensures the existence of such an ownership interest in every piece of land,[26] and the existence of an estate suitable for registration.

1. In possession

[3.10] Legal status is restricted to a fee simple which is in possession, the right to the land accruing now.[27] This is in contrast to a future fee where, for example, a beneficiary is to take the land only when he attains 30. Possession is not necessarily related to physical occupation. A freehold estate remains in possession for the duration of a lease, giving a right to the receipt of rents and profits for the duration of the lease and a right to physical occupation on termination of the lease, the freehold and leasehold estates running side by side.[28]

2. A fee simple

[3.11] Section 1(1) plucks out for stardom just one of the pre-1926 cast of freehold estates. If all estates in land were interests in land of defined duration, the term freehold was reserved for uncertain periods of time based on numbers of lives.[29] Different groups of lives marked out different estates. A life estate was self-explanatory. Fees, by way of contrast, were estates which survived death and so could be inherited. A fee

---

[22] See below **[4.19]**, **[4.30]**.
[23] Cheshire & Burn (16th ed) ch 8; Grays' *Elements* (3rd ed), 66–67; Megarry & Wade (6th ed), **[4.039–4.044]**; Smith's *Property Law* (4th ed), 35–43.
[24] JG Ballard, *Super Cannes* (Flamingo, 2001) ch 16.
[25] LPA 1925 s 1(1)(a).
[26] Several competing fees simple may arise by adverse possession; see below **[10.28]**.
[27] Derived from seisin, the possession of a freeholder: Megarry & Wade (6th ed), **[3.018–3.0121]**.
[28] LPA 1925 s 205(1)(xix); *Re Morgan* (1883) 24 Ch D 114, 116, North J; *Wakefield & Barnsley Union Bank* v. *Yates* [1916] 1 Ch 452, 460, Warrington LJ; *District Bank* v. *Webb* [1958] 1 WLR 148, 150, Danckwerts J; *Pearson* v. *IRC* [1981] AC 753, 772D, Viscount Dilhorne.
[29] In contrast to leaseholds which are fixed periods of years.

simple is a "time without end".[30] Historically it was an estate which passed to any heir of the current tenant – including direct descendants and those taking through collateral lines, such as brothers and sisters.[31] This last point marked out the wider scope of the fee simple as compared to the more limited devolution of the fee tail which could pass only to direct descendants. Changes to the law of succession have reduced all this to the realm of historical explanation, since a modern fee simple never passes to an heir.

3. Absolute

[3.12] Any fee simple is potentially perpetual, but modern legal freeholds must be actually perpetual, the distinction being that an absolute fee is never liable to be cut short in the future. Fees which are terminable are called modified fees and must now be equitable interests.[32] An absolute fee (which is potentially legal) must be undivided, forming one estate which will continue for ever, so that a person buying the land can deal with the estate owner knowing that ownership has not and will not switch to someone else. Modified fees are divided, for if the terminating event occurs estate ownership passes without any document, the possibility of termination raising doubts about whether it is safe to buy the land. Legal ownership is limited to absolute ownership of an indivisible estate.

E. DIVISION BY TIME IN EQUITY

1. Law and equity

[3.13] Modern English land law is an amalgam of the common law and equity. The common law developed the system of legal estate ownership. Equity, which was originally administered in the Court of Chancery, developed a set of equitable interests in land, particularly beneficial interests under trusts. Fusion of the administration of the two sets of courts in 1875 did not alter the basic schema of two parallel sets of interests.[33] In particular the trust continued as before – legal title in the trustees separated from equitable entitlement in the beneficiaries.

A trust divides legal ownership of the property held by the trustee from the equitable or beneficial ownership, apportioning the totality of ownership between the trustees and the beneficiaries. Trusteeship implies management rights over and control of the trust property consisting, after 1996, of all the powers of an absolute owner,[34] but also duties to act in the interests of the beneficiaries. They, the beneficiaries, have the equitable entitlement to the land, representing the right to enjoyment of the property, the right to occupy it[35] or to receive the income from it.

---

[30] *Walsingham's case* (1573) 2 Plowd 547, 555, 75 ER 805; *Fraser* v. *Canterbury Diocesan Board of Finance* [2001] Ch 669, [42], Mummery LJ.

[31] *Quia Emptores* 1290 refers to *in feodo simpliciter*: A Underhill (1911) 27 *LQR* 173, 179n.

[32] LPA 1925 s 1(3).

[33] See below [12.02].

[34] TLATA 1996 s 6(1), unless excluded under s 8.

[35] Ss 12, 13.

2. Settlements under the 1925 legislation

[3.14] Section 1 of the Law of Property Act 1925 is based on the fundamental premise that legal division of ownership by lives should be prohibited. To take the simplest case:

to B1 for life, remainder to B2 absolutely.

A split in the legal title of this form complicated the sale of the land. Our law achieves saleability by ensuring that any division occurs only in equity. The freehold estate must be vested in trustees, the continuing legal estate being distinct from the equitable interests divided by time. Thus the division above can be achieved quite legitimately under section 1 of the Law of Property Act 1925 in this way:

to T1 and T2 in fee simple on trust for B1 for life, remainder to B2 absolutely.

Where beneficial entitlement is split by time in this way, there is said to be a settlement.[36]

The joint interest of T1 and T2 is legal and perpetual, in contrast to the equitable interests held by B1 and B2. The trustees hold management power whereas the equitable interests represent beneficial enjoyment. These do not prevent sale by the trustees, quite the reverse, sale is facilitated by section 2 of the Law of Property Act 1925 which confers on the trustees the power of overreaching – the ability to sell the land and to convert the beneficial interests into interests in the proceeds of sale.[37] The implications of the legislation were so serious that Oxford University was compelled to start teaching equity.[38]

Reallocation of the prohibited legal estates to equity is coupled with a change of terminology: the word "estate" is reserved for legal rights whereas equitable rights are "interests" – life interests, entailed interests (shortened to entails), future interests and so on.[39]

3. Beneficial co-ownership

[3.15] Some 40% of people live alone – the young, the old, the sad, and the ultra-hip – but this still leaves a majority who choose to share a home with a partner. Men and women expect equal treatment, so these homes are co-owned. Our law is based on a radical change made in 1925, quite parochial, and still controversial. Whenever land is held by two or more people concurrently there must be a trust.[40]

The legal estate must be held in a joint tenancy so that, if one of the legal owners dies, title passes to the survivor. Both traditional forms of co-ownership – joint tenancy and tenancy in common – are allowed to continue but only as beneficial interests

---

[36] Contrast a strict settlement, a variant with a special conveyancing machinery under the SLA 1925; see below **[14.10ff]**.

[37] See below **[13]**.

[38] WM Geldart (1923) 39 *LQR* 286, 292.

[39] Dixon's *Principles* (3rd ed) ch 5; Grays' *Elements* (3rd ed), 630ff; Megarry & Wade (6th ed), [3.022–3.032]; Panesar's *General Principles* ch 7; Thompson's *Modern LL* ch 8.

[40] See below **[12]**, **[16]**.

behind a trust. A joint tenancy passes automatically to the survivor on death – the arrangement for example that a happy couple would want. A tenancy in common creates shares in the property – equal or unequal – and that share survives the death of the tenant in common. This is the sort of arrangement by which the partners in a firm of solicitors might hold their business offices, and how a family home might be held after the couple's separation. Thus:

> *to A and B as joint tenants on trust for A and B as beneficial joint tenants;*
> *to T1 and T2 as joint tenants on trust for A and B as beneficial tenants in common.*

The trust imposed in the first case seems bizarre but it does secure saleability, at a price of increased and unnecessary complexity.

4.   Trusts of land

[3.16] Trusts of land were introduced in 1996[41] to replace the trust for sale favoured by the Law of Property Act 1925. The object is simply to make sure that there is a machinery in place which will enable the sale of land held in any trust, perhaps a settlement, a beneficial co-ownership, or a trust used for management of a minority or a deceased's estate. The rearrangement of interests by section 1 depends for its success upon the existence of a mechanism to allow the trustees to sell the trust property free of the beneficiaries, the "overreaching" machinery of section 2 which provides for equitable interests to be detached from the land and converted into a corresponding interest in the proceeds of sale.

F.   IDENTIFICATION OF THE ESTATE

1.   Words of limitation for unregistered land

[3.17] Unregistered conveyancing requires rules to determine which estate or beneficial interest is created in any particular case[42] – whether it is the fee simple, a term of years absolute,[43] an entail or a life interest. Words of *limitation* define the estate to be created, whereas words of *purchase* define the people who are to take the estate. In a gift *to A and his son for their joint lives*, the grantees of the estate are A and his son jointly for these are words of purchase, whereas "for life" are words of limitation defining the estate to be taken.

2.   The fee simple

[3.18] Words of limitation for an unregistered freehold estate are the words "in fee simple."[44] It is a sufficient commentary on the old common law of estates that a con-

---

[41] See below **[13]**.

[42] Cheshire & Burn (16th ed), 168–171; Megarry & Wade (6th ed), [3.022–3.032].

[43] Leasehold estates are created by any words indicating a maximum period of years for which the lease can endure.

[44] LPA 1925 s 60(4); Conveyancing Act 1881 s 51; as from 1882.

veyance to A "in fee simple" did not in fact create a fee simple estate, since until 1882 it was essential to use the time-honoured phrase "and his heirs".[45] Since 1925, it has not been necessary to include any words of limitation in order to create a fee simple. "*To A*" suffices. Section 60(1) of the Law of Property Act 1925 provides that:[46]

> "A conveyance of freehold land to any person without words of limitation . . . shall pass to the grantee the fee simple or other the whole interest which the grantor had power to convey in such land, *unless a contrary intention appears in the conveyance.*"

It is still proper and invariable practice, to avoid the risk of a contrary indication, to add *in fee simple*.[47] Essentially the same rules operate where a fee simple is created by will, the only difference being that the utility of the modern words of limitation was established earlier in 1837.[48]

3. Corporations sole

[3.19] A corporation is a separate legal person, created by Act of Parliament or royal charter, which is capable of owning land. Limited companies and other bodies corporate are made up of a number of individuals, for example shareholders. A corporation sole consists of a single individual, often an ecclesiastical office holder such as a bishop, a rector, or a vicar, and also the Public Trustee. Corporate capacity is perpetual and separate from the personal capacity of the individual currently holding the office. How is one to give land to the church? And how is a bishop to buy his own private house? In the past, *and his successors* indicated church land passing to successive bishops, whereas a conveyance to a bishop *and his heirs* indicated private ownership. The abolition of heirs has led modern law to provide for acquisition of land in the corporate capacity by use of corporate designation without any need for the word "successors", unless a contrary intention appears in the conveyance.[49] An ambiguity arises with gifts such as *to Alfred, Bishop of Wight, in fee simple*, perhaps best seen as a gift to Alfred personally, the reference to his position as Bishop being a description rather than a primary inclusion of the corporate designation.[50]

4. Lesser interests

[3.20] Life interests and entails are now equitable and the words of limitation used to create them are considered in the context of beneficial interests under trusts of land.[51]

---

[45] Query whether this should be effective after 1925 since the fee simple now always passes to personal representatives and never to an heir.

[46] A new provision in 1925 which solves the problem of aberrant formulae such as "in simple fee": A Underhill (1911) 27 *LQR* 173, 179.

[47] *AJ Dunning (Shopfitters)* v. *Sykes & Sons (Poole)* [1987] Ch 287, 302C, Dillon LJ.

[48] Wills Act 1837 s 28.

[49] LPA 1925 s 60(2); ie *to the Bishop of Wight*.

[50] Megarry & Wade (6th ed), [3–029].

[51] See below **[18]**.

5.   Redundancy of words of limitation after registration of title

[3.21] A positive advantage of the registered system is the ease of identification of the estate being dealt with. The property register states whether land is freehold or lease-hold. A transfer merely passes whatever title is identified by the title number from one proprietor to the next, and it is never necessary to include words of limitation to define the estate being dealt with[52] and these are omitted from the prescribed forms.[53] Leases, mortgages, grants of easements and other derivative transactions use distinctive prescribed forms[54] which speak for themselves.

G. TRANSFER OF THE FREEHOLD ESTATE

[3.22] Today's legal freehold estate[55] is best described in terms of how it reacts to the various operations performed on it – sale, gift, inferior transactions and the transmissions which occur on death or bankruptcy.

1.   Sale by substitution

[3.23] Ownership of property carries with it the right to realise the property by turning it into cash, most obviously by sale of the freehold estate to a buyer. So the current owner is allowed to transfer the whole of his ownership right to another person who becomes owner for the future. This is a given for any capitalist system of property law.

Historically the right of sale had to be wrested from the Crown. The fee simple began as a feudal grant by a lord to a vassal (A) on the terms that when A died the land passed automatically to his eldest son as heir.[56] The son's potential right prevented sale by A. However, the heir could be disinherited by *subinfeudation*, that is by making a new feudal grant of the land to B and his heirs in turn. This logic was broken by the statute *Quia Emptores* 1290,[57] which prohibited subinfeudation but instead permitted unhindered sale by *substitution*. This means that the existing estate is transferred. If A sells to B, B's family become notionally entitled to the land in place of A's, though their entitlement is only notional because B may in turn sell the land before he dies or make a will leaving nothing for his family to take. Sale by substitution occurs today whenever freehold land is transferred. Thus:

---

[52] *AJ Dunning (Shopfitters)* v. *Sykes & Son (Poole)* [1987] Ch 287, 302E, Dillon LJ.
[53] Eg a transfer required LR Form TR1.
[54] DLRR 2003 sch 1.
[55] Much of what is said also applies to leasehold estates.
[56] *To A and his heirs*; see above [3.18].
[57] Statute of Westminster III, 18 Edw I (1290) ch II; later extended to tenants in chief: 1 Edw 3 (1327) st 2 chs 12–13; 34 Edw 3 (1360) ch 5; Megarry & Wade (6th ed), [2.040–2.043].

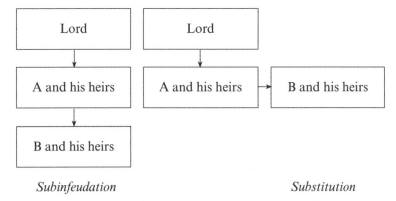

Subinfeudation   *Substitution*

Figure 3-1 Subinfeudation and substitution

[3.24] *Quia Emptores* was not consolidated in 1925 and remains one of the oldest extant property law statutes,[58] operating whenever freehold land is sold to divert the freehold estate from seller to buyer. In practice the feudal tenure has been emasculated and has disappeared from view, and the link between freehold land and the heir was broken in 1925, leaving a perpetual fee simple. Thus in practice:

Figure 3-2 Sale by substitution

Even a transfer of registered land is technically a feudal substitution. Any sale now requires completion by registration of the buyer's title.

As explained elsewhere[59] *Quia Emptores* also guarantees the saleability of freehold land by invalidating restrictions on sale.

2.   Other substitutions

[3.25] Any transfer of a freehold estate effects a substitution, for example where a gift is made.[60] When a freehold estate owner dies,[61] the estate will not end, but rather it will devolve on his personal representatives. Estate owners can choose how their land is to pass after their death by making a gift of the land by will, or otherwise they can leave beneficial entitlement to be determined by the intestacy rules. If the estate owner

---

[58] WS Holdsworth (1926) 42 *LQR* 158; it is beaten by *De Donis Conditionalibus* 13 Edw I (1285) ch 1.
[59] See below **[3.26]**.
[60] An important element of a gift is the donee's consent: J Hill (2001) 117 *LQR* 127; W Swadling "Property" ch 4 in Birks' *English Private Law*, [4.379–4.398].
[61] See below **[14.23]**.

becomes bankrupt the estate will transfer to his trustee in bankruptcy.[62] In a few anomalous and now rare cases these devolutions may cause the estate to end and the land to escheat to the Crown.[63]

H. FREEDOM OF SALE

[3.26] Where possible the policy of the law is to prefer alienability to inalienability.[64]

1. Preservation of transactional power

[3.27] Quia Emptores 1290[65] established the right of free sale of land, which we take for granted today and by implication also invalidates conditions which prevent or restrict dispositions. In *Merttens* v. *Hill*[66] there was a custom in the manor of Rothley, Leicestershire, by which the Lord of the Manor exacted a fine on any sale to a foreigner (meaning any person from outside the village). The fine was fixed at one shilling for each pound of the price (5%), a sum was so large that it could not have been in existence in 1189, the notional legal origin of customs. Hence, the Lord of the Manor was asserting a right to restrict any sale, in contravention of *Quia Emptores*,[67] a condition which the court held to be repugnant[68] to the freehold interest and so void. A landlord has a genuine interest in the financial health of his tenant, so the law has always allowed restrictions to be put on the sale and dealings with a lease.[69]

Land is given to the National Trust on the basis that it will be inalienable, though this restriction can be overcome by a court order authorising a lease.[70]

2. Conditions attached to gifts

[3.28] The common law regarded all attempts to restrict sale with extreme disfavour,[71] but the case-law on conditions in wills reveals a lack of consistency. A condition which completely excludes any power of disposition is void[72] – for example to let at a fixed rent, to cultivate in certain manner, or not to mortgage[73] – whether disposition is prevented for ever or for life.[74] Nor can the right to sell be restricted to

---

[62] See below [28.46].

[63] See below [3.60].

[64] *Bettison* v. *Langton* [2000] Ch 54, 71H, Robert Walker LJ.

[65] See above [3.23].

[66] [1901] 1 Ch 842, Cozens-Hardy J.

[67] Fines on alienation of land held directly of the Crown were abolished in 1660 and on copyhold land in 1925.

[68] It would be better to say that it infringed the rule of public policy which allows free sale: GL Williams (1943) 59 *LQR* 343.

[69] See below [27.05ff].

[70] National Trust Act 1907 s 21; *Wentworth* v. *National Trust* [1985] Conv 134.

[71] *Re Ashforth* [1905] 1 Ch 535, 542, Farwell J.

[72] *Re Dugdale* (1888) 38 Ch D. 176; *Bradley* v. *Peixoto* (1797) 3 Ves 324, 30 ER 1034.

[73] *Corbett* v. *Corbett* (1888) 14 PD 7, CA; *Ware* v. *Cann* (1830) 16 B & C 433, 109 ER 511.

[74] *Re Rosher* (1884) 26 Ch D 801 (son not to sell during widow's lifetime); *Re Dugdale* (1888) 38 Ch D 176, Kay J.

a particular class of buyers. In *Re Brown*[75] a father left property after the death of his widow, to their four sons (when all were adult) in equal shares, subject to a condition which forfeited the share of any son who tried to sell other than to one of his brothers. The permitted class of buyers was small and diminishing, and so the condition restricting sale was held to be void.

Illogically, partial restraints are sometimes valid,[76] provided they avoid being racially or sexually discriminatory.[77] Thus a covenant preventing sale to a specified person is valid, as is a restriction on sale to a particular class. In *Re Macleay*,[78] a devise "to my brother John on condition that he never sells out of the family" was accepted, since forms of disposition other than sale were possible and the family was reasonably large. Though this case has been subject to strong criticism,[79] it was accepted as a definitive statement of the law in *Re Brown*.[80]

A person seeking to impose a condition on the sale of land is likely to use a trust. The law of settlements displays a deep schizophrenia about the extent to which sale can be restrained. Its historical function of preventing the sale of land has been replaced by a modern attitude favouring sale, though it is not carried through with absolute consistency.[81]

I. RENTCHARGE CONVEYANCES

[3.29] Rent represents payment by time for the use of the land. A rent is usually a rent-service payable to a landlord under a lease, but when it is reserved out of freehold land it is called a rentcharge.[82] In the past, before the ready availability of building society mortgage finance, legal rentcharges were used to facilitate the purchase of freehold land. This form of tenure was concentrated in South Wales and Manchester. A house would be sold by a builder freehold, taking some of the purchase price as a capital sum at the time of sale, but also reserving a rentcharge in perpetuity.

Creation of new legal rentcharges as a source of profit was prohibited by the Rentcharges Act 1977.[83] Pre-existing rentcharges may continue until most are extinguished 60 years after the passing of the Rentcharges Act 1977,[84] though many are redeemed either by agreement or under compulsory provisions.[85] The 1977 Act was intended to remove an obsolete form of tenure, but it has in fact led to explosion in the use of "estate rentcharges", a safe and sure way to impose the cost of repairs on

---

[75] [1954] Ch 39, Harman J; *Caldy Manor Estate* v. *Farrell* [1974] 1 WLR 1303.
[76] Authorities are summarised in *Re Brown* [1954] Ch 39, Harman J.
[77] Race Relations Act 1976 s 21; Sex Discrimination Act 1975 s 30.
[78] (1875) LR 20 Eq 186; *Attwater* v. *Attwater* (1853) 18 Beav 330, 52 ER 131, distinguished.
[79] Doubted in *Re Rosher* (1884) 26 Ch D 801, 814–821, Pearson J; E Jenks (1917) 33 *LQR* 11.
[80] [1954] Ch 39, 47–48, Harman J.
[81] See below **[14.10ff]**.
[82] Rentcharges Act 1977 s 1 defines a rentcharge as any annual or other periodic sum charged on or issuing out of land except (a) rent reserved by a lease or tenancy or (b) interest payments.
[83] S 2(1)(2), in force August 22nd 1977; see below **[3.29ff]**.
[84] S 3(1); the 60 year period runs from July 22nd 1977 or the date when rentcharge is first payable if later.
[85] Ss 8–10.

landowners.[86] Family rentcharges designed to provide an income to a family member for life can still be created under a trust.[87]

Rentcharges are invariably paid if the rent owner presses for payment, since a Victorian rent of £10 a year is a minor irritant to the owner of a house now worth perhaps £100,000. In reality the rent owner's interest in the house is trivial, but in theory he enjoys a number of remedies over the land,[88] including the right to re-enter the land and terminate the fee simple estate of the estate owner in the event of non-payment. In theory there are two fee simple estates in the land, one for the owner while the rent is paid and the other for the rent owner if it falls into arrears for 21 days (or whatever).[89] A buyer of the land must obtain a receipt for previous rentcharge payments,[90] and protect his position for the future by paying the rentcharge promptly or by redeeming it.

The 1925 legislation created an unforeseen difficulty since, under the original drafting, a fee simple subject to a rentcharge was not absolute (perpetual) and so it ceased to be legal. Many people who thought they owned their homes found themselves restricted to an equitable interest. Popular agitation in the areas of the country most affected led to an amendment in 1926, an amendment that was successful if in elliptical terms:

"A fee simple subject to a legal or equitable right of entry or re-entry is, for the purposes of this Act, a fee simple absolute."[91]

When categorising a fee simple subject to a rentcharge, the fee simple now has legal status.[92]

It is arguable[93] that this late amendment may inadvertently have let back all in other conditional fees simple. Consider:

A to B in fee simple on condition that St Paul's Cathedral does not fall down, in which event A may re-enter the land and terminate B's interest.

The condition operates through the mechanism of a right to take back the land when the condition is broken, an equitable right of re-entry.[94] B's fee simple appears to fall fairly and squarely within the saving in section 7(1), is deemed to be a fee simple absolute, and so is legal. This remains a hypothesis rather than an established state-

---

[86] S Bright [1988] *Conv* 99; see below [32.53].

[87] Rentcharges Act 1977 s 2(3) also excepts statutory charges to pay for works and rentcharges created by court order.

[88] LPA 1925 s 121; hence the rentcharge is an interest in land, rather than a contractual debt.

[89] The rentcharge is saleable; it qualifies as "land" though it is of course an intangible right in land; hence a rentcharge can issue out of a rentcharge: LPA 1925 s 122.

[90] A clear receipt for the last instalment is conclusive that there were no arrears.

[91] LPA 1925 s 7(1); LP (Amendment) A 1926 s 7, sch ; *Re Rowhook Mission Hall* [1985] Ch 62, 79D, Nourse J.

[92] If the rentcharge is legal, so is the right of entry; similarly an equitable rentcharge is matched by an equitable right of entry: LPA 1925 s 1(2)(e).

[93] Megarry & Wade (6th ed), [4.041].

[94] It is outside LPA 1925 s 1(2)(e).

ment of law but, if true, it was an unintended effect of the 1926 amendment,[95] and one greatly destructive of the conceptual purity of the 1925 legislation.

The whole problem would be best solved by substituting a power to sell the land to recover arrears of rentcharge in place of the right of re-entry – to treat a rentcharge like a mortgage – since if surplus proceeds had to be handed back to the landowner, the "unjust" enrichment of a rentcharge owner which occurs after a successful re-entry would be removed.

J.   UNDOCUMENTED SHIFTING OF LEGAL ESTATES

1.   Termination of the freehold

[3.30] A freehold estate can end in two ways. Escheat occurs when the duration for which the land has been granted by the Crown expires and, so[96] the land passes up the feudal chain and back to the Crown. Shifting occurs when the legal estate in land[97] passes from citizen Smith to citizen Jones, on the occurrence of an event which causes the land to pass without any document to mark the change of ownership. Only a few exceptional cases of legal shifting are left post-1925, that is:

1. Land held subject to a rentcharge after re-entry by the rent-owner on account of non-payment and, possibly, a fee simple held subject to any other condition after re-entry for breach;[98]
2. Reverter of school sites where the school closed before 1987 and of other determinable fees simple in cases outside the Reverter of Sites Act 1987 where reverted can still occur at law, for example where a public highway is closed.[99]

There is a similar problem, though less severe, when a single freehold estate continues but it is moved in an undocumented owner from one owner to another – most notably where a freehold is not sent in for first registration within the two months allowed.[100]

2.   Determination of registered estates

[3.31] The cases of shifting just described are a particularly serious menace when title is registered, because the register suggests that Smith is proprietor when actually the land has shifted off the register to Jones. If a registered estate is both determinable *and* determined this fact must be entered in the register. The title will have to be closed and a new one opened.[101]

---

[95] A trust of land may arise because the land is held in trust for the person entitled after the condition is broken; but a right of re-entry is a burden rather than a trust-based equitable interest: TLATA 1996 sch 3 amends SLA 1925 s 1(1)(ii)(c) (determinable fees) not (b) (conditional).

[96] See below **[3.43]**.

[97] There is no problem when equitable entitlement passes; the legal estate in the trustees is unaffected and the only difficulty is for the trustees to ensure that they pay the proceeds to the correct beneficiary.

[98] See above **[3.29]**.

[99] See below **[14.28]**.

[100] See below **[9.27]**.

[101] LRA 2002 s 64; Law Com 271 (2001), [9.34–9.35]; DLRR 2003 r 79.

K. THE CROWN

1. Feudal grants

[3.32] When Charlemagne dominated most of Western Europe around the year 800, it just so happened that he chose to organise his empire by means of a feudal system. It became common to most of Europe. And, so it happened that when England fell to a single invader in 1066, William introduced his familiar Norman system of social organisation, showing the character that made him a Conqueror by imposing it with a rigour quite unknown elsewhere.[102] All land was held of the King. "Allodial" land outside the system was not permitted.[103] Feudal landholding was based on a grant of land by the lord to a vassal[104] in return for the provision of services. Thus:

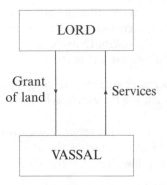

Figure 3-3 Feudal tenure

Feudal society was highly undemocratic, since power was concentrated in the hands of the King and a small group of powerful nobles while the vast majority of the population were condemned to a form of serfdom similar in its essentials to slavery. At some time between 1066 and the twenty-first century, all European countries have neutered or destroyed that system of land holding. In England the final break occurred in 1660, long after it had become obsolescent, when Charles II was restored to the throne. The Channel Island of Sark remains a pure fief ruled over by a feudal seigneur, a system now threatened by a sharp right hook from the human rights lobby.

---

[102] Megarry & Wade (6th ed), ch 2; F Barlow, *The Feudal Kingdom of England 1042–1216* (Longman, 4th ed, 1988); Marc Bloch, *Feudal Society* (Routledge, 2nd ed, 1962) vol 1, 145–279; RC Douglas (1939) 9 *Economic Hist Rev* 128; FM Stenton, *The First Century of English Feudalism 1066–1166* (Clarendon, 2nd ed, 1961).

[103] F Pollock & FW Maitland, *History of English Law* (Cambridge, 2nd ed, 1898) vol 1, 232; Holdsworth's *History* vol 2, 199; SFC Milsom, *The Legal Framework of English Feudalism* (Cambridge, 1976).

[104] "Tenant" is reserved in this book for a person holding under a lease from a landlord; "vassal" is used in the feudal context.

Destruction of the feudal system in England has been so complete that in 999,999 cases its position as the theoretical basis of landownership can be ignored in complete safety, but in the millionth case an understanding of the special standing of the Crown makes all the difference.

2. Abolition of tenures and services

[3.33] Until 1290, the process of grant and regrant could be repeated so as to create a pyramid of tenure, with a few large land holdings at the top and many small ones at the bottom. At its apex stood the King, a lord but not a vassal. Up to eight sub-tenures were reported. Creation of new tenures by subinfeudation was prohibited in the reign of Edward I by *Quia Emptores* 1290, after which the Crown alone could create new fees simple and a cap was imposed on the total number of tenures. Since then there has been a tendency for all intermediate lordships to become unprovable, so much so that by 1851 the possibility was so remote that it could be wholly ignored.[105]

Medieval law was marked by diversity of tenure reflecting the diversity of services required of the vassal. At the top of the feudal pyramid, immediately beneath the King, stood the tenants in chief who were likely to provide military services or services personal to the Crown.[106] Lower down in the pyramid, at the level of a village, vassals would provide agricultural services to a lord of the manor, who would buy their services with land. The Tenures Abolition Act 1660 expunged knight service,[107] leaving a uniform system of socage tenure, the form of tenure that originally involved agricultural services.[108]

Feudal landholding in England collapsed almost as soon as it had been imposed. The feudal system applied with full rigour only for a century or so after the conquest (to c 1166) and then for another century of so with services transmuted into monetary payments. After that inflation reduced the monetary value of the payment substituted for the services which gradually ceased to be collected, and limitation statutes barred those not exacted over a twenty year period.[109] Perquisites called feudal incidents survived longer, for example wardship gave the lord the right to take the profits from land which had passed to an heir who was under age. As overlord, the king benefitted most, but tenures were "much more burdensome, grievous and prejudicial to the kingdom than beneficial to the King",[110] and Charles II's was restoration in 1660 was conditional on his accepting the termination of all his feudal privileges.[111] Land might

---

[105] *Re Lowe's WT* [1973] 1 WLR 882, 886G, Russell LJ.

[106] SE Thorne [1958] *CLJ* 193.

[107] S 1.

[108] S 7; frankalmoign (spiritual tenure of saying prayers for the soul of a dead person) was finally abolished in 1925: AEA 1925 sch 2; D Postles [1991] *CLJ* 330. Query the position of tenancy in ancient demesne (a manor held direct of the crown at the time of Domesday): *Iveagh* v. *Martin* [1961] 1 QB 232, 241, Paull J.

[109] Real Property Limitation Act 1833 s 1 (but not mentioned in modern Limitation Acts); *Humphrey* v. *Gery* (1849) 7 CB 567, 137 ER 225 (arrears); *De Beauvoir* v. *Owen* (1850) 5 Exch 166, 155 ER 72 (bar of title); *Howitt* v. *Harrington* [1893] 2 Ch 497 (copyhold quit rents). Irregular services did not count as "rent" and were not barred: *Bevil's case* (1583) 4 Co Rep 6a, 76 ER 860 (homage and fealty); *Zouche* v. *Dalbiac* (1875) LR 10 Exch 175 (heriots).

[110] Tenures Abolition Act 1660, preamble.

[111] S 1; *Att-Gen for Alberta* v. *Huggard Assets* [1953] AC 420, 441–442, PC.

still be subject to honorary services personal to the sovereign (grand serjeanty) such as attendance at the Coronation.[112] It was an Act for the landowners rather than for the workers since the King was compensated by a tax on beer.[113]

Abolition of the feudal system itself is a logical next step, a process which may be assisted by a human rights assault.

3. Abolition of copyhold in 1925

[3.34] Copyhold land calls for special mention since it was the last tenure to lose its distinctive face. At Domesday (1086) the vast mass of the population who were unfree did not even make it into the feudal pyramid. Villeins were owned by the Lord of Manor, were not free to move, held land at his will, owed unspecified agricultural services, and stood outside the protection of the King's courts. The Black Death (1346) caused a dramatic shift in the balance of power towards the agricultural labour force. A holding "according to the custom of the manor" gradually evolved into villein tenure, itself the progenitor of copyhold tenure. Untouched in 1660,[114] copyhold continued except where enfranchisement occurred by agreement[115] so late as 1925, and the land continued to be transferred by surrender and admittance enrolled the lord's court. This was anomalous long before the Birkenhead legislation converted all to freehold socage tenure.[116] Most services were abolished immediately[117] or in 1950,[118] with a few quasi-public rights being preserved indefinitely.[119] The link with the lord of the manor was broken,[120] so that ex-copyhold land is usually indistinguishable from longer-established freeholds.

4. *Dominium* and ownership

[3.35] When Justinian divided land that was heritable from goods that were moveable, he imposed a system of Western legal philosophy which insisted that land must carry with it an ultimate right of ownership and control called *dominium*. A great French lawyer[121] said: *"C'est la domination complète et exclusive d'une personne sur une chose corporelle"*. This emphasised its ultimate character, with nothing behind or above.[122] Application of this terminology to English land in say 1250 appeared to give *dominium* to the Crown, and this is the basis of modern English theory,[123] but that tells us little except that English land ownership should not be analysed in Latin, nor

---

[112] Tenures Abolition Act 1660 s 7; serjeanty = service; CR Jessel [1997] *NLJ* 34.

[113] Tenures Abolition Act 1660 ss 15–47.

[114] Tenures Abolition Act 1660 s 2.

[115] HJ Randall (1905) 21 *LQR* 150.

[116] AW Withers (1946) 62 *LQR* 167, 167.

[117] LPA 1922 sch 12 para (1).

[118] Ss 128–129, 138–40, sch 13 part II; SI 1949/836.

[119] LPA 1922 s 128(2), sch 12(4)–(6) (mines; fairs; markets; sporting rights; common rights; liability in respect of dykes, ditches, sea walls and hedges).

[120] *Hampshire CC* v. *Milburn* [1991] 1 AC 325, 339G, Lord Templeman.

[121] PF Girard, *Droit Roman*, 267.

[122] WW Buckland, *A Textbook of Roman Law* (Cambridge, 3rd ed by P Stein, 1963), 188; R Gertler "Roman Ideas of Land Ownership" ch 3 in Bright & Dewar.

[123] *Att-Gen of Ontario* v. *Mercer* (1883) 8 App Cas 767, 772, Selborne LC.

even in French.[124] Civilian systems allowed European feudalism to sit side by side with Roman law, but avoiding the absurdity of giving ownership to the lord: Scots law divided the totality of ownership between a *dominium directum* and a *dominium utile* – the real ownership of the vassal[125] – whereas French law placed *dominium* in the vassal with the Lord having an incumbrance against the land. Given that civilian systems could not agree it is not a helpful way to address the ownership of English land. Can the Queen drop in, uninvited, for tea? She cannot, though she would be most welcome by invitation. Can she arbitrarily take away land or demand arbitrary payments? No, to each, nor would she try. Estate ownership is absolute ownership. To deny that is to know some, but too little, Roman law;

"Drink deep or taste not the Pierian spring."[126]

L. REGISTRATION OF THE CROWN ESTATE

1. The Crown as landowner

[3.36] The previous section has demonstrated the unique position of the Crown, perched on the top of a feudal tree. No estate exists when the Crown has land in its own hands, since it cannot be at once both lord and vassal.[127] While the Queen holds land herself, any earlier feudal tenure collapses and the ownership is allodial. This has implications for the acquisition and sale of land as well as its holding. If land is transferred to the Crown, any existing freehold estate must end. This calls for amendment of our fundamental conception of the fee simple absolute in possession as a interest in the land for ever, a miniscule footnote amendment in practice but one that is conceptually important. On a resale the Crown would need to regrant[128] the land to a new vassal in socage tenure.[129]

2. Controls on the sale of Crown land

[3.37] Sale of Crown estate is controlled by a special regime that would not apply to land owned privately. These controls were imposed by Parliament in 1702[130] to prevent William of Orange joining in the frenzy of property speculation then prevalent. Land can only be disposed of by lease and only for 31 years. This has created a problem for a Royal Garden Hotel in Kensington built by Richard Seifert in the 1970s so as to encroach onto a tiny plot six by 60 metres belonging to a Royal palace. When the

---

[124] JE Hogg (1909) 25 *LQR* 178; FW Maitland, *Constitutional History of England* (Cambridge, 1908), 142; JL Barton (1976) 92 *LQR* 108.

[125] FL Ganshof, *Feudalism* (Longmans, 3rd ed, 1964), 129–133; Craig's *Jus Feudale* (c 1600), as described in Stair's *Institutions* (1681); DM Walker, *Scottish Legal System* (Edinburgh, W Green, 6th ed, 1992) ch 3.

[126] A Pope, *Essay on Criticism*, 216.

[127] Except in the rare cases where there is a mesne lordship.

[128] *Quia Emptores* 1290 does not apply to the Crown.

[129] *Belize Estates & Produce Co* v. *Quilter* [1897] AC 367, 372, Lord Watson in PC; *Att-Gen for Alberta* v. *Huggard Assets* [1953] AC 420, 441, PC; services were not essential: J Hurstfield (1949) 65 *LQR* 72.

[130] Crown Lands Act 1702 s 5.

initial 31 year term expired it became necessary to obtain a private Act[131] to facilitate
the sale of this plot to the hotel. The Crown realised £100,000 and this suggests that
there is considerable value to be unlocked by relaxing the controls on the disposal of
Crown land.

3. Categories of Crown land

[3.38] Government is a major landowner, with an asset base worth £14 billion, not
counting the £4 billion or so of land held by the Crown as such. This last falls into a
number of overlapping categories:[132]

(1) Ancient lands of the Crown.
(2) Land such as Buckingham Palace held by the Crown in its political capacity.
(3) Private estates of the Crown, notably Sandringham and Balmoral, held under
    legislation which creates a private capacity by which the sovereign can own
    landed estates.[133]
(4) Royal Duchy of Lancaster. This ancient Dukedom now contains 20,000
    hectares, including such prime sites as Regent Street – where rentals were £450
    a square metre in 2001 – and, out of London, the Worcester Crown Gate shop-
    ping centre. The Duchy was once held by the sovereign in person to provide
    funds for running the kingdom, but any income is now handed over to the
    Government in return for civil list payments of £8 million a year.[134]
(5) Royal Duchy of Cornwall. Another ancient Dukedom, this one designed to
    provide an income for the heir to the throne. It covers 60,000 hectares including
    Dartmoor, the Oval cricket ground, and the Prince's interesting experiment in
    rural suburbanisation at Poundbury, Dorchester. The Duchy is sub-infeudated
    to the Prince of Wales as a tenant in chief, who sells the houses developed by the
    Duchy by normal substitution.[135]

4. Crown privileges

[3.39] Favourable treatment for the Crown survives in fields such as planning law,
adverse possession, and prescription.[136] These privileges may be vulnerable to human
rights challenges.

5. Foreshore and sea bed

[3.40] Foreshore forms part of the Crown Estate, unless it falls into the half which has
been granted away to private owners.[137] Also included are tidal waters such as estu-
aries and the seabed out to the limit of the territorial waters. These last do not form

---

[131] Land at Palace Avenue, Kensington (Acquisition of Freehold) Act 2002, c ii.
[132] Law Com 271 (2001), [11.3].
[133] Crown Private Estate Act 1800.
[134] See also LRA 2002 s 84, below [3.42].
[135] Law Com 271 (2001), [11.5] n 13.
[136] J Sweetman (1988) 132 SJ 1016.
[137] Saundersfoot beach Pembrokeshire was put on the market for nearly £380,000 in autumn 2002.

part of the administrative districts into which local government is organised and so have traditionally fallen outside the ambit of the land registration legislation, but there is now[138] provision to extend the scope of the register to cover sea beds as and when they are mapped. Profit lies ahead in the shape of profits to be extracted from companies laying communications cables.

6. Registration of the Crown as landowner

[3.41] Before 2003, registration was restricted to legal estates, a fact which precluded applications by the Crown,[139] but this meant that the register could never be satisfactory since vast swathes of the Crown estate were off limits.[140] A strong incentive now exists for Crown registrations, since registered land is secure against encroachments by adverse possessors.[141] A programme of registration will take place over the next 10 years or so.[142]

The Crown may now grant itself a freehold estate, thus creating a registrable estate.[143] Her Majesty may grant an estate in fee simple absolute in possession out of demesne land either to herself or to herself on trust for another.[144] The whole process is voluntary in the sense that the Crown decides whether to implement the procedure,[145] but having progressed to the stage of making a grant registration is then compulsory.[146] Rest assured that she will not need to grapple with the forms herself. The mechanics will be undertaken by the appropriate authority which may, depending upon the particular type of land, be a Government department, the Chancellor of the Duchy of Lancaster, a person appointed by Duchy of Cornwall,[147] or a nominee appointed to act for the Queen. The usual two months available for the application may be extended.[148] Rules will enable others claiming rights against the Crown to caution against first registration.[149]

7. Effect of registration

[3.42] As a registered proprietor the Crown will have absolute powers of disposal unless there is a restriction on the register noting some limitation. Legislation affecting the Duchies of Lancaster or Cornwall will not impact on a purchaser in the absence of such a restriction.[150]

---

[138] LRA 2002 s 128; Law Com 271 (2001), EN [555–558].
[139] *Scmlla Properties* v. *Gesso Properties (BVI)* [1995] BCC 793, 798.
[140] Law Com 271 (2001), [11.10].
[141] See below **[11.28ff]**.
[142] Law Com 271 (2001), EN [363].
[143] LRA 2002 ss 79–85; Law Com 271 (2001), EN [351ff].
[144] LRA 2002 s 79(1).
[145] Law Com 271 (2001), [11.13]. Draft rules will be subject to a consultation exercise.
[146] Compulsion does not apply to mines and minerals held apart from the surface: LRA 2002 s 80. The triggers may be amended.
[147] LRA 2002 s 83; Law Com 271 (2001), [11.31–11.32].
[148] LRA 2002 s 79(2)–(5).
[149] LRA 2002 s 81; Law Com 271 (2001), [11.17].
[150] LRA 2002 s 84; Law Com 271 (2001), [11.33].

M. ESCHEAT TO THE CROWN

1. Nature of escheat

[3.43] Escheat was the process by which on the expiration of the duration of time for which land had been granted to a vassal, the land reverted to the feudal lord. Ownership shifted in an undocumented way. Escheat was highly inconvenient in that mortgages burdening the estate fell when the land escheated, a risk against which no title was wholly safe until statutory protection was provided.[151] Ending escheat was a vital stage on the road to modern commercial ownership. No escheat occurs on a criminal conviction after 1870,[152] nor on intestacy without heirs, nor on breach of the mortmain legislation which regulated gifts to charities.[153] Freehold estates became more or less perpetual. If the vassal's interest can never end, one might as well ignore his feudal status and call him a freehold owner. But beware the very exceptional cases now discussed.

2. Intestacy without next of kin

[3.44] A grant in fee simple was made by a feudal lord *to A so long as he had heirs*. This could be a lengthy period, but it was always delimited, as a duration of time during which the current holder[154] of the fee simple would be succeeded on his death by an heir. Termination was easily avoided by making a will, but it was not always possible to forestall it in the case of an unexpected death. Death intestate without an heir led to the expiration of the duration of the estate, causing the land to revert to the feudal lord, usually that is to the Crown.[155]

This final impediment to the perpetual freehold was removed by the Administration of Estates Act 1925. All relatives descended from a person's grandparents are potential next of kin.[156] If all these fail, the land passes as *bona vacantia* to the Crown, the ultimate next of kin of every subject.[157] The change is largely cosmetic in that the destination of the land is unchanged, but it is conceptually important: expiration of the time limited for an estate (when there are no more heirs) cannot occur on death intestate since 1925.[158] Termination of the estate is avoided because the land no longer passes to the Queen in person but rather it vests in the Treasury Solicitor[159] for the

---

[151] *Hackney LBC* v. *Crown Estates Commissioners* (1990) 72 P & CR 233, Knox J (local land charge lost on escheat).

[152] Corruption of Blood Act 1814; Forfeiture Act 1870.

[153] *Re Suarez* (No 2) [1924] 2 Ch 19, 24, Romer J (registered land); FW Hardman (1888) 4 *LQR* 318, 336.

[154] Descent used to be traced from the last "purchaser", a person who acquired title under a deed.

[155] *Att-Gen of Ontario* v. *Mercer* (1883) 8 App Cas 767, 771–772, Selborne LC; Intestate Estates Act 1884 ss 4, 7 (equitable interests); FW Hardman (1888) 4 *LQR* 318, 330–336.

[156] *The Times*, leader, January 1st, 1926, criticised this as being too restrictive.

[157] AEA 1925 s 46(1)(vi). Depending on the location of the land, it may pass to the Queen, the Duchy of Lancaster, or the Duchy of Cornwall: s 46(1)(ix).

[158] *Att-Gen* v. *Parsons* [1956] AC 421, 437.

[159] ND Ing, *Bona Vacantia* (Butterworths, 1971) ch 2. In some parts of the country it will be the Solicitor to the Duchies of Lancaster or Cornwall.

benefit of the Crown, and he takes the pre-existing estate in the land as formerly held by the deceased.[160]

3. Escheat

[3.45] A true escheat occurs in an estimated 500 cases a year of insolvency or corporate dissolution. Until 2002, the unfortunate and anomalous result was that registered land had to be removed from the register,[161] but escheated land will now be kept on the register,[162] subject to a restriction entered to prevent any dealing without an order of the court, at least until the land is sold.

(1) Land left after corporate dissolution

[3.46] Corporations are not usually dissolved until all the land that it owns has been sold, but problems of escheat arise when land owned beneficially[163] has been overlooked. When a company is removed from the register, unsold land passes to the Crown as *bona vacantia*.[164] The same occurs on the dissolution of corporations incorporated by charter and or otherwise, but in such cases there is no legislative assistance. Blackstone's opinion – that a corporation held land for a determinable fee coterminous with its corporate status[165] – is now known to have been wrong, and dissolution does cause an escheat.[166]

(2) Land burdensome to owner, but of value to another

[3.47] Land may lose its value because burdens divert the real value to someone other that the estate owner. For example, freehold land may be let at such a low rent that the freehold is worthless, or leasehold land may be held subject to a very high rent or burdensome repairing covenants. Negative equity arises when land is mortgaged for more than it is worth so that the borrower owns nothing but debt.[167] In such cases a trustee in bankruptcy of an individual[168] or the liquidator of a company may disclaim the land, causing it to pass to the Crown as *bona vacantia*. Others interested in the land retain their rights, and will probably apply to the court for an order vesting the property in them on such terms as the court thinks fit.[169]

---

[160] *Re Lowe's WT* [1973] 1 WLR 882, CA (death before 1926).

[161] Law Com 271 (2001), [11.5].

[162] LRA 2002 s 85; Law Com 271 (2001), [11.29–11.30], EN [369].

[163] *Re Strathblaine Estates* [1948] Ch 228; *Walji* v. *Mount Cook Land* [2002] 1 P & CR 13 at 163.

[164] Companies Act 1985 ss 618–620; *Toff* v. *McDowell* (1995) 69 P & CR 535, Evans-Lombe J; *Bath & Wells DBF* v. *Jenkinson* [2002] EWHC 218, [2002] 3 WLR 202, Etherton J (school site reverting to dissolved company).

[165] Blackstone's *Commentaries* vol 1, 298; WS Holdsworth (1933) 49 *LQR* 160; FE Farrer (1933) 49 *LQR* 240; MW Hughes (1935) 51 *LQR* 347; FE Farrar (1935) 51 *LQR* 361.

[166] LPA 1925 s 7(2); *Re Wells* [1933] Ch 29, 54, CA.

[167] See below **[29.01]**.

[168] *British General Insurance Co* v. *Att-Gen* [1945] LJNCCR 113; RE Megarry (1946) 62 *LQR* 223 (this pre-dates the modern legislation).

[169] IA 1986 ss 178–182 (company), 315–321 (individual bankruptcy); *Hackney LBC* v. *Crown Estates Commissioners* (1996) 72 P & CR 233, Knox J; *Lee* v. *Lee* [1998] 1 FLR 1018, Fam D (surplus after sale by secured lender to be divided between wife and husband's trustee in bankruptcy, since disclaimer only affects rights between bankrupt and his trustee).

(3) Land without value

[3.48] Land may lose all its value, for example if it consists of a cemetery full to capacity and with onerous maintenance obligations,[170] or a listed building worth £200,000 which is subject to a statutory obligation to spend £1m on its maintenance.[171] Disclaimer of such property will pass it to the Crown as *bona vacantia* burdened by the repairing obligations.[172] Subordinate interests survived, however illogical that was.[173] There is no longer an inquisition,[174] but the Crown only accepts liability on the burdens if it takes possession or manages the land,[175] and even then the Treasury Solicitor can serve a notice to disclaim it,[176] which ends the former estate in the land. If he does so it will then return once more to the Crown, this time by escheat and shorn of the onerous obligations formerly attached to the estate.[177]

4. Other cases of escheat

[3.49] Escheat could also occur[178] on a breach of the conditions attached to a conditional Crown grant or as a Crown reverter after the expiration of an entail.

---

[170] *Re Nottingham General Cemetery Co* [1955] Ch 683.

[171] *Hackney LBC* v. *Crown Estates Commissioners* as above.

[172] Companies Act 1985 s 654.

[173] *Scmlla Properties* v. *Gesso Properties (BVI)* [1995] BCC 793; *Att-Gen of Ontario* v Mercer (1883) 8 App Cas 767; *Toft* v. *McDowell* (1993) 69 P & CR 535, 539, Evans-Lombe J (failure to disclaim within 12 months).

[174] Crown Estate Act 1961.

[175] Halsbury's *Law* (4th ed) vol 12(1), [234].

[176] Companies Act 1985 ss 656–658; Friendly Societies Act 1992 s 23(1), sch 10 part II para 68(1)–(3); Companies Act 1985 s 686; DW Elliott (1954) 70 *LQR* 25 (Eastville Cemetery, Bristol).

[177] *Hackney LBC* v. *Crown Estates Commissioners* (1996) 72 P & CR 233, Knox J (local land charge lost on escheat).

[178] Law Com 271 (2001), [11.20–11.32].

4

HOUSES, FLATS AND COMMONHOLDS

Absolute ownership. Fragmentation of ownership. Houses. Flats. Commonholds.

A. FRAGMENTATION AND ABSOLUTE OWNERSHIP

1. Can land be owned?

[4.01] Of pre-1926 law, Joshua Williams wrote that:

"The first thing the student has to do is to get rid of the idea of absolute ownership."[1]

Maitland added that "the next thing the student has to do is painfully to reacquire it."[2] Today this circuitous voyage can be avoided. Ordinary people understand what is meant by saying that they own a house to a level quite sufficient to guide their day to day conduct, so ownership must be at bottom a very simple concept. Why should lawyers deny what every client knows?

2. Full liberal ownership

[4.02] Ownership of land is a slippery concept because it varies so much from case to case, a product of the ease with which the totality of ownership can be divided between different people, perhaps a freeholder and a leaseholder granted a 99 year term. Each is in some sense an "owner". English jurisprudence suggests that this fissility argues against any commonality in the concept of an owner. Property is not a thing but a power relationship, relative, defeasible, with gradations, and susceptible of multiple claims.[3]

Professor Honoré suggested a very simple side step in an essay at once simple and profound.[4] All one needs to do, Honoré pointed out, is to concentrate on one particular exemplar of ownership, the kind that is "absolute" or, in other words:

---

[1] His reasons were the system of Crown tenure and the pre-1926 rule that paper ownership was useless unless supported by possession: FW Maitland (1886) 2 *LQR* 481, 482; Grays' *Elements* (3rd ed), 21; SFC Milsom [2002] *CLJ* 561.

[2] Megarry & Wade (6th ed), [3–041] n 53, [3.115–3.126]; TC Williams 75 *SJ* 843; Cheshire & Burn (16th ed), 172–183.

[3] Grays' *Elements* (3rd ed), ch 2; K Gray and SF Gray "The Idea of Property in Land" ch 1 in Bright & Dewar, 1; CB Macpherson, *Property Mainstream & Critical Positions* (Toronto, 1978), 9–11; JE Penner *The Idea of Property in Law* (Clarendon, 1997), 23–31; A Pottage (1998) 18 *OJLS* 331; Panesar's *General Principles* ch 2.

[4] P Kohler [2000] *CLP* 237.

"the greatest possible interest in a thing which a mature system of law recognises."[5]

Ownership consists of the rights given in this paradigm case.[6] Suppose that a squatter moves in to a house and the owner seeks to evict him. First, we should establish the right of action when the house is owned outright and then we can use this case to guide us where, say, the house has an outstanding mortgage of £50,000 or it is subject to a trust. Fragmentation will not alter the answer to many simple questions.

3.   Absolute ownership in English law

[4.03] Our paradigm of outright ownership consists of land registered with freehold title absolute held by a proprietor as beneficial owner free from incumbrance – that is without any entries in the charges register or overriding interests. Before first registration its equivalent is holding an unregistered estate in fee simple absolute in possession as beneficial owner free from incumbrances. Almost all land has some adverse interest on the title so a full Honoré owner will be rare in real life.

4.   Basis of reform

[4.04] Alexander Pope thought that the world created by God was,

"a mighty maze, but not without a plan"[7]

He might have characterised property law in the same way, and in fact there is a very clear plan in the first few sections of the Law of Property Act 1925, the very pith and marrow of the legislation.[8] In essence the basis is:

(1) A special role for an absolute ownership interest called an estate in fee simple absolute in possession, the novelty lying in the sense that an indivisible estate should exist in every piece of land.
(2) Legal division is permitted between landlord and tenant. The facility is exploited in flat management schemes, but it can be avoided by setting up a commonhold.
(3) Other legal divisions by time are prohibited.
(4) Division by time is permitted in equity under the vehicle of a trust of land.[9]

So after a consideration of ownership and titles to houses the scheme of this chapter is to consider in turn the divisions between

ground landlord and leaseholder;
flat management company and leaseholder; and
commonhold association and commonholder.

---

[5] AM Honoré "Ownership" ch 5 in AG Guest *Oxford Essays in Jurisprudence* (OUP, 1961), 108.
[6] At 110–111.
[7] *Essay on Man*, Epistle i.
[8] *A Concise Explanation of Lord Birkenhead's Act* (Butterworths, 1922), 1.
[9] See below **[18.01ff]**.

B. COMPONENTS OF "ABSOLUTE" OWNERSHIP

[4.05] Ownership, Honoré asserts, is best defined by describing its standard incidents. Ownership is what you can do with the land.[10]

1. Recoverability

[4.06] A baby instinctively holds on to its own toys. Landowners are the same, only bigger.[11] They wish to exclude outsiders and to do so require an action by which the right to the land can be asserted against an intruder or anyone else and which leads to an order for recovery of the land itself. A quirk of history has left an action in tort to achieve the recovery of land, being that form of trespass formerly called *quare clausum fregit* or ejectment.[12] One size fits all. It is used to evict a squatter[13] and also resolves disputes about the substance of ownership, this last use depending on the rule that trespass is actionable per se without proof of damage.[14] Trespass asserts a better right to possession, but a better right to possession is conferred by a freehold estate and, conversely, legal ownership can be equated with the best right to possession.[15] Although personal against an individual defendant, the judgment in trespass is real – for recovery of the land.[16] Further, a true vindication of the title can be achieved in equity, not least by a declaration of ownership[17] or a declaration that a title is registrable.

2. Right to value represented by the land

[4.07] Land is a repository of wealth which can be realised (turned into money) by letting it or by sale – the owner being entitled both to income and to capital.[18]

3. Use

[4.08] Land has a value above and beyond the financial. A person with a half share in a £100,000 home has a home to live in whereas his share of £50,000 would not buy a comparable home. Use is a cardinal feature. A house is of value precisely because it meets the human need for accommodation. Farmland can be nurtured and value added by manuring and so forth precisely because the owner is secure in the knowledge that he will be safe to reap the benefits of his own work. Absolute ownership

---

[10] AM Honoré "Ownership" ch 5 in AG Guest *Oxford Essays in Jurisprudence* (OUP, 1961), 112–123.
[11] At 114–116.
[12] Megarry & Wade (6th ed), appendix; Grays' *Elements* (3rd ed), 287 ff.
[13] An order for possession may be coupled with an order for damages for the value of the occupation called mesne profits.
[14] *Entick* v. *Carrington* (1765) 19 St Tr 1029, 1066.
[15] Apparently a true owner wrongly excluded from the register of title can sue without first obtaining rectification of register: *Malory Enterprises* v. *Cheshire Homes (UK)* [2002] EWCA Civ 151, [2002] Ch 216, [65], Arden LJ.
[16] See above [2.10].
[17] PBH Birks [2000] *King's College LJ* 1.
[18] AM Honoré "Ownership" ch 5 in AG Guest *Oxford Essays in Jurisprudence* (OUP, 1961), 118.

would imply an absolute power of destruction. If Sutherland paints an unflattering portrait why not destroy it, as Lady Churchill did? An eighteenth century owner might move an entire village to improve the view from the main house, and trees might be cut and left to rot or a house pulled down for no reason.[19] A note of caution is required because Honoré defines ownership is the greatest degree of freedom allowed within a particular society, recognising that the use of land is always controlled and in fact many acts would be constrained by twentieth century planning legislation,[20] and this would certainly impact on the demolition of a home.

4.   Management and disposition

[4.09] Today these elements can be considered together since implies both the power of decision and the power to implement that decision by carrying out a transaction and now brought together in the person of an estate owner.[21] Management involves the power to decide how land will be used, to decide when and if transactions should be carried out, and to make contracts to give effect to those decisions. The transactional power is the power to execute the document which gives effect to the transaction. Estate ownership includes the power of transfer on sale, the power of gift, the power to enter into derivative transactions such as leases and mortgages, and the power to choose a successor to take after one's death – positively by making a will or negatively by allowing the land to pass to the next of kin on intestacy.[22]

C. HOUSES

1.   Freehold

[4.10] A house can be seen in two dimensions, a building on a plot of the good earth with boundaries in a vertical plane. So long as no part of the house is above or below any part of one adjoining the title is quite straightforward. Most houses are more or less isolated from their neighbours in legal terms. Communal facilities are limited to a shared garden fence, access drive or telephone line, matters which can be dealt with by easements and covenants. Freehold tenure is also used for much farmland, moorland and some business premises.

2.   Leasehold

[4.11] There are 9000,000 leasehold houses, half in the Northwest and Merseyside region.[23] A leasehold estate is the ownership interest created in the tenant by the grant of a term of years absolute – a period of years. It is therefore permissible to have a freehold estate in the ground landlord but his right to possession is removed by the

---

[19] *Re Denton* [1981] 1 WLR 1446, 1448G, Lord Lane CJ; *Phipps* v. *Pears* [1965] 1 QB 76, 83E–F, Lord Denning MR.
[20] See below **[5.05ff]**.
[21] AM Honoré "Ownership" ch 5 in AG Guest *Oxford Essays in Jurisprudence* (OUP, 1961), 116–123.
[22] See below **[14.25]**.
[23] *Commonhold CP* (DETR, 1998), [1.4]

existence of a grant of the right to possession to a leaseholder for a number of years. Terms used for houses might be 99 or 999 years, generally in return for a small annual rent called a ground rent.[24] The law allows this well recognised division between the freehold which confers the right to receive rent and also to possess the land at some time in the future, along with the right of the leaseholder to possess the land now in return for ground rent. Both freehold reversion and leasehold estate are commerciable interests – they can be valued, bought and sold – but most of the value resides in the leasehold.[25] There is a problem of leakage of value from any leasehold house which can become acute if the examining term falls below 90 years or so. Hence there are statutory procedures for enfranchisement[26] which enable the leaseholder to acquire the freehold by compulsion.

D. FLATS

[4.12] There are one million flats,[27] half of them in London and the South East. A flat[28] is a part of a building constructed so that it lies above or below other flats in the block, perhaps a substantial villa converted into separate units or a monster new build residential complex. No one flat has any value in isolation and to secure proper repairing obligations it is essential to use a leasehold flat management scheme. We must now explain successively the problem and the solution – commonholds.

1.   Individual flats and the problem of wastage

[4.13] Leasehold tenure is not markedly inferior to freehold ownership provided that the lease is very long and the ground rent is low. However a serious problem of wastage of value affects shorter leasehold terms – where the outstanding term is less than about 100 years. This difficulty is addressed by the individual enfranchisement scheme which allows a leaseholder to obtain a 90 year extension of his existing term.[29]

2.   Block ownership

[4.14] In some blocks of flats freehold estate may be retained by the original developer or vested in an outside investor. Such a ground landlord may become a nuisance if he exploits his ownership by demanding excessive interest on arrears of ground rent or by extracting large commission payments on the premiums to insure the block. Properly organised blocks avoid these problems by ensuring that the freehold in the block, the grounds and other common parts are vested in a management company controlled by

---

[24] Contrast renting of residential premises for a short term (less than 21 years) which is generally at a market rent (rack rental) – in this book the parties to such a relationship are called landlord and tenant; P Sparkes *NLT* chs 1–13; see below **[26.01ff]**.

[25] See below **[26.03]**.

[26] L Ref A 1967; Chold and L Ref A 2002; *James* v. *UK*, 8795/97, (1986) 8 EHRR 123; P Sparkes *NLT* ch 15.

[27] *Consultation CP* (DETR, 1998), [1.4]

[28] A maisonette is a flat on several levels.

[29] P Sparkes *NLT* ch 15.

the flat owners collectively. When development is complete[30] title should be transferred to such a management company. There are a number of compulsory mechanisms for leaseholders to take over collective ownership and management.[31]

A company is used to hold the freehold since the corporate vehicle has perpetual succession which avoids the need for repeated vestings of the freehold. Ownership of the flats has to be kept in step with the ownership of the corresponding shares in the management company, so share transfers are required as part and parcel of every sale of every flat.

3.   Management

[4.15] Leases are used for flats because the value of each one is dependent upon the condition of the block as a whole and of every other flat. Positive covenants are needed to cope with repair and the payment of service charges, and these are not enforceable between freeholders[32] but only between leaseholders, so repairing obligations in a leasehold scheme are always enforceable between the current parties,[33] facilitating proper maintenance and repair of the structural parts of the block and common parts. The value of each flat in a block depends upon all other parts of the block being properly maintained with mutuality of obligation and each tenant being liable to contribute to the cost through a service charge. The scheme will also include easements for access and restrictive covenants regulating the use of the flats.

E.   COMMONHOLD

1.   The introduction of commonhold

[4.16] The Commonhold and Leasehold Reform Act 2002 enacts a scheme of commonholds.[34] They are a means of reconciling the freehold ownership of units within a development with the need for common arrangements for the management of the whole. The English scheme builds on the strata titles in Australasia, the condominium laws in North America and the copropiété of France and the continent. The case for reform is best pursued in an essay[35] by David Clarke, the leading expert,[36] but it may be convenient now to forget the 15 year slog towards the legislation.[37]

---

[30] The builder or developer needs to retain control until the last flat has been sold, particularly to collect the premiums, and also so that marketing of the flats can proceed.

[31] P Sparkes *NLT* ch 16

[32] See below **[32.44ff]**.

[33] See below **[27.18ff]**.

[34] Rules are subject to consultation: *Commonhold Consultation* CD 11/02 (LCD, 2002).

[35] D Clarke "Occupying 'Cheek by Jowl': Property Issues Arising from Communal Living" ch 15 in Bright & Dewar.

[36] DN Clarke *Commonhold The New Law* (Jordans, 2002); Clarke on *Commonhold – Law Practice and Precedents* (Jordans, 2002). See also PH Kenny [2001] *Conv* 216; PH Kenny [2002] *Conv* 206; N Roberts [2002] *NLJ* 887.

[37] *Commonhold* Cm 179 (1987) (the "Aldridge Report"); *Commonhold – a CP*, Cm 79 (1987); *Commonhold* Cm 1345 (1990); *Commonhold CP* (July 1996); *Commonhold and Leasehold Reform – Draft Bill and CP* (Cm 4843, September 2000).

Commonhold is a new form of tenure for blocks of flats and other multi-unit properties. Flats are owned individually, the main advance being the tenurial reform which allows the creation of freehold units. Common parts will be owned and managed collectively helped by the scheme of reciprocal positive covenants and a more cohesive corporate management vehicle in the form of a commonhold association. Consideration of the individual aspect will precede the collective.

2. Constitution

[4.17] The constitution[38] of the commonhold will consist of:

the certificate of incorporation of the commonhold association, and its memorandum and articles of association;[39] and
a commonhold community statement[40] which defines the units and the common parts and lays down the reciprocal scheme of obligations and provisions for collective management of the development.

It will become a commonhold when the title is registered as an estate in commonhold land.[41] After registration, buyers will be able to get access to the constitution because the land registry will maintain a comprehensive register including:[42]

details of the commonhold association;
the proprietors of the commonhold units;
the commonhold community statement;
the memorandum and articles of association; and
any other filed documents.

Once set up and registered the constitution can only be challenged by an application for rectification.[43]

F. COMMONHOLD UNITS

1. Atomic theory

[4.18] A unit is the basic indivisible atom of a commonhold. There must be at least two units.[44] This neutral term could describe flats in a block, houses on an estate, shops, or light industrial units on a commercial estate. A unit could be residential or commercial. Division within a commonhold could be vertical (terraced houses) or horizontal (flats and maisonettes) or the units could be free-standing (detached houses or units on an industrial park). No doubt flats will be the most common type each in

[38] Chold and L Ref A 2002 s 1.
[39] S 2, sch 1.
[40] S 31.
[41] S 1(1).
[42] S 5. Rules will flesh out the details: s 65; these are subject to consultation at the time of writing: CP on *Draft Commonhold (Land Registration) R 2003* (LR, 2002).
[43] Chold and L Ref A 2002 ss 40, 66.
[44] Chold and L Ref A 2002 s 11(2).

individual ownership and potentially including physically separate areas such as a garage or an individual garden.[45] Individual units will be described and defined by a commonhold community statement.[46] Once set up the basic integrity of the unit will be protected against non-consensual variations at the behest of the other flat owners.[47]

2. Freehold basis of unit-holding

[4.19] The person registered as proprietor of an individual flat is described as a unit-holder.[48] Commonhold will facilitate the freehold ownership of units, since the whole point is that the ownership of the unit-holder will be perpetual. There will be no risk of the loss of a unit because of non-payment of service charge as there is with a leasehold flat,[49] though other powerful remedies will ensure that service charge contributions are paid. A commonhold is a special variant of the common law freehold estate, subject for example to claims to a matrimonial home right,[50] and only a few trivial amendments to the existing property legislation are required to accommodate commonholds.[51]

3. Transactions with units

[4.20] Free transferability will be inherent in the nature of a commonhold unit and it will not be permissible for the commonhold constitution to impose any restriction on sales, gifts, dealings, or transmission by law.[52] A residential commonhold scheme will not be allowed to degenerate into a quasi-leasehold scheme because there will be an outright ban on the grant of long leases.[53] Dealings, mortgages and sales by lenders must relate to the whole unit and so that the atomic unit is not sub-divided.[54] Units will be subject to normal compulsory purchase procedures.[55] Transfer of a unit will automatically pass the burdens and liabilities to the buyer[56] and will have immediate implications for the membership of the commonhold association.[57]

---

[45] S 11(3)(d). A unit may not even be a part of a building: s 11(4).

[46] S 11(1).

[47] Ss 23–24.

[48] S 12. More accurately it is the person entitled to be registered – including the buyer from the moment of purchase, ignoring for these purposes the registration gap. S 13 provides for joint holders and indicates whether liability is joint only or joint and several.

[49] S 31(8).

[50] S 61.

[51] Sch 5; there are minor amendments to the formality provisions in LPA 1925 s 55 and to the provisions for alteration of a register.

[52] Chold and L Ref A 2002 ss 15, 19. Grants of easements etc require participation by the commonhold association after a 75% vote in favour.

[53] Ss 17–19. The exact length of lease permitted (perhaps 7 years) will be defined by regulations. Leases of commercial developments will be allowed though with some formal requirements.

[54] Ss 21–22.

[55] S 60.

[56] S 16.

[57] See below **[4.22]**.

G. COMMUNAL MANAGEMENT

1. Common parts

[4.21] Common parts are every part of commonhold land which is not a commonhold unit.[58] These might include the structure of the block, communal services, and parts used in common – such as hallways, staircases, communal gardens and shared parking areas. Use of some parts may be restricted.[59] They will be owned by the commonhold association and hence by the unit holders collectively. Legal title to the commonhold parts will be vested in the commonhold association by registration after sale of the first unit.[60]

2. Commonhold association

[4.22] Just as a leasehold scheme requires a flat management company, so a corporate vehicle to be called a commonhold association will be required for communal ownership, management, and decision-making within a commonhold. It will be a conventional company – a private company limited by a members' guarantee of £1[61] – registered at Companies House in the usual way,[62] and regulations will provide for a distinctive form of name.[63] A model set of memorandum and articles of association will be provided with restrictions on alterations.

Membership of the commonhold association will be coincident with the ownership of units: only unit-holders will be allowed to be members and conversely membership will be imposed automatically after acquisition of the ownership of a unit. It will not be necessary as it is with flat companies to issue share certificates nor to transfer shares.

3. Commonhold community statement

[4.23] This is the document which will lay down the mutual scheme of regulation between the unit-holders, making provision for the rights and duties of a commonhold association and the unit-holders.[64] A form for it will be prescribed and so will many of the contents. It will regulate the property law aspects of the development – in particular the inter-relationship of all the unit-holders. Variations will be limited.[65]

4. Reciprocal obligations

[4.24] A commonhold will be a sophisticated form of development involving reciprocal obligations, the revolutionary feature of commonholds being the facility with

---

[58] Chold and L Ref A 2002 s 25.
[59] S 35.
[60] S 9.
[61] S 34, sch 3.
[62] *Commonhold and Leasehold Reform – Draft Bill and CP* (Cm 4843, September 2000) Part I, [1.3.1].
[63] Chold and L Ref A 2002 sch 3 para 16.
[64] Ss 31–33.
[65] S 33.

which positive covenants may be imposed and passed on.[66] Unit holders will have duties to pay for works.[67] The association will prepare a commonhold assessment[68] taking into account the global sums spent on repairs and these will be allocated to individual units in accordance with a scheme contained in the commonhold community statement. The remedy of forfeiture will not be available, but arrears could be charged on units.[69]

5. Dispute resolution

[4.25] An ombudsman scheme will be available for the resolution of disputes.[70] Money can be made available for the provision of advice to commonholders.[71]

H. COMMONHOLD CREATION, VARIATION AND TERMINATION

1. Forms of development – the freehold and ground up rules

[4.26] Although it could be used for commercial blocks or industrial estates,[72] the primary aim of the reform is to improve the position of residential leaseholders in blocks of flats.

The developer who constructs the site must originally be registered with a freehold title that is absolute, or at least be in a position to apply to be registered.[73] Consents will be needed from all other parties interested in the land.[74]

In a simple case, a commonhold development will be used for a block of flats standing in its own grounds, with parking spaces and communal gardens, but isolated from its neighbours so that no part of it lies above or below non-commonhold land. Relationships with neighbouring land can be dealt with by easements and restrictive covenants. It could include non-contiguous parcels of land.[75] Positive covenants cannot run with freehold land and for this reason flying freeholds will not be allowed. All land from the ground level upwards must be subject to the same application. A commonhold development cannot itself be a flying freehold.

2. Development mechanics

[4.27] Any new flat development has three phases – (1) planning and construction, (2) the period after the sale of the first flat, when construction of other parts of the

---

[66] S 16.
[67] S 31(3)–(5).
[68] S 38.
[69] S 31(8).
[70] S 42.
[71] S 62.
[72] *Commonhold and Leasehold Reform – Draft Bill and CP* (Cm 4843, September 2000) Part I, [1.3.1]. Agricultural land is excluded: Chold and L Ref A 2002 s 4, sch 2 para 2. Multi site commonholds are allowed by s 57.
[73] Chold and L Ref A 2002 s 2(1).
[74] S 3. School sites and other land with a defeasible title excluded: sch 2 para 4. Any leases will be extinguished when the registration proceeds: s 10.
[75] S 25.

development may well be continuing and (3) when all flats are sold and the development is handed over to the commonholders.

Period (1) is described as a transitional period during which the land is registered as a commonhold, but without unit holders.[76] This phase would last during the construction of the building condominium and until the first unit is sold. The developer will appear as registered proprietor but without any details of the proprietors of commonhold units. The developer will be allowed to withdraw during this transitional period with the consent of all proprietors and of all others interested in the land.[77]

When the first unit is sold the unit-holder is registered as proprietor, the commonhold association is registered as proprietor of the common parts and the developer will be registered as proprietor of the unsold units. A sales period (unnamed in the Act) lasts until all units have been sold, and during this period the developer has special rights to complete the development and to market unsold units.[78]

The completed development will be "handed over" to the commonholders after the sale of the last unit and from then on they will be responsible for running the commonhold association.

3.   Conversions from leasehold schemes to commonhold

[4.28] In theory it will be possible to apply to convert a leasehold scheme to a commonhold, but the requirement for unanimous consent of all parties (the leaseholders, all secured lenders and the ground landlord or flat management company) will make this conversion very difficult to achieve in practice. The 100% rule is much criticised.

4.   Change

[4.29] Variations or additions[79] to a commonhold impact on the integrity of existing owners and their mutual obligations so there are special safeguards and entrenched voting rights.[80] Individual units as defined by a commonhold community statement[81] are protected against non-consensual variations at the behest of the other flat owners.[82]

5.   Voluntary winding up

[4.30] Buildings rarely have a useful life exceeding 100 years or so, and a chance accident might destroy any construction at any time.

A commonhold association will be able to make a termination resolution that all the land over which it exercises functions should cease to be commonhold land. If it were to be passed unanimously, the association would be free to apply for termination.[83] If

---

[76] Ss 7–8.
[77] S 8(4)–(5).
[78] Ss 9, 58–59, sch 4.
[79] S 41.
[80] S 36.
[81] S 11(1).
[82] Ss 23–24.
[83] Chold and L Ref A 2002 s 44; curiously there is no provision for mortgage-lenders to consent. All unit holders must be given a chance to vote but majorities are of those voting: s 36.

it is passed by 80 per cent of the members voting in favour, the association would have to apply to the court to determine the terms of a termination application, after which there would be another vote on the terms on offer.[84] That statement would deal with the distribution of the assets of the association; the contents would be pre-determined to some extent by the commonhold community statement. The termination resolution and termination statement will need to be noted in the register and at that time the freehold estate in the units is transferred to the commonhold association. A member's voluntary winding up will follow with the liquidator realising the assets of the commonhold association and distribute them to the former unit holders in accordance with the termination statement.[85]

If the commonhold is terminated the registration as commonhold land must be ended.

6. Insolvency

[4.31] It is to be hoped that commonhold associations would not often become insolvent. Normal company procedures will apply.[86] However it is proposed to offer protection to unit holders who have met their individual obligations through the formation of a "phoenix association", or more prosaically a successor association, whose members would consist of all the non-defaulting unit-holders and all new unit holders who had purchased the units of defaulting members from the liquidator.[87]

---

[84] S 45.
[85] Ss 46–49.
[86] Ss 50, 54.
[87] Ss 51–53.

5

SOCIAL CONTROL AND HUMAN RIGHTS

Social interest in land. Compulsory purchase. Planning. Human rights.
Horizontality. Deprivation of possessions. Controls on use. Respect for the
home. Discrimination. Fundamental trial rights.

A. SOCIAL INTEREST IN LAND

1. Private ownership limited in the public interest

[5.01] Coke coined a proverb when he reported that *Semayne's* case had decided that
a person's house

> "is to him as his castle and fortress, as well for his defence against injury and violence as for
> his repose."[1]

Few proverbs are quite so wrong. Coke's cosy image of a landowner putting up the
shutters and bolting the door to the outside world was not true at the start of the
Stuart era and 150 years on, in the middle of the eighteenth century, the Chief Justice
thought it obvious that property could be:

> "taken away or abridged by some public law for the good of the whole."[2]

In truth ownership is never absolute. Tony Honoré has defined it as the greatest possible interest in a thing which a mature system of law recognises, a form of definition
which acknowledges that every liberal system prohibits harmful uses and imposes
similar controls on land owners for the greater good.[3]

English people do not own castles, but homes that are hedged around with restrictions for the public benefit; a householder must pay taxes, avoid creating a nuisance
to neighbours, keep his property safe for visitors, yield up criminals, and much more
besides.[4] In particular the public enjoys two vital interests in private land – the right
of compulsory purchase and the right to impose a (town and country) planning
regime.

---

[1] (1604) 5 Co Rep 91a, 91b, 77 ER 194.
[2] *Entick* v. *Carrington* (1765) 19 St Tr 1029, 1066, Camden CJ.
[3] AM Honoré "Ownership" ch 5 in AG Guest *Oxford Essays in Jurisprudence* (OUP, 1961), 108, 123,
144; PBH Birks "Before We Begin: Five Keys to Land Law" ch 18 in Bright & Dewar, 459.
[4] ED Brown (1965) 18 *CLP* 169.

B. EXPROPRIATION (COMPULSORY PURCHASE)

1. Compulsory purchase powers

[5.02] Modern government requires the power to force a landowner to sell his land when it is needed,[5] a procedure generally referred to as compulsory purchase. Human rights law uses the Continental term expropriation but the American term eminent domain is even more evocative of the overarching and superior rights of the public at large.

The state should only take land with lawful authority, to meet a public need. Statutory authority exists for the purchase of land for a long list of worthy public causes.[6] There must be an opportunity for objections. An acquisition can be challenged in administrative law if the power of acquisition is exceeded or abused. Procedure opens with the making of a compulsory purchase order,[7] which identifies a general area of land intended to be acquired. Objections about whether the land is needed are resolved by a public inquiry or a written objection procedure.

2. Completion of the acquisition and compensation

[5.03] After confirmation of a compulsory purchase order, the acquiring authority is required to treat with each individual owner of land within the area affected in accordance with a statutory procedure.[8] Acquisition is usually completed by normal conveyancing procedures though there is also a streamlined procedure using vesting declarations.

Compensation has to be paid to a landowner whose land is acquired compulsorily.[9] A principle of equivalence crystallised in *Director of Buildings and Lands* v. *Shun Fung Ironworks*[10] requires that the compensation paid must be equal to the landowner's actual loss – taking into account the value of the land, though ignoring the effect of the scheme itself,[11] and also any "injurious affection" of his land.

C. PLANNING

[5.04] Overwhelmingly the most important social control of land is the planning system,[12] dating from 1948, but currently enforced under the provisions of the Town and Country Planning Act 1990 as amended.[13]

---

[5] Cheshire & Burn (16th ed) ch 31; Megarry & Wade (6th ed), [22.056–22.061]. Contrast requisition in war time, which involves temporary taking of possession without the acquisition of ownership.

[6] Acquisition of Land Act 1981 s 1.

[7] Acquisition of Land Act 1981.

[8] Compulsory Purchase Act 1965.

[9] Land Compensation Act 1973 ss 29–63.

[10] [1995] 2 AC 111, 125, Lord Nicholls (on Hong Kong legislation).

[11] *Pointe Gourde Quarrying & Transport Co* v. *Superintendent of Crown Lands* [1947] AC 565, PC; *Rugby Joint Water Board* v. *Foottit* [1973] AC 202, HL; Waters v. *Welsh Development* Agency [2002] EWCA Civ 924, [2002] 2 EGLR 107; Law Com CP 165 (2002).

[12] Cheshire & Burn (16th ed) ch 30; Megarry & Wade (6th ed), [22.009–22.055].

[13] Planning and Compensation Act 1991.

1. Work permitted by planning permission

[5.05] Planning permissions are issued by the local planning authority, usually the District Council.[14] Permission is required for any development, a concept which includes:

> any building operations;
> demolition of dwellings or of any buildings within conservation areas;
> engineering and other forms of operation, and
> any material change of use.[15]

A grant of planning permission does not guarantee the private property rights necessary to carry out a development and is not a defence to a nuisance action.

2. Limitation after operational development

[5.06] Planning breaches are subject to a regime of limitation,[16] which exempts building and other operational development if no enforcement action is taken against a breach for four years.

3. Permitted development

[5.07] The Town and Country Planning (General Permitted Development) Order 1995[17] permits some forms of development without express planning permission. It permits, for example, modest extensions to an existing house, loft conversions, dishes for satellite tv, as well as minor alterations within the curtilage[18] of a dwelling house.

4. Building regulations approval

[5.08] Whether or not building work requires planning permission it will need to comply with Building Regulations.[19] These cover new building work, alterations, and work causing a material change of use. Alterations to older buildings are judged by whether they make the building more or less satisfactory by modern standards. All aspects of building work are regulated, including structural integrity, fire safety, foundations, toxicity of cavity insulation, sound insulation, ventilation, hygiene of sanitary appliances, drainage and waste disposal, heating equipment, guarding of stairs and ramps, conservation of fuel, access for the disabled,[20] and glazing.

---

[14] Major changes are underway for major infrastructure projects: Planning and Compulsory Purchase Bill 2002.

[15] TCPA 1990 s 57(1).

[16] TCPA 1990 s 171B, as amended in 1991.

[17] SI 1995/418 as amended.

[18] *SS for Environment T&R v. Skerritts of Nottingham* (2000) 80 P & CR 516, CA.

[19] Building Act 1984; Building Regs SI 2000/2531, as amended.

[20] Disability Discrimination Act 1995 (banning the traditional doorstep), as amended.

5. Use

[5.09] Use is any activity which is done on land but which does not interfere with its physical characteristics.[21] Change of use is a form of development for which permission is required, if the change is "material"[22] judged in the context of a planning unit. Uses are grouped into classes, the main residential group being Class C3.[23] Changes between use classes generally require permission.

Limitation operates to legitimate a change of use[24] four years after it has occurred in the case of a change of use to use as a single dwelling, or after 10 years in the case of other breaches, including breach of an agricultural occupancy condition.[25]

6. Planning conditions

[5.10] Planning permissions are usually subject to conditions,[26] perhaps for example stating the materials to be used for a building or its external appearance. Occupancy conditions are often imposed to make housing acceptable in a green belt or to restrict houses in rural areas to agricultural occupiers.[27]

7. Planning enforcement

[5.11] Unauthorised development is not itself criminal, but it leaves land vulnerable to enforcement procedures under the Planning and Compensation Act 1991.[28] If the authority considers that operational development or change of use has occurred without authority, it has a discretion to issue an enforcement notice. Notices are frequently challenged. Failure to observe an enforcement notice is an offence.[29]

8. Special regimes

[5.12] There are numerous special planning regimes, covering conservation areas, listed buildings, historic buildings, ancient monuments and archaeological areas. Tight controls apply to trees, advertisements and caravan parks. Many rural environments attract special protection such as green belts around cities, areas of outstanding natural beauty, national parks, sites of special scientific interest and so on.

Special rules for major developments and industrial and commercial development. A rigorous new regime applies to contaminated land.[30] Enterprise zones were set up

---

[21] *Parkes* v. *SS for Environment* [1978] 1 WLR 1308, 1311, Lord Denning MR.

[22] TCPA 1990 ss 55, 57(2)–(4), sch 4.

[23] SI 1987/764 sch; *R(JR) Hossack* v. *Kettering BC* [2002] EWCA Civ 886, [2002] JPEL 1206.

[24] TCPA 1990 s 171B.

[25] *Newbury DC* v. *SS for Environment* (1993) 67 P & CR 68, CA.

[26] TCPA 1990 ss 60, 70. These can be discovered by a local search.

[27] *Fawcett Properties* v. *Buckinghamshire CC* [1961] AC 636, HL; *R* v. *Kensington & Chelsea RLBC ex p Lawrie Plantation Services* [1999] 1 WLR 1415, HL.

[28] R Carnwath, *Enforcing Planning Control* (HMSO, 1989); *Thrasyvoulou* v. *SS for Environment* [1990] 2 AC 273, 292B–C, Lord Bridge; SIs 2002/2682–2686.

[29] TCPA 1990 s 179, as amended; *R* v. *Wicks* [1998] AC 92, HL.

[30] Environmental Protection Act 1990 ss 78A–78YC, inserted by Environment Act 1995 s 57; *Buckinghamshire CC* v. *Briar* [2002] EWHC 2821 (Ch), [2002] December 20th, Lawrence Collins J.

to relax the normal planning restrictions and so encourage commercial development in places such as London's Canary Wharf.

D. HUMAN RIGHTS

1. Rights brought home

[5.13] Today the balance between public and private landowners is maintained by the European Convention on Human Rights. The Human Rights Act 1998 "brought home"[31] rights from Strasbourg, the seat of the European Court of Human Rights, so that they became enforceable in the UK courts.[32] It came into force on October 2nd 2000 its force being prospective only in civil matters.[33] Incorporation applies exclusively to "Convention rights" already recognised by the United Kingdom,[34] excluding for example any commitment to abolish imprisonment for private debt. Our domestic law is aligned with the constitutional arrangements in most continental countries.

Cases since the introduction of the Act have tended to confirm the conservative view[35] of the Act in relation to property, despite one or two headline grabbing changes. A more radical potentiality remains which may result in a second coming at some future time.

2. Rights to property

[5.14] The Convention provides a substantive guarantee of property rights in article 1 of the First Protocol to the Convention.[36] Three distinct but interlocking rights[37] are, in order of application,[38] rights to:

(1) freedom from arbitrary deprivation of possessions;
(2) freedom from unjustified controls on the use of property; and
(3) peaceful enjoyment of possessions.

None of these rights is absolute since interferences with the rights may be, and commonly are, justified in the wider public interest. The right to property is available to

---

[31] *Rights Brought Home* (Cm 3782, 1997).

[32] A stay should not be granted pending a decision of the European Court of Human Rights, since the remedy against the Government is damages for failing to observe the Convention rights: *Locabail UK* v. *Waldorf Investment Corp (No 4)* [2000] Times June 13th, Evans–Lombe J.

[33] *JA Pye (Oxford)* v. Graham [2002] UKHL 30, [2002] 3 All ER 865, [73], Lord Hope; D Beyleveld, R Kirkham & D Townend (2002) 22 *LS* 185. In criminal cases see: *R* v. *Kansal* [2001] UKHL 62, [2002] AC 69.

[34] HRA 1998 s 1, sch 1, as amended.

[35] A Arden & C Baker [1998] 03 *Legal Action* 8; J Howell [1999] *Conv* 287; J Alder [1999] *JHL* 67; R Buxton (2000) 116 *LQR* 48; M Davies [2000] 27 *LSG* 30; D Rook *Property Law and Human Rights* (Blackstones, 2001); D Rook [2002] *Conv* 316; P Halstead [2002] *Conv* 513; J Luba *Housing and Human Rights* (Jordans, 2002); Smith's *Property Law* (4th ed), 16–19.

[36] Agreed at Paris, March 20th 1952.

[37] *Mellacher* v. *Austria*, 10522/83, (1990) 12 EHRR 391, 408. Cases repeat this so often that it has become a Strasbourg cliché.

[38] The right to peaceful enjoyment appears first in the text but the cases treat it as a residual sweeper up with relatively small content.

"every natural or legal person",[39] so that companies and building societies[40] may seek protection just as much as any individual.

3.   Qualifications to the convention right to property

[5.15] Private interests often have to yield to the public good to the extent that this proves necessary.[41] Analytical techniques are provided by the human rights jurisprudence to determine which should prevail in ordinary cases. Article 1 of Protocol 1 is subject to three major limitations:

(1) Deprivation of possessions is permitted: "in the public interest and subject to the conditions provided for by the law and by the general principles of international law."

(2) The right to property "shall not . . . in any way impair the right of a State to enforce such laws as it deems necessary to control the use of property in accordance with the general interest."

(3) States may enact laws "to secure the payment of taxes or other contributions or penalties."[42]

Most people who reach the stage of a legal complaint have indeed been victims of an interference with a property right protected by the Convention, so the battleground is the justification for that interference.

Interferences must be lawful, that is they must be justified by some statute or case law principle. In addition any interference should seek to achieve a legitimate purpose and be necessary in a democratic society. A (wide) margin of appreciation is allowed to the state, this being an area of discretion in which the state is left to determine whether or not particular legislation is useful. Proportionality is the principle used by a court to retain a balance between the interference with private property rights as against the social problem requiring the interference: legislation must be reasonably commensurate with the problem being tackled.[43]

4.   Other human rights to property

[5.16] Ancillary and procedural protections are also important in property law. These include the article 6 guarantee of fair trial of claims to property rights and other civil claims, the article 8 right to respect for the home and for family life, and the article 14 freedom from discrimination in the exercise of Convention rights. All of these rights are qualified by the possibility of public interest justification. These other rights appear to be restricted by the text of the Convention to humans, though states have not in practice taken this point when companies have taken cases to Strasbourg.

---

[39] Art 1 of Protocol 1.
[40] *National and Provincial BS* v. *UK*, 21319/93, (1998) 25 EHRR 127.
[41] *Sporrong* v. *Sweden*, 7151/75, (1983) 5 EHRR 35, [1], Judge Walsh.
[42] *National and Provincial BS* v. *UK*, 21319/93, (1998) 25 EHRR 127; *Gasus Dosier und Fördertechnik* v. *Netherlands*, 15375/89, (1995) 20 EHRR 403.
[43] *Mellacher* v. *Austria*, 10522/83, (1990) 12 EHRR 391.

5. Defences

[5.17] Human rights of others are safeguarded by the principle that one person's reliance on convention rights should not infringe any other right or freedom, with especial safeguards for freedom of expression, and for freedom of thought conscience and religion.[44]

E. VERTICAL AND HORIZONTAL HUMAN RIGHTS

1. Control of public landowners

[5.18] Public authorities are subject to administrative law in that decisions made when acting in a public capacity can be challenged by judicial review. In particular a decision is open to challenge if it is one that no reasonable authority acting properly could have reached.[45] This could include public aspects of land ownership. A council is free to decide for itself when to sell its land without being subject to judicial review, since the council is undertaking a private function,[46] but a council must act within its powers and ensure that it meets its public law obligation to get the full market value.[47]

2. Obligation of public authorities to respect human rights

[5.19] The 1998 Act greatly strengthens the position of individuals affected by the decisions of public bodies. It is unlawful for any public authority to act in a way which is incompatible with any Convention right,[48] unless compelled to do so by primary legislation. Decisions in breach of the Convention will be open to judicial review, and hence the decision may be quashed, or damages awarded. It will also be possible for a victim to defend an action by an offending authority or to sue it directly for an act in breach of his Convention rights.[49]

Authorities subject to control will include the central government, executive agencies, local government, and privatised utilities, and any private person exercising a function of a public nature.[50] This includes a parochial council when it imposes chancel repair liabilities,[51] and drainage authorities,[52] but not private bodies housing the

---

[44] HRA 1998 ss 11–13; *Chassagnou* v. *France*, 25088/94, (2000) 29 EHRR 615.
[45] *Associated Provincial Picture Houses* v. *Wednesbury Corp* [1948] 1 KB 223, 228, Lord Greene MR. Proportionality is now considered.
[46] *R* v. *Leeds CC ex p Cobleigh* [1997] COD 69; *R(JR) Pepper* v. *Bolsover DC* [2000] EGCS 107 November 10th, Keene J.
[47] *R(JR) Structadene* v. *Hackney LBC* [2001] 1 EGLR 15, QBD; *R(JR) Lemon Land* v. *Hackney LBC* [2001] EWHC Admin 336, [2002] 1 EGLR 81, Lightman J; K Lanaghan [2001] 32 *EG* 84; J Bosworth [2001] 26 *EG* 158.
[48] HRA 1998 s 6(1).
[49] Ss 6–8.
[50] S 6(3)–(7).
[51] *Aston Cantlow etc PCC* v. *Wallbank* [2001] EWCA Civ 713, [2002] Ch 51.
[52] *Marcic* v. *Thames Water Utilities (No 1)* [2000] EWHC Techno 421, [2002] QB 929.

homeless such as a housing association[53] or charitable foundation.[54] The position of a local authority acting as a landlord remains open.[55]

3. Horizontal applications

[5.20] The Human Rights Act 1998 is used in a "horizontal" fashion when the Act is used between two private property owners, the one complaining that the other has violated his human rights in reliance on legislation or property ownership rules laid down by a public body. Two propositions seem clear: (1) horizontal effect was not intended;[56] but (2) it has been the effect of the Human Rights Act 1998.[57]

(1) Strasbourg cases

[5.21] Of the few cases supporting horizontality,[58] the clearest is *James* v. *United Kingdom*.[59] A ground landlord took action against the government arguing that enfranchisement rights violated his right to his property. He could only pursue a "vertical" action against the Government in the Strasbourg court. There was jurisdiction, though the case failed on the merits. A ground landlord could argue that the enfranchisement legislation contravened the Convention. The state may be liable for enacting legislation that enables one private individual to expropriate the property of another private individual. Human rights can attack basic property principles.

(2) Human Rights Act 1998

[5.22] The 1998 Act goes beyond the Strasbourg jurisprudence because its definition of the public authorities obliged to observe Convention rights includes the House of Lords as a judicial body, the Supreme Court, all lower courts and tribunals.[60] Judgments of lower courts can only be corrected by an appeal. It seems that the courts must issue judgments in accordance with the Convention ignoring inconsistent case law principles.

(3) Legislation

[5.23] Legislation which impinges on Convention rights can often be made compliant by using interpretation techniques to ensure that primary and secondary legislation is construed, if possible, so as to be compatible with the Convention.[61] However, if this

---

[53] *Poplar Housing and Regeneration Community Ass* v. *Donoghue* [2001] EWCA Civ 604, [2002] QB 48.

[54] *Heather* v. *Leonard Cheshire Foundation* [2002] EWCA Civ 366, [2002] 2 All ER 936.

[55] *Pemberton* v. *Southwark LBC* [2000] 1 WLR 1672, CA.

[56] Lord Irvine, *Hansard* HL vol 583 (November 24th 1997) cols 783–785.

[57] M Hunt [1998] *PL* 423; R Buxton (2000) 116 *LQR* 48; HWR Wade (2000) 116 *LQR* 217; J Howells "The Human Rights Act 1998: the 'Horizontal Effect' on Land Law" ch 9 in E Cooke *Modern Studies in Property Law 1 – Property 2000* (Hart, 2001); D Beyleveld & SD Pattinson (2002) 118 *LQR* 623.

[58] *Hunter* v. *Canary Wharf* [1997] AC 655, 714, Lord Cooke dissenting (human rights principles alter standing to sue in nuisance).

[59] 8795/79, (1986) 8 EHHR 123; see below **[5.27]**.

[60] HRA 1998 ss 4(5), 6(3), 8(6) (Tribunals). Damages for judicial acts in good faith are limited by s 9.

[61] HRA 1998 s 3(1); *Mendoza* v. *Ghaidan* [2002] EWCA Civ 1533, [2002] 4 All ER 1162.

is not possible, the courts do not have power to strike down primary legislation (Acts of Parliament) but should make a declaration of incompatibility.[62] This will prompt the government to change the law using a fast track procedure.[63]

F. DEPRIVATION OF POSSESSIONS

1. Fundamental rights to property

[5.24] Most fundamental to the three limbs of the right to property in article 1 of Protocol 1 of the European Convention is the right to freedom from deprivation:

"No one shall be deprived of his possessions . . .".

Deprivation guards against actual loss of the property itself, the target being arbitrary confiscation.

Fundamental rights are directly in play when the state acquires the right,[64] or if the state acts indirectly, as where thugs apparently supported by the Zimbabwean government forced farmers off their land.[65] State liability is also attracted by legislation which enables one private landowner to expropriate another's property,[66] a limited "horizontal" effect.[67]

2. Ownership of "possessions"

[5.25] What is protected are "possessions", a term which clearly includes land and personal property,[68] but also intangible things like a right to receive a fair rent[69] or a right of restitution.[70] There are limits and overpayments by credit card at a restaurant are not possessions of the waiters even if they are intended by the diners to be a tip.[71]

A human rights complaint can only be brought by the victim[72] of an interference, that is generally an owner whose property has been taken,[73] and taken without his consent.

3. Compensation

[5.26] If an interference is a deprivation of property, as opposed to a control on its use, compensation is generally required. In relation to straightforward deprivations,

---

[62] HRA 1998 s 4; *Wilson* v. *First County Trust (No 2)* [2001] EWCA Civ 633, [2002] QB 74.

[63] HRA 1998 s 10, sch 2; new Bills will require a statement of compatibility.

[64] 1194/86 (forfeiture claim inadmissible); *Adam* v. *Czech Republic* (1997) 1 BHRC 451.

[65] *Commercial Farmers' Union* v. *Minister of Lands etc* (2000) 10 BHCR 1, Supreme Court of Zimbabwe.

[66] *James* v. *UK*, 8795/79, (1986) 8 EHRR 123; see below **[5.27]**.

[67] See above **[5.20ff]**.

[68] *Vasilescu* v. *Romania*, 27053/95, (1999) 28 EHRR 241.

[69] *R* v. *SS for Environment T&R ex p Spath Holme* [2000] 1 All ER 884, 905b, Lord Bingham MR in CA; reversed on appeal on other grounds [2001] 2 AC 349, HL.

[70] *National and Provincial BS* v. *UK*, 21319/93, (1998) 25 EHRR 127; *Gasus Dosier und Fördertechnik* v. *Netherlands*, 15375/89, (1995) 20 EHRR 403; *Matos e Silva* v. *Portugal*, 15777/89, (1997) 24 EHRR 573.

[71] *Nerva* v. *UK*, 42295/98, (2002) 36 EHRR 4 at 31.

[72] HRA 1998 s 7(1), (3), (6); ECHR art 34; *Bryan* v. *UK*, 19178/91, (1995) 21 EHRR 342.

[73] Shareholders lack standing to sue for the taking of property from their company: *Agrotexim* v. *Greece*, 14807/89, (1996) 21 EHRR 250.

the key case is the *Former King of Greece* v. *Greece*.[74] When a republic was declared in Greece in the 1970s, King Constantine was forced into exile and his estates were confiscated, a taking finally confirmed in 1994. The King lost his palace at Tatoi outside Athens and Mon Repos, a summer retreat on Corfu including the house in which the Duke of Edinburgh was born. The Strasbourg court ruled that the Greek government had violated the ex-King's rights. The estates belonged to Constantine as an individual and not to the state, with only two dissenters. Given that the first declaration of Human Rights was directed against the French King Louis XVI, it seemed off for a King to be using human rights arguments, but in fact Constantine ended up with very little.[75] Against a market value of the assets taken – 272m €–the court deducted the value of the tax concessions received by the Greek royal family and made an award of only 12m €. Touché! The case does suggest that in a normal case compensation needs to be at the full market value.[76]

4. Public interest justification

[5.27] At least some compensation has to be paid. Provided that is the case, deprivation of possessions may be justified:

> "in the public interest and subject to the conditions provided for by the law and by the general principles of international law."

States often invoke these limitations and derivative case-law principles to defend property legislation and a margin of appreciation gives each state an area of discretion in which it may determine whether particular legislation is useful. This margin is wide but the principle of proportionality requires that a fair balance must be struck between the right to property and the social needs of the community: the legislative remedy must be reasonably commensurate with the problem being tackled.[77]

The Leasehold Reform Act 1967 enables the owners of leasehold houses to acquire the freehold reversion at the site value well below the full market value. Its motivating philosophy was that tenants under long leases had the moral right to the bricks and mortar for which they had paid when acquiring the lease and landlords should only have the moral right to the undeveloped site. This undoubtedly involved expropriation. Was this justified in the public interest? Enfranchisement withstood a strong attack from the Duke of Westminster in *James* v. *United Kingdom*.[78] James was one of the trustees of the Duke's Grosvenor estate in Central London, consisting of 2,000 leasehold houses, the leaseholders of 80 of which sought to enfranchise in four years in the early 1980s, each with a potential windfall in the range £32,000 to £182,000. The estate stood to lose this amount. Legislation to remove social injustice could satisfy the public interest test, even if its effect was to transfer private rights from one individual to another rather than to achieve direct public ownership. Enfranchisement legislation was fair since occupying leaseholders are morally entitled to ownership,

---

[74] 25701/94, (2001) 33 EHRR 21
[75] *Former King of Greece* v. *Greece (No 2)* [2002] November 28th.
[76] At [78].
[77] *Mellacher* v. *Austria*, 10522/83, (1989) 12 EHRR 391; Y Winisdoerffer (1998) 19 *HRLJ* 18.
[78] 8795/97, (1986) 8 EHHR 123; S Bright [1994] *Conv* 211.

landlords collectively having exploited a monopoly to create a form of tenure which was disadvantageous to tenants. Sales of long leases should be based on the value of the land itself and not the market value of the land carrying the house. The tenant should not be required to buy again what he has already bought, and "unjust enrichment" of landlords should be reversed. The Act was appropriate to this end and not disproportionate. Anomalies in the legislation require separate justification, as they tended to discriminate between different property owners,[79] but the court accepted that objective reasons were available to justify the form of the English legislation.

If this overtly socialist legislation passed muster, it is difficult to see much prospect of successful human rights challenges. The Wilson government's nationalisation of the aircraft and shipbuilding industries survived in *Lithgow* v. *UK*,[80] and challenges to the compulsory purchase legislation have also failed.[81]

5. Deprivation by retroactivity in legislation

[5.28] One certain area for attack is retroactivity in legislation. The common law recognised the need for stability of property rights – even Lord Denning![82] Owners can now complain about any reform that removes existing rights.[83] Taken to extremes this could paralyse the process of reforming and simplifying property law but an attack on retroactive taxation of building society profits failed in *National & Provincial Building Society* v. *United Kingdom*.[84] In the particular case the legislation merely closed a loophole. Human rights theory should not be allowed to prevent changes needed to secure tidy development of the law.

6. Interference with peaceful enjoyment

[5.29] If property is taken from an individual and used by the state without a formal deprivation of legal title there may nevertheless be an interruption of the peaceful enjoyment of property. One case if where a public authority takes possession of land without instituting compulsory purchase procedures and without offering compensation.[85] Other examples are planning blight extending over 23 years,[86] failure to enforce a landlord's right to possession,[87] a long delay in settling compensation claims after expropriation,[88] and refusal to respect succession rights to property.[89]

---

[79] Contrary to art 14.

[80] 9006/86, (1986) 8 EHRR 329.

[81] *Lock* v. *SS for Environment T&R* [2002] EWHC 1654, [2002] 46 EG 203; *Fearon* v. *Irish Land Commission* [1984] ECR 3677, EuCtJ (Irish cpo legislation not discriminatory under EU law).

[82] *Hagee (London)* v. *AB Erikson & Larson* [1976] QB 209, 215, Lord Denning MR; *Phillips* v. *Mobil Oil Co* [1989] 1 WLR 888, 893–894, Nicholls LJ; *Otter* v. *Norman* [1989] AC 129, 146, Lord Bridge.

[83] A 10 year transitional period was thought to avoid the need for compensation when some of the old categories of overriding interests were removed: Law Com 271 (2001), [8.82–8.89].

[84] 21319/93, (1998) 25 EHRR 127.

[85] *Holy Monasteries* v. *Greece*, 13092/87, (1995) 20 EHRR 1; *Papamichalopoulos* v. *Greece*, 14556/89, (1993) 16 EHRR 440, (1996) 21 EHRR 439; *Agrotexim* v. *Greece* 14807/89 (1996) 21 EHRR 250; *Iatridis* v. *Greece*, 31107/96, (2000) 30 EHRR 97; *Pialopoulos* v. *Greece*, 37095/97, (2001) 33 EHRR 39 at 977.

[86] *Sporrong* v. *Sweden*, 7151/75, (1983) 5 EHRR 35.

[87] *Immobiliare Saffi* v. *Italy*, 22774/93, (2000) 30 EHRR 756.

[88] *Erkner* v. *Austria*, 9616/81, (1987) 9 EHRR 464. *Piron* v. *France*, 36436/97, (2002) 34 EHRR 14.

[89] *Marck* v. *Belgium*, 13092/87, (1979) 2 EHRR 330.

G. CONTROLS ON USE

1. Controls

[5.30] A state is allowed to:

"enforce such laws as it deems necessary to control the use of property in accordance with the general interest."[90]

An unjustified control on the use of property is therefore an infringement of the rights of the property owner. The rule interacts[91] with the prohibition on arbitrary deprivation of possessions and with the residual rule securing peaceful enjoyment of possessions.[92] Any controls must be a proportionate response to the social problem requiring legislation. However, a justified control will not generally require compensation.

2. Payment of taxes

[5.31] States may also:

"secure the payment of taxes or other contributions or penalties."

The imposition of a financial burden on land by a public authority may be seen as a form of taxation. This issue was litigated most memorably in *Aston Cantlow etc PCC* v. *Wallbank*.[93] A liability to contribute £95,000 to the cost of repairing the chancel of the parish church[94] of St John the Baptist, Aston Cantlow, was imposed on the owners of Glebe Farm in this Warwickshire parish. This was not only an interference (with the owners' money rather than their house) but also one that was unjustified. The lucky Wallbanks escaped a bill for £95,000. The imposition of a burden by a public authority like the Parochial Church Council was seen as a form of taxation.[95] The question was whether this particular form of taxation met the requirements of the public interest justification.[96] There is clearly a general interest in securing the repair of parish churches but it was quite disproportionate to load liability on to the Wallbanks.[97] It was arbitrary to impose liability on the owner of one house just because the land had formerly belonged to the church but to exempt other freehold land that did not differ in any relevant way.[98] It was also held to be an unfair discrimination.[99]

---

[90] Protocol 1 art 1.
[91] *Mellacher* v. *Austria*, 10522/83, (1989) 12 EHRR 391, 408; *Lithgow* v. *UK*, 9006/86, (1986) 8 EHRR 329.
[92] *National and Provincial BS* v. *UK*, 21319/93, (1998) 25 EHRR 127 (right in restitution); *Gasus Dosier und Fördertechnik* v. *Netherlands*, 15375/89, (1995) 20 EHRR 403; *Matos e Silva* v. *Portugal*, 15777/89, (1997) 24 EHRR 573.
[93] [2001] EWCA Civ 713, [2002] Ch 51.
[94] Chancel Repairs Act 1932 ; abolition was proposed by Law Com 152 (1985).
[95] At [40].
[96] At [41].
[97] At [43].
[98] At [44–50].
[99] At [51].

3. Public justification

[5.32] Laws are permitted to control the use of property: a state may:

"enforce such laws as it deems necessary to control the use of property in accordance with the general interest."

States often invoke these limitations and derivative case-law principles to defend property legislation. A margin of appreciation gives each state an area of discretion in which it may determine whether particular legislation is useful. Proportionality requires a fair balance between the right to property and the social needs of the community: the legislative remedy must be reasonably commensurate with the problem being tackled.[100]

4. Controls on use types

[5.33] Two important controls which are usually justified in the public interest are:

planning and zoning laws;[101]
rent regulation and security of tenure regimes.[102]

Details of legislation are open to scrutiny, and in extreme cases contraventions may be found.[103]

5. Unjustified controls – hunting

[5.34] A second hit was scored in *Chassagnou* v. *France*.[104] She farmed land just north of the Dordogne near the Chateau of Hautefort. French legislation required small farmers to allow local hunting associations to operate over their land. Owners could normally prevent others hunting over their land and the loss of this right was clearly a control on the use of the land.[105] Was it justified? The scheme for compulsory pooling of hunting rights went way beyond a fair balance and was outside the wide margin of appreciation allowed to the state.

---

[100] *Mellacher* v. *Austria*, 10522/83, (1989) 12 EHRR 391; *Scollo* v. *Italy*, 19133/91, (1996) 22 EHRR 514 (Italian security of tenure regime beyond margin of appreciation); Y Winisdoerffer (1998) 19 *HRLJ* 18.
[101] *Katte Klitsche* v. *Italy*, 12539/86, (1995) 19 EHRR 368; *Sporrong* v. *Sweden*, 7151/75, (1982) 5 EHRR 35; *Buckley* v. *UK*, 20348/92, (1996) 23 EHRR 101; and many, many, others.
[102] *Mellacher* v. *Austria*, 10522/83, (1990) 12 EHRR 391; *Spadea* v. *Italy*, 12868/87, (1996) 21 EHRR 482; *Scollo* v. *Italy*, 19133/91, (1996) 22 EHRR 514; *Immobiliare Saffi* v. *Italy*, 22774/93, (2000) 30 EHRR 756; *GL* v. *Italy* 22671/93 (2002) 34 EHRR 41
[103] *Scollo* v. *Italy*, 19133/91, (1996) 22 EHRR 514.
[104] 25088/94, (2000) 29 EHRR 615.
[105] At [71].

6. Controls that interfere with peaceful enjoyment

[5.35] Controls may infringe the guarantee of peaceful enjoyment of property, a protection in play, for example, in relation to planning blight,[106] the creation of a nature reserve,[107] or modification of restrictive covenants.[108]

H. RESPECT FOR THE HOME AND FAMILY LIFE

1. The article 8 right to the home

[5.36] Disputes affecting domestic property invoke article 8(1) of the Convention which guarantees that:

> "Everyone has the right to respect for . . . his home . . ."

It is clearly in play with domestic repossessions and planning decisions affecting homes,[109] even a home which breaks planning rules,[110] but also the office of a professional person.[111] Property never occupied as a home does not count.[112]

2. Justification of interferences with the home

[5.37] The right to respect for the home is heavily qualified by the public interest justification set out in paragraph 2 of Article 8 in these terms:

> "There shall be no interference by a public authority with the exercise of this right except such as in accordance with the law and is necessary in a democratic society in the interests of national security, public safety, or the economic well being of the country, for the prevention of disorder or crime, for the protection of health or morals or for the protection of the rights and freedoms of others."[113]

Examples of interferences that are usually justified are:

(1) Planning enforcement

[5.38] Human rights are in play in relation to a home occupied in breach of planning regulations.[114] But planning rules are generally within the wide margin of appreciation which States enjoy in the sphere of planning permission and the availability of procedural safeguards.[115]

---

[106] *Sporrong* v. *Sweden,* 7151/75, (1982) 5 EHRR 35 (compulsory purchase blocked use of land for 23 years).
[107] *Matos e Silva* v. *Portugal,* 15777/89, (1997) 24 EHRR 573, 590–593.
[108] *Scott* v. *UK,* 10741/84, (1984) 41 Decisions and Reports 226; N Dawson [1986] *Conv* 124.
[109] *Qazi* v. *Harrow LBC* [2001] EWCA Civ 1834, [2002] 1 HLR 14 at 274; J Luba (2002) 6 *LT Rev* 9.
[110] *Buckley* v. *UK,* 20348/92, (1996) 23 EHRR 101.
[111] *Niemietz* v. *Germany,* 13710/88, (1993) 16 EHRR 97.
[112] *Loizidou* v. *Turkey,* 15318/89, (1997) 23 EHRR 513.
[113] *Howard* v. *UK,* 10825/84, (1987) 9 EHRR 116.
[114] *Bryan* v. *UK,* 19178/91, (1995) 21 EHRR 342; *Buckley* v. *UK,* 20348/92, (1996) 23 EHRR 101.
[115] *McGonnell* v. *UK,* 28488/95, (2000) 30 EHRR 289.

(2) Residence conditions – justification

[5.39] Residence conditions designed to protect local populations against outside buyers of homes have been allowed in Guernsey[116] and are now legislative in Wales.[117]

(3) Repossession of a home

[5.40] A court order for repossession of domestic property is a state interference with a house, but the interference involved in a lawful repossession is justified. Proper exercise of the judicial discretion is a sufficient display of respect towards the home of the defendant tenant[118] or borrower.[119] However, it is possible for substantive laws to infringe a home, for example rules about notices to quit,[120] and also rules about access to housing benefit.[121] Procedures with no room for the exercise of a judicial discretion have also survived scrutiny – where a warrant for possession is issued[122] or where Parliament has laid down mandatory grounds for possession.[123]

(4) Searches

[5.41] Homes can always be searched in connection with the investigation of criminal offences and judicial processes such as freezing orders, but violations may occur if the terms of the lawful authority are exceeded.

3. Environmental pollution

[5.42] Environmental pollution could in theory be sufficient to constitute an interference with the home, but only when it is severe.[124] Human rights principles cannot be used to reverse the law of domestic repairs[125] – a landlord of a home rendered uninhabitable by condensation cannot be ordered to make it inhabitable if the cause of the problem is an inherent defect rather than a disrepair. One successful case was *Marcic v. Thames Water Utilities*[126] at first instance in which damages were awarded against

---

[116] *Gillow v. UK*, 9063/80, (1989) 11 EHRR 335; *Fearon v. Irish Land Commission*, EuCtJ Case 182/83, [1984] ECR 3677.

[117] Housing (Wales) Act 2001 ss 4–6.

[118] *Lambeth LBC v. Howard* [2001] EWCA Civ 468, (2001) 33 HLR 58.

[119] *Albany Home Loans v. Massey* [1997] 2 All ER 609, 612g–h.

[120] *Qazi v. Harrow LBC* [2001] EWCA Civ 1834, [2002] 1 HLR 14 at 274; J Luba (2002) 6 *LT Rev* 9.

[121] *Tucker v. SS for Social Security* [2002] HLR 27 at 500; *R(JR) Painter v. Carmarthenshire CC* [2002] HLR 23 at 447.

[122] *St Brice v. Southwark LBC* [2002] EWCA Civ 1138, [2002] 1 WLR 1537 (fresh exercise of discretion not required for an administrative step to give effect to an existing court order).

[123] *Poplar Housing and Regeneration Community Ass v. Donoghue* [2001] EWCA Civ 604, [2002] QB 48 (removal of interim accommodation from those found to be intentionally homeless); *Sheffield CC v. Smart* [2002] EWCA Civ 4, [2002] HLR 34 at 639 (eviction of homeless from temporary accommodation).

[124] *Lopez Osta v. Spain*, 16798/90, (1995) 20 EHRR 277 (air pollution); *R(JR) Malster v. Ipswich BC* [2001] EWHC Admin 711, [2002] P & CR 14, Sullivan J.

[125] *Lee v. Leeds CC* [2002] EWCA Civ 6, [2002] HLR 17 at 367.

[126] [2001] EWHC Techno 421, Judge Harvey QC, on appeal [2002] EWCA Civ 64, both reported at [2002] QB 929; *(No 2)* [2002] QB 2003.

a drainage authority which failed to implement works to prevent Marcic's home being flooded whenever there was heavy rain. Noise is also an important issue which, in a severe case like *Hatton* v. *UK*,[127] concerning flights out of Heathrow between 5 and 5.30 in the morning, may violate the rights of the homeowners in the flight path.

4. Respect for family life

[5.43] States must respect the right of humans to a family life, including the right to marry and to found a family.[128] Article 8 was successfully invoked by the Barclay brothers to challenge the feudal inheritance laws of the island of Sark. The brothers had bought the island of Brecqhou but the law of primogeniture required that it be left to the eldest son of David, since he happened to be the elder of the two twins born some ten minutes before Frederick. This artificial and absurd rule infringed the brothers' fundamental right to make wills as they chose.[129] A whole series of cases following *Marckx* v. *Belgium*[130] has removed the discrimination suffered under the succession laws of many European states by illegitimate children.

I.   DISCRIMINATION

1.   Article 14

[5.44] Discrimination as such does not offend the European Convention though a freestanding protocol attacking discrimination itself is under discussion.[131] Article 14 guarantees freedom from discrimination in the enjoyment of Convention rights.[132] but it is autonomous[133] in the sense that a breach of article 14 may occur the underlying Convention right has not been broken in isolation.

Legislation differentiating between two classes of property owners requires objective justification. In *Larkos* v. *Cyprus*[134] a civil servant was allocated rented accommodation by the government under the terms of an administrative order but when he retired they evicted him, arguing that his right to accommodation ended with his employment. Given that the tenancy agreement was silent as to the consequences of his retirement, this discriminatory treatment lacked any reasonable or objective justification.

---

[127] 36022/97, (2002) 34 EHRR 1.

[128] Art 12; *X, Y, Z* v. *UK*, 21830/93, [1997] 2 FLR 892 (not just within marriage).

[129] The issue was widely reported in October 1998; the whole feudal system in which membership of the legislative assembly is associated with ownership of a fief is now under attack: Guardian, August 24th 2002.

[130] 13092/87, (1979) 2 EHRR 330.

[131] Protocol 12; C McCafferty [2002] 03 *HR* 20.

[132] *Mellacher* v. *Austria*, 10522/83, (1989) 12 EHRR 391, 413; *National and Provincial BS* v. *UK*, 21319/93, (1998) 25 EHRR 127, 173–175.

[133] *Weidlich* v. *Germany*, 19048/91, [1996] March 4th.

[134] 21515/95, (2000) 30 EHRR 597; *Chassagnou* v. *France*, 25088/94, (2000) 29 EHRR 615 (large and small landowners treated differently).

2. Variant rules of property law

[5.45] Property law consists of a set of rules which differentiate between different cases applying one set of outcomes to one group of people and another set of outcomes for another. For example, a right of enfranchisement is given to a leaseholder with a long leasehold term exceeding 21 years but not to a tenant with a 20 year lease, a leaseholder paying a low rent qualifies to buy at one price while a leaseholder with higher rent has to pay more.[135] Attacks on discrimination under article 14 have such great potentiality because the human rights of those excluded may be infringed if the lines are drawn arbitrarily or without sufficient objective justification. The details of the enfranchisement legislation survived in *James*[136] and of the nationalisation legislation in *Lithgow*.[137] However, exemption of large landowners from the scheme to provide compulsory hunting rights over open land in rural France created an unjustified discrimination against the owners of small estates who were caught in the net, whether they liked it or not, and it was also dubious that the scheme applied to a random selection of French départements.[138]

3. Gays

[5.46] Discrimination against homosexuals is gradually being eliminated by repeated recourse to human rights law. Many gays forced out of the armed forces have obtained redress in Strasbourg and another recent case has led to the equalisation of the age of consent.[139] Government proposals will provide legal recognition to homosexual partnerships after registration,[140] though this will not extend to unmarried heterosexual cohabitees because of Treasury opposition to the cost.

The striking potentiality of human rights jurisprudence is illustrated by *Mendoza* v. *Ghaidan*[141] in which the Court of Appeal revisited and "overruled" the decision of the Lords in *Fitzpatrick* v. *Sterling Housing Association*.[142] The earlier case decided that a homosexual partner could not succeed to a Rent Act 1977 tenancy on the death of his partner as a "spouse" of the deceased tenant, but only as a family member at a less favourable rental and with inferior security of tenure.[143] The claim by *Mendoza* has established that this discriminated unfairly against homosexual partners. The succession provisions of the Rent Act 1977 are to be read so that the phrase "as his wife or husband" now includes a homosexual partner.[144] Sexual orientation as a

---

[135] P Sparkes *NLT* ch 15.

[136] 8795/79, (1986) 8 EHRR 123.

[137] 9006/86, (1986) 8 EHRR 329. Exemption from CPO on the basis of residence in Ireland did not discriminate against the nationals of other EU states: *Fearon* v. *Irish Land Commission* EuCtJ Case 182/83, [1984] ECR 3677.

[138] *Chassagnou* v. *France*, 25088/94, (2000) 29 EHRR 615.

[139] *Sutherland* v. *UK*, 25186/94, [2001] Times April 13th.

[140] Announcement by Barbara Roche, Minister for Social Exclusion and Equalities, ODPM, December 6th 2002; a CP is promised for Summer 2003.

[141] [2002] EWCA Civ 1533, [2002] 4 All ER 1162.

[142] [2001] 1 AC 257, HL; SM Cretney & FMB Reynolds (2000) 116 *LQR* 181; K McNorrie [2000] 4 *Edin L Rev* 256; N Roberts [2000] 30 *Fam Law* 417; A Bainham [2000] *CLJ* 39; A Samuels (2001) 22 *Stat L Rev* 154.

[143] P Sparkes, *NLT*, 118–120.

[144] As suggested in *Fitzpatrick* [1998] Ch 304, 338–339, Ward LJ dissenting in CA.

ground for differentiation has no proper and rational justification. Anomalies will arise unless the human rights jurisprudence is widened to prevent any discrimination between heterosexuals who are married and those in de facto relationships. Transsexuals form another disadvantaged group that has recently scored several successes in Strasbourg.[145]

4. Gypsy building restrictions and discrimination

[5.47] Gypsies favour a nomadic lifestyle that often brings then into conflict with the communities in which they stop and one which may well cut across the rules of property law and planning regimes, especially enforcement procedures, since results are often indirectly and unintentionally discriminatory. Most article 8 cases have failed,[146] but there have also been major successes.[147]

5. Accommodation of the disabled

[5.48] Substantial damages may be awarded for failing to meet domestic law standards for disabled accommodation.[148]

J. FUNDAMENTAL TRIAL RIGHTS

1. Trial rights

[5.49] Article 6 guarantees due process for the resolution of civil claims,[149] that is the right to a fair and public hearing, without undue delay, and before an independent and impartial tribunal.[150] The event which brings into play the article 6 guarantee is the determination of an individual's civil rights. Any litigation affecting rights to land or other property is certainly within the scope,[151] though only the primary determination of the right is covered and not subsidiary procedural steps.[152] Domestic law

---

[145] *Goodwin* v. *UK*, 28957/95, (2002) 35 EHRR 447; *I* v. *UK*, 25690/94, [2002] 2 FCR 613. But the Government is fighting a case for recognition of the right to marry, *Beringer* v. *Beringer* which is before the HL in January 2003.

[146] *Buckley* v. *UK*, 20348/92, (1997) 23 EHRR 101; *Andrew Smith* v. *UK*, 26666/95, (2001) 33 EHRR 20.

[147] *Coster* v. *UK*, 24876/94, (2001) 33 EHRR 20 at 479; *Beard* v. *UK*, 24883/94 (2001) 33 EHRR 19 at 442; *Lee* v. *UK*, 25289/94, (2001) 33 EHRR 29 at 677; *Jane Smith* v. *UK*, 25154/94, (2001) 33 EHRR 30 at 712; *Chapman* v. *UK*, 27238/95, (2001) 33 EHRR 18 at 399; *South Buckinghamshire DC* v. *Porter* [2001] EWCA Civ 1549, [2002] 1 All ER 425; *Clare* v. *SS for Environment T&R* [2002] EWCA Civ 819, [2002] JPEL 1365.

[148] *R(JR) Bernard* v. *Enfield BC* [2002] EWHC 2282, [2002] Times November 8th.

[149] Criminal trial procedure is subject to additional controls under art 6(2); anti-social behaviour orders are civil rather than criminal: *R(JR) McCann* v. *Manchester Crown Ct* [2002] UKHL 39, [2002] 3 WLR 1313; so are orders to confiscate the proceeds of crime: *Phillips* v. *UK*, 41087/98, (2001) 11 BHRC 290; there are many UK cases.

[150] *Scollo* v. *Italy*, 19133/91, (1996) 22 EHRR 514, 530–532; *National and Provincial BS* v. *UK*, 21319/93, (1998) 25 EHRR 127, 175–183; *Terra Woninger* v. *Netherlands*, 20641/92, (1997) 24 EHRR 456; *Vacher* v. *France*, 20368/92, (1997) 24 EHRR 482.

[151] *Sporrong* v. *Sweden*, 7151/75, (1982) 5 EHRR 35; *Lafarge Redland Aggregates* v. *Scottish Ministers* [2000] SLT 1361, 1368, [26], Lord Hardie; and many other cases.

[152] *St Brice* v. *Southwark LBC* [2001] EWCA Civ 1138, [2002] 1 WLR 1537.

determines what rights are guaranteed so the Convention is not a vehicle for complaints about irrationalities in the property system.[153]

2. Administrative decisions

[5.50] Case law[154] has extended article 6 to encompass the making of administrative decisions such as the grant of a gaming licence,[155] or a decision to expropriate land. The public authority making such a decision necessarily does not meet the conditions to be an independent judicial tribunal but the entire procedure is compliant if there is a full appeal to an independent court.

Planning procedures must therefore comply with article 6. Especial difficulty is caused by cases where a minister has power to call in a planning decision for personal decision. An enforcement decision called in to the Department of Environment survived scrutiny in *Bryan* v. *United Kingdom*[156] because the minister's decision was subject to judicial review in the High Court, a conclusion supported by the leading domestic case, *Regina (Alconbury Developments)* v. *Secretary of State for Environment Transport and the Regions*.[157] It explores the calling in procedures which apply to large scale projects such as the proposed development of 1000 acres of Alconbury airfield near Huntingdon, just off the London to Edinburgh main line; following a refusal of permission by the council, the Secretary of State then recovered the decision for himself on the ground that it was a major proposal of more than local importance. His decision was a "determination of a civil right" of the developer, and the ministerial involvement was not independent, but article 6 was nevertheless complied with because of the possibility of judicial review of the decision. The grounds for judicial review must be wide enough to include a consideration of proportionality.

3. Full review

[5.51] Many procedures fail to meet Convention standards at the first instance stages. Independence may be sufficiently assured by a provision for an appeal to the courts, which are independent, providing that the grounds of appeal are sufficiently wide. If a homeless person is refused an allocation of housing he can request a review by a panel composed of officers of the housing authority, who clearly lack independence. Human rights compliance is ensured by the provision for an appeal to a county court which has full jurisdiction to review the matter for errors of law.[158]

Another problem arises where Parliament has laid down a procedure which precludes judicial consideration of the merits of the case. A notable example is the

---

[153] Domestic law may fall foul of art 13 if it fails to provide an adequate remedy for a breach of a human right.

[154] *Le Comte* v. *Belgium*, 6878/75, (1982) 4 EHRR 1; *Albert* v. *Belgium*, 7299/75, (1983) 5 EHRR 533, [29]; *Golder* v. *UK*, 4451/70, (1975) 1 EHRR 524.

[155] *Kingsley* v. *UK*, 35605/97, (2002) 35 EHRR 177.

[156] *Bryan* v. *UK*, 19178/91, (1995) 21 EHRR 342; *R(JR) Alconbury*, [2001] UKHL 23, [2001] 2 All ER 929, [101–117], Lord Hoffmann.

[157] [2001] UKHL 23, [2001] 2 All ER 929.

[158] *Begum* v. *Tower Hamlets LBC* [2002] EWCA Civ 239, [2002] 2 All ER 668; confirmed [2003] UKHL 5; *Adan* v. *Newham LBC* [2001] EWCA Civ 1916, [2002] 1 WLR 2120.

procedure for introductory tenancies in the public sector by which a public sector tenant obtains a probationary tenancy without full security of tenure for the first year. The housing authority has an unfettered discretion to end the tenancy during that year, though it is subject to a review procedure and that is subject to judicial review. This procedure has survived several challenges and appears to be Convention compliant.[159]

Judicial review is available of any act of a public authority that is incompatible with any Convention right,[160] unless, that is, the act is in accordance with incompatible primary legislation.[161] Grounds for judicial review will take into account the proportionality principle of human rights jurisprudence.

4.   Access to court

[5.52] Access to a court is a fundamental entitlement to allow a person's civil rights to be determined.[162] Where property rights can be determined by self help procedures like forfeiture of a lease by the landlord's peaceable re-entry[163] distress for rent by the seizure and sale of the tenant's goods,[164] or the removal of trespassers from land by the order of a senior police officer.[165] Access to the court could also be removed by issuing a public immunity certificate,[166] by requiring security before proceedings are issued[167] or by restrictions on legal aid. Enforcement of time limits is perfectly proper,[168] and by extension so is the limitation principle that hands title to an adverse possessor after 12 years is permitted[169] and this is not a deprivation of possessions. The right to a court can be waived, for example by an arbitration clause.

5.   Adequate trial procedure

[5.53] The basic complaint under article 6 is that the state has failed to provide an adequate court.[170] Hearings must be public,[171] "equality of arms" must be maintained between litigants, and remedies must be effective and enforced adequately.[172] Delay is a problem in other jurisdictions but the new case management functions of the Woolf

---

[159] *R(JR) McLellan* v. *Bracknell Forest BC* [2001] EWCA Civ 1510, [2002] 1 All ER 899.

[160] HRA 1998 s 6(1).

[161] As defined in s 21.

[162] *Wilson* v. *First National Trust (No 2)* [2001] EWCA Civ 633, [2002] QB 74.

[163] G Watt "Property Rights and Wrongs: The Frontiers of Forfeiture" ch 7 in E Cooke *Modern Studies in Property Law 1 – Property 2000* (Hart, 2001).

[164] *Fuller* v. *Happy Shopper Markets* [2001] 1 WLR 1681.

[165] Criminal Justice and Public Order Act 1994 s 61; *R(JR) Fuller* v. *Dorset Chief Constable* [2001] EWHC Admin 1017, [2002] 3 All ER 57, Stanley Burnton J.

[166] *Devlin* v. *UK*, 29545/96, [2002] Times November 9th.

[167] *R* v. *Lord Chancellor ex p Lightfoot* [2000] QB 597, CA (no breach on facts).

[168] *Arogundade* v. *Brent LBC* [2002] HLR 18 at 397.

[169] *JA Pye (Oxford)* v. *Graham* [2002] UKHL 30, [2002] 3 All ER 865, [65], Lord Browne-Wilkinson; *Family H Ass* v. *Donellan* [2002] 1 P & CR 34 at 449, Ch D

[170] *Locabail UK* v. *Waldorf Investment Corp (No. 4)* [2000] Times June 13th, Evans-Lombe J.

[171] CPR 39; *R(JR) Pelling* v. *Bow Ct Ct* [2001] UKHRR 165, QBD Admin.

[172] *Immobiliare Saffi* v. *Italy*, 22774/93, (2000) 30 EHRR 756 (eviction took 13 years and after 11 unsuccessful attempts); *Spadea* v. *Italy*, 12868/87, (1996) 21 EHRR 482; *Scollo* v. *Italy*, 19133/91, (1996) 22 EHRR 514.

reforms should ensure that strikes against the UK remain isolated.[173] Adherence to the Civil Procedure Rules should ensure compliance with the Convention.[174]

6. Independent tribunal

[5.54] A determination of civil rights is only fair if it is made by a court, the real meaning of the continental term "tribunal", composed of members independent of the parties and of the executive, and they must also be impartial. There is a voluminous case law that lies beyond the scope of this work.

---

[173] *Davies* v. *UK*, 42007/98, [2002] Times August 1st; *Mitchell* v. *UK*, 44808/98, [2002] Times December 28th.
[174] *Daniels* v. *Walker* [2000] Times May 17th, CA.

6

PROPERTY RIGHTS

Classification. Property law issues. Dovetailing of registered and unregistered land law. New property rights. A taxonomy of burdens. Priority.

A. CLASSIFICATION OF INTERESTS

1. Ownership interests and burdens

[6.01] Roman law divided property interests into two categories. Rights *in re proprieta* are ownership rights in one's own land, right which confer the enjoyment of land, the power to use, sell and bequeath. In English law these are estates and beneficial interests under trusts. Rights *in re aliena* are limited rights over another's land, such as a lease, mortgage or easement. This classification is not a perfect fit for English land because of the wide scope for the division of ownership. A duality is illustrated by interests such as a leasehold estate which from the point of view of the leaseholder is an ownership right conferring possession of the land but which acts as a burden when the ground landlord sells the freehold estate.

2. Endurability of burdens

[6.02] The second category – rights over another's land – are variously described by common lawyers as incumbrances, charges, or third party rights but the term "burdens" as used by *New Land Lawyers* is now also used by the registry.[1] A burden should be visualised as an encrustation attached to a legal estate. If a barnacle attaches itself to the hull of a ship in Sydney harbour it will still be there when the ship docks in Southampton. In the same way, a long lease granted by the owner of a piece of land in 1700 will still bind it in the year 2000, unless the term has expired or the leaseholder has agreed to surrender it. Endurability is the key characteristic, the capacity of a burden to bind the land through successive ownerships.

B. PROPERTY LAW ISSUES

1. The triangle of property law

[6.03] Burdens must be capable of binding a purchaser of the land. A buyer has to accept the blot on the title, or clear it off by agreement, or buy elsewhere. Endurability

---

[1] LRA 2002 s 32(1).

is the main characteristic of a property right, since personal rights are binding only between the original parties, a linkage strictly a non-sequitur[2] but deeply rooted in the common law.

Land law's (decidedly unsexy) threesome can be illustrated thus:

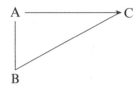

Figure 6-1 A property law triangle

The owner of a piece of land (A) creates a property right in favour of B, which then binds a purchaser (C). If in 1970[3] A promised to pay B a rentcharge of £52 a year secured on A's land a property right was created, but if A merely promised B that whoever lived in A's house would pay B £1 per week for 20 years for the supply of a dozen free range eggs, the contract was personal.[4]

2.   Property law between the original parties

[6.04] It is vitally important to determine whether a particular issue arises between the holder of an adverse interest and the person who created it (B–A) or as against a future owner of the land (B–C). In the former case a personal contract often suffices but property issues may also arise between the original parties. Formality is required for the creation of property rights, even between the original parties,[5] and also vitally because any claim to a share of a home can only be by way of a property claim to a constructive trust. If any interest exists it must be a property interest.

3.   Endurability

[6.05] Property law is always in play when the question of enforcement arises against a successor to the person who originally created the burden. Privity of contract exists between the original parties (A–B), but a proprietary right is required when enforcement is sought against C. Personal rights are differentiated from property rights by the forced transfer that follows bankruptcy and also, more particularly, by a sale. The correct principle is that property rights may endure because a question of priority is

---

[2] K Gray & SF Gray "The Idea of Property in Land" ch 1 in Bright & Dewar, 36; S Bright "Of Estates and Interests: A Tale of Ownership and Property Rights" ch 21 in Bright & Dewar, 541-546; Panesar's *General Principles* ch 10.

[3] Before the Rentcharges Act 1977.

[4] A purchaser takes free of personal claims to damages: *Att-Gen* v. *Biphosphated Guano Co* (1879) 11 Ch D 327, CA; *Reeves* v. *Pope* [1914] 2 KB 284; *National Provincial Bank* v. *Ainsworth* [1965] AC 1175, 1225, 1237-1238, 1259.

[5] See below **[7]**, **[22]**.

raised between the holder of a burden and a subsequent owner of the land, that is between B and C. Priority is introduced below.

It cannot be emphasised sufficiently how important it is to determine which set of questions are being raised. The key is this: has the land potentially affected by the right changed hands?

4. Assignability

[6.06] If the burden of a property right endures it is usually also true that the benefit is assignable.[6] A leasehold estate or the right to receive a secured loan or the benefit of a contract to buy land can all be sold. But this is less fundamental. Property rights can be envisaged that can be enjoyed only by an original party, such as a lease with an absolute covenant against assignment.

C. BURDENS ON REGISTERED AND UNREGISTERED LAND

[6.07] Proprietary status is awarded in unregistered conveyancing to all legal estates, legal interests, equitable interests and equities, that is to the class of rights recognised at law and in equity.

Registered land law can only dovetail properly with its older sister if it operates on the same set of property interests.[7] Interests that were proprietary should not lose that status on first registration, nor, conversely, should registration of the title act to confer endurability on rights that previously lacked this status. Two principles ensure that substantive property law runs in tandem. (1) Entries can only be made in the register in respect of a burden[8] or, in old money, where a person was "interested in any land or a charge".[9] If a right is incapable of binding a purchaser there is nothing to warn him about so personal rights have never been protectible.[10] (2) Overriding status is conferred only on "an interest"[11] or in the older terms if an overriding interest had to "subsist in relation to the land.[12] The Land Registration Act 2002 states that a right of pre-emption is proprietary,[13] as is an equity created by proprietary estoppel and an equity of rectification.[14] These are intended to be declaratory of the unregistered land law but there is a severe risk that the two systems may become decoupled.

Classification of burdens in the two systems also matches, actually much more closely than is generally believed.

---

[6] LPA 1925 s 4(2).

[7] *Elias* v. *Mitchell* [1972] Ch 652, 659F (on LRA 1925); this more or less remains true under the LRA 2002, but see immediately below.

[8] LRA 2002 s 32(1).

[9] Old law for cautions: LRA 1925 ss 54(1), 55(1); *Murray* v. *Two Strokes* [1973] 1 WLR 823 (pre-emption); *Observatory Hill* v. *Camtel Investments* [1997] 1 EGLR 140, Ch D (party wall award).

[10] *Calgary & Edmonton Land Co* v. *Dobinson* [1974] Ch 102, Megarry J (shareholder's right to company's land); *Barnes* v. *Cadogan Developments* [1930] 1 Ch 479 (indemnity); *Cator* v. *Newton* [1940] 1 KB 415, CA (maintenance of estate roads).

[11] LRA 2002 s 29(1).

[12] LRA 1925 s 70(1); see below [15.32].

[13] LRA 2002 s 115; contrast under the old law: *Murray* v. *Two Strokes* [1973] 1 WLR 823, 827H, Goulding J. For unregistered land law see below [24.08].

[14] LRA 2002 s 116.

D. DIVISION BY BURDENS

[6.08] The transactional power of the landowner contains an inherent contradiction, for the landowner with full powers of disposition can create rights which destroy the value of the land for future owners.[15] Curiously, given the invalidity of direct restrictions on saleability, it is possible using the property law powers of disposition to cripple the estate completely. A freeholder may grant a lease for 3,000 years[16] at a rent of £50[17] with an absolute prohibition on sale of the lease. Freehold land worth £100,000 is used as security for a loan of £150,000, the negative equity of the owner ensuring that all the value in the land resides in the lender. A restrictive covenant could impose an obligation not to occupy a house. A building estate developer may grant a strip of land giving access to the development site to another person without reserving access rights, shifting much of the value of the site to the ransom strip. A freeholder may grant an option to purchase land worth £1 million at a price of £1.

E. NEW PROPERTY RIGHTS

1. New burdens

[6.09] So a balance is required. Property law must make available all rights needed for full enjoyment of land ownership, while ensuring that land is not so burdened by adverse rights as to discourage its sale.[18] It does this by limiting the range of accepted property rights.[19] Landowners may not dream up their own burdens, as Pollock CB said in *Hill* v. *Tupper*:[20]

"A new species of incorporeal hereditament cannot be created at the will and pleasure of the owner of property . . . A grantor may bind himself to allow any right he pleases over his property, but he cannot annex to it a new incident . . .".

The facts show why. Hill, who owned a tea rooms on the bank of the canal, obtained from the canal company the grant of an exclusive right of hiring out pleasure boats on it. This right was like a business franchise, rather than an easement which must benefit the land to which it is attached.[21] So when the court asked whether Hill has an easement (a recognised property right) or merely a licence, the decision fell on the personal side. Tupper, the interloper, had not infringed any property right of Hill so Hill's trespass action against him failed.

---

[15] JF Garner (1958) 22 *Conv (NS)* 33.
[16] Long terms have always been valid: *Lamb* v. *Archer* (1692) Carth 266, 90 ER 758.
[17] Above the financial limit of the compulsory enlargement provision: LPA 1925 s 153; see below [25.89].
[18] *Keppell* v. *Bailey* (1834) 2 My & K 517, 535-536, 39 ER 1042, Lord Brougham LC.
[19] The common law equivalent of the civilian "*numerus clausus*".
[20] (1863) 2 H & C 121, 127-128, 159 ER 51; *Bankhart* v. *Tennant* (1870) LR 10 Eq 141, 148-149; Megarry & Wade (6th ed), [4.090-4.091], [13.005] n 53.
[21] See below [32.20].

2.   Equitable child-bearing

[6.10] A snapshot of any legal system taken in three dimensions inevitably suggests that the categories of property rights are fixed, but a moving picture that adds the fourth dimension of time reveals a completely different picture. Medieval owners cared much about manors[22] and advowsons, but had to make do without the lease. Leases were let in during the late medieval period, but the common law could not expand further afterwards, and this early onset of inflexibility[23] passed the task of development to equity. Flexibility was restored by equity's preparedness to fashion new remedies and to grant remedies in novel situations, a dose which, if repeated, gradually crystallises particular sets of facts into a new right. Boy though, does equity work slowly, adding trusts in the seventeenth century and the equity of redemption in the eighteenth, with restrictive covenants as a nineteenth century[24] response to the Victorian fashion for suburban development.

Birkenhead capped the overall range of property rights,[25] so that statutory additions apart, Edwardian case-law should be decisive of the property law of the second Elizabeth. "Equity", said Harman LJ extra-judicially, "is past the age of child-bearing." In *National Provincial Bank* v. *Ainsworth*,[26] Mrs Ainsworth was deserted by her husband and left in occupation of the matrimonial home with her children. As a non-contributor she had to rely on her right as a deserted wife to the provision of a house by her husband. This right was held to be personal, valid against her husband and not capable of binding a lender, the focus of the decision being the fact that proprietary status had not previously been recognised. Contractual licences were another innocent slaughtered in infancy.[27] But proprietary estoppel was conceived, hatched, and brought to maturity during Lord Denning's tenure as Master of the Rolls,[28] so it would be wrong to diagnose equity as having become totally infertile and somehow or another a blind eye has been turned to the legislative prohibition on equitable procreation.

3.   Interests lacking proprietary status

[6.11] Piecemeal development has left one remarkable gap – the inability of one property owner to impose a financial burden on his land in the shape of a positive covenant to spend money so that the burden would bind future owners.[29] Our law is tilted rather too much towards the conservative.

---

[22] It is an irony that the last substantive speech on the LRB 2002 was about its impact on manors.
[23] Now confirmed by LPA 1925 s 1(1)-(2).
[24] *Tulk* v. *Moxhay* (1848) 2 Ph 774, 41 ER 1143.
[25] LPA 1925 s 4(1) proviso; JS Anderson, *Lawyers and the Making of English Land Law 1832–1940* (Clarendon Press, 1992), 309.
[26] [1965] AC 1175, HL.
[27] *Ashburn Anstalt* v. *Arnold* [1989] Ch 1, CA; see below [19.76].
[28] *Inwards* v. *Baker* [1965] 2 QB 29, CA; see below [23].
[29] *Rhone* v. *Stephens* [1994] 2 AC 310, HL; see below [32.34].

4.   Quasi-property

[6.12] Reich identified a new property in the American law of the 1950s,[30] consisting of rights to occupation without ownership (licences[31]), and entitlement to security of tenure and social security benefits. A similar development in the agricultural field is the milk quota, a vital adjunct to dairy land of which the proprietary status is now recognised.[32]

F.   A TAXONOMY OF BURDENS

1.   Forms of burdens

[6.13] There is no universal agreement about how to classify burdens, since so much depends upon what is convenient in a particular context but there are broadly three main types.

2.   Overreachable interests

[6.14] Many adverse interests are removed from land when it is sold by the process of overreaching. A full list will be given in the chapter of this book relating to trusts[33] but of course the most important are beneficial interests under a trusts of land on a sale by two trustees. Protection is inappropriate for rights which will be swept off the land on sale: such interests do not fall into the classes of land charge, and neither is a land registry notice allowed.

3.   Redeemable money charges

[6.15] A mortgage secures the payment of a sum of money on land. If that sum is not repaid, the proprietary character of a secured loan becomes all important. The lender has the right to sell the land and to take the money owed out of the proceeds of sale (another form of overreaching[34]), so the debt is secured in the sense that a first charge is given on the value of the land. In technical terms an arrangement by which money is secured on land is a charge, but this book uses the term "money charge" to avoid possible ambiguity. These interests can be redeemed – the land can be freed of the burden by repayment of the money secured.

4.   True burdens

[6.16] True burdens are interests which cannot be overreached or redeemed so they bind the land in the hands of a purchaser.

---

[30] CA Reich (1964) 73 *Yale LJ* 733. The article has generated a substantial volume of commentary.
[31] See below **[19]**.
[32] *Faulks* v. *Faulks* [1992] 1 EGLR 9, Chadwick J; and numerous later cases.
[33] LPA 1925 s 2; see below **[13.10]**.
[34] See below **[29.20ff]**.

(1) Leases

[6.17] If a freeholder grants a lease to a tenant the leasehold estate is from the point of view of the landlord a burden detracting from his freehold ownership.

(2) One trustee trusts

[6.18] A one-trustee trust may arise where land is registered in the name of T with the aid of a contribution to the purchase price by B. Sale by a single trustee will not overreach the beneficial interest, which acts as a burden against the legal title.[35]

(3) Neighbour obligations

[6.19] An important group of property rights regulate the relationship between neighbouring owners. Easements are rights to use land, for example to gain access along a right of way. Restrictive covenants limit the use to be made of the land, for example maintaining the residential character of a neighbourhood by limiting building to houses. These rights are distinctive because the minus represented by the burden of one neighbour's obligation is matched by a plus consisting of the benefit to an adjoining neighbour, that plus also being attached to the land.

(4) Rights to transfer

[6.20] An important group of rights consist of the right to acquire and estate – such as the rights under a transfer of registered land not yet registered, a contract to buy, a claim to a transfer of rights in the matrimonial home, or, conversely, a right to upset a transfer on the grounds of misconduct practised on the previous owner to induce him to make the transfer. By extension the right may be to obtain an interest in the land, for example a contact for a lease. These give rights to the land itself and are not overreachable.

(5) Pure burdens

[6.21] A small calls of residuals do not fall into the above classes such as rentcharges, which bind and encumber land without any functional reason to do so. These incorporeal hereditaments are gradually being extinguished.[36]

G. PRIORITY

1. Priority

[6.22] A proprietary right *is capable of* binding a purchaser, but whether it will actually do so depends upon which interest has priority.[37] Land law determines which of

---

[35] See below **[15]**.
[36] See below **[34.05]**.
[37] Burdens are overridden by a compulsory purchase: *R* v. *City of London Corp ex p Mystery of the Barbers of London* (1997) 73 P & CR 59; *Shewu* v. *Hackney LBC* [1999] 1 EGLR 1, CA.

two competing interests prevails, with the loser relegated to taking any scraps left after the winner has been satisfied, or pursuing his complaints in the lesser legal subjects of contract, restitution and tort. As Captain Scott wrote at the South Pole after finding the Norwegian flag left by Amundsen:

> "Great God! this is an awful place, and terrible enough for us to have laboured to it without the reward of priority."[38]

Much as the English psyche adores a gallant loser, the truth is that second is nowhere. Once the claim with the highest priority is satisfied there is often nothing left to satisfy secondary claims. There is no balancing act. One person wins and the other is deferred. At least clear cut definitive advice can be given on the state of a title for, as that great adherent of fixed rules, Alfred Denning, once said:

> "In land, certainty is of paramount importance. It does not matter so much what the rule is, so long as it is certain."[39]

Property law priorities can be varied by agreement[40] or by estoppel.[41]

2. First in time

[6.23] There are two approaches to priority, one crude and the other more sophisticated. The former is to line interests up in a queue based on the order of their creation. The first in time prevails. This applies to

legal interests in unregistered land (other than mortgages);
equitable interests between themselves;
interests noted against a registered title between themselves;
overriding interests as against later registered interests; and
overriding interests between themselves.

To describe this as crude is to say that it can be very unfair in operation. If you want to buy land it is impossible to know whether you will get a good title or whether the land will turn out to be subject to earlier interests that you are unaware of. In other words one does not necessarily get what has been paid for.

3. Protected purchasers

[6.24] Most interests are subject to a more sophisticated system which provides a balance between the interests of the members of our property law triangle:

---

[38] *Journal*, January 17th 1912.
[39] (1952) 5 *CLP* 1, 8; *Otter* v. *Norman* [1989] AC 129, 146, Lord Bridge.
[40] *Cheah* v. *Equiticorp Finance Group* [1991] 4 All ER 989, PC; *Re British & Commonwealth Holdings (No 3)* [1992] 1 WLR 672; *Re Maxwell Communication Corp (No 2)* [1993] 1 WLR 1402.
[41] See below **[23]**.

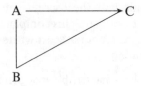

Figure 6-2 A priority triangle

The two principles are:

One: Usually the first in time prevails (B–C); but
Two: A purchaser who is protected can defeat an earlier interest (C–B). In such a case this book describes C as a protected purchaser.

In terms of rule one, means are provided to protect interests – deposit of title deeds, registration of land charges, entry of a notice occupation of registered land. If the interest is properly protected it is perfectly safe. The order is B–C. Valuation of the land is easy because the buyer knows what interests will affect him. Protection is provided for buyers against other, unprotected, interests, reversing the priorities, C–B.

4. Rules for protected purchasers

[6.25] The requirements for protection vary from context to context, but can be summed up in four basic elements, of which the first three are essential in all cases:

(1) Acquisition of a protected interest

[6.26] Basically a protected purchaser (C) buys a legal estate and this trumps an earlier equitable interest (B).

(2) Value

[6.27] The point is to free up the market in land, removing unprotected burdens, but there is only justice in doing this in favour of a buyer. There is no consistency between the various priority principles about what counts as value.

(3) Diligence

[6.28] Purchasers can only claim protection if they have been diligent, that is they have carried out all conveyancing procedures properly in the attempt to discover adverse interests. What steps are required varies from context to context:

equitable interests affecting unregistered land[42] – all reasonable enquiries and a check for occupiers;

---

[42] Other than land charges.

mortgages of unregistered land – check that the seller holds the title deeds and that these have not been deposited with a lender;

land charges affecting unregistered land – conduct a land charges search; and registered land – conduct an official search and check for occupiers.

(4) Honesty

[6.29] Sometimes a purchaser cannot be protected if he knows of an earlier interest. That is the rule for notice doctrine affecting unregistered land. But registration schemes tend to focus on whether or not an adverse interest is registered and not to care what a buyer knows off the register. Hence honesty is not a requirement for reliance on a land charges search nor on an official search of a registered title.

7

DEEDS

Legal formality of a deed. Deeds made on "paper". E-Documents. E-transfers. Documents executed by companies.

A. LEGAL FORMALITY OF A DEED

1. Utility of and requirement for a deed

[7.01] Land lies in grant,[1] meaning that it is transferable by document. Medieval law considered that land lay in livery, which meant that a physical transfer of possession was required to give or sell it.[2] Holding a public ceremony on the land to transfer possession was a sound method of proving that a sale had occurred at a time when many landowners were unable to write, but it was inconvenient for major landowners were often too busy to visit their land for minor conveyancing transactions. Subterfuges were needed to evolve a method of documentary conveyancing and so to undermine the requirement for a physical transfer of possession.[3] This coincidentally achieved privacy in ownership. Deeds-based conveyancing was a long-established fact when it was legitimised by Act in 1845. Ownership is too serious a matter to be left to "depend on the slippery testimony of human memory."[4] Formality maintains a record of transactions and ensures that documentary titles are comprehensive.

Creation or transfer of legal estates and interests can only be accomplished by deed.[5] Section 52 of the Law of Property Act 1925 provides that:

> "All conveyances of land or of any interest therein are void for the purpose of conveying or creating a legal estate unless made by deed."

Land is widely defined,[6] so as to include within section 52 the grant of a mortgage, rentcharge or other interest.

---

[1] LPA 1925 s 51, replacing Real Property Act 1845 s 3; PBH Birks "Before We Begin: Five Keys to Land Law" ch 8 in Bright & Dewar, 482–486; A Critchley "Taking Formalities Seriously" ch 9 in Bright & Dewar.

[2] Possession of the freehold estate was described as "seisin"; a leaseholder enjoyed possession but not seisin. The repeal of the Statute of Uses 1535 in 1925 has robbed this distinction of all significance.

[3] AWB Simpson, *A History of the Land Law* (Clarendon, 2nd ed, 1986), 119–143, 188–190.

[4] *Hill* v. *Hill* [1897] 1 QB 483, 492, Chitty LJ.

[5] Or of course by statute, eg Land at Palace Avenue, Kensington (Acquisition of Freehold) Act 2002, c ii.

[6] LPA 1925 s 205(1)(ix); "conveyance" is also widely defined by para (ii); s 201(1) includes as "land" manors and other incorporeal hereditaments.

2. Exceptional cases of informality

[7.02] Three groups of informal transactions are allowed to impact directly on the legal estate. Some transactions have always required a document *other than a deed* and these survive as anomalies in modern law, examples being assents by personal representatives,[7] disclaimers on bankruptcy, and receipts.[8] A useful simplification would be to require a deed in each of these cases. *Transmissions* pass a legal estate automatically, a situation which obviously makes any documentary formality impossible. One example is the surrender by operation of law – when a landlord grants a new lease to his existing tenant causing the old lease to terminate.[9] Others are the transfer made by a deceased landowner to his personal representatives on his death or by a bankrupt to his trustee in bankruptcy, corporate insolvency, and court vesting orders.[10] Finally, a *short lease* for a term not exceeding three years can be created orally.[11]

3. Failure to use a deed

[7.03] Formality favours the monied, the strong and the well advised, so flexibility is required to correct the imbalance created against the poor and weak. Failure to use a deed renders a conveyance *void at law*, a phrase which seems to presuppose that it can operate in equity.[12] Much ingenuity has been directed, first to evading the requirements, and second, to keeping the techniques of evasion within limits:[13] formality cannot be displaced completely without destroying the value of the register.

B. DEEDS MADE ON "PAPER"

1. Deeds

[7.04] A deed is a particularly formal type of document used to mark some "solemn and authentic act"[14] such as entry into a covenant,[15] a land registry transfer,[16] or any dealing with a legal estate. Section 1 of the Law of Property (Miscellaneous Provisions) Act 1989[17] carries into effect Law Commission proposals[18] "to make new provision with respect to deeds and their execution".[19]

---

[7] Transferring legal title to a beneficiary entitled under a will or on an intestacy.

[8] LPA 1925 s 52(2) paras (a), (b) and (e), as amended.

[9] See below **[25.63]**.

[10] LPA 1925 s 52(2) paras (c), (f), (g).

[11] LPA 1925 ss 52(1)(d), 54(2); LP (MP) A 1989 s 2(5)(a) (contracts); for the exact requirements see below **[25.24]**.

[12] *Parker* v. *Taswell* (1858) 2 De G & J 559, 44 ER 1106 (acts as contract); *Walsh* v. *Lonsdale* (1882) 21 Ch D 9, CA; see below **[24.05]**.

[13] See below **[17]**.

[14] Blackstone's *Commentaries* vol 2, 295.

[15] PJ Horn [1992] 32 *LSG* 25.

[16] DLRR 2003 sch 8.

[17] HW Wilkinson [1990] *Conv* 1; G Virgo & C Harpum [1991] *LMCLQ* 209; R Oerton (1990) 134 *SJ* 1089, 1118; RE Annand (1989) 105 *LQR* 553, 553–555; Smith's *Property Law* (4th ed), 91–92.

[18] Law Com 163 (1987); Law Com WP 93 (1985); JE Adams [1987] *Conv* 325.

[19] Preamble; in force July 31st 1990: s 1(11); SI 1990/1175.

2.   Formal requirements

[7.05] When a deed is made by an individual the essentials are: (1) a document; (2) a formal statement of the intention to create a deed; (3) signature and attestation by a witness; and (4) delivery.[20]

A deed must be written[21] – which includes typing or printing – though there is no longer any restriction of the substances on which a deed is made; it could be the archaic parchment, prosaic paper,[22] or avant garde glass, metal, or set concrete.[23] Why not enter a set of deeds for the Turner prize? The document must contain on its face a formal expression of an intention by each person making it to create a deed. This requirement is new.[24] It may be manifested by the formal description of the document ("This deed") or by stating that the document is executed or signed as a deed ("Signed by me as a deed").

Sealing was the hallmark of a deed before 1989,[25] the classic mantra being "Signed, sealed, and delivered".[26] Many medieval people were unable to write, so a deed had to be authenticated by dripping wax onto the document and impressing a seal into the wax, but now that everyone can write, a signature is much better way of ensuring authenticity. Sealing remained essential until mid-1990,[27] but it was often symbolic, in the shape of a small red wafer of paper[28] or a printed black circle.[29] Even this truncated form was too much to sit comfortably with the generation of documents by computer. So the 1989 Act abolished the requirement to attach a seal to a deed,[30] though sealing is still allowed.[31]

3.   Execution by an individual

[7.06] A deed or land registry transfer[32] requires valid execution when it is made and again when it is altered.[33] In the case of an individual this means signature, witnessing

---

[20] Before August 1990, the requirements were: a document, writing or typing, on the proper substances, signature after 1925 (LPA 1925 s 73), sealing, and delivery.

[21] LP (MP) A 1989 s 1(3)(a) (signature required).

[22] *Goddard's case* (1584) 2 Co Rep 4b, 5a, 76 ER 396; *Fox* v. *Wright* (1598) Cro Eliz 613, 78 ER 855; G Virgo & C Harpum [1991] *LMCLQ* 209, 210.

[23] HW Wilkinson [1990] *Conv* 321.

[24] LP (MP) A 1989 s 1(2)(a); Law Com 163 (1987), [2.16].

[25] *Goddard's case* (1584) 2 Co Rep 4b, 5a, 76 ER 396.

[26] JE Adams [1987] *Conv* 12.

[27] *Re Sandilands* (1871) LR 6 CP 411; *Re Balkis Consolidated Co* (1888) 58 LT 300; *National Provincial Bank of England* v. *Jackson* (1886) 33 Ch D 1.

[28] *Stromdale & Ball* v. *Burden* [1952] Ch 223, 250, Danckwerts J.

[29] *First National Securities* v. *Jones* [1978] Ch 109, CA; D Hoath (1980) 43 *MLR* 415; JE Adams [1988] *Conv* 86.

[30] LP (MP) A 1989 s 1(1)(b), Law Com 163 (1989), [2.4]. It is clearly intended that the new form of deed should be a specialty so as to attract a 12 year limitation period; this point is to be clarified for companies: LCD CD 09 (2002), point K.

[31] HW Wilkinson [1990] *Conv* 1.

[32] DLRR 2003 sch 8.

[33] *Lombard Finance* v. *Brookplain Trading* [1991] 1 WLR 271, CA; *Bank of Credit & Commerce International* v. *Aboody* [1990] 1 QB 923, CA (execution in blank of dubious validity).

and delivery.[34] Signature first became a formal requirement in 1925,[35] using the mantra "Signed as a deed by . . ." or some similar formulation.[36] Permanent ink should be used.

A person unable to sign may make a mark,[37] but a blind or illiterate person[38] usually directs another to sign in his presence, that other usually using his own signature but adding to it the words "at the direction of and on behalf of" the real party.[39] Words of execution are essential to avoid land registry requisitions explaining, for example that a document has been read over to and approved by a blind person.[40] In such cases two witnesses are required.[41]

A copy of a deed is now admissible in evidence without distinction from originals and at however many removes.[42]

4. Attestation

[7.07] Attestation is required by a person who is physically present at the time of signing and who adds his signature as a witness.[43] Except for land registry transfers this was not essential before the 1989 Act,[44] though it builds on earlier practice.[45] Words of attestation which state that signature of the deed occurred "in the presence of" the witness avoid the need for other proof of proper attestation.[46] Safety first: only non-parties should be used as witnesses.[47]

Outside parties are able to reply on a common law estoppel which prevents the parties to a deed which appears to be perfect on its face from disputing that the manner of execution was correct after they have delivered it. In *Shah* v. *Shah*[48] this estoppel was used to uphold a deed of guarantee. Proof that the witness signed after the borrowers and not in their presence did not affect the bank's right to enforce the guarantee. Attestation has the purpose of limiting the scope for disputes about whether the document has been signed. Pill LJ considered that the legislators intended to allow the common law estoppel to continue to operate.[49]

---

[34] LP (MP) A 1989 s 1(3). "Execution" is used inconsistently but usually so as to exclude delivery: *Longman* v. *Viscount Chelsea* [1989] 2 EGLR 242, 245E, 246F, Nourse LJ; G Virgo & C Harpum [1991] *LMCLQ* 209, 209 n 4.

[35] LP (MP) A 1989 s 1(3)(a); LPA 1925 s 73(1). At common law: *Goddard's case* (1594) 2 Co Rep 4b, 5a, 76 ER 396 (unnecessary); *Goodman* v. *J Eban* [1954] 1 QB 550 (rubber stamp ok on solicitor's bill of costs).

[36] LP (MP) A 1989 s 1(2)(a); *Encyclopaedia FP* (5th ed, 1994 reissue) vol 12, [1691–1745].

[37] LP (MP) A 1989 s 1(4); the execution clause should be amended to state that the document has been read over and explained.

[38] *Thoroughgood's case* (1584) 2 Co Rep 9a, 76 ER 408.

[39] Or the deed could be signed in the name of the party to the deed, adding "by his agent".

[40] The deed may be void for *Non est factum*, as described below [30.80].

[41] LP (MP) A 1989 s 1(3)(a)(ii).

[42] Civil Evidence Act 1995 s 38.

[43] LP (MP) A 1989 s 1(3)(a)(i).

[44] *Buckeridge* v. *Flight* (1826) 6 B & C 49, 108 ER 371; Law Com 163 (1987), [2.12].

[45] HW Wilkinson [1990] *Conv* 321, 323.

[46] *Wright* v. *Wakeford* (1811) 17 Ves 455, 34 ER 176.

[47] HW Wilkinson [1990] *Conv* 321, 323.

[48] [2001] EWCA Civ 527, [2002] QB 35; PH Kenny [2001] *Conv* 443.

[49] At [33], Pill LJ.

5. Delivery

[7.08] Deeds are always dated. What is written on the deed is presumed to be correct, but it is not decisive about when a deed is brought into force,[50] since this depends upon delivery.[51] In rare cases a deed may have immediate effect, in which case it should be "Signed *and delivered* as a deed".

Otherwise the operation of a deed is delayed by the requirement of delivery.[52] Whether this principle retained a valuable function was hotly debated.[53] Physical handing over of the deed,[54] the original basis, has now given way to reliance on the underlying intention to be bound, either inside or outside the deed.[55] Modern law thus permits constructive delivery of a document without any change in its physical control. In *Longman* v. *Viscount Chelsea*[56] Nourse LJ identified two means of delayed delivery. One is as an escrow, that is a conditional deed which depends upon some later event for its force,[57] such as payment of the purchase price. Satisfaction of the condition brings the deed into full effectiveness.[58] Two problems are that the deed is backdated[59] and that the validity of the deed during the period of suspension precludes a change of mind by the person making it.[60] These problems do not arise if the deed is handed to an agent with authority to deliver, leaving it in a state of suspense until the agent acts.[61] Before the 1989 Act authority to deliver a deed could only be given by deed,[62] but that rule is now abrogated.[63] Ordinary workaday agency principles now apply. Purchasers[64] may assume that professional conveyancers have authority to deliver a document in the course of a transaction with land, and so the land registry will assume that a document lodged by a purchaser is a valid deed.

Practice on the sale of a house has evolved to take account of the fact that a person who is moving house cannot attend on completion to execute the transfer, so signature takes place a few days in advance but on the basis that that the deed will only become effective on completion day with the money safely in the bank. Pre-1989

---

[50] *Hedley* v. *Joans* (1572) 3 Dyer 307a, 73 ER 693; *Goddard's case* (1584) 2 Co Rep 4b, 5a, 76 ER 396; *Oshey* v. *Hicks* (1610) Cro Jac 263, 79 ER 227.

[51] LP (MP) A 1989 s 1(2)(b).

[52] JE Adams [1987] *Conv* 325, 325.

[53] Law Com 163 (1987), [3.4].

[54] Blackstone's *Commentaries* vol 2, 307.

[55] DEC Yale [1970] *CLJ* 52; *Goddard's case* (1584) 2 Co Rep 4b, 5a, 76 ER 396; *Xenos* v. *Wickham* [1866] LR 2 HL 296, 323, Lord Cranworth; *Vincent* v. *Premo Enterprises (Voucher Sales)* [1969] 2 QB 609, 619E, Lord Denning MR, 622, Winn LJ.

[56] [1989] 2 EGLR 242, 245E.

[57] *Xenos* at 323, Lord Cranworth; *Alan Estates* v. *WG Stores* [1982] Ch 511, 520, Lord Denning MR; JT Farrand (1961) 25 *Conv (NS)* 126.

[58] This is presumed after physical transfer of the deed: *Hare* v. *Horton* (1833) 5 B & Ad 715, 110 ER 954.

[59] *Alan Estates* v. *WG Stores* [1982] Ch 511 (rent payable); PH Kenny [1982] *Conv* 409; *Graham* v. *Graham* (1791) 1 Ves 272, 274–275, 30 ER 339.

[60] *Beesly* v. *Hallwood Estates* [1961] Ch 105, CA.

[61] *Foundling Hospital Governors* v. *Crane* [1911] 2 KB 367, CA.

[62] *Powell* v. *London & Provincial Bank* [1893] 2 Ch 555, 563, Bowen LJ, 565, Kay LJ; *Windsor Refrigerator Co* v. *Branch Nominees* [1961] Ch 88, 98, Cross J; *Phoenix Properties* v. *Wimpole St Nominees* [1992] BCLC 737. Query the converse dictum in *Longman* v. *Viscount Chelsea* [1989] 2 EGLR 242, 246F–H; G Virgo & C Harpum [1991] *LMCLQ* 209, 222.

[63] LP (MP) A 1989 s 1(1)(c); Law Com 163 (1987), [2.11].

[64] LPA 1925 s 205(1)(xxi), LP (MP) A 1989 s 1(5)–(6).

authority treated execution of a transfer as a delivery in escrow, the condition being that the price should be paid.[65] However, Nourse LJ ruled in *Longman* v. *Viscount Chelsea*[66] that a deed handed over to a solicitor before completion was handed over complete, undelivered certainly, but so that the solicitor had authority to deliver it. It remains a non-deed, until the conveyancer gives life to it on completion.

Leases create special problems, because there is generally no contract in advance of completion. Arrangements should not become binding on either party at the instant that the landlord executes the lease.[67] Two cases have treated leases as executed in escrow and so not recallable,[68] but a change of heart was allowed in *Longman* v. *Viscount Chelsea*.[69] A tenant on the Cadogan Estate who wished to extend his lease had agreed all the terms informally, the tenant had executed a surrender of his existing lease and the counterpart of the new lease, and the original lease had been executed by the landlord. At the last moment the landlord withdrew unless the premium and ground rent were increased eightfold! Successfully so, because the failure to effect delivery meant there was as yet no lease.

Unilateral alteration of a deed by one party does not invalidate a deed after it has been properly executed.[70]

C. E-DOCUMENTS

1. Replicating paper formalities electronically

[7.09] Once titles are available online at the registry, it is one short and inevitable step to full electronic conveyancing. A conveyancer will create a document in his word processor, insert a smart card into a reader on his computer, start the signature software, click to sign and then transmit it to the recipient. Hey presto! A deed is created, the land is transferred and, even better, the transfer is registered automatically and instantaneously. The dream is to switch from paper-based documentation to documents created and authenticated electronically.[71]

Signature of a paper based document fulfils a number of important functions, above and beyond the obvious one of providing a record of the terms of the transaction. The signature authenticates the document in the sense that it shows that the party signing affirms and accepts the transaction recorded. Documents are dated so as to make it clear when the document is to have effect. Signature also provides a guarantee against tampering since it is usually obvious that a signed document has been

---

[65] *Beesly* v. *Hallwood Estates* [1960] 1 WLR 549, Buckley J; on appeal [1961] Ch 105, CA; *Kingston* v. *Ambrian Investments Co* [1975] 1 WLR 161, CA; *Glessing* v. *Green* [1975] 1 WLR 863, CA.

[66] [1989] 2 EGLR 242, CA; HW Wilkinson [1990] *Conv* 1; P Luxton [1990] *JBL* 242; DN Clarke [1990] *Conv* 85; G Virgo and C Harpum [1991] *LMCLQ* 209, 221–222 (strong criticism).

[67] *Vincent* v. *Premo Enterprises (Voucher Sales)* [1969] 2 QB 609, CA; *Venetian Glass Gallery* v. *Next Properties* [1989] 2 EGLR 42; DN Clarke [1990] *Conv* 85.

[68] *Beesly* v. *Hallwood Estates* [1960] 1 WLR 549; on appeal [1961] Ch 105, CA; *D'Silva* v. *Lister House Developments* [1971] Ch 17; M Albery (1978) 89 *LQR* 14.

[69] [1989] 2 EGLR 242, CA; HW Wilkinson [1990] *Conv* 1; P Luxton [1990] *JBL* 242; DN Clarke [1990] *Conv* 85; G Virgo & C Harpum [1991] *LMCLQ*, 209, 221–222.

[70] *Raiffesien Zentralbank* v. *Cross-seas Shipping* [2000] 1 WLR 1135, CA.

[71] Smith's *Property Law* (4th ed), 104–107; D Capps [2002] *Conv* 443.

altered. Confidentiality is easy to achieve since a paper document can be sent using a secure postal system.

Procedures for the electronic creation of documents must seek to secure these same objectives:[72]

> to establish the identity of the person executing a document;
> to make clear their consent to the transaction and understanding of its import;
> to create clear proof of receipt;
> to ensure confidentiality; and
> to guarantee against tampering.

It may seem from the description that follows that the procedures are more complex, but much is done automatically by computer, and the procedures should be simplicity themselves to operate.

2. Basis of e signature is logical association

[7.10] A European Directive promotes inter-operability of electronic signatures across Europe.[73] The Act applying it in the UK defines an electronic signature as anything in electronic form:

(1) incorporated in or logically associated with any electronic communication;
(2) purporting to be incorporated or associated for the purpose of establishing the integrity, authenticity or date, of the communication; and
(3) acting as a guarantee of these things.[74]

A signature is a series of symbols just like any other part of a computer file, so the crucial thing is the intention with which that code is linked to the document.

3. Proof of identity

[7.11] Entry of a numerical code into a computer can never by itself prove that a particular person assented to the contents of a computer file, without additional third party validation of identities. Two functions are involved – registration and certification – which may be carried out by one authority or which may be split. Registration is the process of investigation to confirm the identity of the person seeking access to a digital signature. His address will be checked using bills from utility companies, with cross checks against electoral rolls, council tax records, and so on. Once identity is established, certification will be carried out by certification authorities which will issue the keys and certificates necessary to conduct electronic conveyancing. A person will be entitled to apply for the issue of a signature and supporting documentation after his identity has been established by registration. The UK will rely on industry self regulation,[75] the main player at present (2003) being t-Scheme,[76] which involves the

---

[72] T Travers [2001] 36 *LSG* 45.
[73] 1999/93/EC, OJ L013, 12–20. English law does not yet provide fully for advanced digital signatures.
[74] Electronic Communications Act 2000 s 7.
[75] Residual powers of compulsion are included in the Electronic Communications Act 2000 part I.
[76] <www.tscheme.org>; E Thompson, J Kelsey & R Chapman [2001] 48 *EG* 142; T Travers [2001] 36 *LSG* 45; M O'Conor and E Brownsdon [2002] *NLJ* 348.

participation of over 250 members including Microsoft, BT, and the CBI. Inaccurate certification will give rise to liability based on common law contract principles.[77]

4. Method of signature

[7.12] "Keys" are codes, similar to but longer than the PIN numbers used with cash cards. Each key will be stored on a smart card[78] provided by a certification authority which can be inserted into a reader on the computer and which will allow access to the e-conveyancing functions. This procedure is much less vulnerable to hacking than if the code were stored on the computer's hard disk, and provides a guarantee that the owner of the signature was the person who attached the code to a document. The owner of a signature will be responsible for the security of the card:[79] if it is stolen the certification authority must be notified, just as Barclaycard must be told if their credit card is stolen. After creation of a document in a word processor, the signature smart card will be inserted into a reader on the computer, the signature software opened and a click with the mouse will act to sign the document. After that it can be scrambled and sent to the recipient.

5. Authenticating the signature

[7.13] What is to prevent the person receiving a document reading the signature code and then using it to sign a version of the document that has been tampered with or indeed to sign a completely different document? The answer lies in the use of dual key cryptography. There private and public keys are asymmetric, different from each other but related mathematically. With the public key the recipient can authenticate that the sender's private key was used to effect the signature, but it is not possible with present computing capabilities to work out the sequence of numbers which make up the private key working only from the public key, but it is easy and quick to relate them in the reverse direction. Not even the certification authority keeps the private key.[80] The public key cannot be used to deduce the code contained on the private key.

6. Confidentiality

[7.14] Encryption involves scrambling information using an algorithm (that is a mathematical function) to keep it private. Normal text in a document is coded into a set of symbols.[81] No system of coding can ever be completely secure, as the Bletchley enigma team so happily proved, but it should be infeasible to break the system with current mathematical knowledge and current computing capacity. Encryption procedures are secure enough, for now,[82] to safeguard the confidentiality necessary for conveyancing. The key used to scramble documents will be distinct from the one used

[77] T Travers [2001] 36 *LSG* 45.
[78] D Capps [2002] *Conv* 443, 445.
[79] E Thompson, J Kelsey & R Chapman [2001] 48 *EG* 142.
[80] T Travers [2001] 36 *LSG* 45.
[81] S Singh, *Digital Signature Guidelines* (Judicial Studies Board, <www.jsboard.co.uk>, 2000), appendix 1.
[82] T Travers [2001] 36 *LSG* 45.

for signature so that a secretary can be given the encryption key in order to conduct private correspondence without giving away the power to make a signature. After a sender has encrypted text with his private key, it will only be possible for the recipient to de-jumble it using the sender's public key, obtained from the certification authority.[83]

7.   Authenticity

[7.15] What is to prove that a document to which an electronic signature is attached is still in the same form as it was when signed? An independent check is needed that a document has not been tampered with as it is transmitted over the internet. The check is a "fingerprint", scrambled, and then attached to its document as a means of verification. Authenticity is guaranteed if the fingerprint re-emerges when the document is unscrambled. It works like this.

After a document has been prepared in electronic form, it is passed through a hash function which converts it to its digital fingerprint. This is unique to the document but much shorter, allowing faster processing. It is encrypted using the sender's private key. The recipient passes it once more through the hash function to recreate the digital fingerprint, which is then decrypted using the sender's public key. Two techniques used in this process are factorisation of numbers based on multiples of primes, and modular arithmetic – taking the remainder left over after a number is divided by a base number. Both are difficult to crack and yet two similar documents give very different fingerprints, so that any tampering is self-evident.[84]

8.   Certificate and public signature key

[7.16] Electronic signatures do not require to be witnessed because they are authenticated. This is done by certification,[85] the process which links together the key and the person who uses it, a process guaranteed by the certifying authority which confirms that the electronic signature is the one allocated to the person who purports to make use of it.[86] Digital certificates take the form of a computer file in a format marked out into a number of fields, for which there is an accepted international standard.[87] One field will indicate the permitted key usage – probably for a single use within a narrow completion window.[88] Others indicate financial limits on transactions and identity attributes.

What if the signature smart card is stolen? The thief could use it to sign transactions and it would appear to be the true owner who had signed. The owner of the digital signature will not be allowed to repudiate liability on documents to which the signature is attached. The issuer must be notified of the theft immediately and they will cancel it. The currency of the certificate (that is non-revocation) will need to be checked online at the time of completion.

---

[83]   See below **[7.16]**.
[84]   E Thompson, J Kelsey & R Chapman [2001] 48 *EG* 172.
[85]   Electronic Communications Act 2000 s 7.
[86]   R Perry [2001] 39 *LSG* 45; E Thompson, J Kelsey & R Chapman [2001] 48 *EG* 142.
[87]   International Telecommunication Union's X509 v3.
[88]   T Travers [2001] 36 *LSG* 45.

There is a problem of potential misuse by third party.[89] Revocation of the certificate may not be in time if theft of signature not apparent.[90]

9. Proof of execution or exchange

[7.17] In e-conveyancing it will be important to know the precise date and time at which a particular document is completed. The clock on the computer of the person signing will not be a reliable guide, since clocks can be changed easily enough. So the date of a document will have to be certified by passing it through a trusted third party (the certification authority) who will date stamp all communications.

D. E-TRANSFER

1. Electronic conveyancing

[7.18] Electronic formalities for transfers, conveyances leading to first registrations, and registrations are a key component of the Land Registration Act 2002. Part 8[91] makes greater changes than any other part of the Act for, as the Lord Chancellor said when introducing it into Parliament:

> "In a few clauses the Bill will also hugely increase the attractions of registration. It will open the way for radical changes in the way in which formal documents required in conveyancing are prepared, in the quality and speed of services which conveyancers are able to provide and in the relationship between conveyancers and the land registry."[92]

In truth the cost savings may be a paltry £16 per conveyance.[93] But, just as the CREST scheme has revolutionised the stock exchange,[94] so new technology will revolutionise conveyancing. The timescale is slipping, but thinking current at the time of writing is that there should be an operational pilot in 2005 with widespread use set for 2006.[95] No date has been given for the introduction of compulsion.

2. E-transactions

[7.19] If a transaction affecting registered land satisfies the technical rules laid down, the e-document will meet all formality requirements.[96] Where a person[97] attaches his electronic signature to a file, the document is deemed to be in writing,[98] to be signed by the party executing him, and to have effect as if it was a deed.[99] Modes of

---

[89] R Perry [2002] 11 *LSG* 43.

[90] R Perry [2001] 39 *LSG* 45.

[91] LRA 2002 ss 91–95; Law Com 271 (2001), Part XIII, EN [396–431].

[92] Hansard HL, July 3rd 2001, cols 777–778, Lord Irving LC.

[93] D Capps [2002] *Conv* 443, 444.

[94] Megarry & Wade (6th ed), [1.001] n 6.

[95] *e-conveyancing* (LR CP, 2002), [2.4], pilot version early 2006 to be "rolled out" in 2006; D Capps [2002] *Conv* 443, 455.

[96] LRA 2002 s 91; Law Com 271 (2001), EN [398 ff]; *e-conveyancing* (LR CP, 2002), [8.2].

[97] Or his agent, who need not be appointed by deed: Law Com 271 (2001), EN [410].

[98] LRA 2002 s 91(4)(a).

[99] LRA 2002 s 91(5).

execution will be the same for a deed, a written contract,[100] and a declaration of trust,[101] these documents being distinguished merely by their wording. E formality will be sufficient for transactions of the following kinds:[102]

a transfer or other disposition of a registered estate;

a disposition of a registered charge;

postponement of a charge;[103]

a disposition of an interest protected by notice;[104]

a disposition triggering compulsory first registration; and

any other transaction for which electronic disposition is authorised by rules.[105]

Unregistered land may thus be transferred electronically to the extent that the completed disposition will call for first registration of the title, but electronic means will not be available for transactions which will leave the land unregistered, such as the grant of a second mortgage or the creation of a restrictive covenant.[106]

Rules will determine how e-documents are communicated and stored.[107] Electronic forms will be based on the existing paper forms, with a standardised electronic element.[108] Other conditions will be introduced in response to the experience of computerising particular forms of disposition.[109]

E-documents are likely to lead to greater logic in the development of conveyancing forms. When, for example, land is transferred to joint proprietors, the existing practice is to include the declaration of trust, stating how the buyers will hold beneficially, in the transfer document, whereas it will be more sensible to use two separate electronic documents, the transfer e-signed by the sellers and the declaration of trust e-signed by the buyers.[110]

3.   Signature, certification and commencement

[7.20] Each person executing a transfer must attach his electronic signature,[111] which must be authenticated by proper certification,[112] after which it is deemed to be executed as a (deemed) deed.[113] There is no role for attestation by a witness. If an agent authenticates a document the written authority of his principal will be presumed.[114]

Dating and delivery are concepts inapplicable to an electronic document which is completed when all parties attach their electronic signatures and these are authenti-

---

[100] Law Com 271 (2001), EN [399].

[101] LPA 1925 s 53(1)(a); Law Com 271 (2001), EN [412].

[102] LRA 2002 s 91(1)(a), 91(2).

[103] LRA 2002 s 93(6).

[104] LRA 2002 s 91(2)(b); Law Com 271 (2001), [13.22–13.23], EN [427].

[105] LRA 2002 s 91(2).

[106] Law Com 271 (2001), EN [396].

[107] LRA 2002 s 94. PISCES is a protocol for the exchange of information between conveyancing software packages launched in 2002

[108] Law Com 271 (2001), EN [402]; DLRR 2003 rr 56-61, sch 1.

[109] LRA 2002 s 91(3)(d); Law Com 271 (2001), [13.32], EN [403(iv)].

[110] Law Com 271 (2001), EN [403(ii)].

[111] LRA 2002 s 91(10), adopting the definition in Electronic Communications Act 2000 s 7(2)–(3).

[112] LRA 2002 s 91(3)(b)-(c).

[113] Law Com 271 (2001), [13.18–13.19].

[114] LRA 2002 s 91(6); Law Com 271 (2001), [13.20–13.21].

cated. It will therefore be essential for an electronic transfer to provide a time and date on which it is to take effect.[115]

4. Making e-transfer compulsory

[7.21] The perils of the registration gap will be eliminated by a further step – validity will be removed from the conveyancing document and attached instead at the time of its registration. Sequential completion and registration will be replaced by a unified stage in which both steps are instantaneous.[116] Electronic transfer will then be compulsory. This power will not be exercised lightly.[117] Any transitional period during which the two systems operate side by side will be kept to a minimum in order to assist the development of electronic chain management.[118] Rules will introduce compulsion in relation to specific types of dispositions.[119] From that time forwards a disposition will only have effect if it:[120]

is made electronically;
is communicated electronically to the registrar when it purports to take effect; and
meets the relevant registration requirements.[121]

A document which does not meet these e-formality requirements has effect neither at law nor in equity.

5. Registration gap

[7.22] Electronic conveyancing will finally close the registration gap. It will no longer be possible to create or transfer any interest in registered land except by simultaneous registration of the electronic instrument that effects the transaction.[122] Hence there will no longer be any room for a *Walsh* v. *Lonsdale*[123] equity arising under a defective transfer since without formality and registration there will be no property interest in the land.[124] As and when the new system becomes compulsory, it will address the problem of *Brown & Root Technology*[125] – that the registered proprietor remained legal owner after he had completed a sale of the land until the buyer had made a proper application to register his title. Instantaneous creation and registration will leave no gap.

---

[115] LRA 2002 s 91(3)(a); Law Com 271 (2001), [403].
[116] Law Com 271 (2001), EN [423]; Law Com 254 (1998), [11.2].
[117] Law Com 271 (2001), EN [421].
[118] See below **[22.21]**.
[119] LRA 2002 s 93.
[120] LRA 2002 s 93(2).
[121] LRA 2002 s 93(2)(b), 93(3), sch 2; DLRR 2003 rr 51–79. A model is described in *e-conveyancing* (LR CP, 2002), [6].
[122] Law Com 271 (2001), EN [396–397]; *e-conveyancing* (LR CP, 2002), [3.4].
[123] (1882) 21 Ch D 9, CA.
[124] LRA 2002 s 93(4), disapplying s 27(1); Law Com 271 (2001), EN [429]. Presumably an estoppel might arise if the right had been acted on. If so the effect of the change might be very small.
[125] *Brown & Root Technology* v. *Sun Alliance Ass Co* [2001] Ch 733, CA; Law Com 271 (2001), [13.754–13.77], EN [428]; Law Com 254 (1998), [11.5–11.6].

6.   Authority to conduct e-conveyancing

[7.23] Conveyancers will generally authenticate electronic documents on behalf of their clients.[126] Further when an agent uses the network to register a document which states that he is acting on the authority of a principal, that principal for whom he purports to act is presumed to have given his authority.[127] So the buyer will not need to see the seller's solicitor's authority to act for the seller, and vice versa.[128] The risks are greatly increased because there is no outside key to lock or unlock access to the register, the function formerly performed by the land certificate.

The Law Society found it unacceptable that conveyancers should take the risk of misuse of the key code.[129] Non-repudiation will be the principle: a client must accept responsibility for what his conveyancer has done. Any one licensed can certify that he has authority and so a client could be bound by a contract of which he is unaware.[130] Conveyancers will have to ensure that they obtain written authority from the client,[131] probably by getting the client to sign a paper copy of the contract.[132]

7.   Safety of e-conveyancing

[7.24] The one imponderable is whether e-conveyancing will be safe. Under the paper based system it is believed that each District Land Registry had about five fraud cases a month and a very sharp rise must be expected. If it is possible to hack into the Pentagon computer system, one has an uncomfortable feeling that the e-register may provide an opportunity for cyber-crime on a vast scale.

E. DOCUMENTS EXECUTED BY COMPANIES

[7.25] Formalities for execution of deeds by companies[133] were reviewed at the same time as the rules of individual execution,[134] but they remain complex,[135] and are now subject to deregulatory reform.[136] Execution by sealing or signing is distinguished from the process of delivery of a deed to bring it into effect.[137]

---

[126] Law Com 271 (2001), EN [676–677].

[127] LRA 2002 sch 5 para 8; cases disapplied are: *Smith* v. *Webster* (1876) 3 Ch D 49; *H Clark Doncaster* v. *Wilkinson* [1965] Ch 694, 702.

[128] Law Com 271 (2001), [13.60–13.62], EN [677].

[129] HC Standing Committee, December 11th 2001, col 42; *Hansard* HL, vol 626, July 17th 2001, cols 1611–1620.

[130] M Dowden [2001] 41 *EG* 180.

[131] *Hansard* HC vol 380, February 11th 2002, col 24.

[132] R Perry [2002] 11 *LSG* 43.

[133] On the position of contract by a company in course of formation see Companies Act 1985 s 36C; *Braymist* v. *Wise Finance Co* [2002] EWCA Civ 127, [2002] 2 All ER 333; PH Kenny [2002] *Conv* 304.

[134] Companies Act 1985 s 36A, introduced by Companies Act 1989 s 130; DN Clarke [1990] *Conv* 85, 91–92; as from the end of July 1990: SI 1990/1392. Similar rules for Scottish (s 36B), foreign (SI 1994/950) and unregistered companies (SI 1990/2571).

[135] RT Oerton (1990) 134 *SJ* 1118; [1992] 01 *LSG* 28; DN Clarke [1990] *Conv* 85, 412; [1991] *Conv* 243; G Virgo & C Harpum [1991] *LMCLQ* 209, 225.

[136] LCD CD 09 (2002).

[137] LCD CD 09 (2002), point I.

1.   Signature as a deed by two officers

(1) Execution

[7.26] This method, new in 1989, mirrors the new formalities for deeds made by individuals – that is signature as a deed by officers of the company. A *document*[138] can be executed by the company signature being either by a director and secretary or by two directors. Either form of signature will work if the document is expressed in whatever form of words to be executed by the company.[139] Execution specifically as a *deed* is achieved by making clear on its face that it is intended to be a deed.[140]

A company can only act by its officers, so it is important to establish that people executing a document have authority to act. The easiest way to create a deed is to have it executed in this form:

"Signed[141] as a deed by [C] and [D] acting as two directors."

This is beneficial because there is a presumption in favour of a purchaser[142] that a deed has been duly executed if it purports to be signed by a *director and secretary or by two directors*.[143]

(2) Delivery

[7.27] Proof is required that an executed deed has been delivered as a deed, and that this was authorised by the company. A purchaser[144] is protected by a presumption[145] that delivery occurred immediately on the execution of a new-style deed signed by the officers. Preventing delivery is, therefore, more of a problem than achieving it, since a company risks being bound by deed immediately unless positive steps are taken to prevent this. The document should omit to state that it is delivered and should include a statement,[146] such as "Executed as a deed but not delivered until this deed is dated".[147]

Statutory presumptions do not validate a forgery.[148]

---

[138] Widely defined by Companies Act 1985 s 744.
[139] S 36A(4).
[140] S 36A(5).
[141] "Signed and delivered" if delivery is intended on execution.
[142] Who must act in good faith and provide valuable consideration.
[143] Companies Act 1985 s 36A(6).
[144] In favour of the company delivery at the time of execution is presumed unless a contrary intention is proved: Companies Act 1985 s 36A(5).
[145] S 36A(6).
[146] *Derby Coal Co* v. *Wilmot* (1808) 9 East 360, 103 ER 610.
[147] DN Clarke [1990] *Conv* 412, but see [1991] *Conv* 243. The account in the text assumes that the presumption in s 36A(6) is rebuttable.
[148] *Ruben* v. *Great Fingall Consolidated* [1906] AC 439, HL.

2   Affixing company seal

(1) In presence of a director and the secretary

[7.28] Since deeds can now be signed by the officers, a company no longer needs a common seal.[149] The old practice was to create a deed by affixing the company seal in the presence of the officers of the company,[150] there being no requirement for outside witnesses. The deed will state that: "The Common Seal of AB Ltd[151] was affixed in the presence of [C] Director and [D] Secretary." Those outside the company are assisted by the internal management rule, a common law presumption in favour of innocent purchasers that acts have been properly carried out.[152] Its statutory reincarnation applies where a document purported to be executed in the presence of *a director and the secretary* of the company.[153] A seal retains utility in creating a contract under seal which is not intended to be a deed.[154]

(2) Affixing company seal in presence of two directors

[7.29] If the corporate seal was affixed in the presence of *two directors*, before 1989, there was no statutory presumption about due execution, and delivery, and it remains problematical to this day with a document executed with the company seal. Proof of the director's authority to execute is a vital part of the title, either under the articles of association of the company or by delegation by the board of directors. Consultation is taking place on a proposal to amend the law to remove this anomaly.[155]

(3) Delivery

[7.30] Proof is required that an executed deed has been delivered as a deed, and that this was authorised by the company. It is presumed that an old fashioned deed made under the common seal of the company is delivered immediately on the execution of a deed.[156] Execution of a deed in the presence of a director and the secretary gave rise to a rebuttable[157] presumption of delivery on affixing the company seal.[158] This did not assist where two directors executed or any other authorised signatories and in such cases proof of delivery was required.

---

[149] Companies Act 1985 s 36A(3).

[150] S 36A(2).

[151] On the use of incorrect names see W Evans [1994] *Conv* 384.

[152] *Royal British Bank* v. *Turquand* (1856) 6 El & Bl 327, 119 ER 886; *Mahony* v. *East Holyford Mining Co* (1875) LR 7 HL 869.

[153] LPA 1925 s 74; G Virgo & C Harpum [1991] *LMCLQ* 209, 214.

[154] LCD CD 09 (2002), point J.

[155] LPA 1925 s 74; Law Com 253 (1998); LCD CD 09 (2002), point A.

[156] This is presumed in favour of a purchaser by Companies Act 1985 s 36A(6).

[157] LPA 1925 s 74; *Longman* v. *Viscount Chelsea* [1989] 2 EGLR 242, 245M–246C, 246H–K, Nourse LJ; *Longman* overruled two dicta of Buckley J: (1) *Beesly* v. *Hallwood Estates* [1960] 1 WLR 549, 562; (2) *D'Silva* v. *Lister Homes Developments* [1971] Ch 17, 29D–30A.

[158] *Staple Merchants Co* v. *Bank of England* (1887) 21 QBD 160, 165, 166 Wills J; *Venetian Glass Gallery* v. *Next Properties* [1989] 2 EGLR 42, 45M, Harman LJ. This is to be extended to any document (not just a deed) and LPA 1925 s 74 will be aligned in wording with Companies Act 1985 s 36A(6): LCD CD 09 (2002), point D.

3.   Other means of execution

[7.31] Additional means of execution may be allowed by the statute or charter creating the corporation. Sealing is still required for a deed made by a corporation sole such as a bishop or one of the Royal Duchies.[159]

4.   Miscellaneous reforms

[7.32] Consultation is underway on proposals to make a number of deregulatory reforms[160] to clarify a number of dubious points. Where a company is an officer of another company it can sign by a person who is authorised to do so. An individual must sign separately for each company of which he is an officer that is executing a particular document. A conveyancer's presumed authority to deliver a deed will apply not only to land but to all forms of property. It will be made clear that an attorney can act for a company. Also a liquidator will be given a clear power to act for a company even if there is no seal or the seal has been lost.

5.   E-documents by companies

[7.33] Formalities for contracts[161] and deeds entered into by companies are amended in line with those created by individuals.[162] A company can have electronic signature and this can be authenticated by the company officers who would have to sign a paper document or deed. Corporations which currently have to use the company seal will be able to use a power of attorney to delegate the power of signature to named officers.

Land registry documents executed electronically by a company – any company – will also be authenticated by attaching the electronic signatures of the appropriate officers of the company.[163] A company is deemed to seal a document by attaching its electronic signature.[164] An electronic document that is authenticated will fall within the new provision which creates a presumption of due execution.

---

[159] LP (MP) A 1989 s 1(10); SI 1994/1130 (no mention).
[160] CD 09 (LCD, 2002).
[161] LP (MP) A 1989 s2A, to be inserted by Draft LP (Electronic Communications) O 2001.
[162] Companies Act 1985 s 36A, to be inserted by Draft LP (Electronic Communications) O 2001.
[163] LRA 2002 s 91(9); Law Com 271 (2001), [13.29–13.30], EN [406–409].
[164] LRA 2002 s 91(4)(b).

8

TRANSFER

Dematerialisation of the register. Title by registration. Information. Searches. Off register matters. LR Forms. Transfer. Application for registration. Queues. Electronic applications. Derivative transactions.

[8.01] Transfer is the process by which the ownership of land held by A is passed by A's act to B. If the law imposes the transfer there is said to be a transmission – for example because A dies or becomes bankrupt. Most transfers are sales in which money is paid for the land, but in many ways gifts are similar.[1] The word itself is usually reserved for the switch of a registered estate from A to B,[2] the word transfer referring both to the process and to the document that carries it out. Transfer is essentially a matter of changing the name of the registered proprietor if attention is confined to dealings with a whole title. Additional complexities are associated with a transfer of part, these topics being relegated to the chapter on physical division.[3]

A. COMPUTERISATION OF THE REGISTRY

1. The paper and postal register

[8.02] Registration on the sale of land throughout England and Wales inevitably requires a bureaucracy to carry out the detailed work, including a staff of nine thousand,[4] to cope with the sheer volume of business. The year 2000–2001[5] saw approximately 300,000 first registrations, over 3.4 million dealings, and more than 9.6 million requests for preliminary services, with a corresponding volume of enquiry work. The Land Registry has gone to great lengths to reduce processing times to very short periods, so that dealings take only eight days on average[6] and 80% of first registrations are completed within 25 days.[7]

Day to day contact is with the appropriate District Land Registries, of which there are more than 20, each one allocated land in particular London boroughs, counties,

---

[1] A voluntary transfer is presumed to be a gift of beneficial ownership unless it is made clear that a resulting trust is intended: LPA 1925 s 60(3); *Hodgson* v. *Marks* [1971] Ch 892, CA; *Lohia* v. *Lohia* [2001] EWCA Civ 1691, affirming [2001] WTLR 101, Ch D; *Ali* v. *Khan* [2002] EWCA Civ 974, [2002] 30 EG 131 (CS).

[2] An unregistered estate is conveyed by a conveyance.

[3] See below [31].

[4] LRA 2002 sch 7 para 3; CLR *Report 1995–1996*, 13.

[5] LR *Annual Report 2001–2002*, 83.

[6] CLR *Report 1995–1996*, 10.

[7] LR *Annual Report 2001–2002*, 8.

and unitary authorities, each one controlled by a District Land Registrar.[8] It is vitally important to deal with the correct office when making postal applications for registration: sending papers to the Plymouth District Land Registry to register land in Birmingham is ineffective and the papers will be returned, possibly causing loss of priority.

Conventional applications to the land registry are by post to the appropriate District Land Registry.[9] Higher tech variants are by fax, by telephone, or by direct computer access. Rules lay down a general framework, which is fleshed out by means of notices issued by the registrar, under which the land registry provides additional services.[10] Personal attendance at the public counter of a land registry office remains possible.

2.   Dematerialisation of the register

[8.03] Computers and registration were made for each other. When the land registry was first set up in 1862[11] scriveners wrote out indentures by quill pen on pig skins, business was conducted at a leisurely pace by post, and it was envisaged that completions would occur at the registry. Successive registrars have responded to the invention of telephones, typewriters, and faxes. Now, at last, computer technology is available to provide a truly efficient conveyancing system. A programme of computerisation[12] started in 1988 and all titles will be available on-line by 2005.[13]

Registers on blue cards are being converted to a digital format, and held on a computer, the process known as dematerialisation.[14] Some 98% of plans have been scanned into electronic form, and the remainder will be digitised.[15] It will take rather longer to scan in all the deeds held by the registry – a mammoth task involving some 90 million pages.[16]

3.   Land Registry Direct

[8.04] A conveyancer can obtain direct access to the register via a computer terminal in his office linked to a secure computer by a network called LR Direct, a system developed since the register was opened in 1993.[17] Conveyancers connected to it can pay for download details of any register and also print out official copies, conduct searches, or transact any other business involving the open register. Current usage is for preliminary services, but some experiments are also being made with the delivery of substantive applications over the Network. As at 2001, about 40% of services are capable of electronic delivery,[18] a percentage which may explain the low take-up of

   [8] LRA 2002 s 100(3); SI 2001/3424; the list and explanatory leaflets are available from the LR website.
   [9] DLRR 2003 rr 14, 130.
   [10] DLRR 2003 sch 2; LR website.
   [11] Land Registry Act 1862 s 64.
   [12] CAPS = Computerised Application Processing System.
   [13] LR *Annual Report 2001–2002*, 8; LR *Annual Report 2000–2001*, 12, 23.
   [14] LRA 2002 s 1(2); DLRR 2003 r 2.
   [15] LR *Annual Report 2000–2001*, 20; LR *Annual Report 2001–2002*, 20.
   [16] LR *Annual Report 2000–2001*, 20.
   [17] LRA 2002 sch 5; DLRR 2003 r 131, sch 2; LR Practice Leaflet 13 (1999).
   [18] LR *Annual Report 2001–2002*, 21.

electronic services. Of 4 million office copies supplied in 2001–2002, 2.3 million were ordered by post, another 1.4 million by telephone and less than 200,000 by computer.[19] There is, however, a growing use of the facility for registry views, including index map searches.[20] On line searches are currently running at about 400,000 a month.[21]

4. Land Registry Network

[8.05] E-conveyancing will involve preliminary services provided on line followed by on-line applications. It will require a superior electronic communications network, to be called the LR Network.[22] This will provide secure procedures for the following aspects of conveyancing:

communication;
posting or retrieval of information;
making of changes to the register and the cautions register;
issue of official search certificates;
issue of official copies of the register; and
other facilities decided by the registrar.[23]

Network transaction rules will lay down the procedures to be followed,[24] that is the technical framework within which electronic conveyancing is to be conducted.[25] Terms will include monitoring, official management, and ongoing training.[26] Practitioners will be enabled to set in chain the changes to the register caused by a transaction.[27]

Conveyancers[28] will be able to connect to the LR Network under the terms of a network access agreement, will be entitled to access if they meet published criteria,[29] and may then be required to use the network.[30] A conveyancer using the Network will have to adopt a quasi-official position, not unlike the continental notary, with duties to the users of the Network which override those to his client.[31] Breaches will not directly affect the validity of the transaction.[32] Rather they will call into question the conveyancer's continued use of the Network, but given how serious the consequences of the withdrawal of the facility will be for a practitioner there will be a rigorous procedure and an appeal to the Adjudicator.[33]

---

[19] LR *Annual Report 2001–2002*, 83.
[20] Around 2.2 million a year.
[21] LR *Annual Report 2001–2002*, 83
[22] LRA 2002 s 92, sch 5.
[23] LRA 2002 sch 5 para 1(2).
[24] LRA 2002 sch 5 para 5.
[25] Law Com 271 (2001), [13.52], EN [669].
[26] Law Com 271 (2001), [13.66–13.71], EN [681].
[27] LRA 2002 sch 5 para 1(3); Law Com 271 (2001), [13.66–13.71].
[28] Solicitors and licensed conveyancers and possibly, in future, mortgage lenders: DLRR 2003 r 215.
[29] LRA 2002 sch 5 para 1; Law Com 271 (2001), [13.37].
[30] Law Com 271 (2001), EN [651–658].
[31] LRA 2002 sch 5 para 6; Law Com 271 (2001), [13.58–13.59], EN [672–673].
[32] Law Com 271 (2001), EN [670].
[33] LRA 2002 sch 5 paras 3–4; Law Com 271 (2001), [13.55–13.57], EN [659–668]; LRA 2002 s 108.

5. Electronic payment system

[8.06] Computerised completions will require a system of electronic settlement,[34] that is procedures for the electronic transfer of funds, the exact details of which are yet to be agreed with the banks. Legislation will be required to provide for documents to be e-stamped.[35]

6. DIY conveyancing

[8.07] Do it yourself conveyancers will be provided with access to the network, registry staff carrying out the transaction as instructed in return for a fee.[36] Nevertheless, the system will create a substantial and undesirable barrier to independent conveyancing.

B. TITLE BY REGISTRATION

1. Registered titles

[8.08] The Land Registration Act 2002 effects a radical shift. The ultimate proof of ownership of registered land becomes the register itself. Title by registration replaces the concept of registering titles obtained in other ways. A person selling the land can prove definitively his entitlement to sell by showing that he is on the register as proprietor. Previously registration as proprietor was not conclusive because there was the possibility that someone else had acquired title, but as adverse possession of registered land declines in importance, the need to check that the proprietor has possession of the land will be progressively reduced. Control of the land certificate was previously a vital prerequisite of the ability to sell, but it will no longer be necessary to produce the land certificate on a dealing. So registration emerges as the one key determinant of title.

2. Substantive proof of title

[8.09] Title to land means the right to an estate in the land. Proof is required that the seller has the ownership he claims, the substance of which has to be proved does not change in any way once the title is registered,[37] but the mechanics of proving title are vastly superior to the unregistered system. Good title must be shown to the estate. The contract states whether a freehold or a leasehold estate is being sold and in what land and it is then up to the seller to prove that he is the holder of that estate and is entitled to sell it. If title is registered this means that he is registered as proprietor and, unless the contract says otherwise his title must be absolute.[38] Title is established by the fact

---

[34] LRA 2002 s 94; Hansard HC vol 1916, February 11th 2002, col 23; PH Kenny [2002] *Conv* 431; *e-conveyancing* (LR CP, 2002), [5.6.3], [7].

[35] The promised framework has not materialised in the Finance Act 2002.

[36] LRA 2002 sch 5 para 7; Law Com 271 (2001), [13.72–13.73], EN [674–675].

[37] *Re Evan's* [1970] 1 WLR 583.

[38] For possessory and qualified titles see below **[11.09]**.

of registration and even wrongful registration gives title to sell.[39] Physical proof of title is also simplified since the register gathers together all the relevant information in two or three pages and almost all the necessary information can be provided by official copies of the register.

Misdescription is unlikely on the sale of a complete plot to which title is absolute. What is sold is whatever land is included within the title, which means that the physical extent of the land sold must correspond to the extent of the land to which title is shown. The seller has to do no more than to show that he is registered as proprietor to the title referred to in the contract.

3. Other aspects of proof of title

(1) Right to vacant possession

[8.10] Land is sold with the right for the buyer to take occupation of it unless the contract says otherwise. The land must not be subject to any undisclosed lease. Vacant possession can be obtained on the basis of the register if no lease is noted against it, though the land itself has to be checked for the presence of a tenant under a short term lease since such a tenancy is overriding.[40] Any beneficial interest will be overreached if there is a restriction[41] or overridden if there is none,[42] though again a check needs to be made for occupiers.[43]

(2) Freedom from incumbrances

[8.11] Burdens affect the land in the hands of future owners, and most land will be affected by some adverse rights. Mortgages are redeemable, that is the loan can be paid off and the land discharged from the mortgage, and it is assumed that this will occur at the time of completion. If so a mortgage need not be abstracted. Other rights such as contracts, easements and restrictive covenants continue to bind the land indefinitely, and the land must be sold subject to them. A seller must prove his right to the land free from all incumbrances which are not disclosed in the contract. Adverse burdens are listed on the charges register and must be disclosed; the land will be transferred free of any right which is not entered. However, there is a category of overriding interests which bind off the register and it will be necessary to show that such a right exists.

Evidence of benefitting rights may also be necessary.

C. INFORMATION FROM THE REGISTER

[8.12] We must now turn to the physical means of proving a registered title.

---

[39] LRA 2002 s 24.
[40] See below **[25.55ff]**.
[41] Hence it is not necessary to provide an abstract of a trust or settlement; see below **[13.30ff]**.
[42] See below **[13.09]**.
[43] See below **[15.33]**.

1. Official copies

[8.13] Official copies[44] are copies of an individual register[45] generated in such a way as to be authenticated by the land registry and within the registry guarantee. Originally called office copies, they took the form of official photocopies with a registry stamp obtained by postal application but already now, and increasingly so in future, official copies will be generated by a conveyancer using a computer to secure direct access to the register.[46] A complete set consists of copies of the register, the filed plan,[47] and any documents filed at the registry. If office copies are sought of land for which there is a pending application, the buyer has a choice either to accept official copies backdated to the position before the pending application or to wait for completion of the registration process.

Official copies are admissible in evidence as to the state of the register, and conveyancers are entitled to assume their accuracy, but the register remains decisive against inaccurate copies, however official.[48] Reliance on inaccurate copies will give rise to an indemnity for any loss suffered in consequence,[49] but there are few claims of this type.[50] It is an offence to tamper with official copies.[51]

2. Proof of title by official copies

[8.14] Access to the register is now open,[52] and there is no longer any provision about the title to be shown to registered land. It is intended to replace the old law which is prescriptive and heavy handed[53] with a much simpler rules framework.[54] All will be left to the contract between the parties. No doubt buyers will continue to insist on official copies, including the entries on the register, the filed plan, and documents referred to on the register. It is invariable practice to supply a copy of the register entries before exchange of contracts. There seems to be nothing to prevent a buyer insisting on the pre-registration title.[55] A search updates the picture provided by the office copy entries just before completion, and the buyer must then complete within the priority period of the search.[56]

---

[44] DLRR 2003 r 133; DLRR CD ch 9, [32–34]; LR Form OC1; DLRR 2003 r 133(3) (application covering several titles).

[45] For caution titles see below **[9.15]**.

[46] Law Com 271 (2001), [9.44–9.47].

[47] On building estates a title plan is lodged at the registry and buyers of individual plots rely upon a certificate of inspection of the title plan: DLRR 2003 r 143; see below **[31.01]**.

[48] LRA 2002 s 67.

[49] LRA 2002 sch 8 para 1(1)(d)–(e).

[50] CLR *Report 1995–1996*, 20.

[51] LRA 2002 ss 123–125; Law Com 271 (2001), [16.26–16.33], EN [532–546].

[52] There is no longer any need to give a buyer any authority to inspect the register.

[53] Law Com 271 (2001), [12.7].

[54] LRA 2002 sch 10 para 2; Law Com 271 (2001), [12.2], EN [760–764].

[55] This is an unintended consequence of the repeal of LRA 1925 s 110. This might be way over the top for a suburban semi; but it might be sensible for a valuable development site to guard against the risk of becoming embroiled in rectification proceedings. A provision like s 110 is needed.

[56] See below **[8.21]**.

3. Documents lodged at the registry

[8.15] Now that the register is open, there is no restriction on securing copies of filed documents. Copies are conclusive and a buyer is not entitled to ask for the original.[57] The registry will retain all documents unless a paper copy or an e-copy is available.[58] If a document contains prejudicial commercial information, it is possible to apply to the registry for an order designating it as an exempt commercial information document. This protects against disclosure in the ordinary way but information must still be disclosed when needed in relation to criminal proceedings, insolvency or tax liability. For the future leases and charges will be included in the open register. Pre-2002 Act documents of these kinds are transitional period documents, which means that they are exempt for one year and during that year application can be made for a permanent designation.[59]

4. History

[8.16] If a nation is happy "that has not history",[60] the same must apply even more to titles. Registration should record a current snapshot and make it irrelevant how the ownership arrived where it is. Our substantive land law does not sit happily with this, and it may be very important to know the sequence of past transactions when determining, for example, what easements have been created on earlier divisions.[61] Titles are computerised in such a way as to keep a record of previous version of the register. The registry will provide such information as it has available about the history of a registered title.[62] This is a backward step but one that is inevitable until the substantive law is corrected to make it irrelevant.

5. Index map

[8.17] Information about particular land is obtained via an index which records all registered estates and land affected by cautions against first registration.[63] A major use of it is to check an unregistered title to see whether the land is in fact registered, or whether there is any caution to prevent first registration, a check conducted by an index map search.[64] Physical parcels of land continue to be recorded on the Index Map, coloured to show the extent of every registered title.[65] This search, or a search of the verbal index covering franchises and similar rights,[66] may occasionally be use-

---

[57] LRA 2002 s 120.
[58] DLRR 2003 sch 5; SI 2002/2539, sch 1 para 4.
[59] DLRR 2003 rr 135–140; LR Form EX 1; DLRR CD ch 9, [12–18], [35–36].
[60] Cesare Beccaria *On Crimes and Punishments* (1764), introduction.
[61] See below **[34]**.
[62] LRA 2002 s 69; Law Com 271 (2001), [9.58–9.60], EN [306–309]; DLRR 2003 rr 144–145; DLRR CD ch 9, [11], [51]; Megarry & Wade (6th ed), [6.001] n 7.
[63] LRA 2002 s 68; Law Com 271 (2001), [9.54–9.57]; DLRR 2003 r 10. It also includes information about profits etc.
[64] See below **[9.17]**.
[65] DLRR 2003 r 10. References to the General Map were finally expunged by SI 2002/2539 sch 1 para 1.
[66] DLRR 2003 r 147; DLRR CD ch 9, [37–47].

ful when title is registered – for example to reveal the title to neighbouring land over which access rights are claimed.

6. Name

[8.18] The open register provides a ready means of ascertaining the name of the proprietor of registered land, especially if property can be adequately described from its postal address. Assuming that the target land is indeed registered, the result will reveal the title number and the name and address of the proprietor. If, conversely, a name is known, a search of the Index of Proprietor's Names will reveal details of all land held by that person. It can be searched by the proprietor or any other person establishing a sufficient interest.[67]

7. Fees

[8.19] There are nominal fees for the delivery of Land Registry services and searches, which are cheaper by direct access, though index map searches are free.[68]

D. SEARCHES OF THE REGISTER

1. Search without priority

[8.20] A search of the register without priority enables any person[69] to check for changes, updating since official copies of the register were last issued. Priority is unnecessary if all that is wanted is an up to date picture. Searches will reveal any adverse entries or pending applications.[70]

2. Protective searches

[8.21] Searches carried out in the course of a conveyancing transaction are made with priority,[71] updating title based on recent official copies obtained by post or by direct computer access, the date on which they were issued being the "search from" date. The result is shown in an official search certificate.[72] Searches made at a late stage of a conveyancing transaction should rarely produce surprises because the proprietor should be notified of an application for a unilateral notice or a unilateral restriction,[73] and the proprietor will now be warned of matrimonial home registrations or other

---

[67] DLRR 2003 r 11; DLRR CD ch 9, [48]. Excluded are corporate names, joint proprietors of estates and proprietors of charges, if registered before mid 1972.

[68] SI 2001/1179 – generally £2 or £4.

[69] DLRR 2003 rr 156–157. The need to be interested in the land and to have the authority of the proprietor to inspect was removed when the register was opened in 1990.

[70] DLRR 2003 r 148.

[71] LRA 2002 s 72; Law Com 271 (2001), [9.62–9.75]; DLRR 2003 r 148; LR Form OS1. A search can be made against an unregistered title which is subject to an application for first registration.

[72] DLRR 2003 r 150, sch 6 parts I–II.

[73] LRA 2002 s 35.

rare cases in which a final notice can be entered on a unilateral application.[74] An unexpected entry thrown up by a search at a late stage may have a devastating effect on a transaction.

Priority can be obtained by any intending purchaser, including a tenant, mortgage-lender, or anyone acquiring any legal estate for value.[75] The person searching is invited to identify what form of transaction is under way – perhaps a purchase, lease, charge, convert to charge, or a purchase of part. A lender protects both himself and the borrower (the buyer) but a search in the buyer's name will not protect the lender, and two searches are required for two independent loans. Honesty is not required.[76] Priority may also be needed by a lender: obtaining a search which reveals no matrimonial home right gives the lender 14 days in which to institute possession proceedings without having any obligation to inform the borrower's spouse of the proceedings.[77]

Searches must be made in time to be available on completion.[78] A priority period is marked on the search certificate, which is a period beginning from the time of the search and ending after 30 days,[79] with no procedure for extension.

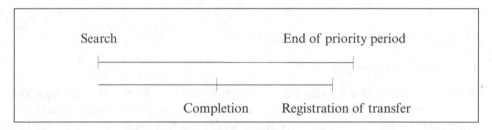

Figure 8-1 Registration within a priority period

Searches guard against registrations made after the search is issued but before the purchaser can apply for registration.[80] Protection depends upon applying to register the dealing in proper form[81] to the correct district registry within the priority period.[82] Clashing official searches form a queue in order of issue,[83] later searches revealing the existence of earlier ones.

---

[74] DLRR 2003 r 82; this is a reversal of the old practice.

[75] DLRR 2003 r 152.

[76] LRA 2002 s 72(2); this reverses the old law: *Smith* v. *Morrison* [1974] 1 WLR 659, 670A, 676E–F, Plowman J.

[77] FLA 1996 s 56(3); DLRR 2003 rr 159–160; LR Form MHB or electronic.

[78] They currently take 2 working days: LR *Annual Report 2001–2002*, 8.

[79] DLRR 2003 r 152; it is assumed that the old period of 30 days will continue though the draft rules do not give a period; the end date is included: DLRR 2003 r 155.

[80] *Leeman* v. *Mohammed* (2001) 82 P & CR 14 at 159, CA; JE Adams [2001] *Conv* 299.

[81] Ie one substantially in order, but not necessarily perfect: *Smith* v. *Morrison* [1974] 1 WLR 659 (error in name of company).

[82] LRA 2002 s 72; DLRR 2003 rr 154–155; on old law: *Mortgage Corp* v. *Nationwide Credit Corp* [1994] Ch 49, 53C, Dillon LJ.

[83] DLRR 2003 r 154.

Once the priority period has expired, it is as if the search had never been made and there is simply a dash to the register.[84] This applies to an 60% of applications, an extraordinary proportion.

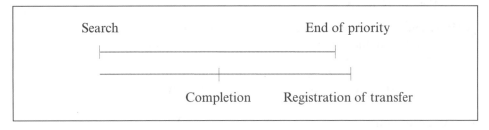

Figure 8-2 An expired priority period

3. Land charges search before a mortgage of registered land

[8.22] Land charges searches are redundant if title is registered, but many lenders do insist on a "bankruptcy only" search in order to ascertain whether the borrower is, or ever has, been bankrupt before committing themselves to lending money.

4. Methods of searching

[8.23] Searches were traditionally made by post and this is still perfectly possible, using the appropriate land registry form to identify the title and the period of the search[85]. Searches can be made by telephone[86] and a clear result can be issued or, if there have been entries, an oral indication can be given of that fact though not precise details of what the entries are.[87] Hi-tech searches can also be delivered by fax, or through direct computer access.[88] Low tech searches can be made by request at the public counter of any district land registry.[89]

5. Errors in searches

[8.24] Errors in searches are not uncommon, cautions being missed in both *Parkash*[90] and *Clark*.[91] The register is the final determinant of title and so entries which are not disclosed are still binding, leaving the buyers with compensation while, conversely, if an entry is erroneously omitted from the register it will not bind purchasers. Errors in

---

[84] On old law: *Watts* v. *Waller* [1973] 1 QB 153; *Bridges* v. *Mees* [1957] Ch 475; *City of London BS* v. *Flegg* [1988] AC 54, HL; *Howell* v. *Montey* (1990) 61 P & CR 18, CA; P Coughlan [1990] *Conv* 392 (*Howell* wrong).

[85] DLRR 2003 sch 1; LR Form OS.

[86] DLRR 2003 sch 2.

[87] DLRR 2003 r 158; R Hewitson, [1994] 27 *LSG* 25.

[88] Under DLRR 2003 r 158; R Hewitson, [1994] 27 *LSG* 25. The terms of a notice issued under DLRR 2003 sch 2.

[89] There are 36 in one recent year: LR *Annual Report 2001–2002*, 83.

[90] *Parkash* v. *Irani Finance* [1970] Ch 101, Plowman J.

[91] *Clark* v. *Chief Land Registrar* [1994] Ch 370, CA.

searches give rise to a claim for an indemnity against loss,[92] though claims are relatively few.

6. Outline applications

[8.25] Where an application cannot be protected by an official search it is possible to make an outline application which reserves priority for a four day period.[93]

E. PROOF OF MATTERS OFF THE REGISTER

1. Overriding interests

[8.26] Some matters operate off the register, usually as overriding interests, and these may impinge on the three elements necessary to show good title – the estate owner-ship, the right to vacant possession and, particularly, freedom from incumbrances. It follows that the contract must disclose all overriding interests and their existence should be proved as if title was unregistered. One example is a short lease (a legal lease for seven years or less) which binds a purchaser without entry on the register. Others are rights of way, any easement created by use, loss of title to a squatter (pre-2002 Act), and any right held by an occupier. A full list of overriding interests must wait until the chapter on burdens.[94]

2. Extent of the land

[8.27] Another matter requiring careful proof is the physical extent of the land sold if the contract contains its own plan or description. A misdescription arises if this does not match the physical extent of the title registered. In *AJ Dunning & Sons (Shopfitters)* v. *Sykes & Son (Poole)*[95] the plan on a land registry transfer included land in an adjoining title. The majority of the Court of Appeal[96] took this to be an attempt to transfer land not owned by the seller. Official copies are only sufficient proof of title to the land in an individual register of the title in the ownership of the seller, and further proof is required of the ownership of adjoining land.

3. Benefitting rights

[8.28] Benefitting rights may not be shown on the register and if so they need to be proved as in unregistered land.

---

[92] LRA 2002 s 103, sch 8; *Prestige Properties* v. *Scottish Provident Institution* [2002] EWHC 330, [2003] Ch 1, Lightman J (reduced by 90% because of faulty conveyancing).
[93] DLRR 2002 r 52.
[94] LRA 2002 sch 3; see below [20].
[95] [1987] Ch 287 CA.
[96] Dillon and Croom–Johnson LJJ, Lord Donaldson MR dissenting.

4. National Land Information Service

[8.29] Before buying one needs to check all sorts of other matters such as local land charges, planning history, mining history, location of power lines, contamination with pollutants etc etc. This has been done by a local search, along with mining searches etc. The National Land Information Service[97] provides much of this information, though it is not yet truly on line – a search is submitted by e-mail with the result issued a few days later. Heavy investment is being made to deliver a truly instantaneous on-line system by 2007.

F. LAND REGISTRY FORMS

[8.30] Many forms are prescribed,[98] the 2002 review aiming to avoid unnecessary changes, but to simplify the forms and to increase the number that are prescribed.[99] Schedule 1 forms are mandatory,[100] the paper forms replicating those produced during the overhaul that took place in 1999.[101] Schedule 3 gives model forms for some other forms of transaction which may be modified, altered, or adapted as necessary.[102] Forms of execution are also prescribed.[103] All forms are available in English or Welsh.[104]

Forms must be easily legible and produced on A4 paper following the printed models,[105] though forms completed with conveyancing software may be modified to omit certain details that are irrelevant.[106]

G. TRANSFER

1. Power to transfer

[8.31] Transfer is the most obvious of the "owner's powers"[107] – those powers exercisable by a registered proprietor[108] which give rise to transactions which must be

---

[97] M Riddick [2002] 3 *Legal IT* 34; N Fulwood (2002) 146 *SJ* 1028.

[98] LRA 2002 s 100(4).

[99] DLRR CD ch 1, [5–6]. Potential difficulties are the increase in prescribed forms and the failure to provide any transitional period: PH Kenny [2002] *Conv* 518, 521–522.

[100] DLRR 2003 r 203(1), sch 1. R 206 permits variations where use of the prescribed form is not possible or would involve excessive expense.

[101] LRR 1999 SI 1999/128; C West [1999] 24 *LSG* 42.

[102] DLRR 2003 sch 3. If no form is provided for a particular transaction, the form will be such as the registrar directs or allows: r 209.

[103] DLRR 2003 sch 8.

[104] DLRR 2003 r 205. For Welsh forms see the Welsh Language LR website.

[105] Panels can be continued on LR Form CS: DLRR 2003 r 207.

[106] Eg instructions for completion of the form in italics, marginal lines, and inappropriate certificates, statements and panels (though the numbering of the official forms must be kept); the plural may stand for the singular and vice versa: DLRR 2003 r 208.

[107] LRA 2002 s 23; Law Com 271 (2001), [4.1–4.31]; *State Bank of India* v. *Sood* [1997] Ch 276, 284, Peter Gibson LJ.

[108] LRA 2002 s 24. Also by a person entitled to be registered.

completed by registration,[109] and which will not operate at law until registration. In favour of a purchaser, it is presumed that a registered proprietor has these power unless a restriction appears on the register.[110]

2. Form of transfer

[8.32] Registered title is passed from A to B by the process called transfer, and the document used being a land registry transfer. Two stages are required, a transfer in the correct form[111] and its registration. Forms are pared down enormously as compared to unregistered conveyances, so that Theodore Ruoff was rightly able to boast that the typed content of a straightforward transfer is less than the Inland Revenue stamp on it.[112]

Land registry form TR1[113] is used for transfers of the whole of the freehold or leasehold land in a title. Stamping details appear first – either a stamp or a certificate of value or an exempting certificate.[114] The second element is identification of the title affected (by title number and postal address). After the date and a definition of the parties, the operative part states simply (if inelegantly) that "the Seller transfers the property to the Buyer".[115] This is supplemented by a consideration clause, used to distinguish sales from gifts and to provide a receipt for any purchase money,[116] as well as a title guarantee.[117] Special adaptations may be required to reflect sales of part or different capacities.[118] Finally execution as a deed is required using the correct land registry form of words.[119]

3. Substitution by transfer

[8.33] A land registry transfer substitutes[120] a buyer for a seller. Before, the proprietorship register will look like this:

---

[109] LRA 2002 s 27, sch 2. Registration requirements do not apply to transfers on death or bankruptcy, dissolution of corporate proprietor, or creation of a local land charge.

[110] LRA 2002 s 26.

[111] But registration of an incorrect form overrides objection to the form: *Smith* v. *Morrison* [1974] 1 WLR 659; *Morelle* v. *Wakeling* [1955] 2 QB 379, 414, Evershed MR.

[112] TBF Ruoff (1953) 17 *Conv (NS)* 105.

[113] TR1 transfer (sale or gift); DLRR 2003 sch 1; DLRR CD ch 1, [21].

[114] LR transfers must be stamped in the normal way: *P & O Overseas Holdings* v. *Rhys Braintree* [2002] EWCA Civ 296, [2002] 2 P & CR 27 at 400, [24–23], Morritt V-C.

[115] Happily for *New Land Lawyers*, "seller" and "buyer" may be substituted for "transferor" and "transferee".

[116] Gifts are less effective than sales in securing priority over previous interests; see below **[15.10]**, **[15.28]**, **[20.39]**, **[21.34]**.

[117] See below **[11.59ff]**.

[118] Eg a declaration of beneficial capacity is required when co-owners acquire land, to state whether they take as joint tenants or as tenants in common, and then whether in equal or unequal shares; see below **[16.13]**.

[119] DLRR 2003 sch 8.

[120] See above **[3.23]**.

> HM LAND REGISTRY
> PROPRIETORSHIP REGISTER of Title no XYZ 12345
> (10th January 1954) Catherine Earnshaw of [address]

Figure 8-3 Proprietorship register before a transfer

A transfer to a buyer should make use of Form TR1:[121]

> HM LAND REGISTRY
> [Stamp duty exemption or certificate of value]
> Title No XYZ 12345.
> Property Wuthering Heights, Haworth, West Yorkshire.
> Date January 21st 2002.
> Parties Catherine Earnshaw (Seller) and Heathcliff (Buyer)
> The Seller transfers the Property to the Buyer.
> [Consideration and receipt clause].
> [Full title guarantee.]
> Signed as a deed by Catherine Earnshaw in the presence of [witness]

Figure 8-4 A transfer form

A pure transfer has no impact on the property or charges register, but merely substitutes the new name on the proprietorship register, and gives the address for service of notices,[122] thus:

> HM LAND REGISTRY
> PROPRIETORSHIP REGISTER of Title no XYZ 12345
> (24th February 2002) Heathcliff of [address]

Figure 8-5 A proprietorship register after a transfer

4. Registered transfer based on registration as proprietor

[8.34] A pre-1926 Court of Appeal held in *Capital & Counties Bank* v. *Rhodes*[123] that a *legal* estate in registered land could be passed off the register, a decision which was totally destructive of the registration system.[124] The case had to be reversed in 1925: registered estates "shall only be capable of being disposed of or dealt with" by the

---

[121] DLRR 2003 sch 1.
[122] DLRR 2003 rr 195–196.
[123] [1903] 1 Ch 631, Cozens-Hardy & Romer LJJ, Collins LJ dissenting.
[124] F Pollock (1903) 19 *LQR* 251; JE Hogg (1904) 20 *LQR* 292, 294.

registered proprietor in the manner authorised by the Land Registration Act.[125] Even wrongful registration as proprietor confers the ability to pass title. In *Re Leighton's Conveyance*[126] a daughter defrauded her mother in order to secure her own registration as proprietor, and this improper registration was sufficient to confer on her the statutory powers of disposition. Innocent lenders obtained valid mortgages. The curtain imposed on the earlier title by registration is explored in full in a subsequent chapter.[127]

H. APPLICATIONS

1.   Application

[8.35] Substantive applications[128] are those made to register transfers and other dealings, as opposed to requests for official copies, searches and other information. A single form is used as a default for almost any full, paper based[129] application for which there is no specific form. Applications must identify the property affected and be made to the correct district land registry.

Commonly the form is used to list several applications, for example a transfer followed by a mortgage, which should be listed in order, and it also requires a list of documents lodged with the registry.[130] All related applications must be listed, but separate applications will now be required for each aspect of a transaction, for example for the registration of a transfer to the buyers and for entry of a restriction recording the capacity in which they hold as joint proprietors.

2.   Removal of the need to deposit the land certificate

[8.36] Ultimate proof of the ownership of registered land is provided by the register itself. A proprietor was formerly issued with a Land Certificate which included a copy of the Register. If the land was mortgaged, the Land Certificate was withheld and a Charge Certificate was issued to the lender. Certificates in circulation usually presented an accurate portrait of the register, but it was possible for them to fall out of date, for example because of a caution or a notice of a type that could be entered without production of the Certificate.[131] In any event the requirement for production of a certificate is not compatible with a system of electronic conveyancing,[132] and they will no longer be issued. It seems that a certificate of registration will be provided rather

---

[125] LRA 1925 s 69(4); now LRA 2002 s 58; Law Com 271 (2001), [9.3–9.9], EN [25].

[126] [1937] Ch 149, CA; see below **[24.29]**.

[127] See below **[11]**.

[128] Law Com 271 (2001), [9.76–9.82].

[129] LR Form AP1; DLRR 2003 r 13. Though excluding the removal of a deceased joint proprietor; also electronic and outline applications: DLRR CD ch 1, [18].

[130] DLRR 2003 r 213; LR Form AP1 should be accompanied by (1) DS1 discharge of the existing mortgage (2) stamped transfer (or if no duty is payable, the transfer and a particulars delivered form); (3) charge; (4) certified copy charge; and (5) a scale fee. See also rr 201–202 (return of documents after registration); rr 211–212 (documents).

[131] P Sparkes *NLL* (1st ed), 10–11, 189–193.

[132] Law Com 271 (2001), [9.83–9.91].

like a receipt to confirm that registration of the transaction has been completed, but without a copy of the entries.[133]

This change is a mistake. There are inevitably problems with keeping any form of copy up to date, but that is to miss the point of the Certificate. Its value was not as a duplicate of the information on the register, but rather as a key used to lock and unlock access to the register itself. In the past a sale could only proceed after production to the registry of the certificate.[134] This important guarantee of the security of the proprietor's holding is now removed. It seems surprising that institutional lenders are prepared to accept the abolition of the charge certificate,[135] surely an important protection against fraudulent sales by the borrower.

3. Land registry fees

[8.37] The land registry has to be self-financing,[136] and so fees[137] are charged on the value of the land (*ad valorem*).[138] Scale 1 applies to transfers for value, and applications to register the grant of a new lease. Sub-sales effect a saving, since only one fee is payable.[139] Scale 2[140] is used for separate mortgage applications[141] and also for transfers lacking a monetary consideration, such as gifts, surrenders, transmissions on death or bankruptcy, assents, and transfers of the matrimonial home.

Fixed fees are specified for a whole list of *applications*, such as entry of a caution or restriction, conversion of title and replacing a lost land certificate.[142] Fees for on-line applications by direct access are generally lower. Many transactions and services are exempt, such as discharge of a registered mortgage, renewal of cautions, entry and withdrawal of notices of deposit, recording the death of a joint proprietor, dispositions by personal representatives, many cancellations,[143] and the approval of estate layout plans. Entry of the compulsory joint proprietor restriction[144] is also free.

4. Completion of applications

[8.38] When a registration is made it is backdated to the time of making the application to register a disposition.[145] Documents will generally be retained in the registry.[146]

---

[133] DLRR CD ch 2, [7–23]; PH Kenny [2002] *Conv* 518, 519.

[134] *Re de Leeuw* [1922] 2 Ch 540, 554, Peterson J. If the certificate was stolen, an inhibition prevented the thief making use of the certificate.

[135] Law Com 271 (2001), [9.86].

[136] It produces a healthy 6% return on capital: *LR Annual Report 2001/2002*, 8.

[137] LRA 2002 s 102; Law Com 271 (2001), EN [467–469]; SI 2001/1179 art 2. They change frequently but the LR website has online fees calculator software.

[138] Eg on a £150,000 house the current fee is £200; and below £1m it is £500.

[139] SI 2001/1179 art 3(3)–(4).

[140] For example up to £100,000 value, the scale 2 is a bargain £40.

[141] There is no fee for a mortgage lodged with a transfer on which a scale fee is paid; fees can be avoided by creating equitable mortgages.

[142] SI 2001/1179, s3; most fixed fees are currently £40.

[143] Except leases (scale fee) or rentcharges (fixed fee).

[144] See below [13.36].

[145] LRA 2002 s 74; Law Com 271 (2001), EN [335–337]; DLRR 2003 r 20.

[146] DLRR 2003 rr 201–202, 211–213.

5. Defective applications

[8.39] Some 50% of applications contain a substantial defect. Electronic conveyancing will depend upon the conveyancer getting things right and so, in order to smooth the transition, the land registry have tightened their rejection policy for paper based applications.[147] An application will be returned if it contains the following substantial defects:

> unstamped documents or the absence of a Particulars Delivered form;
> failure to lodge an original lease etc;
> a transfer of part lacks a plan;
> failure to use a compulsory form;
> an application is made to note a variation of a lease that is substantively registered;
> applications previously rejected which have not been corrected;
> failure to meet a requisition within one month; or
> failure to honour a cheque in payment of fees.

Applications are often delayed by the absence of a discharge for the seller's mortgage, delays arising from the high volume of business undertaken by the large lenders or by ability to stamp the document in time. Extension of the time limits for registration will be allowed in these circumstances.[148]

6. Objections to applications

[8.40] There is a right to object to any application.[149] Disputes can be referred for adjudication.[150]

I. QUEUE OF APPLICATIONS

1. The queue of applications

[8.41] Applications are held in a queue, ranking in the order in which they are made to the land registry,[151] provided they are proper applications made to the correct district land registry.[152] The sequence can be discovered from the day list[153] which lists all pending applications, first registrations, dealings, searches with priority, and applications relating to certificates and their deposit, decisions by the registry to make an alteration of the register, and applications to designate commercially sensitive

---

[147] DLRR 2003 rr 16–17; LR Public Information Leaflet 34–35 (2002); PH Kenny [2002] *Conv* 203.

[148] Amended policy, LR September 2002.

[149] LRA 2002 s 74; DLRR 2003 r 19.

[150] LRA 2002 s 73(1); Draft LR (Referral to the Adjudicator to HM Land Registry) R 2003 (LR, January 2003).

[151] *Gartside* v. *Silkstone* (1882) 21 Ch D 762, Fry J; *Keith Bayley Rogers & Co* v. *Cubes* (1975) 31 P & CR 412; *Michaels* v. *Harley House (Marylebone)* [2000] Ch 104, CA.

[152] DLRR 2003 rr 14, 16, 215.

[153] DLRR 2003 r 12. However, if entry is omitted, the application is deemed to be received at midnight on the day of a morning application or the day after one made in the afternoon: DLRR 2003 r 15.

information.[154] The true state of the register at any moment is its current physical state as amended by all pending applications and objections. Real time priority is applied so that applications and searches by computer are accorded priority as of the precise time they are made.[155] Applications survive death.[156]

2. Priority between applications

[8.42] Where two applications coincide and neither has priority according to the day list, it will usually be possible to sort out the order in which they are to be dealt with because one will be dependent on the other – for example where a house is transferred and then mortgaged by the buyer, but otherwise the order can be agreed between the applicants, or determined by the registrar subject to an objection procedure.[157]

3. The registration gap

[8.43] The gap which exists between completion of a transaction and its registration was already identified as a problem in 1886.[158] Simultaneous creation and registration of interests effected electronically will eventually eliminate the registration gap. For the mean time, until compulsion is introduced, it will remain a problem.

It is axiomatic[159] that a transfer gives the right to apply for registration, but it does not operate to pass the legal estate. In the interim period, before registration a transfer passes only beneficial (that is equitable) ownership of the property,[160] which gives the buyer the right to move in, and the right to apply for registration of the transfer after it has been stamped.[161]

Applications are held in a queue, and when registration is finalised it will be backdated to the date of application[162] provided that it is a proper application properly delivered, so that the critical moment is when papers are lodged at the land registry. Abnormal applications could take years to complete,[163] but usually the delay in waiting for physical registration is no more than a couple of weeks.

Pending registration of the transfer the seller remains legal owner of the property holding on trust for the buyer.[164] Potential difficulties emerged from *Brown & Root Technology* v. *Sun Alliance & London Assurance Co.*[165] A tenant company transferred a registered lease to a wholly owned subsidiary company, but this subsidiary was not

---

[154] See above **[8.15]**.
[155] SI 2000/3225; LR *Annual Report* 2000–2001, 23.
[156] DLRR 2003 r 18.
[157] DLRR 2003 r 53.
[158] T Key (1886) 2 *LQR* 324, 342.
[159] *Pourdanay* v. *Barclays Bank* [1997] Ch 321, 322.
[160] *Crumpton* v. *Unifox Properties* [1992] 2 EGLR 82, CA (no power to forfeit lease).
[161] As between borrower and lender a mortgage effectively charges the loan on the land from the date of the mortgage: LRA 1925 s 27; *Lloyd* v. *Nationwide Anglia BS* [1996] EGCS 80. But the lender might lose priority and legal remedies depend upon registration: LRA 2002 s 51; see below **[28.05]**.
[162] LRA 2002 s 74; Law Com 271 (2001), [9.76–9.82], EN [335–337]; DLRR 2003 r 15. On the old law see: *Crumpton* v. *Unifox Properties* [1992] 1 EGLR 82, 84J–K, Staughton LJ; *Chattey* v. *Farndale Holdings* (1998) 75 P & CR 298, 311, Morritt LJ.
[163] *City of London BS* v. *Flegg* [1988] AC 54 (application delayed while case litigated to HL).
[164] N Hopkins (1998) 61 *MLR* 486.
[165] [2001] Ch 733, CA; *Gentle* v. *Faulkner* [1900] 2 QB 267, CA; *Re Rose* [1952] Ch 449 distinguished.

yet registered as proprietor. The parent company remained the "tenant" under the lease, and so, as the court held, the correct party to serve a break notice to end the lease. Notice served by the subsidiary company did not destroy the lease. The case highlights the unfortunate division between the person appearing on the register as proprietor and the "owner". A seller who remains as registered proprietor is liable for use of the land in breach of a planning enforcement notice until after the registration of the buyer.[166]

An official search is an essential protection against adverse entries being made for the duration of the priority period, but there is no protection against overriding interests. It is in this area that the problems of the registration gap are most pressing, but the Land Registration Act 2002 provides at best a promise of jam tomorrow.

	Completion		Registration
Legal title/ the register	AAAAAA|AAAAAAAAAAAAAAAAAAAA|BBBBBBBBBBB		
	|	registration gap	|
Beneficial Entitlement	AAAAAA|BBBBBBBBBBBBBBBBBBBBBBBBB|BBBBBBBBBBB		

Figure 8-6 The registration gap

J.   ELECTRONIC APPLICATIONS

1.   Pre 2002 Act electronic applications

[8.44] Some experiments are being made with lodging dealings electronically. At present these operate under the terms of a notice issued by the registrar under the LR Direct Enhanced and LR Direct Access Service. Substantive applications of the following kinds have been lodged since February 2002:[167]

> change of name marriage or deed poll;
> change address for service;
> change of property description;
> death of joint proprietor; and
> entry of a restriction after severance of a joint tenancy by notice.

Appropriate documents must be seen by the conveyancer, but the registry will accept his certificate that he has seen the appropriate documentation. Receipt is confirmed electronically and the application is stored. Experiments are continuing with more significant applications with a direct effect on the register, for example the electronic

---

[166] *East Lindsey DC* v. *Thompson* [2001] EWHC Admin 81, [2001] 08 EG 165; *Buckinghamshire CC* v. *Briar* [2002] EWHC 2821 (Ch), [2002] December 20th, [151–152], Lawrence Collins J.
[167] LR *Annual Report* 2000–2001, 20.

entry of a matrimonial home right,[168] and with e-discharge of mortgages.[169] Also on the way are paperless mortgage offers.[170]

2. Electronic applications

[8.45] In future it will be possible to make any substantive[171] application in electronic form,[172] under the terms of a facility notice.[173] This will link into other developments such as e-notices of assignment,[174] e-filing of court documents,[175] and e-grants of probate.[176]

K. DERIVATIVE TRANSACTIONS

1. Declaration of trust by new proprietors

[8.46] An application for registration must state the capacity in which the new proprietor is to hold the property, so that the registrar may determine whether any restriction is necessary. An individual entitled to the land as beneficial owner appears on the proprietorship register without any restriction. Joint proprietorship generally calls for an obligatory restriction, the one exception being where joint proprietors hold for themselves as beneficial joint tenants.[177] The applicants' conveyancer is required to certify how the land is held beneficially, the certificate being based on the declaration made by the buyers about how they are to hold between themselves, probably within the transfer document itself.

2. Derivative transactions

[8.47] Transactions which confer partial or derivative interests include leases, mortgages, and grants of easements. Many transactions are subject to registration requirements, for example the grant or transfer of a legal mortgage, and any express grant or reservation of legal easement or profit. Legal title only passes when title is registered.[178] Proprietors have all the other powers of an owner in the general law. Medium term leases, equitable mortgages, contracts and so forth will need to be protected by notice, which will also require an application.[179]

---

[168] LRR 2001, SI 2001/619; now DLRR 2003 r 51.

[169] DLRR 2003 r 142; re-enacting LRR 2000 SI 2000/429; M Heighton [2000] 19 *EG* 132. At present this is an e-mail notification but direct changes to the register should be possible by the middle of 2003: [2002] 46 *EG* 15.

[170] P Rohan [2002] 36 *LSG* 1.

[171] DLRR 2003 r 15; requests for information are made under DLRR 2003 part 13, rr 129–161.

[172] DLRR 2003 r 52; DLRR 2003 r 208; DLRR CD, ch 7, [8], [15].

[173] DLRR 2003 sch 2.

[174] LRA 2002 s 91(7).

[175] SI 2002/2058. A trial is under way in Walsall: PD 5B.

[176] *Review of Probate Business – a CP* (LCD, November 2002).

[177] See below **[13.37]**.

[178] LRA 2002 s 27(1).

[179] In both cases priority is protected, but a notice does not guarantee the validity of the right.

3.   Mortgages

[8.48] It is normal practice for the buyer to mortgage the land before securing registration. Thus

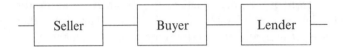

Figure 8-7 Contemporaneous purchase and mortgage

In a case such as this where a transfer of an existing registered title is contemporaneous with a mortgage, the borrower is entitled to registration but not yet registered. Rules permit such a mortgage.[180] Application forms for registration of a dealing also provide for a sequential list of associated transactions, to enable the transfer to be registered before the mortgage.

4.   Subsales

[8.49] A person who has a contract to buy land may sell it without first completing his purchase contract, a process known as a subsale. Two or more sales can be completed by one document, passing legal title direct from the estate owner to the ultimate buyer without any intermediate documentation, saving land registry fees[181] and stamp duty.[182] Thus:

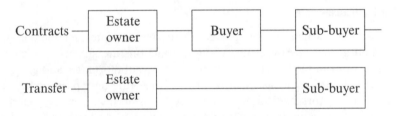

Figure 8-8 Sub-sale of a registered title

The subsale of an existing registered titles occurs where the second contract is made at a time when the first buyer remains off the register. Previously title could be forced on the sub-buyer who was not entitled to insist on the registration of the intermediate purchaser,[183] but now title is a matter of contract between the various parties.

---

[180] LRA 2002 s 24; DLRR 2003 r 35.
[181] See above **[8.37]**.
[182] JE Adams [1989] *Conv* 232, 317.
[183] LRA 1925 s 110(5); JFarrand [1979] *Conv* 1, 2; P Sparkes [1990] *NLJ* 1077; *P & O Overseas Holdings* v. *Rhys Braintree* [2002] EWCA Civ 296, [2002] 2 P & CR 27 at 400 (Development site held on bare trust. Completion 5 days after transfer from developer to vendor. Question was stamping of the first transfers. Too late to raise s 110(5) on facts, and anyway special contractual provision).

5. Chains of transactions

[8.50] Chains of transactions occur where there is a sequence of transfers, the resale occurring while the seller's title is still being registered at the land registry, thus:

Figure 8-9 A chain of dealings with a registered title

Problems arise where title is registered. Where the original proprietor remains regis-tered, and the person selling has an off-register transfer, the second transfer form requires adaptation to show that the disposition is not by a current registered propri-etor.[184] The land registry view is that the registration machinery can be implemented without much modification.[185] Title consists of official copies of the register entries (which show the first seller as registered proprietor), a copy of the transfer which is pending at the land registry, and an official search, which will reveal the pending application to register the first transfer.[186] Whether the ultimate buyer can insist if he chooses to be awkward on waiting for the immediate seller to be registered as propri-etor, as he could under the old law,[187] now depends on the contractual arrangements between the parties.

---

[184] *ES Schwab & Co* v. *McCarthy* (1976) 31 P & CR 196, 201; derivative transactions may be validated after registration by estoppel: *First National Bank* v. *Thompson* [1996] Ch 231, CA.

[185] LR Practice Leaflet 2.

[186] LR (Official Searches) R 1993 r 7.

[187] *Urban Manor* v. *Sadiq* [1997] 1 WLR 1016, CA (too late to requisition on facts); *P & O Overseas Holdings* v. *Rhys Braintree* [2002] EWCA Civ 296, (2002) 2 P & CR 27 at 400; P Sparkes [1990] *NLJ* 1077; EJ Pryer [1990] *NLJ* 1327.

9

FIRST REGISTRATION

Unregistered titles. Proof. Epitomes. LR checks. Cautions against first registration. Conveyance. Compulsion. Voluntary registration. First registration machinery. Derivative transactions.

A. PROOF OF UNREGISTERED TITLE

1. Deeds based conveyancing

[9.01] Unregistered titles are based on title deeds, a collection of documents affecting the land, mainly conveyances by which it is sold from one person to another.[1] A good title is shown by tracing title back to a good root.[2] Title is derivative. What Z now holds depends on what X held in the past and what was transferred on through Y. Indeed one might chase title back through previous owners all the way back to A, producing a chain of title formed of various documents which evidence the passage of the legal estate from one person to another. Most of the links will be deeds,[3] the majority consisting of conveyances on sale, but spiced up with an occasional deed of gift, devolution on death, or mortgage followed by a sale by the lender. Collected together, these are the title deeds to the land.

2. Good title

[9.02] Proof of title to unregistered land involves demonstration, first and foremost, of good title to the estate. The contract states what estate is being sold – whether freehold or leasehold – and in what land and it is then up to the seller to prove that he does indeed hold that estate and is entitled to sell it. The title deduced must be documentary unless the contract says explicitly that reliance is placed on adverse possession.[4]

---

[1] Cheshire & Burn (16th ed), 91–110, ch 23; Goo's *Sourcebook* (3rd ed) ch 3; Grays' *Elements* (3rd ed), 218–226; Megarry & Wade (6th ed), ch 5; A Pottage, "Evidencing Ownership" ch 5 in Bright & Dewar; W Swadling "Property" ch 4 in Birks' *English Private Law*, [4.416–4.444]; MP Thompson *Modern LL* ch 6.

[2] See below **[9.04]**.

[3] LPA 1925 s 52; see above **[8]**.

[4] *Re Atkinson & Horsell's C* [1912] 2 Ch 1, CA; *George Wimpey & Co* v. *Sohn* [1967] Ch 487, CA.

3.   Derivative nature of unregistered estate

[9.03] Unregistered title passes from one owner to another. What passes to B is coextensive with what A had to pass. When considering *estates*,[5] modern[6] English land law adheres strictly to the principle that the title of the recipient is only as good as the title of the giver, that "one can give only what one holds".[7] Only the holder of a legal estate is able to pass a legal title and only a freeholder can pass a freehold. Thus:

(1) If X holds for life under a trust of land, a transfer of his interest to Y passes only an equitable interest *to Y for X's life.*[8]
(2) If land is vested in *H and W on trust for themselves as beneficial joint tenants* legal title is held jointly, so that a sale by H alone (or a forgery by H and a new partner masquerading as W) passes no legal title to the buyer but will assign H's equitable share in the house which he holds on his own account.[9]

Unregistered freehold estates pass only from a person who himself held a freehold estate. That previous owner must have obtained the estate from an earlier estate owner. So title is proved by checking back through a chain, usually by starting at the oldest division of the land and moving forward, though of course a chain can be traversed in either direction, up or down.

4.   The root

[9.04] In theory, any title could be traced backwards indefinitely. A legendary, but exasperated, reply to a requisition about land in Louisiana referred title back through acquisition of the state by the French from the Spanish, via the explorer Christopher Columbus, acting at the command of the Catholic King of Spain, who was supported by the Pope and so derived title from God.[10] William I acquired title by Conquest in 1066, but real life conveyancing could not possible work on the basis of proof of title of anywhere near that length.[11] Some limit has to be imposed on the historical checks on the title, though the short period accepted by modern English land law pulls the reader up short.

An open contract is one containing no special provision about title. A good root of title under such a contract is a document which:

(1) contains a sufficient description of the property;
(2) deals with the entire legal estate and beneficial interests;

---

[5] The principle does not apply to equitable burdens, since these can be destroyed by a protected purchaser, see above **[6.24]**.

[6] Before 1926 there were one or two cases of "tortious assurances", that is of sale of a greater title than the one held: Megarry & Wade (6th ed), [3.115].

[7] A cumbersome translation of the Latin maxim *nemo dat quod non habet*, frequently abbreviated to *nemo dat*; Megarry & Wade (6th ed), [3.115]; G Battersby & AD Preston (1972) 35 *MLR* 268; Panesar's *General Principles* ch 9.

[8] An interest *pur autre vie*.

[9] See below **[16.24]**.

[10] RE Megarry, *Miscellany-at-Law* (Stevens, 1955), 149–150.

[11] The claimants in *Smith* v. *Andrews* [1891] 2 Ch 678, North J, showed title for 700 years, and still lost! Lord Goodhart has encountered a case where deeds were destroyed in the Great Fire of London: *Hansard* HL, vol 623, July 3rd 2001, col 791.

(3) casts no doubt on the title;[12] and

(4) is at least 15 years old.[13]

Best of all is a conveyance on sale. Gifts fall within the technical definition, but they are doubtful in practice since title is not investigated by a donee who is given the land and he is not a protected purchaser. A mortgage does not deal with the entire legal and equitable interest and is technically not a root, even though practice dictates a thorough investigation of title before a mortgage. Assents by personal representatives and specific devises in wills of testators dying before 1926 are also acceptable.[14]

A root of title usually indicates that the land is subject to burdens created earlier, such as easements or restrictive covenants, in which case the document creating the burden in the first place must be produced but not intervening transactions.[15] Investigation before the statutory root of title is not usual,[16] for

"Where ignorance is bliss, tis folly to be wise."[17]

Suppose, by way of example, that the complete title deeds available for a house are as follows:

1865	Conveyance by A to B of one of a pair of semi-detached houses creating restrictive covenants in favour of A.
1928	Deed of gift by B to C subject to the 1865 covenants.
1948	C conveyed the house to D subject to the 1865 covenants.
1980	D conveyed the house to E subject to the 1865 covenants.

Figure 9-1 An epitome of an unregistered title

If title is proved by E in 2003, the root of title is the 1980 conveyance – the most recent deed which is at least 15 years old, though the title will also need to include the 1865 conveyance to give details of the covenants mentioned in the root. Since compulsory first registration was extended to the whole country in 1990, we will reach the extraordinary position late in 2005 that the most recent conveyance is almost always the root.

---

[12] *Re Duce & Boots the Cash Chemists (Southern)'s C* [1937] Ch 642 (the "root" suggested that the land was subject to a strict settlement though it was dealt with by trustees as if there was a trust for sale); H Potter (1938) 54 *LQR* 19.

[13] LPA 1969 s 23; Law Com 9 (1967); S Cretney (1969) 32 *MLR* 477; AM Prichard (1975) 28 *CLP* 125; JW Harris (1967) 30 *MLR* 559. The period was reduced in 1969 from 30 years and it was 40 years before 1926: Vendor & Purchaser Act 1874 s 1.

[14] Unsatisfactory roots are leases, equitable mortgages, gifts by the will of a person dying after 1925, disentailing deeds, and grants of probate (which do not describe the land of the deceased).

[15] LPA 1925 s 45; the buyer can also insist on production of powers of attorney under which the root is executed and documents creating any trust referred to in the abstract.

[16] On the consequences see *Re Scott & Alvarez's C* [1895] 2 Ch 603.

[17] T Gray *Ode on a Distant Prospect of Eton College*, l 99.

5.   Estate ownership – links in the chain

[9.05] Various deeds and documents evidence the passage of the legal estate from one person to another. Undocumented shifting of the legal estate is prohibited a principle which ensures that the legal estate can always be located precisely.[18] A continuous chain must be proved, grounded in the root of title and running forward to the time of sale. Conveyances on sale will preponderate, interspersed by the occasional deed of gift, devolution on death, sale by a mortgage lender or settlement and associated deeds of appointment of trustees.

6.   Vacant possession and freedom from incumbrances

[9.06] A buyer must be given the right to take up occupation of the property (vacant possession) and without any undisclosed burdens (freedom from incumbrances).[19]

(1) Vacant possession

[9.07] It is assumed that land will be sold with vacant possession unless the contract says otherwise. The land must not be subject to any undisclosed lease, and if there is a trust it must be demonstrated that any beneficiaries entitled to the land will be overreached.

(2) Freedom from incumbrances

[9.08] A seller must prove his right to the land free from all incumbrances which are not disclosed in the contract. This may be done by showing that the burden will be overreached[20] or that a money charge will be redeemed before or at the time of sale.[21] Other burdens must be disclosed in the contract. They are usually apparent from the most recent conveyance, since each sale of unregistered land is made subject to all existing incumbrances, but the purchaser is also required to check the deeds back to a good root.

(3) Land charges registration

[9.09] This is a method of registering individual burdens against unregistered titles. Most land is subject to mortgages, easements and restrictive covenants, and there may also be contracts or matrimonial home rights. There is no collection point (corresponding to the charges register of a registered title), so the burdens have to be registered in the land charges register[22] against the name of the person who owns the unregistered estate at the time that the burden is created. No attempt is made to

---

[18] Subject to (1) adverse possession see below [10.28]; and (2) rare cases of slicing see above [3.30ff].

[19] See above [8.09].

[20] See below [13].

[21] See below [28].

[22] See below [21.11]. The register mainly relates to equitable burdens, though some legal mortgages are also registrable.

collate the burdens affecting any particular piece of land, nor to determine the owner-ship of the land itself. On first registration, certificates of land charges searches must be produced and the charges register is prepared from this information. So land charges registration affects only titles which are unregistered. As registration of title has increased since 1997[23] so the volume of new land charges registrations has greatly declined. The register remains important primarily for finding the burdens affecting the land when it is sold just before first registration of the title.[24]

7.   Possession of the title deeds

[9.10] Physical possession of the title deeds is an important part of the proof of own-ership of the land. A stranger is prevented from selling a house which he does not own by the fact that he will not be able to produce the title deeds to the buyer.[25] When unregistered land is mortgaged for the first time, the title deeds are invariably handed over to the lender, so that if the true owner of a house cannot produce the title deeds it will almost certainly mean that there is a mortgage.[26]

B. EPITOME OF AN UNREGISTERED TITLE

[9.11] Physical proof of title is much less convenient while a title remains unregis-tered. The seller has to make up his own copy of the documents of title, xerography being a gift from God to conveyancers. Old time conveyancers had to prepare a copy of all the contents of the title deeds, often using the abbreviations and contractions of standard terms which gave the name to the traditional "abstract", at first handwritten and later typed. This is now replaced by an epitome, that is a photocopy of all relevant title deeds with a front cover listing the documents in date order.[27]

An epitome should begin with a good root of title and should include all documents impacting on the legal estate, that is:

conveyances since the root;
memoranda endorsed on the title deeds;
documents affecting pre-root burdens;
legal mortgages and evidence of their discharge;
grants of easements and restrictive covenants;
settlements and appointments of trustees;
death certificates where survivorship occurs between joint owners;[28]
grants of representation (probate or administration) to the estate of a sole owner;
memoranda endorsed on the grant;

---

[23] See below **[9.23]**.
[24] See below **[21.23]**.
[25] For possessory titles based on adverse possession, see below **[11.13ff]**.
[26] See below **[28]**.
[27] Modern practice is to submit the title for approval along with the draft contract and so to exclude the right to raise requisitions on the title after contracts are exchanged. The Standard Conditions of Sale (3rd ed) set out strict time limits for each stage in the process.
[28] See below **[9.15]**.

assents to beneficiaries; and

land charges searches and certificates relating to revealed entries.

There should be no details of interests that will be overreached (wills and trust instruments) nor are equitable mortgages generally included after they have been discharged.

C. LAND REGISTRY CHECKS ON UNREGISTERED TITLES

1. Index map

[9.12] Information about particular land is obtained from an index which records all registered estates and land affected by cautions against first registration.[29] Physical parcels of land will continue to be recorded on the Index Map, coloured to show the extent of every registered title,[30] but computerisation opens up new ways of accessing information so the index no longer needs to be in the form of a map. Urban properties are identified by means of a postal address, but in rural areas and for open land an identifying plan will be needed.[31] From it can be determined whether land is registered, whether the title is freehold or leasehold, whether cautions prevent first registration, and the title numbers of individual registers. A verbal index will cover franchises and similar rights.[32] The index map can be searched,[33] by post or electronically, and the result may be paper or electronic. A plan may be issued with the result where the search result affects a part or multiple titles.[34]

2. Fees for index map searches

[9.13] Index map searches have been free since 1997.[35]

3. Check for missed first registrations

[9.14] Where the seller offers an unregistered title, it is necessary to consider whether the title should have been registered earlier, since if a compulsory event has been missed legal effect will have been stripped from the abstracted conveyances.[36] If the epitome reveals any sale since the beginning of December 1990 the title should already have been registered. If the most recent sale was before that, the buyer should check its date against the date on which registration became compulsory for the district where the land is sited.[37]

---

[29] LRA 2002 s 68; Law Com 271 (2001), [9.54–9.57]; DLRR 2003 r 10. It also includes information about profits etc.

[30] DLRR 2003 r 10.

[31] DLRR 2003 r 146(3).

[32] DLRR 2003 r 147; DLRR CD ch 9, [37–47].

[33] DLRR 2003 r 146; LR Form SIM; r 147 relates to franchises and manors. If title is registered (free) copies of the register will be supplied on request.

[34] A Sutherland [2000] 42 *PLJ* 6.

[35] SI 2001/1179 art 11, sch 4.

[36] See below **[9.36]**.

[37] Registration of Title Order 1989, SI 1989/1347. The relevant date is revealed by an index map search.

D. CAUTIONS AGAINST FIRST REGISTRATION

1. Reform

[9.15] Any person claiming an interest in unregistered land may apply for a caution against first registration,[38] a facility that has been rewritten[39] and amplified, with the framework now moved to primary legislation.

2. Cautions register

[9.16] Entry of a caution against first registration is not intended to be a substitute for registration, and may not be used to protect an estate which should itself be registered.[40] Nor is it appropriate for an interest which could be protected by a land charges registration. Within those two constraints, the power to accept a caution should be interpreted liberally to allow protection of any other estate, rentcharge, profit, franchise, or interest affecting any legal estate.[41]

An application to the registrar[42] must make the case for entry of the caution, establishing the existence of the interest cautioned, or at least an arguable case for its existence. There is a duty of care.[43] A cautions register[44] will be opened for each caution and this will include a property register – to describe the land and the interest claimed – and the cautioner's register – with details of the cautioner, such as his name, legal adviser, and address for service, and also an indication whether any other person has consented (in writing) to the lodging of the caution.[45]

3. Discovery of a caution

[9.17] A person intending to buy unregistered land will discover the caution from a search of the index map, the result of which will direct him to the caution title.[46] Cautions revealed by the search will cause serious concern to a potential buyer of unregistered land, usually to the extent of blocking a sale until they are removed.

The cautions register is part of the open register so the details of any individual cautions register can be revealed by an official copy,[47] either an official photocopy or increasingly copies generated by direct computer access.[48] The general protections applying to official copies[49] apply.

---

[38] LRA 2002 ss 15–22; Law Com 271 (2001) [2.14], [3.65]; DLRR 2003 rr 36–50; DLRR CD ch 4, [10ff].
[39] Cautions entered under the LRA 1925 continue: LRA 1925 s 53; LRA 2002 sch 12 para 4.
[40] DLRR 2003 r 39.
[41] LRA 2002 s 15(2)–(3).
[42] LRA 2002 s 15(4); DLRR 2003 r 39; LR Form CT1.
[43] LRA 2002 s 77.
[44] LRA 2002 s 19; DLRR 2003 r 38.
[45] DLRR 2003 r 44.
[46] DLRR 2003 r 37.
[47] DLRR 2003 r 133; LR Form OC1.
[48] Law Com 271 (2001), [9.44–9.47].
[49] See above **[8.13]**.

4. Effect of a caution

[9.18] Cautions do not themselves confer any priority but merely the right to be notified of and to object to any application for first registration.[50] There is a duty to act reasonably.[51] Unless the caution is withdrawn,[52] a warning off procedure will be followed, in which the owner of the legal estate[53] may seek the cancellation of the caution,[54] a procedure leading to a determination of the priority between the two competing claims by adjudication.

New provisions enable the court or the registrar to alter the cautions register to correct any mistake or to bring the register up to date.[55] This will be done if the cautioner does not own the interest claimed or the interest did not exist or has come to an end.

5. Fees for cautions

[9.19] A fixed fee is specified for entry of a caution.[56] A much lower fee is charged for official copies of a cautions register.[57]

E. CONVEYANCE OF LAND SUBJECT TO FIRST REGISTRATION

1. Conveyance of registrable land

[9.20] An unregistered title is passed by a conveyance[58] made between vendor and purchaser – or by *New Land Lawyers* between a seller and a buyer.

---

[50] LRA 2002 s 16. For this reason the benefit of the caution can only be claimed by the person who lodged the caution or his personal representative: DLRR 2003 rr 48–49; if the interest protected is sold the new owner of it must lodge his own caution.

[51] LRA 2002 s 77; Law Com 271 (2001), EN [347–349].

[52] LRA 2002 s 17; DLRR 2003 r 40; LR Form WCT.

[53] DLRR 2003 r 42; also the holder of any derivate legal estate or any person who consented to the lodging of the caution: r 43. An appeal will lie to the adjudicator: LRA 2002 s 73.

[54] LRA 2002 s 18; DLRR 2003 r 41; LR Form CCT.

[55] LRA 2002 ss 20–21; Law Com 271 (2001), [3.66]; DLRR 2003 rr 45–47.

[56] SI 2001/1179 s3; currently £40.

[57] SI 2001/1179 sch 3; most are £2 or £4.

[58] LPA 1925 s 205(1)(ii) defines the term more widely to include formal documents effecting any transaction including leases and mortgages.

> THIS CONVEYANCE is made the 21st day of February 2003 between (1) Jane Eyre (the Seller) and (2) Edward Rochester (the Buyer)
> WHEREAS (1) The Seller is seised of the property described below for an estate in fee simple absolute in possession subject as hereafter mentioned but otherwise free from incumbrances
> (2) The Seller has agreed to sell the same to the Buyer in consideration of £100,000
> NOW THIS DEED WITNESSES that in consideration of the sum of one hundred thousand pounds (the receipt of which the seller hereby acknowledges) the Seller hereby conveys with full title guarantee ALL THAT piece or parcel of land known as Thornfield Hall, Halifax, West Yorkshire contained in a conveyance between (1) Jane Fairfax and (2) John Eyre dated 6th June 1916 and shown on the plan annexed thereto and thereon coloured red, together the right of way therein referred to TO HOLD unto the Buyer in fee simple subject to the covenants and easements referred to in the said conveyance of 6th June 1916
> [Stamp duty – exempting clause or certificate of value].
> SIGNED by the Seller as his deed the day and year first before mentioned in the presence of [witness]

Figure 9-2 An unregistered conveyance

2. Land registry transfer form

[9.21] An alternative which was formerly used for sales attracting compulsory registration of titles was to use the land registry transfer form,[59] adapted to define the land conveyed by a traditional unregistered parcels clause and to include other standard clauses required in the unregistered system.

F. COMPULSION

[9.22] First registration is the process by which unregistered titles are brought into the registration of title system, the grey squirrel occupying the territory of the red,[60] and is to be contrasted with the registration of transfer of an existing registered titles.[61]

1. Completing the register

[9.23] Compulsion is essential to overcome consumer resistance to land registry fees. It depends upon the occurrence of a trigger (called a compulsory event) after the

---

[59] DLRR 2003 r 35; this more or less reflects LRR 1925 r 72; but r 35 is drafted to refer to a dealing with land by a person under an obligation to apply for first registration and it is not clear that it applies to the transfer leading to first registration, nor does it appear to apply to a voluntary registration.

[60] See above **[1.01]**.

[61] *Buckley* v. *SRL Investments* (1971) 22 P & CR 756, 767.

district in which the land is situated has become a compulsory area. Until recently only sales triggered compulsion. By this means 75% of the estimated total of 21.4 million potential titles had been registered by 1997.[62] The tide has truly turned, with significantly more titles registered than unregistered, and the sea will now come in rapidly to engulf most unregistered titles.

The Land Registration Act 1997[63] increased the pace of progress towards a universal register by requiring registration of gifts, transfers on death, and first legal mortgages. First registrations have increased by around one third,[64] given a register that was 85% complete in 2001.[65] A stubborn residue of titles are never traded – for example parks and houses handed down from generation to generation within a family – which will remain off the register indefinitely under the current legislation.

Although it is intended to give the quietus to unregistered land as soon as possible, the 2002 scheme does not expand the triggers further. An opposition amendment designed to bring all unregistered land on to the register by the end of 2003 was rejected for a number of reasons:[66] registration had been made more attractive by the protection against adverse possessors; there is a practical difficulty of enforcing registration where no disposition has occurred; and the registry could not cope with the extra load. Matters will be reviewed after five years.

2. Compulsory events

[9.24] Any transaction affecting a freehold estate[67] in unregistered land now triggers compulsory first registration of the estate created or transferred. Sales are, and always have been,[68] registrable; this includes any sale for money, a sale in exchange for other assets,[69] or for land (with or without[70] equality money). Specific reference is now made to sales under court order and also to transfers of a mortgaged estate which suffers from negative equity.[71] Gifts attract compulsion for the first time in 1997, including lifetime gifts, assents to give effect to a will or intestacy, and Settled Land Act vesting documents.[72]

A major innovation in 1997 was the provision that mortgages may trip the wire, that is a legal mortgage to be protected by the deposit of title deeds and ranking before any other mortgage affecting the estate; this embraces a first legal mortgage and any re-financing involving the discharge of all existing mortgages, but second mortgages

---

[62] *Completing the Land Register* (LR, 1992), 9.
[63] Law Com 235 (1995); L Tee [1996] *CLJ* 241; JE Adams [1997] *Conv* 180; HW Wilkinson [1997] *NLJ* 925; PH Kenny [1997] *Conv* 245.
[64] R Hudson [1996] *NLJ* 1751.
[65] LR *Annual Report 2000–2001*, 52.
[66] Law Com 271 (2001), [2.9–2.13].
[67] For the triggers affecting leasehold land see below **[25.38ff]**.
[68] LRA 2002 s 4(1)(a)(i).
[69] There is no longer a specific provision, compare LRA 1925 s 123(6)(a), as amended.
[70] A pure exchange without any balancing payment has only been registrable since LRA 1997.
[71] LRA 2002 s 4(6).
[72] LRA 2002 s 4(1)(a), 4(9); R Towns [1998] *Conv* 380; DG Barnsley [2002] *Conv* 103.

of unregistered land will not impose any obligation to register.[73] New triggers can be added under rules made by the Lord Chancellor.[74]

3. Souvenir land

[9.25] Souvenir land is land divided into tiny plots and sold for the honour of owner-ship rather than for use, primarily it seems (or is this just snobbishness) to Americans. In 1968 parts of West Sussex were on offer in one square foot plots at $10 each. Three years later the registry was aware of nine schemes which were capable of creating 1 million transfers of part. The registrar was given power to designate souvenir schemes which removed this nonsense from the register.[75]

4. Permitted applicants

[9.26] A person may apply to register the title where he is the estate owner[76] of unreg-istered land[77] or is a person entitled to require the unregistered estate to be vested in him, though not a person who has contracted to buy.[78]

5. Failure to register

[9.27] The risk of a resale and the difficulty lenders experienced in selling the land without legal title were always sufficient practical inducements to register title, but since 1997[79] first registration has been truly compulsory after the occurrence of a trigger.[80] The estate owner responsible must apply to be registered within two months from the date of the trigger, that requirement being imposed on a buyer,[81] donee or borrower.[82] There is no longer power to register in the name of a nominee, but noth-ing to prevent a transfer to a bare trustee.

Registration must be sought within the "period for registration", that is two months from the date of the disposition.[83] The legal estate is passed under the con-veyance, and the buyer is able to deal with the land,[84] but at the end of the two month

[73] LRA 2002 s 4(1)(g); see also s 4(4)–(8); mortgages by demise are not treated as leases for this purpose; Law Com 271 (2001), [3.35].

[74] LRA 2002 s 5; Law Com 271 (2001), [3.37].

[75] LR & LCA 1971 s 4; SI 1972/985; as amended by LRR 2002, SI 2002/2539, r 5, sch 4. This will pre-sumably find a place in the final version of the new rules. See also: (1968) 112 *SJ* 323; (1971) 115 *SJ* 161; TBF Ruoff & P Meehan (1971) 35 *Conv (NS)* 390, 397.

[76] An "estate" is not defined though a "legal estate" is: LRA 2002 s 132.

[77] LRA 2002 s 3(2), (6).

[78] This is to avoid loss of fees if a contracting purchaser opted for voluntary registration: Law Com 271 (2001), [3.7].

[79] LRA 2002 s 6; this replaces LRA 1925 s 123A, inserted by LRA 1997 s 1.

[80] LRA 2002 s 4(1).

[81] LRA 2002 s 6(3); costs will be borne by the buyer etc, subject to contrary agreement: s 8; Law Com 271 (2001), [3.38–3.41].

[82] LRA 2002 s 6(2). The lender will be able to insist on registration at the cost of the borrower: LRA 2002 s 6(6); DLRR 2003 r 21; DLRR CD ch 3, [11–13].

[83] LRA 2002 s 6(4). Time should run from the date of unconditional delivery of the conveyance; inser-tion of an incorrect date should not extend the period.

[84] LRA 2002 s 7. The scheme was introduced in 1925 to make it possible to mortgage land at the time of the purchase that attracts compulsion: A Underhill (1911) 27 *LQR* 173, 176–177. Query whether it would not be better to adopt the same scheme as for a transfer – no legal title passing in advance of registration.

period (or any extension) the unregistered estate is divested and returned to the person who transferred it, so that the unregistered conveyance becomes void to pass the legal estate in the land.[85] The divesting does not terminate the freehold estate, which might call into question its legal status,[86] but merely shifts a continuing estate from buyer back to seller.[87] The practical sanction is often small. Even after legal title passes back to the seller, he holds the land on trust for the buyer,[88] as if there were a contract for value. Priority is generally protected by occupation. The buyer may call for a new disposition to make good the effects of the original non-registration, a replacement which itself attracts compulsion.

An order may extend the time allowed on the request of any person interested in the land who is able to show a good reason for the delay. The compulsion provisions then read as if the extended period had always been allowed.[89] Prospective orders can be made in advance of completion if it is clear that an application cannot be made in time or only at unreasonable expense. Most extension orders are retrospective, made after the two month period has expired, when some "accident or other sufficient cause" – some excuse – is provided which satisfies the registrar. Normally the procedure is simply administrative, but there is provision for appeal to the court against the registrar's refusal to accept a late application, and disputes might arise if someone else had bought the land in the interim.[90]

G. VOLUNTARY REGISTRATION

[9.28] Voluntary registration of title has a fluctuating history depending on the degree of pressure at the registry to extend the compulsory areas, but since 1995[91] voluntary registration is allowed, free of restriction, cheap,[92] and encouraged. Of course it is confined to registrable estates and to estate owners.

H. FIRST REGISTRATION MACHINERY

1. Application for first registration

[9.29] Rules set out the mechanics.[93] After completion and stamping, it will be necessary to apply for first registration.[94] Application is made on the prescribed Form[95]

---

[85] LRA 2002 s 7(1); Law Com 271 (2001), [3.38–3.41]. This has no impact on boundary disputes: *Proctor* v. *Kidman* (1985) 51 P & CR 67, 72, Croom-Johnson LJ.

[86] LPA 1925 s 1(1)(a), 7; see above **[3.06]**.

[87] LRA 2002 s 7(4).

[88] LRA 2002 ss 7(2), 8 (cost of buyer etc); DG Barnsley (1968) 32 *Conv (NS)* 391; *Buckley* v. *SRL Investments* (1971) 22 P & CR 756, 767.

[89] LRA 2002 s 6(5), 7(3); there is currently no fee.

[90] *British Maritime Trust* v. *Upsons* [1931] WN 7, Clauson J, appeared to allow an order to prejudice titles acquired honestly; this was wrong in principle.

[91] Statute Law (Repeals) Act 1995, repealing LRA 1966 s 1.

[92] SI 2001/1179 sch 1 col 2 (fees 75% of those for compulsory first registration).

[93] LRA 2002 s 14; Law Com 271 (2001), [3.53].

[94] The application enters a queue with any cautions against first registration: LRA 2002 s 74; Law Com 271 (2001), EN [335–337]; DLRR 2003 rr 15, 39; see also above **[8.41ff]**.

[95] DLRR 2003 r 22, sch 1; DLRR CD ch 3, [6]; LR form FR1 is used for freehold or leasehold land, and as amended for use with rentcharges.

accompanied by all original deeds and documents, a list in duplicate of documents delivered[96] and the appropriate fee. The form consists primarily of an application to register the title, with a brief description of the land identified by plan or otherwise, details of the deed inducing registration, and details of the applicant and his conveyancer.

The rejection of defective applications is considered in the context of transfers.[97]

2.   Fees for first registration

[9.30] A fee is required for first registration[98] based on the value of the land (*ad valorem*).[99] Scale 1 applies to applications for first registration, including applications to register the grant of a new lease. Scale 2[100] is used for transfers lacking a monetary consideration, such as gifts, surrenders, transmissions on death or bankruptcy, assents, and transfers of the matrimonial home.

3.   Proof of title to the registry

[9.31] An applicant is required to state what class of title he wants and for what physical extent of land and then to prove his right to it. The stamped conveyance of the land[101] must be accompanied by all the unregistered title deeds back to a good root, including land charges search certificates and so on.[102] An application by a conveyancer should include a certificate of title, confirming that he acted on the purchase, and confirming the undisputed possession of the applicant, stating that all relevant deeds had been examined, indicating burdens and land charges, and identifying any matters ending by merger. Existing mortgages need to be discharged. (3) Post registration matters.

Registration is almost always completed on the basis of the documentary title without advertisement. Neighbours have a right to object to first registration, but they will rarely know that they have the chance. A discretion remains to order advertisements,[103] which is most likely if the applicant has not bought the land for value. Where all objections are disposed of, the time for any advertisements has passed and the title has been determined, the registrar is required to complete the registration with the priority of the application.[104]

The unregistered title deeds are largely redundant, but they may retain importance in cases of forgery, boundary disputes, and double conveyancing, where easements are created to determine the order of division, or where the title is possessory or qualified. It seems that they will be retained in the registry.[105]

---

[96] LR Form DL.
[97] See above **[8.39]**.
[98] SI 2001/1179 art 3, sch 1; the LR website has an on line calculator.
[99] Eg on a £150,000 house the current fee is £200; and below £1m it is £500.
[100] For example up to £100,000 value, the scale 2 is a bargain £40.
[101] This will generally be retained: DLRR 2003 rr 201–202; DLRR CD ch 3, [8].
[102] DLRR 2003 r 23; if the title is leasehold the lease and a certified copy will be required. R 26 will apply where the title deeds are unavailable.
[103] DLRR 2003 rr 28–29.
[104] DLRR 2003 r 15.
[105] DLRR 2003 rr 201–202, 211–213.

4. Burdens

[9.32] The first charges register must record all burdens affecting the land[106] and as many as possible of the burdens which are overriding[107] there being a duty to disclose unregistered interests when applying for first registration.[108]

5. Post registration matters

[9.33] The applicant must ensure that any necessary restriction is entered,[109] that application is made to register any new mortgage,[110] and that an arrangement is made for the issue of a certificate of registration.

6. First registration curtain

[9.34] First registration creates a curtain, not quite impenetrable.[111]

I. DERIVATIVE TRANSACTIONS

1. Trusts

[9.35] The conveyance triggering first registration will often contain a declaration of trust which may call for a restriction.[112]

2. Mortgages

[9.36] It is normal practice for the buyer to mortgage the land before securing registration. Thus

Figure 9-3 A mortgage created before first registration

If title is unregistered, it becomes potentially registered on completion of the purchase but legal title passes to the buyer and he is a person with the right to apply for

---

[106] DLRR 2003 rr 32–34 (burdens, leases and mortgages respectively).
[107] DLRR 2003 r 55.
[108] LRA 2002 ss 37, 71; Law Com 271 (2001), EN [315–316]; DLRR 2003 r 27.
[109] This shows whether the applicant is beneficial owner or a trustee, in this last case a restriction is required. If a nominee, his consent in writing is required with a statement that he is not a fiduciary (that is a trustee-like capacity).
[110] The lender has a right to apply: DLRR 2003 r 21.
[111] See below **[11]**.
[112] See above **[13.35ff]**.

registration.[113] The form used to apply for first registration has a space to list transactions in order, and thus to show the conveyance before the mortgage. Only later will
the buyer become registered proprietor, thus permitting entry of the mortgage on the
charges register and registration of the lender as its proprietor. The security of the
lender will be threatened if registration is not obtained within the two month "period
for registration".[114] The legal estate is passed under the conveyance, and the buyer is
able to deal with the land. Searches can be made against a potential registered title
created by an application for first registration.[115]

3. Subsales

[9.37] A person who has a contract to buy land may sell it without first completing his
purchase contract, a process known as a subsale. Two or more sales can be completed
by one document, passing legal title direct from the estate owner to the ultimate buyer
without any intermediate documentation, saving land registry fees[116] and stamp
duty.[117] Thus:

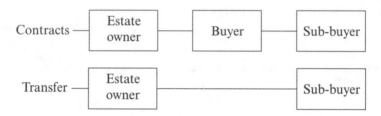

Figure 9-4 A sub sale before first registration

The first contract for sale does not detonate the requirement of compulsory registration, and so it is the sub-buyer as legal estate owner under the transfer who is bound
to apply for first registration.[118]

4. Chains of transactions

[9.38] Chains of transactions occur where land which is subject to first registration is
resold while the seller's title is still being registered at the land registry, thus:

---

[113] LRA 2002 s 7; DLRR 2003 r 35. The scheme was introduced in 1925 to make it possible to mortgage
land at the time of the purchase that attracts compulsion: A Underhill (1911) 27 *LQR* 173, 176–177. It
would now be better to adopt the same scheme as for a transfer – no legal title passing in advance of registration.
[114] LRA 2002 s 6(4). Time should run from the date of unconditional delivery of the conveyance: insertion of an incorrect date should not extend the period.
[115] DLRR 2003 r 148(2); P Sparkes [1990] *NLJ* 1077.
[116] See above at **[9.30]**.
[117] JE Adams [1989] *Conv* 232, 317.
[118] LRA 2002 s 3(2).

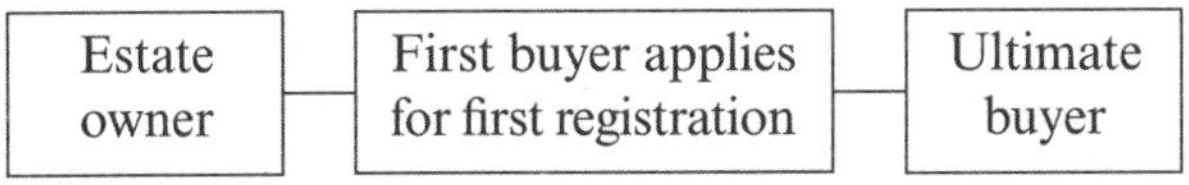

Estate owner	First buyer applies for first registration	Ultimate buyer

Figure 9-5 A transaction after first registration

The land becomes registered as soon as first registration is sought, but there is power[119] to deal with the legal title in advance of registration, and there is no longer[120] a period during which the title is sterilised by statute: whether title can be proved will depend upon the terms of the sale contract.

---

[119] DLRR 2003 r 35.

[120] Contrast on the old law: *Pinekerry* v. *Kenneth Needs (Contractors)* (1992) 64 P & CR 245 CA; AJ Oakley [1993] *CLJ* 22; J Howell (1994) 57 *MLR* 121; P Sparkes [1990] *NLJ* 1077; EJ Pryer [1990] *NLJ* 1327. LRA 1925 s 110 which prevented proof of title except by office copies is not replicated in the 2002 scheme.

10

ADVERSE POSSESSION

Paper title. Possession: factual and intention. Permissive occupation. Limitation. Extended limitation periods. Reform. Title derived from possession. Mechanics. Burdens. Trusts and equitable claimants. (For adverse possession against registered land see chapter 11.)

A. PAPER TITLE AGAINST SQUATTER

1. Adverse possession as theft or quasi-theft

[10.01] Proudhon said that *"la propriété c'est le vol"* ("Property is theft").[1] Few landowners today would view themselves as stealing from the rest of society, but a proprietor will most certainly think that a squatter who obtains title by adverse possession has "stolen" it. A person who takes adverse possession of the land and holds it for 12 years will be able to defeat the title of the dispossessed owner.[2] Theft occurs only in a metaphorical sense, since the criminal law does not in fact allow land to be stolen.[3] Lord Denning attempted a literal equation of adverse possession and theft in *Hayward* v. *Challoner*,[4] but on this he formed a minority of one. The facts show clearly what alarmed him, and how a sound policy of avoiding the cruelty of stale claims[5] can lead the courts to morally dubious decisions. Smallholdings had been let to the rector of a parish at 10s a year, but as an indulgence to the church rent was not claimed after May 1942, generosity for which the landowner was punished by loss of his title after 12 years.[6] All members of the Court of Appeal criticised the conduct of the rector, but Lord Denning was alone in translating moral outrage into a ruling that the law could prevent the rector from taking the land which he knew belonged to a parishioner.

---

[1] *Qu'est-ce que la Propriété?* (1840), ch 1; GB Shaw thought this the only truism; *Maxims for Revolutionists*, an appendix to *Man and Superman*.

[2] G Battersby, "Informally Created Rights in Land" ch 19 in Bright & Dewar, 490–494; PBH Birks "Before We Begin: Five Keys to Land Law" ch 18 in Bright & Dewar, 481; Chapelle's LL (5th ed) ch 2; Dixon's *Principles* (3rd ed), ch 11; Goo's *Sourcebook* (3rd ed) ch 6; Gravells *LL – Text* (2nd ed), 79–104; Grays' *Elements* (3rd ed), 239–282; K Green "Citizens and Squatters: Under the Surfaces of Land Law" ch 9 in Dewar & Bright; Hopkins, *Informal Acquisition*, 217–250; Maudsley & Burn *LL – Cases* (7th ed) ch 3; Megarry & Wade (6th ed) ch 21; Panesar's *General Principles* ch 8; Swadling in Birks' *Private Law*, [4.554–4.558]; Smith's *Property* Law (4th ed), 64–83; Thompson *Modern LL* ch 7.

[3] Theft Act 1968 s 4.

[4] [1968] 1 QB 107, CA; M Goodman (1968) 31 *MLR* 82.

[5] *Cholmondeley* v. *Clinton* (1820) 2 Jac & W 1, 140, 37 ER 527, Willes CJ; *A'Court* v. *Cross* (1825) 3 Bing 329, 332, 130 ER 540, Best CJ.

[6] At 123, Russell LJ.

In the first edition of this work it was stated that "quasi-theft of land is relatively rare",[7] the reason given being that land is of such value that few landowners will allow a complete plot, as opposed perhaps to a boundary sliver,[8] to be lost without taking action to recover it. This hostage to fortune was duly captured in *Pye*,[9] a high-profile case widely reported in the press: the House of Lords handed 25 hectares of prime building land in Berkshire to a farmer who was making hay on it while the development company which owned the land struggled to obtain planning permission. Adverse possession of a sizeable site is only likely in a case such as this when it is standing vacant, earmarked for some future use. No doubt the Court of Appeal would have categorised this case as quasi-theft, since it decided for the developer,[10] and some of the Lords felt unease at the decision they reached,[11] but the farmer's entitlement was clear, the developer's claim impossible,[12] and the family acted honourably throughout.[13]

Other developments that caused dissatisfaction in some quarters included the opening of a Squatters Estate Agency in Nottingham, and cases in which squatters claimed, with varying degrees of success, a number of properties left empty and unmanaged in London, particularly under the shambolic management of the public housing stock in Lambeth.[14] Sneaking respect displayed in the popular press for squatters who had put one over the bureaucrats turned to outrage when those same squatters then proceeded to realise their gains by selling the properties in which they had squatted.

2. Revolution in the law of adverse possession

[10.02] Of the main legislative developments, the first is relatively low key. As part of a wide-ranging review by the Law Commission, the existing law for limitation of personal actions will be swept away and replaced by a new core regime. The Commission's report and draft Bill[15] propose only modest adjustments to the regime applied to land, but the second change could not be more radical. The Land Registration Act 2002,[16] also emanating from the work of the Commission,[17] provides that for the future[18] a registered proprietor will not face the loss of his registered title until he has been given notice that an adverse possessor is claiming to have been in possession of the land for more than 10 years; a proprietor will only be stripped of his title against his will if he remains inactive for a further two years after receiving

---

[7] P Sparkes *NLL* (1st ed), 678.

[8] *Plimmer* v. *Pearson* (2000) 79 P & CR D21, D22, Robert Walker LJ (3" sliver).

[9] *JA Pye (Oxford)* v. *Graham* [2002] UKHL 30, [2002] 3 All ER 865 (hereafter "*Pye*").

[10] [2001] Ch 804, CA.

[11] *Pye* [2002] UKHL 30, [2002] 3 All ER 865, [1–2], Lord Bingham.

[12] *Pye* at [61], Lord Browne-Wilkinson.

[13] *Pye* at [2], Lord Bingham.

[14] *Ellis* v. *Lambeth LBC* (2000) 32 HLR 596, CA; *Lambeth LBC* v. *Archangel* [2002] 1 P & CR 18 at 230, CA (a performance poet who had acknowledged the council's title); *Lambeth LBC* v. *Blackburn* [2001] EWCA Civ 912, (2001) 33 HLR 74, CA; *Battersea Freehold & Leasehold Co* v. *Wandsworth LBC* [2001] 2 EGLR 75, Rimer J.

[15] Law Com 270 (2001).

[16] LRA 2002 part 9, ss 96–98 and sch 6.

[17] Law Com 271 (2001), part XIV.

[18] Vested rights acquired before the implementation of the legislation will be preserved.

that notice. In practice, therefore, registered titles will be immune from adverse possessors in all but the most extreme circumstances. Unregistered and registered land law are no longer aligned, so that three mechanisms for limitation require exposition, applying respectively to unregistered land, registered titles up until 2003, and the 2002 scheme. Reader must be left to judge, as this tale unfolds,[19] just how this radical change will work out in practice.

B. FACTUAL POSSESSION

1. True owners and squatters

[10.03] Title to unregistered land is barred under the Limitation Act 1980 after someone has taken adverse possession of land against the true owner for the statutory limitation period and the same quality of possession is relevant to the operation of the new machinery for registered land.[20] It is easiest to think, at least at first, of two known characters, a squatter moving in to oust a "true" or "paper" owner who can show a registered or paper title.[21] To negate this title the squatter must prove over a limitation period that he held (1) factual possession, with (2) the intention to possess.

2. Possession that is adverse

[10.04] Only one person or group of co-owners[22] has possession at any one time.[23] Adverse possession must be held against the interest of the paper owner,[24] since possession cannot be shared between the paper owner and a person intruding.[25] It need not necessarily *inconvenience* the paper owner, since anyone actually incommoded would be goaded into taking legal action,[26] so possession can be "adverse" without any suggestion of aggression, hostility or subterfuge on the part of the squatter.[27]

Possession involves the exercise of exclusive control over a thing for oneself, the full use of an owner.[28] The squatter may possibly only use part[29] but he must certainly occupy to the exclusion of everyone else, that is the rest of the world as well as the owner. A person who occupied a bombed out pub site but then allowed neighbouring

---

[19] Registration mechanics are considered below **[11.13ff]**.

[20] *Pye* at [68], Lord Hope; see below [11.19].

[21] *Powell* v. *McFarlane* (1979) 38 P & CR 452, 470, Slade J; this statement of the law "cannot be improved": *Pye* at [31], Lord Browne-Wilkinson. However if a person holds lawful possession (eg as tenant) but fails to return the land, it is not necessary to satisfy Slade J's tests – the question is merely whether there has been a dispossession: *Williams* v. *Jones* [2002] EWCA Civ 1097, [2002] 40 EG 169.

[22] For the unity of possession between co-owners, see below **[16.01]**.

[23] *Pye* at [70], Lord Hope.

[24] Latin = *corpus possessionis*.

[25] *Powell* v. *McFarlane* (1979) 38 P & CR 452, 470, Slade J ("conclusive" should read "exclusive"); *Buckinghamshire CC* v. *Moran* [1990] Ch 623, 640H–641E, Slade LJ; approved in *Pye* at [41], Lord Browne-Wilkinson.

[26] *Treloar* v. *Nute* [1976] 1 WLR 1295, 1302E, Sir John Pennycuick.

[27] *Pye* at [69], Lord Hope.

[28] H Bond (1890) 6 *LQR* 259, 270; *Pye* at [70], Lord Hope, [75–76], Lord Hutton.

[29] *West Bank Estates* v. *Arthur* [1967] 1 AC 665, PC; *Pavledes* v. *Ryesbridge Properties* (1989) 58 P & CR 459, Knox J (not small scale parking on part).

tenants to have keys to the site showed by allowing others to have access that he had no intention to hold exclusive possession himself.[30] Acts of exclusion are required: a declaration of intent however plain will not on its own amount to possession.[31]

3. Possession of buildings

[10.05] Factual possession signifies an appropriate degree of physical control, but what is appropriate must, as Slade J has said,[32] depend on the circumstances, "in particular the nature of the land and the manner in which land of that nature is commonly used or enjoyed." It is usually self-evident when possession is taken of a building, for someone will be working from a suite of offices,[33] or living in a house,[34] and a true owner can sense his exclusion when he sees that a squatter has padlocked the front door.[35]

4. Open land

[10.06] Reported cases usually concern open land. *JA Pye (Oxford)* v. *Graham*[36] involved 25 hectares of potential building land near Newbury adjoining the Graham's farm. At first the Grahams occupied this additional land under a grazing licence, but after September 1984 this licence was not renewed and they occupied it as if owners. They padlocked the only access, farmed the land as if it was a part of their farm, harrowing, rolling and liming the land[37] before stocking it with up to 140 cattle, and they trimmed the hedges. An owner would not have done anything more.[38]

Possession may be more difficult to prove if the land is open, so one might turn to acts such as shooting,[39] fishing,[40] or reaping a harvest of wheat;[41] land in the wilds of Canada can be possessed simply by paying tax on it.[42] Erection of no parking signs, or even active steps to prevent parking, is not sufficient in the absence of fencing.[43] Conversely, enclosure is strong evidence of adverse possession,[44] certainly by padlocking the sole access,[45] though possibly even by erecting corner posts[46] though any fencing must have some degree of permanence. Fencing to keep in stock failed on the

---

[30] *Battersea Freehold & Leasehold Co* v. *Wandsworth LBC* [2001] 2 EGLR 75, Rimer J.
[31] *Simpson* v. *Fergus* (2000) 79 P & CR 398, 402, Robert Walker LJ.
[32] *Powell* v. *McFarlane* (1979) 38 P & CR 452.
[33] *Mount Carmel Investments* v. *Peter Thurlow* [1988] 1 WLR 1078, 1082.
[34] *BP Properties* v. *Buckler* (1987) 55 P & CR 337.
[35] *Lambeth LBC* v. *Blackburn* [2001] EWCA Civ 912, (2001) 33 HLR 74.
[36] [2002] UKHL 30, [2002] 3 All ER 865, [6–24], Lord Browne-Wilkinson.
[37] On cultivation: *Jones* v. *Williams* (1837) 2 M & W 326, 150 ER 78.
[38] *Pye* at [19]. Paper acts by the developer were not relevant since they were not in possession.
[39] *Red House Farms* case [1977] 2 EGLR 125, CA.
[40] *Lord Advocate* v. *Lord Lovat* (1880) 5 App Cas 273, Lord Blackburn; *Beaufort* v. *John Aird & Co* (1904) 20 TLR 602 (Wye fishery).
[41] *Cadija Umma* v. *S Don Manis Appu* [1939] AC 136, PC; *Powell* v. *McFarlane* (1979) 38 P & CR 452, 471, Slade J.
[42] *Kirby* v. *Cowderoy* [1912] AC 599, PC.
[43] *Simpson* v. *Fergus* (2000) 79 P & CR 398, CA.
[44] *Williams* v. *Usherwood* (1981) 45 P & CR 235, CA; M Dockray [1983] *Conv* 398; HW Wilkinson (1984) 134 *NLJ* 144.
[45] *Buckinghamshire CC* v. *Moran* [1990] Ch 623, 641B–C, Slade LJ.
[46] *Wuta-Ofei* v. *Danquah* [1961] 1 WLR 1238, PC; RE Megarry (1961) 77 *LQR* 481.

facts of *Batt* v. *Adams*[47] to demonstrate the intention to exclude others. *Treloar* v.
Nute[48] involved acts said to lie on the borderline of what could constitute (adverse)
possession; a buyer who wrongly thought that a derelict plot of 1/7th an acre was
included with his garden grazed three animals and filled a gulley with spoil, the latter
being the more important act. On the other hand,[49] placing an oil tank on the land
and planting shrubs and trees was more than enough. *Prudential Assurance Co* v.
Waterloo Real Estate[50] shows that it is possible to take adverse possession of a party
wall by repairing it and by including the wall in a grant of a lease.

Fleeting acts do not count to create a title. Fencing for one day is not sufficient.[51] In
Marsden v. *Miller*[52] a plot of land between two houses was originally the site of a
derelict cottage with an unknown owner. Both neighbours made limited use of it.
Successive owners of No 3 Preston Nook had used it for access to their garage, parking, hanging out washing and keeping hens, acts which were insufficient to establish
title. The neighbours at No 2 also hung out their washing, played games and parked on
it. In 1981 workmen employed by the owner of No 3 erected a fence with a notice
claiming possession of the land, but this lasted for only one day before being removed
by the owners of No 2. The application three years later for a declaration of ownership
was hopeless. Also equivocal is minimal grazing by goats[53] or irregular parking.[54]

5. Illegality as a defence

[10.07] Possession which is illegal should not create adverse possession by analogy
with the rule for prescription[55] – for example where there is a case of criminal trespass
on defence land. However, failure by a squatter to pay rates or community charge is
not a sufficient illegality.[56]

C. INTENTION TO POSSESS

1. How to prove intention

[10.08] Possession is assumed to reside with the holder of the paper title.[57] Where
someone else claims to be in possession that person, the squatter, must pass tests in
Powell v. *McFarlane*.[58] Acts of possession must be supported by an intention to

---

[47] [2001] 2 EGLR 92, Laddie J.
[48] [1976] 1 WLR 1295, CA.
[49] *Green* v. *Wheatley* [1999] May 19th, CA.
[50] [1999] 2 EGLR 85, CA (7 metre stretch of wall in Knightsbridge with a paper title back to 1710).
[51] *Marsden* v. *Miller* (1992) 64 P & CR 239, CA; *Bills* v. *Fernandez-Gonzalez* (1981) 132 NLJ 66, CA;
Wilson v. *Martin's Executors* [1993] 1 EGLR 178, CA (cutting timber, repairing fence).
[52] (1992) 64 P & CR 239, CA; *Daniells* v. *Mendonca* (1999) 78 P & CR 401, CA.
[53] *Boosey* v. *Davis* (1988) 55 P & CR 83, CA.
[54] *Pavledes* v. *Ryebridge Properties* (1989) 58 P & CR 459, Knox J; *Pulleyn* v. *Hall Aggregates* (1992) 65
P & CR 276, CA; *Williams* v. *Usherwood* (1981) 45 P & CR 235, CA.
[55] See below **[36.16]**.
[56] *Ellis* v. *Lambeth LBC* (2000) 32 HLR 596, CA.
[57] *Pye* at [40], Lord Browne-Wilkinson.
[58] (1979) 38 P & CR 452, 471–472, Slade J; approved in *Pye* at [31], Lord Browne-Wilkinson.

possess.[59] Acts of the mind can often only be demonstrated by acts of the body.[60] In other words, the requisite intention has to be deduced from the evidence of unequivocal acts[61] – controlling access,[62] leaving the owner to squeeze through a hedge to get to his field,[63] or enclosure.[64]

2. What intention?

[10.09] What is required is now much clearer as a result of the exhaustive review conducted by the House of Lords in *Pye*.[65] The intention to be shown by a squatter is to exclude the paper owner and the rest of the world, to the extent that is reasonably practicable and so far as the law allows.[66] He must also intend to exclude the rest of the world. It is the intention of the squatter that matters,[67] and not that of the true owner, who indeed may be wholly unaware of the occupier.[68]

Although older authorities suggested that an intention to own the land was required,[69] the squatter is likely to be aware that he is not the owner,[70] but the relevant intention is to possess the land.[71] A squatter may hold adverse possession while mistakenly believing that he is paying rent,[72] or when he admits that he will be bound to leave the land when it is required for some future use.[73]

3. Proof of intention in *Pye*

[10.10] The facts in *JA Pye (Oxford)* v. *Graham* provoked considerable judicial disagreement. The squatters having succeeded before the trial judge,[74] lost in the

---

[59] Latin = *animus possidendi*; *Buckinghamshire CC* v. *Moran* [1990] Ch 623, 641E–644, Slade LJ; K Green, "Citizens & Squatters: Under the Surfaces of Land Law" ch 9 in Bright & Dewar, 235–241.

[60] *Pye* at [70], Lord Hope.

[61] *Tecbild* v. *Chamberlain* (1969) 20 P & CR 633, 642, Sachs LJ.

[62] *Wallis's Cayton Bay Holiday Camp* v. *Shell-Mex & BP* [1975] QB 94, 106, Stamp LJ.

[63] *Marshall* v. *Taylor* [1895] 1 Ch 641, 645, Halsbury LC.

[64] *Seddon* v. *Smith* (1877) 36 LT 168, 169; *George Wimpey & Co* v. *Sohn* [1967] Ch 487, 511; *Leigh* v. *Jack* (1879) 5 Ex D 264, 271.

[65] *JA Pye (Oxford)* v. *Graham* [2002] UKHL 30, [2002] 3 All ER 865.

[66] *Powell* v. *McFarlane* (1979) 38 P & CR 452, 471–472, Slade J; P Jackson (1980) 96 *LQR* 38; *BP Properties* v. *Buckler* (1987) 55 P & CR 337, 343, Dillon LJ; *Pye* at [42], Lord Browne-Wilkinson.

[67] *Buckinghamshire CC* v. *Moran* [1990] Ch 623, 644D–E, Nourse LJ; *Pye* at [32], Lord Browne-Wilkinson.

[68] *Red House Farms (Thorndon)* v. *Catchpole* [1977] 2 EGLR 125, CA; *Wilson* v. *Martin's Executors* [1993] 1 EGLR 178, 180L, Ralph Gibson LJ; MJ Goodman (1970) 33 *MLR* 281; Law Com 271 (2001), [14.5].

[69] *Littledale* v. *Liverpool College* [1900] 1 Ch 19, 23; *George Wimpey & Co* v. *Sohn* [1967] Ch 487, 510; *Hughes* v. *Griffin* [1969] 1 WLR 23, 28F, Harman LJ.

[70] *Ocean Estates* v. *Pinder* [1969] 2 AC 19, PC; M Dockray [1982] *Conv* 256, 345; *Prudential Assurance Co* v. *Waterloo Real Estate* [1999] 2 EGLR 85, 87E–K.

[71] *Powell* v. *McFarlane* (1979) 38 P & CR 452, 471; *Buckinghamshire CC* v. *Moran* [1990] Ch 623, 643, CA; *Pye* at [42], Lord Browne-Wilkinson.

[72] *Lodge* v. *Wakefield MBC* [1995] 2 EGLR 124 CA.

[73] *Buckinghamshire CC* v. *Moran* [1990] Ch 623, CA.

[74] [2000] Ch 676, Neuberger J.

Court of Appeal,[75] but their victory was restored in the Lords.[76] Those judges who ruled in favour of the squatters did express some reservations about that decision.[77]

Pye bought land adjoining the Grahams' farm, intending to seek residential planning permission. In February 1983 a grazing licence was entered into but this expired that December. Although there was no physical change in the nature of the occupation, its legal character changed.[78] On August 31st 1984 Graham bought a cut of grass from the land for £1100. Pye then wanted the land vacant as that was believed to assist the planning application. From that date the Grahams were in possession adverse to the developer's title. It made no difference that Graham indicated in evidence that he would have paid for his use of the land had he been approached for payment:[79] any candid squatter would admit has much if asked, but possession can be adverse until a request for payment is made.[80]

4.   Earmarked land

[10.11] *Pye* makes quite clear the irrelevance, once a paper owner has lost possession, of the fact that he had plans for the land, that it had been earmarked it for some future use. In *Pye* the intention was to build on the land when planning permission was obtained, but many other cases have involved strips of land set aside for road widening. In some cases it was implied that the true owner granted a licence for the use of strips earmarked for future roads.[81] These cases undermined the policy of securing titles by possession by proof of 15 years' exclusive possession of land,[82] and so were reversed by statute[83] and *Buckinghamshire CC* v. *Moran*[84] shows that 12 years possession of an earmarked strip will now effect a change of ownership. Adverse possession is determined from the quality of the intruder's possession without consideration being given to the paper owner's intended future uses.[85]

Earmarking may make it more difficult to prove both factual possession and the intention to exclude the world.[86] Trivial acts of ownership by the paper owner may prevent the possession of a squatter being seen as adverse.[87] In *Leigh* v. *Jack*,[88] Jack

[75] [2001] Ch 804, CA.
[76] [2002] UKHL 30, [2002] 3 All ER 865; W Batstone [2002] *NLJ* 1234; PH Kenny [2002] *Conv* 429; O Rhys [2002] *Conv* 470; MP Thompson [2002] *Conv* 480.
[77] *Pye* at [1], Lord Bingham.
[78] *Pye* at [55–58], Lord Browne-Wilkinson.
[79] Pye at [46]; *Lambeth LBC* v. *Blackburn* [2001] EWCA Civ 912, (2001) 33 HLR 74.
[80] *Pye* at [46], Lord Browne-Wilkinson; he doubted *R* v. *SS for Environment ex parte Davies* (1990) 61 P & CR 487, CA.
[81] *Leigh* v. *Jack* (1879) 5 Ex D 264; *Wallis's Cayton Bay Holiday Camp* v. *Shell-Mex and BP* [1975] QB 94, CA. Wider dicta in the former and the decision in the latter were overruled by *Pye* at [32], Lord Browne-Wilkinson.
[82] *Ramnarace* v. *Lutchman* [2001] UKPC 25, [2001] 1 WLR 651, [13] Lord Millett; *Buckinghamshire CC* v. *Moran* [1990] Ch 623, 639C–640F, Slade LJ; G McCormack [1986] *Conv* 434; G McCormack [1989] *Conv* 211, 212; JA Omolota (1974) 38 *Conv (NS)* 172.
[83] Limitation Act 1980 sch 1 para 8(4); M Dockray [1982] *Conv* 345. This will be replicated under the new proposals: Law Com 270 (2001); Draft Limitation Bill 2001 sch 1 para 1(8)–(9).
[84] [1990] Ch 623, CA; G McCormack [1989] *Conv* 211; C Harpum [1990] *CLJ* 23; *Hounslow LBC* v. *Minchinton* (1997) 74 P & CR 221 CA.
[85] L Tee [2000] *Conv* 113; O Radley Gardner & C Harpum [2001] *Conv* 155; L Tee [2002] *Conv* 56.
[86] *Buckinghamshire CC* v. *Moran* [1990] Ch 623, 639H–640A, Slade LJ.
[87] *Wallis's* case [1975] QB 94, 109–110, Stamp LJ dissenting.
[88] (1879) 5 Ex D 264.

acquired factories on either side of a strip of land reserved for the site of a proposed street, but he blocked the way to pedestrians with piles of materials destined for use at his factories, and later on the road site was fenced and blocked off. Although this use continued for the 20 year limitation period (under the law at that time) Leigh preserved his paper title by carrying out work on the fence.[89]

D. PERMISSIVE OCCUPATION

1. Exercise of property rights

[10.12] Possession is never adverse if it is enjoyed under a lawful title,[90] whether a lease, trust, agency, easement[91] or profit, or where a purchaser is allowed possession of land under a contract before completion.[92]

2. Licence

[10.13] Acts done by permission of a paper owner do not exclude him.[93] Occupation held under an express informal licence as from 1974 was not adverse.[94] A licence could protect the owner indefinitely.[95] Since 1980, a tenancy at will has had the same effect.[96] It is a question of fact when the licence or tenancy at will is actually terminated,[97] and as from that time limitation can begin to operate.

3. No licence from earmarking

[10.14] A licence may be implied. This should not be simply because the land is earmarked by its owner for some future purpose such as a building site or a road.[98] The

---

[89] *Pye* at [45], Lord Browne-Wilkinson.

[90] *Thomas* v. *Thomas* (1855) 2 K & J 79, 83, 69 ER 701, Page Wood V-C; *Buckinghamshire CC* v. *Moran* [1990] Ch 623, 636G; *Cobb* v. *Lane* [1952] 1 All ER 1199; *British Railways Board* v. *GJ Holdings* (1974) 230 EC 973, CA; *Wallis's* [1975] QB 94, 103G, Lord Denning MR; *Hughes* v. *Griffin* [1969] 1 WLR 23, 30A, Harman LJ; (1969) 85 *LQR* 170.

[91] *Williams* v. *Usherwood* (1981) 45 P & CR 235, CA; M Dockray [1983] *Conv* 398; *Bath & NE Somerset DC* v. *Nicholson* [2002] 10 EG 156 (CS).

[92] *Hyde* v. *Pearce* [1982] 1 WLR 560; M Dockray (1983) 46 *MLR* 89; JE Martin [1982] *Conv* 383; contrast *Bridges* v. *Mees* [1957] Ch 475, Harman J (after purchase money paid).

[93] *Doe d Thompson* v. *Clark* (1828) 8 B & C 717, 108 ER 1209.

[94] *BP Properties* v. *Buckler* (1988) 55 P & CR 337; HW Wilkinson (1988) 138 *NLJ* 238; H Wallace [1994] *Conv* 196; *Wallis's* case [1975] QB 94, CA.

[95] *Cobb* v. *Lane* [1952] 1 All ER 1199; *Hughes* v. *Griffin* [1969] 1 WLR 23, CA; *Heslop* v. *Burns* [1974] 1 WLR 1241 CA.

[96] A tenancy at will is no longer deemed to terminate after a year: Limitation Act 1980 s 9; contrast *Ramnarace* v. *Lutchman* [2001] UKPC 25, [2001] 1 WLR 1651.

[97] *Hyde* v. *Pearce* [1982] 1 WLR 560 (purchaser's licence revoked by request for return of keys; occupation still permissive under contract). Contrast *Foster* v. *Robinson* [1951] 1 KB 149, CA (life interest) and *Palfrey* v. *Palfrey* (1974) 229 EG 1593 (oral gift so adverse possession); *ER Ives Investment* v. *High* [1967] 2 QB 379, 398G, Danckwerts LJ (indefinite).

[98] Limitation Act 1980 sch 1 para 8(4); M Dockray [1982] *Conv* 345; *Buckinghamshire CC* v. *Moran* [1990] Ch 623, 639C–640F, Slade LJ; G McCormack [1986] *Conv* 434; G McCormack [1989] *Conv* 211, 212; JA Omolota (1974) 38 *Conv (NS)* 172; *Hounslow LBC* v. *Minchinton* (1997) 74 P & CR 221, CA; *Pye* at [44–45], Lord Browne-Wilkinson. See above **[10.11]**.

implication of permission may be justified (even after the 1980 Act) on the facts of particular cases[99] such as *Pulleyn* v. *Hall Aggregates*.[100] These cases are few and implied licence is an improbable defence.[101]

4. Payment and acknowledgement

[10.15] These acts also prevent possession being adverse.[102] Payment for land, like part payment of a debt, is an admission of the right of the recipient,[103] and thus of the owner's title.[104] Cessation of payments does not necessarily set the limitation period running immediately,[105] for example when a promissory estoppel prevents the collection of rent.[106] Once the limitation period has run, payment of rent does not revive the title barred.[107] Acknowledgement of the title of the paper owner will also prevent adverse possession by the person making it and his successors,[108] but for sound reasons[109] acknowledgments must occur in writing.[110] Examples are payment of rent,[111] a recital of the true owner's title in a deed, an offer to buy the property,[112] and signature of a petition opposing sale by a local authority landlord.[113] In *Buckinghamshire CC* v. *Moran*, a letter written "without prejudice"[114] stated that the squatter understood that he had the right to the ground unless and until a by-pass was built on it was not an acknowledgement, though this must have been preciously close to the line. A letter asserting that the writer of it is in adverse possession obviously does not amount to an acknowledgement.[115]

In principle an acknowledgment given after the limitation period has elapsed does not revive a title once barred.[116] However, *Colchester BC* v. *Smith*[117] qualifies this

---

[99] Limitation Act 1980 sch 1 para 8(4).

[100] (1992) 65 P & CR 276, CA; *Boosey* v. *Davis* (1988) 55 P & CR 83, CA.

[101] *Pye* at [32], [45], Lord Browne-Wilkinson.

[102] Limitation Act 1980 ss 29–31. No substantive change is proposed: Draft Limitation Bill 2001 cl 27; Law Com 270 (2001), [8.27–8.48].

[103] Law Com 270 (2001), [3.146–3.155]; *Maber* v. *Maber* (1867) LR 2 Exch 153; *Harlock* v. *Ashberry* (1882) 19 Ch D 539, 545, Jessel MR; *Edgington* v. *Clark* [1964] 1 QB 367. On payments to agents see: *Re Beavan* [1912] 1 Ch 196; *Wright* v. *Pepin* [1954] 1 WLR 635; *Re Transplanters (Holding) Co* [1958] 1 WLR 822.

[104] *Sanders* v. *Sanders* (1881) 19 Ch D 373, CA; *Doe d Milburn* v. *Edgar* (1836) 2 Bing NC 498, 132 ER 195; *Lodge* v. *Wakefield MCC* [1995] 2 EGLR 124, CA.

[105] *Lakshmijit* v. *Sherani* [1974] AC 605, PC; AL Goodhart (1974) 90 *LQR* 2.

[106] *Smith* v. *Lawson* (1998) 75 P & CR 466, CA.

[107] *Nicholson* v. *England* [1926] 2 KB 93; *Sanders* v. *Sanders* (1881) 19 Ch D 373, CA.

[108] *St Ives Corp* v. *Wadsworth* (1908) 72 JP 73 (acknowledgement to predecessor). Acknowledgement of a landlord's title cannot be used by a dispossessed tenant: *Sze To Kung* v. *Kung Kwok Wai David* [1997] 1 WLR 1232, PC.

[109] *Browne* v. *Perry* (1991) 64 P & CR 228, PC (Antigua).

[110] Limitation Act 1980 s 30(1).

[111] Even by a true owner: *Bligh* v. *Martin* [1968] 1 WLR 804, Pennycuick J.

[112] *Edgington* v. *Clark* [1964] 1 QB 367, CA.

[113] *Lambeth LBC* v. *Bigden* (2001) 33 HLR 43, CA; *Lambeth LBC* v. *Archangel* [2002] 1 P & CR 18 at 230, CA.

[114] [1990] Ch 623, 634D–635D, Slade LJ; *Hillingdon LBC* v. *ARC (No 2)* [1998] Ch 139, CA; *Llanelec Precision Engineering* v. *Neath Port Talbot CBC* [2000] 3 EGLR 158, L Tr.

[115] *Mount Carmel Investments* v. *Peter Thurlow* [1988] 1 WLR 1078, 1083–1086.

[116] *BP Properties* v. *Buckler* (1988) 55 P & CR 337.

[117] [1992] Ch 421, CA; M Dixon [1992] *CLJ* 420; M Welstead [1991] *Conv* 280.

when there was a genuine dispute since effect has to be given to agreements designed to settle litigation.[118]

E. LIMITATION

1. Personal actions

[10.16] Personal actions must be brought within six years, though only three years are allowed to pursue personal actions and a special relaxation allows 12 years for action on a speciality – that is a contract under seal.[119] This basic six year period will apply to many actions connected with land, for example for rent due under a lease.[120] These are "long-stop" provisions in the sense that the stale claim is squashed even if the owner if unaware of his right.[121]

2. Actions for the recovery of land

[10.17] Limitation is the process by which a stale claim to land is barred extinguished after the period allowed to the paper owner to challenge the squatter. A freehold owner dispossessed by a squatter may not bring an action to recover his land after the expiration of twelve years from the date on which the right of action accrued, provided only that the defence is pleaded.[122]

Limitation is the statutory process by which an owner is dispossessed by a squatter, a limitation period runs, and, acts to bar the owner's title to the land after time has expired without an assertion of title by the owner. Proof of adverse possession for 12 years at any time in the past will suffice: it does not have to be period next before action.[123] Periods based on the deaths of monarchs[124] have been superseded, since 1623,[125] by fixed limitation periods, the familiar 12 year period dating from 1874.[126]

Possession need not necessarily be hostile. Adverse possession is simply possession taken from the true owner, who therefore has a right of action to recover the land until that right of action is barred. The word "adverse" does not carry any connotation of hostility in the quality of the acts required of the squatter and the old concept of non adverse possession[127] abandoned in 1833[128] was not surreptitiously

---

[118] At 435, Butler Sloss LJ.

[119] A deed under LP (MP) A 1989 s 2 is not a specialty (limitation period 6 years not 12).

[120] Law Com CP 151 (1999), [1.6–1.7]; *Romain* v. *Scuba TV* [1997] QB 887, CA (6 years even if lease under seal).

[121] *RB Policies* v. *Butler* [1950] 1 KB 76, 81; M Dockray [1985] *Conv* 272.

[122] *Dismore* v. *Milton* [1938] 3 All ER 762; *Danford* v. *McAnulty* (1883) 8 App Cas 456, HL; *Cole* v. *Heyden* (1860) 1 LT 439 (onus).

[123] *Pye* at [26], Lord Browne-Wilkinson.

[124] First the death of Henry 1 (1135) by statute of 1237, and afterwards the accession of Richard I (1189), and afterwards by the Statute of Limitation 1540: Law Com CP 151 (1999), [1.6–1.7].

[125] Limitation Act 1623.

[126] Real Property Limitation Act 1874.

[127] Limitation Act 1623 s 1; *Nepean* v. *Doe d Knight* (1837) 2 M & W 894, 911, 150 ER 1021; *Paradise Beach and Transportation Co* v. *Price-Robinson* [1968] AC 1072, 1081–1083, Lord Upjohn; *Pye* at [35], Lord Browne-Wilkinson.

[128] Real Property Limitation Act 1833; *Bryant* v. *Foot* (1867) LR 2 QB 161, 179–181; Real Property Limitation Act 1874; *Ramnarace* v. *Lutchman* [2001] UKPC 25, [2001] 1 WLR 1651.

reintroduced in 1939[129] along with the word "adverse" to describe the squatter's possession.

An Act of 1833[130] established the modern system by which limitation removes title to unregistered land. Failure to sue within the limitation period extinguishes the title of the potential claimant,[131] so conclusively that the title can no longer be revived by an acknowledgement,[132] and claims to mesne profits in trespass are barred.[133] A squatter's title is not cast in iron because of the cases where longer than 12 years are allowed, and because of the rule that limitation operates separately against each burden: barring the title does not necessarily bar all the adverse interests affecting the land. A possessory title is much less secure than a documentary title.

3.   Triggers

[10.18] If possession has been held for 30 or 40 years, the exact starting date may be unimportant and it may be sufficient to work backwards from the date of a writ.[134] However where possession has been held for just about twelve years it may be important to work out the exact moment at which the right of action accrued.[135] Whatever the trigger, the crucial date is always when some person takes adverse possession of the land.[136]

(1) *Possession* is relevant where the land is vacant and no one is in possession of it, so that time begins to run when the squatter takes adverse possession of it.[137] (2) *Dispossession* (often inaccurately called ouster[138]) occurs "where a person comes in and drives out the others from possession."[139] Since the true owner is evicted, he is likely to take action immediately to recover land which was in use. The right of action accrues "on the date of the dispossession".[140] Where a person is in possession as licensee and then continues in occupation after his permission to be there is ended, as in *Pye*,[141] this is not a discontinuance of the owner's possession but rather a dispossession. Earmarked land[142] taken over by a squatter is another example of dispossession.[143] (3) *Discontinuance followed by possession* was added in 1833,[144] where "the person in possession goes out and is followed into possession by other persons."

---

[129] Limitation Act 1939; Law Reform Committee (21st Report) Cmnd 6923; Limitation Act 1980.

[130] Real Property Limitation Act 1833 s 34; N Curwen [2000] *Conv* 528.

[131] Limitation Act 1980 s 17.

[132] *BP Properties* v. *Buckler* (1987) 55 P & CR 337, CA.

[133] *Re Jolly* [1900] 2 Ch 616; *Mount Carmel* at 1088–1089, Nicholls LJ.

[134] *Treloar* v. *Nute* [1976] 1 WLR 1295, 1300, Sir John Pennycuick; *Wallis's* [1975] QB 94, 114F, Ormrod LJ (strictly inaccurate).

[135] Limitation Act 1980 sch 1; Law Com 270 (2001), [2.52–2.61].

[136] *Treloar* at 1300F, Sir John Pennycuick; PF Smith (1978) 41 *MLR* 204.

[137] Limitation Act 1980 sch 1 para 1.

[138] *Pye at* [36], Lord Browne-Wilkinson; he disapproved *Rains* v. *Buxton* (1880) 14 Ch D 537, 539, Fry J.

[139] Limitation Act 1980 sch 1 para 8(1).

[140] Limitation Act 1980 sch 1 para 1.

[141] *Pye* at [28–30], Lord Browne-Wilkinson.

[142] *Treloar* v. *Nute* [1976] 1 WLR 1295, 1300F; PF Smith (1978) 41 *MLR* 204; *Wallis's* [1975] QB 94, 114H, Ormrod LJ; *Williams Brothers Direct Supply* v. *Raftery* [1958] 1 QB 159, CA; RN Gooderson [1958] *CLJ* 34.

[143] Limitation Act 1980 sch 1 para 8(4); *Buckinghamshire CC* v. *Moran* [1990] Ch 623, 644H, Nourse LJ.

[144] Limitation Act 1980 sch 1 para 1; *Nepean* v. *Doe d Knight* (1837) 2 M & W 894, 150 ER 1021; *Paradise Beach & Transportation Co* v. *Price-Robinson* [1968] AC 1072; *Hughes* v. *Griffin* [1969] 1 WLR 23, 29E–F, Harman LJ.

Mount Carmel Investments v. *Peter Thurlow*[145] arose because two shareholders in Mount Carmel ceased to take an active interest in a valuable mews property in 1962 – one of them going so far as to withdraw to a Carmelite nunnery – so that by 1970 it had deteriorated to the point where it was almost uninhabitable. Time runs only from the later date on which some person takes adverse possession of the land.[146]

4. Assertion of title

[10.19] Paper title must be asserted within the limitation period. It is not sufficient to protest or to write demanding possession.[147] Physical repossession suffices when it is lawful,[148] but proceedings are more usual. The owner must issue a claim form within the time limit unless the squatter vacates or gives a written acknowledgement to the owner.[149] Service must generally occur within four months.[150] There is very limited scope for service out of time.[151] Actions will be brought and time will stop running on the day a claim form is received in the court office.[152] The limitation period starts again from the date of assertion of title, if, for example, a court order for possession is not enforced.[153]

According to the controversial decision in *Markfield Investments* v. *Evans*,[154] the mere issue of proceedings is not sufficient if the case is subsequently dismissed for want of prosecution. This is difficult to accept. It has been reversed for the purposes of the new registered land scheme,[155] and will be reversed more generally.[156] *Pye* left open the question whether the issue of an originating summons by the registered proprietor for cancellation of a caution lodged by the squatter was a sufficient assertion of title; surely this was in principle sufficient to assert title.[157]

5. Human rights

[10.20] Removal of title by limitation defines the terms on which ownership is allowed by our legal system, and so it cannot be seen as an interference with or deprivation of the owner's possession. It is a deprivation of the owner's right of access to a court, but time limits are readily justifiable.[158]

---

[145] [1988] 1 WLR 1078, CA; *Buckinghamshire CC* v. *Moran* [1990] Ch 623, 635H, Slade LJ.
[146] Limitation Act 1980 sch 1 para 8(1).
[147] *Mount Carmel Investments* v. *Peter Thurlow* [1988] 1 WLR 1078, 1084B, 1085H, Nicholls LJ.
[148] *Worssam* v. *Vendenbrande* (1868) 17 WR 53; *Bryan* v. *Cowdal* (1873) 21 WR 693.
[149] *Mount Carmel Investments* v. *Peter Thurlow* [1988] 1 WLR 1078, 1086, Nicholls LJ.
[150] CPR 7.11.
[151] CPR 6.7; *Anderton* v. *Clwyd CC* [2002] EWCA Civ 933, [2002] 1 WLR 3174.
[152] PD 7.5.1.
[153] *BP Properties* v. *Buckler* (1988) 55 P & CR 337, CA.
[154] [2001] 2 All ER 238, CA (occupation taken in 1977; action in 1990 but discontinued in 1999); MP Thompson [2001] Conv 341.
[155] LRA 2002 sch 6 para 11; Law Com 271 (2001), [14.23].
[156] Law Com 270 (2001), [5.1–5.4].
[157] *Pye* at [22], Lord Browne-Wilkinson.
[158] *Stubbings* v. *UK*, 22083/93, (1996) 23 EHRR 213; Law Com 270 (2001), [1.19]; *JA Pye (Oxford)* v. *Graham* [2001] Ch 804, CA, [36–43], Mummery LJ, [46–48], Keene LJ; this point was not appealed: [2002]

F. EXTENDED LIMITATION PERIODS

1. Disability

[10.21] A person secures capacity at 18, but will lose it by becoming of unsound mind, so as to be unable by reason of mental disorder to manage and administer his property and affairs.[159] Time is extended where the person able to take action was under a disability when the right accrued, time running out six years after the termination of the incapacity or death of the person incapacitated,[160] with a long-stop maximum of thirty years.[161] Once time begins, it continues come what may, throughout subsequent disabilities.[162] Property will usually be vested in trustees who can take action where appropriate.

Where title is registered it is now made clear that there is a defence while the registered proprietor is an enemy or detained in enemy territory and also when his mental disability is such that he cannot give or cannot communicate a proper decision.[163] Further general reform is proposed:[164] the current law will continue with a new provision for children.[165]

2. Fraud, concealment or mistake

[10.22] Where facts necessary to raise the cause of action are hidden from the person with the right to sue, the limitation period does not begin until the fact is discovered or was discoverable.[166] This applies to three forms of action: (1) actions based on fraud;[167] (2) actions based on facts which have been deliberately concealed;[168] and (3) actions for relief from a mistake. Extension of time is available against the fraudulent person and any people deriving title from him,[169] but not against honest buyers.[170] Where concealment occurs after accrual of the landlord's cause of action, a new period runs from the date of discovery.[171]

UKHL 30, [2002] 2 All ER 865, [73], Lord Hope; *Family H Ass* v. *Donnellan* [2002] 1 P & CR 34 at 449, Park J.

[159] Limitation Act 1980 s 38(2)–(4).

[160] No further extension occurs if the right of action passes on death to a person also under a disability: s 28(3), a change since *Cotton's case* (1591) 1 Leon 211, 74 ER 194.

[161] Limitation Act 1980 s 28(1), (4); *Thomas* v. *Plaistow* [1997] Times May 19th, CA (same meaning in s 33(3)(a).)

[162] Limitation Act 1980 s 28(1)–(2); *Stowel* v. *Zouch* (1569) 1 Plowd 353, 75 ER 536; *St John* v. *Turner* (1700) 2 Vern 418, 23 ER 868; *Hamfray* v. *Scroope* (1849) 13 QB 509, 116 ER 1357.

[163] LRA 2002 sch 6 para 8; Law Com 271 (2001) [14.29ff]. The suspension of the period can be noted in the register when the registrar is aware of it.

[164] Law Com 270 (2001), [3.114–3.127], [3.134–3.145], [4.152–4.153], [8.11–8.26],

[165] Draft Limitation Bill 2000 cls 26–30.

[166] Limitation Act 1980 s 32(1).

[167] Eg procuring a conveyance from a mentally incapable person, misrepresenting a right of succession, or wrong entry under a false gift.

[168] Limitation Act 1980 s 32(2); *Willis* v. *Earl Howe* [1893] 2 Ch 545 (not entry by the wrong heir in 1798).

[169] Limitation Act 1980 s 32(1).

[170] S 32(3)–(4).

[171] *Sheldon* v. *RHM Outhwaite (Underwriting Agencies)* [1996] AC 102, HL.

3.   Crown and corporations sole

[10.23] Statute provides favourable treatment[172] based on the identity of the plaintiff seeking to recover the land. Predictably an extended period is allowed to the Crown:[173] the Foreign Secretary was allowed thirty years to evict squatters from the Cambodian embassy.[174] Less meritoriously the same extension is also allowed to charitable and religious corporations sole.[175] The law will be tidied up.[176]

G.   REFORM OF THE LAW OF LIMITATION

1.   Personal actions

[10.24] The Law Commission review of *Limitation of Actions*[177] proposes to sweep away the confusing mess of limitation periods developed piecemeal over the years and replace them with a new core regime, intended to apply to any civil remedy, for restitution, of for the enforcement of any right, including specialties brought into the normal regime so that the period of action is reduced from 12 to three years. The core regime will also apply to claims for arrears of rent, the current six year period falling to three. A limitation defence will operate after three years from discovery of the cause of action, but with a 10 year long stop.[178] Outside the core regime will be family proceedings, insolvency and bankruptcy.

2.   Actions for the recovery of land

[10.25] Law Commission proposals[179] would tidy the provisions on actions to recover land, without radical shifts of policy. Abolition of adverse possession against unregistered titles is not on the agenda.[180] Actions for the recovery of land will be subject to a long stop period of 10 years, the reduction from 12 years being the one really significant change. Special provision will be made for claims to monetary compensation derived from land.

---

[172] Foreshore 60 years: Limitation Act 1980 sch 1 paras 10–11; *Alfred F Beckett* v. *Lyons* [1967] Ch 449; DEC Yale [1968] *CLJ* 195. Reform: (1) registered land: LRA 2002 sch 6 para 13; Law Com 271 (2001), [14.97–14.100], EN [724–726]; (2) general: Law Com 270 (2001), [4.145–4.147]; Draft Limitation Bill 2001 16(2).

[173] Limitation Act 1980 sch 1 para 10 (30 years); Law Com 270 (2001), [4.138–4.150], [6.42]. The period was 60 years until 1939: *Emmerson* v. *Maddison* [1906] AC 569, PC. Where the Crown or corporation conveys to an individual, the period is 30 years or 12 years from the conveyance: sch 1 paras 10–12.

[174] *SS for Foreign and Commonwealth Affairs* v. *Tomlin* [1990] Times, December 4th.

[175] Limitation Act 1980 s 15(7), sch 1 part 2; also for derivative claims. Until 1939 it was 2 incumbencies + 6 years to a maximum of 60 years; *Ecclesiastical Commissioners for England and Wales* v. *Rowe* (1880) 5 App Cas 736; *Blackett* v. *Ridout* [1915] 2 KB 415, CA; see also Draft Limitation Bill 2001 cl 17(5).

[176] Law Com 270 (2001), [4.138–4.144], [4.148–4.150], [6.42]; Law Com CP 151 (1999), [13.122–13.127], [15.54–15.55].

[177] Law Com 270 (2001); Draft Limitation Bill 2001.

[178] Law Com 270 (2001), [1.12].

[179] Law Com 270 (2001), part VI; Draft Limitation Bill 2001 cl 38.

[180] Law Com 270 (2001), [4.131].

3. Triggers

[10.26] The period in which it will be possible to recover land under the Law Commission proposals[181] will be 10 years from the date that the action accrued to the claimant.[182] The existing provisions relating to accrual of causes of action for the recovery of land will be expressly extended to equitable interests but otherwise are more or less reproduced in a re-ordered form.[183]

H. TITLE DERIVED FROM POSSESSION

[10.27] Adverse possession depends upon two coincident events – a bar to the paper title by limitation and at the same time possession creating a title to land in the squatter. These two aspects, one negative and the other positive, combine to leave the adverse possessor as owner of the land.

1. Possession gives a title

[10.28] Substantial acts of possession give a title to land, good against the whole world except a person with a better legal right to possession. The "true" owner could evict any person with a later title. If the true owner chooses not to enforce his rights or they are barred by limitation, the next possessor becomes the effective owner. Theoretically infinite, in practice the number of titles is limited, and it is rare for more than two titles to be in court. A classic involving three titles is *Asher* v. *Whitlock*, the very first case in the official Law Reports![184] In 1842 and 1850 A enclosed two parcels of manorial waste and built a cottage on it. He died in occupation, leaving the cottage by will to his widow during her widowhood, but passing entitlement to their daughter if his widow remarried. In fact she did in 1861, but she retained possession in defiance of the terms of the will giving the cottage to the daughter. Both died. The widow's second husband was required to move out by the heir of the daughter. Thus:

---

[181] Law Com 270 (2001) part VI; Draft Limitation Bill 2001 cl 16(2).
[182] Draft Limitation Bill 2001 cl 16(2).
[183] Draft Limitation Bill 2001 cl 17(1), sch 1.
[184] (1865) LR 1 QB 1, Exch Ch.

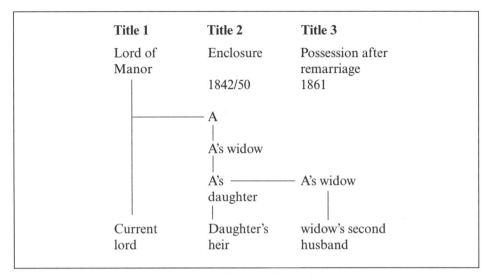

Figure 10-1 Possession based titles

Title 2 is vindicated over title 3.[185] Most cases involve two identified parties, one with paper title (who may be viewed as the "true" owner) and a squatter who claims the land. A decision in favour of the squatter establishes him for practical purposes as owner of the land, since he holds a legal title which cannot be challenged by any other known person.

2.   Succession to squatter's title

[10.29] Periods of adverse possession may be lumped together to make up a full 12-year period. Each possessory title forms a chain, rooted in the adverse possession, which can be sold,[186] given[187] or can pass on death[188] in the same way as a documentary title. Priority is given to the earliest claim to possession.

If one squatter is dispossessed by another, the combined period of adverse possession is available to bar the title of the paper owner,[189] but a competition remains between the two trespassers[190] until the second squatter has served 12 years

---

[185] The case does not establish whether or not the Lord of the Manor was barred. Presumably not, though there is a persistent rumour of a customary right to a house sited on waste land of a manor and occupied all within a single night: AR Everton (1971) 35 *Conv (NS)* 249, (1972) 36 *Conv (NS)* 241, (1975) 39 *Conv (NS)* 426.

[186] The paper title can also be sold: *Wallis's* [1975] QB 94, 106F–H, Stamp LJ (Avis to Shell Mex in 1961).

[187] *Mount Carmel Investments* v. *Peter Thurlow* [1988] 1 WLR 1078, 1086E–F, Nicholls LJ; *Treloar* v. *Nute* [1976] 1 WLR 1295, CA (gift of possessory title); *Buckinghamshire CC* v. *Moran* [1990] Ch 623, CA.

[188] *Asher* v. *Whitlock* (1865) LR 1 QB 1; *Pye* at [24], Lord Browne–Wilkinson (succession in February 1998 when Michael Graham was killed in a shooting accident).

[189] *Mount Carmel* at 1086E–F, Nicholls LJ; *Dixon* v. *Gayfere (No 1)* (1853) 17 Beav 421, 430, 51 ER 1097, Romilly MR.

[190] *Asher* v. *Whitlock* (1865) LR 1 QB 1; *Wallis's* [1975] QB 94, 106, Stamp LJ.

unaided. If the first squatter moves out and abandons possession back to the paper owner,[191] time will run only from when a second person takes possession.[192]

I.   UNREGISTERED MECHANICS

[10.30] Adverse possession of unregistered land creates a legal estate in land as before,[193] and one which is a freehold estate even if it is liable to be cut short by the true owner.[194] At first it is very feeble, but its value increases progressively as previous owners and those with adverse interests are barred. It has long been axiomatic that there is no "Parliamentary conveyance",[195] a point re-emphasised by Lord Radcliffe in *Fairweather* v. *St Marylebone Property Co*,[196] so the squatter is not a successor to the previous paper title. For example, an adverse possessor of leasehold land is not liable on the covenants in the lease,[197] a tenant retains the ability to surrender his unregistered lease even after adverse possession has barred his title to it,[198] and a squatter cannot claim relief from forfeiture.[199] No easements are created on the division of a title caused by adverse possession of a part.[200]

Documentary proof of a possessory title is based on a statutory declaration by the possessor the land showing how possession began at least 12 years before, proving acts sufficient to establish title by possession, stating that no other person has sought to exercise ownership rights, and that no superior title has been acknowledged by rent payments or by letter. Legal title to the freehold estate in the property is subject to the qualifications appearing below.

A contract for sale of any possessory title requires a special condition[201] and care is needed to ensure that terms of it are complied with exactly.[202] Under an open contract the buyer cannot be forced to accept title based solely on possession,[203] though he must accept a paper title with a gap covered by proof of possession.[204] First registration will be required.

---

[191] *Trustees Executors & Agency Co* v. *Short* (1888) 13 App Cas 793, PC; *Willis* v. *Earl Howe* [1893] 2 Ch 545, 553, Kay LJ; *Samuel Johnson & Sons* v. *Brock* [1907] 2 Ch 533, 538, Parker J.

[192] Limitation Act 1980 sch 1 para 8(1).

[193] LPA 1925 ss 12, 55(c).

[194] B Rudden (1964) 80 *LQR* 63, 70–71.

[195] *Doe d Jukes* v. *Sumner* (1845) 14 M & W 39, 42, 153 ER 380, Parke B.

[196] [1963] AC 510, 535; *Bryant* v. *Foot* (1867) LR 2 QB 161, 179–180, Cockburn CJ.

[197] *Tichborne* v. *Weir* (1892) 67 LT 735, CA; *Taylor* v. *Twinberrow* [1930] 2 KB 16.

[198] *Fairweather* [1963] AC 510, HL.

[199] *Tickner* v. *Buzzacott* [1965] Ch 426; DG Barnsley (1965) 28 *MLR* 364.

[200] *Wilkes* v. *Greenway* (1890) 6 TLR 449, CA; *Palace Court Garages (Hampstead)* v. *Steiner* (1958) 108 LJ 274 (registered lease).

[201] Varying the statutory title of 15 years under LPA 1925 s 44.

[202] *George Wimpey & Co* v. *Sohn* [1967] Ch 487, CA (special condition for statutory declaration proving 20 years possession, which in fact showed only 12 years; rescission).

[203] *Moulton* v. *Edmonds* (1859) 1 De GF & J 246, 45 ER 352; *Jacobs* v. *Revell* [1900] 2 Ch 858.

[204] *Re Atkinson & Horsell's C* [1912] 2 Ch 1, CA; *Games* v. *Bonner* (1884) 54 LJ Ch 517 (where a known documentary flaw is corrected).

J. BURDENS

[10.31] Ownership derived from possession only becomes absolute once the possessor has extinguished the right of every other person entitled to challenge it.[205] Limitation applies independently to each adverse interest affecting the land, but only after a trigger has caused that particular right of action to accrue. All this means that limitation is miserably ineffective as a technique for perfecting titles to unregistered land.

1. Burdens

[10.32] Destruction of the previous title by squatters still leaves the land subject to restrictive covenants. The argument against that position in *Re Nisbet & Pott's Contract*[206] was "so startling a proposition, and so wide-reaching, that it must be wrong." Hence the true position, that a squatter takes subject to all burdens – such as easements,[207] land charges, and restrictive covenants – which remain unbarred until the occurrence of an event triggering the need to assert them.[208] Collins MR referred throughout his judgment to incumbrances affecting the land, though properly they affect an estate in the land. This creates an awkward problem of visualisation. Apparently one should see the pre-limitation title as a shell once there is no owner able to enforce it, but with valid incumbrances still hanging on to it. Adverse possession by the squatter creates a new title, but one which is subject to the burdens affecting the paramount shell of the pre-squatting title.

2. Mortgages

[10.33] The law is complex but at least we have the guidance of a recent and superb account by Hugh Beale.[209]

(1) Squatter occupying mortgaged property

[10.34] The squatter's claim is only to the equity of redemption, meaning the land subject to the mortgage.[210] It would be necessary for the squatter to bar the mortgage separately.

(2) Borrower barring the lender – unregistered land

[10.35] A mortgage charges a sum of money on the borrower's land on condition that it will be repaid on the contractual redemption date. After that,[211] the mortgage has

---

[205] *Re Atkinson & Horsell's C* [1912] 2 Ch 1, 9, Cozens-Hardy MR.
[206] [1906] 1 Ch 386, 409, Cozens-Hardy LJ; also at 407–408, Romer LJ; contrast *Tichborne* v. *Weir* (1892) 67 LT 735, 737, Bowen LJ; Dart's *Vendor and Purchaser* (Stevens, 5th ed, 1876) vol 1, 463.
[207] At 411, Cozens-Hardy LJ.
[208] At 401, Collins MR, 406, Romer LJ.
[209] Law Com 270 (2001), [2.62–2.66].
[210] *Carroll* v. *Manek* (2000) 79 P & CR 404, Ch D.
[211] If contractual redemption is postponed indefinitely, as in *Knightsbridge Estates* v. *Byrne* [1939] Ch 441, CA, the mortgage is unbarrable.

to be kept on foot by regular payments of interest, each payment renewing the limitation period.[212] Arrears of payments can be recovered for six years,[213] though if the borrower seeks to redeem, he can do so only by paying all arrears.[214] If no payment is made for 12 years, the lender's mortgage is barred, unless his security is acknowledged in some other way,[215] and time also bars the action for debt[216] and the remedies of sale, foreclosure,[217] or taking possession.[218] Limitation cannot operate so as to create a charge of part of a commonhold unit.[219] If repayment is on demand, time runs from the date of a demand,[220] a point to be made clear by legislation.[221] The position where title is registered is considered elsewhere.[222]

(3) Lender in possession barring the borrower

[10.36] A lender has a right to take possession of the mortgaged property, which is usually done as a preliminary to sale. Time begins to run against the borrower,[223] though the period is extended each time any money is paid. For 12 years, the borrower can apply to redeem his mortgage, by paying back the capital and interest, in order to recover his land free of the mortgage.[224] Once 12 years have passed without the borrower's interest in the land having being acknowledged, the lender acquires title, barring the borrower's equity of redemption.[225]

(4) Mortgages – reform proposals

[10.37] It would perhaps be logical to require the recovery of arrears of mortgage interest within three years,[226] but the Law Commission has shied away from this radical change, and instead has recognised the need for a special regime for mortgages to

---

[212] *Hatcher* v. *Fineaux* (1701) 1 Ld Raym 740, 91 ER 1395; *Harlock* v. *Ashberry* (1882) 19 Ch D 539, CA.

[213] Limitation Act 1980 s 20; *Lowsley* v. *Forbes* [1999] 1 AC 329, HL (execution not limited to six years).

[214] *Mathura Das* v. *Nanindar Bahadur Pal* (1896) 12 TLR 609, PC; *Re Lloyd* [1903] 1 Ch 385, CA; *Holmes* v. *Cowcher* [1970] 1 WLR 834 (after sale); *Ezekiel* v. *Orakpo* [1997] 1 WLR 340, CA.

[215] *Wright* v. *Pepin* [1954] 1 WLR 635

[216] *Bristol & West* v. *Bartlett* [2002] EWCA Civ 1181, [2002] Times September 9th.

[217] *Re Clifden* [1900] 1 Ch 774; *Purnell* v. *Roche* [1927] 2 Ch 142; *Lewis* v. *Plunket* [1937] 1 All ER 530, 534, Farwell J; *Cotterell* v. *Price* [1960] 1 WLR 1097, Buckley J.

[218] *Samuel Johnson & Sons* v. *Brock* [1907] 2 Ch 533 (second lender); *National Westminster Bank* v. *Powney* [1991] Ch 339.

[219] LA 1980 s 19A, as amended by Chold and L Ref A 2002 sch 5.

[220] *Young* v. *Clarey* [1948] Ch 191; *Lloyds Bank* v. *Margolis* [1954] 1 WLR 644; *Cotterell* v. *Price* [1960] 1 WLR 1097; *Holmes* v. *Cowcher* [1970] 1 WLR 834.

[221] Draft Limitation Bill 2001 s 32; Law Com 270 (2001), [4.4–4.6], [6.46–6.50].

[222] See below **[11.20]**.

[223] *Raffety* v. *King* (1836) 1 Keen 601, 48 ER 439, Langdale MR; *Harrison* v. *Hollins* (1812) 1 Sim & St 471, 57 ER 187; *Charter* v. *Watson* [1899] 1 Ch 175, Kekewich J; *Re Loveridge* [1904] 1 Ch 518, Buckley J; *Alderson* v. *White* (1858) 2 De G & J 97, 44 ER 924 (informal conveyance treated as mortgage).

[224] After a sale by the lender, the borrower had 12 years to claim any surplus proceeds of sale at common law: *Re Fox* [1913] 2 Ch 75, Warrington J; but there is now a trust under LPA 1925 s 105. The period for claiming that a sale was at an undervalue is 6 years: *Raja* v. *Lloyds TSB* [2001] EWCA Civ 210, [2001] 82 P & CR 16 at 191, CA.

[225] Limitation Act 1980 s 16; *Young* v. *Clarey* [1948] Ch 191, Harman J; *Cotterell* v. *Price* [1960] 1 WLR 1097.

[226] Law Com CP 151 (1999), [13.130–13.135], [15.56–15.57].

apply the 10 year land period to money claims arising from mortgages secured on land, as well as the proprietary remedies of sale, redemption and foreclosure.[227]

3. Leases

[10.38] It is relatively easy to dispossess a tenant, but much more difficult to acquire a title good against his landlord.

(1) Barring the tenant

[10.39] A tenant evicted from a leasehold estate must take action within twelve years, as otherwise his title to the leasehold estate is barred.[228] *Tichborne* v. *Weir*[229] presents a startling illustration of the negative effect of limitation. A squatter took possession for 40 years against a tenant holding under an 89 year term, paying the agreed rent to the landlord. That squatter assigned his possessory title to Weir, who continued in possession until the end of the 89 year term. The landlord was not allowed to sue Weir for breach of a covenant to give up the property in good repair at the end of the lease.[230] Weir's interest in the property was based on the adverse possession, was not as a successor to the tenant's lease and did not attract liability on the covenants.[231] Rights are not transferred, but rather the original tenant is barred. Presumably the original tenant could be sued.[232]

Tichborne v. *Weir*[233] leaves unclear the nature of the squatter's title. Weir was certainly freed from any claim from the paper tenant for the duration of the lease. He apparently "acquired an absolute title to the land as against everybody but the landlord",[234] but, by paying rent, Weir admitted that his estate was not freehold.[235] This fact should mean that he was unable to claim the benefit of the 89 year term and it seems that he probably became a yearly tenant.[236] Had the landlord sought to evict him during the term he should have had no defence, leaving a squatter paying rent in a very precarious position.

The landlord is obliged to try to get back the land at the end of the original term of the lease,[237] so that if the tenant holds over for 12 years after the end of the lease,

---

[227] Law Com 270 (2001), [4.158–4.197].

[228] *Fairweather* v. *St Marylebone Property Co* [1963] AC 510, HL; *Spectrum Investment Co* v. *Holmes* [1981] 1 WLR 221, Browne-Wilkinson J; *Sze To Keung* v. *Kung Kwok Wai David* [1997] 1 WLR 1232, PC; *Chung Ping Kwan* v. *Lam Island Development Co* [1997] AC 38, PC (option in the lease also barred).

[229] (1892) 67 LT 735, CA.

[230] An estoppel might prevent the squatter denying that he was an assignee of the term, but not on the facts of the case.

[231] Contrast *Abbahall* v. *Smee* [2002] EWCA Civ 1831, [2002] Times December 28; below at **[32.32]**.

[232] *Fairweather* [1963] AC 510, 539, Lord Radcliffe.

[233] (1892) 67 LT 735, CA; *Abbahall* v. *Smee* [2002] EWCA Civ 1831, [2002] Times December 28th (squatter in flat not paying rent had a flying freehold and was not liable on the repairing covenants).

[234] At 737, Bowen LJ.

[235] At 738, Kay LJ; contrast *Fairweather* where no rent was paid.

[236] *Fairweather* v. *St Marylebone Property Co* [1963] AC 510, HL; *Taylor* v. *Twinberrow* [1930] 2 KB 16, Div Ct; *Lam Island* [1997] AC 38, 47F, Lord Nicholls.

[237] *Doe d Davy* v. *Oxenham* (1840) 7 M & W 131, 151 ER 708, Parke B; approved in *Fairweather* [1963] AC 510, 543, Lord Denning.

without paying rent or otherwise acknowledging the title of the landlord, he will secure the freehold by limitation.

(2) Barring the landlord

[10.40] One landlord can dispossess another by taking adverse possession of the rent for 12 years, but only if the lease is in writing and the rent exceeds £10 a year.[238] A tenant cannot dispossess his landlord by stopping rent payments.[239] Since the landlord's right is a right in reversion,[240] it only accrues when the term ends. Non-payment of rent will give rise to an action in debt, enforceable for six years[241] and a right to forfeit (that is to terminate the lease for breach of covenant) within 12 years.[242] If he chooses to tolerate non-receipt of the rent, the landlord can still recover possession at the end of the lease.[243] Indeed the landlord can extend his right of action still further by the grant of a reversionary lease.[244]

(3) Removing the squatter by shortening the term – unregistered land

[10.41] A landlord is able to accelerate his claim to possession against the squatter by shortening the term of the lease. *Fairweather* v. *St Marylebone Property Co*[245] provides a harsh illustration in the context of a hut in a Hampstead back garden straddling the boundary of two neighbouring leasehold titles. The owner of one house took adverse possession of the part of the hut built on the neighbour's garden (No 315) for 30 years,[246] so that by 1932 the neighbour's title was extinguished. What was the effect against the freehold owner of No 315, now the St Marylebone Property Co? Their right to recover that part of the hut at some time was indisputable, but the question was when? St Marylebone sought to hasten along their right to possession by taking an express surrender of the leasehold term from the original (dispossessed) tenant. A surrender made in 1959 allowed, according to a majority of the House of Lords, an action at that stage, long before the lease was due to expire in 1992. It seems that the original tenant retained a shell of an estate which could still be surrendered so as to accelerate the landlord's right to possession.

---

[238] Limitation Act 1980 sch 1 para 8(3)(b).

[239] *Roe d Pellatt* v. *Ferrars* (1801) 2 Bos & P 542, 126 ER 1429; *Doe d Cook* v. *Danvers* (1806) 7 East 299, 103 ER 115; *Chadwick* v. *Broadwood* (1840) 3 Beav 308, 49 ER 121; *Grant* v. *Ellis* (1841) 9 M & W 113, 125–126, 152 ER 49, Rolfe B.

[240] *Doe d Davy* v. *Oxenham* (1840) 7 M & W 131, 151 ER 708; *Ecclesiastical Commissioners for England* v. *Treemer* [1893] 1 Ch 166; *Canterbury Corp* v. *Cooper* (1909) 100 LT 597, CA. Also a contract for a lease (= an equitable lease): *Drummond* v. *Sant* (1871) LR 6 QB 763; *Warren* v. *Murray* [1894] 2 QB 648, CA.

[241] Limitation Act 1980 s 19; *Re Jolly* [1900] 2 Ch 616, CA (rent); *Romain* v. *Scuba TV* [1995] QB 887, CA (guarantor).

[242] Limitation Act 1980 sch 1 para 6; *Barratt* v. *Richardson* [1930] 1 KB 686, 693, Wright J (new right for each breach).

[243] Limitation Act 1980 sch 1 para 4.

[244] *Corpus Christi College* v. *Rogers* (1879) 49 LJ QB 4, CA. If L grants a lease to T for 10 years and a reversionary lease to X for 100 years, X's right to recover possession accrues in 10 years and L's in 100 years.

[245] [1963] AC 510, HL; *Chung Ping Kwan* v. *Lam Island Development Co* [1997] AC 38, PC.

[246] First by the tenant, then a sub-tenant; Fairweather was an assignee of the sub-lease.

Lord Morris dissented,[247] as many academics would have done.[248] Why should a tenant be able to pass a better title than he has himself? Surely the surrender was a transfer of the leasehold estate subject to the squatter's right to bar it?[249]

(4) Removing the squatter by shortening the term – registered land

[10.42] The mechanics of land registration leads to the reverse result.[250]

(5) Holding over

[10.43] A tenant can secure title against his landlord by holding over at the end of the term without paying rent.[251]

(6) Oral periodic tenancies

[10.44] A special rule applies to *oral* periodic tenancies,[252] including short tenancies granted orally and confirmed in writing.[253] The tenancy expires at the end of the last period for which a rent payment is made and the former tenant holds possession adverse to his landlord, and after 12 years this can ripen into ownership.[254] Thus in *Jessamine Investments Co* v. *Schwartz*[255] a weekly subtenant obtained title against his immediate landlord after 12 years and one week.[256]

(7) Encroachment

[10.45] If the tenant encroaches on other land (whether belonging to the landlord or a neighbour) the land is added to the lease. The landlord cannot claim it during the term, but the tenant has no right to it at the expiration of the term.[257] These long established principles have been reconfirmed in two recent cases.[258]

---

[247] *Fairweather* at 548.

[248] HWR Wade (1962) 78 *LQR* 541; RE Megarry & HWR Wade (1962) 78 *LQR* 33; DG Valentine (1962) 25 *MLR* 249; *Lam Island* [1997] AC 38, 47F.

[249] An argument considered and rejected: *Fairweather* at 545–547, Lord Denning.

[250] See below [11.16].

[251] *Williams* v. *Jones* [2002] EWCA Civ 1097, [2002] 40 EG 169.

[252] Limitation Act 1980 sch 1 para 5. Tenancies at will are now assimilated to licences, see above [10.13].

[253] *Long* v. *Tower Hamlets LBC* [1996] Ch 197; J Perkins (1997) 113 *LQR* 394; S Bright [1998] *Conv* 229; Law Com 270 (2001), [6.14].

[254] *Spectrum Investment Co* v. *Holmes* [1981] 1 WLR 221 (oral sub-tenant had ceased to pay rent); *Price* v. *Hartley* [1995] EGCS 74, CA; but limitation does not occur if a promissory estoppel prevents the landlord collecting rent: *Smith* v. *Lawson* (1998) 75 P & CR 466, CA. On void leases contrast: (1) *Magdalen Hospital* v. *Knotts* (1879) 4 App Cas 324, HL; (2) *Webster* v. *Southey* (1887) 36 Ch D 9.

[255] [1978] QB 264, CA; *Re Jolly* [1900] 2 Ch 616; *Hayward* v. *Challoner* [1968] 1 QB 107, CA; M Goodman (1968) 31 *MLR* 82; *Pollard* v. *Jackson* (1994) 67 P & CR 327, CA.

[256] No title was acquired against the freehold since the head lease was for a fixed written term. It seems from this case, and also *Moses* v. *Lovegrove* [1952] 2 QB 533, CA, that a tenant with security of tenure can acquire title as adverse possessor but retain security of tenure as against superior landlords: *Spectrum Investment Co* v. *Holmes* [1981] 1 WLR 221, 225D, Browne Wilkinson J, but query this last point.

[257] *Smirk* v. *Lyndale Developments* [1975] Ch 317, Pennycuick J; *Kingsmill* v. *Millard* (1855) 11 Exch 313, 318–319, 156 ER 849, Parke B; *Att-Gen* v. *Tomline* (1880) 5 Ch D 750, Fry J; *Tabor* v. *Godfrey* (1895) 64 LJ QB 245, Charles J; *King* v. *Smith* [1950] 1 All ER 553, CA; *JF Perrott & Co* v. *Cohen* [1951] 1 KB 705, CA.

[258] *Battersea Freehold & Leasehold Co* v. *Wandsworth LBC* [2001] 2 EGLR 75, Rimer J; *Batt* v. *Adams* [2001] 2 EGLR 92, Laddie J (principle may not apply to third parties).

(8) Reform

[10.46] There are detailed proposals for reform.[259]

K. TRUSTS AND EQUITABLE CLAIMS

1. Equitable remedies

[10.47] The Limitation Act 1980 applies to equitable claims as it does to legal ones, usually by express provision but otherwise by analogy.[260] In many cases,[261] claims to equitable remedies will be barred by delay (that is by the principle of *laches*) much sooner than 12 years,[262] a principle that will be retained.[263]

2. Trust property

[10.48] The Law Commission report on proposed changes in this area is an indispensable guide to the complexities of the current law.[264]

(1) Barring beneficial interests in possession

[10.49] An outsider can bar a beneficial interest in possession by taking adverse possession of the trust property for 12 years, as in *Pollard* v. *Jackson*.[265] A mother and daughter emigrated in 1946, losing touch with the girl's father. He was registered as proprietor of a house, of which he occupied the top floor and let the ground floor to the defendant, but after his death intestate in 1971 the top floor was left vacant. The tenant of the ground floor stopped paying rent and took over possession of the whole house, subsequently making a successful claim to rectification of the register in his favour. The daughter's claim as next of kin on intestacy had been barred by adverse possession for 12 years after 1971.

(2) Barring future interests

[10.50] Where trustees hold for beneficiaries entitled to future interests, limitation operates separately against each beneficial interest and at the final stage, but only then, against the legal title of the trustees.[266] Trustees have the right to take action to recover land lost to the trust within twelve years from the dispossession. Later benefi-

---

[259] Law Com 270 (2001), [6.36–6.39].

[260] *Beckford* v. *Wade* (1805) 17 Ves 87, 96–97, Grant MR; *Poole Corp* v. *Moody* [1945] KB 350.

[261] An exception where there is a bare trust is considered below at **[10.52]**.

[262] Law Com 270 (2001), [4.114–4.119]; *Allcard* v. *Skinner* (1887) 36 Ch D 145; *Knox* v. *Gye* (1872) LR 5 HL 656, 674; *Shaw* v. *Applegate* [1977] 1 WLR 970; *Re Diplock* [1948] Ch 465; *Kleinwort Benson* v. *Sandwell BC* [1994] 4 All ER 890, 943, Hobhouse J.

[263] Draft Limitation Bill 2001 cl 34(2).

[264] Law Com 270 (2001), part IV.

[265] (1994) 67 P & CR 327, CA.

[266] Limitation Act 1980 s 15(5); if land is limited *to A for life, remainder to B for life, remainder to A in fee simple*, A can sue for the fee simple only after B has taken possession.

ciaries, however, have a delayed right to sue for possession, each beneficiary having a distinct action accruing when their interest falls into possession.[267] The legal estate vested in the trustees is preserved until all beneficial interests have been extinguished.[268] In other words the pre-1926 scheme for future legal estates continues to apply under the Limitation Act 1980 even though the legal title to sue is now vested in trustees.[269] Why not require the trustees to sue within twelve years of dispossession, leaving a dispossessed beneficiary to bring an action later when his beneficial entitlement accrues for breach of trust against the trustees? A logical working through of the estate theory of the 1925 legislation[270] would greatly strengthen titles to unregistered land against future beneficiaries. The current reform proposals retain the present unsatisfactory bit by bit approach.[271]

(3) Beneficiary barring trust title

[10.51] A beneficiary cannot generally claim adverse possession *against* a trustee, since he occupies by licence of the trustee.[272]

(4) Beneficiary under a bare trust

[10.52] If *T holds on trust for B*, B is owner in all but legal form and limitation should be allowed to perfect a title lacking only paper formality.[273] Thus in *Bridges* v. *Mees*[274] a sale of a tiny sliver of land for £7 was completed without formality when the purchaser handed over £7 in cash and took occupation, but his title was perfected by adverse possession between 1937 and 1955, the squatter's overriding interest being good against a person who had later secured registration as proprietor.[275] Specific performance is available, however long the delay in seeking it, if an interest has been acquired by contract and the buyer has taken possession.[276] In future it is proposed that an action for the recovery of property held by a bare trustee will not accrue unless and until he acts in breach of the trust.[277]

---

[267] S 18(1), sch 1 para 4. If the previous beneficiary had lost possession, the period is reduced to six years from the later interest falling into possession, or twelve years from the date of dispossession of the previous beneficiary: s 15(2)–(3).

[268] S 18(3)–(4) (trust of land, a bare trust or a trust for sale; special provisions apply to strict settlements); *Llewellin* v. *Mackworth* (1740) 2 Eq Cas Abr 579, 22 ER 488; *Williams* v. *Papworth* [1900] AC 563, PC.

[269] Preston & Newsom *Limitation of Actions* (Longman, 4th ed by J Weeks, 1989), 41.

[270] LPA 1925 s 1.

[271] Draft Limitation Bill 2001 22(1).

[272] Limitation Act 1980 sch 1 para 9 (as amended by TLATA 1996 sch 3); *Garrard* v. *Tuck* (1849) 8 CB 231, 250–253, 137 ER 498, Wilde CJ; *Drummond* v. *Sant* (1871) LR 6 QB 763; *Melling* v. *Leak* (1855) 16 CB 652, 139 ER 915; *Earnshaw* v. *Hartley* [2000] Ch 155, CA.

[273] Limitation Act 1980 sch 1 para 9; *Re Cussons* (1904) 73 LJ Ch 296, Kekewich J.

[274] [1957] Ch 475, Harman J.

[275] As to further extension: C Sweet (1914) 30 *LQR* 158; MJ Goodman (1965) 29 *Conv (NS)* 356; G Battersby (1971) 35 *Conv (NS)* 6.

[276] Law Com 270 (2001), [4.268–4.278]; *Lindsay Petroleum Co* v. *Hurd* (1874) LR 5 PC 221, 226; *Nelson* v. *Rye* [1996] 1 WLR 1378.

[277] Draft Limitation Bill 2001 22(5).

(5) Claims for breach of trust

[10.53] Actions by a beneficiary against a trustee for breach of trust[278] have a limitation period of six years.[279] Claims to receive property from a deceased estate have a limitation period of twelve years,[280] subject to the principle that a trustee who distributes to himself as a beneficiary is only liable for the surplus over his proper share.[281] Each beneficial interest must be considered separately since limitation does not begin to run against a beneficiary until that beneficial interest falls into possession.[282] A beneficiary who is barred may not profit from an action by one who is not.[283] A uniform core regime will be applied in future.[284]

However in a number of cases there is no limitation period and claims are unlimited in time, subject only to laches. (1) *Attorney-General* v. *Cocke*[285] held that charitable trustees were never protected against an action by the Attorney General to protect the interests of the public. (2) There is no period of limitation for actions based on fraud or a fraudulent breach of trust.[286] (3) Trustees who retain[287] or convert[288] trust property are liable without time limit. In *James* v. *Williams*,[289] a family home passed to the children equally on intestacy of the mother, but it was occupied by a brother and unmarried sister to the exclusion of another sister who had married and left home 20 years earlier. The brother held title as an executor de son tort and there could be no time barring.

(6) Co-owners

[10.54] Imposition of a statutory trust on co-owners in 1925[290] ensured that one beneficial co-owner could no longer[291] bar another and neither can the trustees bar the beneficiaries. Old learning on trusts[292] was applied to the statutory co-ownership

---

[278] Limitation Act 1980 s 38(1) included express and constructive trusts, and presumably also fiduciaries: Law Com 270 (2001), [4.1] ("law complex").

[279] Limitation Act 1980 ss 21(3), 23 (accounts); *Tito* v. *Waddell (No 2)* [1977] Ch 106, 250B–252B, Megarry V-C; *Att-Gen* v. *Cocke* [1988] Ch 414, 420–421.

[280] Limitation Act 1980 s 22(a)–(b) (6 years for arrears of interest on legacies); *Re Diplock* [1948] Ch 465, 512; Law Com 270 (2001), [4.94], [4.120–4.125]. Periods run from death and not the later grant of representation: s 26.

[281] Limitation Act 1980 s 21(2) (a change).

[282] Limitation Act 1980 s 21(3); *Thorne* v. *Heard* [1894] 1 Ch 599; *Re Somerset* [1894] 1 Ch 231; *Armitage* v. *Nurse* [1997] 2 All ER 705, 720, Millett LJ.

[283] Limitation Act 1980 s 21(4).

[284] Law Com 270 (2001), [4.10].

[285] [1988] Ch 414; this will continue: Draft Limitation Bill 2001 cl 22(4).

[286] Limitation Act 1980 s 21(1)(a). According to Law Com 270 (2001), [4.97–4.101] only conduct relevant to the limitation regime should disapply the 10 year long stop.

[287] Limitation Act 1980 s 21(1)(b); Law Com 270 (2001), [2.39], [4.17–4.26]; *Paragon Finance* v. *DB Thakerar* [1999] 1 All ER 400, CA; *BCCI* v. *Tan* [1999] November 19th, Ch D; *Coulthard* v. *Disco Mix Club* [2001] 1 WLR 707, Ch D.

[288] On knowing receipt of trust property see Law Com 270 (2001), [4.3]; C Harpum (1986) 102 *LQR* 114, 267, 287–291.

[289] 2000] Ch 1, CA.

[290] LPA 1925 ss 34–36.

[291] *Culley* v. *Doe d Taylerson* (1840) 11 Ad & E 1008, 113 ER 697.

[292] *Knight* v. *Bowyer* (1858) 2 De G & J 421, 44 ER 1053.

trusts in *Re Landi*[293] and to a mortgage lender secured on the interest of a beneficial co-owner in *Re Milking Pail Farm*.[294] Results are now identical whether the trustees are the same as, or different from, the beneficiaries.[295] This was illustrated in *Earnshaw* v. *Hartley*.[296] Legal title to a Yorkshire farmhouse was vested in the President of the Family Division after the intestacy of a mother. One son who lived at home could not oust the rights of his brothers and sisters who had left home. Time had not run because all along they were all next of kin and the claimant was in possession of land as a beneficiary under a trust. Adverse possession could not operate between beneficial co-owners.

3. Reform proposals for trust property

[10.55] The provisions described above will be reproduced under the Law Commission's draft Bill, though in the context of a 10 year long-stop limitation period.[297]

---

[293] [1939] Ch 828, CA; RE Megarry (1941) 57 *LQR* 26 (approval); M Goodman (1965) 29 *Conv NS* 356 (doubts).

[294] [1940] Ch 996; RE Megarry (1941) 57 *LQR* 26 (doubting the decision, but query, for once, Megarry's doubts).

[295] G Battersby (1971) 35 *Conv* (NS) 6. A beneficial co-owner could only acquire good title if he is also a trustee who acquired title before 1940 and before becoming a beneficiary.

[296] [2000] Ch 155, CA.

[297] Law Com 270 (2001), [6.30–6.41]; Draft Limitation Bill 2001 cls 16–18.

11

THE REGISTRATION CURTAIN

Indefeasibility. Title absolute. Possessory and qualified titles and upgrading. Adverse possession against registered titles: vested rights under the 1925 Act; successful cases under the 2002 Act; normal 2002 Act cases. Alteration: pure alterations; rectification (prejudicial alterations). Indemnity. Covenants for title.

A. INDEFEASIBILITY

1. Indefeasibility registered

[11.01] There is no point in having a register unless it is to some extent conclusive as to the title. But it has proved very difficult to get the correct balance with the need to be able correct mistakes.

Before 1926 titles were registered indefeasibly,[1] and this is also the basis of the Torrens system adopted in many Commonwealth countries.[2] Title is guaranteed with a high degree of certainty, but only after a correspondingly complex investigation of title. Even so only the legal title is guaranteed.[3] Before 1926, an exhaustive investigation of title preceded English registrations: of the 34,000 titles granted between 1898 and 1901, only 69 were absolute or qualified, leaving registration an "utter failure".[4] Indefeasibility was a "false god".[5] Greater liberality was essential when granting registered titles, but this necessarily opened the possibility of alterations (the new name for rectification) to bring in earlier titles. Some degree of insecurity affects all registered titles, even those registered pre-1926.[6]

---

[1] Land Registry Act 1862 ss 20–24; Land Transfer Act 1875 ss 95–97; *Chowood* v. *Lyall (No 2)* [1930] 2 Ch 156, 164–165, Lord Hanworth MR; A Underhill (1911) 27 *LQR* 173, 177–178; *Re Suarez (No 2)* [1924] 2 Ch 19.

[2] *Frazer* v. *Walker* [1967] 1 AC 569, PC; *Gardener* v. *Lewis* [1998] 1 WLR 1535, PC; *British American Cattle Co* v. *Caribe Farm Industries* [1998] 1 WLR 1529, PC.

[3] Equitable title is not guaranteed in the face of fraud, prior registered titles, wrong parcels, erroneous boundaries, trusts, and personal claims.

[4] W Strachan (1904) 20 *LQR* 427; W Strachan (1915) 31 *LQR* 404, 407; H Humphry (1887) 3 *LQR* 263, 263–264.

[5] TBF Ruoff (1969) 32 *MLR* 121, 137; DC Jackson (1972) 88 *LQR* 93, 126.

[6] The current legislation is silent: LRA 2002 s 65, sch 4; but this was clear from LRA 1925 s 82, re-enacting LPA 1922 ss 173–175, LP (Amendment) A 1924 sch 8; *Chowood* v. *Lyall (No 2)* [1930] 1 Ch 426, 439, Luxmoore J; [1930] 2 Ch 156, CA.

2. Guarantee

[11.02] Innocents abroad commonly assume that they are absolutely safe buying on the strength of the register. According to the official puff "registration of title gives finality and certainty".[7] Title absolute is really a guarantee of *either* the land *or* monetary compensation. As the official leaflet continues, "A registered title is guaranteed because there is express provision for an indemnity should any person suffer loss through an error or omission that occurs in the register."[8]

B. FIRST REGISTRATION WITH TITLE ABSOLUTE

1. Freehold absolutes

[11.03] A curtain is imposed on first registration but only if the registrar issues a title absolute. This is a guarantee of title both prospectively from the date of registration and retrospectively for the past.

2. Proof of entitlement to an absolute title

[11.04] Title absolute is granted for more than 99% of freehold titles brought in for first registration.[9] Applicants invariably ask for an absolute title, leaving it to the registrar to decide that a lesser title is appropriate. Documentary title is backed up by a conveyancer's certificate that the title has been investigated, that an undisputed right to possession has been obtained, and that all known incumbrances disclosed,[10] though there is power for the registrar to carry out additional searches and advertisements.[11]

Many titles have minor flaws but the registry may ignore any that raise no prospect of a successful challenge.[12] A title can be registered which a competent adviser could properly recommend to a willing buyer.[13] *MEPC* v. *Christian-Edwards*[14] shows that a contract made in 1912 was not a serious defect in 1973 because the contract had either been abandoned or at the very least was no longer specifically performable. There is no reason why the registry should not choose to offer an indemnity to a party with a dubious title,[15] but exercise of the discretion may give a substantive boost to a title.[16]

---

[7] *Registration of title to land: its characteristics and advantages*, LR Explanatory Leaflet 1 (2002), [1].
[8] At [2].
[9] Ruoff & Roper (6th ed, 1996), [32.01].
[10] DLRR 2003 r 27.
[11] R 29.
[12] LRA 2002 s 9(3); eg on pre-1926 intestacy: *Re Suarez (No 2)* [1924] 2 Ch 19.
[13] LRA 2002 s 9(2).
[14] [1981] AC 205, HL.
[15] LRA 2002 s 9(2)–(3); Ruoff & Roper (6th ed, 1996), [2.10]. Doubts were expressed by C Emery (1976) 40 *Conv* (NS) 122.
[16] By protecting against rectification: see below **[11.48]**.

3. First registration

[11.05] Registration has no point unless it writes off the history and presents an up-to-date snapshot of the current state of the title, so that registration must be implemented by means of a curtain. First registration of a freehold title vests an estate in fee simple in possession[17] in the proprietor.[18] This is subject to any entries shown on the register and to any interests that override first registration, and to the rights of adverse possessors of which bind the first registered proprietor, and also to any beneficial interest under a trust of which he has notice. Apart from those matters, first registration takes effect free from all other estates and interests.[19] However there is one unarticulated but crucial limitation on the scope of the vesting by registration, since the estate vested on first registration may be removed or burdened through the process of rectification (that is by prejudicial alteration) of the register[20] though there is a presumption against rectifying mistakes against a proprietor in possession, so that off- register claimants may be forced to make do with an indemnity.[21]

4. Effect of first registration

[11.06] Registration with absolute title[22] vests the estate in the proprietor with all appurtenant interests subject to:

interests protected by entry on the register;
unregistered interests overriding first registration;
interests acquired under the Limitation Act 1980[23] of which he has notice; and
any beneficial interest of which he has notice.[24]

5. Support for the curtain: transfer for value

[11.07] A sale which triggers first registration will defeat unregistered land charges and trusts, either by overreaching or the bona fide purchaser rule. Formerly sale was the usual trigger,[25] meaning that the applicant to register the title was almost always a purchaser protected against any interests not appearing on the documentary title. Now

---

[17] This not the same as vesting possession in the first proprietor, despite *Kingsalton* v. *Thames Water Developments* [2001] EWCA Civ 20, [2002] 1 P & CR 15 at 184, [21], Peter Gibson LJ.

[18] LRA 2002 s 11(3)–(4); this makes clear that equitable title is also vested, subject to overriding interests and the possibility of rectification. On the old law see: Hayton's *Registered Land*, 57–58; *Epps* v. *Esso Petroleum Co* [1973] 1 WLR 1071, 1075A, Templeman J; DG Barnsley *Conveyancing Law & Practice* (Butterworths, 4th ed, 1997), 27–29; *Claridge* v. *Tingey* [1967] 1 WLR 134, 137, Pennycuick J; *Malory Enterprises* v. *Cheshire Homes (UK)* [2002] EWCA Civ 151, [2002] Ch 216, [64–65], Arden LJ (LRA 1925 s 69, but only legal estate).

[19] LRA 2002 s 11(4) Personal liability on covenants and other non-proprietary rights are not affected.

[20] *Chowood* v. *Lyall (No 2)* [1930] 1 Ch 426, 433, Luxmoore J; [1930] 2 Ch 156, 166, Lord Hanworth MR; TBF Ruoff (1955) 19 *Conv (NS)* 350; TBF Ruoff (1969) 32 *MLR* 121, 137.

[21] See below **[11.53ff]**.

[22] LRA 2002 s 11; Law Com 271 (2001) [3.45–3.47], EN [59].

[23] This only applies where the 12 year period has run before the 2002 Act commencement: see below **[11.14]**.

[24] LRA 2002 s 11(5). This is odd. If the first registered proprietor is a donee he apparently takes free of a beneficial interest that bound his donor.

[25] LRA 1925 s 123 before the 1997 amendments.

that registration is triggered by gifts,[26] the first proprietor is not necessarily a protected purchaser. Title is often vested free of interests which were binding before registration of the title. Only the first registered sale will the register match the true legal position.[27] This first sale shears off all rights not shown on the register[28] and alteration is restricted to overriding interests which continue to bind the land after sale.

Despite some blips,[29] protection of purchasers is decisive. In *Freer* v. *Unwins*[30] a restrictive covenant affecting the unregistered title to a shop was omitted from the title of the burdened land on first registration,[31] and the tenant under a registered lease secured title free of the unprotected restrictive covenant.[32] This protection should also have secured the tenant against rectification. Scott LJ confirmed in *Norwich & Peterborough BS* v. *Steed*[33] that a protected purchaser was proof against rectification, since rectification rights turned on substantive law principles. The law would be improved if the right to rectification of the register was stated to be a mere equity which could be defeated by a protected purchaser if not overriding.

C. LESSER TITLES: REGISTRATION AND UPGRADING

[11.08] Freeholds[34] not worthy of receiving the accolade of title absolute can be registered with possessory or qualified titles.

1. Possessory title

[11.09] Possessory title may be granted when the claimant is in actual occupation of the land, or in receipt of rents and profits, when no other class of title is appropriate.[35] The guarantee operates from the date of first registration, prospectively only. Registration does not prejudice the enforcement of any right adverse to the title of the first proprietor "subsisting ... at the time of registration of that proprietor."[36] Possessory title is given in 1% of freehold cases, for example a squatter's title based on twelve years pre-2002 Act adverse possession, after loss of the title deeds,[37] or where the paper title has flaws.[38]

---

[26] See above [9.24].
[27] Of course so should the sale leading to first registration.
[28] LRA 2002 s 29; see below [20.42].
[29] *Orakpo* v. *Manson Investments* [1977] 1 WLR 347, 359H–360E, 361B, Buckley LJ; *Epps* v. *Esso Petroleum Co* [1973] 1 WLR 1071, 1077F, 1078G, 1079C, Templeman J; *Proctor* v. *Kidman* (1986) 51 P & CR 67, 73, Croom-Johnson LJ obiter.
[30] [1976] Ch 288, Walton J; DJ Hayton [1976] *CLJ* 211; J Masson (1976) 39 *MLR* 582; RJ Smith (1976) 92 *LQR* 338; DJ Hayton [1980] *CLJ* 380; S Cretney (1976) 126 *NLJ* 523. Also *Att-Gen* v. *Parsons* [1956] AC 421, 441, Earl Jowitt; Lord Morton dissented (at 448) and the other Lords expressed no opinion; *Morelle* v. *Wakeling* [1955] 2 QB 379, CA.
[31] It was registered as a class D(ii) land charge, but did not appear on the registered title; this error or mistake opened the way for discretionary rectification against the freehold proprietor.
[32] Non-registrable since it was for precisely 21 years.
[33] [1993] Ch 116, CA.
[34] For leaseholds see below [25.46ff].
[35] LRA 2002 s 9(5); Law Com 271 (2001), [3.42–3.53].
[36] LRA 2002 s 11(7).
[37] DLRR 2003 r 26.
[38] *Spectrum Investment Co* v. *Holmes* [1981] 1 WLR 221.

2. Qualified titles

[11.10] Title may also be qualified where it is only established for a limited period or subject to certain reservations which cannot be disregarded.[39] Roughly one title in 100,000 has to be qualified. The guarantee operates subject to a particular qualification stated on the register, perhaps that the title is not guaranteed before a certain date, or that a particular transaction is doubtful – for example where a trustee has sold to himself and so made the title voidable.[40]

3. Challenging possessory titles

[11.11] Applicants usually ask for a title absolute, but modification of the conveyancer's certificate of title may be tantamount to asking for a possessory title. The registrar would be bound by a declaration after a vendor and purchaser summons[41] that a good title has been shown, particularly so thought Lord Russell – when delivering the main speech in the House of Lords in *MEPC* v. *Christian-Edwards*[42] – if the opinion was expressed in the House of Lords! The court should be able to declare that a title is or is not registrable.[43]

4. Upgrading possessory titles

[11.12] Possessory titles are gradually upgraded to superior forms of title on the application of the proprietor or a subsequent buyer.[44] Application is made by a proprietor, a person entitled to be registered, a proprietor of a charge or any other person interested. Any outstanding claim must be dealt with first. If the upgrade is granted, title vests as on first registration.[45]

Upgrading to an absolute title is possible if title can be shown to the satisfaction of the registrar.[46] Otherwise a proprietor who is in possession of the registered land may apply to upgrade after possessory title has been registered for at least twelve years.[47] Twelve years' possession does not necessarily bar all claims to the land, and rectification remains a possibility but a proprietor in possession with title absolute is well against rectification[48] and so the adverse claimant usually has to be satisfied with a claim to monetary compensation.[49]

A qualified title can only be upgraded if the registrar is satisfied as to the title and there is no outstanding claim.[50]

---

[39] LRA 2002 s 9(4).
[40] LRA 2002 s 11(6); Law Com 271 (2001), [3.49].
[41] LPA 1925 s 49.
[42] [1981] AC 205, 221A–B, Lord Russell.
[43] As with transfers: *National Provincial BS* v. *Ahmed* [1995] 2 EGLR 127, CA.
[44] DLRR 2003 r 123.
[45] LRA 2002 s 62(6)–(8).
[46] LRA 2002 s 62(1); Law Com 271 (2001), [9.17]. All documents showing title must be produced: LRA 2002 s 62; DLRR 2003 r 123; LR Form UT1.
[47] LRA 2002 s 62(4); Law Com 271 (2001), [9.17]. The length can be amended by rules.
[48] See below at **[11.48]**.
[49] See below at **[11.53ff]**.
[50] LRA 2002 s 62(1), (6); Law Com 271 (2001), [9.18].

D. ADVERSE POSSESSION RIGHTS UNDER THE 1925 ACT

1. History

[11.13] Adverse possession against a registered title was prohibited by the Land Transfer Act 1875,[51] but the result was a disaster,[52] so the process was restored tentatively in 1897[53] and fully in 1925. It was removed again in 2002 and it will be interesting to see whether the abolition sticks this time.

2. Registered mechanics under the 1925 Act

[11.14] Between 1925 and October 2003 the law was simply that:

> "the Limitation Acts . . . apply to registered land in the same manner and to the same extent as . . . to land not registered".[54]

Rights acquired by limitation completed before the commencement of the 2002 Act will continue under transitional provisions.[55] Let us consider a squatter who took possession in 1990 and so had served his time by the end of 2002.

3. Mechanics

[11.15] Acquisition of title proceeded with the same quality of possession as in unregistered land.[56] Title is not yet registrable during the 12 year limitation period.[57] After the period has run, the registered proprietor remains on the register,[58] but the squatter holds an overriding interest in the property,[59] which he can choose to protect on the register.[60] His adverse possession gives a right to be registered. The 1925 Act said that the registered title was held on trust for the squatter[61] but it was wrong to impose fiduciary obligations on the proprietor,[62] and this trust is now abrogated.[63] The squatter can apply to register his title after the full twelve years[64] by production of proof of

---

[51] Land Transfer Act 1875 s 21.
[52] T Key (1886) 2 *LQR* 324, 338; CH Sargant (1887) 3 *LQR* 272; A Underhill (1911) 27 *LQR* 173.
[53] Land Transfer Act 1897 s 12.
[54] LRA 1925 s 75(1); LR Practice Advice Leaflet 15 (2002); [2002] 09 *LSG* 42.
[55] LRA 2002 sch 12 para 18.
[56] *Williams Brothers Direct Supply* v. *Raftery* [1958] 1 QB 159, CA.
[57] LRA 1925 s 75(2).
[58] Limitation Act 1980 s 17 is subject to LRA 1925 s 75.
[59] LRA 1925 s 70(1)(f); *BP Properties* v. *Buckler* (1987) 55 P & CR 337, 342.
[60] *JA Pye (Oxford)* v. *Graham* [2002] UKHL 30, [2002] 3 All ER 865, [26], Lord Browne-Wilkinson (formerly a caution, now a unilateral notice).
[61] LRA 1925 s 75(1); *Mount Carmel Investments* v. *Peter Thurlow* [1988] 1 WLR 1078, 1089C–D; *Pye* at [26], Lord Browne-Wilkinson.
[62] EJ Cooke (1994) 14 *LS* 1.
[63] LRA 2002 sch 12 para 18(1) says merely that "he is entitled to be registered as proprietor"; Law Com 271 (2001), [14.104–14.105].
[64] LRA 1925 s 75(1)–(3). P Sparkes *NLL* (1st ed), 689–690, points out that the trust implies a right to a transfer, and that a transfer can also be achieved by applying for rectification: *Bridges* v. *Mees* [1957] Ch 475, 487, Harman J; *Re Chowood (No 2)* [1930] 1 Ch 426, Luxmoore J; [1930] 2 Ch 156, CA; *Epps* v. *Esso Petroleum Co* [1973] 1 WLR 1071, 1078E, Templeman J; *Pollard* v. *Jackson* (1994) 67 P & CR 327, CA. This is a non-prejudicial alteration: see below **[11.35]**.

the adverse possession[65] in the shape of a statutory declaration by the squatter himself (possibly supplemented by other declarations) stating the date on which adverse possession began or is first established, the acts of possession, and all other available facts, and a statement that no acknowledgement or payment has been made.[66]

The land registry give a possessory title,[67] closing the old register and opening a new one and so treating the application by the squatter as a first registration, though the squatter is registered subject to any estates or interests not extinguished by adverse possession,[68] such as restrictive covenants. Sedley J applied the trust principle correctly in *Central London Commercial Estates* v. *Kato Kaguku*[69] in a case where the squatter had served his time but had not been registered. Axa surrendered their registered title to the headlease of a car park to the freeholder, but this was ineffective because Kato had adverse possession of the land, a car park in the West courtyard of the BBC's Bush House on the Strand, and so Axa held on trust for Kato, whose interest overrode[70] the surrender. Squatting on registered land was fundamentally distinct from unregistered squatting, because the squatter was entitled to be placed in the position previously held by the proprietor.[71]

4. Leases

[11.16] A squatter on unregistered leasehold land can defeat a tenant after 12 years, but he has not effectively barred the freeholder. He has 12 years from the end of the lease to sue to recover the land, and can frustrate the squatter's title by taking a surrender of the estate held by the dispossessed tenant.[72] Registered land mechanics are quite different and lead to quite different substantive results. Adverse possession does not destroy a title but causes it to be transferred to the squatter. In *Spectrum Investment Co* v. *Holmes*[73] T was the registered proprietor of a 99 year lease. From 1951 to 1968 a "sub-tenant" remained in occupation, without paying rent, so securing registration as proprietor of the leasehold title. A purported surrender by the dispossessed tenant (T) was ineffective because it was not a registered disposition (which can only be made by a proprietor). Registration of the squatter's title vested the powers of disposition of the land in the registered proprietor alone, and stripped all powers from an ex-proprietor who had lost his place on the register. *Spectrum* has been further extended in *Central London Commercial Estates* v. *Kato Kaguku*[74] – the BBC car park case – the doctrinal extension arising from the fact that the squatter was not yet registered. Sedley J based himself on the trust of registered land in favour of the squatter.

---

[65] LRA 1925 s 75(3).

[66] DLRR 2003 r 187; Ruoff & Roper (6th ed), [29.07].

[67] *Spectrum Investment Co* v. *Holmes* [1981] 1 WLR 221, Browne-Wilkinson J.

[68] LRA 1925 s 75(1).

[69] [1998] 4 All ER 948; C Harpum (1999) 115 *LQR* 187; EJ Cooke [1999] *Conv* 136; S Pascoe [1999] *Conv* 329; MG Draper (1998) 142 *SJ* 1102; HW Wilkinson [1999] *NLJ* 118; *Spectrum Investment Co* v. *Holmes* [1981] 1 WLR 221, 228H–229D, 229D–230C, 230C, Browne-Wilkinson J (where squatter registered).

[70] LRA 1925 s 70(1)(f).

[71] It seems that the 2002 Act "right to transfer" achieves the same result.

[72] *Fairweather;* see above at **[10.41]**.

[73] [1981] 1 WLR 221, Browne-Wilkinson J; C Sydenham [1981] *Conv* 157; RE Annand [1981] *Conv* 154; H Wallace (1981) 32 *NILQ* 254; PF Smith (1981) 131 *NLJ* 718; PH Kenny [1982] *Conv* 201 (criticism for ignoring trusteeship).

[74] [1998] 4 All ER 948, Sedley J.

5. Alteration of the register to record 1925 Act squatters

[11.17] All registered titles are subject to overriding interests existing at first registration, or arising during subsequent ownership, or at the time of a subsequent sale.[75] When they become known, the register should be corrected to take account of them, a form of automatic alteration,[76] since it is a non-prejudicial updating of the register.[77]

There were three main categories under pre-2002 law. Adverse possessors held an overriding interest under the old law,[78] and after the 12 year limitation period the registered proprietor's title is barred, so that the squatter can seek rectification by deletion of the proprietor's name and insertion of his own. Case-law examples concern strips of woodland[79] and land bought under an oral contract for £10 but never registered.[80] Actual occupiers override the register anyway.

E. ADVERSE POSSESSION SUCCESSFUL UNDER THE 2002 ACT

1. Substantive nature of adverse possession

[11.18] Adverse possession now takes 10 years, but only in rare cases will it succeed. When it does the quality of possession that it adverse is unaltered, with the minor modifications now outlined.[81]

(1) Triggers where title is registered

[11.19] Adverse possession cannot be taken from over from an earlier squatter on registered land.[82] So the following works:

  10 years by Z;
  5 years by Y followed by 5 years by Z as Y's successor;
  10 years by Z interrupted for a period of time by Y.[83]

But not:

  5 years by Y after which Z dispossessed Y for 5 years;[84]
  4 years by Y followed by a one year gap followed by 5 years by Z.

---

[75] LRA 2002 schs 1, 3; previous cases were decided on LRA 1925 s 70(1).
[76] *Chowood* v. *Lyall (No 2)* [1930] 2 Ch 426, 156, 159; *Bridges* v. *Mees* [1957] 1 Ch 475, 486; *Epps* v. *Esso Petroleum Co* [1973] 1 WLR 1071, 1078E, Templeman J.
[77] Law Com 271 (2001), [10.16].
[78] LRA 1925 s 70(1)(f).
[79] *Chowood* v. *Lyall (No 2)* [1930] 1 Ch 426, Luxmoore J; [1930] 2 Ch 156, CA; TBF Ruoff (1954) 18 *Conv* (NS) 130, 137, (1956) 20 *Conv* (NS) 302, 306–310; *Pollard* v. *Jackson* (1994) 67 P & CR 327, 332, CA.
[80] *Bridges* v. *Mees* [1957] Ch 475, Harman J.
[81] LRA 2002 sch 6 para 11, applying Limitation Act 1980 s 15.
[82] LRA 2002 sch 6 para 11; Law Com 271 (2001), [14.20], EN [717–721].
[83] The periods must follow continuously.
[84] Limitation will run to protect Z against Y after 12 years: Law Com 271 (2001), EN [436(iv)].

(2) Mortgages of registered land

[11.20] Where a mortgage charges a registered estate there will be no period of limitation in relation to redemption, a significant change in the law.[85] A lender in possession will never bar the borrower.

(3) Trust of registered land

[11.21] Adverse possession cannot be taken of land subject to a trust unless the interest of each of the beneficiaries is entitled in possession. The 10 year registered land limitation period only runs from when any life interest falls in. A trustee cannot be in adverse possession against his beneficiary nor the beneficiary against the trustee.[86]

2. Application

[11.22] In most cases this will fail but it may succeed in the residual cases now considered. In three cases the squatter applicant acquires an independent fee simple estate and is entitled to registration as proprietor,[87] that is

(1) estoppel;
(2) independent title to the estate; and
(3) boundary disputes.

Each case requires explication, as do:

(4) general principles apply to all three; and
(5) adverse possession that does not relate to a registered estate.

(1) Estoppel

[11.23] An adverse possessor may insist on registration where it would be unconscionable for the registered proprietor to dispossess the applicant who ought in the circumstances to be registered as proprietor; this is a statutory statement of the principle of proprietary estoppel.[88]

(2) Independent right to estate

[11.24] A squatter who seeks to displace a registered proprietor may have some property claim to the estate quite apart from being a squatter.[89] One common example would be where the registered proprietor has made an agreement to sell a small plot of land, the buyer has paid the price, and has taken occupation. After 12 years the

---

[85] LRA 2002 s 96(2); Law Com 271 (2001), EN [439].
[86] LRA 2002 sch 6 para 12; Law Com 271 (2001), EN [686], [706–709], [722–723].
[87] Law Com 271 (2001), [14.7], [14.63ff].
[88] LRA 2002 sch 6 para 5(2); Law Com 271 (2001), [14.36–14.42], EN [695ff]. S 108(4) enables the adjudicator to apply minimum equity theory.
[89] LRA 2002 sch 6 para 5(3); Law Com 271 (2001), EN [698].

buyer's title would formerly have been perfected by adverse possession.[90] Now he will be treated as a contracting purchaser with a title perfected by squatting and as such entitled to seek registration.

(3) Boundary disputes

[11.25] Boundaries laid out on building estates rarely match the theoretical boundaries shown on the register or, to put it another way, it is common for houses to be built and fences erected in the wrong place. Possession of the land has a vital role to play in settling the boundaries of registered land since land registry plans only show a general boundary, the precise line being fixed by the boundary structures on the land itself. After ten years adverse possession ensures that the legal boundary matches the physical boundary structures.[91] Registration will occur on the application of an adverse possessor if:[92]

(1) the applicant owns land adjacent[93] to that for which application is made;
(2) the exact line of the boundary has not been determined;[94]
(3) the applicant has held adverse possession for a period of ten years ending on the date of the application
(4) throughout that period the applicant (or his predecessor in title) reasonably believed that the land belonged to him;[95] and
(5) the estate to which the application relates was registered more than one year prior to the application.[96]

Adverse possession of the boundary strip in these cases is also a defence to an action in trespass.

(4) General principles applying to the three exceptional cases

[11.26] Registration of a squatter in these three cases takes effect subject to registered charges since lenders do not have a chance to object.[97] A mortgage may need to be apportioned between the two estates according to value, and parts can then be redeemed.[98]

Any disputes will be referred to the adjudicator.[99]

---

[90] *Bridges* v. *Mees* [1957] Ch 475, Harman J.

[91] LRA 2002 s 98(1), sch 6 para 5(4). This will be brought into force 1 year after the rest of the Act to give 1 year for proceedings in these circumstances: Law Com 271 (2001), [14.101ff].

[92] LRA 2002 sch 6 para 5(4); Law Com 271 (2001), [14.7], EN [699–703].

[93] This concept is undefined.

[94] A fix will then be required: DLRR 2003 r 120.

[95] In most boundary disputes the parties will be unsure about the ownership, which is not, apparently, sufficient.

[96] Where the boundary is between registered and unregistered land, it seems that the period is 10 years on one side and 12 on the other (!).

[97] LRA 2002 sch 6 para 9(4); Law Com 271 (2001) [14.77–14.84].

[98] LRA 2002 sch 6 paras 9–10.

[99] S 108; Law Com 271 (2001), [14.41].

(5) Cases outside the new regime

[11.27] Adverse possession can operate as in unregistered land against an interest that is not a registered estate,[100] for example:

adverse possession against a short-term tenant;
cases involving a licensee or tenant at will;
rights of entry which are not estates in land;
dispossession of one squatter by another; or
action by a lender against a borrower in possession who has not paid interest.[101]

F.   REGISTERED LAND MECHANICS UNDER THE 2002 ACT

1.   Reform

[11.28] Part 9 of the Land Registration Act 2002 consists of three brief provions[102] which signal a major departure for registered land, since basically:

> "adverse possession of an estate in land will never of itself bar the registered proprietor's title."[103]

This creates a substantial and substantive rupture between registered and unregistered conveyancing.[104] There is no transitional saving for squatters unless their rights are fully matured by 12 years possession when the 2002 Act is brought into force.[105] A squatter who has held title adverse to the proprietor for say 11 years possession moves straight into the 2002 Act scheme,[106] so he will be most unlikely to secure registration.[107]

2.   New mechanics

[11.29] A squatter will be entitled to apply for registration after 10 years, chosen as the new long-stop period to be applied to all actions for the recovery of land,[108] but only in rare cases will that application succeed. For this reason the role of adverse possession will be residual, for example where needed to perfect title to land after a death or where a proprietor simply disappears.

When title is registered it is not essential to validate the title by checking it against the possession on the ground, since the register provides a definitive statement of ownership and should be the final arbiter. Adverse possession can only ever weaken the

---

[100] Law Com 271 (2001), [14.10], EN [436].
[101] This is subject to the 12 year limitation period: LRA 2002 s 96(1); Limitation Act 1980 ss 15, 20, 29, sch 1; Law Com 271 (2001), [14.12–14.14], EN [437].
[102] LRA 2002 ss 96–98, sch 6; DLRR 2003 rr 186–189; DLRR CD ch 11, [1–20].
[103] Law Com 271 (2001), EN [432–434], also [14.5]; Law Com 254 (1998), [10.43–10.78]; *Hansard* HL vol 1847, July 17th 2001, cols 1621–1631.
[104] K Cartmell [2002] 33 *EG* 90; MP Thompson [2002] *Conv* 480, 492.
[105] Ie October 13th 2003.
[106] LRA 2002 sch 12 para 7 overriding for 3 years.
[107] A squatter in possession will have an overriding interest anyway.
[108] Law Com 270 (2001), [4.133]; Law Com 271 (2001), [14.19].

register[109] and it seems wrong to allow "theft".[110] Reasoning such as this led many Commonwealth jurisdictions to abandon the principle of limitation in favour of the indefeasibility of the Torrens system.[111] Some 60% of the Commission's consultees favoured the proposal to change towards the conclusiveness of registration,[112] which will eventually ensure that land is kept in commerce by making the title clear in every case.[113]

3.   New registered land machinery

[11.30] The basic technique of the Land Registration Act 2002[114] is to disapply the limitation periods on actions for the recovery of land[115] if the title affected is registered. This new scheme applies if title is registered when the issue arises – it is not necessary for it to have been registered throughout the 10-year period.[116] It follows that voluntary registration of title is a sound tactic to defeat a squatter – probably much cheaper than litigation.

No title will accrue from possession as such, and accordingly a registered title will no longer be extinguished when that period of time has run.[117] Instead a person who has been in adverse possession of an estate for ten years may apply to be registered as proprietor.[118] The applicant will usually be in possession on the date of his application. An application will also be permitted where a 10 year squatter has been physically dispossessed by the registered proprietor within the previous six months, though an application in those circumstances will be a complete waste of time and money. Indeed any application for registration of title by an adverse possessor of ten years standing will rarely succeed, outside the exceptional cases already discussed.[119] When an application is received, the registrar will notify the registered proprietor of the estate, who is likely to object.[120] Other people to be notified and who may be able to block the registration include the proprietor of any registered charge, the proprietor of any superior title, and a person who has registered a right to receive notice.[121] Objectors will be given three months to complain,[122] during which time the adverse possessor will be entitled to be registered as proprietor.[123]

---

[109]   Law Com 271 (2001) [14.2–14.3].

[110]   *JA Pye (Oxford)* v. *Graham* [2000] Ch 676, 709–710, Neuberger J; *Pye* [2002] UKHL 30, [2] Lord Bingham, [39] Lord Hope; Law Com 271 (2001), [14.1].

[111]   Law Com 271 (2001), EN [433]; *Belize Estates & Produce Co* v. *Quilter* [1897] AC 367, PC; *Frazer* v. *Walker* [1967] 1 AC 569, PC; *Gardener* v. *Lewis* [1998] 1 WLR 1535, PC.

[112]   Your author was among the 40%. A more formidable opponent was Lord Goodhart: *Hansard* HL vol 1847, July 17th 2001, cols 1621–1631.

[113]   Law Com 271 (2001), [14.6], [14.54].

[114]   LRA 2002 s 96; Law Com 271 (2001), [14.9].

[115]   Limitation Act 1980 s 15.

[116]   LRA 2002 sch 6 para 1(4).

[117]   LRA 2002 s 96(3), disapplying Limitation Act 1980 s 95(3).

[118]   LRA 2002 sch 6 para 1(1)–(3); Law Com 271 (2001), EN [684–688].

[119]   See above **[11.18ff]**.

[120]   LRA 2002 sch 6 para 3(2); DLRR 2003 rr 188–189; LR Form NAP; 3 months are allowed.

[121]   LRA 2002 sch 6 para 2; Law Com 271 (2001), [14.32–14.33], EN [689–691]; DLRR 2003 r 186; LR Form ADV2; the entry will be in the proprietorship register.

[122]   LRA 2002 sch 6 para 3; Law Com 271 (2001), EN [692].

[123]   LRA 2002 sch 6 para 2(2), 4; Law Com 271 (2001), [14.34].

Normally, no doubt, the previous proprietor will object to being displaced from the register, and that objection will prevent the squatter being registered, but the burden of taking action is cast on the proprietor, because the squatter will have the right to make a further application to be registered after being in adverse possession[124] without challenge for two years beginning with the date of the rejection of the previous application. Procedure will be laid down in rules,[125] with disputes referred to the Adjudicator.[126] A further application must be accepted, the adverse possessor will be entitled to be registered,[127] taking the title of the dispossessed proprietor subject to all existing priorities[128] but free of any registered charge.[129] This last exception arises because the proprietor of a charge receives notice of the application to register the adverse possessor and can object if he wishes to do so.[130]

4. Application for registration

[11.31] The application for registration[131] must be accompanied by a statutory declaration giving evidence of adverse possession for not less than 10 years before the application and confirmation of the various facts needed to identify special cases,[132] for example if the estate is subject to a trust it must be stated whether all beneficiaries are interested in possession.

5. Possession proceedings

[11.32] Rules for possession proceedings have been changed to bring them into line with the new rules to determine who is owner of a registered title where it has been subject to adverse possession. Normally a registered proprietor will be able to succeed in an action against a trespasser.[133] Even adverse possession of the land for an unlimited period of time will no longer be a valid defence, since the proprietor's title is never extinguished. His right to sue will only cease if he is displaced as proprietor in the exceptional cases where adverse possession operates, or because the adverse possessor has applied for registration and the previous proprietor has not taken any action to displace him for two years. Where a squatter seeks registration and the proprietor responds by suing for and obtaining a judgment for possession, that judgment will be enforceable for two years, but if the proprietor sits on his judgment for two years, the squatter can then claim registration,[134] and has a defence to a claim for possession.[135]

---

[124] Unless the applicant is: (1) being sued as defendant in possession proceedings; (2) has a possession order made against him; or (3) is evicted pursuant to judgment for possession: LRA 2002 sch 6 para 6(2); Law Com 271 (2001), [14.59]. Registration will be possible where proceedings are discontinued or struck out for want of prosecution.

[125] LRA 2002 sch 6 para 15; DLRR 2003 rr 186–189.

[126] LRA 2002 ss 73, 108(1)(a); Law Com 271 (2001), EN [694].

[127] LRA 2002 sch 6 para 7.

[128] Law Com 271 (2001), EN [712].

[129] LRA 2002 sch 6 para 9; Law Com 271 (2001), [14.74], EN [713–716].

[130] At present the whole mortgage must be redeemed: *Carroll* v. *Manek* (2000) 79 P & CR 173, Ch D.

[131] LRA 2002 sch 6; DLRR 2003 r 187; LR Form ADV1.

[132] LRA 2002 sch 6 paras 1(2), 1(3), 5, 6 (a second application after adverse possession for 2 additional years), 8.

[133] Subject to the exceptions set out above, **[11.18ff]**.

[134] LRA 2002 s 98(2), sch 6 para 1; also s 99(3)–(4), sch 6 para 6; DLRR 2003 r 187; LR Form ADV1.

[135] LRA 2002 s 97(5); Law Com 271 (2001), [14.25], [14.82].

6. Rentcharges – new scheme

[11.33] Title to a rentcharge which is substantively registered will be subject to a modified form of the new (non) limitation scheme[136] subject to transitional provisions.[137]

G. ALTERATION OF THE REGISTER

1. Basic concepts

[11.34] The introduction of the register creates complexities lacking from the innocent world of unregistered land. Suppose land held by A is ripped off by X and sold to B. If title is unregistered the two innocent victims, A and B, must engage in a priority battle, from which one emerges the victor and the other is vanquished, left to a useless action against the fraudster. It is all or nothing. Introduce a register and the picture changes. Two people may end up with rights to the land that appear equally legitimate. For example A may be displaced from the register without his knowledge and the land sold to B, who has relied on the register and done everything right so it would appear that his title is correct on registration principles. The contest between A and B may be seen as a priority clash or it might now be seen that X's registration was an error created by his fraud leaving the registry to sort out the consequences of that error for the two innocent victims, A and B.

The basic concept is alteration of the register, the possibility of changing the register to correct a mistake. Where this prejudices the title of a proprietor it is described as rectification. Qualified indefeasibility is the principle that there is a presumption against rectification of a register to remove a proprietor in possession of the land. Indemnity is the way of compensating an innocent victim who suffers form reliance on the register. Protection against rectification and the indemnity rights are removed by certain types of fault.

2. Reform

[11.35] The Land Registration Act 2002[138] recasts a subject once horrendously complex and vague into a form that is concise, relatively simply, and reasonably transparent.[139] Yet it creates uncharted territory, not at all easy to relate to what has gone before. Coherence has been lost by separating the provisions about alterations to the register from the re-enactment of the 1997 scheme for indemnity, when these are two sides of a single coin.[140]

---

[136] LRA 2002 s 96(2)–(3), 98(7), sch 6 para 14; Law Com 271 (2001), EN [727]; DLRR 2003 rr 190–192; DLRR CD ch 11, [21–27].

[137] LRA 2002 sch 12 para 18.

[138] LRA 2002 s 65, sch 4. P Sparkes *NLL* (1st ed) ch 26, set out the old law in a form similar to its recasting, reading "Pure Alterations" for my headings "Technical Rectification" and "Prejudicial Rectification" for "Discretionary Rectification".

[139] Law Com 271 (2001), [10.1], EN [628].

[140] Law Com 271 (2001), [10.3].

3. 2002 Act terminology

[11.36] Most changes to the register result from an application. Alteration is a new term[141] used to describe any abnormal change in the register which did not proceed from an application.[142] Some changes that ought to have occurred as a result of an application may be made by way of alteration of the register. Suppose that the land appears to be held on trust for a contributor, but the claim is litigated and it is decided that no constructive trust interest exists, the restriction now needs to be removed from the register to give effect to the court judgment – by alteration if there is no application. However, most often, alteration will occur to correct a mistake in the register, where correct entries have not been made on registration principles.

Rectification becomes a subset of the wider class of alterations, the term now being reserved for any alteration which (1) involves the correction of a mistake which (2) prejudices the title of a registered proprietor.[143] Confusion is inevitable, so this book uses three terms (1) alterations, (2) prejudicial rectification, and (3) non-prejudicial or pure alteration – a category previously unnamed.

H. PURE ALTERATIONS

[11.37] A "pure alteration" does no injury is done to the title of the proprietor, so special protection for proprietors is redundant. No indemnity is required since no loss is suffered,[144] though there is a new power to pay costs.[145] Once a case for a pure alteration is made out it should be made with little scope for discretion. All this gives formal expression to the practice which has emerged over the years. Pure alterations fall into four main categories.

1. Non-prejudicial errors

[11.38] The registry will continue to correct many obvious errors where no prejudice occurs to any party or where all parties consent.[146] So-called "slips"[147] could include errors in either a document or in the register, as well as minor changes like changes of name after marriage, updating the name of a lender after a corporate restructuring, new street names, minor changes to plans, and so forth. Alteration now go beyond these slips to include correction of a substantive mistake which has no effect on priorities.

---

[141] Older cases refer to this as "rectification".

[142] Including for the first time a cautions register: LRA 2002 ss 20–21; DLRR 2003 rr 45–46; Law Com 271 (2001), [10.26].

[143] LRA 2002 sch 4 para 1.

[144] *Re Chowood's Registered Land* [1933] Ch 574; *Re Boyle's Claim* [1961] 1 WLR 339, Wilberforce J.

[145] See below **[11.56]**.

[146] DLRR 2003 r 128; Law Com 271 (2001), [10.27–10.28].

[147] LRA 2002 sch 10 para 6(e); DLRR 2003 r 128.

2. Updating to give effect to existing priority

[11.39] The register should be altered to give effect to a decision based on registration principles about the priority of rights affecting the land. This is non prejudicial, since the decision merely reflects existing entitlement and the prejudice has already occurred with the loss of priority.[148] If a transfer leading to registration of the proprietor is rectified, that rectification of the document will be followed automatically by a decision to rectify the register.[149] Further examples involve priority disputes between mortgage-lenders,[150] decisions about the existence of a cautionable interest,[151] the effect of non-registration of a land charge,[152] the enforceability of restrictive covenants,[153] the endurability of interests,[154] the need for a restriction to reflect a trust interest created informally,[155] and questions of capacity.[156]

Rectification was allowed where "any entry in register has been obtained by fraud", meaning fraud on the registration process itself.[157] The modern tendency is to see problems arising from forgeries or voidable conveyances as raising a question of priority. Registered land law is the same as unregistered. A forged transfer can be upset and no rights acquired under it, even by an innocent buyer – though an innocent victim will be able to obtain an indemnity.[158] A voidable transfer passes title but it can be set aside because of some misconduct practised by the recipient on the person making the transfer, such as fraudulent misrepresentation.[159] There is a simple priority issue with the title vulnerable to technical rectification[160] unless and until it reaches the hands of a protected purchaser.[161] Occupation by the true owner prevents a purchaser securing protection.[162]

---

[148] This is a non-prejudicial alteration: Law Com 271 (2001), [10.1]. Old law: LRA 1925 s 82(1)(a)–(b); *Chowood* v. *Lyall (No 2)* [1930] 2 Ch 156, 165, Hanworth MR; *Norwich & Peterborough BS* v. *Steed* 1993] Ch 116, 132H, 133A–C, Scott LJ; *Kingsalton* v. *Thames Water Developments* [2001] EWCA Civ 20, [2002] 1 P & CR 15 at 184 (declaration of location of boundary).

[149] *Blacklocks* v. *JB Developments (Godalming)* [1982] Ch 183; *Holow (470)* v. *Stockton Estates* (2001) 81 P & CR 404, Ch D.

[150] *Orakpo* v. *Manson Investment* [1977] 1 WLR 347, 361H, Buckley LJ; *Mortgage Corp* v. *Nationwide Credit Corp* [1994] Ch 49, CA.

[151] *Calgary & Edmonton Land Co* v. *Discount Bank (Overseas)* [1971] 1 WLR 81, 84G, Brightman J; and many others.

[152] *Horrill* v. *Cooper* (1999) 78 P & CR 336, Ch D (first register corrected to include restrictive covenant omitted on first registration as a result of erroneous search).

[153] *Re Sunnyfield* [1932] 1 Ch 79; *Freer* v. *Unwins* [1976] Ch 288.

[154] *Peffer* v. *Rigg* [1977] 1 WLR 285, Graham J.

[155] *Noble* v. *Ferdinand* [1992] CLYB 564.

[156] *Hounslow LBC* v. *Hare* (1992) 24 HLR 9, 23, Knox J.

[157] Old law: LRA 1925 s 82(1)(d); *Norwich & Peterborough BS* v. *Steed* [1993] Ch 116, 134B–F, Scott LJ; *Buckinghamshire CC* v. *Briar* [2002] EWHC 2821 (Ch), [2002] December 20th, [143–150], Lawrence Collins J.

[158] *Norwich & Peterborough BS* v. *Steed* [1993] Ch 116, Scott V-C.

[159] *Collings* v. *Lee* [2001] 2 All ER 332, CA.

[160] *Re Leighton's Conveyance* [1937] Ch 149, CA; *Kemmis* v. *Kemmis* [1988] 1 WLR 1307, CA; *Norwich & Peterborough BS* v. *Steed* [1993] Ch 116, CA (proprietors removed).

[161] *Norwich & Peterborough BS* v. *Steed* [1993] Ch 116, CA (lenders protected).

[162] *Malory Enterprises* v. *Cheshire Homes (UK)* [2002] EWCA Civ 151, [2002] Ch 216.

3.   Bringing on rights excepted from the effect of registration

[11.40] Where title is possessory or qualified,[163] the registry guarantee does not extend to the pre-registration title and alteration of the register to reflect rights off the register will follow as a matter of course.

Much more common will be an updating of the register designed to implement an overriding interest. All registered titles are subject to overriding interests existing at first registration[164] or of a subsequent sale.[165] The register should be corrected to take account of them when they become known, the alteration being non-prejudicial and automatic.[166] Pre-2002 Act adverse possessors are considered elsewhere.[167] Actual occupiers override the register, so as between two innocent victims of double conveyancing possession occupation likely to be decisive, and indeed more generally in boundary disputes.[168]

4.   Removal of surplus entries

[11.41] Where an interest protected on the register ceases to exist, the court can order that the register be brought up to date[169] but in the majority of cases it will fall to the registrar[170] to tidy up the register by removal of the spent entry. Official examples are when a freezing order is no longer needed in litigation, where a lease has been forfeited, when an entry has been superseded by another form of entry, or when a restriction has blown itself out.[171] This laundry function will increase as electronic conveyancing develops.[172]

5.   Pure alterations and derivative interests

[11.42] Alterations make the register reflect the true position for the future and, it seems, that a non-prejudicial alteration might also be retrospective.[173]

---

[163] Law Com 271 (2001), [10.10]; although these are no longer "overriding" the practical effect is exactly the same.

[164] LRA 2002 sch 1.

[165] LRA 2002 sch 3; previously LRA 1925 s 70(1).

[166] Previously this was almost automatic: *Chowood* v. *Lyall (No 2)* [1930] 2 Ch 426, 156, 159; *Bridges* v. *Mees* [1957] 1 Ch 475, 486; *Epps* v. *Esso Petroleum Co* [1973] 1 WLR 1071, 1078E, Templeman J; Law Com 271 (2001), [10.15].

[167] See above **[11.13]**.

[168] *Blacklocks* v. *JB Developments (Godalming)* [1982] Ch 183; *Epps* v. *Esso Petroleum Co* [1973] 1 WLR 1071, Templeman J; *Nurdin & Peacock* v. *DB Ramsden & Co* [1991] 1 WLR 1249, Neuberger J; *Malory Enterprises* v. *Cheshire Homes (UK)* [2002] EWCA Civ 151, [2002] Ch 216.

[169] LRA 2002 sch 4 para 2(1)(b).

[170] LRA 2002 sch 4 para 5.

[171] Law Com 271 (2001), [10.19].

[172] Law Com 271 (2001), [10.20].

[173] LRA 2002 sch 4 para 8; contrast a prejudicial rectification below at **[11.44]**.

6. Court order

[11.43] The decision for or against (old style technical) rectification developed into an almost automatic response[174] to the decision for or against the validity of the property right before the court or registrar. There is now a duty to make an alteration (other than a rectification) when the ground for it is discovered, unless the circumstances are exceptional.[175]

I. RECTIFICATION (PREJUDICIAL ALTERATION)

1. Rectification

[11.44] Rectification is an alteration of the register made (1) to correct a mistake,[176] in circumstances (2) where the alteration prejudices the title of a registered proprietor.[177] Powers of rectification are exercisable by the court,[178] or by the registrar.[179]

Two claimants compete. One is the proprietor of a registered freehold, a registered leasehold, a registered charge, or a right benefiting a registered title.[180] Qualified indefeasibility is the principle which ensures that the proprietor will not normally be stripped of title. To the victor the land while to loser the possibility of an indemnity if he is not at fault. Since rectification is by definition prejudicial, the land registry guarantee may need to be invoked. Loss by rectification should coincide with entitlement to indemnity. [181]

Discretionary rectification involves a deprivation of the loser's title, but the old law was human rights complaint,[182] and so presumably is the new.

2. Examples of discretionary rectification old law

[11.45] Rectification is confined to the correction of errors – where the current state of the register does not correctly reflect registration principles. This applies to slips that go beyond the trivial so as to prejudice existing registered estates.[183] It also covers a series of errors no longer enumerated in the legislation – where two parties have been

---

[174] *Hodges* v. *Jones* [1935] Ch 657, 671, Luxmoore J; *Norwich & Peterborough BS* v. *Steed* [1993] Ch 116, 138E–139A. But see *Kingsalton* v. *Thames Water Developments* [2001] EWCA Civ 20, [2002] 1 P & CR 15 at 184 (so far as it relates to LRA 1925 s 82(1)(a)); criticised for this reason by Law Com 271 (2001), [10.1].

[175] DLRR 2003 rr 125–126. There is an appeal to the adjudicator: LRA 2002 ss 73, 108; Law Com 271 (2001), [10.21].

[176] This does not include either rights acquired since registration or cases where the register was correct but has become incorrect.

[177] LRA 2002 sch 4 para 1; Law Com 271 (2001), [10.6]. This use of "rectification" is narrower than under the existing law, a point to be borne in mind in reading earlier cases.

[178] LRA 2002 sch 4 para 3.

[179] LRA 2002 sch 4 para 6; DLRR 2003 rr 126–127; there is an appeal to the adjudicator at least where alteration occurs after an application: LRA 2002 ss 73, 108.

[180] LRA 2002 sch 4 paras 3(4), 6(4).

[181] Law Com 271 (2001), [10.3], [10.7(2)].

[182] *Kingsalton* v. *Thames Water Developments* [2001] EWCA Civ 20, [2002] 1 P & CR 15 at 184, [30–32], Peter Gibson LJ.

[183] DLRR 2003 r 128. Old law: LRR 1925 r 14; *Chowood* v. *Lyall (No 2)* [1930] 1 Ch 426, 438–439.

registered in respect of the same land, where lender and proprietor have been transposed, or where registration has occurred in the name of a person who should not be the estate owner.[184] Most cases of new-style rectification would formerly have been dealt with under the sweeper up provision which allowed rectification in any case of "error or omission in the register" or "any entry made under a mistake".[185] The most likely causes are innocent errors, double conveyancing,[186] erroneous first registration,[187] or an incapacity.[188]

3. Retrospectivity

[11.46] Rectification should not alter pre-existing priorities, but there is power to change the priority of derivative interests from the date of rectification for the future.[189] This restates what appeared to be the old law.[190]

4. Rectification where proprietor out of possession

[11.47] When a dispute about a property right is taken to court, the court makes a substantive decision about the dispute, for example it may grant a declaration that a particular disputed document does indeed create a lease. As a result the register needs to be altered and so the court will order an alteration of the register.[191] Where a ground is discovered the courts must make an order for rectification unless exceptional circumstances justify the decisions not to do so.[192]

Other reported cases concern mortgage lenders (apparently unprotected by the borrower's occupation),[193] forged mortgages,[194] and voidable mortgages.[195] No doubt the equities favour the innocent lender, though money charges could often be satisfied by an indemnity.[196] Delay in seeking rectification may be prejudicial as it was before.[197]

---

[184] LRA 1925 s 82(1)(g); *Steed* [1993] Ch 116, 134G–135A, Scott LJ; *Batt* v. *Adams* [2001] 2 EGLR 92, Laddie J; *Kingsalton* v. *Thames Water Developments* [2001] EWCA Civ 20, [2002] 1 P & CR 15 at 184.

[185] LRA 1925 s 70(1)(h); *Norwich & Peterborough BS* v. *Steed* [1993] Ch 116, 135D–G, Scott LJ.

[186] *Epps* v. *Esso Petroleum Co* [1973] 1 WLR 1071, 1078G, Templeman J; *Re 139 High Street, Deptford* [1951] Ch 884, 888, Wynn Parry J.

[187] *Chowood* v. *Lyall (No 2)* [1930] 2 Ch 156, 168, Lawrence LJ.

[188] *Hounslow LBC* v. *Hare* (1992) 24 HLR 9, 23, Knox J.

[189] LRA 2002 sch 4 para 8; Law Com 271 (2001), [10.8].

[190] LRA 1925 s 82(2); Law Com 271 (2001), [10.8]; *Freer* v. *Unwins* [1976] Ch 288, 296–299, Walton J; *Clark* v. *Chief Land Registrar* [1993] Ch 294, Ferris J; *Clark* [1994] Ch 370, 378, 385; *Malory Enterprises* v. *Cheshire Homes (UK)* [2002] EWCA Civ 151, [2002] Ch 216, [71–84], Arden LJ; Clarke and Schiemann LJJ reserved the point.

[191] LRA 2002 sch 4 para 7.

[192] LRA 2002 sch 4 paras 3, 4, 6; this codifies the old law in LRA 1925 s 82(3); Law Com 271 (2001), [10.1].

[193] *Argyle BS* v. *Hammond* (1985) 49 P & CR 148, CA; A Sydenham [1985] *Conv* 135; *Kemmis* v. *Kemmis* [1988] 1 WLR 1307, CA.

[194] *Hammond* again.

[195] *Norwich & Peterborough BS* v. *Steed* [1993] Ch 116, 138E–139A.

[196] At 136G–138C, Scott LJ.

[197] *Claridge* v. *Tingey* [1967] 1 WLR 134, Pennycuick J; TBF Ruoff (1969) 32 *MLR* 121.

5. Qualified indefeasibility

(1) The jurisdiction

[11.48] A registered proprietor is guaranteed against changes to the register, to the extent that he is innocent of wrongdoing. This is a vital buttress for the registration curtain.[198] Non-prejudicial alteration can occur in two cases:

A. where the alteration is non-prejudicial eg to give effect to an overriding interest[199]; or

B. where the proprietor consents.

Rectification can occur to the prejudice of a proprietor's title in two further cases, where:

C. the proprietor has caused or substantially contributed to the mistake by fraud or lack of proper care;[200] or

D. it would be unjust not to make the alteration.

A rectification should normally be made but rule (D) retains the overriding discretion.

(2) Who is protected?

[11.49] Protection is available to a proprietor or person entitled to registration, but not to a 2002 Act squatter.[201]

(3) What is possession?

[11.50] The requirement is that the land should be in the possession of the proprietor.[202] Occupation is sufficient, and will usually give priority anyway via an overriding interest. One dispute about rectification of title to a development plot in Fallowfield, Manchester, was resolved when it was found that the proprietor was in occupation by fencing the land, boarding up the windows of a broken down building on the land and that this had been used for storage. Presence was what put a person inspecting the land on notice that someone was in occupation.[203] However, it is now clear beyond peradventure that the crucial requirement is possession and that this is much wider than occupation. In any event occupation by one party may be transferred notionally to another in certain circumstances. If a tenant is in occupation his

---

[198] LRA 2002 sch 4 paras 2, 6; this reflects: LRA 1925 s 82(3); Law Com 271 (2001), [10.13].

[199] See above at **[11.39]**.

[200] See below at **[11.57]**.

[201] LRA 2002 s 131; Law Com 271 (2001), EN [559–562]; An adverse possessor whose title vested before the 2002 Act would be entitled. Old law: S Cretney & G Dworkin (1968) 84 *LQR* 528, 539–540; Ruoff & Roper, (6th ed) [40–10].

[202] LRA 2002 s 131; this is rather narrower than LRA 1925 s 82(4); *Bridges* v. *Mees* [1957] Ch 475, Harman J.

[203] *Malory Enterprises* v. *Cheshire Homes (UK)* [2002] EWCA Civ 151, [2002] Ch 216, [10–40], Arden LJ.

landlord is protected as a possessor,[204] and the same applies to a lender who has taken possession from his borrower, and protection can also be claimed by a licensor via his licensee and a trustee via his beneficiary. Presumably possession is transferred up a chain from a sub tenant to his head landlord.[205]

(4) Protection of a possessor

[11.51] A person in occupation of the land should be entitled to the land itself and should not be required to settle for compensation for its loss. Physical occupation of the disputed land is generally decisive of double conveyancing and boundary disputes.[206] A very pure illustration is provided by *Kingsalton* v. *Thames Water Developments*.[207] The judge decided a boundary dispute in favour of Kingsalton, but the Court of Appeal refused to upset the title of Thames Water who were both registered as proprietors and in possession of the disputed strip.

(5) Cases where a possessor may lose title

[11.52] A proprietor in possession may lose his land through rectification if it would be unjust not to make the alteration.[208] The effect is to reverse the burden of proof and throw the onus for justifying rectification on to the claimant. An innocent mistake should be ignored for these purposes.[209] Factors are the length of undisturbed possession, need for the land and expenditure on it, and the indemnity position.[210]

J. INDEMNITY

1. The shape of the law

[11.53] Rectification and indemnity are complementary remedies.[211] The rectification issue needs to be decided first. The loser suffers loss, and if free of fault[212] should obtain an indemnity. Compensation rights were improved in 1997,[213] and this amended scheme is now re-enacted without further substantive changes.[214]

---

[204] But not if he has the right to rents but no actual receipt: contrast LRA 1925 s 3(xviii); *Freer* v. *Unwins* [1976] Ch 288, 294, Walton J. Query the position where rent is paid to a beneficiary under a trust as in *UCB Group* v. *Hedworth* [2002] EWCA Civ 708, [2002] 46 EG 200; see above at **[15.47]**.

[205] Law Com 271 (2001), [10.17ff].

[206] *Re 139 High Street, Deptford* [1951] Ch 884, Wynn Parry J (Dobkins a trespasser of only four weeks' standing!); TBF Ruoff (1954) 18 *Conv (NS)* 130.

[207] [2001] EWCA Civ 20, [2002] 1 P & CR 15 at 184, [22–34], Peter Gibson LJ; *Epps* v. *Esso Petroleum Co* [1973] 1 WLR 1071, Templeman J; S Palk [1974] *CLJ* 60; *Chowood* v. *Lyall (No 2)* [1930] 2 Ch 156, 167, Lawrence LJ, overruling [1930] 1 Ch 426, 438, Luxmoore J.

[208] LRA 2002 sch 4 para 3(2)(b); S Cretney & G Dworkin (1968) 84 *LQR* 528, 540–545.

[209] See below **[11.57]**.

[210] *Re 139 High Street, Deptford* [1951] Ch 884, Wynn Parry J; *Epps* v. *Esso Petroleum Co* [1973] 1 WLR 1071, 1080–1083 Templeman J; *Hounslow LBC* v. *Hare* (1992) 24 HLR 9, 23, Knox J.

[211] *Freer* v. *Unwins* [1976] Ch 288, 295H, Walton J; S Cretney and G Dworkin (1968) 84 *LQR* 528, 528.

[212] See below **[11.57]**.

[213] LRA 1925 s 83; LRA 1997 s 2; Law Com 235 (1995); JE Adams [1997] *Conv* 180; HW Wilkinson [1997] *NLJ* 925.

[214] LRA 2002 s 103, sch 8; Law Com 271 (2001) [10.4], [10.29–10.52], EN [470], EN [729–757]. Sch 8 applies to all claims begun on or after April 17th 1997: sch 12 para 19.

2. Matters for which an indemnity is available

[11.54] A person is entitled to be indemnified for loss arising out of:

rectification of the register;
removal of title from an innocent victim of a forgery;[215]
loss remaining after rectification of the register;[216]
refusal to correct a mistake;[217]
a mistake in an official search,[218] or copy document;
loss of a document lodged at the registry;
a mistake in the cautions register;
failure to notify an overriding statutory charge;[219]
upgrading of a title; or
loss of mines and mineral rights expressly included.[220]

3. Statistics

[11.55] Indemnity claims are surprisingly low in number compared to the volume of business transacted at the land registry. Few claims arise from forgery and fraud, though those that do can be expensive. Numerically the largest number of claims are from the delivery of land registry services, errors in register entries, mapping, and boundaries. A substantial number of claims arise from administrative errors, such as loss of documents, mistakes in searches or inaccurate office copies. The low level of claims might be thought to show the benefits of land registration, but it is closer to the mark to say that the rules are so restrictive that many genuine claims go uncompensated.

4. Insurance principles

[11.56] A claim for indemnity must be brought promptly since the right to it will be lost after a limitation period of six years from the time that the claimant knows, or ought to have known, of his claim.[221]

Quantification rules are potentially unfair. After rectification, indemnity is allowed to the full value of the estate or interest then lost. If rectification is refused, the amount recoverable is artificially restricted to the value of the interest at the time of the error.[222] Interest[223] is added at the rate set for court judgment debts.[224]

---

[215] LRA 2002 sch 8 para 1(2).

[216] Old Law: LRA 1925 s 83(1)(b); *Freer* v. *Unwins* [1976] Ch 288, 298H, Walton J.

[217] Old law: *Clark* v. *Chief Land Registrar* [1994] Ch 370, CA.

[218] Index map search: *Prestige Properties* v. *Scottish Provident Institution* [2002] EWHC 330, [2003] Ch 1, Lightman J.

[219] LRA 2002 s 50.

[220] LRA 2002 sch 8 para 2.

[221] LRA 2002 sch 8 para 8; Law Com 271 (2001), EN [700–701].

[222] LRA 2002 sch 8 para 6; Law Com 271 (2001), EN [746–748]; *Epps* v. *Esso Petroleum Co* [1973] 1 WLR 1071, 1081F–G, Templeman J (claim in 1973 limited to the 1959 value under old law). Contrast land charges where compensation is fixed as at the date of the compensation hearing: *Smith* v. *South Gloucestershire* C [2002] EWCA Civ 1131, [2002] 38 EG 206.

[223] Law Com 235 (1995), [4.7] (but price inflation need not be linear).

[224] LRA 2002 sch 8 para 9; Law Com 271 (2001), EN [752–753]; DLRR 2003 r 193.

If the registrar pays an indemnity he has subrogation rights against any causing the loss.[225]

Costs may be paid either as determined by a court,[226] or those incurred in a claim even if no substantive indemnity is paid.[227] Approval to incur costs should be obtained from the registrar, but other costs are covered in cases of urgency or where securing his consent not practicable.[228]

5. Fault

[11.57] Penalties attach to a person who secures registration but is at fault, either through fraud[229] or lack of proper care.[230] Rectification is likely to occur against such a person,[231] and without any indemnity. Compensation is denied to a claimant (1) wholly or partly responsible for the loss[232] by his own fraud or (2) wholly responsible though his lack of proper care.[233] Part responsibility results in a reduction of indemnity according to the principle of contributory negligence.[234]

Negligence or fraud of a predecessor from whom the claimant derives title is also considered if the current owner derives title by way of gift but a sale for value clears the stain of the earlier misconduct.

The innocent[235] will not usually lose their land if in possession, even if they unwittingly cause or contribute to a mistake,[236] and if they do they will be entitled to an indemnity.[237] As a result of the convoluted legislative history,[238] earlier cases[239] need to be handled with great care.

K. COVENANTS FOR TITLE

[11.58] When a buyer of land loses a priority argument he will be bound by the adverse interest but will often be able to claim damages from the person who sold

---

[225] LRA 2002 sch 8 para 10.

[226] LRA 2002 sch 8 para 7.

[227] LRA 2002 sch 8 para 4.

[228] LRA 2002 sch 4 para 9.

[229] Examples from the old case law: *Re Beaney* [1978] 1 WLR 770 (daughter ripped off house of mother suffering from senile dementia); *Peffer* v. *Rigg* [1977] 1 WLR 285; DJ Hayton [1977] *CLJ* 227; FR Crane (1977) 41 *Conv (NS)* 210, 354; *Norwich & Peterborough BS* v. *Steed* [1993] Ch 116, 134B–F, Scott LJ.

[230] LRA 2002 sch 8 para 5.

[231] See above at **[11.52]**.

[232] A "but for" test should not be substituted for the statutory test: *Dean* v. *Dean* (2000) 80 P & CR 457, CA.

[233] *Claridge* v. *Tingey* [1967] 1 WLR 134, Pennycuick J (failure to endorse a memorandum of a sale-off on the unregistered title deeds); *Racoon* v. *Turnbull* [1997] AC 158, PC (duty to inspect title of neighbouring land burdened by right of way).

[234] LRA 2002 sch 8 para 5(2); Law Com 235 (1995), [4.5]; *Prestige Properties* v. *Scottish Provident Institution* [2002] EWHC 330, [2003] Ch 1, Lightman J.

[235] Ie (1) those totally innocent, and (2) those partly negligent, but only to the extent they are innocent.

[236] See above **[11.48]**.

[237] *Hounslow LBC* v. *Hare* (1992) 24 HLR 9, 24–25, Knox J.

[238] S Cretney & G Dworkin (1968) 84 *LQR* 528; P Sparkes *NLL* (1st ed), 716.

[239] *Chowood* v. *Lyall (No 2)* [1930] 1 Ch 426 Luxmoore J; *Chowood* on appeal [1930] 2 Ch 156, 167, CA; *Sheffield Corp* v. *Barclay* [1905] AC 392; *Att-Gen* v. *Odell* [1906] 2 Ch 47; *Re 139 High Street, Deptford* [1951] Ch 884; *Claridge* v. *Tingey* [1967] 1 WLR 134, Pennycuick J.

him the land or one of the previous owners under the long stop of a covenant for title.[240]

1. Statutory schemes

[11.59] Under the medieval system of conveyancing, a seller gave a warranty that his title was valid, so that a buyer who was dispossessed had an action for damages.[241] These turned into covenants for title, implied by statute since 1881. The original form[242] was replaced by part I of the Law of Property (Miscellaneous Provisions) Act 1994.[243] Use of the new trigger words after mid 1995[244] implements the new scheme, possibly increasing the guarantee contracted for under an old contract.

2. Trigger words

[11.60] Covenants are implied into a document transferring or disposing of land (whether a sale or gift) according to the trigger words it contains[245] – either "with full title guarantee"[246] or "with limited title guarantee."[247]

3. Registered titles

[11.61] Covenants for title have a limited role when title is registered, since the registered title is virtually conclusive, innocent victims rarely suffer rectification, and anyway receive an indemnity. The land registry may be able to pursue a claim for reimbursement. Transfer forms now include the statutory trigger words of the 1994 Act.[248] They should not be included in the register.[249]

Covenants for title give no rights in relation to matters entered on the register and known overriding interests.[250] The scope is undisclosed overriding interests of which the buyer does not know,[251] as well as boundary errors where the title is not guaranteed and miscellaneous omissions from the register, or any error reducing the class of title registered.[252] If land is included in a transfer when the seller had no title to it, there will be an action on the covenants for title.[253]

---

[240] *Hodgson* v. *Marks* [1971] Ch. 892, 932B, Russell LJ.

[241] AWB Simpson, *A History of the Land Law* (Clarendon, 2nd ed, 1986) 52–53, 126–137.

[242] LPA 1925 s 76(1), sch 2. There have been few C20th cases: RJ Smith (1986) 39 *CLP* 111, 117.

[243] Ss 1–13; Megarry & Wade (6th ed), [6.102–6.104].

[244] For transitional provisions see P Sparkes *NLL* (1st ed), 719.

[245] S 1(1), as defined by s 1(4).

[246] S 1(2)(a). This replaces the old "beneficial owner" covenants; *Harwood* v. *Harwood* [1991] 2 FLR 274, 286B–G, Slade LJ obiter.

[247] LP (MP) A 1994 s 1(2)(b). LPA 1925 s 76 used "as trustees", "as mortgagee", "as personal representative", or "under court order".

[248] LP (MP) A 1994 s 2(1)(b); LR Form TR1; LRA 2002 sch 10 para 2; DLRR 2003 r 68; D Partington [1989] *Conv* 18.

[249] DLRR 2003 r 68(6)–(7).

[250] DLRR 2003 r 68(3)(b), (4).

[251] *Hissett* v. *Reading Roofing Co* [1969] 1 WLR 1757; MJ Russell [1982] *Conv* 145; TBF Ruoff (1969) 32 *MLR* 121, 139.

[252] LP (MP) A 1994 s 2(2)(a).

[253] *AJ Dunning & Sons (Shopfitters)* v. *Sykes & Sons (Poole)* [1987] Ch 287, CA; *Watts* v. *Waller* [1973] 1 QB 153, 171, Orr J.

4. Guarantee of title

[11.62] The interest transferred should be the registered title or an unregistered title acceptable for registration, which is either freehold or for the unexpired portion of a leasehold estate.[254] Both full and limited title guarantees imply two covenants about the estate. Right to dispose implies just that: the person making the transfer or disposition has the right to dispose of the property. The limitation period continues to be 12 years from the date of the transfer. Further assurance requires the seller to do all that is reasonable to give the title he purports to, costs being borne by the seller, an assurance that can be enforced for 12 years after the demand.[255]

5. Guarantee against burdens

[11.63] Title guarantees also extend to burdens[256] not mentioned in the transfer or known to the buyer. The seller is not liable for rights about which he could not reasonably be expected to know. The guarantee extends to monetary charges, adverse easements, and statutory rights, but excluding potential statutory liabilities and those affecting all property generally.

The full guarantee against incumbrances provides an indemnity against all burdens[257] whenever created. A personal guarantee extends to defects created by any past owner.[258] The first port of call is therefore the immediate seller.[259]

Limited title guarantee covers only burdens created since the last sale of the land. It is a covenant that the person selling or giving the land has not charged or incumbered it personally, or suffered it to be burdened, and that he is not aware that anyone else has done so.[260] Trustees and others with limited capacities should covenant in this limited way.

---

[254] LP (MP) A 1994 s 2.

[255] *Jones* v. *King* (1818) 4 M & S 188, 105 ER 804.

[256] LP (MP) A 1994 s 6(1).

[257] S 3(1).

[258] *Nottidge* v. *Dering* [1909] Ch 647, affirmed [1910] 1 Ch 247; *Spoor* v. *Green* (1874) LR 9 Ex 99, 111, Bramwell B.

[259] The benefit runs with the land: LP (MP) A 1994 s 7.

[260] S 3(3).

12

TRUSTEESHIP/LEGAL CO-OWNERSHIP

Trusts. Joint legal ownership. Collective powers. Trustees. Survivorship.
Co-proprietors of registered land.

A. TRUSTS

1. A simple picture

[12.01] Let us start with a simple picture, even if revisualisation will be needed as detail accumulates. A trust is a device by which the legal title to property is separated from beneficial entitlement. Legal title confers management control on the trustees – the power to sell and make title and the right to decide whether and when to sell. The equitable interests of the beneficiaries include the right to occupy the land, the right to take income, and the right to capital. Thus:

Figure 12-1 A simple trust

Although these parties need to be separated for purposes of analysis they often over-lap as in the most common form of trust:

to H and W as joint tenants on trust for H and W as beneficial joint tenants.

In diagrammatic form this trust can be illustrated thus:

Figure 12-2 A co-owned matrimonial home

Trusts are divided in this book into their two constituent elements. Trusteeship is considered in this and the succeeding three chapters. After that there follow four further chapters on beneficial entitlement.[1]

2. Law and equity fused

[12.02] Two systems of law exist today because there were two sets of courts until 1875. Common law actions such as trespass and debt were heard in Queen's Bench, Common Pleas, and Exchequer. Long before, even before the end of the medieval period, the common law had already became rigid and unjust as it had failed to evolve new writs to match changes in society. This gave rise to the ability of equity[2] to correct individual injustices, first through a system of informal petitions to the Lord Chancellor, but soon crystallised into a Court of Chancery.[3] There the Lord Chancellor heard actions involving title to land, trusts, and mortgages, and provided superior remedies in the shape of injunctions and specific performance. By the mid 19th century the two systems caused unnecessary duplication of effort. As Dickens wrote in *Bleak House*:

> "Equity sends questions to Law, Law sends questions back to Equity; Law finds it can't do this, Equity finds it can't do that; neither can so much as say it can't do anything, without this solicitor instructing and this counsel appearing . . .".[4]

After long discussion of fusion,[5] the Supreme Court of Judicature Act 1873[6] created the modern Supreme Court. Equity business is assigned to the Chancery Division, but all divisions of the High Court should apply both common law and equitable principles.[7]

Equity's function was to rectify common law injustices. As the *Dialogues between Doctor and Student* recorded in 1523:[8]

> "Equity . . . is an exception . . . from the general rules of the law of man, when they, by reason of their generality would in any particular case judge against the law of God or the law of reason . . .".

From this rationalisation it followed that equitable rules had to prevail over the common law.[9] This settlement was confirmed by a personal judgment of James I[10] and never seriously challenged after Lord Coke left the common law bench. Procedurally

---

[1] See below **[16ff]**.

[2] Cheshire & Burn (16th ed) ch 3; Goo's *Sourcebook* (3rd ed) ch 4; Grays' *Elements* (3rd ed), 77–93; Megarry & Wade (6th ed) ch 4; Panesar's *General Principles*, 60–81; Smith's *Property Law* (4th ed) ch 3; Swadling in Birks' *Private Law*, [4.225–4.325]; Thompson *Modern LL* ch 3.

[3] The first court room had a latticed partition = *cancelli*: HA Holland (1945) 9 *CLJ* 17, 17.

[4] Chapter VIII "Covering a Multitude of Sins".

[5] Holdsworth's *History* vol XII, 583–605; AH Manchester *Modern Legal History of England and Wales 1750–1950* (Butterworths, 1980), 144–156; PBH Birks "Before We Begin: Five Keys to Land Law" ch 18 in Bright & Dewar, 476–482.

[6] 36 & 37 Vict c 66.

[7] Supreme Court Act 1981 s 49(2).

[8] TFT Plucknett & JL Barton (Selden Society, 1974), 94–97.

[9] WN Hohfeld *Fundamental Legal Conceptions* (1964 reprint, Goodwood Press); J Tiley *A Casebook on Equity* (1968), 5.

[10] *Earl of Oxford's Case* (1616) Rep CC App 1, 49, 21 ER 485; Holdsworth's *History* vol 1, 459–465.

equity vindicated its superiority by issuing an order (called a common injunction) threatening imprisonment of suitors in common law courts who refused to submit their judgments to equitable review. Hence the rule that equity acted *in personam*, that is against individuals.[11] The Judicature Act 1873 provided for procedural fusion of the administration of legal and equitable rights in one set of courts without fusing the two systems of law.[12] In the rare cases in which the two systems still had conflicting rules in 1875, the equitable rule will continue to prevail.[13]

3. Evolution of the trust

[12.03] An express trust arises when a legal estate is transferred to a person on the basis that he will hold it as trustee for named beneficiaries.[14] After the trustee has accepted his trust, it would be against conscience for him to live in the house himself or to spend the proceeds after selling it.[15] A trustee who was sued in the common law courts could have done just that, for they saw only the legal estate owner and were blind to the trust. Beneficiaries could only protect their position by going to Chancery: equity followed the common law in recognising the legal estate owner as having management power, but corrected the common law by viewing the beneficiary as owner when deciding about entitlement to occupation or receipt of income. After fusion of the two sets of courts, the same practical results are achieved in modern English law. Management powers and the right to sell are recognised in the trustee because the common law and equity both took that view. A beneficiary's entitlement to actual enjoyment of the property arose from the equitable view taken in contradistinction to the common law rule.[16]

A trust usually[17] divides legal ownership of the property held by the trustee from the equitable or beneficial ownership, apportioning the totality of ownership between the trustees and the beneficiaries. Trusteeship, after 1996, implies all the powers of an absolute owner.[18] Beneficiaries can hold the trustees to account for their management if they fail to carry out their duties properly, or derive a personal profit, or they deny the beneficiaries enjoyment, through occupation[19] or the receipt of income. The traditional balance was shifted more towards the beneficiaries in 1996,[20] giving them stronger rights to be involved in decision making.

---

[11] Maitland's *Equity*, 322.

[12] Supreme Court of Judicature Act 1873 s 24; Supreme Court of Judicature (Consolidation) Act 1925 ss 36–43; Supreme Court Act 1981 s 49(2).

[13] 1873 Act s 25(11); 1925 Act s 44; 1981 Act s 49(1); A Burrows (2002) 22 *OJLS* 1.

[14] Definitions are considered by WG Hart (1899) 15 *LQR* 294.

[15] *Carter* v. *Carter* (1857) 3 K & J 617, 644, 69 ER 1256 Page Wood V-C.

[16] *Joseph* v. *Lyons* (1884) 15 QBD 280, 287, Lindley LJ; Maitland's *Equity*, 19 and Lecture IX.

[17] But not necessarily: *West Deutsche Bank* v. *Islington LBC* [1996] AC 669, 709C, Lord Browne-Wilkinson; Grays' *Elements* (3rd ed), 89; L Smith (2002) 116 *LQR* 412; P Parkinson [2002] *CLJ* 657 (required reading).

[18] TLATA 1996 s 6(1), unless excluded under s 8.

[19] Ss 12, 13.

[20] See below at **[19.02ff]**.

4.   Uses of trusts

[12.04] Succeeding chapters discuss the main uses of trusts:

settlement of land on successive generations;
co-ownership;
management during incapacity; and
giving effect to informal contributions.

5.   Trusts of land

[12.05] Trusts of land ensure that there is a machinery in place which will enable land held in trust to be sold. A universal trust, called a "trust of land", and modelled on a slimmed down version of the trust for sale, applies to all post-1996 trusts and to all pre-1997 trusts other than strict settlements.

The next chapter introduces the concept of overreaching by which the beneficial interests can be removed from the land and satisfied instead from the proceeds of sale, as well as the two trustee receipt rule for purchase money and the use of restrictions on registered title and the curtain which conceals beneficial interests from the gaze of purchasers. The following chapter considers certain specialised trusts used for management of land. Hopefully that the basic trusts of land scheme becomes easier to understand with these refinements filtered out. Where a single individual acts as trustee, under a "one trustee trusts" as we shall call them, the doctrine of notice applies if title is unregistered while actual occupiers of registered land enjoy an "overriding interest".[21]

B.   JOINT LEGAL OWNERSHIP

1.   Legal estates must be held by joint tenancy

[12.06] Joint proprietorship and joint holding of unregistered legal estates must be in the form of a joint tenancy. The legislation uses the term "undivided shares" as a statutory "shorthand" for a tenancy in common,[22] so the prohibition on a legal estate being held in this way[23] ensures that there is always a legal joint tenancy. The legislation also prohibits severance of a legal estate.[24] Two or more persons holding the same legal estate must do so as joint tenants.

---

[21] It is convenient to continue to use the term adopted by LRA 1925 s 70(1)(g) even though it is dropped by LRA 2002 sch 3 para 2 – the correct term now is an interest that overrides the register.

[22] LPA 1925 s 34, as amended by TLATA 1996 sch 2; LPA 1925 s 1(6).

[23] There were four methods of co-ownership before 1926: *Hindmarsh* v. *Quinn* (1914) 17 CLR 622, 630, Barton ACJ. However, the other two cannot affect the legal estate: (1) co-parceny – the co-ownership which existed between two or more female tenants in tail; and (2) tenancy by entireties – an unseverable joint tenancy between husband and wife abolished in 1925.

[24] LPA 1925 s 36(2), as amended in 1996. Severance is the process of converting an existing joint tenancy to a tenancy in common.

2. Abolition of legal tenancies in common

[12.07] Before 1926, legal tenancies in common created such substantial conveyancing difficulties that Sir Arthur Underhill considered them a greater threat to free saleability than settlements.[25] Undivided shares tended to fragment as deaths occurred. Suppose that A and B were legal tenants in common when A died intestate, leaving his 10 children to succeed him. The children now held twentieth shares with B keeping his half share, and all eleven signatures were required on a conveyance of the land. The process of subdivision could be repeated, down to and beyond one-millionth shares.[26] More and more owners held smaller and smaller shares. This increased the difficulty of securing agreement to a sale, of investigation of multiple titles, and in securing execution of a conveyance. Tenancy in common was unfit for those who could not agree between themselves.[27]

Lord Birkenhead's legislation adopted a neat solution. The legal estate in land had to be held by joint tenants,[28] and so, since survivorship occurs on death, the legal title is concentrated in fewer hands. An unfortunate corollary was that beneficial ownership had to be separated from legal ownership, though the scheme is cleaner now that the original trust for sale is replaced by a trust of land. Buyers dealing with the trustees can overreach all the fragments of beneficial interest,[29] guaranteeing saleability at the price of some loss of security for beneficial owners.

3. Co-ownership involves a trust

[12.08] Some 40% of people live alone – the young, the old, the sad, and the ultra-hip – but this still leaves a majority who choose to share a home with a partner. Both traditional forms of co-ownership – joint tenancy and tenancy in common – are allowed to continue but only as beneficial interests behind a trust.[30] A joint tenancy passes automatically to the survivor on death – the arrangement for example that a happy couple would want. A tenancy in common creates shares in the property – equal or unequal – and that share survives the death of the tenant in common. This is the sort of arrangement by which the partners in a firm of solicitors might hold their business offices, and how a family home might be held after the couple's separation. Thus:

to A and B as joint tenants on trust for A and B as beneficial joint tenants;
to T1 and T2 as joint tenants on trust for A and B as beneficial tenants in common.

The trust imposed in the first case seems bizarre but it does secure saleability. The price is a quite unnecessary complexity.

---

[25] A Underhill (1920) 36 *LQR* 107, 116.
[26] Brickdale, cited by S Anderson, *English Lawyers and the Making of English Land Law* (Clarendon Press, 1992), 290; *Cresswell* v. *Hedges* (1862) 1 H & C 421, 158 ER 950 (48/315ths).
[27] *Leigh* v. *Dickeson* (1884) 15 QBD 60, 67, Lindley LJ.
[28] LPA 1925 s 1(6). Transitional provisions: LPA 1925 sch 1; TLATA 1996 sch 2 para 7 (now trusts of land); *Re King's Theatre, Sunderland* [1929] 1 Ch 483; *Re Hind* [1933] Ch 208; *Re Ryder & Steadman's C* [1927] 2 Ch 62; *Re Cook* [1948] Ch 212; *Buehler* v. *Chronos Richardson* [1998] 2 All ER 960, CA.
[29] LPA 1925 ss 34–36, as amended by TLATA 1996.
[30] LPA 1925 ss 34–36 as amended; see below **[16.03]**.

4. Legal and beneficial joint tenancy

[12.09] Most shared homes are held by a couple who hold as joint tenants both at law and in equity – the first of the two limitations immediately above. This case is distinct from a normal trust in one important particular – the survivor will be entitled to sell as an absolute owner.[31] So there is no restriction on the register, a precaution required and compulsory in every other case of joint proprietorship.[32]

5. Identity of the initial trustees

[12.10] A transfer or conveyance to co-owners will vest the land in the named co-owners as joint tenants and as trustees. Thus a conveyance "to A and B in fee simple as tenants in common" will pass the legal estate to A and B as joint tenants as trustees of the land, the beneficial tenancy in common operating behind the trust.[33] On first registration or a transfer, this will lead to the registration of A and B as co-proprietors and – although the register does not deign to say so – they will hold as joint tenants.

Trustees are limited to a maximum of four.[34] A conveyance to more than four people will vest the land in the first four adults named.[35] For example, if unregistered land is conveyed *to A, B, C, D, E and F as tenants in common*, it will vest in A, B, C, and D (assuming all are adult) and the beneficial tenancy of all six of them in common will exist behind a trust of land.[36] On a subsequent death, those left off the legal estate will not come on to the legal estate automatically, but only if a deed of appointment of new trustees is made by the surviving trustees. Trustees may also retire.[37]

6. Majority

[12.11] Like all other legal estate owners, trustees must be adult.[38] Majority is attained in law at 18, and gives the capacity to hold and deal with land. A minor (used in preference to the 1925 insult "an infant") does not have capacity to receive or sell a legal estate in land.[39] Trusts are often used to confer benefits on minors and for management during the minority.

---

[31] Purchasers need to guard against a hidden severance; see below **[16.32ff]**.
[32] See below **[13.36]**.
[33] LPA 1925 s 34, as amended.
[34] TA 1925 s 34(1)–(2); Supreme Court Act 1981 s 114(1).
[35] LPA 1925 s 34(2), as amended.
[36] *Persey* v. *Bazley* (1984) 47 P & CR 37.
[37] TA 1925 s 36; less usual is a release: *Re Schär* [1950] 2 All ER 1069; LPA 1925 s 36(2); or a deed of grant: s 72.
[38] LPA 1925 s 1(6).
[39] LPA 1925 ss 1(6), 19.

C. COLLECTIVE POWERS

1. Preservation of four unities

[12.12] A legal joint tenancy must display the four unities.[40] (1) Unity of possession means that all legal estate owners must share the right to the same physical land. (2) Unity of interest requires all legal estate owners to share the same interest in the land, for example a freehold estate. Legal co-ownership cannot arise between a freeholder and a leaseholder, nor between a legal estate owner and a life tenant. (3) Unity of title requires all estate owners to derive title from the same act or document, that is a transfer, conveyance, registration of title, deed of appointment of trustees or act of seizing adverse possession. Finally, (4) unity of time means that the legal estate must vest in all trustees at the same time.[41] For legal estates the four unities cannot be fractured, since severance to create a legal tenancy in common is not permitted.[42]

2. Collective powers

[12.13] Littleton's Norman French has it that joint tenants hold *"per my et per tout"*.[43] The last two words obviously mean that joint tenants take the whole collectively,[44] holding by one title and one right,[45] in a thorough and intimate union of interest and possession. All must unite together in any act affecting or dependant upon legal estate ownership. Doubt surrounds the phrase *"per my"*. Blackstone read it to mean "half", so that the joint tenant holds by the half and by the whole,[46] that is with unity of possession. A better solution is to read *"my"* as *mie*, meaning nothing,[47] so that the joint tenant holds nothing alone, but the whole collectively.[48] Why bandy about half-understood foreign maxims? Littleton provided an excellent exegesis in English – a joint tenant "is seised of every parcel and by the whole . . . for in every parcel and by every parcel and by all the lands and tenements he is jointly seised with his companion."[49] Lord Coke added a note to the effect that:

> "The essential difference . . . is that joyntenants have the lands by one joint title and in one right, and tenants in common by severall titles, or by one title and by severall rights; . . . joyntenants have one joint freehold."[50]

---

[40] Blackstone's *Commentaries* vol 2, 174.
[41] Contrast beneficial entitlement; see below **[16.18ff]**.
[42] LPA 1925 ss 1(6), 36.
[43] Littleton's *Tenures*, [282].
[44] *Doe d Aslin* v. *Summersett* (1830) 1 B & Ad 135, 140, 109 ER 738, Tenterden CJ; *Leek & Moorlands BS* v. *Clark* [1952] 2 QB 788, CA.
[45] *Pullen* v. *Palmer* (1693) 3 Salk, 207 pl 155, 91 ER 780.
[46] Blackstone's *Commentaries* vol 2, 175, 183; Littleton's *Tenures*, [323]; *Sutton* v. *Robertson* (1564) Dal 60, 123 ER 272; *Pullen* v. *Palmer* (1693) 3 Salk 207, pl 155, 91 ER 780; *Nielson-Jones* v. *Fedden* [1975] Ch 222, 228C–D, Walton J.
[47] Grays' *Elements* (3rd ed), 462 n 14; Megarry & Wade (6th ed), 418 n 8.
[48] Bracton fo 430: *"totum tenet et nihil tenet"* translated in Thornton's edition (vol IV, 336) as: "he holds the whole and holds nothing, that is he holds the whole in common and nothing separately by himself."
[49] Littleton's *Tenures*, [288].
[50] Coke on *Littleton* [186].

So, all joint tenants must act in a disposal.[51] If A, B and C are trustees or personal representatives,[52] a sale by A alone cannot pass legal title – and nor can A and B acting without C.[53] Only the three acting in concert can pass title and overreach. The same rule applies when taking action at common law,[54] to judgments for possession,[55] and actions on joint covenants.[56] However, a helpful act by one joint tenant can be called in aid by all the others.[57] Application of these principles to the termination of periodic leases leads to a surprising result.[58]

3. Unity of possession

[12.14] The collective nature of the joint tenancy can also be characterised as a unity of possession.[59] Where this is lost so part of the land belongs to one person exclusively, the land is held in two separate ownerships and there is said to be a partition.[60]

4. Agency

[12.15] The need for an act by all co-owners cannot be overcome by a power of attorney executed by one in favour of the others. In *Walia* v. *Michael Naughton*[61] a transfer of land registered in three proprietors was executed by P, M, and M again (the second time as attorney for A). This was not a valid transfer and no title was shown on a sub-sale. Execution of a conveyance requires compliance with strict Trustee Act 1925 powers of delegation.[62]

D. TRUSTEES

1. General rules

[12.16] Trustees of land[63] should number between two and four, except that a trust corporation can act alone. Thus an attempt to appoint five trustees in fact only appoints the first four named.[64] Collectively trustees form a single continuing body,

---

[51] *Lord Abergavenny's case* (1607) 6 Co Rep 78b, 77 ER 373.
[52] AEA 1925 s 2(2).
[53] *Simpson* v. *Gutteridge* (1816) 1 Madd 609, 616, 56 ER 224, Plumer V-C; *Re Schär* [1950] 2 All ER 1069 (disclaimer); *Robson-Paul* v. *Farrugia* (1969) 20 P & CR 820, CA (one joint tenant might grant or revoke a licence).
[54] *Weston* v. *Keighley* (1673) Cas temp Finch 82, 23 ER 44; Blackstone's *Commentaries* vol 2, 175; Littleton's *Tenures*, [311].
[55] *Gill* v. *Lewis* [1956] 2 QB 1, CA.
[56] *Slingsby's case* (1587) 5 Co Rep 18b, 19a, 77 ER 77.
[57] *Tooker's case* (1601) 2 Co Rep 66b, 76 ER 567.
[58] See below [25.17].
[59] Blackstone's *Commentaries* vol 2, 182.
[60] Blackstone's *Commentaries* vol 2, 185; see below [16.47].
[61] [1985] 1 WLR 1115; NS Price [1986] *Conv* 136; *Green* v. *Whitehead* [1930] 1 Ch 38, CA; *Fountain Forestry* v. *Edwards* [1975] Ch 1 (personal representatives); *Watts* v. *Spence* [1976] Ch 165; *Malhotra* v. *Choudhury* [1980] Ch 52; PW Smith [1980] *Conv* 191.
[62] TA 1925 s 25; Powers of Attorney Act 1971 s 9(2); T Delegation A 1999; see below at [14.44ff].
[63] Cheshire & Burn (16th ed), 889; Megarry & Wade (6th ed), [10.052-10.076].
[64] TA 1925 ss 34, 36, 37. No limits apply to charities or personalty settlements. Vacancies need not be filled.

but the identity of the individuals may change over the life of a trust, with deaths, retirements and new appointments. Statutory powers permit the replacement of dead trustees, retirements,[65] additional appointments, and the removal of those unable to act.[66] Purchasers must accept a statement of the ground on which an appointment is made and are protected against errors.[67] Difficult cases can be solved by application to the Crown.[68]

Appointments are made by a person designated by the trust[69] instrument, or otherwise by the continuing trustees, but if all have died the torch passes to the personal representatives of the last surviving trustee.[70] A purchaser is entitled to deal with the people actually appointed, even if the trust instrument called for other appointments.[71] A deed of appointment vests the legal estate in the new trustees.[72]

2. Beneficiary control

[12.17] A taster of beneficiary control, no more, was introduced in 1996.[73] It applies only where *all* beneficiaries are ascertained and are of full age and capacity,[74] so that acting collectively they would be entitled to terminate the trust.[75] *Re Brockbank*[76] decided that the beneficiaries had no power to control appointments of trustees, but this is reversed by part II of the 1996 Act which permits the beneficiaries to sack an existing trustee.[77] Beneficiaries may also nominate a proper[78] person for appointment as a trustee[79] if there is no one with an express power of appointment.[80] Directions must be given in writing to the trustees[81] – either jointly or by all beneficiaries separately nominating the same trustee[82] – and are revocable until implemented.[83] A trustee must retire when directed to do so, provided that enough trustees are left to satisfy the statutory rules about numbers, but he may insist upon an adequate indemnity against tax and similar liabilities.[84] Similar rights of beneficiary control apply after a trustee becomes incapable, if there is no one able and willing to exercise a

---

[65] S 39. Retirement may not reduce the trustees to one: *Adam & Co International T* v. *Theodore Goddard* [2000] Times March 17th, Evans-Lombe J.

[66] TA 1925 s 36; grounds are absence from the UK exceeding 12 months, refusal or unfitness to act, incapacity, infancy, or dissolution of a trust corporation.

[67] S 38.

[68] S 41.

[69] *Re Walker & Hughes C* (1883) 24 Ch D 698; but note *Re Wheeler & De Rochow* [1896] 1 Ch 315; *Re Sichel's S* [1916] 1 Ch 358.

[70] TA 1925 s 36; *Re Stoneham's ST* [1953] Ch 59.

[71] LPA 1925 s 24(1) as amended.

[72] TA 1925 s 40; DLRR 2003 r 162(2).

[73] TLATA 1996 part II, ss 19–21. Existing trusts are included, unless excluded by a deed executed by the surviving creator(s); application of Part II to new trusts can also be excluded: s 21(5)–(7).

[74] TLATA 1996 s 19(1)(b).

[75] *Saunders* v. *Vautier* (1841) Cr & Ph 240, 41 ER 482.

[76] [1948] Ch 206, Vaisey J.

[77] TLATA 1996 s 19(2)(a).

[78] S 21(4).

[79] S 19(2)(b).

[80] S 19(1)(a).

[81] Or the personal representative of a last survivor: s 19(2)(b).

[82] S 21(1)–(2).

[83] S 21(1).

[84] S 19(2)–(4).

power of replacement; the beneficiaries may direct a replacement by giving a direction to the incapable trustee's receiver, attorney, or Mental Health Act 1983 minder.[85]

When a trustee is appointed it must be formal, at least in writing.[86] Appointments are invariably made by deed to take advantage of vesting provisions, since an appointment or retirement by deed will vest the estate in the new body of trustees automatically.[87] If the trust property is a lease which requires the consent of the landlord to an assignment, this consent should be obtained before the deed of appointment is executed.[88]

E. SURVIVORSHIP

1.   Identity and devolution by survivorship

[12.18] Joint tenancy is ideally suited to the holding of legal title, since its characteristic is survivorship. If one trustee dies, the legal estate passes automatically to the remaining trustees. The current state of the legal title is easily determined from official certification of the death.[89]

The numbers can be replenished by appointments, and this should be done to prevent the number of trustees falling to one. If this is not done the land will eventually stand in the name of a single trustee. On the death of that sole surviving trustee, the land will pass to his personal representatives.[90] If the last trustee leaves a will naming executors who prove the will, those executors will be legal estate owners who may themselves act as trustees,[91] or who may select replacements.[92] Executors of executors may claim by a chain of representation.[93] Otherwise administrators will have to be appointed, and the Public Trustee holds the land in the interim.[94]

2.   Corporations as legal joint tenants

[12.19] The old common law felt a difficulty about allowing a human to be a joint tenant with a corporation, which has perpetual succession and cannot die. In a contest of longevity the company would survive a mortal human and claim the property. But in relationship to a trusteeship it does not much matter who is trustee and using a company avoids repeated vestings as human trustees die or retire. For this reason the common law impediment to a co-ownership between a natural person and a trust

---

[85] S 20.

[86] TA 1925 s 36.

[87] S 40(1)–(2).

[88] S 40(4).

[89] Problems of *commorientes* arise if death is certified on the same date; the younger is presumed to survive the elder; see below **[16.09]**.

[90] AEA 1925 ss 1–3.

[91] TA 1925 s 18(2)

[92] TA 1925 s 36(1)(b); *Re Shafto's T* (1885) 29 Ch D 247; unless there is an express power: *Re Routledge's T* [1909] 1 Ch 280.

[93] AEA 1925 s 7; PF Smith [1977] *Conv* 423.

[94] LP (MP) A 1994 s 14, amending AEA 1925 s 9. Between 1971 and July 1995 title was held by the President of the Family Division.

corporation[95] had to be removed, a trick effected by the unlikely sounding but much used Bodies Corporate (Joint Tenancy) Act 1899.[96]

3. Contemporaneous deaths

[12.20] Deaths in quick succession give rise to difficulty in establishing the correct sequence, facts needed to apply survivorship correctly. Floods and shipwrecks were the old hazards, now joined by car crashes, plane disasters and bombings. Section 184 of the Law of Property Act 1925[97] presumes that deaths occur in the order of seniority if the sequence of deaths is uncertain, so that a younger joint tenant is deemed to have survived the older.[98] The section applies where persons "have died in circumstances rendering it uncertain which of them survived the other or others", including deaths in an unknown sequence and also instantaneous deaths. In *Hickman* v. *Peacey* five people were killed when a bomb demolished their house in Chelsea at the height of the Battle of Britain,[99] and it was held that the estate of the youngest joint tenant took all. The presumption can be excluded by definite evidence of the actual sequence of deaths.[100]

4. Severance by killing

[12.21] Trusteeship can pass by survivorship even if one trustee kills another,[101] though a forfeiture will occur to prevent beneficial inheritance.[102]

F. CO-PROPRIETORS OF REGISTERED LAND

[12.22] Co-ownership of registered titles is simplicity itself since the register shows only legal title and the registrar polices the curtain to keep beneficial entitlement off the register.[103] Joint proprietors are limited to four. If the land is accidentally registered in more than four names it is presumably the first four who are proprietors.[104] The register has no need to state that the proprietors are legal joint tenants, since that is the only form of co-ownership that can reach the register. Existence of a trust may

---

[95] *Law Guarantee & Trust Society* v. *Bank of England* (1890) 24 QBD 406.

[96] S 1(1); *Re Thompson's ST* [1905] 1 Ch 229. On dissolution of a corporation a "survivorship" passes its property to the other joint tenants: s 1(2); the Act also applies beneficially, see below **[16.06]**.

[97] Pre-1926 law was based on the need to prove a case: *Hickman* v. *Peacey* [1945] AC 304, 321, Lord Macmillan; *Wing* v. *Angrave* (1860) 8 HLC 183, 11 ER 397; *Re Phené's T* (1870) LR 5 Ch App 139; *Re Aldersey* [1905] 2 Ch 181; *Re Lindop* [1942] Ch 377.

[98] The rule does not operate on intestacy between a person and his or her spouse: AEA 1925 s 46(3). Otherwise if a married couple were killed together in a crash the family of whichever spouse happened to be younger would inherit all excluding completely the family of the elder spouse.

[99] [1945] AC 304, 337, Lord Porter, 325, Lord Macmillan, 343, Lord Simonds.

[100] *Re Bate* [1947] 2 All ER 418; RE Megarry (1947) 63 *LQR* 423; *Re Rowland* [1963] Ch 1, CA; *Re Pringle* [1946] Ch 124.

[101] *Re K* [1985] Ch 85, 100F–H, Vinelott J.

[102] See below **[16.10ff]**.

[103] LRA 2002 s 78.

[104] If these are not the same as the first four on the transfer there may be a case for alteration or rectification of the register: see above **[11.38]**, **[11.48]**.

be deduced from the presence of a restriction, which is mandatory unless the proprietors are also beneficial joint tenants.[105]

Devolutions should be reflected by the appropriate changes in the register. On the death of a joint proprietor the death certificate should be produced to the registry, so that the survivor can be recorded as proprietor. On the death of the last joint tenant his personal representative is entitled to registration,[106] though it is not essential to register since survivorship can be proved by production of a death certificate, and the title of a personal representative can be proved by production of his grant of representation; in fact, proof of deaths off the register is normal.[107]

[105] See below [13.36].
[106] See below [14.24].
[107] DLRR 2003 rr 163–165; see below [14.24].

13

TRUSTS OF LAND

Flegg. Forms of trusts of land. Overreaching. Curtain. Restrictions. Consent trusts and restriction on powers. Delegations. Interests overreached. Power-based overreaching. Defective overreaching.

A. INTRODUCTION

[13.01] *City of London BS* v. *Flegg*[1] confirmed that trustees are able to pass title to the land without the approval of the beneficiaries and, very likely, against their wishes. The case was decided in 1988 when there was a statutory trust for sale, but its effect is duplicated for post-1996 trusts of land. The scheme of the Law of Property Act 1925 is to enable a buyer to take a transfer without any reference to the equitable interests of the beneficiaries, the land being discharged from the beneficial interests which are transferred to the proceeds of sale.[2] This is the process known as overreaching which is explained in detail in this chapter. The trust of land is a conveyancing device designed to ensure that an overreaching sale is possible.

Overreaching may only occur if the purchase money is paid to two trustees.[3] *Williams & Glyn's Bank* v. *Boland* (1981)[4] concerned a mortgage by a single trustee, who was not therefore able to overreach, and so the House of Lords held that the beneficiary retained priority against the lender who had failed to overreach him. In registered land this happens where the beneficiary is in occupation of the land since the beneficiary then has an overriding interest.[5] The whole problem of one-trustee trusts is the subject of a subsequent chapter.[6] This re-opened the question of whether *Boland* did[7] or did not[8] apply when two trustees effected a sale. *City of London BS* v. *Flegg* decided that the occupiers are not protected since a sale by two trustees overreaches.

A property known as Bleak House[9] was bought jointly by a young couple (the Maxwell-Browns) and by the wife's parents (the Fleggs). The parents put in £18,000

---

[1] [1988] AC 54, HL.

[2] At 78H–79A, Lord Oliver.

[3] LPA 1925 s 27(2).

[4] [1981] AC 487, HL.

[5] LRA 2002 sch 3 para 2, re-enacting LRA 1925 s 70(1)(g).

[6] See below **[15]**.

[7] C Sydenham [1980] *Conv* 427.

[8] *Boland* [1979] Ch 312, 321D, 330C, Lord Denning MR, 334C, Ormrod LJ; JE Martin [1980] *Conv* 361, [1981] *Conv* 219; WT Murphy (1979) 42 *MLR* 567; S Freeman (1980) 43 *MLR* 692, 695; AM Prichard [1980] *Conv* 458.

[9] Dickens' novel recounts the interminable litigation in an imaginary Chancery suit of *Jarndyce* v. *Jarndyce*.

or so in cash,[10] leaving the younger couple to borrow £20,000 in order to finance the purchase. However the property was transferred only to the names of the younger couple, the parents keeping off the title to avoid liability to repay the loan. As a result, legal title was registered in the names of the two Maxwell-Browns on a trust for all four contributors.[11] Later the mortgage that had been used to fund the initial acquisition of the house was paid off and the younger couple remortgaged the property to secure a much larger loan from the City of London Building Society. Which was the more fundamental principle – overreaching or the protection of occupation?[12] The Court of Appeal ruled in favour of the occupation of the Fleggs[13] but, after universal academic execration,[14] that decision was unanimously reversed by the Lords. Their occupation rights had indeed been overreached.[15] Possible complexities explored later in this chapter should not obscure the essential simplicity of the decision. Two trustees effected what appeared to the lenders to be a proper mortgage, so that the rights of the beneficiaries were swept off the title and transferred to the mortgage money. The Fleggs could not enforce their rights against the lenders.[16]

B. FORMS OF TRUSTS OF LAND

[13.02] Trusts of land[17] were introduced by the Trusts of Land and Appointment of Trustees Act 1996,[18] which came into force on January 1st 1997[19] to implement Law Commission proposals[20] intended to "make new provision about trusts of land",[21] and to extend overreaching to bare trusts.[22] Management of trust property was subject to major reform, but here scrutiny is restricted to the reforms dealing with the institutional framework, that is the conveyancing mechanisms adopted for trusts. Old overreaching mechanisms have been purged and purified so that the pre-existing law is restated more clearly without any real substantive change.

---

[10] For resulting and constructive trusts from contribution see below [17].

[11] A statutory trust for sale; it would now be an implied (= statutory) trust of land; see below [16.03].

[12] See below [15.32ff].

[13] [1986] Ch 605, CA.

[14] DJ Hayton [1986] *Conv* 131; WJ Swadling [1986] *Conv* 379; PV Baker (1986) 102 *LQR* 349; C Harpum [1986] *CLJ* 212; RJ Smith (1986) 49 *MLR* 519; MP Thompson (1986) 6 *LS* 140.

[15] [1988] AC 54; RJ Smith (1987) 103 *LQR* 520; C Harpum [1986] *CLJ* 392; WJ Swadling [1987] *Conv* 451; MP Thompson [1988] *Conv* 108; S Gardner (1988) 51 *MLR* 365.

[16] At 83H–84A, Lord Oliver. The Fleggs were interested in the equity of redemption (= the land subject to the mortgage) and could have recovered the house had they been able to pay off the mortgage.

[17] Chapelle's *Land Law* (5th ed) ch 8; Cheshire & Burn (16th ed) ch 10; Goo's *Sourcebook* (3rd ed) ch 13; Gravells *LL – Text* (2nd ed) ch 4; Gray's *Elements* (3rd ed), 878–904; Maudsley & Burn *LL – Cases* (7th ed) ch 4; Megarry & Wade (6th ed), [8.123ff].

[18] PH Kenny [1996] *Conv* 77; R Wallington [1996] *NLJ* 959; AJ Oakley [1996] *Conv* 401; N Hopkins [1996] *Conv* 411; LN Clements (1998) 61 *MLR* 56.

[19] SI 1996/2974; hence "pre-1997" and "post-1996".

[20] Law Com 181 (1989); A Pottage (1989) 52 *MLR* 683; RJ Smith [1990] *Conv* 12.

[21] Preamble.

[22] Law Com 188 (1989) (remaining parts now dropped); S Gardner (1988) 104 *LQR* 367.

1. Definition

[13.03] Terminology is utilitarian in the Law Commission style: a trust of land is any trust of property consisting of or including land.[23] It makes no difference whether the trust was created formally or informally, and whether it is implied, resulting, or constructive.[24] The legislation is much too widely drawn and may now even catch a constructive trust imposed to make a burden bind a purchaser who expressly accepts the obligation.[25] The legal estate is vested in "trustees of land."[26] Most pre-1997 trusts were trusts for sale,[27] and these have been incorporated into the trusts of land scheme with no functional change. By phasing out strict settlements and bare trusts, the Act creates a single conveyancing machinery,[28] including all post 1996 trusts and most old ones which are converted to the new format.[29] Only earlier strict settlements stand outside the new scheme.[30]

Trusts of money or company shares are usually simple trusts in which the trustees are under no obligation to sell.[31] They are free to retain the shares until it becomes appropriate to switch investments. It was an old dream to match trusts of land to trusts of shares, and so to facilitate a settlement of the paintings and other valuable contents of a house on the same trusts as the house itself, an opportunity missed in 1925[32] but the difficulty evaporates under the scheme of the 1996 Act. Legal title must be vested in the trustees, so that if the land is registered it is the trustees who should appear as proprietors. Trusts are created by transferring legal title *to T1 and T2 on trust for* named beneficiaries.[33] A power of sale is conferred on the trustees by statute,[34] but they have no duty to sell. Until they choose to do so, the beneficiaries have rights in the land itself. This form of trust corresponds with clients' natural expectations. Thus:

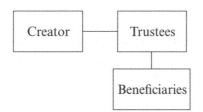

Figure 13-1 A trust of land

[23] TLATA 1996 s 1(1)(a).

[24] S 1(2)(a).

[25] *Lloyd* v. *Dugdale* [2001] EWCA Civ 1754, [2002] 2 P & CR 13 at 167, [55], Peter Gibson LJ; see below **[19.79ff]**.

[26] S 1(1)(b). TA 2000 s 16 makes it possible to have a trust in which legal title is vested in a nominee of the trustees.

[27] See below **[14.02]**.

[28] An old idea: H Potter (1943) 8 *Conv* (NS) 147; GA Grove (1961) 24 *MLR* 123.

[29] TLATA 1996 ss 1(1)(a), 1(3), 2.

[30] Pre-1997 trusts are considered below **[14.01ff]**.

[31] E Scammell (1957) 10 *CLP* 152, 162.

[32] C Sweet (1908) 24 *LQR* 26; JE Hogg (1908) 24 *LQR* 290; A Underhill (1935) 51 *LQR* 221, 227; S Anderson, *Lawyers and the Making of English Land Law 1832–1940* (Clarendon Press, 1992), 67.

[33] Until that occurs the trust is said to be incompletely constituted, and is not generally enforceable: see standard equity texts.

[34] TLATA 1996 s 6.

The top line of the diagram represents legal title passing from the creator of the trust (often called a settlor) to the trustees while the lower line represents the separation of the beneficial interest from the legal title, that is the equitable interests of the beneficiaries.

2. Trusts for sale

[13.04] Trusts for sale were the normal form of trust used for holding land before the 1996 reforms. The land is vested in trustees who have a duty to sell the land. To take a simplified unregistered form of trust:

> *to T1 and T2 in fee simple on trust to sell the property and to hold the proceeds of sale or the net rents and profits until sale on trust for X for life, with remainder to Y absolutely.*[35]

(1) Pre-1997 trusts for sale

[13.05] The simple and workable structure of the trust for sale was used in preference to the more complex strict settlement machinery in 99.9% of trusts involving land between 1925 and 1996.[36] Most trusts for sale were express, but statute imposed a trust for sale on co-ownership and in many other cases. In most cases it was not intended that the land should be sold immediately. Harold Potter observed,[37] long ago, how difficult it was to explain this mechanism to clients, who generally wanted to make a trust of the land itself. Strictly speaking the beneficiary did not have rights in the land itself, but only an interest in the proceeds raised by selling the land. This was the so-called doctrine of conversion: because there was a duty to sell, the beneficiaries' interests were converted to the money secured by sale. Fortunately conversion doctrine was first modified and then the 1996 Act abolished it.[38] However, the price of ducking out of a settlement before 1997 was to accept a theoretical duty of immediate sale. In practice the obligation to sell was not a great inconvenience because it was balanced by a power to postpone sale, and so long as the trustees chose to exercise their right to delay sale, the trust was a perfectly viable means of holding land. The real price was an uncalled for complexity.

(2) Post-1996 trusts for sale

[13.06] Trusts for sale continue after 1996 as trusts of land, but with all their distinctive characteristics stripped away. There is little practical distinction between a trust for sale and a simple trust. It would be eccentric and inappropriate today to create a trust for sale of a house intended for occupation – a "simple" trust is better suited to this job. Trusts for sale retain utility where land is intended as an investment, to

---

[35] LPA 1925 s 35 (now repealed); "net" here means subject to the payment of expenses.

[36] This figure is based on applications for land registry restrictions, but it understates the popularity of trusts for sale because it excludes the most numerous case of beneficial joint tenancy which did not require any restriction.

[37] (1928) 44 *LQR* 227.

[38] Pre-1997 trusts are explained below **[14.01ff]**.

create a monetary income for the beneficiaries, and also where sale is genuinely intended. Suppose a parent dies, intending that the family home be sold and the proceeds split between all his children equally. A trust for sale is tailor-made to achieve this wish, the conveyancing machinery ensures that the land can be sold free of the beneficial interests and imposition of the duty to sell makes clear that beneficiaries are not intended to have occupation rights.[39]

The 1996 Act formalises the position established by the old case-law about the nature of the beneficial interests, which take effect in the land itself,[40] and are no longer regarded as personal property.[41] Power to postpone sale is implied automatically,[42] whether or not it is appropriate.

3.   Bare trusts and "strict settlements"

[13.07] Two special cases, which called for special conveyancing procedures when created before 1997, now create straightforward trusts of land. These are:

(1) Bare trusts – where a single adult beneficiary is absolutely entitled to the land:

  To T1 and T2 on trust for an adult B absolutely;[43]

(2) Former strict settlements – where there was a succession of beneficial interests but no trust for sale, for example:

  to T1 and T2 on trust for A for life, remainder to B in fee simple;[44] *or*

  to A for life, remainder to B in fee simple.

If created today each is subsumed within the overarching category of trusts of land.

C.   OVERREACHING

1.   Sales which override and those which overreach

[13.08] John Aubrey equates "overreaching" with trickery in this passage:

> "At the Innes of Court they do not learn the Rules of Justice . . . but instead . . . the art of wrangling and ill aquation, overreaching and oppression."

This old-fashioned sense is now obsolete. Today overreaching is the process by which an interest (particularly a beneficial interest under a trust) is removed from the land on sale and transferred to the proceeds of sale. The first element is the overriding force of the sale and the second is the overreaching element. The second concept is much older than 1925, though the label was attached to it at that time, largely by accident.[45]

---

[39] See below **[19.03]**.
[40] TLATA 1996 s 3.
[41] TLATA 1996 s 3(1); the section applies retrospectively except where a testator died before 1997: ss 3(2)–(3), 26; but see: PH Pettit (1997) 113 *LQR* 207; R Town (1998) 142 *SJ* 378.
[42] TLATA 1996 s 4(1).
[43] See below **[14.06]**.
[44] See below **[14.10]**.
[45] JM Lightwood (1927) 3 *CLJ* 59, 64–69; S Bailey (1944) 8 *CLJ* 36; C Harpum [1990] *CLJ* 277, 287–304.

2.   Overriding sales

[13.09] Implicit in the existence of a power of sale is the existence of a person with the power to sell the land and override the interests to which it is paramount. Sale of trust land overrides the interests of the beneficiaries,[46] and sale by a mortgage lender removes the interest of the borrower. Pre-1926 drafts of the property legislation referred to the power to override beneficial interests. The word "overriding" was mainly dropped in 1925 to avoid the risk of confusion with overriding interests, [47] two direct opposites: overriding sales defeat existing interests affecting the land whereas overriding interests bind later purchasers without any entry on the register. Overriding sales occur without the concurrence of the beneficiaries who do not need to join in the sale. A sale can be imagined which is overriding but not overreaching, so that prior beneficial interests are defeated but are not transferred from land to money, for example where:

> *T1 and T2 hold on trust to allow A to occupy until sale and to hold the proceeds of sale on trust for B.*[48]

Sale discharges the land from the beneficial interests so the buyer gets a clean title, and A's beneficial interest evaporates.[49]

3.   Overreaching sales

[13.10] Overreaching detaches beneficial interests from land when the land is sold and transfers them instead to the proceeds of sale. It is a necessary counterbalance to the overriding element to ensure that the beneficiaries are compensated with a corresponding interest in the proceeds of sale.[50] Seeing land purely as an investment and the trust property as a fund, the ability to sell ensures that trustees can change the form of investment of the trust property, preserving the rights of the beneficiaries in the value represented by the trust fund whatever its current form.[51]

Suppose that *T1 and T2 hold land on trust for A for life, with remainder to B absolutely*. If the trustees transfer this land to a buyer, their receipt discharges the land from the trusts, giving the purchaser both legal and equitable title to the land. Trustees can only sell at the best price reasonably obtainable, so the proceeds should correspond to the value of the land, ensuring that beneficiaries are not short-changed by an honest sale.[52] Before sale, A could occupy the land, and B would acquire the right to occupy it when A died. After overreaching, their interests both exist in a fund

---

[46] *Re Mansel* (1885) 54 LJ Ch 883 (administration action overreached); *Bernhardt* v. *Galsworthy* [1929] 1 Ch 549.

[47] But see LRA 1925 s 3(xv)(a).

[48] Trusts of the land are usually identical to the trusts of the proceeds of sale and LPA 1925 s 24 (as amended in 1996) imposes a duty to appoint the same trustees.

[49] *Lantsbery* v. *Collier* (1856) 2 K & J 709, 69 ER 967.

[50] The two senses were confused in *State Bank of India* v. *Sood* [1997] Ch 276, 281D.

[51] FH Lawson & B Rudden, *Introduction to Property Law* (Clarendon Press, 2nd ed, 1982), 57.

[52] *Truell* v. *Tysson* (1856) 21 Beav 437, 52 ER 928.

of money, which the trustees would be obliged to invest, paying income to A[53] and retaining the capital fund to pay to B when A dies. If, for example, the house is sold for £100,000, and the trustees invest £100,000 at 5% they will receive £5,000 income per year (less income tax). A is entitled to this net income. When A dies the investment of £100,000 (hopefully increased by good management) will be handed over to B.

Is overreaching fair? In a period of low inflation and stable house prices, a switch from land to money, or vice versa, may be a fair exchange but in unstable economic conditions money may not be an adequate compensation for loss of the beneficiary's home. Anyway, a home often has more significance than its strict monetary value, and if a person has, say, a one-quarter share in a £100,000 house, the £25,000 he receives on sale may not be enough to buy any replacement.

4.   Two trustee rule for capital receipts

[13.11] Successful overreaching occurs only when statutory rules about the payment of the purchase money are observed. The old law applying to trusts for sale is now adapted to trusts of land.[54] Section 27(2) of Law of Property Act 1925 states that:

> "proceeds of sale or other capital money shall not be paid to or applied by the direction of fewer than two persons as trustees . . .".

Trust documents cannot exclude this requirement.[55] Since the powers of trustees of land are joint, all existing trustees must combine together in selling the property. *All* trustees[56] and personal representatives[57] must sell, to which section 27 adds that there must be *at least* two of them: sale by T2 and T3 (without T1) passes no legal title to the buyer.

Nineteenth century practice facilitated fraud by enabling beneficial interests to be overridden by a single trustee. It was too easy for a single trustee to sign a cheque in his own favour and disappear with the proceeds of sale.[58] Insistence on two trustees ensures that money can only be ripped off by trustees who conspire together. Accidental mixing is wholly avoided since money paid to joint trustees and received jointly must necessarily be kept in an account distinct from the trustee's own personal money. Nothing can prevent fraud by a trustee willing to forge the signature of his co-trustee.

As an exception to the general rule, a sole *trust corporation*,[59] acting alone, can receive and give a receipt for purchase money. Examples are the Public Trustee, a trustee in bankruptcy, any corporation appointed as a trustee by the court, and

---

[53]   *Mills* v. *Dugmore* (1861) 30 Beav 104, 54 ER 828; *Burrell* v. *Delevante* (1862) 30 Beav 550, 54 ER 1003.

[54]   LPA 1925 s 27(2), substituted by LP (Amendment) A 1926 sch, now as amended by TLATA 1996 sch 3.

[55]   If legal title is vested in X, the trust may direct the payment of purchase money to Y: *Re Wright & Best's Brewery Co C* [1929] WN 11.

[56]   *Anon* (1363) Jenk 43, 145 ER 33.

[57]   AEA 1925 s 2; LP (MP) A 1994 s 18.

[58]   S Anderson, *Lawyers and the Making of English Land Law 1832–1940* (Clarendon Press, 1992), 292; *Pilcher* v. *Rawlins* (1872) LR 7 Ch App 259, 266, Lord Hatherley LC.

[59]   LPA 1925 s 205(1)(xxviii); SLA 1925 s 117(1)(xxx); TA 1925 s 68(18); AEA 1925 s 55(1)(xxvii); Supreme Court Act 1981 s 128; Public Trustee Act 1906; SR & O 1912/348 r 30, as substituted by SI 1975/1189; LP (Amendment) A 1926 s 3.

numerous individual corporations named in statutory instruments. A generic defini-tion[60] embraces any corporation based anywhere in the EU, with power to undertake trust business, a place of business within the United Kingdom, and a sufficiently large share capital.[61] Trust corporations should be especially trustworthy, safe to trust with extended overreaching powers. If not immune from fraud, there should be at least sufficient assets to meet any claims. A second, ancient, exception permits a sale by a single executor,[62] a practice which is particularly convenient where that person is also the sole beneficiary of the deceased.

5. Transactions with no purchase money

[13.12] Rules requiring money to be paid to two trustees apply only to capital money,[63] for example sale proceeds, a loan, or the premium received on the grant of a lease.[64] Income due to a trust can be paid to a single trustee, examples being rent, rentcharges, compensation for planning decisions,[65] profits from the land,[66] etc. This should be handed over to the adult life tenant, or accumulated for a minor until he reaches 18.[67]

A novel point arose recently in *State Bank of India* v. *Sood*.[68] A husband and wife charged their matrimonial home in Sutton, Surrey in 1983 as security for the discharge of an overdraft to a bank, a mortgage which was later transferred to the State Bank of India. At the time of the mortgage the overdraft stood at nil – there was no capital money payable at the time of the transaction – but by 1993 the bank was owed £1 million. Not unnaturally this bankrupted Mr Sood, whose trustees in bankruptcy did not defend possession proceedings by the bank. However their children (the five young Soods) claimed to have contributed and argued that their beneficial interests had not been overreached. The Court of Appeal decided that overreaching had occurred. Any capital money had to be paid to the trustees but if, as in the case, there was none overreaching will occur anyway.[69] This makes sense: an overdraft mortgage should overreach irrespective of whether £100 was advanced immediately or the overdraft facility remained unused until after the completion of the mortgage.[70]

6. One-trustee trusts

[13.13] Although a single trustee cannot *override* beneficiaries, this in no way affects the possible existence of a trust while legal title is held by a single person,[71] as in the

[60] SR & O 1912/348 r 30, as substituted in 1975.

[61] A company with limited liability must have an issued share capital of at least £250,000, with at least £100,000 of that paid up in cash.

[62] There will usually be at least two administrators of an intestate estate.

[63] LPA 1925 s 205(1)(xxvi); SLA 1925 s 117(1)(ii); *Sood* [1997] Ch 276, 282F–283A.

[64] *Re Brown* (1886) 32 Ch D 597, Kay J.

[65] *Re Meux* [1958] Ch 154.

[66] *Miller* v. *Miller* (1872) LR 13 Eq 263; *Re North* [1909] 1 Ch 625.

[67] TA 1925 s 32.

[68] [1997] Ch 276, CA.

[69] At 286F–287H.

[70] At 289A–C.

[71] LPA 1925 s 27(2); *Re Myhill* [1928] Ch 100, Astbury J.

leading case, *Williams & Glyn's Bank* v. *Boland*.[72] The competition between beneficiary and a purchaser from a sole trustee will be played out under the doctrine of
notice if title is unregistered, and applying the overriding interest arising from actual
occupation if title is registered. *Boland* and "one trustee" trusts are the subject of a
subsequent chapter.[73]

7. Factors which do not affect overreaching

(1) Notice of the trusts

[13.14] Buyers are enabled to take free of the interests of the beneficiaries irrespective
of notice of their rights, or even express knowledge.[74] Indeed knowledge of the trust
facilitates sale by alerting the buyer to the need to pay his money to two trustees.[75]
Beneficial interests are kept behind a curtain. There is no duty to inquire about interests which will be removed on sale.

(2) Concurrence of the beneficiaries

[13.15] Trustees make title to land without requiring the consent of the equitable
owners to sale.[76] Sale is based on the legal title held by the trustees, and any right the
beneficiaries may have to be consulted[77] or to restrain a sale before it happens, cannot
encumber a purchaser's title after a sale is completed. Overreaching takes place
without any implied[78] necessity for consent to be given by the beneficiaries, since an
overreaching sale renders the decision making process leading up to that sale quite
irrelevant.

(3) Attempts to prevent overreaching

[13.16] In *Flegg* a caution had been lodged by the defendant occupiers to protect their
interests,[79] but they still lost the case. Their caution required the entry of an appropriate restriction before the mortgage could be registered, and this in turn required
that the loan should be paid to at least two trustees, but it had no impact on the mortgage actually made, since the borrowers were the two Maxwell Browns. This principle
applies with equal vigour to trusts of land.

---

[72] [1981] AC 487, HL.
[73] See below **[15]**.
[74] LPA 1925 s 27(1), now as amended by TLATA 1996.
[75] *Flegg* [1988] AC 54, 83F, Lord Oliver; FH Lawson & B Rudden, *Introduction to the Law of Property*
(Clarendon Press, 2nd ed, 1982), 57.
[76] *Flegg* [1988] AC 54, 72, Lord Templeman. The Fleggs chose not to go on the title and surely bore the
risk of what happened afterwards.
[77] TLATA 1996 s 16(1); *City of London BS* v. *Flegg* [1988] AC 54, 78; *Sood* [1997] Ch 276, 283C.
[78] For express consent trusts, see below **[13.40]**.
[79] [1988] AC 54, 91E–G; P Sparkes [1988] *Conv* 141. A trust must now be protected by a (unilateral or
mutual) restriction; see below **[13.36]**.

8. Occupiers can be overreached

[13.17] One or more of the beneficiaries is likely to be in occupation of trust property. Physical presence of a beneficiary will usually prevent a *sale* since the trustees have to secure vacant possession,[80] but mortgages do not disturb possession. If any transaction does proceed to completion with the beneficiaries in occupation, *Flegg* shows that they will be overreached.

Whether title is registered or unregistered, section 14 of the Law of Property Act 1925 applies to provide that part 1[81] shall not "prejudicially affect the interest of any person in possession or in actual occupation of land to which he may be entitled in right of such possession or occupation."[82] *Flegg* shows that overreaching removes all rights of the beneficiary from the land leaving nothing for occupation to protect. The exact function of section 14 remains obscure.

When title is registered the rights of actual occupiers are overriding, so that every transaction takes effect subject to them.[83] *Boland*[84] established that the rights of a beneficiary under a trust could be an overriding interest that survived a mortgage by one trustee. However, the interest must relate to the registered land and the Lords decided in *Flegg*[85] that an interest which is overreached no longer subsists in the land. *Boland* is properly limited to a mortgage by a single trustee and occupiers of registered land can be overreached by two trustees. A report by the Law Commission[86] proposing reversal of this rule will not now be implemented. The 1925 legislation ensured that good title to land could be acquired following set conveyancing procedures.[87] Honest purchasers who have carried out proper conveyancing procedures should be guaranteed to acquire an unimpeachable title. The Trusts of Land and Appointments of Trustees Act 1996[88] confirms the law established by *Flegg*. that the new statutory right to occupy trust.

D. UNREGISTERED LAND CURTAIN

[13.18] "Close up his eyes and draw the curtain close", wrote Shakespeare,[89] but how could even that genius have foreseen the basis of Birkenhead's property legislation 400 years later? A curtain implies division into two areas, one showing the legal title open to the light of public gaze and the other (the beneficial interests[90]) concealed

---

[80] Possession is now subject to the court's discretion: TLATA 1996 s 14; contrast *Re Bagot's Settlement* [1894] 1 Ch 177.

[81] LPA 1925 ss 1–39.

[82] M Friend & J Newton [1982] *Conv* 213, 217; DJ Hayton [1986] *Conv* 131, 134–136; RJ Smith (1987) 103 *LQR* 520; C Harpum [1986] *CLJ* 392; PH Kenny [1987] *LSG* 1952.

[83] LRA 2002 sch 3 para 2; see below **[15.32]**.

[84] [1981] AC 487, HL; see below **[15.33]**.

[85] [1988] AC 54, HL.

[86] Law Com 188 (1989); Law Com WP 106 (1987); S Gardner (1988) 104 *LQR* 367; C Harpum [1990] *CLJ* 277.

[87] JE Adams [1998] *Conv* 349.

[88] TLATA 1996 s 12.

[89] Henry VI Part 2, act 3 scene 3.

[90] Not requiring investigation: *Flegg* [1988] AC 54, 79A, Lord Oliver.

"behind the arras".[91] Unfortunately there is also a penumbra, consisting of matters properly hidden in the shadows but liable to full illumination at the most inconvenient moments.[92] So, as *Henry VI* continues, "let us all to meditation".

1. The 1925 unregistered curtain

[13.19] A compromise was reached in 1925[93] by which full overreaching required a receipt by two trustees, but this made it necessary to alert the purchaser to the existence of the trust. The Law of Property Act curtain reveals the names of the trustees and the fact that they are trustees, so a buyer can check that they (the trustees) are at least two in number. Thus:

> *to T1 and T2 in fee simple on trust for . . .*

Beneficiaries are deemed to be adequately protected against fraud by the two-trustee receipt rule. As amended,[94] section 27(1) of the Law of Property Act 1925 exonerates a purchaser of a legal estate from trustees of land from concern with the trusts affecting the land or the proceeds of sale. The curtain keeps the beneficial interests hidden from view, ensuring that a buyer is not distracted by irrelevant details.

In the private domain are details of those equitable interests, trusts, and powers that are transferred to the proceeds on sale, including the identity of the person who is beneficiary in each contingency, occupation rights, rights to income, and powers of appointment. In the case of a beneficial co-ownership, the legal title will not reveal the shares held and whether the parties are beneficial joint tenants or beneficial tenants in common. Also within the private sector are management powers and decision making rules (consent provisions apart), including the requirement that trustees have considered the interests of the beneficiaries,[95] have consulted them,[96] or have obtained their consent to partition.[97] The curtain does not affect burdens – such as restrictive covenants and mortgages and estoppel rights[98] – which are not overreached.

2. Unregistered curtain mechanics

[13.20] Ideally the curtain should be physical, the title being divided into two sets of documents, one public and the other private. Unregistered titles often use a curtain that is notional, both private and public elements being included in the title deeds, but on the basis that the buyer should avert his gaze from those parts of the documents which are private. Laissez-faire is adopted for trusts of land, mirroring the self-regulation formerly allowed to those creating trusts for sale.[99]

---

[91] *Hamlet* act 3 scene 4.
[92] See below [13.53].
[93] Contrast the full curtain proposed in 1922: P Sparkes *NLL* (1st ed), 105–106.
[94] TLATA 1996 sch 3 para 4(8)(a).
[95] Ss 16(1), 6(5).
[96] Ss 16(1), 11(1).
[97] Ss 16(1), 7(3).
[98] *Birmingham Midshires* v. *Sabherwal* (2000) 80 P & CR 256, CA; C Harpum (2000) 116 *LQR* 341.
[99] Compare the rigid rules for strict settlements, see below [14.10].

(1) Acquisition by co-owners

[13.21] Most trusts arise where land is bought by a couple (A and B) as beneficial co-owners. They fulfil multiple roles as buyers, as creators of the trust, as trustees, and also as beneficiaries. Thus:

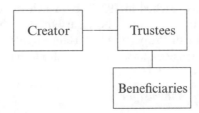

Figure 13-2 Acquisition of land by co-owners

Separate trust deeds are rare, so that the curtain is an abstraction rather than a physical reality.

(2) Lifetime transfer to trustees

[13.22] Next simplest case is the creation of an express trust by a living settlor who transfers the legal estate in his land to trustees.[100] The title deed should record the fact that a trust has been created, and refer to a trust deed[101] of the same date. If two documents are used, as is usual, there is a physical curtain. An epitome of the title includes only deeds passing the legal estate and excludes the trust deed, so a purchaser will never see the private details.[102]

(3) Lifetime declaration of trust

[13.23] A land owner[103] may constitute himself a trustee. Two documents should be used, one declaring that the settlor holds the legal estate as a trustee and the other declaring the trusts of the land. Fraudulent concealment of the existence of the trust can be avoided by endorsing a note of the existence of the trust on the earlier unregistered title deeds.

(4) Trusts created by will

[13.24] Settlements are most commonly created on the death of a property owner. Devolution of property after the settlor's death is directed by a will, which requires

---

[100] *Encyclopaedia FP* (5th ed, 2001 reissue) vol 40 (2), [3544]. Until legal title is vested in the trustees, the trust is unconstituted and so unenforceable; see standard equity texts.

[101] Only a written memorandum is required: LPA 1925 s 53(1)(b).

[102] LPA 1925 s 42.

[103] A trust is validly created even though there is a single trustee, though a second trustee will be required before sale.

testamentary formalities.[104] If a will creates successive interests, it will operate to impose a trust of land. Legal title consists of a grant of probate to the executors who are administering the deceased's estate,[105] and a written assent[106] of the legal estate to the trustees – needed even if the executors and trustees are the same individuals[107] – which will show that the legal estate is passed to the trustees. The will does not form part of the title shown to a buyer, since a sale will overreach whatever beneficial interests it creates.

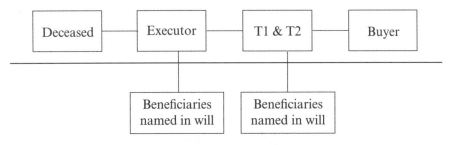

Figure 13-3 The curtain

It is easy for a buyer to break the curtain if he wants to, since the original grant of probate (public) contains within it a copy of the will (private), but the conveyancing curtain obliges the buyer to ignore these intimate details.

3.   Transfer to beneficiaries

[13.25] Sometimes an adult beneficiary becomes absolutely entitled under the terms of the trust. The trust ends and the former beneficiary is entitled to call on the trustees to transfer the land to him.[108] This transfer is not a sale since no money is given, and later buyers will be concerned that the trustees may have defrauded the true beneficiary by transferring the land to a false choice. The trustees should execute a deed of discharge[109] at the end of a trust when conveying land to an adult beneficiary who is absolutely entitled. It might be used at the end of a successive settlement, to partition land, or to transfer it to co-owners, and whether the land is registered[110] or unregistered.[111]

---

[104] Wills Act 1837 s 42.

[105] TLATA 1996 s 18; formerly AEA 1925 s 33; a sole personal representative can act: LPA 1925 s 27(2).

[106] LPA 1925 sch 5 form 9; LPA 1925 s 52(2)(a). A memorandum should be endorsed on the grant of probate. This prevents the personal representatives making a second assent or reselling the property.

[107] Absence of an assent is a common flaw in unregistered titles, revealed in *Re King's WT* [1964] Ch 542.

[108] Eg *on trust for A until B attains 30, provided that if B dies under 30, A shall become absolutely entitled*. B's death converts A's determinable life interest into an absolute beneficial entitlement.

[109] TLATA 1996 s 16(4), drawing on SLA 1925 s 17.

[110] It can be used to cancel a caution under DLRR 2003 r 99, when the trust will cease to affect a buyer.

[111] TLATA 1996 s 16(5).

4.   First registration after a declaration of trust

[13.26] Title will have to be registered since compulsion is triggered by voluntary transfers, gifts, settlements, transfers to beneficiaries, court vesting orders and assents.[112] Title will vest in the first proprietor subject to any trust protected by a restriction and also to any trust of which the first proprietor has notice.[113]

E.   REGISTERED LAND CURTAIN AND RESTRICTIONS

1.   Furniture: the mirror

[13.27] It is intended that the register should mirror the state of the title, though the existence of overriding interests detracts from the purity of the reflection.[114] Thus, when land is held in trust, the mirror principle requires that trustees of land should be registered as proprietors. A lifetime trust is implemented on the register by a transfer of the estate to the trustees followed by their registration as proprietors for the duration of the trust. If a proprietor dies having created a trust by will, he will usually appoint his executors to act as his trustees. It will be rare for the executors to seek registration as such, so the trust will be constituted when the trustees of the will produce to the registrar the probate to the deceased proprietor's estate and a written assent passing title from the executor to the trustees.

2.   Furniture: the curtain

[13.28] Lord Oliver said in *City of London BS* v. *Flegg*[115] that:

> "the philosophy behind both the Land Registration Act 1925 and the Law of Property Act 1925 was that they should operate in parallel and it would, therefore, be surprising if it were found that the two systems were not constructed so as to dovetail into one another. In fact they do."

The Land Registration Act 2002 moves the two systems even closer together. The register is determinative of the state of the legal title (the mirror), whilst the trusts are hidden by the act of registration (the curtain). Trusts are indicated on the register only by a restriction. If the mesh between the two systems is not perfect, it is because the 1925 provisions about registration were not amended to reflect the full force of Lord Cave's attack on the unregistered land provisions of the Law of Property Bill 1922.[116] So the registration legislation continues to provide for a full, absolute, curtain about which Ruoff & Roper find "little to say."[117]

---

[112] LRA 2002 s 4 (1)(a)(i).
[113] LRA 2002 s 11(4), (5); the former binds purchasers whereas the latter may be overridden by a protected purchaser.
[114] *Overseas Investments* v. *Simcobuuild Construction* (1995) 70 P & CR 322, 327, Peter Gibson LJ.
[115] [1988] AC 54, 84G; *Sood* [1997] Ch 276, 283E–284J, Peter Gibson LJ.
[116] P Sparkes *NLL* (1st ed), 105–106.
[117] (6th ed), [32–01].

3. The curtain

[13.29] Section 78 of Land Registration Act 2002 imposes the curtain in one brusque statement, that the registrar shall not be affected with notice of a trust. Its predecessor[118] added that "reference to trusts shall, so far as possible, be excluded from the register". This remains the policy.[119] No space is allocated on the register for entry of beneficial interests, which are kept strictly within the private domain since they are capable of being overridden by the proprietors. Purchasers of registered land can guess that they are dealing with trustees of land from the presence of a restriction on the register, but to acquire good title they merely need to comply with any restriction.[120]

4. Restriction theory

[13.30] Proprietors enjoy full powers of disposition unless a restriction signals some departure from this assumed pattern.[121] Restrictions may only limit dealings with registered estates or mortgages, and not beneficial interests. Entry of a restriction on the proprietorship register places in the public domain any limitation on the power of the proprietor to deal with the registered legal title.[122] In relation to trusts[123] possible uses[124] are to:

prevent invalidity of transactions;
secure overreaching; and
protect a right or claim which is incapable of protection by notice.

The entry may be indefinite, or for a stated period or until a certain event.[125]

If the proprietors are trustees the register must record by restriction how purchase money is to be paid, that is it must reiterate the two trustee rule. A restriction might require prior notice before registration of a dealing, that a consent should be obtained, that the registrar should make an order in a particular case or more generally that some other matter or thing be done before registration.[126] Unreasonable restrictions which are calculated to cause inconvenience may be refused.[127] Later transactions will only be registered if they conform to the restriction, but any doubt can be avoided by a certificate obtained in advance from the registrar that he will register a proposed transaction.

---

[118] LRA 1925 s 74; Land Transfer Act 1897 sch 1; Land Transfer Act 1875 s 83(1).
[119] LR Quinquennial Review (LCD, June 2001), [5.3], proposed that details of beneficial entitlement should be included to help the register become universal, a new Domesday. This is now dropped.
[120] The problem of defective sales is considered below, **[13.53ff]**.
[121] LRA 2002 s 26.
[122] LRA 2002 s 40(4); Law Com 271 (2001), [6.33ff]. Creation of overriding interests off the register (such as leases up to 7 years) is also circumscribed.
[123] Other uses are considered below **[14]**.
[124] LRA 2002 s 42.
[125] LRA 2002 s 40(2). Law Com 271 (2001), [6.33ff].
[126] LRA 2002 s 40. Often the requirement is to obtain a certificate from a conveyancer: DLRR 2003 r 95.
[127] LRA 2002 s 43(3)(b).

The previous opener, "Except under an order of the registrar . . .", is now redundant since the registrar has a general power for the registrar to remove or modify any restriction on the application of any person with a sufficient interest.[128]

5. Restrictions with and without the consent of the proprietor

[13.31] Since 1996[129] restrictions entered with consent of the registered proprietor have been differentiated from those without his consent.

(1) Agreed restrictions

[13.32] Restrictions most commonly appear on the register because the registrar regards a restriction to be necessary or desirable.[130] Otherwise, the proprietor may apply for the entry of a restriction,[131] stating precisely what restriction is required. Commonly the two methods overlap, because when trustees apply to register the transfer to them and so become proprietor of the land, they tick a box on the application form which indicates their limited status, and the registrar responds by entering their names on the proprietorship register subject to a restriction. Application may also be made by any other person able to demonstrate a sufficient interest – for example a beneficiary or a person with a charging order against a beneficial interest[132] – in which case the registered proprietor gives his consent by co-signature of the application form.[133]

Apart from the restriction required in cases of joint proprietorship[134], discussed below, restrictions are mainly voluntary and so can be withdrawn[135] by the people interested in them, and the registrar must cancel it if the land is no longer subject to the trust.[136]

(2) Unilateral restrictions

[13.33] Hostile or "notifiable" restrictions entered without the consent of the proprietor,[137] date from 1996.[138] Application is allowed by any person interested,[139] who must state what restriction is required, justify the need for it, and provide acceptable

---

[128] LRA 2002 s 41; DLRR 2003 r 97; LR Form RX2; DLRR CD ch 6, [32].

[129] LRR 1996, SI 1996/2975.

[130] Notice must be given to the proprietor in a form to be prescribed: LRA 2002 s 42(3), 44(2). The registry may require an application: s 43(2)(a).

[131] LRA 2002 s 43(1)(a); also a person entitled to be registered; DLRR 2003 r 91; DLRR CD ch 6, [7–9]; LR Form RX1.

[132] LRA 2002 s 42(4); DLRR 2003 r 91; this requires evidence of entitlement, either submitted to the registry or certified by a conveyancer.

[133] LRA 2002 ss 42(3), 43; DLRR 2003 r 91; either LR Form RX1 or a separate application; a certificate that a conveyancer holds this will suffice. Signature replaces production of the land certificate as the key.

[134] See below [13.36].

[135] LRA 2002 s 47; DLRR 2003 r 98; DLRR CD ch 6, [33ff].LR Form RX4.

[136] DLRR 2003 r 100. R 101 provides for the court to determine priorities.

[137] LRA 2002 s 45.

[138] LRR 1925 r 236, as amended in 1996. Control of the Land Certificate was crucial before the LRA 2002.

[139] LRA 2002 s 43(1)(c); DLRR 2003 r 92; DLRR CD ch 6, [10–13].

evidence of his right, perhaps, an off-register contribution.[140] There is a duty to act reasonably when entering a restriction.[141] Hostile restrictions do everything previously done by a caution against dealings[142] plus they confer priority.

An application for a non-consensual restrictions is notifiable: notice must be given to the proprietor and others listed in the rules and a period allowed for objections. The entry will only be made if the proprietor consents or if a dispute is resolved in favour of the legitimacy of the interest claimed.[143]

6. Restrictions and trustees

[13.34] Restrictions not in a standard form it should be reasonable and straightforward and should not impose an unreasonable burden on the registry.[144] Specimen forms of restriction will be prescribed for the most common cases involving trustees.

(1) Normal trusts

[13.35] A restriction is usually entered at the same time as the transfer to the trustee,[145] but a freestanding application may be required after an existing proprietor has declared himself to be a trustee. A box on the form of application for registration has to be ticked to indicate the capacity in which the land is taken, for example as a trustee or as a beneficial tenant in common, from which cases entry of the appropriate restriction then follows automatically.[146]

(2) Joint proprietor restriction

[13.36] Joint proprietors are necessarily trustees,[147] and a restriction is needed in almost all cases,[148] for example where land is held by trustees of land under a settlement giving successive interests in land or for beneficial tenants in common. The obligatory form is as follows:

> "No disposition by a single proprietor under which capital money arises should be registered without an order of the court."[149]

This should be entered as soon as joint proprietorship arises, even though the restriction only bites once the trustees are reduced by deaths to a single survivor. The joint proprietor restriction is now refined so as to be targeted specifically at this objective,

---

[140] Other suggested uses are: donee of special power of appointment; to protect the Charity Commissioners in relation to charitable land; to protect the Church Commissioners in relation to ecclesiastical land; and for receivers and administrators etc: DLRR 2003 r 92; r 96 gives various restrictions for use with public sector housing.
[141] LRA 2002 s 77; Law Com 271 (2001), EN [347–349].
[142] LRA 1925 s 54; *City of London BS* v. Flegg [1988] AC 54, 76A.
[143] LRA 2002 s 45; Law Com 271 (2001), [6.54–6.57]; DLRR 2003 r 94; DLRR CD ch 6, [22–26].
[144] LRA 2002 s 43(1).
[145] LRA 2002 s 44(1).
[146] Law Com 271 (2001), [6.40], EN [196–202]; DLRR 2003 r 93.
[147] See below **[16.03]**.
[148] LRA 2002 s 44.
[149] DLRR 2003 r 93; LR Form A.

so that it will no longer impact on dealings by a trust corporation[150] or by a single personal representative, appointments of trustees, vestings of land in a beneficiary, or on a partition. A survivor of joint proprietors may legitimately carry out certain transactions – such as the transfer of the land to the sole remaining beneficiary – so in such a case the land registry will prompt for an application to remove the restriction accompanied by a certificate from a conveyancer establishing the necessary facts.

This restriction remains obligatory so long as there are joint proprietors and so it cannot be withdrawn.

(3) Beneficial joint tenancy

[13.37] Beneficial joint tenancy does not require a joint proprietor restriction.[151] Take a case with three joint tenants – A, B and C. When A dies, no restriction is needed because B and C still have overreaching powers. If B then dies, leaving C as sole proprietor, he holds not as a trustee but as sole beneficial owner who is entitled by survivorship on his own account. No restriction is ever needed so long as the parties remain joint tenants beneficially. If there is a severance of the beneficial joint tenancy so as to convert it into a beneficial tenancy in common this will call for a restriction.[152]

(4) Charging orders against beneficial interests

[13.38] A restriction may now be used to protect a charging order against a beneficial interest under a trust.[153] The beneficial interest can be overreached by a sale by the trustees, and so the charging order is transferred to the proceeds of sale held by the trustees; the restriction ensures that payment is made to the secured creditor rather than to the beneficiary who incurred the debt.

F. CONSENTS AND RESTRICTED POWERS

[13.39] A person creating a private trust can crab the powers of the trustees (and so protect the beneficiaries) by a provision of the trust document restricting the trustees' powers or by a consent provision.

1. Express consents

[13.40] Any private trust of land may require the consent of any person to the exercise of any management function,[154] as was the case before 1997 with trusts for sale.[155] Thus:

---

[150] LRA 1925 s 58(3).

[151] DLRR 2003 r 93(1).

[152] See below **[16.32]**.

[153] LRA 2002 s 42(4); Law Com 271 (2001), EN [202]; DLRR 2003 r 92; LR Form L. A caution is no longer appropriate for this purpose.

[154] TLATA 1996 ss 8, 10. Consents are not allowed in charitable, ecclesiastical or public trusts: s 10(2); DLRR 2003 r 93(6).

[155] This was an immediate trust for sale rather than a strict settlement: LPA 1925 s 205(1)(xxix); *Re Goodall's S* [1909] 1 Ch 440, Swinfen Eady J; *Re Horne's SE* (1888) 39 Ch D 84, CA; *Re Hotchkys* (1886) 32

*to T1 and T2 in fee simple on trust to sell with the consent of Q and to hold the land
until sale and the proceeds after sale on trust for B for life.*

Consent powers would generally be given, as in this example, to a named beneficiary,
often a life tenant,[156] or to any person answering a description such as "my eldest
living child", or possibly even to one of the trustees. A request trust enabled a named
beneficiary to precipitate a sale, but it is unclear whether this form of trust survives the
1996 reform.[157]

Consent provisions have always bound purchasers,[158] so trustees of unregistered
land are required to do all reasonable to bring the consent provision to the knowledge
of a purchaser. If title is registered, a restriction is required.[159] Purchasers are offered
considerable protection: a purchaser is only bound when he has actual knowledge of
the requirement,[160] a buyer need see only two consents[161] and consent is not needed
from a minor.[162] A receiver has power to consent on behalf of a person who is not
mentally competent.[163] Where the consent provision is protected on the register by
restriction, the register will name the person entitled to grant or withhold consent, but
the registrar has power to override the restriction in appropriate cases where, for
example, the named person has died or cannot be traced.[164]

Provisions for consents confer a right of veto, if the person named is adult.[165] There
is power to dispense with an unobtainable consent,[166] but the court will not overrule
a competent adult who has decided it is not in his interests to agree to sale.[167] A beneficiary was overruled in *Re Beale's ST* after he had become bankrupt and so lost his
beneficial interest in the property.[168]

2. Abolition of implied consent provisions

[13.41] The Trusts of Land Act 1996 requires consent provisions to be express.[169]
Implied consent requirements[170] were an undiscoverable trap for buyers and lenders
before 1997, but the trap is abolished where land is held under a trust of land.

Ch D 408, CA; *Re Ffennell's S* [1918] 1 Ch 91; *Duke of Marlborough* v. *Att-Gen* [1945] Ch 145, 154–155,
Morton LJ; see below **[14.03]**.

[156] *Truell* v. *Tysson* (1856) 21 Beav 437, 52 ER 928; *Robertson* v. *Walker* (1875) 44 LJ Ch 220 (annuitant).

[157] P Sparkes *NLL* (1st ed), 112–113.

[158] *Greetham* v. *Colton* (1865) 34 Beav 615, 55 ER 773.

[159] LRA 2002 s 26; DLRR 2003 r 92.

[160] TLATA 1996 s 16(3).

[161] TLATA 1996 s 10(1); LPA 1925 s 26(1). Trustees should obtain the consent of the guardian of a
minor or the receiver of a person under mental disability.

[162] TLATA 1996 s 10(3); LPA 1925 s 26(2); *Re Neave & Chapman & Wren* (1880) 49 LJ Ch 642 (express
clause). Legitimacy is irrelevant: Family Law Reform Act 1987 s 19; this reverses: *Butler* v. *Gregory* (1902)
18 TLR 370; *Re M* [1955] 2 QB 479.

[163] Mental Health Act 1983 ss 95, 96, 99; LPA 1925 s 26(2).

[164] LRA 2002 s 41(2)–(3); Law Com 271 (2001), EN [195].

[165] *Duke of Marlborough* v. *Att-Gen* [1945] Ch 145, CA; *Re Tweedie & Miles' C* (1884) 27 Ch D 355.

[166] TLATA 1996 s 14(2)(a).

[167] *Re Herklot's WT* [1964] 1 WLR 583, CA; *Abbey National* v. *Moss* (1994) 26 HLR 249, CA.

[168] [1932] 2 Ch 15, Maugham J; *Re Cooper* (1884) 27 Ch D 565.

[169] TLATA 1996 s 8(2) requires exclusion to be by express provision.

[170] *Re Herklot's WT* [1964] 1 WLR 583, CA; *Abbey National* v. *Moss* (1994) 26 HLR 249, CA; *Harris* v.
Harris (1996) 72 P & CR 408, CA; *Bank of Baroda* v. *Dhillon* [1998] 1 FLR 524, CA; S Pascud [1998] *Conv*
415; P Sparkes *NLL* (1st ed), 113.

3. Purchasers

[13.42] Purchasers of a beneficial interest can generally override rights of occupation enforceable between the original beneficial co-owners. A purpose trust might arise between parties who buy a home to house their family,[171] but these rarely survive a change of parties. Devlin LJ thought it obvious in the leading case, *Jones* v. *Challenger*, that the matrimonial home would have to be sold if the wife died and left her interest to a third party.[172] A purpose between multiple co-owners may survive some changes, but after sufficient alterations in the parties the presumption will shift in favour of sale.[173] Since assignment of a beneficial interest may severely prejudice the interest of the other co-owner, there was a logic in Lord Denning's desire to restrain dispositions of the beneficial interests by injunction,[174] but, Russell LJ's denial of this jurisdiction was technically correct.[175]

Purchasers acting in consort with a beneficial co-owner may not be seen as having an interest distinct from the party who sells to them. A classic illustration is *Chhokar* v. *Chhokar*.[176] The husband sold the matrimonial home to a purchaser who paid less than the market value for the husband's share and was party to a campaign to try to oust the wife. The purchaser stood in the shoes of the husband, and was bound by the purpose; this should have been so even if the wife had not forgiven her husband and taken him back(!). A scoundrel should not get equitable assistance.

4. Restrictions on powers

[13.43] Trustees of land have all the dispositive powers of absolute owners,[177] power to transfer the land to the beneficiaries when all are adult,[178] power to purchase land,[179] and the power to partition.[180] However, limitations may be imposed by the trust document on any of these powers available to private trustees of land, either by exclusion of the power, a limitation, or the imposition of an express consent requirement.[181]

In the case of unregistered land, limitations will only affect a purchaser of unregistered land who has actual knowledge of the limitation. The trustees should take reasonable steps to bring the limitations to the attention of a buyer.[182] After the title has been registered, any limitation of the powers of disposition of the registered proprietors must be drawn to the attention of the registrar (whenever it arises) in order that a restriction can be entered on the register, since until that occurs otherwise the

---

[171] See below **[19.08ff]**.
[172] [1961] 1 QB 176, 183; *Re Citro* [1991] Ch 142, 158H–159A, Nourse LJ.
[173] *Re Buchanan-Wollaston's Conveyance* [1939] Ch 738, CA; see above **[19.09]**.
[174] *Bedson* v. *Bedson* [1965] 2 QB 666, 678E–G, 687C, Davies LJ; *Bull* v. *Bull* [1955] 1 QB 234, 239; *Smith* v. *Smith* [1945] 1 All ER 584, 586D, Denning J; *Brown* v. *Brown* [1959] P 86, 91, Hodson LJ.
[175] At 698F–700E.
[176] [1984] FLR 313, CA.
[177] TLATA 1996 s 6(1).
[178] S 6(2).
[179] S 6(3)
[180] S 7. This cannot be used to divide a commonhold unit: Chold and L Ref A 2002 sch 5.
[181] TLATA s 8(1)–(2); G Watt [1997] *Conv* 263; exclusion is not possible if the trust is charitable.
[182] TLATA 1996 s 16(3).

proprietor retains all powers of registered disposition.[183] Restrictions generally require the conveyancer acting for the trustees to certify when applying to register the transaction that it complies with the trust deed.

5. Exclusion of the power of sale

[13.44] A major novelty of the Trusts of Land Act 1996 was the provision permitting total exclusion of the power of sale, thus reversing a policy that had endured for centuries, and which reached its culmination in the legislation designed to break strict settlements by imposing a power of sale out of court.[184] A paterfamilias is, once again, allowed to keep his inherited land within the family by the creation of an unsaleable trust. Proponents of the reform assume that the court would retain an overriding power to order the sale of the land, but this is to overlook the fact that a court order must relate "to the exercise by the trustees of any of their functions".[185] If the trust is created in T1 and T2 "without the power to sell", the functions of the trustees do not include sale, and sale could not be ordered under a literal reading of the legislation. Unsaleable trusts are likely to be a serious obstacle in conveyancing and it is predicted that section 8 will eventually need to be changed.

G. DELEGATIONS

[13.45] The Trusts of Land Act 1996[186] permits trustees of land to delegate *any* function[187] to any beneficiary of full age entitled to an interest in possession. If powers to sell or to mortgage are delegated, the purchase money must be paid to at least two trustees.[188] All trustees must join in the act of delegation, which remains vulnerable to revocation at the whim of any one of the trustees, as well as on any change of trustees, or the loss of beneficial entitlement.[189] Trustees avoid liability for the acts of delegates provided that they exercise reasonable care when deciding to delegate.[190] Delegations are made by power of attorney with purchasers, purchasers relying on the usual statutory protections for people buying from an attorney.[191]

---

[183] DLRR 2003 r 92; LR Form B.
[184] See below [14.10].
[185] TLATA 1996 s 14(2)(a).
[186] TLATA 1996 s 9; it is not permissible to use an enduring power: s 9(6).
[187] S 9(1). The pre-1997 power in LPA 1925 s 29 was limited to powers of leasing, accepting surrenders of leases, and management. Existing delegations continue: TLATA 1996 s 9(9).
[188] TLATA 1996 s 9(7); this is clearly intended despite a slight ambiguity.
[189] S 9(2), (6).
[190] S 9(8).
[191] S 9(2); see below [14.44ff].

H. INTERESTS OVERREACHED

1. Overreachable interests

[13.46] Statute mentions four specific cases when *equitable* interests may be over-reached,[192] thus reinforcing the common but inaccurate perception that *legal* interests cannot be overreached. It is true that *trustees* overreach only equitable interests after 1925,[193] but legal rights were overreached under pre-1926 strict settlements and this continues to be the case when a lender exercises the power of sale in a legal mortgage.[194]

The creator of a trust confers a mandate on the trustees to sell the property free of interests created by the settlement, but he cannot improve the title of his trustees by purporting to free the land of interests which bound him at the moment of settlement. Equitable interest which can be overreached by trustees include all beneficial interests and powers affecting the land under the trust,[195] even a trust which is being adminis-tered by the court.[196] including beneficial co-ownerships, life interests,[197] voluntary leases for life,[198] future interests, remainders and reversions,[199] interests of a discre-tionary class of beneficiaries, powers of appointment, licences to occupy under the trust, and rights to income. There is no magic in it: the process is repeated in four million or so sales every year.

2. Non-overreachable burdens

[13.47] Burdens are adverse rights which bind the land in the hands of a purchaser. Easements, restrictive covenants and many others cannot be rendered in money. Money charges could be converted to money, but only by destroying the whole concept of the security provided by a mortgage, that the debt is guaranteed against the land itself.[200] Burdens created by the trustees cannot be overreached because subse-quent dealings implicitly take effect subject to the earlier ones.[201] No precise category of burdens exists, but those safe from extended overreaching must also be exempt from normal overreaching.[202]

---

[192] LPA 1925 s 2: (1) strict settlement, (2) trustees of land, (3) mortgage-lenders or personal representa-tives, and (4) under court order. This applied to transactions by trustees for sale before 1997: *Birmingham Midshires* v. *Sabherwal* (2000) 80 P & CR 256, CA; C Harpum (2000) 116 *LQR* 341.

[193] LPA 1925 s 1(1)–(3).

[194] See below **[29.24]**.

[195] Before 1926 called equitable estates, a phrase abandoned for no good reason in 1925: FH Lawson & B Rudden, *Introduction to Property Law* (Clarendon Press, 2nd ed, 1982), 101.

[196] *Re Mansel* (1885) 54 LJ Ch 883; *Bernhardt* v. *Galsworthy* [1929] 1 Ch 549.

[197] *Mills* v. *Dugmore* (1861) 30 Beav 104, 54 ER 828, Romilly MR.

[198] Outside LPA 1925 s 149(6), and so operating as life interests.

[199] TLATA 1996 sch 3 para 4(2)(b), inserts LPA 1925 s 2(1A), to make it clear that implied reversions are overreachable.

[200] Suppose a mortgage for £100,000 is secured on land worth £75,000; were overreaching to be allowed the lender would lose his security for the final £25,000.

[201] LPA 1925 s 3(1)(ii).

[202] See below **[14.09]**.

Most difficult to categorise are estoppel rights, but these were considered in *Birmingham Midshires* v. *Sabherwal*[203] and correctly classified as burdens, and not, therefore, overreachable.

3. When does overreaching occur?

[13.48] A normal sale of registered land involves three stages: contract to buy, completion, and registration of the transfer. At this last stage overreaching has indisputably occurred. Professor Thompson argued[204] that since legal title only passes on registration, overreaching cannot occur earlier. He disputed the result of *Flegg*[205] which allowed overreaching on completion of a mortgage, even though a caution prevented a legal mortgage being created by registration. Lord Oliver thought that overreaching had occurred because the building society was "a purchaser in proper form from the trustees of statutory trusts",[206] so that there is a potential for overreaching on execution of the charge,[207] which becomes full overreaching when registration follows.[208] Indeed, as soon as the trustees have contracted to sell, there has been a tentative form of overreaching which the courts should facilitate by ordering the beneficiaries to give up possession. In just the same way, an overreaching sale by a lender cannot be blocked by tender of the redemption money after a lender has made a contract to sell.[209] Priorities of adverse interests are finally determined when a legal transfer is registered and until that time there is merely a queue to get on to the register. If a transfer in that queue will cause overreaching then the beneficiaries have effectively already lost their rights in the land.

I. POWER-BASED OVERREACHING

1. Failure to provide statutory basis for overreaching

[13.49] Statute does not provide any basis for normal overreaching. A draft provision[210] was lost from the final consolidated form of the 1925 legislation,[211] leaving no statutory clarification of how overreaching is achieved by trustees for sale[212] or trustees of land.[213]

---

[203] (2000) 80 P & CR 256, CA; C Harpum (2000) 116 *LQR* 341. An interest which creates a share in property must be treated as a constructive trust and not an estoppel: see below **[17.29]**.

[204] [1988] *Conv* 108, 112.

[205] [1988] AC 54, HL.

[206] At 1279F.

[207] LRA 1925 s 27(3).

[208] P Sparkes [1988] *Conv* 141.

[209] *Waring* v. *London & Manchester Assurance Co* [1935] Ch 310; *Property & Bloodstock* v. *Emerton* [1968] Ch 94.

[210] LPA 1922 s 3(3)(i).

[211] LP (Amendment) A 1924 sch 2 part II; C Harpum [1990] *CLJ* 277, 291.

[212] LPA 1925 s 2(2) applies only to trustees approved by the court.

[213] TLATA 1996 sch 3 para 4.

2.   Rejection of conversion theory

[13.50] Text writers tended to see overreaching as a new and nobler function for conversion theory.[214] Abolition of that doctrine in 1996[215] had no impact on overreaching so it is necessary to discard this as an explanation for overreaching. Harold Potter found "nothing novel in the overriding powers of a tenant for life . . . but only in their very moderate extension by the new legislation."[216]

3.   Power based overreaching

[13.51] Potter's thesis was that a power to sell land implies the power to free it of interests affecting the land that would impede the sale. Medieval law allowed executors to sell the estate to raise money to pay off the deceased's debts[217] and recognises testamentary trusts for sale.[218] Bare powers of sale were facilitated by the Statute of Uses 1535.[219] Trusts for sale to meet debts were recognised by Bridgman's precedents,[220] and genuine holding trusts only became fully established after 1840.[221] Strict settlements that could tie up family estates for many generations could be broken by express powers of sale after about 1850[222] and by statutory powers after 1882.[223] Sales of shares and other personal property also involve pure power-based overreaching.[224]

Charles Harpum[225] adopted power based overreaching in his critique of *City of London Building Society* v. *Flegg*.[226] Overreaching occurs because trustees have a *power* of (as opposed to a *trust* for) sale though strictly this only explains why trustees may *override* beneficial interests. The overreaching effect calls for more explanation. A trust for sale contains an express trust of the proceeds of sale which explains why the beneficiaries obtain interests in the fund created by sale: the trust says so.[227] *Trusts of land* are usually simple trusts which lack any separate trust of the proceeds of sale, but it seems obvious that the trustees must be prevented from taking beneficially, which can only be achieved by allowing the beneficiaries a claim against the proceeds.

---

[214] HG Hanbury, *Essays in Equity* (Clarendon Press, 1934), 33; S Anderson (1984) 100 *LQR* 86, 108n, attributes this to Cheshire's second edition; other adherents were Williams, Lightwood, Hargreaves, the various editors of Snell, and Megarry.

[215] TLATA 1996 s 3.

[216] (1928) 44 *LQR* 227, 233. The main innovation is that the legal estate is now vested in the trustee with power of sale.

[217] Holdsworth's *History* vol 7, 153.

[218] M Lewis (1949) 13 *Conv* (NS) 429 (will trust 1387); *Anon* (1363) Jenk 43, 145 ER 33.

[219] G Farwell, *Powers* (Stevens, 2nd ed, 1893), 1; *Cluette* v. *Storey* [1911] 1 Ch 18, 30 Farwell J; SJ Bailey (1944) 8 *CLJ* 36; S Anderson (1984) 100 *LQR* 86, 89.

[220] *Popham* v. *Hobert* (1676) 1 Cas in Ch 280, 22 ER 801; common by mid C18th: JM Lightwood (1927) 3 *CLJ* 59, 60.

[221] SJ Bailey (1944) 8 *CLJ* 36; JM Lightwood (1927) 3 *CLJ* 59, 62–63; earlier was *Pechel* v. *Fowler* (1795) 2 Anst 549, 145 ER 963.

[222] A Underhill (1935) 51 *LQR* 221, 225; SJ Bailey (1944) 8 *CLJ* 36; Holdsworth's *History* vol 7, 151.

[223] SLA 1882 s 3; SLA 1925 s 72.

[224] CJ Harpum [1990] *CLJ* 277, 303; *Re Pope's C* [1911] 2 Ch 442; *Hume* v. *Lopes* [1892] AC 112; *Re Roth* (1896) 74 LT 50; *Re Hilton* [1909] 2 Ch 548; *Harrold* v. *Harrold* (1861) 3 Giff 192, 66 ER 378.

[225] CJ Harpum [1990] *CLJ* 277; CJ Harpum [1987] *CLJ* 392; WJ Swadling [1987] *Conv* 451; *Whitlock's case* (1609) 8 Co Rep 69b, 77 ER 580.

[226] [1988] AC 54, HL

[227] *Sood* [1997] Ch 276, 281D, Peter Gibson LJ.

However the Trusts of Land Act 1996 needed to say so[228] and to create a clear trust of the sale proceeds.

J. DEFECTIVE OVERREACHING

[13.52] *Flegg* suggests that overreaching is a matter of black and white, but really there is sun, full shade, and half shade, and into that last area, the penumbra, fall cases where the trustees have breached their duties to the beneficiaries, so that a fastidious buyer who knew would decline to have anything to do with the land offered. Let us consider one representative example which is central to the success or failure of the Trusts of Land Act 1996.

> Suppose that land worth £100,000 is held *by T1 and T2 for B1 for life with remainder to B2 absolutely*, where B1 is an adult in occupation of the land. The trustees sell the land to a purchaser (P) for £25,000. Has overreaching occurred?

Clearly the beneficiaries will be entitled to pursue the trustees for breach of trust, and it is conceivable that there may be personal remedies against the buyer for knowing receipt of trust property. Does the breach of trust impinge on and invalidate the title to the land in the hands of the buyer? This may depend whether title is registered or unregistered.

1. Trusts of unregistered land

[13.53] Trustees of land must exercise powers "for the purpose of exercising their functions as trustees"[229] and that trustees must observe the rights of the beneficiaries[230] and general rules of equity,[231] unless exempted by an express provision of the trust.[232] Trustees have fiduciary obligations to act for their beneficiaries rather than for themselves. Their duties to perform competently include an obligation to get the best price[233] for the land when selling,[234] or at least a price that appears to them to be reasonable,[235] with only very limited exceptions for works of public benefit.[236] So strong is this duty that trustees are obliged to gazump by accepting a higher offer if one is received before exchange of contracts.[237] At auction a reserve ought to be fixed.[238] After completion[239] of the sale, a beneficiary can only upset the sale if the

---

[228] TLATA 1996 s 17.
[229] TLATA 1996 s 6(1).
[230] S 6(5).
[231] S 6(6).
[232] S 8(1).
[233] This is no longer a pre-condition to legal validity that the sale.
[234] *Ord* v. *Noel* (1820) 5 Madd 438, 56 ER 962; *Taylor* v. *Tabrum* (1833) 6 Sim 281, 58 ER 599 (refused £6,000 before selling for £3,600); *Robinson* v. *Briggs* (1853) 1 Sm & G 188, 217–218, 65 ER 81, Stuart V-C; *Franks* v. *Bollans* (1867) 37 LJ Ch 148, 158, Stuart V-C; A Samuels (1975) 39 *Conv (NS)* 117.
[235] *Mortlock* v. *Buller* (1804) 10 Ves 292, 32 ER 857; *Grove* v. *Search* (1906) 22 TLR 290.
[236] SLA 1925 ss 54–57.
[237] *Buttle* v. *Saunders* [1950] 2 All ER 193, Wynn-Parry J; (1950) 66 *LQR* 295.
[238] *Re Peyton's S* (1862) 30 Beav 252, 54 ER 885.
[239] Specific performance could be refused before completion: *Dance* v. *Goldingham* (1873) LR 8 Ch App 902, 911, James LJ, 913, Mellish LJ; *Bridger* v. *Rice* (1819) 1 Jac & W 74, 37 ER 303; *Shrewsbury &*

purchaser and trustees were acting in collusion.[240] Equally fundamental is the requirement to sell to an independent purchaser, for if the buyer is someone connected to the trustee he will be liable to account for any profit made and more importantly the buyer's title will be voidable. This prevents sale to any of the trustees, family members, or the family solicitor.[241]

Purchasers of unregistered land are exempted purchasers from the need to consider breaches of the trustees' duties.[242] A purchaser who knows of a breach of trust cannot, nevertheless, overreach or even override the beneficiaries since only a purchaser[243] in good faith is protected: there is a requirement of honesty. In this way, trustees of land are required to get a fair price for the land before being granted the power to overreach. Restrictions on powers imposed by statute,[244] court orders, and orders of Charity Commissioners[245] must also be observed, but other restrictions are binding only when the purchaser has actual knowledge of a breach.[246]

2. Trusts of registered land

[13.54] Protection for buyers from trustees of land is not needed when title is registered.[247] There is a pure (pre-Cave) curtain, subject only to any restriction on the register. Standard restrictions require purchase money to be paid to two trustees, but do not indicate how much money must be paid.[248] Sale at an undervalue gives title, honesty in relation to known trusts not being a requirement.[249] Amendment of the 1925 scheme in 1996 may have created a problem,[250] but this is eradicated by the provision that a proprietor can exercise all owner's powers apart from any restriction on the register.[251] A person who buys from the proprietor and complies with the terms of any restriction gets good title and the beneficiary loses any overriding status.

Birmingham Rly v. *London & NW Rly* (1853) 4 De G M & G 115, 43 ER 451; *Turner* v. *Harvey* (1821) Jac 169, 37 ER 814.

[240] TA 1925 s 13(2); *Davies* v. *Hall* [1954] 1 WLR 855.
[241] *Robinson* v. *Briggs* (1853) 1 Sm & G 188, 65 ER 81.
[242] TLATA 1996 ss 6(5), 16(1).
[243] S 23(1); LPA 1925 s 205(1)(xxi).
[244] TLATA 1996 s 6(8).
[245] S 6(6)–(7); separate protections are available for a person buying charity land, see below **[14.17ff]**.
[246] S 6(6)–(8).
[247] S 16(7). The reason according to Law Com 181 (1989), [6.1], was that protection for registered land had to be tied to the general review of overreaching which followed from *Flegg*. Given that this has now been scrapped, the trusts of land scheme is left imbalanced.
[248] There ought to be a standard restriction on the register requiring full value to be obtained whenever the proprietors are trustees, unless perhaps they are themselves beneficially entitled. This restriction is allowed under DLRR 2003 r 92, but is neither usual nor mandatory.
[249] LRA 2002 s 29.
[250] G Ferris & G Battersby: [1998] *Conv* 168; [2001] *Conv* 221; (2002) 118 *LQR* 270.
[251] LRA 2002 s 26(1); this provision may be much wider than is intended; see below **[15.03]**.

14

MANAGEMENT TRUSTS

Pre 1997 trusts: trusts for sale, bare trusts, and strict settlements.
Management during incapacity. Charities. death. School sites. Restrictions.
Insolvency. Powers of attorney: ordinary and enduring, delegation of trusts
and purchase from attorneys.

A. INTRODUCTION

[14.01] Were titles mainly unregistered, this chapter might appear to consist of an appalling ragbag of unconnected matters, but in the crazy world of registration there is a clear and underlying logic – the use of a restriction. If the rules for straightforward trusts of land can now be taken as read,[1] a number of anomalous or special forms of trusts still require consideration. These include pre-1997 trusts, strict settlements, charitable trusts, school sites, extended overreaching powers applied to family charges, and trusts imposed on after-acquired land trusts for management on death, minority and incapacity. Also included are special uses of restrictions to cover quasi-corporate landowners, landowners with restricted powers and on insolvency. The chapter concludes with a discussion of the use of power of attorney to pass management functions to an attorney without the division of legal and equitable ownership involved in a trust, and also the delegation of trusts and trust functions by way of power of attorney.

B. PRE-1997 TRUSTS FOR SALE

1. Nature of a trust for sale

[14.02] A trust for sale was the normal form of trust used for land holding before the 1996 reforms[2] and it retains utility even today for investment property or where sale is really intended. The land is vested in trustees, who have a duty to sell the land. To take a simplified unregistered form of trust:

> '*to T1 and T2 in fee simple on trust to sell the property and to hold the proceeds of sale or the net rents and profits until sale on trust for X for life, with remainder to Y absolutely.*'[3]

---

[1] See above **[13]**.
[2] Cheshire & Burn (16th ed), 78–79, 215–225; Megarry & Wade (6th ed), [8.109–8.122].
[3] This is drawn from the now repealed LPA 1925 s 35 (now repealed) "net" here means subject to the payment of expenses.

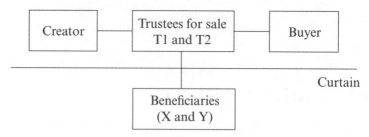

Figure 14-1 A trust for sale

The trustees held the legal estate and control of the basic management functions.

2. Existence of a trust for sale

[14.03] Between 1925 and the end of 1996 it was necessary to create expressly an *immediate binding trust for sale*[4] in order to avoid being drawn into the cumbersome machinery of the strict settlement. This remains important when proving title to unregistered land involving an old trust; proper proof of the absence of a strict settlement is of vital importance in establishing that title has passed as it has appeared to do.[5]

A trust required a pre-emptory direction imposing a mandatory duty of sale on the trustees, though this could be balanced by a power to postpone sale or a requirement to proceed to sale only with the consent of named people.[6] If, instead, trustees were given a power they had a discretion whether or not to sell,[7] and this created a strict settlement.[8] Trusts *to sell or retain* land were treated as trusts for sale with a power of postponement both before 1926 and afterwards.[9]

A trust for sale also had to be immediate, in contrast to a trust arising at some time in the future – for example when a duty to sell arose when a life tenant died,[10] a lender demanded payment,[11] or after a fixed time.[12] In *Re Hanson*[13] trustees were directed to purchase a house for the testator's widow to live in until their son attained 25, and only then to sell, but until that time this was a strict settlement. The difference was largely semantic. For example in *Re Herklots' WT*[14] a will passed a house to trustees for sale, and even though a Miss Gordon was given the right to live in house for life "without prejudice to the trust for sale", the duty of sale was nevertheless still held to be immediate.

---

[4] LPA 1925 s 205(1)(xxix), based on cases on SLA 1882 s 63(1) and SLA 1884 s 7; the exemption for trusts for sale was an afterthought: SLA 1925 s 1(7); LP (Amendment) A 1926 sch; SLA 1925 s 117(1)(xxx).

[5] *Re Bryant & Barningham's C* (1890) 44 Ch D 218, CA.

[6] LPA 1925 s 205(1)(xxix).

[7] *Re Hotchkys* (1886) 32 Ch D 408.

[8] See below **[14.10]**.

[9] LPA 1925 s 25(4); *Re Crips* (1906) 95 LJ 865; *Re Johnson* [1915] 1 Ch 435; *Re White's S* [1930] 1 Ch 179.

[10] *Want* v. *Stallibrass* (1873) LR 8 Exch 175; *Carlyon* v. *Truscott* (1875) LR 20 Eq 348.

[11] *Rooke* v. *Kensington* (1856) 25 LJ Ch 567.

[12] *Re Horne's SE* (1888) 39 Ch D 84; *Re House* [1929] 2 Ch 166.

[13] [1928] Ch 96, Astbury J; *Bevan* v. *Johnston* [1990] 2 EGLR 33, CA.

[14] [1964] 1 WLR 583, CA; *Ayers* v. *Benton* (1967) 204 EG 359; *Abbey National BS* v. *Moss* (1994) 26 HLR 249, CA. Query the correctness of *Bacon* v. *Bacon* [1947] P 151.

Trusts were binding if the trustees were obliged to sell the estate in all circumstances and not just to pay debts or as building plots.[15] It was necessary to give the trustee power to sell free of any legal estates affecting the land[16] but it was not essential that they could overreach all equitable interests.[17]

3.   Transactions exceeding the powers of pre-1997 trustees for sale

[14.04] Trustees for sale used to have limited power and often effected transactions which were breaches of trust. Examples occurred when land was mortgaged to secure business debts,[18] where the house was remortgaged to pay the trustees' private debts,[19] and even (curiously) where the mortgage was used to finance the initial acquisition of the house.[20] When the trust land was registered, a restriction was required,[21] but the registry wrongly discouraged such entries and so the problem was invariably overlooked.[22] This official view confused the protected position of a buyer with the limited status of the trustees, though fortunately the 1996 Act gives trustees of land the full powers of an absolute owner. This aligns the law with earlier registry thinking.

Unregistered trustees for sale obviously had power to sell their land,[23] but pre-1997 they were limited to Settled Land Act 1925 powers.[24] Transactions which they lacked power to effect included gifts,[25] undervalued sales, long leases, the grant of options[26] and almost all mortgages.[27] Charles Harpum suggested that power-based overreaching required strict compliance with the terms of an authorised power. It was, he said, a misconception that "overreaching will take place whenever trustees for sale make *any* disposition, whether it is within their powers or not."[28] On his view, an unregistered *Flegg*[29] would not be overreached. Brilliant as the general thesis is, this particular criticism proceeds on a false analogy with bare powers. Before 1926, a bare power of sale could be vested in a person who held no estate, and to pass title it was necessary to observe precisely the terms of his power of sale,[30] a "blundering execution" passing nothing.[31] But modern trusts vest the legal estate in the trustees, so that legal title can pass either under a sale authorised by the trust deed (as before) *or* under an *un*authorised sale to a purchaser who is protected, that is one without notice of any

---

[15] *Re Smith & Lonsdale's C* [1934] WN 36.

[16] *Re Parker's SE* [1928] Ch 247, 263, Romer J; query the correctness of this dictum.

[17] *Re Leigh's SE* [1926] Ch 852; *Re Leigh's SE (No 2)* [1927] 2 Ch 13; *Re Ryder & Steadman's C* [1927] 2 Ch 62, CA. Such interests could be removed by extended overreaching powers.

[18] *Williams & Glyn's Bank* v. *Boland* [1981] AC 487, HL.

[19] *City of London Building Society* v. *Flegg* [1988] AC 54, HL.

[20] *Abbey National BS* v. *Cann* [1991] 1 AC 56, HL.

[21] LR Form 10.

[22] *Sood* [1997] Ch 276, 281F, 286D.

[23] Amplified by TA 1925 s 12.

[24] LPA 1925 s 28.

[25] *Davey* v. *Durrant* reported in G Farwell, *Powers* (Stevens, 2nd ed 1893), 548.

[26] *Oceanic Steam Navigation Co* v. *Sutherberry* (1880) 16 Ch D 236, CA.

[27] *Stroughill* v. *Anstey* (1852) 1 De GM & G 648, 42 ER 700; *Walker* v. *Southall* (1887) 56 LT 882, North J.

[28] [1990] *CLJ* 277, 279.

[29] [1988] AC 54 HL; C Harpum [1990] *CLJ* 277, 306.

[30] G Farwell *Powers* (Stevens, 2nd ed, 1893) ch V; *Hawkins* v. *Kemp* (1803) 3 East 410, 440, 102 ER 655, Ellenborough CJ; S Anderson (1984) 100 *LQR* 86, 89.

[31] *Whitlock's case* (1609) 8 Co Rep 69b, 77 ER 580.

defect.[32] That second alternative, the "great leap forward" in 1925, ensures that an unauthorised mortgage now passes legal title to the lender, the only question being whether or not the beneficial interests stick to the lender.[33]

Even if a transaction was unauthorised, manifold protections were available to purchasers.[34] They could rely on an express provision in the trust deed, or insist that a defective transaction should be remedied by the trustees,[35] and statute protected against improper use of loans,[36] false receipts,[37] and general defects in leases.[38]

Beneficial co-owners acted both as trustees and as beneficiaries under the same trust, so that collectively they constituted one absolute owner of the house. Before 1997, it was important to extend (ideally on the face of the legal title) the limited powers available to trustees for sale, so as to confer on the trustees all the powers of absolute owners. Additional powers were often limited to 80 years, even though there was no perpetuity problem – after the middle of 1964 pure management powers can be exercised indefinitely.[39] Today trustees of land have all powers[40] so extension is not required.

4. Termination of the trust for sale

[14.05] A pre-1997 title depends both on the existence of a valid trust for sale and also on its continued existence at the time of the sale. Termination of a trust for sale might be followed by a strict settlement or bare trust,[41] and also happened if trustees sold all their land.[42] But, so far as regards the safety and protection of any purchaser, a trust for sale was deemed to continue to subsist until the land was conveyed to (or under the direction of) those interested in the proceeds of sale.[43] It was arguable that a buyer was not protected if he had actual knowledge that the trust for sale had ended.

C. OTHER PRE-1997 TRUSTS

1. Bare trusts

[14.06] Bare trusts require special consideration because before the Trusts of Land and Appointment of Trustees Act 1996 they lacked a proper power of sale. The Act

---

[32] *Lloyds Bank* v. *Bullock* [1896] 2 Ch 192; *Bailey* v. *Barnes* [1894] 1 Ch 25, CA. Notice doctrine is discussed below **[15.06]**.

[33] *Caunce* v. *Caunce* [1969] 1 WLR 286; *Boland* [1981] AC 489 HL; etc.

[34] W Ambrose (1947) 11 *Conv (NS)* 86.

[35] G Farwell *Powers* (Stevens, 2nd ed, 1893) ch 7.

[36] TA 1925 s 17; *Flegg* [1988] AC 54, HL.

[37] TA 1925 s 14; LPA 1925 s 67 (payment to trustees' conveyancer).

[38] LPA 1925 s 152; *Pawson* v. *Revell* [1958] 2 QB 360, CA.

[39] Perpetuities and Accumulations Act 1964 s 8.

[40] TLATA 1996 s 6.

[41] *Re Cook* [1948] Ch 212 (there was a reconversion to land); *Re Grimthorpe* [1908] 2 Ch 675, CA.

[42] *Re Wakeman* [1945] Ch 177; *Re Wellsted's WT* [1949] Ch 296, CA; *Re Power* [1947] Ch 572. This problem is solved by TLATA 1996 ss 6(3)–(4), 17.

[43] LPA 1925 s 23; *Peters* v. *Lewes & District Rly* (1881) 18 Ch D 429; *Re Lord Sudeley & Baines & Co's C* [1894] 1 Ch 334; *Re Dyson & Fowke's C* [1896] 2 Ch 720.

embraces them as just one more species of trust of land[44] with the object of conferring a clear statutory power of sale.

A bare trust arose where one or more trustees held land on trust for a single beneficiary who was a competent adult,[45] and absolutely entitled to the land in possession. Bare trusts include both land held by a single trustee (*T holds on trust for B absolutely*) as in *Hodgson* v. *Marks*,[46] and also cases with two or more trustees,[47] and arose whether the trust was passive or active[48] since any active duty terminated when one adult beneficiary claimed the land.[49] If T buys land with money provided by B, T holds on resulting trust for B. Bare trusts also arise if B transfers land to T with an express provision that T is to hold on trust for B,[50] if a transfer is invalidated by undue influence, pending registration of a transfer, or where title is divested after the two month period allowed for first registration.[51] But a contract does not create a trust in this sense.[52] The death throes of many settlements involve a period when a single adult beneficiary becomes absolutely entitled.

The 1996 regime readily incorporates bare trusts, since the trustees hold the legal estate with a power of sale and all the other powers of an absolute owner.[53] The beneficiary is protected by consultation provisions[54] and by the rule that the beneficiary can direct the trustees how to exercise their administrative powers.[55] Transitional provisions in 1925 had sought to execute bare trusts existing at the commencement of the legislation by passing the legal estate to the beneficial owner,[56] but the possibility of bare trusts arising after 1925 was overlooked.[57] This left a doubt about whether bare trustees could overreach their beneficiaries,[58] and although it could be argued that a power of sale was implied by statute,[59] it was only safe to rely on an express power of sale.[60]

[44] S 6; Law Com 188 (1989), [1.7], [2.17], [3.10]; S Gardner (1988) 104 *LQR* 367.

[45] *Re Douglas & Powell's C* [1902] 2 Ch 296; *Re Jump* [1903] 1 Ch 129.

[46] [1971] Ch 892, CA; *Wilson* v. *Wilson* [1969] 3 All ER 945, 949C, Buckley J.

[47] C Harpum [1990] *CLJ* 277, 302, Law Com 188 (1989), [2.17]. The beneficiary might be one of the trustees; contrast in other contexts: *Morgan* v. *Swansea Urban Sanitary Authority* (1878) 9 Ch D 582; *Re Blandy Jenkins Estate* [1917] 1 Ch 46.

[48] Hanbury & Martin, *Modern Equity* (Sweet & Maxwell, 16th ed, 2001), 71–72; *Inland Revenue Commissioners* v. *Silverts* [1951] Ch 521, CA; this despite *Christie* v. *Ovington* (1875) 1 Ch D 279; *Re Docwra* (1885) 29 Ch D 693; *Re Cunningham & Frayling* [1891] 2 Ch 567.

[49] *Re Johnston* [1894] 3 Ch 204; *Re Nelson* [1928] Ch 920n, CA.

[50] *Hodgson* v. *Marks* [1971] Ch 892, CA (oral trust).

[51] See above [9.27].

[52] *Lloyds Bank* v. *Carrick* [1996] 4 All ER 630, CA.

[53] TLATA 1996 s 6.

[54] S 11.

[55] *Saunders* v. *Vautier* (1841) 4 Beav 115, 49 ER 282, affirmed Cr & Ph 240, 41 ER 482; TLATA 1996 s 6(5)–(6).

[56] LPA 1925 sch 1 part II paras 3, 6(d).

[57] Maitland's *Equity*, 140; JF Garner (1971) 35 *Conv NS* 92.

[58] Sale was possible where trustees had been appointed by the court: LPA 1925 s 2(2); WJ Swadling [1986] *Conv* 379; LPA 1922 s 3(3)(iii) was clearer; see below [14.09].

[59] C Harpum [1990] *CLJ* 277, 302–304; *Re Pratt* [1943] 2 All ER 375 (shares).

[60] H Potter (1928) 44 *LQR* 227, 233–234.

2. Trusts of after acquired land

[14.07] Since 2001,[61] trustees have had a general power to investment in land, whether for investment, for occupation, or for any other reason. This is restricted to the purchase of a legal estate in freehold or leasehold land in the UK.[62] The powers of an absolute owner can be restricted by the trust instrument and are subject to any statutory provision.

Before the recent Act trustees of land could acquire substitute land[63] but personalty trustees required authorisation from their trust instrument. Where that authorisation existed, statute imposes a trust of land on a purchaser[64] — where land is acquired by trustees of a personalty settlement or where trustees have lent money secured by a mortgage of land but the borrower has later lost the right to redeem by his delay.[65] It was therefore possible, even common, to have a situation where land had been bought without the power to do so. Before 1997 this could also arise where trustees for sale sold all their land and only afterwards – when they had ceased to hold any land – did they acquire replacement land; this replacement was not authorised and this lack of authorisation could also create problems for a purchaser who had notice of the want of authority.[66]

3. Family charges

[14.08] The Trusts of Land Act 1996 imposes a trust of land when a document made after 1996 causes land to be charged with payment of a family charge. These are defined to be a rentcharge for life or a shorter period or any capital, annual, or periodic sum charged on land, whether the charge arises immediately or only after an interval, provided that it is created voluntarily, in consideration of marriage or by way of family arrangement.[67] The beneficiary usually waives his right in order to facilitate a sale. However a recalcitrant beneficiary cannot be forced to agree to this, and in such a case formal overreaching will be required. Instruments creating a family charge operate as a declaration of trust,[68] enabling the trustees to sell the burdened land[69] free of the family charge, leaving the beneficiary to look to the proceeds of sale. Pre-1997 family charges could be imposed behind an express trust for sale but otherwise created an optional strict settlement.[70]

---

[61] Trustee Act 2000 ss 8–10; in force February 1st 2001.

[62] The duty of care applies under TA 2000 sch 1 para 2 subject to any express exclusion.

[63] TLATA 1996 s 6, as amended by TA 2000 sch 2 para 45.

[64] LPA 1925 s 32; *Power* v. *Banks* [1901] 2 Ch 487; *Re Jenkins & HE Randall & Co's C* [1903] 2 Ch 362; TLATA 1996 sch 2 para 2.

[65] LPA 1925 s 31; TLATA 1996 sch 2.

[66] *Re Wakeman* [1945] Ch 177; *Re Wellsted's WT* [1949] Ch 296, CA; *Re Power* [1947] Ch 572. This problem is solved by TLATA 1996 ss 6(3)–(4), 17.

[67] TLATA 1996 sch 1 para 3.

[68] As above.

[69] S 6; a second trustee may be needed.

[70] See below **[14.10]**.

4. Extended overreaching

[14.09] The creator of a trust confers a mandate on the trustees to sell the property free of interests created by the settlement, but neither he nor his trustees may improve his title by purporting to free the land of interests which bound him at the moment of settlement.

> Suppose that family estates were held in fee simple subject to an equitable rentcharge in favour of a family member created in 1930 but otherwise absolutely. In 1960, the freehold was then settled on trustees for sale subject to the existing equitable rentcharge. The trustees can now use *normal* overreaching to sell free of the beneficial interests under the 1960 settlement, but require *extended* overreaching powers to sell free of the 1930 rentcharge.

This is highly abnormal today though the very word "overreaching" was reserved for this case before 1926,[71] where there was some special contract or statutory power to justify an extended power.[72]

Original proposals to allow all trustees extended overreaching powers proved too drastic to pass the Lords,[73] and it is now restricted to ad hoc trusts of land.[74] Trustees have this power only if they have been approved or appointed by the court[75] or if sale is made by a trust corporation.[76] Many burdens are safe even from extended over-reaching[77]; these are interests protected by a deposit of the title deeds, restrictive covenants, equitable easements, estate contracts, and most registered land charges. However, it is possible to overreach registered annuities and general equitable charges (equitable mortgages) despite the potential prejudice of loss of security to a lender.

D. PRE-1997 STRICT SETTLEMENTS

1. Conveyancing machinery

[14.10] A strict settlement[78] was made before 1997 by creating a succession of beneficial interests without imposing any duty of sale. The simplest possible settlement benefitted *X for life, with remainder to Y absolutely*. The Settled Land Act 1925 vested the land, the right to sell, and all management powers in the tenant for life, that is an adult

---

[71] Jowitt's *Dictionary of English Law* (2nd ed by J Burke, 1995) vol 2, 1299; JM Lightwood (1927–1929) 3 *CLJ* 59, 68.

[72] Eg a compound settlement: SLA 1925 s 31; *Re Leigh's SE (No 2)* [1927] 2 Ch 13; *Re Parker's SE* [1928] 1 Ch 247; *Re Sharpe's Deed of Release* [1939] Ch 51.

[73] JM Lightwood (1927) 3 *CLJ* 59, 68.

[74] LPA 1925 s 2(2)–(3), as amended by TLATA 1996 sch 3; Cheshire & Burn (16th ed), 892–894; Megarry & Wade (6th ed), [4.073–4.082].

[75] LPA 1925 s 2(2)(a); extended powers continue for successors.

[76] The "or" in s 2(2)(a) is apparently disjunctive, however absurd it may be to deny extended powers to an approved trustee (T1) holding with a trust corporation (T2).

[77] LPA 1925 s 2(3); LPA 1922 s 3 was clearer.

[78] Chapelle's *LL* (5th ed), ch 7; Cheshire & Burn (16th ed), ch 4, 188–215, 883–889; Goo's *Sourcebook* (3rd ed), ch 12; Grays' *Elements* (3rd ed), 646–653; Maudsley & Burn *LL – Cases* (7th ed), ch 6; Megarry & Wade (6th ed), [8.003–8.108]; Thompson's *Modern LL* ch 8.

beneficiary with a life interest in possession, here X. Trustees of the settlement were appointed, primarily, to receive the capital money arising on sale.

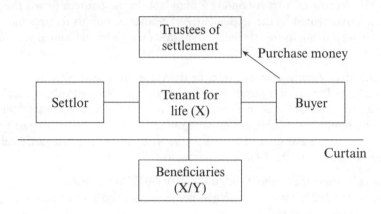

Figure 14-2 A strict settlement

Complex certainly, but with its own internal logic. It was useful as a vehicle for the management of family estates where land was vested in successive members of family. Suppose, for example that X is current Lord of Xanadu and on his death, the title, the land and the family estates would descend to his eldest son, the next Lord Xanadu. Under a strict settlement, X (the current lord) is effective owner of the land as tenant for life, a legal structure which reflects the reality on the ground.

Changes in society and in the taxation regime has made this legal fabric of aristo-cratic settlements irrelevant.[79] No new strict settlements may be created after 1996 and a limitation which would have created a strict settlement now creates a trust of land.[80] If land is passed *to T on trust for X for life with remainder to Y absolutely* the land and the management powers are vested in the trustee, T. Pre-existing strict settlements continue indefinitely.

2.   Strict settlements in proper form

[14.11] Properly created strict settlements are easy to recognise. Where title is regis-tered the terms of the settlement are not revealed by the proprietorship register, but its existence is easily deduced from a restriction which contains the names of the Settled Land Act trustees as the proper recipients of sale proceeds and other capital money.[81] This is a signal that the registered proprietor is a tenant for life,[82] a person who can control sale of the land but is not entitled to receive the sale proceeds.

A buyer needs to know little of the Settled Land Act in order to obtain a good title. Changes of ownership within the settlement (that is a change in the person entitled as

---

    [79] A Pottage (1998) 61 *MLR* 162.
    [80] TLATA 1996 s 2(1).
    [81] SLA 1925 s 119(3); LRA 2002 s 89; DLRR 2003 sch 7.
    [82] SLA 1925 s 19. A tenant for life must be an adult with a life interest in possession in the whole income: *Peasley* v. *Haileybury & Imperial Service College* [2001] WTLR 1365, Ch D. If there is none (eg because the life tenant was a minor) the land should be vested in statutory owners as defined in s 20.

tenant for life) are supervised by the registrar and a purchaser deals with whoever is registered. If a settlement ends, this must be proved to the registrar who will then remove the Settled Land Act restriction. Beneficial interests under a strict settlement can only be minor interests,[83] so that occupation of the land is no protection.

Strict settlements of unregistered land are flagged by a vesting document. A vesting deed is used for a settlement created during the settlor's lifetime or a vesting assent after a settlement created by will. The policy of the Settled Land Act 1925 was to ensure that all settlements were made by two documents,[84] a vesting deed and a trust instrument,[85] the latter being curtained off the title. So buyers must act on the basis of the vesting deed, even if it contains errors.[86] Again, the function of the vesting deed is to identify the tenant for life who holds the legal estate and can sell; it also identifies the trustees of the settlement who are required to receive and invest the purchase money.

Changes in ownership occur when, for example, a life tenant dies and the property passes to a new life tenant. Special documents mark out these changes. A vesting deed is required for a lifetime change[87] and a special grant of probate limited to settled land and a vesting assent on death.[88] These documents will now trigger compulsory first registration.[89] Buyers must assume that the settlement continues so long as there is any reference in the latest vesting document to the Settled Land Act trustees, but he must assume it has ended when there is a plain conveyance without mention of the trustees.[90]

Overreaching occurs on a sale under a strict settlement[91] by the tenant for life or statutory owners, but purchase money[92] has to be paid to the trustees of the settlement;[93] a receipt is required from two trustees or a trust corporation, or purchase money may be paid into court.[94]

3. Inadvertent strict settlements

[14.12] The Trusts of Land Act 1996 removes, at last,[95] the notorious trap of accidental strict settlements created in home made wills.[96] What is the problem with this, innocuous looking, testament?

---

[83] LRA 2002 sch 1 para 2, sch 3 para 2(a).
[84] If a lifetime settlement was created by one document: the legal estate was paralysed until the problem was rectified, and ever afterwards there was no curtain: SLA 1925 s 13; *Re Alefounder's WT* [1927] 1 Ch 360; *Davies* v. *Hall* [1954] 1 WLR 855.
[85] SLA 1925 s 4(1).
[86] S 5(3); *Re Curwen* [1931] 2 Ch 341; *Re Cayley & Evan's C* [1930] 2 Ch 143.
[87] S 8.
[88] AEA 1925 ss 22–24; SLA 1925 s 7(1). An ordinary grant and assent are used when the settlement ends.
[89] LRA 2002 s 4(1)(a), (9).
[90] SLA 1925 s 110(5); it should be supplemented by a deed of discharge: s 17.
[91] LPA 1925 s 2(1)(i); SLA 1925 s 72.
[92] *Mortlock* v. *Buller* (1804) 10 Ves Jun 292, 308, 32 ER 837, Eldon LC.
[93] Trustees are defined in a complex way by SLA 1925 s 30.
[94] SLA 1925 s 72.
[95] H Potter (1944) 8 *Conv (NS)* 147, 165; GA Grove (1961) 24 *MLR* 123, 128.
[96] *Muir* v. *Lloyds Bank* [1992] LSG July 22nd, 32; EC Ryder (1962) 15 *CLP* 194; Law Com WP 94 (1985), [3.3].

> This will is made the 1st January 1990 by me Attlee:
> 1. I give all my property, including my freehold house, to my wife for life and after her death to my child.
> 2. I appoint my wife to be my sole executor.
> [Signed by Attlee in the presence of two attesting witnesses.]

Two equitable interests were created in succession and the testator omitted to opt expressly for a trust for sale. On a death occurring before 1997 this will created a strict settlement and subsequent title should be based on a Settled Land Act vesting document, though it rarely was.

The problems were even greater where a settlement was created by a single document executed by a living settlor. This paralysed the legal title, preventing any dealing with the land until the settlement had been rectified by the execution of the two proper documents, although an honest purchaser without notice of the settlement was protected against the consequences of such a defect.[97] This problem could also arise from unguarded drafting of matrimonial orders – for example if a wife was given a right to occupy a former matrimonial home for life[98] – and again from oral licences.[99]

In terms of definition, a strict settlement arose when land was "limited in trust for persons by way of succession."[100] There could be an express trust, a trust imposed on limited interests,[101] or a succession created when a reversion arises after creation of a limited interest, for life,[102] an entail, or a determinable, base, or conditional fee. Additional forms of settlement were introduced in 1925: where there was no interest in possession – for example where land is given *to my first child to attain 30*[103] – where land was passed to a minor entitled absolutely in possession,[104] and where land was owned absolutely subject to family charges.[105]

4.   Concealed settlements

[14.13] Unless the trustees of a strict settlement collect the purchase money, the tenant for a life is not authorised to sell and any attempt to do so is void as to the legal estate.[106] Protection is provided for an honest purchaser against minor defects: he is conclusively taken to have given the best price that could reasonably have been obtained by the tenant for life, and also "to have complied with all the other require-

---

[97] SLA 1925 s 13, as amended in 1926.

[98] *Bacon* v. *Bacon* [1947] P 151; RE Megarry (1947) 63 *LQR* 421; *Morss* v. *Morss* [1972] Fam 264, CA (no trust on facts); *Martin* v. *Martin* [1978] Fam 12 (point missed); P Smith [1978] *Conv* 229.

[99] *Peasley* v. *Haileybury & Imperial Service College* [2001] WTLR 1365, Ch D; see below [19.59].

[100] SLA 1925 s 1(1)(i).

[101] LPA 1925 s 1(3); SLA 1925 s 16.

[102] SLA 1925 s 1(4); this reproduces the pre-1926 law: *Re Hunter & Hewlett's C* [1907] 1 Ch 46.

[103] SLA 1925 s 1(1)(iii). Before 1926 the land was unsaleable during any gap in the beneficial entitlement: *Re Horne's SE* (1888) 39 Ch D 84.

[104] Ss 1(1)(ii)(d), 27(1).

[105] See above [14.08].

[106] SLA 1925 s 18; *Bevan* v. *Johnston* [1990] 2 EGLR 33, CA; J Hill (1991) 107 *LQR* 596; R Bartlett [1992] *Conv* 425.

ments of this Act".[107] This protection may not apply if the tenant for life suppresses the settlement completely and purports to sell it as if he was a beneficial owner. Such a fraud enables him to collect the whole purchase price even though he has some limited beneficial interest.

Where title is registered, a buyer will get a good title since the beneficial interests are minor interests which are overridden if not protected on the register at the time of a sale. If title is unregistered the position is less satisfactory. Danckwerts J held in *Weston* v. *Henshaw*[108] that the buyer's protection broke down in this case just where it was needed most. Settled Land Act 1925 protection is only available to a buyer who knows he is dealing with a tenant for life.[109] However, a more recent case doubts this restrictive interpretation and is more lenient to the purchaser.[110] Had the settlement been created by only one document, an honest purchaser without notice of the existence of a defective settlement would be safe.[111] Clearly such a purchaser should always be protected against the suppression of an undiscoverable settlement.

E. MANAGEMENT DURING INCAPACITY

1. Minors

[14.14] Since 1970,[112] a minor has been a person under 18 years of age, majority being attained at the beginning of the eighteenth birthday. Previously majority was attained at 21,[113] and a person below that age is described as an infant throughout the 1925 legislation. A minor does not have capacity to receive or sell a legal estate in land.[114] Conferring a benefit on an underage person necessarily creates a trust, the capacity of the trustees to sell overcoming the contractual deficiency of the minor.[115] All trusts involving minors created after 1997 fall within the trusts of land scheme.

Children are the most common objects of settlements. Trustees administer the property and pay some of the income to the parents to use for the maintenance of the child, and accumulate surplus income to provide a nest egg on their majority;[116] the trustees can also make capital advancements.[117] Alternatively the trustees may allow the beneficiary to occupy the property as a home, a possibility more clearly stated under the new scheme.[118] After 1996 a straightforward trust of land suffices, that is *to T in trust for M for life*, but before 1997 the default was a strict settlement.[119]

---

[107] SLA 1925 s 110(1).

[108] [1950] Ch 510.

[109] EH Scammell [1957] *CLP* 152; GA Grove (1961) 24 *MLR* 123, 129; P Stone [1984] *Conv* 354; R Warrington [1985] *Conv* 377.

[110] *Re Morgan's Lease* [1972] Ch 1; DW Elliott (1971) 87 *LQR* 338; RH Maudsley (1973) 36 *MLR* 25; Hurrell v. *Littlejohn* [1904] 1 Ch 689.

[111] SLA 1925 s 13, as amended in 1926.

[112] Family Law Reform Act 1969 ss 1, 9.

[113] The day before the 21st anniversary: *Re Shurey* [1918] 1 Ch 263.

[114] LPA 1925 s 1(6), 19; Cheshire & Burn (16th ed), ch 29.

[115] Contracts are voidable at the instance of the minor: *Chaplin* v. *Leslie Frewin (Publishers)* [1966] Ch 71; *Cornell* v. *Harrison* [1916] 1 Ch 328; *Edwards* v. *Carter* [1893] AC 360.

[116] TA 1925 s 31. Income can be paid to a minor who is married: LPA 1925 s 21.

[117] TA 1925 ss 32.

[118] TLATA 1996 ss 12, 13.

[119] SLA 1925 s 1(1)(ii)(d).

On transfer to a minor, a trust is imposed in order to secure saleability where an absolute interest is given to or sold to a minor. No legal estate can pass, and instead an attempt to convey land to a minor operates as a declaration that the land is held on trust for him. A trust of land also arises where a minor becomes entitled on intestacy or in any other circumstance.[120] If land is passed jointly to two people – one an adult and the other a minor – a trust of land is imposed by which the adult will hold the land on trust for both of them jointly.[121] A minor cannot act as trustee, so the legislation deletes any attempt to make him one.[122]

2. Mental patients

[14.15] The Mental Health Act 1983[123] provides for the management of the property and affairs of a patient, that is a person whose mental disorder renders him incapable of managing and administering his property and affairs.[124] Management is undertaken by the Court of Protection, headed by a designated High Court judge, which assumes full control over the patient's property, including sale and purchase, mortgaging, and management control,[125] and directing provision for those whom the patient might have been expected to benefit.[126] Management is carried out by the Public Trustee acting under the supervision of the court[127] or by a receiver[128] appointed by the court to look after the affairs of an individual patient.[129] Further reform is proposed.[130]

F. CHARITIES

[14.16] Charity land may be held by individuals as charitable trustees, by an incorporated body supervised by the Charity Commissioners,[131] or by the Official Custodian of Charities[132] a course which avoids the need to vest and revest land on every change of trustees.[133] Charitable trustees now draw their managerial powers from the trusts

---

[120] TLATA 1996 sch 1 paras 1–2; similarly if land is acquired by a group of people who are all minors. Before 1997 there was a strict settlement, but if the settlement remained defective in 1996 (that is there was no vesting deed in favour of statutory owners) a trust of land arises.

[121] TLATA 1996 sch 1 para 1(2), replacing the LPA 1925 s 19 trust for sale.

[122] TLATA 1996 sch 1 paras 1(1)–(2), amending LPA 1925 s 19(5).

[123] Ss 93–113; Cheshire & Burn (16th ed) ch 29. Note also enduring powers of attorney, below **[14.39ff]**.

[124] *Imperial Loan Co* v. *Stone* [1892] 1 QB 599; AH Hudson [1984] *Conv* 32; *Hart* v. *O'Connor* [1985] AC 1000, PC; AH Hudson [1986] *Conv* 178.

[125] Mental Health Act 1983 s 97.

[126] Ss 96–97; *Re C* [1991] 3 All ER 866 Hoffmann J; *Re S* [1997] 1 FLR 96; *Re Beaney* [1978] 1 WLR 770.

[127] SI 1994/3046 r 6.

[128] Receivers have all powers of trustees of land: TLATA 1996 sch 3 amending LPA 1925 s 22; *Pritchard* v. *Briggs* [1980] Ch 338, CA (sale was subject to burdens which would bind a purchaser if there was no mental disability).

[129] Mental Health Act 1983 ss 95–96, 99; SI 1994/3046 r 8. A restriction should be placed on the register to prohibit registration of any disposition not authorised by the Court of Protection.

[130] Law Com 231 (1995); *Who Decides?* (HMSO, December 1997).

[131] Charities Act 1993 ss 50–69; DLRR 2003 r 177.

[132] Charities Act 1993 s 2; DLRR 2003 rr 176(4)(b), 178.

[133] Charitable trustees execute transactions in the name of the Official Custodian, a fact recorded on the register by a restriction: DLRR 2003 r 178.

of land scheme,[134] but with a conveyancing machinery derived from charities legislation.[135]

Acquisition of land by charities was restricted by the mortmain legislation,[136] rules concerned with accumulations of land outside the feudal net and obsolescent long before their abolition in 1960.[137] Sales of land by charities are also restricted to prevent breaches of trust,[138] but the regime established by the Charities Act 1993[139] is quite relaxed. The new rules for land registration require that a transfer must be accompanied by a free standing application for a restriction.

(1) Acquisition of land by a charity

[14.17] Since sales of charity land are restricted, potential buyers and the land registry must be alerted to the fact that the land is held for a charity by a statement made in the transfer *to* the charity. New forms of certificate were provided in 1993[140] which must state whether the charity is or is not exempt.

(2) Sale by exempt charity

[14.18] Charities exempted from full regulation include universities, grant maintained schools, colleges,[141] the large national museums, the Church Commissioners, and prescribed additions.[142] Transfers and contracts must state that the recipient is an exempt charity, a certificate which protects future purchasers.[143] The land registry restriction requires only that the transaction is authorised by the trusts of the charity.[144]

(3) Charities which are not exempt

[14.19] Restrictions apply to almost all dealings[145] with the land of non-exempt charities.[146] A certificate in the document transferring title to the charity leads to the entry of an appropriate restriction on the register.[147] Before selling, the trustees must carry out certain obvious steps, though care is needed to comply with the statutory detail. A

---

[134] TLATA 1996 sch 1 para 4; consent requirements are not permitted: s 10(2). See: Cheshire & Burn (16th ed), 78–79, 215–225; Megarry & Wade (6th ed), [8.109–8.122].

[135] GA Grove (1962) 24 *MLR* 123, 125 (bare trusts).

[136] Mortmain & Charitable Uses Acts 1888 and 1891; *De Viris Religiosis* 1279 (7 Edw 1 stat 2).

[137] Charities Act 1960 s 38.

[138] S 29.

[139] Charities Act 1993 ss 36–40; White Paper, *Charities: A Framework for the Future* Cm 694 (HMSO, 1989).

[140] Charities Act 1993 s 37(5); DLRR 2003 r 179. If unregistered, the transaction will now attract first registration: s 37(7)–(8), as amended by LRA 2002 sch 11.

[141] Universities & College Estates Acts 1925–1964 (Oxford, Cambridge, Durham, Eton & Winchester).

[142] Charities Act 1993 ss 3, 96, sch 2.

[143] Charities Act 1993 ss 37(1)–(2), 39 as amended (mortgage); DLRR 2003 r 180(1)(a).

[144] Charities Act 1993 s 37(9)–(10) as amended; DLRR 2003 r 182.

[145] But not (1) transactions permitted by a statute or scheme; (2) transfers permitted by the trust from one charity to another; (3) leases granted to a beneficiary to permit occupation, where authorised; (4) release or redemption of a rentcharge: Charities Act 1993 ss 36(9), 37(1)(ii), 40; DLRR 2003 r 180(5).

[146] Charities Act 1993 s 36(1).

[147] S 37(1), (8); DLRR 2003 r 176; LR Form E. This is also required if an exempt charity becomes non-exempt.

written report on the proposed transaction must be commissioned from a qualified and experienced surveyor, who must advise about advertisement.[148] The trustees must consider the terms and decide that the best possible price will be obtained.[149] If the trusts require land to be used for the purposes of the charity, and it is not proposed to buy replacement land, there is a public notice and consultation procedure must be followed.[150] Purchasers are protected by the trustees' certificate that the transaction is not a breach of trust and that they have followed the procedural formalities.[151]

(4) Transactions authorised by the Charity Commissioners

[14.20] The Commissioners may authorise transactions, override statutory prohibitions,[152] and give directions.[153] Purchasers are protected by the trustees' certificate that the transaction has been sanctioned by the Commissioners.[154]

G. DEATH

1. Assimilation

[14.21] A previous chapter has explained how the 1925 legislation assimilated the two pre-1926 systems for succession into a single unified system that applies to all property, land and chattels, real and personal.[155]

2. Two effects of death

[14.22] It is vitally important to distinguish two different effects of the death of an estate owner or registered proprietor. Thus

(1) Land is held by a single proprietor, RP. In this case the effect of his death is to vest the land in his personal representatives.[156]

(2) Land is held by joint proprietors, RP1 and RP2. The effect of death of one of them (RP1) is to vest the land in the other (RP2) by survivorship,[157] a transmission proved by the death certificate of the proprietor who has died.

This passage is concerned only with the former of these effects.

---

[148] Charities Act 1993 s 36(3)–(4).
[149] Ss 36(3)(c), 36(5)–(6) (leases), 38–39; DLRR 2003 r 180.
[150] Charities Act 1993 s 36(6)–(7); short leases for up to 2 years at a rack rental do not require notice; nor do transactions exempted by the Commissioners.
[151] S 37(3)–(4).
[152] S 26(1)–(2).
[153] S 26(3)–(4).
[154] S 37(2)–(4).
[155] See above **[2.12]**.
[156] If RP was himself a personal representative see below **[14.24]**.
[157] See above **[12.18]**.

3. Devolution on death

[14.23] The entire estate of a deceased person passes at the moment of death to the personal representatives,[158] and this includes both legal title to his land and all other forms of personal property.

A person dies testate if there is a valid will which names effective executors, in which case legal title will pass to them on death. The executors will prove the will and secure a grant of probate which acts as their proof of legal title.

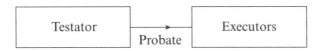

Figure 14-3 Transmission to executives

Most people die intestate. There is no will to appoint executors, but still an intestate's property must have a home. Today, it vests temporarily in the Public Trustee, but that is a recent change;[159] at the time of the 1925 legislation it would have passed to the Probate judge.[160] Thereafter the relatives of the deceased can apply for appointment as administrators; legal title is vested in them by a grant of administration to the deceased's estate.

Figure 14-4 Transmission to administrators on intestacy

The personal representatives must then administer the deceased's estate. Usually this involves *sale* of the land and distributing the money raised by sale. Alternatively the land may be passed to the person entitled to it under the deceased's will or on his intestacy by a document called an *assent*. Devolution of title to *registered land* on death may be proved either on or off the register; the personal representative may elect to be sell off the register (which is usual) or they may decide to become registered proprietors themselves before selling.[161]

4. Title to registered land after death

[14.24] Title is based on the register, including any restriction on the register, but on no other fact. Thus if the personal representative sells or assents, the registrar is not

---

[158] Cheshire & Burn (16th ed), 879–882; R Kerridge "Succession and Trusts" ch 7 in Birks' *Private Law*; Megarry & Wade (6th ed), [11.122–11.133].

[159] LP (MP) A 1994 s 14, amending AEA 1925 s 9.

[160] The President first of the Probate Divorce and Admiralty Division, and later the Family Division. Originally the Bishop had acted as "ordinary".

[161] It should be noted on the register that they are personal representatives and a restriction in Form C is compulsory: DLRR 2003 rr 92–93.

investigate his authority to do so, but merely that his act falls within any restriction on the register.[162]

If, as is usual, personal representatives remain off the register, it will be necessary to produce the original grant, of probate or letters of administration, in order to establish title to sell.[163] If they decide to secure registration, this will require production of the original grant or a certificate by their conveyancer that he holds the original.[164] The register will reveal that the proprietor is an executor or administrator.[165]

5. Beneficial entitlement on death

[14.25] A fundamental of modern ownership is that the owner can make a will directing who is to succeed to his property. The ability to devise land was recognised by medieval law, and after a brief hiatus was re-established by statute in the reign of Henry VIII;[166] the power to make a will is now enshrined in the Wills Act 1837.[167] *Freedom of testation* permits the testator to choose who is to benefit after his death. Modern law circumscribes this freedom to ensure that dependants are properly provided for, whether by will or on intestacy. A successful application by a person dependent on a deceased for *family provision*[168] overrides the will or the operation of the intestacy rules. These matters raise no classification issues since most succession law applies impartially to all forms of property. Historically the greatest problems were presented by intestate succession. *Intestacy* arises where a person dies without a will or, at least, without an effective will.

6. Deathbed gifts

[14.26] It is possible to make a deathbed gift of land by handing over the title deeds at a time when one is in contemplation of death.[169]

7. Intestate succession after 1925

[14.27] On deaths after 1925 the new assimilated law of intestate succession applies. An intestate's entire estate, including all freehold and leasehold land, is divided between the next of kin.[170] Land never passes to the heir of the deceased,[171] male

---

[162] DLRR 2003 r 163.

[163] DLRR 2003 r 163(2).

[164] R 164. R 164(3) requires the same information on registration of an additional pr, and afterwards notice will be given to the existing prs.

[165] R 164(2).

[166] Wills Act 1540.

[167] S 9, as amended by the Administration of Justice Act 1982 s 17; A Borkowski [2000] *Conv* 31; Cheshire & Burn (16th ed) ch 25; R Kerridge ch 7 "Succession and Trusts" in Birks' *Private Law*; Megarry & Wade (6th ed), [11.001–11.082].

[168] Inheritance (Provision for Family and Dependants) Act 1975; *Re B* [2000] Ch 662 (care of mother).

[169] *Sen* v. *Headley* [1991] Ch 425, CA; P Sparkes [1992] *NILQ* 35; N Hopkins *Informal Acquisition*, 21–26; Megarry & Wade (6th ed), [11.083–11.086].

[170] Cheshire & Burn (16th ed) ch 26; R Kerridge ch 7 "Succession and Trusts" in Birks' *Private Law*; Megarry & Wade (6th ed), [11.087–11.121].

[171] Entails are the solitary exception, below **[18.04]**.

primogeniture is abolished, and the law secures equal division between children. Very often this means that the land has to be sold, so that what is actually divided is the proceeds of sale. Next of kin are entitled on intestacy. They must share at least grand parents in common, but the people entitled in a particular case are those closest to the deceased, according to a statutory list which identifies the various permutations of relatives who survive.[172] The problem caused by cases where there is no living relative sufficiently closely related to the deceased to qualify as a personal representative are considered elsewhere.[173]

H. SCHOOL SITES

1. Rights of reverter

[14.28] Land was often given for a public purposes so that it is held only so long as it is needed, but on the terms that cessation of the use will cause ownership of the land to revert to the donor or to his modern day successor. A particular example was the School Sites Acts 1841–1852. Today a local education authority or a school trust would buy a site for a school in the commercial market in the same way as any other business,[174] but before the public role in education was established, sites for schools were provided by local benefactors. A school board[175] held the site for a determinable fee simple, retaining the legal estate so long as the school remained open,[176] but losing legal ownership automatically if it was closed.[177] No litigation was reported in the secure world before the First War,[178] but serious difficulties emerged afterwards as more schools were amalgamated or closed. Local education authorities commonly wanted to close village schools and move the children to a larger school built to serve a group of villages. Such schemes depended for their viability on the ability of the authority to sell the existing school site but under the School Sites Acts the sites actu-ally belonged to the former owner after closure of the village school. Reverter might or might not occur if the original school was replaced by another educational use.[179]

2. Reverter to whom?

[14.29] It is now settled by *Fraser* v. *Canterbury Diocesan Board of Finance*[180] that the destination of reverter is back to the fee simple. The land reverts to the person of the

---

[172] AEA 1925 s 46, as amended most recently by the Law Reform (Succession) Act 1995.

[173] See above [3.44].

[174] BR Howell [1991] *Conv* 327.

[175] Local education authorities often took over the running of village schools.

[176] LPA 1925 s 7(1).

[177] A reverter has to be confined to a perpetuity period; if this was not done the reverter was void and the charitable gift to the school board was absolute: *Re Cooper's Conveyance* [1956] 1 WLR 1096, 1103; *Bath & Wells DBF* v. *Jenkinson* [2002] EWHC 218, [2002] 3 WLR 202, Etherton J.

[178] G Baughen Graham (1951) 15 *Conv (NS)* 151, 266.

[179] *Fraser* v. *Canterbury Diocesan Board of Finance* [2001] Ch 669, [27–35], Mummery LJ. See also: *Att-Gen* v. *Shadwell* [1910] 1 Ch 92, Warrington J; *Re Clayton's Deed Poll* [1980] Ch 99, Whitford J; *Habermehl* v. *Att-Gen* [1996] EGCS 148, Rimer J; *Brewers of City of London (Master of)* v. *Att-Gen* [2000] ELR 117, Ch D.

[180] [2001] Ch 669, [40–48], Mummery LJ; *Marchant* v. *Onslow* [1995] Ch 1, which applied a different rule to sites forming part of a larger estate, was wrongly decided.

landowner who gave the site in the 19th century, and so (after his death) it is necessary to trace the devolution of his estate under his will or on his intestacy, possibly through several generations.[181] Where a successor sold the estate to which the right of reverter attaches the purchaser acquires the rights.[182]

3.   Reverter behind a trust

[14.30] The Reverter of Sites Act 1987[183] ensures that legal title[184] is no longer affected by a reverter, which operates instead as an equitable reverter hidden behind a trust of land.[185] Closure of a school has no effect on the legal title held by the school trustees, or their management powers, but it shifts beneficial (equitable) entitlement to the person entitled by reverter.[186] Beneficial entitlement to the site includes the right to the proceeds from sale of the site, and the trustees are obliged to locate the person entitled. The Secretary of State for Education must ensure adequate protection for potential beneficiaries when considering closures.[187] This change works very much in favour of the families of original donors, since limitation can no longer act to bar equitable rights. Gifts affected by the 1987 Act include the sites of schools for the poor, schools for the middle classes, libraries, museums, churches, and chapels.[188]

4.   Reverter at law

[14.31] Reverter of school sites occurred at law until 1987. In *Re Rowhook Mission Hall*[189] a school had been closed in 1904 so that legal ownership reverted to the previous landowner, but a limitation period for bringing claims ran for 12 years from the moment of closure, and barred a claim by the family made in 1985. Legal title continued to shift under the Birkenhead reforms, for example when the Old National School, Ladypool Road, Birmingham[190] was shut in 1938. Again 12 years were allowed to make a claim from the date of closure.

The old law continues for any land acquired by statutory authority for a public use subject to reverter on termination of the use which is outside the Reverter of Sites Act 1987.[191] Examples are rifle ranges,[192] and land acquired under old compulsory pur-

---

[181] *Fraser* at [49–53]; *Re Cawston's Conveyance* [1940] Ch 27 CA.
[182] *Bath & Wells DBF* v. *Jenkinson* [2002] EWHC 218, [2002] 3 WLR 202 (great nephew of donor sold as tenant for life to a company, now dissolved; so title to the reverter vested in the Crown as bona vacantia).
[183] D Evans [1987] *Conv* 408; Jeffreys & Powell [1981] *Conv* 161; CJ Allen & S Christie [1981] *Conv* 186; C Sydenham [1981] *Conv* 454; CLR Ingram [1982] *Conv* 391.
[184] LPA 1925 s 3(3) was partially repealed by Reverter of Sites Act 1987 s 8, sch.
[185] As from TLATA 1996 sch 2; LR Practice Advice Leaflet 3 (1995).
[186] S 1(2); Charities Act 1993 s 23.
[187] School Standards and Framework Act 1998 sch 3 para 2(9), sch 6 para 16(8).
[188] School Sites Act 1841–1852; Literary and Scientific Institutions Act 1854; Places of Worship Sites Act 1873; Law Com 111 (1981), [4–10].
[189] [1985] Ch 62, Nourse J; *Dennis* v. *Malcolm* [1934] Ch 244, Clauson J; *Re Chavasse's Conveyance* [1954] April 14th, Harman J; *Re Ingleton's Charity* [1956] Ch 585, Danckwerts J; *Fraser* v. *Canterbury Diocesan Board of Finance* [2001] Ch 669, [27–35], Mummery LJ (church character lost 1874, sale 1998).
[190] [1985] Ch 62, 76B–84G; D Evans (1984) 100 *LQR* 527; [1987] *Conv* 408, 409–410.
[191] SLA 1925 s 1(1)(ii)(c), as amended by TLATA 1996 sch 3.
[192] Volunteer Act 1863; Law Com 111 (1981), [54–55].

chase legislation.[193] A major example is a highway which vests in the local authority on a determinable fee simple so long as the public use continues, but so that the land reverts to the neighbouring land owner if the road is shut.[194] The authority's fee simple is legal.[195]

I. RESTRICTIONS

1. Restriction theory

[14.32] Entry of a restriction on the proprietorship register places in the public domain any limitation on the power of the proprietor to deal with the registered legal title. Proprietors enjoy full powers of disposition except to the extent that a restriction signals some departure from this assumed pattern. Restrictions must limit dealings with registered estates or mortgages, as opposed to beneficial interests.[196] Apart from their use to impose a curtain on trusts of land and settlements,[197] restrictions may be used:[198]

to prevent invalidity of transactions;
to secure overreaching; or
to protect a right or claim incapable of protection by notice.

The limitation imposed may be indefinite, for a stated period or until a certain event,[199] and might require various procedures before a registration proceeds,[200] including:

prior notice to a named person;
obtaining the consent of a named person;
obtaining an order by the registrar; or
some other matter or thing.

Unreasonable restrictions which are calculated to cause inconvenience will be refused.[201] Later transactions will only be registered if they conform to the restriction,[202] though any doubt can be avoided by a certificate obtained in advance from the registrar that he will register a proposed transaction.

---

[193] Land Clauses Consolidation Act 1845 (reverter after non-use for 10 years). Reverter rights in old railway tracks were withdrawn by the British Railways Act 1968 s 18; *British Railways Board* v. *Pickin* [1974] AC 765, HL.
[194] Highways Act 1980 s 263; *Rolls* v. *St George the Martyr, Southwark Vestry* (1880) 14 Ch D 785, CA.
[195] *Tithe Redemption Commissioners* v. *Runcorn UDC* [1954] Ch 383, CA
[196] LRA 2002 s 40(4). A restriction also circumscribes the creation of overriding interests off the register, such as leases shorter than 7 years.
[197] See above [13.34ff].
[198] LRA 2002 s 42.
[199] S 40(2).
[200] S 40.
[201] S 43(3).
[202] S 58(2).

2.   Restrictions with and without the consent of the proprietor

[14.33] Since 1996[203] restrictions entered with consent of the registered proprietor have been differentiated from those without his consent, a scheme which is now continued but has been explained in the context of trusts of land.[204]

3.   Corporate and other special landowners

[14.34] Optional restrictions are used to denote landowners with limited powers under special statutory regimes.[205] Companies can of course be registered. If they are registered under the Companies Act 1985 the register must state the company's registered number.[206] Corporations limited by charter have powers which depend upon its charter and the register must record by restriction any limit on its powers of dealing with its land.[207] In the case of a dealing by a non-registered company it will be necessary to produce evidence that the transaction is within its powers.[208]

Restrictions are also needed with partnerships, limited liability partnerships,[209] and clubs. Specialised restrictions are used for building societies, development corporations, ecclesiastical landowners, – especially Church of England incumbents[210] – European bodies, housing associations, liquidators, the National Trust and many others.[211]

J.   INSOLVENCY

[14.35] Insolvency of an individual leads to his bankruptcy. If a company becomes insolvent it will be put into liquidation. In each case all property is removed from the insolvent and applied for the benefit of the creditors. The person who looks after the interests of the creditors is either a trustee in bankruptcy of an individual or a liquidator if it is corporate. The use of restrictions to record the process of the insolvency is considered elsewhere,[212] as are the rare exceptional cases in which insolvency cause an estate in freehold land to terminate.[213]

---

[203] LRR 1996, SI 1996/2975.
[204] LRA 2002 ss 42–43; see above **[13.34]**.
[205] DLRR 2003 rr 95–96.
[206] R 181.
[207] Law Com 271 (2001), [6.40], EN [196–202].
[208] DLRR 2003 r 183.
[209] Limited Liability Partnership Act 2000; SI 2000/1090; M Rodrigues [2001] 12 *EG* 219; [2001] 16 *LSG* 37 (LR guidance); SI 2002/2539 sch 1 para 10; DLRR 2003 r 181(4).
[210] DLRR 2003 rr 174–175.
[211] *Encyclopaedia FP* (5th ed, 1999 reissue) vol 25 (1), [3599–3643].
[212] See below **[28.51]**.
[213] See above **[3.46ff]**.

K. ORDINARY POWERS OF ATTORNEY

[14.36] A trust vests management power in a trustee whilst separating the rights of enjoyment in the beneficiaries. Management control can also be passed by a landowner to an outside person by a power of attorney, the difference being that legal and equitable ownership is retained in the hands of the landowner – he has merely ceded the right to deal. The power of attorney passes to the donee (the attorney) the ability to deal with the property belonging to and vested in the donor. The attorney does not have the duties of a trustee, but he is a fiduciary, that is he is obliged to act in the interests of the donor.

1. Ordinary powers

[14.37] Any property owner can give an attorney a mandate to carry out transactions with his land. What transactions are covered depends upon the wording but most are general powers putting the attorney in the same position as the donor.[214] The attorney usually executes a sale in his own name acting by the authority of the landowner, but he may also sign using the donor's name.[215] Authority for the attorney to act continues only so long as the person creating the power (the donor) has capacity, so that it will be revoked by death, bankruptcy or loss of mental competence, or by a change of mind. This is a trap for the attorney, for whom protection is provided,[216] and even more so for buyers.[217]

2. Irrevocable powers of attorney

[14.38] Powers are irrevocable when given to secure a proprietary interest of the attorney or an obligation owed to him. Almost always this means that the donor of the power is a borrower who has mortgaged his land to the donee of the power (the lender) who has been given a power of attorney permitting him to sell the land if the borrower defaults in repaying the loan. Such a power in an equitable mortgage cannot be revoked by the borrower so that death, mental incapacity or bankruptcy become irrelevant.[218] A purchaser's title is safe unless he knows that the power was not in fact given as security for a property interest.

L. ENDURING POWERS OF ATTORNEY

[14.39] Lack of mental capacity will remove a property owner's ability to deal with his property and will also revoke any ordinary power of attorney he has created.[219]

---

[214] PAA 1971 s 10, sch; SI 2000/215 (Welsh forms). Delegation of the functions of trustees or personal representatives is a specialised topic calling for extended treatment below **[14.44ff]**.

[215] S 7.

[216] S 5.

[217] See below **[14.50ff]**.

[218] S 4.

[219] *Drew* v. *Nunn* (1879) 4 QBD 661, CA.

Senility often creeps in as a person ages, and considerable expense and embarrassment is involved in formal application to the Court of Protection for appointment of a receiver.[220] Enduring powers of attorney[221] avoid this problem by providing an inexpensive method of selecting in advance a person to look after an elderly person's property if, unfortunately, he loses grip.[222]

1. Capacity

[14.40] The object of an enduring power is to confer management powers on the attorney in the event of loss of capacity, but this delegation can only be made at a time that the donor of the power is mentally capable. It is often appropriate to take this action during a lucid interval after the first signs of mental instability have manifested themselves.[223] It is wise to have a doctor present at the execution of the document. According to Hoffmann J[224] the donor must be able to understand that the attorney could assume complete control of his affairs if he becomes incapable, with power to do anything which he (the donor) could have done, and that the delegation is irrevocable without confirmation by the court. Disputed capacity is a ground for objection to registration of the power.[225]

2. Selection of the attorney

[14.41] An enduring power must be in a prescribed form[226] with prescribed explanatory material. It requires execution by the donor and the attorney in the presence of witnesses. Usually the court will accept the donor's choice of attorney, who should be a competent adult or trust corporation,[227] but there remains a discretion to refuse an unsuitable choice.[228] Attorneys cannot be substituted, so it is wise to appoint several, either to act collectively (jointly) or to have power to act individually (severally as well as jointly).[229] Each nominated attorney must execute[230] the power to indicate his acceptance of office,[231] to acknowledge his duty to register when the donor becomes incapable, and to accept any limitations on the scope of his authority.

---

[220] *Re R* [1990] Ch 647, 650B, Vinelott J.
[221] Enduring PAA 1985; Law Com 122 (1983).
[222] *Re K* [1988] Ch 310, 311–312, Hoffmann J.
[223] At 315G, Hoffmann J.
[224] At 316C–F.
[225] Enduring PAA 1985 s 5(5); *Re K* [1988] Ch 310; *Re R* [1990] Ch 647; *Re W* [2001] Ch 609, [21–22], Sir Christopher Staughton (onus on objectors); *Re C* [2000] 2 FLR 1, CA.
[226] SI 1990/1376; *Encyclopaedia FP* (5th ed, 1999 reissue) vol 31, [4601]. An earlier power does not necessarily revoke an earlier one: *Re E* [2001] Ch 364, Arden J.
[227] Enduring PAA 1985 ss 2(7), 13. Bankruptcy terminates an appointment: s 2(10).
[228] S 6(5)(e).
[229] Ss 2(9), 11, sch 3.
[230] Defects: ss 2(6), 5(5)(a); Practice Direction [1989] 2 All ER 64.
[231] Disclaimer requires notice to the donor: s 2(12).

3. Statement of authority

[14.42] Mandated authority stated in an enduring power will usually be general.[232] If it is limited to particular acts or parts,[233] the donor's intentions cannot be overridden by the court, which is limited to interpretation,[234] giving consents, directing management, ordering accounts, and allowing payment to the attorney. Attorneys must generally act for the benefit of the donor. Birthday presents and similar gifts must be reasonable in amount in relation to the size of the donor's estate.[235] Benefits to others, including the attorney, are limited to what the donor might have been expected to provide for their needs or to meet his obligations.[236] In *Re R*[237] the applicant had been employed as a resident housekeeper, cook, and companion, who had accepted low pay in the expectation that she would be provided for. A nephew (acting under an enduring power) terminated the companion's employment and asked her to leave the house. The court declined to order payment where the only obligation to make them was moral.

It is proposed to replace enduring powers with continuing powers, which would extend to health care and general welfare as well as dispositions of property. Living wills will allow advance directions refusing particular treatments and also, for the future, advance consent to positive treatments.[238]

4. Registration on impending incapacity

[14.43] The donor retains control of his affairs after executing an enduring power, but he has given his attorney the authority to take over when mental instability emerges. A duty to register arises when the attorney has reason to believe that the donor is becoming incapable by reason of mental disorder of managing and administering his property and affairs.[239] Written notice[240] must be given to the donor, to the three closest relatives of the donor, and to other nominated attorneys,[241] with application following immediately after the last notice.[242] Registration usually occurs without a hearing.[243] Grounds for objection are invalidity of the power, fraud or undue pressure, mental capacity of the donor, and unsuitability of the attorney.[244] The Court of Protection will adjudicate on any objections[245] and may appoint a Mental Health Act receiver instead.[246]

---

[232] Even here there are limits: for example a notice to enfranchise must be signed by a leaseholder personally and so not by his attorney, an odd result: *St Ermins Property Co* v. *Tingay* [2002] EWHC 16733, [2002] 40 EG 174, Lloyd J.

[233] S 3(1)–(2).

[234] S 8.

[235] S 3(5).

[236] S 3(4).

[237] [1990] Ch 647, Vinelott J.

[238] Law Com 231 (1995); *Who Decides? (HMSO, December 1997)*.

[239] Enduring PAA 1985 ss 4(1), 13; disclaimer requires consent of the court: s 4(6).

[240] S 13; SI 1994/3047 r 7; Form EP1.

[241] Enduring PAA 1985 s 4(3), sch 1.

[242] S 4(2), (4); SI 1994/3047 rr 8, 9; Form EP2; amended by SI 2002/1944.

[243] Enduring PAA 1985 s 6(1); SI 1994/3047 r 11.

[244] Enduring PAA 1985 ss 5(5), 13; SI 1994/3047 rr 11–25.

[245] Enduring PAA 1985 s 6(4); SI 1994/3047 rr 10–13.

[246] Enduring PAA 1985 s 6(2).

Registration shifts management power from the donor to the attorney.[247] The donor requires permission from the court to revoke the power,[248] and recovery of capacity will not automatically revive his powers, though it is certainly a ground on which registration can be cancelled.[249]

M. DELEGATION OF TRUSTS

1. Collective delegation of management functions

[14.44] Trustees may delegate any management function to an agent. This might for example allow trustees to appoint an estate agent to market the land held by the trust, or a solicitor to conduct the conveyancing. It will also allow the appointment of a stockbroker to conduct investment and (subject to a policy document drawn up by the trustees) to choose investments for the trust fund. Attorneys may only be given delegable functions,[250] a concept which does not allow them to select between beneficiaries, appoint trustees, or set fees.

It is possible for the trustees to delegate to one of their number.[251] A delegate may also be a nominee or custodian. However, a beneficiary cannot be a delegate and substitutes are not generally allowed

The trustees will be under a duty of care when delegating and are required to review delegations[252] and also to consult with the beneficiaries of a trust of land.[253] Trustees who act properly in the appointment and review properly will not be liable for the acts of the delegate,[254] though the corresponding statutory duty is imposed on the delegate.[255]

2. Collective delegation to a beneficiary

[14.45] Trustees of land may delegate the functions of their trust to a beneficiary of full age entitled to an interest in possession.[256] This might include both administrative functions and execution of the trust itself. One ends up with an arrangement rather similar to a strict settlement in which the life tenant who is most intimately concerned with the estate has management control of it. The delegation is of indefinite duration, not limited to one year at a time, but it is always revocable. Since the power to delegate is collective all trustees must join in making the delegation and it follows that this can be revoked by any one trustee, as well as on any change of trustees, or the loss of

---

[247] Until bankruptcy of the attorney or appointment of a receiver: s 2(10)–(11).
[248] S 7.
[249] Ss 7(3), 8(4); SI 1994/3047 r 26.
[250] TA 2000 s 11; this is a considerable improvement on the earlier law in TA 1925 ss 23, 30. The trust instrument may extend or restrict the statutory power.
[251] TA 2000 s 12.
[252] TA 2000 sch 1 para 3.
[253] TLATA 1996 s 11(1); TA 2000 s 13(3)–(5).
[254] TA 2000 s 23.
[255] Terms restricting liability of the agent or authorising a conflict of interest are only permitted where they are reasonably necessary: TA 2000 s 23.
[256] TLATA 1996 s 9.

beneficial entitlement.[257] Trustees avoid liability for the acts of delegates provided that they exercise reasonable care when deciding to delegate.[258] Delegation is by ordinary[259] power of attorney and the purchaser is protected in the same way as any other person buying from an attorney.[260] Purchase money must be paid to at least two trustees.[261]

3. Unilateral delegation of trust functions – non-beneficiaries

[14.46] The Trustee Delegation Act 1999[262] allows a unilateral delegation of the functions of trusteeship, that is a delegation by one trustee (T1) to a person selected by that trustee (A to work with T2). There is a more generous rule, discussed below,[263] for a trustee who is also beneficially entitled under the trust, but first we must consider the normal rule for pure trustees, that is a trust in the form:

To T1 and T2 on trust for B1 and B2.

The trustees here are different individuals from the beneficiaries. Under the Trustee Delegation Act 1999[264] a trustee function can be delegated to an attorney under a power of attorney, but any such delegation[265] must comply with the statutory power in the Trustee Act 1925:[266] a delegate can only be given authority for a limited period, with a maximum of one year at a time. Delegation commences on date stated in the power of attorney[267] or, if none, the date of its execution and then continues for that 12 months maximum, or any shorter period stated.[268] Written notice should be given before or within seven days after the delegation by the donor to the person entitled to appoint trustees, and to the other trustees,[269] but failure to give notice does not affect title.

It will probably be normal to effect a general delegation, meaning that T1 steps out of the trust for a year and allows A to act in his stead as trustee. A form is prescribed for this general type of delegation,[270] though it is also possible to use any form to like effect which makes clear which statutory power of delegation is being exercised. Variations from the prescribed form would be needed if the intention is to delegate

---

[257] S 9(2), (6).

[258] S 9(8).

[259] An enduring power is not allowed: s 9(6).

[260] S 9(2). There is no need to produce evidence of the delegation: LRR 2002, SI 2002/2539 sh 1 para 3; LRA 1925 r 82A; LR Form 115; DLRR 2003 r 64.

[261] TLATA 1996 s 9(7); this is clearly intended despite a slight ambiguity.

[262] In force March 1st 2000: SI 2000/216; Law Com 220 (1994).

[263] See below **[14.47]**.

[264] S 1(1).

[265] A delegate may not delegate further: TA 1925 s 25(8).

[266] TA 1925 s 25, as redrawn by T Delegation A 1999 s 5 for powers executed after March 1st 2000. It has not been necessary since 1971 for the trustee to be abroad.

[267] Query whether it is possible in 2002 to execute a series of powers of attorney each for one calendar year – 2002, 2003, 2004 etc. This infringes the spirit but not the letter of the new law. The legislation also leaves open an inconvenient possibility that the commencement could be on a contingency, eg when the trustee is certified incapable by a GP.

[268] TA 1925 s 25(2).

[269] S 25(4); ss (10) provides for notices by prs or SLA owners.

[270] S 25(5)–(6).

particular functions, where several trustees are delegating their functions, or where several trusts are included.

The new law more or less follows the pre-existing law for ordinary powers of attorney,[271] but narrows it for enduring powers.[272] Use of an enduring power ensures that the delegate can sell the land when the trustee has become incapable,[273] but an enduring power affected by the new law only permits delegation of trust functions for a maximum period of one year.

4. Unilateral delegation of trust functions – beneficiary trustees

[14.47] Wider powers of delegation are allowed under a trust involving land[274] where the trustee is also a beneficiary

X and Y hold as trustees for themselves (X and Y) as beneficial joint tenants.

A purchaser needs to be sure that the trustee was also a beneficiary and so is entitled to the wider powers. Hence there is provision enabling a purchaser to rely on an appropriate statement made by the attorney,[275] which is conclusive evidence provided it is made at the time of sale or up to three months afterwards.

If a joint tenant such as X executed a normal power of attorney in favour of A this delegate acquired authority over X's beneficial interest but not, it was decided in 1985,[276] authority to deal with X's interest as legal co-owner of the property. This was very inconvenient! It severely circumscribed the value of an ordinary power of attorney since the authority it gave excluded any co-owned house, but the new law widens the power of delegating to trustee-beneficiaries.[277] It is not necessary to use a Trustee Act delegation[278] and so any delegation may extend beyond one year to an indefinite duration.

5. Two trustee rule

[14.48] An attorney of a trustee proves title in the same way as any other attorney, but in addition sales must comply with the two trustee rule to ensure that overreaching occurs.[279] New rules dating from 1999[280] ensure that two separate individuals receive

---

[271] PAA 1971 s 10; *Walia* v. *Michael Naughton* [1985] 1 WLR 1115.

[272] See below [14.49].

[273] T Delegation A 1999 s 6; LPA 1925 s 22(2), s 22(3) added by T Delegation A 1999 s 9; A Hawes [1993] *NLJ* 1360.

[274] T Delegation A 1999 s 1. Land is defined by ss 10, 11. An interest in the proceeds of sale suffices in those rare cases in which conversion continues to apply despite TLATA 1996 s 3. The exclusion of chattels is unfortunate: M Mallender [2000] 12 *LSG* 16.

[275] T Delegation A 1999 s 2; LR Practice Leaflet 32 suggests: "I [Attorney] confirm that [donor of power] has a beneficial interest in the property on the date of this document"); it also suggests an alternative varying the form of execution of the deed.

[276] *Walia* v. *Michael Naughton* [1985] 1 WLR 1115.

[277] T Delegation A 1999 s 1(1).

[278] TA 1925 s 25.

[279] R Oerton [1995] 12 *LSG* 18; PR Saunders [1993] *NLJ* 1360; RT Oerton [1993] *NLJ* 840.

[280] T Delegation A 1999 s 7. This applies both prospectively and retrospectively. For the two trustee rule see above [13.11].

the money, although they may be acting in different capacities eg as trustee and as attorney. Thus:

(1) if there are two trustees and T1 delegates to T2, T2 cannot act to receive the purchase money;

(2) if both trustees (T1 and T2) delegate separately to A, A cannot receive purchase money;

(3) if T2 delegates to T3, T1 may sell with T3.

There is the usual exception for a trust corporation to act alone.[281]

6. Earlier enduring powers

[14.49] An enduring power survives the incapacity of the trustee. The rules described above apply to any enduring power of attorney executed in or after March 2000, and they also apply to any older enduring power if the incapacity of the trustee causing the power to be registered occurs in or after March 2001.

Earlier, a much wider authority[282] allowed the delegation of any trust by an enduring power, whether or not the trustee was also a beneficiary, and unlimited in time. This earlier power may continue to apply to an older (pre-March 2000) enduring powers if the incapacity and registration occurred before March 2001, and indefinitely so unless the trustee recovers capacity and the registration is cancelled. The changes to the two trustee rule described above do not apply,[283] but there is a new power[284] for the attorney under an enduring power to appoint an extra trustee to meet the two trustee rule where he is the only active "trustee".

N. PURCHASE FROM ATTORNEYS

1. Proof of a power of attorney

[14.50] After a sale the attorney will usually retain the original power for future use, so a buyer has to prove title with a copy which is acceptable evidence of the existence of the power if it is certified as a true copy by a solicitor, notary public, or stockbroker.[285]

2. Protection of purchasers – sale within 12 months of delegation

[14.51] Protection is available for purchasers against the risk that the power of attorney had been revoked at the time that the land is bought from the attorney, so long as the buyer did not know at that time of an act causing a revocation.[286] A later buyer

---

[281] A proper delegate under TA 1925 s 25(3).

[282] Enduring PAA 1985 s 3(3); this was a response to *Walia* v. *Michael Naughton* [1985] 1 WLR 1115, decided as the 1985 Bill was in Parliament.

[283] T Delegation A 1999 s 7.

[284] T Delegation A 1999 s 8. This must be produced to the registry: DLRR 2003 r 62.

[285] PAA 1971 s 3; DLRR 2003 r 62; also a copy of a copy; Evidence and Powers of Attorney Act 1940. It will no longer be necessary to lodge the original if a conveyancer certifies that he holds this.

[286] PAA 1971 s 5.

depends for his title upon the knowledge of the first buyer at the time of the initial acquisition from the attorney. If the first sale occurs within 12 months of the execution of the power of attorney, all subsequent purchasers are protected by a conclusive presumption that the first purchaser had no knowledge of revocation.

3. Protection of purchasers – sale more than 12 months after delegation

[14.52] Where a sale occurs more than 12 months after execution of the power future security of the title requires that the first purchaser execute a statutory declaration – before the purchase or within three months afterwards – stating that he did not have knowledge of any revocation or event terminating the power when he bought.[287] This statutory declaration will be required by the registrar before the initial purchase can be registered. The precise contents of the declaration will vary according to the type of power. Under an ordinary power, it must affirm the absence of knowledge of revocation or death, incapacity or bankruptcy of an individual donor, or the winding up of a corporate donor.[288]

4. Enduring powers

[14.53] Enduring powers can also be proved by an office copy sealed by the Court of Protection, which is evidence of the contents of the power and the fact of registration.[289]

Under an enduring power[290] the statutory declaration must assert absence of knowledge of (1) revocation by the court,[291] (2) any event causing loss of power in the attorney such as the death or bankruptcy of the donor or bankruptcy of the attorney, and (3) any ground for avoiding the registration such as fraud or lack of capacity.[292]

5. Delegation under trusts

[14.54] In the case of a delegation of powers under a trust of land[293] it will be absence of knowledge that the power has been revoked by the donor of the power, or that new trustees had been appointed, or of any other revoking event.[294] On a sale by a beneficiary under powers delegated by trustees of land, evidence will be required by statutory declaration that the buyer acted in good faith with no knowledge that it was not a proper delegation.[295]

---

[287] S 5(4); for post-1971 dealings.

[288] DLRR 2003 r 63; but since 2002 it has not been necessary to produce evidence of non-revocation if a conveyancer certifies that he holds adequate evidence: SI 2002/2539 sch para 2; LRA 1925 s 82A; LR Form 114.

[289] Enduring PAA 1985 s 7; searches for registration are allowed under SI 1994/3047.

[290] Enduring PAA 1985 s 9; DLRR 2003 r 62.

[291] Only a confirmed revocation counts: s 9(5).

[292] S 9(3)–(4).

[293] TLATA 1996 s 9. Note also the more general declaration referred to above at [14.51].

[294] DLRR 2003 r 64.

[295] DLRR 2003 r 64; since 2002 it is not necessary to produce this to the registry if a conveyancer certifies that they hold the evidence: LRR 2002/2539 sch 1 para 3; LRR 1925 r 82A; LR Form 115.

15

ONE-TRUSTEE TRUSTS

Endurability. Beneficial entitlement. Unregistered land: protected interests; honesty; diligence; occupiers. Registered land: priority; occupiers; when do occupiers bite? Removal of protection from occupiers.

A. BENEFICIAL INTERESTS NOT OVERREACHED

1. Maitland and endurability of beneficial interests

[15.01] Maitland introduced the Cambridge classes of the 1900s to his thesis that beneficial interests under trusts are personal in character in these words:

> "Equitable estates and interests are rights *in personam* but they have a misleading resemblance to rights *in rem*."[1]

Maitland's insistence that the trust was a species of personal property placed emphasis on the form of judgment used to enforce a trust – a personal action for damages for breach of trust – and depends upon his supposition that the form of judgment is the most important diagnostic feature. In fact equity could replace trustees or order an official to execute a transfer, means of securing the land just as effective as any legal remedy. It is better to focus on the substantive nature of the rights created and the real question, whether a right binds a purchaser of the land. Mrs Boland[2] could enforce her rights against a lender, which demonstrates conclusively the proprietary character of her interest. Equitable rights are proprietary,[3] as Maitland himself recognised towards the end of his life.[4]

Maitland's lectures remain of value because of the emphasis he placed on the need to establish personal liability against an individual defendant, a point developed below.[5]

2. Boland

[15.02] First instincts are usually right, but occasionally time for reflection gives rise to face saving second thoughts. So it was for the protection of beneficiaries. Only after the 1925 legislation has passed through Parliament was it amended to restrict

---

[1] Maitland's *Equity*, 117.
[2] *Williams & Glyn's Bank* v. *Boland* [1981] AC 487, HL.
[3] GW Keeton (1937) 1 *MLR* 86.
[4] FW Maitland, *Collected Papers III* (Cambridge UP, 1911), 349–350.
[5] See below [15.06].

overreaching to cases where the capital money was paid to two trustees.[6] It seems obvious to us now that the legislators also needed to pause for a third thought so as to make clear what was to happen on a sale or mortgage by a single individual as trustee.

In *Williams & Glyn's Bank* v. *Boland*[7] a matrimonial home was transferred to the husband's name and later registered in his name. Finance for the purchase came partly from a mortgage, but partly also from selling the previous matrimonial home, which was shared beneficially by husband and wife, from which Mrs Boland's existing equity was transferred to the new house. Hence she contributed to the new house and her husband held the registered title as a statutory trustee.[8] Neither contribution nor trust was apparent from the register. After the couple had moved in, Mr Boland re-mortgaged the matrimonial home to Williams & Glyn's Bank without his wife's knowledge, to secure the debts of his company, Epsom Contractors. He failed to repay the second borrowing, but it was unnecessary to decide whether *he* had a defence to the possession proceedings,[9] since *she* had priority over the bank and they could not obtain possession against her.[10] Mrs Boland's beneficial interest under a trust for sale was a proprietary interest, capable of binding a purchaser, and in fact binding the lender against whom she was protected by occupation. Any suggestion that her interest took effect only in the proceeds of sale was firmly rejected.[11]

The result follows more obviously after 1996, since conversion is abolished for trusts of land and beneficiaries are interested in the land itself until overreached.[12]

Many trusts now arise through payments of mortgage instalments and other contributions. In the past homes of married couples were often taken in the sole name of the husband, and informal trusts are even more common between cohabiting couples. It is still usually the case that the legal title is in the man's name and a woman is claiming the protection of an overriding interest, though very likely that pattern will change. Lord Birkenhead could not have envisaged in 1925 such dangerous innovations as women earning money, wanting to share ownership of property, and couples living together without marrying. So it is no surprise that the property Acts made hopelessly inadequate[13] provision for these modern social phenomena.[14]

3.   *Boland* and the Land Registration Act 2002

[15.03] We must pause briefly to consider whether *Boland*[15] remains a good authority on the Land Registration Act 2002.

---

[6] LPA 1925 s 27(2), as amended by LP (Amendment) A 1926 sch; *City of London BS* v. *Flegg* [1988] AC 56, HL.

[7] [1981] AC 487, HL; JE Martin [1980] *Conv* 361; JE Martin [1981] *Conv* 219; RJ Smith (1981) 97 *LQR* 12; C Sydenham [1980] *Conv* 427; A Nicol & R Rawlings (1980) 43 *MLR* 692; MJ Prichard [1980] *CLJ* 243.

[8] LPA 1925 s 34, now as amended by TLATA 1996 sch 3 to create a simple trust.

[9] [1981] AC 487, 509.

[10] The bank could have applied for sale as a beneficial co-owner; see below **[19.26]**.

[11] P Sparkes *NLL* (1st ed), 137.

[12] TLATA 1996 s 3.

[13] JS Anderson *Lawyers and the Making of English Land Law 1832–1940* (Clarendon, 1992), 331.

[14] Feminist analysis suggests that occupation has a vital role to play in protecting the rights of women: K Green (1993) 3 *Fem LS* 131. Surely, a conveyancing system should be gender neutral and should not be caught up in righting the property imbalance between men and women.

[15] *Williams & Glyn's Bank* v. *Boland* [1981] AC 487, HL.

Suppose land is vested in T as registered proprietor but T holds on trust for himself and another who has the right to block a sale thus:

to T on trust to sell with the consent of B and otherwise to hold for T & B as tenants in common.

If title is registered a restriction should appear on the register to protect B's power of consent. In the absence of a restriction, title to the land can be made without B's consent. Occupation by B is no protection. This is because the title of the registered proprietor is, in favour of a purchaser, taken to be free from any limitation affecting the validity of a disposition.[16] That case is clear because it is more or less the example given by the Law Commission.[17]

Now take this extension, most emphatically not intended, to a *Boland* trust:

to T on trust for T & B as tenants in common.

The register is free of restriction. When T sells to a purchaser, we know that B's interest can override the disposition if B is in occupation of the land. A sale or mortgage of the land is an exercise of the owner's powers vested in the registered proprietor.[18] It needs to be in the correct form and it needs to be registered.[19] In these circumstances

"a person's right to exercise owner's powers in relation to a registered estate . . . is taken to be free from any limitation affecting the validity of a disposition.[20]

A sole trustee is not entitled to sell, but the issue is whether the disponee's title can be questioned.[21]

What is stop the buyer arguing that T's power to exercise the owner's powers should be taken to be free of any restriction; that the proprietor, instead of selling as a trustee and being required to overreach, actually sells as an ordinary proprietor free of restriction. The limitation affecting the validity of the disposition – the requirement to pay purchase money to two trustees – derives from the Law of Property Act 1925[22] and is not imposed by or under the Land Registration Act 2002.[23] So if B lacks an overriding interest in the case of a consent provision, there seems to be no logic in allowing him one in a *Boland* type trust.

No doubt some limitation will be read into section 26 to confine it to its intended ambit. It seems unlikely that subsequent courts will treat *Boland* as having been overruled by a Report that obviously did not intend to do so. The remainder of this chapter makes the assumption that some way will be found to confine owners' powers as apparently intended.

---

[16] LRA 2002 s 26.
[17] Law Com 271 (2001), [4.10], EN [121].
[18] LRA 2002 ss 23–24.
[19] Ss 25–27.
[20] S 26(1).
[21] S 26(3).
[22] S 27.
[23] LRA 2002 s 26(2)(b).

4. Structure of this chapter

[15.04] Priority rules are considered below in the chronological order of their development – unregistered notice doctrine followed by the priority rules for registered
land and overriding interests affecting registered land.

B. BENEFICIAL ENTITLEMENT REQUIRED

[15.05] An occupier claiming protection against a purchaser of the land must show a
proprietary interest in the land, whether title is unregistered or registered.

The point was more debatable if title was registered. The old law made registered
dispositions subject to such overriding interests "as may be for the time being subsisting in reference" to the land,[24] a provision now restated in the requirement that it
must be an "interest" and that it must "relate to" the land.[25] Most emphatically this
does *not* protect occupiers as such.[26] Rather actual occupation acts as a means of
giving notice of a right. How could it be otherwise? A tramp who moves into a house
just as it is sold, without having paid for any interest, cannot say "I am an occupier"
and demand the right to stay indefinitely. Interests capable of overriding the register
are inherently limited to rights capable of binding purchasers. Although registration
alters the method by which notice is given of rights, Lord Wilberforce emphasised that
the Land Registration Acts were framed against a background of interests and rights
of known transmissible character.[27] Interests which override the register must be
capable of enduring through different ownerships.[28]

National Provincial Bank v. *Ainsworth*[29] established this definitively. A matrimonial
home, owned by and registered in the name of the husband, was also financed exclusively by him. When he deserted his family, he left behind his wife and children in
occupation of the home. Later he transferred the legal title to his company – the
Hastings Car Mart – which was registered as proprietor, in order that the matrimonial
home could be mortgaged as security for the company's business debts. He was
unable to pay what had been borrowed. Did Mrs Ainsworth have an overriding interest which would bind the company and the bank? She was undoubtedly in occupation,
but she held no property right which was capable of being matured by occupation into
an overriding interest. The only postulant was the deserted wife's equity – the right to
remain in her husband's house after his desertion. Earlier Court of Appeal decisions
had suggested a proprietary character for this right, but the House of Lords decided
in *Ainsworth* in favour of the view that this right was purely personal and, having
resolved that question in that way, it followed immediately that the wife's right was
not an overriding interest.

---

[24] LRA 1925 s 70(1).
[25] LRA 2002 sch 3 para 2; Law Com 271 (2001), [4.36–4.37].
[26] *National Provincial Bank* v. *Hastings Car Mart* [1964] Ch 665, 692, Donovan LJ; L Tee [1998] *CLJ*
328.
[27] *National Provincial Bank* v. *Ainsworth* [1965] AC 1175, 1261E.
[28] [1964] Ch 665, 696, Russell LJ.
[29] [1965] AC 1175, HL.

Lloyds Bank v. *Rosset*[30] provides a second illustration of the same principle. A dilapidated farm house was bought in a husband's name with the aid of a cash contribution from his family's trust fund, and renovated with money borrowed in the husband's name. His wife claimed a beneficial interest through the joint venture involved in renovating the house fit to live in as a family home and her work in supervising the builders. She was successful in the Court of Appeal,[31] but the House of Lords unanimously reversed this decision.[32] No constructive trust arose since the trustees of the husband's family trust fund insisted that she should not have any beneficial interest and nor had she made any significant financial contribution.[33] Lacking beneficial entitlement she had no claim to an overriding interest.

C. PROTECTED INTERESTS IN UNREGISTERED LAND

1. Notice doctrine for unregistered land

[15.06] Notice doctrine lay at the very heart of equity,[34] until the 1925 legislation virtually abolished it, but it retains a residual application on a failure to overreach a beneficial interest affecting unregistered land.[35]

Maitland[36] emphasised the need to establish personal liability against an individual defendant. Equity could only issue its orders against a person whose conscience was infected by wrong doing, a principle which explains precisely the scope of the enforcement of a trust. A trustee who breaks his trust obviously has a bad conscience. Outsiders who might also be prevented from withholding the land from the true beneficiaries may be infected include: (1) those inheriting on death, (2) creditors, (3) donees, (4) purchasers who know of the trusts (actual notice), and (5) purchasers who ought to have known (constructive notice). Maitland[37] was wrong to suggest that this was an historically true picture of the chronological order in which liability extended, since the full *bona fide* purchaser defence was recognised for uses in the reign of Edward IV (1461)[38] before trusts were ever invented. Metaphorically, however, his analysis enshrines an important truth, that an equitable interest is dependent upon a raft of personal actions against individuals, each defendant bound in conscience by the trust. Total innocents could, in all good conscience, deny the trust, and so lay was outside the reach of equitable remedies and they were able to take the land free of the trust.

---

[30] [1991] 1 AC 107, HL; *Winkworth* v. *Edward Baron Developments Co* [1986] 1 WLR 1512, HL.
[31] [1989] Ch 350, CA; PG McHugh [1989] *CLJ* 180; S Bright (1988) 138 *NLJ* 685.
[32] [1991] 1 AC 107, HL; S Gardner (1991) 54 *MLR* 126; *Barclays Bank* v. *Khaira* [1993] 1 FLR 343, CA.
[33] See below **[17]**.
[34] *Barclays Bank* v. *O'Brien* [1994] 1 AC 180, 195G, Lord Browne-Wilkinson.
[35] Cheshire and Burn (16th ed) 59–66; Grays' *Elements* (3rd ed), 86–90; Maitland's *Equity*, 111–146; Maudsley & Burn *LL – Cases* (7th ed), 25–30; Megarry & Wade (6th ed), [5.015–5.025]. See also undue influence, below **[30.42ff]**.
[36] Maitland's *Equity*, 117.
[37] At 112–113.
[38] J Williams, *Real Property* (Sweet & Maxwell, 24th ed by RA Eastwood, 1926), 54; J Howell [1997] *Conv* 431.

2. Notice doctrine today

[15.07] Practical application of the rule breaks down into two stages.[39] First, proof of a trust raises a presumption that the beneficial interests bind people who later acquire title through the trustees: equitable interests bind the world except a protected purchaser. Second, the protected purchaser rule can be pleaded as a defence, so that the onus switches to the purchaser to establish freedom from the trust.[40] Once satisfied a successful plea is an unanswerable defence to the jurisdiction of equity.[41] Protection is given to a *bona fide* purchaser for value of a legal estate without notice of the equitable interest. In more malleable language, a purchaser must: (1) provide value, (2) acquire a protected interest, (3) be honest; and (4) display diligence. The duty of diligence relating to unregistered land extends to the contents of all documents, to occupiers, and to the investigation of any other suspicious circumstances. Conversely, beneficiaries can protect themselves against buyers by taking occupation, though only until overreaching.

3. Protection of legal purchasers of unregistered land

[15.08] Protection against an earlier property interest depends on the later acquisition of an interest superior in the hierarchy of interests in land.[42] Legal estates defeat earlier equitable interests.[43] Interests which are at the same level in the hierarchy rank in order of their creation: *First in time is first in right*,[44] the rule applied between equal legal rights.[45]

Only the historical division between the common law courts and Chancery can explain the special protection afforded to the stronger legal estate. Equity recognised the common law ownership of the trustee, but enforced the trust against the conscience of the trustee and also against people claiming through the trustee who were in some sense at "fault": a person could not in conscience deny the trust if he was given the land, or had bought with notice of the trust. Wholly "innocent" buyers were left in undisturbed possession of the legal estate. All rights are now enforced in the one court, but the Victorian hierarchy of legal and equitable rights remains in place.[46]

The protected interest could be a freehold estate or some lesser interest:[47] a purchaser of a lease for 99 years is proof against trusts for the duration of the lease,[48] and

---

[39] *Anon* (1465) Cary 10, 21 ER 5; YB 5 Edw 4, 7.

[40] *Phillips* v. *Phillips* (1862) 4 De GF & J 208, 45 ER 1164; *Att-Gen* v. *Biphosphated Guano Co* (1879) 11 Ch D 327, CA; *Royal Bank of Scotland* v. *Etridge* [2001] UKHL 44, [2002] 2 AC 773, [145], Lord Scott.

[41] *Pilcher* v. *Rawlins* (1872) LR 7 Ch App 259, 269; *Re Nisbett & Potts' C* [1905] 1 Ch 391, 402, Farwell J.

[42] Full notice doctrine does not apply to personal property: *Nelson* v. *Larholt* [1948] 1 KB 339; Maitland's *Equity*, 139–146.

[43] For mere equities see below **[24.30]**.

[44] *Qui prior est tempore, potior est jure.*

[45] *Williams* v. *Lambe* (1791) 3 Bro CC 264, 29 ER 526; *Collins* v. *Archer* (1830) 1 Russ & M 284, 39 ER 109.

[46] *Ind Coope & Co* v. *Emmerson* (1887) 12 App Cas 300, HL.

[47] LPA 1925 s 205(1)(xxi); *Re Alms Corn Charity* [1901] 2 Ch 750, 761 (on Conveyancing Act 1882 s 3); *Midland Bank Trust Co* v. *Green* [1981] AC 513, 529D, Lord Wilberforce; *Hunt* v. *Luck* [1902] 1 Ch 428, 433, Vaughan Williams LJ.

[48] *Re King's Leasehold Estates* (1873) LR 16 Eq 521.

a lender is protected until the mortgage is paid off.[49] Protection accrues after acquisition of the legal estate on unconditional delivery of a conveyance and payment of the price.[50] A buyer who is innocent of notice at the time of the contract but who learns of the adverse interest before completion should refuse to complete and rescind the contract.[51] Suppression of a trust of land or of a trust for sale calls for the application of notice doctrine.[52] Trusts created by contribution are often ignored when the land is mortgaged and if so a legal estate passes to the lender in breach of trust, and an innocent purchaser is protected against the trust. In *Pilcher* v. *Rawlins*[53] the sole surviving trustee concealed an original mortgage of the Whitchurch property,[54] by effecting a reconveyance of the legal estate to the borrower and suppressing it. This left the borrower free to mortgage the land to innocent lenders as if he was an outright owner. The deeds showed an apparently perfect title[55] and lack of notice protected the lender against the breach of trust. However, a seller without any title cannot pass a legal estate and so the basic prerequisite for protection of the buyer is lacking.[56]

4. Competition between two equitable interests affecting unregistered land

[15.09] Transfers of equitable interests are "innocent" transfers: they give only what the grantor is justly entitled to, that is the land subject to all existing equities.[57] Priorities between equitable interests are based on time alone[58] with no attempt to weigh the merits of the equal[59] equitable claims, and no special weight attached to later acquisition of the legal estate.[60] In *Cave* v. *Cave*[61] a solicitor fraudulently stole trust funds and used them to buy land in his brother's name, which the brother then mortgaged. Firstly there was a *legal* mortgage to a lender without notice of the trust: this lender was protected from the rights of the beneficiaries under the trust. The same property was remortgaged, secondly, to a lender who took only an *equitable* mortgage. He was equally innocent, but the earlier claims of the beneficiaries were held to prevail over his equitable mortgage.

---

[49] *Willoughby* v. *Willoughby* (1756) 1 Term Rep 763, 99 ER 1366; *Taylor* v. *London & County Banking Co* [1901] 2 Ch 231, 256, Stirling LJ; *Kingsnorth Finance Co* v. *Tizard* [1986] 1 WLR 783, 792.

[50] If the payment is innocent, it is possible that legal title may be got in later: *Blackwood* v. *London Chartered Bank of Australia* (1874) LR 5 PC 92; *Taylor* v. *Russell* [1892] AC 244, HL.

[51] *Caballero* v. *Henty* (1874) LR 9 Ch App 447; *Shaw* v. *Foster* (1872) LR 5 HL 321.

[52] As to strict settlements, see above **[14.13]**.

[53] (1872) LR 7 Ch App 259; E Jenks (1908) 24 *LQR* 147; *Clouette* v. *Storey* [1911] 1 Ch 18, CA (fraud on a power of appointment.)

[54] Different frauds were used for the Smithfield and New Street properties.

[55] An invalid estate may secure protection if clothed with possession: *Jones* v. *Powles* (1834) 3 My & K 581, 40 ER 222, Leach MR; *Young* v. *Young* (1867) LR 3 Eq 801; *Pilcher*, at 266.

[56] Eg under a forgery: Maitland's *Equity*, 125; *Lloyd's Bank* v. *Bullock* [1896] 2 Ch 192.

[57] *Phillips* v. *Phillips* (1862) 4 De GF & J 208, 45 ER 1164. But see D O'Sullivan (2002) 118 *LQR* 296.

[58] *Penn* v. *Browne* (1697) Freem Ch 214, 22 ER 1168; *Willoughby* v. *Willoughby* (1756) 1 Term Rep 763, 99 ER 1366; *Cave* v. *Cave* (1880) 15 Ch D 639, 647, Fry J; *Bailey* v. *Barnes* [1894] 1 Ch 25, CA; *Taylor* v. *London & County Banking Co* [1901] 2 Ch 231, CA.

[59] Inequality might arise from fraud or gross negligence.

[60] LPA 1925 s 94(3); *Assaf* v. *Fuwa* [1955] AC 215, PC; *McCarthy & Stone* v. *Julian S Hodge & Co* [1971] 1 WLR 1547, Foster J.

[61] (1880) 15 Ch D 639.

5. Unregistered land: buyers and donees

[15.10] In modern law, a purchaser is a person who has bought for value,[62] but the mantra "bona fide purchaser for value" is used, despite its apparent tautology, because purchaser here is used in a technical sense meaning any person who took under a deed. This excluded inheritors and squatters, but included both buyers and, curiously, also donees.[63] So it makes sense, after all, to add that a purchase must be "for value". After paying for the land, a buyer is able to defeat unknown trusts, for his conscience cannot be impugned if he has not discovered a trust when he has acted both honestly and diligently. Equity's support for a buyer was settled by precedents already numerous and ancient in 1705.[64] Transactional safety of commerce in land requires favouritism to be displayed towards a person who pays for the land. After saving up to buy a house, the purchaser expects to get his money's worth, that is an unincumbered title which he can sell freely and at its full value. A person who is given land has to accept it as it stands:[65] after all, *one cannot look a gift house in the mouth*!

Provided the consideration is valuable, it is not necessary to show the adequacy of the price paid, which could be above or below market value.[66] A purely nominal consideration should provide no protection,[67] since the suspicions of an honest purchaser would be aroused if the land is very cheap.[68]

6. Extended meaning of value for unregistered land

[15.11] Land is usually bought with money, but value includes anything else of monetary worth such as shares. Also accepted by equity is the payment of an existing debt, despite the contract law rule that it is a past consideration.[69] A mortgage taken out to cover a new loan is on an equal footing with a mortgage to secure an existing debt.[70] Also included is a marriage consideration. Today we have the namby-pamby fashion of marrying for love, so it seems strange to us to treat a future marriage as "value".[71] Jane Austen style marriages of convenience involved a pact between two landed families, the father of each spouse settling land to the benefit of the spouses and later their children, so that each side of the family entered a "contractual" arrangement.[72] On

---

[62] LPA 1925 s 205(1)(xxi).

[63] *Re Nisbet & Potts' C* [1905] 1 Ch 391, Farwell J. The decision is convenient but unorthodox. If the estate held by the former owner is extinguished by adverse possession, all estates and interests attached to it fall; on escheat see Maitland's *Equity*, 115. *Nisbet* ignores the theory of estate ownership and assumes that rights attach to the land itself.

[64] *Dudley & Ward* v. *Dudley* (1705) Prec Ch 241, 249–250, 24 ER 118.

[65] *Mansell* v. *Mansell* (1732) 2 P Wms 678, 24 ER 913.

[66] *Bullock* v. *Sadlier* (1776) Amb 763, 27 ER 491 (interest worth £1,232 bought for £200); *Kettlewell* v. *Watson* (1882) 21 Ch D 685, Fry J.

[67] Statutes vary: LPA 1925 s 205(1)(xxi); LCA 1972 s 17(1); LRA 1925 s 3(xxi); *Midland Bank Trust Co* v. *Green* [1982] AC 513, 529D, 532 (£500 not nominal (!)).

[68] *Pilcher* v. *Rawlings* (1871) LR 7 Ch App 259, 269, James LJ.

[69] *Re McArdle* [1957] Ch 669.

[70] *Ex p Knott* (1806) 11 Ves 609, 32 ER 1225; *Taylor* v. *Blakelock* (1886) 32 Ch D 560, CA; *Taylor* v. *London & County Banking Co* [1901] 2 Ch 231, CA; RE Megarry (1943) 59 *LQR* 208.

[71] LPA 1925 s 205(1)(xxi).

[72] *Lord Keeper* v. *Wyld* (1682) 1 Vern 139, 23 ER 372; *Att-Gen* v. *Jacobs Smith* [1895] 2 QB 341, CA; *Salih* v. *Atchi* [1961] AC 778.

this model, spouses, children, and grandchildren come within the marriage consideration, are "purchasers", and are thus enabled to override earlier equitable interests affecting the land. This rule has been discarded for registered titles.[73]

7. Transactional security: later buyers

[15.12] Protection is given to transactions rather than to individual purchasers.[74] A purchaser who pays £100,000 for a house which, unbeknown to him, belongs to a trust is only adequately protected by the bona fide purchaser rule if he is free to sell the house and realise his £100,000 investment back into money. The slate has to be wiped clean. So if a purchaser without notice sells on to a purchaser with notice, the second purchaser is not bound by the trust, a rule laid down with remarkable consistency[75] and reiterated in *Wilkes* v. *Spooner*.[76] A tenant entered into a restrictive covenant against competition with a neighbouring butcher. His lease was surrendered to the landlord, who was unaware of the restrictive covenant, before being re-granted to the son of the original tenant, who did know, but was nevertheless entitled to hold this new lease free of the covenant. Had it been regranted to the original tenant, he would have been bound by the trust; the *original trustee* is prevented from laundering the land by passing it through an innocent party; if he repurchases it himself he is bound by the trust.[77]

D. HONESTY (ACTUAL NOTICE) AND UNREGISTERED TITLES

1. Bona fide

[15.13] The requirement for a purchaser to act bona fide, that is in good faith or with honesty, largely restates the requirement to recognise interests of which one knows.[78]

2. Actual notice

[15.14] *Knowledge* that someone else is claiming a beneficial interest naturally attracts liability on the basis of bad faith,[79] but actual *notice* is a more extensive concept: it would include knowing of the existence of a settlement from which there would be deemed knowledge of all its contents.[80] A buyer will only be affected by circumstances which appear to be relevant,[81] but it would no longer be safe to ignore information

---

[73] See below **[15.28]**.

[74] *Wallwyn* v. *Lee* (1803) 9 Ves 24, 34, 32 ER 509, Eldon LC.

[75] *Bennett* v. *Walker* (1737) West temp Hard 130, 25 ER 857; *Att-Gen* v. *Biphosphated Guano Co* (1879) 11 Ch D 327, CA; and many others.

[76] [1911] 2 KB 473, CA.

[77] *Re Stapleford Colliery* (1880) 14 Ch D 432, CA; *Gordon* v. *Holland* (1913) 82 LJPC 81, PC.

[78] *Midland Bank* v. *Farmpride Hatcheries* [1981] 2 EGLR 147, 151C, Oliver LJ. But the two requirements are distinct: *Midland Bank Trust Co* v. *Green* [1981] AC 513, 528E, Lord Wilberforce.

[79] *Northern Counties of England Fire Insurance Co* v. *Whipp* (1884) 26 Ch D 482, 487–488, Fry J.

[80] LPA 1925 s 199(1)(ii)(a); *Ware* v. *Lord Egmont* (1854) 4 De GM & G 460, 473, 43 ER 586, Lord Cranworth LC; *Polly Peck International* v. *Nadir (No 2)* [1992] 4 All ER 769, 781; *Eagle Trust* v. *SBC Securities* [1992] 4 All ER 488, 497–498.

[81] *Lloyd* v. *Banks* (1868) LR 3 Ch App 488, 490.

garnered from a casual conversation,[82] or newspaper advertisement.[83] In marginal cases, dishonesty (ignoring actual knowledge) merges into carelessness (constructive notice),[84] but reckless disregard for obvious facts may be tantamount to dishonesty.[85] There is some confusion in the case law about whether a person has *knowledge* of a matter he has forgotten,[86] but whatever the truth of that it seems clear on principle that he would have *notice*.

3. Imputed notice

[15.15] Knowledge is imputed from a conveyancer or other agent to the principal who employs him. "He . . . who trusts most ought to suffer most."[87] This is a form of actual notice.[88] Knowledge can be imputed where a solicitor acts for a number of parties to a transaction, so that it has become very difficult to act for multiple parties;[89] however imputation does not infect a client who is being cheated by his solicitor.[90]

Imputation applies to the knowledge of a counsel, solicitor, or other agent "acting as such".[91] Imputation should only occur if there is a duty to communicate a particular piece of information. This is so, for example, if a surveyor inspects a property which it is intended to mortgage and discovers the fact that the borrower is separated.[92] That same test also determines when information is deemed to pass from a person in one capacity to himself in another.[93] Imputation of knowledge is limited to the transaction with respect to which the question of notice arises.[94] A solicitor must be employed as solicitor and on the same business. Knowledge will not necessarily be imputed when a solicitor is instructed to act merely to secure the execution of a mortgage.[95] In general where a solicitor is instructed to act both for a bank and for a surety giving a security to the bank, these are two separate transactions and no question of imputation of knowledge will arise.[96]

---

[82] *Barnhart* v. *Greenshields* (1853) 9 Moo PCC 18, 36–38, 14 ER 204; *Cornwallis' case* (1595) Toth 186, 21 ER 163.

[83] *Lloyd* v. *Banks* (1868) LR 3 Ch App 488; LPA 1925 s 199(1)(ii)(a).

[84] *Wilde* v. *Gibson* (1848) 1 HLC 605, 9 ER 897; DC Jackson (1978) 94 *LQR* 239, 252.

[85] *Bailey* v. *Barnes* [1894] 1 Ch 25, 35, Lindley LJ; *English & Scottish Mercantile Investment Co* v. *Brunton* [1892] 2 QB 700, 707–708, Esher MR.

[86] Megarry & Wade (6th ed), [5.016] n 67.

[87] *Le Neve* v. *Le Neve* (1747) 3 Atk 646, 26 ER 1172.

[88] *Espin* v. *Pemberton* (1859) 3 De G & J 547, 554, 44 ER 1380, Chelmsford LC; *Cave* v. *Cave* (1880) 15 Ch D 639, 643, Fry J.

[89] *Rolland* v. *Hart* (1871) LR 6 Ch App 678; *Kettlewell* v. *Watson* (1882) 21 Ch D 685; *Goody* v. *Baring* [1956] 1 WLR 448.

[90] *Kennedy* v. *Green* (1834) 3 My & K 699, 40 ER 266, Brougham LC; *Re European Bank* (1870) LR 5 Ch App 358, Giffard LC; *Cave* v. *Cave* (1880) 15 Ch D 639, 643, Fry J; *Davis* v. *Hutchings* [1907] 1 Ch 356.

[91] LPA 1925 s 199(1)(ii)(b); *Lloyds Bank* v. *Marcan* [1973] 1 WLR 339, 348, Pennycuick V-C, on appeal [1973] 1 WLR 1387, CA; *B* v. *B (No 2)* [1995] 1 FLR 374, 380D–G, Hoffmann LJ (not between different solicitors in the same firm); *Halifax Mortgage Services* v. *Stepsky* [1996] Ch 207, CA; *Royal Bank of Scotland* v. *Etridge (No 2)* [1998] 4 All ER 705, 718d–g, Stuart-Smith LJ.

[92] *Kingsnorth Finance Co* v. *Tizard* [1986] 1 WLR 783, Ch D.

[93] *Simpson* v. *Molson's Bank* [1895] AC 370, PC; *Re Hampshire Land Co* [1896] 2 Ch 743; *Re Fenwick Stobart & Co* [1902] 1 Ch 507; TA 1925 s 28 (two trustees).

[94] LPA 1925 s 199(1)(ii)(b); *Meyer* v. *Chartres* (1918) 34 TLR 589. Maitland's *Equity*, 117 (earlier case-law restricted).

[95] *Wyllie* v. *Pollen* (1863) 3 De GJ & Sm 596, 46 ER 767, Lord Westbury LC; Megarry & Wade (6th ed), [5.023].

[96] See below **[30.62]**.

E. DILIGENCE IN RELATION TO UNREGISTERED TITLES

[15.16] Diligence is the obligation to investigate title and the fact that a purchaser is bound by matters which he ought to have discovered.

1. Constructive notice

[15.17] Constructive notice is knowledge by a purchaser of any document or fact which "would have come to his knowledge if such inquiries and inspections had been made as ought reasonably to have been made",[97] which may be personal or via his solicitor or agent.[98] Diligent inquiry is required to discover rights which were reasonably discoverable.[99] This duty of inquiry crystallised in 1882[100] and the new law was wider than what went before.[101]

The section is interpreted to impose a positive duty to make reasonable inquiries,[102] despite its negative phraseology,[103] but nevertheless notice doctrine has not yet lost its elasticity[104] so that new inquiries may be required by social changes.

2. Investigation of unregistered title

[15.18] A buyer or lender has constructive notice of all facts discoverable from a proper investigation of title.[105] Extraordinary circumspection is not required. Suspicions should be raised by a hurriedly written receipt on a mortgage,[106] unexplained parties to title deeds,[107] or a sale subject to undisclosed incumbrances.[108]

A purchaser is safe from a fact which no inquiry would reveal,[109] and a false answer may let the purchaser off the hook,[110] but if inquiry is wholly omitted it must be assumed that a correct answer would have been given.[111] A full statutory title must be

---

[97] "Inquiry" (eg a planning inquiry, and in unregistered land: LPA 1925 s 199) is more formal than "enquiry" (eg at a railway station or with registered land: LRA 1925 s 70(1)(g); LRA 2002 sch 3 para 2).

[98] LPA 1925 s 199(1)(ii); *Hunt* v. *Luck* [1902] 1 Ch 428, 433.

[99] *Midland Bank* v. *Farmpride Hatcheries* [1981] 2 EGLR 147, 151C, Oliver LJ.

[100] *Oliver* v. *Hinton* [1899] 2 Ch 264, 274, Lindley MR.

[101] *Re Nisbet & Potts' C* [1905] 1 Ch 391, 400, Farwell J; *Molyneux* v. *Hawtrey* [1903] 2 KB 487, CA; *Midland Bank Trust Co* v. *Green* [1981] AC 513, 528E, Lord Wilberforce; *Kemmis* v. *Kemmis* [1988] 1 WLR 1307, 1333.

[102] *Bailey* v. *Barnes* [1894] 1 Ch 25, 35, Lindley LJ.

[103] *Taylor* v. *London & County Banking Co* [1901] 2 Ch 231, 258; LPA 1925 s 199(3) side note; *English & Scottish Mercantile Investment Co* v. *Brunton* [1892] 2 QB 700, 707–708, Esher MR; *Joseph* v. *Lyons* (1884) 15 QBD 280, 287, Lindley LJ; *The Birnam Wood* [1907] P 1, 14, Farwell LJ; Maitland's *Equity*, 119, wrongly suggests that the doctrine was narrowed in 1882.

[104] *Boland* [1981] AC 487 HL; *Kemmis* v. *Kemmis* [1988] 1 WLR 1307, 1324B, Purchas LJ.

[105] LPA 1925 s 199(1)(ii).

[106] *Kennedy* v. *Green* (1834) 3 My & K 699, 40 ER 266, Brougham LC.

[107] *Steadman* v. *Poole* (1847) 16 LJ Ch 348.

[108] *Re Alms Corn Charity* [1901] 2 Ch 750, 760.

[109] *Wilkes* v. *Spooner* [1911] 2 KB 473, CA; *Taylor* v. *London & County Banking Co* [1901] 2 Ch 231, 258, CA; *Rowell* v. *Satchell* [1903] 2 Ch 212, 221.

[110] *Jared* v. *Clements* [1903] 1 Ch 428, CA, but see *Hodgson* v. *Marks* [1971] Ch 892, 932D, Russell LJ (reliance on untrue *ipse dixit* insufficient).

[111] *Jones* v. *Williams* (1857) 24 Beav 47, 53 ER 274, Romilly MR; *Knight* v. *Bowyer* (1858) 2 De G & J 421, 450, 44 ER 1053.

investigated back to a good root of title – now possibly as recent as 15 years old[112] –
and accepting a short title gives constructive notice of anything on the documents not
demanded.[113] All links in the title after the root must be investigated.[114] However a
tenant is not entitled to see his landlord's title, and has no constructive notice of
adverse interests affecting it.[115]

3. Land charges search

[15.19] Registration of a land charge gives notice of a burden affecting unregistered
land, so a diligent purchaser must effect a land charge search.[116]

4. Suspicious facts off an unregistered title

[15.20] Notice of suspicious facts relevant to the property being bought[117] imposes a
duty to go on and ascertain the truth.[118] A buyer told of two mortgages on a property
was bound to make inquiries and discover a third.[119] Problems arise from the fluctuating nature of domestic relationships; for example in *National Provincial Bank* v.
Ainsworth[120] one question was whether a bank had notice of the fact that a husband
had deserted his wife. In fact no, even though the manager's secretary lived in the
same road, and the address given by the husband indicated that he no longer lived at
the matrimonial home.[121] However *Kingsnorth Finance Co* v. *Tizard* reached an opposite conclusion.[122] A married man living in the former matrimonial home with his
children stated in his mortgage application that he was single, but told the lender's
surveyor the truth that he was separated. This discrepancy should have alerted the
lender to the wife's interest or at the least needed further inquiry.

F. OCCUPIERS OF UNREGISTERED LAND

[15.21] Inquiry of occupiers is required in order to avoid constructive notice of their
rights. In *Barnhart* v. *Greenshields*[123] Lord Kingsdown referred to notice derived from
actual occupation by a tenant.[124]

---

[112] LPA 1969 s 23; Law Com 9 (1967); see above [9.04].

[113] *Patman* v. *Harland* (1881) 17 Ch D 353, 355; *Imray* v. *Oakshette* [1897] 2 QB 218, CA; *Matthews* v.
Smallwood [1910] 1 Ch 777, Parker J; *Re Nisbett & Potts' C* [1905] 1 Ch 391, 402, Farwell J.

[114] *Pilcher* v. *Rawlins* (1872) LR 7 Ch App 259, 272, Mellish LJ.

[115] LPA 1925 s 44(3); overruling *Patman* v. *Harland* (1881) 17 Ch D 353; *Shears* v. *Wells* [1936] 1 All ER
832; *White* v. *Bijou Mansions* [1937] Ch 610, 619, Simonds J; DW Logan (1940) 56 *LQR* 361.

[116] See below [21.26].

[117] *West* v. *Reid* (1843) 2 Hare 249, 260, 67 ER 104; *Wyllie* v. *Pollen* (1863) 3 De GJ & S 596, 604, 46 ER
767, Westbury LC (not if other property).

[118] *Jones* v. *Smith* (1841) 1 Hare 43, 66 ER 943; *Knight* v. *Bowyer* (1858) 2 De G & J 421, 450, 44 ER
1053; *Espin* v. *Pemberton* (1859) 3 De G & J 547, 554, 44 ER 1380: *Bailey* v. *Barnes* [1894] 1 Ch 25, CA.

[119] *Jones* v. *Williams* (1857) 24 Beav 47, 53 ER 274, Romilly MR.

[120] [1965] AC 1175, 1234, Lord Upjohn.

[121] [1964] Ch 665, 700, Russell LJ; [1965] AC 1175, 1250, Lord Wilberforce.

[122] [1986] 1 WLR 783; MP Thompson [1986] *Conv* 283; Peter Luxton (1986) 136 *NLJ* 771; P McHugh
[1987] *CLJ* 28. It accords with earlier cases: Megarry & Wade (6th ed), [5.019] n 82.

[123] (1853) 9 Moo PCC 18, 14 ER 204.

[124] LPA 1925 s 14; *City of London BS* v. *Flegg* [1988] AC 54, 90F–G.

1. Tenants

[15.22] Possession by a tenant is notice of the tenant's interest[125] and of all the contents of the lease,[126] but not of defects in the lease since a buyer is entitled to assume that the tenancy agreement states the agreed terms correctly.[127] Similarly the presence of a wife in the matrimonial home is not notice of her right to apply for a transfer of it on divorce.[128] Occupation also protects equitable rights enjoyed by the tenant outside the lease,[129] and gives notice of other rights, such as the licence of an employee.[130]

2. Occupiers discoverable by inspection

[15.23] Modern buyers must inspect the land to look for occupiers, a duty of reasonable inquiry settled in *Hunt* v. *Luck*, equating the equitable duty applied at first instance[131] with the statutory duty on appeal.[132]

The buyer should inquire of the seller who is in occupation of the property and by what right. The Law Society's National Protocol[133] requires the solicitor acting for the seller to ascertain the identity of all adults[134] living in the dwelling and ask about any financial contribution they or anyone else may have made towards its purchase or subsequent improvement. Inspection must be used to verify this information.

Occupation must be discoverable, since unless it is obvious, the whole equitable basis of notice collapses.[135] Case-law appears to impose an unrealistically high duty of inspection. In one case a discrepancy between the 14 visible chimney pots and the 12 flues inside the house, was notice of a neighbour's easement to use two flues.[136] Count your fireplaces! *Kingsnorth Finance Co* v. *Tizard*[137] concerned a mortgage of a matrimonial home after the breakdown of the marriage. The husband lived in the house, but although the wife had left home and slept elsewhere, she returned every day to care for the children. A surveyor appointed by the finance company was on the lookout for signs of the existence of a girlfriend but properly drew the line at opening

---

[125] *Barnhart* v. *Greenshields* (1853) 9 Moo PCC 18, 14 ER 204; *Knight* v. *Bowyer* (1858) 2 De G & J 421, 449, 44 ER 1053, Turner LJ; *Jones* v. *Smith* (1841) 1 Hare 43, 60, 66 ER 943, Wigram V-C; *Hodgson* v. *Marks* [1971] Ch 892, 915G, Ungoed-Thomas J at first instance; *Kemmis* v. *Kemmis* [1988] 1 WLR 1307, 1333.

[126] *Taylor* v. *Stibbert* (1794) 2 Ves 437, 440, 30 ER 713, Loughborough LC; *Hollington Brothers* v. *Rhodes* [1951] 2 TLR 691, 694–695, Harman J.

[127] *Smith* v. *Jones* [1954] 1 WLR 1089, Upjohn J; *Hunt* v. *Luck* [1901] 1 Ch 45, 51, Farwell J at first instance.

[128] *Kemmis* v. *Kemmis* [1988] 1 WLR 1307.

[129] *Meux* v. *Maltby* (1818) 2 Swanst 277, 36 ER 621 (contract).

[130] *Midland Bank* v. *Farmpride Hatcheries* [1981] 2 EGLR 147, CA; RE Annand [1982] *Conv* 67; HW Wilkinson (1982) 132 *NLJ* 68. The case wrongly assumed that a contractual licence was proprietary.

[131] [1901] 1 Ch 45, 50, Farwell J; *Green* v. *Rheinberg* (1911) 104 LT 149, 150 Vaughan Williams LJ; *Reeves* v. *Pope* [1914] 2 KB 284, 290, Buckley LJ; *Caunce* v. *Caunce* [1969] 1 WLR 286, 293, Stamp J.

[132] [1902] 1 Ch 428, 433, Vaughan Williams LJ; *Smith* v. *Jones* [1954] 1 WLR 1089, 1091, Upjohn J.

[133] *Encyclopaedia FP* (5th ed, 1997 reissue) vol 35, [1326].

[134] [1979] 1 WLR 440, 444D, Templeman J; on registered land see *Hypo-Mortgage Services* v. *Robinson* [1997] 2 FLR 71, CA.

[135] *Hodgson* v. *Marks* [1971] Ch 892, 915G, Ungoed-Thomas J at first instance.

[136] *Hervey* v. *Smith* (1856) 22 Beav 299, 52 ER 1123.

[137] [1986] 1 WLR 783.

cupboards. However, inspection took place by appointment one Sunday, which gave the man an opportunity to eliminate signs of his wife's occupation, and there ought, held the judge, to have been more than this pre-arranged inspection. Perhaps this application of notice doctrine was too severe,[138] since professional people must work to diary appointments and repeated inspection would be unrealistically expensive. It should not be necessary to call in the CID.

3. Joint occupiers

[15.24] It might be occupation to the exclusion of the seller or joint with him, whether or not the presence of the claimant is inconsistent with the title.[139] Husbands often held legal title in a matrimonial home occupied jointly by husband and wife. Until the 1960s it was probable that the wife was living in a house owned by her husband,[140] but a purchaser can no longer rely on that outdated assumption. Today there is a strong possibility that a spouse or cohabiting partner has a beneficial interest through contribution. Dicta in *Williams & Glyn's Bank* v. *Boland*[141] repudiated the old law and indicated that, had title been unregistered, notice would have arisen from Mrs Boland's joint occupation with Mr Boland.

4. Recipients of rent from unregistered land

[15.25] Occupation of unregistered land by a tenant does not give notice of the rights of his landlord, or whoever else is the recipient of the rent. There is no obligation to ask the tenant to whom he pays rent.[142] However natural such an inquiry may seem, a line in the sand was drawn to exclude it by *Hunt* v. *Luck*.[143] Dr Hunt had, apparently, been induced by fraud to convey 27 tenanted houses at Wimbledon to his agent Gilbert, who passed them by will to Luck, who in turn mortgaged them. After Dr Hunt's death his widow sought to recover the houses, which required her to prove that the lenders had constructive notice of Dr Hunt's beneficial entitlement. Rents were collected by a local estate agent, Woodrow, and the lenders may have known this fact, but even so it did not give constructive notice of Hunt's interest.[144] Lenders are not required to establish who collects rent and on whose behalf. Occupation by tenants is no notice of the landlord's title.[145] It would have been different had the lender known of rent payments to a person known to be claiming an interest adverse to the title offered by the borrower.[146]

---

[138] MP Thompson [1986] *Conv* 283; P Luxton (1986) 136 *NLJ* 771.

[139] *Cavander* v. *Bulteel* (1873) LR 9 Ch App 79.

[140] *Caunce* v. *Caunce* [1969] 1 WLR 286, Stamp J (unregistered); *Bird* v. *Syme-Thomson* [1979] 1 WLR 440; *Williams & Glyn's Bank* v. *Boland* (1979) 26 P & CR 448 Ch D (both registered).

[141] [1981] AC 487, 505, Lord Wilberforce, 511, Lord Scarman; see below **[15.38]**.

[142] *Barnhart* v. *Greenshields* (1853) 9 Moo PC 18, 34, 14 ER 204; *Hunt* v. *Luck* [1902] 1 Ch 428, 433, [1901] 1 Ch 45, 51; *Knight* v. *Bowyer* (1858) 2 De G & J 421, 44 ER 1053.

[143] [1902] 1 Ch 428, CA; [1901] 1 Ch 45, Farwell J.

[144] [1902] 1 Ch 428, 433.

[145] [1902] 1 Ch 428, 432, Vaughan Williams LJ; [1901] 1 Ch 45, 49, Farwell J; *Green* v. *Rheinberg* (1911) 104 LT 149, 151, Vaughan Williams LJ.

[146] *Knight* v. *Bowyer* (1858) 2 De G & J 421, 449, 44 ER 1053, Turner LJ; [1901] 1 Ch 45, 50, Farwell J.

G. PRIORITY IN REGISTERED LAND

[15.26] This section analyses the three factors relevant to becoming a protected purchaser of registered land: (1) the need for a protected interest; (2) value; and (3) diligence. It also considers (4) the absence of any requirement of honesty.

1. Protected interests in registered land

[15.27] Protection of a purchaser of registered land depends upon acquisition of a legal estate under a registered disposition. This in turn depends upon substantive registration. Equitable interests are created at the time of completion of a sale[147] but these only mature into legal rights by registration so that protection of a buyer is dependent upon his becoming registered proprietor.[148] A buyer hands over his money on completion, but only secures protection on the date of his application for registration.[149] The registration gap between these two dates, during which time the buyer is at severe risk, needs to be covered by an official search with priority.[150]

2. Provision of value

[15.28] Protection is provided only for dispositions "for valuable consideration", a concept now defined to exclude marriage.[151] A nominal consideration in money is not sufficient.[152] In *Peffer* v. *Rigg* a house was transferred by the proprietor to his ex-wife when they divorced in consideration of £1 as part of their divorce settlement. Graham J used the express consideration (£1), which was nominal, and so he refused to treat Mrs Rigg as a purchaser.[153] Donees must take the land in the condition in which they find it, that is subject to all existing equities.[154]

3. Diligence

[15.29] Diligence is required in determining the state of the register. The register will reveal notices which protect burdens and which will bind the purchaser. There may also be restrictions to protect overreachable interests, which will be removed from the title if the terms of the restriction are complied with. Beneficial interests under trusts will normally be overreached on sale, but even if this was not the case they are likely to overridden on a sale.[155] A purchaser takes free from other estates and interests

---

[147] Priority is based on first in time: LRA 2002 s 28.
[148] S 29.
[149] S 74.
[150] See above **[8.21]**.
[151] LRA 2002 s 132(1); this reverses LRA 1925 s 3 (xxxi).
[152] LRA 2002 s 132(1); *Re de Leeuw* [1922] 2 Ch 540 (not a foreclosure order under pre-1926 law).
[153] [1977] 1 WLR 285, 293G, Graham J.
[154] LRA 2002 s 28; *Peffer* was decided on LRA 1925 s 20(4).
[155] LRA 2002 s 29; *De Lusignan* v. *Johnson* (1973) 230 EG 499, 499, Brightman J; *Abbey National BS* v. *Cann* [1991] 1 AC 56, 79A, Lord Oliver; *City of London BS* v. *Flegg* [1986] Ch 605, 617C, Dillon LJ.

which are registrable but are unprotected when he buys unless protected on the register[156] or by occupation.[157]

Diligence is also required to discover overriding interests, and particularly those which override through occupation, and any other matters which take effect off the register.

It is axiomatic that a purchaser of registered land has no further duty to investigate title, to find non-occupiers,[158] or to check suspicious circumstances or matters off the register.[159] Registration is the only form of notice, purchasers being freed from the hazards of constructive notice and the need to make elaborate inquiries.[160] An unfortunate gap is opened between the two conveyancing systems, with the unregistered system looking fairer.

4. Irrelevance of honesty

[15.30] Honesty is not a requirement of a buyer under the registered system.[161] A person giving value is allowed to defeat an interest of which he knows. The reform process of report and counter-report wavered on this central and crucial issue, with a proposal to introduce a requirement of good faith at every stage[162] except the last two. Finally the rule adopted and legislated was that the knowledge was made wholly irrelevant,[163] harsh cases being resolved by the personal liability for interference with a trust or knowing receipt of trust property.[164]

This legislative provision is misguided. The crunch case is *Peffer* v. *Rigg*.[165] Peffer and Rigg were the husbands of two sisters who agreed to buy a house for occupation by their joint mother-in-law (Mrs Bingle). The house was transferred to Rigg's name since he would have the financial status to obtain a mortgage and an improvement grant, but he held on trust for both of himself and Peffer equally. Since the house was occupied by Mrs Bingle and a tenant, the contributor (Peffer) had no overriding interest. When the Riggs divorced, title was transferred to the ex-wife in consideration of a nominal payment of £1 which did not defeat Peffer's contribution. Another way of looking at the case was that the former Mrs Rigg provided substantial consideration

---

[156] The only appropriate entry is a restriction (unilateral or mutual) which will merely facilitate overreaching by requiring two trustees to give the receipt. Many informal trusts will not be protected in this way.

[157] LRA 2002 sch 3 para 2.

[158] *National Provincial Bank* v. *Ainsworth* [1965] AC 1175, 1261E.

[159] LRA 2002 s 78 states that the *registrar* is not affected by any trust to which s 29 adds that a *purchaser* is not affected by matters unprotected on the register; LRA 1925 s 74 referred both to the registrar and to purchasers.

[160] *Williams & Glyn's Bank* v. *Boland* [1981] AC 487, 503, Lord Wilberforce; *Parkash* v. *Irani Finance* [1970] Ch 101, 109.

[161] LRA 2002 s 29(1); *De Lusignan* v. *Johnson* (1973) 230 EG 499, Brightman J (estate contract); *Hodges* v. *Jones* [1935] Ch 657, Luxmoore J; *Strand Securities* v. *Caswell* [1965] Ch 373, 390, Cross J, 958, 987, Russell LJ.

[162] Law Com 158 (1987), [4.14–4.15].

[163] Law Com 254 (1998), [2.5], [3.39–3.50].

[164] At [3.48]. This non-proprietary remedy is unlikely to be successful after the insolvency of the defendant.

[165] [1977] 1 WLR 285, Graham J; FR Crane (1977) 41 *Conv (NS)* 207; RJ Smith (1977) 93 *LQR* 341; DJ Hayton [1977] *CLJ* 227; JE Martin [1978] *Conv* 52; S Anderson (1977) 40 *MLR* 602; DC Jackson (1978) 94 *LQR* 239.

in settling her claims arising from the couple's divorce. On that assumption, considered obiter by Graham J, Mrs Rigg was a purchaser for valuable consideration with notice of her brother-in-law's contribution. Graham J[166] found ways to finesse the language of the Land Registration Act 1925 to find a requirement that a purchaser of registered land must be honest before claiming to be a protected purchaser. That decision is much criticised for technical error, but is self evidently just.[167] Mrs Rigg would have lost even if she had been a purchaser.

That is no longer the case. No room for doubt is left by the Land Registration Act 2002: a known but unprotected beneficial interest is destroyed by a purchaser for value. The purchaser is not required to be honest, nor to act in good faith. Honesty was required in order to place reliance on a search under pre-2002 law,[168] but there is no longer any trace of this requirement.

H. OCCUPIERS OF REGISTERED LAND

[15.31] Occupation is a method of protection of an interest affecting registered land. A right overrides a disposition of the land if it is:

"an interest belonging to a person . . . in actual occupation."[169]

If the main thrust of the old law is preserved, there are also significant differences, so the encrustation of jurisprudence which attached itself to the notorious and much litigated paragraph (g)[170] must be carried forward with care. As re-enacted in the less euphonious paragraph 2 of schedule 3, registered land law is brought into close alignment with unregistered notice doctrine, a re-alignment long argued for by *New Land Lawyers*.[171] It now becomes much easier to expound the law as one coherent whole.

1. Interests protected

(1) Occupiers without any interest

[15.32] Overriding status is awarded only to those claiming an interest, so it is not available to a person living in another's house without having contributed or being promised any beneficial interest in it.[172]

(2) Beneficial interests under trusts of land

[15.33] Beneficial interests under trusts of land are one of the major kinds of interest protected by occupation.

---

[166] At 293H–294A citing Brickdale & Stewart Wallace's, *Land Registration Act 1925* (Stevens, 4th ed 1939), 107 note (1).
[167] P Sparkes *NLL* (1st ed), 150.
[168] SI 1993/3276 rr 2, 6; *Smith* v. *Morrison* [1974] 1 WLR 659, Plowman J.
[169] LRA 2002 sch 3 para 2 (dispositions); sch 1 para 2 (first registration).
[170] LRA 1925 s 70(1)(g); Megarry & Wade (6th ed), [6.047–6.064].
[171] P Sparkes [1989] *Conv* 342; P Sparkes *NLL* (1st ed), 152–157.
[172] *National Provincial Bank* v. *Ainsworth* [1965] AC 1175, HL; *Lloyds Bank* v. *Rosset* [1991] 1 AC 107, HL; see below [17].

Protection for tenants[173] was extended to include all occupiers in 1925.[174] Beneficial interests are essentially overreachable, but a dual status was established for bare trusts in *Hodgson* v. *Marks*.[175] Beneficial interests used to be assigned to the category of minor interests (interests requiring protection on the register), but "dual status" ensured that such an interest could transfer to the category of overriding interests (enforceable off the register) when protected by occupation. Dual status was extended further by *Williams & Glyn's Bank* v. *Boland*[176] to trusts for sale, short shrift being given to the argument that the beneficial interest was inherently restricted to rights in the proceeds of sale. Three changes have occurred. All these trusts are treated as trusts of land, conversion to the proceeds has been abolished,[177] and the two distinct categories of minor[178] and overriding interests have been abolished.

So it is now indisputable[179] that occupation can protect a beneficiary under a trust of land.

(3) Beneficial interests under two trustee trusts

[15.34] Beneficial interests under trusts of land should be protected by restriction, an entry which facilitates overreaching by ensuring that the transaction complies with the terms of the restriction. A beneficial interest held by an occupier appears to be overriding even while it is protected on the register by restriction. If the transaction overreaches properly the beneficial interest is transferred to the proceeds of sale and no longer attaches to the land, so it ceases to override.[180]

Under the 1925 scheme, overriding status was lost at the time of a protective entry on the register by restriction or a notice requiring the appointment of a second trustee, but not, apparently, by entry of a caution against dealings.[181] Under the 2002 Act the entry must be a restriction – unilateral or mutual – but this does not affect the overriding status of an occupier.[182]

(4) Strict settlements

[15.35] Beneficial interests arising under pre-1997 strict settlements[183] do not enjoy dual status and can only be protected on the register by a restriction.

---

[173] Land Registry Act 1862 s 27; Land Transfer Act 1875 s 18.
[174] LPA 1922 sch 16 para 5(3)(i); LRA 1925 s 70(1)(g).
[175] [1971] Ch 892, 926E–H, Micklem's argument rejected by CA.
[176] [1979] Ch 312, 331D–F, Lord Denning MR; [1981] AC 487, 506E–G, Lord Wilberforce. This is not what the 1925 legislators intended: P Sparkes *NLL* (1st ed), 151.
[177] See above **[13.05]**.
[178] *UCB Group* v. *Hedworth* [2002] EWCA Civ 708, [2002] 46 EG 200.
[179] *Wallcite* v. *Ferrishurst* [1999] Ch 355, 370E, Robert Walker LJ.
[180] *City of London BS* v. *Flegg* [1988] AC 54, HL.
[181] *Flegg* [1988] AC 54, HL; P Sparkes [1988] *Conv* 141.
[182] LRA 2002 s 29(3) removes overriding status only from interests protected by notice.
[183] LRA 2002 sch 3 para 2(a); SLA 1925 ss 2, 117(1)(xxiv).

(5) Burdens

[15.36] Any interest belonging to an occupier and relating to the land may be overriding, so this includes all endurable burdens such as leases, the interests of adverse possessors, contracts, proprietary estoppel rights, rights to avoid voidable transfers, rights of rectification and so on.[184] Occupation does not need to be indicative of the right claimed to be overriding, so an occupier could claim protection for an option.[185] Overriding status is lost if the interest once becomes protected by notice.[186]

2. Actual occupation

[15.37] What constitutes occupation? The only real guidance in the Lords was given by Lord Wilberforce when he said in *Williams & Glyn's Bank* v. *Boland*[187] that:

> "If there is actual occupation, and the occupier has rights, the purchaser takes subject to them. If not, he does not. No further element is material."

If one took this literally, it might seem that a purchaser would be bound by an undiscoverable occupier, but it now appears that Lord Wilberforce's wider statement of principle was incorrect.

The occupation based overriding interest was clearly intended as a statutory restatement in 1925 of the unregistered notice doctrine of *Hunt* v. *Luck* (1902).[188] "Actual occupation" itself was pasted in from *Barnhardt* v. *Greenshields*, a notice case decided by the Privy Council in 1852.[189] This suggests therefore that the crucial quality of the occupation is that it should alert the purchaser to the need to make enquiry of the occupier. Subsequent cases vacillated between a notice based interpretation[190] and a literal interpretation,[191] but the Land Registration Act 2002 accepts the former view.[192]

That occupation of registered land must be "actual" merely emphasises the requirement of physical presence.[193] Uncertainties of notice are replaced in registered land by a simple factual enquiry about occupation.[194]

---

[184] See below **[20.16ff]**.

[185] *Wallcite* v. *Ferrishurst* [1999] Ch 355, 372D, Robert Walker LJ.

[186] LRA 2002 s 29(2)–(3).

[187] [1981] AC 487, 504E; *Kling* v. *Keston Properties* (1985) 49 P & CR 212 (car in garage).

[188] [1902] 1 Ch 428, CA; [1901] 1 Ch 45 Farwell J; *Wallcite* v. *Ferrishurst* [1999] Ch 355, 372C, Robert Walker LJ.

[189] (1853) 9 Moo PCC 18, 14 ER 204, PC; *Taylor* v. *Stibbert* (1794) 2 Ves Jun 437, 440, 30 ER 713.

[190] *National Provincial Bank* v. *Hastings Car Mart* [1964] Ch 665, 689, Lord Denning in, CA; on appeal as *Ainsworth* [1965] AC 1175, 1259F–1261, Lord Wilberforce; *Boland* [1979] Ch 312, 335H, Ormrod LJ; *Boland* [1981] AC 487, 493B–C, Lord Wilberforce; *City of London* BS v. Flegg [1988] AC 54, 88B, Lord Oliver; *Strand Securities* v. *Caswell* [1965] Ch 958, CA.

[191] C Fortescue-Brickdale & J Stewart-Wallace, *The Land Registration Act* (3rd ed, 1927); *Hodgson* v. *Marks* [1971] Ch 892, 915, Ungoed-Thomas J; *Boland* [1981] AC 487, 504F, Lord Wilberforce; *Kling* v. *Keston Properties* (1985) 49 P & CR 212, 219; JE Martin [1985] *Conv* 406.

[192] See below **[15.42]**.

[193] *Boland* at 504F, Lord Wilberforce.

[194] At 505–506, Lord Wilberforce, 511, Lord Scarman.

3. Joint occupation

[15.38] A beneficiary who is in occupation jointly with the registered proprietor will be protected. The lodger (Evans) in *Hodgson* v. *Marks*[195] was registered as proprietor but it was held that Mrs Hodgson was also in occupation of the house. *Boland* finally nailed the outdated heresy that regarded husband and wife as one[196] which was inconsistent with the standing of women in our society today.[197] The House of Lords was equally emphatic. Occupation can be relevant even if shared and even if an explanation can be imagined that would be consistent with the title of the seller.[198] Rejection of the sexist explanation for a woman's presence in the matrimonial home means that a woman can be in actual occupation, alone or joint, just as much as any man. Mr Boland mortgaged to Williams & Glyn's Bank a matrimonial home at a time when it was occupied by both himself and Mrs Boland and so the lender took subject to Mrs Boland's overriding interest in the house. The same is true with the genders reversed, or if the title is unregistered.[199]

4. Fleeting occupation

[15.39] Preparatory acts do not confer protection. In *Abbey National Building Society* v. *Cann* completion of the Cann's purchase and mortgage took place at 12.20 one Monday lunchtime, 35 minutes after the seller had allowed carpet layers to begin laying carpets on behalf of Mrs Cann,[200] and furniture removers had begin to move in Mrs Cann's belongings. The Court of Appeal considered that Mrs Cann was in actual occupation at the time of completion[201] but the House of Lords decided that fragmentary acts of this kind could not amount to occupation.[202] Sneaking in 35 minutes early would not have put a lender on enquiry had title been unregistered, and the registered system simply had to follow suit. In another case a Saudi princess who had not set in foot in London for year was held not to be in actual occupation of her home there.[203]

5. Derivative occupation

[15.40] Derivative occupation creates problems for registered land. Occupation by a licensee is insufficient,[204] and there is a recent decision which suggests[205] that when a

[195] [1971] Ch 892, 934H, Russell LJ.
[196] *Caunce* v. *Caunce* [1969] 1 WLR 286, Ch D; FR Crane (1968) 32 *Conv (NS)* 254; JF Garner (1969) 33 *Conv (NS)* 240.
[197] [1979] Ch 312, 332E–F, Lord Denning MR.
[198] [1981] AC 487, 505, 510, Lord Wilberforce; [1979] Ch 312, 338, Ormrod LJ.
[199] *Hodgson* v. *Marks* [1971] Ch 892, 934–935; *Boland* [1979] Ch 312, 322D, Lord Denning, 334D–E, Ormrod LJ; *Boland* [1981] AC 487, 505E, Lord Wilberforce, 511G, Lord Scarman; *Midland Bank* v. *Farmpride Hatcheries* [1981] 2 EGLR 147, 151D–E, Oliver LJ; *Kingsnorth Finance Co* v. *Tizard* [1986] 1 WLR 783.
[200] Query whether occupation taken without the permission of the owner could be overriding.
[201] *Cann* (1989) 57 P & CR 381, 388–389.
[202] [1991] 1 AC 56, 93D–94B, Lord Oliver; contrast M Beaumont [1989] *Conv* 158, 160–161.
[203] *Stockholm Finance* v. *Gordon Holdings* [1995] NPC 162; Grays' *Elements* (3rd ed), 1030.
[204] *Strand Securities* v. *Caswell* [1965] Ch 958, CA.
[205] *Lloyd* v. *Dugdale* [2001] EWCA Civ 1754, [2002] 2 P & CR 13 at 167, [40–49], Sir Christopher Slade; M Dixon [2002] *Conv* 384.

company is in occupation of a shopping unit in a mill it does not give notice of the rights of the managing director of the company who had been promised a lease and spent £15,000 on refitting. However, occupation by a housekeeper or paid agent does protect,[206] and *Lloyds Bank* v. *Rosset*[207] suggests that the test is whether a person inspecting the land would discover the right. A majority of the court held that occupation via a builder employed jointly by husband and wife was sufficient to amount to "actual occupation" by the wife. Unregistered land notice doctrine gives a clear and coherent test to answer such questions – would a reasonable person discover it?

6. Inquiry

[15.41] Protection for an occupier is removed if inquiry is made of that person before the disposition and he fails to disclose his interest when he could reasonably have been expected to do so.[208]

7. Undiscoverable occupation

[15.42] The Land Registration Act 2002 contains a new provision[209] that removes protection by occupation which is not reasonably discoverable by the purchaser. This should cope easily with cases which had the potential to could create enormous injustice before.[210] It is perfectly possible for a buyer to act diligently and honestly and yet fail to discover an occupier. A borrower may deliberately conceal traces of a contributor's occupation,[211] in which case the lender's liability ought to depend upon what he knew or could discover. As one unregistered case shows, an inspection may be arranged at a fixed time giving the seller a chance to make the property appear "clean".[212] At the crucial moment of inspection, the occupier may be on holiday or out shopping, and there would, of course, be no opportunity to discover a person who moves in after the purchaser's inspection. The exception in the current law[213] refers to a particular buyer before a particular disposition, that person being entitled to become a protected purchaser if two conditions are satisfied:

(1) Honesty – the purchaser must not have actual knowledge[214] of the interest at the time of the disposition.[215]

---

[206] Not unpaid relatives: *Strand Securities* [1965] Ch 958, 981, Lord Denning MR; *Abbey National BS* v. *Cann* [1991] 1 AC 56, HL.

[207] [1989] Ch 350, CA; on appeal on different grounds [1991] 1 AC 107, HL.

[208] LRA 2002 sch 3 para 2(b); this reproduces the saving under LRA 1925 s 70(1)(g); *Habermann* v. *Koehler (No 2)* [2000] EGCS 125, CA; see below **[15.53]**.

[209] LRA 2002 sch 3 para 2(c); Law Com 271 (2001), [8.60–8.62]; also Law Com 254 (1998), [5.71–5.73], Law Com WP 37 (1971), [74]; compare: Law Com 158 (1987) part II, Law Com 173 (1988), draft Bill.

[210] P Sparkes [1989] *Conv* 342; L Tee [1998] *CLJ* 328.

[211] *Kingsnorth Finance Co* v. *Tizard* [1986] 1 WLR 783, 793B.

[212] *Tizard* again, at 794H–795C.

[213] It seems to imply that undiscoverable occupation does fall within the main part of sch 3 para 2 and is only removed by sub para (c); this is important because if so undiscoverable occupation could override first registration: sch 1 para 2 has no equivalent exception.

[214] Rather than actual notice, so what is known by the buyer's solicitor is not imputed?

[215] So an interest known about but forgotten can be defeated by the buyer. Why?

(2) Occupation not discoverable by diligence – a purchaser can be protected against an occupier if the occupation would not have been obvious on a reasonably careful inspection of the land. The statute says that the inspection should take place at the time of the disposition, but this clearly means when the land would normally be inspected before the occupation.

The focus is correct since diligent purchasers are fully protected. Modern registered land law is strikingly similar to unregistered notice doctrine. So it should be.

8. Undiscoverable occupation between 1925 and 2003

[15.43] A question that must be addressed is whether this was always so. It is noteworthy that the Land Registration Act 2002 contains no transitional provision to protected vested rights and priorities acquired under the 1925 legislation.[216] No change was thought to have occurred. Is this true? The Law Commission based itself on the Court of Appeal decision in *Lloyds Bank* v. *Rosset*.[217] Mrs Rosset was held in that court to have a half beneficial interest through contribution to the renovation of a dilapidated farmhouse. She was present on many days supervising the work of the builders but did not sleep at the property and in the end her claim to actual occupation depended on the presence of the builders at the property.[218] Marginal occupation was to be resolved by the result of the notional enquiry: "Are you in occupation?", a test that looks at the effect of acts on the mind of an enquirer.[219] Actual occupation alone was irrelevant, unless appropriate inquiries made by the bank have elicited the fact of her interest[220] Nicholls and Purchas LJJ held that if a representative of the mortgage-lender had inspected the property before completion of the mortgage he would have seen that someone was there and the bank only had itself to blame if it did not enquire further.[221] Mustill LJ, dissenting on this point, held that no one arriving on the site would suppose that the masons and plasterers could be in occupation of the site[222] and that the daily presence of the wife at an uninhabitable house did not disclose anything about the possibility of an adverse interest in the house.[223] Criticism of the notice-based test[224] was misconceived.[225] This has been followed in *Malory Enterprises* v. *Cheshire Homes (UK)*:[226] a fraudulent sale of a development site in the suburbs of Manchester was upset because the true owner retained occupation of the property through use for the storage of goods, boarding it up and changing the lock, acts which should have put a purchaser on notice.

---

[216] LRA 2002 sch 12 provides transitional protection in relation to recipients of rent but not occupiers.

[217] [1989] Ch 350; RJ Smith (1988) 104 *LQR* 507; MP Thompson [1988] *Conv* 453. Reversed on other grounds [1991] 1 AC 107, HL.

[218] *McCarthy & Stone* v. *Julian S Hodge & Co* [1971] 1 WLR 1547, 1557.

[219] At 376G–377E, Nicholls LJ, 394F–G, Mustill LJ; *Malory Enterprises* v. *Cheshire Homes (UK)* [2002] EWCA Civ 151, [2002] Ch 216, [80–82], Arden LJ.

[220] At 404H.

[221] At 379F, 405H–406D.

[222] At 398F, Mustill LJ.

[223] At 399A, Mustill LJ.

[224] RJ Smith (1988) 104 *LQR* 507, 509; MP Thompson [1988] *Conv* 453, 458.

[225] P Sparkes [1989] *Conv* 342.

[226] [2002] EWCA Civ 151, [2002] Ch 216, [10–12], Arden LJ.

Contrary authorities are legion. In *Hodgson* v. *Marks*[227] the Court of Appeal explicitly repudiated[228] the notice analogy adopted by the trial judge, Ungoed-Thomas J.[229] Russell LJ stated that "However wise a purchaser may be he may have no ready opportunity of finding out; yet the law will protect the occupier."[230] This appears to be ratio. Lord Wilberforce supported this view, obiter, in *Williams & Glyn's Bank* v. *Boland*[231] and it became the academic orthodoxy. Robert Walker LJ suggested in *Wallcite* v. *Ferrishurst*[232] that the onus of enquiry was *heavier* (a reversal of the normal understanding) where title is registered. It is hard to accept that the old law for registered land was identical to notice doctrine. The true position is that the cases were split. The new legislation takes the right side but it needed a transitional saving.

9.   Occupation of parts

(1) New law

[15.44] A person with an interest in part of the land can only protect it by occupation if he is in occupation of that part. This principle applies to unregistered land,[233] to overriding rights on first registration,[234] and when overriding a transfer[235] – the last two principles stemming from the restriction on the scope of protection "so far as relating to land of which he is in actual occupation". If a person is in occupation of plot 1 on a housing development, one would never dream that he may have an option to purchase plot 100; such occupation is simply not directed towards giving notice of that right.[236]

(2) Old law

[15.45] The controversial decision in *Wallcite* v. *Ferrishurst*[237] has been reversed and the earlier Court of Appeal decision in *Ashburn Anstalt*[238] restored to favour. Somewhere off a cul de sac in Hampstead there is the building which became the subject of the litigation in *Wallcite*. The whole formed part of a single registered sub-leasehold title. Ferrishurst was in occupation of an office building (3/5ths of the whole) as tenant, but had an option to purchase a lock-up garage (the remaining 2/5ths). The question of protection of the option arose because it was being exercised

---

[227] [1971] Ch 892, CA; JL Barton (1972) 88 *LQR* 14; I Leeming (1971) 35 *Conv (NS)* 235. A case with strikingly similar facts is *Collings* v. *Lee* [2001] 2 All ER 332, CA; R Nolan [2001] *CLJ* 477.

[228] At 931F. But how could Russell LJ have based his decision on the notice analogy at the same time?

[229] [1971] Ch 892, 915G (a brilliant judgment deservedly vindicated).

[230] At 932D.

[231] [1981] AC 487, 506, Lord Wilberforce, 511, Lord Scarman.

[232] [1999] Ch 355, 372C.

[233] *Wallcite* v. *Ferrishurst* [1999] Ch 355, 371G, Robert Walker LJ.

[234] LRA 2002 sch 1 para 2.

[235] LRA 2002 sch 3 para 2.

[236] Law Com 254 (1998), [5.70]; Law Com 271 (2001), [8.55–8.58].

[237] [1999] Ch 355, CA; L Tee [1999] *CLJ* 483; PH Kenny [1999] *Conv* 73; S Pascoe [1999] *Conv* 144; J Hill (2000) 63 *MLR* 113.

[238] [1989] Ch 1, CA. Robert Walker LJ ruled at [1999] Ch 355, 364–368, 372D, that *Ashburn Anstalt* was given *per incuriam* several HL decisions.

against Wallcite, who had now bought both the leasehold title and the freehold, with no entry on the register to warn them of the option. Results can be capricious because all depends upon which parcels happen to be lumped together in a single registered title.[239] The Court of Appeal may have been technically correct in their interpretation of the Land Registration Act 1925 but the decision was undesirable because it called for very extensive and inappropriate enquiries on a building estate, as Robert Walker LJ himself recognised.[240]

10. Removal of protection for recipients of rent

(1) New law

[15.46] Receipt of rent no longer gives protection and the ability to override the register either on first registration or at the time of a transfer.[241] Hence registered and unregistered land law[242] are once again aligned.

(2) Old law

[15.47] In addition to occupiers, the 1925 Act protected "the rights of every person . . . in receipt of the rents and profits" of the land.[243] This did not apply, as *Strand Securities* v. *Caswell*[244] showed, to rent-free occupation by a licensee.[245] Another curiosity is the result in *UCB Group* v. *Hedworth*.[246] A matrimonial home registered in the name of a husband was, as a result of matrimonial proceedings, held by him on trust for his wife, but she granted him a tenancy to remain in occupation. His rent payments to her as beneficiary did not count as a receipt of rents from the land, land being defined so as to exclude a beneficial interest under a trust of land, and the receipt of rent therefore excluding rent received by a beneficiary.

When it was discovered that rent was being paid to a landlord, enquiry had to be directed to that recipient in order to ascertain whether he claimed any rights over the land.[247] This created a distinction between the registered and unregistered systems. Transitional protection is provided for vested rights[248] in recognition of the fact that the law has been changed. If receipt of rent ceases a protective entry will be required on the register.

---

[239] *Celsteel* v. *Alton House Holdings* [1985] 1 WLR 204, Scott J; on appeal [1986] 1 WLR 512, CA. It would no longer be possible as in this case to protect claims to an easement by occupation of neighbouring benefitted land.

[240] At 372A.

[241] LRA 2002 sch 1 para 2, sch 3 para 2 (each limited to occupiers); Law Com 271 (2001), [8.64], EN [802–803].

[242] See above **[15.25]**.

[243] LRA 1925 s 70(1)(g); Hayton's *Registered Land*, 91–93. Payment of a deposit is not a rent payment: *Eden Park Estates* v. *Longman* [1982] Conv 239.

[244] [1965] Ch 958, 980A, Lord Denning MR, 984F–G, Russell LJ.

[245] [1965] Ch 958,

[246] [2002] EWCA Civ 708, [2002] 46 EG 200.

[247] *Lloyds Bank* v. *Rosset* [1989] Ch 350, 396H, Mustill LJ; *Strand Securities* v. *Caswell* [1965] Ch 958, 980A, Lord Denning MR.

[248] LRA 2002 s 131, sch 12 para 8, inserting transitionally sch 3 para 2A; Law Com 271 (2001), EN [802–803]; LRA 1925 s 70(1)(g).

I. WHEN DO OCCUPIERS BITE?

1. Protection of finance for initial acquisition

[15.48] Notice doctrine and the overriding interest of occupiers apply to determine rights between buyers and contributors, but in fact most cases concern mortgages. Sale of a property intended for occupation as a home involves its vacation by the seller to enable possession to be delivered. Mortgages do not disturb existing occupiers so most priority cases concern lenders.

Williams & Glyn's Bank v. *Boland*[249] established the possibility that a beneficiary may have an overriding interest as against a lender. Subsequent cases have sapped the strength of the decision. *Boland* itself concerned a *remortgage* of the property to secure the business overdraft of Mr Boland's company, Epsom Contractors. The decision will not apply to lenders who provide the finance for the purchase of a house (such as Pearl Assurance Co who lent to the Bolands). Usually a beneficiary has not had time to take occupation in time to get protection against the lender who funds the purchase and, if by chance occupation precedes completion, even so the lender is safe.

Post-*Boland* case-law establishes that if a person buys a house with the aid of a mortgage, any equitable interests created by the buyer bite only on the equity of redemption. Occupiers are prevented from gaining priority over the initial acquisition mortgage. This is made clear by *Abbey National Building Society* v. *Cann*.[250] A competition arose Mrs Cann as a contributor to the deposit on a flat bought for her by her son and the lender from whom he borrowed most of the price. When completion occurred there was a transfer to the son and a first mortgage to the Abbey National. The Lords[251] preferred a line of authority[252] which held that the conveyance and advance were a single, simultaneous, transaction. So the house was acquired subject to the mortgage. There was no gap between transfer and mortgage so as to allow Mrs Cann's contribution right to attach to the land in priority over the lender's interest.[253] *Cann* eliminates occupiers holding interests derived from the borrower as a significant problem for lenders who provide the finance for the initial acquisition of land.[254]

2. Unregistered conveyancing

[15.49] Completion of a sale of unregistered land occurs virtually instantaneously when the purchase money is paid and the conveyance executed. Occupation is certainly required at that time to fix the buyer with notice of an adverse right, and in practice will be required much earlier before the purchaser inspects.

---

[249] [1981] AC 487, HL; see the acerbic comments in *Winkworth* v. *Edward Baron Developments Co* [1986] 1 WLR 1512, 1515, Lord Templeman (who heard *Boland* at first instance).

[250] [1991] 1 AC 56, HL; *Lloyds Bank* v. *Rosset* [1989] Ch 350, CA; J Jeremie [1994] *JBL* 363; G Goldberg (1992) 108 *LQR* 380; compare *Coren* v. *Keighley* [1972] 1 WLR 1556.

[251] [1991] 1 AC 56, 91A–D, 93A–B, Lord Oliver.

[252] *Re Connolly Bros (No 2)* [1912] 2 Ch 25, CA; *Security Trust Co* v. *Royal Bank of Canada* [1976] AC 503, 519, Lord Cross.

[253] *Abbey National BS* v. *Cann* [1991] 1 AC 56, 89G, 93B; they overruled *Church of England BS* v. *Piskor* [1954] Ch 553, CA.

[254] *Nationwide Anglia BS* v. *Ahmed* (1995) 70 P & CR 381, CA.

3. First registration

[15.50] First registration occurs as of the date on which an application for registration is delivered to the land registry,[255] and the land is registered subject to overriding interests operative on that date. First registration is subject to rights which were binding under the doctrine of notice at the time of the unregistered sale which called for registration of the title. Unregistered doctrine applies at the time of the sale and the same interest becomes an overriding interest at the moment that the land becomes registered. A separate schedule 1 list of overriding interests applies on first registration, an important conceptual innovation rather messily implemented.[256]

Re Boyle's Claim is authority for taking the date of first registration.[257] Boyle purchased some unregistered[258] vacant freehold land, and he was registered as proprietor in July 1952. His neighbour's garage stood on a small triangle of land within Boyle's registered title, so the title had to be rectified by removing this triangle from Boyle's title. He received no indemnity: his neighbour's overriding interest bound Boyle's title at the moment of first registration.[259]

4. Transfer of registered title

[15.51] "When do occupiers bite?"[260] At what time must a person be in occupation of registered land in order to secure protection against a transfer? It was possible to argue that it should be the date of registration of the dealing,[261] in which case there was a registration gap between completion and registration during which occupiers could secure protection.[262] Panic measures were considered; perhaps it was necessary to keep every property empty until an application for registration could be lodged, or to revert to the 1862 practice of completing at the land registry![263] That was obvious nonsense and it is now settled by statute[264] that occupation is required as of the date of the sale or mortgage.

This confirms the cases on the 1925 legislation which ultimately settled on the date of the transfer or mortgage as the crucial date. Nicholls LJ observed in *Rosset*, that any other rule would lead to "a conveyancing absurdity",[265] and *Abbey National*

---

[255] DLRR 2003 r 15; *Smith* v. *Morrison* [1974] 1 WLR 659.

[256] LRA 2002 sch 1 para 2. The legislation is untidy in creating two lists in schs 1 and 3 despite the large duplication in content.

[257] [1961] 1 WLR 339, Wilberforce J.

[258] A land registry transfer form was used in anticipation of first registration: LRR 1925 r 72; DLRR 2003 r 35.

[259] P Sparkes [1986] *Conv* 309, 312–315; *Abbey National BS* v. *Cann* [1991] 1 AC 56, 83, Lord Oliver; *Lloyds Bank* v. *Rosset* [1989] Ch 350, 355G, 360D.

[260] *Boland* [1979] Ch 312, 319, Michael Essayan QC.

[261] *Re Boyle's Claim* [1961] 1 WLR 339, Wilberforce J; *Paddington BS* v. *Mendelsohn* (1985) 50 P & CR 244, CA. This overlooked the fact that *Boyle* concerned first registration: P Sparkes [1986] *Conv* 309, 312 nn 33–34.

[262] Registration remained the correct date for other classes of overriding interest until the 2002 Act, see below **[20.18]**.

[263] Land Registry Act 1862 s 64.

[264] LRA 2002 sch 3 para 2; Law Com 254 (1998), [5.112–113].

[265] *Lloyds Bank* v. *Rosset* [1989] Ch 350, 374B (builders began work on November 7th; contracts were exchanged on the 23rd; completion and the mortgage took place on December 17th; registration was sought on February 7th the following year); MP Thompson [1988] *Conv* 453; RJ Smith (1988) 104 *LQR* 507; S Bright (1988) 138 *NLJ* 685.

Building Society v. *Cann*[266] rules decisively in favour of the time of completion. A son bought a house for occupation by his mother and stepfather, with the aid of a cash contribution by the mother. Purchase and mortgage were both completed one August, when Mrs Cann was on holiday in the Netherlands, but she took up occupation on her return, well before application was made for registration of the transfer and charge in September. Mrs Cann claimed that her contribution was protected by occupation on the date of registration. No, held the House of Lords, the relevant date was completion when Mrs Cann was absent.[267]

Once protection of a right has crystallised against a new proprietor,[268] it is unnecessary to continue in occupation, as Brightman J held in *London & Cheshire Insurance* v. *Laplagrene*.[269] If the occupier moves out, it does of course put at risk his priority over a future purchaser unless he protects himself on the register.

J.   REMOVAL OF PROTECTION FROM OCCUPIERS

[15.52] This section applies whether title is registered or unregistered.

1.   Enquiry

[15.53] A purchaser of *unregistered land* is bound only by rights he discovers after reasonable enquiry. Diligent enquiry discharges his responsibilities, though it may be necessary to probe further after a reply which gives rise to any suspicion. Protection against purchasers of *registered land* is lost where enquiry is made of the occupier and the rights are not disclosed. One recent case concerned an unpaid seller's lien, and the consequences of failure to disclose it when asked.[270] The right was lost. Physical presence provides full protection if the seller's occupation is not investigated.[271] An agent involved in negotiating a sale cannot himself assert an overriding interest if he fails to disclose it.[272]

Rights are removed only if enquiry was made and the rights were not disclosed[273] but are protected on a total failure of enquiry. This reproduces precisely the doctrine of constructive notice.[274]

According to *Hypo-Mortgage Services* v. *Robinson*[275] enquiry is only required of adult occupiers: children living with their parents are not in actual occupation and so do not put a purchaser under a duty of enquiry. Enquiry must be made "of that

---

[266] [1991] 1 AC 56, HL; RJ Smith (1990) 106 *LQR* 545; AJ Oakley [1990] *CLJ* 397; S Baughen [1991] *Conv* 116; S Gardner (1991) 54 *MLR* 126; J Greed [1990] *NLJ* 815, 867; PT Evans [1991] *Conv* 155; A Pottage (1995) 15 *OJLS* 371.

[267] P Sparkes [1986] *Conv* 309, 317.

[268] Query if occupation is also required at the moment of registration.

[269] [1971] Ch 499.

[270] *UCB Bank* v. *Beasley* [1996] CLYB 4951, CA.

[271] *Barclays Bank* v. *Estates & Commercial* [1997] 1 WLR 415, CA.

[272] *Midland Bank* v. *Farmpride Hatcheries* [1981] 2 EGLR 147, CA.

[273] *UCB Bank* v. *Beasley* [1996] CLYB 4951, CA; *Habermann* v. *Koehler (No 2)* [2000] EGCS 125, CA (failure to disclose option).

[274] Contrast [1989] Ch 350, 396H, Mustill LJ (a slip?).

[275] [1997] FLR 71, CA.

person", that is the person in actual occupation, so asking the vendor will not do.[276] Although this has its origin in unregistered land doctrine,[277] it must be doubtful as a general proposition of unregistered land law,[278] since there must be many cases in which it would be reasonable to rely on what the seller says.

Enquiry is only required of a person with authority to provide an answer.[279] Priorities are fixed at completion.[280] Hence if an incumbrance is discovered before completion, it will be necessary to seek rescission of the contract or damages for non-disclosure.[281] This in turn means that a purchaser should inspect before contracting to buy. Otherwise he runs the risk that the rights of an occupier might be treated as a patent defect, leaving no contractual remedy. That inspection is not necessarily sufficient to give him priority over rights discoverable before completion. However, conveyancers cannot make repeated inspections, and few insist that their clients should do so.

2. Implied waiver

[15.54] A beneficiary may be postponed to a later mortgage if the beneficiary is aware that the mortgage is to occur and that money must be borrowed to finance the acquisition. Any contributor loses priority to the lender in these circumstances. Implied waiver severely qualifies the protection afforded by *Boland*.

Bristol & West BS v. *Henning*[282] concerned a couple who lived together in a villa in Devon, sharing a self-sufficiency project. He put in £2,000 or so in cash, and raised a mortgage of £11,000 from the Bristol & West. The woman did much work on a previous property, on the small holding, and in building and decoration work on the villa. After the man left and stopped paying the mortgage, the building society succeeded in an action for repossession of the property. The woman's claim to priority over the lender was defeated by the fact that she knew that a mortgage was required to buy the house. Her beneficial interest under a constructive trust depended upon the agreement that could be inferred between the parties,[283] which was an agreement to contribute to the equity of redemption – that is the property subject to the mortgage. Mary Welstead[284] criticised a decision which she felt undermined the traditional requirement that the later party is left to establish the absence of notice. Certainly contribution rights are eroded.

Henning applies just as much if the title is registered. In *Paddington BS* v. *Mendelsohn*[285] a flat with registered title in Sneyd Park in Bristol. *Boland* was

---

[276] LRA 2002 sch 3 para 2(a); *Hodgson* v. *Marks* [1971] Ch 892, 932D, Russell LJ; Hayton's *Registered Land*, 88–90, 102.

[277] *Hunt* v. *Luck* [1901] 1 Ch 45, 53, Farwell J.

[278] *Goody* v. *Baring* [1956] 1 WLR 448; *Northern Bank* v. *Henry* [1981] IR 1.

[279] *Kling* v. *Keston Properties* (1985) 49 P & CR 212, Vinelott J.

[280] Contrast *Rosset* [1989] Ch 350, 402C–D, Purchas LJ.

[281] *Rignall Developments* v. *Halil* [1988] Ch 190; JF Garner (1959) 23 *Conv (NS)* 129.

[282] [1985] 1 WLR 778, CA; P Todd [1985] *Conv* 361; MP Thompson [1986] *Conv* 57; MP Thompson (1986) 49 *MLR* 245.

[283] The use of "imputed" is a slip: M Welstead [1985] *CLJ* 354 (she also criticised the decision on the broader ground that contribution rights are eroded); MP Thompson [1992] *Conv* 206, 209–210.

[284] [1985] *CLJ* 354.

[285] (1985) 50 P & CR 244, CA; MP Thompson [1986] *Conv* 57.

therefore limited to the case of subsequent mortgages taken out without the consent or knowledge of the occupying contributor.[286]

Waiver can only be implied with knowledge of the mortgage. A contributor like the wife in *Lloyds Bank* v. *Rosset* who is unaware of it cannot be subordinated to the mortgage.[287] If knowledge is absent recourse may be had to the doctrine of estoppel where the lender has relied to its detriment on an expectation of priority.[288] However it is not necessary to know the exact amount borrowed. *Abbey National BS* v. *Cann*[289] also concerned a house bought in a son's name for occupation by his mother. She knew that the sale of a previous home would leave a shortfall, which her son would have to borrow to make up. Since she left it to her son to raise the balance, she took subject to the subsequent mortgage.[290] On the particular facts of *Cann* the mother thought the loan would be only £4,000, but she was postponed to the extent of the full £25,000 actually borrowed. Possibly this was because the building society was not put on enquiry as to the amount it could advance,[291] though this ground for decision has been criticised.[292]

Refinancing should neither improve nor worsen the position of the beneficiary. In *Prestidge*,[293] a property was acquired in the name of Mr Prestidge with the aid of a mortgage securing a loan of £30,000 from the Britannia Building Society. His partner who contributed was postponed for that amount. When Mr Prestidge later negotiated a refinancing from Equity & Law for £42,000, the contributor was postponed to the new lender only to the extent of £30,000.[294]

3.   Express waiver

[15.55] A person can waive the priority of his interest, since any express agreement regulates priority,[295] and makes the question of implied consents irrelevant.[296] A lender which discovers a beneficiary should secure a written waiver of his known equitable interest. If a tenant agrees to a mortgage he does not necessarily waive other rights such as an option to purchase.[297] An express consent cannot waive Rent Act

[286] At 248–249, Browne-Wilkinson LJ.

[287] [1989] Ch 350, 387E, Nicholls LJ; on appeal [1991] 1 AC 107, HL. Also on express waiver: *Skipton BS* v. *Clayton* (1993) 66 P & CR 223, CA.

[288] *Midland Bank* v. *Farmpride Hatcheries* [1981] 2 EGLR 147, 150H, Shaw LJ (Willey failed to disclose licence re West Hall House; held estopped from asserting it against lender). Estoppel doctrine is discussed below **[23]**.

[289] [1991] 1 AC 56, HL; J Greed [1990] *NLJ* 815, 867; S Baughen [1991] *Conv* 116; PT Evans [1991] *Conv* 155; M Beaumont [1989] *Conv* 158. Distinguished in *Skipton BS* v. *Clayton* (1993) 66 P & CR 233, CA.

[290] (1989) 57 P & CR 381, 392, 394, CA; approved *obiter* [1994] 1 AC 56, 94, Lord Oliver.

[291] At 392.

[292] M Beaumont [1989] *Conv* 158, 161–163; S Baughen [1991] *Conv* 116; MP Thompson [1992] *Conv* 206. *Le Foe* v. *Le Foe* [2001] EWCA Civ 1870; affirming [2001] 2 FLR 970, Fam Div.

[293] *Equity & Law Home Loans* v. *Prestidge* [1992] 1 WLR 137, CA; RJ Smith (1992) 108 *LQR* 371; J Greed (1992) 142 *NLJ* 539; SH Goo (1993) 44 NILQ 51; *Locabail (UK)* v. *Bayfield Properties (No 1)* [1999] Times March 31st, Ch D.

[294] MP Thompson [1992] *Conv* 206.

[295] M Dixon "Consenting Away Proprietary Rights" ch 11 in E Cooke (ed) *Modern Studies in Property Law 1 – Property 2000* (Hart, 2001); C Sawyer "A World Safe for Mortgagees?" ch 12 in E Cooke, as above.

[296] *Nationwide Anglia BS* v. *Ahmed* (1995) 70 P & CR 381, CA; *Barclays Bank* v. *Estates & Commercial* [1997] 1 WLR 415, 425, Millett LJ; *Castle Phillips Finance Co* v. *Piddington* (1995) 70 P & CR 592, CA.

[297] *Habermann* v. *Koehler* (1996) 72 P & CR D10, CA.

1977 or other rights to residential security of tenure.[298] One case has held that a consent was not binding unless it was noted on the register,[299] but this seems to be wrong in principle.

A consent is not necessarily vitiated by a misunderstanding of its terms, but waivers are inherently disadvantageous to the person making them and this renders the mortgage vulnerable to the finding that it was secured by pressure (undue influence) or misrepresentation.[300] The lender should insist on the provision of independent legal advice to the party making the waiver.

---

[298] *Woolwich BS* v. *Dickman* [1996] 3 All ER 204, CA; L Tee [1997] *CLJ* 37.
[299] *Dickman* at 211j–h Waite LJ, 214c–d, Morritt LJ; Law Com 254 (1998), [5.109–5.111].
[300] *Kings North Trust* v. *Bell* [1986] 1 WLR 119, CA; *Skipton BS* v. *Clayton* (1993) 66 P & CR 223, CA; L Crabb [1993] *Conv* 478; see below **[30.65ff]**.

16

BENEFICIAL CO-OWNERSHIP

Unity of possession. Legal co-ownership recapped. Statutory trusts.
Beneficial co-ownerships. Survivorship. Express and implied creation.
Severance. Partition.

A. UNITY OF POSSESSION

[16.01] Most family homes are shared. Beneficial co-ownership[1] arises where entitlement to an estate in land[2] is held concurrently by a number of people. Both basic forms of beneficial co-ownership – joint tenancy or tenancy in common – are each characterised by unity of possession.[3] "Only this propertie is common to them both, viz that their occupation is undivided and neither of them knoweth his part in severall."[4] Blackstone's suggestion that they must occupy promiscuously may be going too far.[5] Neither can exclude the other.[6] Even if the shares are unequal,[7] entitlement to occupation arises equally: a quarter share in a four bedroomed house does not give ownership of any one bedroom, since each has an "undivided share" in the whole.[8] Unity of possession is common to the joint tenancy and the tenancy in common, and defines the existence of a co-ownership.

If any part of the land belongs to one person exclusively, so they have the *right* to exclude all others, the land is held in two separate ownerships and not one co-ownership. Partition is the process of division of a co-ownership so as to create two or more single ownerships, by division both of the physical accommodation and, more importantly, of the legal right to share.[9]

---

[1] Littleton's *Tenures* book 3 chaps I–IV; Blackstone's *Commentaries* vol 2 ch XII; Cheshire & Burn (16th ed) ch 11; Dixon's *Principles* (3rd ed) ch 4; Goo's *Sourcebook* (3rd ed) ch 14; Grays' *Elements* (3rd ed) ch 8; Maudsley & Burn *LL – Cases* (7th ed) ch 5; Megarry & Wade (6th ed), ch 9; Smith's *Property Law* ch 13; Swadling in Birks' *Private Law*, [4.326–4.375]; Thompson *Modern LL* chs 8, 10.

[2] Co-ownership can exist in a whale: *Fennings* v. *Lord Grenville* (1808) 1 Taunt 241, 127 ER 825; a lake: *Menzies* v. *Macdonald* (1856) 2 Macq 463 HL; or a mausoleum: *Galasso* v. *Del Guercio* 276 A 2d 186, 189f (1971); Grays' *Elements* (3rd ed), 835 n 11.

[3] Blackstone's *Commentaries* vol 2, 182.

[4] Coke on *Littleton*, 186.

[5] Blackstone's *Commentaries* vol 2, 185.

[6] *Wiseman* v. *Simpson* [1988] 1 WLR 35, 42E–H, Ralph Gibson LJ; *JA Pye (Oxford)* v. *Graham* [2002] UKHL 30, [70], Lord Hope.

[7] As is possible with a beneficial tenancy in common.

[8] Contrast on business tenancy renewal: *Mayer* v. *Roddick* (1990) 60 P & CR 50, 54, Fox LJ.

[9] Blackstone's *Commentaries* vol 2, 185; see below **[16.47]**.

B. LEGAL CO-OWNERSHIP RECAPPED

[16.02] Legal co-ownership has been considered in the context of trusteeship. Co-ownership involves a trust. Instead of the pre-1926 straight joint tenancy or straight tenancy in common a statutory trust is imposed as a management vehicle, thus:

> *to H and W as joint tenants on trust for themselves as joint tenants;*
> *to T1 and T2 as joint tenants on trust for B1 and B2 as joint tenants.*

Points drawn out in the previous discussion[10] are these:

> the legal estate is held by joint tenants;
> survivorship therefore applies;
> trusteeship is limited to four adults;
> corporate trustees are allowed by statute;
> there is a statutory trust of land;
> severance of the legal estate is not allowed;
> transactions which would sever or destroy any of the four unities may affect beneficial entitlement but have no impact on the legal estate;
> powers to deal with the legal estate are collective;

This chapter explores the beneficial entitlement which exists in equity behind the trust of the land.

C. IMPOSITION OF THE STATUTORY TRUST

[16.03] Beneficial co-ownerships must occur under a trust of land, either express or implied. If parties are legally advised, express trusts are invariably used. After 1996 a simple trust suffices, thus:

> *to H and W as joint tenants on trusts for themselves as beneficial joint tenants.*

Express trusts permit the exclusion or modification of management powers.[11] It is still possible to create a traditional trust for sale where sale and division is really intended, thus:

> *to T1 and T2 on trust to sell and to hold the net proceeds of sale on trust for A and B as beneficial tenants in common.*

However, this will be decidedly eccentric where a home is intended for occupation but would be appropriate if sale is genuinely intended. Power to postpone sale is implied, whether wanted or not, but the terms of the trust may modify the normal occupation rights and so ensure there is a duty to sell.[12] Pre-existing express trusts for sale are now

---

[10] See above **[12.06ff]**.
[11] TLATA 1996 ss 6, 8; see above **[13.43]**.
[12] S 4(1).

treated as trusts of land, without conversion[13] but with the automatic implication of a power to postpone sale.[14]

A trust of land is implied by statute if there is no express trust,[15] on all beneficial co-ownerships created since 1996, and statutory trusts existing at the end of 1996 are converted to become implied trusts of land. Trusts of land allow the trustees either to hold the land or to dispose of it by exercising the power of sale,[16] but the very existence of the trust in simple co-ownership of a family home remains remote from reality.[17] A trust of land is imposed however a beneficial co-ownership arises. Thus:

transfer *to A and B as joint tenants*.[18]
beneficial joint tenancy, later severed;[19]
transfer *to A and B as tenants in common*;[20]
gift by will *to A and B as tenants in common*;[21]
co-ownership *between A and B* (as a sub-trustee or personal representative for C);[22]
transfer *to A* who holds for A and B by contribution either as joint tenants[23] or as tenants in common.[24]

D. FORMS OF BENEFICIAL CO-OWNERSHIP

1. "Tenancies"

[16.04] Beneficial co-ownership takes one of two basic forms – joint tenancy or tenancy in common. The use of the word "tenancy" here is an inappropriate throwback to the feudal origin of freehold ownership, since the interest owned jointly could be a freehold, a leasehold, a short tenancy,[25] or a life interest.[26]

2. Effect of death

[16.05] The two forms of holding are differentiated mainly by the effect of death. Joint tenancy carries a right of survivorship, meaning that the remaining joint tenants take the property on the death of one of them. The property never falls into the estate

---

[13] S 3.
[14] S 4(1).
[15] Under pre-1997 law it was never quite clear whether the express or the statutory trust for sale prevailed: P Sparkes *NLL* (1st ed), 298.
[16] *Notting Hill HT* v. *Brackley* [2001] EWCA Civ 601, [2001] 3 EGLR 11, [23], Peter Gibson LJ.
[17] *Burton* v. *Camden LBC* [2000] 2 AC 399, 404H, Lord Nicholls.
[18] LPA 1925 s 1; TLATA 1996 sch 2 para 4.
[19] LPA 1925 s 36(2); *Bernard* v. *Josephs* [1982] Ch 391, CA.
[20] LPA 1925 ss 34 (2); TLATA 1996 sch 2 para 3.
[21] LPA 1925 s 34(3).
[22] TLATA 1996 sch 2 para 3(4). These parties cannot claim occupation rights: s 22(2).
[23] TLATA 1996 s 1(2)(a).
[24] TLATA 1996 s 1(2)(a); SLA 1925 s 36(4); *Bull* v. *Bull* [1955] 1 QB 234, 237, Denning LJ; *Williams & Glyn's Bank* v. *Boland* [1981] AC 487, 503D, Lord Wilberforce, 510G, Lord Scarman; *City of London BS* v. *Flegg* [1988] AC 54, HL; *Hammersmith & Fulham LBC* v. *Monk* [1992] 1 AC 478, 493B–E, Lord Browne-Wilkinson.
[25] See below [25.16].
[26] Beneficial co-ownership of interests under trusts of land is discussed below [18.09].

of the deceased joint tenant, so a gift by will is ineffective, and his next of kin have no claim on his intestacy. Land held by A, B and C as joint tenants passes, on C's death, to A and B as joint tenants. On B's death it will pass to A alone.[27]

3. Joint tenancy

[16.06] Wharton[28] defined survivorship[29] as the concentration of property from more to fewer by the accession of parts belonging to those that die to the survivors, until it passes to a single hand and the joint tenancy ceases. Death of a joint tenant has the same effect in equity as at law.[30] During the joint lives the form of co-ownership is irrelevant,[31] since a beneficial joint tenancy can always be converted into a tenancy in common by severance, but leaving the tenancy unsevered during one's lifetime is an agreement to submit to the chance of survivorship.[32] This is so even if a deceased joint tenant left a will: this has no effect on beneficial entitlement in the absence of a severance. A joint tenancy creates a sort of tontine,[33] in other words a gamble on the life of the survivor, so that the longest survivor scoops the pool. Equity is maintained by the requirement of initial unity of interest which ensures that the stakes are equal.[34] The gamble between a company and an individual was previously thought to be unequal, but statute now allows corporate beneficiaries to be joint tenants with individuals.[35]

Joint tenancy is a very suitable means for a couple to hold a matrimonial or family home, since if one of them dies, he will wish it to pass to the other and vice versa.[36] Simple estates can pass without the need for any grant of administration. Severance is essential if the couple fall out, and for business partnerships and house sharing.[37] Mark Thompson[38] has suggested that abolition of beneficial joint tenancy would simplify title and avoid the problems which are caused by survivorship after a relationship turns sour. But many people are attracted to the simplicity of survivorship which eases devolution of title on death. After all a majority of us still enjoy happy relationships.[39]

---

[27] Littleton's *Tenures*, [280]; *Farah* v. *Moody* [1998] 1 EGCS 1, CA.

[28] *Law Lexicon* (11th ed, 1911), 471; Blackstone's *Commentaries* vol 2, 179–180; *Samme's case* (1609) 13 Co Rep 54, 77 ER 1464; *Goddard* v. *Lewis* (1909) 101 LT 528; *Cunningham-Reid* v. *Public Trustee* [1944] KB 602; *Jones* v. *Jones* [1972] 1 WLR 1269.

[29] In Latin, a *ius accrescendi*.

[30] *Aston* v. *Smallman* (1706) 2 Vern 556, 23 ER 960, Cowper LK; *R* v. *Williams* (1735) Bunb 342, 145 ER 694.

[31] *Re Rushton* [1972] Ch 197, 202H–203A, Goff J.

[32] *Staples* v. *Maurice* (1774) 4 Bro Parl Cas 580, 2 ER 395, HL.

[33] *Dealex Properties* v. *Brooks* [1966] 1 QB 542, 551A, Harman LJ; [1993] *Conv* 446, 447–448.

[34] *Staples* v. *Maurice* (1774) 4 Bro Parl Cas 580, 2 ER 395, HL.

[35] Bodies Corporate (Joint Tenancy) Act 1899 s 1(1); on dissolution the property will devolve on the other joint tenants.

[36] *Bedson* v. *Bedson* [1965] 2 QB 666, 675, 675.

[37] D Green [1990] 4 *LSG* 23; M Wilkie [1991] 2 *LSG* 23; J Leigh [1990] 14 *LSG* 31 (tenancy in common between cohabitees).

[38] [1987] *Conv* 29; S Bandali (1977) 41 *Conv (NS)* 243.

[39] AM Prichard [1989] *Conv* 273; [1987] *Conv* 275.

4. Tenancy in common

[16.07] A tenancy in common is used where it is desired to give a notional share in the property. When a tenant in common dies, this beneficial[40] share passes to his estate, so that his personal representatives can pass it on to the beneficiary named in his will or to the next of kin who take on his intestacy. Thus, if[41]

  (1) land is held *on trust for 1/4 to A and 3/4 to B as tenants in common*;
  (2) A dies intestate, leaving X and Y as his next of kin;
  (3) then *on trust for 1/8 to X, 1/8 to Y and 3/4 to B as beneficial tenants in common.*

One divorce court, intending to pass the husband's beneficial interest in the matrimonial home to his wife, ordered the variation of a beneficial tenancy in common as if the husband were dead, but the family lawyers had misunderstood a most basic tenet of property law: the husband's share in a tenancy in common did not pass by survivorship.[42]

Beneficial tenancy in common is appropriate for holding property where the parties are at arm's length, since each undivided share is held by each tenant in common on his own account.[43] On death, it passes first to the personal representatives and then to the beneficiary named in the will of the deceased tenant in common or for his next of kin in the event of an intestacy.[44]

5. Custom made co-ownerships

[16.08] Apart from joint tenancy and tenancy in common, other forms of *equitable* co-ownership are possible by express limitation. There is no reason why parties cannot tailor their own forms of co-ownership by express limitations, mixing up elements of the beneficial joint tenancy and the tenancy in common. Co-owners could hold in unequal shares but with the benefit of survivorship.[45] A joint tenancy could be mixed with a tenancy in common where two couples buy a house, each couple being joint tenants, but with a tenancy in common between the two couples. Beneficial joint tenancy and tenancy in common are merely convenient shorthands to describe the most common forms of beneficial arrangement.

---

[40] A *legal* tenancy in common cannot exist in land: LPA 1925 s 34, as amended by TLATA 1996 sch 2 para 3.

[41] *McGrath* v. *Wallis* [1995] 2 FLR 114, CA.

[42] *Jones* v. *Jones* [1972] 1 WLR 1269, CA.

[43] Blackstone's *Commentaries* vol 2, 173; Littleton *Tenures*, [292].

[44] *McGrath* v. *Wallis* [1995] 2 FLR 114, CA.

[45] *Haddelsey* v. *Adams* (1856) 22 Beav 266, 52 ER 1110; Megarry & Wade, (6th ed), [9.011]; *Taafe* v. *Conmee* (1862) 10 HLC 64, 11 ER 949; *Doe d Borwell* v. *Abey* (1813) 1 M & S 428, 105 ER 160. The 1925 legislation does not prohibit such forms of trust, despite *Cowcher* v. *Cowcher* [1972] 1 WLR 425, 430H.

E. SURVIVORSHIP

1. Contemporaneous deaths

[16.09] Deaths in quick succession give rise to difficulty because one needs to establish the correct sequence in which they have occurred in order to apply survivorship correctly. Floods and shipwrecks were the old hazards, now joined by car crashes, plane disasters and bombings. Section 184 of the Law of Property Act 1925[46] presumes that deaths occur in the order of seniority if the sequence of deaths is uncertain, so that a younger joint tenant is deemed to have survived the older.[47] The section applies where persons "have died in circumstances rendering it uncertain which of them survived the other or others", including deaths in an unknown sequence and also instantaneous deaths. *Hickman* v. *Peacey* illustrates this last point, by a bare majority of the Lords after five people had been killed when a bomb demolished their house in Chelsea at the height of the Battle of Britain.[48] The estate of the youngest joint tenant took all. The statutory presumption can be excluded by definite evidence of the actual sequence of deaths.[49] It may be fairer in a case of "commorientes" to pass the land equally to the estate of all deceased joint tenants.[50]

2. Severance by killing

[16.10] A person convicted of *murder* cannot inherit any property from his victim and so cannot take joint property by survivorship,[51] at least beneficially.[52] Relief against forfeiture is not available to a murderer.[53]

The bar on beneficial survivorship applies to any unlawful killing, so conviction of *manslaughter* will usually cause a forfeiture. *Re K*[54] concerned a wife subjected to repeated physical attacks by her husband, a retired Naval Commander leading her eventually to shoot him. It was not a serious case of homicide: the wife's sentence for manslaughter was two years' probation. The act of killing was held to preclude survivorship to his beneficial interest in the matrimonial home, the beneficial joint

---

[46] Pre-1926 law was based on the need to prove a case: *Hickman* v. *Peacey* [1945] AC 304, 321, Lord Macmillan; *Wing* v. *Angrave* (1860) 8 HLC 183, 11 ER 397; *Re Phené's T* (1870) LR 5 Ch App 139; *Re Aldersey* [1905] 2 Ch 181; *Re Lindop* [1942] Ch 377.

[47] The rule does not operate on intestacy between a person and his or her spouse: AEA 1925 s 46(3). Otherwise if a married couple were killed together in a crash the family of whichever spouse happened to be younger would inherit all excluding completely the family of the elder spouse.

[48] [1945] AC 304, 337 Lord Porter, 325, Lord Macmillan, 343, Lord Simonds.

[49] *Re Bate* [1947] 2 All ER 418; RE Megarry (1947) 63 *LQR* 423; *Re Rowland* [1963] Ch 1, CA; *Re Pringle* [1946] Ch 124.

[50] *Re Grosvenor* [1944] Ch 138, CA; *Hickman*, Lords Simon & Wright; Uniform Simultaneous Deaths Act of United States; Grays' *Elements* (3rd ed), 826.

[51] *Davitt* v. *Titcumb* [1990] Ch 110 Scott J; JE Martin [1991] *Conv* 50; JB Ames, *Lectures on Legal History* (Harvard, Cambridge, Massachussets, 1931), 310; TG Youdan (1973) 89 *LQR* 235; *Re Crippen* [1911] P 108, 112, Evans P. In old times there was an escheat to the Crown: *Dunbar* v. *Plant* [1998] Ch 412, [1998] Ch 412, 429, Phillips LJ.

[52] Trusteeship can pass: *Re K* [1985] Ch 85, 100F–H, Vinelott J.

[53] Forfeiture Act 1982 s 5.

[54] [1986] Ch 180, CA; *Re Dellow's WT* [1964] 1 WLR 451.

tenancy was severed,[55] and his share was forfeit to the Crown,[56] though she obtained relief as described below. Manslaughter arising from negligence will not occasion forfeiture,[57] but any deliberate and intentional crime will prevent survivorship.[58] In *Dunbar* v. *Plant*[59] a woman was convicted of assisting her fiancé in a suicide pact, and, although she was not prosecuted for it, the offence occasioned a forfeiture and loss of his share of the house and insurance money. The availability of relief makes it unnecessary to limit forfeiture to cases of intentional violence.[60]

Following a conviction for manslaughter (as opposed to murder), it is open to the court to grant relief from forfeiture.[61] Relief is discretionary: the court should consider whether justice requires the rule to be modified, balancing the conduct of the offender and of the deceased and taking into account other circumstances.[62] Relief restores the beneficial interest, but cannot be granted after another person has acquired an interest.[63] In *Re K*, the killing followed provocation, and was at the bottom of the range of manslaughter cases in terms of seriousness,[64] so the Naval Commander's battered wife did take the entire interest in the matrimonial home. Relief was also allowed by a majority in *Dunbar* v. *Plant*[65] to the woman who survived participation in a suicide pact. In *Re S*[66] the children were allowed to benefit from an endowment policy held on the couple's house, rather than the wife who had been convicted of her husband's manslaughter.

3.   Claim for family provision

[16.11] Family and dependants of a deceased person may claim under the Inheritance (Provision for Family and Dependants) Act 1975, which prevents a person cutting a dependant out of his will without reasonable cause. Reasonable provision can be sought from his estate, including any interest as a beneficial joint tenant which has passed by survivorship on his death. In such circumstances, a successful claim for family provision causes a severance.

---

[55] *Re Giles* [1972] Ch 544, Pennycuick V-C; (1972) 88 *LQR* 12; *Re S* [1996] 1 FLR 910.

[56] The killer is not deemed to be dead for the purposes of a condition in a will: *Jones* v. *Midland Bank Trust Co* [1997] 3 FCR 697, CA.

[57] *Ex p Connor* [1981] QB 758.

[58] *Gray* v. *Barr* [1970] 2 QB 626, 640, Geoffrey Lane J; on appeal [1971] 2 QB 554, CA; *Re Royse* [1985] Fam 22, CA; NS Price (1985) 48 *MLR* 723; *Jones* v. *Roberts* [1995] 2 FLR 422.

[59] [1998] Ch 412, CA; MP Thompson [1998] *Conv* 45.

[60] *Re H* [1990] 1 FLR 441, Peter Gibson J; JE Martin [1991] *Conv* 48.

[61] Forfeiture Act 1982 s 1; PH Kenny (1983) 46 *MLR* 96; SM Cretney (1980) 10 *OJLS* 289; *Ho Young* v. *Bess* [1995] 1 WLR 350, PC; a claim for relief must be brought within 3 months of the death.

[62] S 2(2). The test is not what is a fair between the parties to the litigation: *Dunbar* v. *Plant* [1998] Ch 412, 438F, Phillips LJ.

[63] S 2(7); *Re K* [1986] Ch 180, CA.

[64] [1986] Ch 180, 193–194.

[65] [1998] Ch 412, CA; MP Thompson [1998] *Conv* 45; S Bridge [1998] *CLJ* 31.

[66] [1996] 1 FLR 910.

F. EXPRESS CO-OWNERSHIP

1. Formality requirement

[16.12] Express trusts require formal declaration in writing. Section 53(1)(b) of the Law of Property Act 1925 provides that:

> "a declaration of trust respecting any land or any interest therein must be manifested and proved by some writing signed by some person who is able to declare such trust or by his will."[67]

A later memorandum suffices.[68] It must prove both the existence of a trust, and details of its precise terms.[69] Writing provides solid proof of the existence of the trust, and justifies proprietary enforcement outside the confines of the immediate parties.

An express oral trust may be enforced in exceptional cases because it is fraudulent to rely on the formality requirement.[70]

2. Need for formal declaration on joint purchase

[16.13] When land is passed to joint buyers, they must declare the beneficial capacity in which they are to hold.[71] It may be negligent to omit this. No presumption of beneficial entitlement arises from a transfer of land to two or more joint legal owners that each is to have a beneficial interest,[72] even though it is likely that they intend to share equally.

Who is able to declare the trust?[73] If a seller transfers land to A and B, safety suggests that the declaration must be signed by A and B.[74] However in several cases[75] the declaration has been valid even though only the seller signed. It has been assumed that it has been inserted at the request of the buyers, unless a case for rectification is made out.

The declaration must relate to *beneficial* ownership. Land registry transfer forms have given most difficulty. Early forms for transfers to joint proprietors did not provide for execution by the buyers, so trusts may not have been validly declared,[76] but in 1974 the form was amended to provide for execution by the buyers and to include

---

[67] Megarry & Wade (6th ed), [10.039–10.045]; DC Wilde "Formalities for Declaring Trusts of Land" ch 10 in Jackson and Wilde; the Law Com will review the law: Law Com 268 (2001), [5.9]. Land is widely defined by LPA 1925 s 205(1)(ix).

[68] *Forster* v. *Hale* (1798) 3 Ves 696, 707, 30 ER 1226, Arden MR; *Gardner* v. *Rowe* (1828) 5 Russ 258, 38 ER 1024.

[69] *Smith* v. *Matthews* (1861) 3 De GF & J 139, 45 ER 831.

[70] Eg *Hodgson* v. *Marks* [1971] Ch 892, 907F, 933A–B.

[71] *Bernard* v. *Josephs* [1982] Ch 391, 403E–F, Griffiths LJ; *Cowcher* v. *Cowcher* [1972] 1 WLR 425, 442C, Bagnall J.

[72] *Bernard* v. *Josephs* [1982] Ch 391, CA; *Walker* v. *Hall* [1984] FLR 126, CA; *Springette* v. *Defoe* [1992] 2 FLR 388.

[73] LPA 1925 s 53(1)(b).

[74] *Robinson* v. *Robinson* [1977] 1 EGLR 80, Div Ct; *Gross* v. *French* (1974) 232 EG 1319, 1321, Walton J; JT Farrand (1977) 41 *Conv (NS)* 78–79; K Gray [1983] *CLJ* 30.

[75] *Pink* v. *Lawrence* (1977) 36 P & CR 98, 101, Buckley LJ; *Re Gorman* [1990] 1 WLR 616, 623E–624B, Vinelott J; *Roy* v. *Roy* [1996] 1 FLR 541, CA.

[76] *Walker* v. *Hall* [1984] FLR 126, 129D, 136E (transfer May 1972).

a declaration about whether the survivor of the proprietors could or could not give a receipt for capital money.[77] Definition of the legal capacity of a surviving proprietor was not necessarily deciding the beneficial capacity in which they held during their joint lives. In *Huntingford* v. *Hobbs*[78] a transfer included the statement:

> "The transferees hereby declare that the survivor of them can give a valid receipt for capital money arising on a disposition of the land."

This was held not to be a valid declaration of beneficial joint tenancy, since the statement of legal capacity could be explained by other beneficial arrangements.[79] and a resulting trust arose to reflect the unequal contributions. Many millions of joint transfer forms executed since 1974 were shown to be defective. Since 1997 a new land registry transfer form (TR1) has included a declaration that joint proprietors hold on trust for themselves as beneficial joint tenants or as tenants in common in equal shares or in some other capacity which they state.[80] This solves the problem for the future.

3. Express declaration of trust conclusive

[16.14] An express declaration settles the form and extent of the beneficial interests,[81] as between the parties to it,[82] precluding any variation as a result of contributions or informal agreement.[83] "The declaration contained in the document speaks for itself", as *Goodman* v. *Gallant*[84] shows. A husband and wife, who held as beneficial joint tenants, split up. The wife remained in the matrimonial home and later lived there with Gallant. Later still the husband conveyed the property to his ex-wife and Gallant "as beneficial joint tenants". She fell out in turn with Gallant, and then argued that she was now entitled to three quarters of the equity – her original half plus half the equity transferred by her ex-husband. However, their entitlement was held to be equal, as stated in the express declaration. *Barton* v. *Morris*[85] was an extreme illustration; a man who contributed £900 took an entire house costing £40,000 by survivorship under an express beneficial joint tenancy.

4. Express declaration conclusive as to quantification

[16.15] The written declaration of the trust should address the capacity in which co-owners hold and, a separate though related issue, quantification of the beneficial

---

[77] TBF Ruoff (1975) 39 *Conv (NS)* 152.
[78] [1993] 1 FLR 736, CA; HE Norman [1992] *Conv* 347.
[79] *Harwood* v. *Harwood* [1991] 2 FLR 274, CA (parties husband, wife and partnership).
[80] LRR 1925 r 98, as substituted by SI 1997/3037; now DLRR 2003 sch 1.
[81] *Pettitt* v. *Pettitt* [1970] AC 777, 813 Lord Upjohn; *Gissing* v. *Gissing* [1971] AC 886, 905, Lord Diplock; *Bernard* v. *Josephs* [1982] Ch 391, 403C, Griffiths LJ; *Lohia* v. *Lohia* [2001] EWCA Civ 1691; *Grindal* v. *Hooper* [2000] Times February 8th, John Jarvis QC.
[82] *City of London Building Society* v. *Flegg* [1988] AC 54, HL (declaration between the Maxwell-Browns did not affect the contributing Fleggs); DJ Hayton [1986] *Conv* 131, 132; MP Thompson [1988] *Conv* 108, 109.
[83] *Turton* v. *Turton* [1988] Ch 542, 552C, Nourse LJ.
[84] [1986] Fam 106, 111A, Slade LJ; S Juss (1986) 45 *CLJ* 205. See also: *Wilson* v. *Wilson* [1963] 1 WLR 601; *Re John's Assignment T* [1970] 1 WLR 955; *Leake* v. *Bruzzi* [1974] 1 WLR 1528; *Pink* v. *Lawrence* (1977) 36 P & CR 98; *Brykiert* v. *Jones* (1981) 125 SJ 323, CA; *Bernard* v. *Josephs* [1982] Ch 391, 403, Griffiths LJ.
[85] [1985] 1 WLR 1257.

interests. Each party gets what has been promised,[86] with no necessary relation to the financial contributions. One of two joint tenants receives a half,[87] whether he has paid all, or nothing, or one half. Any outstanding mortgage debt is deducted from the proceeds of sale before a division of the equity.[88]

Judicial advice to declare the beneficial interests in writing is often ignored[89] leaving beneficial entitlement to depend upon proof of a resulting or constructive trust.

5. Rectification

[16.16] An expressly declared trust may be undone by a successful claim for rescission, perhaps as a response to a misrepresentation,[90] or may be corrected by rectification in a clear case[91] so as to make the declaration of trust correspond,[92] retrospectively,[93] to the preceding informal arrangement,[94] or a unilateral intention of the giver.[95] In *Gross* v. *French*,[96] a house was intended for a mother alone, but the transfer was made to herself, her daughter, and her son-in-law and included a mistaken declaration that all three were beneficial tenants in common. Rectification excluded those not intended to benefit. It will be too late to seek rectification once title has passed to a protected purchaser.

6. Words used

[16.17] Transfers invariably refer to "joint tenancy" or "tenancy in common" but wills commonly use informal words. They must be certain.[97] Wills often define the size of the beneficial interests but not the capacity of joint beneficiaries. A tenancy in common is created by words of severance, indicating an intention to create undivided shares. Equity was so antagonistic to the joint tenancy that slight words swung the issue. Examples of words of severance are *among, equally*,[98] *equally to be divided*,[99] in

---

[86]   *Turton* v. *Turton* [1988] Ch 542, 546F, Nourse LJ.

[87]   *Turton* v. *Turton* [1988] Ch 542; J Montgomery [1988] *Fam Law* 72.

[88]   *Abbey National BS* v. *Cann* [1991] 1 AC 56, 93A, Lord Oliver; *Rodway* v. *Landy* [2001] EWCA Civ 471, [2001] Ch 703, [21], Peter Gibson LJ.

[89]   *Gissing* v. *Gissing* [1971] AC 886, 900H, Lord Diplock; *Lloyds Bank* v. *Rosset* [1991] 1 AC 107, 129C, Lord Bridge; *Roy* v. *Roy* [1996] 1 FLR 541, CA; *Carlton* v. *Goodman* [2002] EWCA Civ 545, [2002] 2 FLR 259, [44], Ward LJ.

[90]   Invalidating a transaction but not giving effect to the intended gift: *Gibbon* v. *Mitchell* [1990] 1 WLR 1304, Millett J; *Schnieder* v. *Mills* [1993] 3 All ER 377.

[91]   *Joscelyne* v. *Nissen* [1970] 2 QB 86, CA; *Banks* v. *Ripley* [1940] Ch 719, Morton J; *Goodman* v. *Gallant* [1986] Fam 106, 117B.

[92]   Not if it already reflects their intentions: *Roy* v. *Roy* [1990] 1 FLR 541, CA.

[93]   *Malmesbury* v. *Malmesbury* (1862) 31 Beav 407, 418, 54 ER 1196, Romilly MR.

[94]   *Joscelyne* v. *Nissen* [1970] 2 QB 86, CA; *Re Colebrook's C* [1972] 1 WLR 1397; *Lake* v. *Lake* [1989] STC 865.

[95]   *Whiteside* v. *Whiteside* [1950] Ch 65, CA; *Kemp* v. *Neptune Concrete* [1989] 2 EGLR 87, CA (unsuccessful); *Re Butlin's ST* [1976] Ch 251, 260–261.

[96]   [1976] 1 EGLR 129, CA.

[97]   *Cowcher* v. *Cowcher* [1972] 1 WLR 425, 430E.

[98]   *Morley* v. *Bird* (1798) 3 Ves 628, 30 ER 1192.

[99]   *Rigden* v. *Vallier* (1751) 3 Atk 731, 26 ER 1219, Lord Hardwicke.

equal shares,[100] or *on trust to divide,*[101] though a reference to a "share" was not by itself sufficient to sever.[102]

Wills and settlements often include inconsistent descriptions. *Slingsby's case* applied an artificial presumption that the first words were taken in a deed (later words being repugnant) whereas the last words were taken in a will (being the testator's last wish).[103] Another solution is to treat a transfer containing irreconcilable expressions as if it was two deeds, the first passing property to the trustees as legal and equitable joint tenants, whereas the second effected an immediate severance by words to convert the beneficial interest to a tenancy in common. This was the result in *Martin* v. *Martin*[104] of the words *on trust for themselves as beneficial joint tenants in common in equal shares.*

G. THE FOUR UNITIES

1. Unities characteristic of beneficial joint tenancy

[16.18] Joint tenancy implies a holistic ownership, traditionally evidenced by the presence of the four unities of possession, interest, title, and time.[105] Dissection of any tenancy in common will reveal the absence of one of the last three of these unities. Time is probably an illegitimate interloper, a question addressed in the context of settlements.[106] It is best to rely on the two central requirements stated long ago in *Pullen* v. *Palmer*:[107]

> "tenants in common hold their lands either by several titles or by several rights, but joint tenants hold them by one title and one right."

2. Absolute co-ownerships

[16.19] Absolute co-ownership arises where co-owners hold collectively for the duration of a legal estate. Joint tenancy must display one right, that is when all co-owners hold the same estate or interest in the property, as in:

> *to A and B in fee simple as beneficial joint tenants;*
> *to A and B for a term of 80 years as beneficial joint tenants.*

Common entitlement to a single estate gives rise to a joint tenancy so long as the stakes are equal. Unity of title is required, since the joint interest in the property must

---

[100] *Brown* v. *Oakshot* (1857) 24 Beav 254, 53 ER 355; *Re North* [1952] Ch 397; *Re Davies* [1950] 1 All ER 120, 123.

[101] *Barclay* v. *Barclay* [1970] 2 QB 677.

[102] *Re Schofield* [1918] 2 Ch 64; contrast *Jones* v. *Jones* (1881) 44 LT 642; *Re Woolley* [1903] 2 Ch 206, 210–211, Joyce J.

[103] (1587) 5 Co Rep. 18b, 19a, 77 ER 77; *Joyce* v. *Barker Bros (Builders)* (1980) 40 P & CR 512, 513; *Martin* v. *Martin* (1987) 54 P & CR 238, 243.

[104] (1987) 54 P & CR 238, 244, Millett J (the offending words in earlier cases were not in the habendum); JE Adams [1987] *Conv* 405; JE Martin [1988] *Conv* 57; also *Cowcher* v. *Cowcher* [1972] 1 WLR 425, 430H, Bagnall J.

[105] Blackstone's *Commentaries* vol 2, 174.

[106] See below **[18.07]**.

[107] (1693) 3 Salk 207, pl 155, 91 ER 780.

derive from one document of title and (if you accept Blackstone's fourth unity) at the same time, and it must not have been broken by a severance.

Tenancy in common arises if the beneficiaries hold by several titles or by several rights. Unity of interest is lacking if the co-owners hold unequal shares, for example if *A holds 1/4 and B holds 3/4 absolutely*. Contribution trusts are commonly unequal, and so the parties must take as beneficial tenants in common.[108] Another method is to use words of severance, for example *as beneficial tenants in common* or *in equal shares*.[109] Another method is assignment of the beneficial interest of a joint tenant, which breaks the single equitable title. The continuing beneficiaries trace their title from the creation of the joint tenancy, but those joining later trace title from the assignment and cannot come on board as joint tenants.[110]

3.   Limited co-ownerships

[16.20] Limited co-ownerships arise when what is shared is an equitable interest created by a will or settlement, such as a shared life interest, pre-1997 entail or other interest under a trusts of land. These are analysed below.[111]

H. IMPLIED CO-OWNERSHIP

1.   Co-ownership implied from contribution

[16.21] Joint tenancy is implied from equal contributions. In medieval law, joint tenancy simplified the collection of feudal payments, so it was preferred at common law, and the presumption in favour of it survived[112] long after this reason had become obsolete.[113] It continues to apply where property is purchased with equal contributions,[114] or under a common intention to give equal interests.[115] Survivorship is an equal chance, so there is nothing inequitable in giving all to the longest liver.[116] Tenancy in common is implied from unequal shares, reflecting unequal contributions or a common intention to give shares which are unequal.[117] It would be unfair to create a lottery on the life of fellow beneficiaries,[118] to give a larger contribution to a longer liver.[119] In this case equity favours the tenancy in common, and prevails over the contrary legal rule.

---

[108] *Williams & Glyn's Bank* v. *Boland* [1981] AC 487, HL.
[109] See below [16.42].
[110] See below [16.44].
[111] See below [18.09].
[112] Blackstone's *Commentaries* vol 2, 186.
[113] *Staples* v. *Maurice* (1774) 4 Bro Parl Cas 580, 2 ER 395, HL.
[114] *Morley* v. *Bird* (1798) 3 Ves 628, 30 ER 1192; *Cowcher* v. *Cowcher* [1972] 1 WLR 425, 430F, Bagnall J.
[115] *Bernard* v. *Josephs* [1982] Ch 391, 403G, Griffiths LJ.
[116] *Lake* v. *Gibson* (1729) 1 Eq Cas Abr 290, 21 ER 1052; *Aveling* v. *Knipe* (1815) 19 Ves 441, 34 ER 550.
[117] *Bull* v. *Bull* [1955] 1 QB 234, CA; *Williams & Glyn's Bank* v. *Boland* [1981] AC 487, HL; *City of London BS* v. *Flegg* [1988] AC 54, HL; *Abbey National BS* v. *Cann* [1991] 1 AC 56, HL.
[118] *Partriche* v. *Powlet* (1740) West t Hard 4, 26 ER 430; *Gould* v. *Kemp* (1834) 2 My & K 304, 39 ER 959; *Burgess* v. *Rawnsley* [1975] Ch 429, 438, Lord Denning MR.
[119] *Lake* v. *Craddock* (1733) 3 P Wms 158, 24 ER 1011.

2. Joint business ventures

[16.22] A tenancy in common is also implied in those business ventures where the gamble involved in survivorship is inappropriate. Joint lenders are presumed to advance money as tenants in common,[120] even if there is a joint account clause binding the borrower.[121] Again, survivorship has no place in a business partnership, where people carry on a business in common and share profits,[122] and hence the statutory rule that partnership property[123] is held in a beneficial tenancy in common. Examples occur when land is used for farming,[124] land speculation,[125] or for a club,[126] but not from joint holding of land or sharing rental income.[127]

The equitable presumption of a tenancy in common was extended to other joint ventures,[128] in *Malayan Joint Credit* v. *Jack Chia*[129] a suite of business offices let on a joint lease was divided so that A occupied 3,614 square feet and B took 2,306 square feet. Although closely analogous to existing categories, the absence of profit sharing and absence of purchase money meant that the Privy Council had the stretch the existing equitable rules when it found a tenancy in common in the proportions 3614:2306.[130] Further extensions may occur in future. Factors considered included the separate commercial interests, an agreement in advance about space allocation, an agreement to divide the rent and service charge, separate invoicing of the deposit, and actual division of rent and service charge payments.[131]

I. CREDITORS ACQUIRING BENEFICIAL INTERESTS

1. Mortgage by assignment

[16.23] A mortgage of an equitable interest in land is made by assigning it to the lender, who becomes an equitable co-owner. Thus if *T1 and T2 hold land on trust for A and B as beneficial co-owners*, A alone cannot touch the legal estate,[132] but he can transfer his beneficial interest to a lender as security for a loan. The form is an assignment of the interest being mortgaged, with a provision for reassignment on

---

[120] *Edwards* v. *Fashion* (1712) Prec Ch 332, 24 ER 156 (words of severance anyway).
[121] *Re Jackson* (1887) 34 Ch D 732; *Steeds* v. *Steeds* (1889) 22 QBD 537, 541; LPA 1925 s 111; LRA 2002 s 56.
[122] Partnership Act 1890 s 1(1).
[123] Partnership Act 1890 ss 20–21; Limited Liability Partnership Act 2000; *Barton* v. *Morris* [1985] 1 WLR 1257.
[124] *Jeffreys* v. *Small* (1683) 1 Vern 217, 23 ER 424; *Morris* v. *Barrett* (1829) 3 Y & J 384, 148 ER 1228; but *Ward* v. *Ward* (1871) LR 6 Ch App 789 (farming as joint tenants).
[125] *Dale* v. *Hamilton* (1846) 5 Hare 369, 67 ER 955; *Darby* v. *Darby* (1856) 3 Drew 495, 61 ER 992; *Re Hulton* (1890) 62 LT 200.
[126] *Brown* v. *Dale* (1878) 9 Ch D 78; Megarry & Wade (6th ed), [9.093–9.096].
[127] Partnership Act 1890 s 2(1).
[128] *Lake* v. *Gibson* (1729) 1 Eq Cas Abr 290, 21 ER 1052; on appeal *Lake* v. *Craddock* (1733) 3 P Wms 158, 24 ER 1011.
[129] [1986] AC 549, PC; JE Martin [1986] *Conv* 354.
[130] At 560F.
[131] At 561.
[132] Even if A and B are also trustees.

redemption of the loan,[133] Writing is required whatever form of property is held in the trust.[134] If the loan is not repaid, the lender could sell the equitable interest which is mortgaged,[135] but the real remedy is to apply for an order for sale of the legal estate.

2. Fraudulent mortgage by one co-owner

[16.24] One co-owner may be tempted to defraud the other by arranging for a friend to forge the other's signature on a mortgage. If husband and wife are joint owners or a matrimonial home, H may induce his new girlfriend to masquerade as his wife when mortgaging the house. Such a forgery has no effect on the legal estate, but does mortgage H's beneficial interest. Husband and wife are left holding the legal estate jointly on trust for the lender and wife. Just this happened in *Ahmed* v. *Kendrick*.[136] A failed attempt to mortgage a legal estate operates as a valid mortgage of the equitable interest under a statutory all-estate clause: a mortgage or conveyance is effectual to pass any estate or interest held by the conveying parties.[137] Hence if A purports to transfer or mortgage a legal estate vested in A and B, only the beneficial interest actually held by A will pass. The beneficial interest under a trust of land is clearly an interest in the land,[138] but the law was the same under a trust for sale before 1997.[139] Otherwise an innocent purchaser could be severely prejudiced.

A problem may remain where the mortgage takes the form of a contract to mortgage. *Cedar Holdings* v. *Green*[140] held that specific performance should not be ordered of a contract for an equitable charge so as to prejudice a third party title. The point was not expressly disapproved in *Boland*,[141] but the Court of Appeal which decided *Green* misunderstood the equitable position. A mortgage is executed once the money is lent, a fact which greatly reduces the defences to specific performance. Later cases have avoided the difficulty by relying on a well-known exception where hardship is caused to the third-party lender.[142]

---

[133] *Ex p Kensington* (1813) 2 V & B 79, 35 ER 249 (stocks).

[134] LPA 1925 s 53(1)(c); notice must be given to the trustees to secure priority; ss 85–87 (forms of mortgages of legal estates) do not apply.

[135] LPA 1925 s 102.

[136] [1988] 2 FLR 22; *Bankers Trust Co* v. *Namdar* [1997] EGCS 20, CA; A Dunn [1996] *Conv* 371.

[137] LPA 1925 s 63; *Bridges* v. *Harrow LBC* [1981] 2 EGLR 143, 145 (tree roots); *Deen* v. *Andrews* [1986] 1 EGLR 262, Hirst J; *Kijowski* v. *New Capital Properties* (1990) 15 Con LR 1 (not benefit of NHBC agreement); *Boots the Chemist* v. *Street* [1983] 2 EGLR 51, 52 (right to rectify); *Brackenbank Lodge* v. *Peart* (1994) 67 P & CR 249 257–258, Russell LJ (soil passed with grazing); *Bank of Ireland* v. *Bell* [2001] 2 FLR 809; R Probert [2002] *Conv* 61.

[138] TLATA 1996 s 3.

[139] *Williams & Glyn's Bank* v. *Boland* [1981] AC 487, 507G, Lord Wilberforce; *Thames Guaranty* v. *Campbell* [1985] QB 210, 239, Slade LJ; *Ahmed* v. *Kendrick* [1988] 2 FLR 22, 28D–E; *Re Ng* [1998] 2 FLR 386.

[140] [1981] Ch 129, CA.

[141] [1981] AC 487 HL.

[142] *Thames Guaranty* v. *Campbell* [1985] QB 210, 235, 239G–240H, Slade LJ; JE Adams [1985] *Conv* 165; *Ahmed* v. *Kendrick* [1988] 2 FLR 22, 28 (left open).

3. Severance by mortgage etc

[16.25] A mortgage of a beneficial interest or an attempt at a fraudulent mortgage of a legal estate severs just as much as an outright assignment.[143] For example, in *First National Securities* v. *Hegerty*[144] the husband forged his wife's signature on a mortgage of a matrimonial home held by the couple as beneficial joint tenants. Acting as a charge on the husband's beneficial interest, this caused a severance.

An involuntary transfer also effects a severance of the beneficial interest.[145] A charging order enforcing a debt against the share of a beneficial co-owner would also sever.[146] If a family home is held by beneficial joint tenants and a debt is incurred by one party alone, (say H, since insolvent husbands figure more often in the cases) a charging order affects only H's beneficial interest.[147]

4. Bankruptcy and its severing effect

[16.26] Any beneficial interest held by a bankrupt passes to the trustee in bankruptcy,[148] thus converting a beneficial joint tenancy to a tenancy in common. Bankruptcy has no direct effect on the holding of the legal estate.[149]

Pre-1986 a bankruptcy order was backdated in its effect to the act of bankruptcy which precipitated the proceedings. Hence, if a person died without having been adjudicated bankrupt in his lifetime, a severance would nevertheless occur if he became bankrupt posthumously. This happened in *Re Dennis*, a case which only reached the Court of Appeal in 1995.[150] Dennis committed an act of bankruptcy in September 1982 (before 1986) leading a creditor to submit a petition in bankruptcy in December of that year and to the adjudication of his bankruptcy in November 1983. According to the Elizabethan principle of relation back,[151] this dated from the act of bankruptcy in September 1982, and caused a severance at that date. Meanwhile his wife died in February 1983 and did so as a tenant in common. Her share she left to her children by will, and it evaded the clutches of the trustee in bankruptcy, who could claim only Dennis' beneficial share.

The Insolvency Act 1986 abolished relation back.[152] In *Re Palmer*[153] a solicitor stole money from his firm to such an extent that his liabilities would make him insol-

---

[143] *York* v. *Stone* (1709) 1 Salk 158, 91 ER 146; *Denne d Bowyer* v. *Judge* (1809) 11 East 288, 103 ER 1014 (conveyance by 3 of 5 joint tenants severed interest of 3 at law); *Williams* v. *Hensman* (1861) 1 John & H 546, 70 ER 862; *Re Pollard's E* (1863) 3 De G J & Sm 541, 557–558, 46 ER 746; *Re Sharer* (1912) 57 SJ 60.

[144] [1985] QB 850, CA; *Ahmed* v. *Kendrick* (1987) 56 P & CR 120; not a sham where the lender is a complicit party: *Penn* v. *Bristol & West BS* [1995] 2 FLR 938.

[145] Eg appointment of an equitable receiver: *Hills* v. *Webber* (1901) 17 TLR 513, CA; or a voluntary arrangement: *Johnson* v. *Davies* [1999] Ch 117, CA.

[146] *Irani Finance* v. *Singh* [1971] Ch 59, CA.

[147] *First National Securities* v. *Hegerty* [1985] QB 850, 854, Bingham J; J Price [1989] *Conv* 133.

[148] *Thomason* v. *Frere* (1809) 10 East 418, 103 ER 834; *Re Gorman* [1990] 1 WLR 616, Vinelott J; *Lee* v. *Lee* [1998] 1 FLR 1018.

[149] *Re Solomon* [1967] Ch 573; it is a ground for removal as a trustee.

[150] [1996] Ch 80, CA; L Tee [1996] *CLJ* 21.

[151] [1996] Ch 80, 89–104, Millett LJ; *Ex p Smith* (1800) 5 Ves 295, 31 ER 595; *Smith* v. *Stokes* (1801) 1 East 363, 102 ER 141; *Morgan* v. *Marquis* (1853) 9 Exch 144, 156 ER 62.

[152] IA 1986 s 278.

[153] [1994] Ch 316, CA; M Haley [1995] *Conv* 68; L Tee [1995] *CLJ* 52; *Abergavenny's case* (1607) 6 Co Rep 78b, 77 ER 373.

vent. He died in November 1990 before he could be sued by his creditors. In 1991 his
executors applied for an insolvency administration order, which was held to apply
from its date and not to be backdated. Hence the interest in Palmer's matrimonial
home had passed by survivorship to his wife and his creditors had no claim to it.[154]
Survivorship applies when a joint tenant dies after 1986 and none of the joint tenants
has faced a bankruptcy petition at the moment of his death.

5.   Charging orders

[16.27]   Under a trust of land, the debt of a beneficiary can be charged on the equitable
interest under the trust though not on the legal estate.[155] A beneficial interest under a
trust of land can be overreached, and so too can a mortgage or charging order affecting it. In particular a charging order is registrable.[156] To allow registration of a land
charge or caution "cuts right across the system of conveyancing."[157]

6.   Priority of claims

[16.28]   Priority of mortgages of equitable interests of land is decided primarily by the
order of notices received by the trustees, who constitute in a sense a register.[158] The
rule in *Dearle* v. *Hall*[159] had always applied to personalty and choses in action. In
1925[160] it was extended to apply to a mortgage of any equitable interest in *unregistered*
land,[161] including all beneficial interests under trusts of land, and formerly encom-
passing trusts for sale,[162] strict settlements and rights in capital money.[163] Since 1987
it has also applied to *registered* land.[164] An experiment with a minor interests index to
record dealings with beneficial interests in registered land was abandoned.[165]

   Dearle v. *Hall* governs priority between two competing dealings after the creation
of the trust,[166] such as mortgages, charges,[167] assignments, settlements, and transfers
by operation of law.[168] According to *United Bank of Kuwait* v. *Sahib*,[169] it does not

---

[154] SI 1986/1999, sch 1 part II para 12, appeared to provide to the contrary, but these regulations were
ultra vires the IA 1986.

[155] TLATA 1996 s 3.

[156] *Perry* v. *Phoenix Assurance* [1988] 1 WLR 940; JE Martin [1988] *Conv* 286; now confirmed by
TLATA 1996 sch 3 para 12. Nor is notice to the trustees needed.

[157] At 945B, Browne-Wilkinson V-C.

[158] *Ward* v. *Duncombe* [1893] AC 369, 393, Lord Macnaghten.

[159] (1828) 3 Russ 1, 38 ER 475; *Foster* v. *Cockerell* (1835) 3 Cl & Fin 456, 6 ER 1568 HL; EC Firth (1895)
11 *LQR* 337; J de Lacy [1998] *Anglo-American* 87.

[160] LPA 1925 s 137 (some parts amend the law of personalty); J Howell [1993] *Conv* 22.

[161] *Lee* v. *Howlett* (1856) 2 K & J 531, 69 ER 893; *Re Richards* (1890) 45 Ch D 589, Stirling J.

[162] *Gresham Life Assurance Society* v. *Crowther* [1915] 1 Ch 214, CA.

[163] LPA 1925 s 137(1); reversing *Ward* v. *Duncombe* [1893] AC 369, 389–390.

[164] LRA 1986 s 5.

[165] LRA 1925 s 102(2). Existing entries at the end of 1986 are treated as a notice to the trustees and an
indemnity is provided.

[166] LPA 1925 s 137(10).

[167] *Rhodes* v. *Allied Dunbar Pensions Services* [1987] 1 WLR 1703, 1707.

[168] LPA 1925 s 137(1), (10).

[169] [1997] Ch 107, 118, 120 (Sogenal's equitable mortgage against Kuwait Bank's charging orders); this
point was not argued on appeal; AJ Oakley (1996) 112 *LQR* 215; *Scott* v. *Lord Hastings* (1858) 4 K & J 633,
637–638, 76 ER 633.

apply to the competition between a mortgage and a later charging order. Chadwick J thought that notice should not promote a judgment creditor who had been content to advance credit without any security.

Between mortgages the main issue is the order by which notices are received by the trustees. However a lender with notice of a prior mortgage at the time of making his loan[170] cannot sneak priority by giving the first notice to the trustees.[171] Notice secures priority, and ensures that the trustees meet the claim.[172] It is not necessary to create a valid mortgage between the parties.[173] If the mortgage relates to a *legal* estate in land, notice is unnecessary and does not give any priority.[174]

Notice to secure priority must now be in writing.[175] Oral notice is sufficient to protect the lender against payment by the trustee to the borrower, but written notice is necessary to secure priority against a later lender. It must be served on the trustees. It is advisable to serve notice on *all* trustees, since the statute refers to "trustees" in the plural, though it also continues the effect of the old rules about notices. Once given a notice continues its effectiveness following the death or retirement of any trustee. If notice was given to a single trustee who then retired, continuing effect for the notice was dependent upon communication between them,[176] but the trustee receiving notice is now required to deliver it to the custody of all trustees.[177] An alternative (and superior) procedure is to indorse notice on the trust instrument notices of dealings.[178] Any person affected may seek production of the trust instrument.[179]

J. SEVERANCE

[16.29] Severance is the process of converting a joint tenancy into a tenancy in common.[180] It is encouraged both by equity[181] and also as a matter of legislative policy.[182]

---

[170] Later notice is irrelevant: *Mutual Life Association Society* v. *Langley* (1886) 32 Ch D 460, 486, Cotton LJ.

[171] *Re Holmes* (1885) 29 Ch D 786; *Rhodes* v. *Allied Dunbar Pension Services* [1989] 1 WLR 800, 806, Nicholls LJ.

[172] *Ward* v. *Duncombe* [1893] AC 369, 392, Lord Macnaghten; *Hodgson* v. *Hodgson* (1837) 2 Keen 704, 48 ER 800.

[173] *Ward* v. *Duncombe* [1893] AC 369, 392, Lord Macnaghten.

[174] *Wiltshire* v. *Rabbits* (1844) 14 Sim 76, 60 ER 285; *Union Bank of London* v. *Kent* (1888) 39 Ch D 238, CA; *Assaf* v. *Fuwa* [1955] AC 215, PC; HWR Wade [1955] *CLJ* 32.

[175] LPA 1925 s 137(3).

[176] *Ward* v. *Duncombe* [1893] AC 369, HL; *Re Phillip's Trusts* [1903] 1 Ch 183; *Lloyds Bank* v. *Pearson* [1901] 1 Ch 865.

[177] LPA 1925 s 137(8).

[178] S 137(4)–(6). Or a trust corporation can be appointed to receive notices and its appointment indorsed: s 138. For the pre-1926 law see: *Phipps* v. *Lovegrove* (1873) LR 16 Eq 80; *Hill* v. *Peters* [1918] 2 Ch 273, 278.

[179] LPA 1925 s 138(9)–(11); this reverses *Low* v. *Bouverie* [1891] 3 Ch 82.

[180] HW Wilkinson (1984) 134 *NLJ* 63.

[181] *Burgess* v. *Rawnsley* [1975] Ch 429, 438D, Lord Denning MR; *Partriche* v. *Powlet* (1740) West t Hard 4, 26 ER 430; *Gould* v. *Kemp* (1834) 2 My & K 304, 39 ER 959.

[182] *Burgess* v. *Rawnsley* [1975] Ch 429, 448B, Sir John Pennycuick.

1. Severance restricted to beneficial interests

[16.30] Lord Birkenhead's prohibition of severance of a joint tenancy of the *legal* estate,[183] merely serves to confirm the possibility of severing the *equitable* interests.[184] A transfer to A and B to hold the freehold estate as joint tenants on trust for themselves as beneficial joint tenants, which is followed by a severance, will leave A and B still holding the legal estate as joint tenants but on trust for themselves *as beneficial tenants in common*. The implied trust continues.[185]

When a marriage or relationship deteriorates the first step should often be a severance,[186] but care is needed because a notice of severance can inflame passions and lead to the flinging of pots and pans and the slamming of doors.[187] A tenancy in common should always be used for business property. A person may also wish to sever if, as Jekyll MR once said, he "has an ill opinion of his own life".[188]

Severance destroys survivorship, since it converts an existing joint tenancy to a tenancy in common, the parties thenceforth holding undivided shares as tenants in common,[189] and necessarily in equal shares.[190] Severance must occur during the lifetime of the joint tenant,[191] with no effect being given to an attempt to sever by will,[192] though the Law Commission has recommended a change in this rule.[193]

Can a joint tenancy be made unseverable? This was once achieved by a tenancy by entireties between husband and wife, "the most intimate union known to law."[194] New creations were prohibited after 1882 and those few left in 1925 were converted to normal joint tenancies.[195] An attempted revival by Lord Denning MR in *Bedson* v. *Bedson*[196] was contrary to authority[197] and heretical.[198] Tailor-made co-ownerships could achieve something similar, but there are many taxation traps.[199]

2. Severance on the legal title

[16.31] Where land is vested in beneficial joint tenants, the survivor becomes solely entitled, thus:

---

[183] LPA 1925 ss 1(6), 36(2)–(3).

[184] S 36(2).

[185] *Ali* v. *Sandwell MBC* (1990) 60 P & CR 374, 375.

[186] Despite *McDowell* v. *Hirschfield Lipson & Rumney* [1992] 2 FLR 126, 129H.

[187] *Re 88 Berkeley Road, London NW9* [1971] Ch 648, 651E.

[188] *Cray* v. *Willis* (1729) 2 P Wms 529, 22 ER 453.

[189] *Harris* v. *Goddard* [1983] 1 WLR 1203, 1210, Dillon LJ.

[190] *Nielson-Jones* v. *Fedden* [1975] Ch 222, 228D, Walton J.

[191] Apart from unlawful killing and claims by dependants.

[192] *Carr-Glynn* v. *Frearsons* [1999] Ch 326, CA; *Swift d Neale* v. *Roberts* (1764) 3 Burr 1488, 1496, 97 ER 941; *Gould* v. *Kemp* (1834) 2 My & K 304, 309, 39 ER 959; Littleton's *Tenures*, [287]; Coke on *Littleton* [185b]; Blackstone's *Commentaries* vol 2, 184; L Tee [1995] *Conv* 105, 111–113.

[193] Law Com WP 94 (1985).

[194] Challis, *Real Property* (Butterworths, 3rd ed by C Sweet, 1911), 377.

[195] Married Women's Property Act 1882 s 1; LPA 1925 sch 1 part VI.

[196] [1965] 2 QB 666, 678B.

[197] At 690E, Russell LJ; RE Megarry (1966) 82 *LQR* 29; S Roberts (1966) 29 *MLR* 334.

[198] *Radziej* v. *Radziej* [1967] 1 WLR 659 at first instance; *Re Draper's Conveyance* [1969] 1 Ch 486, 492E–494B; *Cowcher* v. *Cowcher* [1972] 1 WLR 425; IA Saunders (1973) 37 *Conv (NS)* 270, 272; *Harris* v. *Goddard* [1983] 1 WLR 12093, 1208F–H.

[199] *Penn* v. *Bristol & West BS* [1995] 2 FLR 938.

to A and B in fee simple as joint tenants on trust for A and B as joint tenants;

When A dies:

To B in fee simple on trust for B in fee simple = to B in fee simple.

The position is quite different is a severance occurs before A's death. The end result in that case is

to B in fee simple as joint tenants on trust for A's personal representatives and B as tenants in common.

The ultimate beneficiaries of A's share will be those named in his will or entitled as his next of kin on his intestacy. In this second case the survivor (B) is not in a position to sell, but only to overreach by the appointment of a second trustee.

So although severance affects the equitable title it has an important impact on the legal title. It is important that the change is recorded on the legal title by the endorsement of a memorandum of the severance on the conveyance which passed the land to the beneficial joint tenants or, if title is registered, by entry of a restriction.

The survivor can now sell and give a receipt for the purchase money, unfettered by the former trust. If title is registered, the two appeared on the register as proprietors without any restriction to bite on death, so B is able to sell on proof of A's death.

3. Effect of severance

[16.32] Severance of the beneficial joint tenancy creates a tenancy in common, with quite different conveyancing procedures following death. Legal title vests in the sole surviving co-owner, since legal co-owners are necessarily joint tenants, but the undivided beneficial share of a deceased tenant in common passes under his will or under his intestacy – immediately to his personal representatives, and ultimately to his successor nominated by will or to his next of kin on intestacy. The trust continues and an overreaching sale is required by two trustees, the survivor needing to appoint an additional trustee in order to achieve this. Proper conveyancing practice is to mark the severance on the legal title, in registered land by applying to the registrar for a joint proprietor restriction,[200] or if title is unregistered by endorsing a memorandum on the title deed creating the beneficial joint tenancy.

4. Hidden severance: registered land

[16.33] If no restriction is entered following a severance, registration confers full powers of disposition on the surviving proprietor. A good title is obtained by a purchaser as if the survivor is really beneficially entitled on death. Informal acts not notified to him have no effect on a purchaser, unless they happen to create overriding interests.[201]

---

[200] See above **[13.36]**.

[201] LP (Joint Tenants) A 1964 has no application where title is registered: s 3 (as amended by LRA 2002 sch 11). Honesty is not required: see below **[20.45]**. But a purchaser might be bound by the severed share of a person in occupation: G Ferris & G Battersby [1998] *Conv* 168, 183–184.

5. Hidden severance: unregistered land

[16.34] If unregistered title deeds show a conveyance to beneficial joint tenants but no trace of a memorandum of severance, the purchaser is left unsure whether the case is one of beneficial joint tenancy (example 1 above – survivor can sell) or of tenancy in common after a hidden severance (example 2 above – second trustee required). It is impossible to prove the negative that no severance has occurred, but a purchaser is protected by being able to assume a beneficial survivorship if the three conditions of the Law of Property (Joint Tenants) Act 1964[202] are satisfied.

(1) Conveyance by beneficial owner

[16.35] The seller must be expressed to convey as beneficial owner or the conveyance must recite that he is so entitled.[203] Before 1995 the necessary statement would usually have been included in the conveyance in order to trigger the beneficial owner covenants for title. If for some reason they were missing from a pre-1964 conveyance, a written statement could be obtained afterwards from the seller or his personal representative.[204] After 1995, covenants for title are triggered by the words "with full title guarantee"[205] so that an extra statement is required to bring into play the protection of the 1964 Act. Protection is also provided where a survivor of beneficial joint tenants dies and it is his personal representatives who are selling.[206]

(2) No bankruptcy registration

[16.36] Bankruptcy passes the beneficial interest to the trustee in bankruptcy and so works a severance. A purchaser is required to obtain a clean land charges search.[207]

(3) No memorandum of severance

[16.37] Protection is removed if there is a memorandum of severance endorsed on the conveyance to the beneficial joint tenants.[208] This requirement is concerned with the protection of purchasers and failure to endorse the memorandum does not remove the validity of the notice of severance as between the joint tenants – even under an express clause.[209]

The 1964 Act imposes no duty of diligence to discover a severance beyond checking for a memorandum. In the first edition of this work[210] it was stated that:

---

[202] P Jackson (1964) 30 *Conv (NS)* 27; PH Kenny and A Kenny (1980) 80 *LSG* 1473, 1475.
[203] LP (Joint Tenants) A 1964 s 1(1).
[204] S 2. The Act applies retrospectively from the start of 1926.
[205] See above **[11.60]**.
[206] S 1(2). The pre-1995 covenants for title trigger "as personal representatives" was not sufficient.
[207] S 1(2)(b), as amended by IA 1985.
[208] LP (Joint Tenants) A 1964 s 1(2)(a).
[209] *Grindal* v. *Hooper* discussed immediately below.
[210] P Sparkes *NLL* (1st ed), 317.

"Honesty is a requirement,[211] and it would not be safe to take title if the buyer knows of a severance. In such a case he should insist on an overreaching conveyance."

That may in fact have been over dogmatic of the law as it stood in the time, but it has turned out to be correct. When the beneficial joint tenancy between S and V in *Grindal* v. *Hooper*[212] was severed by V's notice, this was not, as the express terms of the conveyance required, endorsed on the conveyance. After V died, Sheila Hooper conveyed the unregistered title to Brian Hooper (who knew of the severance) for £600. Title derived from Brian was not absolute, as they would have done if rather they held a half share on trust for V's executors. In other words the 1964 Act had not protected Brian because he was not an honest purchaser without notice.

K. METHODS OF SEVERANCE

[16.38] Severance converts a beneficial joint tenancy into a beneficial tenancy in common. *Unilateral severance* occurs by the act of one joint tenant without the concurrence of the others, either by:

1. written notice under section 36 of the Law of Property Act 1925; or
2. a disposition destroying one of the unities.

If there are more than two joint tenants, it is only a partial severance, which slices off the share of the person causing the severance but leaves the joint tenancy intact between the other beneficiaries.[213] *Mutual severance* must involve the agreement or conduct of all the joint tenants and leading to a complete severance. Methods are:

1. a written agreement to sever; or
2. a course of conduct showing a mutual intention to sever.

The present law is clearly unsatisfactory. The Law Commission suggested almost 20 years ago that[214] there should be a statutory formulation of a single method of severance by written notice, and that a gift by will should suffice.

1. Written notice

[16.39] The possibility of effecting severance of a *beneficial* joint tenancy by written notice was first enacted in 1925:

"[W]here a legal estate . . . is vested in joint tenants beneficially, and any tenant desires to sever the joint tenancy in equity, he shall give to the other joint tenants a notice in writing of such desire . . .".[215]

---

[211] S 4(1) incorporates the LPA 1925 definition of purchaser in s 205(1)(xxi), that is a purchaser in good faith for valuable consideration.

[212] [2000] Times February 8th, John Jarvis QC.

[213] Littleton's *Tenures*, [294]; *Williams* v. *Hensman* (1861) 1 John & H 546, 70 ER 862 (mortgage authorised by 8 children, 5 adults and 3 minors; effect was {5/8ths to the adult children as joint tenants} and {3/8ths to the minors as joint tenants} with a tenancy in common between those two interests); *Napier* v. *Williams* [1911] 1 Ch 361; *Bedson* v. *Bedson* [1965] 2 QB 666, 689D, Russell LJ.

[214] Law Com WP 94 (1985), [16.11–16.14]; L Tee [1995] *Conv* 105.

[215] LPA 1925 s 36(2); minor textual amendment by TLATA 1996 sch 2 para 4; this method is not available to joint tenants for life under a strict settlement.

Written notice is restricted to land.[216] It was not available for personal property before 1926,[217] nor afterwards,[218] though the exclusion of personalty is most unfortunate.[219]

(1) Must legal and beneficial joint tenants be identical?

[16.40] Written notice works "where a legal estate is vested in joint tenants beneficially".[220] At face value this states a condition that the trustees of the legal estate must be identical to the beneficial joint tenants, since only in that case is the legal estate *vested in* the beneficial joint tenants.[221] Thus if A and B hold the legal estate on trust for themselves as beneficial joint tenants, A could sever by written notice, but not if the legal estate was vested in T1 and T2. The courts should try to read the notice provision expansively.

(2) Giving of notice

[16.41] Written notice must be given "by the joint tenant wishing to sever" and with his authority[222] "to the other joint tenants." Correspondence between advisers will not do.[223] A notice can be left at the last known place of abode or business in the United Kingdom or sent by registered post.[224] A bizarre possibility is that a notice by A is properly served by posting it to B at the property, even if it is taken in by A,[225] as demonstrated by *Kinch* v. *Bullard*.[226] A married couple remained joint tenants of the matrimonial home though their relationship had deteriorated. When the wife received a diagnosis of a terminal cancer she decided to end the joint tenancy and instructed her solicitor to post a notice to her husband at the property. He had a heart attack on August 6th, the day before the notice was pushed through the letter box. His wife, now favouring her chances of survivorship, picked up the letter containing the notice and destroyed it. The husband in fact died that same month whereas the wife survived until the following January. But, despite the destruction of the notice, a severance had occurred. Once given the notice is binding.

---

[216] *Nielson-Jones* v. *Fedden* [1975] Ch 222, 229C; *Burgess* v. *Rawnsley* [1975] Ch 429, 447, Sir John Pennycuick; *Harris* v. *Goddard* [1983] 1 WLR 1203, 1208E. Land is defined by LPA 1925 s 205(1)(x).

[217] *Williams* v. *Hensman* (1861) 1 John & H 546, 70 ER 862; P Luther (1995) 15 *LS* 219.

[218] Lord Denning MR in *Burgess* v. *Rawnsley*, [1975] Ch 429, 438, 439G–440B, mistook the force of the word "other" in s 36(2).

[219] *Nielson-Jones* v. *Fedden* [1975] Ch 222, 229B, Walton J; *Burgess* v. *Rawnsley* [1975] Ch 429, 440A, Lord Denning MR.

[220] LPA 1925 s 36(2).

[221] Wolstenholme & Cherry (13th ed by JT Farrand) vol 1, 98.

[222] *Harris* v. *Goddard* [1983] 1 WLR 1203 (notice given while husband in coma by his solicitors ineffective); PV Baker (1984) 100 *LQR* 161; S Coneys [1984] *Conv* 148.

[223] At 1207F–H; *Nielson-Jones* v. *Fedden* [1975] Ch 222, 230, despite [1975] Ch 429, 440C, Lord Denning MR.

[224] LPA 1925 s 196(3)–(4). The service provided for a century and a half by the Royal Mail is now opened to any "postal operator": Postal Services Act 2000.

[225] *Re 88 Berkeley Road, London NW9* [1971] Ch 648; (1971) 87 *LQR* 155.

[226] [1998] 1 WLR 421, Neuberger J; M Percival [1999] *Conv* 60.

(3) Statement of intention to sever

[16.42] Where "any tenant desires to sever the joint tenancy in equity" section 36(2) gives effect to a "notice of such desire". A model for a *formal* notice is provided by *Re 88 Berkeley Road, London NW9*:

> "I hereby give notice of my desire to sever the joint tenancy in equity of and in the property described in the schedule hereto now held by you and me as joint tenants both at law and in equity."[227]

Case-law generally considers whether *informal* documents have stated the desire to sever effectively. Decisions are consistent, just, but contain fine distinctions.[228] *Re Draper's Conveyance*[229] held that a court application by a divorcing wife under section 17 of the Married Women's Property Act 1882 was a written notice of severance. The application was for an order for sale of the matrimonial home and division of the proceeds of sale according to the parties' respective interests, and it had led to an order for sale[230] and a declaration of the wife's entitlement to a half interest in the property, though the property remained unsold at the husband's death. The application occasioned severance when served on the husband.[231] A second case chronologically was *Nielson-Jones* v. *Fedden*.[232] On separation of a married couple, who were beneficial joint tenants, both signed a DIY memorandum[233] stating as follows:

> "The [husband] to use his entire discretion to sell [the matrimonial home] and employ the funds realised to his new home if it is decided to sell in order to provide a home for . . . himself . . . to live".

This did not cause severance, so when the husband was killed in an accident, the wife became entitled, quite fortuitously, by survivorship. The memorandum dealt solely with the use by the husband of the proceeds of sale and had nothing to say about ownership. Surely this was a strange reading of the memorandum but, given that aberration, the decision is right. Finally, *Harris* v. *Goddard*[234] concerned a divorce petition which invited the court to consider exercising its property adjustment jurisdiction and "that such order may be made . . . as may be just". This spoke in general and unparticularised terms[235] of the future, whereas a severance notice must take

---

[227] [1971] Ch 648, 650–651; *Goodman* v. *Gallant* [1986] Fam 106, 109B.

[228] *Burgess* v. *Rawnsley* [1975] Ch 429, 4448B.

[229] [1969] 1 Ch 486, 491G, 492E Plowman J; *Burgess* v. *Rawnsley* [1975] Ch 429, 440A; *Harris* v. *Goddard* [1983] 1 WLR 1203, 1210A, Lawton LJ, 1210G, Dillon LJ; FR Crane (1968) 32 *Conv (NS)* 65; PV Baker (1968) 84 *LQR* 462.

[230] On court orders: *Re Wilks* [1891] 3 Ch 59 (affected by LPA 1925 s 36); *Burgess* v. *Rawnsley* [1975] Ch 429, 440D, 447F; *Harris* v. *Goddard* [1983] 1 WLR 1203, 1210D, Dillon LJ; PV Baker (1968) 84 *LQR* 462; MJ Prichard [1975] *CLJ* 28; FR Crane (1974) 38 *Conv (NS)* 363; PV Baker (1984) 100 *LQR* 161.

[231] *Harris* v. *Goddard* [1983] 1 WLR 1203, 1210G, Dillon LJ.

[232] [1975] Ch 222; MJ Prichard [1975] *CLJ* 28.

[233] FR Crane (1974) 38 *Conv (NS)* 363.

[234] [1983] 1 WLR 1203, CA; PV Baker (1984) 100 *LQR* 161; S Coneys [1984] *Conv* 148; *McDowell* v. *Hirschfield Lipson & Rumney* [1992] 2 FLR 126; *Hunter* v. *Babbage* (1995) 69 P & CR 548, 556–557, 560–561.

[235] At 1210H, Dillon LJ.

effect immediately.[236] No alteration in the shares was implied in advance of a decision by the court to exercise its property adjustment powers.

To conclude, a notice works if it is to sever immediately, but a notice to sever in the future does not. An intention to retain the property but to treat it as held in shares will sever. A notice requesting a sale will not sever, since it is possible to have a joint tenancy in the proceeds of sale, but a notice is effective if it requires both sale and division of the proceeds.

(4) No severance by unilateral declaration

[16.43] Plowman J considered in *Re Draper's Conveyance*[237] that an oral declaration by one of a number of joint tenants of his intention to sever operates as a severance." A formidable array of authority against this view starts in 1740[238] runs through the leading severance case, *Williams* v. *Hensman*,[239] and proceeds to Walton J's observation that no essential unity is shattered by a unilateral oral statement.[240] This is supported by a rare unanimity among academics.[241] So it is clear that an uncommunicated declaration or verbal notice cannot sever.[242]

2. Severance by unilateral disposition

[16.44] Since all four unities are essential for the continuation of a joint tenancy, destruction of any one will lead to a severance. Unilateral severance is effected by the act of one joint tenant, without the concurrence or consent of the others, and even if concealed.[243] Unity of possession cannot be removed without destroying the co-ownership and time, once present, is present for ever.[244] So an intended severance must strike at unity of title or unity of interest.[245] Until 1926 there was no other means to sever, so an artificial transaction was needed by which A assigned his beneficial interest from A to *T on trust for A*.[246]

Sale of the beneficial interest of one[247] joint tenant destroys the unity of title[248] and so severs his share. The principle applied to sales of shares in the legal estate since the reign of Edward IV,[249] now applies to beneficial shares under a trust of land.[250]

---

[236] At 1209B, Lawton LJ; *Gore & Snell* v. *Carpenter* (1990) 60 P & CR 456, 462.

[237] [1969] 1 Ch 486, 491G; *Hawkesley* v. *May* [1956] 1 QB 304, Havers J; RN Gooderson [1956] *CLJ* 25 ("erroneous"); *Burgess* v. *Rawnsley* [1975] Ch 429, 440C, Lord Denning MR.

[238] *Partriche* v. *Powlet* (1740) West t Hard 4, 26 ER 430.

[239] (1861) 1 John & H 546, 558, 70 ER 862, Page Wood V-C.

[240] *Nielson-Jones* v. *Fedden* [1975] Ch 222, 230. The other view was "wholly unwarranted" and renders s 36 otiose: at 234, 236–237.

[241] DJ Hayton [1976] *CLJ* 20, 22–23; MJ Prichard [1975] *CLJ* 28; FR Crane (1968) 32 *Conv (NS)* 65; PV Baker (1968) 84 *LQR* 462; PV Baker (1984) 100 *LQR* 161.

[242] *Burgess* v. *Rawnsley* [1975] Ch 429, 447C, Sir John Pennycuick.

[243] *First National Securities* v. *Hegerty* [1985] QB 850.

[244] *Nielson-Jones* v. *Fedden* [1975] Ch 222, 228F, Walton J; contrast TS Eliot in the opening lines of Burnt Norton!

[245] Blackstone's *Commentaries* vol 2, 179.

[246] Self-dealing does not sever: *Rye* v. *Rye* [1962] AC 496, 514.

[247] As opposed to a dealing by all joint tenants: *Palmer* v. *Rich* [1897] 1 Ch 134.

[248] *Sym's case* (1584) Cro Eliz 33, 78 ER 299; Littleton's *Tenures*, [292].

[249] Littleton's *Tenures*, [292]; Blackstone's *Commentaries* vol 2, 179.

[250] TLATA 1996 s 3, sch 2 para 4.

Assignments of beneficial interests require writing[251] though just as good is a contract for value to assign[252] or a declaration of trust[253] will do just as well. Lesser transactions also sever, such as leases,[254] covenants to settle,[255] mortgages of the beneficial interest and fraudulent mortgages. It was generally thought that a mortgage would effect a permanent severance in the same way as a sale, but two recent and persuasive articles argue that the effect is temporary and that the joint tenancy will revivify if the mortgage is discharged.[256]

Bankruptcy and charging orders also sever,[257] as does a successful claim for family provision as a dependent of a deceased person.[258]

Acquisition of a larger share effects a severance. Suppose, for example that A, B and C hold as beneficial joint tenants[259] when A assigns his interest to B. B holds the 1/3rd share received from A as a tenant in common but B and C remain joint tenants of the original 2/3rds share.[260] Taking payment of a share in a trust fund of personalty will sever, as will an advancement of the share before vesting.[261] If there are 20 houses, of which one is sold and the proceeds divided, there is a tenancy in common in the one, but a joint tenancy left in the 19.[262]

3. Mutual agreement for severance

[16.45] As Page-Wood V-C said simply in *Williams* v. *Hensman*, "A joint tenancy may be severed by mutual agreement."[263] When a monetary share of a trust fund was advanced to one of the eight children in the class, the others covenanting not to sue if too much had been advanced, all children participated and the entire class was severed. The agreement may be to execute mutual wills,[264] to sever, or to deal with the land in a way which implies a severance,[265] though not simply an agreement to sell.[266]

---

[251] LPA 1925 s 53(1)(c).

[252] *Brown* v. *Raindle* (1796) 3 Ves 256, 30 ER 998; *Gould* v. *Kemp* (1834) 2 My & K 304, 39 ER 959; *Kingsford* v. *Ball* (1852) 2 Giff App 1, 66 ER 294.

[253] [1994] *NLJ* 1698 (precedent).

[254] Littleton's *Tenures*, [289]; *Anon* (1560) Dyer 187, 73 ER 412; *Shelley's case* (1581) 1 Co Rep 88b, 76 ER 199; *Clerk* v. *Clerk* (1694) 2 Vern 323, 23 ER 809; *Doe d Marsack* v. *Read* (1810) 12 East 57, 104 ER 23; *Cowper* v. *Fletcher* (1865) 6 B & S 464, 122 ER 1267; *Napier* v. *Williams* [1911] 1 Ch 361.

[255] *Caldwell* v. *Fellowes* (1870) LR 9 Eq 410; *Burnaby* v. *Equitable Reversionary Interest Society* (1885) 28 Ch D 416; *Re Hewett* [1894] 1 Ch 362.

[256] S Nield [2001] *Conv* 462; BC Crown (2001) 117 *LQR* 477.

[257] See below **[28.44ff]**.

[258] *Gratton* v. *McNaughton* [2001] WTLR 1305, Ch D.

[259] Littleton's *Tenures*, [304]; Blackstone's *Commentaries* vol 2, 180. But a release increases the entitlement as joint tenants: *Gore & Snell* v. *Carpenter* (1990) 60 P & CR 456.

[260] *Doe d Hutchinson* v. *Prestwidge* (1815) 4 M & S 178, 105 ER 800; *Wiscot's case* (1599) 2 Co Rep 60b, 76 ER 555; *Newman* v. *Edmunds* (1611) 1 Bulst 113, 80 ER 809; *Napier* v. *Williams* [1911] 1 Ch 361. Merger is no longer automatic: LPA 1925 s 185.

[261] *Williams* v. *Hensman* (1861) 1 John & H 546, 70 ER 862; *Hawkesley* v. *May* [1956] 1 QB 304, 314, held that a request for payment was insufficient to sever, but this seems illogical.

[262] *Leak* v. *Macdowall* (1862) 52 Beav 28, 55 ER 11. Contrast *Re Wilks* [1891] 3 Ch 59 (now a severance by written notice).

[263] (1861) 1 John & H 546, 70 ER 862; P Luther (1995) 15 *LS* 219.

[264] *Re Wilford's Estate* (1879) 11 Ch D 267; *Re Heys* [1914] P 192.

[265] *Burgess* v. *Rawnsley* [1975] Ch 429, 446B, Sir John Pennycuick.

[266] *Nielson-Jones* v. *Fedden* [1975] Ch 222; *Mills* v. *Mifsud* [1996] 2 CLYB 5033, CA (severance).

How should this principle be applied to informal agreements relating to land? In *Burgess* v. *Rawnsley*[267] Honick agreed to buy the freehold reversion of his house from the landlord for £800. Payment of the price was shared by Honick and a friend (Mrs Rawnsley) each paying £400 and the reversion was conveyed to them as beneficial joint tenants. Honick intended to marry Mrs Rawnsley, though he had not told her.[268] Her rejection of his proposal made it apparent that she just wanted the upstairs flat. Honick naturally, but improperly, turned Mrs Rawnsley out. He negotiated to buy out her interest and they settled orally on a price of £750, which under the decision of fact at first instance must be assumed to have been an oral agreement for sale, however flimsy the evidence.[269] Their agreement only lasted overnight, because next day Mrs Rawnsley increased the price to £1,000. With negotiations stalled, Honick died. Mrs Rawnsley was not entitled to the whole house by survivorship because their conduct amounted to a severance. The agreement was unenforceable by action, but its existence was held to be sufficient to create a mutual severance.

Since 1989, a valid contract relating to land requires writing.[270] *Burgess* appeared to focus on the display of intention rather than the formality position,[271] so *Hunter* v. *Babbage*[272] is correct in applying the earlier case to the new formality regime. After Mr Gordon Babbage's divorce, solicitors acting for himself and his ex-wife were in desultory negotiations to settle his ex-wife's claims for property adjustment. The house was worth £100,000 but it was proposed that she would be paid £40,000 in satisfaction of the half share. No final agreement had been reached when he died. A severance had occurred and gave rise to *equal shares*; the informal agreement did sever[273] but was not an enforceable agreement to alter the size of the shares.

4.   Course of conduct

[16.46] *Williams* v. *Hensman* recognised as a distinct[274] head of severance any mutual course of dealing treating the interests as held under a tenancy in common.[275] Knowledge that they were joint tenants is not essential because the relevant intention is to act as tenants in common.[276] Successful case-law falls into three, non-exhaustive, groups. (1) In *Nielson-Jones* v. *Fedden* negotiations falling short of final agreement were held not to sever,[277] but doubts expressed by Lord Denning suggest that this was in fact a sufficient course of conduct to effect a severance.[278] A proposal or offer to

---

[267] [1975] Ch 429, CA; DJ Hayton [1976] *CLJ* 20; FR Crane (1975) 39 *Conv (NS)* 44; JF Garner (1975) 40 *Conv (NS)* 77; SM Bandali (1977) 41 *Conv (NS)* 243.

[268] Lord Denning MR (at 435) made play of the circumstances of their introduction.

[269] Browne LJ (at 443G) and Sir John Pennycuick (at 446A) found the evidence unsatisfactory; Lord Denning MR appeared to feel no doubt.

[270] LP (MP) A 1989 s 2.

[271] [1975] Ch 429, 440C, 444A–C, 446C.

[272] (1995) 69 P & CR 548, Ch D.

[273] At 557–560; query the result in *Pearce* v. *Bulteel* [1916] 2 Ch 544, 556–557.

[274] *Burgess* v. *Rawnsley* [1975] Ch 429, 447, Sir John Pennycuick.

[275] (1861) 1 John & H 546, 557, 70 ER 862 (third head).

[276] At 560–561.

[277] [1975] Ch 222, 230C–D, Walton J; MJ Prichard [1975] *CLJ* 28.

[278] *Burgess* v. *Rawnsley* [1975] Ch 429, 439D, 447A–B, Sir John Pennycuick; *Hunter* v. *Babbage* (1995) 69 P & CR 548, 560, *obiter*.

purchase will not sever.[279] (2) Physical division of a house into two maisonettes might sever, but only[280] if coupled with an intention to hold separately. (3) If property held by joint tenants begins to be used as partnership property this will sever, a principle accepted if not applied , in *Barton* v. *Morris*.[281]

L. PARTITION

[16.47] Unity of possession[282] is necessary to support a co-ownership. Partition is a method of ending co-ownership by creating two or more single ownerships.[283] Division of occupation, say of a house into two flats, will not cause a legal partition but will leave the co-ownership intact.[284] Co-ownership ends when the *right* to share possession is removed by agreement between the parties. One title is split to form two.

Under the pre-1926 law, any legal tenant in common could insist on physical division of the land by a partition action in equity.[285] The result could be ruinous. In *Turner* v. *Morgan*[286] a mill had to be divided into two, leaving each part useless. How could you split chimney stacks, fireplaces, staircases, and toilets?[287] In practice it was often necessary to exercise the statutory discretion to order sale instead.[288]

Lord Birkenhead's reforms made partition redundant after 1925,[289] since co-owned land was held on trust for sale, and the court could execute the trust by ordering sale in preference to physical division. Partition required consent, but if all adult tenants in common did agree, a statutory procedure enabled the trustees to partition.[290] A similar provision for trusts of land[291] allows land to be divided between beneficial tenants in common. Beneficiaries must consent to accept a particular share,[292] though the court also has power to impose a partition.[293] The terms may include equality money, and mortgages may either be settled or left outstanding.[294] Legal title is passed to beneficiaries who are all of full age and absolutely entitled to undivided shares, but if any beneficiary is a minor the trustees must retain that share, and if a share is held in trust that share must be conveyed to the appropriate trustee.[295] Partition may be excluded

---

[279] [1975] Ch 429, 446 (argument not accepted by the court?).

[280] *Greenfield* v. *Greenfield* (1979) 38 P & CR 570; *Gore & Snell* v. *Carpenter* (1990) 60 P & CR 456, 462.

[281] [1985] 1 WLR 1257; *Brown* v. *Oakshot* (1857) 24 Beav 254, 53 ER 355; *Re Hulton* (1890) 62 LT 200; *Jackson* v. *Jackson* (1804) 9 Ves 591, 32 ER 732, Eldon LC.

[282] See above **[16.01]**.

[283] Blackstone's *Commentaries* vol 2, 185; Megarry & Wade (6th ed), [9.098–9.100].

[284] *Greenfield* v. *Greenfield* (1979) 38 P & CR 570; *Sanders* v. *McDonald* [1981] CLYB 1534. Division usually requires planning permission.

[285] Partition at law was possible by statute (though the writ of partition was abolished in 1833), but it always occurred in equity.

[286] (1803) 8 Ves 143, 145, 32 ER 307, Eldon LC.

[287] *Bailey* v. *Hobson* (1869) LR 5 Ch App 180 (waste after partition).

[288] Partition Acts 1868 to 1876; *Dennis* v. *McDonald* [1982] Fam 63, 74, Purchas J at first instance; EH Bodkin (1970) 34 *Conv (NS)* 123; R Cocks [1982] *Conv* 415.

[289] *Re Warren* [1932] 1 Ch 42, 47, Maugham J; *Bull* v. *Bull* [1955] 1 QB 234, 237, Denning LJ.

[290] LPA 1925 s 28(3); *Re Brooker* [1934] Ch 610 Eve J; *Re Gorringe & Braybon's C* [1934] Ch 614n; *Re Thomas* [1930] 1 Ch 194 (not life tenants); TA 1925 s 57 (court order).

[291] TLATA 1996 s 7(1). A commonhold unit must not be divided: Chold and L Ref A 2002 sch 5.

[292] TLATA 1996 s 7(3).

[293] S 14; *Rodway* v. *Landy* [2001] EWCA Civ 471, [2001] Ch 703; see below **[19.06]**.

[294] TLATA 1996 s 7(4).

[295] S 22.

or subjected to the consent of a named person.[296] After a partition the land is shown to be free of the trusts by execution of a deed of discharge, which protects a purchaser's title.[297] If the beneficiaries refuse to agree, the trustee can escape from their positions when each of the beneficiaries is an adult of full age and capacity absolutely entitled, by insisting that the beneficiaries accept a conveyance of the land.[298]

---

[296] S 8(1)–(2).

[297] S 16(4)–(5) (unregistered land); purchasers are not concerned to check that the beneficiary consented: s 16. This can be used to apply to the registry for withdrawal of a restriction affecting a registered title, after which the land can be dealt with by the proprietor as beneficial owner.

[298] TLATA 1996 s 6(2) unless excluded.

17

INFORMAL CO-OWNERSHIP

Family homes. Resulting trusts. Contribution-based constructive trusts. Other explanations for cash injections. Intention based constructive trusts. Holistic trusts. Family homes. Alternatives to common intention.

A. SHARED FAMILY HOMES

1. Trust basis

[17.01] *Pettitt* v. *Pettitt* decided in 1970[1] that the ownership of a family home must be based on a trust,[2] this in turn depending upon what has been agreed, expressly and in writing. The principles applied to registered and unregistered land law are the same.[3] In property law spouses should not be differentiated from those in any other relationship.[4] The categories are contributors and those promised interests. Family law often allows the rearrangement of interests created and recognised in property law.

2. Express trusts

[17.02] Most trusts are express trusts properly evidenced in writing,[5] the declaration being conclusive both of the form of beneficial co-ownership and also the quantification of the beneficial interests. This last follows the formally expressed intention: each party gets what has been promised, with no necessary relation to the financial contributions.[6] Only when the judicial advice to declare the beneficial interests in writing is ignored[7] is beneficial entitlement left to depend upon proof of a resulting or constructive trust.

---

[1] *Pettitt* v. *Pettitt* [1970] AC 777, 795, Lord Reid, 809–810, Lord Hodson, 817, Lord Upjohn.
[2] *Gissing* v. *Gissing* [1971] AC 886, 904H, Lord Diplock, 900B, Viscount Dilhorne; *Burns* v. *Burns* [1984] Ch 317, 326, Fox LJ; *Grant* v. *Edwards* [1986] Ch 638, 659G, Mustill LJ.
[3] Query D Wilde [1999] *Conv* 382.
[4] [1971] AC 886, 899G.
[5] LPA 1925 s 53(1)(b); see above **[16.12ff]**.
[6] *Turton* v. *Turton* [1988] Ch 542, 546F, Nourse LJ.
[7] *Gissing* v. *Gissing* [1971] AC 886, 900H, Lord Diplock; *Lloyds Bank* v. *Rosset* [1991] 1 AC 107, 129C, Lord Bridge; *Roy* v. *Roy* [1996] 1 FLR 541, CA; *Carlton* v. *Goodman* [2002] EWCA Civ 545, [2002] 2 FLR 259, [44], Ward LJ.

3. Informal trusts

[17.03] Shortly after *Pettitt* had settled the trust basis of shared homes, *Gissing*[8] provided the opportunity for Lord Diplock to identify a form of constructive trust based on the common intention of the parties to the purchase of property. In *Lloyd's Bank* v. *Rosset*[9] Lord Bridge subdivided constructive trusts into two categories – those quantified by contributions and those quantified by express agreement – a classification which forms the basis of the current law explained in this chapter.

B. RESULTING TRUSTS

1. Purchase in the name of another

[17.04] Resulting trusts imposed on a purchase in the name of another were already ancient when they were articulated by Eyre CB in *Dyer* v. *Dyer* (1788)[10] thus:

> "[T]he trust of a legal estate, whether freehold . . . or leasehold results to the man who advances the purchase-money."

Purchase in the name of another occurs where the money to buy a property is provided by one person (B) while legal title is conveyed to another (A), so that A holds on resulting trust for B.[11] Modern cases usually concern contribution to the purchase money by two or more people jointly, which creates proportionate beneficial shares,[12] the pattern in *Bull* v. *Bull*,[13] where a mother paid for an extension of her son's house, and *Boland*,[14] where Mrs Boland put in cash from the sale of a previous matrimonial home. Contribution often creates a one-trustee trust in which the beneficial interest cannot be overreached, though the principles are the same in the less troubling cases involving multiple trustees.[15] Resulting trust principles also apply where two trust funds contribute to a joint purchase.[16]

2. Irrelevance of destination of legal title

[17.05] Equity works the same whether legal title is transferred to A alone[17] or to A and B jointly. Transfer to joint names may suggest that both parties are intended to benefit equally, but beneficial entitlement is not presumed from appearance on the legal title, which may be solely to assist in management. Unmarried cohabitants

---

[8] [1971] AC 886, HL.

[9] [1991] 1 AC 107, HL.

[10] (1788) 2 Cox 92; 30 ER 42 (obiter); R Cheung, *Resulting Trusts* (Clarendon, 1997).

[11] *Lloyds Bank* v. *Carrick* [1996] 4 All ER 630, CA.

[12] *Wray* v. *Steele* (1814) 2 V & B 388, 35 ER 366; *Gissing* v. *Gissing* [1971] AC 886, 902E, Lord Pearson.

[13] [1955] 1 QB 234, CA.

[14] [1981] AC 487, HL; *Abbey National BS* v. *Cann* [1991] 1 AC 56, HL (mother-son); *Halifax BS* v. *Brown* [1996] 1 FLR 103, CA.

[15] *Dyer* v. *Dyer* as above.

[16] *Foskett* v. *McKeown* [2001] 1 AC 102 HL, [1998] Ch 265 CA; R Grantham & C Rickett (2000) 63 *MLR* 905; CE Rickett & R Grantham (2000) 116 *LQR* 15.

[17] If B pays all, equitable title will result to B: *Re Share* [2002] BPIR 194, Patten J.

bought a house jointly in *Bernard* v. *Josephs*[18] were equal co-owners because the woman contributed half and not because she was put on the legal title.[19] Unequal entitlement results from unequal contribution to the purchase price by the joint holders of the legal title.[20] A transfer to joint names ought to be treated as a promise of equal beneficial entitlement unless the contrary was clearly proved.[21] This one simple change would avoid much unnecessary litigation.

3. Resulting trust technique

[17.06] Capital contribution gives rise to a corresponding beneficial share under a resulting trust[22]:

> "The fact of advancement of money as between these persons, standing in no relation to each other, . . . raises a trust in the person, vested with the interest, for the benefit of the person, who paid the money."[23]

Shares are proportionate,[24] and mathematical: suppose A pays £50,000 out of a price of £75,000, and the house is later sold for £300,000, then A receives £200,000. Resulting trust technique matches cash contributions to an exactly equivalent beneficial interest, without passing the facts through any conceptual filter. Beneficiaries receive what they pay for.[25] Classical doctrine allowed a resulting trust only from contribution to the initial purchase, but as will be explained below constructive trusts have evolved to overcome this limitation.[26] Purchase money resulting trusts arising from contribution are imposed to carry out the *presumed intention* of the parties, and so contrary evidence can be used to rebut the presumption and to remove the resulting trust.[27] Cash injections might be explained as rent payments, loans, or gifts, and an advancement (that is a gift) might also be presumed from the fact of a close family relationship.[28]

C. CONTRIBUTION-BASED CONSTRUCTIVE TRUSTS

[17.07] Claims to an informal trust failed in *Gissing*, but Lord Diplock's speech fashioned a "new-model" constructive trust, which provides a solid theoretical

---

[18] [1982] Ch 391, CA; JM Thomson (1982) 98 *LQR* 517; J Warburton [1982] *Conv* 444; K Gray [1983] *CLJ* 30; *Carlton* v. *Goodman* [2002] EWCA Civ 545, [2002] 2 FLR 259.

[19] At 404H–405A, Griffiths LJ; *Ivin* v. *Blake* [1995] 1 FLR 70, CA.

[20] *Walker* v. *Hall* [1984] FLR 126, CA; *Springette* v. *Defoe* [1992] 2 FLR 388, CA; HE Norman [1992] *Conv* 347; *Savill* v. *Goodall* [1993] 1 FLR 755, CA.

[21] Law Com WP 94 (1985), [16.5].

[22] *Murless* v. *Franklin* (1818) 1 Swans 13, 18, 36 ER 278, Eldon LC; *Sekhon* v. *Alissa* [1989] 2 FLR 94, 99D, Hoffmann J; *Harwood* v. *Harwood* [1991] 2 FLR 274, 292C, Slade LJ.

[23] *Rider* v. *Kidder* (1805) 10 Ves 360, 366, 32 ER 884, Eldon LC; *The Venture* [1908] P 218, CA.

[24] *Goodman* v. *Gallant* [1986] Fam 106, 110H, Slade LJ, citing *Pettitt* v. *Pettitt* [1970] AC 777, 813–814, Lord Upjohn.

[25] DJ Hayton, *The Law of Trusts* (Sweet & Maxwell, 1989), 145.

[26] *Drake* v. *Whipp* [1996] 1 FLR 826, CA (improvements).

[27] *Re Vandervell's T (No 2)* [1974] Ch 269, 294E–F, Megarry J.

[28] See below **[17.18ff]**.

basis to explain why equity requires that recognition be given to the interest of a contributor.[29]

1. Classification of informal trusts

[17.08] *Gissing* trusts now fall into two categories, even if this technical analysis is often blurred.[30] Trusts based on contribution (those considered here and apparently most common[31]) give a claimant what he has paid for, whereas intention-based trusts[32] give the claimant what has been promised, often more than has been paid for.

Terminology is important and a potent source of confusion,[33] because there are two categories for three types of trust, and judges are more concerned to establish a valid claim than to describe it accurately.[34] Some commentators describe all trusts based on contribution as resulting trusts,[35] so that classification follows from the method of quantification. Orthodox terminology focuses rather on the means of creation, treating a resulting trust as one arising from a cash payment towards acquisition and a constructive trust arising from a common intention.[36] All agree that a trust based on an expressed common intention is constructive, the claimant receiving what he has been promised. This book adopts a threefold classification: (1) resulting, (2) contribution-based constructive, and (3) intention-based constructive.[37] A less certain addition, (4), is the holistic trust.

2. Technique for constructive trusts based on contribution

[17.09] Contribution is evidence of a common intention to give a share and is also the evidence used to quantify the share.[38] Unless it is expressly agreed in advance that particular contributions are to give a particular share,[39] the court must infer an arrangement from the contributions and other conduct, the judicial function being to unravel an arrangement that was actually made at the time but not articulated.[40] The court may not impute an arrangement, it may not impose a solution which it would

---

[29] A Bottomley "Women and Trust(s): Portraying the Family in the Gallery of Law" ch 8 in Bright & Dewar; Grays' *Elements* (3rd ed), ch 7; J Dewar "Land, Law, and the Family Home" ch 13 in Bright & Dewar; JW Harris "Justice, Informality and Home-sharing" ch 5 in Jackson and Wilde; N Hopkins *Informal Acquisition* 87–125; Megarry & Wade (6th ed), [10.017–10.033]; Smith's *Property Law* (4th ed), 129–164; Thompson's *Modern LL* (Oxford, 2001), ch 9; MP Thompson "Reform of the Law relating to Property Rights on the Breakdown of Cohabitation" ch 6 in Jackson and Wilde.

[30] New categories are possible: *James* v. *Williams* [2000] Ch 1, CA.

[31] *Lloyds Bank* v. *Rosset* [1991] 1 AC 107, 132H, Lord Bridge.

[32] See below [17.22].

[33] *Drake* v. *Whipp* [1996] 1 FLR 826, 827C, Peter Gibson LJ.

[34] DJ Hayton, *Law of Trusts* (Sweet & Maxwell, 1989), 145.

[35] *Allen* v. *Snyder* [1977] 2 NSWLR 685, 692A Glass JA; Hanbury & Martin *Modern Equity* (16th ed, Sweet & Maxwell, 2001), 264–271; DJ Hayton as above, 144.

[36] This is usual terminology: *Rosset* [1991] 1 AC 107, Lord Bridge, *Gissing* [1971] AC 886, Lord Diplock; *Cowcher* v. *Cowcher* [1972] 1 WLR 425, 431, Bagnall J; Megarry & Wade, (6th ed), [10.028].

[37] P Sparkes (1991) 11 *OJLS* 39.

[38] *Grant* v. *Edwards* [1986] Ch 638, 646H–647B, Nourse LJ, 655B, Browne-Wilkinson V-C. Contribution gives a share as under a right rather than a life interest: *Ivin* v. *Blake* [1995] 1 FLR 70, CA.

[39] *Gissing* v. *Gissing* [1971] AC 886, 905D, 906A.

[40] *Lloyds Bank* v. *Rosset* [1991] 1 AC 107, 132H, Lord Bridge; M Dixon [1991] *CLJ* 38; JD Davies (1990) 106 *LQR* 539; S Gardner (1991) 54 *MLR* 126; MP Thompson [1990] *Conv* 314.

have been reasonable for the couple to adopt if they had applied their minds to the matter.[41]

Special justification is required to enforce a trust lacking a written memorandum,[42] the basis being that is unconscionable to deny a promised beneficial interest after the claimant has incurred, in general terms, a detriment,[43] or more specifically after he has made a substantial contribution. Payment is easily proved and protects creditors from excessive claims.[44]

3. Patterns of contribution

[17.10] Beneficial interests should usually be fixed, once and for all, on acquisition,[45] though evidence of the intention at that time can be gathered from everything done up to the time that the couple separate.[46] If a couple arrange to buy a house equally, the shares are unaffected by the fact that one party is afterwards unable to make payments, while out of work or while caring for a child.[47] But the need for a common intention can also be used to deny interests. In *Pettitt* v. *Pettitt*[48] work done to improve a matrimonial home did not operate to create a constructive trust, because there was no intention to create such a trust at the time of acquisition. Payments of mortgage interest in another case between 1966 and 1968 showed nothing about the state of the mind of the parties when a house was bought in 1962.[49]

Decisive breaks in the pattern should raise an inference that the arrangement had been altered, adapting the beneficial interests to changes in the course of a relationship,[50] reflecting events.[51] A breach should occur where a cohabitant moves in and starts making mortgage repayments after the initial purchase by the other cohabitee, or where the couple agree to fund a major extension.[52] Beneficial interests fixed by an express trust require formal variation by written disposition.[53]

The need for a shared intention at the moment of acquisition can be overcome by a *contribution variable* constructive trust.[54] In *Gissing* Lord Diplock thought it not unlikely that parties would agreed to such beneficial interests as could be seen in

---

[41] *Rosset* at 132H, Lord Bridge; but see below at **[17.26]**, **[17.31]**.

[42] LPA 1925 s 53(2).

[43] *Gissing* v. *Gissing* [1971] AC 886, 905B, Lord Diplock; *Burns* v. *Burns* [1984] Ch 317, 326, Fox LJ; *Grant* v. *Edwards* [1986] Ch 638, 654D, Browne-Wilkinson V-C.

[44] *Re Gorman* [1990] 1 WLR 616, Div Ct; *Re Pavlou* [1993] 1 WLR 1046, Millett J.

[45] *Lloyds Bank* v. *Rosset* [1991] 1 AC 107, 132F, Lord Bridge; *Burns* v. *Burns* [1984] Ch 317, 327, Fox LJ; *Bernard* v. *Josephs* [1982] Ch 391, 404E–F, Griffiths LJ.

[46] *Bernard* [1982] Ch 391, 399F, 404C–D, 404G; approved *Burns* [1984] Ch 317, 327A.

[47] *Bernard* at 404A, Griffiths LJ.

[48] [1970] AC 777, HL.

[49] *Cowcher* v. *Cowcher* [1972] 1 WLR 425, 441A.

[50] *Gissing* v. *Gissing* [1971] AC 886, 906A, Lord Diplock; *Grant* v. *Edwards* [1986] Ch 638, 651h, Mustill LJ; *Lloyds Bank* v. *Rosset* [1991] 1 AC 107, 132F, Lord Bridge.

[51] *Austin* v. *Keele* (1987) 72 ALR 651–652, Lord Oliver; JD Davies (1990) 106 *LQR* 539.

[52] *Bernard* v. *Josephs* [1982] Ch 391, 404, Griffiths LJ; *Mollo* v. *Mollo* [2000] WTLR 227, Ch D.

[53] LPA 1925 s 53(1)(c); *Cowcher* v. *Cowcher* [1972] 1 WLR 425, 432E, Bagnall J; *Ivin* v. *Blake* [1995] 1 FLR 70, 87E, Glidewell LJ.

[54] Apparently this is sufficiently certain: *Cowcher* v. *Cowcher* [1972] 1 WLR 425, 430D, Bagnall J; *Richards* v. *Dove* [1974] 1 All ER 888, 894d, Walton J; *Jeffries* v. *Stevens* [1982] STC 639, 651, Walton J; *Walker* v. *Hall* [1984] FLR 126, 136, Lawton LJ. See equity texts for a general discussion of certainty. See also the holistic trust, below at **[17.31]**.

retrospect to be fair,[55] and this provides a convenient intellectual device to cope with spasmodic mortgage repayments or where an express agreement promises an unquantified share.[56] Equity weighs all cash inputs, later mortgage repayments, and indirect contributions to the family budget which enable the mortgage to be paid, as well as major improvements.[57]

4. Contributions referable to acquisition

[17.11] A common intention about the ownership of a house can only be inferred from contributions which are strictly referable to its acquisition. When Lord Bridge said in *Rosset*[58] that "it is extremely doubtful whether anything less will do", he accepted the restrictive decision in *Winkworth* v. *Edward Baron Developments Co*,[59] that a payment by a director to a company which had already bought, the payment being made after completion of the company's purchase, was not a contribution to the acquisition of title. Simon Gardner has argued that removal of the referability filter would improve the law without excessive technical dislocation.[60]

No beneficial interest arises from payments of rent, partially because a capital contribution is required,[61] but mainly because rent pays for the use and occupation of the land:[62] in *Passee* v. *Passee*[63] two women contributors each paid £2.50 a week towards *the mortgage* and secured a beneficial interest, whereas the owner's son who paid £3 weekly *as rent* and so secured no beneficial interest.[64] Indeed the court can take into account the value of occupation received as a deduction from monetary contributions.[65]

Contributions must be substantial. *Pettitt* v. *Pettitt*[66] concerned a matrimonial home vested in the wife's name in which her husband claimed a share based on work in redecoration and improvement which, although costing £1,000, enhanced the value by only £300. This was too insubstantial. So too was Mrs Rosset's investment of time in supervising the builders who were renovating a farmhouse to make it fit for her family. Express arrangements can be supported by relatively small acts of detriment.[67]

---

[55] [1971] AC 886, 909D–E.

[56] *Stokes* v. *Anderson* [1991] 1 FLR 391, 399, Nourse LJ; *Passee* v. *Passee* [1988] 1 FLR 263, CA.

[57] *Midland Bank* v. *Cooke* [1995] 4 All ER 562, 574d–e, Waite LJ; P Wylie (1995) 25 *Fam Law* 633; S Gardner (1996) 112 *LQR* 378.

[58] [1991] 1 AC 107, 133; *Gissing* [1971] AC 886, 909G, Lord Diplock.

[59] [1986] 1 WLR 1512, 1516, Lord Templeman; J Warburton [1987] *Conv* 217; *Kowalczuk* v. *Kowalczuk* [1973] 2 All ER 1042, CA Contrast the successful piercing of the corporate veil in *Re Schuppan (No 2)* [1997] 1 BCLC 256. Also *Winsper* v. *Perrett* [2002] WTLR 927, Ch D (reimbursement of part of price was a contribution).

[60] S Gardner (1993) 109 *LQR* 263; S Wong (1998) 18 *LS* 369.

[61] *Savage* v. *Dunningham* [1974] Ch 181; FR Crane (1973) 37 *Conv (NS)* 440; but see *Malayan Joint Credit* v. *Jack Chia* [1986] AC 549, 560G–H, Lord Brightman.

[62] *Annen* v. *Rattee* [1985] 1 EGLR 136, CA.

[63] [1988] 1 FLR 263, 266G–267B, CA; J Warburton [1988] *Conv* 361.

[64] *Cracknell* v. *Cracknell* [1971] P 356, CA; *Davis* v. *Vale* [1971] 1 WLR 1022, 1028C; *Hazell* v. *Hazell* [1972] 1 WLR 301, 303B; *Bernard* v. *Josephs* [1982] Ch 391, 410C, Kerr LJ; *Ivin* v. *Blake* [1995] 1 FLR 70, CA.

[65] *Thomas* v. *Fuller-Brown* [1988] 1 FLR 237, CA.

[66] [1970] AC 777 HL; J Tiley [1969] *CLJ* 191; G Jones [1969] *CLJ* 196; PV Baker (1969) 85 *LQR* 330.

[67] *Lloyds Bank* v. *Rosset* [1991] 1 AC 107, 133F–H, Lord Bridge.

5. Direct and indirect contributions

[17.12] Cash injections used[68] to buy a house give a corresponding share,[69] for example money derived from the sale of a previous house,[70] or savings put towards a deposit.[71] A council tenant has the right to buy his property at a discount calculated according to the length of time that it has been his home, and this should normally be seen as a cash contribution by the qualifying tenant,[72] or at least as evidence of a common intention that he should benefit from it.[73] In applying these rules the ownership of the money which is used may well become the vital question.[74]

Indirect contributions are filtered through an inferred intention which allows a more flexible approach to the kinds of contributions which register. Equity is able to find a cash equivalent to indirect contributions,[75] that is any "material sacrifice by way of contribution to or economy in the general family expenditure",[76] such as payments by a wife of household expenses in order to free the husband to pay the mortgage.[77] Contributions from a business built up by joint efforts are themselves joint.[78] An express agreement may be needed if anything indirect is to be counted.[79] Certainly effort expended in building up the couple's relationship is too indirect to give any interest in the family home.

6. Mortgage repayments

[17.13] Mortgage payments technically repay a debt, but constructive trust theory is based on the economic reality[80] that a mortgage is used to buy a house. Any regular pattern of mortgage repayments will readily justify the inference necessary for the

---

[68] Money advanced for a purchase but not used will be held on resulting trust: *Briggs* v. *Rowan* [1991] EGCS 6.

[69] *Gissing* v. *Gissing* [1971] AC 886, 905D; *Lloyds Bank* v. *Rosset* [1991] 1 AC 107, 133.

[70] *Williams & Glyn's Bank* v. *Boland* [1981] AC 487 HL; *Abbey National BS* v. *Cann* [1991] 1 AC 56 HL; *Tinsley* v. *Milligan* [1994] 1 AC 340, HL.

[71] *Halifax BS* v. *Brown* [1996] 1 FLR 103, CA (half a deposit of £150 against a loan of £330,000).

[72] *Springette* v. *Defoe* [1992] 2 FLR 388, CA; HE Norman [1992] *Conv* 347; *Savill* v. *Goodall* [1993] 1 FLR 388, CA (left open); *Evans* v. *Hayward* [1995] 2 FLR 511, CA. The presumption that the discount is to be treated as a contribution to the price may be rebutted by establishing that the transaction was a sham to protect a bankrupt against his creditors: *Ashe* v. *Mumford* (2000) 33 HLR 67, CA.

[73] *Marsh* v. *Von Sternberg* [1986] 1 FLR 526, Bush J; JE Adams [1989] *Conv* 155; *Evans* v. *Hayward* [1995] 2 FLR 511, 516D–516C, Dillon LJ.

[74] Married Women's Property Act 1964 s 1 (housekeeping); MC Cullity (1969) 85 *LQR* 530 (joint bank accounts).

[75] *Gissing* v. *Gissing* [1971] AC 886, 896, Lord Reid, 903, Lord Pearson.

[76] *Gissing* at 905D, Lord Diplock.

[77] *Hargrave* v. *Newton* [1971] 1 WLR 1611, 1613 (reward for finding Great Train Robbery money); *Cooke* v. *Head* [1972] 1 WLR 518, CA (income pooled in joint kitty); *Hazell* v. *Hazell* [1972] 1 WLR 301, CA; J Eekelaar (1972) 88 *LQR* 333; *Burns* v. *Burns* [1984] Ch 317, 328, Fox LJ.

[78] *Nixon* v. *Nixon* [1969] 1 WLR 1676, CA; *Windeler* v. *Whitehall* [1990] 2 FLR 505; *Chan Pui Chun* v. *Leung Kam Ho* [2002] BPIR 7233, Ch D.

[79] *Rosset* [1991] 1 AC 107, 133A, Lord Bridge; *R* v. *Robson* (1991) 92 Crim App R 1, CA; *Howard* v. *Jones* (1989) 19 Fam Law 231, CA; *Ivin* v. *Blake* (1994) 67 P & CR 263, CA.

[80] *Diwell* v. *Farnes* [1959] 1 WLR 624, CA; *Gissing* v. *Gissing* [1971] AC 886, 906F; *Bernard* v. *Josephs* [1982] Ch 391, 404D, Griffiths LJ.

creation of a constructive trust,[81] though nothing can be inferred from isolated payments.[82] Acceptance of liability as a joint borrower will not give any interest if it is done to help a friend obtain mortgage finance and the friend makes all repayments.[83] No importance attaches to the form of the mortgage: a repayment mortgage more obviously buys an interest in the house, but so too do monthly payments towards an endowment policy intended to repay the loan.[84]

Should repayments be assessed on their gross value, including interest, or only on the capital element? In the early years of an instalment mortgage most of what is repaid is interest,[85] so it is not fair to balance an interest payment against hard cash used for a deposit,[86] though the point is open.[87] There is no objection to the aggregation of gross mortgage repayments over a period of time to give a proportionate share of that part of the property which is attributable to the mortgage.[88]

A large sum used for a substantial one-off reduction in the debt should give a proportionate interest in the property.[89]

7.   Balancing the deposit and the mortgage

[17.14] Resulting trust technique[90] is to view the introduction of a mortgage advance as a cash contribution to the purchase price equal to the amount of the loan.[91] On the first day, the beneficial interest arising from the mortgage contribution will be zero, as the redemption figure will be debited against the share arising from the mortgage advance. In later years, when the loan has been fully discharged, the mortgage contribution will come to stand at its full proportion as against the deposit, with nothing to debit.[92]

Constructive trust technique is less satisfactory as a means of balancing a cash deposit and a mortgage advance. Unless beneficial entitlement is equal,[93] it is not correct to deduct the mortgage redemption figure from the sale proceeds and then to

---

[81] *Gissing* v. *Gissing* [1971] AC 886, 905D, 907E, Lord Diplock; *Lloyds Bank* v. *Rosset* [1991] 1 AC 107, 133, Lord Bridge; *Bernard* v. *Josephs* [1982] Ch 391, 404, Griffiths LJ; *Burns* v. *Burns* [1984] Ch 317, 329B, Fox LJ, 344F–345A, May LJ.

[82] *Young* v. *Young* [1984] FLR 375, CA (man had paid only £175).

[83] *Carlton* v. *Goodman* [2002] EWCA Civ 545, [2002] 2 FLR 259.

[84] *Smith* v. *Clerical Medical & General Life Assurance Society* [1993] 1 FLR 47, CA; *Cowcher* v. *Cowcher* [1972] 1 WLR 425, 441G, 441H–442B, Bagnall J; *Heseltine* v. *Heseltine* [1971] 1 WLR 342, 345E; *Ulrich* v. *Ulrich* [1968] 1 WLR 180, 186E–F, Lord Denning MR.

[85] *Falconer* v. *Falconer* [1970] 1 WLR 1333, CA (debt reduced in 8 years from £2,660 to £2,500); *Young* v. *Young* [1984] FLR 375, CA (£200 over 16 months).

[86] *Rimmer* v. *Rimmer* [1953] 1 QB 63, 74; *Cowcher* v. *Cowcher* [1972] 1 WLR 425; J Levin (1972) 35 *MLR* 547; *Diwell* v. *Farnes* [1959] 1 WLR 624, 633; *Cracknell* v. *Cracknell* [1971] P 356, 361C–D, Lord Denning MR; *Cooke* v. *Head* [1972] 1 WLR 518; *Hall* v. *Hall* (1982) 3 FLR 379; *Walker* v. *Hall* [1984] FLR 126, 130E.

[87] *Passee* v. *Passee* [1988] 1 FLR 263, 267G–268A, Nicholls LJ; J Warburton [1988] *Conv* 361.

[88] *Turton* v. *Turton* [1988] Ch 542, 548F, Nourse LJ; J Warburton [1987] *Conv* 378.

[89] *Burns* v. *Burns* [1984] Ch 317, 328, Fox LJ.

[90] P Sparkes (1991) 11 *OJLS* 39.

[91] If there is an agreement to service it equally then in equal cash contribution: *Marsh* v. *Von Sternberg* [1986] 1 FLR 526, 534G, Bush J.

[92] *Huntingford* v. *Hobbs* [1993] 1 FLR 736, CA; also *Harwood* v. *Harwood* [1991] 2 FLR 274, CA; *McHardy & Sons* v. *Warren* [1994] 2 FLR 338, CA; *Halifax BS* v. *Brown* [1996] 1 FLR 103, CA.

[93] *Rimmer* v. *Rimmer* [1953] 1 QB 63, 74; *Ulrich* v. *Ulrich* [1968] 1 WLR 180, 186E–F; *Bernard* v. *Josephs* [1982] Ch 391, 400F–H.

determine the beneficial shares in the divisible equity.[94] The numerical fraction representing each share necessarily varies according to the amount of the mortgage that has been discharged and so a specific date is required for quantification,[95] but the correct method remains to be settled.[96]

8. Improvements

[17.15] There is no direct liability to pay for improvements,[97] but an obligation may arise to pay over a proportion of the value of a property when the land is sold, under modern law as under the old law of partition.[98] In other words there may be a lien for repayment of the cost of the work.[99] Substantial[100] works of improvement may also give rise to a beneficial share under a constructive trust. Do not expect a share from putting up a shelf, touching up paint-work, or gardening,[101] nor from any other work normally carried out by members of a family on the family home.

Substantial[102] improvements to matrimonial property will normally give entitlement to an enhanced beneficial interest[103] without any express or inferred agreement under section 37 of the Matrimonial Proceedings and Property Act 1970. This confirms the majority decision in *Jansen* v. *Jansen*.[104] A husband spent so much time and effort converting a house owned by his wife into self-contained flats, that he had to give up his university course to concentrate on the renovation work. He took a share of the profit his work had created. The section has been applied[105] to partial installation of central heating,[106] major works of internal renovation,[107] repairs and improvements.[108] The enhanced beneficial interest is such "as may seem in all the circumstances . . . just".[109]

No share is acquired by substantial improvement of non-matrimonial property. In *Thomas* v. *Fuller-Brown*[110] an unemployed man did work to improve the house owner

[94] *Cooke* v. *Head* [1972] 1 WLR 518, CA; *Falconer* v. *Falconer* [1970] 1 WLR 1333; *Cracknell* v. *Cracknell* [1971] P 356, 361C; *Hargrave* v. *Newton* [1971] 1 WLR 1611. Query the approach in *Midland Bank* v. *Cooke* [1995] 4 All ER 562, CA.

[95] *Passee* v. *Passee* [1988] 1 FLR 263, 272A, CA.

[96] *Equity & Law Home Loans* v. *Prestidge* [1992] 1 WLR 137, 142D–E, Mustill LJ; *Marsh* v. *Von Sternberg* [1986] 1 FLR 526, 533D, Bush J; *Huntingford* v. *Hobbs* [1993] 1 FLR 736, Steyn LJ dissenting.

[97] *Thomas* v. *Thomas* (1850) 5 Exch 28, 155 ER 13; *Re Coulson's T* (1907) 97 LT 754; *Leigh* v. *Dickeson* (1884) 15 QBD 60, CA.

[98] *Re Jones* [1893] 2 Ch 461; *Re Cook's Mortgage* [1896] 1 Ch 923; *Kenrick* v. *Mountsteven* (1890) 48 WR 141; *Leigh* v. *Dickeson* (1884) 15 QBD 60, CA; *Re Pavlou* [1993] 1 WLR 1046, Millett J.

[99] *Lake* v. *Craddock* (1733) 3 P Wms 158, 24 ER 1011; *Gross* v. *French* [1976] 1 EGLR 129.

[100] *Pettitt* [1970] AC 777, HL.

[101] *Button* v. *Button* [1968] 1 WLR 457, CA; *Pettitt* v. *Pettitt* [1970] AC 777, HL.

[102] *Pettitt* is unaffected: Law Com 25 (1969), [58].

[103] The claim is proprietary rather than a personal claim in restitution: *Firth* v. *Mallender* [2001] WTLR 1109, CA.

[104] [1965] P 478, CA, Denning MR and Davies LJ; J Tiley [1969] *CLJ* 81; *Pettitt* [1970] AC 777, minority view of Lords Reid and Diplock; Law Com 25 (1969), [57], *Davis* v. *Vale* [1971] 1 WLR 1022, 1025G–1026D, CA.

[105] *Samuel's Trustees* v. *Samuels* [1975] 1 EGLR 94, Walton J; *Kowalczuk* v. *Kowalczuk* [1973] 2 All ER 1042, CA; *Griffiths* v. *Griffiths* [1973] 1 WLR 1454 Arnold J.

[106] *Re Nicholson* [1974] 1 WLR 476, Pennycuick V-C (replacement of gas cooker ignored).

[107] *Davis* v. *Vale* [1974] 1 WLR 1021, CA.

[108] *Re Pavlou* [1993] 1 WLR 1046, Millett J.

[109] Matrimonial Proceedings and Property Act 1970 s 37.

[110] [1988] 1 FLR 237, CA; *Rosset* [1991] 1 AC 107, HL; *Ungurian* v. *Lesnoff* [1990] Ch 206, Vinelott J.

by his female partner in return for his keep, but acquired no interest. An agreement or common intention to give a share is essential, and it must usually be express to permit clear quantification,[111] unless it can be inferred from very substantial work[112] or expense.[113]

Interests gained by improvement that fall to be quantified on constructive trust principles will depend upon what common intention can be inferred.[114] A financial equivalent has to be discovered,[115] a question of some nicety where the improvement obviates the need for repair.[116] However, the real problem is to decide between the cost of the improvement work or the increase in value of the house.[117] *Re Nicholson* supports the added value approach.[118]

D. OTHER EXPLANATIONS FOR CASH INJECTIONS

1. Loan

[17.16] This is distinct from a contribution, since a loan has to be repaid and usually with interest.[119] A lender should not be paid twice over, so that a finding that money is lent precludes a finding of trust.[120] In real life the distinction blurs, because of inaccurate use of language,[121] inaccurate documentation,[122] or the drift of human affairs. In *Hussey* v. *Palmer*[123] an elderly widow was invited to live with her daughter and son-in-law provided she paid for construction of a bedroom extension. After the parties had fallen out, she sued for return of the money, but it was decided that it had not been a loan. In a second action, this time posited on the assumption that the sum was a contribution, the woman inconveniently gave evidence that she had provided the money as a loan! One view was that this precluded a finding of a beneficial interest under a resulting or constructive trust but a majority of the Court of Appeal took pity on a plaintiff who clearly had a valid claim to something and allowed her payment to stand as a contribution. Too much emphasis can be placed on the initial finding of fact.

---

[111] *Davis* v. *Vale* [1971] 1 WLR 1022, CA.
[112] *Davis* v. *Vale* [1971] 1 WLR 1022, CA; *Cooke* v. *Head* [1972] 1 WLR 518, CA; *Re Nicholson* [1974] 1 WLR 476, 482H, Pennycuick V-C; *Eves* v. *Eves* [1975] 1 WLR 1338, CA; *Drake* v. *Whipp* [1996] 1 FLR 826, CA. Unsuccessful cases are *Rosset* [1991] 1 AC 109, HL; *Ungurian* v. *Lesnoff* [1990] Ch 206, Vinelott J.
[113] *Hussey* v. *Palmer* [1972] 1 WLR 1286; *Bernard* v. *Josephs* [1982] Ch 391, 404E, Griffiths LJ; *Burns* v. *Burns* [1984] Ch 317, 327D, Fox LJ; *Spence* v. *Brown* (1988) 18 Fam Law 291, CA; *Sekhon* v. *Alissa* [1989] 2 FLR 94, Hoffmann J; *Briggs* v. *Rowan* [1991] EGCS 6.
[114] Commonly it is to give whatever interest is fair: *Cooke* v. *Head* [1972] 1 WLR 518, CA.
[115] *Passee* v. *Passee* [1988] 1 FLR 263, CA (plaintiff's share increased from 40% to 60%); J Warburton [1988] *Conv* 361.
[116] *Lloyds Bank* v. *Rosset* [1991] 1 AC 107, 131C, 131F.
[117] *Re Pavlou* [1993] 1 WLR 1046, Millett J.
[118] [1974] 1 WLR 476, Pennycuick V-C; also *Pettitt* at first instance.
[119] *Bennet* v. *Bennet* (1879) 10 Ch D 474, CA.
[120] *Re Sharpe* [1980] 1 WLR 219, Browne-Wilkinson J; *Richards* v. *Dove* [1974] 1 All ER 888; *Noble* v. *Ferdinand* [1992] CLYB 564.
[121] *Spence* v. *Brown* (1988) 18 Fam Law 291, CA (not really loan but part of price for living in house).
[122] *Risch* v. *McFee* (1990) 61 P & CR 42, CA (loan agreement drawn by solicitor); *Stokes* v. *Anderson* [1991] 1 FLR 391, CA (promissory note).
[123] [1972] 1 WLR 1286, CA; (1973) 89 *LQR* 2.

2. Proved gift

[17.17] No capital share arises from money provided as a gift. Oral evidence is allowed to prove a gift, particularly cogent evidence being receipt of income from the land[124] and possession,[125] though payment of interest favours a finding of loan.[126] All acts, contemporaneous and later, are admissible both for[127] and against[128] the person who made them.

3. Gift (advancement) presumed from family relationship

[17.18] A presumption of advancement (that is of gift) may arise from the family relationship between the person paying the price and the person in whose name title is taken.[129] Nineteenth century equity adopted a rigid doctrine based on set relationships, but changes in social organisation in the intervening years have left those rules looking most unjust.[130] The strength of the presumption has diminished[131] to the extent that four members of the Lords in *Gissing* thought that it rarely had a role to play, certainly not between a couple sharing a house.[132] Paradoxically its vitality has been reasserted in a recent illegality case.[133]

(1) Parental gifts

[17.19] Transfers of property from father to child are presumed to be as a gift,[134] there being a "moral obligation to give",[135] even if the child is wealthy[136] or middle-aged.[137] The presumption was much less clear with an illegitimate child,[138] but modern statutes make it irrelevant whether a child's parents are or are not married, and this should have a knock-on effect in advancement. Mother to child is more problematic. Older cases referred neutrally to parents, but during the nineteenth century the presumption of gift was limited to fathers to correlate with the moral obligation to

---

124 *Rider* v. *Kidder* (1805) 10 Ves 360, 32 ER 884; *Re Gooch* (1890) 62 LT 384. But a reservation of income for life is consistent with a gift of capital.

125 *Stock* v. *McAvoy* (1872) LR 15 Eq 55, 59, Wickens V-C.

126 *Bennet* v. *Bennet* (1879) 10 Ch D 474.

127 Civil Evidence Act 1968 s 2, now superseded by Civil Evidence Act 1995 s 7 (1).

128 *Shephard* v. *Cartwright* [1955] AC 431, HL; RE Megarry (1953) 69 *LQR* 169; *Sidmouth* v. *Sidmouth* (1840) 2 Beav 447, 455, 48 ER 1254, Langdale MR; *Warren* v. *Gurney* [1944] 2 All ER 472.

129 *Tinsley* v. *Milligan* [1994] 1 AC 340, 372B, Lord Browne-Wilkinson.

130 *Pettitt* v. *Pettitt* [1970] AC 777, 824A–D, Lord Diplock.

131 At 793E–G, Lord Reid, 811G, Lord Hodson, 824A–D, Lord Diplock.

132 [1971] AC 886, 907, Lord Diplock; *Falconer* v. *Falconer* [1970] 1 WLR 1333, 1335H–1336A, Lord Denning MR; *McGrath* v. *Wallis* [1995] 2 FLR 114, CA.

133 *Tinsley* v. *Milligan* [1994] 1 AC 340, HL.

134 A selection: *Grey* v. *Grey* (1677) 1 Ch Cas 296, 22 ER 809; *Dyer* v. *Dyer* (1788) 2 Cox 92, 30 ER 42; *Sidmouth* v. *Sidmouth* (1840) 2 Beav 447, 48 ER 1254 (Lord Eldon's brother); *Re Engelbach's E* [1924] 2 Ch 348 (daughter); *Warren* v. *Gurney* [1944] 2 All ER 472 (rebutted on facts); *Shephard* v. *Cartwright* [1955] AC 431, HL; *Webb* v. *Webb* [1991] 1 WLR 1410; *McGrath* v. *Wallis* [1995] 2 FLR 114, CA.

135 *Bennet* v. *Bennet* (1879) 10 Ch D 474, 477, Jessel MR.

136 *Elliot* v. *Elliot* (1677) 2 Ch Cas 231, 22 ER 922.

137 *Hepworth* v. *Hepworth* (1870) LR 11 Eq 10.

138 *Beckford* v. *Beckford* (1774) Lofft 490, 98 ER 763; *Soar* v. *Foster* (1858) 4 K & J 152, 70 ER 64 (unsatisfactory).

provide capital to a child to set him up in life, a dominant historical tradition[139] which survives to this day,[140] though the base presumption is of little moment given how easy it is to prove that a mother intends a gift.[141] Modern law does not distinguish the maintenance obligations of mother and father and advancement ought to be gender neutral.[142]

A person adopting the position of parent is said to stand "in loco parentis", and a presumption of advancement can arise.[143] The giver might be a stepfather,[144] a widowed mother,[145] or a grandfather who has taken over the parental role.[146]

(2) Spouses and cohabitants

[17.20] Advancement may have been presumed from husband to wife either because of the frequency with which men did make gifts to their wives, or, more probably, because of the former economic dependency of married women.[147] It seemed natural to match the common law obligation to provide for a wife with a presumption that transfers to her were meeting this obligation, whether by direct transfer to her name,[148] by paying mortgage instalments,[149] or by transfers of property to joint names.[150] Engaged couples stand on the same footing as spouses,[151] so a gift is presumed from a male fiancé to a female fiancée,[152] even if the marriage plans subsequently fall through. No gift is presumed by a wife to her husband, so the husband holds the property on resulting trust for his wife, whether he purchases in his wife's name[153] or she makes a voluntary transfer to him.[154] The lack of gender neutrality can only be explained historically.

If moral obligation was the basis of advancement, one would expect a strong presumption of advancement by a man to a woman with whom he was living out of marriage, especially given the severity of the social the penalties attaching to a cohabiting woman under Victorian settlements, but in fact no advancement was

---

[139] *Re De Visme* (1863) 2 De GJ & Sm 17, 46 ER 280; *Bennet* v. *Bennet* (1879) 10 Ch D 474, CA; *Bull* v. *Bull* [1955] 1 QB 234, CA (rebuttal on the evidence). For gift see *Batstone* v. *Salter* (1875) LR 10 Ch App 431.

[140] *Sekhon* v. *Alissa* [1989] 2 FLR 94, Hoffmann J; G Kodilinye [1990] *Conv* 213; *Ivin* v. *Blake* (1994) 67 P & CR 263, CA; A Dowling [1996] *Conv* 274.

[141] *Bennet*, at 479, Jessel MR; *Dewar* v. *Dewar* [1975] 1 WLR 1532, Goff J.

[142] *Gross* v. *French* [1976] 1 EGLR 129, 132L, Scarman LJ.

[143] *Bennet* at 477, Jessel MR.

[144] *Re Paradise Motor Co* [1968] 1 WLR 1125, CA (stepson).

[145] *Sayre* v. *Hughes* (1868) LR 5 Eq 376; *Batstone* v. *Salter* (1875) LR 10 Ch App 431; *Re Orme* (1883) 50 LT 51, Kay J.

[146] *Ebrand* v. *Dancer* (1680) 2 Ch Cas 26; 22 ER 829; contrast *Re Vinogradoff* [1935] WN 68 (surely unreal?).

[147] *Pettitt* v. *Pettitt* [1970] AC 777, 793E–G, Lord Reid.

[148] *Harrods* v. *Tester* [1937] 2 All ER 236, 239C.

[149] *Moate* v. *Moate* [1948] 2 All ER 486; *Silver* v. *Silver* [1958] 1 WLR 259; *Richards* v. *Richards* [1958] 1 WLR 1116; however a husband paying a mortgage should not be seen as making a gift to his wife.

[150] *Re Eykyn's Ts* (1877) 6 Ch D 115 (spouse and stranger); *Re Harrison* (1920) 90 LJ Ch 186; *Re Figgis* [1969] 1 Ch 123.

[151] Law Reform (MP) Act 1970 s 2(1).

[152] *Moate* v. *Moate* [1948] 2 All ER 486; *Mossop* v. *Mossop* [1989] Fam 77, 84F, Sir F Lawton; *Shaw* v. *Fitzgerald* [1992] 1 FLR 357.

[153] *Re Dixon* [1900] 2 Ch 561, CA; *Mercier* v. *Mercier* [1903] 2 Ch 98, CA.

[154] *Heseltine* v. *Heseltine* [1971] 1 WLR 342, CA.

presumed,[155] even where there was a high degree of emotional commitment, for example after an invalid attempt to marry.[156] Usually today there will be proof of the actual intention.[157] Advancement was never presumed between two lesbians. The House of Lords applied the old presumptions in *Tinsley* v. *Milligan*,[158] though it was a novelty to apply them to a *Gissing* constructive trust.[159] Milligan introduced about £3,500 cash, but her successful counterclaim for an equal share of the beneficial interest could only arise under a constructive trust,[160] and the court should have found what common intention existed without any regard to artificial presumptions, but ignoring all evidence of illegality.

4. Rebuttal by proof of contribution

[17.21] Without any presumptions there would be a very wide sea without a chart, but the rules can be displaced by hard evidence, even so as to create a trust.[161] Any evidence is now considered by the courts (illegality apart[162]), so it should be rare to have to decide a case on the presumption alone. Frequently the presumption is vindicated by the actual evidence,[163] but it is equally possible that the evidence will contradict the presumption.[164] Evidence may show that a different name was used for convenience[165] that oral statements negated a gift,[166] or that there was an unexecuted trust deed.[167] Possession of the land may provide important evidence.

E. INTENTION-BASED CONSTRUCTIVE TRUSTS

1. Common intention

[17.22] Intention-based constructive trusts give the claimant what he has been promised, as a supplement to any interest already bought by contribution. In *Re Densham* the wife contributed £585 out of a purchase price of £5,650, thus acquiring by contribution a beneficial interest amounting to perhaps 1/9th,[168] but

---

[155] *Rider* v. *Kidder* (1805) 10 Ves 360, 32 ER 884 (cohabitant); *Lowson* v. *Coombes* [1998] Ch 373, CA.

[156] *Soar* v. *Foster* (1858) 4 K & J 152, 70 ER 64 (marriage to deceased wife's sister).

[157] Avoidance of a transfer for undue influence obviously negates any intention to give: *Simpson* v. *Simpson* [1992] 1 FLR 601; B Dale [1989] *Conv* 63; *Re Figgis* [1969] 1 Ch 123.

[158] [1994] 1 AC 340, HL.

[159] [1992] Ch 310, 340B, Lloyd LJ.

[160] [1994] 1 AC 340, 371E, Lord Browne-Wilkinson; [1992] Ch 310, 340A–C, Lloyd LJ. Query whether there was a resulting trust on these facts: Law Com CP 157 (1998), [3.63–3.64].

[161] Ashburner's *Equity* (Butterworths, 2nd ed by D Browne, 1953), 110 n 2.

[162] *Tinsley* [1994] 1 AC 340 HL; *Webb* v. *Webb* [1992] 1 All ER 17 at first instance; A Briggs (1994) 110 *LQR* 526.

[163] *Dyer* v. *Dyer* (1788) 2 Cox 92, 30 ER 42.

[164] *Hatley* v. *Liverpool Victoria Legal Friendly Society* (1918) 88 LJKB 237 (insurance to cover burial expenses obviously not gift); *Jones* v. *Jones* [1977] 1 WLR 438, CA.

[165] *Marshall* v. *Crutwell* (1875) LR 20 Eq 328; *Hoddinott* v. *Hoddinott* [1949] 2 KB 406; *Re Figgis* [1969] 1 Ch 123, 144–6; MC Cullity (1969) 85 *LQR* 530.

[166] *Warren* v. *Gurney* [1944] 2 All ER 472, CA.

[167] *McGrath* v. *Wallis* [1995] 2 FLR 114, CA.

[168] [1975] 1 WLR 1519, 1531B, Goff J; F Webb (1976) 92 *LQR* 489.

the evidence showed clearly that the parties intended the property to be held equally.[169]

2. Proof of a common intention

[17.23] Direct proof of a common intention is required,[170] usually[171] at the time of acquisition.

(1) Express agreement

[17.24] A constructive trust of this type is based on an oral declaration of trust,[172] and indeed is particularly easy to prove if a declaration is prepared but left unsigned,[173] but generally the penalty for failure to use formality may be small. Quantification is based on the interest promised, possibly a half share,[174] but possibly some other definite share, or a share of indeterminate size.[175] It is no matter that the arrangement is imperfectly remembered or imprecise, provided the couple together[176] have "entered into an agreement", "made an arrangement", or "reached an understanding" to share[177] or have always shared everything.[178] *Hammond* v. *Mitchell*[179] concerned a £400,000 bungalow at the junction of the M11 and M25 in Essex shared by a 40 year old second-hand car dealer and a 21 year old former bunny. After "a painfully detailed retrospect" the judge found that the man had promised the woman that they would share the house equally. Endearments did indeed cost him dear.

(2) Excuse cases

[17.25] Two classic excuses were mentioned in *Rosset*.[180] In *Eves* v. *Eves*[181] Janet and her cohabitee Stuart Eves bought a house to live in following the birth of a daughter. Title was taken in his sole name, because, he told her, she could not hold legal title while she was under 21. Stuart said in evidence that he never intended that the house should be in joint names, and she was in any event of age by the time of completion.

---

[169] The agreement for the larger share was void against the husband's trustee in bankruptcy: IA 1986 s 339.

[170] *Lloyds Bank* v. *Rosset* [1991] 1 AC 107, 132F, Lord Bridge; *Grant* v. *Edwards* [1986] Ch 638, 654, Browne-Wilkinson V-C.

[171] Possibly later: *Austin* v. *Keele* (1987) 61 AJLR 605, 609, Lord Oliver.

[172] A formal express trust or enforceable contract precludes a constructive trust: *Lloyds Bank* v. *Carrick* [1996] 4 All ER 630, CA.

[173] *Re Gorman* [1990] 1 WLR 616, Div Ct; *McGrath* v. *Wallis* [1995] 2 FLR 114, CA.

[174] *Tinsley* v. *Milligan* [1992] Ch 310, 337H, [1994] 1 AC 340, 371C–D; *Savill* v. *Goodall* (1993) 25 HLR 588, 592–593, Nourse LJ; *Clough* v. *Killy* (1996) 72 P & CR D22, CA (express agreement determines quantification).

[175] *Stokes* v. *Anderson* [1991] 1 FLR 391, CA.

[176] *Savill* v. *Goodall* (1993) 25 HLR 588, 593, Nourse LJ.

[177] *Lloyds Bank* v. *Rosset* [1991] 1 AC 107, 127G, 132F, Lord Bridge; *Halifax BS* v. *Brown* [1996] 1 FLR 103, CA (no discussion).

[178] *Midland Bank* v. *Dobson* [1986] 1 FLR 171, 174; *McHardy & Sons* v. *Warren* [1994] 2 FLR 338, CA.

[179] [1991] 1 WLR 1127, Waite J; L Clarke & R Edmunds (1992) 22 *Fam Law* 523; A Lawson [1992] *Conv* 218; P O'Hagan (1993) 56 *MLR* 224.

[180] [1991] 1 AC 107, 133, Lord Bridge; P Milne (1995) 145 *NLJ* 423, 456.

[181] [1975] 1 WLR 1338, CA.

He provided all the money. Her contribution consisted of heavy work in the house, breaking up concrete with a 14 lb. sledgehammer, and demolishing a garden shed. The case is supported today on the majority view:[182] there was a bargain between the parties that the claimant would contribute her labour in return for an agreed beneficial interest (found to be one-quarter) which was proved on the facts by the excuse. Similar was *Grant* v. *Edwards*,[183] where a house was conveyed into the name of the male cohabitee, the excuse given to the woman being that the presence of her name on the legal title would prejudice her pending divorce proceedings.[184] This also implied that the woman was to have a beneficial interest,[185] this time a half.

3. Failure to establish a common intention

[17.26] According to *Rosset*,[186] acquisition of a larger share than is contributed depends upon an express common intention, a view which casts doubt on many earlier cases.[187] With her husband, Mrs Rosset had bought a derelict farmhouse to renovate, but all the money was provided by the husband, much of it coming from a Swiss family trust fund on the (very unsound) terms that his wife was to have no beneficial interest. Her claim to a half beneficial share failed in the absence of substantial money contributions and of any common intention. A tourniquet was applied by the Lords to constrict intention-based trusts to cases where the intention is clearly proved.

Inference of a common intention is permitted, in the sense of making explicit an agreement which the parties did actually make but left uncrystallised. Imputation, in the sense of the imposition of a fair solution on parties who did not decide in advance how they should own their home, is now way out of court,[188] although the original decision to reject that technique was narrow.[189]

Some attempts have been made to revive imputation theory after *Pettitt* by relying on the minority speeches.[190] In *Midland Bank* v. *Cooke*[191] a property was conveyed to a husband, a mortgage was obtained in his name, and he made the repayments. The deposit was provided as a wedding present to the couple, giving the wife 6.5% of the value of the house. Each party denied on oath having made any arrangement about

---

[182] Brightman J and Browne LJ.

[183] [1986] Ch 638, CA; B Sufrin (1987) 50 *MLR* 94; DJ Hayton [1986] *CLJ* 394; J Warburton [1986] *Conv* 291.

[184] No common intention is inferred from the use of joint names; see above at **[17.05]**.

[185] At 649A, 653D, Mustill LJ.

[186] [1991] 1 AC 107, 133A, Lord Bridge; JD Davies (1990) 106 *LQR* 539; MP Thompson [1990] *Conv* 314; M Dixon (1991) 50 *CLJ* 38; S Gardner (1991) 54 *MLR* 126; P O'Hagan (1991) 42 *NILQ* 238.

[187] Eg dicta in *Grant* v. *Edwards* [1986] Ch 638, CA; *Re Nicholson* [1974] 1 WLR 476; numerous Denning cases.

[188] *Re Densham* [1975] 1 WLR 1519, 1525D, Goff J; *Grant* v. *Edwards* [1986] Ch 638, 652D, Mustill LJ; *Hammond* v. *Mitchell* [1991] 1 WLR 1127, Waite J (Spanish house).

[189] *Pettitt* [1970] AC 777, 810E, Lord Hodson, 816E, Lord Upjohn, 804G–H, Lord Morris; *Gissing* [1971] AC 886, 904E, Lord Diplock, 900D, Viscount Dilhorne, 898, Lord Morris; for imputation were Lord Reid (at 896F) and Lord Pearson (at 902G).

[190] *Hussey* v. *Palmer* [1972] 1 WLR 1286, Phillimore LJ; *Richards* v. *Dove* [1974] 1 All ER 888; *Eves* v. *Eves* [1975] 1 WLR 1338, 1342G, Lord Denning MR; *Burns* v. *Burns* [1984] Ch 317, 325C, Waller LJ.

[191] [1995] 4 All ER 562, CA; *Drake* v. *Whipp* [1996] 1 FLR 826, CA.

ownership of the house, but Waite LJ felt that the court could still infer one. This was in truth an illegitimate exercise in imputation.[192]

4. Detriment

[17.27] An oral declaration of trust cannot be enforced without detriment. When Mr Gissing left the matrimonial home he told Mrs Gissing not to worry because the house was hers, but her failure to act on that oral declaration meant that she could not enforce it.[193] *Gissing*[194] recognises that a common structure lies behind all claims to a beneficial interest arising from joint acquisition, since it must be unconscionable for the estate owner to deny the claimant a beneficial interest, unconscionability that is only demonstrated if the claimant has acted to his detriment in the reasonable belief that by so acting he was acquiring a beneficial interest in the land.[195] After an irrevocable change of legal position,[196] it is no longer possible to go back to square one, so one is forced to go forwards and enforce the promise.

5. Reliance

[17.28] This acts as a filter for conduct during a relationship, sorting out relevant acts and discarding others from consideration.[197] The need for a link emerged from *Eves* v. *Eves*.[198] Janet was given an excuse for her exclusion from the legal title, which showed a common intention that she was to have a share. Was this promise linked to the heavy work of renovation she carried out to make the home they had bought fit to live in? The Court of Appeal found no difficulty in treating this as "part of the bargain" from the nature of the work itself.[199]

Direct contributions may be assumed to be made in reliance on the promise of a share,[200] unless they are tiny.[201] Indirect contributions can also act as detriment, where there is an express agreement or where payments of household expenses by a woman frees her man to pay mortgage instalments.[202] Wider acts, not referable to acquisition of the house, may nevertheless constitute a detriment,[203] where, for

---

[192] N Glover & P Todd (1996) 16 *LS* 325; M Oldham [1996] *CLJ* 194; P O'Hagan (1997) 60 *MLR* 420; S Gardner (1996) 112 *LQR* 378.

[193] *Gissing* v. *Gissing* [1971] AC 886, 905D–E, Lord Diplock; *Re Densham* [1975] 1 WLR 1519, 1524E, Goff J; *Midland Bank* v. *Dobson* [1986] 1 FLR 171, 175, CA; *Lloyd's Bank* v. *Rosset* [1991] 1 AC 107, 132, 132G, Lord Bridge.

[194] [1971] AC 886, 905D–G, Lord Diplock; *Lloyds Bank* v. *Rosset* [1991] 1 AC 107, 132–133, Lord Bridge.

[195] *Burns* v. *Burns* [1984] Ch 317, 326, Fox LJ; *Grant* v. *Edwards* [1986] Ch 638, 654E, Browne-Wilkinson V-C.

[196] *Austin* v. *Keele* (1987) 61 AJLR 605, 610, Lord Oliver.

[197] A Lawson (1996) 16 *LS* 218.

[198] [1975] 1 WLR 1338, CA.

[199] At 1345D, Brightman J, 1343C–E, Browne LJ.

[200] *Austin* v. *Keele* (1987) 61 ALJR 605, 610, Lord Oliver.

[201] *Eves* v. *Eves* [1975] 1 WLR 1338, CA; *Grant* v. *Edwards* [1986] Ch 638, CA; *Lloyds Bank* v. *Rosset* [1991] 1 AC 107, 133, Lord Bridge.

[202] *Grant* v. *Edwards* [1986] Ch 638, 649F, 654B, 656D–F.

[203] At 657A–C, Browne-Wilkinson V-C; he cited: *Jones* v. *Jones* [1977] 1 WLR 438, CA; *Pascoe* v. *Turner* [1979] 1 WLR 431, CA.

example, a woman provides emotional support for a man's risky business ventures,[204] or a person continues to work for an employer,[205] or gives up work, forgoes pension rights, gives up a tenancy with security of tenure, or has children.[206] Non-financial contributions can be taken into account,[207] and this may particularly benefit women.

No precise test for reliance has been formulated, but the means of inferring a link in the law of proprietary estoppel is almost identical, and cross-fertilisation should occur.[208] Once detriment is proved reliance may be presumed,[209] unless the legal owner can show some other explanation for the claimant's conduct.[210] Relevant factors in establishing reliance are a conscious decision to act on the common intention,[211] conduct which would not otherwise have been carried out,[212] the legal owner's knowledge of the acts of detriment,[213] and the degree of material sacrifice.[214]

6. Exclusion of proprietary estoppel claim

[17.29] Restrictions on the recognition of constructive trust claims cannot be avoided by recasting a claim in proprietary estoppel.[215] A person who has made no contribution and has not been promised any share,[216] cannot plead that he had an expectation of a share induced by the owner of the house. To put it another way a claim to a beneficial share by way of proprietary estoppel is a claim to a constructive trust.[217] Were that not so, a switch of field could potentially let in new claims[218] – based on unilateral expectations[219] and agreements inferred from acts other than contribution. Professor Hayton argued that the distinction between constructive trust claims and estoppel claims is illusory,[220] but *Rosset* has shut the front door, and it seems that estoppel claims will not be allowed to creep in by the back.[221] It can be most unfair, but there it is. One day the House of Lords should assimilate the two doctrines.[222]

---

[204] *Hammond* v. *Mitchell* [1991] 1 WLR 1127, Waite J; L Clarke & R Edmunds (1992) 22 *Fam Law* 523; A Lawson [1992] *Conv* 218.

[205] *Austin* v. *Keele* (1987) 61 AJLR 605, PC.

[206] JD Davies (1990) 106 *LQR* 539.

[207] J Montgomery [1987] *Conv* 16.

[208] *Grant* v. *Edwards* [1986] Ch 638, 656G–H, Browne-Wilkinson V-C, 653B, Mustill LJ; B Sufrin (1987) 50 *MLR* 94; DJ Hayton [1986] *CLJ* 394; J Warburton [1986] *Conv* 291; see below at **[23.28ff]**.

[209] *Greasley* v. *Cooke* [1980] 1 WLR 1306, CA.

[210] [1986] Ch 638, 656B, Browne-Wilkinson V-C; *Austin* v. *Keele* (1987) 61 ALJR 605, 610, Lord Oliver (domestic rather than commercial contexts).

[211] At 656B, Browne-Wilkinson V-C.

[212] At 656B, Browne-Wilkinson V-C.

[213] *Lloyds Bank* v. *Rosset* [1989] Ch 350, 379, Nicholls LJ.

[214] *Gissing* v. *Gissing* [1971] AC 886, 905D, Lord Diplock.

[215] This passage can only be fully understood after reading the explanation of estoppel; see below **[23]**.

[216] Eg *Burns* v. *Burns* [1984] Ch 317, CA.

[217] *Birmingham Midshires* v. *Sabherwal* (2000) 80 P & CR 256, CA; C Harpum (2000) 116 *LQR* 341; *Austin* v. *Keele* (1987) 72 ALR 579, 587, PC; *Gissing* [1971] AC 886, 905C, Lord Diplock; *Lloyd's Bank* v. *Rosset* [1991] 1 AC 107, 129D, 133C–G, Lord Bridge; also in CA: *Grant* v. *Edwards* [1986] Ch 638, 656B–657D, Browne-Wilkinson V-C; *Sen* v. *Headley* [1991] Ch 425, 439, Nourse LJ; *Stokes* v. *Anderson* [1991] 1 FLR 391, 399, Nourse LJ.

[218] J Eekelaar [1987] *Conv* 93; MP Thompson [1990] *Conv* 314; DJ Hayton [1990] *Conv* 370.

[219] Constructive trusts require a common intention.

[220] DJ Hayton [1990] *Conv* 370; DJ Hayton (1993) 109 *LQR* 485.

[221] P Ferguson (1993) 109 *LQR* 114; J Hayes (1993) 137 *SJ* 606.

[222] *Stokes* v. *Anderson* [1991] 1 FLR 391, 399D, Nourse LJ.

7. Quantification

[17.30] Constructive trusts based on an express oral intention give whatever beneficial interests were agreed, whether equally or in some other fixed proportion, irrespective of contribution. Proof of the agreement quantifies the share. In *Grant* v. *Edwards*[223] money to settle a fire insurance claim was paid into a joint account which demonstrated that the property was held equally. An agreement to share an ex-council house equally was established in *Savill* v. *Goodall*[224] by evidence of a discussion between the couple, their children and social workers.

F. HOLISTIC TRUSTS

[17.31] Often an agreement to share leaves the exact proportions undefined, so that the agreement is for the shares to be fixed later. In *Eves* v. *Eves*[225] the work done was worth less than the share claimed, and alone would not have justified any claim,[226] but Janet Eves was held to be entitled to a quarter share.[227] The decision to award one quarter is unprincipled, and it could just as well have been one half or one eighth.[228] Nourse LJ found the same type of trust in *Stokes* v. *Anderson*[229] and found no practical alternative but to decide what was fair, on the facts one half of the ex-wife's one half share being acquired. *Midland Bank* v. *Cooke*[230] reasserted the need for "broad brush" quantification in a case where there was some contribution, but also other acts which justified a larger share. *Rosset* apparently requires an express agreement before larger acts can be taken into account, but Waite LJ's brush was so large as to sweep aside this principle; *Rosset*, he said, imposes a barrier which must be overcome in order to claim *any* share, but that once over that hurdle the court can review *all* conduct in order to assess the size of the share. The judge shall "undertake a survey of the whole course of dealing between the parties relevant to their ownership and occupation of the property." Lord Denning also favoured looking at a whole range of factors, including earnings and contributions, statements made to outsiders, savings, repayments, cash inputs, work done on the property, planning and design, and the history of the transaction.[231] That conflicted with *Gissing*,[232] as *Cooke* conflicts with *Rosset*.[233] However *Le Foe* v. *Le Foe*[234] follows the new vogue for the lower courts overruling inconvenient House of Lords decisions. Lord Bridge was too restrictive to be followed, so the court applied the *Cooke* holistic trust. Once some contribution had been discovered, the court could determine what the parties would have decided,

---

[223] [1986] Ch 638, CA.
[224] [1993] 1 FLR 755, CA.
[225] [1975] 1 WLR 1338, CA; JD Davies (1990) 106 *LQR* 539.
[226] *Lloyds Bank* v. *Rosset* [1991] 1 AC 107, 133G, Lord Bridge.
[227] [1975] 1 WLR 1338, 1345G, Brightman J.
[228] *Grant* v. *Edwards* [1986] Ch 638, 657, Browne-Wilkinson V-C.
[229] [1991] 1 FLR 391, 399F, Nourse LJ; *Hammond* v. *Mitchell* [1991] 1 WLR 1127, 1137F–G.
[230] (1995) 27 HLR 733, CA.
[231] [1972] 1 WLR 518, 521H–522B, CA.
[232] *Re Densham* [1975] 1 WLR 1519, 1530G, Goff J.
[233] It implies a fixed date for quantification, on separation, followed by equitable accounting.
[234] [2001] EWCA Civ 1870; affirming [2001] 2 FLR 970, Fam Div.

and so on the facts a half share was awarded to a woman who had contributed much less.

There is no automatic assumption that family assets are held equally,[235] but equal shares are commonly awarded simply because that is the most likely agreement to be made between cohabitants.[236]

G. ILLEGALITY

[17.32] Factually *Tinsley* v. *Milligan*[237] can be encapsulated in a few sentences. Two lesbians purchased a lodging house as a joint business venture. When it was registered in the sole name of one of them, Tinsley, their joint object was to enable Milligan to make fraudulent claims for social security benefits. After a quarrel, the legal owner claimed possession. The House of Lords refused possession, and instead declared that the contributor was entitled to joint beneficial ownership and an order for sale. Milligan's hands were unclean, but this was irrelevant since she was able to plead her case without revealing that fact.[238]

1. Common law rules

[17.33] Illegality[239] is an absolute bar to an action to enforce an executory contract.[240] That does not prevent property passing under an illegal contract between A and B, to give B sufficient ownership to maintain an action against C.[241] Actions are permitted if founded on rights acquired under the contract, provided that the case can be pleaded without placing any reliance on the illegality.[242]

2. Equitable rule

[17.34] A party to an illegal transaction has unclean hands, which one might expect to bar any equitable claim.[243] However, Lord Browne-Wilkinson and a majority of the Lords applied common law principles to Milligan's equitable counter-claim, and thought that the rules should be fused.[244] An equitable claim is allowed if it can

---

[235] *Pettitt* v. *Pettitt* [1970] AC 777, HL.

[236] *Cobb* v. *Cobb* [1955] 1 WLR 731, CA; *Gissing* v. *Gissing* [1971] AC 886, 908D, Lord Diplock.

[237] [1994] 1 AC 340 HL; ALG Berg [1993] *JBL* 513; H Stowe (1994) 57 *MLR* 441; N Enonchong (1995) 111 *LQR* 135; N Enonchong (1994) 14 *OJLS* 295; M Halliwell [1994] *Conv* 62.

[238] *Mortgage Express* v. *Robson* [2001] EWCA Civ 887, [2001] 2 All ER (Comm) 886.

[239] Law Com CP 157 (1998).

[240] *Holman* v. *Johnson* (1775) 1 Cowp 341, 343, 98 ER 1120, Lord Mansfield CJ; *Thomson* v. *Thomson* (1802) 7 Ves 470, 32 ER 190.

[241] *Bowmakers* v. *Barnet Instruments* [1945] KB 65, CA; *Sajan Singh* v. *Sardara Ali* [1960] AC 167, 176–177, Lord Denning; [1992] Ch 310, 326B, 335E.

[242] *Simpson* v. *Bloss* (1816) 7 Taunt 246, 249, 129 ER 99, Gibbs CJ; *Tinsley* v. *Milligan* [1994] 1 AC 340, 377A–B, Lord Browne-Wilkinson; *Tribe* v. *Tribe* [1996] Ch 107, 134H, Millett LJ.

[243] *Cottington* v. *Fletcher* (1740) 2 Atk 155, 26 ER 498, Lord Hardwicke LC; *Muckleston* v. *Brown* (1801) 6 Ves 52, 69, 31 ER 934, Lord Eldon LC.

[244] *Tinsley* v. *Milligan* [1994] 1 AC 340, 375B–C; JE Martin [1992] *Conv* 153; *Silverwood* v. *Silverwood* (1997) 74 P & CR D9, CA (transfer); *Mortgage Express* v. *Robson* [2001] EWCA Civ 887, [2001] 2 All ER (Comm) 886.

pleaded without reliance on any improper purpose. Earlier cases on express trusts,[245] voluntary transfers with no presumption of advancement,[246] pre-1926 voluntary conveyances without advancement,[247] purchase money resulting trusts[248] and estoppel[249] were ambivalent. As analysed by the majority, Milligan had contributed money to a property raising a presumption of resulting trust, proved by pleading the contribution.

This reasoning depends upon the assumption that a resulting trust arose between the two cohabitants. *Tinsley* v. *Milligan* actually concerned a constructive trust. Each of them introduced £3,500 cash from a previous home, and the rest of the price was raised by a bank loan of £12,000 in Tinsley's name. Milligan's counterclaim for an equal share required the loan to be treated as an equal contribution, that is a constructive trust.[250] So, her counterclaim did, in truth, rely upon an express[251] and illegal[252] agreement.

3. Repentance

[17.35] Both law[253] and equity[254] give the opportunity of repentance (a *locus poenitentiae*[255]) before a fraud is carried into effect at all.[256] It was too late in *Tinsley* v. *Milligan*, but not in *Tribe* v. *Tribe*.[257] The plaintiff stood to lose his shares in the family company if the company's landlord was successful in a claim for damages for disrepair. To avoid this claim he made a notional transfer of the shares to his son. Actually the disrepair claim was settled and the shares were not imperilled. The father then sued for their return. He needed to rebut the presumption of advancement by leading evidence that the transfer was merely a nominal transfer to defeat creditors, and the Court of Appeal upheld his right to do so. He had to rely on evidence of his illegal intention, but he had repented in time.[258] Genuine contrition is not required.[259]

---

[245] *Ayerst* v. *Jenkins* (1873) LR 16 Eq 275; *Phillips* v. *Probyn* [1899] 1 Ch 811 North J.

[246] *Chettiar* v. *Chettiar* [1962] AC 294, PC; *Gascoigne* v. *Gascoigne* [1918] 1 KB 223 DC; *Tinker* v. *Tinker* [1970] P 136, CA, rejected at [1994] 1 AC 340, 353D–E, 361E–G; *Lowson* v. *Coombes* [1998] Ch 373, CA.

[247] *Benyon* v. *Nettlefold* (1850) 3 Mac & G 94, 101, 42 ER 196, Truro LC; *Haigh* v. *Kaye* (1872) LR 7 Ch App 469; *Coultwas* v. *Swan* (1870) 20 LT 539, on appeal (1871) 19 WR 485.

[248] *Curtis* v. *Perry* (1802) 6 Ves 739, 31 ER 1285, Lord Eldon; *Cantor* v. *Cox* [1976] 2 ECLR 104, Plowman V-C (said to be wrongly decided in *Lowson* v. *Coombes* [1998] Ch 373, CA); *Tinsley* v. *Milligan* [1994] 1 AC 340, 366G–367D, 367G, Lords Jauncey and Lowry.

[249] *Maharaj* v. *Chand* [1986] AC 898, PC (licence to occupy a hut).

[250] [1994] 1 AC 340, 371–372C, Lord Browne-Wilkinson; [1992] Ch 310, 340A–C, Lloyd LJ. The opposite conclusion is reached in Law Com CP 157 (1999), [3.59–3.64].

[251] [1992] Ch 310, 337H, Lloyd LJ.

[252] R Thornton [1993] *CLJ* 394, 396.

[253] *Tappenden* v. *Randall* (1801) 2 Bos & P 467, 126 ER 1388; *Taylor* v. *Bowers* (1876) 1 QBD 291, CA; *Tribe* v. *Tribe* [1996] Ch 107, 125C–H.

[254] *Birch* v. *Blagrave* (1755) Amb 264, 27 ER 176; *Platamone* v. *Staple* (1815) Coop G 250, 35 ER 548; *Cecil* v. *Butcher* (1821) 2 Jac & W 565, 37 ER 744; *Symes* v. *Hughes* (1870) LR 9 Eq 475.

[255] [1994] 1 AC 340, 374A–E, Lord Browne-Wilkinson; *Chetty* v. *Servai* (1908) 24 TLR 462, 462, PC.

[256] *Re Great Berlin Steamboat Co* (1884) 26 Ch D 616.

[257] [1996] Ch 107, CA; G Virgo [1996] *CLJ* 23; FD Rose (1996) 112 *LQR* 545; P Creighton (1997) 60 *MLR* 102.

[258] JK Grodecki (1955) 71 *LQR* 254; B Elkan (1955) 91 *LQR* 317; R Merkin (1981) 97 *LQR* 420.

[259] At 259–260 Millett LJ, 247h, Nourse LJ.

Had the father chosen someone to whom he was unrelated, he could have relied on his resulting trust.[260]

4. Discretion

[17.36] If so there was merit in Nicholls LJ's "public conscience test" enabling the court to balance the adverse consequences of granting relief against the adverse consequences of refusing relief,[261] to work out just how unclean they were. This test was unanimously rejected by the Lords as an approach to property cases or equitable claims.[262]

The Law Commission are consulting about whether to allow the courts a discretion to determine the weight to be given to illegality.[263]

H. FAMILY HOMES

1. Husband and wife

[17.37] Before 1970, Lord Denning's Court of Appeal developed the concept of the family asset[264] which assumed that a house and other property belonging to a family was held equally for husband and wife. The spouses in *Rimmer* v. *Rimmer* held equally even though the husband contributed £2,000 and his wife only £280.[265] This doctrine dealt easily with one stereotypical case, of a young couple without much money who shared their lives and shared the adventure of buying a joint home. Though fair to women involved in child rearing, its apparent simplicity proved illusory in cases involving short term relationships, remarriage later in life, and couples of unequal wealth. It was demolished by *Pettitt* in 1970[266] which established that the ownership of a family home must be based on a trust.[267] Shortly afterwards *Gissing*[268] provided the opportunity for Lord Diplock to identify a form of constructive trust based on the common intention of the parties to the purchase of property. This forms the basis of the current law explained in this chapter. Viscount Dilhorne deprecated the error of differentiating spouses from people in any other relationship.[269] The legal principles used in a case like *Boland* apply to any case between an estate owner and a contributor,[270] as opposed to specifically between husband and wife.

---

[260] *Rowan* v. *Dann* (1991) 64 P & CR 202, CA.

[261] *Tinsley* v. *Milligan* [1992] Ch 310, 319H.

[262] *Tinsley* v. *Milligan* [1994] 1 AC 340, 353C–361G; H Stowe (1994) 57 *MLR* 441, 442–446.

[263] Law Com CP 157 (1999); this is much like the public conscience test: *Tinsley* v. *Milligan* [1992] 310, 317–321, Nicholls LJ.

[264] *Hine* v. *Hine* [1962] 1 WLR 1124, 1127; *Fribance* v. *Fribance (No 2)* [1957] 1 WLR 384; *Gissing* v. *Gissing* [1969] 2 Ch 85, 93; *Ulrich* v. *Ulrich* [1968] 1 WLR 180, 189H, Diplock LJ.

[265] [1953] 1 QB 63, CA.

[266] *Pettitt* v. *Pettitt* [1970] AC 777, 795, Lord Reid 809–810, Lord Hodson, 817, Lord Upjohn.

[267] *Gissing* v. *Gissing* [1971] AC 886, 904H, Lord Diplock, 900B, Viscount Dilhorne; *Burns* v. *Burns* [1984] Ch 317, 326, Fox LJ; *Grant* v. *Edwards* [1986] Ch 638, 659G, Mustill LJ.

[268] [1971] AC 886, HL.

[269] [1971] AC 886, 899G.

[270] [1981] AC 487, 502F, Lord Wilberforce.

It is only acceptable to distinguish married and unmarried couples as a result of a statutory provision. In relation to matrimonial homes, property law is supplemented by the courts' power to redistribute family property on divorce or judicial separation.[271] It is much less important to determine whether husband or wife owns the matrimonial home, or how it is shared, since what matters is whether a divorce court will think that it should be transferred by the wife to her husband, or by him to her. Provision is often made for an ex-wife who is left to bring up the children in what was the family home.

2. Spouses and outsiders

[17.38] Contribution to a family home will secure an equitable interest which is capable of binding purchasers, or the trustee in bankruptcy of the legal owner. *McHardy & Sons* v. *Warren*[272] is an archetypal case in which the contest was between a wife and her husband's trade creditors. Something was salvaged for the family by treating the deposit provided by the husband's father as a present to the couple in equal shares, giving the wife a share proportionate to half the deposit. Proprietary claims to the home must meet strict criteria so that there is a clear reason why a lender should be bound. It might be consistent with this policy to allow a more generous claim against the other spouse personally, but in fact English law links the two claims together, and a wife can only claim against her husband the same share that she could claim against his creditors.[273]

3. Unmarried couples

[17.39] One million or more couples live together without marrying, thereby opting (usually unconsciously) to sit outside the family law powers of redistribution on divorce, and to rely solely on trust law principles. Equitable rules[274] are based primarily on money and so are entirely gender-neutral in formulation. Given the historical imbalance in earning capacity between the sexes, practical results tilt in favour of men and against women, though the extent of the discrimination can be exaggerated.[275]

The unmarried woman claimant in *Burns* v. *Burns*[276] had done everything which did not count towards an interest in the house, but had failed to do anything which equity would register. *Burns* directs a spotlight on the injustice of constructive trust doctrine.[277] The couple had lived together and raised a family without marrying, but the home was acquired in 1963 in the sole name of the man. He provided all the finance for its acquisition and paid the mortgage, while the woman looked after the

---

[271] Matrimonial Causes Act 1973 part II.
[272] [1994] 2 FLR 338, CA.
[273] *Midland Bank* v. *Cooke* [1995] 4 All ER 562, 574f, Waite LJ. But query if this dictum is correct.
[274] J Mee *The property rights of unmarried cohabitees* (Hart, 1998).
[275] R Probert (2001) 13 *CFLQ* 275.
[276] [1984] Ch 317, CA; R Ingleby [1984] *CLJ* 227.
[277] It may be so grotesque as to be an infringement of the human right to family life under European Convention on Human Rights art 8: *Times* June 5th 1998.

children and the house.[278] When the children had grown up and she found work as a driving instructor, her earnings were not applied directly to the house, but rather to the following items:

gifts of clothing to the man and the children;
housekeeping (using an allowance of £60 per week);
payment of rates and telephone bills; and
purchase of a dishwasher, washing machine, and armchairs.[279]

Fox LJ concluded that none of these payments was referable to the acquisition of the house. For most of the eighteen years that they lived in the house, she had nothing to contribute.[280]

No particular rights are acquired through cohabitation.[281] Griffiths LJ confirmed this gender neutral doctrine in *Bernard* v. *Josephs*, but added that the nature of the relationship is a very important factor in determining what inferences should be drawn from the way that the parties have conducted their affairs,[282] and a degree of commitment to the relationship may be vital. Less can be inferred from the "undetermined and indeterminable"[283] relationship of a couple who choose not to marry in order to retain their independence.[284] "What might be sensible between husband and wife might not be so between two brothers".[285] Cases fail consistently if there is neither express agreement nor contribution.[286] In *Windeler* v. *Whitehall*,[287] for example, a woman living with a theatrical agent acted as hostess when he entertained business clients, but these were not financial contributions and he had not promised her any share explicitly.[288]

4. Unmarried couples with children

[17.40] Power to redistribute property exists where cohabitees have children.[289] The order may be sought by a parent or a person who has a residence order, that is an order regulating the housing of the child. Commonly an unmarried mother will seek the order against the father[290] of the child. The object of property adjustment is to provide for children as dependants. The order must be sought while the child is under

---

[278] *Nixon* v. *Nixon* [1969] 1 WLR 1676, CA, considered a wife's services to be equal to financial contributions, but this was discredited by *Pettitt* and *Gissing*.

[279] *Gissing* v. *Gissing* [1971] AC 886, 909G (furniture, cooker, fridge and turfing); *Richards* v. *Dove* [1974] 1 All ER 888 (furniture).

[280] [1984] Ch 317, 327F, Fox LJ.

[281] *Dennis* v. *MacDonald* [1981] 1 WLR 810, 814B, Purchas J; *Grant* v. *Edwards* [1986] Ch 638, 651F, Mustill LJ.

[282] [1982] Ch 391, 402E–F, Griffiths LJ, 408D, Kerr LJ; J Warburton [1982] *Conv* 444.

[283] At 400A–B Lord Denning MR (were a couple "engaged"?); C Harpum (1982) 2 *OJLS* 277, 277.

[284] At 403B–C.

[285] *Gordon* v. *Douce* [1983] 1 WLR 563, 565H–566A, Fox LJ.

[286] *Thomas* v. *Fuller-Brown* [1988] 1 FLR 237, CA; *Howard* v. *Jones* (1989) 19 Fam Law 231; *Hammond* v. *Mitchell* [1991] 1 WLR 1127; *Ivin* v. *Blake* (1994) 67 P & CR 263, CA.

[287] [1990] 2 FLR 505, Millett J.

[288] No interest is derived from a promise of a roof over one's head or of financial security: *Coombes* v. *Smith* [1986] 1 WLR 808; *Layton* v. *Martin* [1986] 2 FLR 227, Scott J.

[289] Children Act 1989 s 15, sch 1; *Hager* v. *Osborne* [1992] Fam 94, Ward J; see below at **[24.18]**.

[290] Not an unmarried cohabitee who is not the natural father: *J* v. *J* [1993] 2 FLR 56, Eastham J.

18, but once made it can continue until the termination of full time education, or longer if the child is disabled. The mother only benefits coincidentally through rent-free occupation.[291] This merely reconfirms the vulnerability of an unmarried cohabitee, since she may be left in middle age with nothing at all.[292]

5. Other relationships

[17.41] Equity is amoral, being concerned simply with what has been agreed or contributed. For parent and child,[293] aunt and niece,[294] yuppies sharing, or sleeping together, or homosexuals,[295] it is the pull of money that counts.

I. ALTERNATIVES TO COMMON INTENTION

1. Remedial constructive trusts

[17.42] Trust analysis is a natural when two companies share the purchase of a development site,[296] but it is a very artificial way of analysing the relationship of a couple who shack up together in a house. Whether or not they have formed a common intention in advance is almost irrelevant in assessing the weight of non-financial contributions to family life. However, trust law is now firmly settled unless and until it is replaced by legislation.[297]

It would be possible to allow personal remedies to a cohabitant without allowing proprietary force against lenders and unsecured creditors.[298] American law is based upon the concept of unjust enrichment, a principle used to provide "palimony" to support an unmarried cohabitant at the end of a personal relationship.[299] These claims are not recognised here:[300] no rights are acquired by living with a partner for a long period of time, looking after children, or contributing to the living expenses or family life.[301] American law goes further and recognises a proprietary claim. A constructive trust arises where a person holding title to property is subject to an equitable duty to convey it to another because he would be unjustly enriched[302] if he were permitted to retain it.[303] The remedial constructive trust was proposed by Lord Denning

---

[291] *A* v. *A* [1994] 1 FLR 657.
[292] *T* v. *S* [1994] 2 FLR 883.
[293] *Bull* v. *Bull* [1955] 1 QB 234; *Sekhon* v. *Alissa* [1989] 2 FLR 94 (mother and daughter).
[294] *Re Sharpe* [1980] 1 WLR 219 (a loan case).
[295] *Tinsley* v. *Milligan* [1994] 1 AC 340, HL; *Wayling* v. *Jones* (1995) 69 P & CR 170, CA; L Flynn & A Lawson [1995] *Fem LS* 105.
[296] *Walker* v. *Hall* [1984] FLR 126, 133, Dillon LJ.
[297] *Burns* v. *Burns* [1984] Ch 317, 330G, Fox LJ.
[298] C Harpum (1982) 2 *OJLS* 272; S Wong (1999) 7 *Fem LS* 47.
[299] *Marvin* v. *Marvin* 557 P 2d 953 (1976).
[300] *Windeler* v. *Whitehall* [1990] 2 FLR 505, 506C, Millett J.
[301] *Burns* v. *Burns* [1984] Ch 317.
[302] *Gissing* trusts are not restitutionary because they are intention-based: W Swadling (1996) 16 *LS* 110, 111; PBH Birks (1990) 16 QULJ 1.
[303] *Restatement of the Law of Restitution* (St Paul, USA, American Law Institute, 1937), [160].

MR particularly in *Hussey* v. *Palmer*,[304] imposed by law because good conscience requires it. In *Eves* v. *Eves*[305] Janet Eves made no financial contribution but she did heavy work to assist with renovation after which Lord Denning wanted to impose a trust because she was in all fairness entitled to share, looking in retrospect rather than looking for a common intention agreed prospectively. Lenders can be protected by imposing the remedial trust for the future, that is only from the date of the court order. This is now the dominant tradition in the common law world,[306] but remediation and futurity[307] remain heretical here.

2. Need for reform

[17.43] The case for reform of the law set out in this chapter is self-evident. Home-sharing is widespread and most cohabitants believe that the law confers rights to their partner's property on death or the dissolution of the relationship. This is not the case unless they have children.[308] It creates a gender imbalance against women[309] not least because bringing up children is not seen as a contribution. The main beneficiaries of cohabitant's homes are lawyers, since every litigated case requires a "painfully detailed retrospect".[310]

3. No reform

[17.44] The Law Commission's marathon review resulted in a decision not to proceed with any reform.[311] In the light of the conclusion that the current law contained defects this is disappointing. The Commission pins its hope on holistic trusts, which seem to have a shaky doctrinal base,[312] but anyway small changes could make a significant change – the most obvious being that a transfer to the joint names of people sharing a home should raise a presumption of joint and equal beneficial entitlement, irrespective of the money contributions. That alone would eliminate many disputes. There is a huge social problem way outside the ambit of non-contentious reform. What is needed is a scheme based on registration of civil relationships. A Government Bill is promised for 2003[313] but restricted to homosexual couples. The

---

[304] [1972] 1 WLR 1286, 1289, CA; TC Ridley (1973) 36 *MLR* 436; PV Baker (1973) 89 *LQR* 2; K Hodkinson [1983] *Conv* 420; J Montgomery [1987] *Conv* 16; AJ Oakley (1973) 26 *CLP* 17. Also *Cooke* v. *Head* [1972] 1 WLR 518, CA; *Binions* v. *Evans* [1972] Ch 359, CA; *Burke* v. *Burke* [1974] 2 All ER 944, CA.

[305] [1975] 1 WLR 1338, 1342, Lord Denning MR; disapproved in *Grant* v. *Edwards* [1986] Ch 638, 647G, Nourse LJ who preferred Brightman J's ground.

[306] *Pettkus* v. *Becker* (1980) 117 DLR (3d) 257; *Baumgartner* v. *Baumgartner* (1988) 164 CLR 137; *Gilles* v. *Keogh* [1989] 2 NZLR 327; F Bates [1982] *Conv* 424 (Australia); M Bryan (1990) 106 *LQR* 213 (New Zealand); C Harpum (1982) 2 *OJLS* 272 (Australia).

[307] *Re Sharpe* [1980] 1 WLR 219; *Westdeutsche Landesbank Girozentrale* v. *Islington LBC* [1996] AC 669, 716G–H, Lord Browne-Wilkinson.

[308] See below **[24.18]**.

[309] M Halliwell, (1990) 19 Anglo-American 500; S Gardner (1993) 109 *LQR* 263; G Battersby, "Informally Created Rights in Land" ch 19 in Bright & Dewar; A Bottomly, "Women & Trusts: Promoting the Family" ch 10 in Bright & Dewar.

[310] *Hammond* v. *Mitchell* [1991] 1 WLR 1127, 1129D, Waite J (costs of £125,000).

[311] Law Com 278 (2002), [4.1–4.2].

[312] See above **[17.31]**.

[313] Announcement by Barbara Roche, Minister for Social Exclusion and Equalities, ODPM, December 6th 2002; a CP is promised for Summer 2003.

cost of addressing succession rights, pension entitlement, and equalisation of tax treatment for heterosexual couples is apparently too great. The cost of not legislating will be far greater.

18

BENEFICIAL SETTLEMENT

Settlements. Beneficial interests: life interests, entails, future fee simples,
conditional interests. Limited co-ownership. Perpetuities: fixed periods,
Royal lives clauses, reform, life-based rules.

A. SETTLEMENTS

[18.01] A settlement is a means of holding land for the benefit of future generations, of creating a succession of beneficial interests, of slicing ownership by uncertain time. Until 1882 land could be settled at law in an unsaleable settlement. Since then it has been possible to break a settlement by sale of the land,[1] since 1925 the succession has taken effect only in equity,[2] and since 1996[3] the only permitted vehicle has been a trust of land. In it simplest form a settlement is created by transferring land:

> *to T1 and T2 on trust for A for life, B absolutely.*

However, a settlement provides a vehicle of great flexibility for allocation and reallocation of property within a family, and there is only space here to consider those forms of beneficial interest originally derived form common law estates. Real settlements make much use of powers, discretionary trusts and class gifts. They are most often created by wills.

B. BENEFICIAL INTERESTS

[18.02] Many beneficial interests modelled on the old estates are a time in the land or land for a time.

> "[D]iversities of estates . . . are no more than diversities of time, for . . . he who has land in tail has a time in the land for as long as he has issues of his body, and he who has an estate in land for life has no time in it longer than his own life . . ."[4]

Section 1(1) of the Law of Property Act 1925 prohibits any legal division of ownership on death, and any legal springing or shifting of interests, but the prohibited legal

---

[1] SLA 1882; SLA 1925.

[2] LPA 1925 s 1(1)–(3).

[3] TLATA 1996 s 1; previously a trust for sale or strict settlement under the SLA 1925; only in the last case is it technically correct to speak of "settled land"; see above **[14.10]**.

[4] *Walsingham's case* (1573) 2 Plowd 547, 555, 75 ER 805; *Fraser* v. *Canterbury Diocesan Board of Finance* [2001] Ch 669, [42], Mummery LJ.

estates are merely reallocated to equity and allowed to continue as beneficial interests under trusts. This change is marked by a change of terminology: the old estates should now be called life interests, entailed interests (shortened to entails), future interests and so on.[5]

1. Life interests

[18.03] Before 1926, it was possible to create a legal life estate by granting the land *to A for life*.[6] On the death of A the life estate would terminate and legal ownership would pass to the person entitled afterwards. This undocumented shifting of legal title is prohibited under modern law. So life interests are necessarily equitable and necessarily operate under a trust. A trust can be used to give a person a beneficial interest in land for his lifetime only.[7]

Originally a document or will was presumed to pass a life estate, unless the words of limitation appropriate for some other common law estate were used. Even *to A in fee simple* passed a life estate to A before 1882 rather than the fee simple. Changes, outlined above,[8] have reversed the presumption in favour of the fee simple, so that it is now necessary to demonstrate by clear words an intention to create a life interest – invariably and obviously by giving land *to A for life*.[9]

2. Entails

[18.04] Legal fees tail were also abolished in 1925. Fee was the word used to describe an estate which could pass on death to a descendant, that is, it was an estate of inheritance.[10] The French *taillé* means cut down, this referring to its characteristic of passing only to *direct* descendants of the original tenant in tail.[11] Under a grant *to A and the heirs of his body* the land passed to A's eldest son, to that son's eldest son, and so on; if the eldest male line died out, it could follow the lines of younger sons, and then daughters, but it could only ever pass to direct descendants of A. This mimics the devolution of the Crown, which was entailed by Act in 1406.[12] The fee tail could terminate, since it was not able to pass through A's brothers and sisters or parents. Legal entails involved an undocumented shift of legal ownership on the death of the last lineal descendant of A, since the land passed to whoever was entitled on termination of the entail. The shift of the legal estate was undocumented, in contravention of the principles of the 1925 legislation, and so legal entails were abolished.

---

[5] Dixon's *Principles* (3rd ed) ch 5; Grays' *Elements* (3rd ed), 630ff; Megarry & Wade (6th ed), [3.022–3.032]; Panesar's *General Principles* ch 7; Thompson's *Modern LL* ch 8.

[6] Megarry & Wade (6th ed), [10.077–10.102].

[7] Cheshire & Burn (16th ed) ch 13; Megarry & Wade (6th ed), [3.092–3.096].

[8] See above **[3.17]**.

[9] An estate for the life of another (= *pur autre vie*) is created by the words *to A for the life of B*.

[10] Entails were created by statute *De Donis Conditionalibus* 1285; J Brancalano *The Fee Tail and the Common Recovery in Medieval England 1176–1502* (CUP, 2001).

[11] Contrast a fee simple which also passed to collateral heirs.

[12] Under an entail all daughters held equally as co-parceners. Obviously the Crown has to pass to a single female heir.

Equitable entailed interests could be created using trusts[13] between 1925 and 1996. However, new entails are prohibited by the Trusts of Land Act 1996.[14]

Entails were created by a gift *to A and the heirs of his body*, terminology still possible after 1925 since this is the one exceptional case in which land does in fact pass to the heir of the previous estate owner. However, in practice the words "in tail" were used between 1881[15] and 1996, the date when new entails were prohibited.[16]

The characteristic of a entail is that it can be barred by its holder. Where the entail is in possession, the effect is to bar the rights of all future generations and all those interested when the entail ends. The entail is converted, in other words into a fee simple absolute in possession. Barring an entail which is not yet in possession has a less dramatic effect: the rights of future generations of the family are barred but not those entitled when the entail ends.[17]

3. Future fees simple

[18.05] Future fees are equitable, that is they operate behind a trust. One example is where there is a prior interest which prevents the fee giving immediate rights to the land. Thus:

B to A for life, reversion to B in fee simple;
B to A for life, remainder to C in fee simple.

Note the terminology: a reversion comes back to the person who gave away a smaller interest, whereas a remainder is something left over to a third person after the gift of a smaller interest. A fee simple will also be equitable if there is some condition (a condition precedent)[18] which has to be satisfied before the interest takes effect. Parents often want to defer entitlement of their children until the age of 25 or 30, which leaves a gap in beneficial ownership until that age is reached. Thus:

to A in fee simple on condition that she qualifies as a solicitor

an encouragement to her to enter the profession. Until she does so, her interest is not in possession, and has no legal effect.

4. Modified fees

[18.06] Modified fees are ones which are liable to be cut short at some time in the future. They are now equitable interests.[19] Unfortunately there are two different

---

[13] CP Sanger (1924) 2 *CLJ* 212 (the sole concession in the nascent CLJ to the 1925 changes!); Megarry & Wade *The Law of Real Property* (6th ed), [3.033–3.038].

[14] TLATA 1996 sch 1 para 5, sch 4 (repeal of LPA 1925 s 130). For arguments that abolition was not complete: EB Histed (2000) 116 *LQR* 445; S Pearce [2001] *Conv* 396.

[15] LPA 1925 s 60(4)(b) replacing Conveyancing Act 1881 s 51; it can be qualified "in tail male" or "in tail female" to restrict succession to one sex.

[16] TLATA 1996 schs 1, 4.

[17] Procedure is regulated by the Fines & Recoveries Act 1833; the holder of the entail executes a deed of disentailment. After 1925 it creates an equitable fee simple, and the right to obtain the legal estate from the trustees.

[18] Contrast conditions subsequent, see below at **[18.06]**.

[19] LPA 1925 s 1(3).

mechanisms by which a fee could be cut short.[20] Determinable fees continue until a specified determining event occurs, when the right to possession will shift without the next owner having to take any action. The classic example, sanctified by repeated citation in the texts, is:

> to A in fee simple until St Pauls Cathedral falls down, in which event to B.[21]

Determinable fees could probably be legal before 1926,[22] but afterwards they are clearly equitable. Conditional fees are similar except that the next owner has to choose to bring the prior fee simple to an end by exercising a right to enter the land. Substantially the same estate rendered as a conditional fee simple[23] would be:

> to A in fee simple on condition that St Paul's Cathedral does not fall down, in which event B may enter the land and hold it in fee simple.

Conditional fees are equitable today operating to give beneficial entitlement behind a trust.[24] It is unlikely that a settlor will choose the collapse of St Paul's as a contingency for redistribution of assets within his family. More likely contingencies are attainment of a set age, bankruptcy, or marriage.[25]

C.   LIMITED CO-OWNERSHIP INTERESTS

1.   Unities characteristic of a beneficial joint tenancy

[18.07] Joint tenancy traditionally requires the four unities of possession, interest, title, and time.[26] Dissection of any tenancy in common will reveal the absence of one of the last three of these unities.

Is time a legitimate addition to the longer-established trinity of possession, interest and title? Blackstone, who first used the four unities,[27] was a common lawyer, who took the undoubted rules for *legal* estates and wrongly applied them to *equitable* joint tenancies. Unity of time was not required for uses and gifts by will,[28] so it should not now be needed for equitable interests.[29] Challis lambasted Blackstone's analysis as having "attracted attention rather by reason of its captivating appearance of symmetry and exactness than by reason of its practical utility"[30] and the judiciary have

---

[20] Cheshire & Burn (16th ed) chs 15–16; Megarry & Wade (6th ed), [3.062–3.076].

[21] *Walsingham's case* (1573) 2 Plowd 547, 557, 75 ER 805.

[22] *Quia Emptores* 1290 prohibited reversions after a fee simple: JC Gray (1887) 3 *LQR* 399; HW Challis (1887) 3 *LQR* 403.

[23] A condition subsequent; contrast a condition precedent: see above [18.05].

[24] For an argument that conditional fees retain legal status by mistake see above [3.29].

[25] There is a complex case-law about the validity of conditions and determining events: Megarry & Wade (6th ed), [3.062–3.077].

[26] Blackstone's *Commentaries* vol 2, 174.

[27] Halsbury's *Laws* (4th ed, reissue) vol 39, (2), [193].

[28] *Kenworthy* v. *Ward* (1853) 11 Hare 196, 203, 68 ER 1245, Page Wood V-C; *Mutton's* case (1568) 3 Dyer 274b; 73 ER 613 (bachelor *to the use of himself and any wife he may marry* created a joint tenancy); Megarry & Wade (6th ed) [9.006].

[29] H Potter (1930) 46 *LQR* 71.

[30] Challis, *Real Property* (Butterworths, 3rd ed by C Sweet, 1911), 367; Bacon's *Abridgment* by Gwillim (1798) vol III, 677 sidenote.

agreed.[31] When looking at beneficial entitlement, it is better to rely on the two central requirements stated long ago in *Pullen* v. *Palmer*:[32]

> "tenants in common hold their lands either by several titles or by several rights, but joint tenants hold them by one title and one right."

2. Absolute co-ownerships

[18.08] Beneficial co-ownership of a legal estate is considered in the chapter on co-ownership.[33]

3. Limited co-ownerships

[18.09] The unities are most important when determining the nature of limited co-ownerships, that is of equitable interests created by wills and settlements, including shared life interests, pre-1997 entails and other interests under trusts of land.[34] Joint tenancies must display unity of interest. All must hold the same estate or interest in the property, for example gifts to children for their joint lives,[35] and (it seems clear in modern law) a gift to a class.[36] They must claim by one title, under a single settlement, trust, or will. However, their interests need not vest at one time. A gift *to my children at 25* must necessarily vest at separate times unless the children are twins – in defiance of the supposed unity of time,[37] but still as joint tenants.[38]

Tenancy in common arises when unity of interest is lacking. Thus if land is given by will *to A for life and to B in fee simple*, survivorship is clearly impossible,[39] as it is if land is given to all children for life, but with a gift over to the survivors when the first child dies.[40] Words of severance also create separate shares.[41] Any gift providing for the maintenance of one beneficiary must create a tenancy in common, since money is drawn from one share to maintain another beneficiary.[42]

D. PERPETUITIES

[18.10] It is natural for parents to distrust their children, and so to want to reach out into the future in order to control their property after their deaths. However, a gift

---

[31] *Burgess* v. *Rawnsley* [1975] Ch 429, 438F; *Nielson-Jones* v. *Fedden* [1975] Ch 222, 228C.

[32] (1693) 3 Salk 207, pl 155, 91 ER 780.

[33] See above **[16]**.

[34] Before 1997 this created joint tenants for life and a statutory trust: SLA 1925 s 36; *Mayo* v. *Mayo* [1943] Ch 302.

[35] *Stratton* v. *Best* (1787) 2 Bro CC 233, 29 ER 130; *Berens* v. *Fellowes* (1887) 56 LT 391.

[36] *Re Gansloser's WT* [1951] Ch 30, 43, Evershed MR; *Re Kilvert* [1957] Ch 388.

[37] Blackstone's *Commentaries* vol 2, 175; Halsbury's *Laws* (4th ed, reissue) vol 39, (2), [193].

[38] *Stratton* as above; *Samme's* case (1609) 13 Co Rep 54, 77 ER 1464; *Sussex* v. *Temple* (1698) 1 Ld Raym 310, 91 ER 1102; *Oates d Hatterley* v. *Jackson* (1742) 2 Stra 1171, 93 ER 117; *Kenworthy* v. *Ward* (1853) 11 Hare 196, 68 ER 1245; *Morgan* v. *Britten* (1871) LR 13 Eq 28; *Binning* v. *Binning* [1895] WN 116.

[39] (1) Joint tenancy: Littleton's *Tenures*; *Wiscot's* case (1599) 2 Co Rep 60b, 76 ER 555; (2) tenancy in common: Challis, *Real Property* (3rd ed by C Sweet, 1911), 370.

[40] *Surtees* v. *Surtees* (1871) LR 12 Eq 400, 406.

[41] *Re Kilvert* [1957] Ch 388.

[42] *Re Gardner* [1924] 2 Ch 243.

to my first descendant to be born after the year 2300

obviously casts its shadow too far forward into the future. The rule against perpetuities requires a contingent interest to vest within a perpetuity period.[43]

1. Vesting of contingent interests

[18.11] A contingent interest vests when the uncertainty surrounding the destination of the interest is removed and that is the moment which must not be delayed too long. Three requirements must be satisfied before an interest is vested, that is:[44]

(1) the beneficiary is alive and ascertained;
(2) any pre-condition to his entitlement[45] has been fulfilled; and
(3) the size of the beneficial share is ascertained.[46]

If land is given to *A for life, with remainder to B absolutely*, A's interest is *vested in possession* since it gives an immediate right to enjoyment, whereas B's interest is *vested in interest* (also called a future vested interest). Until it vests a gift is *contingent*. If the gift is

to A's first child to reach 21

the gift vests when B becomes the first child of A to make 21. At the moment of vesting, the description of potential beneficiaries can be eliminated, and replaced by the name of the actual beneficiary. It is only then that the threat from the rule against perpetuities is lifted. No control is imposed on the duration of an interest once it has vested.[47]

2. Fixed statutory perpetuity periods

[18.12] Section 1 of the Perpetuities and Accumulations Act 1964 provides a simple and much used means of guaranteeing the validity of future gifts made on or after July 16th 1964. A donor may specify a perpetuity period of any fixed duration, up to a maximum of 80 years. The period must be identified as a period of time fixed in years,[48] but it need not be written down in numerical terms. Thus, in *Re Green's WT*, a codicil made in 1973 validly provided a perpetuity period from the date of the female testator's death until January 1st, 2020. On her death in 1976 this was fixed as a period of 43 11/12ths years, but it could not in any event have exceeded 80 years.[49] Current

---

[43] Cheshire & Burn (16th ed) ch 14; Maudsley & Burn *LL – Cases* (7th ed) ch 7; Megarry & Wade (6th ed) ch 7.

[44] Fearne, *Contingent Remainders* (10th ed) vol ii, 27; *Re Ashforth* [1905] 1 Ch 535, 546, Farwell J; *Mann Crossman & Paulin* v. *Land Registrar* [1918] 1 Ch 202, Neville J.

[45] The event which causes vesting must be certain: *Re Wightwick's WT* [1950] Ch 260, Wynn Parry J (gift over "from time vivisection abolished by law in Great Britain, Ireland, the continent of Europe and elsewhere" void for uncertainty); *Re Engels* [1945] 1 All ER 506 (termination of war); *Re Grotrian* [1955] Ch 501 (does not consider perpetuity, and surely wrong).

[46] This third condition relates to class gifts, and only for perpetuity purposes. A share which can be passed on death arises when the first two conditions are satisfied.

[47] *Re Cassel* [1926] Ch 358, 368, Russell J.

[48] A period of 80 years from the death of a living donor is not a fixed time.

[49] [1985] 3 All ER 455, Nourse J.

law imposes one fundamental restriction. A fixed perpetuity period must be adopted as such by the instrument creating the disposition,[50] for example by providing that

> *the period from the date of my death to 1st January 2020 is hereby specified as the Perpetuity Period for the purposes of the trusts of the residue of my estate.*[51]

Guaranteed vesting clauses allow the postponement of gifts whether or not they are sensible. Mr James Digweed, a retired schoolteacher who lived in a tent in his sitting-room, died in 1977 leaving £26,000 to *Jesus Christ if, during the next 80 years He comes to reign on earth*. In *Re Green's WT*[52] a member of an aircrew who went missing in a bombing raid was certified dead in January 1943. But his mother refused to accept that he had died, and so on her death in 1976 left £700,000 *to her son if he claimed it at any time before the year 2020*. The court issued a direction that the son had predeceased her and allowed the trustees to distribute the estate.

3. Royal lives clauses

[18.13] Royal lives clauses were used before 1964 to guarantee vesting and continue to be used to secure a longer period than the statute allows. Life-based perpetuity periods are 21 years from the death of the last life which is in being at the time of the gift. A gift *to such of my descendants as are born within twenty-one years of the death of Annabel* cannot fail for perpetuity, since Annabel is a life in being. Multiplication of the lives gives the longest possible perpetuity period; candles lighted together last until the last one burns out.[53] Nine lives were allowed in *Thellusson* v. *Woodford*[54] and dicta indicate that it could have been 1000 lives.[55] The lives selected may be unconnected with the beneficiaries.[56]

Royal lives clauses use a large class of readily ascertainable lives defined as the descendants of a particular member of the Royal family. In *Re Villar*,[57] a testator had died in 1926 leaving a gift:

> *to such of my descendants as are living 20 years after the death of the last survivor of the lineal descendants of Queen Victoria living at my death.*

By 1929 there were 120 such lives. Morton J hinted in 1943[58] that there may be too many lives, and that practice should move on to more manageable descendants of George V. However, a clause based on the lives of Queen Victoria was upheld in 1944,

---

[50] S 1(1).

[51] *Re Green's WT* [1985] 3 All ER 455, 458g.

[52] [1985] 3 All ER 455, Nourse J; R Warrington (1986) 49 *MLR* 258; P Luxton [1986] *Conv* 138.

[53] *Love* v. *Wyndham* (1605) 1 Mod 50, 54, 86 ER 724; *Duke of Norfolk's case* (1685) 3 Ch Cas 1, 20, 32, 22 ER 931; *Thellusson* v. *Woodford* (1799) 4 Ves 227, 285, 31 ER 117 (argument of Lord Eldon when Scott Att-Gen).

[54] (1805) 11 Ves 112, 32 ER 1030, HL, affirming (1799) 4 Ves 227, 31 ER 117.

[55] *Robinson* v. *Hardcastle* (1786) 2 Bro CC 22, 30, 29 ER 11, Lord Thurlow (the "not" inserted by the editor is a mistake; Thurlow says it would be within the line of a perpetuity, that is valid); *Duke of Norfolk* (1681) 3 Ch Cas 1, 22 ER 931 (20 successive lives in being); *Berry* v. *Green* [1938] AC 575, HL (40 annuitants).

[56] *Cadell* v. *Palmer* (1833) 1 Cl & Fin 372, 6 ER 956.

[57] [1929] 1 Ch 243.

[58] *Re Leverhulme* [1943] 2 All ER 274, 280–281 (death 1925).

when there were 194 legitimate issue and three of more dubious provenance.[59] King Olav V was born in 1903 and died in 1991, after which the torch passed to obscure German princelings.[60]

Care must be taken to avoid uncertainty caused by selecting too many lives. "Property may be so limited as to make it unalienable during any number of lives, not exceeding that, to which testimony can be applied, to determine, when the survivor of them drops."[61] In *Re Moore*[62] the period adopted was 21 years from the death of the last survivor of all people living at the testator's death; this gift failed for uncertainty rather than for perpetuity.

4. Perpetuities reform

[18.14] The Law Commission Report on the *Rule against Perpetuities and Excessive Accumulations*[63] proposes a new universal fixed period of 125 years for new gifts made after the new legislation. Research which guided the American uniform code[64] concluded that 90 years was the average duration of a life-based period, and the Commission reckon that the maximum attainable under the current law is about 120 years.[65] Statute will provide a single universal perpetuity period which could not be excluded or modified by the Act, and the maximum fixed period should be extended from 80 years to 125 years. Novel and welcome features are that it would no longer be necessary to incorporate the period expressly and it would not be possible to shorten it. The period should be long enough to allow any sensible gift to vest.

It is also proposed to allow a let-out for trustees operating existing Royal lives clauses. Apparently the survivorship of descendants of Queen Victoria is difficult to determine and many practitioners have taken to using an arbitrary number of years as the termination point of the trust.[66] Trustees will be allowed to switch to the new 125-year period whenever an existing instrument specifies an unascertainable group of lives in being.[67]

5. Life-based rules

[18.15] The *Duke of Norfolk's case* (1681)[68] provided the common law limit for the vesting of a gift. The period ran from the date of a lifetime gift or the date of death of a testamentary donor. The basic elements were (1) a period of a life or lives in being at the time that the gift takes effect, (2) a period of 21 years and (3) any relevant pregnancy. This forms the basis for the common law rule which applied to gifts made

---

[59] *Re Warren's WT* (1961) 105 SJ 511, CA.
[60] Law Com CP 133 (1993), [4.6].
[61] *Thellusson* v. *Woodford* (1805) 11 Ves 112, 146, 32 ER 1030, Lord Eldon.
[62] [1901] 1 Ch 936.
[63] Law Com 251 (1998); P Sparkes (1998) 12 *TLI* 148; T Gallanis [2000] *CLJ* 284. The rule against excessive accumulations is to removed as a matter of deregulation: LCD CP 10 (2002).
[64] LW Waggoner [1982] *CLJ* 234, 235; Law Com 251 (1998), [8.11].
[65] Law Com 251 (1998), [8.2–8.13].
[66] At [8.4]; surely this is a clear breach of trust.
[67] Draft Bill cl 12.
[68] (1681) 3 Ch Cas 1, 22 ER 931.

before the 1964 statute became operational. It was necessary at common law for a gift to be limited in advance so that it was certain to vest within the time allowed. However, unlikely eventualities were often overlooked by those drafting trusts causing sensible gifts to fail.

The Perpetuity and Accumulations Act 1964 applies to gifts made on or after July 16th 1964. The fundamental change is the introduction of a wait and see provision for gifts which fail the common law test, enabling perpetuity to be assessed according to events which actually occur.[69] This rescues many gifts. More minor changes are child-bearing presumptions and trap saving provisions.[70]

Details of life-based rules lie beyond the scope of this work.[71]

[69] S 3; the section specifies the lives in being to be considered.
[70] Ss 4, 5; this particularly saves gifts requiring attainment of an age exceeding 21 and class gifts.
[71] Law Com 251 (1998); Cheshire & Burn (16th ed) ch 14; Megarry & Wade (6th ed) ch 7.

19

OCCUPATION RIGHTS

Co-ownership occupation rights. Purpose trusts. The decision to sell. Rent and equitable accounting. Sale applications by creditors. Occupation orders. Matrimonial home rights and proprietary enforcement. Trust licences. Occupational licences. Equitable licences. Proprietary licences. Constructive trust doctrine.

[19.01] "Land law is . . . also a different ownership, unrecognised in the old books, a having by using, a possession by sharing".[1] The subject of this chapter is this new property,[2] the value of being able to settle down in a house as a family home.

A. CO-OWNERS OCCUPYING UNDER TRUSTS OF LAND

1. Who is entitled to occupy?

[19.02] The Trusts of Land and Appointment of Trustees Act 1996 formalises the balance achieved by case law on trusts for sale, notably *Bull* v. *Bull*.[3] A co-ownership trust is a simple trust,[4] attaching to the land itself rather than the proceeds,[5] a perception reinforced by conferring a statutory right of occupation until sale where the land is intended for occupation. A person claiming occupation must be entitled to possession, as opposed to the income, and for himself beneficially rather than as a sub-trustee or personal representative.[6]

2. When occupation rights arise

[19.03] Occupation rights arise[7] if:

(1) the purposes of the trust include making the land available for occupation by the beneficiary;

---

[1] K Green (1993) 3 *Fem LS* 131, 156–157.
[2] CA Reich (1964) 73 *Yale LJ* 733; see above **[6.12]**.
[3] [1955] 1 QB 234, CA.
[4] TLATA 1996 s 1 (express), sch 2 paras 3–4 (implied trusts).
[5] S 3. Contrast a trust for sale where the beneficial interest was realised in the proceeds of sale.
[6] S 22(3).
[7] S 12(1)–(2); DG Barnsley [1998] *CLJ* 123 (strong criticism). Formerly a beneficiary occupied as licensee: *Grace* v. *Taylor* [1998] 4 All ER 17, CA. Now it is as an incident of beneficial entitlement.

(2) the purposes of the trust include making land available for occupation by a class of which he is a member; or

(3) the trustees decide that it is available for occupation.

Trustees may prevent occupation by deciding that the land is either unavailable or unsuitable for occupation. However, the courts have an overriding discretion.[8]

3.   Multiple occupiers

[19.04] Trustees may select between multiple potential occupiers[9] if the trust gives beneficial interests in possession to a number of named individuals or creates a class from which the trustees may select who is to benefit. Where two or more people entitled to a right of occupation, the trustees may exclude or restrict the entitlement of some, but not of all. In making a choice, they are required to act reasonably, considering the settlor's intention, the purposes for which the land is held, and the circumstances and wishes of other entitled beneficiaries.[10] There is a duty to be even handed between the various beneficiaries.[11] Reasonable conditions can be imposed, such as a requirement to pay outgoings, to assume an obligation, or to pay an excluded beneficiary.[12] A beneficiary already in occupation can only be excluded in favour of another against his wishes by a court order.[13]

4.   The court

[19.05] Any decision made by the trustees is subject to the supervision of the court, with powers in the Trusts of Land Act 1996[14] which now governs all court proceedings. Those entitled to apply to the court are the trustees and any other person interested in the trust land. A beneficiary can apply to control the trustees in the exercise of any of their functions. In particular the court might order sale, override any consent provision, ignore the result of a consultation process, declare the beneficial interests, or deal with the proceeds of sale.[15] The court has a discretion but should take into account certain factors:[16] the settlor's intentions, the purposes for which the property is held, any express direction for sale, the welfare of any minor who may expect to use it as home, the interests of any secured creditor, and the wishes of any adult beneficiary.[17]

Case law under the 1925 legislation[18] established the broad principles of the so called "purpose trust" but it differs in important details from the 1996 scheme.

---

[8] See below at [19.05].

[9] TLATA 1996 s12(1)–(2); DG Barnsley [1998] *CLJ* 123 (strong criticism).

[10] TLATA 1996 s 13(1)–(2).

[11] *Rodway* v. *Landy* [2001] EWCA Civ 471, [2001] Ch 703, [33], Peter Gibson LJ.

[12] TLATA 1996 s 13(3)–(6); CJ Whitehouse (1997) 113 *LQR* 211 (tax).

[13] S 13(7).

[14] TLATA 1996 s 14. County courts have unlimited jurisdiction, including District Judges: Practice Direction [1999] 3 All ER 192.

[15] TLATA 1996 s 17(2).

[16] S 15.

[17] S 15(2)–(3).

[18] LPA 1925 s 30.

5.   Partition

[19.06] Land held in a trust for beneficial co-owners can be apportioned, that is split by physical division into two or more parts. This power was established by *Rodway* v. *Landy*.[19] The Vitason Clinic in Sevenoaks was held in common by two doctors in partnership. When the joint practice broke down, one of the doctors wanted sale but the other counterclaimed for partition, into a right hand side and left hand side, an outcome supported by the trustees and the other beneficiary. Powers which extended to the exclusion of a beneficiary or restriction of occupation by any beneficiary, obviously also allowed the court to evict a co-owner from one of two adjoining houses.[20] Physical division was thus approved.

6.   Trusts for division

[19.07] A trust for division cannot be created directly, since a power to postpone sale is imposed automatically,[21] but the practical effect can be achieved by creating a trust of which the purpose is division, which succeeds in excluding rights of occupation and consultation rights.[22]

B.   OLD CO-OWNERSHIP PURPOSE TRUSTS

1.   The history of occupation rights

[19.08] Before 1926 sharing of land was generally undertaken as a *legal* co-ownership and a necessary ingredient of the unity of possession enjoyed between co-owners was co-equal[23] rights of occupation. It was not necessary to formulate occupation rights between people who were simply joint owners.[24]

This simple position had to be re-established in 1996 by statue. The reforms of 1925 had cast doubt on whether entitlement to occupation followed from holding a beneficial interest under a statutory trust for sale imposed on co-ownership.[25] Beneficial co-ownership attached to the proceeds of a sale, an application of conversion doctrine,[26] and this did not necessarily imply any right to live in the property itself. After a tussle it came to be recognised that the trust for sale was a pure conveyancing device and that a trust to allow occupation pending sale could arise where land was acquired with the object of providing a home. This purpose trust pushed aside the principle of conversion. It was greatly developed and articulated in the context of matrimonial homes and the homes of cohabitants. The Trusts of Land Act 1996 continues to differentiate trusts where occupation was intended and those genuinely intended to lead to sale.

---

[19] [2001] EWCA Civ 471, [2001] Ch 703.
[20] At [33], Peter Gibson LJ.
[21] TLATA 1996 s 4(1).
[22] Ss 8(2), 11, 12(1)(a).
[23] Whether the beneficial ownership is equal or unequal.
[24] R Cocks [1984] *Conv* 198, 206.
[25] LPA 1925 ss 34–36, as originally enacted.
[26] See above **[15.02]**.

2. Trusts to prevent development

[19.09] Purpose trusts were developed as a justification for refusing to order sale, though this was only relevant where a challenge was made before completion of an overreaching sale.[27] The theoretical duty to sell was pushed aside by having regard to the purpose for which the property was initially purchased. Section 14 of the Trusts of Land Act 1996 is drafted to reflect the purpose trust case law though there is no longer any presumption in favour of sale.[28]

Re Buchanan-Wollaston's Conveyance[29] was the seminal case. Four people (A to D) each owned a house near the sea at Lowestoft. Collectively they bought a piece of vacant land between their houses and the sea with the object of keeping it free from development, a purpose recited in an express trust deed which required any sale to be agreed by all parties.[30] B had bought out A's interest and sold his house, so that he now wanted the cliff-top plot sold in order to realise his share of its development value. C refused to agree to the sale, a decision supported by the executors of D, who had succeeded to his share. One trustee for sale could ordinarily compel sale, but the court refused to oblige. Development could be prevented and the view preserved, as the original buyers intended, only by blocking a sale, at least in the circumstances as they stood at the time of the court hearing: things might change when all the original parties were dead or had all assigned their interests.[31] *Buchanan-Wollaston* is a case between parties who were not associated with each other,[32] so pure property law principles would still be applied today.

3. Residential purposes

[19.10] *Bull* v. *Bull*[33] extended the purpose trust to trusts to provide a home. A son bought a house with his mother in 1949 in order to share it as a home, the son taking the legal estate in his sole name. His mother made a smaller, but significant contribution to the purchase price, so as to create an implied beneficial tenancy in common in the proceeds under a trust for sale. When the son married in 1953, his wife came to share the house, and it was agreed that the mother should have the use of two rooms. Relations between the two women soon deteriorated and the son served notice to quit on his mother and sued for possession. The son had the misfortune to come before a Court of Appeal including Denning LJ, a judge scarcely likely to destroy the security of a home on the basis of an arbitrary theory like conversion, but the court was in fact unanimous in its ruling that the mother could stay.

---

[27] *City of London Building Society* v. *Flegg* [1988] AC 54, HL.

[28] TLATA 1996 s 15(1)(a)–(b); S Baughen [1996] *Fam Law* 736; W Massey (1997) 141 *SJ* 1158.

[29] [1939] Ch 738, CA; H Potter (1939) 55 *LQR* 178, 348 ("may prove to be important"!); (1938) 3 *Conv* (NS) 328, 439.

[30] Unanimity was required for sale of the north land; a vote was required for the south land, but no vote had been held.

[31] *Re Hyde's Conveyance* (1952) 102 LJ 58 (purchase of land for business of company); *Miller* v. *Lakefield Estates* [1989] 1 EGLR 212, CA.

[32] FLA 1996 s 62.

[33] [1955] 1 QB 234, CA; HR Gray (1955) 18 *MLR* 408 (criticism); GA Forrest [1955] *CLJ* 155; GA Forrest (1956) 19 *MLR* 312; H Forrest [1978] *Conv* 194, 203–5.

This was orthodox in terms of the earlier equity. Life tenants under trusts for sale had no automatic right to occupy,[34] but there was a judicial discretion. Equitable entitlement under a trust for sale was a proper case to allow possession against suitable undertakings, unless some reason existed to justify withholding possession.[35] Rights of equitable tenants in common had not been defined, pre-*Bull*, but their position was if anything stronger than a beneficiary for life because equitable entitlement will usually be coupled with a share of the legal estate.[36] Imposition of the statutory trust in 1925 was designed to facilitate conveyancing and was not intended to prejudice the substantive rights of the co-owners,[37] so much so that the statutory trust was subject to all powers and provisions needed to give effect to the rights of those interested in the land.[38]

Jones v. *Jones*[39] was a case like *Bull* v. *Bull* where the issue was whether to order sale. A father bought a house for his son's family with the aid of a contribution of one quarter of the price from the son. Following the father's death the step-mother sought sale, but she was unsuccessful since the father had promised his son a home for life and sale should not be ordered to defeat that promised right. In *Harris* v. *Harris*[40] it was held that an express trust to provide a home for father and son continued so long as either of them wished to stay. Beneficial co-owners are now associated parties, whose disputes are resolved by application for an occupation order.[41]

4. Matrimonial homes – old property law principles

[19.11] It was a short step from *Bull* v. *Bull* to full protection of residence rights in family homes, preventing sale while a house is still needed to provide accommodation. Case-law principles have been superseded by statutory jurisdictions where the couple are married,[42] or are unmarried parents,[43] though these build on purpose trust principles. Sale was first sought between spouses under ordinary co-ownership rules[44] in *Jones* v. *Challenger* (1961).[45] A matrimonial purpose prevented sale during the continuance of the marriage, but the purpose was held to end on divorce, so that a duty to sell reasserted itself on divorce. In *Rawlings* v. *Rawlings*[46] the end point was moved forward to the breakdown of the marriage, that is at the time of separation.[47] The

---

[34] *Re Stamford and Warrington* [1925] Ch 162.

[35] *Re Wythes* [1893] 2 Ch 369, 374, Kekewich J; *Re Bagot's Settlement* [1894] 1 Ch 177; *Re Newen* [1894] 2 Ch 297.

[36] *Re Stamford and Warrington* [1925] Ch 162, 171, Russell J.

[37] *Hammersmith & Fulham LBC* v. *Monk* [1992] 1 AC 478, 493D–E, Lord Browne-Wilkinson; *Re Warren* [1932] 1 Ch 42, 47, Maughan J; *Bull* v. *Bull* [1955] 1 QB 234, CA.

[38] LPA 1925 s 35(1), now repealed.

[39] [1977] 1 WLR 438; J Alder (1978) 41 *MLR* 208.

[40] (1996) 72 P & CR 408, CA.

[41] See below **[19.30]**.

[42] *Williams* v. *Williams* [1976] Ch 278, 285D, Lord Denning MR.

[43] Children Act 1989 sch 1.

[44] LPA 1925 s 30. This was an improvement on the Married Women's Property Act 1882 s 17, even after its amendment in 1896 to allow sale.

[45] [1961] 1 QB 176, CA; DG Valentine (1960) 23 *MLR* 703; SJ Bailey [1960] *CLJ* 167.

[46] [1964] P 398, CA; JC Hall [1964] *CLJ* 210; RE Megarry (1964) 80 *LQR* 477; (1964) 80 *LQR* 31; *Crawley BC* v. *Ure* [1996] QB 13, 27, Hobhouse LJ.

[47] Resurrected by a resumption of cohabitation: *Chhokar* v. *Chhokar* [1984] FLR 313, CA.

unfortunate implication that the matrimonial home should be sold before the financial details of a divorce settlement were finalised, has been avoided by transferring jurisdiction to the Family Division and requiring all aspects of a matrimonial breakdown to be settled in one set of proceedings.[48] Cases like this would now call for an occupation order.[49]

Sale was deferred while a house was providing a home for *dependent children*, since this is one of the objects of buying a matrimonial home.[50] The period of deferral might be until the youngest child reached 16, or longer while any child remained in education which might be disrupted by sale of the family home. In *Williams* v. *Williams* the youngest son was 12 and still at school and Lord Denning MR insisted that steps should be taken to preserve the property as a home for the remaining spouse and children.[51] When the dependency ended, a fresh application could be made for sale.

5. Co-habitants – property law principles

[19.12] Purpose trust principles also protected cohabitants who set up home together,[52] though today these associated parties will need to seek an occupation order.[53] Separation was usually the trigger for a demand for sale,[54] as in *Bernard* v. *Josephs*,[55] where a woman forced out of the home by her male partner's violence was able to force a sale: preservation of the house as a home for one of two cohabitees singly was not an object of the trust. A short period should be allowed to give time to find alternative accommodation.[56] There is no reason to attempt to repair the relationship, and no power to weigh the conduct of the parties.[57] Longer postponement required proof that it was inequitable for one party to want to realise his interest.[58] Relevant factors were the financial position of the parties, the size of the accommodation, and the housing needs of the other parties.

Cohabitants cannot insist on sale while the property is providing a home for dependent children.[59] In *Re Ever's Trust*[60] the man was refused sale of a property occupied by his ex-partner and their child of four. He had not shown a need to realise the

---

[48] *Rawlings* v. *Rawlings* [1964] P 398; *Bedson* v. *Bedson* [1965] 2 QB 666, 680; *Appleton* v. *Appleton* [1965] 1 WLR 25; *Williams* v. *Williams* [1976] Ch 278, 286, Lord Denning MR.

[49] For a case between husband, wife and wife's sister see *Laird* v. *Laird* [1999] 1 FLR 791, CA.

[50] *Rawlings* v. *Rawlings* [1964] P 398, 418, Salmon LJ.

[51] [1976] Ch 278, 285G; MW Bryan (1977) 93 *LQR* 176; *Rawlings* v. *Rawlings* [1964] P 398, 419, Salmon LJ.

[52] *Bedson* v. *Bedson* [1965] 2 QB 666, 678, Lord Denning MR; *Re Evers' T* [1980] 1 WLR 1327, CA; *Bernard* v. *Josephs* [1982] Ch 391, 402A Griffiths LJ; *Turton* v. *Turton* [1988] Ch 542, CA; *Re Citro* [1991] Ch 142, 147, Nourse LJ.

[53] See below [19.30ff].

[54] *Jones* v. *Challenger* [1961] 1 QB 176, 183, Devlin LJ; *Turton* v. *Turton* [1988] Ch 542, 554C, Kerr LJ.

[55] [1982] Ch 391, CA; JM Thomson (1982) 98 *LQR* 517; K Gray [1983] *CLJ* 30; *Jackson* v. *Jackson* [1971] 1 WLR 1539, CA (sale ordered).

[56] Four months in *Bernard* v. *Josephs*.

[57] *Dennis* v. *McDonald* [1982] Fam 63, 68A–D, Purchas J at first instance; contrast *Bedson* v. *Bedson* [1965] 2 QB 666 (wife).

[58] *Jones* v. *Challenger* [1961] 1 QB 176, 183, Devlin LJ; *Rawlings* v. *Rawlings* [1964] P 398, 420, Salmon LJ; *Bedson* v. *Bedson* [1965] 2 QB 666, 678, Lord Denning MR; *Oke* v. *Rideout* [1998] CLYB 4876.

[59] *Williams* v. *Williams* [1976] Ch 278, CA; *Rawlings* v. *Rawlings* [1964] P 398, 419 Salmon LJ; *TSB Bank* v. *Marshall* [1998] 3 EGLR 100, Ct Ct.

[60] [1980] 1 WLR 1327, CA.

property and sale would be very awkward for the mother. The same principle was applied in *Dennis* v. *McDonald*[61] where three children were living with the man. The ejected partner was free to reapply when the children reached 16 though deferral generally continued throughout periods of full time education.

6. Adult children

[19.13] It is possible for a purpose trust to arise in favour of adult children.[62]

7. Trusts for division

[19.14] Under pre-1997 *trusts for sale* a land owner could impose a duty to sell without a power of postponement where he wanted his land sold and the proceeds divided, for example to pay debts or to divide land between the children of a testator. For example, in *Barclay* v. *Barclay*[63] a father left his bungalow on trust for sale because he wanted the value of the house divided between his five sons and daughters-in-law after his death. Wills frequently created express testamentary trusts for sale, and if the duty to sell was not balanced by a power to postpone sale,[64] the trustees were under an immediate duty to sell. In *Re Atkins WT*[65] trustees of a farm were directed to sell when the testator's stepson ceased to work the farm, and to divide the net proceeds equally among the beneficiaries living at the date of sale. Prompt sale was clearly intended, rather than postponement. Statute has created division trusts on intestacy[66] and for the administration of the estate of a deceased person by personal representatives.[67]

C. CO-OWNERSHIP: THE DECISION TO SELL

1. Unanimous trustees

[19.15] Beneficial co-owners stand to lose their home if the trustees decide on sale, since rights of occupation are equitable and overreachable if sale is made by two or more trustees.[68] Consultation is required, so it may be a breach of trust to sell without considering the wishes of the beneficiaries, but a purchaser is unaffected.[69]

2. Divided trustees under a trust of land

[19.16] Trusts of land are usually "simple" trusts which leave the trustees free to decide either to sell the land or to hold it. Their power of sale is subject to any express

---

[61] [1982] Fam 63, 68C, Purchas J at first instance. Property adjustment is now possible; see below at **[24.18]**.

[62] *TSB Bank* v. *Marshall* [1998] 3 EGLR 100, Ct Ct.

[63] [1970] 2 QB 677, CA; FR Crane (1970) 34 *Conv (NS)* 344; MJ Prichard [1971] *CLJ* 44; PV Baker (1970) 86 *LQR* 443; *Nickisson* v. *Cockill* (1863) 3 De G J & Sm 622, 46 ER 778; *Re Ball* [1930] WN 111.

[64] This point no longer holds good since TLATA 1996 s 6 implies a power of sale, see above **[13.43]**.

[65] [1974] 1 WLR 761; *Re Rooke's WT* [1953] Ch 716.

[66] AEA 1925 s 47, as amended by TLATA 1996 sch 2 para 5.

[67] LPA 1925 s 33, as amended by TLATA 1996 s 18; R Mitchell [1999] *Conv* 84.

[68] *City of London Building Society* v. *Flegg* [1988] AC 54, HL; see above **[13]**.

[69] See above **[19.18]**.

restriction in the trust document.[70] Since an even balance is struck between sale and postponement, indecision will point to retention. Any one trustee can in practice block a sale by declining to execute the transfer until ordered to do so by the court.

3. Divided trustees under a trust for sale

[19.17] A decision to postpone sale involves the exercise of a discretion. The court will not override a proper decision,[71] either to proceed with a sale[72] or to retain as in *Re Steed's WT*:[73] a settlor had created a protective trust to guard against the bankruptcy of Steed but the court refused to order sale in defiance of an honest exercise of the trustees' discretion to postpone sale.

If a trust of land includes a duty of sale on the trustees, a power of postponement is imposed by statute whatever the trust deed says.[74] The same applies to a trust created before 1997 which is now fitted into the trust of land scheme.[75] Further the balance of power established by the trust is important because of the rule requiring unanimity among the trustees before a power is exercised. Of the three trustees for sale in *Re Mayo*,[76] two wished to retain the house while one wanted it sold, but the decision was for sale because the one dissident trustee precluded a discretionary decision to postpone. This shows the basic balance between a trust to sell and a power of postponement.

4. Consultation

[19.18] Consultation is the most important check on trustees of land. It applies to all post-1996 trusts of land unless excluded by a provision of an express trust.[77] Trusts imposed before 1997 will also require consultation if the trust was imposed by statute,[78] or where, as was done occasionally, an express trust adopted the principle of consultation.[79] Otherwise they will become subject to the new consultation requirements unless the requirement was excluded by execution of an irrevocable deed during a transitional period of one year.[80] A disclaimer can be executed by the creator of the trust (or those living and capable) or by a beneficiary to the extent of his interest.[81]

---

[70] TLATA 1996 ss 6(1), 8.

[71] *Re Norrington* (1879) 13 Ch D 654, 659, Bacon V-C; *Re Boston's WT* [1956] Ch 395. As to decisions not taken in good faith see: *Re Blake* (1885) 29 Ch D 913, 917 Cotton LJ; *Norrington* at 659.

[72] *Re Crips* (1906) 95 LT 865, 867, Kekewich J; *Re Johnson* [1915] 1 Ch 435; distinguished in *Re White's S* [1930] 1 Ch 179.

[73] [1960] Ch 407, 418–419, CA; *Re Horsnaill* [1909] 1 Ch 631.

[74] S 4(2).

[75] This included a trust to "sell or retain land": LPA 1925 s 25(4). For pre-1997 postponement see P Sparkes *NLL* (1st ed), 321–322.

[76] [1943] Ch 302 (co-ownership of life interests under a settlement, no purpose trust); *Re Roth* (1896) 74 LT 50; *Re Hilton* [1909] 2 Ch 548.

[77] TLATA 1996 s 11(2)(a). Exclusion is not possible in a trust implied by statute.

[78] LPA 1925 s 26(3), as substituted by LP (Amendment) A 1926 s 7, sch.

[79] As in *Re Buchanan-Wollaston's Conveyance* [1939] Ch 738, CA.

[80] TLATA 1996 s 11(3)–(5)(a); ie during 1997.

[81] S 11(4); in practice a beneficiary of age could disclaim at any time.

Consultation must take place before sale or before the exercise of any other function in relation to the trust land.[82] However, in *Crawley BC* v. *Ure*[83] service of a notice to quit by a periodic tenant was held not to be a positive act, but a negative one which did not call for a consultation exercise. Those entitled to be consulted are all persons of full age for the time being beneficially entitled to an interest in possession.[84] An injunction can be obtained to restrain a sale without any consultation with the adult co-owners if it is discovered in time,[85] but beneficiaries can only impose their will on reluctant trustees by court proceedings,[86] and it will be too late once a sale has been completed.[87] Trustees are only required to consult[88] "so far as practicable" and they may decide that it is impossible. Trustees should give effect to the wishes of the *majority* by value[89] but *only so far as consistent with the general interests of trust*,[90] a qualification which removes much of the sting from consultation.

5.   Other checks on beneficiaries

[19.19] Beneficiaries may also be trustees, in which case refusal to sign a conveyance will require the others to seek an order for sale. By declining to vacate the property, a beneficiary can effectively block a sale without a court order.[91] The trust may give a beneficiary a right to refuse consent to a sale, which confers a veto, unless the court finds a clear reason to override the beneficiary's objection.[92]

D. RENT AND EQUITABLE ACCOUNTING

[19.20] Equity has developed a jurisdiction to order an account between co-owners in any case where it would be just to do so.[93] It may be an order to account for profits, to pay an occupation rent, or to make allowance for mortgage payments. Compensation is discretionary, and should not, for example, be ordered after the outrageous conduct by the husband in *Chhokar* v. *Chhokar*.[94] An account must be sought within a reasonable time and once agreed can only be upset for fraud or serious error.

---

[82]   S 11(1), except a transfer of the land to the beneficiaries under s 6(2).

[83]   [1996] QB 13, CA; *Notting Hill HT* v. *Brackley* [2001] EWCA Civ 601, [2001] 3 EGLR 11; see below at **[25.17]**.

[84]   TLATA 1996 s 11(1)(b). Annuitants are now excluded: s 23(3).

[85]   *Waller* v. *Waller* [1967] 1 WLR 451; RE Poole (1967) 31 *Conv (NS)* 259; *Re Jones* [1931] Ch 375.

[86]   TLATA 1996 s 14.

[87]   S 16(1); *City of London BS* v. *Flegg* [1988] AC 54, 78D.

[88]   Query whether the public law concept of consultation provides any analogy.

[89]   TLATA 1996 s 11(1)(b); *Bull* v. *Bull* [1955] 1 QB 234, 238; *Re Warren* [1932] 1 Ch 42, 47, Maugham J; *Re Davies' WT* [1932] 1 Ch 530; *Re Parker's SE* [1928] Ch 247, 259, Farwell J.

[90]   TLATA 1996 s 11(1)(b).

[91]   *Bull* v. *Bull* [1955] 1 QB 234, 238, Denning LJ.

[92]   See above **[13.40]**.

[93]   *Re Pavlou* [1993] 1 WLR 1046, 1050D, Millett J; *Dennis* v. *McDonald* [1982] Fam 63, 70H–71A; *Hill* v. *Hickin* [1897] 2 Ch 579, 581, Stirling J.

[94]   [1984] FLR 313, 323A, 332B, 332E (husband deserted wife in India; dishonest sale to defeat wife's occupation.)

1. Account for profits

[19.21] The common law[95] allowed one tenant in common to harvest all the hay on jointly owned fields, to work out a coal mine, or to cut trees,[96] though some unilateral acts may now be a breach of trust[97] and wanton destruction could be stopped.[98] However, equity insists that profits of a joint enterprise[99] must be split in proportion to the beneficial shares,[100] and there is a general equitable right to demand an account.

2. Occupation rent following ouster

[19.22] Compensation equivalent to rent[101] should be awarded in equity between either tenants in common[102] or joint tenants[103] in any case where this is necessary to do equity between the parties. Equitable principles can be seen as a settlement of accounts between beneficiaries, or a specific application of the general fiduciary duty of a trustee,[104] but since the payments are only "rent" in a loose sense, quantification is based solely on trust law.[105]

A party who leaves voluntarily, but would be welcome back, should not normally charge his partner with a rent he never expected to pay.[106] "Rent" is called for where one co-owner has *ousted* any of the others from the property – the rule for the common law trespass action[107] applied to the modern co-ownership trust by *Jones v. Jones*.[108] All too often a violent man has forced his female partner to leave, and until a sale he should be made to pay for her exclusion.[109]

---

[95] No fiduciary relationship existed between legal co-owners: *Kennedy* v. *De Trafford* [1897] AC 180, 190.

[96] *Fennings* v. *Lord Grenville* (1808) 1 Taunt 241, 127 ER 825 (whale turned into blubber); *Jacobs* v. *Seward* (1872) LR 5 HL 464; *Job* v. *Potton* (1875) LR 20 Eq 84, 93.

[97] *Tyson* v. *Fairclough* (1824) 2 Sim & St 142, 144, 57 ER 300, Leach V-C; *Re Landi* [1939] Ch 828, CA; *Bull* v. *Bull* [1955] 1 QB 234, 237, Denning LJ; *Re Warren* [1932] 1 Ch 42, 47, Maugham J.

[98] *Bailey* v. *Hobson* (1869) LR 5 Ch App 180.

[99] Not profits earned by the industry of one: *Henderson* v. *Eason* (1851) 17 QB 701, 117 ER 1451.

[100] *Job* v. *Potton* (1875) LR 20 Eq 84, 93, Bacon V-C; *Jones* v. *Jones* [1977] 1 WLR 438, 442A; *Chhokar* v. *Chhokar* [1984] FLR 313, 332G.

[101] G Miller (1971) 35 *Conv (NS)* 332, 345–351.

[102] *Dennis* v. *McDonald* [1982] Fam 62, 70–71, Purchas J.

[103] *Re Pavlou* [1993] 1 WLR 1046, 1048F, Millett J.

[104] *Dennis* v. *McDonald* [1982] Fam 63, 80G–H, Arnold P; F Webb (1982) 98 *LQR* 519; *Re Landi* [1939] Ch 828; RE Megarry (1941) 57 *LQR* 26, 29.

[105] [1982] Fam 62, 80G–H, Arnold P; R Cocks [1984] *Conv* 198, 205.

[106] *Re Pavlou* [1993] 1 WLR 1046, 105E, Millett J; *Wright* v. *Johnson* [2001] EWCA Civ 1667, [2002] 2 P & CR 15 at 210.

[107] *M'Mahon* v. *Burchell* (1846) 2 Ph 127, 41 ER 889; *Murray* v. *Hall* (1849) 7 CB 441, 137 ER 175; *Henderson* v. *Eason* (1851) 17 QB 701, 117 ER 1451; *Stedman* v. *Smith* (1857) 8 El & Bl 1, 6, 120 ER 1 (ouster from a wall!); *Jacobs* v. *Seward* (1872) LR 5 HL 464; *Kennedy* v. *De Trafford* [1897] AC 180, HL; *Jones* v. *Jones* [1977] 1 WLR 438, 443, Roskill LJ.

[108] [1977] 1 WLR 438, 441, Lord Denning MR; JE Martin [1982] *Conv* 305; J Alder (1978) 41 *MLR* 208; *Dennis* v. *McDonald* [1982] Fam 62, 71A, Purchas J; *Chhokar* v. *Chhokar* [1984] FLR 313; *Re Pavlou* [1993] 1 WLR 1046, 1050D, Millett J.

[109] *Bernard* v. *Josephs* [1982] Ch 391, CA; *Dennis* v. *McDonald* [1982] Fam 62, Purchas J.

3. Compensation when deferring sale

[19.23] When a sale of trust property is deferred, rent should be paid by the person allowed to continue in occupation,[110] usually as an adjustment when splitting the proceeds of sale. Suppose that A leaves the house he has been sharing with B and wants to realise his share by sale but B successfully opposes sale on the ground that there are children living there. A has chosen not to occupy but the sterilisation of his asset derives from the court order deferring sale so it is fair to order rent,[111] now under the provisions relating to trusts of land[112] or occupation orders.[113]

Equitable accounting may also be required following bankruptcy,[114] death,[115] or partition.[116]

4. After separation, pending sale

[19.24] When a relationship deteriorates and the family home has to be sold, it is necessary to determine how much money each partner is entitled, possibly a half but possibly more or less, applying the shares fixed, usually, at the moment of acquisition. As house prices inflate, so does the monetary worth of the share.[117] Equitable accounting fills the gap between separation and sale, dealing with receipts and payments made during that gap.[118] *Bernard* v. *Josephs*[119] is a typical case in which a violent man forced out his female partner. If he had to account for the value of his occupation, it was only fair to make allowance to him for his mortgage repayments. Credits reflect payments of mortgage instalments,[120] improvements and repairs. Debits reflect receipts, such as rents received from letting rooms.[121] Monetary adjustment is required unless the credits and debits happen to balance each other out.[122]

Sale causes a *realisation* of the monetary value of a beneficial interest, such as £50,000.[123] If one party is left in the family home, that person often wishes to buy out

---

[110] *Re Warren* [1932] 1 Ch 42, 47, Maugham J.

[111] *Turner* v. *Morgan* (1803) 8 Ves 143, 145, 32 ER 307; *Bedson* v. *Bedson* [1965] 2 QB 666, 697F–698A, Lord Denning MR; *Appleton* v. *Appleton* [1965] 1 WLR 25; JE Martin [1982] *Conv* 305, 309; *Dennis* v. *McDonald* [1982] Fam 63, 73–74, Purchas J; *Bernard* v. *Josephs* [1982] Ch 391, CA.

[112] TLATA 1996 s 13(5)(6).

[113] FLA 1996 s 40.

[114] *Re Pavlou* [1993] 1 WLR 1046, Millett J.

[115] *Re Landi* [1939] Ch 828; *Williams* v. *Holland* [1965] 1 WLR 739, CA.

[116] *Re Warren* [1932] 1 Ch 42, 47, Maugham J.

[117] *Turton* v. *Turton* [1988] Ch 542, 548E–G; J Warburton [1987] *Conv* 378; J Montgomery [1988] *Fam Law* 72; *Gordon* v. *Douce* [1983] 1 WLR 563, CA; *Walker* v. *Hall* [1984] FLR 126, 131G, 136D; *Passee* v. *Passee* [1988] 1 FLR 263, CA; *Hall* v. *Hall* (1982) 3 FLR 379, CA.

[118] *Re Gorman* [1990]1 WLR 616; also on a bankruptcy order.

[119] [1982] Ch 391, CA.

[120] *Cobb* v. *Cobb* [1955] 1 WLR 731, CA; *Cracknell* v. *Cracknell* [1971] P 356; *Davis* v. *Vale* [1971] 1 WLR 1022, CA; *Crisp* v. *Mullings* [1976] 2 EGLR 103, CA (unequal); *Bernard* v. *Josephs* [1982] Ch 391, 400, Denning MR, 405, Griffiths LJ; *Hembury* v. *Peachey* (1996) 72 P & CR D47, CA (no prior agreement); query whether to allow capital or capital and interest.

[121] *Davis* v. *Vale* [1971] 1 WLR 1022, CA; *Coley* v. *Coley* (1975) 5 Fam Law 195, CA; *Bernard* v. *Josephs* [1982] Ch 391, 400.

[122] *Dennis* v. *McDonald* [1982] Fam 63, 74–75, affirmed at 79, CA; *Bernard* v. *Josephs* [1982] Ch 391, 401B, Lord Denning MR; *Re Gorman* [1990] 1 WLR 616; *Re Pavlou* [1993] 1 WLR 1046 (not if any party objects).

[123] When the co-owned property is let it should be valued on a tenanted basis, not with vacant possession: *Butcher* v. *Wolfe* [1998] EGCS 153, CA.

the one who has left, and a short postponement of sale is in order to facilitate this.[124] Otherwise a global sum is produced by the sale from which are deducted the costs of sale, and the redemption figure for any mortgage[125] to arrive at the divisible equity. Equitable accounting adjusts that sum.

E. BENEFICIARIES AS AGAINST CREDITORS

"If a household is divided against itself, the house will never stand."[126]

1. Interests of creditors

[19.25] Creditors may become involved in the matrimonial home in various ways. In this passage we are concerned with cases where a creditor becomes entitled as a beneficial co-owner of the matrimonial home against the interests of the family who remain beneficially interested. Suppose two spouses were beneficial joint tenants, thus

to H and W on trust for H and W as beneficial joint tenants.

Let us further assume that it is H who has been imprudent, though it could, of course, just as well be W. Creditors may become entitled to a charge on H's share in various ways:

a mortgage by H of his beneficial interest;
a fraudulent attempt by H to mortgage the legal estate by forging W's signature, which cannot charge the legal estate but will change H's beneficial interest;
the bankruptcy of H;
the making of a charging order against H's beneficial interest.

Creditors will be keen to force a sale of the property, realising its value in cash which can be used to pay H's debts. His wife is likely to oppose sale on behalf of herself and their children and must be joined in the proceedings.[127]

2. Creditors' sale – old law for trusts for sale

[19.26] Almost invariably creditors were able to obtain an immediate order for the sale of any property over which they had a charge on a beneficial interest. Money talked. Matrimonial purposes were subordinated to the interests of creditors in *Re Citro*.[128] Two brothers had become bankrupt.[129] Carmine lived in the matrimonial

---

[124] *Bernard* v. *Josephs* [1982] Ch 391, 401; *Turton* v. *Turton* [1988] Ch 542, CA.

[125] *Bernard* at 400; *Turton* v. *Turton* [1988] Ch 542, CA; J Montgomery [1988] *Fam Law* 72; *Abbey National BS* v. *Cann* [1991] 1 AC 56, 93B, Lord Oliver.

[126] *St Mark* ch 3, v 25.

[127] *Judd* v. *Brown* [1999] 1 FLR 1191, CA.

[128] [1991] Ch 142, CA; JC Hall [1991] *CLJ* 45; S Cretney (1991) 107 *LQR* 177; D Brown (1991) 55 *MLR* 284; A Lawson [1991] *Conv* 302; *Barclays Bank* v. *Hendricks* [1996] 1 FLR 258; *Zandfarid* v. *Bank of Credit and Commerce International* [1996] 1 WLR 1420, Parker J; *Bankers Trust Co* v. *Namdar* [1996] EGCS 20, CA; A Dunn [1996] *Conv* 371; *Re Ng* [1998] 2 FLR 386; *Bowe* v. *Trustee of Bowe* [1998] 2 FLR 439.

[129] The case was decided before the changes to bankruptcy law in 1986 discussed below.

home with his wife and children,[130] whereas Domenico had left his wife and the children, the youngest of whom was aged 10.[131] The Court of Appeal ordered immediate sale of both properties over the heads of the children.[132]

Short term deferment was allowed to allow a spouse to find alternative accommodation or to allow the remaining wife to buy out the bankrupt's interest.[133] In *Re Gorman*[134] sale was deferred for six months for the wife to pursue a negligence claim, but any longer delay in sale would have required very exceptional circumstances. No doubt the court had power to adjudicate upon "whose voice ought to prevail?"[135] But the answer was always the trustee in bankruptcy or creditor unless there were really compelling reasons absent from the ordinary run of cases for refusing sale.[136] In *Re Holliday*[137] there was plenty of equity available to clear the debt and the creditors would eventually get their money in full since the husband himself had petitioned as a tactical move to prevent a property transfer order on divorce.[138] Immediate sale was refused. His wife was allowed to continue in occupation with her three young children until the youngest child attained 17. Another exceptional circumstance was the fact that the husband was terminally ill and was expected to die within six months.[139]

Re Citro was a case between bankrupts under the pre-1986 law. Its principles applied to most claims by creditors for the exercise of a pre-1997 trust for sale, though ironically no longer to trustees in bankruptcy. Examples are mortgage-lenders,[140] receivers appointed to enforce a debt,[141] and creditors with charging orders.[142]

How was priority determined between a purchaser of a beneficial interest and a beneficiary claiming a purpose trust? Generally the trust could be overreached, but not where, as in *Chhokar* v. *Chhokar*,[143] the purchaser was acting in consort with a beneficial co-owner may not be seen as having an interest distinct from the party who sells to them. The husband sold the matrimonial home to a purchaser who was party to a conspiracy to oust the wife. He paid less than the market value for the husband's share and was party to a campaign to try to oust her. The purchaser stood in the shoes of the husband, and was bound by the purpose; this should have been so even if the wife had not forgiven her husband and taken him back(!). A scoundrel should not get equitable assistance.

---

[130] *Boydell* v. *Gillespie* (1970) 216 EG 1505; *Re Turner* [1974] 1 WLR 1556; *Re Densham* [1975] 1 WLR 1519; *Re Lowrie* [1981] 3 All ER 353.

[131] *Re Solomon* [1967] Ch 573; *Re Bailey* [1977] 1 WLR 278.

[132] *Re Lowrie* [1981] 3 All ER 353; *Re Bailey* [1977] 1 WLR 278, Megarry V-C.

[133] *Re Turner* [1974] 1 WLR 1556 (2 months).

[134] [1990] 1 WLR 616, Div Ct.

[135] *Re Solomon* [1967] Ch 573, 588, Goff J; C Palley (1969) 20 *NILQ* 132; *Re Turner* [1974] 1 WLR 1556; *Re Densham* [1975] 1 WLR 1519; A Lawson [1991] *Conv* 302, 304–306.

[136] *Re Citro* [1991] Ch 142, 156–157, Nourse LJ, 160E, 161E, Bingham LJ; *Harman* v. *Glencross* [1986] Fam 81, 104, Fox LJ.

[137] [1981] Ch 405; A Sydenham [1981] *Conv* 79; C Hand (1981) 97 *LQR* 200; *Re Citro* [1991] Ch 142, Waller LJ dissenting; *Re Mott* [1987] CLYB 212, Hoffmann J.

[138] *Re Lowrie* [1981] 3 All ER 353, 355, Walton J.

[139] *Re Bremner* [1999] 1 FLR 912.

[140] *Kemmis* v. *Kemmis* [1988] 1 WLR 1307; *Lloyds Bank* v. *Byrne* (1991) 23 HLR 472, 478, Parker LJ.

[141] *Levermore* v. *Levermore* [1979] 1 WLR 1277, Balcombe J.

[142] *Thames Guaranty* v. *Campbell* [1985] QB 210, CA; *First National Securities* v. *Hegerty* [1985] QB 850; *Harman* v. *Glencross* [1986] Fam 81, CA; NP Gravells (1985) 5 *OJLS* 132; PF Smith [1985] *Conv* 129; J Warburton [1986] *Conv* 218; *Midland Bank* v. *Pike* [1988] 2 All ER 434, Ch D.

[143] [1984] FLR 313, CA.

3. Creditors under trust of land

[19.27] *Mortgage Corporation* v. *Shaire*[144] is a crucially important case which determines whether *Citro* principles continue to apply in the post-1996 world to a trust of land. It was held that the trusts of land scheme is significantly different.

A matrimonial home was vested in the joint names of Mr and Mrs Shaire, when Shaire mortgaged his interest to secure his business debts, along with his partners, Fox, Blaxhill, and Silkin. The Mortgage Corporation sought an order for sale of the property and so an order for vacant possession against Mrs Shaire. The issue was determined under section 15 of the Trusts of Land Act 1996. Neuberger J held that this was more favourable to the wife than the 1925 legislation. Under section 15 the court had to consider the following four factors:

(1) the intentions of the creator of the trust;
(2) the purposes of the trust;
(3) the welfare of any minor whose home is in the property; and
(4) the interests of any secured creditor.

This requires a balance between the interests of the family (2 and 3) and the interests of the creditor (4), with nothing to say that the interests of creditors should automatically prevail.[145] On the particular facts the court refused to order sale on the facts, though a sale is appropriate if the wife has only a very small beneficial interest.[146] The fundamental shift from *Re Citro* creates a division between mortgages and bankruptcy.[147]

It may be necessary to grant a stay pending the decision about whether to grant ancillary relief to the wife, that is whether or not to make a property adjustment order over the head of the lender.[148]

4. Bankruptcy

[19.28] A general review of bankruptcy law led to new provisions in the Insolvency Act 1986.[149] Payments for the occupation of premises cannot give the bankrupt any beneficial interest.[150] New rights cannot accrue after the presentation of a bankruptcy petition from a marriage or purchase of a matrimonial home after the bankruptcy petition. Any matrimonial home right continues in force,[151] but control of sale and occupation passes to the bankruptcy court, which may continue or terminate it.[152]

---

[144] [2001] Ch 743 Neuberger J; M Oldham [2001] *CLJ* 43; *A* v. *B* [1997] May 23rd, Cazalet J.
[145] Nor was there under LPA 1925 s 30. It may be doubted whether this decision will survive at appellate level.
[146] *Bank of Ireland* v. *Bell* [2001] 2 FLR 809; R Probert [2002] *Conv* 61.
[147] IA 1986 as amended by TLATA 1996 continues to apply *Citro;* see below **[19.28]**.
[148] *Le Foe* v. *Le Foe* [2001] 2 FLR 970, Fam Div; on appeal *Woolwich* v. *Le Foe* [2001] EWCA Civ 1870; J James [2001] 23 *JSWFL* 353.
[149] S 336; C Hand [1983] *Conv* 219; JG Miller [1986] *Conv* 393; S Wheeler [1989] *JSWL* 101.
[150] IA 1986 s 338.
[151] A change made in 1986.
[152] S 336(1)–(2).

A bankrupt has a right of occupation of his home on behalf of his *minor children*[153] with whom he is sharing a home, so that they can only be evicted by court order, or if they are living elsewhere, they have a right against the trustee in bankruptcy to enter with leave of the court. The court has jurisdiction to enforce or terminate the rights.

Contests involving a co-ownership between a trustee in bankruptcy and a spouse over occupation and sale of the matrimonial home – a modern replaying of *Re Citro*[154] – would now be fought out in a bankruptcy court,[155] applying provisions introduced by the trusts of land legislation.[156] Applications *within one year* of bankruptcy by the trustee in bankruptcy for sale of a matrimonial home[157] will take into account the interests of the creditors as a weighty factor, but this will not necessarily outweigh all other considerations. The court has to balance all relevant factors, including any conduct by the spouse contributing to the bankruptcy,[158] the needs and financial resources of the claimant, the needs of any children and all other circumstances.[159] *After one year*, the court is required to consider the interests of the bankrupt's creditors,[160] and where an application for sale is made more than a year after vesting of the property in the trustee in bankruptcy, the court must assume that these interests outweigh all other considerations. Sale will be usual, but a residual jurisdiction remains[161] to defer sale if "the circumstances of the case are exceptional".[162]

5. Consent trusts

[19.29] In some cases in the past creditors had to be balanced against a person with an implied power to refuse consent to a sale. *Abbey National Building Society* v. *Moss*[163] shows that the continuing occupation right created by the consent provision could not be overridden in the interests of creditors, but Hirst LJ dissented and in *Bank of Baroda* v. *Dhillon*[164] the court ordered sale, favouring *Re Citro* over *Moss*.

---

[153] S 337.
[154] [1991] Ch 142, CA (bankruptcy in 1985).
[155] IA 1986 s 336(3).
[156] S 335A, inserted by TLATA 1996 sch 3, and retrospective.
[157] S 335(2)(b).
[158] *Re Densham* [1975] 1 WLR 1519 (participation in reckless spending).
[159] IA 1986 ss 335A(2), 336(4), 337(5).
[160] Ss 335(2)(a), 336(4)(a), 337(6).
[161] Ss 335A(3), 336(5), 337(6); *Re Citro* [1991] Ch 142, 159G, Nourse LJ (old law).
[162] *Judd* v. *Brown* [1999] 1 FLR 1191, CA (cancer); *Re Raval* [1998] 2 FLR 718 (mental illness of wife, postpone 12 months); C Wagstaffe (1998) 28 *Fam Law* 99; *Claughton* v. *Charalambous* [1998] BPIR 558, Ch D (severe disability).
[163] [1994] 1 FLR 307, CA; DN Clarke [1994] *Conv* 331; *Re Mott* [1987] CLYB 212, Hoffmann J; *Harris* v. *Harris* (1996) 72 P & CR 408, CA.
[164] [1998] 1 FLR 524, CA; S Pascud [1998] *Conv* 415.

F. OCCUPATION ORDERS

1. Co-owners

[19.30] Part IV of the Family Law Act 1996 gives powers to make occupation orders affecting family homes.[165] It may be the current home, or one used in the past or intended for the future. Disputes about occupation should be resolved by application for an order in preference to the enforcement of pure property law rights.[166] Occupation orders will be in play where two conditions apply:

(1) Each party has a property law entitlement to occupy a family home, for example as a beneficial co-owner or as a joint licensee or under shared security of tenure.

(2) The parties are associated.[167] This will be the case if they are spouses,[168] former spouses, heterosexual cohabitants, former heterosexual cohabitants, people who live in the same household under a non-commercial arrangement,[169] relatives of defined classes, people who had agreed to marry, or parties to other family proceedings. Proposals to extend protection to all those who had enjoyed (or indeed not enjoyed) sexual relations were dropped because of the difficulty of proof!

2. Spouses

[19.31] Occupation orders are available to any spouse who is entitled to occupy a matrimonial home[170] under a matrimonial home right.[171] They may be indefinite.[172] The court is *required* to make an order where harm is likely to be suffered by the applicant or a relevant child living with him which outweighs the harm likely to be suffered by the other spouse and any children living with him.[173] In other cases the court *may* make an order taking into account:[174] (1) the housing needs and resources of each party including relevant children, (2) the financial resources of each party, (3) the likely effect on the health, safety and well being of the parties and any relevant child, and (4) conduct in relation to each other and generally.

Matrimonial home rights and occupation orders between spouses will end on the death of either spouse,[175] and on divorce,[176] unless the court has prolonged it.[177] The

---

[165] FLA 1996 ss 33(3)–(4); J Dewar "Land, Law, and the Family Home" ch 13 in Bright & Dewar; M Humphries (2001) 31 *Fam Law* 542.

[166] *Nwogbe* v. *Nwogbe* [2000] 2 FLR 744, CA.

[167] FLA 1996 ss 33(1), 62; *G* v. *F* [2000] Fam 186, Wall J.

[168] Derived from MHA 1983 s 9 and earlier Acts; *Scott* v. *Scott* [1992] 1 FLR 529, CA.

[169] Not as employee, tenant, lodger or boarder, but including house sharers and homosexual partners.

[170] Orders can be made for renewable periods of 6 months where occupation is under a bare licence (FLA 1996 s 37) or of a caravan, houseboat or other structure (s 63).

[171] FLA 1996 s 33(1)(a). *Hoggett* v. *Hoggett* (1980) 39 P & CR 121, 128, decided under the old law that this applied when the right was unregistered.

[172] FLA 1996 s 33(10).

[173] S 33(7). This stiffens the old law.

[174] S 33(6).

[175] S 33(9)(b).

[176] *O'Malley* v. *O'Malley* [1982] 1 WLR 244, CA; *Lucas* v. *Lucas* [1992] 2 FLR 53, CA.

[177] FLA 1996 ss 31(8), 33(5), 33(8).

position of *former spouses* is improved by the 1996 Act, since temporary occupation orders can be obtained by a former spouse where inadequate provision was made by the divorce court.[178] This can be done while both spouses remain alive, but after the other spouse has died the only possibility is a claim for family provision as a dependant left inadequately provided for.[179]

3. Non-entitled co-habitants

[19.32] A sharp distinction is drawn between entitled applicants (spouses and equitable co-owners) and cohabitants who have no property entitlement. Any occupation order made in favour of the latter category will be temporary and made only after account is taken of the degree of emotional commitment to the relationship.[180] A heterosexual cohabitant may obtain an occupation order to stay in a home in which he has no property law right, but only in the short term (six months with at most one renewal).

4. Children

[19.33] Children[181] will not usually be able to obtain an occupation order against their parents,[182] since the children usually occupy as bare licensees.[183] An order could be made if the child has a property interest in the family home.[184]

5. Scope of occupation orders

[19.34] Occupation orders may be sought by a freestanding applications or along with a divorce petition or other family applications when all proceedings should be determined together.[185] There is power to make orders before notice has been given to the other party where there are significant risks to the applicant or any relevant child.[186] Innumerable cases demonstrate how the family courts should exercise the powers within the family but this book concentrates on proprietary enforcement against lenders and buyers.

(1) Conferring occupation

[19.35] The court may

enforce one person's right to occupation against the other;
require the occupier to admit the non-occupier;

---

[178] S 35 (6 months, renewable).
[179] Inheritance (Provision for Family and Dependants) A 1975; *Andrew* v. *Andrew* [1990] 2 FLR 376.
[180] FLA 1996 s 36.
[181] Except those with a trust interest in the home.
[182] FLA 1996 s 59.
[183] *Metropolitan Properties Co* v. *Cronan* (1982) 44 P & CR 1, 18; *Waterhouse* v. *Waterhouse* (1905) 95 LT 133; *Stevens* v. *Stevens* (1907) 24 TLR 20; *Egan* v. *Egan* [1975] Ch 218.
[184] FLA 1996 s 59.
[185] Ss 39–40.
[186] S 45.

regulate the terms of occupation – requiring rent or repair and covering the cost of outgoings;[187]
declare the existence of a matrimonial home right;[188] and
vary or discharge orders.[189]

For example in one case in which a wealthy politician cohabited with an impecunious student who had contributed to the development of his career, the court delayed sale of the property until she had finished her studies.[190]

(2) Exclusion orders

[19.36] Negative impacts might include:

prohibiting occupation by the owner;[191]
ordering an occupier to leave;
excluding him from a defined area of the house; or
restricting or terminating the matrimonial home right.

A balance has to be made between harm to the applicant and harm caused by exclusion to the respondent, the interests of children being most prominent,[192] though details of the way that the jurisdiction is exercised lie beyond the scope of this book. After domestic violence has occurred an injunction may be supported by a non-molestation order[193] and/or a power of arrest.[194]

G. MATRIMONIAL HOME RIGHTS

"Wedlock and a padlock much the same".[195]

[19.37] Part IV of the Family Law Act 1996[196] is a reconsolidation of the matrimonial homes legislation dating from 1967. The matrimonial home right[197] is given only to "spouses",[198] a terms which applies neutrally to husbands[199] and wives, though no doubt protection is most commonly needed by women, as a result of the hangover of old marriages in which the matrimonial home was held in the husband's sole name.[200] Cohabitants cannot take advantage of matrimonial home rights.

[187] See below **[19.21ff]**.
[188] FLA 1996 s 33(4).
[189] S 49.
[190] *Chun Pui Chun* v. *Leung Kam Ho* [2002] BPIR 723, Ch D.
[191] FLA 1996 ss 33(3), 36(5), 36(5), 37–38; formerly "ouster injunctions".
[192] Ss 33(7), 35(8).
[193] S 42.
[194] S 47.
[195] Byron *Don Juan* v, clviii.
[196] Ss 30–32, sch 4; Law Com 207 (1992); M Hayes (1990) 53 *MLR* 222; M Horton [1996] *Fam Law* 49; Megarry & Wade (6th ed), [17.021–17.027].
[197] FLA 1996 s 30(2).
[198] S 30(1); polygamous marriages were included in 1981: s 63(5).
[199] *Barnett* v. *Hassett* [1981] 1 WLR 1385.
[200] By 1983, 73% of all homes were held by a man and woman jointly, though this figure fell by 1996 to 61% as a result of the rise of "girl power", not the Spice Girls but women as sole owners. According to the Halifax survey (August 2002) 40% of homes are now held by sole owners.

1.   Bare spouses

[19.38] A "bare" wife[201] with no legal or equitable property right in the family house was stripped of all defences against a lender when the Lords rejected Mrs Ainsworth's claim in 1965.[202] This gap was plugged by Matrimonial Homes Act 1967,[203] which enabled Lord Denning to lay claim to victory in his battle over the rights of women with the Lords.[204] To use the modern statutory terminology, protection exists where one spouse (the beneficial owner) is entitled to occupy a matrimonial home and the other spouse (the claimant) is not so entitled.[205] This involves several rights. (1) If the claimant spouse already occupies the matrimonial home it is a right not to be evicted or excluded by the other spouse, except by court order. (2) A spouse who is out of occupation has a right to take up occupation with the leave of the court.[206] (3) A matrimonial home right gives standing to apply for an occupation order against the other spouse, so the court has power to prevent sale in appropriate cases. (4) The claimant may register the right, so as to give proprietary protection against buyers and lenders.

2.   Equitable co-owners

[19.39] Many a spouse who is not on the legal title has contributed to the purchase so as to become an equitable tenant in common. Thus *to H in fee simple on trust for H and W as beneficial tenants in common.* The pioneer legislation in 1967 did not protect a spouse like W who was an equitable co-owner,[207] but protection was just as necessary because of the vulnerability to overreaching. Since 1970 a woman in the position of Mrs Boland[208] has been protected, because when determining entitlement of a claimant to occupy against the legal owner, any equitable interest is ignored. Unconsidered consolidation has not improved this messy terminology.[209] Duplicate protection is provided – in addition to the claim to a share as a beneficial co-owner, the spouse can also register a matrimonial home right to prevent sale.

3.   Exclusion of legal and equitable co-owner

[19.40] Matrimonial homes are generally vested in husband and wife at law as beneficial joint tenants, but in this archetypal case neither has a matrimonial home right. It is thought to be sufficient protection that either party can block an undesirable dealing by the other by refusing to execute the transfer or mortgage. In fact spouses on the legal title are not adequately protected against a loan secured on the other spouses'

---

[201] *Gurasz* v. *Gurasz* [1970] P 11, 17, Lord Denning MR.
[202] *National Provincial Bank* v. *Ainsworth* [1965] AC 1175, HL; see above **[15.05]**.
[203] MHA 1967; Royal Commission on *Marriage and Divorce*, Cmnd 9678; OM Stone (1968) 31 *MLR* 305.
[204] *Gurasz* v. *Gurasz* [1970] P 11, 16H.
[205] FLA 1996 s 30(1).
[206] S 30(2)(a)–(b).
[207] *Gurasz* v. *Gurasz* [1970] P 11, CA.
[208] *Williams & Glyn's Bank* v. *Boland* [1981] AC 487, HL.
[209] FLA 1996 s 30(9).

beneficial share, given that the lender will be able to force a sale,[210] and additional protection is needed in this case.

4. Beneficiaries

[19.41] Matrimonial home rights are now recognised where one spouse is entitled to occupy as a beneficiary under a trust, but the amendment to plug this gap is awkwardly worded,[211] so much so that it is proposed to depart, with apologies, from gender neutral language and to assume that the wife is seeking protection against her husband who occupies as a beneficiary. There are four rules. *One*: H must be entitled to a beneficial interest under a trust while W is not so entitled.[212] But *two*: if W also holds an equitable interest she still has a matrimonial home right provided she is not also on the legal title.[213] *Three*: if the right exists (under rules 1 and 2) and H is the only beneficiary under the trust the matrimonial home right is a charge on the legal estate held by the trustees.[214] *Four*: if H is one of several beneficiaries, H's beneficial interest is charged, but not the legal estate. Thus:

(1) if *T1 and T2 hold on trust for H and W*, no matrimonial home right is available to W[215] – a serious gap;
(2) if *T1 and H hold on trust for H and X*, there is a matrimonial home right against the other spouse, but not against the trustees;[216]
(3) If *T1 and H hold on trust for H and W*, there is a matrimonial home right against the legal estate, which is not overreachable.[217]

Literally, no matrimonial charge arose in favour of a wife with an exclusive contractual licence, even if her husband was a beneficial co-owner. Common sense suggests that a matrimonial right should exist both against the husband and against the property by registration.[218]

5. Borrowers

[19.42] Most couples borrow money to buy their home. The existence of the mortgage makes no difference either way to any matrimonial home right.[219] Repayments of instalments must be accepted from the spouse who is entitled to a matrimonial home right[220]: a "connected person" is entitled to be made a party to proceedings and to take on the borrower's liabilities, provided application is made before a final

---

[210] See above **[19.27]**.
[211] MH and Property A 1981 s 1(1).
[212] FLA 1996 s 30(1).
[213] S 30(9).
[214] S 31(4)–(7). Ignore for this purpose potential beneficiaries under a power of appointment exercisable by either spouse.
[215] S 30(1), (9).
[216] S 31(4); *Chaudhry* v. *Chaudhry* [1987] 1 FLR 347, CA.
[217] FLA 1996 ss 30(9), 31(4)–(7), 31(13).
[218] *Kalsi* v. *Kalsi* [1992] Fam Law 333, CA.
[219] FLA 1996 ss 54, 63.
[220] S 30(3)–(6); also against a purchaser: s 34(1).

repossession order.[221] A spouse who has registered a matrimonial home right is entitled to a notice from the lender before the lender commences possession proceedings.[222]

6. Rented homes

[19.43] What if a couple live in rented accommodation? Matrimonial home rights of occupation exist where one spouse is the legal or contractual tenant and the other is not,[223] whatever the form of lease or tenancy and whatever the security of tenure regime in operation,[224] but not under a bare licence from parents or employers.[225] Tenders of rent must be accepted from the spouse claiming the right of occupation[226] and occupation counts for the purposes of claiming security of tenure.[227]

If (say) the wife remains in occupation of accommodation rented in her husband's name when they separate, there is a danger that the husband will not have sufficient occupation to keep a statutory tenancy alive, that he will not bother to pay the rent, and that he may surrender his tenancy. The wife should seek a transfer of a tenancy by a property adjustment order made on divorce. There is also power to order the transfer of *statutory* tenancies in the public or private sectors,[228] a transfer which includes a notional transfer of the occupation necessary to keep the statutory tenancy on foot.[229]

7. Homes other than matrimonial homes

[19.44] Protection is confined to a dwelling house,[230] and one either occupied together by the married couple as their home,[231] or at least *intended* for joint use:[232] a house bought for occupation by one spouse alone is not covered.[233] If several homes qualify, one may be selected by registration.[234]

---

[221] S 55.

[222] A search is required and proceedings must be commenced within the priority period of the search: s 56; SI 1997/1964 r 6; DLRR 2003 rr 159–161; see below **[30.28]**.

[223] FLA 1996 s 30(1). Protection applies between spouses and not as against the landlord: *Sanctuary H Ass* v. *Campbell* [1999] 1 WLR 1279, CA.

[224] *Tarr* v. *Tarr* [1973] AC 254, HL; *Richards* v. *Richards* [1984] AC 174, HL.

[225] See below **[19.61]**.

[226] FLA 1996 s 30(3).

[227] S 30(4). Results can be capricious: *Hoggett* v. *Hoggett* (1980) 39 P & CR 121; *Hall* v. *King* (1988) 55 P & CR 307; *Griffiths* v. *Renfree* (1989) 21 HLR 338, CA.

[228] FLA 1996 sch 7 para 2; *Crago* v. *Julian* [1992] 1 WLR 372; P Sparkes [1992] *Conv* 375.

[229] FLA 1996 s 53, sch 7; *Jones* v. *Jones* [1997] Fam 59, CA. Liability for arrears of rent may also transfer: *Church Commissioners for England* v. *Al Emarah* [1997] Fam 34, CA.

[230] FLA 1996 s 63(1), (4) (caravans and houseboats excluded). A commonhold unit is included: Chold and L Ref A 2002 s 61.

[231] *Collins* v. *Collins* (1973) 4 Fam Law 133, CA; *Whittingham* v. *Whittingham* [1979] Fam 9, 16B; *Kemmis* v. *Kemmis* [1988] 1 WLR 1307, 1321A.

[232] FLA 1996 sch 4 para 2; Law Com 207 (1992), [4.4]; *Syed* v. *Syed* (1980) 1 FLR 129 (old law).

[233] *Nanda* v. *Nanda* [1968] P 351; *Chaudhry* v. *Chaudhry* [1987] 1 FLR 347; *Hall* v. *King* (1988) 85 P & CR 307. The deserted wife's equity also fails.

[234] FLA 1996 sch 4 para 2.

H. MATRIMONIAL HOME RIGHT: PROPRIETARY ENFORCEMENT

1. A registrable charge

[19.45] The matrimonial home right provides proprietary protection for a spouse's occupation against a purchaser. It creates a new kind of equitable interest,[235] which operates as a charge (that is a burden) on the legal estate owned by the other spouse. Registration must affect the legal estate in the matrimonial home.[236] Protection against purchasers and lenders[237] is dependent on registration,[238] which is allowed even if the spouse claiming protection is out of occupation.[239] Occupation is irrelevant: the right cannot be an overriding interest[240] and notice is also irrelevant. An essential first step is to discover by means of an index map search whether or not title to the matrimonial home is registered.[241]

If title to the home is unregistered, the matrimonial home right requires registration as a land charge of class F[242] which must be against the name of the other spouse as it appears on the unregistered title deeds. Most matrimonial homes have registered titles, in which case a class F is useless,[243] and protection depends upon entry of a land registry notice.[244] A full notice will be entered even without the consent of the registered proprietor (contrary to the practice for other forms of notice), though a warning will now be given to the proprietor. Notices can be lodged electronically.[245]

The court has power to extend protection past the death or divorce of either spouse, and if it does so this extended right must also be registered.[246]

Termination of the charge is caused by the death of either spouse, a divorce decree absolute, or a court order ending the right to occupy.[247] Any registration needs to be cancelled if the underlying right is terminated,[248] and also if protection of a right in a first home is superseded by registration of a second charge.[249]

2. Defects of registration

[19.46] The blot on an unregistered title created by a Class F registration may be unknown to the owner, though proprietors of registered homes are now being given

[235] WT Murphy (1983) 46 *MLR* 330.
[236] FLA 1996 s 31(10). The charge survives surrender of a leasehold interest: s 31(9).
[237] *Hastings & Thanet BS* v. *Goddard* [1970] 1 WLR 1544, CA; *Williams & Glyn's Bank* v. *Boland* [1981] AC 487, HL.
[238] FLA 1996 s 31(2); FR Crane (1968) 32 *Conv (NS)* 85.
[239] *Watts* v. *Waller* [1973] 1 QB 153, 177, Sachs LJ.
[240] FLA 1996 s 31(1), as amended by LRA 2002 sch 11.
[241] The search should indicate its purpose so that the land registry need not investigate boundaries; see above **[8.20]**.
[242] LCA 1972 s 2(7).
[243] *Miles* v. *Bull* [1969] 1 QB 258; *(No 2)* [1969] 3 All ER 1585; *Hastings & Thanet BS* v. *Goddard* [1970] 1 WL 1544, CA.
[244] FLA 1996 s 31(10); DLRR 2003 r 82.
[245] See above **[8.04]**.
[246] FLA 1996 sch 4 paras 4(2)–(5).
[247] Ss 31(8), 33.
[248] Sch 4 para 4.
[249] Sch 4 para 2.

warning of a matrimonial home notice. Violence is only too likely if a man becomes aware of a hostile registration by his wife. There is no practical way to control spite registrations,[250] unless an improper motive can be proved.[251] A disaffected spouse is handed a "weapon of great power and flexibility",[252] which can be used to vicious effect to block sale.

Registration is a hostile procedure inherently unsuitable for family interests, and anyway the need for it is often overlooked by spouses who have not heard of registration, and would not understand it.[253] Protection will only occur where legal advice is sought as a result of matrimonial difficulties, when it may well be too late to stop a mortgage.[254] Millions of possible registrations result in very few actual registrations,[255] so that the practical result is mass invalidity of charges.[256] No practicable alternative has been found.[257] Might a register of marriages be a solution?

3. Procedure on sale – registered charges

[19.47] Any contract for the sale of a house with vacant possession has implied into it a term that the seller will procure cancellation of any matrimonial home registration before completion. Any application for cancellation must be checked most carefully by the buyer to ensure that it will be effective and has been signed by the registering spouse personally.[258]

A seller may easily put himself in the impossible situation of the husband in *Wroth* v. *Tyler*.[259] A civil servant in London decided that, on his retirement, he would sell the bungalow in Surrey and buy a similar bungalow free of mortgage in Norfolk. His wife appeared to support the move, for example by showing potential buyers how to work the cooker, until after her husband had exchanged contracts for the sale of the Surrey bungalow. Then she registered, apparently because their daughter had decided that she did not wish to move away from her friends. The husband was forced to break his sale contract. Megarry J declined to order specific performance, on the principle that a contracting party is not compelled to engage in hazardous litigation to secure removal of an incumbrance, but instead ordered damages for failure to sell the house with vacant possession. Since the contract price was £7,500 and the value of the bungalow had increased to £11,500, the award was in the order of £5,000, an order which might well have bankrupted the husband.

---

[250] *Wroth* v. *Tyler* [1974] Ch 30, 64, Megarry J; *Wicks* v. *Wicks* [1998] Fam 65, CA.

[251] *Barnett* v. *Hassett* [1982] 1 WLR 1385.

[252] *Wroth* v. *Tyler* [1974] Ch 30, 46, Megarry J.

[253] *Boland* [1979] Ch 312, 328E–F, Denning MR, 339F, Ormrod LJ.

[254] An injunction can be obtained if the need for it is known in time: *Sherry* v. *Sherry* [1991] 1 FLR 307, CA.

[255] In 1995–1996 there were less than 2,000 class F registrations according to the CLR *Report 1995–1996*. There seems to be no public record of the number of registrations affecting registered titles.

[256] If all charges were registered, most would be useless: *Wroth* v. *Tyler* [1974] Ch 30, 64B, Megarry J.

[257] Law Com 86 (1978), [2.83].

[258] FLA 1986 sch 4 para 5; *Holmes* v. *Kennard & Son* (1984) 49 P & CR 202; NS Price [1985] *Conv* 293.

[259] [1974] Ch 30; DJ Hayton (1974) 38 *Conv (NS)* 110; DG Barnsley (1974) 27 *CLP* 76.

4. Procedure on sale – potential registrations

[19.48] Where a house vested in a single name is being sold by a person who may be married, action is needed to prevent the sale being snagged by a subsequent matrimonial home registration. A written release must be obtained from the non-contracting spouse,[260] who either joins in the contract or signs a separate waiver.[261] There is no reported example of loss of priority by an implied waiver.[262]

5. Purchase subject to a registered charge

[19.49] Registration of a matrimonial charge will bind any purchaser. However, there remains a discretion about enforcement in the court between a registering spouse and a buyer,[263] a discretion illustrated in *Kashmir Kaur* v. *Gill*.[264] After marrying in India, the wife came to join her husband at a house in Gravesend in July 1985. She left the following January driven out, as the judge found, by the husband's conduct while she was pregnant. While she was living elsewhere, the husband completed the sale of the house to the purchaser, despite the fact that the wife lodged a land registry notice a few days before completion. The buyer's solicitors relied upon a telephone search which did not (at that time) provide priority, so the buyer was bound by the wife's entry on the register.

A majority held that the court could balance the buyer's circumstances against the wife's, and this must be right:[265] buyers can apply for the termination of the rights of occupation just as much as the other spouse can. Very rarely would a purchaser win after buying subject to a registered charge, since his conveyancing has almost inevitably been at fault.[266] In *Kashmir Kaur* however the buyer was blind and had exceptional housing needs. The judge found in his favour and no appeal was made against this exercise of discretion. Personal sympathy for the buyer should not obscure the real cause of his problems, which was the inadequate search conducted on his behalf. Little weight should be given to the interests of a person who buys subject to a registered charge.[267]

6. Priorities

(1) Basic rules

[19.50] A matrimonial home right notice binds those taking under a registered disposition, but if it is unprotected a registered disposition defeats it when the transfer is

---

[260] FLA 1996 sch 4 paras 5–6 (release and deferral).
[261] On avoiding undue influence see below **[30.65]**.
[262] *Wroth* v. *Tyler* [1974] Ch 30, 47; *Barnett* v. *Hassett* [1982] 1 WLR 1385; JE Martin [1983] *Conv* 70.
[263] FLA 1996 s 34. Orders can be varied: s 49(3).
[264] [1988] Fam 110; C Harpum [1988] *CLJ* 355; M Welstead [1988] *Conv* 295; P Sparkes (1988) 52 *MLR* 110.
[265] FLA 1996 s 34.
[266] *Watts* v. *Waller* [1973] 1 QB 153, CA (search allowed to expire); *Holmes* v. *Kennard & Son* (1984) 49 P & CR 202 (ineffective withdrawal).
[267] [1988] Fam 110, 117D, Bingham LJ.

registered. Occupation is no protection.[268] A class F registration binds the world,[269] but the charge is void against a purchaser of a legal estate *or equitable interest* in unregistered land unless registered before completion of the purchase.[270] Between a matrimonial home right and other equitable interests, the principle is (whether title is registered or unregistered) that the first in time prevails. However (and this is of central importance) a matrimonial home right will usually secure priority over other equitable interests because the commencement date is backdated. The right is created on the last of three dates:[271]

(1) the acquisition of the estate or interest in the matrimonial home;
(2) the date of the marriage; and
(3) January 1st, 1968 (when the 1967 Act came into force).[272]

Suppose for example a home was bought by H in 1965, he married W in 1975 and she registered a class F land charge in 1986. Her right of occupation dates on these facts from the marriage in 1975, unless defeated before 1986 by a dealing while it remained vulnerable through non-protection.

(2) Mortgages

[19.51] A matrimonial home right will not be enforceable against a mortgage taken out on initial acquisition of the home, since it will be void for non-registration, and further advances will also secure priority.[273] A matrimonial home right will invariably be lost to a subsequent lender who follows correct conveyancing procedures, since no lender would advance money with a registration in place and will insist on removal of a registered charge, and if it is unregistered it will be lost on completion of the loan. A lender secured on *registered land* may need a legal mortgage to be safe, since in a competition between two equities, the back-dated matrimonial right will have priority over any equitable mortgage created after acquisition.[274] However with *unregistered land*, class F charges can be defeated by a purchaser of an equitable interest,[275] so a lender with an equitable mortgage will be able to take free of an unregistered class F.

(3) Contract

[19.52] Here is the crux.[276] Suppose a charge of a matrimonial home dates from the husband's purchase in 1970. H contracts to sell the house in 1998 to a buyer,[277] but in 1999 W registers a matrimonial home right, before the contract is completed. In *registered land*, the matrimonial registration has priority over the contract, the

---

[268] See above **[20.20]**.
[269] LPA 1925 s 198.
[270] LCA 1972 s 4(8).
[271] FLA 1996 s 31(3).
[272] *Wroth* v. *Tyler* [1974] Ch 30, 43.
[273] FLA 1996 s 31(12).
[274] LRA 2002 ss 28–30.
[275] LCA 1972 s 4(8).
[276] DJ Hayton [1976] *CLP* 26, 29.
[277] It is irrelevant whether the *contract* is registered; query *Watts* v. *Waller* [1973] 1 QB 153, 177, Sachs LJ; see DJ Hayton (1974) 38 *Conv* (NS) 110, 118.

competition being on a first in time basis but modified by the backdating, which pushes the occupation right in the example back to 1970, earlier than the contract.[278] If title is *unregistered*, it is generally assumed that the result is the same. But, a buyer under a contract is a purchaser of an equitable interest and so ought to be allowed to invalidate an unregistered matrimonial home right.[279]

I.   OCCUPATION RIGHTS CREATED BY DIVORCE COURTS

[19.53] Exercise of the court's powers on divorce may create a co-ownership between the spouses, but on the terms that one spouse is entitled to occupy to the exclusion of the other. Sale is regulated under a custom drawn provision.[280] Occupation rights are created for the period of deferral under a trust of land. Rent may be awarded in favour of a spouse excluded who is a beneficial co-owner.[281]

The order of the divorce court may be to prevent realisation during the dependency of a child – a *Mesher* order[282] – or for the life of the wife – a *Martin*[283] order. A family court[284] has power to regulate the sale of matrimonial property.[285] Wide-ranging powers include orders for payments out of the proceeds,[286] that the house be offered to a named person, or to suspend sale on terms,[287] or to order possession.[288] However, variations are limited by the principle that property adjustment is a one-off settlement of affairs at the time of a divorce. If the divorce court states a date on which sale is to occur, this cannot be reviewed,[289] but timing can be reviewed if the property adjustment order is expressed to be subject to further order.[290]

J.   TRUST LICENCES

1.   Licences

[19.54] A licence[291] may confer a right to occupy land. If it is sufficiently extensive it may amount to a full beneficial interest operating as a trust and if so the proprietary

---

[278] LRA 2002 s 28; *Wroth* v. *Tyler* [1974] Ch 30, Megarry J; RJ Smith [1973] *CLJ* 223; DJ Hayton (1974) 38 *Conv* (NS) 110.

[279] LCA 1972 s 4(8); DJ Hayton [1976] *CLP* 26, 29 (option).

[280] MCA 1973 s 24A.

[281] *Harvey v Harvey* [1982] Fam 83; K Gray [1982] *CLJ* 228.

[282] *Mesher* v. *Mesher* [1980] 1 All ER 126, CA; *Dinch* v. *Dinch* [1987] 1 WLR 252, HL.

[283] *Martin* v. *Martin* [1978] Fam 12, CA; *Harvey* v. *Harvey* [1982] Fam 83, CA; *Suter* v. *Suter* [1987] Fam 111, CA; *Clutton* v. *Clutton* [1991] 1 WLR 359, CA; M Hayes (1994) 110 *LQR* 124.

[284] Decisions must not be based on TLATA 1996: *Tee* v. *Tee* [1999] 2 FLR 613, CA.

[285] MCA 1973 s 24A; Law Com 99 (1980).

[286] *Scallon* v. *Scallon* [1990] 1 FLR 194, CA.

[287] MCA 1973 s 24A(4).

[288] *Crosthwaite* v. *Crosthwaite* [1989] 2 FLR 86, CA, reversed by SI 1991/1247 r 2.64(3).

[289] *R* v. *Rushmoor BC ex p Barrett* [1987] QB 275 Reeve J; on appeal [1989] QB 60, CA; *M* v. *M* [1993] 2 FLR 723, CA; *Omielan* v. *Omielan* [1996] 2 FLR 306, CA.

[290] *Thompson* v. *Thompson* [1986] Fam 38, CA.

[291] Dixon's *Principles* (3rd ed) ch 9; Goo's *Sourcebook* (3rd ed) ch 11; Gravells' *LL – Text* (2nd ed) ch 6; Grays' *Elements* (3rd ed), 119–190; Maudsley & Burn *LL – Cases* (7th ed) ch 9; Megarry & Wade (6th ed) ch 17; Smith's *Property Law* (4th ed) ch 19; Thompson's *Modern LL* ch 15. The lease/licence distinction is considered below **[25.73ff]**.

character which many have sought will be created despite the truism that an occupational licence is essentially a personal arrangement between licensor and licensee

2.   Formal licence equivalent to life interest

[19.55] A grant of an interest in land to the exclusion of all others for any indeterminate time created a common law estate,[292] whether for life or determinable on events such as remarriage or giving up occupation. Legal status was withdrawn in 1925, so that in modern law the effect is an equitable life interest or determinable life interest, taking effect behind a trust of land. Since then licences have only been used by mistake.[293] Settlors commonly directed trustees to buy a house and then to permit a named person to occupy it as a residence for as long as that person wanted. An option to reside in a particular[294] house was treated as a full life interest, whether or not a positive election was required before taking up residence,[295] the only practical difference being the dependence upon continued residence and the consequential termination if the beneficiary moved out.[296]

3.   Informal licence as a life interest

[19.56] Extension of this same principle to informal arrangements was decided upon in *Bannister* v. *Bannister*.[297] A widow sold two cottages to her brother-in-law subject to an arrangement that she could live in No 30 for as long as she wanted, rent-free. No 30 was therefore held in trust to permit this and that fact precluded an order for possession.[298] Proprietary protection was needed in *Binions* v. *Evans*.[299] Mr Evans was employed as chauffeur by the Tredegar estate and was provided with a tied cottage from 1922 until his death. Afterwards, "in order to provide a temporary home", they agreed to allow his widow to occupy the cottage as a tenant at will, rent-free, for the remainder of her life. A majority[300] felt bound by authority to treat Mrs Evans as having a life interest under a trust.

True such a trust is informal, but it is created under a constructive trust.[301] As in *Bannister*[302] Mrs Binions took subject to an express condition that they would observe the licence, each paying a reduced price to reflect that burden which made it unconscionable to retain title without admitting the licence. Estoppel is another means of informal creation, arising from an expectation of a life interest created by a

[292] Coke on *Littleton*, [42a]; *Re Carne's SE* [1899] 1 Ch 324, 329, North J.
[293] *Bacon* v. *Bacon* [1947] P 151, Wilmer J. On rectification see: *Dent* v. *Dent* [1996] 1 WLR 683; *Costello* v. *Costello* (1994) 70 P & CR 297, CA.
[294] Contrast a right to live in any house a son should select: *Re Bond's Estate* (1904) 48 SJ 192.
[295] *Re Gibbons* [1920] 1 Ch 372; *Re Anderson* [1920] 1 Ch 175.
[296] *Re Paget's SE* (1885) 30 Ch D 161; *Re Carne's SE* [1899] 1 Ch 324; *Re Trenchard* [1902] 1 Ch 378; *Re Llanover's WT* [1903] 2 Ch 16.
[297] [1948] 2 All ER 133; DC Potter (1948) 11 *MLR* 477 (nothing new!); CPH (1948) 10 *CLJ* 278; AJ Hawkins (1964) 30 *Conv (NS)* 256; E Scammell (1957) 10 *CLP* 152, 161.
[298] *Ivory* v. *Palmer* [1975] ICR 340, 355, Browne LJ.
[299] [1972] Ch 359, CA; PV Baker (1972) 88 *LQR* 338; DJ Hayton (1972) 36 *Conv (NS)* 266; JE Martin (1972) 36 *Conv (NS)* 277; AJ Oakley (1972) 35 *MLR* 551; RJ Smith [1973] *CLJ* 123.
[300] At 370, Megaw LJ, 372, Stephenson LJ.
[301] LPA 1925 s 53(1)(b), (2).
[302] [1948] 2 All ER 133, 136A, Scott LJ.

promise of security[303] and an exercise of the discretion to satisfy that expectation by ordering a full life interest.[304]

4. Trust or licence?

[19.57] If trust analysis has often been applied, it has equally often been ignored. Common law estates were characterised by *exclusive possession* of the land[305] for a particular duration of time, so a licence must be exclusive if it is to confer a life interest under modern law.[306] Hornsby argued[307] that an additional requirement was an intention to create an estate in the land, so that a land owner could create a purely personal licence by demonstrating their intention clearly,[308] for example where personal undertakings have been given to settle divorce proceedings.[309] Domestic arrangements between spouses or cohabiting couples have generally been treated as licences, so the intention to create personal status may perhaps be inferred.[310]

5. Formal strict settlements (pre-1997)

[19.58] Exclusive licences created before 1997 would be equivalent to the grant of a life interest under the Settled Land Act 1925,[311] the licensee being treated as tenant for life and so having the power of sale. This scheme was reinforced by section 106 of the Settled Land Act 1925[312] guarding the statutory powers from attempts to hamper their exercise,[313] direct[314] or indirect.[315] Residence clauses were common, for example *Encombe House to John Scott for life until he ceases to reside there*. In *Re Acklom*[316] a tenant for life subject to a residence clause remained entitled to the income for her life despite letting the property between 1925 and 1927. The attempted forfeiture on non-residence was knocked out by the prohibition of indirect restrictions on leasing.[317] On

---

[303] *Ungurian* v. *Lesnoff* [1990] Ch 206, 223C–D, Vinelott J; M Oldham [1990] *CLJ* 25; P Sparkes [1990] *Conv* 223; *Griffiths* v. *Williams* [1978] 2 EGLR 121, CA (expectation of inheritance).
[304] *Dodsworth* v. *Dodsworth* (1973) 228 EG 1115, CA (repayment of amount spent with occupation until repayment); *Jones* v. *Jones* [1977] 1 WLR 438, CA (time not ripe to order full life interest).
[305] *Street* v. *Mountford* [1985] AC 809, HL.
[306] *Bannister* v. *Bannister* [1948] 2 All ER 133, CA; *Binions* v. *Evans* [1972] Ch 359, CA; *Costello* v. *Costello* (1995) 76 P & CR 297, CA. Query the decision in *Ungurian* v. *Lesnoff* [1990] Ch 206, 224C, Vinelott J; P Sparkes [1990] *Conv* 223, 226.
[307] (1977) 93 *LQR* 561.
[308] *Buck* v. *Haworth* [1947] 1 All ER 342, CA.
[309] *Morss* v. *Morss* [1972] Fam 264, CA; *Dent* v. *Dent* [1996] 1 WLR 683, Ch D.
[310] *Errington* v. *Errington* [1952] 1 KB 290, CA; *Inwards* v. *Baker* [1965] 2 QB 29, CA; *Tanner* v. *Tanner* [1975] 1 WLR 1346, CA; *Chandler* v. *Kerley* [1978] 1 WLR 693, CA; *Hardwick* v. *Johnson* [1978] 1 WLR 683, CA; *Greasley* v. *Cooke* [1980] 1 WLR 1306, CA.
[311] *Costello* v. *Costello* (1996) 70 P & CR 297, CA; *Re Hanson* [1928] Ch 96 (widow entitled to occupy house until son 25 could sell it). Joint licensees were viewed as joint tenants for life: *Re Boyer's SE* [1916] 2 Ch 404; but not individually: *Peasley* v. *Haileybury & Imperial Service College* [2001] WTLR 1365, Ch D.
[312] Effectively re-enacting SLA 1882 s 51: *Re Orlebar* [1936] Ch 147.
[313] *Re Mundy & Roper's C* [1899] 1 Ch 275, 288, CA.
[314] SLA 1925 s 106(1)(a); *Re Paget's SE* (1885) 30 Ch D 161 (subletting). Determinable and conditional interests are valid, as such, with the fetter on sale dropping off: s 106(2)–(3).
[315] SLA 1925 s 106(1)(b).
[316] [1929] 1 Ch 195; *Re Smith* [1899] 1 Ch 331; *Re Richardson* [1904] 2 Ch 777; *Re Sarah Dalrymple* (1901) 49 WR 627; *Re Adair* [1909] 1 IR 311.
[317] *Re Paget's SE* (1885) 30 Ch D 161; *Re Edwards S* [1897] 2 Ch 412.

the other hand, if the tenant for life simply moved out and left the property empty, section 106 was not in play and the forfeiture operated.[318] Similar rules apply to trust funds settled with a house,[319] though there was a controversial exception for trusts to pay the outgoings of land.[320] A licence survives sale, is overreached, and so is converted to a right to income from the proceeds of sale.[321]

Under a trust for sale the licensee risked being overreached by the trustees unless he also had a right to refuse consent to a sale, a protection so essential that it was commonly implied.[322]

6. Informal strict settlements (old law)

[19.59] Where land was limited in a succession created expressly before 1997[323] a strict settlement was created. The decision in *Bannister* v. *Bannister*,[324] followed by the majority in *Binions* v. *Evans*,[325] to extend this to a succession created impliedly stretched the Settled Land Act 1925 to the limits.[326] It is nevertheless followed[327] or accepted as valid and side-stepped.[328]

The impact of the Settled Land Act 1925 was most unhappy. Managerial control and the power of sale was conferred on the licensee, as tenant for life, contrary to the intention of the licensor. In *Costello* v. *Costello*[329] a son financed his parent's acquisition of their council house, but allowed them to occupy the house for as long as they wished rent-free under an express trust deed. When his father died, it was held that legal title should pass to his mother since she was tenant for life. Worse still, settlements of this type were necessarily defective in failing to meet the requirement for two documents, leaving a licensee of registered land very vulnerable to a sale.[330] Conversely, if title was unregistered, all dealings with the legal estate[331] were (and for

---

[318] *Re Haynes* (1888) 37 Ch D 306; *Re Levy's WT* (1885) 30 Ch D 119; *Re Bliss* [2001] 1 WLR 1973, Ferris J (moved out to nursing home).

[319] SLA 1925 s 106(1)(b); *Re Eastman's SE* (1898) 68 LJ Ch 122 (reduction in annuity); *Re Carne's SE* [1899] 1 Ch 324; *Re Ames* [1893] 2 Ch 479; *Re Orlebar* [1936] Ch 147; *Re Herbert* [1946] 1 All ER 421.

[320] *Re Aberconway's ST* [1953] Ch 647, CA. Since outgoings were no longer needed if the house was sold, loss of income from a trust for repair was said not to be a disincentive to sale, but Lord Denning's dissent is much more convincing: loss of a house with repairs paid for is a real loss. See also *Re Simpson* [1913] 1 Ch 277; *Re Patten* [1929] 2 Ch 276; *Re Burden* [1948] Ch 160; *Raikes* v. *Lygon* [1988] 1 WLR 281 (Madresfield House, a model for *Brideshead*).

[321] *Ungurian* v. *Lesnoff* [1990] Ch 206, 226, Vinelott J; *Costello* v. *Costello* (1996) 70 P & CR 297, 305, Henry LJ.

[322] *Re Herklot's WT* [1964] 1 WLR 583; *Ayer* v. *Benton* (1967) 204 EG 359, Buckley J; *Abbey National BS* v. *Moss* [1994] 1 FLR 307, CA.

[323] TLATA 1996 s 1(3).

[324] [1948] 2 All ER 133, CA; *Re Trafford's SE* [1915] 1 Ch 9, 21, Warrington J.

[325] [1972] Ch 359, Megaw and Stephenson LJJ.

[326] [1972] Ch 359, 366F, Lord Denning MR dissenting; *Ivory* v. *Palmer* [1975] ICR 340, 347, Cairns LJ; *Griffiths* v. *Williams* [1978] 2 EGLR 121, 123F–J; *Chandler* v. *Kerley* [1978] 1 WLR 693, 697F, Lord Scarman.

[327] *Ungurian* v. *Lesnoff* [1990] Ch 206, Vinelott J; *Costello* v. *Costello* (1995) 76 P & CR 297, CA.

[328] *Morss* v. *Morss* [1972] Fam 264, CA; *Dodsworth* v. *Dodsworth* (1973) 228 EG 1115, CA; *Griffiths* v. *Williams* [1978] 2 EGLR 121, CA (licence for life); *Dent* v. *Dent* [1996] 1 WLR 683.

[329] (1994) 70 P & CR 297, CA; MP Thompson [1994] *Conv* 391.

[330] Interests under a strict settlement cannot override: LRA 2002 sch 3 para 2(a).

[331] The tenant for life could deal with his beneficial interest: SLA 1925 s 18; *Bevan* v. *Johnston* [1990] 2 EGLR 33, CA.

pre-1997 strict settlements continue to be) paralysed until the settlement is corrected by execution of a vesting deed in favour of the licensee, and occupation of the land by the licensee would give notice and so prevent title to unregistered land passing to a purchaser.[332] Hence in *Binions* v. *Evans*,[333] when the Tredegar Estate appeared to "sell" the cottage occupied by Mrs Evans to the developer, the conveyance was in fact totally nugatory. Mrs Evans was entitled to receive legal title as tenant for life and all dealings were blocked until she did. Despite Lord Denning MR's doubts he was bound by *Bannister*,[334] and the House of Lords never got a chance to squash this settlement analysis.

7.   Trust of land

[19.60] A licence created after 1996 will operate as a trust of land, a term which embraces any trust whether express, implied, resulting or constructive.[335] Management control is vested in trustees, with an occupation right conferred on the licensee.[336] This may be overreached unless coupled with a right to refuse consent to a sale,[337] and so it can be converted into a right to enjoy the income after sale.[338] The law is not satisfactory since overreachability is scarcely appropriate to a right which aims to protect the use value of land. Non-trust licences create a burden against the legal estate owner's title consisting of the right to occupy land, but not to give any stake in the property – no share in the fund realised by sale.

K. OCCUPATIONAL LICENCES

1.   Basic nature

[19.61] A licence is a permission given by a property owner (or licensor) to another person (a licensee) to be on land of another. As was explained in *Thomas* v. *Sorrell* (1673):

> "A dispensation or licence properly passeth no interest, nor alters or transfers property in any thing, but only makes an action lawful, which without it had been unlawful. As a licence . . . to hunt in a man's park [or] to come into his house, are only actions, which without licence had been unlawful."[339]

Such a licence can be used as a defence to an action in trespass.

---

[332] SLA 1925 s 13.
[333] [1972] Ch 359, CA.
[334] [1948] 2 All ER 133, CA.
[335] TLATA 1996 s 1(1)–(2).
[336] S 12.
[337] Ss 10(1), 16 (only express right affects purchasers).
[338] *Ungurian* v. *Lesnoff* [1990] Ch 206, 224D, Vinelott J; *Costello* v. *Costello* (1995) 70 P & CR 297, 299, Dillon LJ, 305, Leggatt LJ.
[339] (1673) Vaugh 330, 124 ER 1098. This dictum is cited regularly: *Wood* v. *Leadbitter* (1845) 13 M & W 838, 844, 153 ER 351; *National Provincial Bank* v. *Ainsworth* [1965] AC 1175, 1223, Lord Hodson.

Occupational licences give the right to occupy a family home, without creating any estate,[340] no stake in the property, no liability for council tax,[341] and no co-ownership. The burden cannot be overreached.[342] In a typical licence case, a couple set up home together and have children, a fact which implies a licence to provide a home for the duration of the dependency of the children. When the relationship breaks down, can the legal owner stand on his proprietary rights and insist on possession? Many women who have been unable to contribute to acquisition of the family home have been thrown back to licence law.

2.   Revocation of bare licences

[19.62] A permission to occupy land is called a bare licence if it lacks special supporting characteristics – such as a contract or an estoppel. It is revocable at any time and has no proprietary force, as illustrated by *Heslop* v. *Burns*.[343] A couple made the acquaintance of the owner of a cottage when the wife worked as his office cleaner. The owner developed an affection for the wife, and offered the cottage as a home for the couple rent-free for life, without any formal arrangement as to terms of occupation. They lived there for 14 years, during which time the owner visited the couple daily and had his meals at the house, but when the owner died, his executors sued successfully for possession. Death revoked the licence which, lacking proprietary status, was incapable of binding successors.[344] The benefit of the licence is incapable of assignment, and the burden of it is incapable of binding a purchaser of the land to which the licence relates.[345] It could have been revoked by notice at any time.

Bare licence reasoning is adopted when the other forms of licence are inappropriate.[346] One case is where a licence gives exclusive occupation of a house against a backcloth of charity, friendship or family relationship,[347] for example where a father handed the keys to a house to his son and daughter in law for them to occupy for as long as they wanted.[348] Cohabitants[349] or parents[350] who share living expenses but make no financial contribution to acquisition of the home will also be seen as bare licensees.[351] No right to stay can be implied from the licensee's unilateral belief that he was unlikely to be asked to move,[352] nor from cohabitation with a person to whom no security of occupation has been promised.[353]

---

[340] *Street* v. *Mountford* [1985] AC 809, 814G, Lord Templeman.

[341] *Norris* v. *Birmingham CC* [2001] RVR 89.

[342] *Birmingham Midshires* v. *Sabherwal* (2000) 80 P & CR 256, CA; C Harpum (2000) 116 *LQR* 341.

[343] [1974] 1 WLR 1241, CA.

[344] *Wood* v. *Leadbitter* (1845) 13 M & W 838, 844, 153 ER 351, Alderson B.; *Wallis* v. *Harrison* (1834) 4 M & W 538, 544, 150 ER 1543, Parke B; *Street* v. *Mountford* [1985] AC 809, 814, Lord Templeman.

[345] *Terunnanse* v. *Terunnanse* [1968] AC 1086, 1095–6, Lord Devlin.

[346] J Warburton, *Sharing Residential Property* (Sweet & Maxwell, 1990), 20–24 refers to numerous unreported cases.

[347] *Booker* v. *Palmer* [1942] 2 All ER 674 (evacuees).

[348] *David* v. *Lewisham LBC* (1977) 34 P & CR 112 (no value on compulsory purchase).

[349] *Richards* v. *Dove* [1974] 1 All ER 888; *Horrocks* v. *Forray* [1976] 1 WLR 230; *Metropolitan Properties Co* v. *Cronan* (1982) 44 P & CR 1.

[350] *Hannaford* v. *Selby* [1976] 2 EGLR 113.

[351] *Horrocks* v. *Forray* [1976] 1 WLR 230, CA.

[352] *E & L Berg Homes* v. *Grey* [1980] 1 EGLR 103, CA.

[353] *Stilwell* v. *Simpson* (1983) 133 NLJ 894; *Savva* v. *Costa* (1981) 131 NLJ 1114, CA; *Layton* v. *Martin* [1986] 2 FLR 227; *Coombes* v. *Smith* [1986] 1 WLR 808.

3. Packing up time

[19.63] The burden of proving revocation is on the person alleging that it has occurred.[354] Packing up time applies to a *bare licence* to give a licensee a reasonable period to move.[355] *Canadian Pacific Railway Co* v. *The King*[356] concerned telegraph lines erected alongside a railway track in the maritime provinces of eastern Canada, on land belonging to the Crown,[357] these circumstances entitled the railway company to an allowance of time on revocation of the licence to make alternative arrangements.[358] Some contractual licences are also terminable at will under the terms of the contract,[359] for example where a service occupancy of residential accommodation ends on the dismissal of an employee.[360] Frequently, however, the court will imply a term that a reasonable period of notice should be given,[361] the so-called packing up time.[362]

The time allowed no longer runs from termination of the licence, giving a reasonable period for making alternative arrangements.[363] *Minister of Health* v. *Bellotti*[364] held that the packing up time ran from the date of the notice without the owner having to state a length of time in the notice. Time ticks away while the case is pending so that by the time it reaches court the owner will normally be entitled to immediate possession.[365] Against that, *Canadian Pacific Railway Co* v. *The King*[366] held that the notice had to state a period of reasonable duration and, if he failed to do so, would have to start over with a fresh notice and fresh proceedings. Carnwath J had to consider the conflict in *Re Hampstead Garden Suburb Institute*.[367] Notice to terminate the licence of the governors of a school in Hampstead was given by the trustees of the land to the school governors (a distinct body) in March 1993 to expire in December 1993. Two years would have been a reasonable period of notice, and the unreasonably short period of notice actually given rendered the notice totally ineffective. The distinction between public[368] and private cases is unconvincing for reasons stated by Tamara Kerbel.[369] *Bellotti* is more logical, but *Canadian Pacific* more just.

---

[354] *Llanelly Rly & Dock Co* v. *London & NW Rly* (1875) LR 7 HL 550, 567, Lord Selborne.

[355] Eg to remove stored goods: *Wood* v. *Leadbitter* (1845) 13 M & W 838, 153 ER 351; *Cornish* v. *Stubbs* (1870) LR 5 CP 334.

[356] [1931] AC 414, PC; DNS (1930) 4 *CLJ* 391.

[357] There was no estoppel, because the railway company had no mistaken belief, or at least none known to the Crown: *Plimmer* v. *Wellington Corp* (1884) 9 App Cas 699, PC, distinguished.

[358] At 432–433, Lord Russell.

[359] *Australian Blue Metal* v. *Hughes* [1963] AC 74, PC; *Norris* v. *Checksfield* [1991] 1 WLR 1241, 1247.

[360] *Ivory* v. *Palmer* [1975] ICR 340, CA.

[361] [1963] AC 74, 98, Lord Devlin; *Hannaford* v. *Selby* [1976] 2 EGLR 113 (family arrangement).

[362] *Winter Garden Theatre (London)* v. *Millennium Productions* [1948] AC 173, 198, Lord Uthwatt, 203, Lord Macdermott.

[363] *Mellor* v. *Watkins* (1874) LR 9 QB 400; *Aldin* v. *Latimer Clark Muirhead & Co* [1894] 2 Ch 437, 447–448, Stirling J; *Hannaford* v. *Selby* [1976] 2 EGLR 113; *Greater London Council* v. *Jenkins* [1975] 1 WLR 155, 158, Lord Diplock; J Hill [2001] *CLJ* 89.

[364] [1944] 1 KB 298, CA; *E & L Berg Homes* v. *Grey* [1980] 1 EGLR 103, CA.

[365] Unless the contract states a particular duration: *Wallshire* v. *Advertising Sites* [1988] 2 EGLR 167.

[366] [1931] AC 414, PC; DNS (1930) 4 *CLJ* 391.

[367] [1995] 93 LGR 470.

[368] [1931] AC 414, 432, Lord Russell.

[369] [1996] *Conv* 63, 67; [1996] *CLJ* 229.

4. Irrevocable licences

[19.64] Not all licences are revocable at will. Preventing revocation is the vital first step towards the protection of licensees, though it needs to be accompanied by rights that are also secure against future owners of the land. Limits on revocation may exist in the case of: (1) contractual licences; (2) licences coupled with an interest; and (3) equitable licences, particularly those supported by proprietary estoppel.

5. Revocation of contractual licences

[19.65] Suppose a licensor contracts to allow a licensee to occupy his land for a given period – perhaps 10 years or while the licensee has dependant children. He will be prevented from breaking his contract, so that revocation must conform to the contract, this equitable rule prevailing over the laxer common law principle.

(1) Ticket cases at common law

[19.66] After reasonable notice, a licence terminated at common law and the former licensee became a trespasser. Revocation was even permitted in breach of contract. In *Wood* v. *Leadbitter*[370] a racegoer had paid a guinea for a season at the Doncaster Races, but was later evicted, without any improper conduct being alleged against him. He could have sued in contract for the return of the price of his ticket,[371] but his action failed since it was formulated in tort[372] for damages for assault by the stewards who evicted him. Alderson B held in Exchequer[373] that the licence to enter the racecourse had been revoked, and that reasonable force used in the eviction of a trespasser did not amount to an assault.

(2) Injunction to restrain revocation

[19.67] Equity only allows a contract to be revoked in accordance with the contract. This rule should now prevail in all courts. *Winter Garden Theatre (London)* v. *Millennium Productions*[374] concerned a non-exclusive licence to use a theatre for an unspecified period, determinable by the licensee by one month's notice. The House of Lords held unanimously that the owner was also entitled to terminate by one month's notice. What if, as the Court of Appeal had thought, the contract had been irrevocable? Lord Greene MR said[375] that breach of a licence agreement could be restrained

---

[370] (1845) 13 M & W 838, 153 ER 351.

[371] *C & P Haulage* v. *Middleton* [1983] 1 WLR 1461; *Arthur Maiden* v. *Patel* [1990] 1 EGLR 269, Mummery J (removal of advertising hoarding).

[372] Simply a case of wrong pleading? *Winter Gardens* [1948] AC 173, Viscount Simon and Lord Uthwatt, contrary to Lord Porter; *Hurst* v. *Picture Theatres* [1915] 1 KB 1, 10, 13.

[373] *Adams* v. *Andrews* (1850) 15 QB 284, 117 ER 466; *Taplin* v. *Florence* (1851) 10 CB 744, 138 ER 294.

[374] [1948] AC 173; HWR Wade (1948) 64 *LQR* 57; C Fletcher-Cooke (1948) 11 *MLR* 93; EO Walford (1948) 12 *Conv (NS)* 121.

[375] (1946) 115 LJ Ch 297, 303; *Hurst* v. *Picture Theatres* [1915] 1 KB 1, Buckley and Kennedy LJJ; JC Miles (1915) 31 *LQR* 217; contrast *Booker* v. *Palmer* [1942] 2 All ER 674, 677, Greene MR. See also *Llanelly Rly & Dock Co* v. *London & NW Rly* (1873) LR 8 Ch App 942, CA.

by injunction,[376] and three of the Lords agreed.[377] "This infusion of equity means that contractual licences now have a force and validity of their own and cannot be revoked in breach of contract."[378]

A contractual licence is an inherent part of the contract with no independent existence, so the right to occupy the land depends entirely upon the contract, and terms may be implied to protect it.[379]

Entitlement to equitable remedies may be lost by misconduct.[380]

6.   Licence where act completed

[19.68] A licence cannot be revoked once the act permitted by it has been completed: it is too late to turn back the clock so as to refuse permission retrospectively for a licensee who has been and gone. In *Armstrong* v. *Sheppard & Short*[381] a manhole and sewer could not be removed after construction, though the continuing licence to drain effluent through the sewer could be terminated. Earlier cases allowing irrevocability to a licence for the future once it had been acted on were probably overruled in *Wood* v. *Leadbitter*,[382] but it remains arguable that rule was a recognised exception and, if so, it survives as a rule of modern law.[383]

7.   Specific performance of executory licence

[19.69] Licences to enter land in the future can be enforced in equity by an award of specific performance. Yarmouth Town Hall had been booked in *Verrall* v. *Great Yarmouth BC*[384] for a meeting of the National Front, an extreme right-wing organisation. Political control of the council changed, and the new (but old) Labour council wanted to renege on the contract. They were compelled to carry out the agreement.[385]

Specific performability should not be allowed to turn a licence into a property right. A contract for a lease creates an equitable lease because specific performance gives a

---

[376] Or interim injunction: *Arthur Maiden* v. *Patel* [1990] 1 EGLR 269, Mummery J.

[377] [1948] AC 173, 189, Viscount Simon, 194, Lord Porter, 202, Lord Uthwatt; Lords MacDermott and Simonds made no reference to the point.

[378] *Errington* v. *Errington* [1952] 1 KB 290, 299, Denning LJ; *Bendall* v. *McWhirter* [1952] 2 QB 466, 480; *Hounslow LBC* v. *Twickenham Garden Developments* [1971] Ch 233, 245, Megarry J; *Tanner* v. *Tanner* [1975] 1 WLR 1346, 1350H, Lord Denning MR; *Verrall* v. *Great Yarmouth BC* [1981] QB 202, 216, Lord Denning MR, 219, Roskill LJ.

[379] *Winter Gardens case* [1948] AC 173, 198–199, Lord Uthwatt; *Hounslow* [1971] Ch 233, 246C, Megarry J; *DHN Food Distributors* v. *Tower Hamlets LBC* [1976] 1 WLR 852, Goff LJ; D Powles (1977) 40 *MLR* 339; DJ Hayton [1977] *CLJ* 12.

[380] *Thompson* v. *Park* [1944] KB 408, CA (riot and affray); (1944) 9 *Conv (NS)* 111. This decision may be wrong: *Errington* v. *Errington* [1952] 1 KB 290, 298, Denning LJ; *Verrall* v. *Great Yarmouth BC* [1981] QB 202, 215G–216G, Lord Denning MR, 219E, Roskill LJ.

[381] [1959] 2 QB 384; HWR Wade [1960] *CLJ* 42.

[382] *Webb* v. *Paternoster* (1619) Pop 151, 79 ER 1250; MC Cullity (1965) 29 *Conv NS* 19; P Sparkes *NLL* (1st ed), 379.

[383] *Winter Garden Theatre (London)* v. *Millennium Productions* [1948] AC 173, 194, Lord Porter; *Armstrong* v. *Sheppard & Short* [1959] 1 QB 384, 399; *Hounslow LBC* v. *Twickenham Garden Developments* [1971] Ch 233, 255B, Megarry J.

[384] [1981] QB 202, CA; A Briggs [1981] *Conv* 212.

[385] A licence to share may not be susceptible of specific performance: *Thompson* v. *Park* [1944] KB 408, CA; *Hounslow* [1971] Ch 233, 248, Megarry J.

route towards the legal estate,[386] but a contract for a licence creates a mere licence. Buckley LJ thought[387] that an informal licence was made to operate as if it was a licence under seal, but this was fallacious: a formal licence is no more or less revocable than one that is informal.[388] Fusion of law and equity itself cannot elevate a non-endurable interest to proprietary status.

8. Licences coupled with an interest

[19.70] Irrevocability is well established in the case of a licence which is coupled with an interest. As Alderson B explained in *Wood* v. *Leadbitter*:[389]

> "That which is called a licence is often something more than a licence; it often comprises or is connected with a grant, and then the party who has given it cannot in general revoke it, so as to defeat his grant, to which it was incident."

Permitted legal grants are delimited by the rules defining easements and profits. A profit à prendre may grant the right to take fish caught in a river, ore that has been mined,[390] or grass that is grazed by cows. Access to the land by the angler, the miner or the cows takes place under an associated licence, but this incidental licence takes on the character and endurability of the legal profit with which it is associated.[391] The grant to which the licence is attached is a legal interest, but it could also be an equitable interest – one possible explanation of *Errington* v. *Errington*.[392] In *Webb* v. *Paternoster*[393] Plummer allowed Webb to keep his hay on Plummer's land until it could be sold, but two years later the land was leased to Paternoster, whose cattle ate Webb's hay. Webb's licence had expired, but earlier he had an oral licence coupled with a property right in the hay, one which according to Montague CJ "chargeth the land into whose soever hands it comes". A licence cannot be coupled to an ephemeral right such as the spectator's interest in viewing a sporting event[394] or theatrical production.[395]

L. EQUITABLE LICENCES

[19.71] An equitable licence is an irrevocable right to stay in a family home spelled out of an informal discussion,[396] formed of an amalgam of contract law and estoppel.

---

[386] *Walsh* v. *Lonsdale* (1882) 21 Ch D 9, CA.
[387] *Hurst* v. *Picture Theatres* [1915] 1 KB 1, 7–10; GC Cheshire (1953) 16 *MLR* 1, 13.
[388] *Hurst* at 17–19, Phillimore LJ; *Cowell* v. *Rosehill Racecourse Co* (1937) 56 CLR 605, 617–618, Latham CJ (High Ct of Australia); (1937) 53 *LQR* 318; HG Hanbury [1954] *CLJ* 201, 210 (*"ignis fatuus"*).
[389] (1845) 13 M & W 838, 153 ER 351.
[390] *Muskett* v. *Hill* (1839) 5 Bing NC 694, 132 ER 1267; *Woods* v. *Donnelly* [1982] NI 257.
[391] *Wood* v. *Leadbitter* at 844; *James Jones & Sons* v. *Tankerville* [1909] 2 Ch 440, 442, Parker J.
[392] [1952] 1 KB 290 (estate contract); *National Provincial Bank* v. *Ainsworth* [1965] AC 1175, 1239A, Lord Upjohn; *Ashburn Anstalt* v. *Arnold* [1989] Ch 1, 17 (possibility 1); *Camden LBC* v. *Shortlife Community Housing* (1992) 25 HLR 330, 341, Millett J.
[393] (1619) Pop 151, 79 ER 1250.
[394] *Wood* v. *Leadbitter* (1845) 13 M & W 838, 153 ER 351.
[395] *Hurst* v. *Picture Theatres* [1915] 1 KB 1; but see *Hounslow LBC* v. *Twickenham Garden Developments* [1971] Ch 233, 243–244, 254E, Megarry J.
[396] *Re Sharpe* [1980] 1 WLR 219, Browne-Wilkinson J; JE Martin [1980] *Conv* 206; G Woodman (1980) 96 *LQR* 336.

It requires a common assumption of residential security, acted upon by expenditure in reliance, from which the court will imply an irrevocable licence or trust to give effect to that common assumption.[397] It should only involve an occupation right and not a claim to a share of the fund represented by the house.[398] As between the original owner and his licensee, the intervention of trust doctrine is unnecessary and unhelpful.[399]

1. Contractual analysis

[19.72] Contractual analysis was tried out for family interests, the vogue starting with *Errington* v. *Errington*[400] in 1952. When a father bought a house for his son and daughter-in-law, he promised them that if they paid off all the mortgage instalments, the house would be theirs. From this unpromising material the court discovered a contract and manufactured its terms. Personal and non-assignable it may have been, but this licence could not be revoked by the father once the couple had entered on performance of the contract.[401] Contractual analysis has been found wanting even more when applied to cohabitation arrangements.[402] In *Tanner* v. *Tanner*,[403] a married man set up home with another woman, but, after the birth of twins, the couple grew apart and the man purported to terminate the woman's right to stay in the house with the children. It was odd to regard as contractual an arrangement for a man to provide the woman with accommodation so long as their children were of school age, and also to regard her act of giving up a protected tenancy and a claim to maintenance as consideration.[404] A contractual term was implied to prevent revocation, but the evidence of the duration of the licence was hazy in the extreme. In *Chandler* v. *Kerley*,[405] a similar arrangement was held to be terminable on six months notice, the difference being that the relationship broke down after only six weeks, though no doubt intended to be permanent. In truth, neither couple were negotiating a contract when they shacked up together.[406] Informal sharing arrangements almost always lack one or more essentials of a contract[407] – an agreement on certain terms, consideration, or especially the intention to create legal relations.

---

[397] At 223E

[398] *Hussey* v. *Palmer* [1972] 1 WLR 1286, CA; PB Fairest [1973] *CLJ* 41; TC Ridley (1973) 36 *MLR* 436; *Re Basham* [1986] 1 WLR 1498 (licence or inheritance?); DJ Hayton [1987] *CLJ* 215; JE Martin [1987] *Conv* 211.

[399] *Re Sharpe* at 223C; *Canadian Imperial Bank of Commerce* v. *Bello* (1992) 64 P & CR 48, 52, Dillon LJ.

[400] [1952] 1 KB 290, CA.

[401] At 292–293, Somervell LJ, 295, Denning LJ.

[402] P Robson & Q Watchman [1980] *Conv* 27; S Moriarty (1984) 100 *LQR* 376.

[403] [1975] 1 WLR 1346, CA; JL Barton (1976) 92 *LQR* 168; E Ellis (1979) 95 *LQR* 11; M Richards (1976) 40 *Conv (NS)* 351, 361–365; J Masson [1979] *Conv* 184; G Battersby [1991] *Conv* 36, 46.

[404] At 1352B, Brightman J.

[405] [1978] 1 WLR 693, CA.

[406] *Horrocks* v. *Forray* [1976] 1 WLR 230, 235, Megaw LJ.

[407] At 236, Megaw LJ; M Richards (1976) 40 *Conv (NS)* 351, 361.

2. Estoppel analysis

[19.73] A shift to estoppel doctrine[408] was seen in *Hardwick* v. *Johnson*.[409] A mother helped her son and his wife buy a house, they paying £28 a calendar month for the right of occupation. The mother's possession action against her daughter in law, after she had been deserted by the son, failed. Lord Denning MR now preferred to treat such a loose family arrangement as an equitable licence, contractual analysis being discarded because of the absence of an intention to create legal relations.[410] Similarly in *Horrocks* v. *Forray*,[411] a house provided by a man for his mistress and their child, while he continued to live with his wife, was not contractual, there being no meeting of minds, no intention to effect legal relations, and no consideration. An estoppel did arise, satisfied by 12 months' security against termination, but other possible durations[412] might be for a fixed number of years, or during the dependency of children, or for life.

Estoppel doctrine is better suited to dealing with vague expectations than is contract law.[413] After discovery of the scope of the licensee's expectation, there is a discretionary matching of that expectation to a remedy, a process which reduces the importance of any inadequacy in the way that the parties have expressed their legal relationship.[414] Maximum entitlement is fixed by the expectation, but the court retains a discretion to reduce the award to take into account the value of benefits received, to satisfy the expectation in a smaller way[415] or a quite different way,[416] and to find the minimum equity consistent with justice.[417]

3. Binding the landowner

[19.74] The landowner is bound by a contract because he has made a promise capable of acceptance by the other party, so that the owner is properly held to his promise. Estoppel-based inducement is less precise, but occurs where it is unconscionable for the owner to deny the licence which is expected. Detrimental reliance by the licensee could take the form of contractual consideration or of a monetary or non-monetary detriment linked to the owner's promise by reliance upon it, which shows that it forms a price for the promise.

---

[408] See below **[23.07]**.

[409] [1978] 1 WLR 683, CA.

[410] *Balfour* v. *Balfour* [1919] 2 KB 571; *Pettitt* v. *Pettitt* [1970] AC 777, 804, Lord Morris, 806, Lord Hodson; *Cowcher* v. *Cowcher* [1972] 1 WLR 425, 436D; *Burns* v. *Burns* [1984] Ch 317, 335D, May LJ; *Horrocks* v. *Forray* [1976] 1 WLR 230, 239F–240A, Scarman LJ; AAS Zuckerman (1980) 96 *LQR* 248; S Hedley (1985) 5 *OJLS* 391.

[411] [1976] 1 WLR 230, 236; *Coombes* v. *Smith* [1986] 1 WLR 808, 814.

[412] A surrender should not be implied from non-residence alone: *Bone* v. *Bone* [1992] EGCS 81, CA.

[413] J Hill (1988) 51 *MLR* 226, 233; G Battersby [1991] *Conv* 36, 37.

[414] P Todd [1981] *Conv* 347, 350.

[415] *Dodsworth* v. *Dodsworth* (1973) 228 EG 1115, CA (expectation of home for life satisfied by a lien for expenditure.)

[416] *Burrows* v. *Burrows & Sharp* (1991) 23 HLR 82, CA.

[417] *Baker* v. *Baker* (1993) 25 HLR 408, CA.

M. PROPRIETARY FORCE OF LICENCES

1. Bare and proprietary licences

[19.75] Introduce an outsider into the game between owner and licensee and one needs to find a proprietary status for the licensee. A simple licence is revoked as soon as ownership of the land changes hands, as *Heslop* v. *Burns* has shown,[418] a non-proprietary licence could not bind successors on death.

During the 1960s and 1970s, Lord Denning MR explored a wide variety of routes towards the goal of proprietary status, but orthodoxy has broadly re-established itself:[419] an equitable interest must be coupled with an appropriate property law protection, for example by occupation of registered land. Discussion is required of contractual licences (now known to be non-proprietary), licences coupled with an interest, licences by estoppel, and constructive trusts.

2. Endurability of contractual licences

[19.76] A contractual licence is personal in nature and cannot bind a purchaser of the land. Traditional principles have reasserted themselves though with a modified constructive trust doctrine.

Orthodox property law is based on the principle of privity of contract, which ensures that the burden of a contractual licence can only affect the original licensor. The House of Lords held in *King* v. *David Allen & Sons Billposting*[420] that a licence to put up an advertising billboard was not enforceable against a purchaser of the free-hold on which the sign was sited. *Clore* v. *Theatrical Properties*[421] refused to enforce front of house rights at a theatre (a concession to provide refreshments) against a purchaser of theatre.[422] Earlier law appeared to have been entrenched in the 1925 legislation.[423]

Shortly after *Winter Gardens* had established irrevocability between the original parties,[424] Denning LJ proposed in *Errington* v. *Errington* that endurability against purchasers should be recognised.[425] The right of the daughter-in-law to stay as licensee while paying mortgage instalments bound the licensor's widow, who inherited all his property. Possession was refused. How the licence came to bind the new owner was never properly articulated since all Denning LJ had to say was that:

---

[418] [1974] 1 WLR 1241, CA; *Terunnanse* v. *Terunnanse* [1968] AC 1086, PC.

[419] A Briggs [1981] *Conv* 212; S Moriarty (1984) 100 *LQR* 376, 376.

[420] [1916] 2 AC 54, HL.

[421] [1936] 3 All ER 483, CA. There is no objection to an assignment of the benefit of a contract.

[422] *Webb* v. *Paternoster* (1619) Pop 151, 79 ER 1250; *National Provincial Bank* v. *Hastings Car Mart* [1964] Ch 665, 697, Russell LJ; *Re Solomon* [1967] Ch 573, 585, Goff J.

[423] LPA 1925 s 4.

[424] See above **[19.67]**.

[425] [1952] 1 KB 290, CA. Academic reaction was mixed: FR Crane (1952) 16 *Conv (NS)* 323; D Pollock (1952) 16 *Conv (NS)* 436; AD Hargreaves (1953) 69 *LQR* 466; HWR Wade (1952) 68 *LQR* 337; C Farran (1952) 15 *MLR* 236.

"Neither the licensor nor anyone who claims through him can disregard the contract, except a purchaser for value without notice."[426]

No authority was cited since there was none to cite.[427]

Lord Denning MR returned to the assault when he dissented in *Binions* v. *Evans*.[428] Tredegar Estate provided for the widow of its chauffeur by allowing her to remain living in their tied cottage, rent free for the rest of her life, on her promise to maintain it in good condition and to cultivate the garden. The Tredegar Estate sold the house at a low price, reduced to reflect the widow's contractual licence, but the builder who bought it sought possession six months later with the widow still alive. Lord Denning MR held that her contractual right to reside in the house gave her an equitable interest in the land, which bound any purchaser with knowledge of her right. By 1981 the impact of Lord Denning's judicial activity was such that the Court of Appeal could assume that a contractual licence enjoyed proprietary force.[429]

Rejection of proprietary character is technically *obiter* in *Ashburn Anstalt* v. *Arnold*,[430] but Fox LJ's reasoning is carefully considered and authoritative. A company sold its shop to developers but with a licence (the *obiter* discussion assumes) to occupy the shop until needed by the developers for redevelopment. The freehold was sold. Could the new owners dispossess the licensees? Fox LJ decided that a contractual licence was inherently incapable of binding freehold purchasers. He emphasised the settled state of the law before *Errington*,[431] and rejected the central dictum by Denning LJ as unnecessary, unsupported by authority, and given *per incuriam*.[432] Proprietary status could not attach to contractual obligations. The contrary view, heretical as it was, was finally repudiated.[433]

Some remnants of proprietary character have not been expunged. Damages for breach of a contractual licence may be awarded if the land increases in value through an unlawful revocation.[434] Statutory compensation is payable on compulsory purchase.[435]

3. Licence coupled with an interest

[19.77] A licence coupled with an interest enjoys the proprietary character of the right with which it is associated. Thus a legal profit to fish in a river carries with it a licence

---

[426] [1952] 1 KB 290, 299. For hostile comment see: RH Maudsley (1956) 20 *Conv (NS)* 281; HWR Wade (1952) 68 *LQR* 337.

[427] *Ashburn Anstalt* v. *Arnold* [1989] Ch 1, 17, Dillon LJ.

[428] [1972] Ch 359, CA; SM Bandali (1973) 37 *Conv (NS)* 402.

[429] *Midland Bank* v. *Farmpride Hatcheries* [1981] 2 EGLR 147, CA; RE Annand [1982] *Conv* 67; *Heslop* v. *Burns* [1974] 1 WLR 1241, 1251G, Scarman LJ; S Moriarty (1984) 100 *LQR* 376, 388–397.

[430] [1989] Ch 1, CA; MP Thompson [1988] *Conv* 201; AJ Oakley [1988] *CLJ* 353; J Hill (1988) 51 *MLR* 226; P Sparkes (1988) 104 *LQR* 175; G Battersby [1991] *Conv* 36.

[431] At 15H.

[432] At 17, 22.

[433] *Camden LBC* v. *Shortlife Community Housing* (1992) 25 HLR 330, 341, Millett J; *Sparkes* v. *Smart* [1990] 2 EGLR 245, CA; *IDC Group* v. *Clark* [1992] 1 EGLR 187, 189 on appeal [1992] 2 EGLR 184, CA; *Nationwide Anglia BS* v. *Ahmed* (1995) 70 P & CR 381, CA (no rights against lender).

[434] *Tanner* v. *Tanner* [1975] 1 WLR 1346, CA; *W* v. *W* [1976] Fam 107, 113A–B, Baker P.

[435] Compulsory Purchase Act 1965 ss 5, 10; *DHN Food Distributors* v. *Tower Hamlets LBC* [1976] 1 WLR 852, CA; *Pennine Raceway* v. *Kirklees MBC* [1983] QB 382, CA; *MacDougall* v. *Wrexham Maelor BC* (1993) 33 RVR 141.

to use the river bank from which to fish, which is itself essentially a legal interest in the land. If this was not so the profit would be useless, for the licence could be revoked after sale of the burdened land, leaving a profit that could not be exploited. The licence must take on the character of the property right to which it is attached.[436] A licence is proprietary if coupled with an interest which is proprietary.

4. Estoppel licences

[19.78] An interest created by proprietary estoppel has the characteristic of endurability against future owners of the land, including purchasers: notice doctrine applies to informal burdens affecting unregistered land.[437] Proprietary status is now confirmed if the estoppel affects registered land,[438] and it then usually be overriding through occupation.[439]

Estoppel can be used to give proprietary status to an occupational licence. As it happens almost all of the cases have concerned enforcement against the recipient of a gift rather than against a purchaser. *Inwards* v. *Baker*[440] is an archetype. An estoppel was raised against a father who encouraged his son to build a bungalow on his land and who raised in his son's mind the expectation that he would be allowed to stay for life. When the father died, this right was held binding on his personal representatives, who sued on behalf of the successors entitled on the fathers death. The decision to refuse possession shows that the estoppel created an unprotectible and novel equitable interest.[441]

It is also possible to reassign contractual licences – which are personal – to estoppel doctrine.[442] Enforcement against a successor may be allowed if the previous owner created an expectation of residential security on which the licensee has acted to his detriment.

N. CONSTRUCTIVE TRUST DOCTRINE

[19.79] The property law objection to enforcement of a contract[443] or licence against a purchaser can be side-stepped by imposing a constructive trust on a person who accepts the burden of it when he buys.[444] This proprietary novation requires more than the mere existence of a contractual licence,[445] since, as *Ashburn Anstalt* v. *Arnold*

---

[436] See above **[19.70]**.

[437] *ER Ives Investment* v. *High* [1967] 2 QB 379, CA; see below **[23.40]**.

[438] LRA 2002 s 116.

[439] LRA 2002 sch 1 para 2, sch 3 para 2.

[440] [1965] 2 QB 29, CA.

[441] S Moriarty (1984) 100 *LQR* 376, 393; J Hill (1988) 51 *MLR* 226, 233; J Dewar (1986) 49 *MLR* 741, 742; G Battersby [1991] *Conv* 36, 46.

[442] *Lloyds Bank* v. *Carrick* [1996] 4 All ER 630, CA, holds this reassignment to be illegitimate if the contract is registrable, but this has no impact on licence cases where the contract is not to create a legal estate, and is not registrable. Reassignment of *Errington* [1952] 1 KB 290, CA, began early: RH Maudsley (1956) 20 *Conv (NS)* 281.

[443] AJ Oakley (1972) 35 *MLR* 551, 557; MP Thompson [1988] *Conv* 201.

[444] *Gissing* v. *Gissing* [1971] AC 886, 905, Lord Diplock.

[445] Despite *DHN Food Distributors* v. *Tower Hamlets LBC* [1976] 1 WLR 852, 859, Lord Denning MR, 860–861, Goff LJ.

demonstrates, a contractual licence is not itself proprietary.[446] A burden, such as a contractual licence, needs to have some added factor X.[447] Case-law eliminates certain possible Xs – notice,[448] occupation,[449] and actual knowledge by itself.[450] This leaves two recognised grounds for imposing a constructive trust.

1. Payment of a reduced price

[19.80] It is legitimate to impose a constructive trust where the price paid for the land is reduced to reflect the fact that vacant possession will not be given, since such a purchaser could not without gross inequity defeat the licence. In *Bannister* v. *Bannister*[451] the owner of two cottages sold them to a buyer who gave an oral undertaking that the seller would be allowed to live in her existing cottage for as long as she wanted. The conveyance did not refer to this arrangement. The buyer secured both cottages at a bargain price, since he was only obtaining vacant possession of one of them. It was a fraud by the buyer to insist on the absolute character of the conveyance to defeat her interest,[452] and a constructive trust was imposed to protect her licence.[453] In *Binions* v. *Evans*[454] the purchasers had been supplied with a copy of the agreement covering Mrs Evans occupation, they paid a reduced price, and then "it would be utterly inequitable for the plaintiffs to turn the defendant out contrary to the stipulation subject to which they took the premises."

2. Purchase subject to a specific burden

[19.81] The acceptance of a new obligation is crucial.[455] In *Lyus* v. *Prowsa Developments*[456] a development site was sold by a lender[457] subject to a contract for the sale of the house built on one of the plots. The developer who bought the whole

---

[446] *Ashburn Anstalt* v. *Arnold* [1989] Ch 1, 24E; *Lyus* v. *Prowsa Developments* [1982] 1 WLR 1044, Dillon J; J Hill (1988) 51 *MLR* 226. Query *Re Sharpe* [1980] 1 WLR 219; see JE Martin [1980] *Conv* 206.

[447] *Ashburn Anstalt* v. *Arnold* [1989] Ch 1, 23C, 26E, Fox LJ; *IDC Group* v. *Clark* [1992] 1 EGLR 187, 189 on appeal [1992] 2 EGLR 184, CA. It is not necessary to show that a trust is intended: *Bannister* v. *Bannister* [1948] 2 All ER 133, 136, Scott LJ; *Lyus* v. *Prowsa Developments* [1982] 1 WLR 1044, 1053A. Query *Re Schebsman* [1944] Ch 83, 89, Lord Greene MR; *Canadian Imperial Bank of Commerce* v. *Bello* (1992) 64 P & CR 48, 51; *IDC Group* v. *Clark* [1992] 1 EGLR 187, 189 on appeal [1992] 2 EGLR 184, CA.

[448] *Lyus* v. *Prowsa Developments* [1982] 1 WLR 1044, 1051D, Dillon J; *London CC* v. *Allen* [1914] 3 KB 642, CA (covenant); *Miles* v. *Bull (No 2)* [1969] 3 All ER 1585, Bridge J; *Kewal Investments* v. *Arthur Maiden* [1990] 1 EGLR 193, Ch D; *Canadian Imperial Bank of Commerce* v. *Bello* (1992) 64 P & CR 48, 51, Dillon LJ.

[449] *Lyus* at 1051, Dillon J; but see *Binions* v. *Evans* [1972] Ch 359, 368–369.

[450] *Lyus* at 1051; *Chattey* v. *Farndale Holdings Inc* (1998) 75 P & CR 298, 313, Morritt LJ.

[451] [1948] 2 All ER 133, CA.

[452] The conveyance itself need not be fraudulent.

[453] *Booth* v. *Turle* (1873) LR 16 Eq 182; *Chattock* v. *Muller* (1878) 8 Ch D 177; *Re Duke of Marlborough* [1894] 2 Ch 133; *Rochefoucauld* v. *Boustead* [1897] 1 Ch 196.

[454] [1972] Ch 359, 368–369, Lord Denning MR. Less clear is *Sparkes* v. *Smart* [1990] 2 EGLR 245, 249H–250F, Purchas LJ, but see at 251M–252D, Ralph Gibson LJ.

[455] *Lloyd* v. *Dugdale* [2001] EWCA Civ 1754, [2002] 2 P & CR 13 at 167, [52–53], Peter Gibson LJ.

[456] [1982] 1 WLR 1044, Dillon J; TG Youdan [1984] *CLJ* 306; PH Kenny (1983) 46 *MLR* 96; C Harpum [1983] *CLJ* 54; P Jackson [1983] *Conv* 64; P Bennett (1984) 47 *MLR* 476. Another contract case is *Lloyd* v. *Dugdale* [2001] EWCA Civ 1754, [2002] 2 P & CR 13 at 167.

[457] They chose to honour a contract which they had priority to override had they chosen to do so.

site was held to take subject to this uncompleted sale of a single plot under a constructive trust. Later purchasers were also bound.[458]

Conscience is not affected when a sale is made subject to general unspecified burdens affecting the land. Such a clause is a protection for the seller rather than an attempt to impose new burdens on the buyer. Sale subject to a specific burden standing alone it is not sufficient.[459] Coupled with it needs to be evidence that the price has been reduced to reflect the existence of the licence, in which event the buyer's conscience will be affected.

3.   Proprietary status

[19.82]   Clearly the object of this trust is to make an interest bind a purchaser, but the most recent case has left open the uncomfortable possibility that the trust may be a straightforward trust of land, like any other constructive trust interest, and so overreachable.[460] This would destroy the whole point of the trust.

---

[458] If a purchaser asks, the right must be asserted: *Re Sharpe* [1980] 1 WLR 219; *Ashburn Anstalt* [1989] Ch 1, 25; *IDC Group* v. *Clark* [1992] 1 EGLR 187, 189.

[459] *Ashburn Anstalt* v. *Arnold* [1989] Ch 1, CA; MP Thompson [1988] *Conv* 201; AJ Oakley [1988] *CLJ* 353; J Hill (1988) 51 *MLR* 226; P Sparkes (1988) 104 *LQR* 175; G Battersby [1991] *Conv* 36.

[460] *Lloyd* v. *Dugdale* [2001] EWCA Civ 1754, [2002] 2 P & CR 13 at 167, [55], Peter Gibson LJ.

20

BURDENS ON REGISTERED LAND

LR Notices. Agreed and unilateral notices. Removal of spent entries.
Restrictions. Protective occupation. Overriding interests: nature; a list.
Burdens on first registration. Priority: first in time; protection of pur-
chasers.

A. LAND REGISTRY NOTICES

1. Burdens

[20.01] The Land Registration Act 2002 adopts a category of burdens, which will
bind a purchaser if properly protected. No purpose would be served by alerting a
purchaser to an interest affecting the title that is, in its nature, incapable of enduring
to bind him. Endurability is central to registered land law, with the same proprietary
categories as in the unregistered system, and the same proscription of equitable child
bearing.[1] A non proprietary interest cannot be protected on the register.[2] It is now
made clear, for the registered system alone, that proprietary status is conferred on
rights of pre-emption, estoppel rights and mere equities.[3]

2. Notices

[20.02] Protection of a burden is by a notice entered in the charges register of the title
or charge affected.[4] This will be described in this book as a land registry notice where
this is needed to avoid confusion.

3. The taxonomy of registered land

[20.03] Although the substantive law dovetails, it is not helpful to use the unregistered
categories to analyse burdens affecting a title once it is registered.[5] Any burden
involves a benefit (a plus) and a burden (a minus). When title is registered the primary
categories are:

---

[1] See above [6].
[2] *Blenheim Estates* v. *Ladbroke Retail Parks* [1993] 4 All ER 157.
[3] LRA 2002 ss 115–116; Law Com 271 (2001), [5.26–5.38].
[4] LRA 2002 s 32(1)–(2); DLRR 2003, 32.
[5] *Elias* v. *Mitchell* [1972] Ch 652, 664, Pennycuick V-C.

(1) guaranteed protectible burdens – interests substantively registered so that the registrar guarantees the validity of the right (the plus) of which the burden (the minus) is recorded against the title affected by it by a notice;

(2) protectible burdens – the validity of these is not guaranteed but the burden (the minus) is protectible by a notice on the charges register of the title affected or, alternatively, through occupation;

(3) overreachable interests – beneficial interests and burdens on beneficial interests which can be protected by restriction;[6] and

(4) overriding interests – these bind without any entry on the register, though it is desirable for them to be entered on the register when they fall into class (2) above.

It will be seen that the negative aspect of categories (1) and (2) is very similar, protected in both cases by entry of a notice. In the absence of a legislative descriptor for this category,[7] interests which can be protected by notice are described by *New Land Lawyers* as "protectible burdens".

4. Guaranteed burdens

[20.04] Some rights are guaranteed by the registrar because the positive aspect of the right, that is the benefit of the interest, is substantively registrable. The most obvious example is a mortgage entered on the charges register as a burden against the title mortgaged, but guaranteeing the lender his rights in the land.[8] A more tactile example is the long lease.[9] This is a burden on the landlord's title (assuming it is a head lease), recorded against anyone buying the freehold estate by entry of a notice against it. If the leasehold estate created is for more than seven years,[10] the tenant must apply for substantive registration of the leasehold title, and in the course of that process when it is accepted for registration with its own separate title, the registrar guarantees the tenant's holding for the future. A shorter lease (below seven years but of at least three years[11]) is not registered with its own title, and its validity is not in any way confirmed, but the notice recording the lease as a burden on the landlord's title will look very similar.

Just the same might apply to the benefit of any right which appears in the property register of the title,[12] such as an easement granted by the proprietor of title XY01 to the proprietor of title XY02, this burden should appear as a notice on XY01 as well as being an appurtenant right to the property register of XY02.[13] The same would apply to other rights capable of substantive registration for which a separate register is

---

[6] These are excluded "interests" ie not protectible by notice: LRA 2002 s 33; Law Com 271 (2001), [6.9], EN [165]; see below **[20.05]**.

[7] Unfortunately the proposal to create clearly defined categories was not adopted: Law Com 254 (1998), [3.2].

[8] DLRR 2003 r 34; see below **[28.06]**.

[9] LRA 2002 s 38; DLRR 2003 r 33; see below **[25.02]**.

[10] See below **[25.36]**.

[11] See below **[25.53]**.

[12] DLRR 2003 r 5.

[13] *Willies-Williams* v. *National Trust* (1993) 63 P & CR 359, 361, Hoffmann LJ.

created – rights to mines, rentcharges, franchises, profits in gross, and manors.[14] Only by registration is legal status conferred and the land registry guarantee of entitlement brought into force.[15]

5. Non-guaranteed burdens

[20.05] In all other cases – where the right is not the subject of a substantive registration, a notice records a claim to the interest. Entry is made in the charges register of the title affected,[16] but it does not by itself guarantee anything other than the *priority* of the claim.[17] Anyone buying the land will take subject to the interest noted, but only if it proves to be valid.[18] In *White* v. *Bijou Mansions*,[19] a restrictive covenant on a building estate was noted against the freeholder's title and this bound a person who bought a leasehold estate in one plot, without knowledge of the freeholder's title or the covenant. A notice will not revivify an interest already void for non-protection as a land charge before first registration.[20]

Interests that are proprietary and not overreachable may be protected by notice, including the following wide range:

(1) "Land charges"
Interests within the classes of land charge for unregistered land are protectible by land registry notice. Examples are equitable mortgages,[21] debentures and other equitable money charges, estate contracts and options, restrictive covenants,[22] equitable easements, and matrimonial home rights.

(2) Litigation rights
The same applies to litigation rights such as pending land actions and writs or orders, creditor's notices, and charging orders though in some cases a restriction is appropriate.[23]

(3) Statutory rights.
A number of statues require entry of a notice to protect, for example, manorial incidents, acquisition orders for blocks of flats, access orders to neighbouring land, orders confiscating the proceeds of crime,[24] and notices connected with leasehold enfranchisement.[25]

---

[14] LRA 2002 ss 2(1), 3(1), 88; Law Com 254 (1998), [3.13–3.23]. No new manors may be registered and those that are may be deregistered: LRA 2002 s 119; Law Com 271 (2001), EN [521–522].

[15] LRA 2002 s 27.

[16] LRA 2002 s 32; DLRR 2003 r 32.

[17] LRA 2002 s 32(3); *Duke* v. *Robson* [1973] 1 WLR 267; Law Com 271 (2001) [6.6]. Previously the same effect was achieved by deemed notice: LRA 1925 s 52(1); *Clark* v. *Chief Land Registrar* [1994] Ch 370, 381, Nourse LJ.

[18] LRA 2002 ss 29–30.

[19] [1937] Ch 610, Simonds J; H Potter (1937) 53 *LQR* 467; appeal on different points [1938] Ch 351, CA. Compare *Patman* v. *Harland* (1881) 17 Ch D 353 for unregistered titles, above [15.18].

[20] *Kitney* v. *MEPC* [1977] 1 WLR 981, CA.

[21] *Bristol & West BS* v. *Brandon* [1995] Times March 9th, Colman J.

[22] With the exception of restrictions affecting landlord and tenant affecting land: LRA 2002 s 33(d).

[23] LRA 2002 s 87; Law Com 271 (2001) [6.61]; see below [20.15].

[24] Proceeds of Crime Act 2002; Terrorism Act 2000 part II.

[25] L Ref A 1967 s 5(5); L Ref HUDA 1993 s 97(1).

(4) Off-register transfers etc.

Rights which require substantive registration such as an off-register transfer or an unregistered legal mortgage may be protected, though a notice should only be allowed where for some good reason an application for full registration is not possible.

(5) Residual rights affecting registered title.

Some residual rights are omitted from the list of the classes of land charges but, however much these dog unregistered land law,[26] they are no problem when title is registered: protection by notice is allowed to cover the burden of any interest.[27] This all-embracing category includes all proprietary interests, without any residual category, including estoppels and other rights now declared to be proprietary.[28]

(6) There is a category of "excluded interests"[29] that are incapable of any form of protection on the register, which are:

overreachable interest;[30]
leasehold estates for three years or less if not substantively registrable;
PPP leases;
restrictive covenants between landlord and tenant so far as affecting the property let;
interests registered under the Commons Registration Act 1965; and
coal and mineral rights.

B. AGREED AND UNILATERAL NOTICES

[20.06] The old duality of notice and caution has been replaced with a much improved system of agreed and unilateral notices.[31] In fact there are four categories for consideration.

1. Agreed notices

[20.07] Normally a notice will be called for on completion of a registered disposition.[32] Most adverse rights are created expressly by the registered proprietor by execution of a deed of grant. An agreed notice should be entered. Application[33] is normally made by the registered proprietor or a person entitled to be registered, and otherwise it must include the proprietor's consent. Entry of an agreed notice is also possible where the registrar is satisfied as to the validity of the claim.[34]

---

[26] See below **[21.20]**.
[27] LRA 2002 s 32(1); *Newman* v. *Real Estate Debenture Corp* [1940] 1 All ER 131.
[28] LRA 2002 ss 115–116.
[29] LRA 2002 s 33; Law Com 271 (2001), [6.8–6.16], EN [164–172].
[30] See below **[20.14]**.
[31] LRA 2002 ss 32–39; Law Com 271 (2001) part VI, EN [173–183]; entries are made in the charges register. It will be possible to transfer the benefit: DLRR 2003 r 89; LR Form UN1.
[32] LRA 2002 s 38. Law Com 271 (2001), [6.17ff].
[33] DLRR 2003 r 81; LR Form AN1; DLRR CD ch 5, [11].
[34] LRA 2002 s 34(3).

Pre-2002 Act notices[35] are preserved, and continue as agreed notices.[36]

2.   Agreed notice entered unilaterally

[20.08] The old practice continues of granting a full (or, in new money, an agreed) notice of a matrimonial home right where application is made by the claimant spouse without the consent of the other spouse as registered proprietor.[37] Applications may be lodged electronically.[38] In contrast to the old procedure, a warning of the entry will now be given to the spouse affected.

3.   Unilateral notice

[20.09] A unilateral notice[39] will be used to protect disputed rights. It will perform much of the work previously done by a caution against dealings.[40] One common use would be where B says he has contracted to buy from the registered proprietor (A) who disputes the existence of the contract.[41] A unilateral notice will indicate it is unilateral and will identify the person with the benefit of the notice, but details of the interest claimed will be withheld in the interests of commercial confidentiality, for example to maintain the secrecy of a disputed corporate liquidation.[42]

Notice of the application for the notice will be given to the proprietor and to others interested.[43]

It will be possible to challenge a unilateral notice by a "warning off" procedure.[44] If an application is made for registration of a dealing, notice of the dealing will be served on the person entitled to the benefit of the unilateral notice who will have an (extendible) period of 21 days to object. If he does so the objection has to be resolved with any dispute referred for adjudication.[45]

A unilateral notice has one vital distinction from a pre-Act caution against dealings, which is that the notice now provides priority for the claim noted. If it is challenged and the interest claimed stands up to scrutiny, then the interest will bind a purchaser by virtue of the notice.

---

[35] A notice was only entered (leases apart) if the land certificate was sent with the application (or was available in the registry). Land certificates will play a much smaller part in future and consent is now crucial.

[36] LRA 2002 sch 12 paras 1–2; Law Com 271 (2001), EN [791–794]; including applications pending when the legislation comes into force: sch 12 paras 5–6.

[37] Law Com 271 (2001), EN [177].

[38] LRR 2001, SI 2001/619; DLRR 2003 rr 80–82; DLRR CD ch 5, [1–9]; P Booth & H Brayne [2001] *NLJ* 715.

[39] LRA 2002 s 35; DLRR 2003 rr 83–84; LR Form UN1; DLRR CD ch 5, [11].

[40] See below **[20.10]**.

[41] Not a claim to a beneficial interest by contribution – which requires a restriction; see below **[20.14]**.

[42] Law Com 271 (2001), EN [179–180].

[43] LRA 2002 s 73; Law Com 271 (2001), EN [327–334].

[44] LRA 2002 s 36; DLRR 2003 r 86. DLRR CD ch 3, [19–22]; LR Form UN4.

[45] LRA 2002 s 77(1)(b).

4. Transitional continuation of cautions against dealings

[20.10] For the future, land registry use of the word "caution" is reserved for entries restricting first registrations but before the 2002 Act there was a category of cautions against dealings,[46] used for the protection of disputed rights. Existing cautions will continue in force,[47] the entry appearing on the proprietorship register.[48]

A caution gives no priority[49] but merely an entitlement to notification of a later transaction and the right to an opportunity to assert the validity of the interest before the registration of any dealing. In theory this should have been more than enough to protect burdens adequately, but the machinery was defective because the need to warn off cautions was often overlooked by the registry, so the priority bearing unilateral notice is a much better solution.

Protection by caution is temporary, until warning off.[50] Unless he consents to a dealing being entered the cautioner[51] will challenge the registration of any later dealing, whereupon the interest will either fall or will be converted into a permanent protective notice.[52] A warning notice is served by the registry giving the cautioner a fixed time (typically 14 days) to apply to preserve his entry[53] by establishing that he has a valid proprietary interest in the land with priority.[54] Disputes will in future be resolved by the adjudicator.[55]

5. Action to prevent or remove a unilateral notice or caution (vacation)

[20.11] Entry of a caution or unilateral notice does not give rise to any right of action against the registry.[56] An injunction can be issued to prohibit entry of a notice or a caution to protect an interest which has been rejected by the court,[57] and vexatious cautioners or noticers can be required to obtain leave from the court before applying for a caution.[58]

There is a duty to act reasonably when entering a notice or caution, so damages can be awarded for any loss. [59]

---

[46] LRA 2002 sch 12 para 17, continuing LRA 1925 s 53.

[47] LRA 1925 ss 55–56; LRA 2002 sch 12 para 2(4); DLRR 2003 rr 216–219.

[48] Beware a contract to sell subject to entries in the charges register, which does not catch cautions.

[49] LRA 1925 s 56(2); *Clark* v. *Chief Land Registrar* [1994] Ch 370, CA.

[50] DLRR 2003 r 219; LR Form CCD.

[51] The benefit of a caution can pass to personal representatives; but after sale the buyer needs to enter his own caution – the benefit does not transfer.

[52] Or, in the case of a beneficial interest, into a restriction.

[53] A proprietor (a husband) has no right to stop a bank making a loan from informing the cautioner (H's trustee in bankruptcy) of an application to warn off the caution: *Christofi* v. *Barclays Bank* [1999] 4 All ER 437, CA.

[54] LRA 1925 ss 54(1), 55(1); DLRR 2003 r 218; *Parkash* v. *Irani Finance* [1970] Ch 101, 110H Plowman J; *Chancery* v. *Ketteringham* [1994] 1 Ch 370, CA; *Clark* v. *Chief Land Registrar* [1993] Ch 294, 310D–E, Ferris J; on appeal [1994] Ch 370, CA. Cautions can be supported on grounds not in the statutory declaration: *Atombrook* v. *Heather Weston* [1988].

[55] LRA 2002 ss 73(7), 108.

[56] Subject to the possibility of judicial review: *Nationwide Anglia BS* v. *Ahmed* [1995] 2 EGLR 127, CA.

[57] *McLean Homes* v. *Dace* [1997] EGCS 120, Blackburne J.

[58] *Wren* v. *Meacock* [1997] CLYB 4226, CA.

[59] LRA 2002 s 77; Law Com 271 (2001), EN [347–349]; LRA 1925 s 56(3) (caution); *Willies-Williams* v. *National Trust* (1993) 65 P & CR 359, CA.

Removal will be ordered of a unilateral notice or caution if the right protected by it does not exist. In the case of a notice this will be a non-prejudicial alteration of the register, which can be ordered by the court or by the registrar.[60] In the case of a caution it will be by court proceedings for vacation of the entry.[61] This could be done on an interlocutory application if there is no fair or arguable case.[62] Sterilisation of the land can be avoided by ordering vacation of the register – thus freeing the title to dealings – against an undertaking by the registered proprietor not to impede the success of the action cautioned,[63] and a cross undertaking in damages from the cautioner.[64] Presumably by analogy the court should free the register of a unilateral notice at any early stage of a hopeless case.

C. REMOVAL OF SPENT ENTRIES

[20.12] Entries can be withdrawn by the person entitled to the protection. Cancellation follows from proof that the right protected has ceased to exist to the registrar's satisfaction.[65] Forms differ for agreed notices,[66] unilateral notices,[67] and cautions,[68] so it is vitally important to a buyer's title that he ensures that the correct form is used.[69]

D. RESTRICTIONS

1. Notices and restrictions

[20.13] One great merit of the new legislation is that it creates a clear functional distinction[70] between notices and restrictions. Notices are used to protect burdens against legal estates whereas restrictions are used for beneficial interests and for burdens against beneficial interests which are themselves overreachable.[71] A notice may not be used to protect an interest under a trust of land or strict settlement[72] whereas,

---

[60] See above [11.37].

[61] LRA 1925 s 56(3); P Sparkes *NLL* (1st ed), 185–186.

[62] *Rawlplug Co* v. *Kamvale Properties* (1969) 20 P & CR 32, Megarry J; *Lester* v. *Burgess* (1973) 26 P & CR 536; *Calgary & Edmonton Land Co* v. *Dobinson* [1974] Ch 102, Megarry J; *Northern Developments (Holdings)* v. *UDT Securities* [1976] 1 WLR 1230, Megarry J; *Alpenstow* v. *Regalian* [1985] 1 WLR 721, 728, Nourse J; *Hynes* v. *Vaughan* (1985) 50 P & CR 444, 461, Scott J.

[63] *Clearbrook Property Holdings* v. *Verrier* [1974] 1 WLR 243, Templeman J. (property on the Old Kent Road worth £750,000, in contradiction of the Monopoly board); *Tiverton Estates* v. *Wearwell* [1975] Ch 146, 161, Lord Denning MR; *Carlton* v. *Halestrap* (1988) 4 BCC 538, Morritt J; *Willies-Williams* v. *National Trust* (1993) 65 P & CR 359, CA.

[64] *Alpenstow* v. *Regalian* [1985] 1 WLR 721, Nourse J; *Clowes Developments (UK)* v. *Mulchinock* [1998] 1 WLR 42, Carnwath J.

[65] LRR 1925 r 16 inserted by SI 1996/2975 in force January 1st 1997.

[66] DLRR 2003 rr 87–88; LR Form CN1.

[67] DLRR 2003 r 85; LR Form UN2.

[68] DLRR 2003 r 218; LR Form WTC.

[69] *Holmes* v. *Kennard & Son* (1984) 49 P & CR 202, CA.

[70] The portmanteau term "minor interests" defined by LRA 1925 s 3(xv) covered both true burdens binding on sale and overreachable interests transferred to the proceeds of sale. This is now discarded.

[71] See below [20.14].

[72] LRA 2002 s 33(a).

conversely, a restriction cannot be used to protect a burden for which the proper means of protection is a notice.[73] This reconstruction has introduced much needed coherence.

2. Overreachable burdens

[20.14] A burden against an equitable interest is also overreachable. Thus if a charging order is obtained against the matrimonial home of H and W it should be protected by notice against their legal title, but a charging order made against H as a sole debtor which charges his beneficial interest, and is overreachable, should be protected against the legal title by restriction.[74]

3. Restrictions to protect rights of creditors etc

[20.15] Very occasionally a restriction[75] (unilateral or mutual as appropriate) may be used to record a true, non-overreachable, burden against a legal registered title. This can only be done in cases in which a notice is inappropriate[76] – no longer after the 2002 Act commencement[77] to protect estate contracts.[78] Under the more limited scheme now in force a restriction may only be used to record limits to the circumstances in which a disposition of a registered estate or charge may be the subject of an entry in the register.[79] Proper cases are to protect some of the litigation rights – pending land actions and writs or orders[80] – in particular the appointment by creditors of a receiver or sequestrator, and also a deed of arrangement or a bankruptcy petition,[81] as well as to freeze dealings with the assets of a defendant to litigation[82] or to implement an order for the confiscation of the proceeds of crime.[83]

4. Conversion of inhibitions to restrictions

[20.15A] An inhibition was an order prohibiting any dealing with a title, but new entries are prohibited and existing inhibitions are to operate as restrictions.[84]

---

[73] S 42(2).
[74] S 42(4); Law Com 271 (2001), EN [202]. A caution may no longer be used.
[75] LRA 2002 ss 40–47; Law Com 271 (2001), [6.33 ff], EN [190].
[76] LRA 2002 ss 42(1)(c), 46; Law Com 271 (2001), [6.40], EN [196–202].
[77] LRA 2002 sch 12 paras 1–2, 5–6 (applications pending at commencement); Law Com 271 (2001), [6.32], EN [791–794].
[78] Compare LRA 1925 s 57; LRR 1925 rr 230–231; JE Adams [1994] *Conv* 265.
[79] LRA 2002 s 40.
[80] S 87; Law Com 271 (2001) [6.61].
[81] LRA 2002 s 86(4).
[82] A freezing order; formerly a *Mareva* injunction: *Mareva Compania Naviera* v. *International Bulk Carriers* [1980] 1 All ER 213, CA.
[83] Proceeds of Crime Act 2002.
[84] LRA 2002 sch 12 paras 1–2, 5–6 (applications pending at commencement); Law Com 271 (2001), [6.32], EN [793].

E. PROTECTIVE OCCUPATION

1. Occupiers of registered land

[20.16] Interests which generally require protection by notice can also, in the alternative, be protected by occupation of the land, since the register is overridden by

"an interest belonging to a person in actual occupation . . .".[85]

Almost any burden may acquire overriding status in this way. Informally created
estoppels and such like, can be protected informally by occupation – the point at
which the substantive law of the two systems diverges most markedly.

2. Protection requires actual occupation

[20.17] The general rules set out in the context of one-trustee trusts apply:[86]

the basis is actual occupation – possibly joint but not too fleeting;
occupation may be personal or derivative;
protection against a transfer is limited to rights which are reasonably discoverable;
overriding status is lost if enquiry goes unanswered;
also by an express or implied waiver;
receipt of rent which starts after the 2002 Act commencement does not protect, but
overriding status for burdens continues if receipt started before the 2002 Act commencement and continues uninterrupted.[87]

One vital limit to the protection of the burden is the rule that occupation only protects
burdens affecting that part of the land which is occupied.[88] For the future, an occupier
who holds the benefit of an interest over other parts of the title needs a protective
notice.[89]

3. When occupiers bite

[20.18] Occupation works on an interest that is protectible to give an alternative
means of making the right safe against particular purchasers. Protection crystallises at
the time of a transaction, so if the person entitled to the burden moves out it becomes
vulnerable to any subsequent dealing,[90] and a protective notice will be needed.

---

[85] LRA 2002 sch 3 para 2; replacing LRA 1925 s 70(1)(g); Law Com 271 (2001), [8.14ff], [8.53ff].
[86] See above **[15.31ff]**.
[87] LRA 2002 sch 3 para 2A, inserted transitionally by sch 12 para 8; *Nurdin & Peacock* v. *DB Ramsden
& Co* [1999] 1 WLR 1249, Ch D; G Virgo [1999] *CLJ* 478; S Pascoe [1999] *Conv* 421; Law Com 271 (2001),
EN [609]. In the event of interruption a protective notice is required.
[88] LRA 2002 sch 3 para 2; Law Com 271 (2001), [8.19], EN [612].
[89] *Wallcite* v. *Ferrishurst* [1999] Ch 355, CA, is reversed with no transitional protection(!).
[90] See above **[15.51]**.

4. Trigger

[20.19] Occupation of the land acts as a "trigger" for the protection of a property right. Any interest enjoyed by an occupier can be overriding, with no requirement for any causal connection between the occupation and the interest being protected. Thus in *London & Cheshire Insurance* v. *Laplagrene Property*[91] a company in occupation as tenant under a lease was entitled to additional protection for its unpaid seller's lien. Leases are overriding through the tenant's actual occupation, for short term legal leases,[92] when enjoying statutory security of tenure,[93] under equitable leases operating as contracts for leases,[94] and even if the lease exceeds seven years and so ought to have its own title. Protection extends to any additional rights over the land, such as an option to purchase the freehold.[95] Registrable estates which are unregistered may become overriding in the period before registration as they could under the old law,[96] despite the fact that there is now a compulsion to register.[97]

General protection by occupation for equitable[98] "land charges" was enacted for the first time in 1925,[99] though the courts did not recognise the dual status of an estate contract held by a person in actual occupation until 1957.[100] Even an easement of parking might be protected by actual occupation.[101] Protection is also afforded to residual rights falling outside the classes of land charges, such as estoppel rights[102] and mere equities consist of a discretionary right to an equitable remedy – examples are a right to rectification of a document[103] or rectification of the register,[104] and the right to avoid a fraudulent transfer.[105]

---

[91] [1971] Ch 499.

[92] *Ashburn Anstalt* v. *Arnold* [1989] Ch 1, CA; *Canadian Imperial Bank of Commerce* v. *Bello* (1991) 24 HLR 155, CA; *Crumpton* v. *Unifox Properties* [1992] 2 EGLR 82, CA; *Pourdanay* v. *Barclays Bank* [1997] Ch 321, Scott V-C; but for an exception see below **[25.55ff]**.

[93] *National Provincial Bank* v. *Hastings Car Mart* [1964] Ch 665, 689, Lord Denning MR; left open in *Pourdanay* v. *Barclays Bank* [1997] Ch 321, 329B, Scott V-C.

[94] *City Permanent BS* v. *Miller* [1952] Ch 840, CA; *Strand Securities* v. *Caswell* [1965] Ch 958, CA; *Lloyd* v. *Dugdale* [2001] EWCA Civ 1754, [2002] 2 P & CR 13 at 167.

[95] *Webb* v. *Pollmount* [1966] Ch 584; *Kling* v. *Keston Properties* (1985) 49 P & CR 212; *Habermann* v. *Koehler* (1996) 72 P & CR D10, CA; *Wallcite* v. *Ferrrishurst* [1999] Ch 355, 372D, Robert Walker LJ.

[96] *Bridges* v. *Mees* [1957] Ch 475 (unregistered transfer).

[97] When electronic creation becomes compulsory, no interest will exist in advance of registration so there will be nothing to be overriding. The change may be minimal because informal rights may often raise an estoppel.

[98] *City Permanent BS* v. *Miller* [1952] Ch 840.

[99] LRA 1925 s 70(1)(g), re-enacting LPA 1922 sch 16 para 5.

[100] *Bridges* v. *Mees* [1957] Ch 475.

[101] *Saeed* v. *Plustrade* [2001] EWCA Civ 2011, [2002] 2 EGLR 19.

[102] LRA 2002 s 116; *Lloyd* v. *Dugdale* [2002] 2 P & CR 13 at 167, CA; J Skovron [2002] *PLJ* 11; M Dixon [2002] *Conv* 584; see below **[23.42]**.

[103] *Collings* v. *Lee* [2001] 2 All ER 332, CA; R Nolan [2001] *CLJ* 477; *Holow (470)* v. *Stockton Estates* (2001) 81 P & CR 404, Ch D.

[104] *Blacklocks* v. *JB Developments (Godalming)* [1982] Ch 183, Mervyn Davies QC; *Nurdin & Peacock* v. *DB Ramsden & Co* [1999] 1 WLR 1249, Ch D; *Bhullar* v. *McArdle* [2001] EWCA Civ 510, (2001) 82 P & CR 38 at 481; *Malory Enterprises* v. *Cheshire Homes (UK)* [2002] EWCA Civ 151, [2002] Ch 216, [68–70], Arden LJ.

[105] *Collings* v. *Lee* [2001] 2 All ER 332, CA.

5.   Limits to occupation as a means of protection

[20.20] Certain burdens must be protected by entry on the register and not by actual
occupation, notably:

enfranchisement notices;[106]
matrimonial home rights;[107]
beneficial interests under old strict settlements;[108] and
future leases where possession is delayed more than three months from the grant.[109]

Rights entered on the register by notice at any time after the 2002 Act commencement
are deprived of their overriding status.[110] It is very curious that overriding status is
consistent with entry of a restriction.

F.   OVERRIDING INTERESTS

1.   Nature

[20.21] Rights which are overriding are automatic since they bind a purchaser without entry on the register.[111] An innovative and irritating feature of the 2002 Act is that
there are two different lists: schedule 1 lists interests overriding first registration;
whereas schedule 3 sets out interests overriding a transfer. Occupiers apart, the lists
are similar.

Overriding interests are freestanding property rights. Most are legal,[112] though this
is not necessarily true of rights protected by occupation.

2.   Overriding reform

[20.22] Overriding interests which bind off the register substantially reduce the value
of the register. They are a major obstacle to registered conveyancing and should be
kept to a minimum.[113] Overriding status should be grudgingly conceded when protection against purchasers is really needed if it is not sensible to expect an entry on the
register, and the attempt to reduce the category has been a disappointing tinkering at
the edges.[114]

---

[106] L Ref HUD A 1993 ss 13, 42.
[107] FLA 1996 s 31(1)(b).
[108] LRA 2002 sch 3 para 2(a). Protection is by restriction and not by notice: LRA 2002 s 33(a)(ii).
[109] LRA 2002 sch 3 para 2(d).
[110] S 29(3); *Webb* v. *Pollmount* [1966] Ch 584, 594G.
[111] The rights are outside the guarantee; see above **[11.40]**.
[112] *City Permanent BS* v. *Miller* [1952] Ch 840, 850, Cozens Hardy MR; FR Crane (1958) 22 *Conv (NS)*
14, 17; H Potter, *The Principles of Land Law under the Land Registration Act 1925* (Sweet & Maxwell, 1941),
268–269.
[113] Law Com 271 (2001), [8.1]; *SS for Environment T&R* v. *Baylis (Gloucester)* (2000) 80 P & CR 324,
338, Kim Lewison QC.
[114] LRA 2002 ss 29–30, sch 3; Law Com 271 (2001), [8.35–8.46], [8.74–8.95], EN [599–627]; E Cooke
[2002] *Conv* 11; PH Kenny [2001] *Conv* 216; PH Kenny [2002] *Conv* 3.

3. Priority

[20.23] Priority of overriding interests against future holders of the registered title is clear; they are automatic burdens which affect the title without special protection.[115] Relative priority between two overriding interests will be decided on the first in time principle.[116]

4. Completion of the register

[20.24] The register should be made as comprehensive as possible, so interests overriding the register should be got onto the register when possible. It is certainly no longer appropriate to delete a notice of an overriding interest such as a right of way.[117] The registrar will have[118] a much more extensive discretion than before[119] to note any known overriding interests on the register at the time of registration, notice being given to registered proprietor and others appearing to be protected.[120] Unregistered interests must be disclosed on first registration[121] or at the time of any subsequent registered disposition.[122]

G. OVERRIDING INTERESTS: A LIST

1.   Short-term leases under the 2002 Act

[20.25] In essence the 2002 Act provides that leases exceeding seven years are substantively registrable and leases for between three and seven years can be protected by notice. There are also a few forms of lease which must be substantively registered,[123] and which cannot be overriding.[124] Otherwise legal leases[125] for a term not exceeding seven years are overriding, as more generally, is any lease held by a tenant in possession.[126]

2.   Short-term leases – transitional continuation of the old law

[20.26] Until the 2002 Act commencement, leases were only substantively registrable if the unexpired term exceeded 21 years, so overriding status was conferred on any

---

[115] LRA 2002 s 29(2); *Marks* v. *Attallah* (1966) 110 SJ 709, Ungoed-Thomas J.
[116] Now irrespective it seems of whether the right is legal or equitable; see below **[20.40]**.
[117] *Re Dances' Way, West Town, Hayling Island* [1962] Ch 490, CA; *Willies-Williams* v. *National Trust* (1993) 65 P & CR 359, 362, Hoffmann LJ.
[118] LRA 2002 s 37.
[119] LRA 1925 s 70(3); Law Com 271 (2001), [8.90–8.95], EN [184].
[120] DLRR 2003 r 90; DLRR CD ch 5, [35–38].
[121] DLRR 2003 r 27.
[122] LRA 2002 s 71; Law Com 271 (2001), EN [315–316]; DLRR 2003 rr 27, 55. This does not apply to "excluded interests".
[123] See below **[25.37]**.
[124] LRA 2002 schs 1/3 para 1; Law Com 271 (2001), [8.9–8.10], EN [517]; EN [603–605].
[125] See below **[25.55ff]**.
[126] LRA 2002 schs 1/3 para 2. At the time of transfer a lease to be granted more than 3 months afterwards is not protected by occupation under another interest: para 2(d).

legal lease "granted for a term not exceeding twenty-one years".[127] This only applied to leases "granted", a term interpreted to limit the protection to legal leases.[128] Equitable leases require protection by notice, caution or occupation. It would be wrong to clutter the register with numerous ever-changing short term leases, but the effect could be very unfair if the tenant was not in occupation.[129] Protection is continued by a transitional provision,[130] the relevant date for checking the existence being the date of first registration, the date of registration of a transfer pre-commencement,[131] or the date of transfer post-commencement.[132]

3. Easement

(1) General rule

[20.27] Legal easements and profits à prendre are overriding.[133] At the time of first registration this includes documentary easements, but once title is registered legal status only attaches to an easement made by registered disposition and recorded on the register,[134] so a formal easement cannot be legal off the register and cannot override a subsequent transfer. However, this class will include inherently unregistrable easements, those created by prescription (long use)[135] or by implied grant or reservation on physical division of the land.[136]

(2) Limitation to easements discoverable on transfer

[20.28] Overriding status on a transfer will be restricted – after a transitional three year period to allow for entry of a protective notice[137] – to an easement[138] of one of the following four kinds:

registered under the Commons Registration Act 1965;
within the actual knowledge of the purchaser;
obvious on careful inspection of the land; or
exercised within the year preceding the transfer.

---

[127] LRA 1925 s 70(1)(k), as amended in 1986.
[128] *City Permanent BS* v. *Miller* [1952] Ch 840, CA.
[129] Or where the flat to which protection attaches has been destroyed: *Prince* v. *Robinson* (1999) 31 HLR 89, CA, obiter.
[130] LRA 2002 sch 12 para 12.
[131] *Pourdanay* v. *Barclays Bank* [1997] Ch 321, Scott VC.
[132] LRA 2002 ss 11(4), 29(2).
[133] Schs 1/3 para 3; Law Com 271 (2001), EN [620–627]. This reproduces LRA 1925 s 70(1)(a).
[134] LRA 2002 s 27(1).
[135] See below [35].
[136] See below [34].
[137] LRA 2002 sch 12 para 10; Law Com 271 (2001), EN [623–627].
[138] LRA 2002 sch 3 para 3; Law Com 271 (2001), EN [620–627].

(3) Equitable easements

[20.29] These were unwontedly overriding under the 1925 rules, according to the decision of Scott J in *Celsteel* v. *Alton House Holdings*,[139] since the rules included any right appurtenant or reputed to appertain to registered land.[140] In *Celsteel* itself Djafarian had been promised a lease of garage 52 with access rights. These unprotected equitable easements were overriding against Mobil Oil's registered leasehold title and blocked their plan to install a car wash. Had title been unregistered land charges registration would have been required, so *Celsteel* caused the two systems to diverge. The new Act brings them once more into proper alignment, but with transitional protection for pre-Act vested rights.[141]

4. Customary and public rights

[20.30] The overriding status of customary and public rights is maintained.[142]

5. Local land charges

[20.31] Local land charges are public burdens recorded by the district councils,[143] including for example liability to contribute to the cost of making up a road, and road building agreements. There is a separate registration system, so they override the register of titles.[144]

6. Certain mineral rights

[20.32] Mineral rights granted overriding status are rights to coal, mines under land first registered before 1898, and mines separated from the surface before a first registration which occurred before 1925.[145]

7. Overriding interests abolished after a transitional period of 10 years

[20.33] Chancel repair liabilities are no longer enforceable and their overriding status is removed.[146] Five other interests of ancient origin are unusual, difficult to discover, and exceptionally onerous.[147] These are abolished after 10 years,[148] viz:

[139] [1985] 1 WLR 204, Scott J; on appeal [1986] 1 WLR 512, CA; MP Thompson [1986] *Conv* 31; PH Kenny (1985) 82 *LSG* 339; AM Prichard, [1987] *Conv* 328.

[140] LRR 1925 r 258; M Davey [1986] *Conv* 296. Query whether this was, as Scott J decided, within the rule-making power; *Thatcher* v. *Douglas* [1996] NLJ 282, CA.

[141] LRA 2002 sch 12 para 9.

[142] LRA 2002 schs 1/3 paras 4–5; definition: Law Com 271 (2001), [8.23], EN [588]; *Overseas Investments* v. *Simcobuild Construction* (19951) 70 P & CR 322.

[143] LRA 2002 schs 1/3 para 6; also any protected before the 1975 definitional changes: sch 12 para 13.

[144] *Overseas Investment Services* v. *Simcobuild Construction* (1995) 70 P & CR 322, CA. They bind the estate and are lost on escheat (unless preserved by the vesting order): *Hackney LBC* v. *Crown Estates Commissioners* (1996) 72 P & CR 233, Knox J.

[145] LRA 2002 schs 1/3 paras 7–9.

[146] Chancel Repairs Act 1932; Law Com 152 (1985); *Aston Cantlow etc PCC* v. *Wallbank* [2001] EWCA Civ 713, [2002] Ch 51; Law Com 271 (2001), [8.75]; see above **[5.31]**.

[147] Law Com 271 (2001), [8.35].

[148] LRA 2002 s 115; Law Com 271 (2001), [8.81–8.89]; during the 10 years the right requires protection by caution against first registration or LR notice; no fee will be charged.

franchises;

manorial rights;[149]

Crown rents;

non statutory rights to embankment sea or river wall; and

payments in lieu of tithe.

8. Squatters rights protected transitionally

[20.34] Rights acquired under the Limitation Act 1980 before the 2002 Act commencement[150] may be overriding (1) indefinitely if the squatter is in occupation,[151] or (2) for a transitional period of three years if the squatter is out of occupation.[152]

H. BURDENS ON FIRST REGISTRATION

1. Notice

[20.35] At the time of first registration, it will be necessary to enter notices[153] to reflect any burden revealed by the investigation of title and binding on the first proprietor, as well as restrictions to deal with overreachable interests. There is a duty to disclose interests to make the first register as comprehensive as possible.[154] Any cautions against first registration need to be reconciled and, if valid, turned into appropriate register entries.[155]

Entry of a notice does not guarantee the existence of a burden – it merely gives notice of a claim to a right; so if the interest was void against the unregistered pre-registration title it will not be revivified by first registration. Thus an option void against a purchaser for non-registration as a class C(iii) land charge is also void against the registered proprietor when the title is later registered.[156]

2. Occupiers

[20.36] Interests can be protected by occupation at the time of first registration of the land. The requirements are (1) an interest (2) held by a person in actual occupation (3) which relates to the land occupied (4) which is not a beneficial interest under a strict settlement.[157] Much of the detail affecting this form of protection at the time of a transfer is omitted at the earlier stage of first registration.[158]

---

[149] As defined in LPA 1922 sch 12 paras 5–6.
[150] See above **[11.13]**.
[151] LRA 2002 schs 1/3 para 2.
[152] LRA 2002 schs 1/3 para 15, inserted by sch 12 paras 7, 11, 18; Law Com 271 (2001), [8.76ff]. The title should be registered within those 3 years.
[153] LRA 2002 s 34.
[154] See above **[9.32]**, **[20.24]**.
[155] See above **[9.15]**.
[156] *Freeguard* v. *Royal Bank of Scotland* (2000) 79 P & CR 81, CA.
[157] LRA 2002 sch 1 para 2.
[158] See above **[20.16]**.

3. Overriding interests

[20.37] A large number of interests override first registration.[159] The list is now separated from that applying to a transfer but, occupiers apart, the two lists are practically identical:

Short leases;[160]
Legal easement and profits;[161]
Customary and public rights;
Local land charges;
Mines and minerals and coal;
Miscellaneous old and tenurial rights for a transitional period of 10 years – franchises, manorial rights, Crown rents, sea wall etc repairs, and corn rents.

I.   PRIORITY: FIRST IN TIME

1.   Priority and the first in time principle

[20.38] Priority principles for registered land, once horrendously complicated,[162] are greatly simplified by the 2002 consolidation,[163] which states two universals:

priorities are determined by the first in time; but
protected purchasers may claim priority over unprotected interests.[164]

Where interests are not affected by a disposition of the estate priority is based on the date of creation.[165]

2.   Donee against earlier burden

[20.39] A person who receives land under a gift (who cannot be protected as a purchaser) is bound by all burdens existing when he is given the land. They, the burdens, are earlier in time that the gift. The same applies to any person who pays only a nominal consideration, for example Mrs Rigg who paid £1 in *Peffer* v. *Rigg*.[166] Once the money paid rises above the nominal protection as a purchaser may kick in, even if the price paid is still an undervalue.[167]

---

[159] LRA 2002 sch 1; Law Com 271 (2001), EN [472, EN [570ff]; compare above **[20.25]**.
[160] As for transfer except for the omission of the qualification about registered dispositions.
[161] The proviso for easements undiscoverable on transfer does not apply.
[162] P Sparkes *NLL* (1st ed), 148–157, 208–213.
[163] LRA 2002 ss 28–29; Law Com 271 (2001), [5.1–5.38]; also Law Com 254 (1998), part VII; also above **[15.26]**.
[164] See below **[20.41]**.
[165] LRA 2002 s 28; Law Com 271 (2001), [5.5], EN [147].
[166] [1977] 1 WLR 285, 293G, Graham J; see above **[15.28]**.
[167] See below **[20.43]**.

3. Priority as between burdens off the register

[20.40] The first in time principle is applied between two burdens whether or not they are protected by notices. Leading cases on the 1925 legislation would be decided the same way today. *Mortgage Corporation* v. *Nationwide Credit Corporation*[168] involved a competition between:

1. a mortgage in the form of a legal charge but neither registered nor protected by notice; and
2. a second mortgage properly protected by notice.

Although unprotected, the first of two equitable lenders[169] was held to have priority. *Barclays Bank* v. *Taylor*[170] showed the same for a competition between (1) an unprotected[171] equitable mortgage and (2) a later contract. Interest (1) had priority despite the caution protecting the contract. Finally, in *Parkash* v. *Irani Finance*[172] there were successively:

1. a charging order protected by caution; and
2. a transfer and mortgage, unregistered because of the caution.[173]

The charging order had priority and the creditor could insist on entry of a notice before the transfer and mortgage were registered.

In *Freeguard* v. *Royal Bank of Scotland*[174] an option to repurchase a ransom strip should have secured priority over a later transfer and charge which were held off the register by the existence of a caution. However, this was held to be a case in which the two equities were unequal, and so a case in which priority had been waived by allowing the impression to be created of absolute ownership of the strip free of the option. The absence of registration of a thoroughly artificial transaction led to postponement.[175] This case should not be decided the same way today since the intention of the 2002 Act was to make priorities strictly temporal without any process of weighing the equities for equality.[176]

These cases demonstrate that protection on the register does not secure priority.[177] If a legal registered title is subject to X's unprotected burden and Y's protected burden, X wins. A first in time of registration principle is required, but the Law Commission intend to wait for the evolution of electronic conveyancing before proposing it.[178]

---

[168] [1994] Ch 49, CA; *ES Schwab & Co* v. *McCarthy* (1975) 31 P & CR 196 (transfer and charge both unregistered as against a surrender).
[169] The result would have been reversed if the second mortgage had been substantively registered, thus creating a *legal* security.
[170] [1974] Ch 137, CA; PV Baker (1973) 89 *LQR* 170.
[171] Barclays had entered a notice of deposit of the land certificate when (the discussion of priority assumes) they needed the (now redundant) mortgage caution.
[172] [1970] Ch 101, Plowman J.
[173] Failure of an official search to reveal the caution did not affects its validity: LRR 1930 r 1; LR (Official Searches) R 1993 r 6.
[174] (2000) 79 P & CR 81 CA.
[175] At 89, Robert Walker LJ.
[176] LRA 2002 s 28; Law Com 271 (2001), [5.5].
[177] *Barclays Bank* v. *Taylor* [1974] Ch 137, 147 ; *Clark* v. *Chief Land Registrar* [1994] Ch 370, 384–385.
[178] Law Com 254 (1998), [7.32].

J.   PRIORITY: PROTECTION OF PURCHASERS

[20.41] A person who buys and secures substantive registration of his title can destroy the interests of those off the register. The priority principle of the 2002 consolidation is painfully simple. The three essentials are simple to learn:

1. acquisition of a protected interest;
2. value; and
3. diligence.

There is no additional element of (4) honesty. This is excluded so clearly as to leave no room for escape in circumstances where the scheme may work most unjustly. Therein lies the pain.

1.   Protected interest

[20.42] First in time (AB) operates between any pair of interests, unless B can trump A by acquiring a registered estate. This depends upon substantive registration of B's title derived from a registered disposition,[179] though priority is also conferred on a tenant under a short-term, non registrable, lease.[180] Completion of a sale creates equitable interests, full protection being dependent upon legal rights which pass only when title is registered.[181] The registration gap must be closed by obtaining an official search and applying to be registered during its priority period.[182]

2.   Value

[20.43] Protection is provided for a person who takes under a registered disposition of a registered estate for value.[183] A person who provides money to buy land needs protection to ensure that he can realise his investment for the same value, and this implies that he must have priority over unknown burdens, which would otherwise detract from the value of the land. This concept excludes a nominal consideration in money and also (a new provision) a marriage – a wedding gift is no longer made for value.[184] Value may be provided by a person who provides nothing other than an indemnity to the person transferring against liability on the covenants in a lease.[185]

---

[179] LRA 2002 s 29; *Abbey National BS* v. *Cann* [1991] 1 AC 54, 79A, Lord Oliver; correspondingly for derivative interests such as leases and charges: s 30.

[180] LRA 2002 s 29(4); Law Com 271 (2001), [5.15]; *Freeguard* v. *Royal Bank of Scotland* (2000) 79 P & CR 81, [24], Robert Walker LJ; *Leeman* v. *Mohammed* (2001) 82 P & CR 14 at 159, CA.

[181] LRA 2002 s 27.

[182] In fact some 60% of transfers lodged are outside priority period. For searches see above **[8.21]**.

[183] LRA 2002 s 29.

[184] LRA 2002 s 132(1); Law Com 271 (2001), [5.8–5.10]; this reverses LRA 1925 s 3(xxxi). Pre-1926 law excluded a foreclosure order: *Re de Leeuw* [1922] 2 Ch 540.

[185] *DB Ramsden & Co* v. *Nurdin & Peacock* [1999] 1 WLR 1249 (yes).

3. Diligence

[20.44] A person who registers a disposition of a registered estate for value takes subject to the following interests:[186]

> registered mortgages;
> any interest protected by a land registry notice;
> the interest of any person in actual occupation at the time of the transfer[187];
> any other overriding interest;[188] and
> any incidents of leasehold estates.

Dovetailing can be observed because most of the overriding interests are legal and so
bind automatically if title is unregistered, though of course protection is then by land
charges registration. As Hoffmann LJ observed in *Willies-Williams* v. *National
Trust*,[189] the hazards of constructive notice are removed from registered land. The
duty to make inquiry is limited to a search of the register and for occupiers. It is
axiomatic that any other form of notice of suspicious circumstances is irrelevant once
title is registered.[190] The only cases in which knowledge or notice of an adverse interest is relevant are:

> a trust at the time of first registration;[191]
> an Inland Revenue charge;[192]
> bankruptcy – where good faith is relevant;[193] and
> a legal easement at the time of transfer.[194]

4. Honesty

[20.45] Buyers of registered land, as of unregistered land,[195] can take the land free of
unprotected burdens of which they know. Protection on the register supersedes any
requirement of honesty.[196] There is a gut feeling that a person should not ignore rights
of which he knows,[197] but the policy is instead to uphold the integrity of the register.[198] Good faith is not relevant as the Land Registration Act 2002 makes very

---

[186] LRA 2002 ss 29, 30 (charge).

[187] LRA 2002 sch 3 para 2.

[188] LRA 2002 sch 3. Overriding status is lost if the interest has been protected by notice at any time since
the 2002 Act implementation date: s 29(3).

[189] (1993) 65 P & CR 359, 362; *Williams & Glyn's Bank* v. *Boland* [1981] AC 487, 503, Lord Wilberforce.

[190] Law Com 271 (2001), [5.16].

[191] LRA 2002 s 11(5); see above **[11.05]**.

[192] S 31; see below **[28.37]**.

[193] S 86(5)(c)(ii); see below **[28.51]**.

[194] Sch 3 para 3; see above **[20.28]**.

[195] *Midland Bank Trust Co* v. *Green* [1981] AC 502, HL; see below **[21.39]**.

[196] *Hodges* v. *Jones* [1935] Ch 657, Luxmoore J; *Strand Securities* v. *Caswell* [1965] Ch 373, 390, Cross J,
958, 987, Russell LJ; *Miles* v. *Bull (No 1)* [1969] 1 QB 258, Megarry J; *(No 2)* [1969] 3 All ER 1585,
1585–1590, Bridge J; *Parkash* v. *Irani Finance* [1970] Ch 101, 109.

[197] *Rolland* v. *Hart* (1871) LR 6 Ch App 678, 683, Lord Hatherley. For older cases decided on this principle see P Sparkes *NLL* (1st ed), 210–211.

[198] *Ashburn Anstalt* v. *Arnold* [1989] Ch 1, 25; *Markfaith Investments* v. *Chia Hua Flashlights* [1991] 2 AC
43, PC.

explicit. In *De Lusignan* v. *Johnson*[199] an unprotected estate contract was void on sale and Brightman J dismissed an attempt to plead bad faith as an utter irrelevance. The decision is distressing. Dr Lusignan, who owed money to his wife and had already agreed to sell a property to her, mortgaged the land to his solicitor (Johnson) who was aware of the wife's contractual right. The solicitor still won. Bad faith short of fraud could not assist the wife.[200] One "rogue"[201] decision, *Peffer* v. *Rigg*,[202] discovered a requirement of honesty in the interstices of the Land Registration Act 1925 but after fierce criticism[203] it is clear that there is no role for honesty under the brutally clear terms of the Land Registration Act 2002.[204] A loser may well have a personal action for knowing receipt, but no proprietary remedy. [205]

In relation to burdens there may be merit in the clear scheme adopted,[206] and in this context registered and unregistered land law dovetail.

5. Priority: other solutions

[20.46] The chapter on unregistered land charges contains discussion of the following topics:[207]

variation by agreement;
estoppel;
constructive trusts; and
personal actions.

These apply equally where title is registered.

---

[199] (1973) 230 EG 499.
[200] At 499.
[201] Grays' *Elements* (3rd ed), 1062.
[202] [1977] 1 WLR 285, Graham J.
[203] FR Crane (1977) 41 *Conv* (NS) 207; RJ Smith (1977) 93 *LQR* 341; DJ Hayton [1977] *CLJ* 227; JE Martin [1978] *Conv* 52; S Anderson (1977) 40 *MLR* 602; DC Jackson (1978) 94 *LQR* 239.
[204] A requirement of good faith was proposed: Law Com 158 (1987), [4.14–4.15]; but this was dropped in 1998: Law Com 254 (1998), [3.39–3.50]; Law Com 271 (2001), [5.16].
[205] Law Com 271 (2001), [4.11].
[206] Contrast one-trustee trusts where the two systems do not dovetail; see above **[15]**.
[207] See below **[21.41]**.

21

BURDENS ON UNREGISTERED LAND

Legal burdens. Classes of land charge. Residual burdens. Vacation of land charges. Land charges: registration; searches. Priority: land charges; other solutions.

A. LEGAL BURDENS ON UNREGISTERED LAND

1. Nature

[21.01] Most legal burdens are "automatic burdens", that is ones which bind purchasers simply because they exist without any steps being needed to protect them or to bring them to a buyer's attention. "Legal rights bind the world." In other words, "The first in time prevails". If a legal easement is granted to B and this is followed by a legal lease granted to C, the tenant is bound by B's easement. This is the essence of a legal estate[1] and if we exclude mortgages[2] is fully true of legal rights in unregistered land. Overriding interests are automatic against registered titles. So most legal burdens bind purchasers come what may, whether or not they were discovered or discoverable.

2. A list of automatic legal burdens

[21.02] Legal interests are incumbrances which attach like a leech to a legal estate, sucking some of the value from it. They give limited rights over another's land. The Law of Property Act 1925[3] reduces them to a short list.

(1) Legal leases

[21.03] Legal leases are estates,[4] brought and sold in their own right, but they act as burdens on a sale of the reversionary estate; if freehold land is sold subject to a 99 year lease, the lease derogates from the title in much the same way as an easement or mortgage.

---

[1] *Bruton* v. *London & Quadrant HT* [1998] QB 834, 845E, Millett LJ; Grays' *Elements* (3rd ed) ch 5; Megarry & Wade (6th ed), [4.047–4.054].
[2] See below **[28.15ff]**.
[3] LPA 1925 s 1(2).
[4] S 1(1)(b).

(2) Easements

[21.04] Legal status is conferred on an "easement, right or privilege over land",[5] particularly easements to use a neighbour's land for access or drainage, rights to light and profits à prendre consisting of grazing or fishing rights. In order to secure legal status the duration of the easement must match one of the legal estates – it must be either in fee simple absolute in possession or for a term of years absolute. A right of way for life or to commence in the future is necessarily equitable.

(3) Rentcharges

[21.05] Rentcharges are legal interests[6] charging a rent on freehold land, though since 1977 newly created rentcharges have been restricted to estate rentcharges designed to secure the performance of obligations and not as a source of profit.[7] A legal rentcharge must be "in possession", but this concept is extended to include any case where payments commence at some future time![8] Once it vests, a legal rentcharge must endure perpetually or for a term of years, so a rentcharge *to B for life* is equitable.

(4) Money payments like a tithe rentcharge

[21.06] "Other similar charge" still appears in the legislation[9] but the repeal of land tax and tithe rentcharges leaves the question: similar to what?

(5) Rights of entry

[21.07] Finally, independent legal status is granted to certain rights of entry, that is a right to enter on the land as a remedy to secure performance of an obligation attached to a legal lease – that is rights of forfeiture – or legal rentcharge. Other rights of entry are equitable.[10]

3. Mortgages

[21.08] Mortgages[11] are no longer automatic, even if legal, since the Birkenhead legislation introduced a new regime which requires mortgages to be protected either by retention of the title deeds (first mortgages) or otherwise by land charges registration.[12]

---

[5] LPA 1925 s 1(1)(a).

[6] S 1(2)(b).

[7] See above **[3.29]**, below **[32.53ff]**.

[8] LP (Entailed Interests) A 1932 s 2.

[9] LPA 1925 s 1(2)(d).

[10] S 1(2)(e). Equitable rights of re-entry include those attached to a conditional fee simple or attached to a lease on an assignment: *Shiloh Spinners* v. *Harding* [1973] AC 691, HL.

[11] Mortgages in the technical sense are leases within LPA 1925 s 1(1)(b), but most are actually legal charges, that is charges by deed by way of legal mortgage, a form of legal interest in s 1(2)(c); see below **[28.15]**.

[12] See below **[21.11]**.

4.   Documentary and non-documentary legal burdens

[21.09] Legal incumbrances are generally created by deed,[13] so the existence of the right should be apparent from the title deeds, the more so if, as is the correct practice, grants of easements and other adverse rights are noted on the most recent title deed by memorandum. Sellers invariably reveal the existence of adverse legal rights to avoid contractual liability for non-disclosure. Attempts to introduce negligence as a factor have failed other than for first mortgages protected by deposit:[14] it is not negligent to fail to register a transfer[15] or to give notice of a mortgage.[16] Burdens created by pre-scription (long use)[17] are non-documentary, but are nevertheless legal and so bind the world whether or not they are discoverable.

B.   CLASSES OF LAND CHARGE

[21.10] Land charges are the matters requiring registration against the name of an estate owner who creates them while title remains unregistered. All these rights require protection by notice once title is registered.[18]

1.   Mortgages

[21.11] Registration is an obvious means of giving tangible protection to an invisible mortgage, and one which is required for all mortgages of unregistered land unless the title deeds are deposited.[19]

A puisne[20] mortgage of class C(i)[21] is a *legal* mortgage which is not protected by a deposit of documents relating to the legal estate affected.[22] Usually a first lender retains the title deeds, so second mortgage will have to be registered. An equitable mortgage is registrable in class C(iii)[23] as a general equitable charge if it charges a loan[24] on specific property and binds the legal estate.[25] Equitable mortgages usually rank after to a legal mortgage secured by deposit,[26] and so are registrable.

Equitable mortgages take the form of a contract to create a legal mortgage. However, if a mortgage creates an immediate equitable charge on land it is registrable

---

[13] LPA 1925 s 52, 54; see above **[7.01]**.

[14] See below **[28.23ff]**.

[15] *Mortgage Corp* v. *Nationwide Credit Corp* [1994] 1 Ch 49.

[16] *Grierson* v. *National Provincial Bank* [1913] 2 Ch 18.

[17] See below **[35]**.

[18] See above **[20.05]**.

[19] Mortgages were added to the existing registrable interests in 1925: LPA 1922 sch 7; LP (Amendment) A 1924 sch 6; LCA 1925 s 10; LCA 1972 s 2; *Ministry of Housing & Local Government* v. *Sharp* [1970] 2 QB 223, 280, Cross LJ.

[20] Pronounced "puny".

[21] CLR *Report 1995–1996* shows less than 30,000 C(i) registrations and 1,500 in class C(iii); very few C(i)s have been registrable since 1997 because a first mortgage now triggers registration.

[22] LCA 1972 s 2(4)(i); local land charges are not registrable under the central system.

[23] Law Com 18 (1969), [63].

[24] Not an agreement to divide the proceeds of sale: *Thomas* v. *Rose* [1968] 1 WLR 1797, 1807, Megarry J; nor an indemnity.

[25] As to mortgages of equitable interests see above **[16.28]**.

[26] LCA 1972 s 2(4)(iii).

as an general equitable charge – class C(iii).[27] If the *only* security is a right to request the creation of a legal mortgage in the future, class C(iv) registration is required as an estate contract by *Williams* v. *Burlington Investments*.[28] Safety first may suggest that equitable mortgages are best entered under both classes.

2.   Other money charges as land charges

[21.12] A lien arises automatically by operation of law,[29] and if title is unregistered it requires protection in class C(iii). An unpaid seller's lien arises when some of the price[30] is left outstanding at the time of sale, giving the seller a charge on the land to secure the payment of the remainder of the price, unless he takes a formal mortgage.[31] In *Chattey* v. *Farndale Holdings*[32] 400 flats were to be constructed near the West London Air Terminal and two potential purchasers of individual flats each paid 20% deposits. Even though the contracts were conditional on planning permission being obtained, it was held that the purchasers had a lien for the return of their deposits with proprietary force against a purchaser of the whole development.[33]

Statutory charges of classes A and B are imposed by an Act of Parliament with the object of enabling a person who has been forced to spend money to recoup it from the land owner, acting when registered as if mortgages.[34] Class A dating from 1888 applies to rare cases of charges created by personal application, whereas Class B charges arise automatically, the most numerous being the legal aid charge imposed on property recovered as a result of a successful publicly funded action. [35] Class D(i) is for the Inland Revenue charge securing unpaid inheritance tax.[36]

3.   Estate contracts

[21.13] Estate contracts are the first example of true incumbrances[37] which burden the land itself, are not convertible to money, and never overreachable. Before 1926 many equitable interests were reliant on the doctrine of notice, so that holders lived in fear of the loss of their interest to a purchaser and buyers feared being caught by undiscovered rights. Hence the introduction of the requirement to register in 1925.[38]

---

[27] *Property Discount Corp* v. *Lyon Group* [1981] 1 WLR 300, CA.

[28] (1977) 121 SJ 424, HL.

[29] *UCB Bank* v. *Beasley* [1996] CLYB 4951, CA. (loss by non-disclosure on inquiry); MP Thompson [1996] *Conv* 44.

[30] *Uziell-Hamilton* v. *Keen* (1971) 22 P & CR 655; *Woolf Project Management* v. *Woodtrek* [1988] 1 EGLR 179 (not contract to pay additional sums if extra land developed); *Barclays Bank* v. *Estates & Commercial* [1997] 1 WLR 415, CA (arrangement to share profits on development was registrable).

[31] *Nationwide Anglia BS* v. *Ahmed* (1995) 70 P & CR 381, CA.

[32] (1998) 75 P & CR 298, CA.

[33] One was binding and the other void for non-registration at the time of first registration of the new developer's title.

[34] LCA 1972 ss 2(2)(3), 4(1)–(3), sch 2; *R* v. *Land Registry* (1889) 24 QBD 178. CLR *Report 1995–1996* records no class A entries, less than 5,000 in class B, and 400 or so Inland Revenue Charges.

[35] Legal Aid Act 1974 s 9; SI 1989/339 reg 95; S Shute (1993) 109 *LQR* 636.

[36] LCA 1972 s 2(5)(i); *Lord Advocate* v. *Countess of Moray* [1905] AC 531, HL.

[37] CLR *Report 1995–1996* (rounded): estate contracts: C(iv) 14,000; restrictive covenants: D(ii) 10,000; equitable easements D(iii) 700; matrimonial home rights: F 1,800.

[38] LPA 1922 sch 7; LP (Amendment) A 1924 sch 6 ("classes"); LCA 1925 s 10; LCA 1972 s 2; *Ministry of Housing & Local Government* v. *Sharp* [1970] 2 QB 223, 282, Cross LJ.

A class C(iv) estate contract is "a contract by an estate owner or by a person entitled at the date of the contract to have a legal estate conveyed to him to convey or create a legal estate."[39] Registration depends for its effectiveness on the underlying contract, so that vacation will be ordered if there was never a valid contract or if a valid contract has terminated.[40] A contract to transfer a legal estate creates a proprietary interest in the land.[41] Enforcement against a purchaser of unregistered land depends upon registration as a class C(iv) land charge,[42] with no fall back in trust law or estoppel.[43]

Contracts for sale of freehold or leasehold estates,[44] contracts to grant leases,[45] and statutory contracts on enfranchisement should be registered. Ordinary contracts for the purchase of land are not generally registered, since the real risk is small, unless completion is delayed or the seller appears to be financially embarrassed. Sub-sale contracts arise when A contracts to sell to B and B contracts to sell to C, and since the sub-seller is a "person entitled at the date of the contract to have a legal estate conveyed to him" the subsale contract falls squarely within the definition of class C(iv). Registration by C must take place against the current legal estate owner (A) and not against the immediate contracting party (B).[46] Registration is required of conditional contracts, for example to offer to surrender a lease before assigning it,[47] to sell subject to planning permission and the consent of the Charity Commissioners,[48] or to provide a legal charge on request.[49]

Registration is required of options, options to renew leases,[50] and rights of pre-emption to the extent that they are proprietary.[51]

4. Obligations between neighbours

[21.14] Many easements are legal, but others are equitable, and these need registration as do restrictive covenants between freeholders. Registration was not retrospective, and pre-1926 rights may continue to affect the land indefinitely,[52] according to the doctrine of notice. Registration applied from 1925 onwards.

---

[39] LCA 1972 s 2(4)(iv).

[40] See below [21.21].

[41] *Walsh* v. *Lonsdale* (1882) 21 Ch D 9, CA.

[42] Not the settlement of a boundary dispute: *Nielson* v. *Poole* (1969) 20 P & CR 909.

[43] *Lloyds Bank* v. *Carrick* [1996] 4 All ER 630, CA.

[44] A contract between A and B to convey to C is registrable: *Turley* v. *Mackay* [1944] Ch 37. Contracts to create legal interests are registrable in other classes: easements in class D(iii) and mortgages in class C(iii).

[45] *Blamires* v. *Bradford Corp* [1964] Ch 585.

[46] *Barrett* v. *Hilton Developments* [1975] Ch 237, CA.

[47] *Greene* v. *Church Commissioners for England* [1974] Ch 467, Sachs LJ; *Beesly* v. *Hallwood Estates* [1960] 1 WLR 549, Buckley J.

[48] *Haslemere Estates* v. *Baker* [1982] 1 WLR 1109, Megarry V-C.

[49] *Williams* v. *Burlington Investments* (1977) 121 SJ 424, HL.

[50] *Beesly* v. *Hallwood Estates* [1960] 1 WLR 549; on appeal [1961] Ch 105, CA; *Phillips* v. *Mobil Oil Co* [1989] 1 WLR 888, 891C–F, Nicholls LJ; assumed in *Greene* v. *Church Commissioners for England* [1974] Ch 467, CA and *Kitney* v. *MEPC* [1977] 1 WLR 981, CA.

[51] For all three, see below [24.07ff].

[52] Class D charges are never registrable if created before 1925; class C charges are registrable only if the benefit is assigned after 1925: LCA 1972 s 4(7).

(1) Restrictive covenant

[21.15] Class D(ii)[53] requires registration of any "covenant or agreement restrictive of the user of land" against the name of the landowner burdened by it, but with three exceptions. First, restrictive covenants entered into with local authorities require entry as local land charges. Second, registration was not retrospective, and notice continues to apply to pre-1926 restrictive covenants[54] – many of which affect towns developed in the Victorian or Edwardian periods. Third, restrictive covenants in leases are not registrable, since parties dealing with a lease will read the lease and so become acquainted with the restrictions it contains.[55]

(2) Equitable easements

[21.16] Registration under class D(iii) applies to any post-1925 equitable easement, and also to easement-like rights and privileges affecting land.[56] A proper easement must benefit the land of a neighbouring owner. In *London & Blenheim Estates* v. *Ladbroke Retail Parks*[57] a right to park could be extended to benefit further land by a notice, but in advance of an extension notice this potential right was not registrable. Class D(iii) is vague and uncertain of definition. Clearly within it fall easements for life or other periods which cannot be legal. Lord Denning MR narrowed the class in *ER Ives Investment* v. *High*[58] to cover only that type, so excluding any equitable easement created by use of contractual formalities.[59] This drastic constriction is inconsistent with the plain wording of the definition of class D(iii), but however shaky technically it achieved a just solution; the formality of registration is inappropriate for informally created rights, and legislative restriction of class D(iii) is needed.[60] Rights which clearly fall outside class D(iii) are proprietary estoppels,[61] a tenant's right to remove fixtures at the expiration of the lease[62] and equitable rights of re-entry.[63]

5. Matrimonial home rights

[21.17] Class F is a spouse's right of occupation of the matrimonial home.[64]

---

[53] LCA 1972 s 2(1)(ii); RG Rowley (1956) 20 *Conv (NS)* 370.

[54] In operation it often allows a purchaser with actual knowledge of a restrictive covenant to defeat it for non-registration.

[55] Even if the benefit of the covenant attaches to neighbouring land of the landlord: *Dartstone* v. *Cleveland Petroleum Co* [1969] 1 WLR 1807, Pennycuick J; literally correct but surely unintended?

[56] *Lewisham BC* v. *Maloney* [1948] 1 KB 50, CA (not requisition).

[57] [1994] 1 WLR 31, CA.

[58] [1967] 2 QB 379, 395, CA; *Poster* v. *Slough Estates* [1969] 1 Ch 495, Cross J; AG Guest & J Lever (1963) 27 *Conv (NS)* 30, 33. Not applied to registered land: *Celsteel* v. *Alton House Holdings* [1985] 1 WLR 204, 220A–D Scott J (on appeal [1986] 1 WLR 291).

[59] CV Davidge (1937) 53 *LQR* 259; HWR Wade [1956] *CLJ* 216, 225–226.

[60] *ER Ives* [1967] 2 QB 379, 395; Roxburgh Committee (Cmnd 9826, 1956), [16]; HWR Wade [1956] *CLJ* 216; Law Com 18 (1969), [63]; S Cretney (1969) 32 *MLR* 477, 487; G Battersby (1995) 58 *MLR* 637, 645–648.

[61] At 405C–F Winn LJ; see below **[23.41]**.

[62] *Poster* v. *Slough Estates* [1969] 1 Ch 495, Cross J.

[63] *Shiloh Spinners* v. *Harding* [1973] AC 691, HL; D Yates (1974) 37 *MLR* 87; PB Fairest [1971] *CLJ* 258, [1973] *CLJ* 218.

[64] FLA 1996 ss 30–31; MHA 1983; MHA 1967.

6. Litigation rights

[21.18] These are considered below.[65]

7. Summary

[21.19] To recap the more important land charges are:

Class C(i)	puisne mortgages;
Class C(iii)	general equitable charges;
Class C(iv)	estate contracts;
Class D(ii)	restrictive covenants;
Class D(iii)	equitable easements; and
Class F	matrimonial home rights.

C. RESIDUAL BURDENS ON UNREGISTERED LAND

[21.20] Rights left without an adequate home are here described as residual burdens. It was likely that some rights would be missed, and in fact some were. These rights are all equitable[66] subject to notice doctrine. This serves the holders of informal rights well, because it is unrealistic to expect formal registration of informal rights, but it is a disaster from the point of view of a buyer. Since the purchaser must continue to conduct all reasonable enquiries, notice has not been side-lined or diminished at all. Once one is engaged on the enquiry process one might as well leave notice doctrine to apply to all non-monetary burdens.

Non-registrable rights fall into three main categories.[67] *(1) Full equitable interests outside the registrable list*, including the equitable right of re-entry imposed on a sale of leasehold land.[68] Lord Wilberforce rejected[69] the need for registration as an estate contract or as an equitable easement. The intention was probably to embrace all residual rights in class C(iii)[70] but in fact the courts have restricted the general equitable charge to money charges,[71] leaving a residue of true incumbrances completely outside the net. *(2) Estoppel rights* appeared to be unregistrable.[72] *(3) Mere equities* are rights to discretionary equitable relief, such as rectification of written document and the right to set aside a document made as a result of undue influence.[73] Such rights are not registrable and modified notice doctrine applies.[74]

---

[65] See below **[24.11ff]**.
[66] LPA 1925 s 1(2) contains a definitive list of legal interests.
[67] JF Garner (1967) 31 *Conv (NS)* 394, 394–397, 401–404.
[68] *Shiloh Spinners* v. *Harding* [1973] AC 691 HL; D Yates (1974) 37 *MLR* 87; PB Fairest [1973] *CLJ* 218, [1971] *CLJ* 258.
[69] At 719.
[70] LCA 1972 s 2(4)(iii).
[71] The introductory words of LCA 1972 s 2(1) make clear that "charge" is to be read as "incumbrance".
[72] *ER Ives Investment* v. *High* [1967] 2 QB 379, CA; see below **[23.41]**.
[73] See below **[30.53]**.
[74] *Smith* v. *Jones* [1954] 1 WLR 1089; see above **[15.08]**.

D. VACATION OF LAND CHARGES

[21.21] Disputes about the validity of a registration are resolved by court proceedings for vacation of the entry. An extended jurisdiction to order vacation dating from 1972 states simply that "registration may be vacated pursuant to an order of the court."[75] Registration of a land charge is invalid if the right it falls outside the definition of the statutory classes. It may also be that the individual interest claimed is invalid:[7]: for example an estate contract if there never was a contract[77] or if a once valid contract has now been terminated[78]

Adverse registrations can seriously damage the wealth of a land owner, so the court should be robust in ordering vacation,[79] even at an interlocutory stage of an unarguable case.[80] An impersonal order for vacation is made.[81]

Vacation of pending land actions affecting unregistered land has been possible since 1973[82] where the action does not relate to land, has no hope of success,[83] or is not being prosecuted in good faith.[84] An appeal stays an order for vacation until it is determined.[85]

E. LAND CHARGES: REGISTRATION

[21.22] A register of land charges is maintained under the Land Charges Act 1972[86] at the Plymouth office of the land registry. Land charges registration[87] is quite different from registration of title,[88] and inferior to it, since entries of individual burdens are made in isolation against the name of the estate owner at the time of registration.

1. Unregistered titles and first registration

[21.23] Registration of land charges is only possible while title remains unregistered, since the registrar will refuse to register any charge over registered land, and will

---

[75] LCA 1972 s 1(6); Practice Direction [1990] 1 All ER 255; *Calgary & Edmonton Land Co* v. *Dobinson* [1974] Ch 102, Megarry J; *Northern Developments (Holdings)* v. *UDT Securities* [1976] 1 WLR 1230, Megarry J; compare vacation of cautions, above **[20.11]**.

[76] Eg *Perry* v. *Phoenix Assurance* [1988] 1 WLR 940, Browne-Wilkinson V-C (no charging order against beneficial interest).

[77] *Tiverton Estates* v. *Wearwell* [1975] Ch 146, CA.

[78] *Clearbrook Property Holdings* v. *Verrier* [1974] 1 WLR 243, Templeman J; and many others.

[79] *Haslemere Estates* v. *Baker* [1982] 1 WLR 1109, 1118G, Megarry V-C.

[80] *Norman* v. *Hardy* [1974] 1 WLR 1048.

[81] *Lester* v. *Burgess* (1973) 26 P & CR 536, Goulding J; *Calgary & Edmonton Co* v. *Dobinson* [1974] Ch 102, 110H–111C, Megarry J; *Northern Developments (Holdings)* v. *UDT Securities* [1976] 1 WLR 1230, Megarry J.

[82] LCA 1972 s 1(6).

[83] *Northern Developments*; *Price Bros (Somerford)* v. *J Kelly Homes (Stoke-on-Trent)* [1975] 1 WLR 1512, CA.

[84] LCA 1972 s 5(10).

[85] *Belcourt* v. *Belcourt* [1989] 1 WLR 195, Morritt J.

[86] S 1(1); LCA 1925 as amended is now split between LCA 1972 and Local LCA 1975.

[87] Chapelle's *LL* (5th ed) ch 3; Goo's *Sourcebook* (3rd ed) ch 7; Maudsley & Burn *LL – Cases* (7th ed) 31–54; Megarry & Wade (6th ed) [4.056–4.065].

[88] *Watts* v. *Waller* [1973] QB 153, 168E, Orr LJ.

cancel any existing entry.[89] A land charge invalid at the time of first registration (because defeated by a purchaser) is not resurrected by inclusion of the right on a registered title.[90]

Land charges created by a document which attracts compulsory registration do not require registration.[91] This substantially reduces the volume of business at the land charges registry, now that almost all dealings trigger compulsory registration.[92] Cover is not required for the short period between completion and applying for first registration, though priority problems could arise if the buyer exceeds the two month period allowed for registration.

2. Procedure for registration of land charges

[21.24] The Land Charges Rules 1974[93] provide a mechanism which is heavily dependent on official forms.[94] Registration is required to be in the full name of the estate owner as recorded on the title deeds of the unregistered estate.[95] The administrative area must be stated, along with a short description of the land. In *Horrill* v. *Cooper*[96] a registration recording the district of a house and field near Totton in Hampshire as Ower was sufficiently precise. In fact the correct parish was Netley Marsh, but the search was conducted in relation to the parish of Eling. The primary means of registration is against the names of the land owners and so the registration was sufficiently clear on facts. Details are required of the document (if any) creating the burden – its date, the parties, and the class of land charge it creates[97] – with a separate application required for each sub-class against each name.[98] Fees are low, essentially £1 per name per registration.[99] An unregistered charge becomes void on sale, so it is necessary to register as soon as the charge is made in order to be absolutely safe, and at least before a buyer searches.[100]

No check is made on the validity of the right registered,[101] though applications not made by professional conveyancers require the support of a statutory declaration.[102] A land owner is often unaware[103] that a land charge has been registered against his name, raising the possibility of tactical and spite registrations, and handing a potent weapon to the claimant. Inappropriate registrations can be removed after an application for vacation of the register.

[89] SI 1974/1286, r 13.
[90] *Kitney* v. *MEPC* [1977] 1 WLR 981, CA.
[91] LCA 1972 s 14.
[92] New registrations are running at below 100,000 a year; there are 1 million searches (unregistered land) as against 4 million insolvency only searches (registered land); LR *Annual Report 2001–2002*, 49.
[93] SI 1974/1286, as amended.
[94] Registrations use LC Form K1 but there are variants for class F, litigation registers, and renewals.
[95] LCA 1972 s 3.
[96] (1999) 78 P & CR 336, Ch D.
[97] LCA 1972 s 3(5)–(6); SI 1974/1286 sch 1 (pending actions).
[98] SI 1974/1286, r 25.
[99] SI 1990/327, as amended by SI 1994/286.
[100] SI 1974/1286, rr 16–18.
[101] Erroneous applications can be corrected by rectification, though safeguarding the position of any honest buyer: SI 1974/1286, r 14.
[102] SI 1974/1286, r 6.
[103] *Watts* v. *Waller* [1973] QB 153, CA; *Taylor* v. *Taylor* [1968] 1 WLR 378, 383, CA; S Cretney (1969) 32 *MLR* 477, 486–487; *Hynes* v. *Vaughan* (1985) 50 P & CR 444, 461, Scott J.

3. Priority notices

[21.25] Land charges created in the course of a rapid chain of transactions needed protection by a priority notice,[104] but the wide extensions of compulsory registration mean that this procedure is now rarely needed.

4. Effect of registration

[21.26] According to section 198 of the Law of Property Act 1925:

> "[R]egistration . . . shall be deemed to constitute actual notice of such . . . matter, and of the fact of such registration, to all persons and for all purposes connected with the land affected . . . ".[105]

Properly registered land charges are secured against the world except where they are overridden on a sale by a lender.[106] Diligent search is necessary so that any buyer discovers all registered charges. Actual notice is only deemed to arise from proper registration under the correct name and in the appropriate class and sub-class: registration of a C(iv) estate contract under class C(iii) has no effect.[107] Incorrect registrations often do bring rights to the attention of a buyer, and may crab completion, so an invalid registration is better than nothing at all.

Actual notice is deemed to arise in the course of a purchase,[108] but it would be very unjust to impose notice on a person who has no cause to make a search, for example when adding further advances to the security of an existing mortgage loan (tacking),[109] or when determining whether a landlord has committed the offence of letting property knowing that it is subject to a closing order.[110] Land charges searches are made before completion of a purchase of unregistered land, but not at an earlier stage, and certainly not before exchanging contracts.[111] Actual notice by registration does not, after 1969,[112] bite against a person contracting to buy the land being removed by the legislature. Knowledge of a contracting party is determined by reference to his actual (or imputed actual) knowledge, without regard to registration, and regardless of any contractual provision.[113] The supposed difficulty may survive for local land charges;[114] but Millett J has disapproved[115] the decision which appeared to create the

---

[104] LCA 1972 s 11; SI 1974/1286, rr 4, 7.

[105] LPA 1925 s 198(1), amended in 1975.

[106] LCA 1972 s 13; LPA 1925 s 43(1); see below **[29.24]**.

[107] LPA 1925 s 199; despite SJ Bailey (1948) 10 *CLJ* 241, 246.

[108] LPA 1925 s 198; *Rignall Developments* v. *Halil* [1988] Ch 190, 202D–E, Millett J.

[109] LPA 1925 ss 94(1)(b), 94(2); see below **[29.07]**.

[110] *Barber* v. *Shah* (1985) 17 HLR 584.

[111] A wise *seller* searches for land charges before drafting a contract; *Newbery* v. *Turngiant* (1991) 63 P & CR 458, CA, is reversed by LP (MP) A 1989 s 3.

[112] LPA 1969 s 24; Law Com 18 (1969), part C; S Cretney (1969) 32 *MLR* 477, 485–486.

[113] LPA 1969 s 24(2).

[114] S 24(3); a local search is usual before exchange of contracts.

[115] *Rignall Developments* v. *Halil* [1988] Ch 190, 199–203, Millett J; C Harpum [1987] *Conv* 291; PG McHugh [1988] *CLJ* 18; HW Wilkinson (1987) 137 *NLJ* 1178; *Citytowns* v. *Bohemian Properties* [1986] 2 EGLR 258, 262B.

problem.[116] Notice of a fact is not the same as knowledge of it, and contractual liability should turn on knowledge.

5. Names registration

[21.27] Land charges must be registered against the "name of the estate owner whose estate is to be affected".[117] Here is one of the weakest features of the whole property legislation,[118] which will only be eradicated when all titles are registered. As a temporary relief, new legislation is needed to permit future registrations against a caution title at the land registry, creating a provisional list of burdens ready for first registration.

The name to use when registering is the name of the estate owner as it appears on the title deeds. Anyone needing to search will usually have access to the deeds, but a wife may not know the precise name that her husband uses.[119] That care is essential as demonstrated by *Oak Co-op Building Society* v. *Blackburn*.[120] A contract to sell by *Francis David* Blackburn was registered against the name of *Frank* David Blackburn – the name under which the seller practised as an estate agent. This registration was held good against a search in a third variant of the name, Francis *Davis* Blackburn.

Subsales provide a further illustration of the dangers lurking in the apparently simple concept of names registration. Registration is required against the name of the estate owner, so *both* contracts have to be registered against the name of the same person. This trap was sprung on the unsuspecting solicitor involved in *Barrett* v. *Hilton Developments*.[121] A contracted to sell land in Blackpool to Barrett, who contracted to sell that land on to C Co; this second contract was registered against the name of Barrett. Eight days later this would have been correct as the legal estate had by then been conveyed to him, but the actual registration against Barrett was premature since it occurred before he held the legal estate. Searches cover a defined period of years, so registration must occur against the name of the person currently holding the legal estate.

6. Registration where estate owner dead

[21.28] After mid-1995[122] a land charge can be registered against the name of a person who has died.[123] The names of the personal representatives must also be searched

---

[116] *Re Forsey & Holleybone's Contract* [1927] 2 Ch 379, Eve J; much criticised, eg by H Potter (1928) 44 *LQR* 18; and most conveyancing texts.

[117] LCA 1972 s 3(1), also ss 5(4), 6(2), 7(1); s 3(2) pre-1926 registrations. Registrations against owners of short leases are unlikely to be picked up by a search; eg *Sharp* v. *Coates* [1949] 1 KB 285, CA (yearly tenant); AM Prichard [1979] *Conv* 249, 251–252.

[118] Law Com 18 (1969), [19] (retrospective changes too complex).

[119] *Diligent Finance* v. *Alleyne* (1971) 23 P & CR 346, Foster J (title deeds and search: Erskine Owen Alleyne; class F registration against Erskine Alleyne held ineffective); *Standard Property Investments* v. *British Plastics Federation* (1985) 53 P & CR 25, Walton J; JE Adams [1987] *Conv* 135 (omission of second Christian etc names).

[120] [1968] Ch 730, CA; PV Baker (1968) 84 *LQR* 303.

[121] [1975] Ch 237, CA.

[122] LP (MP) A 1994 s 15, amending LCA 1972 s 3; also pending actions (amending s 5) and writs and orders (amending s 6); in force July 1st 1995: SI 1995/1317; Law Com 184 (1989), [2.2–2.9]; JGH Sunnucks [1990] *NLJ* 95.

[123] SI 1974/1286 r 19, inserted in 1995.

to discover any land charges that *they* have created in administering the estate. Before statutory clarification, a dead person was probably not an estate owner,[124] but registrations were accepted[125] and common-place, and safety requires a search against the name of a deceased estate owner, his personal representatives, and (if he died intestate) the Public Trustee.[126]

7. Cancellation

[21.29] Redundant entries are usually withdrawn on the application of the person who registered,[127] or a successor who proves his title, or otherwise.[128] A person buying the land should insist on receiving completed applications for the withdrawal of all spent charges or better still a certificate of cancellation.[129]

F. LAND CHARGES: SEARCHES

1. Official searches

[21.30] Land charges registers have always been open to any person who wishes to search.[130] Traditional postal searches[131] are supplemented by telephone (most useful where few entries are revealed), fax,[132] and direct access by computer.[133] Searches can also be made in person at the offices of the land charges registry.[134]

It is essential to identify correctly the administrative area,[135] taking account of any boundary changes over the years for which the persons owned the estate, and the *exact* names to be searched. A short description of the land is used to narrow down the number of entries revealed, and if this is entered incorrectly the search may be worthless.[136] Official searches issued by the registrar confer protection against errors on buyers[137] and for conveyancers relying on them.[138] A search will either be clear

---

[124] Wolstenholme & Cherry, *Conveyancing Statutes* (12th ed) vol 2, 843.

[125] ES Pryer (1986) 83 *LSG* 2127; AM Prichard [1979] *Conv* 249; JE Adams [1986] *Conv* 237.

[126] AEA 1925 s 9, as amended by LP (MP) A 1994 s 14. Earlier land of an intestate vested in the probate judge – the President of the Family Division or, before October 1971, the President of the Probate Divorce and Admiralty Division; JE Adams [1987] *Conv* 135, 137.

[127] SI 1974/1286, rr 9–10.

[128] Eg a matrimonial home right ends on death, a divorce decree absolute or a court order terminating the right of occupation; FLA 1996 sch 4 para 4; SI 1974/1286, rr 10–11.

[129] SI 1974/1286, r 12.

[130] LCA 1972 s 9(1); *Ministry of Housing & Local Government* v. *Sharp* [1970] 2 QB 223, 280, Cross LJ (history).

[131] SI 1974/1286 r 16; LC Form K16. These are now less than 1 million a year: LR *Annual Report 2001–2002*, 49.

[132] SI 1990/485.

[133] SIs 1994/1287, 1995/1355.

[134] LCA 1972 s 9(2).

[135] Land Charges Practice Leaflet (1999); *Du Sautoy* v. *Symes* [1967] Ch 1146, Cross J (search confused two parishes).

[136] *Horrill* v. *Cooper* (1999) 78 P & CR 336, Ch D.

[137] LCA 1972 s 10(4); non-fraudulent employees are exonerated: s 10(5); *Ministry of Housing & Local Government* v. *Sharp* [1970] 2 QB 223, CA; *Stock* v. *Wanstead & Woodford BC* [1962] 2 QB 479, Stevenson J.

[138] LCA 1972 s 12(b) restricted to official searches under s 10.

(revealing no entries) or will list entries against the name searched in the county for the years searched;[139] revealed entries often relate to other land, and the buyer has to rely on a conveyancer's certificate written on the search that some entries are irrelevant. Particulars of the document by which the registrable charge was created can be obtained for further application for an office copy of the registration.[140] Fees are essentially £1 per name per search, or double that for hi-tech methods.[141]

Unregistered land charges are void after the completion of a purchase.[142] An official search certificate guards against registrations occurring in the last few days before completion. A buyer with an official search certificate will be protected against applications to register new land charges for the 15 working days of the priority period,[143] the last protected day being marked on the search certificate. Usual practice is to apply for a search a week or so before the anticipated completion day, and to make a new search if completion is delayed.

2. Names searching

[21.31] A search must be made in the correct name for registration, that is the name used on the title deeds, which is not necessarily what is shown on the birth certificate.[144] Names *searching* is less seriously flawed than names *registration* – since the relevant name is apparent on the epitome of title – but it remains a flaw and one which cannot now be corrected.[145] The internet search engine, Googol, logged 635,000 attempts to find the name "Britney Spears" in three months of 2001, of which only 77% spelt her name correctly, and there were an amazing 594 incorrect variants. In *Diligent Finance* v. *Alleyne*[146] a perfect search secured priority over a flawed registration. However a flawed registration prevails against a flawed search: in *Oak Co-Operative BS* v. *Blackburn*,[147] the title deeds used version 1 of Mr Blackburn's name, registration of a C(iv) occurred against version 2, and the search adopted version 3.

3. Old land charges

[21.32] Burdens have been registrable as land charges since 1925, so a complete search will embrace all names on the title since then, but buyers will only be aware of the names appearing on the title back to a good root. When a root of title was at least thirty years,[148] 1955[149] was the first year in which it was possible for names to disap-

---

[139] SI 1974/1286 r 17. JE Adams [1987] *Conv* 135 gave these figures: 32,000 registrations against Smith, 280 with the sole first name John, and of these 70 were in Lancashire.

[140] SI 1974/1286 r 19; as amended in 1995 to cover hi-tech searching.

[141] SIs 1990/327, 1994/286.

[142] See below [21.35].

[143] LCA 1972 s 11(5)–(6).

[144] *Standard Property Investment* v. *British Plastics Federation* (1985) 53 P & CR 25, Walton J (registration against Roger Caudrelier not revealed by a search against Roger Denis Caudrelier).

[145] Law Com 18 (1969).

[146] (1971) 23 P & CR 346, Foster J (deeds and search: Erskine Owen Alleyne; registration: Erskine Alleyne).

[147] [1968] Ch 730, CA; *Horrill* v. *Cooper* (1999) 78 P & CR 336, Ch D.

[148] LPA 1925 s 44(1).

[149] HWR Wade [1956] *CLJ* 216, 218 (root of title 30 years); R Ainscough (1935) 51 *LQR* 367, 368.

pear behind the root of title. This is even more likely now, almost eighty on, with statutory title reduced to 15 years.[150]

Properly registered land charges[151] continue to bind later owners for ever, however old, since registration is deemed to be actual knowledge of the interest. Compensation has to be accepted. Entitlement to an indemnity depends upon taking an estate or interest in land affected by the charge – whether it is a freehold sale, an assignment of leasehold land, a mortgage, the grant of a sub-lease, a compulsory purchase, or a compulsory enfranchisement.[152] A causal link is required between acquisition of the estate and the loss, but compensation will include the cost of securing the removal of the interest, as well as the cost of the application for compensation.[153] A person dealing with a *leasehold interest* cannot obtain compensation for land charges affecting the *reversionary title*: the old practice when taking a lease was not to investigate the landlord's title, so any loss arises from the landlord's failure to make a full disclosure, and redress should be through action on the covenants for title.[154]

Compensation is restricted to undiscovered and undiscoverable land charges. Most burdens are repeated on the title deeds, so on each sale the buyer acquires actual knowledge of them.[155] Compensatable old charges are those which it is impossible to discover from the statutory title. A person who accepts less than fifteen years title will prejudice his compensation rights.[156]

Claims are made against the land registrar by an action in the High Court, made within six years of the time at which the land charge comes to the notice of the purchaser.[157] The registrar may seek an indemnity from any person whose fraud caused the loss.[158] Entries are made to bring the charge to the attention of future purchasers.[159]

G. PRIORITY: LAND CHARGES

[21.33] Purchasers must be protected against unregistered burdens, since otherwise what is the point of requiring things to be registered? Before 1926 notice doctrine applied to equitable interests, under which purchasers had to show (1) value, (2) acquisition of a protected interest, (3) diligence and (4) honesty. In the case of land charges, diligence is limited to carrying out a land charges search. The impact of the land charges legislation on the other three more debatable elements were settled by the House of Lords in *Midland Bank Trust Co* v. *Green*.[160] Honesty is not a requirement. A buyer may ignore any land charge that is unregistered.[161]

[150] LPA 1969 s 23.
[151] Registrations of pending actions, writs and orders affecting land and bankruptcy matters must be renewed every five years: LCA 1972 s 8.
[152] LPA 1969 s 25(1).
[153] S 25(1), (4); headleases are not included.
[154] S 25(9)–(10); LPA 1925 s 44(2)–(5); see above **[11.58ff]**.
[155] LPA 1969 s 25(1)(b); including imputed knowledge: ss (11).
[156] S 25(1)(c), (10).
[157] S 25(4)–(6).
[158] S 25(8).
[159] SI 1974/1286 r 15.
[160] [1981] AC 513 HL; HE Johnson [1981] *Conv* 361; RJ Smith (1980) 96 *LQR* 8; B Green (1981) 97 *LQR* 518; B Berkovits (1980) 43 *MLR* 225; C Harpum [1981] *CLJ* 213; M Friend & J Newton [1982] *Conv* 213; B Berkovits (1980) 43 *MLR* 225; G Battersby (1995) 58 *MLR* 637, 654–657.
[161] *Lloyds Bank* v. *Carrick* [1996] 4 All ER 630, CA.

1. Value

[21.34] Protection is available to a purchaser,[162] that is a person who provides valuable consideration,[163] usually in money. Future marriage counts as consideration for the creation of a marriage settlement, a rule which enables the husband and wife and issue of the marriage to secure undeserved priority over unregistered mortgages and land actions.[164] Continuing protection of parties to a marriage can no longer be justified, and for commercial incumbrances and bankruptcies[165] the law requires a genuine purchaser providing "money or money's worth".[166]

A gift cannot improve the title to land, but protection for land purchase extends far beyond genuine buyers negotiating in the open market. It included Mrs Green who bought at an undervalue from her husband without negotiating the price, without engaging in the normal leisurely conveyancing exchanges,[167] and acting without any commercial purpose.[168] Read literally, the Land Charges Act 1972 allows protection to anyone who provides any value, irrespective of how its monetary worth measures against the value of the land. He may pay the market value or well below it. This reading is confirmed in *Midland Bank Trust Co* v. *Green*.[169] A father granted an option to his eldest son to purchase Gravel Hill Farm in Lincolnshire, exercisable for ten years, but the son's solicitor omitted to register it as an estate contract of class C(iv). Later, his father decided to break the option and was advised to transfer the farm worth £40,000 to his wife for £500.[170] Thirteen years litigation ensued.

Take first the view of Lord Denning MR to see what is *not* the law. He ruled in the Court of Appeal that sale at an undervalue did not defeat the unregistered land charge.[171] The key phrase, "for money or money's worth", should not on his view be constricted by contract law rules preventing investigation of the adequacy of consideration, since property law would not regard the grotesquely small sum Mrs Green paid as a fair value.[172] The House of Lords rejected this view.[173] Evelyn Green did not have the necessary £500, which she had to borrow it from the bank. Without the fact of borrowing, the conveyance might have been set aside as a sham[174] in which case she

---

[162] LCA 1972 s 4; *Blamires* v. *Bradford Corp* [1964] Ch 585 (compulsory purchase excluded); *Monarch Aluminium* v. *Rickman* [1988] CLYB 1526, Knox J (LPA 1925 definition).

[163] LCA 1972 s 17(1). An indemnity covenant is value: *Price* v. *Jenkins* (1877) 5 Ch D 619, CA; *Johnsey Estates* v. *Lewis & Manley (Engineering)* [1987[2 EGLR 69, CA; *Nurdin & Peacock* v. *DB Ramsden & Co* [1999] 1 WLR 1249, Neuberger J.

[164] Classes A and B (statutory charges) C (i) to (iii) (mortgages), class F (matrimonial homes right), pending land actions, writs and orders affecting land, deeds of arrangement.

[165] Classes C(iv) estate contracts, D (restrictive covenants and equitable easements etc), and petitions in bankruptcy.

[166] LCA 1972 s 4(6) proviso; *Connell Estate Agents* v. *Begej* [1993] 2 EGLR 35, CA; *Midland Bank Trust Co* v. *Green* [1981] AC 513, 531, Lord Wilberforce. The same rule now applies to all burdens when title is registered, see above **[20.43]**.

[167] [1980] Ch 590, 621D.

[168] [1980] Ch 590, 612D, Oliver J; [1980] Ch 590, 633C.

[169] [1981] AC 513, HL.

[170] By 1980 it was worth £450,000, a prize worth a fight: [1980] Ch 590, 623B.

[171] [1980] Ch 590, CA.

[172] At 621C, 624D–F, 629A–B.

[173] At 531D–532C, Lord Wilberforce, supporting Sir Stanley Rees' dissent.

[174] A transfer which is a sham does not pass legal title: *Buckinghamshire CC* v. *Briar* [2002] EWHC 2821 (Ch), [2002] December 20th, [151–152], Lawrence Collins J. See also below **[25.81]**.

would never have received the legal estate needed to give her protection, but on the facts the conveyance was obviously genuine.[175] Given a real price, the only requirement was that it should count as a contract law consideration, no account being taken of adequacy or fairness. Mrs Green's payment was obviously inadequate to an insider, but an outsider looking at the title many years later could not form a judgement about what had been a fair price many years before. The sum of £500 was not nominal[176] but even if it had been it would still have defeated an unregistered land charge.[177]

2. Acquisition of a protected interest

(1) True burdens

[21.35] Purchasers[178] generally require a legal estate in order to override prior equitable interests. This conventional pattern applies to commercial incumbrances – estate contracts, restrictive covenants and equitable easements and bankruptcies. A contract permitting later acquisition of the legal estate is not sufficient.[179] Freehold purchase destroys the unregistered burden for ever, whereas tenants or mortgage-lenders defeat it only to the extent of the interest acquired.[180]

(2) Money charges

[21.36] An experiment was tried before 1926 which would have led to the abolition of the distinction between legal and equitable rights and fragmentary remnants of this experiment survive for money charges – that is classes A, B and C (except estate contracts) and the matrimonial home right (class F).[181] Land charges of these classes are void against a purchaser of *any* interest in such land unless registered before completion. The object of the experiment was to allow any lender to claim protection, irrespective of whether his mortgage was legal or equitable. Consider this sequence of events:

first, a legal mortgage protected by deposit with A;
second, a legal mortgage to B not registered as a C(i);
third, an equitable mortgage to C.

C will take free of B's prior legal mortgage as a protected lender. Within a queue of mortgages, legal or equitable mortgages are not distinguished. There was some logic in this experiment before 1926, but it is less appropriate today when it is possible to create any number of legal mortgages, so that a lender can get a legal right if he wishes to insist, and even less so for land actions and the matrimonial home right.

---

[175] At 611C–E, 613E, Oliver J; disputed at 628B–H, Eveleigh LJ, but restored in the Lords.
[176] At 532B–C, Lord Wilberforce; *Vartoukian* v. *Daejean* (1969) 20 P & CR 983; *Nurdin & Peacock* v. *DB Ramsden & Co* [1999] 1 WLR 1249, Neuberger J (£1 held nominal).
[177] Purchaser has a special meaning in the case of the Inland Revenue Charge: Finance Act 1975 sch 12 para 8.
[178] LCA 1972 s 4(6).
[179] *McCarthy & Stone* v. *Julian S Hodge & Co* [1971] 1 WLR 1547, 1555, Foster J.
[180] LCA 1972 s 17(1).
[181] LCA 1972 s 4(2), (5), (8); see above [19.50ff].

(3) Order of registration of mortgages

[21.37] A second flaw in the scheme for mortgages registered as land charges appears in section 97 of the Law of Property Act 1925:

> "Every mortgage affecting a legal estate in land [made after 1925] whether legal or equitable shall rank according to its date of registration as a land charge . . .".

This may conflict with the land charges legislation[182] which renders an unregistered land charge void at the time of the next sale or mortgage.

Suppose there is a sequence: *A created, B created, A registers, B registers*. Both lenders are at fault, and it is difficult to decide from first principles which should win. On the one hand A has registered his mortgage first, and B afterwards, and where all are registered the sequence of registrations (AB) should be decisive.[183] On the other hand the first lender failed to register at the initial stage and lost priority on the creation of the second mortgage, so that the sequence of priorities should be BA.[184] Looking at the whole scheme of the land charges registration it is relatively clear that the second is the better view, but the point remains unsettled.

With three registrable mortgages a triangle of priorities can be created. Take the sequence: *A created, B created, A registers, C created*. Each lender has some claim to priority over every other lender. A's claim is based on his registration, B's on having defeated A's non-registered mortgage, and C on defeating B who already has priority over A. Priority principle cannot resolve this case, and attempting to apply subrogation principles drives one back to the difficulty that one needs to know where to start. The sanction for non registration[185] ought to be the first principle to apply. The situation can be aggravated by the inclusion of more than one registration, out of sequence, so that section 97 of the Law of Property Act 1925 also becomes relevant.

3. Diligence

[21.38] A proper search for land charges is the beginning and end of the buyer's duty of diligence, with constructive notice being totally irrelevant.[186] Section 199(1) of the Law of Property Act 1925 confirms that a person is not to be prejudicially affected by any matter registrable as a land charge "which is void or not enforceable as against him . . . by reason of the non-registration thereof".[187] Occupation of the land need not be checked.[188]

---

[182] LCA 1972 s 4(5); RE Megarry (1940) 27 *CLJ* 243, 255–256.
[183] LPA 1925 s 97.
[184] LCA 1972 s 4.
[185] S 4(5).
[186] *Coventry Permanent Economic BS* v. *Jones* [1951] 1 All ER 901.
[187] Once void, it will not be revivified by entry of a notice to protect it on first registration: *Kitney* v. *MEPC* [1977] 1 WLR 981, CA.
[188] See below **[21.40]**.

4. Honesty

[21.39] Registration of land charges displaces any role for actual knowledge.[189] Even sale of land subject to a known burden will destroy a land charge which is unregistered. In *Hollington Brothers* v. *Rhodes*,[190] a contract to grant a sub-lease of a suite of offices for seven years was not registered by the sub-tenants as a C(iv): sale of a head-lease of the entire office block destroyed the sub-lease – even though the buyers were expressed to take subject to and with the benefit of all existing tenancies. *Green* extended this to cases where the object of the sale was to destroy the unregistered charge.[191] A son had been given an option under which he could acquire a farm by paying £22,500 when it was worth £40,000, which had grown in value to £450,000 at the time of the litigation. Just why the father decided to exploit the son's oversight in failing to register the option was never fully revealed, since the death of all the parties during the 13 years spent in litigation made it impossible to pin down their motives, but the speed and secrecy of the conveyancing suggest that the father and mother hatched a plot to destroy the option by a sale for £500.[192]

Take first, to see what is *not* the law, the views of the majority of the Court of Appeal led by Lord Denning MR. They found for the son, deciding that a fraudulent sale intended to defeat an option did not succeed. Fraud was "any dishonest dealing done so as to deprive unwary innocents of their rightful dues",[193] a test which included activity far short of the kind which might result in a criminal charge or tortious liability for deceit. Eveleigh LJ adopted a middle course. He felt that title to the land was protected by the Land Charges Act 1972, but that personal liability was imposed on the mother by way of a constructive trust to cancel the effect of the fraud.[194] Either way, the Court of Appeal was firmly reversed in the House of Lords. It is not a fraud to buy land knowing of an unregistered charge. Lord Wilberforce recognised the requirement of honesty when relying on notice doctrine and under some pre-1926 registration schemes but not under the antecedents of the land charges legislation,[195] nor the plain wording of the current legislation.[196] What Parliament had omitted should not be inserted by the courts. Lord Wilberforce articulated the policy reasons for ignoring motives.[197] It would be exceedingly difficult between the parties to dissect the purchaser's mind in order to determine what his motives were. Proof of knowledge was not proof that the purchaser had acted fraudulently. Further difficulties would be caused by death, concealment, and the need to dissect mixed motives.

Unconsidered consolidation has left a confusing and unnecessarily complicated pattern for litigation rights:[198] in some cases (such as pending land actions) express

---

[189] *Green* [1981] AC 513, 529–530; *Kling* v. *Keston Properties* (1985) 49 P & CR 212, 221, Vinelott J.
[190] [1951] 2 TLR 691, 696 Harman J (obiter as no agreement proved).
[191] [1981] AC 513, HL.
[192] Graphically described at [1980] Ch 590, 619–623, Lord Denning MR.
[193] At 625B.
[194] At 626D–F.
[195] LC Registration and Searches Act 1888 s 4; LPA 1922 sch 7; LP (Amendment) A 1924 sch 6.
[196] At 527–528; LCA 1972 s 4; contrast LPA 1925 s 205(1)(xxi); LRA 1925 s 3(xxi).
[197] At 530A–E.
[198] R Ainscough (1935) 51 *LQR* 367.

notice of a claim is sufficient to bind a purchaser, but in other cases *Green* will apply.[199]

5.　Occupation no protection against unregistered titles

[21.40] Lord Birkenhead's legislation was intended to provide wide ranging protection for occupiers of unregistered land. The reforms should not

> "prejudicially affect the interest of any person in possession or in actual occupation of land to which he may be entitled in right of such possession or occupation."[200]

This section qualified the 1922 version of the land charges provisions,[201] but on consolidation in 1925 it was limited to part I of the Law of Property Act 1925 (sections 1 to 39), leaving section 14 almost redundant, and removing the intended protection for the holders of unregistered land charges.[202] The wide divergence this created between the two systems[203] appeared in *Lloyds Bank* v. *Carrick*.[204] A widow who sold her house and gave the proceeds to her brother-in-law on an oral agreement that it would be payment for the leasehold interest he owned in the maisonette, a pre-1989 contract which became enforceable when she paid the price and moved into possession. After her brother in law had mortgaged the lease to a bank and failed to repay what he had borrowed, she was held to have no defence to a possession action. Her only rights were under an estate contract,[205] which was unregistered, and so void against the bank as legal mortgage-lender. Occupation did not overcome her failure to register the land charge. Morritt LJ accepted that she would have been protected if the 1922 enactment had survived but process of splitting the legislation into its constituent parts had removed occupation as a protection against unregistered titles.

H.　PRIORITY: OTHER SOLUTIONS

1.　Variation by agreement

[21.41] Priorities can be varied by agreement.

2.　Estoppel

[21.42] A unregistered land charge can bind successors on the basis of a proprietary estoppel, if: (1) the holder has an expectation that the unregistered charge will nevertheless be enforceable, (2) that expectation has been included by the land owner, either by active encouragement or by passive acquiescence in expenditure, and (3) the holder

---

[199] LCA 1972 s 5(7).

[200] LPA 1925 s 14.

[201] LPA 1922 part I, schs 1–9.

[202] C Harpum (1977) 41 *Conv (NS)* 415, 419 (acknowledging David Ibbetson); Megarry & Wade, *The Law of Real Property* (6th ed), [5.121]; Friend & Newton [1982] *Conv* 213, 216–217.

[203] Law Com 18 (1969), [53] (too early to say which is best).

[204] [1996] 4 All ER 630, CA; MP Thompson [1996] *Conv* 295; P Ferguson (1996) 112 *LQR* 549. In *Midland Bank Trust Co* v. *Green* [1981] AC 513, HL (the son was also in occupation).

[205] Arguments based on bare trusts, constructive trusts and an estoppel were dismissed.

has relied on that expectation to his detriment. A purchaser who could normally insist on treating an unregistered land charge as void, will be estopped from saying it is invalid when these elements are established.[206] One of the plaintiffs (Olds) succeeded in *Taylors Fashions* v. *Liverpool Victoria Trustee Co.*[207] Options to renew leases of two neighbouring shops in Bournemouth were unregistered at the time that enforcement was sought against a purchaser of the reversions, but Olds had installed lifts and made other improvements expecting to have the security of the extended leases, and the freeholders had induced their belief that they would be able t stay by allowing them to spend this money.[208]

3. Constructive trust

[21.43] Non-registration of a land charge can be overcome by imposing a constructive trust on a person who accepts a particular burden, such as a contract, when he buys. This principle is considered in the context of contractual licences where it most often arises but it may equally well apply to a more conventional burden.[209]

4. Personal actions

[21.44] Property law is concerned solely with the proprietary relation.

Figure 21-1 Personal actions

Failure of B's property claim against C leaves the land clear as happened in *Midland Bank Trust Co* v. *Green*.[210] Personal actions were begun and continued by and against their estates, after the three main actors had all died in the course of the litigation.[211] The son's solicitor failed to register the option in the first place, which possibly gave rise to an action in negligence. A limitation period of six years ran only from the date damage occurred, when the sale occurred to break the option.[212] The son's action was settled on the basis that damages would be paid if the option was held void. After the Lords decision in the main action, the solicitors' insurers presumably paid up.[213] The

---

[206] If the previous owner created an expectation of priority, the new owner may be bound by notice (unregistered land) or occupation (registered land). Satisfaction of an estoppel is technically discretionary.

[207] [1982] QB 133n, 157C–159A. Taylors Fashions lost because their expectation of priority had not been induced by the landlords.

[208] At 155D–157C.

[209] *Lyus* v. *Prowsa Developments* [1982] 1 WLR 1044, Dillon J; *Chattey* v. *Farndale Holdings Inc* (1998) 75 P & CR 298, 313, Morritt LJ; *Lloyd* v. *Dugdale* [2001] EWCA Civ 1754, [2002] 2 P & CR 13 at 167; see above **[19.79ff]**.

[210] [1981] AC 513, HL.

[211] HE Johnston [1981] *Conv* 361.

[212] *Midland Bank Trust Co* v. *Hett Stubbs & Kemp* [1979] Ch 384, Oliver J.

[213] They may have had subrogation rights against other parties.

father sold his farm cheaply to break his son's option. In freeing the land of liability under this contract, he incurred personal liability for breach of contract.[214] Judgment was entered in default of defence[215] for damages for which his estate was liable after his death. The father's action in divesting himself of his assets to avoid liability might have been forestalled by timely proceedings.[216] The unknown advisor who prevailed on the father to break his option may have been liable for negligent advice. Tortious inducement of breach of contract may have occurred when the mother encouraged the father to break his contract by accepting a conveyance of the land in breach of the contract.[217] This action was not pursued against Mrs Green's estate in time;[218] just as well because her personal representative had failed to plead that she was defending in a representative capacity, potentially opening up her entire private wealth. Had the right defeated been a trust interest, action would have been for breach of trust[219] rather than in tort.[220]

---

[214] Damages were not reduced on account of the son's failure to register, since he was under no duty to do so: *Lake* v. *Bayliss* [1974] 1 WLR 1073; *Wright* v. *Dean* [1948] Ch 686; *Hollington Brothers* v. *Rhodes* [1951] 2 TLR 691; HWR Wade [1956] *CLJ* 227, n54.

[215] At 611E, Oliver J; *Midland Bank Trust Co* v. *Green (No 3)* [1979] Ch 496 (application to set aside rejected).

[216] [1980] Ch 590, 622, Lord Denning MR.

[217] N Cohen-Grabelsky (1982) 45 *MLR* 241, 260–262; *Murray* v. *Two Strokes* [1973] 1 WLR 823.

[218] Then 6 months from the date of the grant of representation: [1980] Ch 590, 611E, Oliver J.

[219] Dishonest assistance in a breach of trust: *Royal Brunei Airlines* v. *Tan* [1995] 2 AC 378, PC.

[220] *Metall & Rohstoff* v. *Donaldson Lufkin & Jenrette* [1990] 1 QB 391, 481, Slade LJ; left open in *Crawley BC* v. *Ure* [1996] QB 13, 23, Glidewell LJ.

22

CONTRACT FORMALITY

Paper based contracts. Contracts by exchange. Variations. E-contracts and e-chains. Special forms of contract. Completeness. Informal contracts: invalidity; enforcement. Contracts that have been acted upon.

A. FORMATION OF PAPER-BASED CONTRACTS

1. Old law

[22.01] After 1677,[1] a contract relating to land had to be *evidenced by signed writing*. This provision spread around the common law world[2] and was reproduced in section 40 of the Law of Property Act 1925. Its defect was that parties who were negotiating "subject to contract" could become contractually bound by accident if they wrote down the agreed terms in casual correspondence.[3] Leases, options and mortgages[4] entered into before September 28th 1989 may continue to operate under the older, looser, formalities.

2. Law of Property (Miscellaneous Provisions) Act 1989

[22.02] The Law Commission proposed tightening the formalities to ensure that all contracts were reduced to writing.[5] This was thought likely to eliminate disputes about whether a contract has been made and if this seems over ambitious, the new scheme does seem to be working in a fashion that is broadly satisfactory. A contract relating to land should have to be *made in writing*,[6] a reform enacted by section 2 of the Law of Property (Miscellaneous Provisions) Act 1989. All contracts made on or after September 27th 1989[7] are regulated by the new scheme, which is markedly different from what went before.[8]

---

[1] Statute of Frauds 1677 s 4.

[2] Law Com 164 (1987), [2.14–2.21], App C.

[3] *Law* v. *Jones* [1974] Ch 112, CA; the dangers were reduced if not eliminated by *Tiverton Estates* v. *Wearwell* [1975] Ch 146, CA.

[4] MP Thompson [1994] *Conv* 233; *Lloyds Bank* v. *Carrick* [1996] 4 All ER 630, CA (arrangement in 1982).

[5] *Spiro* v. *Glencrown Properties* [1991] Ch 537, 541C, Hoffmann J; *Tootal Clothing* v. *Guinea Properties Management* (1992) 64 P & CR 452, 455, Scott LJ; *Firstpost Homes* v. *Johnson* [1995] 1 WLR 1567, 1571G, Peter Gibson LJ.

[6] Law Com 164 (1987), [1.1], part IV; HW Wilkinson [1987] *Conv* 313; response [1988] *Conv* 71; RE Annand (1989) 105 *LQR* 555; PH Pettit [1989] *Conv* 431; L Bentley & P Coughlan (1990) 10 *LS* 325; G Griffiths "Continuing Problems of Formality in Contracts for the Sale of Land?" ch 9 in Jackson and Wilde.

[7] Ie two months from the Royal Assent: s 5.

[8] *Firstpost Homes* v. *Johnson* [1995] 1 WLR 1567, 1571, Peter Gibson LJ.

3. Signature

[22.03] *Firstpost Homes* v. *Johnson*[9] concerned an informal agreement for the sale of some building land. A letter was signed by the landowner, but the only signature by the building company as buyer was by a director of the company on the plan attached to the letter. Obiter[10] the Court of Appeal decided that the letter itself required a signature.[11] That signature had to be placed so as to authenticate the document.[12] On the facts the company's name typed as addressee of the letter by one the secretaries employed by the company was not equivalent to signature by the company,[13] the old artificial rule which allowed a typed signature[14] being replaced by a strict requirement for a personal signature.[15] A photocopy or fax representation of the signature is probably not sufficient, though properly signed contracts might be *exchanged* by fax and if an original was signed a copy of that original will be admissible as evidence of the proper formation of the contract.[16]

An agent may sign on behalf of a contracting party. He should sign as agent to avoid personal liability on the contract,[17] but if he signs personally and fails to state that he is an agent, the undisclosed principal can nevertheless sue on the contract.[18] A person can be authorised orally to act as an agent.[19] Old case-law[20] suggests that estate agents and solicitors[21] cannot contract without specific authority to do so. A contracting party may ratify any act by an agent in excess of his authority and so adopt the contract.[22]

4. Jointly owned property

[22.04] Joint tenants must all sign when selling jointly owned property and for this purpose one of them should not appoint the other as his agent.[23] In *Malhotra* v. *Choudhury*,[24] for example, a partnership deed relating to a doctor's surgery contained an option agreement allowing the junior partner to buy the surgery on the dissolution

---

[9] [1995] 1 WLR 1567, CA; MP Thompson [1995] *Conv* 488; JE Adams [1995] *Conv* 365; AJ Oakley [1996] *CLJ* 192.

[10] It was held the contract lacked an obligation to buy.

[11] At 1571G, Peter Gibson J.

[12] *Caton* v. *Caton* (1866) LR 1 Ch App 137, 139, Lord Chelmsford; *Ogilvie* v. *Foljambe* (1817) 3 Mer 53, 62, 36 ER 21, Grant MR; *Lobb* v. *Stanley* (1844) 5 QB 574, 582, 114 ER 1366, Coleridge J; *Leeman* v. *Stocks* [1951] Ch 941, Roxburgh J.

[13] *Firstpost Homes* [1995] 1 WLR 1567, 1574C–1576E, Peter Gibson LJ, 1577C–G, Balcombe LJ.

[14] *Evans* v. *Hoare* [1892] 1 QB 593.

[15] *Goodman* v. *J Eban* [1954] 1 QB 550, 561, Denning LJ.

[16] Civil Evidence Act 1995 s 38.

[17] *Long* v. *Millar* (1879) 4 CPD 450, CA.

[18] *Basma* v. *Weekes* [1950] AC 441, PC; *Davies* v. *Sweet* [1962] 2 QB 300, CA.

[19] *Daniels* v. *Trefusis* [1914] 1 Ch 788; *Heard* v. *Pilley* (1869) LR 4 Ch App 548; *Rossiter* v. *Miller* (1878) 3 App Cas 1124, HL; *Gavaghan* v. *Edwards* [1961] 2 QB 220, CA; *Davies* v. *Sweet* [1962] 2 QB 300, CA.

[20] The issue was whether there was authority to sign a memorandum: *North* v. *Loomes* [1919] 1 Ch 378; HW Wilkinson [1988] *Conv* 313; PH Pettit [1989] *Conv* 431, 440.

[21] *Forster* v. *Rowland* (1861) 7 H & N 103, 158 ER 410; *Smith* v. *Webster* (1876) 3 Ch D 49, 57, CA; *Rosenbaum* v. *Belson* [1900] 2 Ch 267; *Elias* v. *George Saheley & Co (Barbados)* [1983] 1 AC 646, 672G, PC.

[22] *Maclean* v. *Dunn* (1828) 4 Bing 722, 130 ER 947.

[23] *Wright* v. *Dannah* (1809) 2 Camp 203, 170 ER 1129; *Bird* v. *Boulter* (1833) 4 B & Ad 443, 110 ER 522.

[24] [1980] Ch 52, CA; PW Smith [1980] *Conv* 191.

of partnership. This was signed only by the senior partner, who was joint tenant with his wife, the absence of whose signature invalidated the option agreement.[25] One joint tenant might authorise the other joint tenant to sign as agent, even orally, but specific performance has generally been refused,[26] leaving the buyer to a remedy in damages.

5. Single signed document

[22.05] This is the more fundamental of the two methods of contractual creation recognised in 1989. One document is used to meet the requirement of writing. That document must incorporate all terms that have been expressly agreed, either expressly or by reference to another document. Further, it must be signed for each party, either in person or by an authorised agent.[27]

When contracting orally, Francis Bacon said[28] "the second worde makes the bargaine". In just the same way a land contract in a single document will be concluded by the second signature, unless the contract defers its effect. The first to sign makes an offer, which could generally be revoked before signature by the second party, unless some contractual term defers the contractual relationship.

Signature in blank may create fundamental problems. In *Smith* v. *Mansi*[29] both parties had signed a single contractual document with the completion date left blank, and the seller made it clear to his solicitor that he did not wish to be bound until a new completion date had been agreed. When the solicitor inserted the old completion date in error, the parties were bound to the contract. Under the old law in force at the time, writing merely recorded the terms of a pre-existing agreement. The 1989 Act makes no provision for this situation. No contract exists in advance of the agreement in writing of all terms. Strictly, a document signed without a completion date is not a proper contract so when the date is inserted the signature needs to be revivified. A purposive approach to the legislation is needed, since it is a convenient and universal practice for a client to sign a contract in advance of exchange subject to the last minute insertion of the date for completion.

B. CONTRACTS BY EXCHANGE

1. Formation by exchange

[22.06] Contracts are usually created by exchange. Two[30] parts of a contract are prepared which are more of less identical and which incorporate all agreed contractual terms. Each part must be signed by (or on behalf of) one of the contracting parties. The contract can then be completed by physical exchange of the two parts.[31] An

---

[25] It was a valid agreement to sell the husband's beneficial interest.

[26] *Fountain Forestry* v. *Edwards* [1975] Ch 1 (personal representatives); *Watts* v. *Spence* [1976] Ch 165; *Malhotra* v. *Choudhury* [1980] Ch 52, CA.

[27] LP (MP) A 1989 s 2(1)–(3).

[28] *Colours of Good and Evill*, [68].

[29] [1963] 1 WLR 26, CA.

[30] Multilateral contracts operate with the appropriate multiplication of parts and of parties.

[31] LP (MP) A 1989 s 2(1), (3).

advantage of this system of exchange is that each side holds proof signed by the other of the existence of the contract.[32]

(1) Nature of exchange

[22.07] An exchange is as easy to recognise as an elephant but just as difficult to define. Stuart Smith LJ set out in *Commission for the New Towns* v. *Cooper (GB)*[33] the essential features of a bilateral contract. Each party is given a document incorporating all agreed terms which is intended to record their proposed contract. It is not necessary to call the documents parts of a contract, but they must be intended to be contracts and able to be fairly described as such. Each party signs in the expectation that the other will execute a corresponding part with a mutual intention to be bound only when contracts are exchanged. Exchange is a formal delivery of each part into the actual or constructive possession of the other party.

Stuart Smith LJ referred to "corresponding parts". The 1989 Act does not require the two parts to be identical, but rather to set out the same terms. In practice both are generated by word processor and should begin life in identical form. Material differences between the two parts will prevent the existence of any agreement,[34] unlike the old law.[35]

(2) Physical exchange

[22.08] Exchange is governed by general contractual principles and earlier case-law.[36] Exchanges commonly occurred face to face, and virtually simultaneously, across a table between the conveyancers of the parties. Modern practice involving chains of related sales and purchases use methods of sequential[37] exchange, for example by post[38] or *via* a document exchange.[39] No contract arises if physical exchange fails, for example where the seller's solicitor returns the buyer's part of the contract mistakenly thinking it to be the seller's part.[40]

(3) Constructive exchange

[22.09] Long chains expand the period of uncertainty, for it is inevitable that there is a moment of time at each link in the chain where the buyer is bound to sell his existing house but does not have a contract to buy his new one. Hi-tech exchanges can minimise these gaps. Telephonic exchanges are sanctioned by *Domb* v. *Isoz*:[41] both

---

[32] Law Com 164 (1987), [4.6].

[33] [1995] Ch 259, 285B–285E, 294F–295F, Evans LJ; AJ Oakley [1995] *CLJ* 502.

[34] *Harrison* v. *Battye* [1975] 1 WLR 58.

[35] *Domb* v. *Isoz* [1980] Ch 548, CA; *New Hart Builders* v. *Brindley* [1975] Ch 342.

[36] *Commission for the New Towns* v. *Cooper (GB)* [1995] Ch 259, 285G–287A, Stuart Smith LJ.

[37] At 285F, Stuart Smith LJ.

[38] Postal acceptance rule (creation on posting of the second part) adopted by Standard Conditions of Sale (3rd ed) cond 2.1.1; no contract arises earlier: *Eccles* v. *Bryant* [1948] Ch 93, 97–98.

[39] *Wilmott* v. *John Read Homes* (1986) 51 P & CR 90.

[40] *Harrison* v. *Battye* [1975] 1 WLR 58 (old law remains valid).

[41] [1980] Ch 548, CA; AG Guest (1989) 96 *LQR* 323; JT Farrand [1980] *Conv* 87; HW Wilkinson [1980] *Conv* 227.

signed parts of the contract were in the possession of the seller's solicitor, but he held the buyer's part to the order of his (the buyer's) solicitor. A contract was formed by a telephone conversation between the two solicitors authorising exchange without any physical manifestation of the change in the possession of the contracts. A whole chain of contracts can be triggered quickly by a series of phone calls.

Law Society guidelines ensure that there is proper evidence of exactly when exchange has taken place.[42] Formula A covers a case like *Domb* v. *Isoz* in which both parts are held by one side's solicitor. Formula B covers cases where each solicitor holds his own client's part of the contract, when a check is needed to ensure that the two parts correspond.[43] These ensure that a completion date is agreed and recorded, that necessary parts are posted immediately after exchange (with a deposit cheque as appropriate), and that an attendance note records details of the telephone call. Formula C[44] is a two part protocol: in the first stage the solicitors agree that they are ready to exchange and that the offer to exchange will not be revoked, whereas the second stage (activated[45] after other links in the chain are agreed) consists of the exchange. Where exchange is by fax, the facsimile message provides documentary evidence of fact triggering exchange – receipt of the second fax message.[46]

2.   Contract races

[22.10] A contract race arises where a seller negotiates with several potential buyers, offering to sell to the first of them to produce a signed contract and deposit. Buyers incur conveyancing charges without any guarantee that they would be able to buy the property, and professional obligations are laid down to protect buyers:[47] the fact that a solicitor is instructed to send out more than one contract must be disclosed to each prospective buyer, and solicitors may only act for one client.[48] Buyers seeking more assurance may try to obtain a contractually binding arrangement by the seller (in writing) to exchange contracts with the first buyer ready and willing to exchange.[49] Potentially even more useful is the "lock-out agreement" recognised in *Pitt* v. *PHH Asset Management*,[50] that is an agreement by the seller not to consider offers from any other person for two weeks.[51]

---

[42] *Encyclopaedia FP* (5th ed) vol 35, [1198].
[43] R Castle [1990] 22 *LSG* 19.
[44] [1991] 45 *LSG* 15 (fax); R Castle [1990] 22 *LSG* 19 (formula C little used).
[45] By fax, telephone, or telex, as agreed.
[46] *Entores* v. *Miles Far East Corporation* [1955] 2 QB 327, CA.
[47] *Encyclopaedia FP* (5th ed) vol 35, [1199].
[48] Solicitors Practice Rules 1988 r 6; this overrides exceptions which would normally allow solicitors to act for both parties to a low value transaction.
[49] *Daulia* v. *Four Millbank Nominees* [1982] Ch 231, 240G.
[50] [1994] 1 WLR 327, CA; C Macmillan [1993] *CLJ* 392. The appropriate remedy is damages: *Tye* v. *House* [1997] 2 EGLR 171 Ch D; F Richards [1998] 1 *PLJ* 21.
[51] A "lock in" agreement – to negotiate with the buyers – is unenforceable as an agreement to agree: *Courtney & Fairbairn* v. *Tolaini Brothers (Hotels)* [1975] 1 WLR 297, CA; *Walford* v. *Miles* [1992] 2 AC 128, HL.

3. Abolition of non-mutual contracts

[22.11] It was a fundamental objection to the old law that contracts were not necessarily mutual. If A signed a memorandum, B could enforce against him but A could not enforce against B if there was no memorandum signed by him. Contracts were frequently unilateral.[52] This is unfair.[53] The 1989 Act avoids this unfairness by requiring signature by both parties,[54] so ensuring that modern land contracts are necessarily reciprocal.

4. Ensuring correct formation

[22.12] Formality is designed to ensure that contractual formation does not occur before the parties are ready to proceed with the sale and purchase.

(1) Writing

[22.13] The old law recognised the validity of an oral contract made, for example, as a buyer looked round a seller's house. Canny buyers would make an offer "subject to contract" to prevent a legally enforceable agreement, but those with less wisdom were saved by the rule that a contract could not be enforced in court until it was evidenced in writing.[55] This did not prevent the seller forfeiting any deposit paid by the buyer.[56] The buyer and seller would invariably refer their oral agreement to their conveyancers who would carry out searches, arrange finance and go through all the necessary checks before allowing either party to commit themselves to the sale and purchase. The Law Commission objective when reforming the law was to decrease the likelihood of contracts becoming binding before parties could obtain legal advice.[57] In practice the rule that there is no contract in advance of a written statement of the terms works well, though the reform provides no safeguard for parties who do write down their agreement but without the saving phrase "subject to contract".

An informal transaction failed in *Firstpost Homes* v. *Johnson*.[58] An offer for the sale of some building land was made by this letter:

> "I now agree to sell you the above land shown on the enclosed plan which extends to 15.64 acres in consideration of £1,000 per acre.
> Yours sincerely, Mrs M Fletcher."

---

[52] *Buckhouse* v. *Crossby* (1737) 2 Eq Cas Abr 32, pl 14, 22 ER 28; *Reuss* v. *Picksley* (1866) LR 1 Exch 342.

[53] *Farrell* v. *Green* (1974) 232 EG 587, 589, Pennycuick V-C; Law Com 164 (1987), [1.7], [4.8].

[54] LP (MP) A 1989 s 2(1).

[55] *Leroux* v. *Brown* (1852) 12 CB 801, 138 ER 1119; *Britain* v. *Rossiter* (1879) 11 QBD 123, CA; *Maddison* v. *Alderson* (1883) 8 App Cas 467, HL.

[56] *Monnickendam* v. *Leanse* (1923) 39 TLR 445, Horridge J (discretion to order return of the deposit); *Low* v. *Fry* (1935) 152 LT 585, Du Parcq J (action on the deposit cheque); *Delaney* v. *TP Smith* [1946] KB 393 (not by forcible entry).

[57] Law Com WP 92 (1985), [5.2]; Law Com 164 (1987), part II; HW Wilkinson (1967) 31 *Conv (NS)* 182, 254.

[58] [1995] 1 WLR 1567, CA; MP Thompson [1995] *Conv* 488; JE Adams [1995] *Conv* 365; AJ Oakley [1996] *CLJ* 192.

Mrs Fletcher's personal representatives were not bound to sell the land. Under the old law, this letter might have been a sufficient memorandum, but under the reformed law it fell at the first hurdle, since it was a single document and not signed by both parties.

(2) Abolition of contracts by correspondence

[22.14] The 1989 reform removes a major trap,[59] which was the possibility of accidental creation of a memorandum. One example was by pleadings in litigation,[60] but much worst was the possibility of contracting by correspondence. If A wrote to B setting out terms informally agreed, A was bound;[61] B could also become bound by writing back confirming the terms.

The 1989 Act abolishes contracts by correspondence. The Law Commission report left open the possibility of a contract created by letter[62] and, although the Act itself is different in form to their draft it remained arguable that a contract by correspondence was valid until this possibility was eliminated by *Commission for the New Towns* v. *Cooper (GB)*.[63] It was held that the statutory method of creating contracts by exchange presupposed two contractual parts and presupposed also that each was intended to be a part of a contract. Two letters exchanged by post failed this last test.[64] Whether or not it is technically sound, the decision has been welcomed[65] as a way of keeping the 1989 Act more or less within its intended ambit.

(3) "Subject to contract" agreements

[22.15] Under the new law the writing needed to contract must itself affirm that it is a contract. McLaughlan defined a written contract as:

> "a contractual instrument which the parties agree or intend is to contain the whole of their contract."[66]

So the writing must say "I agree to sell". If it says "I am negotiating with a view to sale" there is no contract, as the potential tenant found in *James* v. *Evans*.[67] A manager of a flock of sheep was negotiating for the grant of a 10 year lease when the owner died before, unfortunately, signing the contract. No contract arose, and the owner's administrator was entitled to possession, because the potential tenant was aware that negotiations remained subject to contract. This fact also precluded any finding of a constructive trust or estoppel.[68]

---

[59] RE Annand (1989) 105 *LQR* 553.
[60] *Grindell* v. *Bass* [1920] 2 Ch 487, Russell J; *Hardy* v. *Elphick* [1974] Ch 65, CA.
[61] A point settled immediately after the Statute of Frauds 1677: *Moore* v. *Hart* (1682) 1 Vern 110, 201, 23 ER 352.
[62] Law Com 164 (1987), [4.15].
[63] [1995] Ch 259, CA; AJ Oakley [1995] *CLJ* 502.
[64] CJ Davis, NP Gravells, and AM Prichard [1990] *NLJ* 105.
[65] AJ Oakley [1995] *CLJ* 502.
[66] Law Com 164 (1987), [4.5], cites DW McLaughlan's definition in *The Parol Evidence Rule* (1976), 39.
[67] [2000] 3 EGLR 1, CA.
[68] *Edwin Shirley* v. *Workspace Management* [2001] 2 EGLR 16, Ch D; *Att-Gen of Hong Kong* v. *Humphreys Estates (Queen's Gardens)* [1987] AC 114, PC; see below **[23.14]**.

No restitutionary remedy is available for expenses incurred during "subject to contract" negotiations.[69]

(4) Subject to contract cases under the old law

[22.16] This magic formula[70] "subject to contract" enables negotiating parties to reach a provisional arrangement about terms, which remain subject to further negotiation: neither party is bound until a formal contract had been signed by both parties and exchanged. Only very exceptionally will a contract arise in the face of the "subject to contract" formula.[71]

Law v. *Jones*[72] revealed a trap under the old formality regime. A negotiation at stage 1 "subject to contract" was followed at stage 2 by a fresh oral contract, which was evidenced by a letter referring back to a letter written "subject to contract" at stage 1. A binding contract arose at stage 2. This suggested that a memorandum merely needed to record the terms of the contract and did not need to affirm the existence of the contract.[73] Further the "subject to contract" qualification could be removed by a clear oral agreement to expunge it.[74] This last proposition is frankly inconsistent with the whole basis of negotiation subject to contract. In *Tiverton Estates* v. *Wearwell*[75] Lord Denning made the observation, surely intended ironically, that *Law* v. *Jones* was given *per incuriam*(!) – but the earlier decision was reasserted in *Daulia* v. *Four Millbank Nominees*[76] and an important part of conveyancing practice was exposed to doubt.

(5) Statement of a concluded agreement

[22.17] A 1989 Act contract should contain a statement of a concluded agreement,[77] meaning an unqualified acceptance by one party of all the terms proposed by the other party,[78] and contain a clear agreement to be bound.[79] No contract is created by an unequivocal offer to sell which is not matched by any agreement to buy.[80] What

---

[69] *Regalian Properties* v. *London Docklands Development Corporation* [1995] 1 WLR 212, Rattee J; G Virgo [1995] *CLJ* 243; MP Thompson [1995] *Conv* 135.

[70] Other phrases are less definite in meaning: S Robinson (1970) 34 *Conv* (NS) 332, (1975) 39 *Conv* (NS) 251; B Coote (1976) 40 *Conv* (NS) 37; HW Wilkinson [1985] *Conv* 90.

[71] *Chillingworth* v. *Esche* [1924] 1 Ch 97, 114, Sargant LJ; *Richards (Michael) Properties* v. *St Saviour's Parish, Southwark* [1975] 3 All ER 416; *Alpenstow* v. *Regalian Properties* [1985] 1 WLR 721, Nourse J; HW Wilkinson [1987] *Conv* 313; JE Adams [2001] *Conv* 449.

[72] [1974] Ch 112, CA; CT Emery [1973] *CLJ* 214; AM Prichard (1974) 90 *LQR* 55.

[73] Later cases: *Munton* v. *Greater London C* [1976] 1 WLR 649, CA; *Sherbrooke* v. *Dipple* [1980] 2 EGLR 140, CA; *Cohen* v. *Nessdale* [1981] 3 All ER 118, [1982] 2 All ER 97.

[74] *Griffiths* v. *Young* [1970] Ch 675, CA.

[75] [1975] Ch 146, CA; CT Emery [1974] *CLJ* 42; JW Tinnion (1974) 37 *MLR* 695; MJ Perry (1974) 71 *LSG* 340; Law Com 65 (1975).

[76] [1978] Ch 231, CA; HW Wilkinson (1979) 95 *LQR* 7.

[77] Before 1989, a draft could be a sufficient memorandum of an oral agreement: *Toogood* v. *Farrell* [1988] 2 EGLR 233, CA.

[78] *Commission for the New Towns* v. *Cooper (GB)* [1995] Ch 259, 293E, Evans LJ.

[79] This is presumed in commercial contracts: *Kleinwort Benson* v. *Malaysian Mining Corp* [1989] 1 WLR 379, CA.

[80] *Firstpost Homes* v. *Johnson* [1995] 1 WLR 1567; MP Thompson [1995] *Conv* 488; JE Adams [1995] *Conv* 365; AJ Oakley [1996] *CLJ* 192.

earlier case-law considered to be an offer to negotiate will not create a contract to sell. Thus in *Gibson* v. *Manchester City Council*[81] when the treasurer of the council wrote to a tenant, Gibson, stating that the council "may be prepared to sell" a house at a stated price, the letter was an invitation to treat and acceptance could not create a contract.[82] Normal contractual principles require the inclusion of all the vital contractual elements, that is agreement on the parties, the property and the price. Land contracts also require the contractual document to record any other terms expressly agreed between the parties.[83]

C. VARIATION OF CONTRACTS

[22.18] Formal written documents can be varied by signed writing, usually by physical alterations to the original contract which are themselves signed.[84] *McCausland* v. *Duncan Lawrie*[85] established that informal variations do not remove the effect of an existing formal contract. A contract which provided for completion on a Sunday, but this was rapidly rearranged for the preceding Friday, the variation being recorded in correspondence between the two solicitors. A completion notice based on the *varied* completion date was held to be invalid but the *unamended* contract was enforced. What used to be illogical and paradoxical[86] has now acquired a logic under the tightened formalities.[87]

D. E-CONTRACTS AND E-CHAINS

1. E signatures

[22.19] EU obligations[88] require the UK to implement electronic signatures. Recognition of electronic contracts in ordinary commerce is implemented by section 7 of the Electronic Communications Act 2000. The European Directive it is based on excluded most land contracts, but UK implementation is across the board. Innumerable statutes laid down paper based formality requirements, each of which will require individual amendment by statutory instrument.[89] In particular the amendment may related to:

any thing required to be in writing;
any document, notice or instrument;

---

[81] [1979] 1 WLR 294, HL; JT Farrand [1983] *Conv* 85.

[82] In *Harvey* v. *Facey* [1893] AC 552, PC, the words "lowest price for Bumper Hall Pen £900" in reply to a request for a price were not to constitute an offer capable of acceptance.

[83] LP (MP) A 1989 s 2(1)–(2).

[84] The old law allowed initialling or the revival of the existing signatures by appropriate words or gestures, and this still holds good.

[85] [1997] 1 WLR 38, CA; PH Kenny [1996] *Conv* 322; MP Thompson [1996] *Conv* 366; *Morrall* v. *Krause* [1994] EGCS 177, CA. But see *Target Holdings* v. *Priestley* (2000) 79 P & CR 305, Ch D.

[86] *Morris* v. *Baron & Co* [1918] AC 1, 30 HL; Megarry & Wade (5th ed), 581.

[87] PH Pettit [1989] *Conv* 431, 436; RJ Smith (1992) 108 *LQR* 217, 220.

[88] See above [7.09ff].

[89] Electronic Communications Act 2000 ss 8–10.

post and special forms of delivery;
making a statement by oath or statutory declaration;
making any account, record, notice, instrument, document;
provisions for production to public;
making payment; or
the means of showing whether thing done, time or date, place, person, authenticity
and integrity of the contents.

Electronic methods of contracting will be an alternative to paper based methods, and
not a replacement.

2.   Contract formality

[22.20] In terms of land, widespread consultation took place on a draft order[90]
intended to amend the paper based formalities. This has been superseded by the more
far reaching provisions of the Land Registration Act 2002,[91] though the terms of the
draft Order are indicative of how e-contracting is to be implemented for registered
land. The draft Order may eventually by implemented for unregistered land.

It was proposed to amend the 1989 scheme of contract formalities[92] by a matching
section[93] for electronic contracting. The conditions laid down were:

(1) a document in electronic form purporting to be a contract;
(2) incorporating all agreed terms;
(3) containing a provision about its timing and dating;
(4) carrying the electronic signature by each person by whom it purports to be
     authenticated; and
(5) having each signature certified.[94]

A contract in this form will be deemed to have the effect of a contract in writing signed
by each party or sealed by a corporation. Similar requirements will now be enacted
under the legislation governing registration.[95]

This method of contracting may prove to be more suitable for contracts having a
short-term effect, which are followed by a completion by deed, and less suitable for
contracts having long term effect such as options.

3.   Chains

[22.21] Most sales of houses involve a chain – each owner has to sell and buy at the
same time. Delays in the chain are the major source of delays in house buying. There
will be a chain manager for each chain transaction responsible for collating information about what is holding up chain and circulating this to all parties; however he will
have no powers of compulsion.

---

[90] Draft LP (Electronic Communications) O 2001 (see the LCD website).
[91] S 91; Law Com 271 (2001), [13.7–13.10], EN [405]; see above **[7.18ff]**.
[92] Draft LP (Electronic Communications) O 2001 reg 4.
[93] LP (MP) A 1989 s 2A.
[94] On conditions (4) and (5) see the discussion of e-deeds, above **[7.12ff]**.
[95] *e-conveyancing* (LR CP, 2002), [8.2].

Eventually most conveyancing will take place via Network Access Agreements. Any transitional period of parallel operation of the two systems will be kept to a minimum since paper based links are likely to be slow down electronic chains. The registrar will act as chain manager.[96] Draft contracts will be submitted via the network, so that the land registry will have access to them. This will give time for the preparation in advance of completion a notional register showing what effect the contract will have on the existing register entries. Parties to a chain of transactions will be required to disclose information to others involved within the network about their progress with the sale and purchase – receipt of searches, making of mortgage applications, mortgage offers, sale of their own house and so forth. The chain manager will try to identify what is holding up a chain.

Contracts will be made in electronic form, signed and exchanged electronically via the land registry network. Conveyancers will need to obtain the express authority of their clients to proceed with signature and exchange. The contract will be signed on the intranet and passed to the certifying authority for certification of each signature. It will be passed on to the registry who will note the contract on the register. This notice will freeze the register for an agreed protective period to enable the contract to be completed.

E. SPECIAL FORMS OF CONTRACT

1. Auctions

[22.22] Occasionally, where a mortgage-lender is selling or where a particular property is unusual, land will be sold at auction. The owner's conveyancer will prepare a draft contract in the usual way. The auctioneer offers the land to the members of the public present at the auction on the terms of the draft contract. Land is invariably sold with a reserve, that is an undisclosed price below which the seller will not sell, the seller commonly reserving the right to bid up to the reserve.[97] Bidding creates a (revocable) offer to buy. Even after the reserve has been reached the seller can still withdraw the property during the sale, and refuse to sell to the highest bidder,[98] since acceptance occurs only when the auctioneer knocks the property down to the highest successful bidder. Completion of the auction creates a binding contract without writing.[99] It is usual to add documentary proof even if this is strictly unnecessary. The auctioneer signs the contract for the seller[100] and asks the highest bidder to sign a copy of the contract and to pay the deposit.[101]

---

[96] LRA 2002 sch 5 para 9; Law Com 271 (2001), [13.63–13.65], EN [678–680]; *e-conveyancing* (LR CP, 2002), [3.3], [4.1], [6].
[97] Sale of Land by Auction Act 1867 ss 4–6; *Gilliat* v. *Gilliat* (1869) LR 9 Eq 60; *Parfitt* v. *Jepson* (1877) 46 LJQB 529; *Hills & Grant* v. *Hodson* [1934] Ch 53; *Barry* v. *Heathcote Ball* [2000] 3 EGLR 7, CA.
[98] Query if there is no special provision and no reserve price.
[99] LP (MP) A 1989 s 2(5)(b).
[100] *Day* v. *Wells* (1861) 30 Beav 220, 54 ER 872; *Leeman* v. *Stocks* [1951] Ch 941 Roxburgh J.
[101] Old cases on the authority of an auctioneer to sign a *memorandum* at the time of the sale or shortly afterwards: *Emmerson* v. *Heelis* (1809) 2 Taunt 38, 127 ER 989; *Cohen* v. *Roche* [1927] 1 KB 169; *Chaney* v. *Maclow* [1929] 1 Ch 461, CA; *Bell* v. *Balls* [1897] 1 Ch 663; *Phillips* v. *Butler* [1945] Ch 358; *Gavaghan* v. *Edwards* [1961] 2 QB 220, CA (not a clerk, estate agent or solicitor).

2. Options

[22.23] An option is a contract giving one party only the right to insist on a transfer of property. Options to buy give B an option to purchase A's land, so that A is bound to sell if and when B elects to trigger this obligation by giving a notice exercising his option. An option granted after 1964 can be exercised within any period fixed by the option to a maximum of 21 years.[102] All terms must be agreed, and in particular the price must be fixed or ascertainable: a price to be agreed renders an option void,[103] so there must be a formula for fixing the price, and preferably also a machinery.[104]

Contractual formation takes place in two stages. First the grant of the option:

Option agreement dated 2002 between (1) A and (2) B;

In consideration of £1 the receipt of which is acknowledged, A gives B the option to buy the freehold land registered under title number XY 123456 at a price of £100,000 exercisable by written notice given within 5 years.

Signed [A], [B].

Figure 22-1 An option agreement

Protection against purchasers of the land is dependent upon registration of the option.[105] The option is exercised later by notice thus:

Notice dated 2003;

B gives notice to A to exercise the option dated 1996 between (1) A and (2) B relating to the land in title no XY 123456.

Signed [B].

Figure 22-2 Notice to exercise an option

This notice creates a full bilateral contract which binds A to sell and B to buy.[106]

Full 1989 Act formalities are required at stage 1 when the option is granted, but not at stage 2 when the option is exercised by notice. Hoffman J decided this in *Spiro* v. *Glencrown Properties*:[107] an option to buy a house for £745,000 was to be exercisable by written notice served on the same day, and was held to be validly exercised by a notice signed by the buyer alone. Had the decision been to the reverse it would have destroyed the utility of option agreements. Cases[108] which suggested the contrary[109]

---

[102] Perpetuities & Accumulations Act 1964 s 9; if no period is stated it is valid if exercised within 21 years.

[103] *King's Motors (Oxford)* v. *Lax* [1970] 1 WLR 426.

[104] *Sudbrook Trading Estates* v. *Eggleton* [1983] 1 AC 444, HL; there are many cases.

[105] See above at **[20.05]**, **[21.13]**.

[106] *London & SW Rly* v. *Gomm* (1882) 20 Ch D 562, CA.

[107] [1991] Ch 537; PF Smith [1991] *Conv* 140; AJ Oakley [1991] *CLJ* 236.

[108] *Helby* v. *Matthews* [1895] AC 471, 477, 479–480; *United Scientific Holdings* v. *Burnley BC* [1978] AC 904, 945F, Lord Simon.

[109] JE Adams [1990] 06 *EG* 59; JE Adams [1990] 33 *LSG* 19; EW Christie & JW Evans [1990] 28 *LSG* 21 (doubts); S Tromans [1984] *CLJ* 55, 62 (older cases).

were directed to explaining the position of the potential buyer[110] but not the position of the seller.[111] Hoffmann J's commonsense decision has been applauded[112] and followed.[113]

3. Rights of pre-emption

[22.24] A right of pre-emption – that is a right of first refusal exercisable if but only if the landowner decides to sell. If title is registered it creates an interest in land,[114] the pre-emptive right is registrable, and so requires section 2 formality. It seems that none of this is true if title is unregistered.[115]

4. Mixed contracts

[22.25] The 1989 Act affects contracts "for the sale or other disposition of an interest in land".[116] Old case-law remains good as a rough guide to interpretation of the reformed law.[117] Contracts for the sale of the freehold are included as are options and put options which bind the *buyer* to buy at the request of the seller.[118] An obvious exception is a compulsory purchase order.[119] Contracts for leases must be in writing, including furnished lettings,[120] but short leases are excepted from all formality.[121] Contracts to grant mortgages,[122] easements, and other incorporeal interests[123] require writing, as does a contract to dispose of a beneficial interest under a trust of land,[124] or to make a will affecting land.[125] Composite transactions are caught[126] if an essential term provides for the transfer of land.[127] Writing is also required for contracts to sell fixtures,[128] mines and minerals, slag,[129] houses sold as building material,[130] and mixed contracts affecting goods and land.

[110] *Spiro* at 542F; though see *J Sainsbury* v. *O'Connor* [1990] STC 516, Millett J.

[111] *Helby* v. *Matthews* [1895] AC 471, 482, Lord Macnaghten; *London & SW Rly* v. *Gomm* (1882) 20 Ch D 562, 582, Jessel MR; *Griffith* v. *Pelton* [1958] Ch 205; *Re Mulholland's WT* [1949] 1 All ER 460.

[112] Dollar & McGee-Osborne [1991] 03 *LSG* 17; E Dumbill [1991] *NLJ* 124; P Jenkins [1993] *Conv* 13; [1993] *Conv* 244; [1993] *Conv* 485.

[113] M Haley (1993) 22 *Anglo-American* 498, 508–509.

[114] *Pritchard* v. *Briggs* [1980] Ch 338, CA; *Nicholson* v. *Markham* (1998) 75 P & CR 428, CA (does not prevent gift).

[115] See below [24.08].

[116] LP (MP) A 1989 s 2(6)–(7); this is similar to LPA 1925 s 40.

[117] PH Pettit [1989] *Conv* 431, 433.

[118] *Commission for the New Towns* v. *Cooper (GB)* [1995] Ch 259, 283F–H.

[119] *Munton* v. *Greater London C* [1976] 1 WLR 649, CA; *Llanelec Precision Engineering Co* v. *Neath Port Talbot CBC* [2000] 3 EGLR 158, L Tr.

[120] *Inman* v. *Stamp* (1815) 1 Stark 12, 171 ER 386; *Edge* v. *Strafford* (1831) 1 Cr & J 391, 148 ER 1474.

[121] LP (MP) A 1989 s 2(5)(a).

[122] *Driver* v. *Broad* [1893] 1 QB 744, CA; *Simmons* v. *Simmons* [1996] 5 CLYB 2874, CA; *Kumah* v. *Osborne* [1997] EGCS 1, CA (no formality for allowing a borrower back on terms as to payment).

[123] Profit: *Webber* v. *Lee* (1882) 9 QBD 315 (game).

[124] (1) Pre-1989: *Cooper* v. *Critchley* [1955] Ch 431, CA; (2) 1989 to 1996: LP (MP) A 1989 s 2(6); (3) Post 1996: TLATA 1996 s 3.

[125] *Taylor* v. *Dickens* [1998] 1 FLR 806, Ch D.

[126] Eg a share in a partnership holding land: *Hammond* v. *Brearley* [1992], CA, cited by M Haley (1993) 22 *Anglo-American* 498, 503.

[127] *Gray* v. *Smith* (1888) 43 Ch D 208.

[128] *Jarvis* v. *Jarvis* (1893) 63 LJ Ch 10, 13, North J.

[129] *Morgan* v. *Russell & Sons* [1909] 1 KB 357.

[130] *Lavery* v. *Pursell* (1888) 39 Ch D 508.

Transactions which neither create not transfer an interest in land fall outside the statutory control of contract formality. Examples are contractual licences,[131] boarding agreements,[132] tickets for leisure activities,[133] road-building agreements,[134] sales of standing timber,[135] and a separation agreement – even one which settles claims to the matrimonial home.[136]

F. COMPLETENESS

1. Terms written down

[22.26] A term is stated with a sufficient degree of precision if it can be rendered certain.[137] Although the parties are usually named, they could be identified by a descriptor such as "the proprietor".[138] The property is usually defined from the title number or an unregistered parcel clause, but it could be something like "Mr Ogilvie's House".[139] Apparently land to be allocated after the payment of instalments of the price is sufficiently certain.[140] A contract for a lease must state the term, and also the commencement date of the term.[141]

Bargains are enforced rather than promises,[142] and since the seller provides the land, the buyer must reciprocate by paying a certain price or at least by promising to do so. It may be money, or an equivalent of money like shares, or the discharge of an existing[143] debt. Adequacy of consideration is not investigated, so that a nominal consideration of £1 is sufficient to support any contract, but a promise to transfer land without any consideration at all (that is a promise to give) is only binding if a deed is used to create a covenant.[144]

Land contracts will usually contain numerous other terms, such as the date for possession or the fact that the price is payable by instalments, which should all be written down. Terms implied by law need not appear anywhere in the contractual documents.[145]

---

[131] *Ashburn Anstalt* v. *Arnold* [1989] Ch 1, CA.

[132] *Wright* v. *Stavert* (1860) 2 El & El 721, 121 ER 270.

[133] *Tayler* v. *Waters* (1816) 7 Taunt 374, 129 ER 150.

[134] *Jameson* v. *Kinmell Bay Land Co* (1931) 47 TLR 593.

[135] *Marshall* v. *Green* (1875) 1 CPD 35.

[136] *Simmons* v. *Simmons* [1996] CLYB 2874, CA. Also an agreement to accept arrears of mortgage interest by instalments; *Target Holdings* v. *Priestley* (2000) 79 P & CR 305, Ch D.

[137] *Rossiter* v. *Miller* (1878) 3 App Cas 1124, 1141, Cairns LC; PH Pettit [1989] *Conv* 431, 434.

[138] *Rossiter* v. *Miller* (1878) 3 App Cas 1124, HL.

[139] *Ogilvie* v. *Foljambe* (1817) 3 Mer 53, 36 ER 21.

[140] *Bushwall Properties* v. *Vortex Properties* [1976] 1 WLR 591, CA (but Oliver J was surely right); CT Emery [1976] *CLJ* 215.

[141] *Harvey* v. *Pratt* [1965] 1 WLR 1025, CA.

[142] *Eastwood* v. *Kenyon* (1840) 11 Ad & El 438, 113 ER 482.

[143] Past debts cannot form a consideration: *Re McArdle* [1951] Ch 669, CA.

[144] P Jenkins [1993] *Conv* 13, 18–21; response [1993] *Conv* 244.

[145] LP (MP) A 1989 s 2(1); *Farrell* v. *Green* (1974) 232 EG 587, Pennycuick V-C (old law); query where an implied term is expressly agreed: PH Pettit [1989] *Conv* 431, 436.

2. Incorporation and joinder

[22.27] A 1989 Act contract must incorporate all express terms of the contract,[146] a point on which the older authorities[147] retain some vitality.[148] A land contract must incorporate all the terms which the parties have expressly agreed in one document or in each part of an exchanged contract, either by setting out the terms in the document or by reference to some other document.[149] Presumably the 1989 Act adopts the old law on "joinder" of documents. Under both old[150] and new[151] rules one must start with the signed document, since the base document must be signed whereas documents incorporated need not. When joinder is permissible, the documents are laid side by side in order to discern a complete contract from the collective documents. Documents referred to should be in existence at the time of signature of the main contractual document or possibly very shortly afterwards.

Before this can occur one must find some reference in the base document (that is the one which is signed) to link it to the document to be incorporated,[152] so that a cheque drawn in favour of the seller's solicitors cannot be read with a receipt given by the seller to the buyer.[153] Contrast a letter signed by the seller (the base document) which defined the land by reference to an enclosed plan which enabled the plan to be incorporated as a contractual document.[154] Houses are generally sold subject to the Standard Conditions of Sale, which are either printed inside or referred to.[155] Express reference can join the front and back of a contract form,[156] a memorandum to a deed which it mentions,[157] two letters,[158] a contract and a plan mentioned as describing the land[159] or a rent book to the lease.[160] Implied reference from oral evidence[161] may, for example, link a receipt to auction particulars,[162] two letters which did not expressly cross-refer,[163] a receipt and an agreement,[164] a top copy to its carbon,[165] or a letter addressed "Dear Sir" to the addressee on the envelope.[166]

[146] LP (MP) A 1989 s 2(1).
[147] A pre-1989 memorandum had to incorporate all *material* terms: *Stimson* v. *Gray* [1929] 1 Ch 629.
[148] PH Pettit [1989] *Conv* 431, 434–438.
[149] LP (MP) A 1989 s 2(1)–(2).
[150] *Timmins* v. *Moreland Street Property* [1958] Ch 110, CA; RE Megarry (1958) 74 *LQR* 22; HWR Wade [1958] *CLJ* 36; DG Valentine (1958) 21 *MLR* 183.
[151] LP (MP) A 1989 s 2(2), (3).
[152] *Timmins* at 130, Jenkins LJ; *Elias* v. *George Saheley & Co (Bardados)* [1983] 1 AC 646, 655A, Lord Scarman.
[153] *Timmins* v. *Moreland Street Property* [1958] Ch 110, CA.
[154] *Firstpost Homes* v. *Johnson* [1995] 1 WLR 1567, CA (invalid on other grounds).
[155] *British Bakeries* v. *Thorbourne Retail Parks* [1991], Ch D; M Haley (1993) 22 *Anglo-American* 498, 500; PH Kenny & A Kenny [1989] 39 *LSG* 15, 18.
[156] *Coldham* v. *Showler* (1846) 3 CB 312, 136 ER 126.
[157] *Macrory* v. *Scott* (1850) 5 Exch 907, 155 ER 396; *Ridgway* v. *Wharton* (1857) 6 HLC 238, 10 ER 1287.
[158] *Fyson* v. *Kitton* (1855) 24 LT (OS) 232; *Griffiths* v. *Young* [1970] Ch 625, CA.
[159] *Nene Valley Drainage Commissioners* v. *Dunckley* (1876) 4 Ch D 1, CA.
[160] *Hill* v. *Hill* [1947] Ch 231, CA.
[161] *Elias* v. *George Saheley & Co (Bardados)* [1983] 1 AC 646, PC; MP Thompson [1983] *Conv* 78.
[162] *Shardlow* v. *Cotterell* (1881) 20 Ch D 90, CA.
[163] *Wylson* v. *Dunn* (1887) 34 Ch D 569; *Burgess* v. *Cox* [1951] Ch 383.
[164] *Long* v. *Millar* (1879) 4 CPD 450, CA; *Elias* as above.
[165] *Stokes* v. *Whicher* [1920] 1 Ch 411, Russell J.
[166] *Pearce* v. *Gardner* [1897] 1 QB 688, CA.

3. Missing terms

[22.28] The form of the 1989 Act, which reflects last minute drafting changes,[167] requires the inclusion of "all the terms which the parties have expressly agreed".[168] The past tense is unfortunate, because there is no agreement before a written contract.[169] Missing terms under the 1989 Act should often be excluded by the parol evidence rule, which makes a written contract conclusive of the terms of the contract,[170] although exceptions riddle the rule.

Missing terms may render the whole contract void unless the contract can be rectified. In *Robert Leonard Developments* v. *Wright* omission to mention that fixtures were to be sold with a show flat meant that the contract did not comply (as it stood) with the 1989 Act.[171] *McCausland* v. *Duncan Lawrie* held that a completion date was an essential term and without it the contract was void.[172] The law has become even more stringent than it was before, when this effect was only attributable to *material* terms.[173] Now omission of the most trivial term may invalidate the contract.

4. Collateral contracts

[22.29] If there is a collateral contract the question of rectification may not arise.[174] Parties will often enter into a formal contract for the sale of land but support this by a collateral contract about the manner in which the sale will be conducted. As a single contract this would be invalid, since the formal written contract would not include the totality of the express terms, but the courts have allowed the single arrangement to be split into a formal contract for the sale of land and an accompanying collateral contract, which may be informal if it is not a land contract.[175]

If there are to be two agreements, this should be decided by the parties themselves who will be left to determine the content of each contract.[176] A clear case for division was *Record* v. *Bell*.[177] A contract for the sale of No 6 Smith Square in London at £1.3m was due for exchange. The seller offered a warranty that there were no undisclosed entries on the register and confirmed this in correspondence. This "side-letter"

---

[167] Law Com 164 (1987), draft Bill cl 1(1), required that "all the express terms of the contract are incorporated."

[168] S 2(1).

[169] J Greed [1990] *NLJ* 296.

[170] RJ Smith (1992) 108 *LQR* 217, 220.

[171] [1994] EGCS 69; M Haley [1995] *JBL* 176; MP Thompson [1995] *Conv* 484. The difficulty was solved by rectification below. Omission of the vendor's name avoided a written contract drawn up by an estate agent: *Rudra* v. *Abbey National* (1998) 76 P & CR 537, CA.

[172] [1997] 1 WLR 38, CA; A Silverton [1996] 27 *LSG* 32; PH Kenny [1996] *Conv* 322; MP Thompson [1996] *Conv* 366.

[173] *Martin* v. *Pycroft* (1852) 22 LJ Ch 94; *North* v. *Loomes* [1919] 1 Ch 378; *Hawkins* v. *Price* [1947] Ch 645; *Scott* v. *Bradley* [1971] Ch 850; *Tweddle* v. *Henderson* [1975] 1 WLR 1496; *Tiverton Estates* v. *Wearwell* [1975] Ch 146, 161; *Ram Narayan* v. *Shah* [1989] 1 WLR 1349, PC. Contrast on the old law: *Timmins* v. *Moreland Street Property* [1958] Ch 110, CA.

[174] *Walker Property Investments (Brighton)* v. *Walker* (1947) 177 LT 204.

[175] Law Com 164 (1987), [5.7–5.8]; JE Adams [1989] *Conv* 386.

[176] *Godden* v. *Merthyr Tydfil H Ass* (1997) 74 P & CR D1, CA (single contract since no evidence it was split).

[177] [1991] 1 WLR 853; M Harwood [1991] *Conv* 471; C Harpum [1991] *CLJ* 399; M Haley (1993) 22 *Anglo-American* 498, 511; RJ Smith (1992) 108 *LQR* 217.

did not diminish the enforceability of the main sale contract. Other illustrations are an agreement by a side letter that a landlord would accept a surrender if the tenant wished to break the lease rather than pay an increased rent[178] and an agreement collateral to a lease to rectify dampness.[179] Potentially the most significant decision to date is *Pitt* v. *PHH Asset Management*,[180] which allowed an informal "lock-out" agreement – that is an agreement by the seller not to consider offers from any other person for a set period.[181]

Current thinking is that a collateral contract argument should not be used where the parties had agreed all the terms of an agreement as a single package. In *Tootal Clothing* v. *Guinea Properties Management*[182] the Court of Appeal split an agreement by a landlord to allow a rent-free fitting out period from the grant of the lease. However, this case was doubted by a later Court of Appeal in *Grossman* v. *Hooper*.[183] After the separation of a married couple, H agreed to transfer the matrimonial home to G subject to an agreement about the discharge of a debt. Had this been a term of the final agreement, as the judge at first instance thought, it could not have been hived off into a collateral contract. This analysis was not helpful for excess terms.

6. Rectification

[22.30] In *Robert Leonard Developments* v. *Wright*[184] a contract relating to the sale of a show flat was held to be invalid because it contained no reference to an agreement to sell fixtures, but the difficulty was easily cured because it was an appropriate case to rectify the contractual document to insert the missing term. As Mark Thompson observes, the freedom with which rectification is being granted leads to the paradoxical result that tightening the formalities in 1989 has left the law less stringent in relation to omitted terms. Proof of the existence of the omitted term will almost automatically give grounds for rectification, despite the need for "strong irrefragable evidence",[185] that is "convincing proof".[186]

Rectification makes the record of a transaction[187] correspond with its intended effect, for example aligning a transfer with its preceding contract.[188] Though a prior

---

[178] *System Floors* v. *Ruralpride* [1995] 1 EGLR 48, CA.

[179] *Lotteryking* v. *Amec Properties* [1995] 2 EGLR 13, Lightman J.

[180] [1994] 1 WLR 327, CA; C Macmillan [1993] *CLJ* 392.

[181] Contrast *Daulia* v. *Four Millbank Nominees* [1978] Ch 231, 240G, Goff LJ (contract race required formality).

[182] (1992) 64 P & CR 452, 462, CA; D Wilde (1993) 109 *LQR* 191; P Luther [1993] *Conv* 89; M Haley [1993] 22 *Anglo-American* 498, 504–507.

[183] [2001] EWCA Civ 615, [2001] 2 EGLR 82.

[184] [1994] EGCS 69; M Haley [1995] *JBL* 176; MP Thompson [1995] *Conv* 484.

[185] *Shelburne (Countess of)* v. *Earl of Inchiquin* (1784) 1 Bro CC 338, 341, 28 ER 1166, Thurlow LC.

[186] *Joscelyne* v. *Nissen* [1970] 2 QB 86, 98, Russell LJ; *Nurdin & Peacock* v. *DB Ramsden* [1999] 1 WLR 1249 (failed on facts).

[187] *Mackenzie* v. *Coulson* (1869) LR 8 Eq 368, 375, James V-C.

[188] *Blacklocks* v. *JB Developments (Godalming)* [1982] Ch 183; *Berkeley Leisure Group* v. *Williamson* [1996] EGCS 18, CA; *Swainland Builders* v. *Freehold Properties* [2002] EWCA Civ 560, [2002] 2 EGLR 71 (rectify omission from sale of block of flats of agreement to reserve long leases of 2 flats). Rectification is no longer applicable to the contract once the contract has been completed: *Whiteside* v. *Whiteside* [1950] Ch 65, CA; (1956) 66 *LQR* 287; *Eason* v. *Brownrigg* [1998] CLYB 3659.

concluded contract is not an essential,[189] a common intention is, as well as some out-
ward expression of that common intention.[190] The mistake must relate to the effect of
a transaction rather than about its consequences, so a document cannot be corrected
simply because it increases the tax payable.[191] Unilateral mistake, especially if known
to the other party,[192] is a ground to rectify gifts, voluntary settlements[193] and now, by
statute, wills.[194] A number of recent cases provide further illustrations. In *Templiss
Properties* v. *Hyams*[195] a lease was corrected to remove the landlord's liability to non-
domestic rates, since a covenant to pay them had not been agreed in advance and the
tenant who had failed to draw attention to this change had knowingly taken advantage of the landlord's error. Similarly, a break clause was removed from a lease in
Coles v. *William Hill Organisation Ltd.*[196] but a guarantor's covenant was added in
Eason v. *Brewster*.[197]

Rectification is an equitable discretionary remedy and also a defence to a contractual action. Although proprietary, it is easily defeated by a protected purchaser, who
is unaware of the right and could not have discovered it.[198] Rectification was formerly
retrospective to the date of the contract, but there is now a judicial discretion as to the
date from which a rectification order is to operate.[199]

G. INVALIDITY OF INFORMAL CONTRACTS

1. Invalidity

[22.31] Ultimately if all else fails, a contract relating to land that is informal will simply fail to create any rights in the land. In *Jelson* v. *Derby CC*[200] the city council
entered into a development agreement with the owners of two development sites in
Derby, the oral arrangement being that the quota of units of affordable housing
should be provided from the part of the site owner by a development corporation.

---

[189] *Joscelyne* v. *Nissen* [1970] 2 QB 86 (overruling prior dicta); PV Baker (1970) 86 *LQR* 303; *Grand Metropolitan* v. *William Hill Group* [1997] 1 BCLC 390, Arden J (common intention rather than exact agreement).

[190] Doubted by L Bromley (1971) 87 *LQR* 532.

[191] *Gibbon* v. *Mitchell* [1990] 3 All ER 338, Millett J; *Racal Group Services* v. *Ashmore* [1995] STC 1157, CA; S Lacey [1996] *NLJ* 1589.

[192] *JJ Huber (Investments)* v. *Private DIY Co* [1996] 2 CLYB 3756; *Coles* v. *William Hill Organisation* [1998] EGCS 40 (even though solicitor had opportunity to check). As opposed to fraud: *Riverlate Properties* v. *Paul* [1975] Ch 133, CA; AL Goodhart (1974) 90 *LQR* 439; RE Megarry (1961) 77 *LQR* 313 (old law).

[193] *Re Butlin's ST* [1976] Ch 251; (1976) 92 *LQR* 325; *Tankel* v. *Tankel* [1998] 1 FLR 676, Park J; *Re Détente* [2000] 1 WTLR 133; *Pappadakis* v. *Pappadakis* [2000] WTLR 719, Park J.

[194] Administration of Justice Act 1982 s 20(1); *Re Slocock's WT* [1979] 1 All ER 358; (1979) 95 *LQR* 322; *Schneider* v. *Mills* [1993] 3 All ER 377.

[195] [1999] EGCS 60. Where a single solicitor acts for both parties and makes a mistake, this shows a com-
mon intention, which is a ground for rectification: *Mace* v. *Rutland House Textiles* [2000] Times January 11th, ChD; Q Smye [1999] 49 *EG* 92.

[196] [1998] EGCS 40, ChD.

[197] [1997] 1 CLYB 1987.

[198] *Smith* v. *Jones* [1954] 1 WLR 1089 (unregistered); *Blacklocks* v. *JB Developments (Godalming)* [1982] Ch 183 (registered); *Nurdin & Peacock* v. *DB Ramsden & Co* [1999] 1 WLR 1249 (failed on facts).

[199] LP (MP) A 1989 s 2(4).

[200] [1999] EGCS 88, David Mackie QC.

However, the fact that 30 affordable dwellings were to be provided from the housing association owned part of the site was not included in the written agreement signed by the corporation, which was void.

2. Informal mortgages

[22.32] Informal mortgages by deposit of the title deeds were recognised in 1783.[201] Before 1989 it was common to deposit a land certificate or unregistered title deeds with a lender in return for a loan. Usually a written memorandum or deed evidenced the terms, but sometimes the deposit was the only evidence of the transaction. A bank manager might for example request the deposit of title deeds and in return allow an increased overdraft limit. Legal effectiveness for this oral arrangement depended on the doctrine of part performance after deposit of the deeds.[202]

Section 2 of the Law of Property (Miscellaneous Provisions) Act 1989 applies to mortgages.[203] The point had not been considered by the Law Commission,[204] but was decided in *United Bank of Kuwait* v. *Sahib*.[205] Informal mortgages are invalid. Sahib charged his interest in the matrimonial home to the bank in return for a loan of £130,000. There was no written evidence of the mortgage but Sahib held the land certificate of the property for the bank, an arrangement amounting to a contract for a mortgage of Sahib's equitable interest in the property. The Court of Appeal held that such an agreement could only be valid if there was a document signed by both parties and incorporating all agreed terms. So a mortgage by deposit is just a contract[206] requiring contractual formality. A simple deposit of title deeds no longer creates any charge.

H. MEANS OF ENFORCING INFORMAL CONTRACTS

1. Effect of informality after 1989

[22.33] The Law Commission's guiding principle was that reform should not increase the risk of injustice, so that the new law had to be flexible enough to avoid hardship.[207]

2. Contracts not directly affecting land

[22.34] Some contracts do not require formal statement. Examples are contracts for the sale of property other than land, contracts about how land is sold, contracts for

---

[201] *Russel* v. *Russel* (1783) 1 Bro CC 269, 28 ER 1121.

[202] See below **[22.37]**.

[203] Guarantees require writing under Statute of Frauds 1677 s 4: *Elpis Maritime* v. *Marti Chartering* [1992] 1 AC 21, HL; *Carlton* Communications v. *Football League* [2002] EWHC 1650, [2002] August 1st.

[204] Law Com 164 (1987), [4.3].

[205] [1997] Ch 107, CA; M Oldham [1995] *CLJ* 249; see also Davis, Gravells & Prichard [1990] *NLJ* 105, 108; M Haley (1993) 22 *Anglo-American* 498, 501. It would not be safe to follow the dicta in *Target Holdings* v. *Priestley* (2000) 79 P & CR 305, [57–58], Judge Hicks.

[206] *Re Wallis & Simmonds (Builders)* [1974] 1 WLR 391; *Re Alton Corp* [1985] BCLC 27.

[207] Law Com WP 92 (1985), [5.2]; Law Com 164 (1987), pt V; PH Pettit [1989] *Conv* 431, 441–442; J Howell [1990] *Conv* 441.

short leases,[208] sales at auction, contracts for regulated financial services, and contracts for trusts that are resulting, implied or constructive.[209]

3. Other remedies

[22.35] In addition it is possible to rely on alternative remedies, for example damages for misrepresentation, restitutionary remedies, and rectification.[210] However the main reliance is on estoppel.[211] The Commission felt that new remedies were unnecessary.[212]

I. CONTRACTS THAT HAVE BEEN ACTED UPON

1. Executed contracts

[22.36] Arguably, also, formality ceases to be an issue when a contract is executed, that is when all rights it creates have been carried into effect.[213]

2. Part performance before 1989

[22.37] Writing has been required for land contracts since 1677, but as early as 1682 the courts enforced an oral contract which was evidenced by acts of part performance,[214] and the doctrine had statutory force after 1925.[215] The basis of the doctrine for pre-1989 Act contracts was that a person could not deny his contract after allowing the other party to act on it.

Acts of part performance had a twofold function, first to explain why an informal contract should be enforced and secondly to provide evidence of the terms of the contract in the absence of a written memorandum. Acts of part performance had to prove the existence of some contract[216] and be consistent with the one alleged.[217] As the leading cases demonstrated[218] the doctrine was arbitrary and could work very

---

[208] *Target Holdings* v. *Priestley* (2000) 79 P & CR 305, [57–58], Judge Hicks.

[209] LP (MP) A 1989 s 2(5); *Healey* v. *Brown* [2002] 19 EG 147 (CS) (a contract to make mutual wills requires s 2 formality, but an oral arrangement may create a constructive trust).

[210] See below **[22.30]**.

[211] See below **[23.38]**.

[212] Law Com 164 (1987), [5.2].

[213] *Tootal Clothing* v. *Guinea Properties Management* (1992) 64 P & CR 452, CA; D Wilde (1993) 109 *LQR* 191; P Luther [1993] *Conv* 89; *Singh* v. *Beggs* (1996) 71 P & CR 120, 121–122.

[214] *Moore* v. *Hart* (1682) 1 Vern 110, 23 ER 352, *Hollis* v. *Edwards* (1683) 1 Vern 159, 23 ER 385; *Butcher* v. *Stapely* (1686) 1 Vern 363, 23 ER 524, Jeffreys LC; *Lester* v. *Foxcroft* (1701) Colles 108, 1 ER 205.

[215] LPA 1925 s 40(2). Repeal of this section (though not LPA 1925 s 55(d)) must have resulted in abolition of the doctrine despite *Singh* v. *Begg* (1996) 71 P & CR 120, 122, Neill LJ obiter. After 1989 there is no contract without writing to be proved orally.

[216] *Thynne* v. *Glengall* (1848) 2 HLC 131, 158, 9 ER 1042, Lord Brougham; *Daulia* v. *Four Millbank Nominees* [1978] Ch 231, 243B–244D; *Singh* v. *Beggs* (1996) 71 P & CR 120, CA.

[217] *Kingswood Estate Co* v. *Anderson* [1963] 2 QB 169, 189, Upjohn LJ; E Fry *Specific Performance* (Sweet & Maxwell, 6th ed by GR Northcote, 1921), 278.

[218] *Maddison* v. *Alderson* (1883) 8 App Cas 467 HL; *Kingswood Estate Co* v. *Anderson* [1963] 2 QB 169, CA; *Wakeham* v. *Mackenzie* [1968] 1 WLR 1175; *Steadman* v. *Steadman* [1976] AC 536, HL.

unfairly. Payment of the purchase price of a house was not part performance[219] but payment of other sums[220] could be.

Creation of an informal mortgage by deposit of the title deeds before the 1989 Act came into force[221] was an example of part performance.

If doctrinal uncertainty was a central problem of the old law,[222] proprietary[223] estoppel[224] provides a tailor-made replacement. It rests on a similar principle – that it is unconscionable to go back on a promised right after detrimental reliance upon it by the party who expects to receive it – but satisfaction of the equity is discretionary. It remains to be seen whether it operates as a satisfactory alternative.[225]

3. Contracts by estoppel

[22.38] Contractual expectations enforced by a proprietary estoppel require detailed exposition below,[226] but the leading case, *Yaxley* v. *Gotts*,[227] is so important that it cannot be deferred. Yaxley was a small time builder in Norfolk who approached Gotts, investor in a number of properties, with a proposition. Yaxley had wanted to buy a property but lacking the finance had approached Gotts who decided to buy it himself. In fact it was transferred into the name of his son, who was registered as proprietor. Gotts offered Yaxley two ground floor flats in return for his work on the upper four flats, and arrangement agreed orally. Work carried out in 1992 was worth over £9,000. All essential elements of an estoppel were present: the expectation that Yaxley would obtain two flats for himself, the inducement of this expectation by Gotts' promise, and the detriment in labour incurred in reliance on the promise. Yaxley's rights could be phrased in terms of estoppel or in terms of a constructive trust. Robert Walker LJ rejected as unsustainable the suggestion that informal contracts were a no go area for estoppel. Gotts, the son, was ordered to grant Yaxley 99 year leases of the two flats he had been promised. So proprietary estoppel or constructive trust doctrine fills in where previously there would have been a part performance.[228]

4. Joint investment ventures

[22.39] In *Banner Homes Group* v. *Luff Developments*[229] two parties were interested in a development site in Berkshire. They agreed that one would bid for the site and

---

[219] *Chaproniere* v. *Lambert* [1917] 2 Ch 356, CA.
[220] *Steadman* at 541B, 565B–E, 570–572, 553H; *Lloyds Bank* v. *Carrick* [1996] 4 All ER 630, CA; *Wu Koon Tai* v. *Wu Yau Loi* [1997] AC 179, PC.
[221] See above [22.32].
[222] Law Com 164 (1987), [1.7–1.9], [4.13], [5.4–5.5].
[223] Other forms of estoppel will not do: *Godden* v. *Merthyr Tydfil H Ass* (1997) 74 P & CR D1, CA
[224] See below [23].
[225] PH Pettit [1989] *Conv* 431, 441–442; J Howell [1990] *Conv* 441; P Rank (1990) 134 *SJ* 72; L Bentley & P Coughlan (1990) 10 *LS* 325; C Davis (1993) 13 *OJLS* 99; MP Thompson [1994] *Conv* 233; G Woodman (1981) 44 *MLR* 461; GLlH Griffiths [2002] *Conv* 216 (favours part performance).
[226] See below [23.14ff].
[227] [2000] Ch 162 CA; I Moore (2000) 63 *MLR* 912; RJ Smith (2000) 116 *LQR* 11; L Tee [2000] *CLJ* 23.
[228] *Lloyd* v. *Dugdale* [2001] EWCA Civ 1754, [2002] 2 P & CR 13 at 167, [26–39], Sir Christopher Slade.
[229] [2000] Ch 372 CA; N Hopkins [2002] *Conv* 35; MP Thompson [2001] *Conv* 265.

having acquired it would give an interest in it to the other party. The non-acquiring party agreed to omit to do something to the advantage of the acquiring party, in this case keeping out of the market and so reducing the price. Although there was no formal contract there was an arrangement or understanding before the acquisition,[230] best expressed as a joint venture.[231] These circumstances make it inequitable to deny an interest to the non acquiring party. Another good illustration is provided by *Hooper* v. *Garvin*.[232] An action group of tenants was formed to protest about service charges on a freehold industrial estate only to find that their spokesman, Garvin, had bought the freehold on his own account. He had been under a fiduciary obligation towards the other tenants and so after the purchase held the freehold on trust for them.

---

[230] This is essential: *Pridean* v. *Forest Taverns* (1998) 75 P & CR 447, CA.
[231] *Pallant* v. *Morgan* [1953] Ch 43; N Hopkins (1998) 116 *MLR* 486.
[232] [2001] 2 WTLR 575 ChD; PH Kenny [2001] *Conv* 293.

23

PROPRIETARY ESTOPPEL

Doctrinal base. Expectations: negative, positive, contractual. Inducement. Detrimental reliance. Satisfaction. Proprietary force.

A DOCTRINAL BASE

[23.01] Formal property law favours those with money and legal advice who can draft proper documents and register them. Equity intervenes to estop a landowner from relying on informality as a defence where it is unconscionable to do so, and proprietary estoppel doctrine[1] goes even further by allowing the positive creation of new rights.

1. The structure of the modern law

[23.02] Proprietary estoppel has doctrinal requirements which determine when it is unconscionable to insist on strict legal rights. Flexibility is secured by stating the requirements[2] at a high level of abstraction:

(1) **An expectation.** The claimant must expect the creation or enforcement of some property right, such as a gift ("The house is yours"), a contract ("I will sell you the house") or the grant of a right of way.

(2) **Inducement by the property owner.** The expectation must be induced by the property owner, for example by direct encouragement ("Build a house on my field and the house is yours") or by passivity in circumstances in which there is a duty to disabuse the claimant of his expectation (the owner of a field fails to stop a claimant building a house on it).

(3) **Detrimental reliance** by the claimant, for example by spending money building a house, or by working on repairs.

An equity arises through estoppel to fulfil the claimant's expectation, though how it is satisfied is in the discretion of the court.

---

[1] G Battersby "Informally Created Rights in Land", ch 19 in Bright & Dewar; P Birks "Before We begin: Five Keys to Land Law" ch 18 in Bright & Dewar, 482; E Cooke *Modern Law of Estoppel* (OUP, 1999); E Cooke "What are We Going to Do about Estoppel" ch 3 in Jackson and Wilde; P Critchley "Taking Formalities Seriously" ch 20 in Bright & Dewar; Goo's *Sourcebook* (3rd ed) ch 5; Megarry & Wade (6th ed) ch 13; Smith's *Property Law* (4th ed), ch 9; MP Thompson *Modern LL* ch 15.
[2] *Att-Gen of Hong Kong* v. *Humphreys Estate (Queen's Gardens)* [1987] AC 114, 124, Lord Templeman, PC.

2. A typical case of proprietary estoppel

[23.03] Earlier strands of authority crystallised into the modern concept of proprietary estoppel in the nineteenth century. *Dillwyn* v. *Llewellyn*[3] illustrates as early as 1862 many of the modern concerns. A father and his son signed a memorandum saying that the property was left to the son as the site for a new house. This attempted gift conferred no rights on the son: none at law because it was not by sealed deed, and none in equity because the promise was made without consideration and equity was unable to perfect a gift where legal title was not vested is the recipient. However, an *expectation* that the land belonged to the son was created (or *induced*) by the memorandum. *Detrimental reliance* on the father's promise, by building a house with the father's knowledge and approval, overcame the absence of formality and made it inequitable for the father to claim back the land.

Fully fledged, there is the basis of a modern estoppel.[4] The father was estopped from claiming possession of the land, a fact which showed the negative aspect of an estoppel (the shield) which provides a defence to an action inconsistent with the promise that has been made. Equity also compelled the transfer of the fee simple in the plot to the son giving effect to the father's promised gift (the sword), a positive aspect which is diagnostic of an estoppel which is *proprietary*.[5] The father kept his word in *Dillwyn*, but his widow sought possession after his death. Estoppel against the father created an equity in the property, binding on a volunteer like the widow and any other successor, except a protected purchaser without notice.

3. Development of the doctrine

[23.04] All members of the House of Lords recognised the doctrine in *Ramsden* v. *Dyson*,[6] but only Lord Kingsdown's dissent applied it to the facts. Lord Cranworth LC for the majority laid down stricter conditions for the existence of an estoppel, conditions applied by Fry J in *Willmott* v. *Barber*[7] so restrictively that development of the doctrine was temporarily crabbed. Flexibility was restored by the classic judgment of Denning J in the *High Trees* case[8] immediately after the Second World War. That case concerned a promissory estoppel, used to effect a temporary variation of contractual rights, but the wide terms, its obvious justice, and the brilliance of its formulation created a ripple effect which spread out and liberated proprietary estoppel. Case to case development occurred rapidly during Lord Denning's tenure as Master of the Rolls, creating a settled addition to equity jurisprudence, but one he left with unsure doctrinal requirements. Cases since 1980 have laid down clear criteria, secured consistency, and avoided more extreme applications.

---

    [3] (1862) 4 De GF & J 517, 45 ER 1285; *Sen* v. *Headley* [1991] Ch 425, 439H, Nourse LJ.
    [4] DE Allan (1963) 79 *LQR* 238 (an estoppel case, even though it did not use modern estoppel terminology).
    [5] FR Crane (1967) 31 *Conv (NS)* 332, 340; *East India Co* v. *Vincent* (1740) 2 Atk 83, 26 ER 451 (the first case?). Contrast estoppel by representation and promissory estoppel.
    [6] (1866) LR 1 HL 129.
    [7] (1880) 15 Ch D 96, 105–106.
    [8] *Central London Property Trust* v. *High Trees House* [1947] KB 130; see any contract text.

B. NEGATIVE EXPECTATIONS (DEFENSIVE ESTOPPEL)

1. Lesser estoppels

[23.05] According to Les Termes de la Ley,[9]

> "Estoppel is, when one is concluded and forbidden in law to speak against his own act or deed, yea though it be to say the truth."

Lord Coke[10] explained that the French word *estoupe* led to the English equivalent "stopped", where a person's "own act or acceptance stoppeth or closeth up his mouth to allege or plead the truth." Its defensive origin is laid bare. A plaintiff takes action on facts which would normally ensure success, but the defendant can put forward an estoppel to prevent the plaintiff pleading the facts needed to win. Estoppel originated as a rule of evidence.[11]

Numerous off-shoots of estoppel doctrine are limited to a defensive role. Issue estoppel[12] binds each party to accept the result of earlier litigation: it is a defence to a second action to say that the same issue[13] had been decided in favour of the defendant against the plaintiff[14] in earlier proceedings.[15] Waiver of rights occurs where a person with full knowledge of his rights elects not to rely on them, for example to oppose a business renewal,[16] forfeit a lease, enforce a restrictive covenant, or insist on time limits.[17] Promissory estoppel was developed from nineteenth century precursors[18] in the *High Trees* case.[19] If a promise[20] is made which is intended to create legal relations an estoppel arises if the person to whom it is made acts on it. Landlords of a block of flats in London promised during the war that the rent would be halved, so they were entitled to sue for the full rent after the war had ended. But, Denning J indicated *obiter*, they were estopped from claiming full rent for the duration of the war. Promissory estoppel may only create a temporary[21] variation of an existing contract, and of contractual remedies,[22] but it always limited to a defensive

---

[9] W Rastell & T Blount (Portland, 1812).

[10] Coke on *Littleton*, [352a].

[11] *Low* v. *Bouverie* [1891] 3 Ch 82, 105, Bowen LJ.

[12] Estoppel by the record occurs where a person is bound by an official record such as a register of title.

[13] *Lordsvale Finance* v. *Bank of Zambia* [1996] QB 752, Colman J.

[14] *Lloyds Bank* v. *Semmakie* [1993] 1 FLR 34.

[15] *Arnold* v. *National Westminster Bank* [1991] 2 AC 93, HL; *Barber* v. *Staffordshire CC* [1996] 2 All ER 748, CA.

[16] *Kammins Ballrooms Co* v. *Zenith Investments (Torquay)* [1971] AC 850, 883, Lord Diplock; *Stevens & Cutting* v. *Anderson* [1990] 1 EGLR 95, CA; *Bristol Cars* v. *RKH (Hotels)* (1978) 38 P & CR 411, CA; *Watkins* v. *Emslie* [1982] 1 EGLR 81, CA.

[17] *Ogilvy* v. *Hope-Davies* [1976] 1 All ER 683, 687c–j, 689b.

[18] *Hughes* v. *Metropolitan Rly Co* (1877) 2 App Cas 439, HL; *Birmingham & District Land Co* v. *London & NW Rly* (1888) 40 Ch D 268; M Lunney [1992] *Conv* 239, 239–240.

[19] *Central London Property Trust* v. *High Trees House* [1947] KB 130.

[20] Or representation: *James* v. *Heim Gallery (London)* (1980) 41 P & CR 269, 280, Oliver J.

[21] Cheshire Fifoot & Furmston's *Law of Contract* (Butterworths, 2001), 112. Variation may be permanent if it is impossible to resume the original position: *Ajayi* v. *RT Briscoe (Nigeria)* [1964] 1 WLR 1326, PC. Performance of an existing duty may suffice: *WJ Alan & Co* v. *El Nasir Export & Import Co* [1972] 2 QB 189. Proprietary estoppel can create a permanent variation.

[22] MP Thompson [1983] *CLJ* 257, 261.

role between the original parties.[23] The promise cannot be used offensively to found a claim in damages.[24]

2.   Defensive use of proprietary estoppel

[23.06] Proprietary and promissory estoppels overlap when an owner is estopped from asserting his strict legal rights because he has induced an expectation in another that he will not rely on them. Proprietary estoppel requires detrimental reliance for example by the expenditure of money,[25] and comes into its own when a variation is permanent or enforcement is sought against a person who is not an immediate contracting party. *Duke of Beaufort* v. *Patrick*[26] concerned some of the Duke's land taken and dug up for a canal, but it was only after his death that purchasers of his estate secured a common law judgment for recovery of the land forming the site of the canal. Enforcement of this legal right was prevented in equity,[27] since the Duke had allowed the canal company to incur expense in building the canal.

Extinction of the owner's title requires proof of an expectation that the owner will not enforce his rights, not just a hope.[28] *Willmott* v. *Barber*[29] considered whether a landlord was permitted to forfeit a lease after a sub-letting in breach of covenant. The sub-tenant claimed that the landlord was bound by conduct to grant his licence for the sub-letting,[30] but this defence was unsuccessful since the head landlord did not know of any money being spent. Successful pleas may neutralise a restrictive covenant,[31] preclude a landlord from evicting a tenant,[32] or bind a property owner to an informal rearrangement of rights to light.[33] Estoppel may also preclude a claim to adverse possession.[34]

---

[23] *Brikom Investments* v. *Carr* [1979] QB 467, CA; *Canadian Imperial Bank of Commerce* v. *Bello* (1992) 64 P & CR 48, 52, Dillon LJ; *Smith* v. *Lawson* (1998) 75 P & CR 466, CA (defence to adverse possession).

[24] *Combe* v. *Combe* [1951] 2 KB 215, Denning J; *Beesly* v. *Hallwood Estates* [1960] 1 WLR 549, 560–561, Buckley J; *BP Exploration Company (Libya)* v. *Hunt* [1979] 1 WLR 783; *Pacol* v. *Trade Lines* [1982] 1 Lloyds Rep 456; *JT Developments* v. *Quinn* (1991) 62 P & CR 33, 45.

[25] *Crabb* v. *Arun DC* [1976] Ch 179, 188; *Moorgate Mercantile* v. *Twitchings* [1976] QB 225, 242, Lord Denning MR.

[26] (1853) 17 Beav 60, 78, 51 ER 954; *Att-Gen* v. *Baliol College* (1744) 9 Mod Rep 407, 412, 88 ER 538; *Stiles* v. *Cowper* (1748) 3 Atk 692, 26 ER 1198; *Cawdor* v. *Lewis* (1835) 1 Y & C 427, 433, 160 ER 174; *Powell* v. *Thomas* (1848) 6 Hare 300, 67 ER 1180.

[27] It could prevent enforcement of equitable rights: *Habib Bank* v. *Habib Bank Zurich* [1981] 1 WLR 1265, 1285, Oliver LJ.

[28] *Boxbusher Properties* v. *Graham* [1976] 2 EGLR 58.

[29] (1880) 15 Ch D 96, Fry J.

[30] At 104–105, Fry J.

[31] *Shaw* v. *Applegate* [1977] 1 WLR 970.

[32] *Kammins Ballrooms Co* v. *Zenith Investments (Torquay)* [1971] AC 850, HL (unsuccessful); *Hammersmith & Fulham LBC* v. *Tops Shop Centres* [1990] Ch 237.

[33] *Cotching* v. *Bassett* (1862) 32 Beav 101, 55 ER 40.

[34] *Colchester BC* v. *Smith* [1992] Ch 421, CA; see above **[10.15]**.

C. POSITIVE EXPECTATIONS

1. Property rights

[23.07] Even Lord Denning MR expressed initial surprise that the entire claim in one pleaded case relied upon estoppel,[35] but then there are estoppels and estoppels. If the estoppel is proprietary it can be used to create new rights, the sword being its distinctive characteristic. In *Crabb* the whole basis of his right to sue was what might be called an "easement by estoppel", and many other cases rely on "leases" granted by estoppel.[36] Lord Kingsdown referred in *Ramsden* v. *Dyson*[37] to:

"a verbal agreement . . . or, what amounts to the same thing, . . . an expectation . . .".

Ever since the positive aspect of estoppel has been expressed in terms of expectation.[38] The court usually gives effect to the belief in entitlement created in the mind of the claimant,[39] subject to the discretion available in satisfaction.

A proprietary estoppel raises an expectation in relation to the owner's land,[40] or an assurance by the owner.[41] Proprietary estoppel doctrine is widely applied to secure grants of new property rights despite missing formalities. Examples are the perfection of informal gifts,[42] creation of informal easements[43] and the settlement of boundary disputes.[44] Leases offer fruitful opportunities for claims to informal grants,[45] renewals,[46] and licences to assign.[47] However, claims to shared beneficial entitlement have to be raised under constructive trust doctrine.[48] The expectation may be that normal priority will be waived,[49] and estoppel has long been used to determine loss of priority between mortgage-lenders.[50]

---

[35] *Crabb* v. *Arun DC* [1976] Ch 179, 187.

[36] *JT Developments* v. *Quinn* (1991) 62 P & CR 33, 45.

[37] (1866) LR 1 HL 129, 170; *Dann* v. *Spurrier* (1802) 7 Ves 231, 32 ER 94, Eldon LC.

[38] *Inwards* v. *Baker* [1965] 2 QB 29 37A; *ER Ives Investment* v. *High* [1967] 2 QB 379, 394; *Crabb* v. *Arun DC* [1976] Ch 179, 188D; MP Thompson [1983] *CLJ* 257.

[39] *Midland Bank* v. *Farmpride Hatcheries* [1981] 2 EGLR 147, 151K, Oliver LJ; *Taylors Fashions* v. *Liverpool Victoria Trustees Co* [1982] QB 133n, 144; *JT Developments* v. *Quinn* (1991) 62 P & CR 33, 45, Ralph Gibson LJ.

[40] *Lee-Parker* v. *Izzet (No 2)* [1972] 1 WLR 775, 780–781; *Preston & Henderson* v. *St Helens MBC* (1989) 58 P & CR 500, 503; *Brinnard* v. *Ewens* (1987) 19 HLR 415, CA.

[41] *Griffiths* v. *Williams* [1978] 2 EGLR 121, CA; *JT Developments* v. *Quinn* (1991) 62 P & CR 33.

[42] *Dillwyn* v. *Llewellyn* (1862) 4 De GF & J 517, 45 ER 1285; *Voyce* v. *Voyce* (1991) 62 P & CR 290; JE Martin [1992] *Conv* 53, 56.

[43] *Ward* v. *Kirkland* [1967] Ch 194; *ER Ives Investment* v. *High* [1967] 2 QB 379, 394; *Crabb* v. *Arun DC* [1976] Ch 179, CA; *Montague* v. *Long* (1972) 24 P & CR 240.

[44] *Hopgood* v. *Brown* [1955] 1 WLR 213; *Penfold* v. *Penfold* [1978] NLJ 736.

[45] *Ramsden* v. *Dyson* (1866) LR 1 HL 129; *Siew Soon Wah* v. *Yong Tong Hong* [1973] AC 836, PC; *Daejean Properties* v. *Mahoney* (1996) 28 HLR 498, CA.

[46] *Huning* v. *Ferrers* (1711) Gilb Rep 85, 25 ER 59 (the oldest identifiable case?); *JT Developments* v. *Quinn* (1991) 62 P & CR 33, CA.

[47] *Dann* v. *Spurrier* (1802) 7 Ves 231, 32 ER 94; *Willmott* v. *Barber* (1880) 15 Ch D 96 (both unsuccessful).

[48] *Lloyds Bank* v. *Rosset* [1991] 1 AC 107, 132–134, Lord Bridge; see above **[17.29]**.

[49] *Taylors Fashions* [1982] QB 133n, Oliver J; PV Baker (1981) 97 *LQR* 513; P Jackson [1982] *Conv* 450; see above **[21.42]**.

[50] *Steed* v. *Whitaker* (1740) Barn Ch 220, 27 ER 621; see below **[28.23ff]**.

Older cases were concerned with the use of proprietary estoppel to create interests in land, including fixtures.[51] Promissory estoppel suffices for personal licences,[52] but the proprietary form of estoppel *may* create interests in other forms of property,[53] including all forms of personal property,[54] so that land is treated the same as not-land on death.[55] The doctrine is however limited to rights in property, and cannot create a right to continue an existing planning use which would otherwise be a breach of planning control.[56]

2. Expectations of gift

[23.08] *Dillwyn* v. *Llewellyn*[57] demonstrated the use of estoppel to perfect a gift after detrimental reliance on the promise of a gift. The quantum of detriment may be small, as in *Pascoe* v. *Turner*.[58] After the breakdown of the relationship between a couple, the woman stayed in the house and spent £230 or so on redecoration, improvements and repair, after the man had promised her that the house was hers, and he knew that she was improving what she believed to be her property. Transfer of the house was the minimum required to satisfy the woman's equity. Disproportion between the amount spent and the value received is inevitable, but gives an inescapable feeling of injustice to the man.[59]

3. Expectations of inheritance

[23.09] Proprietary estoppel may raise expectations of inheritance, thus overcoming the inadequacies of family provision legislation,[60] but only after a promise or an induced belief that a gift will be made.[61] Lack of precision in the promise will not prevent the creation of an equitable right.[62] In *Re Basham*[63] a couple looked after the woman's father-in-law believing that on his death she would inherit his house, an expectation ultimately fulfilled by the court order against his personal representative. So also in *Wayling* v. *Jones*,[64] after a homosexual man died having promised his part-

---

[51] *Hamp* v. *Bygrave* [1983] 1 EGLR 174.

[52] *Maharaj* v. *Chand* [1986] AC 898, PC.

[53] *Amalgamated Investment & Property Co* v. *Texas Commerce International Bank* [1982] QB 84, 120–122, Lord Denning MR, 102–103, Robert Goff J.

[54] *Re Foster (No 2)* [1938] 3 All ER 610; *Pacol* v. *Trade Lines* [1982] 1 Lloyds Rep 456, 467–468, Webster J; *Moorgate Mercantile Co* v. *Twitchings* [1976] QB 225, 242, Lord Denning; MP Thompson [1983] *CLJ* 257, 272–275.

[55] S Naresh (1980) 96 *LQR* 534, 539–542.

[56] *Western Fish Products* v. *Penwith DC* [1981] 2 All ER 204, CA.

[57] (1862) 4 De GF & J 517; 45 ER 1285; see above **[23.03]**.

[58] [1979] 1 WLR 431, CA, FR Crane [1979] *Conv* 379; B Sufrin (1979) 42 *MLR* 574; S Moriarty (1984) 100 *LQR* 376, 379–382.

[59] See below **[23.36]**.

[60] S Naresh (1980) 96 *LQR* 534, 539–542; CJ Davis [1996] *Conv* 193.

[61] *Windeler* v. *Whitehall* [1990] 2 FLR 505, Millett J.

[62] At 1508.

[63] [1986] 1 WLR 1498; JE Martin [1987] *Conv* 211; DJ Hayton [1987] *CLJ* 215; M Davey (1988) 8 *LS* 92; *Jones* v. *Watkins* [1987], CA; *Burrows* v. *Burrows & Sharp* (1991) 23 HLR 82, CA; S Jones [1992] *NLJ* 320; JE Martin [1992] *Conv* 54.

[64] (1995) 69 P & CR 170, CA; *Morritt* v. *Wonham* [1993] CLYB 553; *Durant* v. *Heritage* [1994] EGCS 134.

ner of 16 years to leave him the hotel they had managed together, the survivor was held to be entitled to the value of the hotel.

One view was that a promise to make a will could not create an estoppel since a will is always revocable so that there was no promise that the inheritance promised would never be revoked.[65] That is no longer the law. A different line was taken in *Gillett* v. *Holt*[66] in which case a promise of inheritance was even enforced against a donor who was still alive. Gillett worked for Holt from the age of 16, becoming farm manager and working for almost 30 years at a reduced salary. In 1964 and periodically thereafter, Holt made unambiguous promises that Gillett would inherit the farm on Holt's death. Holt eventually met a young man who moved into his farmhouse, after which Gillett was cut out of Holt's will and dismissed. Gillett was held to have an exceptionally strong claim on Holt's conscience. Nevertheless, the decision to award him the farm, thus interfering with his freedom of testation, is likely to be highly controversial.[67] Estoppel can also perfect a will where the correct formalities for a will have not been used.[68]

4. No expectation

[23.10] Detriment alone creates no property right. Detriment only counts if it is incurred in response to an expectation, and one that is induced by the property owner. Developers who knew that consent was required from the charity commissioners had no expectation that they could contract without that consent.[69] Neighbours who approved a developer's plans in no way created the expectation that eaves of new houses could overhang.[70] A person who builds on land knowing it is not his raises no equity in his own favour.[71] If terms are never agreed there is no expectation.[72]

D. CONTRACTUAL EXPECTATIONS

[23.11] A formal contract creates rights which can only find expression in a contractual action.[73] Estoppel is useful where there is an arrangement which is essentially contractual but which lacks one of the crucial elements of a valid contract.

---

[65] *Taylor* v. *Dickens* [1998] 1 FLR 806; MP Thompson [1998] *Conv* 210; *Gillett* v. *Holt* [1998] 3 All ER 917, Carnwath J at first instance.

[66] [2001] Ch 210, CA.

[67] M Dixon [1999] *Conv* 46; P Milne [1999] *CLJ* 25; M Dixon [2000] *CLJ* 453; S Nield (2000) 20 *LS* 85.

[68] *Campbell* v. *Griffin* [2001] EWCA Civ 990, [2001] WTLR 981.

[69] *Haslemere Estates* v. *Baker* [1982] 1 WLR 1109, Megarry V–C; *Watkins* v. *Emslie* [1982] 1 EGLR 81, CA.

[70] *Ward* v. *Gold* (1969) 211 EG 155.

[71] *Ramsden* v. *Dyson* (1866) LR 1 HL 129.

[72] *Orgee* v. *Orgee* [1997] EGCS 152, CA; M Pawlowski (1998) 114 *LQR* 351; *Southwark LBC* v. *Logan* (1997) 29 HLR 40, CA; *Pridean* v. *Forest Taverns* (1998) 75 P & CR 447, CA.

[73] *Lloyds Bank* v. *Carrick* [1996] 4 All ER 630, CA.

1. Contractual variation

[23.12] Estoppels have been developed in categories but all are in one sense part of a wider doctrine.[74] Estoppel by convention[75] arises where the parties to a transaction proceed on the basis of a shared assumption which does not correspond strictly with their contractual rights. It may be an error of fact or law, and based on a misrepresentation or a mistake. Neither party can go back on the shared assumption,[76] when it would be unconscionable to do so.[77] Thus if both parties to a lease lose sight of the fact that it included a covenant against assignment, the landlords are estopped from objecting to a sale in breach of covenant.[78] *John* v. *George*[79] is a good example of a shared assumption that a particular scheme for repairing fire damage would be proceeded with as a complete package or not at all. Even a common misunderstanding is insufficient to change the law.[80]

Promissory estoppel varies the rights or remedies[81] under an existing contractual relationship,[82] usually only temporarily.[83] Again it cannot override general principles of law, or negate the operation of a statute.[84] Any alteration of position based on the promise is sufficient, perhaps even performance of an existing contractual duty.[85] Proprietary estoppel overlaps with promissory where a person makes a promise that strict contractual rights relating to property will not be enforced. Detrimental reliance is essential, but if this is established there are advantages in switching to the more macho doctrine: it overcomes imprecision,[86] sanctions permanent variations, and reaches beyond the confines of the privity of contract.[87]

2. Informal contracts

[23.13] The use of proprietary estoppel to enforce contracts lacking proper written formality has already been considered.[88]

---

[74] *Taylors Fashions* v. *Liverpool Victoria Trustee Co* (1979) [1982] QB 133n, Oliver J.

[75] *Johnson* v. *Gore Wood* [2002] 2 AC 1, HL; J Dawson (1989) 9 *LS* 16; H Linnare (1991) 12 *BLR* 185; M Harvey (1995) 23 *ABLR* 45.

[76] *Amalgamated Investment and Property Co* v. *Texas Commerce International Bank* [1982] QB 84, 122.

[77] *Wilson Bowden Properties* v. *Milnes & Bardon 22* [1995] NPC 182, Blackburne J.

[78] *Troop* v. *Gibson* [1986] 1 EGLR 1, CA (rent review).

[79] [1996] 1 EGLR 7, CA; *Crédit Suisse* v. *Beegas Nominees* [1994] 4 All ER 803 Lindsay J; *Dun & Bradstreet Software Services (England)* v. *Provident Mutual Life Assurance Association* [1998] 2 EGLR 175, CA (validity of break notice).

[80] *Keen* v. *Holland* [1984] 1 WLR 251, CA.

[81] MP Thompson [1983] *CLJ* 257, 258–263.

[82] *High Trees* [1947] KB 130, Denning J; *Brikom Investments* v. *Carr* [1979] QB 467, 482G, Lord Denning MR.

[83] *Ajayi* v. *RT Briscoe (Nigeria)* [1964] 1 WLR 1326, PC; *Panoutsos* v. *Raymond Hadley Corp of NY* [1917] 2 KB 473, CA (notice required).

[84] *Beesly* v. *Hallwood Estates* [1960] 1 WLR 549, 560–561, Buckley J.

[85] *WJ Alan & Co* v. *El Nasir Export & Import Co* [1972] 2 QB 189.

[86] *Holiday Inns* v. *Broadhead* (1974) 232 EG 951, 1087, Robert Goff J; P Todd [1981] *Conv* 347, 350; MP Thompson [1983] *CLJ* 257, 275–277. Contrast *Ramsden* v. *Dyson* (1866) LR 1 HL 129, 170, Lord Kingsdown; *Taylors Fashions* [1982] QB 133n, 144, Oliver J.

[87] *Brikom Investments* v. *Carr* [1979] QB 467, CA; *Hazel* v. *Akhtar* [2001] EWCA Civ 1883, [2002] 2 P & CR 17 at 240 (rent always accepted late).

[88] See above **[22.38]**.

3. Contract-like arrangements

[23.14] Proprietary estoppel stands alone when there is an arrangement to create a property right which falls short of being an enforceable contract. The trouble may be lack of formality, a likelihood increased by the recent tightening of formality,[89] since no contract exists without writing, but there may be an equity raised by the expectation of contractual entitlement. The plaintiff in *Lim Teng Huan* v. *Ang Swee Chuan*[90] secured the enforcement of an informal agreement for the exchange of a half interest in land after spending $1m building a house on the site. Other arrangements enforced by estoppel may be too imprecise to be contractual. *ER Ives Investment* v. *High*[91] concerned an arrangement to allow the foundations of flats to remain on High's land in return for a right of way over the forecourt of the flats. Again in *Crabb* v. *Arun DC*[92] an oral arrangement for the council to allow a right of access to Crabb's land fell short of a contract. However, estoppel cannot achieve what an express contract could not.[93]

4. Subject to contract negotiations

[23.15] Where parties are negotiating "subject to contract" neither has an expectation that rights will be created. *Attorney-General of Hong Kong* v. *Humphreys Estate (Queen's Gardens)*[94] demonstrates this *in excelsis*, since the government had demolished a block of flats even though the developers made clear that they retained the right to resile from the arrangement. No expectation, so no estoppel. Worse, any expenses incurred subject to contract are irrecoverable.[95]

Very exceptionally the "subject to contract" qualification might be removed after a direct representation that a contract will be concluded. In *Salvation Army Trustee Co* v. *West Yorkshire MBC*,[96] a contract for acquisition of a new site for a Salvation Army hall was linked to negotiations for the disposal of the site of the old hall for road widening, and, even though negotiations for acquisition of the old site remained "subject to contract", the council became bound to complete the acquisition by estoppel after allowing the trustees to spend money on buying and building a new hall. Similar facts in *JT Developments* v. *Quinn*[97] divided the Court of Appeal, but a majority upheld a claim based on proprietary estoppel.

---

[89] LP (MP) A 1989 s 2.

[90] [1992] 1 WLR 113, PC.

[91] [1967] 2 QB 379; FR Crane (1967) 31 *Conv (NS)* 332; HW Wilkinson (1967) 30 *MLR* 530; SJ Bailey [1968] *CLJ* 26; *Thatcher* v. *Douglas* [1996] NLJ 282 (contractual).

[92] [1976] Ch 179, CA; FR Crane (1976) 40 *Conv (NS)* 156; P Atiyah (1976) 92 *LQR* 174; P Millett (1976) 92 *LQR* 342.

[93] *Daejean Properties* v. *Mahoney* (1996) 28 HLR 498, CA.

[94] [1987] AC 114, PC; *Derby & Co* v. *ITC Pension Trust* [1977] 2 All ER 890, Oliver J; *Mecca Leisure* v. *London Residuary Body* [1988] CLYB 1375, Mervyn Davies J; *James* v. *Evans* [2000] 3 EGLR 1, CA.

[95] *Regalian Properties* v. *London Dockland Development Corp* [1995] 1 WLR 212, Rattee J.

[96] (1981) 41 P & CR 179; JT Farrand [1983] *Conv* 85; *Att-Gen of Hong Kong* [1987] AC 114, 126–128, Lord Templeman.

[97] (1991) 62 P & CR 33, CA.

5.   Contract and estoppel discrete

[23.16] Contract and estoppel may arise on similar facts. Suppose A contracts to transfer his house to B in return for B's promise to pay a price of £19,000, giving rise to an executory contract. If B then pays the price, the position might be analysed in terms of an executed contract or in terms of an expectation created by A's promise on which B has relied to his detriment. It becomes vital to resolve this overlap if A sells the land, for B's contractual entitlement requires registration, whereas an estoppel right might be protected by occupation or notice.

Lloyds Bank v. *Carrick*[98] decided that the buyer's rights arose exclusively under contract. Carrick suggested to his sister-in-law, after she had been widowed, that she should move into one of his leasehold maisonettes. She sold her house, moved into the maisonette, and paid £19,000 to her brother-in-law. After a mortgage of the maisonette to the bank and default in repayment of the loan, the bank's entitlement to possession against Mr Carrick was clear. They were also held to be entitled to possession against his sister-in-law. Mrs Carrick had rights under a valid contract[99] affecting the unregistered leasehold title, which was void against the bank as an unregistered land charge.[100] Morritt LJ rejected arguments in the alternative for Mrs Carrick based on a bare trust, a constructive trust, or an estoppel right, refusing in particular to allow proprietary estoppel to duplicate the trust arising under an enforceable contract. Mrs Carrick's estate contract was defeated by non-registration.

The decision in *Carrick* appears to run directly contrary to the Court of Appeal decision in *ER Ives Investment* v. *High*.[101] An oral contract allowed access to a garage over the forecourt of a block of flats in return for permission to retain encroaching foundations. Equitable easements were registrable as a class D(iii) land charge. Lord Denning justified enforcement of the unregistered estoppel right by narrowing the class of registrable equitable easements to take High's right outside it. Winn LJ preferred to treat any right created by estoppel as an independent equity which was capable of binding a purchaser with notice of it. *Carrick* also casts doubt on Geoffrey Cheshire's[102] characterisation of the unilateral contract case *Errington* v. *Errington*[103] as one of estoppel. Had Mrs Carrick's contract been made under the 1989 Act formalities, she would have won, since no contract would exist without writing so an estoppel could be raised.[104]

---

[98] [1996] 4 All ER 630, CA; MP Thompson [1996] *Conv* 295; P Ferguson (1996) 112 *LQR* 549.

[99] It pre-dated LP (MP) A 1989 s 2, so an oral contract was enforceable on the basis of part performance.

[100] *Midland Bank Trust Co* v. *Green* [1981] AC 513, HL discusses the position under an executory contract before payment of the price, but should not prevent an expectation enforceable by estoppel after the price is paid: MP Thompson [1983] *CLJ* 257, 275.

[101] [1967] 2 QB 379, CA; G Battersby (1995) 58 *MLR* 637, 646.

[102] GC Cheshire (1953) 16 *MLR* 1; A Everton (1976) 40 *Conv* (NS) 416, 421; HWR Wade (1952) 68 *LQR* 337; AD Hargreaves (1953) 69 *LQR* 466; A Briggs [1981] *Conv* 212, 218; MP Thompson [1983] *Conv* 50; A Briggs [1983] *Conv* 285; MP Thompson [1983] *Conv* 471; J Hill (1988) 51 *MLR* 226, 232.

[103] [1952] 1 KB 290, CA.

[104] MP Thompson [1990] *Conv* 295.

E. INDUCEMENT

[23.17] Inducement is the magic ingredient which binds the property owner to meet the claimant's expectation. A spectacular demonstration of non-inducement is provided by *Attorney-General of Hong Kong* v. *Humphreys Estate (Queen's Gardens)*[105] A block of flats was swapped for a development site, each side taking possession before exchange of contracts. Even though it was "impossible for the government to go back and unthinkable for HKL not to go forward,"[106] both parties knew that the matter remained in negotiation and the developers never surrendered the right to withdraw. Hence HKL had neither created nor encouraged any belief in the Government.[107]

1.   Unconscionability as sole test of inducement

[23.18] Possible forms of inducement are so various that hard and fast rules are inappropriate. It might be standing by, passive encouragement, active encouragement, stimulating expenditure, or not objecting to it. Three main case-law compartments (active, passive and mixed) are by no means comprehensive, and they may all be sub-heads of a wider test of unconscionability first proposed by Ungoed-Thomas J[108] but taken up and developed in *Taylors Fashions* v. *Liverpool Victoria Trustees Co.*[109] Oliver J favoured a single question: in the particular circumstances would it be unconscionable for a party to be permitted to deny that which, knowingly or unknowingly, he has allowed or encouraged another to assume to his detriment?[110] Unconscionability is approved as a test for inducement by the Court of Appeal[111] and in the Privy Council.[112] In *John* v. *George*,[113] for example, the owner secured an advantage that he could not otherwise have obtained, by requesting the claimant's co-operation, and knowing that he had not agreed to forego his rights. Older authorities remain indicative of how to apply the new test of unconscionability. Tidy jurisprudential development has been distorted by the restrictive "probanda" set out by Fry J in *Willmott* v. *Barber*.[114]

---

[105] [1987] AC 114, PC; *Haslemere Estates* v. *Baker* [1982] 1 WLR 1109; *Boxbusher Properties* v. *Graham* [1976] 2 EGLR 58 (agents gave no assurance); *Western Fish Products* v. *Penwith DC* [1981] 2 All ER 204, CA; *Taylors Fashions* v. *Liverpool Victoria Trustees Co* [1982] QB 133n (reliance on own solicitors).

[106] *Att-Gen of Hong Kong* at 124F, Lord Templeman.

[107] Contrast *Lim Teng Huan* v. *Ang Swee Chuan* [1992] 1 WLR 113, PC; SH Goo [1993] *Conv* 173.

[108] *Ward* v. *Kirkland* [1967] Ch 194, 239.

[109] [1982] QB 133, 151H, 155C; PV Baker (1981) 97 *LQR* 513; P Jackson [1982] *Conv* 450.

[110] At 151H, 155C.

[111] *Habib Bank* v. *Habib Bank Zurich* [1981] 1 WLR 1265, PV Baker (1981) 97 *LQR* 513; *John* v. *George* [1996] 1 EGLR 7, CA; *Lloyds Bank* v. *Carrick* [1996] 4 All ER 630, CA.

[112] *Lim Teng Huan* v. *Ang Swee Chuan* [1992] 1 WLR 113, PC; SH Goo [1993] *Conv* 173; *Swallow Securities* v. *Isenberg* [1985] 1 EGLR 132, CA.

[113] [1996] 1 EGLR 7, CA.

[114] (1880) 15 Ch D 96, 105–106; MP Thompson [1983] *CLJ* 257, 269–272.

2. Active inducement

[23.19] Lord Kingsdown recognised in *Ramsden* v. *Dyson*[115] that an estoppel may arise "under a verbal agreement". One form of active inducement is to request another to spend money, an example being the jetty built in *Plimmer* v. *Wellington Corporation* at the behest of the New Zealand government for the reception of immigrants.[116] A second is direct encouragement of which *Inwards* v. *Baker* (1965)[117] now ranks as a veteran, and classic, example. A father said to son "Why don't you build the bungalow on my land and make it a bit bigger?" With this encouragement the son's work on the bungalow created an estoppel.[118] Active inducement may also consist of a pseudo-contractual oral agreement,[119] exemplified in *ER Ives Investment* v. *High*.[120] The agreement to permit access over the forecourt of the flats induced an expectation in estoppel terms that an access would be allowed. It was in essence a unilateral promise.[121]

Active encouragement diverged from passive inducement in *Ramsden* v. *Dyson*.[122] Thornton[123] took a building plot in the suburbs of Huddersfield from Ramsden as a tenant at will, but with a promise from the owner's agents that he could have a long lease at any time.[124] Lord Cranworth LC decided that any inducement was purely passive and insufficient to raise any estoppel.[125] Fry J's restrictive probanda[126] derive from this opinion. Lord Kingsdown felt that the agent had actively created an expectation of entitlement to a long lease,[127] the source of the modern consensus that active cases are unaffected by the probanda.[128] Knowledge of the expenditure is not necessary.[129]

---

[115] (1866) LR 1 HL 129, 170; *Midland Bank* v. *Farmpride Hatcheries* [1981] 2 EGLR 147, 151K, Oliver LJ.

[116] (1884) 9 App Cas 699, PC.

[117] [1965] 2 QB 29, CA; RH Maudsley (1965) 81 *LQR* 183; FR Crane (1965) 29 *Conv (NS)* 222; *Voyce* v. *Voyce* (1991) 62 P & CR 290; JE Martin [1992] *Conv* 56.

[118] *Re Basham* [1986] 1 WLR 1498; JE Martin [1987] *Conv* 211; DJ Hayton [1987] *CLJ* 215; M Davey (1988) 8 *LS* 92.

[119] *Ramsden* v. *Dyson* (1866) LR 1 HL 129, 170, Lord Kingsdown; *Devonshire* v. *Eglin* (1851) 14 Beav 530, 51 ER 389; *Beaufort* v. *Patrick* (1853) 17 Beav 60, 78, 51 ER 954.

[120] [1967] 2 QB 379, 394; FR Crane (1967) 31 *Conv (NS)* 332; HW Wilkinson (1967) 30 *MLR* 580; SJ Bailey [1968] *CLJ* 26.

[121] *Crabb* v. *Arun DC* [1976] Ch 179, 187, 188; *Brikom Investments* v. *Carr* [1979] QB 467, CA; *Windeler* v. *Whitehall* [1990] 2 FLR 505, Millett J (unsuccessful).

[122] (1866) LR 1 HL 129; *Plimmer* v. *Wellington Corporation* (1884) 9 App Cas 699, 710–712, Sir A Hobhouse; *Michaud* v. *Montreal City* (1923) 92 LJPC 161.

[123] Dyson was a money lender.

[124] No estoppel is raised simply because of the landlord's long practice of renewing leases: *Keelwalk Properties* v. *Waller* [2002] EWCA Civ 1076, [2002] 48 EG 142.

[125] (1866) LR 1 HL 129, 140–141; *Weller* v. *Stone* (1885) 54 LJ Ch 497, CA; *Att-Gen to Prince of Wales* v. *Collom* [1916] 2 KB 193.

[126] *Willmott* v. *Barber* (1880) 15 Ch D 96, 106, Fry J.

[127] *Ramsden* (1866) LR 1 HL 129, 170–173 (dissenting); *Pascoe* v. *Turner* [1979] 1 WLR 431, 436G, Cumming Bruce LJ.

[128] *Crabb* v. *Arun DC* [1976] Ch 179, 195, Scarman LJ.

[129] *JT Developments* v. *Quinn* (1991) 62 P & CR 33, CA.

3.   Passive inducement

[23.20] Lord Eldon LC said that "the circumstance of looking on is in many cases as strong as using terms of encouragement."[130] The duty to be active to correct a unilateral mistake arises only if the case meets all five of the "probanda" stated by Fry J in *Willmott* v. *Barber*.[131] These deal with (1) expectation, (2) detrimental reliance, and (5) passive inducement by acquiescence, leaving (3) and (4) as the keys, the ones which restrict passive inducement to a known mistake.

> (3): The landowner must have known of the existence of his own right inconsistent with the claimant's right; and
>
> (4): The landowner must know of the claimant's mistaken belief.

(1) Knowledge of the claim (probandum 3)

[23.21] The landowner will generally be alerted to the claimant's mistaken belief of his rights when work is carried out on his land.[132] In the seminal case,[133] the Duke of Beaufort stood by while a canal was built, and could not afterwards ask for it to be filled in. Knowledge of the work must be sufficient to convey the fact of a claim. No right to a long term option arose in *Taylors Fashions* from the installation by the tenants of a lift in the landlord's shop, since they might have been improving their shop for the remainder of their existing term.[134] Conversely a property owner who is unaware of the work is not bound by an estoppel. In *Willmott* v. *Barber* itself[135] direct evidence that the *landlord* knew that the proposed subtenant was spending money did not in any way estop the *head landlord*. In *J Willis & Son* v. *Willis* unknown expenditure on installing central heating and a new bathroom suite could raise no estoppel.[136] Passive inducement occurs only when a landowner stands by with knowledge of the expenditure.

(2) A known mistake (probandum 4)

[23.22] Not only must the landowner know of the claimant's belief, but he must also know that the claimant is mistaken. Fry J's third probandum[137] is that "the owner of the legal right, must know of the existence of his own right which is inconsistent with the right claimed". *Matharu* v. *Matharu*[138] shows that it is possible to establish a

---

[130] *Dann* v. *Spurrier* (1802) 7 Ves 231, 237–238, 32 ER 94.

[131] (1880) 15 Ch D 96, 105–106, Fry J.

[132] *Ramsden* v. *Dyson* (1866) LR 1 HL 129, 140, Cranworth LC.

[133] *Duke of Beaufort* v. *Patrick* (1853) 17 Beav 60, 78, 51 ER 954.

[134] [1982] QB 133n, 156–157; *Willmott* v. *Barber* (1880) 15 Ch D 96, 106.

[135] (1880) 15 Ch D 96, 106–107; *Darnley* v. *London & Chatham & Dover Rly* (1867) LR 2 HL 43; *Evans* v. *Smallcombe* (1868) LR 3 HL 249; *Banque Jacques Cartier* v. *Banque d' Épargne de Montreal* (1887) 13 App Cas 111, PC; *Rees* v. *de Bernardy* [1896] 2 Ch 437.

[136] [1986] 1 EGLR 62, CA; MP Thompson [1986] *Conv* 406; *Swallow Securities* v. *Isenberg* [1985] 1 EGLR 132, CA; *Brinnard* v. *Ewens* (1987) 19 HLR 415, CA; *Ward* v. *Gold* (1969) 211 EG 155; *Gross* v. *French* [1976] 1 EGLR 129, CA.

[137] *Willmott* v. *Barber* (1880) 15 Ch D 96, 105–106, Fry J; *Ramsden* v. *Dyson* (1866) LR 1 HL 129, 141 Lord Cranworth LC; *Dann* v. *Spurrier* (1802) 7 Ves 231, 235, 32 ER 94, Eldon LC.

[138] (1994) 68 P & CR 93, CA; G Battersby (1995) 7 *CFLQ* 59; M Welstead [1995] *Conv* 61.

unilateral mistake. A wife dropped legal proceedings against her husband claiming rights in the matrimonial home, which was actually owned by her father-in-law, but he had stood by and allowed her to withdraw her proceedings knowing that she believed her husband to be owner, so the father-in-law was estopped from asserting ownership.

Many cases like *Kammins Ballrooms Co* v. *Zenith Investments (Torquay)*[139] are unsuccessful because the land owner shares the claimant's mistake. The tenant acted to his detriment by deferring his application for a new tenancy until it was too late to make a timely application, but this undoubted mistake was common to the landlord, who was not estopped.

4. Intermediate inducement

[23.23] Estoppel cases present infinitely variable facts, which often refuse to fall neatly into the active/passive dichotomy.

(1) Active elements

[23.24] *Willmott* v. *Barber* is most easily evaded by finding active elements in apparent passivity. *ER Ives Investment* v. *High*[140] was analysed by Lord Denning MR[141] partly as an expectation created by conduct, but the need for flexibility in the categorisation of inducement is made much more forcibly in *Crabb* v. *Arun DC*. The council failed to stop Crabb selling other land leaving his last plot landlocked and failed to disabuse him of his belief that he had an access at a new point where the council had erected a gate (both passive) but an active element[142] was the oral promise of additional access made by an officer of the council.[143]

(2) Proprietary estoppel by representation

[23.25] Estoppel by representation prevents a person denying the truth of a statement of an existing fact which he has made.[144] It operates at common law, is personal in character, and does not create proprietary rights. After the claimant has acted upon the representation to his detriment a proprietary estoppel can arise. This binds later owners, and includes statements of future intention as well as representations of existing fact.

---

[139] [1971] AC 850, HL; *Taylor's Fashions* [1982] QB 133n, 157A (contrast the *Olds* case); *Michaels* v. *Harley House (Marylebone)* [1997] 1 WLR 967, Lloyd J; on appeal [2000] Ch 104, CA.

[140] [1967] 2 QB 379, CA; FR Crane (1967) 31 *Conv (NS)* 332; HW Wilkinson (1967) 30 *MLR* 580; SJ Bailey [1968] *CLJ* 26.

[141] At 394.

[142] [1976] Ch 179, 187, Lord Denning MR; compare at 196–197, Scarman LJ.

[143] Lack of authority of its officers was no defence: *Crabb* at 189AH, 193C; *Ramsden* v. *Dyson* (1866) LR 1 HL 129; *Att-Gen to Prince of Wales* v. *Collom* [1916] 2 KB 193, 203; *Moorgate Mercantile Co* v. *Twitchings* [1976] QB 225, 243.

[144] *Jorden* v. *Money* (1845) 5 HLC 185, 10 ER 868; DC Jackson (1965) 81 *LQR* 84, 223.

Intermediate inducement cases have often been analysed in terms of a representa-tion.[145] *Hopgood* v. *Brown*[146] found that the erection of a garage by a builder was a representation that it was built on land to be conveyed to the purchaser and not on adjoining plot retained by the builder. Both the builder and the new owner of that adjoining house were bound.

Where inducement is by representation it is generally[147] thought that the *Willmott* v. *Barber* probanda are irrelevant.[148] In *Olds*[149] landlords told Olds that it could have a long term lease of no 20, though in fact it could be broken when the lease of no 21 ended, and the landlord could end it after only 28 years if a neighbouring tenant (Taylors Fashions) did not renew their lease. Unknown to both Taylors Fashions and the landlords, the Taylor Fashions option was actually void for non-registration. An implied representation to Olds of the option's continuing validity took the *Olds* case outside the need for the five probanda and away from the restriction to unilateral mistake.

(3) Common mistake

[23.26] Despite some confusion in the authorities,[150] a common mistake is best treated as an unadulterated issue of unconscionability, as it was in *John* v. *George*.[151] After the uninsured Allt Isaf Farm had burnt down, the landlord was unable to afford the repair. By arrangement between landlord and tenant intended as a single package, planning permission was sought for conversion of the burnt out remains of the farm building to a house and for a small bungalow to house the tenant farmer. Events turned sour on the tenant when planning permission was given for conversion of the old farm buildings, but refused for the bungalow. The landlord exploited this by using the permission for non-agricultural use as a ground for ending the tenant's agricul-tural security of tenure. Morritt LJ decided that an estoppel arose from the common misapprehension, ignoring the *Willmott* v. *Barber* probanda.

---

[145] If the representation is misinterpreted, estoppel is based on the expectation fairly raised in the mind of the claimant, whether or not intended: *Moorgate Mercantile Co* v. *Twitchings* [1976] QB 225, 242, Lord Denning MR.

[146] [1955] 1 WLR 213, CA; *Montague* v. *Long* (1972) 24 P & CR 240; *Brikom Investments* v. *Carr* [1979] QB 467, CA; *JT Developments* v. *Quinn* (1991) 62 P & CR 33.

[147] But see: *Crabb* v. *Arun DC* [1976] Ch 179, 195, Scarman LJ; *E & L Berg Homes* v. *Grey* [1980] 1 EGLR 103; *Swallow Securities* v. *Isenberg* [1985] 1 EGLR 132, 134, CA; *Coombes* v. *Smith* [1986] 1 WLR 808; *Matharu* v. *Matharu* (1994) 68 P & CR 93, CA.

[148] *Hopgood* v. *Brown* [1955] 1 WLR 213, 223, Lord Evershed MR; *Canadian Pacific Rly Co* v. *R* [1931] AC 414, 429, Lord Russell; *Electrolux* v. *Electrix* (1953) 71 RPC 23, 33, Evershed MR; *Shaw* v. *Applegate* [1977] 1 WLR 970, 978, 980, Goff LJ.

[149] Reported with *Taylors Fashions* [1982] QB 133n, 157C–159A; PV Baker (1981) 97 *LQR* 573; P Jackson [1982] *Conv* 450.

[150] *Ramsden* v. *Dyson* (1866) LR 1 HL 129, 141, Cranworth LC; *Crabb* v. *Arun DC* [1976] Ch 179, 195E, Scarman LJ; *Taylors Fashions* [1982] QB 133n, 152, Oliver J.

[151] [1996] 1 EGLR 7, CA.

F. DETRIMENTAL RELIANCE

[23.27] Lord Eldon LC recognised an equity based on laying out money or acts which the claimant would not otherwise have done.[152] Fry J transmuted this principle into his second probandum that "the plaintiff must have expended some money or must have done some act (not necessarily upon the defendant's land) on the faith of his mistaken belief."[153] This element is unquestionable.[154] Without a detriment all cases have failed,[155] though it need not be in money,[156] and proof of detriment created a presumption of reliance.[157] makes it inequitable for the landowner to insist on his strict legal rights. Although the requirement of detriment has been developed separately in the two doctrines, proprietary estoppel and constructive trust doctrine can in future cross-fertilise.[158]

1. Detriment

[23.28] Many reported cases have involved money payments, for example part payment of the purchase price supporting a claim to a licence to reside in the property.[159] Work quantifiable in money also qualifies, for example building a house, an extension, or a garage, effecting improvements,[160] decoration,[161] laying drains,[162] the extension of a jetty[163] or dredging a pond.[164] Substantial acts are equally efficacious,[165] as are minor acts with a cumulative effect,[166] but minimal acts can be ignored.[167] It may be selling land without reserving access rights,[168] or demolition. Failure to make a court application[169] can also be detrimental.

---

[152] *Dann* v. *Spurrier* (1802) 7 Ves 231, 235–236, 32 ER 94.

[153] *Willmott* v. *Barber* (1880) 15 Ch D 96, 105, Fry J; *Ramsden* v. *Dyson* (1866) LR 1 HL 129, 170, Lord Kingsdown.

[154] *Midland Bank* v. *Farmpride Hatcheries* [1981] 2 EGLR 147, 151K, Oliver LJ; *Re Sharpe* [1980] 1 WLR 219, 223E, Browne-Wilkinson J.

[155] *Bristol Cars* v. *RKH (Hotels)* (1978) 38 P & CR 411, 420, Templeman LJ; *Layton* v. *Martin* [1986] 2 FLR 227; *Coombes* v. *Smith* [1986] 1 WLR 808; *Stevens & Cutting* v. *Anderson* [1990] 1 EGLR 95, 97L, Stuart Smith LJ; *Bank of India* v. *Mody* [1998] 12 LSG 29, Ch D.

[156] *Greasley* v. *Cooke* [1980] 1 WLR 1306, 1311F, Lord Denning MR.

[157] At 1311H; *Gillett* v. *Holt* [2001] Ch 210, CA (onus on Holt).

[158] *Grant* v. *Edwards* [1986] Ch 638, 656F–H, Browne-Wilkinson V-C.

[159] *Jones* v. *Jones* [1977] 1 WLR 438, CA; *Preston & Henderson* v. *St Helens MBC* (1989) 58 P & CR 500; *Burrows* v. *Burrows & Sharp* (1991) 23 HLR 82, CA; *Baker* v. *Baker* (1993) 25 HLR 408.

[160] *Willmott* v. *Barber* (1880) 15 Ch D 96, Fry J, and many other cases.

[161] *Re Sharpe* [1980] 1 WLR 219.

[162] *Ward* v. *Kirkland* [1967] Ch 194.

[163] *Plimmer* v. *Wellington Corp* (1884) 9 App Cas 699, PC; *Montague* v. *Long* (1972) 24 P & CR 240 (erection of bridge).

[164] *Watson* v. *Goldsbrough* [1986] 1 EGLR 265, CA.

[165] *Greasley* v. *Cooke* [1980] 1 WLR 1306, 1311G.

[166] *Re Basham* [1986] 1 WLR 1498.

[167] *Penfold* v. *Penfold* [1978] NLJ 736 (erection of a post and wire fence).

[168] *Crabb* v. *Arun DC* [1976] Ch 179, CA; *Lombard North Central* v. *Stobart* [1990] Times March 2nd, CA.

[169] *Hammersmith & Fulham LBC* v. *Tops Shop Centres* [1990] Ch 237.

Suppose that a couple (A and B) shack up together in A's house. Does B suffer a detriment by doing so without acquiring property rights? In *Coombes* v. *Smith*[170] for example, no detriment was suffered when a woman left her husband, became pregnant by another man, moved into his house, and did decorating and gardening. Small acts of redecoration and repair sufficed in *Pascoe* v. *Turner*.[171] Other acts might include making mortgage payments,[172] caring for relatives,[173] and leaving existing accommodation,[174] or a job.[175] In *Greasley* v. *Cooke*[176] a woman, who had moved in as a housekeeper, had worked unpaid for many years, and had cared for a handicapped child, had obviously incurred a major detriment by deciding not to move elsewhere.[177] Carers may do much more than even most friendly lodger. One such in *Campbell* v. *Griffin*[178] was assured by an elderly couple that she would have a home for life. At the discretionary stage of satisfying the equity the weight of the detriment may become relevant.[179]

2. Reliance

[23.29] A detriment must be incurred honestly[180] and *in reliance on* the expectation created by the landowner.[181] The claimant must have spent money or acted in a way which he would not have done if the landowner had not built up an expectation in his mind.[182] In *Inwards* v. *Baker* the son built a bungalow on the father's field relying on the father's promise of security.[183] In *ER Ives Investment* v. *High*[184] High allowed the foundations of neighbouring flats to remain and built a garage facing the forecourt of the flats because he expected a right of access. *Pascoe* v. *Turner*[185] concerned a woman who repaired a house relying on a man's promise that the house was now hers. And so on for each successful case.

---

[170] [1986] 1 WLR 808; DJ Hayton [1986] *CLJ* 394; JE Martin [1988] *Conv* 59; L Flynn & A Lawson (1995) 3 *Fem LR* 105; U Riniker [1998] *Conv* 202.

[171] [1979] 1 WLR 431, CA; FR Crane [1979] *Conv* 379; B Sufrin (1979) 42 *MLR* 574.

[172] *Preston & Henderson* v. *St Helens MBC* (1989) 58 P & CR 500; *Burrows* v. *Burrows & Sharp* (1991) 23 HLR 82, CA.

[173] *Piquet* v. *Tyler* [1978] CLYB 119; *Burrows* as above.

[174] *Jones* v. *Jones* [1977] 1 WLR 438, CA; FR Crane (1977) 41 *Conv (NS)* 279; J Alder (1978) 41 *MLR* 208; *Piquet* as above; *Burrows* as above.

[175] *Jones* as above; *Gillett* v. *Holt* [2001] Ch 210, CA (staying in job at 10% below market salary).

[176] [1980] 1 WLR 1306, CA; RE Annand [1981] *Conv* 154; MP Thompson (1981) 125 *SJ* 539, G Woodman (1981) 44 *MLR* 461.

[177] At 1311E; she also worked without payment.

[178] [2001] EWCA Civ 990, [2001] WTLR 981, CA.

[179] See below **[23.36]**.

[180] *Lombard North Central* v. *Stobart* [1990] Times, March 2nd, CA. However, reliance on an estoppel by representation did not need to be reasonable: *Downderry Construction* v. *SS for Transport LG&R* [2002] EWHC 2, [2002] ACD 62, Richards J.

[181] A Lawson (1996) 16 *LS* 218; A Robertson (1998) 18 *LS* 360. A similar link is required for the change of position defence in restitution: *Scottish Equitable* v. *Derby* [2001] EWCA Civ 360, [2001] 3 All ER 818.

[182] S Nield "Estoppel and Reliance" ch 5 in E Cooke (ed) *Modern Studies in Property Law 1 – Property 2000* (Hart, 2001).

[183] [1965] 2 QB 29, CA.

[184] [1967] 2 QB 379, CA; FR Crane (1967) 31 *Conv (NS)* 332; HW Wilkinson (1967) 30 *MLR* 586; SJ Bailey [1968] *CLJ* 26.

[185] [1979] 1 WLR 431, CA; FR Crane [1979] *Conv* 379; B Sufrin (1979) 42 *MLR* 574.

Claimants rarely articulate their motives, so reliance has to be inferred from prov-
able facts,[186] or presumed. "Once it is shown that a representation was calculated to
influence the judgement of a reasonable man, the presumption is that he was so influenced."[187] So in *Greasley* v. *Cooke*[188] the fact that a live-in maid worked unpaid for
almost 30 years, looking after the family, and a handicapped daughter could only be
explained by a promise that she would be looked after. Lord Denning inferred
reliance in that case,[189] as have many subsequent judges.[190]

Reliance does not occur if the claimant was doing something which he would have
done anyway.[191] In *Willmott* v. *Barber*[192] the claimant laid out money on one acre of
land, which he already owned, and this was not detriment to support an option to
acquire the neighbouring three acre[193] Work done in the hope that a right will be
acquired creates no estoppel.[194] How to apply these principles to cohabitation
arrangements? In *Tanner* v. *Tanner*[195] the Court of Appeal found that a woman had
moved in with a man on an expectation of future security for the defendant and her
twin daughters.[196] As Browne-Wilkinson V-C said in *Grant* v. *Edwards*[197] it is often
impossible to tell how the claimant would have acted without the promise of an interest in the house: a couple in love will set up home together, have a baby, and share
housekeeping, all for love and without bargaining about ownership of the house. So
an expectation has to be proved and, once it is, reliance may be a correct inference.[198]
Similar problems arise in differentiating a person caring for an elderly relative who
merely hopes to inherit from a carer who has been looking after them following a
promise of inheritance.[199] Once again reliance is easy to infer once the expectation is
established.[200]

3. Estoppel without detriment

[23.30] *Promissory* estoppel does not require detriment in the full sense, since any act
based on the promise is sufficient[201] such as performance of an existing contractual

---

[186] *Watson* v. *Goldsbrough* [1986] 1 EGLR 265, CA.

[187] *Brikom Investments* v. *Carr* [1979] QB 467, 483, CA.

[188] [1980] 1 WLR 1306, CA; RE Annand [1981] *Conv* 154; MP Thompson (1981) 125 *SJ* 539;
G Woodman (1981) 44 *MLR* 461.

[189] *Watts* v. *Story* [1983], Dunn LJ; *Stevens & Cutting* v. *Anderson* [1990] 1 EGLR 95, 97L, Stuart Smith LJ.

[190] *Griffiths* v. *Williams* [1978] 2 EGLR 121; *Hamp* v. *Bygrave* [1983] 1 EGLR 174; *Re Basham* [1986] 1
WLR 1498; *Lim Teng Huan* v. *Ang Swee Chuan* [1992] 1 WLR 113, PC; SH Goo [1993] *Conv* 173.

[191] *Dann* v. *Spurrier* (1802) 7 Ves 231, 236, 32 ER 94, Eldon LC; *Wayling* v. *Jones* (1995) 69 P & CR 170,
CA.

[192] (1880) 15 Ch D 96, 106, Fry J.

[193] *Taylors Fashions* v. *Liverpool Victoria Trustees Co* (1979) [1982] QB 133n, Oliver J (*Taylors* case);
Watkins v. *Emslie* [1982] 1 EGLR 81, CA; *Stilwell* v. *Simpson* (1983) 133 NLJ 894; *Brikom Investments* v.
Carr [1979] QB 467, CA.

[194] *Brinnard* v. *Ewens* (1987) 19 HLR 415, CA; *Savva* v. *Costa* (1981) 131 NLJ 1114, CA.

[195] [1975] 1 WLR 1346, 1349G.

[196] At 1350A, Lord Denning MR.

[197] [1986] Ch 638, 657A.

[198] Contrast *Coombes* v. *Smith* [1986] 1 WLR 808; DJ Hayton [1986] *CLJ* 394; JE Martin [1988] *Conv* 59.

[199] See above **[23.09]**.

[200] *Re Basham* [1986] 1 WLR 1498; DJ Hayton [1987] *CLJ* 215; JE Martin [1987] *Conv* 211; *Matharu* v.
Matharu (1994) 68 P & CR 93, CA.

[201] M Lunney [1992] *Conv* 239, 240; but see *Vitol* v. *Esso Australian ("The Wise")* [1989] 2 Lloyds Rep
451, CA.

obligation.[202] Detriment may be relevant in switching from a revocable contractual variation[203] to one which is permanent if it is impossible for the claimant to resume his original position.[204] The fundamental similarity of proprietary estoppel and promissory estoppel has led some judges[205] and academics[206] to suggest that a common doctrine is emerging. However, assimilation is not yet achieved in English law,[207] with detriment standing as the boundary marker.

mention ✳

G. SATISFACTION

[23.31] Proof of an expectation, inducement and detrimental reliance establishes a right to an inchoate equity.[208] A second stage follows in which "the court must look at the circumstances in each case to decide in what way the equity can be satisfied",[209] or, in other words, the court exercises a discretion.[210]

1.   Matching to a property right

[23.32] Estoppel is an informal method of creating or protecting established property rights,[211] with the satisfaction process matching an expectation to a corresponding property right. Different expectations lead to different remedies: in *Dillwyn* v. *Llewellyn*[212] a son was promised a gift of a plot and secured a transfer after building a house, but in *Inwards* v. *Baker*[213] the son was promised a right to occupy a bungalow for life if he built it on the father's plot, which was satisfied by a licence for life.[214] Surely in this last case the expectation was wrongly identified, since people in fact only build on land which they own.[215] If the expectation is uncertain or at least is not expressed in neat conveyancing language, this is no hindrance to estoppel doctrine,[216] and indeed lack of precision may be an important essential distinction between

---

[202] *WJ Alan & Co* v. *El Nasir Export & Import Co* [1972] 2 QB 189.

[203] *Central London Property Trust* v. *High Trees House* [1947] KB 130, Denning J.

[204] *Ajayi* v. *RT Briscoe (Nigeria)* [1964] 1 WLR 1326, PC; *Austin* v. *Keele* (1987) 61 ALJR 605, 610, Lord Oliver; A Duthie (1988) 104 *LQR* 362, 365–366.

[205] *Amalgamated Investment & Property Co* v. *Texas Commerce International Bank* [1982] 1 QB 84, 122, Lord Denning MR; *Crabb* v. *Arun DC* [1976] Ch 179, 193, Scarman LJ; *Taylors Fashions* [1982] QB 133n, 153D, Oliver J; *Habib Bank* v. *Habib Bank Zurich* [1981] 1 WLR 1265.

[206] MP Thompson [1983] *CLJ* 251, 277; A. Duthie (1988) 104 *LQR* 362; M Halliwell (1994) 14 *LS* 15.

[207] PT Evans [1988] *Conv* 346, 348, 355; PV Baker (1981) 97 *LQR* 513, 515.

[208] *Low* v. *Bouverie* [1891] 3 Ch 82, 105, Bowen LJ.

[209] *Plimmer* v. *Wellington Corp* (1884) 9 App Cas 699, 714, Sir A Hobhouse; *Ramsden* v. *Dyson* (1866) LR 1 HL 129, 170, Lord Kingsdown; the decision of Lord Thurlow to which he refers is obscure; M Pawlowski (1997) 113 *LQR* 232; M Pawlowski (2002) 118 *LQR* 519.

[210] *Crabb* v. *Arun DC* [1976] Ch 179, 188C, Lord Denning MR, 193, Scarman LJ; *Amalgamated Investment & Property Co* v. *Texas Commerce International Bank* [1982] QB 84, Robert Goff J; S Gardner (1999) 115 *LQR* 438.

[211] S Moriarty (1984) 100 *LQR* 376; G Battersby [1991] *Conv* 36, 46.

[212] (1862) 4 De GF & J 517, 45 ER 1285.

[213] [1965] 2 QB 29, CA; RH Maudsley (1965) 81 *LQR* 183; FR Crane (1965) 29 *Conv (NS)* 222.

[214] S Moriarty (1984) 100 *LQR* 376, 378, 382–384; G Battersby [1991] *Conv* 36, 42–43.

[215] *Dillwyn* (1862) 4 De GF & J 517, 522, 45 ER 1285, Lord Westbury LC.

[216] *Holiday Inns* v. *Broadhead* (1974) 232 EG 951, 1087; *Plimmer* v. *Wellington Corp* (1884) 9 App Cas 699, 713.

contract and estoppel,[217] but estoppel cannot achieve what an express agreement could not.[218]

Matching is more complex where an expectation is novel and does not neatly relate to some established property right, a problem which arises particularly in the case of a licence giving a right to remain on land for a definite period, since this is not a traditional estate or interest.[219]

2.   Novel expectations matched by creative use of remedies

[23.33] A proprietary estoppel is satisfied by the grant of a discretionary remedy, such as specific performance, an injunction, ordering a transfer, or a declaration of the rights established by the estoppel. A remedy may be awarded in defiance of recognised property law principles. *Plimmer* v. *Wellington Corporation*[220] illustrates the creative possibilities of the injunction. Plimmer moored *Noah's Ark*, an old hulk, in Wellington harbour under a revocable licence from the Government. When the Government asked him after a few years to extend the jetty and to build a warehouse for the reception of immigrants to New Zealand, he naturally believed that his interest would be permanent. Did the claimant have a compensatable interest when the land was requisitioned by the government? Clearly yes. It was not necessary to articulate whether Plimmer had acquired freehold ownership or, more probably, they recognised a new property interest in the shape of a perpetual licence supported by estoppel.

Many modern decisions can only be explained on the assumption that an estoppel can raise a proprietary licence which the parties could not have created in any other way. In *Inwards* v. *Baker*,[221] a father encouraged his son to build a bungalow on the father's land, resulting in a licence by which the son could stay there for as long as he wanted. Enforcement against the widow, following the father's death, shows the presence of a proprietary interest, which was a licence by estoppel, and not a life interest. Numerous later cases[222] have treated a licence by estoppel as a substantive right incapable of direct creation by contract.

3.   Compensation in lieu

[23.34] If the court is unable to satisfy the estoppel by the grant of the expected property right it may be necessary to award compensation instead. This is particularly appropriate if money has been spent on building or improving another's land,[223] possibly coupled with an order securing occupation until the money has been repaid,[224]

---

[217] P Todd [1981] *Conv* 347, 350.

[218] *Daejean Properties* v. *Mahoney* [1995] 2 EGLR 75, 79, Hoffmann LJ.

[219] See above [19.78].

[220] (1884) 9 App Cas 699, 713–714.

[221] [1965] 2 QB 29, CA; RH Maudsley (1965) 81 *LQR* 183; FR Crane (1965) 29 *Conv (NS)* 222.

[222] *Matharu* v. *Matharu* (1994) 68 P & CR 93, CA; G Battersby (1995) 7 *CFLQ* 59; P Milne (1995) 58 *MLR* 412; M Welstead [1995] *Conv* 61; *Bank of India* v. *Mody* [1998] 12 LSG 29, Ch D.

[223] *Unity Joint Stock Banking Association* v. *King* (1853) 25 Beav 72, 53 ER 563.

[224] *Dodsworth* v. *Dodsworth* (1973) 228 EG 1115, CA; *Re Sharpe* [1980] 1 WLR 219; JE Martin [1980] *Conv* 207; G Woodman (1980) 96 *LQR* 336.

and charging the amount on the land.[225] *Burrows* v. *Burrows*[226] concerned an arrangement for a joint exercise of the right to buy the house at a discount, earned by the grandmother's status as a secure tenant. Her granddaughter's family agreed to pay the mortgage and undertake care of a handicapped daughter, in return for being left the house by will. Within two months the arrangement proved to be unworkable and the court had to impose a clean break, achieved by requiring the grandmother to refund the relevant expenditure with interest. Many cases of proprietary estoppel concern what are basically non-formalised contracts where the consideration is reflected in the right acquired, and restitutionary remedies will be available for return of the detriment if the "contract" is not performed.

4. Quantification

[23.35] This is the process of deciding how large a right should be conferred by the court in response to the expectation which have been proved. The maximum entitlement is set what the claimant expected.[227] A claimant who expected a lease of a fishing pond to be terminable at the end of each year cannot obtain a lease for a five year term by dredging the pool and stocking it with fish.[228] Normal entitlement is equal to the expectation – the court orders the implementation of the property right created informally.

Estoppel also perfects gifts if general equity is otherwise unable to compel transfer of the legal title, under a lifetime gift[229] or a promised inheritance.[230] With a gift there is necessarily a disparity between the value of the land and the quantum of detriment needed to secure it. Thus an agreement to make a gift by will of a farm worth £365,000 may be supported by work costing £20,000,[231] but the disparity was greatest in *Pascoe* v. *Turner*,[232] where an outright gift was supported by a detriment of £230 spent by Mrs Pascoe on redecoration, improvement, and repair. Disapproval of the man's general conduct led the court to fulfil the gift after this minor detrimental reliance, though monetary compensation for this level of expenditure would objectively have been a more appropriate remedy.

5. Minimum equity

[23.36] Minimum equity theory permits a court to reduce an award to take account of the fact that the expectation is disproportionately large in comparison to the detriment incurred. In determining whether there is *any* qualifying detriment, it is

---

[225] *Campbell* v. *Griffin* [2001] EWCA Civ 990, [2001] WTLR 981; *Jennings* v. *Rice* [2002] EWCA Civ 159, [2002] WTLR 367.

[226] (1991) 23 HLR 82, CA; S Jones [1992] *NLJ* 320; JE Martin [1992] *Conv* 54.

[227] S Moriarty (1984) 100 *LQR* 376, 376–388.

[228] *Watson* v. *Goldsbrough* [1986] 1 EGLR 265, CA; *Burrows* v. *Burrows & Sharp* (1991) 23 HLR 82, 92, Dillon LJ; *Elitestone* v. *Morris* (1996) 71 P & CR D6, CA (a point not pursued in HL).

[229] *Voyce* v. *Voyce* (1991) 62 P & CR 290; JE Martin [1992] *Conv* 56; *Pascoe* v. *Turner* [1979] 1 WLR 431, CA.

[230] See above **[23.09]**.

[231] *Morritt* v. *Wonham* [1993] CLYB 553.

[232] [1979] 1 WLR 431, CA; FR Crane [1979] *Conv* 379; B Sufrin (1979) 42 *MLR* 574; RD Oughtred (1979) 129 *NLJ* 1193; S Moriarty (1984) 100 *LQR* 376, 382.

necessary to deduct the value of benefits received by the claimant from the amount of his expenditure. Only if there is a debit balance is there an equity requiring satisfaction. Lord Eldon LC observed in *Dann* v. *Spurrier*[233] that the claimant must prove considerable expense showing that a larger interest is expected rather than a smaller one. For illustration take *Lee-Parker* v. *Izzet (No 2)*,[234] where the £200 or so spent on repairs and improvements was far outweighed by the value of rent free occupation, or again in *Sledmore* v. *Dalby*.[235]

A surplus of detriment over benefits received leaves an equity calling for satisfaction, but minimum equity theory permits the expectation to be reduced in order to make the award correspond to the detriment incurred.[236] Great expectations may be cut down to match small detriments. There are few cases where this has actually been done. *Pascoe* v. *Turner* was the most blatant lost opportunity,[237] but when the award was cut in *Baker* v. *Baker*[238], minimum equity theory operated most unjustly. A 75 year old grandfather contributed £34,000 to the acquisition of a house by his son in return for the right to live there rent free for life. Unfounded allegations of sexual molestation of his granddaughter caused the grandfather to leave, but he did not recover the whole of his cash contribution: his expectation was a right to rent-free accommodation for life and he was repaid only the value of that occupation right, less than he had contributed.

6.   Discretionary bars

[23.37] Proprietary estoppel is an equitable doctrine and subject to the usual equitable bars to relief. The right to an interest may be lost by failure to assert the claim when challenged by the property owner,[239] or by delay amounting to laches.[240]

It may also be lost by illegality[241] or misconduct amounting to unclean hands, though the effect of misconduct varies according to whether the licence is inchoate or choate, it being inchoate after detrimental reliance on an expectation but before it is recognised in court. Equitable relief is withdrawn on proof of serious misbehaviour. Part of the detriment alleged in *J Willis & Son* v. *Willis*[242] consisting of the installation

---

[233] (1802) 7 Ves 231, 236, 32 ER 94.

[234] [1972] 1 WLR 775, 780–781; *Appleby* v. *Cowley* [1982] Times April 14th, Megarry V-C; *J Willis & Son* v. *Willis* at first instance, but left open on appeal: [1986] 1 EGLR 62, CA.

[235] (1996) 72 P & CR 196, CA; JE Adams [1997] *Conv* 453; M Pawlowski (1997) 113 *LQR* 232.

[236] *Crabb* v. *Arun DC* [1976] Ch 179, 198G, Scarman LJ; *Baker* v. *Baker* (1993) 25 HLR 408, 412, Dillon LJ; E Cooke (1997) 17 *LS* 258 (should satisfy in full).

[237] [1979] 1 WLR 431, CA; FR Crane [1979] *Conv* 379; B Sufrin (1979) 42 *MLR* 574; *Voyce* v. *Voyce* (1991) 62 P & CR 290; JE Martin [1992] *Conv* 53, 56 (gift also completed); E Cooke (1997) 17 *LS* 258.

[238] (1993) 25 HLR 408, CA; *Campbell* v. *Griffin* [2001] EWCA Civ 990, [2001] WTLR 981. See also on a payment by mistake; estoppel defence only to the amount of the representation made that it was the customer's money: *National Westminster Bank* v. *Somer International (UK)* [2001] EWCA Civ 970, [2002] 1 All ER 194.

[239] *Fryer* v. *Brook* (1984) 81 LSG 2856; contrast *Re Sharpe* [1980] 1 WLR 219 (when aware of right claimant asserted it immediately).

[240] *Re Sharpe* [1980] 1 WLR 219; JE Martin [1980] *Conv* 207; G Woodman (1980) 96 *LQR* 336; *Voyce* v. *Voyce* [1991] 62 P & CR 290; JE Martin [1992] *Conv* 56 (laches not relevant if only step left is to perfect legal title); *Frawley* v. *Neill* [1999] Times April 5th, CA (basis unconscionability).

[241] *Chalmers* v. *Pardoe* [1963] 1 WLR 677, PC; *Maharaj* v. *Chand* [1986] AC 898, PC (illegal leases); *Godden* v. *Merthyr Tydfil H Ass* (1997) 74 P & CR D1, CA.

[242] [1986] 1 EGLR 62, CA; MP Thompson [1986] *Conv* 406.

of a bathroom was fictitious, and all equitable relief was refused, when the case might have succeeded if the true facts had been pleaded.

The licence becomes choate when it is recognised in court. In *Williams* v. *Staite*[243] an equitable licence to occupy a cottage for life under a family arrangement reached in 1960 was articulated by a county court declaration in 1972. The licensees created difficulties about the occupation of an adjoining cottage and paddock after they had been sold, making a false claim to occupation of the paddock, deliberately breaking promises made to the judge who had recognised their licence, and giving false evidence. This conduct was reprehensible, certainly, but not bad enough to forfeit the licence.[244] A licence recognised in court is terminable by extreme misconduct[245] – such as swearing at neighbours, obscene gesturing, joy-riding, and sounding car horns late at night.[246]

H. PROPRIETARY FORCE OF ESTOPPEL

1. General principles

[23.38] Court proceedings to enforce an equity created by proprietary estoppel should be protected as a pending action and any judgment as a writ or order affecting land, though usually the court orders the creation of a formal property right which then requires appropriate conveyancing protection.

Proprietary (as opposed to promissory[247]) estoppel is capable of creating new rights against the current landowner – the sword – and also of carrying them forward against new owners of the land – the proprietary sword. It remains inchoate until the exact property right is finally[248] settled in proceedings[249] but even at that stage the equity is treated as a property right in the land,[250] and occupation under it is not adverse possession.[251] The interest may attract compensation on compulsory purchase.[252]

2. Nature of the interest created

[23.39] The interest created by estoppel does not arise under a trust and is not overreachable:[253] it acts as a burden against the owner's land which can endure against future owners.

---

[243] [1979] Ch 291, CA; FR Crane [1978] *Conv* 386; E Ellis (1979) 95 *LQR* 11; S Anderson (1979) 42 *MLR* 203.
[244] At 297A Lord Denning MR, 299A, Goff LJ.
[245] At 298C, Lord Denning MR; but see at 300A, Goff LJ.
[246] *Brynowen Estates* v. *Bourne* (1981) 131 NLJ 1212, CA.
[247] *Combe* v. *Combe* [1951] 2 KB 215, CA; *Brikom Investments* v. *Carr* [1979] QB 467.
[248] *Jones* v. *Jones* [1977] 1 WLR 438, CA.
[249] S Moriarty (1984) 100 *LQR* 376; G Battersby (1995) 58 *MLR* 637, 640–643; A Everton [1982] *Conv* 118, 177.
[250] If the estoppel is created by a person who does not own an estate in the land at the time, the estoppel may be "fed" thus creating an equitable interest in the land from the time of acquisition of the legal estate; see eg *Watson* v. *Goldsbrough* [1986] 1 EGLR 265, CA; but the equity will probably not secure priority after *Abbey National BS* v. *Cann* [1991] 1 AC 56, HL.
[251] M Welstead [1991] *Conv* 280.
[252] *Plimmer* v. *Wellington Corp* (1884) 9 App Cas 699, PC; *Preston & Henderson* v. *St Helens MBC* (1989) 58 P & CR 500; *Pennine Raceway* v. *Kirklees MBC* [1983] QB 382, 390–391, 394G, 395G.
[253] *Birmingham Midshires* v. *Sabherwal* (2000) 80 P & CR 256, CA; C Harpum (2000) 116 *LQR* 341.

3. Proprietary force in unregistered land

[23.40] Can an estoppel right bind purchasers of unregistered land? Clearly yes, given the number of cases in which proprietary force has been recognised. In *Ramsden* v. *Dyson*[254] the land had passed from Sir J Ramsden to his grandson who was bound by the estoppel as donee,[255] and it also binds inheritors[256] and the owner's trustee in bankruptcy.[257] It can also bind future buyers, like the canal-side landowners in *Duke of Beaufort* v. *Patrick*,[258] certainly those with *express* notice,[259] and almost certainly also those with *constructive* notice.[260] So it seems certain that the inchoate estoppel right creates a full equitable interest[261] which is avoided only by a protected purchaser of a legal estate. This involves sidestepping the attempt by the 1925 legislation[262] to impose a cap on the range of equitable interests and prohibited new creations, perhaps because estoppel had already been established before 1926.[263] It remains arguable that the estoppel creates a mere equity,[264] binding if the holder of the interest is in occupation[265] or on any purchaser with notice by other means, but destroyed by a protected purchaser of a legal estate or equitable interest.[266]

4. Estoppel rights and land charges registration

[23.41] Inchoate estoppel rights are not registrable as land charges, as can be seen from *ER Ives Investment* v. *High*.[267] High claimed a right of way across the forecourt of a neighbouring block of flats, which superficially required registration as a class D(iii) equitable easement, but although informal and unprotected, his right bound Ives, a purchaser with express notice of it. Why? Lord Denning MR decided that the access right was not registrable as an equitable easement under class D(iii) for a highly technical reason, that registrable easements were ones which could exist at law before

---

[254] (1866) LR 1 HL 129, Lord Kingsdown dissenting.
[255] RH Maudsley (1956) 20 *Conv (NS)* 281, 300.
[256] *Dillwyn* v. *Llewellyn* (1862) 4 De GF & J 517, 45 ER 1285; *Inwards* v. *Baker* [1965] 2 QB 29, CA; *Jones* v. *Jones* [1977] 1 WLR 438, CA; *Griffiths* v. *Williams* [1978] 2 EGLR 121; *Greasley* v. *Cooke* [1980] 1 WLR 1306, CA; *Re Basham* [1986] 1 WLR 1498; *Voyce* v. *Voyce* (1991) 62 P & CR 290.
[257] *Re Sharpe* [1980] 1 WLR 219, Browne-Wilkinson J.
[258] (1853) 17 Beav 60, 78, 51 ER 954; *Unity Joint Stock Banking Association* v. *King* (1853) 25 Beav 72, 53 ER 563; S Baughen (1994) 14 *LS* 147.
[259] *Beaufort* at 78–79, Romilly MR; *Inwards* v. *Baker* [1965] 2 QB 29, CA; *Lee-Parker* v. *Izzet (No 2)* [1972] 1 WLR 775, 780–781; *Montague* v. *Long* (1972) 24 P & CR 240; *Dodsworth* v. *Dodsworth* (1973) 228 EG 1115, CA; *Crabb* v. *Arun DC* [1976] Ch 179; *Midland Bank* v. *Farmpride Hatcheries* [1981] 2 EGLR 147, CA.
[260] MP Thompson [1983] *Conv* 50, 53–56.
[261] *Hopgood* v. *Brown* [1955] 1 WLR 213, 223, Evershed MR, 219, Jenkins LJ, 231, Morris LJ.
[262] LPA 1925 s 4(1).
[263] S Baughen (1994) 14 *LS* 147, 148–151; JS Anderson *Lawyers and the Making of English Land Law 1832–1940* (Clarendon, 1992), 330.
[264] S Baughen (1994) 14 *LS* 147, 154; J Alder (1978) 41 *MLR* 208.
[265] A significant doctrinal advantage is that a mere equity binds not from mere occupation, but only from occupation giving notice of the circumstances giving rise to the equity: *Smith* v. *Jones* [1954] 1 WLR 1089.
[266] Superficially it is more like a right to rectification than a trust or a contract.
[267] [1967] 2 QB 379, CA; FR Crane (1967) 31 *Conv (NS)* 332; SJ Bailey [1968] *CLJ* 26; G Battersby [1991] *Conv* 36, 39; G Battersby (1995) 58 *MLR* 637, 643–652.

1926.[268] This achieves the correct result for estoppels at the price of complete distortion of class D(iii) and so Winn LJ's[269] more generalised technique is to be preferred: any expectation by estoppel is a distinct equitable right,[270] which – like Duracell's battery – carries on working after more formal rights had failed.[271] "All this seems to show that there may well be rights of an equitable character outside the provision relating to registration and incapable of being overreached."[272] Winn LJ's approach in *Ives* sidesteps the land charges legislation completely,[273] but is difficult to reconcile with *Lloyds Bank* v. *Carrick*.[274] That Court of Appeal said that a contractual expectation could not co-exist with an estate contract, or in other words that estoppel is an informal method of creation of conventional rights. Many estoppel cases are dubious if *Carrrick* is right, and indeed it would cripple the use of estoppel as a means of informal creation of rights against unregistered land.

5. Estoppel rights in registered land

[23.42] The proprietary status of inchoate rights by estoppel is now resolved[275] where title is registered; the right is capable of binding successors in title and is subject to the general priority principle of first in time. It is treated as a full equitable interest, as are mere equities against registered titles. Transfers for value of registered land take effect free of unprotected burdens,[276] so estoppel rights require protection. Occupation of the land affected is by far the commonest method, which gives an overriding interest.[277] It is too great a protection: a buyer may be bound by rights which are not really brought to his attention, for example where a tenant in occupation under a lease for one year has a right by estoppel to an extension for 999 years. Conversely actual knowledge of an estoppel claim by a non-occupier will not bite, since honesty is not essential for protection of a purchaser of registered land.[278]

6. Expectation of priority

[23.43] Estoppel rights between owner and claimant can bind a new owner of the land if the new owner creates an expectation that his right to priority will not be enforced.[279]

---

[268] This reasoning is surely wrong: see above [21.16].

[269] *Ives* [1967] 2 QB 379, 405G, also at 398, Danckwerts LJ.

[270] At 405.

[271] Or any inchoate equity is unregistrable before the court decides how to satisfy it: argument by PJ Millett [1967] 2 QB 379, 390; G Battersby (1995) 58 *MLR* 637.

[272] *Shiloh Spinners* v. *Harding* [1973] AC 691, 721C, Lord Wilberforce.

[273] JE Martin [1982] *Conv* 80; P Todd [1981] *Conv* 347, 359–360; G Battersby (1995) 58 *MLR* 637, 646.

[274] [1996] 4 All ER 630; *Brocket Hall (Jersey)* v. *Clague* [1998] CLYB 4367 (lease by estoppel not registrable as a land charge).

[275] LRA 2002 s 116; Law Com 271 (2001), [5.36], EN [508–509]; the proposal attracted 55% support but with some academics against.

[276] LRA 1925 s 20(1).

[277] *Dovto Properties* v. *Astell* [1964] CLYB 2067; *Ward* v. *Kirkland* [1967] Ch 194, Ungoed Thomas J.

[278] LRA 2002 s 116; *Re Basham* [1986] 1 WLR 1498.

[279] *Taylors Fashions* v. *Liverpool Victoria Trustees Co* (1979) [1982] QB 133n (*Olds case*), Oliver J; S Baughen (1994) 14 *LS* 147, 148.

24

TRANSFER RIGHTS

Bare trusts. Contracts. Estoppels. Litigation. Bankruptcy. Property adjustment. Gifts to avoid claims. Defective links. Mere equities.

[24.01] Many interests consist of the right to a transfer of land, the right to make a claim against land, or the right to upset a transfer already made. They represent the right to claim legal ownership at some time in the future. These are unified in their characteristic of being true burdens – they only make sense against the land itself and so their proprietary character is undoubted and unreserved. Beyond that it is hard to find coherence in the law – all are equitable but some are overreachable, some are outright, others discretionary and others so contingent that one almost hesitates to call them rights in the land itself. Most interests considered in this chapter require registration.

A. BARE TRUST

1. A bare trust

[24.02] Legal title can be separated from beneficial entitlement by passing land to a nominee, thus

> *to T on trust for B absolutely.*

This *Saunders* v. *Vautier* trust[1] is an oddity because the trustees must observe instructions about the management of the property given by the beneficiary, who is thus empowered to direct a termination of the trust at any moment. The "real" beneficial title is clear even though problems may arise in proving title,[2] and from the fact that the imposition of a trust of land now ensures that the beneficial interest will be overreachable.[3]

2. The registration gap

[24.03] The gap which exists between completion of a transaction and its registration had been identified as a problem as early as 1886.[4] Simultaneous creation and regis-

---

[1] (1841) 4 Beav 115, 49 ER 282; affirmed Cr & Ph 240, 41 ER 482.
[2] *P & O Overseas Holdings* v. *Rhys Braintree* [2002] EWCA Civ 296, [2002] 2 P & CR 27 at 400.
[3] See above **[13.07]**.
[4] T Key (1886) 2 *LQR* 324, 342.

tration of interests effected electronically will eventually eliminate the registration gap but for the time being the problem remains.

It is axiomatic[5] that a transfer gives the right to apply for registration, but it does not operate to pass the legal estate. In the short interim period, before registration, a transfer passes full beneficial ownership of the property,[6] the buyer has the right to move in while tamping and registering the transfer.

Pending registration of the transfer the seller remains legal owner of the property holding on trust for the buyer.[7] Potential difficulties arise because sometimes ownership has to be determined according to the legal title leaving a mismatch with the true position. Thus in *Brown & Root Technology* v. *Sun Alliance & London Assurance Co*,[8] a tenant company transferred a registered lease to a wholly owned subsidiary company, but this subsidiary was not yet registered as proprietor. The parent company remained the "tenant" under the lease, and so, as the court held, the correct party to serve a break notice to end the lease. Notice served by the subsidiary company did not destroy the lease. The proprietor is also the "owner" in the context of planning enforcement notices, for which the seller remains liable until registration of the buyer.[9]

3. First registration

[24.04] A bare trust also arises when first registration is delayed by more than two months and so legal title reverts to the previous owner.[10]

B. CONTRACTS

1. Land contracts

[24.05] Contracts relating to land are distinctive in three main regards, the requirement for formality in creation, the availability of specific performance, and the consequential rule that the buyer acquires an equitable interest in the land in advance of creation. The creation of equitable leases in this way is considered below,[11] but the same principle applies to transfer beneficial ownership of land under a contract to transfer the legal estate:[12] the trust arises under an unconditional contract but not where pre-conditions remain unfulfilled.[13]

---

[5] *Pourdanay* v. *Barclays Bank* [1997] Ch 321, 322.
[6] *Crumpton* v. *Unifox Properties* [1992] 2 EGLR 82, CA (no power to forfeit lease).
[7] N Hopkins (1998) 61 *MLR* 486; see above **[8.43]**.
[8] [2001] Ch 733, CA; *Gentle* v. *Faulkner* [1900] 2 QB 267, CA; *Re Rose* [1952] Ch 449 distinguished.
[9] *East Lindsey DC* v. *Thompson* [2001] EWHC Admin 81, [2001] 08 EG 165; *Buckinghamshire CC* v. *Briar* [2002] EWHC 2821 (Ch), [2002] December 20th, [151–152], Lawrence Collins J.
[10] See above **[9.27]**.
[11] *Walsh* v. *Lonsdale* (1882) 21 Ch D 9, CA; see below **[25.29]**.
[12] *Lysaght* v. *Edwards* (1876) 2 Ch D 499, 506–510, Jessel MR; Megarry & Wade (6th ed), [12.051–12.055].
[13] *Michaels* v. *Harley House (Marylebone)* [2000] Ch 104, 113F–117A, Robert Walker LJ; P Sparkes *NLT*, 530; see below **[25.30]**.

2. Estate contracts

[24.06] Estate contracts are true incumbrances[14] which burden the land itself, are not convertible to money, and never overreachable. Many equitable interests were once reliant upon the doctrine of notice, so that holders lived in fear of the loss of their interest to a purchaser and buyers feared being caught by undiscovered rights. Hence the introduction of the requirement to register in 1925.[15]

A class C(iv) estate contract is "a contract by an estate owner or by a person entitled at the date of the contract to have a legal estate conveyed to him to convey or create a legal estate."[16] Registration depends for its effectiveness on the underlying contract, so that vacation will be ordered if there was never a valid contract or if a valid contract has terminated.[17] Enforcement against a purchaser of unregistered land depends upon registration as a class C(iv) land charge, with no fall back in trust law or estoppel.[18]

Contracts for sale of freehold or leasehold estates,[19] contracts to grant leases,[20] and statutory contracts on enfranchisement should be registered.[21] Ordinary contracts for the purchase of land are not generally registered, since the real risk is small unless completion is delayed or the seller appears to be financially embarrassed. Registration is required of conditional contracts – for example to offer to surrender a lease before assigning it,[22] to sell subject to planning permission and the consent of the Charity Commissioners,[23] or to provide a legal charge on request.[24]

Sub-sale contracts arise when A contracts to sell to B and B contracts to sell to C; the sub-seller (B) is a "person entitled at the date of the contract to have a legal estate conveyed to him" and thus the sub-sale contract falls squarely within the definition of class C(iv). Registration by C must take place against the current legal estate owner (A) and not against the immediate contracting party (B).[25]

3. Options

[24.07] Options are specifically mentioned in the definition of the land charge of class C(iv).[26] A proprietary interest is created since the option holder can compel removal of the legal estate from the existing owner.[27] Many options are conditional.[28] Options

---

[14] CLR *Report* 1995–1996 recorded roughly 14,000 estate contracts registered under class C(iv).

[15] LCA 1972 s 2; *Ministry of Housing & Local Government* v. *Sharp* [1970] 2 QB 223, 282, Cross LJ.

[16] LCA 1972 s 2(4)(iv).

[17] See above **[21.13]**.

[18] *Lloyds Bank* v. *Carrick* [1996] 4 All ER 630, CA.

[19] A contract between A and B to convey to C is registrable: *Turley* v. *Mackay* [1944] Ch 37.

[20] *Blamires* v. *Bradford Corp* [1964] Ch 585. Contracts to create legal interests are registrable in other classes: equitable easements in class D(iii) and equitable mortgages in class C(iii).

[21] Not settlement of a boundary dispute: *Neilson* v. *Poole* (1969) 20 P & CR 909.

[22] *Greene* v. *Church Commissioners for England* [1974] Ch 467, Sachs LJ; explaining *Beesly* v. *Hallwood Estates* [1960] 1 WLR 549, Buckley J; (1975) 91 *LQR* 3.

[23] *Haslemere Estates* v. *Baker* [1982] 1 WLR 1109, Megarry V-C.

[24] *Williams* v. *Burlington Investments* (1977) 121 SJ 424, HL.

[25] *Barrett* v. *Hilton Developments* [1975] Ch 237, CA.

[26] LCA 1972 s 2(4).

[27] *London & SWR* v. *Gomm* (1882) 20 Ch D 562, CA.

[28] Eg subject to planning permission: *Hallam Land Management* v. *UK Coal Mining* [2002] EWCA Civ 982, [2002] 2 EGLR 80; *Smith* v. *Royce Properties* [2001] EWCA Civ 949, [2002] 2 P & CR 5 at 67, CA; P Sparkes NLT, 535–538.

require registration[29] and will be destroyed by a sale at a time that they are unregistered.[30] Exercise of the option creates no additional burden.[31] Registration is also required for options to renew leases, a point which requires special emphasis because the general belief was that options for renewal ran with the land at common law rendering separate protection unnecessary.[32] Buckley J established their registrability in *Beesly* v. *Hallwood Estates*[33] and it is now settled up to the Court of Appeal.[34] If the lease containing the option is surrendered this will destroy the option for renewal.[35]

4. Right of pre-emption

[24.08] A right of pre-emption gives the right to buy the land at a fixed price but only if the estate owner decides to sell it. A right of first refusal is the corresponding right to be offered the land at the price that the owner is prepared to sell it before anyone else can make an offer.[36] It is common for commercial[37] or long-term residential leases to state that if the leaseholder wishes to sell the lease he must first give the landlord the opportunity to acquire it, that is the tenant must offer to surrender the lease before selling it. This is illustrated by a leading case in which the ground landlord of a house in central London had the right to acquire it for £1.7 million.[38]

According to *Dear* v. *Reeves*[39] the benefit of a right of pre-emption is a piece of property, albeit one that is difficult to value, and hence the right of first refusal passes to the trustee in bankruptcy. Back land behind a bungalow on the outskirts of Southampton with development potential could not be sold on the open market without first offering it to a previous owner at a price that has the development value stripped out of it. This was an interest that could pass for the benefit of the creditors of the previous owner, assignability of the benefit being an important characteristic of a property right.[40]

The burden of a pure pre-emption is not, apparently, proprietary. It is one crucial step removed from an option, since the land cannot be taken away from the owner against his will: there is no blank cheque.[41] This distinction was held to be so fundamental by the Court of Appeal in *Pritchard* v. *Briggs*,[42] that a right of pre-emption

---

[29] *Spiro* v. *Glencrown Properties* [1991] Ch 537, Hoffmann J; *Bircham & Co* v. *Worrall Homes* [2001] EWCA Civ 775, [2001] 3 EGLR 83, [41–42], Chadwick LJ; see above **[22.23]**.

[30] *Freeguard* v. *Royal Bank of Scotland* (2000) 79 P & CR 81, CA.

[31] *Armstrong & Holmes* v. *Holmes* [1993] 1 WLR 1482, Ch D; NP Gravells [1994] *Conv* 483.

[32] [1989] 1 WLR 888, 891C–F, Nicholls LJ; *Taylors Fashions* v. *Liverpool Victoria Trustees* [1982] QB 133n.

[33] *Beesly* v. *Hallwood Estates* [1960] 1 WLR 549; on appeal [1961] Ch 105, CA; *Phillips* v. *Mobil Oil Co* [1989] 1 WLR 888, 891C–F, Nicholls LJ; also assumed in: *Greene* v. *Church Commissioners for England* [1974] Ch 467, CA; *Kitney* v. *MEPC* [1977] 1 WLR 981, CA.

[34] *Phillips* v. *Mobil Oil Co* [1989] 1 WLR 888, 891C–F, Nicholls LJ; assumed in *Greene* v. *Church Commissioners for England* [1974] Ch 467, CA; also in *Kitney* v. *MEPC* [1977] 1 WLR 981, CA.

[35] *Plummer* v. *Tibsco* [2002] EWCA Civ 102, [2002] 1 EGLR 29.

[36] *Bircham & Co* v. *Worrall Homes* [2001] EWCA Civ 775, [2001] 3 EGLR 83, [31], Chadwick LJ.

[37] On the impact of the business tenancies legislation see: P Sparkes *NLT*, 558.

[38] *Bircham & Co* v. *Worrall Homes* [2001] EWCA Civ 775, [2001] 3 EGLR 83.

[39] [2001] EWCA Civ 277, [2002] Ch 1.

[40] At [38–40], Mummery LJ; see above **[6.06]**.

[41] *Brown* v. *Gould* [1972] Ch 53, 58F, Megarry J.

[42] [1980] Ch 338; C Harpum (1980) 39 *CLJ* 35; HWR Wade (1980) 96 *LQR* 488; A Everton [1982] *Conv* 177, 180; *Murray* v. *Two Strokes* [1973] 1 WLR 823; M Albery (1973) 89 *LQR* 462; *London & Blenheim Estates* v. *Ladbroke Retail Parks* [1994] 1 WLR 31, 36C, 38B–F, Peter Gibson LJ.

was not registrable[43] even though the statutory definition of class C (iv) mentions pre-emption rights expressly.[44] Pre-emption rights become registrable when the estate owner indicates his intention to sell the land, so that the holder of the pre-emption right has an equitable right to insist on transfer of the estate.[45] The result is unsatisfactory, surely, since it enables the estate owner to break the promised pre-emption before its holder wakes up to the fact that it needs registration. Its correctness has been questioned by the leading text for practitioners[46] and by Mummery LJ,[47] and remains open in the House of Lords[48]

This also has important consequences in terms of formality, where a pre-emption is distinct from an option. With an option the grant of the option requires contract formality, but the exercise is by unilateral notice. No interest is created in the land by conferring a right of first refusal, and it follows that no contract is formed when the owner notifies his intention to sell and the person with the right of refusal accepts informally. The owner is free to withdraw unless and until he enters into a formal contract.[49]

5.   Estate contracts and pre-emption rights affecting registered land

[24.09] Any burden affecting registered land must be protected by LR notice.[50] In the past it was common to protect a right of pre-emption by restriction,[51] though this was of dubious validity given the decision in *Pritchard* v. *Briggs* just discussed.[52] But the new legislation declares that rights of pre-emption are now to be seen as proprietary when title is registered.[53] The reform is welcome but it is unfortunate to split asunder the substantive systems of property law, and unregistered land should now be brought into line.[54]

C. ESTOPPELS

[24.10] Failed contracts can often be rescued by estoppel, where the promised right has been acted upon, that is after detrimental reliance.[55] Proprietary status is now well

---

[43] Also contracts to contract, eg a notice to treat by a compulsory purchase authority: *Capital Investments* v. *Wednesfield UDC* [1965] Ch 774; also a right for an agent to refuse or accept offers for sale: *Thomas* v. *Rose* [1968] 1 WLR 1797.

[44] LCA 1972 s 2(4); *Dear* v. *Reeves* [2001] EWCA Civ 277, [2002] Ch 1, [34], Mummery LJ.

[45] *Kling* v. *Keston Properties* (1983) 49 P & CR 212, 217 (registered land); *Nicholson* v. *Markham* (1998) 75 P & CR 428, CA (defeated by gift).

[46] Megarry & Wade (6th ed), [12.062].

[47] *Dear* v. *Reeves* [2001] EWCA Civ 277, [2002] Ch 1, [32–34], [43], Mummery LJ.

[48] *Bircham & Co* v. *Worrall Homes* [2001] EWCA Civ 775, [2001] 3 EGLR 83, [28–29], Chadwick LJ.

[49] At [41–42], Chadwick LJ; he distinguished *Spiro* v. *Glencrown Properties* [1991] Ch 537, Hoffmann LJ; see above **[22.23]**.

[50] See above **[20.05]**.

[51] P Sparkes *NLL* (1st ed), 192; contrast now above **[20.13]**.

[52] See above **[24.07]**.

[53] LRA 2002 s 115; Law Com 271 (2001), EN [507–509].

[54] See above **[6.07]**.

[55] See above **[23]**.

established whether title is unregistered[56] or registered.[57] However, that small step from formal to informal contract involves an extraordinary conceptual leap: there is no question of specific performance of the promise to create an expectation, and hence no trust, and there is no automatic enforcement of the expectation as there is with a contract since discretionary factors such as minimum equity theory come into play at the stage of satisfaction.[58] This is also the chasm between registrable rights and residual rights reliant on notice[59] or actual occupation.[60]

D. LITIGATION AFFECTING LAND

1. Litigation affecting land

[24.11] Litigation could never be brought to a successful conclusion if it was permissible to dispose of the land affected after litigation had started.[61] If litigation affects a legal estate registration is both possible and required – claims of these kinds cannot be protected by actual occupation.[62]

2. Pending actions

[24.12] Pending actions[63] are ones which are still in progress through the courts. Registrations must be renewed after an initial period of five years.[64]

If title is registered, protection is by a unilateral notice against the title affected by the litigation.[65] While title remains unregistered, an entry must be made in the names-based registers of litigation first created in 1839.[66] Neither type of entry prevents dealings nor creates any charge on the property, but simply gives notice of a right which may or may not be vindicated by the litigation.[67] However, the practical effect is to inhibit all dealings. But litigants are often required to accept the alternative protection of an injunction supported by an undertaking in damages.[68] This frees up the land. After final disposal of a case, including any appeal, the pending action must be vacated,[69] to be followed – if the case has succeeded – by a final order that may itself

---

[56] See above **[23.40]**.
[57] LRA 2002 s 116; Law Com 271 (2001), [5.36].
[58] See above **[23.31ff]**.
[59] See above **[21.20]**.
[60] See above **[20.16ff]**.
[61] Cheshire & Burn (16th ed), 824.
[62] LRA 2002 s 87(3).
[63] LCA 1972 s 5; J Howell [1995] *Conv* 309; LRA 2002 s 87; Law Com 271 (2001), EN [383–388].
[64] LCA 1972 s 8; *Shaw* v. *Neale* (1858) 6 HLC 581, 10 ER 1422; *Re Receiving Order* [1947] Ch 498.
[65] LRA 2002 ss 35, 87; before the 2002 Act commencement a caution was used.
[66] *Willies-Williams* v. *National Trust* (1993) 65 P & CR 359, 362, Hoffmann LJ; *Ministry of Housing & Local Government* v. *Sharp* [1970] 2 QB 223, 280, Cross LJ.
[67] *Bull* v. *Hutchens* (1863) 32 Beav 615, 618, 55 ER 242, Romilly MR.
[68] *Willies-Williams* v. *National Trust* (1993) 65 P & CR 359, CA; *Clearbrook Property Holdings* v. *Verrier* [1974] 1 WLR 243, Templeman J; *Clowes Developments (UK)* v. *Mulchinock* [1998] 1 WLR 42, Carnwath J.
[69] *Sowerby* v. *Sowerby* (1982) 44 P & CR 192, Megarry V-C (property transfer application vacated after decree absolute).

be registrable. Non-registration of litigation rights has less drastic consequences than with land charges, since actual notice makes a claim stick to a purchaser.[70]

3. Writs and orders

[24.13] Many successful actions will lead to the recognition by the court of some property right – perhaps a mortgage, charging order, or easement – which requires normal conveyancing protection. Registration of writs or orders is a means of protecting processes affecting land relating to the enforcement of a judgment or delivery in execution. Against a registered title, protection is by LR notice,[71] whereas for unregistered titles there is a separate register of writs or orders.[72] Again registrations are for an initial period of five years.[73]

4. Actions relating to land

[24.14] Actions are only registrable if they affect a legal estate in land.[74] Most entries relate to claims by creditors – bankruptcies, liquidations, or charging orders. Another common source of registrations is claims to property adjustment after divorce.[75] Other statutory claims relating to land include acquisition orders for blocks of flats in disrepair,[76] orders for access to neighbouring land,[77] claims against drug traffickers,[78] actions to establish that an interest in land has ended,[79] forfeiture of leases, and applications for leave to forfeit.[80] Freezing injunctions can be registered after the final order but not an interim stages.[81]

Proprietary protection is not allowed for personal actions for damages[82] or to enforce repairing covenants, even by mandatory injunction.[83] Nor, surprisingly, is an application for sale[84] or for an injunction to prevent a sale registrable, since it is not an action to assert a proprietary interest.[85]

---

[70] LRA 2002 s 87; LCA 1972 s 5(7)–(8).

[71] LRA 2002 s 87; Law Com 271 (2001), EN [383–388].

[72] LCA 1972 s 6; replacing registers dating from 1839. This could include a receivership incapable of binding a purchaser: LCA 1972 s 6(1)(b); *Clayhope Properties* v. *Evans* [1986] 1 WLR 1223, CA.

[73] LCA 1972 s 8.

[74] LCA 1972 s 17(1); earlier Acts referred to a "*lis pendens*".

[75] See below **[24.18ff]**.

[76] LTA 1987 part 3.

[77] Access to Neighbouring Land Act 1992.

[78] Drug Trafficking Act 1994; Proceeds of Crime Act 2002.

[79] *Allen* v. *Greenhi Builders* [1978] 1 WLR 156; *Willies-Williams* v. *National Trust* (1993) 65 P & CR 359, CA.

[80] *Selim* v. *Bickenhall Engineering* [1981] 1 WLR 1318, Megarry V-C.

[81] *Stockler* v. *Fourway Estates* [1984] 1 WLR 25, Kilner Brown J; *Orwell Steel (Erection & Fabrication)* v. *Asphalt & Tarmac (UK)* [1984] 1 WLR 1097. If title is registered, a restriction should be used.

[82] *Haslemere Estates* v. *Baker* [1982] 1 WLR 1109, 1119C, Megarry V-C; *Simmons* v. *Simmons* [1996] CLYB 2874, CA.

[83] *Regan & Blackburn* v. *Rogers* [1985] 1 WLR 870, 875A, Scott J.

[84] *Taylor* v. *Taylor* [1968] 1 WLR 378, CA.

[85] *Calgary & Edmonton Land Co* v. *Dobinson* [1974] Ch 102, 105, Megarry J; but see *Whittingham* v. *Whittingham* [1979] Fam 9, 21–23, Stamp LJ.

5. Restrictions

[24.15] A restriction is the appropriate means of recording sequestration orders and receiverships or a deed of arrangement – a LR notice should not be entered.[86]

E. BANKRUPTCY

[24.16] Bankruptcy involves a transfer of all property owned beneficially by the bankrupt so it could be seen as a forced transfer, and certainly the bankruptcy petition and bankruptcy order require registration – the first as a pending action and the latter as a writ or order affecting land. However, since the transfer in this case is merely a way of realising land for the benefit of those owed money, insolvency is considered as a specific type of money charge in this book.[87]

F. PROPERTY ADJUSTMENT

1. Declaration of property rights

[24.17] Although the property of married couples can be redistributed on divorce the first step must be to determine the existing resources and property rights of the parties.[88] A simple procedure is provided by the Married Women's Property Act 1882[89] for resolving property disputes between husband and wife during the marriage, on separation, within three years of the end of the marriage, on termination of an engagement to marry, on insolvency, or following sale of matrimonial property. Subsidiary powers include restraining sale, ordering sale,[90] giving directions with respect to the proceeds of sale, assessing the value of a share, and ordering payment of a share.[91] Under the 1882 Act, the court may "make such order with respect to the property as it thinks fit",[92] but it must give effect to the existing legal and equitable property rights of husband and wife.[93]

2. Powers of property adjustment

[24.18] Family courts have powers to adjust the property rights of members of a family in a number of situations:

(1) between spouses when they divorce in ancillary proceedings[94];

---

[86] LRA 2002 s 87(3).
[87] See below **[28.46ff]**.
[88] MCA 1973 s 25(2)(a) as amended; *Calderbank* v. *Calderbank* [1975] 3 All ER 333, CA.
[89] S 17 as amended.
[90] Married Women's Property Act 1882 s 7(7).
[91] *Bothe* v. *Amos* [1976] Fam 46, CA.
[92] Married Women's Property Act 1882 s 17, as amended in 1984.
[93] *National Provincial Bank* v. *Ainsworth* [1965] AC 1175, 1220, 1245. Enjoyment of rights may be deferred.
[94] MCA 1973 s 24.

(2) between spouses at the time of proceedings for judicial separation or a declaration of nullity;

(3) following overseas divorces when the strongest connection is with this country; and

(4) between unmarried parents for the benefit of their minor children.[95]

Property adjustment most commonly follows a divorce.

3. Exercise of adjustment powers

[24.19] One spouse may be ordered to transfer the matrimonial home to the other,[96] either by an outright transfer, or by transfer of an existing share, or the creation of a beneficial co-ownership by conferring a share on a non-owner. Transfer may require the consent of an existing lender[97] or a landlord.[98] Balancing payments are often ordered and may be charged on the house.[99] Instead of an outright transfer, there is power to order the creation of a settlement or to vary a marriage settlement. The court often creates a co-ownership in a former matrimonial home but allows one party to occupy[100] with the children of the marriage.

It is beyond the scope of this work to consider the form of the orders that should be made. [101] A vital factor is the welfare of the children. Where there are minor children, a declaration of beneficial co-ownership is likely to be coupled with an order deferring sale,[102] but in other cases it may be feasible to achieve a clean break.[103] The court has to balance the needs of family members against the resources available, bearing in mind the family setting and the contributions to the marriage, but largely ignoring conduct and pre-nuptial agreements.

Where it is feasible to rehouse both spouses, *Wachtel* v. *Wachtel*[104] is authority for division into thirds, one for the husband, another for the wife, with the final third put towards maintenance of the children. A couple without children would share half and half.[105] However, English law is still based on need rather than any automatic presumption of equal division. Recent "big money" cases have led to larger payments for wives and a closer approach to equality.[106]

---

[95] Children Act 1989 sch 1 para 1(2).
[96] MCA 1973 ss 21, 22A(2), as amended.
[97] *Regan* v. *Regan* [1977] 1 WLR 84.
[98] *J* v. *J* [1980] 1 All ER 156.
[99] This money charge requires protection; see below **[28.12ff]**, **[28.17ff]**.
[100] See above **[19.53]**.
[101] MCA 1973 s 25, as amended in 1984 and 1996.
[102] See above **[19.53]**.
[103] *Piglowsa* v. *Piglowski* [1999] 1 WLR 1360, HL.
[104] [1973] Fam 72, 94–95, Lord Denning MR; *Potter* v. *Potter* [1982] 1 WLR 1255; *Bullock* v. *Bullock* [1986] 1 FLR 372; *Dew* v. *Dew* [1986] 2 FLR 341; *W* v. *W* [1995] 2 FLR 259, Ewbank J.
[105] *Page* v. *Page* (1981) 2 FLR 198, 202D, Dunn LJ.
[106] *White* v. *White* [2001] 1 AC 596, HL; *Cowan* v. *Cowan* [2001] EWCA Civ 679, [2002] Fam 97; *Lambert* v. *Lambert* [2002] EWCA Civ 1685, [2003] 1 FLR 139.

4. Registering property adjustment applications

[24.20] A claim to property adjustment is registrable as a pending land action, though only after matrimonial proceedings have commenced.[107] The application should to be targeted at specific property by registration, after which it binds any purchaser,[108] though an unregistered claim still binds a purchaser with actual notice.[109]

5. Bankruptcy and ancillary relief

[24.21] There are a considerable number of cases about the conflict of priority that exists between the claims of a family to property adjustment and the claims of creditors channelled through a trustee in bankruptcy. A property transfer order creates an equitable interest in the home at the time it is made, in advance of the transfer.[110] A bankruptcy one day later will not remove the right created by the property adjustment order.

If the sequence is reversed – so the spouse is bankrupted, or bankrupts himself, before the property adjustment orders are made, any order of the family court must be ratified by the bankruptcy court.[111] A property adjustment order is a gift or partial gift which can be avoided under the rules discussed below[112] if the spouse ordered to make the transfer becomes bankrupt within five years,[113] though partial protection accrues for a spouse who provides value by giving up claims to maintenance.[114]

G. GIFTS TO AVOID CLAIMS

1. Gifts just before insolvency

[24.22] A debtor should not give away his assets so as to reduce what is left for his creditors, and nor should he sell them too cheaply.[115] The time limit allowed for challenge of a gift or partial gift is five years,[116] running backwards from the moment of presentation of a bankruptcy petition. During that five year period the title of the donee is provisional, and it becomes voidable on the donor's bankruptcy.[117]

---

[107] *Kemmis* v. *Kemmis* [1988] 1 WLR 1307, CA; *B* v. *B* [1994] 2 FLR 739, Bracewell J; on appeal [1995] 1 FLR 374, CA.

[108] *Whittingham* v. *Whittingham* [1979] Fam 9, CA; *Perez-Adamson* v. *Perez Rivas* [1987] Fam 89, CA.

[109] *B* v. *B* [1994] 2 FLR 739, Bracewell J; a point left open on appeal: *B* v. *B (No 2)* [1995] 1 FLR 374, CA.

[110] *Mountney* v. *Treharne* [2002] EWCA Civ 1174, [2002] 3 WLR 1760.

[111] *Re Flint* [1993] Ch 319; *Albert* v. *Albert* [1997] 2 FLR 791, CA.

[112] See below **[24.24]**.

[113] IA 1986 ss 339–340; MCA 1973 s 39.

[114] *Re Abbot* [1983] Ch 45; *Harman* v. *Glencross* [1986] Fam 81; *Re Kumar* [1993] 2 All ER 700, Ferris J.

[115] IA 1986 ss 238, 241, 339; this encompasses (1) a gift, (2) a transfer with no consideration or (3) a transfer for a marriage consideration; and (4) any imbalanced transaction – where the bankrupt received significantly less value than he provided; *Re Densham* [1975] 1 WLR 1519, Goff J (wife acquired larger share than she had paid for); *Reid* v. *Ramlot* [2002] EWHC 2416, [2002] Times November 15th; *Philips* v. *Brewin Dolphin Bell Lawrie* [2001] UKHL 2, [2001] 1 WLR 143.

[116] IA 1986 s 339.

[117] Actual avoidance may be many years later: *Re Dent* [1994] 2 FLR 540, Div Ct.

Other provisions invalidate a preference (which gives payment to one creditor rather than another)[118] or an undervalued conveyance intended to defraud creditors.[119]

2. Protection of buyers from donees

[24.23] It will be too late to upset a gift after the land has passed to an honest purchaser. If title is registered, the only question is whether the register reveals the fact that the land was acquired under a potentially voidable gift, and otherwise the registration curtain protects the purchaser. The register no longer records that the document founding the registration was a gift, since title can be passed by the person recorded as proprietor.[120]

Special protection has been required for purchasers of unregistered land. A check of the title reveals the fact that the later sale is still within five years measured from the date of the gift. The buyer's title was voidable because of the buyer's knowledge of this "relevant circumstance".[121] Insurance against this risk was the only solution. The Insolvency (No 2) Act 1994 cures this problem for all transactions after mid-1994.[122] Relevant circumstances are defined.[123] The purchaser remains vulnerable only if: (1) the buyer is an associate of the giver or of the recipient; or (2) the buyer has knowledge of the bankruptcy or impending bankruptcy. The later buyer protects himself by a bankruptcy search against the original giver. Protection presumably accrues to later owners.

3. Gifts designed to avoid property adjustment

[24.24] The family court may invalidate a transaction which has already occurred[124] in favour of a spouse claiming property adjustment or other financial relief on divorce if this will lead to different financial provision.[125] Reviewable transactions include any form of conveyance or lifetime gift,[126] including an undervalued sale of the matrimonial home,[127] a mortgage,[128] or a waiver of priority.[129] Not, however, a notice to quit a joint periodic tenancy.[130] A transaction is reviewable if it was made with the inten-

---

[118] IA 1986 ss 244–245, 340–341.

[119] IA 1986 ss 423–425. Not a tenancy at the best rent: *National Westminster Bank* v. *Jones* [2001] 1 BCLC 98, CA; nor a gift made on advice for sound fiscal reasons *Law Society* v. *Southall* [2001] EWCA Civ 2001, [2002] WTLR 1151.

[120] [2000] 14 *LSG* 48.

[121] IA 1986 ss 241 (corporate donor), 342 (individual).

[122] IA 1986 s 6 (on or after July 26th 1994); JE Adams [1994] *Conv* 434.

[123] IA 1986 s 241(3), as amended.

[124] There is also power to block proposed transactions: MCA 1973 s 37(2)(a); *Green* v. *Green* [1981] 1 WLR 391; *Hamlin* v. *Hamlin* [1985] 2 All ER 1037, CA (Spanish villa); *Shipman* v. *Shipman* [1991] 1 FLR 250; *Langley* v. *Langley* [1994] 1 FLR 383, CA; *Araghchinchi* v. *Araghchinchi* [1997] 2 FLR 142, CA.

[125] MCA 1973 s 37.

[126] But not a gift by will: MCA 1973 s 37(6).

[127] *Sherry* v. *Sherry* [1991] 1 FLR 307, CA.

[128] *Whittingham* v. *Whittingham* [1979] Fam 9; *Green* v. *Green* [1981] 1 WLR 391; *Perez-Adamson* v. *Perez Rivas* [1987] Fam 89, CA; *B* v. *B (No 2)* [1995] 1 FLR 374, CA.

[129] *Kemmis* v. *Kemmis* [1988] 1 WLR 1307, CA; *H* v. *H* (1979) 10 Fam Law 152.

[130] *Newlon HT* v. *Alsulaimen* [1999] AC 313, HL.

tion of defeating the claim to financial relief,[131] but this intention may be presumed for three years where the practical effect of a dealing is to defeat a claim for financial relief.[132]

Purchasers are protected by the rule that a disposition for valuable consideration cannot be set aside against a purchaser acting in good faith and without notice – actual, imputed, or constructive[133] – of the intention to defeat the spouse's claim for financial relief.

H. DEFECTIVE LINKS

[24.25] A defective transfer operates, when registered, to vest the legal estate in the person to whom the transfer is made, but the title conferred may be upset. It will be crucially important to determine whether the transfer is void or voidable.

1. Transfer void – title of forger

[24.26] A forgery is void, as is any transfer to which *non est factum* applies.[134] Since the deed conveying unregistered land is not executed by the real owner of the estate, no title at all passes. Where title is registered, registration of the forger's title vests legal title in him.[135] However the true owner can establish in court proceedings that the title is void and seek rectification of the register to remove the forger from it. Under the old law rectification could be awarded where any entry in the register was "obtained by fraud", the target being fraud on the registration process itself. [136] So this is a non-prejudicial alteration which is made automatically when a forger or an accomplice is uncovered, with no protection provided by possession and no indemnity.[137]

2. Transfer void – successors to forgery

[24.27] If title is unregistered, a forgery could pass no title to any successor, innocent or guilty. Even an innocent buyer could be duped out of his money by a worthless title in this way. Adverse possession will eventually validate a title but for 12 years the title remains vulnerable to an action by the true owner.[138]

---

[131] *Shipman* v. *Shipman* [1991] 1 FLR 250.

[132] MCA 1973 s 37(5).

[133] S 37(4); *Green* v. *Green* [1981] 1 WLR 391; *Kemmis* v. *Kemmis* [1988] 1 WLR 1307, CA; *Sherry* v. *Sherry* [1991] 1 FLR 307, CA; *B* v. *B (No 2)* [1995] 1 FLR 374, CA; *Le Foe* v. *Le Foe* [2001] 2 FLR 970.

[134] *Norwich & Peterborough BS* v. *Steed* [1993] Ch 116, 125D–128G, Scott LJ (unsuccessful); the leading authority discussed extensively in the following paras.

[135] LRA 2002 ss 23, 27; RJ Smith (1985) 101 *LQR* 79.

[136] LRA 1925 s 82(1)(d); *Argyle BS* v. *Hammond* (1985) 49 P & CR 148, CA; *Norwich & Peterborough BS* v. *Steed* [1993] Ch 116, 134B–F, Scott LJ; *Buckinghamshire CC* v. *Briar* [2002] EWHC 2821 (Ch), [2002] December 20th, [143–150], Lawrence Collins J.

[137] See above [11.39].

[138] He needs to claim promptly after discovery of his right to claim.

So it is with registered land. This was a case of automatic rectification under the old law[139] and is now therefore a case of non-prejudicial alteration. The pleaded facts in *Norwich & Peterborough BS* v. *Steed*[140] were that the owner of a house alleged that while he was abroad a transfer was forged in favour of his sister and brother-in-law. They obtained a mortgage on the strength of that forgery from innocent lenders. Scott LJ held that a person deprived of his land by a forged document was entitled to reclaim it. A court declaration of the forgery would be followed by rectification of the register to remove the lender who relied on the forgery. The building society obtained an indemnity.

3. Transfer voidable – title of defrauder

[24.28] Legal title does pass under a voidable transfer, but the transfer can be set aside because of some misconduct practised by the recipient on the person making the transfer. Examples are transfers made by a senile person under undue influence,[141] fraudulent misrepresentation,[142] and gerrymandering.[143]

Registered titles can be upset in the same circumstances as unregistered titles,[144] since misconduct established in court proceedings[145] leads to automatic non-prejudicial alteration. Examples are attempts to defeat property adjustment applications,[146] a mother ripped off by her daughter, [147] and the fraud been practised on the attorney who executed the transfer by the sister and brother-in-law of the proprietor in *Norwich & Peterborough BS* v. *Steed*.[148]

4. Transfer voidable – innocent buyers

[24.29] If title is unregistered, a valid title can be passed on to subsequent buyers if they obtain title before rescission of a voidable conveyance.[149] parallel law for registered titles to put an innocent purchaser or lender[150] beyond the reach of rectification if they would have a good title on unregistered principles. The old law which treated

---

[139] LRA 1925 s 82(1)(a); *Att-Gen* v. *Odell* [1906] 2 Ch 47; *Re De Leeuw* [1922] 2 Ch 540, 554–557, Peterson J; *Morelle* v. *Wakeling* [1955] 2 QB 379, CA; *Att-Gen* v. *Parsons* [1956] AC 421, HL. Earlier cases also used LRA 1925 s 82(1)(h) under which the court had a discretion and possession was likely to be decisive; in modern terms that is there was a rectification rather than an alteration.

[140] [1993] Ch 116, 133C–G, Scott LJ.

[141] *Re Beaney* [1978] 1 WLR 770; see below **[30.53ff]**.

[142] *Collings* v. *Lee* [2001] 2 All ER 332, CA; R Nolan [2001] CLJ 477. But not innocent misrepresentation or mistake: *Steed* [1993] Ch 116, 132B, Scott LJ.

[143] *National & Provincial BS* v. *Ahmed* [1995] 2 EGLR 127, CA.

[144] Previously LRA 1925 s 114; the failure to re-enact this section might alter some of the explanation in this passage.

[145] Previously LRA 1925 s 82(1)(a).

[146] *Kemmis* v. *Kemmis* [1988] 1 WLR 1307, 1321A–D, Purchas LJ.

[147] *Re Leighton's Conveyance* [1937] Ch 149, CA; H Potter (1937) 53 *LQR* 308; DC Jackson (1972) 88 *LQR* 93

[148] [1993] Ch 116, CA.

[149] *Hayes* v. *Nwajiaku* [1994] NPC 83; *National & Provincial BS* v. *Ahmed* [1995] 2 EGLR 127, CA.

[150] *Norwich & Peterborough BS* v. *Steed* [1993] Ch 116, 136G–138C, Scott LJ; *Re Leighton's Conveyance* [1936] 1 All ER 667, Luxmoore J; on appeal [1937] Ch 149, 152, Wright MR; H Potter (1937) 53 *LQR* 308; DC Jackson (1972) 88 *LQR* 93.

this as a prejudicial rectification[151] may have achieved fairer results. A lender will be bound if the true owner retains occupation and hence has status to override the mortgage.[152]

I. MERE EQUITIES

[24.30] A mere equity is a right to a equitable remedy which is discretionary in character,[153] so that the substance of the right is the possibility of applying to the court for an order to enforce the right. Examples are the right to set aside a transaction for undue influence[154] and the right to rectify a document for mistake.[155] Much academic comment arose from the putative development of the rights of deserted wives as a mere equity[156] before this development was squashed by the House of Lords.[157]

A modified form of notice doctrine applies.[158] Protection against a mere equity could be given by acquisition of an equitable interest,[159] though most cases have concerned legal estates.[160] So if a lease states a rent of £130 when it was agreed at £230, a mortgage lender can insist on paying the lower rent.[161] In principle, protection is also removed against a discoverable mere equity, but a buyer is entitled to rely on apparently valid title deeds, and it will be difficult to dispute the diligence of a buyer.[162]

Mere equities relating to a registered title are now declared to be proprietary.[163] These rights are rarely recorded on the register, so the crucial question is whether there is an overriding interest through actual occupation.[164]

---

[151] See the discussion of the case of Haigh, the acid bath murderer: TBF Ruoff (1969) 32 *MLR* 121, 140–41.

[152] *Collings* v. *Lee* [2001] 2 All ER 332, CA; R Nolan [2001] CLJ 477; *Malory Enterprises* v. *Cheshire Homes (UK)* [2002] EWCA Civ 151, [2002] Ch 216.

[153] HWR Wade [1955] *CLJ* 160.

[154] See below **[30.54]**.

[155] See above **[22.30]**.

[156] *Westminster Bank* v. *Lee* [1956] Ch 7; RE Megarry (1955) 71 *LQR* 481; HWR Wade [1955] *CLJ* 160; FR Crane (1955) 19 *Conv (NS)* 343; VT Delaney (1958) 21 *Conv (NS)* 195; A Everton (1976) 40 *Conv (NS)* 209.

[157] *National Provincial Bank* v. *Ainsworth* [1965] AC 1175, 1226, 1237–1238, 1254.

[158] See above **[15.06ff]**.

[159] *Phillips* v. *Phillips* (1862) 4 De GF & J 208, 45 ER 1164; *Cave* v. *Cave* (1880) 15 Ch D 639, 647–648, Fry J; *Blacklocks* v. *JB Developments (Godalming)* [1982] Ch 183, 196G.

[160] *Smith* v. *Jones* [1954] 1 WLR 1089; RE Megarry (1955) 71 *LQR* 175.

[161] *Garrard* v. *Frankel* (1862) 30 Beav 445, 54 ER 961; *Bainbrigge* v. *Browne* (1881) 18 Ch D 188 (undue influence); *Bulley* v. *Bulley* (1874) LR 9 Ch App 739 (fraudulent conveyance); *De Witte* v. *Addison* (1899) 80 LT 207 (actual notice of undue influence).

[162] *Smith* v. *Jones* [1954] 1 WLR 1089.

[163] LRA 2002 s 116; Law Com 271 (2001), [5.36] 55% (but academics against).

[164] LRA 2002 sch 3 para 2; *Nurdin & Peacock* v. *DB Ramsden & Co* [1999] 1 WLR 1249, Ch D; G Virgo [1999] *CLJ* 478; S Pascoe [1999] *Conv* 421; *Holow (470)* v. *Stockton Estates* (2001) 81 P & CR 404, Ch D; *Bhullar* v. *McArdle* [2001] EWCA Civ 510, (2001) 82 P & CR 38 at 481; see above **[20.19]**.

25

LEASES

Terms of years. Commencement. Periodic tenancies. Certainty. Formality. Equitable leases. Leases of registered land: substantive registration; notices; overriding; "public" leases. Termination: surrender; merger; break clauses. Residential renting. Licences. Negotiations and tenancies at will. Exclusive licences. Renewal and enfranchisement rights.

A. TERM OF YEARS

[25.01] A lease[1] is created when a tenant is given exclusive possession of his landlord's property for a period of time. This duration is called the term of the lease.[2] After 1925 legal status is restricted to the term of years absolute,[3] meaning that leases for life are excluded.

1. The term of years absolute

[25.02] A fixed term is one archetype of the lease.[4] Exclusive possession must be given for a maximum duration in years ascertained at the outset. Any perpetual interest or indefinite interest creates a freehold estate, rather than a lease.[5] If not fixed in the lease, the term may be fixed by reference to some event which is certain at the time of the grant or at least when the lease actually takes effect.[6] English law imposes no limit on how long or short the term may be. Mortgages of freehold land used to employ the device of a 3,000 year lease.[7] Leases for 999 years are common,[8] usually requiring only

---

[1] Chappelle *Land Law* (5th ed) ch 9; Cheshire & Burn (16th ed) ch 17; Dixon's *Principles* (3rd ed) ch 6; Goo's *Sourcebook* (3rd ed) ch 9; Gravells, *LL – Text* (1999) ch 5; Grays' *Elements* (3rd ed) chs 4, 11; Maudsley & Burn *LL – Cases* (7th ed) ch 8; Megarry & Wade (6th ed) ch 14; Smith's *Property Law* (4th ed) chs 16–18; W Swadling "Property" ch 4 in Birks' *English Private Law*, [4.83 ff]; Thompson *Modern LL* ch 11.

[2] Contrast the terms on which the land is held, called the covenants, discussed in the succeeding chapter.

[3] LPA 1925 ss 1(1)(b), 205(1)(xxvii); LRA 2002 s 132(1).

[4] LPA 1925 s 205(1)(xxvii) includes "a term of years . . .". The other is the periodic tenancy, see below at **[25.12]**.

[5] *Sevenoaks Maidstone & Tunbridge Rly Co* v. *London Chatham & Dover Rly Co* (1879) 11 Ch D 625, 635, Jessel MR.

[6] *Bishop of Bath's* case (1605) 6 Co Rep 34b, 35b, 77 ER 303; *Re Midland Railway Co's Agreement* [1971] Ch 725, 731H, Russell LJ.

[7] LPA 1925 s 85(2).

[8] [1982] *Conv* 95 "supposed to last – like the Third Reich – for a 1000 years or so"; NG James (1998) 19 *JLH* 1 (long leases common in old Court of Wards). The duration may be associated with the early Christian assumption that the world would end in a thousand years: *Revelations* xx, 1–7. See also *Att-Gen* v. *Owen* (1805) 10 Ves 555, 560, 32 ER 960, Eldon LC (duration traditionally limited to 40 years); Megarry & Wade (6th ed), [14.004], n 40.

a nominal rent payment so that all the value in the land is transferred to the tenant. However, houses in London are often sold on a 99 year lease and if a substantial rent is reserved, the financial value of the land is divided between the lease and the reversion. The lease is a wasting asset, its value declining with each year that passes and transferring to the ground landlord. Hence the old Irish wisdom that:

The devil never grants long leases.

The damage can be ameliorated by enfranchisement, that is by compelling the landlord to transfer his reversion to a residential leaseholder, but details of those procedures lie beyond the scope of this work.[9] Twenty one years is an important cut off point for enfranchisement rights. It was also important for registrability, but leases as short as seven years now require registration.[10] Very short terms are recognised, including a "term for less than a year or for a year or years and a fraction of a year."[11] Residential tenancies are often weekly or monthly, a lease of a timeshare may be for one week,[12] and why not a lease for one day to watch a Royal procession or a concert?[13]

"Absolute" has a distinct meaning in the two key phrases, the "term of years absolute" and the "fee simple absolute in possession".[14] It excludes from legal status any fee simple interest liable to end early, whether by condition or determination. Leasehold terms may be "absolute" in this sense, but they are extreme rarities and even then the term can be ended by an agreed surrender.[15] So "absolute" when applied to a lease generally means no more than that the *maximum* duration is fixed in years – that one should be able to tell the longest possible commitment of the landlord. Legal status is allowed to a lease which is:

"liable to determination by notice, re-entry, operation of law, or by a provision for cesser on redemption, or in any other event[16] (other than the dropping of a life . . .)".[17]

A lease invariably provides for forfeiture if the tenant fails to perform his covenants so that the landlord can end the term by forfeiture after a sufficiently serious breach of covenant.[18] Another common provision is a break clause, enabling one or other or both of the parties to end the term by notice.

2. Leases for life at a rent or fine

[25.03] Periods of lives must take effect as beneficial interests behind a trust of land. Leases for life were common before 1926 and special provision had to be made to fit

---

[9] Sparkes *NLT* ch 15; Chold and L Ref A 2002 Part II.
[10] See below [25.36].
[11] LPA 1925 s 205(1)(xxvii).
[12] *Cottage Holiday Associates* v. *Customs & Excise Commissioners* [1983] QB 735; M Haley (1995) 24 *Anglo-American* 236.
[13] Licences are more usual: *Krell* v. *Henry* [1903] 2 QB 740, CA.
[14] LPA 1925 s 1(1).
[15] See below [25.62].
[16] Eg *for 10 years or until the next general election if sooner*; *Eton College* v. *Bard* [1983] Ch 321, CA (until the lease shall cease to be vested in a member of the association).
[17] LPA 1925 s 205(1)(xxvii).
[18] See below [26.32ff].

them into the statutory straightjacket. The term of years absolute excludes any interest terminable on "the dropping of a life or the determination of a determinable life
interest". An inherent problem is that the death of the measuring life could leave a
family homeless overnight, as happened to the Winterborne family in Hardy's *The
Woodlanders*[19] after old South died. Although legal leases for life were prohibited in
1925, the change was largely cosmetic.

Section 149(6) of the Law of Property Act 1925 converts a lease for life at a rent or
fine into a term of 90 years. This catches not only a straight lease for life but also any
term of years determinable with life[20] or on marriage. Conversion is:

> "for a term of ninety years determinable after the death or marriage of the original lessee . . .
> by at least one month's notice in writing . . .".[21]

However, this rewritten lease for 90 years is still terminable by notice after the dropping of that same life, so the difference in duration is minimal. The legislation is
arbitrary and unnecessary as these examples show:

(1) *To A for life* is converted to a term of 90 years; an adult would have to live to
    more than 108 to exhaust the statutory duration, an unlikely longevity.
(2) *To B for 99 years if she so long lives*, is reduced from 99 to 90 years for no
    discernible reason.
(3) *To C for 99 years if D so long lives* is converted to 90 years.[22]

(4) *To E for 10 years if he so long remains a bachelor*. Already a term of years
    absolute,[23] this is extended for no good reason from 10 to 90 years.

Any converted lease is terminable by written notice on either side, though the landlord
usually has the greatest interest in ending it. Notice must be of at least one month's
duration, and may expire on any subsequent quarter day.[24] If the lease was granted in
1954 (meaning that the converted term expires in 2044) and the tenant dies on October
28th 2002, it can be terminated by one month's notice to expire on December 25th
2002 or any later quarter day.

3. Equitable leases for life

[25.04] A voluntary lease for life reserves no rent and no premium.[25] Such leases are
overreachable, and are practically identical to a life interest except that repairing
obligations are more easily imposed. Today they operate under a trust of land, but
before 1997 they had to be created under a trust for sale unless the settlor was happy

---

[19] T Hardy chs 13–15. The birthplace near Dorchester was held by his father on a lifehold.
[20] *Bass Holdings* v. *Lewis* [1986] 2 EGLR 40, CA (tenancy terminable by notice after tenant's death not
a lease for life).
[21] Detailed provisions govern the date on which notice must be served. It applies to leases, underleases
and contracts for commercial leases: *Blamires* v. *Bradford Corp* [1964] Ch 585.
[22] LPA 1925 s 149(6)(c).
[23] S 205(1)(xxvii) does not refer to marriage.
[24] Unless special quarter days are agreed (s 149(6)(d)), the quarter days are December 25th, March 25th,
June 24th, and September 29th.
[25] *Skipton BS* v. *Clayton* (1993) 66 P & CR 223, CA (sale below market price subject to rent-free right for
sellers to occupy for life; this was value); *Waite* v. *Jennings* [1906] 2 KB 11 (on 1881 Act).

for the strict settlement machinery to apply.[26] Commercial terms were not converted if they took effect in equity under a (strict?[27]) settlement and in this way a life interest could be made subject to a rent.

B. COMMENCEMENT

[25.05] A perfect lease requires a certain beginning as well as a certain ending.[28]

1. The commencement date

[25.06] Odd as it may seem, the long established rule is that if a lease runs "from" a stated day, that day is not part of the term,[29] though it may be brought in by express words or contrary indications.[30] The length of the term may be measured from a date before the grant of the lease to the tenant, though rent should not predate the right to occupation.[31] Hence it is possible to achieve a common termination date across a leasehold development. When a tenant holds over at the end of a previous lease, new terms can be agreed later to operate from the end of the previous lease.[32]

2. Future leases

[25.07] A legal lease may operate immediately from its grant or it may entitle the tenant to possession of the land only in the future. A future lease[33] which is to operate at law must be created by deed.[34] Section 149(3) of the Law of Property Act 1925 states that:

"A term, at a rent or granted in consideration of a fine . . . to take effect more than 21 years from the date of the instrument purporting to create it shall be void . . .".[35]

A lease in 1999 to confer possession in 2018 is valid, but if possession were deferred until 2025 it would be void. Why aren't gratuitous leases included since the burden is even greater? *Swift v. Macbean*[36] apparently allowed a legal lease to commence on an

---

[26] SLA 1925 s 1; *Binions v. Evans* [1972] Ch 359, CA.

[27] LPA 1925 s 149(6)(a) refers to SLA 1925 s 117(1)(xxiv); this may now be spent.

[28] *Marshall v. Berridge* (1881) 19 Ch D 233, 245, Lush LJ; *Say v. Smith* (1530) 1 Plowd 269, 75 ER 410; Blackstone's *Commentaries* vol 2, 143; *Prudential Assurance Co v. London Residuary Body* [1992] 2 AC 386, 390, Lord Templeman.

[29] *Sidebotham v. Holland* [1895] 1 QB 378, CA; *Whelton Sinclair v. Hyland* [1992] 2 EGLR 158, CA; E Cooke [1993] *Conv* 206; *Yeandle v. Reigate & Banstead BC* [1996] 1 EGLR 20.

[30] *Meadfield Properties v. SS for Environment* [1995] 1 EGLR 39, Ch D.

[31] *Roberts v. Church Commissioners for England* [1972] 1 QB 278, CA (enfranchisement measured from possession date).

[32] *Bradshaw v. Pawley* [1980] 1 WLR 10.

[33] Sometimes called a "reversionary lease", but this term is also used for a lease sitting between an existing lease and the reversion; see below [27.04].

[34] Except for a contract for a short lease: LP (MP) A 1989 s 2(5)(a); see below [25.27].

[35] Exceptions are leases created under settlements, those out of equitable interests, or under equitable powers to mortgage for indemnity.

[36] [1942] 1 KB 375 (overruled by *Lace v. Chantler* [1944] KB 368, CA, on termination); *Bishop of Bath's case* (1605) 6 Co Rep 34b, 35b, 77 ER 303; *Duke of Norfolk's case* (1685) 3 Ch Cas 1, 22 ER 931; *Ex p Voisey* (1882) 21 Ch D 442, CA.

uncertain future date, but the contingency must be fulfilled within a perpetuity period.[37]

3. Contracts for the creation of leases

[25.08] A contract for a legal lease involves three dates, A when the contract is entered into, B when the legal lease is granted, and C when the term of the lease is to commence. Three restrictions arise: (1) Date B must be agreed, since a contract is not valid without stating a commencement date for the term. This cannot be implied,[38] though it may be inferred from taking occupation. (2) The period A–B is regulated by the rule against perpetuities. This limits future vesting of an estate in the tenant.[39] Uncertainty about the entitlement of the tenant to the lease must be removed within a perpetuity period, usually expressly stated to be 80 years.[40] (3) The period B–C is regulated by the future lease provisions.[41] As with legal leases, the legislation focuses on the gap between execution of the lease and its taking effect in possession, that is dates B and C. Once it takes effect in possession, the lease could be for a very long period. Curious anomalies result from section 149(3):

> One: A contract is void if created in 1999 (A) for a commercial lease to be granted in 2000 (B) for 40 years from 2025 (C). Two: a contract is valid if created in 1999 (A) to grant a commercial lease in 2016 (B) for a 40 year term from 2025 (C).

4. Perpetually renewable lease

[25.09] Statute defines this as any lease of which perpetual renewal can be enforced by the tenants, with or without conditions.[42] Provisions in the Law of Property Act 1922 (as opposed to the 1925 Act) convert such leases to a single, non-renewable term of 2000 years.[43] This can be broken by the tenant but not by the landlord. An option to renew once, or to renew when a new rent is agreed[44] presents no danger. What transforms an innocuous looking lease into a 2000 year monster is the inclusion of a provision that the renewed lease is itself renewable, since this creates an indefinite loop,[45] "sowing the seeds of its own reproduction". Before 1926 the tenant had to remember

---

[37] It is open to question whether the period should be 21 years, 80 years, or a full period of lives in being plus 21 years.

[38] *Harvey* v. *Pratt* [1965] 1 WLR 1025, 1027E, Lord Denning MR.

[39] Before 1926, future leases escaped perpetuity problems because the tenant acquired only an *interesse termini*: C Sweet (1914) 30 *LQR* 66; LPA 1925 s 149(1) (abolition).

[40] Perpetuities and Accumulations Act 1964 s 1.

[41] LPA 1925 s 149(6).

[42] LPA 1922 s 190.

[43] LPA 1922 s 145, sch 15; SR & O 1925/857. Special terms of the lease are: (1) assignments must be registered with the landlord; (2) no privity of contract liability; and (3) a fine in a pre-1926 lease was converted to extra rent but a fine in a post-1925 lease is lost.

[44] *Marjorie Burnett* v. *Barclay* [1981] 1 EGLR 41. Renewal may be subject to conditions such as performance of the tenant's covenants but not to agreement of a future rent. Also *Plumrose* v. *Real and Leasehold Estates Investment Society* [1970] 1 WLR 52.

[45] *Parkus* v. *Greenwood* [1950] 1 Ch 644, CA (renewal "on same terms, including the present covenant for renewal"); RE Megarry (1950) 66 *LQR* 22, 162; *Re Hopkin's Lease* [1972] 1 WLR 372, CA (correctness open in HL); (1972) 88 *LQR* 177; *Northchurch Estates* v. *Daniels* [1947] 1 Ch 117 ("on identical terms"); RE Megarry (1947) 63 *LQR* 20; ACT (1945) 9 *CLJ* 379.

to initiate the process for renewal each time, but the 1922 Act reverses the burden, making the lease continue across the millennia at a fixed rent until the tenant chooses to terminate it before one of the old renewal dates. Landlords should avoid this type of lease at all costs.

5. Options

[25.10] Many leases contain options to renew the lease or to allow the tenant to buy the landlord's reversion. Essentials are agreement on the price (a premium or rent), contractual formality, and protection usually by estate contract registration.[46] The only control on renewal (which occurs when an existing lease ends) is that the term must not be renewed so as to exceed 60 years from the termination of an existing lease.[47] Options are usually conditional on observance of the covenants – meaning strict compliance at the date of exercise is required,[48] though spent or remedied breaches may be ignored.[49] Options to purchase the landlord's reversion are valid if contained within the lease provided they are exercisable by the current tenant alone, and only during the term or within one year after its end.[50] Any other option is subject to the rule against perpetuities, which requires actual exercise within 21 years.[51] The benefit probably passes with the lease.[52]

6. Estoppel

[25.11] Renewal rights can be created by estoppel, but not simply from a long practice of renewing leases;[53] there must be a promise of renewal and some detrimental reliance.

C. PERIODIC TENANCIES

[25.12] Most short term tenancies are periodic, a form included in the term of years absolute.[54] A term "from year to year", or yearly tenancy, is an initial grant for one

---

[46] See above [21.13].

[47] LPA 1922 sch 15 para 7(2) for post-1925 options; RE Megarry (1947) 63 *LQR* 280.

[48] *West Country Cleaners (Falmouth)* v. *Saly* [1966] 1 WLR 1485, CA; *Bairstow Eves (Securities)* v. *Ripley* (1992) 65 P & CR 230.

[49] *Bass Holdings* v. *Morton Music* [1988] Ch 493, CA; *West Middlesex Golf Club* v. *Ealing LBC* (1995) 68 P & CR 461, Ch D.

[50] Perpetuities and Accumulations Act 1964 s 9(1).

[51] S 9(2); (options after mid-1964). Old law: *Muller* v. *Trafford* [1901] 1 Ch 54; *Woodall* v. *Clifton* [1905] 2 Ch 257; *Re Hunter's Lease* [1942] Ch 124; *Coronation Street Industrial Properties* v. *Ingall Industries* [1989] 1 WLR 304, 307–308, Lord Templeman.

[52] (1) Pre-1996 leases: *Re Adams & Kensington Vestry* (1883) 24 Ch D 199; affirmed (1884) 27 Ch D 394, CA; *Friary Holroyd & Healey's Breweries* v. *Singleton* [1899] 2 Ch 261, CA; *Batchelor* v. *Murphy* [1920] AC 63, HL; *Griffith* v. *Pelton* [1958] Ch 205, CA; *Coastplace* v. *Hartley* [1987] QB 948; (2) clearly so under the LT (Covenants) A 1995, ss 2–3, 28; (3) but see: *Kumar* v. *Dunning* [1989] 1 QB 193, 207, Browne-Wilkinson V-C.

[53] *Ramsden* v. *Dyson* (1866) LR 1 HL 129; *Keelwalk Properties* v. *Waller* [2002] EWCA Civ 1076, [2002] 48 EG 142; see above [23].

[54] LPA 1925 s 205(1)(xxvii).

year which continues to grow by one year at a time, indefinitely,[55] until terminated by proper notice.[56] A year was the archetypal period for agricultural land, but many residential tenancies are monthly or weekly.

1. Creation

[25.13] *Express* tenancies may be for any period. Negotiation might lead to a period of a calendar month or periods of twenty eight or thirty days, or indeed some random time such as 47 days. This flexible structure can be moulded to individual needs. Provided that the initial period of the lease is for less than three years oral creation is allowed.[57]

Periodic tenancies more commonly arise by implication where a tenant occupies land to the exclusion of the landlord and rent is paid and accepted. A tenancy at sufferance arises where a tenant occupies land to the exclusion of the landlord but without his consent, that is as a trespasser who is tolerated.[58] Acceptance of the tenant by the landlord creates a tenancy at will. According to Littleton:[59]

> "Tenant at will is where lands or tenements are let by one man to another, to have to hold to him at the will of the lessor, by force of which lease the lessee is in possession . . . he hath no certain or sure estate, for the lessor may put him out at what time it pleaseth him."

Express tenancies at will arise[60] where a prospective tenant is let into occupation without a lease while negotiations continue, where a purported lease is void,[61] or where a tenant holds over when his existing lease expires.[62]

A periodic tenancy is inferred from the payment and acceptance of rent by reference to a particular period, where the payment has no other explanation.[63] If a tenant enters a property where no particular term has been agreed, payment of rent leads to the implication of a periodic tenancy. The change from a tenant at will to a periodic tenant has important implications for the onset of security of tenure. As with tenancies at will, so it is with periodic tenancies: implication may derive from allowing exclusive occupation of land during negotiations for a new lease, where an attempted fixed term fails for want of formality or uncertainty,[64] or where an existing tenant holds over.

---

[55] Hence the odd rule that a yearly tenant can create a valid sub-lease for 99 years: *Pennell* v. *Payne* [1995] QB 192, CA; this is surely illogical since the tenancy is only for one year prospectively.

[56] A lease for a year and so on from year to year is for a minimum duration of two years.

[57] LPA 1925 s 54(2); otherwise by deed.

[58] The term "tolerated trespasser" is used for a public sector tenant in breach of the terms of a possession order: P Sparkes *NLT*, 333–334.

[59] Littleton's *Tenures* book I, ch VIII.

[60] *Wheeler* v. *Mercer* [1957] AC 416, HL; *British Railways Board* v. *Bodywright* (1971) 220 EG 651 (parties' label not accepted).

[61] *Dossee* v. *Doe d East India Co* (1859) 1 LT 345, PC; *Meye* v. *Electric Transmission* [1942] Ch 290.

[62] *Hagee (London)* v. *AB Erikson & Larson* [1976] QB 209, CA.

[63] A tenancy at will may continue despite rent payments: (1) if agreed: *Cardiothoracic Institute* v. *Shrewdcrest* [1986] 1 WLR 368, Knox J (query if this really avoids security); (2) if accepted by mistake: *Maconochie Bros* v. *Brand* [1946] 2 All ER 778; *Sector Properties* v. *Meah* (1973) 229 EG 1097, CA; (3) after a computer generated demand issued in error: *Dreamgate Property* v. *Arnot* (1998) 76 P & CR 25, CA; or (4) after isolated payments: *Thompsons (Funeral Furnishers)* v. *Phillips* [1945] 2 All ER 49, CA; *Bennett Properties* v. *H & S Engineering* [1998] CLYB 3683, QBD.

[64] *Prudential Assurance Co* v. *London Residuary Body* [1992] 2 AC 386, HL; Blackstone's *Commentaries* vol 2, 147; see below **[25.18ff]**.

What period is implied?[65] It is not necessarily a yearly tenancy, since the period implied follows from the method by which the rent is calculated. In *Ladies' Hosiery & Underwear* v. *Parker* the example was given, *obiter*, of a tenant holding over at the expiration of a three year term at rent of £2 per week, which, in Maugham J's opinion, led to a weekly tenancy.[66] Similarly in *Prudential Assurance Co* v. *London Residuary Body*[67] rent calculated at the yearly rate of £30 was payable quarterly, so that a yearly tenancy arose.

2. Notice to quit

[25.14] Parties to a periodic tenancy start off on the basis that either of the joint tenants may end the tenancy by notice at any time in the future. Lord Millett has said that:

> "A periodic tenancy comes to an end on the expiration of a notice to quit served by the landlord on the tenant or by the tenant on the landlord. [I]t comes to an end by effluxion of time. In each case the tenancy is determined in accordance with its terms. [T]he parties have agreed at the outset on the manner of its determination. The parties and their successors in title, including those who derive title under them, are bound by their agreement."[68]

A notice to quit is non-consensual in contrast to a surrender, since the notice operates under the terms of the original tenancy agreement and does not require the agreement of the other party.

If the landlord gives notice it is called a notice to quit, whether the landlord genuinely wants possession or whether it is simply a vehicle to secure a rent increase or a variation in the terms.[69] Notice is an election to end the existing lease, so the landlord cannot withdraw it unilaterally.[70] If the landlord accepts rent after a notice to quit has expired, this may well create a new periodic tenancy.[71] A tenant who wishes to leave may give a notice of intention to quit.

Every periodic tenancy must be terminable by notice. The length of notice is decided, first, by any *express provision* in the tenancy agreement, which need not be linked to the period of the tenancy. In *Re Midland Railway Co's Agreement*, a six-monthly tenancy was terminable by three months' notice.[72] Express agreement can also require a longer period of notice, despite theoretical problems with repugnancy, so long as the period of notice is of certain duration.[73] Failing an express agreement, the length of notice to terminate a periodic tenancy is *implied* to reflect the period of the tenancy. Yearly tenancies can be terminated by half a year's notice[74] which must

---

[65] If there is any express agreement this is determinative.

[66] [1930] 1 Ch 304, 325 (a tedious and complex case despite its promising name); left open on appeal.

[67] [1992] 2 AC 386, HL.

[68] *Barrett* v. *Morgan* [2000] 2 AC 264, 270C–E, Lord Millett.

[69] *Ahearn* v. *Bellman* (1879) 4 Ex D 201, CA.

[70] *Lower* v. *Sorrell* [1963] 1 QB 959, CA; RE Megarry (1963) 79 *LQR* 178; DG Barnsley (1963) 27 *Conv (NS)* 335; A Dowling [1994] *Conv* 437 (prefers the Irish view permitting withdrawal).

[71] But in some cases not even a tenancy at will was created, below **[25.82]**.

[72] [1971] Ch 725, CA.

[73] *Breams Property Investment Co* v. *Stroulger* [1948] 2 KB 1, CA (three years' notice); DC Potter (1948) 11 *MLR* 342; *Prudential Assurance* v. *London Residuary Body* [1992] 2 AC 386, 395A.

[74] A full year's notice was considered too long by the old common law.

expire on an anniversary date of the commencement of the tenancy. If rent is paid on October 10th, the tenancy could be terminated at the end of October 9th in any subsequent year by a notice served on or before May 9th in the year of termination.[75] At the worst moment in the cycle termination could be delayed for one day less than two years. If the period is less than a full year, the length of notice required is equal to the period of the tenancy. Thus to terminate a monthly tenancy a full month's notice is required,[76] and for a weekly tenancy it is one week's notice; in each case notice must expire at the end of a full period of the tenancy.[77] A monthly tenancy created on July 15th can be terminated by notice expiring at the end of the 14th day of August, September, October, or any subsequent month.[78] If a house is inhabited, notice must be of at least 28 days or four calendar weeks (on either side) but this period is unrelated to the period of the tenancy.[79] It may be implied that notice should not be served too far in advance.[80]

All derivative interests end if a head lease ends by forfeiture[81] or notice to quit: when a periodic tenant serves notice to quit, this ends the head tenancy, and the effect is to bring to an end any sub-tenancy.[82]

3.   Notice to quit – formal requirements and duration

[25.15] Most notices relating to land must be in writing,[83] including any required by a document made after 1925,[84] although unfortunately this statutory rule does not apply to a periodic tenancy if the term about the length of the notice to quit is implied.[85] Validity of a notice depends upon service by the correct landlord on the correct tenant. Service must be proved either in person or more commonly by post.[86] Notices can be sent by registered post, or recorded delivery for statutory notices,[87] but ordinary post will not do.[88] A notice sent by registered post is deemed to be served if it is not returned even if it never in fact arrived.[89]

---

[75] If the tenancy was created on a traditional quarter day (December 25th, March 25th, June 24th and September 29th) two quarter's notice is required. Otherwise the corresponding date rule is applied; see below [25.15].

[76] But see E Cooke [1992] *Conv* 263.

[77] Where the creation date of the tenancy is unknown, this is assumed to be the date on which the rent is paid. The effect of minor errors is considered in the context of break notices.

[78] See below [25.15].

[79] Protection from Eviction Act 1977 s 5.

[80] Contrast: *Multon* v. *Cardell* [1986] 1 EGLR 44; and *Biondi* v. *Kirklington & Piccadilly Estates* [1947] 2 All ER 59, Roxburgh J.

[81] *Great Western Rly Co* v. *Smith* (1876) 2 Ch D 235, CA, affirmed (1877) 3 App Cas 165, HL. The subtenancy may become liable to forfeiture.

[82] *Barrett* v. *Morgan* [2000] 2 AC 264, HL; L Tee [2000] *CLJ* 25; *Pennell* v. *Payne* [1995] QB 192, CA.

[83] LPA 1925 s 196(1); JE Adams [1980] *Conv* 246, 323; *New Hart Builders* v. *Brindley* [1975] Ch 342, Goulding J (option to renew).

[84] Including a notice of severance: *Re 88 Berkeley Road NW 9* [1971] Ch 648, Plowman J; *Kinch* v. *Bullard* [1999] 1 WLR 423, Ch D.

[85] *Wandsworth LBC* v. *Atwell* [1995] 1 WLR 95, CA; JE Adams [1995] *Conv* 186; J Montgomerie (1952) 16 *Conv (NS)* 98, 107.

[86] LPA 1925 s 196(4); P Sparkes *NLT*, 591–593.

[87] Recorded Delivery Service Act 1962 s 1.

[88] *Holwell Securities* v. *Hughes* [1973] 1 WLR 757, Templeman J; contrast *Yates Building Society Co* v. *RJ Pulleyn & Sons (York)* [1976] 1 EGLR 157, CA.

[89] *Commercial Union Life Assurance Co* v. *Moustafa* [1999] 2 EGLR 44, Smedley J; HW Wilkinson

Months[90] measured from (say) January 20th, expire on the 20th day of February, March, April and so on. The number of days in a particular month is irrelevant, so that if notice is required of so many months duration it may expire on the corresponding date of any later month. In *Dodds* v. *Walker*[91] a business tenant had four months to apply to the court for a renewal of his lease, a period which ran from the date of the landlord's notice on September 30th 1978. The date of service (September 30th) was excluded, so the notice expired on the corresponding day (January 30th 1979). Application on the 31st was out of time.[92] The corresponding date rule applies to years, quarters measured from a quarter day,[93] and quarters measured from other dates (which equal three months).[94] Since a week is a certain period of seven days there is no need for a corresponding date rule.[95]

Where a period is measured "from" a particular date, the rule in *Sidebotham* v. *Holland*[96] operates to exclude that date. So a term from September 20th actually begins on the 21st and ends at midnight on the 20th in a later month.[97] *Sidebotham* is counter-intuitive, and is easily excluded.[98]

The new rule is that notices are to be interpreted in a purposive way so that a notice clear to a reasonable recipient will be valid.[99] This might even overcome[100] the doubts felt at common law about a notice to quit in the alternative.[101]

4. Short tenancies held jointly

[25.16] Co-ownership of short tenancies is common, since it is natural for couples to rent living accommodation together. However, legal analysis of this common arrangement was greatly complicated by the simplifications of 1925.

Apparently, a short term tenancy can only be held by joint tenants. When it is, a statutory trust of the land is created.[102] A tenancy in common is equally possible.

[2001] *NLJ* 275; *WX Investments* v. *Begg* [2002] EWHC 925, [2002] 1 WLR 2849, Patten J; *Blunden* v. *Frogmore Investments* [2002] EWCA Civ 573, [2002] 2 EGLR 29 (notice attached to Arndale Centre Manchester after it had been damaged by an IRA bomb).

[90] The rule for calendar months is given by LPA 1925 s 61(4).

[91] [1981] 1 WLR 1027, HL; JT Farrand [1981] *Conv* 321.

[92] *EJ Riley Investments* v. *Eurostile Holdings* [1985] 2 EGLR 124, CA; (1986) 102 *LQR* 3.

[93] March 25th, June 24th, September 29th, December 25th.

[94] *Samuel Properties (Developments)* v. *Hayek* [1972] 1 WLR 1296, CA; (1972) 88 *LQR* 459.

[95] *Okolo* v. *SS for Environment* [1997] 4 All ER 242, CA.

[96] [1895] 1 QB 378, CA.

[97] Notice to quit at noon is invalid. *Bathavon RDC* v. *Carlile* [1958] 1 QB 461, CA; *Yeandle* v. *Reigate & Banstead BC* [1996] 1 EGLR 20 (notice to give possession on September 28th 1993 implied termination at the end of the 28th or beginning of the 29th).

[98] *Ladyman* v. *Wirral Estates* [1968] 2 All ER 197; *Meadfield Properties* v. *SS for Environment* [1995] 1 EGLR 39; *Burman* v. *Mount Cook Land* [2001] EWCA Civ 1712, [2002] 1 EGLR 61.

[99] See below **[25.65]**.

[100] *Speedwell Estates* v. *Dalziel* [2001] EWCA Civ 1277, [2002] HLR 43 (rule not applying to notice lacking crucial statutory details); *Trafford MBC* v. *Total Fitness UK* [2002] EWCA Civ 1513, 44 EG 169 (CS).

[101] *Barclays Bank* v. *Bee* [2001] EWCA Civ 1126, [2001] 37 EG 153; also: *Bridges* v. *Stanford* [1991] 2 EGLR 265, CA; *Addis* v. *Burrows* [1948] 1 KB 444; *P Phipps & Co (Northampton & Towcester Brewers)* v. *Rogers* [1925] 1 KB 14, CA.

[102] *Hammersmith & Fulham LBC* v. *Monk* [1992] 1 AC 478, HL; *Crawley BC* v. *Ure* [1996] QB 13, CA; *Notting Hill HT* v. *Brackley* [2001] EWCA Civ 601, [2001] 3 EGLR 11.

Joint tenancy implies equal participation and equal obligations. *AG Securities* v. *Vaughan*[103] concerned a four bedroomed furnished flat with a communal sitting room and bathroom. No occupant had exclusive possession of any one room. Each of four men signed an occupation agreement described as a "licence", each arriving on a different date and making various monthly payments, so that at any one time there was a mixture of fixed licences for six months and monthly holdings.[104] A joint tenancy was rejected because the unities of time, title and interest were missing.[105] "Initially several", Lord Bridge could not understand "by what legal alchemy they could ever become joint."[106] So it was impossible to have a tenancy in common of a short term tenancy. This view can just about be justified. The co-ownership trust[107] can only be created by a "conveyance", a concept which involves at least a written document,[108] and so holding an oral tenancy in common is not allowed.[109]

5. Unilateral notice to terminate a joint periodic tenancy

[25.17] *Hammersmith & Fulham LBC* v. *Monk*[110] decides that a periodic tenancy can be ended by one of the joint tenants acting unilaterally. Common law notice given by any one without the concurrence of the others ends a joint periodic tenancy unless the rule is altered by the terms of the tenancy itself.[111] The decision was heavily influenced by the particular facts. Mr Monk was the joint tenant of council property with Mrs Powell. After they fell out, she left the property and sought to be rehoused but the housing authority told her that she would only be rehoused[112] if she terminated her existing tenancy, thus freeing the public accommodation which they had shared.

Dealing with a joint legal tenancy requires a joint act for termination.[113] Examples are the exercise of a break clause, a disclaimer, an option to renew, and applying for relief from forfeiture.[114] A unilateral surrender failed in *Hounslow LBC* v. *Pilling*.[115] Miss Doubtfire wrote a letter on Friday to terminate a weekly tenancy the next Monday, which was invalid as a notice since the duration of the notice was less than 28 days,[116] and invalid as a surrender since any dealing had to be joint.

---

[103] [1990] 1 AC 417, HL; *UHU Property Trust* v. *Lincoln CC* [2000] RA 419, Sullivan J (issue council tax).

[104] House sharing in the style of *The Young Ones* is under threat from rule that any household with more than two unrelated people sharing will be an HMO.

[105] At 472B, Lord Oliver; also in CA at 433, Sir George Waller.

[106] At 454A; PV Baker (1988) 104 *LQR* 173, 174–175.

[107] LPA 1925 s 1(6). Technical co-ownership rules are really inappropriate: *Lloyd* v. *Sadler* [1978] QB 774, 788G, Lawton LJ; *Savage* v. *Dunningham* [1974] Ch 181, 185, Plowman J.

[108] LPA 1925 s 34 (as amended), 62, 205(1)(ii); *Borman* v. *Griffith* [1930] 1 Ch 493, 498–499; *Rye* v. *Rye* [1962] AC 496, HL.

[109] LPA 1925 s 34(1).

[110] [1992] 1 AC 478, HL; J Dewar (1992) 108 *LQR* 375; L Tee [1992] *CLJ* 218.

[111] A release by T1 to T2 is an assignment of the tenancy not a surrender: *Burton* v. *Camden LBC* [2000] 2 AC 399, HL.

[112] Local authorities have used *Monk* to end the tenancy of a violent partner and to regrant a tenancy of the same property to the victim, but surely this reassignment should be made after an exercise of judicial discretion.

[113] Eg enfranchisement: *Wax* v. *Chelsea* [1996] 2 EGLR 80.

[114] *Hammersmith & Fulham LBC* v. *Monk* [1992] 1 AC 478, 490G, Lord Bridge.

[115] [1994] 1 All ER 432, CA; L Tee [1994] *CLJ* 227; *Burton* v. *Camden LBC* [1998] 1 FLR 681, CA (deed of release); *Osei-Bonsu* v. *Wandsworth LBC* [1999] 1 WLR 1011, CA.

[116] Protection from Eviction Act 1977 s 5.

Monk looks suspect in creating a divide between a surrender and a notice to quit.[117] Nevertheless Lord Bridge ruled in *Monk* that a periodic tenancy created an estate in the land for one period at a time, and it continued to the next period only if all parties wished it to do so. Blackstone speaking of a yearly tenancy, observed that it continues during the will of both parties. Nineteenth[118] and twentieth[119] century opinions and authorities support this view because it avoids the inconvenience of holding a joint tenant bound for life by a tenancy he no longer wants.

Although *Monk* enables a local authority to break a public sector "secure" tenancy after domestic violence and relet the property to the victimised partner, it can also work most unfairly. When one party deserts the home, what is to stop him or her then serving notice to quit as a simple matter of spite and forcing the former partner out of the home that they had shared? Or to foil an attempt to exercise the right to buy?[120] Presumably the other joint tenant is not entitled to any period of notice from the landlord at all. A number of attempted solutions have failed. No action is allowed for breach of the statutory co-ownership trust.[121] Family law non-molestation orders failed to help in *Harrow LBC* v. *Johnstone*,[122] even, apparently,[123] if the wording of the injunction had expressly prohibited service of a notice to quit(!) The remaining spouse cannot rely on the divorce legislation. A divorcing spouse could apply for an order transferring the tenancy from joint names to the name of the spouse who wishes to stay,[124] but a notice to quit ends the tenancy so there is nothing left to transfer. In *Newlon Housing Trust* v. *Alsulaimen*,[125] a husband obtained legal aid for his application for a transfer of the tenancy of the former matrimonial home, but his former wife gave notice to quit and the landlord sought immediate possession in advance of the husband's application in the family court. She crabbed his matrimonial application. Her notice was not a disposition intended to preclude matrimonial relief. Nor is the matrimonial home right any protection.[126]

It remains arguable that *Monk* is an unjustified interference with the tenant's right to respect for his home.[127]

---

[117] *Howson* v. *Buxton* (1928) 97 LJKB 749, 752, Scrutton LJ; *Monk* [1992] AC 478, 491, Lord Browne-Wilkinson ("strong and logical").

[118] *Doe d Aslin* v. *Summersett* (1830) 1 B & Ad 135, 109 ER 738; *Doe d Kindersley* v. *Hughes* (1840) 7 M & W 139, 151 ER 711; *Alford* v. *Vickery* (1842) Car & M 280, 174 ER 507.

[119] *Leek & Moorlands BS* v. *Clark* [1952] 2 QB 788; *Smith* v. *Grayton Estates* [1960] SC 349; *Greenwich LBC* v. *McGrady* (1982) 46 P & CR 223, CA; *Parsons* v. *Parsons* [1983] 1 WLR 1390; *Annen* v. *Rattee* [1985] 1 EGLR 136, CA.

[120] *Bater* v. *Bater* [1999] 4 All ER 944, CA.

[121] *Crawley BC* v. *Ure* [1996] QB 13, CA; *Notting Hill HT* v. *Brackley* [2001] EWCA Civ 601, [2001] 3 EGLR 11.

[122] [1997] 1 WLR 459, HL; MP Thompson [1997] *Conv* 288.

[123] At 470H, Lord Mustill, 471, Lord Hoffmann.

[124] Family Law Act 1996 s 53, sch 7 (including cohabitees).

[125] [1998] 1 AC 313, HL; *Harrow LBC* v. *Johnstone* [1997] 1 WLR 459, 471, Lord Hoffman; MP Thompson [1997] *Conv* 288.

[126] *Sanctuary H Ass* v. *Campbell* [1999] 1 WLR 1279, CA.

[127] *Qazi* v. *Harrow LBC* [2001] EWCA Civ 1834, [2002] HLR 14 at 276; I Loveland (2002) 3 *EHRLR* 327.

D. CERTAINTY

[25.18] A tenancy granted until a future event occurs runs the risk that the event may never occur, so that what is intended to be a short term turns into a perpetual burden on the land. This danger is avoided by requiring a term to be certain in advance.

1. Fixed terms

[25.19] A lease must obviously be certain in *retrospect*. When the time comes for the lease to end, this fact must be clear. In addition, the law has insisted since at least 1530[128] that the duration of a lease must be fixed with *prospective* certainty, that is in advance, either by a fixed date or by reference to a certain future event. In *Lace* v. *Chantler*[129] a tenancy "furnished for duration" – that is for the duration of the Second World War – was struck down by the Court of Appeal.[130] In, say 1940, one could not tell for how many years the war would last. At the time of the litigation in 1944, the war was still on with no end in sight, though fortunately the tide had turned.

After some contrary decisions[131] the test of prospective certainty was unanimously approved by the House of Lords in *Prudential Assurance Co* v. *London Residuary Body*.[132] A lease of land fronting Walworth Road in London was granted in 1930 to continue until the land was required for road widening. This single uncertain term was void. By 1992 it had become extremely unlikely that the road would ever be widened and to have allowed the lease to stand would have been to confer a perpetual right of possession at a fixed rent of £30 a year. That injustice was avoided by invalidating the term. A tenancy at will arose, converted to a periodic tenancy by payment and acceptance of rent,[133] which could be terminated to allow the rent increase.

2. Avoiding uncertainty

[25.20] Lord Browne-Wilkinson characterised the result of *Prudential Assurance Co* v. *London Residuary Body* as unsatisfactory, but Lord Templeman provided no hint of unease at the result to which his technical analysis directed him. Academic opinion is also divided.[134]

---

[128] *Say* v. *Smith* (1530) 1 Plowd 269, 75 ER 410; *Bishop of Bath's case* (1605) 6 Co Rep 34b, 35b, 77 ER 303; Coke on *Littleton*, [45b]; Blackstone's *Commentaries* vol 2, 143; T Platt, *Law of Leases* (1847) vol 1, 22.

[129] [1944] KB 368, 370; *Joseph* v. *Joseph* [1967] Ch 78, 86D–G (to give up occupation "by July 31st 1960", valid).

[130] [1944] KB 368; (1944) 60 *LQR* 219; JDGJ (1945) 9 *CLJ* 121; *Eker* v. *Becker* [1946] 1 All ER 721.

[131] *Ashburn Anstalt* v. *Arnold & Co* [1989] Ch 1, CA (until notice that the landlord was ready to begin development); *Canadian Imperial Bank of Commerce* v. *Bello* (1991) 24 HLR 155, CA (until builder paid for building work); *Prudential* [1992] 2 AC 386 in CA.

[132] [1992] 2 AC 386, HL; P Sparkes (1993) 109 *LQR* 93; PF Smith [1993] *Conv* 461; S Bridge [1993] *CLJ* 26; D Wilde (1994) 57 *MLR* 117; M Biles [1994] *NLJ* 156; M Haley (1995) 24 *Anglo-American* 236.

[133] See above **[25.13]**.

[134] [1992] 2 AC 386, 396G. Contrast P Sparkes (1993) 109 *LQR* 93, 110–113 (decision correct); and S Bright (1993) 13 LS 38 (decision unfair).

Two techniques are available to avoid uncertainty if this is thought desirable. In *Great Northern Railway Co* v. *Arnold*,[135] a lease for the duration of the Great War was treated as a lease for 999 years terminable on the cessation of that war, though *Lace* v. *Chantler*[136] suggests that the selection of 999 years was artificial; why not the more optimistic period of 10 years adopted by statute towards the end of the second war?[137] Even 999 years might not be long enough to cover the period *until Scotland wins the World Cup*,[138] or indeed until they reach the second phase. Equity has the same rule,[139] since specific performance of an agreement to create an uncertain term would create an invalid lease of uncertain duration.[140] So a tenant who failed for uncertainty in the common law courts,[141] before transferring to equity and trying again, also failed on this second occasion for uncertainty.[142] However, equity is sometimes able to reinterpret an agreement, for example by treating an uncertain term as a lease for life,[143] which will now act as a term of 90 years.[144]

3.   Certainty of periodic tenancies

[25.21] A periodic tenancy is in its very nature uncertain.[145] Initially for one period, it will roll on from one period to the next until one or other of the parties brings it to an end by notice. A monthly tenancy which has lasted for 50 years is for the future for one month only. The maximum commitment can be fixed at any moment by service of notice. Each occupational unit of time, as it is added to the preceding unit, is of certain duration.[146]

Prudential Assurance[147] has swept away the decision in *Re Midland Railway Co's Agreement*,[148] which allowed periodic terms to have attached to them an uncertain minimum duration. Some railway land – a mere 100 square yards[149] – was granted in 1920 subject to a term which prevented the landlord from serving notice unless the land was required for the purposes of the railway. No need had arisen by 1971, so the tenant had what was effectively an indefinite right to occupy at a fixed rent. This was not a valid tenancy, since *Midland Railway* has been overruled, and prospective certainty is stated as a requirement for periodic tenancies. Thus, in *Prudential*

---

[135] (1916) 33 TLR 114; *Siew Soon Wah* v. *Yong Tong Hong* [1973] AC 836, 844 (*this lease shall be permanent* = 30 years, the maximum allowed under Malaysian law.)

[136] [1944] KB 368, 371, Lord Greene MR; 372, MacKinnon LJ.

[137] Validation of War Time Leases Act 1944 s 1(1); [1992] 2 AC 386, 391G–392A, Lord Templeman.

[138] Compare [1992] 1 EGLR 47, 51A (*until England wins the Davis Cup*, an example happily less striking ten years after Scott LJ suggested it).

[139] *Harvey* v. *Pratt* [1965] 1 WLR 1025, 1026E, Lord Denning MR; *Marshall* v. *Berridge* (1881) 19 Ch D 233, 245, Lush LJ; contrary to *Wallis* v. *Semark* (1951) 2 TLR 222, 226.

[140] *Cheshire Lines Committee* v. *Lewis & Co* (1880) 50 LJQB 121, 129, Brett LJ.

[141] *Doe d Warner* v. *Browne* (1807) 8 East 165, 103 ER 305.

[142] *Browne* v. *Warner* (1808) 14 Ves 156, 33 ER 480.

[143] *Prudential* [1992] 2 AC 386, 409; *Re King's Leasehold Estates* (1873) LR 16 Eq 521, 527, Malins V-C; *Cheshire Lines* (1880) 50 LJQB 121, 126, 129; *Wood* v. *Beard* (1876) 2 Ex D 30, 36.

[144] LPA 1925 s 149(6); *Zimbler* v. *Abrahams* [1903] 1 KB 577, CA; *Binions* v. *Evans* [1972] Ch 359 367E–H, Lord Denning MR.

[145] *Re Midland Railway Co's Agreement* [1971] Ch 725, 732F–G.

[146] *Hammersmith & Fulham LBC* v. *Monk* [1992] 1 AC 478, 484E, Lord Bridge.

[147] [1992] 2 AC 386, 395G, Lord Templeman.

[148] [1971] Ch 725, CA; D Macintyre [1971] *CLJ* 198.

[149] Less than 10 metres by 10 metres.

Assurance,[150] a single term to endure until land was required for road widening was held to be uncertain. Entry under a void tenancy, coupled with the payment and acceptance of a yearly rent meant that the tenant obtained a yearly tenancy. It was not permissible to imply a provision that this yearly tenancy could only be terminated when the land was required for the purposes of road widening. Like any other yearly tenancy, it could be terminated by one half year's notice expiring at the end of *any* period of the tenancy.

4. Repugnancy

[25.22] An express or implied term of a periodic tenancy may be rejected because of an inconsistency with the nature of the periodic tenancy of which it forms a part. Old law prevented any term relating to any time after the end of the very first period, for example, a covenant to paint every three years,[151] or to give two years notice to quit,[152] or to do substantial repairs.[153] Modern law restricts repugnancy to the future, allowing terms to be enforced which apply to a time when the tenant has actually been in occupation.[154] Notice provisions limit termination in the future, but illogically a tenancy can restrict service of notice for a fixed period of time such as five years.[155] A clause becomes repugnant if the landlord can never terminate the lease.[156]

E. FORMALITY FOR LEGAL LEASES

1. Legal leases by deed

[25.23] Leases are "conveyances "[157] which section 52(1) of the Law of Property Act 1925[158] requires to be by deed, unless they fall into the short lease exemption considered below. An informal lease is "void for the purpose of conveying or creating a legal estate".[159] Formality is also required for any legal assignment of any existing legal lease, whether it is long or short.[160]

---

[150] *Prudential Assurance* [1992] 2 AC 386, 394F, Lord Templeman; *Onyx (UK)* v. *Beard* [1996] EGCS 55, Ch D. It is odd that a licence may be created for an uncertain period: P Sparkes (1993) 109 *LQR* 93, 107–110.

[151] *Tooker* v. *Smith* (1857) 1 H & N 732, 156 ER 1396.

[152] *Pinero* v. *Judson* (1829) 6 Bing 206, 130 ER 1259.

[153] *Doe d Thomson* v. *Amey* (1840) 22 Ad & El 476, 479, 113 ER 892.

[154] *Pistor* v. *Cater* (1842) 9 M & W 315, 152 ER 134; *Adams* v. *Clutterbuck* (1883) 10 QBD 403, 406.

[155] *Prudential* [1992] 2 AC 386, 395A, Lord Templeman; *Breams Property Investment Co* v. *Stroulger* [1948] 2 KB 1; DC Potter (1948) 11 *MLR* 342.

[156] *Centaploy* v. *Matlodge* [1974] Ch 1, Whitford J; *Re Midland Railway Co's Agreement* [1971] Ch 725, 733F, Russell LJ.

[157] Including leases of intangible rights such as easements: *Brown* v. *Peto* [1900] 2 QB 653, CA.

[158] Replacing Statute of Frauds 1677 (writing) and Real Property Act 1845 s 3 (deed). For deeds see above **[7]** and short leases see below **[25.24]**.

[159] For the effect in equity see above **[24.05]**, below **[25.29ff]**.

[160] *Botting* v. *Martin* (1808) 1 Camp 317, 170 ER 970; *Crago* v. *Julian* [1992] 1 WLR 372, CA; P Sparkes [1992] *Conv* 375.

2. Informal short-term leases

[25.24] Short leases are exempted from the need for a full formality by the Law of Property Act 1925 in these terms:

"Nothing [in sections 40 to 54] shall affect the creation by parol of leases (1) taking effect in possession, (2) for a term not exceeding three years (whether or not the lessee is given power to extend the term) (3) at the best rent which can reasonably be obtained without taking a fine."[161]

Creation can be purely orally[162] though full formality is required to transfer any existing lease.[163]

(1) Best rent

[25.25] The modern requirement is that an informal tenancy must be at the best rent, so that a deed is required for any lease which reserves a fine.[164]

(2) Term not exceeding three years

[25.26] A legal lease for three years certain can be written or oral, but a legal lease for three years and one week certain must be by deed.[165] The maximum duration determines the necessary formality.[166] Rights for the landlord to forfeit the lease, for the tenant to extend it,[167] or for either side to break it[168] are ignored.

A legal tenancy from leap year to leap year would require full formalities, but periodic tenancies will generally qualify for informal creation[169] – whether yearly, monthly,[170] or weekly.[171] This is despite the obvious fact that [a periodic] tenancy may go on for a great number of years.[172] The touchstone is the length of the lease after each party has tried to terminate it. Despite *Ex p Voisey*,[173] a deed should be required if either party is compellable past three years.[174]

---

[161] S 54(2) (numbering supplied); it re-enacted in a different form the Statute of Frauds 1677 s 2; P Sparkes [1992] *Conv* 252, 337; JE Adams [2001] *Conv* 213.

[162] An oral lease suffers certain disadvantages: *Rye* v. *Rye* [1962] AC 496, HL.

[163] *Botting* v. *Martin* (1808) 1 Camp 317, 170 ER 970; *Crago* v. *Julian* [1992] 1 WLR 372, CA.

[164] Compare *City Permanent BS* v. *Miller* [1952] Ch 840, 846 (original overriding interest).

[165] *Miller* as above, CA.

[166] Not the minimum period: *Hammond* v. *Farrow* [1904] 2 KB 332, 335, Wills J; explained in *Kushner* v. *Law Society* [1952] 1 KB 264, 273, Goddard LCJ.

[167] LPA 1925 s 54(2); *Hand* v. *Hall* (1877) 2 Ex D 355; *Gray* v. *Spyer* [1922] 2 Ch 22, 38–39; *Rollason* v. *Leon* (1861) 7 H & N 73, 158 ER 398.

[168] *Kushner* at 274; query both *Ex p Voisey* (1882) 21 Ch D 442, 456, 459, 464, and *Hammond* v. *Farrow* [1904] 2 KB 332, 335, Lord Alverstone CJ.

[169] *Westminster CC* v. *Peart* (1991) 24 HLR 389, CA (public sector secure tenancy).

[170] Or a tenancy of indefinite duration terminable by a month's notice: *Doe d Lansdell* v. *Gower* (1851) 17 QB 589, 117 ER 1406.

[171] *Hammond* v. *Farrow* [1904] 2 KB 332 (weekly tenancy for less than three months for rating purposes).

[172] *Kushner* [1952] 1 KB 264, 274, Lord Goddard CJ.

[173] (1882) 21 Ch D 442, 456, Jessel MR, 458, Brett LJ, 464 Cotton LJ (the lender/landlord had not executed the mortgage deed).

[174] *Breams Property Investment Co* v. *Stroulger* [1948] 2 KB 1, 7, Scott LJ (landlord restricted for exactly 3 years).

(3) Taking effect in possession

[25.27] This was a new requirement in 1925.[175] In consequence a term for one month arising in one year's time, or one day's time, or on a contingency, cannot be legal without a deed[176] as *Long* v. *Tower Hamlets LBC*[177] demonstrates: a letter written on September 4th granting a tenancy from September 29th was ineffective at law. This need not matter. After 1989 contracts for a short lease do not require writing,[178] so a lease to start in the future may operate as an informal contract for the creation of a legal lease.

3.   Transfer of short tenancies

[25.28] Transfer of an informal short lease requires a deed. In *Crago* v. *Julian*[179] the landlord was seeking possession of a flat against Mrs Julian. Her husband had rented the flat in 1966 but, when they divorced in 1982, he gave a written undertaking to do everything necessary to transfer to the tenancy of the flat to Mrs Julian. She stayed in the flat until 1987 when, having asked the managing agents to change the name shown in the rent book, she was asked to leave. The weekly tenancy of Mrs Julian's former husband was validly terminated by notice to quit, and he had no right to claim security of tenure as he was no longer resident in the flat. Mrs Julian had to prove that she had taken an assignment (and, the court assumed, a legal assignment[180]) of the tenancy before its termination.

Nicholls V-C accepted the traditional view that a deed was required for a legal assignment of an parol lease and even an equitable assignment needs writing.[181] The exemption for short legal leases is limited to parol *creation*.

F.   EQUITABLE LEASES

1.   Equitable leases by contract

[25.29] A person with a contractual right to an interest in land can obtain a decree of specific performance which enables him to get at the land itself, a right which confers

---

[175] Pre-1926 law was better, because it allowed one period of three years from the first grant to the end of the lease, and the date on which possession was taken did not matter: Statute of Frauds 1677 s 2; *Wood* v. *Beard* (1876) 2 Ex D 30, 34; *Rawlins* v. *Turner* (1699) Ld Raym 736, 93 ER 760; *Ryley* v. *Hicks* (1725) 1 Stra 651, 91 ER 1392; *Foster* v. *Reeves* [1892] 2 QB 255, CA; query the decision in *Ex p Voisey* (1882) 21 Ch D 442, 464, Cotton LJ.

[176] *Bowes* v. *East London Waterworks Co* (1821) Jacob 324, 330, 37 ER 873, Lord Eldon (lease on 20th to take effect on 25th is in reversion); *Ex p Voisey* would not be legal today; *Bush Transport* v. *Nelson* [1987] 1 EGLR 71, 73.

[177] [1998] Ch 197, 210–219, James Munby QC; S Bright [1998] *Conv* 229. Hence the squatter was not hindered in his claim to adverse possesson by the status of being a legal tenant.

[178] LP (MP) A 1989 s 2(5)(a); *Target Holdings* v. *Priestley* (2000) 79 P & CR 305, Ch D. This creates too wide a scope for future incumbrances. Protective registration is required.

[179] [1992] 1 WLR 372; P Sparkes [1992] *Conv* 375; G Battersby (1995) 58 *MLR* 637; *Camden LBC* v. *Alexandrou (No 2)* (1998) 30 HLR 534, CA (informal surrender may have same practical effect, though it requires the consent of the landlord).

[180] Presumably the undertaking in the divorce petition was a future promise to assign rather than an immediate written assignment; compare *Croydon LBC* v. *Buston* (1991) 24 HLR 36, CA.

[181] LPA 1925 s 53(1)(a).

an immediate equitable interest in the land. A contract for a lease operates as an equitable lease under *Walsh* v. *Lonsdale*.[182] Lonsdale agreed as landlord to grant a lease of a mill to Walsh for seven years by unsealed writing. The rent was a minimum of £810 a year. After possession was taken in 1879, rent was paid quarterly in arrears for three years. In March 1882 the landlord served notice on the tenant, as he was entitled to do under the contract, requiring a year's rent in advance from that date. He waited only two days before distraining for that rent.[183] Walsh sued his landlord for damages for illegal distress, claiming in other words that rent was not due.

Had the lease been granted by deed, the landlord's case would have been (with apologies for the pun) run of the mill. In fact possession[184] was held under a written agreement for a lease for seven years, with the right to specific performance conceded.[185] The case was reported at an interim stage, but the decision favouring the landlord was in effect a ruling that the distress was proper.[186] Walsh was an equitable tenant for seven years under the terms of his agreement.[187]

Orthodox analysis assumes that Walsh was liable to pay rent quarterly in arrears at common law and to pay a year's rent in advance in equity.[188] In any conflict between common law and equitable rules, the latter prevail. Actually rent probably was owing at law, but the common law position was simply an irrelevance.[189] *Walsh* v. *Lonsdale* governs the effect of a contract in the interim period after formation of a contract but before any court application for specific performance. Equity treats as done that which ought to be done, so specific performance would be backdated.[190] As between the original parties, a contract has the same effect as if a legal lease had been granted.[191] *Walsh* v. *Lonsdale* considered the position immediately after 1875 when law and equity were fused by the (Supreme Court of) Judicature Act 1873.[192] Unfortunately the decision can be seen either as a case of procedural fusion or of a substantive conflict.

(1) Procedural fusion

[25.30] Maitland concluded that:

> "the Court of Appeal in deciding that under the Judicature Acts L[onsdale] could distrain did but give effect to the net result of the previously existing rules of law and equity."[193]

---

[182] (1882) 21 Ch D 9, CA; Grays' *Elements* (3rd ed), 574–586; Hopkins, *Informal Acquisition*, 61–86; Megarry & Wade (6th ed), [14.039–14.053], [14.168–14.171]; Sparkes *NLT*, 521–534.

[183] Ie he seized goods belonging to Walsh.

[184] Taking possession (mentioned at 14, Jessel MR) is not relevant after the abolition of *interesse termini* doctrine: LPA 1925 s 149(2).

[185] Both parties had an interest in securing a legal lease, Lonsdale to ensure his right to distrain and Walsh to keep occupation for all seven years.

[186] An interlocutory application to recover the goods taken by distress; the tenant was required to lodge security for the amount of the rent, implying that rent was owing and that the distress was lawful.

[187] Similarly a contract for a lease for life: LPA 1925 s 149(6); *Kingswood Estates Co* v. *Anderson* [1963] 2 QB 169.

[188] Maitland's *Equity*, 157.

[189] P Sparkes (1988) 8 *OJLS* 350, 351–355.

[190] P Sparkes [1989] *JLH* 29 (a legal distress was not justified).

[191] Liabilities date from entry into the agreement: *Trane UK* v. *Provident Mutual Life Assurance* [1995] 1 EGLR 33.

[192] 36 & 37 Vict c 66; amendments in 1875 did not affect fusion.

[193] Maitland's *Equity*, 157; Holdsworth's *History* vol XV, 134; Supreme Court Act 1981 s 49(2).

In pursuance of this proceduralist vision, Lord Esher MR (who sat in *Walsh* v. *Lonsdale* as Brett LJ) later restricted the scope of the decision to cases "where there is such a state of things that a court of equity would compel specific performance."[194] In most cases in which equitable status has been refused the contract has been conditional, so that the right to specific performance has never accrued, and the future tenant's rights are obviously contractual.[195] Where procedural theory extends beyond that it suggests, for example, that there was no equitable lease in a county court lacking the jurisdiction to grant specific performance.[196] This is quite wrong.

(2) Conflict

[25.31] In a fused system the conflict provision[197] allocates priority to the equitable rule whenever this is different from the common law rule. *Walsh* v. *Lonsdale* can be seen as just such a case. At one level there was a conflict about the estate held by Walsh who, Jessel MR said, had a seven year term in equity rather than the old common law periodic tenancy.[198] On another level, the case seems to decide that distress is allowed under a contract after 1875,[199] whereas earlier cases saw distress as a legal remedy restricted to a legal lease.[200] Most modern cases adopt the true fusion line.[201] For example, the contract continues to regulate the rights of the parties after the lease has ended, when the right to specific performance is lost.[202] Also, a sub-tenant holding from a *Walsh* v. *Lonsdale* head tenant has an equitable sub-tenancy, without the need for any proof that the superior tenancy is specifically performable.[203]

---

[194] *Swain* v. *Ayres* (1888) 21 QBD 289, 293; *Gray* v. *Spyer* [1922] 2 Ch 22, CA. Support comes from cases on equitable charges: *Holroyd* v. *Marshall* (1862) 10 HLC 191, 11 ER 999; *Rose* v. *Watson* (1864) 10 HLC 672, 11 ER 1187; *Howard* v. *Miller* [1915] AC 318, 326, Lord Parker; *Central Trust & Safe Deposit Co* v. *Snider* [1916] 1 AC 266, HL.

[195] *Cornish* v. *Brook Green Laundry* [1959] 1 QB 394, CA; JWA Thorneley [1959] *CLJ* 171; *Warmington* v. *Miller* [1973] QB 877, CA.

[196] *Foster* v. *Reeves* [1892] 2 QB 255, CA. Now limited to claims as opposed to defences and counterclaims: *Cornish* v. *Brook Green Laundry* [1959] 1 QB 394, CA; *Kingswood Estate Co* v. *Anderson* [1963] 2 QB 169 (ratio); S Gardner (1987) 7 *OJLS* 60, 69–70. Widening of the county court jurisdiction has removed much of the sting from *Foster*: P Sparkes (1987) 6 *CJQ* 304.

[197] Now Supreme Court Act 1981 s 49(1).

[198] (1882) 21 Ch D 9, 14; *Cardiothoracic Institute* v. *Shrewdcrest* [1986] 1 WLR 368, 378B, Knox J; *Tinsley* v. *Milligan* [1994] 1 AC 340, 371A–B, Lord Browne-Wilkinson; *R* v. *Tower Hamlets LBC ex p Von Goetz* [1999] QB 1019, CA; *R(JR) Pickering* v. *Bradford MBC* (2001) 33 HLR 38, Munby J.

[199] (1882) 21 Ch D 9, 15; *Re Young ex p Vitale* (1882) 47 LT 480; *Crump* v. *Temple* (1890) 7 TLR 120; *Murgatroyd* v. *Silkstone & Dodsworth Coal & Iron ex p Charlesworth* (1895) 65 LJ Ch 111; *Manchester Brewery Co* v. *Coombs* [1901] 2 Ch 608; *Rickett* v. *Green* [1910] 1 KB 253.

[200] *Vincent* v. *Godson* (1853) 1 Sm & G 384, 390, 65 ER 168, Stuart V-C; *Walters* v. *Northern Coal Mining* (1855) 5 De G M & G 629, 43 ER 1015, Cranworth LC; P Sparkes (1988) 8 *OJLS* 350.

[201] Apart from those mentioned elsewhere; *Allhusen* v. *Brooking* (1884) 26 Ch D 559; *Re Maugham* (1885) 14 QBD 956; *Crump* v. *Temple* (1890) 7 TLR 120; *Zimbler* v. *Abrahams* [1903] 1 KB 577; *Rushton* v. *Smith* [1976] QB 480.

[202] *Tottenham Hotspur Football & Athletic Co* v. *Princegrove Publishers* [1974] 1 WLR 113.

[203] *Industrial Properties (Barton Hill)* v. *Associated Electrical Industries* [1977] QB 580.

(3) Statute

[25.32] Some rights are denied to equitable tenants[204] because the statute conferring the right defines "tenants" too narrowly. A legal tenant in breach of a covenant in his lease is liable to forfeiture, but he has a statutory right to receive a notice warning him what is wrong[205] and to effect a timely remedy of the default. *Coatsworth* v. *Johnson*[206] held that a tenant in breach of a contract for a lease had lost the right to specific performance, so that he had no protection as a tenant and no right to a warning notice. This wrongly applied pre-1875 law,[207] was shown to be wrong in the case of a contract lacking a forfeiture clause,[208] and is contrary to what Jessel MR thought.[209] The underlying cause was the narrow ambit of the early statutory provisions about warning notices, but corrective legislation in 1892[210] ensures that equitable tenants do now benefit from the notice provision.[211]

2. Purchasers and equitable tenants

[25.33] Maitland, in his Lectures on *Equity* stressed that different considerations had to be applied when *Walsh* v. *Lonsdale* doctrine was applied to a case involving third parties:

> "[B]etween the contracting parties an agreement for a lease may be as good as a lease. . . . But introduce the third party and then you see the difference."[212]

This was another case of defective statutory definitions. The old rules for the running of leasehold covenants were restricted to legal tenants,[213] but modern statutes do equate legal and equitable leases.[214] In modern law there should be no difference between a lease by deed and one created by contract, provided only that the agreement is properly protected so as to secure priority over the purchaser.[215]

---

[204] *Borman* v. *Griffith* [1930] 1 Ch 493, 497–498 (not a conveyance); *City Permanent BS* v. *Miller* [1952] Ch 840, CA; *Re Rycroft's S* [1962] Ch 263; S Gardner (1987) 7 *OJLS* 60, 63.

[205] LPA 1925 s 146; see below **[26.35]**.

[206] (1886) 55 LJ QB 220; *Swain* v. *Ayres* (1888) 21 QBD 289; *Bell Street Investments* v. *Wood* (1970) 216 EG 585, O'Connor J.

[207] *Parker* v. *Taswell* (1858) 2 De G & J 559, 44 ER 1106.

[208] *Lowther* v. *Heaver* (1889) 41 Ch D 248, CA; *Gourlay* v. *Duke of Somerset* (1812) 1 V & B 69, 73, 35 ER 27, Eldon LC.

[209] *Walsh* v. *Lonsdale* (1882) 21 Ch D 9, 14.

[210] 55 & 56 Vict c 13; now LPA 1925 s 146(5)(a)–(c). This could also be given by express agreement: *Dream Factory* v. *Crown Estate Commissioners* [2000] 3 EGLR 107, Ch D.

[211] *Sport International Bussum* v. *Inter-Footwear* [1984] 1 All ER 376, 385e, Oliver LJ; S Gardner (1987) 7 *OJLS* 60, 63, 98; C Harpum (1984) 100 *LQR* 369, 372–375; *Re Olympia & York Canary Wharf (No 2)* [1993] BCC 159, Morritt J; Megarry & Wade (6th ed), [14.168–14.171]. Query dicta in the pre-condition case *Greville* v. *Parker* [1910] AC 335, 341, PC.

[212] Maitland's *Equity*, 158.

[213] See below **[27.31]**.

[214] LPA 1925 ss 141–142; LT (Covenants) A 1995 s 28(1); also eg LTA 1988 s 5(1).

[215] Eg by entry of a notice or by occupation.

3. Estoppel

[25.34] A lease can be created by estoppel,[216] but here the right in advance of a court order to enforce it is inchoate.[217]

G. SUBSTANTIVE REGISTRATION OF LEASES

1. Categories after 2002

[25.35] The original 1925 scheme[218] was confused and fragmentary[219] until greater coherence was introduced in 1986.[220] These categories were reworked again in 2002, with much confusion creeping back in. An undoubted defect in the Land Registration Act 2002 is the failure to give convenient labels to the various types of lease recognised by the Act. Basically there are three kinds of lease: (1) leases requiring substantive registration – here called registrable leases; (2) leases requiring protection by notice – here called protectible leases; and (3) short leases which override the register – here called overriding leases. Many but not all leases can migrate from category (3) to category (2). The position is complicated further by the need for transitional provisions to cope with the change from the 1925 to the 2002 system.

These categories are similar on compulsory first registration,[221] on voluntary first registration,[222] on the grant of leases out of existing registered titles, and on the transfer of leases.[223] It would have been better to have defined each category once to avoid the awkward repetition of the 2002 Act.

2. Registrable leases

(1) Seven year leases

[25.36] Registration is required of any legal leasehold estate for a term which has more than seven years to run,[224] this time is measured at the time of the transfer grant or creation calling for registration.[225] The most marked change[226] is the shortening of the length of registrable leases from 21[227] to seven years, a change opposed by the profession[228] but one that will greatly increase the utility and comprehensiveness of the

---

[216] *Tower Hamlets LBC* v. *Sherwood* [2002] EWCA Civ 229, [2002] HER 13.
[217] See above **[23.32]**.
[218] LRA 1925 ss 8–12, 21–24, 48, 70.
[219] Hayton's *Registered Land* ch 3; FRR Burford (1936) 1 *Conv* 344; R Graham Page (1937) 2 *Conv* 98.
[220] LRA 1986 in force January 1st 1987; Law Com 125 (1983).
[221] LRA 2002 s 4(1)(c), (2)(b), (4).
[222] S 3(3)–(4).
[223] S 27(2), sch 2 para 3.
[224] Ss 3(3), 4(2), 27(2). Mortgage terms are not substantively registrable.
[225] This form of legislation does not take full account of the gap between the grant and the term taking effect; if this is more than 3 months registration is compulsory: see below **[25.37]**.
[226] Law Com 271 (2001), [2.6], [3.14].
[227] P Sparkes *NLL* (1st ed), 399–400.
[228] *Hansard* HL vol 1916, February 11th 2002, col 40.

register, since it will bring on to the register many business leases.[229] There is power to reduce the length of registrable leases still further.[230]

(2) Other registrable leases

[25.37] This category is restricted to legal estates,[231] the following of which may attract substantive registration:

(1) a lease for any discontinuous period however short;[232]
(2) any lease to take effect in reversion more than three months after the date of the grant;[233]
(3) certain "public" leases;[234]
(4) any lease of a registered franchise or manor.[235]

3. Events calling for substantive registration

(1) Compulsory first registration on grant of a new lease

[25.38] Compulsion applies on a grant or transfer of a registrable lease, now as already explained basically a lease having more than seven years to run at the time of transfer grant or creation,[236] and subject to the exceptions also outlined above, and also to the principle that registration is not required when a lease is assigned or surrendered to the owner of immediate reversion so as to merge into it.[237]

(2) Grant of a new lease

[25.39] When a registrable lease is granted out of an unregistered reversion, registration of title is compulsory, the triggers[238] being broadly the same as for freeholds and under post-1997 law.[239] It makes no difference whether the grant is for valuable or other consideration or by way of gift or pursuant to a court order.

(3) Compulsory registration on transfer of an unregistered lease

[25.40] Registration is also compulsory following a transfer of a qualifying estate, that is a registrable estate, the length exceeding seven years judged at the date of the

---

[229] There is a trend for shorter terms: J Roberts [1997] 24 *EG* 55 (average in 1995 14 years).
[230] LRA 2002 s 118; Law Com 271 (2001), [3.16], EN [519–520]; transitional protection will be required.
[231] LRA 2002 s 3(1)(a); this is much better than LRA 1925 s 2 which talked of leases capable of existing at law – implying that equitable leases should have been included. Mortgage terms are not substantively registrable.
[232] Registration is voluntary: LRA 2002 s 3(4); Law Com 271 (2001), [3.10–3.16]. This will include timeshare arrangements as in *Cottage Holiday Ass* v. *Customs & Excise Commissioners* [1983] QB 735.
[233] Registration is compulsory: LRA 2002 ss 4(1)(a), 27(2)(b)(ii).
[234] See below [25.58].
[235] LRA 2002 s 27(2)(c).
[236] LRA 2002 s 4(2); PJG Williams [2001] 28 *EG* 138.
[237] LRA 2002 s 4(4)(b).
[238] S 4.
[239] Law Com 271 (2001), [3.30–3.34]; Sparkes *NLL* (1st ed), 399–400; see above [9.24].

event calling for registration. This may therefore bring on to the register a pre-2002 Act lease in the bracket 7–21 years which was not registrable when granted but which will require registration if assigned. The triggers are:[240]

a transfer for any consideration, valuable or otherwise or for a negative value;[241]
a gift, settlement, assent or vesting assent;[242]
a transfer in pursuance of court order; and
transactions with certain "public" leases.[243]

Events which do not act as triggers are:[244]

assignment or surrender of lease to the owner of the immediate reversion so as to cause merger;[245]
death (when the subsequent assent is the trigger); and
bankruptcy (when it is the the court order appointing a trustee in bankruptcy).

(4) Voluntary first registration

[25.41] Voluntary registration is allowed, without any trigger, of[246] any leasehold estate:

with more than seven years unexpired;
which coupled with a subsequent lease taking effect within one month of the end of the first lease creates a term exceeding seven years;[247] or
any discontinuous term however short.

(5) Transfer or grant of a lease out of a registered title

[25.42] Grants of leases out of registered titles are affected by registration requirements, as are dispositions of registrable leases.[248] No legal rights pass in advance of registration.[249] The requirement of registration[250] applies to the following transactions with registrable leases:

a transfer;
a grant of a lease for more than seven years;[251]
a grant of those other leases that are registrable;[252] and
some transactions with "public" leases.

---

[240] LRA 2002 s 4(1)(a), (2).
[241] S 4(6).
[242] S 4(1)(a), (7), (9); except a bare trust for the settlor or a transfer uniting the legal and sole beneficial interest.
[243] See below **[25.58]**.
[244] LRA 2002 s 4(3)–(5).
[245] S 4(4)(b).
[246] S 3(3)–(4).
[247] S 3(7); Law Com 271 (2001), [3.13].
[248] LRA 2002 s 27.
[249] See above **[8.43]**.
[250] LRA 2002 sch 2.
[251] This is a disposition and not a first registration: LRA 2002 s 4(1)(c), (2).
[252] See above **[25.37]**.

Registration requirements do not apply to death, bankruptcy, or corporate dissolution.

4. Rules for substantive registration under the 1925 Act scheme

[25.43] Any legal lease with a term exceeding 21 years remaining unexpired at the time of registration required completion by registration.[253] This applied: (1) to a grant of a new lease by a landlord whose title is registered, when the case is one of dealing; (2) to a grant of a new lease by a landlord with an unregistered title, when it is a case for first registration;[254] or (3) to any transfer of an unregistered lease with at least 21 years of the term unexpired at the time that it passes.[255]

If a long lease was granted before December 1990 (when the last parts of the country became compulsory) and the last sale occurred while the district was non-compulsory, registration may never have been triggered – though it will be if the lease is assigned when more than seven years remain. For grants before 1987[256] further factors come into play. If the landlord's title was unregistered at the time of the grant of the lease, registration of leases (both grants and assignments) was only compulsory where the term was for 40 years or more, and remained voluntary where the term was between 21 and 40 years in length.[257] Further, substantive registration was not allowed for leases containing an absolute prohibition against dealings.[258]

5. Classes of leasehold title

(1) Leasehold absolute

[25.44] Absolute title requires proof of the title to the lease and also proof of the landlord's title to grant the estate.[259] The requirements for first registration with leasehold absolute title are rather similar to the requirements for freehold absolute title, the test being whether a competent professional adviser would advise a buyer to accept the title,[260] but the registrar may disregard any defect which is not likely to lead to the holding being disturbed.[261] The state guarantees both ownership of the lease and that the lease was validly granted and if the tenant is in possession is pretty well secure against prejudicial alteration of the register.[262]

Registration with title absolute has effect[263] to vest the leasehold estate with all easements and other appurtenant rights that benefit it[264] subject to the following burdens:

---

[253] LRA 1925 s 8(1)(b) as amended by LRA 1986 s 2.
[254] LRA 1925 s 123, as amended by LRA 1986 s 2; the period was measured from the grant, not the date of application for registration: LRA 1925 s 8(1A).
[255] LRA 1925 s 8(1) and 8(1A) as amended.
[256] LRA 1986.
[257] LRA 1925 old s 13(1).
[258] LRA 1925 old s 8(2). In fact such a lease could be sold with the consent of the landlord and the anomaly was removed by LRA 1986 s 3.
[259] LRA 2002 s 10(1).
[260] S 10(1).
[261] S 10(4).
[262] See above **[11.48ff]**.
[263] LRA 2002 ss 12(2)–(4), 13(1); DLRR 2003 r 31.
[264] LRA 2002 s 63; Law Com 271 (2001), [9.29–9.35].

covenants, obligations and liabilities incident to estate;

interests protected by an entry on the register;

interests that override first registration;[265] and

squatters' title by limitation if the squatter is in occupation[266] or if the first proprietor has notice.

A leaseholder may secure absolute title by showing a complete title both to the lease *and* all reversionary titles – including the freehold and all intermediate leaseholds. This is simple enough if the superior titles are registered, for the registrar can refer to them, and can then enter a notice of the lease against the landlord's title.[267] Leasehold absolute title can only be obtained against an unregistered freehold title by contracting to extend the statutory title[268] or after voluntary deduction of the superior title. Buyers and lenders should insist upon a full title.

(2) Good leasehold

[25.45] Good leasehold title is granted where the leasehold title is produced to the registrar and so guaranteed, but the freehold title is not approved.[269] Registration is without prejudice to "the enforcement of any estate, right, or interest affecting or in derogation of the title of the lessor to grant the lease".[270] This title was once common because of the statutory restrictions on securing access to superior unregistered titles,[271] but these rules are now amended to allow a derivative tenant to see all the superior titles.[272] Universal modern practice is to require production of superior titles so that absolute title can be obtained and the proportion of good leasehold titles is declining.

(3) Possessory titles

[25.46] Possessory title to leasehold land[273] provides a guarantee limited to operate only from the date of first registration, and leaves open the possibility of enforcement of interests adverse to the title of the first proprietor and subsisting at the time of registration of that proprietor.[274] Possessory title is given in 1% of freehold cases, for example a squatter's title based on twelve years adverse possession, after loss of the title deeds,[275] or where the paper title has flaws.[276]

---

[265] LRA 2002 sch 1; see above **[20.37]**.

[266] Sch 1 para 2.

[267] DLRR 2003 r 33; see above **[20.04]**.

[268] LPA 1925 s 44, as amended by LRA 2002 sch 11.

[269] LRA 2002 s 12(6). Old law: LRA 1925 s 8(ii); *Strand Securities* v. *Caswell* [1965] Ch 958; *White* v. *Bijou Mansions* [1937] Ch 612, [1938] Ch 351, CA.

[270] LRA 2002 s 12(6); Law Com 271 (2001), [9.29–9.35].

[271] LPA 1925 s 44; C Sweet (1912) 28 *LQR* 6, 7–8.

[272] As amended by LRA 2002 sch 11 para 2; Law Com 271 (2001), [12.9–12.13]. The new rules remain defective in that an assignee can only see the immediate lease and not the superior title: s 44(3); I am indebted to a presentation by Sue Bright at Reading for this point.

[273] This dates from 1903: *Re King* [1962] 1 WLR 634, 639, Buckley J.

[274] LRA 2002 s 10(6), based on possession or receipt of rents and profits where no other class of title is appropriate. The effect is stated in s 12(8).

[275] DLRR 2003 r 26.

[276] *Spectrum Investment Co* v. *Holmes* [1981] 1 WLR 221.

(4) Qualified title

[25.47] Title may also be qualified so as to be guaranteed subject to a particular qualification. The defect excluded from the guarantee may be one arising before a certain date, or where a trustee has sold to himself making the title voidable.[277] Roughly one title in 100,000 has to be qualified.

6. Upgrading leasehold titles

[25.48] Upgrading[278] to leasehold absolute occurs on the application of the proprietor, if the superior title to the freehold and any intervening leasehold is deduced,[279] and the registrar can also act on his own initiative. As more and more freehold titles come to be registered, more leasehold titles will be able to migrate to absolute registration.

Possessory titles are gradually upgraded to superior forms of title on the application of the proprietor or a subsequent buyer.[280] Upgrading occurs if title to the lease can be shown to the satisfaction of the registrar.[281] Otherwise a proprietor may apply to upgrade to good leasehold after holding possession and being registered for at least twelve years.[282]

A qualified title can only be upgraded if the registrar is satisfied as to the title.[283]

7. Leasehold registers

(1) Contents

[25.49] The register sets out the bare bones of the relationship (length, date and parties) leaving those interested to obtain an authenticated copy of the lease.[284]

(2) Restrictions on alienation

[25.50] Leases frequently contain some restriction on transfer of the leasehold estate, which should appear by way of restriction on the register.[285] Any infringing sale is excepted from the effect of registration.

(3) Cancellation of entries

[25.51] When a lease ends, it is necessary to cancel the individual register and any notice recording the lease against the landlord's title.[286]

---

[277] LRA 2002 s 10(5); the effect is stated in s 12(7).
[278] S 62; Law Com 271 (2001), [9.16–9.22]. The effect is the same as a first registration: s 62(8).
[279] LRA 2002 s 62(2).
[280] Application is by a proprietor, a person entitled to be registered, a proprietor of charge, or other person interested: LRA 2002 s 62(7); this is wider than the old law: Law Com 271 (2001), [9.23–9.24].
[281] LRA 2002 s 62(3).
[282] S 62(5).
[283] S 62(3); upgrading is to good leasehold or leasehold absolute according to the title shown.
[284] DLRR 2003 r 6.
[285] DLRR 2003 r 93.
[286] See above **[20.12]**.

8.   A prescribed form for leases?

[25.52] It was proposed to prescribe a form for a lease created out of a registered title,[287] but this has proved to be controversial and the initial draft at least has been withdrawn.[288]

H. LEASES NOTED AND OVERRIDING

1.   Interchangeability of categories

[25.53] Unless a lease attracts compulsory first registration it is likely to be inter-changeable between the category of protectible leases which can be protected by entry of a notice on the register and the overriding category. It is desirable to bring on to the register and note as many interests as possible, and when an entry is made the interest ceases to override.[289] A notice cannot be entered in relation to a leasehold estate in land which is granted for a term of three years or less unless it is of those exceptional cases which require entry on the register; these very short leases are overriding only.

2.   Protection by notice (old law)

[25.54] Some leases may be protected against the landlord's title as minor interests, entry of a notice warning all later buyers of the existence of the lease.[290] Protection by notice requires either the consent of the landlord or a court order, but a caution may be used for non-consensual entries.[291] Protection as a minor interest is not allowed if the lease is substantively registered nor if it is an overriding interest, at least if the lease is obvious.[292] Notices are left to protect: (1) certain pre-1987 leases: leases for 21 years or less at a fine; leases for 21 years or less without any rent; and any lease made before 1986[293] with an absolute prohibition on assignment; (2) agreements for leases;[294] and (3) future leases.

3.   Short leases overriding the register
(1) Grants after 2002 Act commencement

[25.55] A leasehold estate granted for a term not exceeding seven years can override the register. This appears to restrict overriding status to legal grants as under the 1925 scheme. Exceptional leases which cannot override are:

---

[287] LRA 2002 s 25; DLRR sch 1; LR draft Form L1; DLRR CD ch 1, [27].
[288] LR Press Notice (January 2003); S Highmore & K Fenn [2002] 41 *EG* 174.
[289] LRA 2002 s 29(2).
[290] LRA 1925 s 48(1).
[291] Or possibly a restriction: JE Adams [1994] *Conv* 200.
[292] LRR 1925 r 199.
[293] LRA 1986 s 3; Law Com 125 (1983).
[294] *Clark* v. *Chief Land Registrar* [1994] Ch 370, CA; *Chancery* v. *Ketteringham* (1995) 69 P & CR 426, Ch D; AKR Kiralfy (1952) 16 *Conv (NS)* 38; JE Adams [1994] *Conv* 265.

a term to take effect in possession more than three months after the grant;[295]
certain "public" type leases;[296]
a lease created out a registered title by disposition.[297]

(2) Grants under the 1925 scheme

[25.56] Transitional provisions[298] will continue the overriding effect of pre-2002 Act commencement leases "granted for a term not exceeding twenty-one years".[299] The crucial word is "granted".[300] In *City Permanent BS* v. *Miller*[301] it was held that an oral agreement to create a lease for three years and then from week to week (that is for a minimum term of three years and one week) was not a legal lease, and so was not a paragraph (k) overriding interest. Certainly a lease by deed is "granted", and it seems to follow from the course of discussion in *Miller* that an informal short lease is also granted if it creates a legal tenancy. It now makes no difference whether the lease is at a rack rent, reserves a fine, or is purely gratuitous.[302]

Protection adheres without occupation of the land and indeed can continue even after physical destruction of the building affected.[303]

Until the 2002 Act commencement the crucial date for the existence of the lease was the registration of a transfer[304] but overriding interests now override particular dealings so it is the date of the transfer that is critical.[305]

4. Tenants as occupiers overriding the register

[25.57] Occupation by a tenant is a means of protecting a lease on first registration,[306] on a post-2002 Act transfer[307] or on a pre-2002 Act transfer.[308] In the past receipt of rents from a sub-tenant could protect the title of the head tenant, but this is now withdrawn for the future.[309] Occupation may protect a tenant in occupation under a registrable but unregistered lease, a short term tenant who overrides anyway, or an equitable tenant in possession. Fortuitous protection is provided for a person with an option for a future lease who happens to be in occupation under some other right. Protection is lost if the lease is not disclosed after enquiry[310] or if occupation is given up before a transaction with the land.

---

[295] Law Com 271 (2001), EN [618].
[296] See above **[25.58]**.
[297] LRA 2002 sch 3 para 1; Law Com 271 (2001), EN [603–605].
[298] LRA 2002 sch 12 para 12; Law Com 271 (2001), [8.50–8.52]; LRA 2002 sch 3 para 12; Law Com 271 (2001), EN [809].
[299] LRA 1925 s 70(1)(k), as amended by LRA 1986 s 4(1).
[300] *City Permanent BS* v. *Miller* [1952] Ch 840, CA.
[301] [1952] Ch 840, CA.
[302] Amendments by LRA 1986 s 4.
[303] *Prince* v. *Robinson* (1999) 31 HLR 89, CA, obiter.
[304] LRA 1925 s 70(1); *Pourdanay* v. *Barclays Bank* [1997] Ch 321, Scott V-C; M Robinson (1998) 114 *LQR* 354.
[305] LRA 2002 s 29(1).
[306] Sch 1 para 2.
[307] Sch 3 para 2.
[308] LRA 1925 s 70(1)(g).
[309] See above **[15.47]**.
[310] See above **[15.53]**.

I. REGISTRATION OF CERTAIN "PUBLIC" LEASES

1.   Grants involving public sector housing

[25.58] Registration is compulsory for:

a right to buy grant of a public sector dwelling;[311]
a grant of legal lease of the landlord's interest in a public sector estate; and
a transfer of such an interest.[312]

2.   Public transport in London

[25.59] Leases connected with public transport in London (PPP leases) are not registrable[313] and override the register.[314]

J. TERMINATION BY COMBINATION OF LEASE AND REVERSION

1.   Lease to oneself

[25.60] It is now possible to convey land to oneself,[315] but *Rye* v. *Rye*[316] decides that one cannot grant an oral lease to oneself and the need for two parties able to contract applies just as much to a formal lease.

If an owner cannot let land to himself as tenant, the problem can easily be avoided by granting the lease *to a nominee*. The legality of this dodge was doubted in the Scottish case *Clydesdale Bank* v. *Davidson*,[317] but the House of Lords has now made clear that a lease by a landlord to his nominee is valid. Lady Ingram, the appellant in *Ingram* v. *Inland Revenue Commissioners*,[318] wanted to give her house to her children but to retain the right to live in the house in her old age. Three transactions took place on successive days. On the first, she conveyed the house to her solicitor; on the second the solicitor granted her a lease rent-free for 20 years, and on the third the freehold was conveyed to trustees for her family. The House decided that for taxation purposes the value of the property transferred to the family trustees was to be valued on the basis of the freehold estate subject to the lease. In other words, the House of Lords held that the lease granted by the solicitor (as nominee for Lady Ingram) to Lady Ingram was valid. Although the speeches concentrate on the taxation issue – now a dead duck since the inheritance tax loophole exploited by Lady Ingram has now been closed[319] – it seems that the Lords affirmed Millett LJ's dissent in the Court of Appeal

---

[311] S 4(1)(e), as under the old law.
[312] S 4(1)(b), reproducing the old law.
[313] S 90; Law Com 271 (2001), [8.11–8.13], EN [393–395].
[314] Greater London Authority Act 1999 s 219; LRA 1925 s 70(1)(k); LRA 2002 s 90.
[315] LPA 1925 ss 72, 82 (covenants).
[316] [1962] AC 496, HL.
[317] [1998] SC 51, HL.
[318] [2000] AC 293, HL.
[319] Finance Act 1986 s 102A, inserted by Finance Act 1999 s 104.

on the property issues.[320] It is possible to vest a freehold estate in a nominee, so why not also a lease?

Two tenants (T1 and T2) can assign to one of their number (T1),[321] and this is not a surrender.

2. Merger

[25.61] A lease may be terminated by a dealing which results in the leasehold estate and reversion passing into a single ownership, an event which sometimes causes the two estates to fuse. Merger describes the case in which both interests are transferred to one person,[322] which under modern law depends upon intention.[323] Surrender occurs when a tenant gives up his lease to his landlord.[324] A deed and land registry application are required for a legal merger or surrender,[325] but a contract operates in equity.[326] The lease is ended prospectively, but liability continues for the past, for example under a rent review not settled at the date of the surrender.[327]

2. Surrender

[25.62] Lord Millett said in *Barrett* v. *Morgan*[328] that:

"A surrender is simply an assurance by which a lesser estate is yielded up to the greater, and the term is usually applied to the giving up of a lease or tenancy before its expiration. If a tenant surrenders his tenancy to an immediate landlord, who accepts the surrender, the tenancy is absorbed by the landlord's conversion and is extinguished by operation of law."

Coke on *Littleton*[329] wrote graphically of a case where the estate:

"may drowne by mutual agreement between them."

Passage of the legal title is usually accompanied by the equitable title.[330]

Formality is required for a legal surrender, but a contract for a surrender ends the lease in equity.[331]

---

[320] *Ingram* v. *IRC* [1997] 4 All ER 395, CA.

[321] *Burton* v. *Camden LBC* [2000] 2 AC 399, HL.

[322] *Southampton Community Health Services NHS Trust* v. *Crown Estate Commissioners* [1997] EGCS 155, Ch D.

[323] LPA 1925 s 185; *Ingle* v. *Vaughan Jenkins* [1900] 2 Ch 368, 370, Farwell J; *Westwood* v. *Heywood* [1921] 2 Ch 130, 140, Astbury J. There are numerous cases.

[324] *Leek & Moorlands BS* v. *Clark* [1952] 2 QB 788; *Featherstone* v. *Staples* [1986] 2 All ER 461. It requires the consent of a lender secured on the landlord's interest: LPA 1925 s 100.

[325] DLRR 2003 r 79, 87–88.

[326] *Take Harvest* v. *Liu* [1993] AC 552, PC (Hong Kong law like LPA 1925 s 40); *Barakat* v. *Ealing LBC* [1996] 36 RVR 138 (not letter spelling out proposed terms). Future agreements to surrender are frequently negated by security of tenure legislation.

[327] *Torminster* [1983] 1 WLR 676, 682H.

[328] *Barrett* v. *Morgan* [2000] 2 AC 264, HL; L Tee [2000] *CLJ* 251.

[329] Coke on *Littleton*, [337b].

[330] *Allen* v. *Rochdale BC* [2000] Ch 221, CA.

[331] By deed; a contract to surrender ends the lease in equity: *Take Harvest* v. *Liu* [1993] AC 552, PC. Agreements to surrender made in advance are invalidated under most security of tenure regimes.

4. Informal surrender

[25.63] Surrender is implied where landlord and tenant conduct themselves in a manner inconsistent with continuation of the lease. This is a long established[332] form of estoppel,[333] with many conflicting authorities.[334] A tenant cannot end his lease by moving out,[335] or handing back the keys without their being accepted by the landlord.[336] The most common indication that a landlord has accepted a surrender is reletting, whether to a new tenant[337] or to the existing tenant on new terms.[338] Other mutual acts may be sufficient, for example advertising for a new tenant,[339] taking possession at the tenant's request[340] or accepting the tenant's return of the key.[341]

Surrender transfers the tenancy to the landlord subject to existing sub-tenancies.[342]

5. Preservation of derivative interests

[25.64] All derivative interests end if a head lease ends by forfeiture[343] by effluxion, or by break instigated by the landlord. In *Pennell* v. *Payne*[344] it was decided that if a periodic tenant serves notice to quit, thus ending the head tenancy, the effect is to bring to an end any sub-tenancy. However on surrender and merger derivative interests are preserved by statute.[345] The next interest takes effect in reversion.[346] Surrenders should generally be analysed as a transfer of the lease rather than as a termination.[347]

---

[332] *Wrotesley* v. *Adams* (1560) 1 Plowd 189, 75 ER 290.

[333] *Lewis* v. *Jenkins R Kerman & Son* [1971] Ch 477, 496, Russell LJ.

[334] P Sparkes *NLT*, 37–41, 298–301, 596–603.

[335] *Preston BC* v. *Fairclough* (1983) 8 HLR 70; *Lyon* v. *Reed* (1844) 13 M & W 285, 130 ER 118; *Chamberlain* v. *Scalley* (1994) 26 HLR 26, CA (possessions left).

[336] *Proudreed* v. *Microgen Holdings* [1996] 1 EGLR 89, CA; *Bhogal* v. *Cheema* [1998] 2 EGLR 50, Ch D (no duty to mitigate). See also *Cannan* v. *Grimley* (1850) 9 CB 634, 137 ER 1040; *Oastler* v. *Henderson* (1877) 2 QBD 575, CA.

[337] *Sidebotham* v. *Holland* [1895] 1 QB 378; *ES Schwab & Co* v. *McCarthy* (1975) 31 P & CR 196, Oliver J; *Tower Hamlets LBC* v. *Ayinde* (1994) 26 HLR 631, CA.

[338] *Smirk* v. *Lyndale Developments* [1975] Ch 317; *Jaskel* v. *Sophie Nursery Products* [1993] EGCS 42, CA.

[339] *Oastler* v. *Henderson* (1877) 2 QBD 575.

[340] *R* v. *Croydon LBC ex p Toth* (1988) 20 HLR 576, CA; *McDougall's Catering Foods* v. *BSE Trading* [1997] 2 EGLR 65 (not if to preserve against squatters). Contrast: *Hoggett* v. *Hoggett* (1979) 39 P & CR 121 (no delivery of possession).

[341] *Barakat* v. *Ealing LBC* [1996] EGCS 67, Brooke J; *Filering* v. *Taylor Cam* [1996] EGCS 95, CA.

[342] LTA 1730 s 6; now LPA 1925 s 150; *Ecclesiastical Commissioners for England* v. *Treemer* [1893] 1 Ch 166, 172, Chitty J; *Plummer & John* v. *David* [1920] 1 KB 326; *Basingstoke & Deane BC* v. *Paice* [1995] 2 EGLR 9, CA; N Hopkins [1996] *Conv* 284.

[343] *Great Western Rly Co* v. *Smith* (1876) 2 Ch D 235, CA, affirmed (1877) 3 App Cas 165, HL.

[344] P Sparkes *NLT*, 596–603; *Pennell* v. *Payne* [1995] QB 192, CA; *Barrett* v. *Morgan* [2000] 2 AC 264, HL.

[345] LPA 1925 s 150; *Ecclesiastical Commissioners for England* v. *Treemer* [1893] 1 Ch 166, 172, Chitty J.

[346] LPA 1925 s 139; *London RT* v. *Brandt* [1997] 2 BCLC 558, CA.

[347] N Hopkins [1996] *Conv* 284.

K. TERMINATION BY BREAK NOTICE

[25.65] Many leases provide that they may be ended by notice, particularly by the tenant.[348] A tenant may choose to break a lease if the initial rent was uneconomic or after receiving an unwelcome rent review.[349]

A break notice must be an unambiguous exercise of the clause.[350] Careful compliance is required with the terms of the lease about when to serve notice and how long it should be. Most conditions are mandatory.[351] A (masculine) lease might, for example, require a notice to be served on blue paper, in which case it would be no good serving it on (feminine) pink paper.[352] However, a more relaxed view stated in *Carradine Properties* v. *Aslam*[353] is now accepted:

> "Is the notice quite clear to a reasonable tenant reading it? Is it plain that he cannot be misled by it?"

An older rule requiring strict literal compliance with the lease[354] was disapproved by a bare majority of the House of Lords[355] in *Mannai Investment Co* v. *Eagle Star Life Assurance Co.*[356] A lease of offices in Jermyn Street allowed termination by notice expiring on the third anniversary of the term commencement date. This was actually January 13th 1995, but the tenant's letter purported to terminate it one day early on January 12th.[357] The House of Lords held that this minor misdescription did not mar the validity of the notice, since the tenant's decision to terminate had been conveyed with sufficient clarity. This convenient decision has rapidly attracted a substantial encrustation of case-law.[358] Plainly erroneous dates can be ignored. An impossible date (1973 in a notice in 1974) can be read as if it said the correct date (1975).[359] In *Micrografix* v. *Woking 8*[360] the tenant's letter and the actual notice stated two different, but equally erroneous, dates, but the notice was held to refer to the correct date

---

[348] Landlords make less use of them since most commercial tenants have security of tenure.

[349] *Nocton* v. *Walter Hall Group* [1997] EGCS 97 (break if no longer viable to quarry; it was, so no break).

[350] *Aylward* v. *Fawaz* (1997) 29 HLR 408, CA , distinguishing *Hankey* v. *Clavering* [1942] 2 KB 326.

[351] An offer can specify the method of acceptance, but some terms are merely directory: *Yates Building Co* v. *RJ Pulleyn & Sons (York)* [1976] 1 EGLR 157, CA.

[352] *Mannai Investment Co* v. *Eagle Star Life Assurance Co* [1997] AC 749, 776B, Lord Hoffmann.

[353] [1976] 1 WLR 442, 444, Goulding J; approved in *Germax Securities* v. *Spiegel* (1978) 37 P & CR 204, 206, CA; *Morrow* v. *Nadeem* [1987] 1 WLR 237, CA.

[354] *Hankey* v. *Clavering* [1942] 2 KB 326, CA.

[355] Lords Steyn, Hoffmann and Clyde, Lords Goff and Jauncey dissenting.

[356] [1997] AC 749, HL; M Biles "Hunting for Allegories on the Banks of the Nile" ch 14 in Jackson and Wilde; PF Smith [1998] *Conv* 326; L Tee [1998] *CLJ* 29; M Robinson (1999) 115 *LQR* 389; A Lovitt & J Martin [2000] 42 *EG* 170; JE Adams [2002] *Conv* 212; HW Wilkinson [2002] *NLJ* 645; J Gaunt & N Cheffings [2002] *NLJ* 424, 460.

[357] Contrast where the notice is to expire at midnight, so the notice could state either the day before or the one after: *Sidebotham* v. *Holland* [1895] 1 QB 378, CA; *Crate* v. *Miller* [1947] KB 946, CA.

[358] *Garston* v. *Scottish Widows Fund & Life Assurance Society* [1998] 1 WLR 1583, CA; *Havant International Holdings* v. *Lionsgate (H) Investment* [1999] 47 LSG 34, Hart J; *Lemmerbell* v. *Britannia IAS* [1998] 3 EGLR 67, CA.

[359] *Carradine* [1976] 1 WLR 442, Goulding J.

[360] [1995] 2 EGLR 32, Jacob J; approved in *Mannai*.

which would be obvious to the landlord reading the lease. There are also a large number of cases on defective shorthold notices.[361]

L. RESIDENTIAL RENTING

1. The housing market

[25.66] Of the 21 million dwellings in England and Wales, roughly 2.7 million are rented from a council, 1.2 million from a social landlord (that is a housing association) and 2.0 million are rented privately.[362] It is time to rationalise the forms of security of tenure[363] and indeed the Law Commission is working towards a division into two main forms – long term tenancies with full residential security and short term tenancies without.[364] In the meantime there is a mess which must be explored elsewhere.

2. Long term residential security

[25.67] Full residential security provides protection against repossession of the property by the landlord. The landlord must serve notice to quit, take court proceedings and prove a ground for possession. A tenant who pays the rent punctually and otherwise behaves himself is usually entitled to stay indefinitely.[365]

Two schemes apply in the private sector, according to the date on which the tenancy was first granted. The Rent Act 1977 applies to private sector residential tenancies granted before early 1989. It confers "lifelong" security of tenure and the right to register a fair rent below the market rent. Many Rent Act tenants are now elderly. On the death of a tenant, the tenancy may pass by succession to a surviving spouse or other resident family member. Fully assured tenancies were granted in the private sector from early 1989 onwards.[366] The quality of the security of tenure is largely unaffected by this change,[367] but a market rent regime was adopted. At first, rents under the new system were dramatically higher, but fair rents have gradually increased so that the gap has narrowed.

Most tenancies with full security are granted by social or public landlords. Housing associations generally grant fully assured tenancies in the private sector. Rents should be "affordable". Public sector landlords are mainly local authorities, and they grant secure tenancies[368] to tenants selected according to strict allocation rules.[369] This is the largest group of tenants with full residential security. Public sector tenants have

---

[361] P Sparkes *NLT*, 47–48; *Ravenseft Properties* v. *Hall* [2001] EWCA Civ 2034, [2002] 1 EGLR 9.
[362] *Annual Housing Statistics* (ODPM, 2000), [8.2].
[363] P Sparkes "Towards a Structure for the Law of Landlord and Tenant" ch 13 in E Cooke *Modern Studies in Property Law 1 – Property 2000* (Hart, 2001).
[364] *Reform of Housing Law: A Scoping Paper* (Law Com, March 2001).
[365] P Sparkes *NLT* ch 5.
[366] HA 1988, operating from January 15th 1989 by s 141(3).
[367] Succession rights are much reduced.
[368] HA 1985; P Sparkes *NLT*, 7–10; for introductory tenancies see below [25.71].
[369] P Sparkes *NLT* ch 4; Homelessness Act 2002.

the right to buy their homes at a discount,[370] and there are some equivalent rights of acquisition for those in the social sector.

Full security is removed from shorthold tenants, those with limited security, or those against whom a ground for possession is established, and from all licensees.

3. Shortholds

[25.68] Shorthold tenancies now dominate the private sector residential letting market. The tenant has the assurance of a short fixed term of occupation, but after that short "hold" the landlord has a guarantee that he will be able to recover possession.

A section 19A shorthold is a tenancy originally created after the commencement of the Housing Act 1996.[371] The guarantee remains for a minimum of six months, but it is no longer necessary to make a contractual grant for any fixed period – a shorthold might be for an initial fixed term, or a holding over, or an open-ended periodic tenancy.[372] The grant should be in writing so that the landlord can take advantage of the accelerated repossession procedures.[373] Termination by the landlord is generally proscribed during the initial six month period. Almost all formalities have now been stripped away, and in particular a shorthold notice is no longer required, so a private sector tenancy is a shorthold unless steps are taken to confer full security of tenure.

Assured shorthold tenancies created between early 1989[374] and early 1997 required more formality. There had to be an initial grant for a term certain of not less than six months,[375] and it was necessary to serve on the proposed tenant in advance a shorthold notice warning that he would not enjoy full security of tenure.[376] Major errors invalidate the notice[377] but the reasonable recipient principle[378] applies to validate notices containing minor defects where the meaning would be obvious to a reasonable recipient.[379]

4. Termination

[25.69] An assured shorthold is brought to an end by a notice giving two months warning[380] followed by a court application for a mandatory possession order under the accelerated repossession procedure.[381]

---

[370] HA 1985 part V; P Sparkes *NLT* ch 18.

[371] HA 1988 s 19A inserted by HA 1996 s 96; for grants on or after February 28th 1997: SI 1997/225.

[372] The six month period runs once and is not triggered again by a contractual renewal of the tenancy.

[373] CPR 55.11ff.

[374] HA 1988 s 20, operating from January 15th 1989.

[375] HA 1988 s 55; *Bedding* v. *McCarthy* (1995) 27 HLR 103, CA; *Marath* v. *MacGillivray* (1996) 28 HLR 484, CA; *Mundy* v. *Hook* (1998) 30 HLR 551, CA; *Goodman* v. *Evely* [2001] EWCA Civ 104, [2002] HLR 53.

[376] HA 1988 s 19A; HA 1996 s 96; *Bedding* v. *McCarthy* (1995) 27 HLR 103, CA; *Demetriou* v. *Panayi* [1998] CLYB 3597; *Yenula Properties* v. *Naidu* [2002] EWCA Civ 719, [2002] 42 EG 162.

[377] *Panayi* v. *Roberts* (1993) 25 HLR 421, CA; *Mundy* v. *Hook* (1998) 30 HLR 551, CA; *Andrews* v. *Brewer* (1998) 30 HLR 203, CA; *Mustafa* v. *Ruddock* (1998) 30 HLR 495, CA; *Manel* v. *Memon* (2001) 33 HLR 24, CA.

[378] *Mannai Investments* [1997] AC 749, HL; see above **[25.65]**.

[379] *Panayi* v. *Roberts* (1993) 25 HLR 421, 425, Mann LJ; *York* v. *Casey* [1998] 2 EGLR 25, CA; *Clickex* v. *McCann* [1999] 2 EGLR 63, CA; *Ravenseft Properties* v. *Hall* [2001] EWCA Civ 2034, [2002] 11 EG 156.

[380] HA 1988 s 21, as amended in 1996; P Sparkes *NLT*, 54–56.

[381] CPR 55.11–55.19; PD 55.18.

5. Termination by the tenant

[25.70] A tenant is entitled to quit at the end of any fixed term, but he must give notice to quit if his tenancy is periodic, the total period of notice being at least four weeks.[382] These restrictions can be avoided by an agreed[383] surrender.

6. Limited residential security

[25.71] Even if a residential tenancy is not a shorthold, security of tenure is very often limited.[384] The Law Commission is working towards creating a universal form of short term tenancy.[385] In the mean time there is a confusing mess of cases where security is limited. In the private sector, for example:

occupation of accommodation that is not self-contained;[386]
accommodation in a house shared with a resident landlord;
luxury property;
property without residential use;[387]
company lets;
property required for an owner occupier;
holiday dwellings and out of season lets; and
lets by educational institutions to students and vacation letting.

Whilst in the public sector, for example:

introductory tenants in their first year;[388] and
property affected by reconstruction work.

Even in these cases the Protection from Eviction Act 1977[389] generally guarantees due process, that is the requirement for notice and court proceedings before repossession is carried out, and protection of occupiers against harassment intended to force them out.[390] Due process does not apply to "excluded tenancies and licences"[391] – including resident landlord tenancies, temporary refuges, holiday accommodation, gratuitous arrangements, and licences in some publicly funded hostels.

---

[382] Protection from Eviction Act 1977 s 5.
[383] *Laine* v. *Cadwallader* (2001) 33 HLR 36, CA.
[384] P Sparkes, *NLT* ch 6.
[385] *Reform of Housing Law: A Scoping Paper* (Law Com, March 2001); R Carnwath [2001] *LT Rev* 3; M Partington [2001] 04 *Legal Action* 10.
[386] *Uratemp Ventures* v. *Collins* [2001] UKHL 43, [2002] 1 AC 301; P Sparkes *NLT* 166–170.
[387] Eg a head tenant who has sub-let the whole: *Ujima H Ass* v. *Ansah* (1998) 30 HLR 831, CA.
[388] HA 1996 s 124–125; *Manchester CC* v. *Cochrane* (1999) 31 HLR 810, CA. This scheme has survived human rights challenges; see above **[5.51]**.
[389] S 3(2B) as amended by HA 1980 s 30.
[390] Protection from Eviction Act 1977 s 1(3) as amended by HA 1988 ss 28–29 (damages increased); *Jones* v. *Miah* (1992) 24 HLR 578, 588–591, Dillon LJ; *Wandsworth LBC* v. *Osei-Bonsu* [1999] 1 WLR 1611, CA.
[391] Protection from Eviction Act 1977 s 3A, inserted by HA 1988 s 31; *Brillouet* v. *Landless* (1995) 28 HLR 837, CA.

M. LICENCES

[25.72] Residential security of tenure applies to self-contained residential accommo-dation which "is let".[392] Licensees are excluded from all protection. Lease/licence litigation took off against the backdrop of the Rent Acts, where on one side there was "life-long" security and fair rents and on the other virtually immediate eviction. The pressure driving it has been released by the general practice of granting shortholds in the private sector, but a trickle of old cases is still reaching the courts as well as a steady stream of cases concerning business security of tenure.[393]

1.   Exclusive possession

[25.73] *Street* v. *Mountford*[394] decides that the acid test for the existence of a tenancy is the presence or absence of exclusive possession.[395] Given that, an occupier is a ten-ant, whereas without it he is merely a licensee. This prevents a landlord from granting rights to self-contained residential accommodation with one hand and with the other denying the occupier the status of a tenant. Earlier Court of Appeal decisions attached importance to the intention of the parties, allowing evasion of the Rent Acts by expression of the intention to do so. Lord Templeman[396] reasserted orthodox doc-trine in forceful terms laying down the three essential *indicia* of a tenancy:

(1) a grant of exclusive possession,
(2) for a term,
(3) at a rent.

Of these, the first is most fundamental.

In *Street* v. *Mountford*, the landlord was a solicitor who entered into an agreement with a Mrs Mountford giving her the right to occupy two furnished rooms in Boscombe for £37 a week. Since the accommodation was self-contained, and she did not have to share it with anyone else, it was conceded in the Lords that Mrs Mountford did have a right to exclusive possession of the flat. She had a weekly ten-ancy and paid a rent. This entitled her to seek registration of a Rent Act 1977 fair rent.[397] The written agreement she signed stated that "this personal licence is not assignable" demonstrating that Street's subjective intention was to create only a licence, and she also signed a statement recognising that she would have no Rent Act protection. But subjective intention was irrelevant, and the test for exclusive

---

[392] RA 1977 s 1; HA 1988 s 1; HA 1985 s 79.

[393] The position is different because protection does not attach to short-term arrangements and business security can be excluded: P Sparkes NLT, 551–558; *JA Pye(Oxford)* v. *Graham* [2002] UKHL 30, [2002] 3 All ER 865, [57], Lord Browne-Wilkinson; *National Car Parks* v. *Trinity Development Co (Banbury)* [2001] EWCA Civ 1686, [2001] 2 EGLR 43, Ch D.

[394] [1985] AC 809, HL; S Anderson (1985) 48 *MLR* 712; S Tromans [1983] *CLJ* 351; R Street [1985] *Conv* 328, HL; S Bridge [1986] *Conv* 344, HL; AJ Waite (1987) 50 *MLR* 226.

[395] It also tests whether a sub-lease has been granted: *Brent LBC* v. *Cronin* (1997) 30 HLR 43, CA. However this is not quite a litmus test, because there are some exclusive licences; see below **[25.83]**.

[396] [1985] AC 809, 816G.

[397] P Sparkes *NLT*, 227–239.

n is substantive.[398] *Street* v. *Mountford* was an easy case, decided unani-
favour of Mrs Mountford.

occupiers are either tenants or lodgers,[399] though the true touchstone
remains exclusive possession.[400] A licensee escapes liability to rating.[401]

2. Possession between landlord and tenant crucial

[25.74] The test for the grant of a lease is applied between the putative landlord and
tenant. An estoppel arises between those two parties if the landlord does not in fact
have power to grant a tenancy.[402] This orthodox principle was applied in an extreme
way in *Bruton* v. *London & Quadrant Housing Trust*.[403] Lambeth LBC granted a
licence of Oval House in Brixton to the Trust, on terms which precluded the grant of
exclusive possession to any occupier. But, in fact, the trust did grant exclusive possession of Flat 2 to Bruton. Temporary accommodation was given in a property earmarked for redevelopment to a person who clearly understood that his occupation
was temporary, but it must be remembered that the proposals had long since been
dropped and that Bruton had been forced to live in inadequate damp conditions for
six years.

3. Rights crucial

[25.75] Exclusive possession is the right to exclude all others from the property, especially the landlord.[404] Undisturbed occupation for many years may not carry the right
to insist that it should continue. Thus, in *Shell-Mex & BP* v. *Manchester Garages*,[405]
commercial occupation of a filling station for four years was quite consistent with the
owner's right to interrupt that occupation, and the same principle applies to residential property. Limited rights of access – perhaps to enter to view the state of repair of
the property[406] – do not affect the tenant's exclusive possession and indeed reempha-
sise it, as do forfeiture clauses.[407]

---

[398] J Hill (1996) 16 *LS* 200.
[399] [1985] AC 809, 817H–818A; *Monmouth BC* v. *Marlog* (1994) 27 HLR 30, CA.
[400] *Brooker Settled Estates* v. *Ayers* (1987) 54 P & CR 165, CA; *AG Securities* [1990] 1 AC 417,
459G–460A; *Aslan* v. *Murphy (No 1)* [1990] 1 WLR 766, 770F–G, Lord Donaldson MR.
[401] *Croydon LBC* v. *Maxon Systems Inc (London)* [1999] EGCS 68, Jowitt J.
[402] Megarry & Wade (6th ed), [14.097–14.101].
[403] [2000] AC 406, HL; S Murdoch [1999] 30 *EG* 90; D. Rook [1999] *Conv* 517; S Bright (2000) 116 *LQR*
7; M Dixon [2000] *CLJ* 25; P Routley (2000) 63 *MLR* 424; M Pawlowski [2002] *Conv* 550; Megarry & Wade
(6th ed), [14.026] (seems to approve?).
[404] *Heslop* v. *Burns* [1974] 1 WLR 1241, 1251G, Scarman LJ; this is confirmed by *Street*.
[405] [1971] 1 WLR 612, CA; *Carroll* v. *Manek* (2000) 79 P & CR 173, Ch D (manager of licensed
premises).
[406] *Street* v. *Mountford* [1985] AC 809 (clause 3); *Huwyler* v. *Ruddy* (1996) 28 HLR 555, CA (genuine
access rights prevent a lease).
[407] *Southampton Community Health Services NHS Trust* v. *Crown Estate Commissioners* [1997] EGCS
155.

4. Serviced accommodation

[25.76] A residential occupier is a licensee if "the landlord provides attendance or services which require the landlord or his servants to exercise unrestricted access to and use of the premises."[408] The extremes are quite clear. A person allowed sole occupation of a whole house or a self-contained flat for an indefinite period is clearly a tenant. But a guest in a hotel taking a room for a week or so is a licensee, since the management reserves the right of access to the room at all times, provides services, and can terminate the arrangement after the week's stay. Between lies what Lord Donaldson MR has described as a "spectrum of exclusivity".[409]

At the non-exclusive end lies the "Emperors Gate Hotel" discussed in *Appah* v. *Parncliffe*.[410] This particular "hotel" was really a set of residential apartments, split into 17 different rooms each with its own Yale lock. The management provided daily cleaning, could ask occupants to vacate without notice, and insisted that visitors leave by 10.30 at night. Occupants were held to be licensees. By way of contrast, *Luganda* v. *Service Hotels*,[411] also concerned a large house in multiple occupation described as a hotel, with a number of rooms each having its own key and gas rings. A student at the Bar was given two days notice to quit after he had been in occupation for three years when he objected to a rent increase. Held on the facts to be a protected tenant, he was able to secure a mandatory injunction to require his reinstatement even after the room had been relet. In *Marchant* v. *Charters*[412] "bachelors" occupying service apartments which were cleaned daily by a housekeeper and provided with clean linen weekly were held to be licensees, though that decision may have been weakened by *Street* v. *Mountford*.[413] Specifically approved by Lord Templeman was *Abbeyfield (Harpenden) Society* v. *Woods*,[414] holding that residents of an old people's home with sole use of a room were licensees, given that the management provided cleaning, meals, heating, and the services of a housekeeper.

Attendance makes a occupier a lodger only if the provision of the particular service requires that the owner should have unrestricted access to the premises.[415] Examples are provision of breakfast, porterage, or management retention of the keys. This last is often used to argue that the occupiers are licensees, but the underlying agreement is crucial: are keys held by the management for the provision of services?[416]

---

[408] *Street* v. *Mountford* [1985] AC 809, 818. Anyway Rent Act 1977 protection was removed by letting at a low rent, or for services, or for board or substantial attendance.

[409] *Aslan* v. *Murphy* [1990] 1 WLR 766, 770F–G.

[410] [1964] 1 WLR 1064, CA (liability of the owners in negligence); *Mehta* v. *Royal Bank of Scotland* [1999] 3 EGLR 153, QBD (some of the dicta in this case are doubtful).

[411] [1969] 2 Ch 209, CA.

[412] [1977] 1 WLR 1181, CA; *Vandersteen* v. *Agius* (1992) 65 P & CR 266, CA; *Brillouet* v. *Landless* (1996) 28 HLR 836, CA.

[413] [1985] AC 809, 825C, Lord Templeman.

[414] [1968] 1 WLR 374; *Street* [1985] AC 809, 824B, Lord Templeman.

[415] *Markou* v. *Da Silvaesa* (1986) 52 P & CR 204 (test is entitlement rather than actual exercise).

[416] *Aslan* v. *Murphy (No 1)* [1990] 1 WLR 766, 773E, Lord Donaldson MR; *Duke* v. *Wynn* [1990] 1 WLR 766, 776.

5. Joint occupation

[25.77] What if a house or flat is provided for occupation by a group of people, per-haps a cohabiting couple or a group of students? They may collectively form a single tenant or they may be individual licensees sharing with each other.

(1) Strangers sharing

[25.78] Residential sharing arrangements led to a mass of inconsistent Court of Appeal decisions, now clarified by the House of Lords in two combined appeals. The scope for sharing arrangements to create genuine licences is shown by *AG Securities* v. *Vaughan*.[417] Four occupants of a shared flat each moved in on a different day, paid a different rent, and were strangers before moving in. The House of Lords held them to be licensees. No one of them had a right to exclusive occupation of the whole flat.[418] Their position was the same as that of the first person let into occupation of a double bed-sit – since the owner can quite legitimately require the first occupier to share when another occupant is introduced.[419]

(2) Couples sharing

[25.79] Artificially splitting the totality of possession between two joint occupiers could yield rich dividends for landlords. In *Somma* v. *Hazelhurst*,[420] the owner entered into two separate agreements with a Mr Hazelhurst and his girlfriend, Miss Savelli, for use of a double bedsitting room for 12 weeks for £120 each. Each was given the right to share the room with each other (which was alright), but also with the owner Somma or another person nominated by the landlord (which was decidedly dubious). The room, it should be said, measured 22 feet by 18 feet and contained two single beds. Neither occupier had exclusive rights, so the Court of Appeal held them to be licensees.

But this decision was absurd. Any landlord could avoid the Rent Act by sharp drafting. The flaw lay in the assumption that the documentation reflected correctly the legal arrangement between the couple, when it patently did not. The whole purpose was that "Hazelhurst and Miss Savelli might live together in undisturbed quasi-connubial bliss".[421] The authority of *Somma* was doubted in *Street* and wholly destroyed by a second burst of fire in *Antoniades*. A Court of Appeal again upheld a clause requiring sharing of a flat containing a bedroom and a small lounge on the basis that the third occupier could sleep in the lounge, a room "not big enough to put the goldfish bowl in". At the time of the letting, the couple opted for a double bed,

---

[417] [1990] 1 AC 417, HL; PV Baker (1989) 105 *LQR* 165; S Bright (1991) 11 *OJLS* 136; C Harpum [1989] *CLJ* 19; J Hill (1989) 52 *MLR* 408; H Wallace (1990) 41 *NILQ* 143; P Sparkes [1989] *JSWL* 293; PV Baker (1989) 105 *LQR* 165; *Parkins* v. *Westminster CC* (1998) 30 HLR 894, CA.

[418] There was a genuine arrangement that the owner could reallocate the rooms when any individual occupier left: [1990] 1 AC 417, 460E, Lord Templeman; *Hadjiloucas* v. *Crean* [1988] 1 WLR 1006, 1023A–B, Mustill LJ; *Stribling* v. *Wickham* [1989] 2 EGLR 35, CA; *Brennan* v. *Lambeth LBC* (1998) 30 HLR 481, CA.

[419] [1990] 1 AC 417, 470G, Lord Oliver.

[420] [1978] 1 WLR 1014, CA; M Partington (1979) 42 *MLR* 331; K Gray (1979) 38 *CLJ* 38.

[421] *Street* [1985] AC 809, 825G, Lord Templeman.

showing most conclusively that their occupation was joint, and so they were joint tenants.

One unwarranted escape route from joint letting arrangements remains. According to *Mikeover* v. *Brady*,[422] splitting the rent of a property may be sufficient to split possession between licensees, though the rents were surely not genuinely separate in that case.

(3) Sharing with the landlord's nominee

[25.80] In both *Somma*[423] and in *Antoniades*, licence agreements included a provision that the occupiers should share with the landlord or (more realistically) with a person nominated by the landlord. This clause may be perfectly valid where strangers share a twin bedsit,[424] so that each occupier arrives and leaves independently, but it is quite unrealistic where a couple share accommodation and, particularly, a bed. By overruling *Somma*,[425] and rejecting this clause in *Antoniades*[426] the House of Lords has shown that this standard form clause will often be treated as a pretence. A sharing provision is only valid if it reflects a real intention that the original occupiers should share with future strangers.

6. Pretences

[25.81] The parties' description of their transaction is not conclusive, because it may be mislabelled.[427] According to Lord Templeman a five pronged digging implement is a fork, even if its manufacturer calls it a spade.[428] In *Street*[429] the House of Lords ignored the statement that "this personal licence is not assignable" as well as the "coda" by which Mrs Mountford recognised that she was signing away her Rent Act protection.

A pretence is a term which mis-states the real agreement reached between the parties. Whole agreements or individual provisions may be excluded leaving genuine terms to be interpreted.[430] "Pretence" has proved to be a better test that "sham", since it includes the usual case in which the intention to deceive is that of the landlord alone, that is it is one-sided.[431] Apart from *Somma* and *Antoniades* there have been a number of more recent illustrations.[432]

[422] [1989] 3 All ER 618, CA; JL Barton (1990) 106 *LQR* 215.

[423] [1978] 1 WLR 1014, CA.

[424] *AG Securities* (four strangers sharing four bedroomed flat).

[425] [1985] AC 809, 825G.

[426] [1990] 1 AC 417, 465A–H; *Mikeover* v. *Brady* [1989] 3 All ER 618, CA.

[427] *Aslan* v. *Murphy* [1990] 1 WLR 766, 770D, Lord Donaldson; *Hadjiloucas* v. *Crean* [1988] 1 WLR 1006, 1019F, Mustill LJ.

[428] *Street* [1985] AC 809, 819F; *Aslan* [1990] 1 WLR 766, 770F–G, Lord Donaldson MR. However, the author uses garden forks with four tines!

[429] [1985] AC 809, HL; see above **[25.73]**.

[430] *Street* [1985] AC 809, 825C, Lord Templeman; *Hadjiloucas* [1988] 1 WLR 1006, 1013–14, Purchas LJ; *Antoniades* [1990] 1 AC 437, 445G, Bingham LJ (CA); *Aslan* [1990] 1 WLR 766.

[431] *AG Securities* v. *Vaughan* [1990] 1 AC 417, 462H, Lord Templeman; *Stribling* v. *Wickham* [1989] 2 EGLR 35, CA; *Aslan* v. *Murphy (No 1)* [1990] 1 WLR 766; *Bhopal* v. *Walia* [1999] 14 LSG 33, CA (sham).

[432] *Nicholaou* v. *Pitt* [1989] 1 EGLR 84, CA; *Skipton BS* v. *Clayton* (1993) 66 P & CR 223, CA; *Huwyler* v. *Ruddy* (1996) 28 HLR 550, CA.

The parol evidence rule only allows proof of the written terms of a contract in writing, and so stacks the dice in favour of the landlord. It is easily avoided by showing that the real relationship between the parties was created by an oral grant which predated the written document, for example where a flat was advertised in a newspaper as "To let".[433]

Relevant factors in determining pretences are a standard form contract,[434] excessive insistence on the fact of personal licences,[435] preceding negotiations,[436] promises that written terms would not be enforced,[437] the relationship of the parties, and the physical size of the accommodation.[438] Later conduct may be relevant[439]: a term that the occupier should vacate each day between 10.30 am and noon *with his belongings* just might be genuine, but the course of events is highly likely to display its artificiality.[440]

N. NEGOTIATIONS/TENANCY AT WILL

[25.82] What happens if a landlord allows a person to take exclusive occupation of land while they negotiate for a lease? Traditional theory is that exclusive occupation indicates a tenancy at will if the landlord assents, or at sufferance if he expresses neither approval nor disapproval. Residential security was a significant risk for either a tenancy at will[441] or tenancy at sufferance,[442] but the courts sought to evade this unfortunate result.

A business tenant can usually insist on renewal of his lease, but entitlement to renewal does not accrue simply from occupation during a period of negotiations. Business tenancies legislation does not apply to a tenancy at will, whether it is express[443] or implied.[444] In particular it has been held that a tenancy at will should be implied where a person holds pending negotiations.[445] Usually payment of rent will convert the tenancy from being at will to being a full periodic tenancy.[446] But even after rent payments, the court may be prepared to hold that occupation is still covered by a tenancy at will, as in *Cardiothoracic Institute* v. *Shrewdcrest*[447] where no security

---

[433] *O'Malley* v. *Seymour* [1979] 1 EGLR 116, CA.

[434] *Hadjiloucas* v. *Crean* [1988] 1 WLR 1006, 1023D; *Demuren* v. *Seal Estates* [1979] 1 EGLR 102, CA.

[435] *Somma* v. *Hazelhurst* [1978] 1 WLR 1014, 1022.

[436] *Antoniades* [1990] 1 AC 417, 463D, Lord Templeman; *Aslan* v. *Murphy (No 1)* [1990] 1 WLR 766, 770F, Lord Donaldson MR.

[437] *Gisborne* v. *Burton* [1989] QB 390, CA.

[438] *Somma* (room 22 by 18 feet); *Antoniades* at 464, Lord Templeman (sitting room). Statutory rules about overcrowding should be relevant despite *Somma*.

[439] *Stribling* v. *Wickham* [1989] 2 EGLR 35, 36H, Parker LJ; *Walsh* v. *Griffiths-Jones* [1978] 2 All ER 1002; *Sturolson & Co* v. *Weniz* [1984] 2 EGLR 121, CA, rejected at [1985] AC 809, 826A.

[440] *Markou* v. *Da Silvaesa* (1986) 52 P & CR 204; *Aslan* as above.

[441] *Francis Jackson Developments* v. *Stemp* [1943] 2 All ER 601 (if express); contrast *Dunthorne and Shore* v. *Wiggins* [1943] 2 All ER 678.

[442] *Artizans Labourers & General Dwellings Co* v. *Whitaker* [1919] 2 KB 301.

[443] *Hagee (London)* v. *A B Erikson & Larson* [1976] QB 209; *BRB* v. *Bodywright* (1971) 220 EG 651.

[444] *Wheeler* v. *Mercer* [1957] AC 416, HL.

[445] *Hagee* at 217, Scarman LJ.

[446] *Bennett Properties* v. *H & S Engineering* [1998] 2 CLYB 3683 (invoice for the first rent was paid).

[447] [1986] 1 WLR 368; JE Martin [1987] *Conv* 55; JE Adams [1988] *Conv* 16; *Longrigg & Trounson* v. *Smith* [1979] 2 EGLR 421; *London & Associated Investment Trust* v. *Calow* (1987) 53 P & CR 340; *Canterbury Cathedral Dean* v. *Whitbread* [1995] 1 EGLR 82; *Dreamgate Properties* v. *Amot* (1998) 76 P & CR 25, CA; *Walji* v. *Mount Cook Land* [2002] 1 P & CR 13 at 163, CA.

arose from occupation pending an application to the court to allow contracting out of business security. A similar result is achieved where a tenant enters into occupation[448] or holds over[449] at a quarterly rent pending negotiations for a lease, which ultimately prove to be abortive. So landlords of commercial property can generally avoid conferring security during negotiations. However, it must be a genuine tenancy at will. "Parties cannot impose upon an agreement by a choice of label a nature or character which upon its proper construction it does not possess."[450]

Direct translation of this case-law to residential property is unhelpful, since tenancies at will are protected. Instead the courts have allowed a diversion into licence doctrine where a potential tenant takes occupation of residential accommodation before making a binding agreement. Parties negotiating for a new residential lease *may* fall into the *Errington* exceptional classes of exclusive licences. It needs to be shown that the arrangement for a tenant remains subject to contract, so that the parties do not yet have the intention to create legal relations.[451] In theory the negotiation phase could be ended by estoppel where the landlord leads the occupier to believe that he will be treated as a tenant, though many cases fail for want of detriment or on the balance of equities.[452]

A tenant holding over and paying rent will usually create a new periodic tenancy, but the circumstances may negative an intention to regrant a lease if the owner is considering his position or negotiating to see whether terms can be agreed for a new tenancy.[453]

O. EXCLUSIVE LICENCES

[25.83] Circumstances surrounding a grant of exclusive possession of separate residential accommodation may make it clear that the occupation is short-term or temporary. Exceptional categories of exclusive licence[454] were identified by Denning LJ in *Errington* v. *Errington*,[455] and approved in *Street* v. *Mountford*.[456] These are based on an objective assessment of the surrounding circumstances rather than any subjective intention.

1. Family relationship and charity

[25.84] After the owner of one house allowed his brother to occupy rent-free, the brother's ungenerous claim to security of tenure was rejected.[457] The most enduring

---

[448] *Javad* v. *Aqil* [1991] 1 WLR 1007, CA; *Mattey Securities* v. *Ervin* [1998] 2 EGLR 66, CA; *James* v. *Evans* [2000] 3 EGLR 1, CA.

[449] *Cricket* v. *Shaftesbury* [1999] 3 All ER 283, Neuberger J.

[450] *Hagee* at 217, Scarman LJ.

[451] *VG Fraulo & Co* v. *Papa* [1993] 2 EGLR 99, CA; *Brent LBC* v. *O'Bryan* [1993] 1 EGLR 59, CA (commercial sector scout hut).

[452] *Southwark LBC* v. *Logan* (1997) 29 HLR 40, CA.

[453] *Marcroft Wagons* v. *Smith* [1951] 2 KB 496; *Vaughan-Armatrading* v. *Sarsah* (1995) 27 HLR 631, CA (South Bank student allowed to stay during exam resit); *Leadenhall Residential 2* v. *Shirley* [2001] EWCA Civ 1011, [2002] 1 WLR 499, [2001] 3 All ER 645.

[454] An exclusive licensee may have sufficient standing to evict a squatter: *Manchester Airport* v. *Dutton* [2000] QB 133, CA.

[455] [1952] 1 KB 290, 296–298.

[456] [1985] AC 809, 823D, Lord Templeman.

[457] *Cobb* v. *Lane* [1952] 1 All ER 1199, CA.

authority is *Errington* v. *Errington*[458] itself, in which a father bought a house for his son and daughter in law with the aid of a building society mortgage, allowing them to occupy on payment of the mortgage instalments; they occupied as contractual licensees rather than tenants at will. A licence also arose from a loose family arrangement that a mother should make monthly payments for accommodation.[459] Family relationship can be overridden by opting for a commercial letting at a market rent.[460]

Charity suggests a licence, including war-time evacuees,[461] those enjoying straightforward generosity,[462] and residents of almshouses.[463]

2.   Exclusive public sector occupation

[25.85] Secure tenancies in the public sector include both leases and exclusive licences of self-contained accommodation,[464] so that security of tenure cannot generally be avoided by the grant of a licence, but there are a number of exceptional cases of exclusive licences lacking any security:

> temporary accommodation for the homeless[465] is given by lease, but so that there is a statutory right to end the occupation.[466]
> short term arrangements;[467] and
> short life property pending demolition[468] or redevelopment;[469]
> temporary exemption from repossession.[470]

3.   Employees

[25.86] Some employers provide accommodation for employees using normal residential leases, but it is also possible to create a service occupancy (a form of licence[471]) where occupation of particular property is necessary for the better performance of the job. Expressed in the older terminology of master and servant:

---

[458] [1952] 1 KB 290, CA.
[459] *Hardwick* v. *Johnson* [1978] 1 WLR 683, CA; also a licence granted by an employer to a retired employee for life: *Foster* v. *Robinson* [1951] 1 KB 149, CA.
[460] *Nunn* v. *Dalrymple* (1989) 21 HLR 569, CA (parents-in-law); *Ward* v. *Warnke* (1990) 22 HLR 496, CA; R Lee [1991] *Conv* 270 (daughter).
[461] *Booker* v. *Palmer* [1942] 2 All ER 674, CA; *Minister of Health* v. *Bellotti* [1944] KB 298, CA (a requisitioning authority allowing possession at a weekly rent).
[462] *Heslop* v. *Burns* [1974] 1 WLR 1241, CA.
[463] *Grace* v. *Taylor* [1998] 4 All ER 17, CA.
[464] HA 1985 s 79(3); *Westminster CC* v. *Clarke* [1992] 2 AC 288, HL (hostel); DS Cowan [1992] *Conv* 285; *Brennan* v. *Lambeth LBC* (1998) 30 HLR 481, CA; *Parks* v. *Westminster CC* [1998] 13 EG 145.
[465] *Eastleigh BC* v. *Walsh* [1985] 2 All ER 112, HL.
[466] HA 1985 sch 1 para 4; shortholds are used in the private and social sectors: HA 1996 s 209(3).
[467] HA 1985 sch 1 paras 5–7; *West Wiltshire DC* v. *Snelgrove* [1997] 2 CLYB 3290; *Northern Ireland Housing Executive* v. *McCann* [1979] NI 39. In the private sector see below [25.88].
[468] HA 1985 sch 1 para 6; *Camden LBC* v. *Shortlife Community Housing* (1992) 25 HLR 330 Millett J; *Shepherds Bush HA* v. *Hats Co-Operative* (1991) 24 HLR 176, CA.
[469] HA 1985 sch 1 para 3; *Attley* v. *Cherwell DC* (1989) 21 HLR 613, CA; *Hyde H Ass* v. *Harrison* (1990) 23 HLR 57, CA; *Brent LBC* v. *O'Bryan* [1993] 1 EGLR 59, CA. But see *Bruton*, HL, below at [25.88].
[470] *Hammersmith & Fulham LBC* v. *Harrison* [1981] 1 WLR 650, CA; PF Smith [1982] *Conv* 218; *Burrows* v. *Brent LBC* [1996] 1 WLR 1448, CA; S Bright (1997) 113 *LQR* 216; *Westminster CC* v. *Basson* (1990) 23 HLR 225, CA (surely close to the line?); *Southwark LBC* v. *Logan* (1997) 29 HLR 40, CA.
[471] *Street* v. *Mountford* [1985] AC 809, 827, Lord Templeman.

"the test is whether the servant requires the premises he occupies in order the better to perform his duties as a servant."[472]

In *Norris* v. *Checksfield*[473] a coach driver was allowed to live in a bungalow to ensure that he was near his place of work and was available to do urgent driving work at short notice. Disqualification as a driver led to his dismissal from his employment, and hence eviction from his bungalow. A caretaker given a flat in the building that he is employed to guard has only a licence,[474] coterminous with his employment contract, but a caretaker given an independent house elsewhere will usually be a tenant.[475]

Occupiers of agricultural tied cottages enjoy special protection.[476]

4. Purchasers allowed possession before completion

[25.87] Sellers often agree to allow possession to their buyers before completion, for example to carry out redecoration or alterations. Security of tenure should not accrue, despite the nineteenth century learning that a purchaser occupied as a tenant at will.[477] Denning LJ avoided the danger of accidental residential security in *Errington* v. *Errington*[478] by finding that a purchaser in possession under an open contract is in fact a licensee, a ruling apparently accepted in *Street* v. *Mountford*.[479] If the Standard Conditions of Sale apply there is an express, revocable,[480] licence,[481] with no security of tenure.[482]

If the buyer has a contractual right to possession before completion, possession is no longer held under a tenancy at will, but rather by force of the contract.[483] This will often be so under an *instalment purchase* contract,[484] but uncertainty in the buyer's position led to Parliamentary intervention so that the buyer does not lose all by

---

[472] *Smith* v. *Seghill Overseers* (1875) LR 10 QB 422, 428, Mellor J.

[473] [1991] 1 WLR 1241, CA. Accepting rent after redundancy will not automatically create a new lease: *Brent LBC* v. *Charles* (1997) 29 HLR 876, CA.

[474] *Methodist Secondary Schools Trustees* v. *O'Leary* (1993) 25 HLR 364, CA.

[475] *Facchini* v. *Bryson* [1952] 1 TLR 1386; *Scrimgeour* v. *Waller* [1981] 1 EGLR 68, CA (gardener); *Royal Philanthropic Society* v. *County* [1985] 2 EGLR 109, CA; PF Smith [1986] *Conv* 215 (care worker).

[476] P Sparkes NLT ch 7.

[477] *Howard* v. *Shaw* (1841) 8 M & W 118, 151 ER 973; *Ball* v. *Cullimore* (1835) 2 Cr M & R 120, 150 ER 51; *Doe d Tomes* v. *Chamberlaine* (1839) 5 M & W 14, 151 ER 7. All cases of contracts providing for possession. But the same rule was applied, after a selective citation of authority, in *Ramnarace* v. *Lutchman* [2001] UKPC 25, [2001] 1 WLR 1651, [15–17], PC.

[478] [1952] 1 KB 290, 296–298, Denning LJ; *Wheeler* v. *Mercer* [1956] 1 QB 274, 284. There was a strong rebuttal in the Lords: [1957] AC 416, 425, Viscount Simonds LC, 435, Lord Somervell.

[479] [1985] AC 809, 827, Lord Templeman.

[480] *Hyde* v. *Pearce* [1982] 1 WLR 560; *Crisp* v. *Fox* (1967) 201 EG 769 (right to mesne profits as if purchaser is trespasser).

[481] Standard Conditions of Sale (3rd ed) cond 5(2).

[482] *Belabel* v. *Mehmet* [1990] 1 EGLR 220, CA. On earlier General Conditions see *Hyde* v. *Pearce* [1982] 1 All ER 1029, CA; *Walters* v. *Roberts* (1981) 41 P & CR 210.

[483] *Ball* v. *Cullimore* (1835) 2 Cr M & R 120, 150 ER 51; *Doe d Tomes* v. *Chamberlaine* (1839) 5 M & W 14, 151 ER 7; *Howard* v. *Shaw* (1841) 8 M & W 118, 151 ER 973; *Crockford* v. *Alexander* (1808) 15 Ves 138, 138, 33 ER 707; *Williams* v. *Greatrex* [1957] 1 WLR 31, 40, Hodson LJ; *Industrial Properties (Barton Hill)* v. *AEI* [1977] QB 580, CA.

[484] B Hoggett (1972) *36 Conv (NS)* 325, 328–332; B Hoggett (1975) 39 *Conv (NS)* 343; HW Wilkinson [1989] *Conv* 307.

missing one or two instalments.[485] The buyer only loses his occupation if the seller can rescind the contract,[486] that is they are treated as buyers rather than as licensees.[487]

5. Irrelevance of absence of power to create tenancy and short-life of property

[25.88] Earlier cases had suggested that a sub-licence would arise where the immediate landlord held as a licensee and occupied short-life property with a view to housing homeless people until redevelopment proceeded. Both grounds were squashed in *Bruton* v. *London & Quadrant Housing Trust*.[488] The trust provided temporary housing for the homeless in short-life properties which they themselves held on licence from Lambeth London Borough Council. Bruton was allowed exclusive rights in a self-contained flat and had a lease as against the trust, meaning that the trust had a repairing obligation.[489] Absence of power to grant a lease can be overcome by estoppel.[490] An intention to make use of short life accommodation is not sufficient to justify the creation of an exclusive licence.[491]

P. RENEWAL AND ENFRANCHISEMENT

1. Enfranchisement

[25.89] Long term residential tenants often have the right to acquire the freehold or extend their lease; there are two schemes for tenants of houses, one for individual tenants of flats and one collective scheme for all tenants in a block.[492]

2. Commercial tenants

[25.90] Business tenants have the right to renew their lease when it expires.[493] There are two schemes protecting agricultural tenants.[494]

---

[485] Housing Act 1980 ss 88–89.

[486] *Errington* v. *Errington* [1952] 1 KB 290, 293, Somervell LJ; *Lakshmijit* v. *Faiz Sherani* [1974] AC 605, PC; *Allen* v. *IRC* [1914] 2 KB 327, 332, Cozens-Hardy MR.

[487] *Errington* [1952] 1 KB 290, 294, 296, 301; *Street* v. *Mountford* [1985] AC 809, 821, Lord Templeman.

[488] *Bruton* [2000] 1 AC 406, HL; P Routley (2000) 63 *MLR* 424; M Dixon [2000] *CLJ* 25; S Bright (2000) 116 *LQR* 7; the HL followed *Family H Ass* v. *Jones* [1990] 1 WLR 779, 794B, Slade LJ.

[489] See below **[26.17ff]**.

[490] *Tower Hamlets LBC* v. *Sherwood* [2002] EWCA Civ 229, [2002] EHLR 13 (kiosk near the Tower of London).

[491] *Westminster CC* v. *Clarke* [1992] 2 AC 288, 300–302, Lord Templeman; *Bruton* [2000] AC 406, 414E–F, Lord Hoffmann.

[492] L Ref A 1967; L Ref HUDA 1993; Chold and Ref A 2002; P Sparkes *NLT* chs 15–16. Termination of very long leases at very low rents may also occur by statutory extension though few leases qualify: LPA 1925 s 153.

[493] LTA 1954 part II; P Sparkes *NLT* ch 20; exclusion is considered at 552–555; see also CPR 56.

[494] Agricultural Holdings Act 1986; Agricultural Tenancies Act 1995; P Sparkes *NLT* ch 22.

26

CONTENT OF LEASES

Covenants. Rent. Repair. Residential repair. Termination by the tenant.
Forfeiture. Flats.

A. COVENANTS

[**26.01**] The terms on which a tenant holds of his landlord are called the covenants.
Although this term is more properly restricted to the terms of a lease by deed the effect
of less formal promises is similar. In this introductory text covenants are treated as
a single whole, proponents of the *New Landlord and Tenant*[1] find no coherence in
the subject and consider that the terms of leases should be treated in three main
groupings.

1. Short term residential leases

[**26.02**] Rents may be regulated, the main repairing burdens are imposed on landlords
and European law recognises the generally inferior position of the tenant by allowing
terms to be challenged for unfairness.[2] A complete consolidation of the rights and
duties of tenants may now be on the cards.[3]

2. Long-term residential leases

[**26.03**] Leaseholders generally pay a low rent called a ground rent and have the obligation to repair – either directly or by contributing to a service charge. They have rights
to enfranchisement and there are important controls over block ownership and management, and there are important statutory controls, recently beefed up, on ground
rents, service charges, and forfeiture.[4]

3. Business leases

[**26.04**] Terms are negotiated in an open market, repairs are down to the tenant, most
rents are subject to review, and there is a move towards contractual analysis of the

---

[1] P Sparkes *NLT* (Hart, 2001); P Sparkes "Towards a Structure for the Law of Landlord and Tenant"
ch 13 in E Cooke *Modern Studies in Property Law 1 – Property 2000* (Hart, 2001).
[2] Unfair Terms in Consumer Contracts Regulations 1999, SI 1999/2083; S Bright & C Bright (1995) 111
LQR 655. OFT Press Release 44/01 (www.oft.gov.uk); D McKibbin [2002] 01 *Legal Action* 6.
[3] *Reform of Housing Law: A Scoping Paper* (Law Com, 2001); M Partington [2001] 04 *Legal Action* 10.
[4] See below [**26.48**].

relationship between landlord and tenant[5] which can be identified in such matters as frustration and repudiation.[6] Agricultural leases form a specialised sub-genre.[7]

B. RENT

1. Three sectors

[26.05] Lord Griffiths has said that:

> "There are basically two ways in which a landlord can obtain moneys worth for a house that he wishes to let on a long lease. Either he can let the premises for the highest annual rent he can obtain in the market, ie the rack rent, or he can accept a lower rent plus the payment of an immediate capital sum – a premium."[8]

Commercial leases tend to reserve a rack rent, that is a rent reflecting the full periodic value of the land,[9] and will almost certainly contain a provision for review of the rent.[10] Short-term residential letting is also based on rack rental letting, though some rents are regulated[11] and others should be affordable.[12] Assured lettings in the private sector are now made at market rents. Longer leases are usual for residential ownership of houses and flats. An initial capital payment (a premium) is used to buy the right to the lease, followed by a much smaller annual rent (called a ground rent).[13] In extreme cases the rent might be nominal, the tradition being to reserve a notional rent as "one peppercorn (if demanded)".

2. The rent obligation

[26.06] A rent is a periodical payment for the use of land. Although usually payable in money, payment could take any other form – rabbits, bottles of wine, red roses, or gold.[14] Rent is payable in arrears unless the lease provides otherwise. Early payment is not advisable since a new landlord who buys the reversion can sue for the same rent again,[15] whereas early payment gives no right to a discount.[16] In practice, almost all leases require rent to be paid in advance, that is at the start of the period for which rent is paid.[17]

---

[5] M Howard (2000) 20 *LS* 503.

[6] See below **[26.30ff]**.

[7] P Sparkes *NLT* ch 22.

[8] *Johnston* v. *Duke of Westminster* [1986] AC 839, 845A.

[9] *Compton Group* v. *Estates Gazette* (1977) 36 P & CR 148.

[10] P Sparkes, *NLT* ch 24.

[11] Fair rents under Rent Act tenancies are capped: Rent Acts (Maximum Fair Rent) Order 1999, SI 1999/6.

[12] P Sparkes *NLT* ch 9.

[13] P Sparkes *NLT*, 366–368; restrictions now apply to the collection of ground rent; see below **[26.48]**.

[14] *Treseder-Griffin* v. *Co-Operative Insurance* [1956] 2 QB 127.

[15] *De Nicholls* v. *Sanders* (1870) LR 5 CP 589.

[16] On insolvency the landlord need not allow a deduction to reflect the fact that payment is made early: *Re Park Air Services* [2000] 2 AC 172, HL.

[17] *City & Capital Holdings* v. *Dean Warburg* [1989] 1 EGLR 90, CA.

A rent covenant[18] is a promise by deed to pay the rent which should be backed up by a proviso for forfeiture in the event of non-payment, which enables the landlord to terminate the lease if the rent is unpaid.[19] Where a tenant holds property without a lease, there is an obligation to pay reasonable compensation for use and occupation or damages for trespass depending upon whether the owner does or does not consent to the occupation.[20]

Tenants are usually obliged to pay rates and taxes and commercial rent may be subject to Value Added Tax.[21]

3. Termination of the rent liability

[26.07] It is a fundamental of the law of landlord and tenant that entitlement to rent ends when the duration of the lease ends – meaning the contractual period and any statutory extension of it. Whether rent is due in the future depends upon whether either party is able to terminate the lease and so stop rent running. As Lord Millett has observed:

> "[R]ent is not a simple debt. It is the consideration for the right to remain in possession. . . . Its existence depends upon future events. Rent in respect of a future rental period may never become payable at all. Rent payable in future under a subsisting lease cannot be treated as a series of future debts making up a pure income stream."[22]

4. Remedies for arrears of rent

[26.08] Arrears of rent can be pursed as a debt by *personal action* through the courts, almost invariably in the County Courts.[23] Short term residential letting will contain a provision for termination in the event of non-payment of rent but the landlord has then to go on and establish a ground for possession under the relevant security of tenure regime.[24] Non-payment of rent will be a ground for forfeiture of a commercial lease.[25] Forfeiture of long residential leases is now severely controlled.[26]

If the rent of a *tenant* is in arrears the head landlord may serve a *rent diversion notice* to claim the rent payable by a *subtenant* directly.[27]

---

[18] A *reddendum* (that is a formal reservation of rent) has the same effect, the traditional phrase "yielding and paying" being equal to an express covenant: *Royton Industries* v. *Lawrence* [1994] 1 EGLR 110, Aldous J.

[19] See below **[26.34]**.

[20] When a former tenant holds over the liability is for double rent: Distress for Rent Act 1737 s 18; *Oliver Ashworth (Holdings)* v. *Ballard (Kent)* [2000] Ch 12, CA; *Lewisham LBC* v. *Masterson* [2000] 1 EGLR 134, CA.

[21] P Sparkes *NLT*, 642–643. The rental limit for stamp duty on short leases was increased from £500 to £5,000 in March 2000: Finance Act 2000 s 115.

[22] *Re Park Air Services* [2000] 2 AC 172, 187E, Lord Millett.

[23] PD 7, [2.1].

[24] P Sparkes *NLT*, 335–340.

[25] See below **[26.34]**.

[26] See below **[26.48]**.

[27] Law of Distress Amendment Act 1908 s 6; *Lawrence Chemical Co* v. *Rubinstein* [1982] 1 WLR 284, CA; *Rhodes* v. *Allied Dunbar Pension Services* [1989] 1 WLR 800, CA; F Oditah [1990] *JBL* 431; JE Adams [1993] *Conv* 11.

5. Distress

[26.09] Distress is the process of seizing goods belonging to a debtor as a means of securing satisfaction of a claim to rent due from a tenant under a lease,[28] the process being called a distraint. There are major limitations on this self help remedy and much property is exempt. Distress is strictly limited against residential tenants,[29] is under more general review[30] and may require modification to make it human rights compliant.[31]

6. Set off

[26.10] It may be a defence to a rent action to prove that the landlord is in breach of his repairing obligations, but there are technical rules. Set off is the process of putting a counterclaim forward as a means of eliminating or reducing a claim. Naturally the defence must be serious, but there is a reluctance to cut off even shadowy defences before trial.[32] Common law recoupment is a right at common law to recover the cost of work which the tenant has actually carried out for which the landlord is liable. This ancient right was lost sight of until *Lee-Parker* v. *Izzet*.[33] Goff J held that the common law right is restricted to cases where there was an ascertained liability, that is that the repair work had been carried out and a fixed sum was being deducted from the rent,[34] and it may be that the sum has also to be indisputable. Equitable set-off is a much broader principle which permits any defendant who faces a claim by action or distress[35] to set off any counterclaim which he has against the claimant,[36] leaving only the net balance owing.[37] If a tenant's claim for damages for disrepair exceeds the landlord's claim for rent, the set-off is a complete defence to the rent action, a principle used successfully in the *British Anzani* case.[38] Claims by subtenants that the floors of a warehouse at Felixstowe were seriously defective gave a right to damages estimated to amount to £1m, though unquantified until the court made a monetary award. It was clear that these claims would far exceed the unpaid rent, so no rent was owing. It made no difference that the claim arose from a free-standing covenant outside the

---

[28] P Sparkes *NLT*, 650–653; SI 2000/2737; *McLeod* v. *Butterwick* [1998] 1 WLR 1603, CA (nature of walking possession).

[29] Leave of the court is required: HA 1988 s 19 (assured tenants); Rent Act 1977 s 147 (Rent Act protected tenants).

[30] Law Com 268 (2001), [1.36].

[31] J Joyce [2001] *EG* 186.

[32] *Maremain* v. *Lewis* [1993] EGCS 130, CA; *Agyeman* v. *Boadi* (1997) 28 HLR 558.

[33] [1971] 1 WLR 1688, Goff J; PM Rank (1976) 40 *Conv (NS)* 196; AJ Waite [1981] *Conv* 199; *Hanak* v. *Green* [1958] 2 QB 9, CA; *Melville* v. *Grapelodge Developments* (1979) 39 P & CR 179, Neill J.

[34] *Lee–Parker* v. *Izzet* [1971] 1 WLR 1688, 1693; *Asco Developments* v. *Gordon* [1978] 2 EGLR 41, Megarry V-C. Set off requires a counter-liability; none exists if no notice has been given on the need for repair: *Holding & Barnes* v. *Hill House Hammond* [2001] EWCA Civ 1334, affirming [2000] 2 P & CR 11 at 145, Neuberger J.

[35] *Lee-Parker* v. *Izzet* [1971] 1 WLR 1688, 1692–1693, Goff J; *Fuller* v. *Happy Shopper Markets* [2001] 1 WLR 1681, Lightman J.

[36] Not other parties: *Mander Taylor* v. *Blaquiere* [2002] Times November 21st, CA.

[37] Supreme Court Act 1981 s 49(2).

[38] *British Anzani (Felixstowe)* v. *International Marine Management (UK)* [1980] QB 137, Forbes J; AJ Waite [1983] *Conv* 373.

lease. The right is also exercisable to challenge the legality of a distress.[39] Set-off is often excluded by a contractual provision requiring payment of the rent without any deduction.[40]

C. REPAIR

1. Balance of covenants

[26.11] A tenant is liable under an old statute[41] for waste under a fixed term[42] lease but not under a periodic tenancy.[43] In a commercial letting, the landlord's liability rests solely on repairing covenants,[44] but most commercial leases are full repairing leases which allocate all responsibility to the tenant; the landlord's rent is pure income.[45] The landlord is under no implied obligation to repair commercial property nor leasehold flats.[46]

2. The standard of repair

[26.12] *Proudfoot* v. *Hart*[47] states that an ordinary repairing covenant imposes an obligation to carry out such repair, having regard to the age, character and locality of the house, as would make it reasonably fit for the occupation of a tenant of the class who would be likely to take it. A higher standard is expected of a new house than of one which is 200 years old, but the remaining commercial life of the building is irrelevant.[48] Location matters since a higher standard was expected of a house in Victorian Mayfair than in Spitalfields.[49] The standard can be altered by contract. For example, "tenantable" repair is limited to keeping the property habitable[50] – excluding painting, decoration and repapering.[51] "Necessary" adds nothing to repair,[52] but "thorough repair" does increase the standard.[53]

---

[39] *Eller* v. *Grovecrest Investments* [1995] QB 272, CA.

[40] The most recent cases are: *Coca-Cola Financial Corp* v. *Finsat International* [1998] QB 43, CA; *Unchained Growth III* v. *Granby Village (Manchester) Management Co* [2000] 1 WLR 739, CA; *Baygreen Properties* v. *Gil* [2002] EWCA Civ 1340, [2002] 49 EG 126.

[41] Statute of Marlborough 1267, 52 Henry 3 c 23.

[42] *Dayani* v. *Bromley LBC* [1999] 3 EGLR 144, QBD.

[43] There is a more limited duty to keep wind and watertight: *Wedd* v. *Porter* [1916] 2 KB 91, CA.

[44] *Demetriou* v. *Poolaction (1982)* [1991] 1 EGLR 100, CA.

[45] *O'May* v. *City of London Real Property Co* [1983] 2 AC 726, HL.

[46] *Adams* v. *Lincoln Grange Management* [1998] 1 EGLR 58, CA; *Yankwood* v. *Havering LBC* [1998] EGCS 75, Neuberger J. Contrast short term residential letting, below at **[26.17ff]**.

[47] (1890) 25 QBD 42, CA.

[48] *Ladbroke Hotels* v. *Sandhu* [1995] 2 EGLR 92.

[49] (1890) 25 QBD 42, 52–53, 55.

[50] *Payne* v. *Haine* (1847) 16 M & W 541, 153 ER 1304.

[51] *Proudfoot* v. *Hart* (1890) 25 QBD 42.

[52] *Truscott* v. *Diamond Rock Brewing Co* (1882) 20 Ch D 251, CA.

[53] *Lurcott* v. *Wakely* [1911] 1 KB 905, 918, Fletcher Moulton LJ.

3. Existing standard or improvement?

[26.13] Whether a tenant is required to improve his property depends upon the form of a particular covenant. If the covenant is simply *to repair* it is necessary to maintain the standard set at the time of the lease – neither more[54] nor less[55] – but this must be done irrespective of the commercial life of the building left at the time of enforcement of the covenant.[56]

A covenant to *put into repair*, discussed in *Proudfoot* v. *Hart*,[57] involves improvement in the standard of the property at the outset to a proper standard of repair. If it is *to keep in repair*, there is a duty first to put it in repair and then to maintain it in repair,[58] an odd interpretation acted upon in very many cases. Thus to keep in good and tenantable repair imposed an obligation on the landlord to repair leaking stone cladding which had never been satisfactory.[59] Similarly *to leave in good condition* involves more than just repair, since it must be kept in good condition.[60]

The Law Society's standard form for commercial letting departs from the usual terminology of repair, by imposing an obligation to maintain the property, that is to conserve the standard existing at the date of the lease.[61]

4. Renewal of parts contrasted with improvement of whole

[26.14] *Lurcott* v. *Wakely*[62] decided that repair may include demolition and reconstruction of a subsidiary part of a building, if this is necessary to put the whole house in repair. After the London County Council had required a landlord to demolish and reconstruct the front wall of a house, the cost was successfully passed on to the tenant under the tenant's express repairing covenant. The wall was a subsidiary part, which had to be renewed completely if the whole house was to be in repair. Other cases have involved rewiring,[63] and complete replacement of a worn-out roof.[64] Complete changes to the character of the property let is a rebuilding outside the repairing covenant.[65]

5. Reconstruction and inherent defects

[26.15] This is outside the scope of a repairing covenant. Thus in *Brew Brothers* v. *Snax (Ross)*[66] when a flank wall tilted as its weight caused the collapse of a drain, the

---

[54] *Shaw* v. *Kay* (1847) 1 Exch 42, 154 ER 175.
[55] *Re London Corp* [1910] 2 Ch 314, Eve J; *Coward* v. *Gregory* (1866) LR 2 CP 153.
[56] *Ladbroke Hotels* v. *Sandhu* [1995] 2 EGLR 92.
[57] (1890) 25 QBD 42, CA.
[58] At 50, Esher MR.
[59] *Crédit Suisse* v. *Beegas Nominees* [1994] 4 All ER 803.
[60] *Lurcott* v. *Wakely* [1911] 1 KB 905, 915.
[61] Standard Business Lease, [5.1].
[62] [1911] 1 KB 905, CA.
[63] *Roper* v. *Prudential Assurance Co* [1992] 1 EGLR 5 QBD; *Creska* v. *Hammersmith & Fulham LBC* [1998] 3 EGLR 35, CA.
[64] *New England Properties* v. *Portsmouth New Shops* [1993] 1 EGLR 84; *Elite Investments* v. *TI Bainbridge Silencers* [1986] 2 EGLR 43.
[65] *City Offices (Regent Street)* v. *Europa Acceptance Group* [1990] 1 EGLR 63, CA.
[66] [1970] 1 QB 612, CA.

cost of remedial work was equal to the cost of a new building, work which, a majority[67] held, went far beyond what a reasonable person would call repair. A commercial tenant is not usually obliged to repair design defects and neither is the landlord.[68] A stalemate was reached in *Post Office* v. *Aquarius Properties*,[69] since neither party was responsible for correcting the fact that the basement of a 1960s office block in the City was often ankle deep in water.

The same rule has been applied, with less justice, to limit the landlord's obligation to provide proper dwellings. In *Quick* v. *Taff Ely BC*[70] houses were uninhabitable as a result of design defects which led to excessive condensation. Solving the problem would have required replacement of the metal windows, which were sound.[71] This work was not required of the landlord. Similarly in *McDougall* v. *Easington DC*[72] the tenant failed because the work needed to prevent water penetration, involved replacement of the front and rear elevations, a new roof and new windows. Work which does fall within a repairing obligation may coincidentally remedy an inherent defect.[73]

6. Landlord's damages for disrepair

[26.16] Damages available to a landlord are capped by the Landlord and Tenant Act 1927[74] so as not to exceed the loss in value of the landlord's reversion. No damages at all are to be awarded if the premises would be pulled down shortly after the end of the lease, nor if there will be such major alterations that the repair is irrelevant. Landlords in the early 1920s would terminate the lease of a soldier returned from the trenches, sue the displaced tenant for failure to deliver up the property in good repair, and then demolish and reconstruct the property. Landlords were able to secure a double profit, from full repairing damages and from the redevelopment. The 1927 Act withholds this double profit from landlords.[75]

If the repairs are to be carried out the extent to which the reversion depreciates is normally identical to the cost of the necessary work. However, a cap is imposed at the diminution in value of the reversion. Thus, if the selling value is £5,000 and the cost of the repairs is £10,000 the damages are limited to £5,000. If there is no diminution in value, there are no damages.[76] Restrictions apply to actions for damages during the term of the lease.[77]

---

[67] At 640, Sachs LJ, 640, Phillimore LJ: Harman LJ's dissent (at 631F) that this was risk which the tenant ought to discover by survey is more convincing; *Adams* v. *Lincoln Grange Management* [1998] 1 EGLR 58, CA.

[68] Except under an express covenant: *BHP Petroleum Great Britain* v. *Chesterfield Properties* [2001] EWCA Civ 1797, [2002] Ch 194.

[69] [1987] 1 All ER 1055, CA; PF Smith [1987] *Conv* 224; S Murdoch [1987] *JBL* 383.

[70] [1986] QB 809, CA.

[71] Contrast *Minja Properties* v. *Cussins Property Group* [1998] 2 EGLR 52 (existing windows sound).

[72] (1989) 58 P & CR 201, CA; PF Smith [1990] *Conv* 335.

[73] *Ravenseft Properties* v. *Davston Holdings* [1980] 1 QB 12, Forbes J; *Elmcroft Developments* v. *Tankersley-Sawyer* [1984] 1 EGLR 47, CA; *Stent* v. *Monmouth DC* (1987) 19 HLR 269; *Eyre* v. *McCracken* (2000) 80 P & CR 220, CA; *Holding & Barnes* v. *Hill House Hammond* [2001] EWCA Civ 1334, affirming [2000] LTR 428, Neuberger J; see also below [26.19].

[74] S 18(1).

[75] *Salisbury* v. *Gilmore* [1942] 2 KB 38, CA; *Re King* [1963] Ch 459, CA.

[76] For the case law see P Sparkes *NLT*, 681–684.

[77] Leasehold Property (Repairs) Act 1938 s 1 as amended; see below [26.37].

D. RESIDENTIAL REPAIR

1. Landlord's obligation to repair dwellings

(1) Short leases of dwellings

[26.17] Much of the benefit of repair work to property let for a short term will accrue to the landlord, so it is right for statute to place the liability for major structural repairs onto private sector landlords.[78] Freedom of contract operates for a lease of exactly seven years[79] or for any longer period, but the landlord is obliged to repair any dwelling let for a shorter period.[80]

The duty only bites after the landlord has made an initial grant of a tenancy. In *Bruton* v. *London & Quadrant Housing Trust*[81] the claimant occupied a flat in a block held by a voluntary homelessness trust under a licence granted by a local authority. The Trust granted exclusive possession to Bruton, creating a tenancy binding between themselves, sufficient to entitle Bruton to enforce the statute. This was so despite the fragility of Bruton's tenure as against the local authority as freeholder.

(2) Work covered

[26.18] There is an implied covenant by the landlord to repair the structure and exterior of the dwelling. With flats the landlord's duties include not only the individual flat, but also the structure of the entire block.[82] Regard is had to the age, character, and prospective life of the dwelling in fixing the standard of repair required.[83] Included in the structure are internal plastering, ceilings, and external doors,[84] as well as windows, sashes, cords and frames,[85] and the steps leading to the back door.[86] Excluded are back-yard, rear footpaths,[87] and an outbuilding containing a WC.[88] The tenant may remain liable for internal decoration.[89]

Installations must also be maintained by the landlord so as to be in repair and proper working order[90] including those for the supply of water (basins, sinks, and baths),[91] electricity, gas, sanitation (including toilets), space heating and water

---

[78] LTA 1985 ss 11–17; P Sparkes *NLT*, 368–371.
[79] *Brikom Investments* v. *Seaford* [1981] 1 WLR 863, CA.
[80] LTA 1985 s 13. Contracting out with the consent of the county court is rare.
[81] [2000] AC 406, HL.
[82] LTA 1985 s 11(1A), inserted in 1988 to reverse *Campden Hill Towers* v. *Gardner* [1977] QB 823, CA.
[83] Applying the rule in *Proudfoot* v. *Hart* (1890) 25 QBD 42, CA.
[84] *Morris* v. *Liverpool CC* [1988] 1 EGLR 47; *Staves* v. *Leeds CC* (1990) 23 HLR 107, CA; *Hussein* v. *Mehlman* [1992] 2 EGLR 87, Stephen Sedley QC.
[85] *Irvine* v. *Moran* (1991) 24 HLR 1, 5.
[86] *Brown* v. *Liverpool Corp* [1969] 3 All ER 1345, CA.
[87] *Hopwood* v. *Cannock Chase DC* [1975] 1 WLR 373, CA; *McAuley* v. *Bristol CC* [1992] QB 134, CA; *King* v. *South Northants DC* [1992] 1 EGLR 53, CA.
[88] *Cresswell* v. *Sandwell MBC* [2001] CLYB 4211, Ct Ct.
[89] *Irvine* v. *Moran* (1991) 24 HLR 1, Ch D.
[90] Minor adaptions to adjust to changes in patterns of supply are also required: *O'Connor* v. *Old Etonians H Ass* [2002] EWCA Civ 150, [2002] Ch 295.
[91] *Sheldon* v. *West Bromwich Corp* (1973) 25 P & CR 360, CA (cold water tank); *Wycombe H Ass* v. *Barnett* (1982) 5 HLR 84 (not lagging pipes).

heaters.[92] Fittings and other appliances for making use of the services[93] remain the tenant's responsibility.

(3) Exclusion of inherent defects

[26.19] The landlord's obligation is limited to repairing damage caused by the natural effects of time, and does not extend to reconstruction. As Lord Hoffmann put it in *Southwark LBC* v. *Mills*:[94]

> "Keeping in repair means remedying disrepair. The landlord is obliged only to restore the house to its previous good condition. He does not have to make it a better house than it originally was."

In *Quick* v. *Taff Ely BC*[95] houses became uninhabitable as a result of design defects caused by condensation, a problem which could only be cured by replacement of the metal windows. Since existing windows were sound, they were not in disrepair and the landlord was not liable.

(4) Tenant's responsibility for repairs

[26.20] Tenants of dwellings may be liable to do minor work such as internal decoration and they are more generally required to use any property in a tenant-like manner,[96] though fair wear and tear is allowed. Breach of these terms may give rise to a ground for possession.[97]

2. Fitness for habitation

[26.21] Fitness for habitation[98] is distinct from disrepair, since it involves such matters as condensation,[99] lack of safety, poor ventilation[100] or disrepair of steps.[101] Some 5% of all homes are unfit, but as many as 20% in the private rented sector. No obligation is imposed on the landlord of an unfurnished house.[102] In *Southwark LBC* v. *Mills*[103] the House of Lords decided that a local authority landlord was not liable to soundproof residential accommodation against the activities of neighbours, even though the tenants could hear all the everyday activities in the neighbouring flats –

---

[92] LTA 1985 s 11(1)(c); *Hussein* v. *Mehlman* [1992] 2 EGLR 87 (gas heaters).
[93] S 11(1)(b).
[94] [2001] 1 AC 1, 8C.
[95] [1986] QB 809, CA; *Palmer* v. *Sandwell MBC* [1987] 2 EGLR 79, CA; *Southwark LBC* v. *McIntosh* [2002] 1 EGLR 25, Lightman J; *Ratcliffe* v. *Sandwell MBC* [2002] EWCA Civ 06, [2002] 2 P & CR 23 at 322; *Welsh* v. *Greenwich LBC* [2000] 3 EGLR 41, CA; *Lee* v. *Leeds CC* [2002] EWCA Civ 6, [2002] HLR 17 at 367 (survived human rights attack); also above **[26.15]**.
[96] *Warren* v. *Keen* [1954] 1 QB 15, 20, Denning LJ.
[97] P Sparkes *NLT*, 344–346.
[98] LTA 1985 s 10; HA 1985 s 604(2); PF Smith [1998] *Conv* 189.
[99] *Quick* v. *Taff Ely BC* [1986] QB 809, CA.
[100] *Summers* v. *Salford Corp* [1943] AC 283, HL.
[101] *McCarrick* v. *Liverpool Corp* [1947] AC 219, HL.
[102] *Cavalier* v. *Pope* [1906] AC 428, HL; *McNerny* v. *Lambeth LBC* (1988) 21 HLR 188, CA.
[103] [2001] AC 1, HL; D Rook [2000] *Conv* 161; J O'Sullivan [2000] *CLJ* 16.

televisions, babies crying, comings and goings, quarrels and lovemaking.[104] Exceptional cases must now be considered.

(1) Obsolete statutory liability to ensure fitness.

[26.22] It is a condition of the lease of a house that it is fit for human habitation at the commencement of the lease and there is an undertaking to keep it in that condition but – and this is a big but – the term is only implied where the rent is less than £80 *a year* in Inner London and £52 elsewhere.[105] Only Parliament can now decide to bring these limits up to date.[106]

(2) Position where property furnished.

[26.23] If property is let furnished,[107] there is an implied condition that is it reasonably fit for habitation. A woman who took a furnished house for the season in Brighton only to find it infested with bugs could repudiate the lease, and quit without notice.[108]

(3) Proposed Housing Fitness Standard

[26.24] It is proposed to introduce a Housing Fitness Standard which will require dwellings to reach a stated standard irrespective of the causes of defects.[109]

3. Notice to repair

[26.25] A landlord's duty to repair arises only when the tenant has given notice of the need for repair and has allowed access to carry out the work. Notice is required whether the repairing duty arises under an express covenant,[110] under the statutory duty to make a house fit for habitation,[111] or under the modern statutory obligation to maintain the structure and installations in a dwelling.[112] Even if the tenant is unaware of the defect requiring repair, notice is still required. In *O'Brien* v. *Robinson*[113] the bedroom ceiling collapsed on tenants while they were in bed, the cause being an inherent defect that was not apparent from inspection. The tenants were unable to recover for their injuries. Notice is not required where the property to be repaired is under the control of the landlord.[114]

---

[104] At 7E, Lord Hoffmann.

[105] LTA 1985 s 8.

[106] *Boldack* v. *East Lindsey DC* (1999) 31 HLR 41, 49, May LJ.

[107] *Sutton* v. *Temple* (1843) 12 M & W 52, 152 ER 1108; *Chester* v. *Powell* (1885) 52 LT 722, CA.

[108] *Smith* v. *Marrable* (1843) 11 M & W 5, 152 ER 693; *Wilson* v. *Finch-Hatton* (1877) 2 Ex D 336; *Collins* v. *Hopkins* [1923] 2 KB 617 (tb).

[109] D Ormandy [2002] 5 *JHL* 50.

[110] *Hugall* v. *M'Lean* (1885) 53 LT 94, CA; *Holding & Barnes* v. *Hill House Hammond* [2001] EWCA Civ 1334, affirming [2002] 2 P & CR 11 at 145, Neuberger J.

[111] *Summers* v. *Salford Corp* [1943] AC 283, HL; *McCarrick* v. *Liverpool Corp* [1947] AC 219, HL.

[112] *O'Brien* below.

[113] [1973] AC 912, HL; *Hussein* v. *Mehlman* [1992] 2 EGLR 87, 91L–M, Stephen Sedley QC.

[114] *British Telecommunications* v. *Sun Life Assurance Society* [1995] 4 All ER 44, CA; *Ladsky* v. *TSB Bank* (1997) 74 P & CR 372, CA (no notice where duty to repair in mortgage).

4. Common parts

[26.26] There may be an implied term to take reasonable steps to keep common parts in repair.[115]

5. Tenant's remedies for landlord's failure to repair

[26.27] The tenant will be entitled to claim as damages the cost of the work and any consequential damage.

Tenants cannot usually cope with the cost and organisational problems involved in major work. The earlier reluctance to award specific performance[116] has been displaced by a statutory jurisdiction to order specific performance of landlord's repairing obligations in favour of residential tenants.[117] The jurisdiction can be exercised in a county court[118] and also where a district judge sits as a small claims arbitrator.[119] Even a tenant can be compelled to carry out a repairing obligation according to *Rainbow Estates* v. *Tokenhold*[120] where other remedies such as damages and forfeiture are inadequate. The court is able to examine the end result of the repair to see whether it meets the required standard.[121]

Where the landlord is required to repair he must be able to gain access to carry out the necessary works.

6. Repair and deduct

[26.28] There is a common law right to repair and deduct the cost from the rent, and a wider equitable right to set off potential, unquantified, claims. Landlords often try to avoid this by a clause that rent is to be paid without deductions.[122]

7. Administrative procedures to enforce repairs

[26.29] Local authorities have powers to require work to unfit or unsatisfactory houses, using powers to abate statutory nuisances[123] and to issue repairs notices.[124]

---

[115] *Liverpool* CC v. *Irwin* [1977] AC 239, HL; *Southwark LBC* v. *Long* [2002] EWCA Civ 403, [2002] 47 EG 150.

[116] *Hill* v. *Barclay* (1810) 16 Ves 402, 33 ER 1037, Eldon LC.

[117] Now LTA 1985 s 17.

[118] *Quick* v. *Taff Ely BC* [1986] QB 809, CA.

[119] *Joyce* v. *Liverpool CC* [1996] QB 252, CA.

[120] [1999] Ch 64, Ch D; PH Kenny [1998] *Conv* 163; M Pawlowski & J Brown [1998] *Conv* 495; S Bridge [1999] *CLJ* 283; O Breen (1999) 50 *NILQ* 102.

[121] *Co-operative Insurance Society* v. *Argyll Stores (Holdings)* [1998] AC 1, 12–16, Lord Hoffmann.

[122] See above **[26.10]**.

[123] Environmental Protection Act 1990 ss 79–90.

[124] HA 1985 s 189.

E. TERMINATION BY THE TENANT

1. Repudiation of the lease

[26.30] A tenant may be entitled to repudiate a lease after a breach of one of its fundamental terms by the landlord. In *Hussein* v. *Mehlman*[125] a tenant held a shorthold for a three year term, but returned the keys with 18 months remaining when it became apparent that the landlord would not maintain the property. One particularly serious breach by the landlord led to the collapse of the ceiling and this by itself was sufficient to vitiate the tenancy agreement. The decision represents a further big step towards recognition of a contractual basis to leasehold law,[126] and appears now to be accepted as sound doctrine.[127] In *Chartered Trust* v. *Davies*[128] a lease in a shopping mall was terminated after the landlord had let a nearby shop to a pawnbroker, whose queue of customers caused a nuisance and interfered with the tenant's light. The landlord had failed in his duty to prevent the nuisance and hence the tenant could repudiate his lease. Breaches of covenant will rarely be so serious as to allow a commercial tenant to walk away in the absence of express contractual provisions. [129]

2. Frustration

[26.31] Frustration is:[130]

"the premature determination of an agreement between the parties . . . owing to the occurrence of an intervening event or change in circumstances so fundamental as to be regarded by the law both as striking at the root of the agreement and as entirely beyond what was contemplated by the parties when they entered into the agreement."

In *Taylor* v. *Caldwell*[131] a licence to allow the use of a concert hall was frustrated when the hall was burnt down, so that both parties were excused performance. Expansion to embrace leases dates only from the later part of the twentieth century as a means to secure escape from injustice, following recognition that tenants may suffer injustice just as much as any other contracting party.

Many circumstances are insufficiently grave to provoke a frustration. In *London & Northern Estates Co* v. *Schlesinger*[132] a flat was leased to an Austrian who was prohibited from occupying it when he was classified as an enemy alien during the Great War. In *Cricklewood Property & Investment Trust* v. *Leighton's Investment Trust*[133]

---

[125] [1992] 2 EGLR 87, Stephen Sedley QC; C Harpum [1993] *CLJ* 212; S Bright [1992] *Conv* 71; W Barr "Repudiation of Leases – a Fool's Paradise" ch 14 in Jackson & Wilde.

[126] Also *Killick* v. *Roberts* [1991] 1 WLR 1146 (can rescind a Rent Act tenancy procured by a fraudulent statement).

[127] *Re Olympia & York Canary Wharf (No 2)* [1993] BCC 159, 166; *Kingston on Thames RLBC* v. *Marlow* [1996] 1 EGLR 101, 102K–L.

[128] [1997] 2 EGLR 83, CA.

[129] *Nynehead Developments* v. *RH Fibreboard Containers* [1999] 1 EGLR 7 Ch D; M Pawlowski & J Brown [1999] *Conv* 150; P Luxton [1999] *JBL* 471.

[130] *Cricklewood Property & Investment* v. *Leighton's Investment Trust* [1945] AC 221, 228, Simon LC.

[131] (1863) 3 B & S 826, 122 ER 309.

[132] [1916] 1 KB 20; *Whitehall Court* v. *Ettlinger* [1920] 1 KB 680.

[133] [1945] AC 221, HL.

building leases could not be implemented because of wartime building restrictions. And in *National Carriers* v. *Panalpina (Northern)*[134] access to a warehouse in Hull was blocked for 20 months out of a total term of 10 years. But a majority of four to one in *Panalpina* indicated that a lease could be ended by frustration if the circumstances were sufficiently exceptional, though "hardly ever".[135] Suitable cases for frustration might be:

obstruction of the commercial venture;[136]
physical destruction of the premises;
outbreak of war;
government interference or supervening illegality – for example building restrictions, dedication of the land as an open space,[137] or the imposition of restrictions on the use of second homes.[138]

Normal contractual principles apply to determine the effect of frustration.[139]

F. FORFEITURE

[26.32] Forfeiture is the right of the landlord to re-enter the premises which he had let to the tenant as a consequence of the tenant's breach of covenant, and to terminate the lease. The present law[140] is a mess and radical reform is likely.[141] This section focuses on forfeiture of commercial premises since there are special controls on the forfeiture of residential flats.[142]

1. Reservation of the right

[26.33] The existence of this remedy is dependent upon the terms of the lease, and it is usual to include a separate proviso for forfeiture on breach of covenant.

2. Arrears of rent

[26.34] Leases generally provide for termination when rent which is owing[143] is left unpaid for (say) 14 or 31 days. This procedure applies to payments of service charge

---

[134] [1981] AC 675, HL; K Hodkinson [1981] *Conv* 227; S Tromans [1981] *CLJ* 217.
[135] At 688H, Hailsham LC.
[136] At 691E, Hailsham LC.
[137] *Cricklewood* at 229, Simon LC.
[138] *Swift* v. *Macbean* [1942] 1 KB 375, Birkett J.
[139] P Sparkes *NLT*, 713–716; W Barr (2001) 52 *NILQ* 82.
[140] Sparkes, *NLT* ch 29.
[141] Law Com 142 (1985); Law Com 221 (1994); *Termination of Tenancies by Physical Re-entry: CD* (Law Com, 1999); Law Com 268 (2001), [5.5]; JE Adams [1998] *Conv* 165; G Watt "Property Rights and Wrongs: The Frontiers of Forfeiture" ch 7 in E Cooke *Modern Studies in Property Law 1 – Property 2000* (Hart, 2001).
[142] See below **[26.48]**.
[143] At common law a formal demand was required but leases invariably exempt from this requirement; otherwise action is only possible when 6 months rent is owing: Common Law Procedure Act 1852 s 210.

which are reserved as rent, the terms of the lease being decisive.[144] A landlord who elects to forfeit then sues for possession without needing to give any prior warning.[145] While proceedings are pending or after judgment, relief will be allowed to a tenant who stumps up the money.

In *Kataria* v. *Safeland*[146] the tenant of a walk-in kiosk on Kingsway in London owed £10,000 in rent at the time that the freehold was sold to Safeland. Even though the terms of the sale were that the arrears would be recoverable by the previous land-lord, Safeland was nonetheless entitled to re-enter and forfeit the lease on the grounds of arrears of rent – the proprietary right to re-enter being distinct from the personal right of action for rent arrears.

3. Notice procedure

[26.35] A landlord may only forfeit for other breaches (other that is than non-payment of rent) after serving on the tenant a notice under section 146 of the Law of Property Act 1925. This tells the tenant what is wrong and gives him an opportunity to rectify any breach and to consider his position.[147] Hence the three essential con-tents of a pre-forfeiture notice: (1) it must specify the particular breach complained of;[148] (2) it must require the tenant to remedy the breach, assuming that it is capable of remedy;[149] and (3) it must require the tenant to make compensation in money for the breach (if compensation is required). Proceedings may only be commenced after a reasonable time has elapsed.[150] In *Expert Clothing Service & Sales* v. *Hillgate House*,[151] the tenants were already 15 months late in completing the reconstruction of a property, but further time had to be allowed.

When the landlord proceeds in the courts the tenant can claim relief from forfeiture by way of defence to the proceedings, whereas after a physical re-entry, the tenant's claim for relief must be made in separate proceedings.[152]

Breaches of a covenant against assignment were brought within the section 146 notice procedure only in 1925.[153] This is a change with little substance, since assigning without permission is an irremediable breach, and a section 146 notice merely gives a short period of notice to quit the property. In *Scala House & District Property Co* v. *Forbes*[154] the Court of Appeal held that 14 days notice was sufficient. Many breaches are waived and there is a theoretical power to relieve an innocent buyer.[155] However,

---

[144] *Escalus Properties* v. *Robinson* [1996] QB 231, CA; *Khar* v. *Delmounty* (1998) 75 P & CR 232, CA; subject to statutory restrictions below **[26.48]**.

[145] LPA 1925 s 146(11).

[146] [1998] 1 EGLR 39, CA.

[147] *Horsey Estates* v. *Steiger* [1899] 2 QB 79, 91, Lord Russell LCJ.

[148] *Adagio Properties* v. *Ansari* [1998] 2 EGLR 69, CA ("making alterations so as to divide flat without permission" was a sufficient definition of the breach).

[149] It must include a claim to forfeit: *Lambeth LBC* v. *Vincent* [2000] 2 EGLR 73, Ch D.

[150] LPA 1925 s 146(1).

[151] [1986] Ch 340, CA.

[152] See below **[26.38]**.

[153] LPA 1925 s 146(8)(i).

[154] [1974] QB 575, CA; PV Baker (1973) 89 *LQR* 460; DJ Hayton [1974] *CLJ* 54; *Savva* v. *Hossein* [1996] 2 EGLR 65, 66G, Staughton LJ. A permanent stigma is created by the use of premises for prostitution, see below [26.45].

[155] *Creery* v. *Summersell* [1949] Ch 751; *Savva* v. *Hossein* [1996] 2 EGLR 65, 66H, Staughton LJ.

Savva v. *Hossein*[156] has shown recently that breaches of any other negative covenants (such as not to erect advertising signs) can be rectified.

4. Special forms of notice

(1) Internal decorative repair

[26.36] A pre-forfeiture notice which relates to internal decorative repair must be proved to be reasonable,[157] so landlords cannot be unduly fussy about painting and wallpapering.

(2) Unfair disrepair claims

[26.37] The Leasehold Property (Repairs) Act 1938 prevents unscrupulous people buying up leases and then putting pressure on tenants by producing exaggerated lists of dilapidations.[158] It bites only if, at the time of service of a pre-forfeiture notice, at least five years of the term remain outstanding.[159] The Act applies both to houses and commercial premises.[160] Leave of the court must be obtained before the landlord may proceed on any one of five grounds[161] where, in essence, immediate enforcement is important. Even if one of the five grounds is established, leave to proceed remains discretionary.

In *Associated British Ports* v. *CH Bailey*[162] the landlords granted a lease of a port, which included a dry dock. Changes in boat repairing practice meant that this was not used after 1983 and it fell into disrepair. A notice asked for remedial work costing £600,000 but the dry dock would have been worn out by the end of the term, changes in working practices had already rendered it obsolete, and the landlord's loss was no more than £3,500. The tenants were being asked to spend £600,000 to no good purpose but the court prevented the landlords from proceeding on this basis. The 1938 Act relies on a clumsy procedure, by which the landlord's pre-forfeiture notice must set out the tenant's right to claim the benefit of the Act by counter notice served within 28 days. It is always correct for a tenant to claim the benefit of the Act.[163]

5. Re-entry

[26.38] Proceedings for trespass[164] are the normal method of forfeiture, and the only lawful method for property with a residential occupier. Leave is not required even if

---

[156] [1996] 2 EGLR 65, CA.

[157] LPA 1925 s 147. There appear to be no reported cases.

[158] [1990] 2 AC 703, 709B, Lord Templeman.

[159] S 1(1).

[160] S 1(1); LTA 1954 s 51; *Associated British Ports* v. *CH Bailey* [1990] 2 AC 703, 709D, Lord Templeman.

[161] Leasehold Property (Repairs) Act 1938 s 1(5).

[162] [1990] 2 AC 703, HL; PF Smith [1990] *Conv* 305; S Bridge [1990] *CLJ* 401.

[163] The right is not, apparently, available to a secured lender: *Smith* v. *Spaul* [2002] EWCA Civ 1830, [2002] Times December 28th.

[164] *Commissioners for Works* v. *Hull* [1922] 1 KB 205.

the tenant is insolvent.[165] The claim for forfeiture should be protected as a pending land action.[166]

It may seem surprising that a complex dispute about whether a breach of covenant has occurred and whether it is so serious as to preclude relief from the forfeiture should be settled by the landlord changing the locks.[167] What is laughingly called "peaceable" re-entry is an undoubted remedy under a commercial lease,[168] and one that will be preserved.[169] Service of a valid section 146 notice is a vital precursor to peaceable re-entry, other than for non-payment of rent.[170] Peaceable re-entry should not be used against a residential occupier since forfeiture can only occur in court,[171] it is an offence to repossess physically,[172] and an offence to forfeit against a residential occupier who is opposed to the repossession.[173] Residential property that is vacant can be repossessed out of court.[174]

Re-entry by starting proceedings or physical re-entry is an election to terminate[175] but the lease continues in force until actual termination by the judgment for possession and the absence of a successful claim for relief. Reletting is another way of exercising that election.[176]

6.   Land registry procedure

[26.39] Procedure has recently changed.[177] An application to reflect a forfeiture on the register may involve closing an independent title[178] or the deletion of a notice of the lease as a burden against the landlord's title.[179] Apart from the fee, it is necessary to lodge the lease and any sub-leases, the land certificates and the consent of the landlord's lender.

Application is allowed at any time after actual re-entry under an order for possession on proof of the order for possession and actual re-entry under it. Peaceable re-entry must also be proved by a statutory declaration. It is no longer necessary to wait six months before deleting the lease after a forfeiture for arrears of rent. It must be shown that the property is not occupied as a dwelling and that the service charge

---

[165] IA 1986 s 383(2); *Razzaq* v. *Pala* [1997] 1 WLR 1336, Lightman J; *Essex Furniture* v. *National Provident Institution* [2001] LTR 3, Ferris J.

[166] *Selim* v. *Bickenhall Engineering* [1981] 1 WLR 1318 (application for leave to forfeit); see above **[24.14]**.

[167] The view of the landlord is decisive: *Eaton Square Properties* v. *Beveridge* [1993] EGCS 91, CA.

[168] Leave of the court may be required after some insolvency procedures.

[169] *Termination of Tenancies by Physical Re-entry: CD* (Law Com, 1999); this is a reversal of policy: Law Com 142 (1985); Law Com 221 (1994); *Kataria* v. *Safeland* [1998] 1 EGLR 39, 41M, Brooke LJ.

[170] *Fuller* v. *Judy Properties* [1992] 1 EGLR 75, CA; *Charville Estates* v. *Unipart Group* [1997] EGCS 36; *Twogate Properties* v. *Birmingham Midshires Building Society* [1997] EGCS 55, CA.

[171] Protection from Eviction Act 1977 s 2.

[172] S 3.

[173] Criminal Law Act 1977 s 6.

[174] *Betterkey* v. *Joseph* [1991] Independent November 1st (forfeiture because windows not cleaned); relief would now be available; see below **[26.45]**.

[175] *Ivory Gate* v. *Spetale* [1998] 2 EGLR 43, CA.

[176] *Cromwell Developments* v. *Godfrey* [1998] 2 EGLR 62, CA; *Bland* v. *Ingram's Estates* [2001] Ch 767, [38], Nourse LJ.

[177] O Christopherson [1999] 37 *LSG* 34, [1999] 39 *LSG* 37.

[178] LR Form AP1 (closure of title – forfeiture). The landlord's title must be proved if it is not registered.

[179] LR Form CN1.

provisions have been complied with. The registry gives notice to anyone who seems to be interested in the lease. *Croydon (Unique)* v. *Wright*[180] is just one example of many where land registry notification is the first a lender knows of a forfeiture, so this may well provoke an application for relief.[181] If the court orders the grant of a new lease by way of relief to a sub-tenant or lender, a first registration will be required.

7. Waiver

[26.40] Landlords are not entitled to blow hot and cold.[182] Waiver is a very substantial and necessary qualification on the landlord's right to terminate the lease, which wipes the slate clean. Waiver is implied if:[183]

(1) the landlord is aware of the acts or omissions of the tenant which make the lease liable to forfeiture; but
(2) the landlord does some unequivocal act recognising the continued existence of the lease.

The most likely acts are demanding or accepting rent. However existing law cannot be said to be satisfactory since it is weighted too heavily in favour of tenants and often acts as a trap for landlords who extend temporary generosity to a tenant.

8. Relief after non-payment of rent

(1) Automatic stay

[26.41] In some rent actions the tenant has an automatic right to stay proceedings by paying what is owed in arrears and costs before proceedings come to court. In the High Court all proceedings are stayed if the tenant owes at least six months' rent and pays all outstanding arrears and costs into court before trial.[184] In a county court the tenant has a right to stay proceedings by paying all arrears and costs into court five clear days before the return date in the action.[185]

(2) Discretionary relief in proceedings

[26.42] A tenant who is not entitled to an automatic stay will often be entitled to discretionary relief from forfeiture. In the High Court this applies before trial where there are small arrears, and also after judgment by an application made within six

---

[180] [2001] Ch 318, CA.

[181] This should be protected by unilateral notice, if necessary after revival of the earlier title.

[182] If a breach has been tolerated, it may be revived as a ground for forfeiture by making clear that it will no longer be tolerated: *Hazel* v. *Akhtar* [2001] EWCA Civ 1883, [2002] 2 P & CR 17 at 240; J Morgan [2002] *Conv* 493.

[183] *Matthews* v. *Smallwood* [1910] 1 Ch 777, 786, Parker J; *Fuller's Theatre & Vaudeville Co* v. *Rofe* [1923] AC 435, PC; *Kammins Ballrooms Co* v. *Zenith Investments* [1971] AC 850, HL; and many other cases: P Sparkes *NLT*, 812–815.

[184] Common Law Procedure Act 1852 ss 210–212; *Standard Pattern Co* v. *Ivey* [1962] Ch 432.

[185] County Courts Act 1984 s 138(1) as amended; *Escalus Properties* v. *Robinson* [1996] QB 231, CA (the *Robinson* case); *Maryland Estates* v. *Joseph* [1999] 1 WLR 83, CA.

months of the execution of the judgment for possession.[186] All arrears and costs must be paid in.[187] The High Court also has a residual power to grant relief from a forfeiture for non-payment of rent in a summary manner.[188] Relief is normal on payment of rent and costs.[189]

In a county court[190] relief is discretionary as from five days before the return date. Possession must be suspended for at least four weeks, and the tenant can avoid repossession during that time by paying in the arrears and costs.[191] Previously a tenant had a much less ample allowance of time than in the High Court,[192] but a 1985 amendment[193] gives the tenant six months after execution of any judgment for possession in which to apply for relief, thus aligning the procedure in all civil courts.

After a peaceable forfeiture for non-payment of rent, the High Court has an equitable power to grant relief,[194] and there is a statutory right to apply to a county court for relief within six months.[195]

The practice of the court is to grant relief on payment of what is due with costs except in exceptional circumstances.[196] Equity treats the right to forfeit as a mere security for the payment of rent, and is generally prepared to allow relief from forfeiture where the tenant pays up to date what is owing to the landlord. Other conduct can be considered, but in a leading case the court was prepared to ignore a conviction for an indecent assault which occurred on the property itself.[197]

The overriding principles of the Woolf reforms have no impact on the established principles on which relief was granted, the old discretion continuing on well-settled principles. [198]

9. Relief to the tenant for other breaches

(1) After notice and proceedings

[26.43] Re-entry must be preceded by a section 146 notice, which must allow a reasonable time for remedy of any breach. Relief may be needed if the period allowed by the notice for remedy has expired, or where the breach is irremediable so that no time has to be allowed. Relief is available to a tenant under section 146(2) "where a tenant is proceeding, by action . . . to enforce such a right of . . . forfeiture." So relief must be sought during the currency of the proceedings and not after the landlord has actually

---

[186] Common Law Procedure Act 1852 s 210.

[187] S 211.

[188] Supreme Court Act 1981 s 38(1); *Escalus Properties* v. *Robinson* [1996] QB 231 (*Cooper-Smith* case); *Standard Pattern Co* v. *Ivey* [1962] Ch 432, Wilberforce J.

[189] *Gill* v. *Lewis* [1956] 2 QB 1, CA.

[190] County Courts Act 1984 s 138(1) as amended in 1985.

[191] S 138(3)–(5); *Narndean Estates* v. *Buckland* (1967) 111 SJ 684, CA (18 months); M Wonnacott (1994) 144 *NLJ* 296.

[192] County Courts Act 1984 s 138; *Di Palma* v. *Victoria Square Property Co* [1986] Fam 150, CA.

[193] Administration of Justice Act 1985 s 55.

[194] *Thatcher* v. *CH Pearce & Sons (Contractors)* [1968] 1 WLR 748, 774–775, Simon P.

[195] County Courts Act 1984 s 139(2); *Bland* v. *Ingram's Estates (No 1)* [2001] Ch 767; *(No 2)* [2001] EWCA Civ 1088, [2002] 1 All ER 264; S Gold [2001] *NLJ* 1177.

[196] *Gill* v. *Lewis* [1986] 2 QB 1, 13, Jenkins LJ.

[197] At 13G, Jenkins LJ.

[198] *Inntrepreneur Pub Co (CPC)* v. *Langton* [1999] 08 EG 169, Arden J.

re-entered under a judgment,[199] a rule now forming settled law. Relief is available while the tenant is proceeding, not where he has proceeded. Application is usually made as a defence to the landlord's possession action as an equitable counterclaim.[200]

(2) After peaceable re-entry

[26.44] Where the landlord forfeits out of court, the tenant has a right to apply to the court for relief. The tenant's right is clear where the landlord has served a section 146 notice but has not yet re-entered. The right to relief following physical re-entry was established by the House of Lords in *Billson* v. *Residential Apartments*.[201] Tenants undertook a major alteration of a property on the Gunton Estate in South Kensington without the landlord's permission. This was a clear deliberate breach of covenant, to which the landlords responded by serving a section 146 notice, and barging in at 6 am one morning. The lease was terminated, despite the tenant's decision to force his way back in four hours later and recommence work, but the issue in the litigation was whether the tenants were in time to claim relief.

Lord Oliver said that a peaceable re-entry was wrongly equiparated with an executed judgment[202] and that a landlord "is proceeding" while he is taking any necessary steps[203] until a final and unassailable judgment,[204] a sale,[205] or until six months have elapsed.

(3) Exercise of discretion

[26.45] A large cash bonus may accrue to the landlord on a successful forfeiture. That is not necessarily an unjust enrichment nor in itself a reason to grant relief,[206] since the court has a very wide discretion indeed.[207] But it is clearly a factor to be weighed and in general a landlord should not profit from a forfeiture.[208] Relief is usual if the breach of covenant has been rectified completely. Poor conduct by the tenant can be penalised by refusing relief or in costs.[209] However relief is likely to be refused after flagrant breaches – such as those in *Billson* v. *Residential Apartments*[210] – after long standing breaches, or where a continuing stigma has been created by use of the

---

[199] *Quilter* v. *Mapleson* (1882) 9 QBD 672, 677, Bowen LJ; *Billson* v. *Residential Apartments* [1992] 1 AC 494, 538, Lord Templeman.

[200] *Morgan & Son* v. *S Martin Johnson & Co* [1949] 1 KB 107, CA; *Sambri Investments* v. *Taborn* [1990] 1 EGLR 61, 62L, Peter Gibson J; *High Street Investments* v. *Bellshore Property Investments* [1996] 2 EGLR 40, CA.

[201] [1992] 1 AC 494, HL; PF Smith [1992] *Conv* 273; S Bridge [1992] *NLJ* 216; S Payne [1992] *NLJ* 22.

[202] At 544B, Lord Oliver.

[203] At 538H–539B, Lord Templeman, 544B, Lord Oliver.

[204] At 542.

[205] *Bhojwani* v. *Kingsley Investment Trust* [1992] 2 EGLR 70.

[206] *Darlington BC* v. *Denmark Chemists* [1993] 1 EGLR 62, CA.

[207] *Hyman* v. *Rose* [1912] AC 623, 631; *Associated British Ports* v. *CH Bailey* [1990] 2 AC 703, 708, Lord Templeman.

[208] *Bland* v. *Ingram's Estates (No 2)* [2001] EWCA Civ 1088, [2002] 1 All ER 244.

[209] *Billson (No 3)* [1993] EGCS 55 (tenant's conduct not bad enough to justify costs on an indemnity basis).

[210] *Billson (No 2)* [1993] EGCS 150 (major alterations begun without the landlord's consent and continued despite a peaceable re-entry; relief refused); *Crawford* v. *Clarke* [2000] EGCS 33, CA; *Fivecourts* v. *JR Leisure Development Co* (2001) 81 P & CR 22, Gray J.

property for prostitution.[211] A residual discretion remains even with wilful breaches, so that relief was granted in *Mount Cook Land* v. *Hartley*[212] even after the tenant had persisted in a sloppy practice of subletting without the landlord's consent. Relief is not available after reletting, in many cases of insolvency or after denial of the landlord's title.[213]

After re-entry, the lease enters a trance-like state, but the lease has not been destroyed, and does not have to be recalled to life. *Escalus Properties* v. *Robinson*[214] concerned four leases of flats held on long leases at low rents. The landlord company argued that it was entitled to damages based on a market rent during the hiatus between the forfeiture and the relief, but the court held that relief was retrospective so the (much lower) ground rent continued.

10. Relief for derivative interests

[26.46] The right to forfeit is a proprietary right,[215] and any subsidiary interest created out of the lease is terminated. A landlord cannot choose to eliminate his tenant whilst retaining his sub-tenant.[216]

Sub-tenants and lenders can seek relief, usually under the tailor-made provisions of section 146(4) of the Law of Property Act 1925.[217] All people known by the landlord to have a right to claim relief should be named in the proceedings to give them an opportunity to apply since any possession order is voidable if a party entitled to relief was not notified of proceedings.[218] Relief can be claimed while proceedings continue, or after a judgment which has not been executed,[219] but also after a physical re-entry.[220] There is much detail, since applications are common.[221] Sub-tenants and lenders may also claim as "tenants", which has the benefit that relief is retrospective as well as prospective from the date of the court order.[222] A majority in *Croydon (Unique)* v. *Wright* decided that a creditor holding a charging order over a lease was entitled to join the proceedings to assert his rights against the landlord.[223] Equitable

---

[211] *Rugby School* v. *Tannahill* [1935] 1 KB 87, CA (the school were landlords!); LGC (1933) 5 *CLJ* 396; *Borthwick-Norton* v. *Romney Warwick Estates* [1950] 1 All ER 798, CA; *Burfort Financial Investments* v. *Chotard* [1976] 2 EGLR 53 Foster J (the facts are racy); *Central Estates (Belgravia)* v. *Woolgar (No 2)* [1972] 1 WLR 1048, CA (relief granted by a majority); *British Petroleum Pension Trust* v. *Behrendt* [1985] 2 EGLR 97, 99G, Purchas LJ.

[212] [2000] EGCS 8, Ch D; *Duarte* v. *Mount Cook Land* [2001] 33 EG 87 (CS).

[213] P Sparkes *NLT*, 831–832; *Abidogun* v. *Frolan Health Care* [2001] 45 EG 138 (CS); M Pawlowski [2002] *Conv* 399.

[214] [1996] QB 231, CA.

[215] See below **[27.20]**.

[216] *Ashton* v. *Sobelman* [1987] 1 WLR 177; *Hall* v. *Griffin* [1987] 1 EGLR 81, CA.

[217] This applies to rent as well as to other breaches.

[218] *Croydon (Unique)* v. *Wright* [2001] Ch 318, CA.

[219] *Hammersmith & Fulham LBC* v. *Top Shop Centres* [1990] Ch 237, Scott J.

[220] *Abbey National BS* v. *Maybeech* [1985] Ch 190, Nicholls J; *Billson* v. *Residential Apartments* [1992] 1 AC 501, Nicholls LJ dissenting in CA, but impliedly approved by HL; *Cardigan Properties* v. *Consolidated Property Investments* [1991] 1 EGLR 64.

[221] *Barclays Bank* v. *Prudential Assurance Co* [1998] 1 EGLR 44.

[222] *Escalus Properties* v. *Robinson* [1996] QB 231, CA. Apparently a lender in possession of mortgaged premises is not a "lessee" and so not entitled to serve notice under the Leasehold Property (Repairs) Act 1938: *Smith* v. *Spaul* [2002] EWCA Civ 1830, [2002] Times December 28th.

[223] [2001] Ch 318, CA.

chargees who lack a right to possession fall outside the statutory scheme for claiming relief, but the inherent jurisdiction of the court will protect them.[224]

11. Forfeiture on insolvency

[26.47] Most leases provide for forfeiture on insolvency. Although permission is needed to enforce a security interest after an insolvency, a right of forfeiture is not a security interest,[225] but a moratorium is imposed by many procedures such as administration orders, administrative receivership or a company voluntary arrangement.[226] Section 146 is excluded altogether and no relief for a forfeiture occurring on insolvency is allowed in leases of agricultural land, mines, pubs, and furnished houses, and also where the personal qualifications of the tenant are important.[227] Section 146 applies for one year in all other cases. This enables the trustee in bankruptcy or liquidator to realise the lease, by sale within one year. However, the period runs from the date of the insolvency, not the date of the section 146 notice, and so the tenant may lose his right to relief before he realises that he is vulnerable to forfeiture.[228] The provision allowing relief to sub-tenants and lenders is available following insolvency irrespective of the above circumstances, and continues even one year after the insolvency.[229]

G. FLATS

[26.48] Substantial controls apply to the following terms of long-term residential leases:

> ground rents;
> service charges;
> administration charges;
> insurance rents; and
> other breaches.

A ground rent demand must be made before any liability accrues.[230] Service charge contributions must be held in trust in a distinct bank account.[231] Consultation is required before costs chargeable to the service charge are incurred.[232] The reasonableness of the costs charged to the leaseholders can be determined by a leasehold

---

[224] *Bland* v. *Ingram's Estates (No 1)* [2001] Ch 767, [2002] 1 All ER 221; *(No 2)* [2001] EWCA Civ 1088, [2002] 1 All ER 264.

[225] *Re Park Air Services* [2000] 1 AC 172, 186B–D, Lord Millett.

[226] IA 2000 ss 1, 9; *Re Lomax Leisure* [1999] 2 EGLR 37, Neuberger J; *Cromwell Developments* v. *Godfrey* [1998] 2 EGLR 62, CA.

[227] LPA 1925 s 146(9).

[228] *Official Custodian of Charities* v. *Parway Estates Developments* [1985] Ch 151, CA; *Hammersmith & Fulham LBC* v. *Tops Shop Centres* [1990] Ch 237, Scott J.

[229] LPA 1925 s 146, as amended by LP (Amendment) A 1929 s 1.

[230] Chold and L Ref A 2002 s 166.

[231] LTA 1987 s 42A; Chold and L Ref A 2002 s 156.

[232] LTA 1985 s 20ff; Chold and L Ref A 2002 s 151.

valuation tribunal[233] and no liability arises until costs are agreed or determined. Liability to pay administration charges – such as fees for consents to assignments – can also be determined by a tribunal.[234]

Forfeiture for non-payment of service charge[235] may not proceed and a section 146 notice may not be served[236] until the amount has been agreed or determined. A moratorium is imposed on forfeiture for small amounts of ground rent, service charge and administration charge; so forfeiture will only succeed where there are substantial arrears or lengthy delays. Any section 146 warning notice must warn the tenant of his rights.[237]

Leaseholders also have important collective rights to acquire ownership of the block (collective enfranchisement) or to take over the management (right to manage).[238]

---

[233] LTA 1985 s 27A; Chold and L Ref A 2002 s 153.
[234] Chold and L Ref A 2002 sch 11.
[235] HA 1996 ss 81, 83; Chold and L Ref A 2002 s 155.
[236] Chold and L Ref A 2002 s 168.
[237] HA 1996 s 82.
[238] P Sparkes *NLT* ch 16; Chold and L Ref A 2002 ss 150–176.

27

TRANSFER OF LEASES

---

*Dealings. Control of dealings. Improper assignments. Estate-based
liability. Physical division. Covenants not running. Tenants unable to pay.
Substitutes. Reimbursement and indemnity.*

A. DEALINGS

1. Assignment as a transfer

[27.01] Transfer of a leasehold estate is usually described as an assignment, with the parties assignor and assignee. A transfer can be legal if made by deed.[1] Legal title to a registered lease passes only on registration.[2] An equitable assignment can occur under a formal contract for value to assign the lease.[3]

2. Sub-lease

[27.02] This arises where the person who holds a leasehold estate confers exclusive possession on another (the sub-tenant). Normal leasehold formalities are required. Two tenures are created. The person creating the sub-lease can be seen to occupy a dual position, as tenant under the head lease and as landlord under the sub-lease.[4] The freeholder is referred to as a head landlord, and the ultimate tenant as the sub-tenant, with no direct relationship between them. The process can be repeated.[5]

A sub-lease must reserve a reversion.[6] If a purported sub-lease disposes of the entire term of the lease it will actually act as a transfer. To put it another way a sub-lease must be shorter than the head lease from which it is created. In *Milmo* v. *Carreras*[7] when a tenant had 13 months of his lease remaining, he purported to grant a sub-lease for one year and then from quarter to quarter, that is for a minimum period of 15

---

[1] LPA 1925 s 52; even for informal short tenancies, see above **[25.28]**.
[2] LR Forms TR1 (whole) and TR2 (part).
[3] *Gentle* v. *Faulkner* [1900] 2 QB 267, CA (this is not a breach of a covenant against assignment).
[4] Ie as head tenant and sub-landlord. In older terminology, head-lessor, head-lessee, sub-lessor, sub-lessee etc.
[5] Ie to a sub-under-tenant.
[6] *Brent LBC* v. *Cronin* (1998) 30 HLR 43, CA.
[7] [1946] KB 306, CA; (1946) 62 *LQR* 212; *Bryant* v. *Hancock* [1898] 1 KB 716, 719, Smith LJ; *Parc (Battersea)* v. *Hutchinson* [1999] 2 EGLR 33, Moore-Bick J; *Stretch* v. *West Dorset DC* [1998] 3 EGLR 62, CA.

months. This in fact transferred the 13 month term. A sub-lease arises if the superior lease is a periodic tenancy,[8] a business tenancy extension[9] or a lease for life.[10]

3. Devolutions

[27.03] Property vests automatically in personal representatives on death,[11] or in a trustee in bankruptcy on insolvency.[12] Involuntary transfers occur under compulsory purchase orders,[13] court orders[14] and executions.[15] The real question is whether the landlord can prevent the *next* dealing. Yes, so it appears, but only if the covenant is clearly worded. The landlord may control sale by a trustee in bankruptcy[16] or liquidator,[17] and also an assent by personal representatives to vest land in a beneficiary after death.[18]

4. Dealings with the landlord's reversion

[27.04] Apart from transfer[19] or physical division,[20] a landlord may also create a lease of the reversion (or concurrent lease), that is a lease which sits between the reversion and the existing lease.[21]

B. CONTROL OF DEALINGS

1. Residential tenancies

[27.05] Short-term residential tenancies always impose an absolute prohibition on transfer and subletting, particularly in the public sector.[22]

2. Commercial freedom to deal

[27.06] This is implied if the lease has no restriction, giving the tenant the right to grant subleases, create mortgages or enter into other transactions.[23] This is common

---

⁸ *Pennell* v. *Payne* [1995] 2 EGLR 592, CA; and many older cases.
⁹ *William Skelton & Son* v. *Harrison & Pinder* [1975] QB 361.
¹⁰ *Bruerton* v. *Rainsford* (1583) Cro Eliz 15, 78 ER 281.
¹¹ AEA 1925 s 1.
¹² *Re Riggs* [1901] 2 KB 16 (voluntary petition).
¹³ *Slipper* v. *Tottenham & Hampstead Junction Rly* (1867) LR 4 Eq 112.
¹⁴ *Marsh* v. *Gilbert* [1980] 2 EGLR 44.
¹⁵ *Doe d Mitchinson* v. *Carter* (1798) 8 Term Rep 57, 300, 101 ER 1264, 1400.
¹⁶ *Re Wright* [1949] Ch 729.
¹⁷ *Re Farrow's Bank* [1921] 2 Ch 164, CA.
¹⁸ *Doe d Goodbehere* v. *Bevan* (1815) 3 M & S 353, 105 ER 644; *Re Birkbeck PBBS* [1913] 2 Ch 34, 38, Neville J; *Re Farrow's Bank* [1921] 2 Ch 164, CA; DG Barnsley (1963) 27 *Conv NS* 159.
¹⁹ Traditionally an "assignment" of the reversion.
²⁰ LPA 1925 s 140(3) applies generally from 1881. A nominee can be used to divide any holding in two.
²¹ *Horn* v. *Beard* [1912] 3 KB 181; *Cole* v. *Kelly* [1920] 2 KB 106; *Adelphi (Estates)* v. *Christie* (1983) 47 P & CR 650, CA.
²² HA 1985 ss 91–95; *Sanctuary H Ass* v. *Baker* [1998] 1 EGLR 42, CA; P Sparkes *NLT* ch 11.
²³ *Doe d Mitchinson* v. *Carter* (1798) 8 Term Rep 57, 60, 101 ER 1284, Kenyon CJ; *Keeves* v. *Dean* [1924] 1 KB 685, 691, Bankes LJ; *Houlder Brothers & Co* v. *Gibbs* [1925] Ch 575, 583, Pollock MR.

for long residential leases with a ground rent, but the landlord will generally want to keep track of the identity of the tenant, by imposing an obligation to register a transfer with the landlord within a set period of time after it has occurred.[24] Consent is not required under building leases for more than 40 years until the tail end of the term, but rather the tenant is required to notify the landlord of dealings within six months.[25]

3. Qualified covenants

[27.07] The most common restriction is a qualified covenant against dealings, which requires the landlord's consent to be obtained. The landlord may object to a buyer with an unsatisfactory financial status, but the tenant is left free to find a suitable buyer. A proviso is implied by section 19(1) of the Landlord and Tenant Act 1927 that the landlord's consent is not to be unreasonably withheld, and the impact of this statute is usually anticipated by express provision.[26]

A landlord has a genuine reason to want to restrict transfer of the lease, since any incoming tenant must be able to pay the rent and carry out the tenant's obligations. There is also the fear that a tenant may extract value from the land by taking a premium when he grants a sub-lease.[27] Express restrictions have always been allowed on the freedom of a tenant to deal with his lease.[28]

Covenants against dealings need to be drawn comprehensively to cover all possible forms of transaction, especially since any covenant will be construed against the landlord.[29] The Landlord and Tenant Act 1988 refers to covenants not to enter into any of the following: assigning, under-letting, charging or parting with possession[30] of the premises comprised in the tenancy.[31] It may also be desirable to try to restrict automatic devolutions.

4. The need to ask for consent

[27.08] *Hendry* v. *Chartsearch* has recently reconfirmed[32] that there is a breach of covenant if the tenant does not ask, even if the circumstances are such that the landlord would be bound to grant consent.

---

[24] Administration charges on dwellings are controlled; see above **[26.48]**.

[25] LTA 1927 s 19(1)(b); not for commercial leases: s 19(1D) inserted in 1995; *Vaux Group* v. *Lilley* [1991] 1 EGLR 60 (surrender valid); P Sparkes [1991] *JBL* 494; JE Adams [1990] *Conv* 332.

[26] Lease is widely defined in LTA 1927 s 25(1), but this does not affect a covenant between head landlord and subtenant; SI 2001/2717; *Williamson* v. *Williamson* (1874) LR 9 Ch App 729. Law Com 141 (1985), [4.61–4.71], proposed that *all* covenants should be fully qualified in this way.

[27] A lower rent is all that is left to the head landlord.

[28] *Dumpor's case* (1603) 4 Co Rep 119b, 76 ER 1110; *Church* v. *Brown* (1808) 15 Ves 258, 264, 33 ER 752, Eldon LC.

[29] *Crusoe d Blencowe* v. *Bugby* (1771) 2 W Bl 766, 96 ER 448.

[30] This catches a licence; but it may be difficult to tell whether the original tenant has given up possession: *Gondal* v. *Dillon Newsagents* [1998] NPC 127, CA.

[31] S 1(1)(a); LTA 1927 s 19.

[32] [1998] Times September 16th, CA.

5. Procedural requirements – qualified covenants

[27.09] Many tenants were in the past treated unjustly by failure to consider applications for consent to dealings promptly.[33] The Landlord and Tenant Act 1988[34] implements Law Commission proposals[35] to remedy these deficiencies. Duties are triggered by a tenant's written request for consent.[36]

The landlord[37] must respond with a written decision within a reasonable time.[38] Information can be required if it is relevant to the decision making process,[39] including details of the proposed new tenant, but not the price he pays.[40] In *Midland Bank v. Chart Enterprises*,[41] the letter asking for consent was sent in mid February, but there was no written response until May 5th. By this time the delay was already excessive, and the decision letter in fact contained an unreasonable condition. On a summons taken out in August, the court made a declaration that consent was unreasonably refused and awarded damages. However, it would be churlish of a tenant to complain that the landlord had acted too swiftly.[42]

The landlord must not behave unreasonably when withholding consent. A decision must be given in writing with reasons[43] for refusal or for imposing any conditions.[44] He is restricted to circumstances known at the time,[45] and has the onus of proof.[46] The test of what is reasonable is not altered.[47]

Tenants would be helped most by deemed consent to a dealing if the landlord failed to respond to the request for consent to dealings within a reasonable time. However, the Law Commission felt that this radical step would be unworkable.[48] Instead there

---

[33] *City Hotels Group* v. *Total Property Investments* [1985] 1 EGLR 253.

[34] LTA 1988 ss 5(4), 7(2); J Gaunt (1987) 284 *EG* 1371; R Shuttleworth (1987) 284 *EG* 1480; R Cullum (1987) 284 *EG* 1580; JE Adams [1988] 32 *EG* 35.

[35] Law Com 141 (1985); AJ Waite [1986] *Conv* 240; HW Wilkinson [1988] *Conv* 1.

[36] LTA 1988 s 1(3); *Barrow* v. *Isaacs & Son* [1891] 1 QB 417, CA; *Eastern Telegraphic Co* v. *Dent* [1899] 1 QB 835, CA; *Cohen* v. *Popular Restaurants* [1917] 1 KB 480; *Creery* v. *Summerskell* [1949] Ch 751; *Marks* v. *Warren* [1979] 1 All ER 29.

[37] Whether (1) express, (2) statutory, or (3) an express covenant of a head landlord not to refuse consent to a subtenant (outside the 1927 Act); notices served on the wrong person must be passed on promptly: LTA 1988 s 2.

[38] Ss 1, 5, 6 (Crown).

[39] *Norwich Union Life Insurance Society* v. *Shopmoor* [1999] 1 WLR 531, Scott V-C; PH Kenny [1998] *Conv* 346; L Crabb (2000) 116 *LQR* 208.

[40] *Kened* v. *Connie Investments* [1997] 1 EGLR 21, CA.

[41] [1990] 2 EGLR 59, Popplewell J; *Fischer* v. *Toumazos* [1991] 2 EGLR 204; L Crabb [1992] *Conv* 213.

[42] *Moss Bros Group* v. *CSC Properties* [1999] EGCS 47, Neuberger J.

[43] LTA 1988 s 1(3)(b); *Footwear Corp* v. *Amplight Properties* [1991] 1 WLR 551; PH Kenny [1998] *Conv* 346.

[44] *Dong Bang Minerva (UK)* v. *Davina* [1996] 2 EGLR 31, CA; K Stepien (1994) 138 *SJ* 910 (undertaking re costs of rent review); see below **[27.14ff]**.

[45] *CIN Properties* v. *Gill* [1993] 2 EGLR 97; L Crabb [1994] *Conv* 314; *Kened* v. *Connie Investments* [1997] 1 EGLR 21, CA; *Blockbuster Entertainments* v. *Leakcliff Properties* [1997] 1 EGLR 28.

[46] Reversing *International Drilling Fluids* v. *Louisville Investments (Uxbridge)* [1986] Ch 513, 520, Balcombe LJ, and many earlier cases.

[47] *Chart Enterprises* [1990] 2 EGLR 59, 60C, Popplewell J; *Air India* v. *Balabel* [1993] 2 EGLR 66, 69, Stuart Smith LJ.

[48] Law Com 141 (1985), [8.106].

is a right of action in tort,[49] for an injunction[50] or damages.[51] Tortious damages should place the tenant as if the tort had not been committed, including reasonably foreseeable losses and loss of bargain. The deterrent effect has been strong.[52]

If the landlord refuses consent unreasonably *after being asked for permission* the tenant may proceed anyway[53] but it is most unlikely that a buyer will accept the risk involved. In practice it is better to obtain a declaration or injunction. Contracts for sale of leases are generally conditional on the landlord's licence being obtained[54] by the time of the contractual completion date, and on refusal there is a contractual right to rescind.[55]

6. Reasonable and unreasonable grounds

[27.10] An identical test applies to express covenants, the statutory implied proviso, and the new statutory duties.[56] It is only possible to give a taste of the voluminous case-law. Landlords are mainly concerned with their own interests rather than to be fair to the tenants.[57] Broadly speaking the landlord may act on two grounds.

(1) Undesirability of the proposed new tenant

[27.11] In *International Drilling Fluids* v. *Louisville Investments (Uxbridge)* Balcombe LJ reiterated that the main purpose of the covenant was to protect the landlord from having his premises pass to an undesirable sub-tenant or assignee.[58] Landlords are entitled to consider the financial stability of proposed new tenants, check financial references,[59] and consider their personal experience of the proposed tenant.[60] Landlords may legitimately wish to control the proposed use to be made of the property; it will be reasonable to object if the new tenant will break the use covenant and may be reasonable to object to a use that is not a breach of covenant.[61] Serious breaches of

---

[49] LTA 1988 s 4.

[50] *Hemingway Securities* v. *Dunraven* (1996) 71 P & CR 30.

[51] New in 1988 for implied covenants: *Ideal Film Renting Co* v. *Nielsen* [1921] 1 Ch 575 (express covenant); *Berkeley Leisure Group* v. *Lee* (1997) 73 P & CR 493, CA (old law still applies to mobile homes).

[52] Law Com 141 (1985), [1.108].

[53] *Treloar* v. *Bigge* (1874) LR 9 Ex 151; *Fuller's Theatre & Vaudeville Co* v. *Rofe* [1923] AC 435, PC. If consent is not requested, the landlord will have an almost automatic right to forfeit.

[54] Standard Conditions of Sale (3rd ed), [8.3.2].

[55] *Barings Securities* v. *DG Durham Group* [1993] EGCS 192, Ferris J.

[56] (1) G Kodilinye [1988] *Conv* 45; (2) LTA 1927 s 19(1); (3) LTA 1988 s 1(3)(5); T Aldridge (1989) 133 *SJ* 1277; *Air India* v. *Balabel* [1993] 2 EGLR 66, CA; *Footwear Corp* v. *Amplight Properties* [1991] 1 WLR 551; PH Kenny [1998] *Conv* 346; *Roux Restaurants* v. *Jaison Property Development Co* (1997) 74 P & CR 357, CA.

[57] *Tredegar* v. *Harwood* [1929] AC 72, 81–82, Lord Phillimore; *Bickel* v. *Westminster* [1977] QB 517, CA; *Martin* v. *Gilbert* [1980] 2 EGLR 44, 46K, Nourse J.

[58] [1986] Ch 513, 519H; *Bates* v. *Donaldson* [1896] 2 QB 241, 247; *Houlder Brothers & Co* v. *Gibbs* [1925] Ch 575, CA.

[59] *Shanly* v. *Ward* (1913) 29 TLR 714, CA; *Ponderosa International Development Inc* v. *Pengap Securities (Bristol)* [1986] 1 EGLR 66, Warner J; *Storehouse Properties* v. *Ocobase* [1998] Times April 3rd, Rimer J (no objection to company with net assets of £38 million).

[60] *Air India* v. *Balabel* [1993] 2 EGLR 66, CA.

[61] *Louisville* [1986] Ch 513, CA; *Ashworth Frazer* v. *Gloucester CC* [2001] UKHL 59, [2001] 1 WLR 2180.

covenant by the tenant justify withholding consent to a sale until they are rectified,[62] though trivial breaches do not.[63]

Refusals on grounds of race or sex are prohibited by statute,[64] and diplomatic immunity is apparently irrelevant.[65]

(2) Interests of landlord

[27.12] *Houlder Brothers & Co* v. *Gibbs* recognised the validity of concerns about due and proper management of the property,[66] an extension recognised by later Court of Appeal decisions.[67] It may be to control the letting scheme on an entire development,[68] preventing the removal of value by premiums on subletting,[69] avoiding new security of tenure,[70] preventing enfranchisement,[71] or to avoid the possibility of a lease being broken.[72] That estate management is a legitimate consideration is confirmed by the House of Lords in *Tredegar* v. *Harwood* in a case relating to consent to fire insurance,[73] but extending to any transaction affecting the letting potential of other units[74] or the landlord's own redevelopment proposals.[75]

(3) Landlord must not seek to achieve a collateral purpose

[27.13] A decision must be reached on grounds connected with the landlord-tenant relationship, and not on collateral grounds.[76] Landlords must not manoeuvre so as to secure occupation of the premises themselves[77] or to take into account the reletting potential of the buyer's existing property.[78]

---

[62] *Goldstein* v. *Sanders* [1915] 1 Ch 549, Eve J; *Orlando Investments* v. *Grosvenor Estate Belgravia* (1990) 59 P & CR 21, CA; P Luxton [1991] *JBL* 57.

[63] *Beale* v. *Worth* [1993] EGCS 135, CA; L Crabb [1994] *Conv* 316.

[64] Race Relations Act 1976 s 24; Sex Discrimination Act 1975 s 31.

[65] *Parker* v. *Boggon* [1947] KB 346 (no real reasons stated); (1947) 63 *LQR* 147.

[66] [1925] Ch 575, 582–583, Pollock MR; G Kodilinge [1988] *Conv* 45.

[67] *Bickel* v. *Duke of Westminster* [1977] QB 517, 523H, 524C–G, Lord Denning MR; *Louisville* [1986] 1 Ch 513, 519–521, Balcombe LJ.

[68] *BRS Northern* v. *Templeheights* [1998] 2 EGLR 182.

[69] *Re Town Investments' Underlease* [1954] Ch 301, 315; *Straudley Investments* v. *Mount Eden Land* (1997) 74 P & CR 306, CA; *Blockbuster Entertainments* v. *Leakcliff Properties* [1997] 1 EGLR 28.

[70] *Brann* v. *Westminster Anglo-Continental Investment Co* [1976] 2 EGLR 72, CA; *West Layton* v. *Ford* [1979] QB 593, 605, Roskill LJ; and many other cases.

[71] *Bickel* v. *Duke of Westminster* [1977] QB 517, CA.

[72] *Re Olympia & York Canary Wharf (No 2)* [1994] 2 EGLR 48, CA; L Crabb [1994] *Conv* 316.

[73] *Tredegar* v. *Harwood* [1929] AC 72, 78, 80; *Crown Estate Commissioners* v. *Signet Group* [1996] 2 EGLR 200.

[74] *FW Woolworth* v. *Charlwood Alliance Properties* [1987] 1 EGLR 53 (Arndale Centre in Manchester); L Crabb [1987] *Conv* 381.

[75] *Pimms* v. *Tallow Chandlers Co* [1964] 2 QB 547; *BRS Northern* v. *Templeheights* [1998] 2 EGLR 182, Neuberger J (two supermarkets).

[76] *Louisville* [1986] Ch 513, 520B, Balcombe LJ; *Rayburn* v. *Wolf* (1985) 18 HLR 1, CA.

[77] *Bates* v. *Donaldson* [1896] 2 QB 241, CA.

[78] *Houlder Brothers & Co* v. *Gibbs* [1925] Ch 575, CA; despite criticism in *Tredegar* [1929] AC 72, 78, 80, 82; see also *Bromley Park Gardens Estates* v. *Moss* [1982] 1 WLR 1019, 1031B, Cumming-Bruce LJ.

7. Express terms restricting the landlord's discretion

[27.14] The lease may limit the landlord more than the statute, perhaps by requiring the landlord to approve a respectable and responsible assignee,[79] and a transaction which is not a breach of covenant must be approved.[80] On the other hand more onerous restrictions cannot be imposed on tenants.[81] So, for example, a tenant cannot be required to offer to surrender the lease to the landlord before being allowed to sell it.[82]

Conditions imposed by the landlord must be reasonable.[83] A lease may require payment of the landlord's reasonable expense, but consents should not be a source of profit:[84] without an express provision[85] the landlord is not allowed to ask for any fine nor any indirect profit,[86] and the tenant is free to assign if the landlord makes an improper demand.[87] Any condition must be included in the written notice of decision,[88] and justified. Consent is deemed to be given free of unreasonable conditions, for example ones which attempt to change the terms of the lease on assignment,[89] but strict compliance is required with reasonable conditions.[90] Conditions are normally formalised in a licence to assign to which the parties are landlord, old tenant, new tenant and any guarantors. But if outright consent is given, stating that it is "subject to formal licence" the condition is meaningless, and the consent is immediately valid.[91]

8. Commercial leases under the 1995 Act

[27.15] The Landlord and Tenant (Covenants) Act 1995 amends the 1927 Act to give the landlord much greater control over the assignment (as opposed to sub-letting) of commercial leases, though it does not apply to residential or agricultural leases.[92] Landlord and tenant may agree the circumstances in which landlord is entitled to withhold his licence to a transfer and also the conditions which may be attached to any grant of consent. This agreement may be contained in the lease or any later writ-

[79] *Moat* v. *Martin* [1950] 1 KB 175, CA; *De Soyson* v. *De Pless Pol* [1912] AC 194, HL; *Re Greater London Property's Lease* [1959] 1 WLR 503; (1959) 75 *LQR* 306.

[80] LTA 1988 s 1(5); T Aldridge (1989) 133 *SJ* 1277; Law Com 161 (1987), [9].

[81] LTA 1927 s 19(1); *Creery* v. *Summersell* [1949] Ch 751, 759–760, Harman J; *Houlder & Brothers Co* v. *Gibbs* [1925] Ch 575, 585, Warrington LJ; G Kodilinye [1988] *Conv* 45.

[82] *Re Smith's Lease* [1951] 1 All ER 346; *Bocardo* v. *S & M Properties* [1980] 1 WLR 17, CA.

[83] *Vaux Group* v. *Lilley* [1991] 1 EGLR 60, Knox J; P Sparkes [1991] *JBL* 494; *Orlando Investments* v. *Grosvenor Estate Belgravia* (1990) 59 P & CR 21, CA; *Kened* v. *Connie Investments* [1995] 1 EGLR 21, CA.

[84] *Waite* v. *Jennings* [1906] 2 KB 11, 17, Fletcher Moulton LJ.

[85] LPA 1925 s 144, replacing Conveyancing Act 1892 s 3; *Lambert* v. *FW Woolworth & Co* [1937] Ch 37, CA.

[86] *Gardner & Co* v. *Cone* [1928] Ch 955 (tied house clause); *Jenkins* v. *Price* [1907] 2 Ch 229 (increased rent); *Comber* v. *Fleet Electrics* [1955] 1 WLR 566 (compensation); but not entry into covenants.

[87] *West* v. *Gwynne* [1911] 2 Ch 1, CA. However if a fine is paid it is not recoverable.

[88] LTA 1988 s 1(3).

[89] *Young* v. *Ashley Gardens Property Investments* [1903] 2 Ch 112; *Mills* v. *Cannon Brewery Co* [1920] 2 Ch 38; *Balfour* v. *Kensington Gardens Mansions* (1932) 49 TLR 29; *Midland Bank* v. *Chart Enterprises Inc* [1990] 2 EGLR 59.

[90] *Allied Dunbar Assurance* v. *Homebase* [2002] EWCA Civ 666, [2002] 27 EG 144.

[91] *Venetian Glass Gallery* v. *Next Properties* [1989] 2 EGLR 42; P Luxton [1990] *JBL* 246; *Prudential Assurance Co* v. *Mount Eden Land* [1997] 1 EGLR 37, CA; *Aubergine Enterprises* v. *Lakewood International* [2002] EWCA Civ 177, affirming [2001] 39 EG 141, Ch D.

[92] Ss 27–28; LTA 1927 s 19(1A); for leases whenever made.

ten agreement.[93] The landlord acts reasonably by withholding consent in accordance with the agreed terms.[94] Most often landlords will want sureties[95] or an authorised guarantee agreement.[96] Any factor left for determination by the landlord must either be determined reasonably or subject to independent review of the landlord's decision.[97]

9. Absolute prohibition

[27.16] This restricts dealing by the tenant completely. Any long term tenant must insist on being able to sell, but absolute bars on physical division are common, and bars on all dealings are normal in residential tenancies and other short leases. Since the landlord may waive the restriction, it really operates as a covenant not to act without the landlord's permission,[98] but there is an enormous difference between the tenant having a *right* to transfer and being required to beg for permission.[99]

C. IMPROPER ASSIGNMENTS

[27.17] Forfeiture is virtually automatic against a person who has taken an assignment or sub-lease in breach of covenant. Assuming that the particular dealing that has occurred is a breach of covenant and that the right to forfeit is reserved, the landlord may terminate the lease where:

there is an absolute prohibition;[100]
there is a qualified covenant but the landlord is not asked;[101]
there is a qualified covenant and the landlord has been asked, has not replied, but would be entitled to refuse consent;[102] or
the landlord has reasonably refused consent.

A section 146 notice must be served specifying the breach though it is not necessary to require a remedy or compensation.[103] The reasonable time which must elapse before re-entry might be as short as 14 days.[104] Relief may be available for example where a

---

[93] LTA 1927 s 19(1B); it must pre-date the application for consent.

[94] S 19(1D).

[95] Reversing *Pakwood Transport* v. *15 Beauchamp Place* (1978) 36 P & CR 112, CA.

[96] See below [27.54].

[97] LTA 1927 s 19(1C); examples are: (1) to assign to a company with a specified capitalisation or to require a director's guarantee; or (2) to provide an acceptable guarantor, or to conduct an appropriate trade.

[98] There is *no* proviso that consent must not be unreasonably withheld: *Vaux Group* v. *Lilley* [1991] 1 EGLR 60, 64C, Knox J. Sexually and racially discriminatory covenants are prohibited.

[99] *FW Woolworth & Co* v. *Lambert* [1937] Ch 37, 58–59, Romer LJ.

[100] *Yorkshire Metropolitan Properties* v. *Cooperative Retail Services* [2001] LTR 26, Neuberger J

[101] *Hendry* v. *Chartsearch* [1998] Times September 16th; P Sparkes *NLT*, 732.

[102] P Sparkes *NLT*, 734. Relief will be granted where the landlord would have been bound to grant consent: *Duarte* v. *Mount Cook Land* [2001] 33 EG 87 (CS).

[103] P Sparkes *NLT*, 796.

[104] *Scala House & District Property Co* v. *Forbes* [1974] QB 575, CA; *Savva* v. *Houssein* [1996] 2 EGLR 65, 66G, Staughton LJ.

tenant engages in the sloppy practice of granting sub-leases without getting consent[105] or to a buyer who is blameless,[106] but in general the breach will be treated as irremediable and so forfeiture will be allowed, especially where the breach is deliberate.[107] Re-entry might be achieved by proceedings, by peaceable re-entry or by re-letting the property.

Illegal assignments and sub-leases are often validated by waiver, where the landlord knows of the breach and demands rent.[108]

D. ESTATE-BASED LIABILITY

[27.18] Parties are so confusing that a standard terminology is required, the following diagram indicates the usage adopted here,

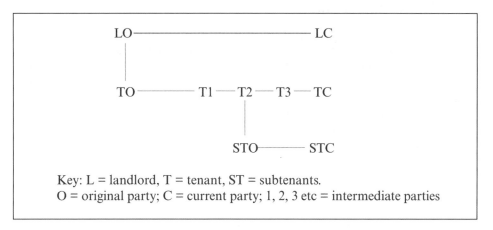

Key: L = landlord, T = tenant, ST = subtenants.
O = original party; C = current party; 1, 2, 3 etc = intermediate parties

Figure 27-1 Assignments and sub-leases

1. New and old leases

[27.19] Radical reform which was prompted by the Law Commission[109] was enacted by the Landlord and Tenant (Covenants) Act 1995,[110] though the purity of the original scheme was distorted by pressure from the landlords' lobby. Almost all of the provisions apply only to those leases which have been granted since the Act came into force on January 1st 1996.[111] The old law continues in force for "old tenancies", –

---

[105] *Mount Cook* v. *Hartley* [2000] EGCS 26; HW Wilkinson [2001] *NLJ* 27, 140.
[106] *Imray* v. *Oakshette* [1897] 2 QB 218, CA.
[107] *Scala House* as above; *Mount Eden Land* v. *Towerstone* [2002] 31 EG 97 (CS).
[108] See above **[26.40]**.
[109] Law Com 174 (1988); D Gordon [1987] *Conv* 103; HW Wilkinson [1989] *Conv* 145, [1992] *Conv* 393.
[110] P Luxton [1996] *JBL* 388; S Bridge [1996] *CLJ* 313; PH Kenny [1996] *Conv* 3, 81, 237; M Davey (1996) 59 *MLR* 78.
[111] SI 1995/2963. Such leases are inelegantly referred to as "new tenancies", though this book refers to "post-1995 leases".

meaning all pre-1996 leases, and leases granted afterwards under old contracts.[112] These divided regimes will last for centuries to come. Terms will require adjustment[113] as leases are renewed (or there is an implied surrender and regrant[114]) and so pass into the new scheme.

Action on covenants in a lease is normally taken on the basis of privity of estate, when the current landlord sues the current tenant for rent, or the current tenant sues the current landlord on his repairing obligations. A tenant who buys a lease is obviously required to pay the rent for the use of the land and to carry out the other covenants in the lease.[115] Old and new law are similar, except that under the old law only covenants which touched and concerned the land passed[116] and a distinction was drawn between legal and equitable leases.[117] The new law is all-embracing, treating the whole lease as a package and all leases alike.

2. Proprietary effect of forfeiture

[27.20] A landlord may secure rent payments by threatening forfeiture, that is termination of the lease if the obligations are not met. This is particularly effective where the tenant paid a premium for a lease so the tenant stands to lose some of the value of the land, but the threat is totally absent if the lease is onerous, since forfeiture simply gives the tenant a chance to bolt. The current[118] landlord's right to forfeit the lease is proprietary in character, binding the original tenant and anyone deriving title from him. Forfeiture therefore affects a buyer of the lease, or of any part of the property let, a sub-tenant or any mortgage-lender, and any derivative interest falls.[119] Relief may be available, but only if the breach is remedied.

3. Covenants: new law

(1) Liability of current tenant

[27.21] The 1995 Act passes the benefit and burden of all covenants in a new lease, which are therefore enforceable between the current parties to the lease.[120] The current tenant (TC) is liable to the current landlord (LC) for the duration of his ownership. Liability attaches at the moment of acquisition of the estate,[121] so that existing arrears require separate assignment.[122] Covenants are annexed and incident to the

---

[112] S 1 (contracts, court orders and options).

[113] PH Kenny [1996] *Conv* 3.

[114] *Friends Provident Life Office* v. *British Railways Board* [1996] 1 All ER 336, CA; F Jenkins [1996] 07 *LSG* 24.

[115] *City of London Corp* v. *Fell* [1994] 1 AC 458, 464G, Lord Templeman.

[116] See below **[27.39ff]**.

[117] See below **[27.31]**.

[118] New: LT (Covenants) A 1995 s 4 ; old: LPA 1925 s 141; equity: *Shiloh Spinners* v. *Harding* [1973] AC 691, 717H–718A, Lord Wilberforce.

[119] Eg *Hall* v. *Griffin* [1987] 1 EGLR 81, CA.

[120] LT (Covenants) A 1995 s 2; covenants with management companies relating to any "relevant function" (excluding a financial guarantee) also pass: s 12.

[121] S 3(2); a personal waiver or release is disregarded: s 3(4).

[122] S 23(2); contrast the old law; see below **[27.28]**.

reversion, so that the new landlord is both bound by the terms of the lease, and also entitled immediately to the benefit of the tenant's covenants.[123]

The terms of the whole lease form a single package. It is no longer necessary to identify covenants that have reference to the subject matter of the lease, and no distinction is made between express and implied covenants.[124] Personal covenants will not run.

(2) Release of previous tenant etc

[27.22] A former tenant is released from liability for all covenants (including personal ones) on an assignment of the whole of a new lease. If only a part is sold, the release relates only to that part.[125] A previous tenant can never be directly liable for the defaults of current tenants, so indemnity covenants are no longer required.[126]

No release occurs on a transmission by operation of law, nor on an assignment in breach of covenant, the two forms of "excluded assignments".[127] If there is a covenant against dealings and the tenant wants a release he must obtain consent to the sale. An unauthorised transfer makes the new tenant liable under the covenants but does not release the former tenant, so that both will have to wait for the next non-excluded assignment for their release.[128]

Release of a landlord after a sale of the reversion is not automatic because a tenant has no vetting power, but a landlord can apply to be released, prospectively,[129] when he assigns the premises. Again release may be complete, or partial if it is only part which is sold. Notice requesting a release may be given to the tenant[130] before, or up to four weeks after, the assignment. Failure on the tenant's part to object[131] within four weeks from receipt will secure the release. A second chance occurs for four weeks after the next sale, though how is the former landlord to know that this second opportunity has presented itself? No release occurs on a transmission of the reversion which occurs by operation of law,[132] but both transmitter and receiver are discharged on a subsequent sale.

4. Old law of privity of estate

[27.23] In medieval law no stranger could take advantage of the benefit of a covenant.[133] The motivating force behind the change made by the Grantees of

---

[123] Ss 3(3), 24 (personal waivers again disregarded). As for many years past, it makes no difference whether the covenant relates to existing buildings or to future additions: s 3(7) (old *in esse* rule abolished).

[124] Ss 2(1); 28(1) (collateral agreements).

[125] S 5(2)–(4); release is prospective, leaving accrued liability unaffected: s 24(1).

[126] S 14 repealed LPA 1925 s 77(1)(c)–(d) and LRA 1925 s 24(1)(b)–(c); see also LRA 2002 sch 11 para 33. An authorised guarantee agreement may be required; see below [27.54].

[127] LT (Covenants) A 1995 s 11(1); the "or" should read "and".

[128] Ss 11(2), 24(3). It is prospective from that time.

[129] S 24(1).

[130] S 6; SI 1995/2964, Forms 3–6; also LTA 1985 s 3(3A); Release only applies to proprietary covenants and not those personal to the original landlord: *BHP Petroleum Great Britain* v. *Chesterfield Properties* [2001] EWCA Civ 1797, [2002] Ch 194; [2002] Ch 12, Lightman J; P Luxton [2002] *JBL* 101. See below [27.34].

[131] Eg because of doubts about the new landlord's financial stability; this will force court proceedings: LT (Covenants) A 1995 s 8.

[132] LT (Covenants) A 1995 s 11(3), (4), (7).

[133] *Re King* [1963] Ch 459, 479, Lord Denning MR.

Reversions Act 1540 was Henry VIII's wish to off-load monastic land seized at the time of the Reformation, much of which was let. However, the legislation also affected common citizens.[134] The 1540 Act and 1881 amendments[135] were consolidated in 1925.[136]

(1) Benefit passing between landlords

[27.24] The benefit of central obligations in a lease passes between landlords by statutory provision.[137] Express mention is made of rights of forfeiture, rent, and every other covenant having reference to the subject matter of the lease. These are "annexed and incident to, and shall go with, the reversionary estate." Action is brought by the person who can show any form of title to the immediate reversionary estate. Rents can be passed for a fixed period by the grant of a reversionary lease.[138]

(2) Original landlord against current tenant

[27.25] This is the archetypal and most common case, in which the original landlord seeks to sue the current tenant (*L0* v. *TC*). Henry VIII was only concerned to deal with the successors to the original monastic landlords, so the 1540 Act left a gap, plugged by the Elizabethan decision in *Spencer's case*.[139] Spencer (L0) had leased to T0 who had assigned to T1, who in turn assigned to Clarke (TC). Spencer would have won, except that the covenant he was trying to enforce was personal. Since Coke's report scarcely mentioned the 1540 Act, the rule for running of covenants between tenants became established as a common law rule,[140] but Wray CJ did decide the case on the equity of the 1540 statute.[141] The Conveyancing Act 1881 did not need to cover the action L0–TC, but a gap was created when the 1925 Act repealed the 1540 Act and re-enacted the 1881 wording in isolation. This gap existed between 1925 and 1996.[142] *Spencer's case* supports a common law rule that the current tenant may be sued by the current landlord – whether as an original tenant, a later tenant by assignment, or a tenant of any part. An estoppel binds a buyer who secures a licence to assign and takes possession.[143]

---

[134] *Hill* v. *Grange* (1556) 2 Dyer 130b, 73 ER 284; *Re King* as above.

[135] Conveyancing Act 1881 s 10; Conveyancing Act 1911 s 2.

[136] LPA 1925 ss 141–142

[137] LPA 1925 s 141 (all leases whenever made); *Dorrell* v. *Wybone* (1561) 2 Dyer 206b, 73 ER 455; *Matures* v. *Westwood* (1598) Cro Eliz 599, 78 ER 842; *Thursby* v. *Plant* (1669) 1 Saund 230, 85 ER 254; *Martyn* v. *Williams* (1857) 1 H & N 817, 156 ER 1430; *Stuart* v. *Joy* [1904] 1 KB 362. It passes subject to any right of set-off: *Panton* v. *St Mary's Estate* [2002] 05 CL 427.

[138] *London & County (A & D)* v. *Wilfred Sportsman* [1971] Ch 764, CA.

[139] (1583) 5 Co Rep 16a, 77 ER 72.

[140] *Williams* v. *Earle* (1868) LR 3 QB 739, Blackburn J; *Muller* v. *Trafford* [1901] 1 Ch 54, 61–62, Farwell J.

[141] At 18a; *Hill* v. *Grange* (1556) 2 Dyer 130b, 73 ER 284; *Hyde* v. *Windsor* (1597) Cro Eliz 457, 552, 78 ER 710.

[142] GD Muggeridge (1934) 50 *LQR* 66.

[143] *Rodenhurst Estates* v. *Barnes* [1936] 2 All ER 3, CA. Contrast *Official Trustee of Charity Lands* v. *Ferriman Trust* [1937] 3 All ER 85.

Intermediate tenants are cleared (prospectively[144]) as soon as they pass on their estate,[145] and indeed tenants were once advised to sell to impecunious assignees to curtail liability.[146]

(3) Enforcement against current tenant

[27.26] This is the archetypal case, in which the current landlord takes action against the current tenant. This was expressly covered by the Grantees of Reversions Act 1540,[147] but slipped out in 1925 by erroneous consolidation. The benefit passes by statute, but the "common law" rule in *Spencer's case* is needed to explain how the burden runs,[148] an accident which prevents passage of the burden of informal and equitable leases.[149]

(4) Burden passing between landlords

[27.27] When a tenant seeks enforcement of repairing or other covenants in an old lease against the landlord, enforcement is fully catered for by section 142 of the Law of Property Act 1925.[150] The obligation under a condition or central covenant entered into by a landlord shall be annexed to and go with that reversionary estate, making it enforceable against any person entitled from time to time to the reversionary estate. Informality of the lease has made no difference since 1925.[151]

Where the current tenant takes action against the current landlord, section 142 passes both the burden between landlords and the benefit between tenants.[152] So the statute justifies the actions TC against L0,[153] and TC against LC.[154]

5.   Existing breaches

[27.28] Estate-based liability should be pursued between the parties who were in privity of estate at the time of the breach for new leases, and this was also the law before 1881[155] Unfortunately this is not the rule for pre-1996 leases where the reversion was

---

[144] *Horley* v. *King* (1835) 2 Cr M & R 18, 150 ER 8.

[145] *Overton* v. *Sydal* (1597) Cro Eliz 555, 78 ER 801; *Gooch* v. *Clutterbuck* [1899] 2 QB 148, CA; *Granada Theatres* v. *Freehold Inn (Leytonstone)* [1959] Ch 592, CA (bites on acquisition of estate).

[146] *Onslow* v. *Corrie* (1817) 2 Madd 330, 56 ER 357; *Hopkinson* v. *Lovering* (1883) 11 QBD 92.

[147] LC – TC is therefore a stronger case than L0 – TC; see above [27.25].

[148] *Moss Empires* v. *Olympia (Liverpool)* [1939] AC 544, HL.

[149] See below [27.31].

[150] Restating Grantees of Reversions Act 1540 s 2 and Conveyancing Act 1881 s 11, and applying to any lease whenever made.

[151] *Breams Property Investments* v. *Stroulger* [1948] 2 KB 1, 7–8, Scott LJ; see below [27.31].

[152] Query *Muller* v. *Trafford* [1901] 1 Ch 54, 61, Farwell J. A person entitled to income from the reversion cannot be sued: *Duncliffe* v. *Caerfelin Properties* [1989] 2 EGLR 38, 39J, Garland J.

[153] *Webb* v. *Russell* (1789) 3 Term Rep 393, 401–402, 100 ER 639 (1540 Act).

[154] *Baylye* v. *Hughes* (1628) Cro Car 137, 79 ER 720 (on 1540 Act); *Ricketts* v. *Enfield Churchwardens* [1909] 1 Ch 544 (1881 Act).

[155] New tenancies: LT (Covenants) Act 1995 ss 23–24; pre 1881 leases: *Flight* v. *Bentley* (1835) 7 Sim 149, 58 ER 793; *Re King* [1963] Ch 459, 479, Lord Denning MR (continuing breaches in case of lease granted before 1882 did pass).

sold after 1881.[156] The property in dispute in *Re King decd*[157] burnt down and remained in a derelict condition when the tenant died, after which it was compulsorily purchased by the London County Council. Their right to damages was nominal (since they intended to knock down the ruined factory) and the original landlord lost his claim on compulsory purchase, when the right to sue passed along with the land.[158] The benefit "is annexed to and incident to and goes with the reversionary estate", that is there is an automatic transfer.[159] The decision on disrepair was extended by *London & County (A & D)* v. *Wilfred Sportsman*[160] to existing arrears *of rent*. Hence, at least to the Court of Appeal, the benefit of existing breaches does pass on a sale of the reversion.[161]

Rights to forfeit pass both for continuing breaches,[162] and for single breaches after 1911.[163] Sale[164] of the reversion subject to the forfeitable lease, passes the right to forfeit which survives the sale.[165] In *Kataria* v. *Safeland*[166] the current landlord was not personally owed any rent because, when he bought the reversion, he had assigned existing arrears to the previous landlord who sold to him. Nevertheless the new landlord was entitled to forfeit the lease for the breach of covenant involved in non-payment of rent to the previous landlord.

6.   Sub-tenants

[27.29] No privity of estate exists between a head landlord and a sub-tenant, so covenants cannot be enforced[167] though a sub-tenant is vulnerable to forfeiture.[168] A reversionary lease ends the landlord's liability to the original tenant.[169]

7.   Mortgage-lenders

[27.30] Lenders commonly wish to blow hot and cold, avoiding liability themselves but having the right to pursue the tenant. The law is not quite as comfortable for

---

[156] LPA 1925 s 141, re-enacting Conveyancing Act 1881 s 10.

[157] [1963] Ch 459, CA.

[158] Upjohn and Diplock LJJ; Lord Denning was more convincing, despite the apparent injustice on the facts; R Thornton (1991) 11 *LS* 47, 51.

[159] At 488, Upjohn LJ.

[160] [1971] Ch 764, CA.

[161] When a tenant sues his landlord (1) the *benefit* passing between tenants does not include the right to sue for earlier breaches: *City & Metropolitan Properties* v. *Greycroft* [1987] 1 WLR 1085; PF Smith [1987] *Conv* 374; (2) a landlord is only liable for his own breaches: *Duncliffe* v. *Caerfelin Properties* [1989] 2 EGLR 38, Garland J; PF Smith [1990] *Conv* 335, 345.

[162] *Rickett* v. *Green* [1910] 1 KB 253.

[163] Conveyancing Act 1911 s 2; now LPA 1925 s 141(3); *Atkin* v. *Rose* [1923] 1 Ch 522.

[164] Including grant of a reversionary lease.

[165] *London & County*, CA, doubting *Davenport* v. *Smith* [1921] 2 Ch 270.

[166] [1998] 1 EGLR 39, CA.

[167] *South of England Dairies* v. *Baker* [1906] 2 Ch 631, Joyce J; *Walters* v. *Northern Coal Mining Co* (1855) 5 De GM & G 629, 43 ER 1015 (not with beneficiaries under a trust of the lease).

[168] Indirect enforcement: (1) as a restrictive covenant; *Hall* v. *Ewin* (1887) 37 Ch D 74, CA (old); LT (Covenants) A 1995 s 3(5) (new); (2) if HL has the benefit of the covenants in the sub-lease under LPA 1925 s 56; *Amsprop Trading* v. *Harris Distribution* [1997] 1 WLR 1025, Neuberger J; (3) by pressure on T to enforce covenants in the sub-lease.

[169] *London & County (A & D)* v. *Wilfred Sportsman* [1971] Ch 764, CA; see above **[27.04]**.

lenders as it used to be. Under post-1995 leases, a lender becomes liable on taking possession.[170] For older leases, lenders could avoid liability if the mortgage took the form of a sub-demise[171] or legal charge.[172] However, lenders are allowed to enforce the right of the landlord against the tenant despite the absence of any direct estate between them, new[173] and old[174] law being the same. The courts have interpreted this as an either/or provision which allocates the right of action to whichever party has possession.

8. Informal leases

[27.31] The Landlord and Tenant (Covenants) Act 1995 applies whether leases are legal or equitable and whether sales are formal or informal.[175] This is a radical change. The Grantees of Reversions Act 1540 was limited to leases by deed,[176] but written leases were included in 1881[177] and oral ones in 1925.[178] Equitable leases – meaning *Walsh* v. *Lonsdale* contracts[179] – were included in the 1881 and 1925 statutes, causing benefits and burdens to be transferred with the reversion.[180] Unfortunately burdens[181] did not run between equitable tenants, either before[182] or after[183] the fusion of law and equity. However, any tenant who wishes to retain his land will be forced to accept the burden of the covenants in a specific performance action. An equitable assignee of a pre-1996 leasehold term was also outside the 1925 scheme, and so escaped liability on the covenants in the lease,[184] though this exemption also depends upon being willing to give up possession.

---

[170] LT (Covenants) A 1995 s 15(3)–(4); F Jenkins [1996] 07 *LSG* 24.

[171] LPA 1925 s 85; *Hand* v. *Blow* [1901] 2 Ch 721; *Re Abbot (JW & Co)* (1913) 30 TLR 13.

[172] LPA 1925 s 87.

[173] LT (Covenants) A 1995 s 15(1)–(2).

[174] LPA 1925 s 141(2), re-enacting Conveyancing Act 1881 s 10(1). This reformed *Webb* v. *Russell* (1789) 3 Term Rep 393, 100 ER 639; *Matthews* v. *Usher* [1900] 2 QB 535, CA (equitable lender no right to rent).

[175] LT (Covenants) A 1995 s 28 (definitions).

[176] *Standen* v. *Christmas* (1847) 10 QB 135, 116 ER 53; *Bickford* v. *Parson* (1848) 5 CB 920, 136 ER 1141; *Smith* v. *Eggington* (1874) 30 LT 521; *Allcock* v. *Moorhouse* (1882) 9 QBD 366, CA.

[177] LPA 1925 s 154; Conveyancing Act 1881 s 10; *Rickett* v. *Green* [1910] 1 KB 253; *Gilbey* v. *Cossey* (1912) 106 LT 607, Div Ct; *Cole* v. *Kelly* [1920] 2 KB 106, CA; *J Betts & Sons* v. *Price* (1924) 40 TLR 589; *Rye* v. *Purcell* [1926] 1 KB 646; *Breams Property Investment Co* v. *Stroulger* [1948] 2 KB 1, 7, Scott LJ; *Weg Motors* v. *Hales* [1962] Ch 49, 73, 76.

[178] LPA 1925 ss 154, 205(1)(xxiii); this reverses *Blane* v. *Francis* [1917] 1 KB 252, CA; *Elliott* v. *Johnson* [1868] LR 2 QB 120.

[179] (1882) 21 Ch D 9, CA.

[180] LPA 1925 ss 141–142, even though an estate contract creates an equitable interest in the land which binds anyone over whom it has priority.

[181] The benefit of a contract is assignable: *Manchester Brewery Co* v. *Coombs* [1901] 2 Ch 608, Farwell J (not deciding argument on Conveyancing Act 1881 s 10); *Dowell* v. *Dew* (1843) 12 LJ Ch 158 (reverse action by TC against L0 permitted).

[182] *Moore* v. *Greg* (1848) 2 Ph 717, 41 ER 1120, Cottenham LC; *Cox* v. *Bishop* (1857) 8 De GM & G 815, 44 ER 604; *Whitton* v. *Peacock* (1836) 2 Bing (NC) 411, 132 ER 161.

[183] *Purchase* v. *Lichfield Brewery Co* [1915] 1 KB 184; *Friary Holroyd & Healey's Brewery* v. *Singleton* [1899] 1 Ch 86, Romer J; RJ Smith [1978] *CLJ* 95. Query *Boyer* v. *Warbey* [1953] 1 QB 234, 245, Denning LJ.

[184] *Cox* v. *Bishop* (1857) 8 De GM & G 815, 44 ER 604; subject to any estoppel: *Rodenhurst Estates* v. *Barnes* [1936] 2 All ER 3, CA.

E. PHYSICAL DIVISION

1.   New law

[27.32] A major objective of the 1995 reforms was to ensure a safe method of physical division of a lease. Where any part is sold or disclaimed, whether it is the lease or the reversion, the covenants and liability to forfeiture[185] are split. If a covenant "falls to be complied with" in relation to a specific part[186] it binds the tenant of that part, but the tenant of the other part takes free of it.[187] Where a covenant affects both parts, liability is apportioned. The two part owners can reach an agreement about how to apportion liability,[188] which can be made binding on the other party to the lease by a notice and counter notice[189] procedure.[190] Sale of a part affected by a binding apportionment should be safe. Control of estate management can be retained if the landlord inserts an absolute covenant against dealing with parts.[191]

2.   Old law

[27.33] So long as one concerns oneself with leases split after 1925,[192] the law on division of the *reversion* is simple. The holder of any part of the reversion can enforce the covenants or forfeit the lease against the tenant of any part.[193] Divisions can have unfortunate effects on the tenant's security of tenure.

On a division of the *lease*, covenants which tended to the support and maintenance of the thing demised followed the reversion and the lease:

> "Let them go where they will. They stick so fast to the thing on which they wait that they follow every part of it."[194]

Hence personal liability on covenants was divided when a lease was divided. Unfortunately the landlord could forfeit the whole lease for a breach of covenant occurring on another part,[195] so that purchasers rarely accepted a division of a leasehold title and sub-leases had to be used instead.

---

[185] LT (Covenants) A 1995 ss 4, 21.

[186] S 28(2).

[187] Ss 3(2)–(3) (reversion).

[188] S 9.

[189] SI 1995/2964 forms 7–8; PH Kenny [1996] *Conv* 324.

[190] LT (Covenants) A 1995 s 10; s 26(3) provides an exception where there is any other statutory procedure for apportionment, eg under the Inclosure Acts.

[191] Sale is then an "excluded assignment": s 11; see above **[27.22]**.

[192] LPA 1925 s 140(3) but not for pre-1882 leases severed before 1926 (Conveyancing Act 1881 s 12 was limited to post-1881 leases).

[193] B Rudden (1961) 25 *Conv (NS)* 384.

[194] *Rally* v. *Wells* (1769) Wilm 341, 346, 97 ER 130; *United Dairies* v. *Public Trustee* [1923] 1 KB 469, 473, Greer J, lists older authorities; *Baynton* v. *Morgan* (1888) 22 QBD 74, CA (surrender).

[195] LPA 1925 s 141.

F. COVENANTS NOT RUNNING: NEW LAW

1. Personal covenants

[27.34] A lease now forms a single package under which all the terms agreed between original landlord and tenant pass, and to avoid this automatic transfer, it is necessary to qualify the covenant so as to make it personal,[196] with liability between the original parties.

2. Options without priority

[27.35] Options require registration and if the seller is not bound, neither is the buyer.[197]

3. Peripheral covenants

[27.36] New leases form a package, under which all the terms agreed between original landlord and tenant pass, a package which also includes covenants with outside parties such as management companies.[198] It remains to be seen whether eccentric or over-zealous landlords will begin to abuse this new found freedom.

G. COVENANTS NOT RUNNING: OLD LAW

1. Personal covenants

[27.37] Lord Oliver stated in *P & A Swift Investments* v. *Combined English Stores Group* that a covenant could not touch and concern the land when expressed to be personal.[199] Covenants were assumed to be proprietary[200] so a clear restriction of contractual scope was required to make them personal[201] – for example by referring to one individual[202] or by using words of personal obligation.[203]

2. Options without priority

[27.38] Options require registration and if the seller is not bound, neither is the buyer.[204]

---

[196] LT (Covenants) A 1995 s 15. *BHP Petroleum Great Britain* v. *Chesterfield Properties BHP* [2001] EWCA Civ 1797, [2002] Ch 194; [2002] Ch 12, Lightman J (personal repair); P Luxton [2002] *JBL* 101. The benefit might be assignable.

[197] LT (Covenants) A 1995 s 3(6)(b); also for old leases.

[198] Ss 3(6)(b), 12.

[199] [1989] AC 632, 642F. But a covenant should be able to run between landlords when expressed to be personal to the original tenant.

[200] LPA 1925 s 79; *Caerns Motor Services* v. *Texaco* [1994] 1 WLR 1249.

[201] *Eccles* v. *Mills* [1898] AC 360, PC; *Hua Chiao Commercial Bank* v. *Chiaphua Industries* [1987] AC 99, PC; *Kumar* v. *Dunning* [1989] QB 193, 197, Browne-Wilkinson V-C.

[202] *Roberts* v. *Tregaskis* (1878) 38 LT 176; *Muller* v. *Trafford* [1901] 1 Ch 54 Farwell J (*in case the said David Austin shall obtain*, personal.)

[203] *Re Royal Victoria Pavilion, Ramsgate* [1961] Ch 581.

[204] See above [25.10].

3. Peripheral covenants

[27.39] Only central covenants were capable of running under the pre-1996 law. Almost all common covenants did run, but one which did not was a covenant to repay a tenant's deposit.[205] A spate of appellate decisions has begun to introduce coherence.[206] *Spencer's case* in 1583 used the phrase "touch and concern"[207] which is exactly equivalent[208] to the statutory phrase "having reference to the subject matter of the lease".[209] Cheshire's test was this: does the covenant affect the landlord in his normal capacity as landlord or the tenant in his normal capacity as tenant.[210] A more precise test was stated by Bayley J in *Congleton Corporation* v. *Pattison*;[211] the covenant must either (1) affect the land itself during the term, or (2) be such as by itself, and not merely from collateral circumstances, affects the value of the land.

(1) Covenants affecting occupation of the land

[27.40] Obvious examples are rent,[212] repair,[213] to build,[214] to insure against fire,[215] use covenants,[216] covenants against assignment,[217] or against serving notice to quit,[218] tied house clauses[219] and landlords' covenants for quiet enjoyment.[220]

(2) Money payments

[27.41] Rent is a money payment, and other sums could be reserved as rent.[221] A heresy suggested that other money covenants were necessarily marginal, but this fallacy was extirpated by *P & A Swift Investments* v. *Combined English Stores.*[222] The

---

[205] *Hua Chiao Commercial Bank* v. *Chiaphua Industries* [1987] AC 99, PC; R Thornton (1991) 11 LS 47, 63.
[206] C Harpum [1988] *CLJ* 180, 182.
[207] (1583) 5 Co Rep 16a, 77 ER 72 (negative form at 163 suggests that "and" is correct); Holdsworth's *History* vol 7, 287–292; *Dewar* v. *Goodman* [1909] AC 72, 75, Lord Loreburn ("touch *or* concern"); HA Bigelow (1914) 30 *LQR* 319.
[208] *Davis* v. *Town Properties Investment Corporation* [1903] 1 Ch 797, 805, Cozens-Hardy LJ; *Breams Property Investment Co* v. *Stroulger* [1948] 2 KB 1, 7, Scott LJ, 9, Asquith LJ.
[209] LPA 1925 ss 141, 142.
[210] Cheshire & Burn (16th ed), 477; *Hua Chiao* [1987] AC 99, 107, Lord Oliver.
[211] (1810) 10 East 130, 103 ER 725; *Hua Chiao* at 107, Lord Oliver; *P & A Swift Investments* v. *Combined English Stores Group* [1989] AC 632, 640, Lord Oliver.
[212] *Kumar* v. *Dunning* [1989] 1 QB 193, 199H, Browne-Wilkinson V-C.
[213] *Spencer's case* (1583) 5 Co Rep 16a, 77 ER 72; *Moss Empires* v. *Olympia (Liverpool)* [1939] AC 544, HL; *Boyer* v. *Warbey* [1953] 1 QB 234, CA.
[214] *In esse* test abolished: LPA 1925 s 79(1); LT (Covenants) A 1995 s 3(7).
[215] *Vernon* v. *Smith* (1823) 5 B & Ald 1, 106 ER 1094.
[216] *Congleton*; *Gibson* v. *Doeg* (1857) 2 H & N 615, 157 ER 253.
[217] *Horsey Estate* v. *Steiger* [1899] 2 QB 79, CA; *Caerns Motor Services* v. *Texaco* [1994] 1 WLR 1249.
[218] *Breams Property Investment Co* v. *Stroulger* [1948] 2 KB 1, CA; *Prudential Assurance* v. *London Residuary Body* [1992] 2 AC 386, HL.
[219] *Clegg* v. *Hands* (1890) 44 Ch D 503, CA; *Manchester Brewery Co* v. *Coombs* [1901] 2 Ch 608, Farwell J; *Regent Oil* v. *Gregory* [1966] Ch 402, CA.
[220] *Middlemore* v. *Goodale* (1638) Cro Car 503, 79 ER 1033; *Campbell* v. *Lewis* (1820) 3 Barn & Ald 392, 106 ER 706; compare *Davies* v. *Town Properties Investment Corp* [1903] 1 Ch 797, CA.
[221] *Vyvyan* v. *Arthur* (1823) 1 B & C 410, 107 ER 152; *Lambeth LBC* v. *Thomas* (1997) 74 P & CR 189, CA.
[222] [1989] AC 632, HL; JE Adams [1989] 47 EG 24; *Kumar* v. *Dunning* [1989] 1 QB 193, 199H, CA; C Harpum [1988] *CLJ* 180, 180 ("remarkable and bold"); P Luxton [1987] *JBL* 299.

House of Lords decided that a surety covenant does touch and concern the land, and so passes to a new landlord on a sale of the reversion. *Coronation Street Industrial Properties* v. *Ingall Industries* applied the same rule to a covenant by a surety to accept a lease if the tenant was in liquidation.[223] *Hua Chiao Commercial Bank* v. *Chiaphua Industries*[224] decided that a promise by the landlord to return a deposit at the end of the lease was held to be personal, so that a buyer of the reversion escaped having to return the deposit to his tenant. The decision is borderline, that is to say, wrong.

Covenants to pay a collateral sum should not touch and concern land.[225] Examples are to pay the landlord's taxes on other land,[226] to pay fees under a building licence, to pay extra rent if the landlord increased the size of the house, to account for profit on wine sold on the land, to pay an annual sum to churchwardens, to repay an unsecured loan and to provide a box in a theatre free of charge.[227]

(3) Covenants affecting neighbouring land

[27.42] Tenants covenants relating to neighbouring land are collateral.[228] The same rule is less just when applied to landlords, since they often own neighbouring property, and it would be convenient for the covenants to run.[229] They will do so where the covenant has a direct impact on the property let to the tenant, for example repair of an adjacent sea-wall.[230] The whole purpose of leasehold developments is to make covenants run. Surely a covenant by an intermediate landlord to observe the covenants in his head-lease should exemplify this principle? The reverse decision in *Dewar* v. *Goodman*[231] must be wrong.[232] Restrictions on the landlord's use of his adjoining property will often qualify as restrictive covenants and pass for that reason.

(4) Covenants affecting the value of the landlord's reversion

[27.43] This is the second head of *Congleton Corporation* v. *Pattison*[233] where a covenant affects the value of the land itself – where the covenant is of value to the land owner from time to time and to no other person.[234] A tenuous effect on the value is not enough to make the covenant touch and concern – for example the covenant in *Congleton* not to employ workers from outside the parish, with the intention of reducing the poor rate levied on the landlord's other property in the parish.

---

[223] [1989] 1 WLR 304, HL.
[224] [1987] AC 99, PC; *Eden Park Estates* v. *Longman* [1982] Conv 239.
[225] (1583) 5 Co Rep 16a, 16b, 77 ER 72.
[226] *Gower* v. *Postmaster General* (1887) 57 LT 527.
[227] *Camden* v. *Batterbury* (1860) 7 CBNS 864, 141 ER 1055.
[228] *Spencer's case* (1583) 5 Co Rep 16a, 77 ER 72.
[229] *Davis* v. *Town Properties Investment Corp* [1903] 1 Ch 797, CA.
[230] *Morland* v. *Cook* (1868) LR 6 Eq 252.
[231] [1909] AC 72, HL
[232] *Kumar* v. *Dunning* [1989] QB 193, 205G, Browne-Wilkinson V-C; he thought it impliedly overruled by *Dyson* v. *Forster* [1909] AC 98, HL (restrictive covenant must touch and concern the *neighbouring* land).
[233] (1808) 10 East 130, 103 ER 725.
[234] *Vyvyan* v. *Arthur* (1823) 1 B & C 410, 107 ER 152; *Vernon* v. *Smith* (1821) 5 B & Ald 1, 9, 10, 11, 106 ER 1094, Best J; *Forster* v. *Elvet Colliery Co* [1909] AC 72, HL; *Kumar* v. *Dunning* [1989] QB 193, 204, Browne-Wilkinson V-C; *Swift* [1989] AC 632, 640–641, Lord Oliver.

H. TENANTS UNABLE TO PAY

1. Insolvent tenants

[27.44] Insolvency is not a defence to an action for rent,[235] but in practice it prevents full recovery since the tenant does not have enough money to pay. The landlord is left to prove for rent in the tenant's insolvency, claiming either against an individual's trustee in bankruptcy or the liquidator of a corporate tenant.[236] Usually only a proportion of the debts are paid and rent abates proportionately. Proofs may relate to existing arrears of rent and also to rent which will become due from the date of the insolvency until the term date of the lease; however future rent payments have to be discounted to take account of the fact that the landlord will receive early payment as well as the possibility of reletting.[237] Actual payments may be appropriated to future rent payments, leaving the whole of the arrears untouched, and leaving sureties vulnerable.[238]

Sometimes a moratorium is enforced to try to give an opportunity for the company to recover from its debts, perhaps by an administration order[239] or a voluntary arrangement between a tenant and his creditors. These procedures are designed to give a breathing space and so to ward off insolvency. Substitutes remain exposed to action.[240]

2. Liability for future rent

[27.45] In *Re Park Air Services*,[241] the House of Lords had to decide whether the landlord could prove for the whole of the aggregate rents due for the remainder of the term, or whether a discount had to be allowed to reflect the fact that payments were accelerated by the tenant's insolvency. In the particular case the liquidators of the tenant company had disclaimed the lease. The decision was that a discount had to be applied, though even so the landlord was awarded £1 million. Lord Millett observed that the right to rent was ended by the disclaimer to be substituted by a claim for compensation by a person suffering loss as a result of a disclaimer, who is deemed to be a creditor of the company and so is entitled to prove "for the loss or damage". Damages should be assessed as if there was a contract that had been wrongfully terminated, and accordingly the landlord had to allow credit for rents that he would obtain from reletting the property and also a discount for early receipt of the rent. The landlord could not sell the lease and on disclaimer the right to end the lease had gone, a right that

---

[235] *St Thomas' Hospital* v. *Richardson* [1910] 1 KB 271.

[236] A liquidator or trustee in bankruptcy can become personally liable for rent, eg by taking steps to sell the lease: *Re Page* (1884) 14 QBD 401; *Re ABC Coupler & Engineering Co (No 3)* [1970] 1 WLR 702, 709; *Re Downer Enterprises* [1974] 1 WLR 1460.

[237] *Re Park Air Services* [2000] 2 AC 172, HL; *Re Hide* (1871) LR 7 Ch App 28.

[238] *Milverton Group* v. *Warner World* [1995] 2 EGLR 28, CA; M Haley [1995] *JBL* 181.

[239] IA 1986 part II; IA 2000 s 9.

[240] *RA Securities* v. *Mercantile Current* [1995] 3 All ER 581; *Mytre Investments* v. *Reynolds* [1995] 3 All ER 588.

[241] [2000] 2 AC 172, HL.

could not be described as a security.[242] The decision would not necessarily have been the same had the contract provided for sums to become immediately payable on breach, nor if the question had been of entitlement to prove in an insolvency (as opposed to on a disclaimer).

3. Dissolution of a company without liquidation

[27.46] Commercial leases invariably provide that dissolution of the tenant company is a termination event entitling the landlord to forfeit the lease; however if he chooses to do so, he must retake possession from whoever is trading there.[243] Very often the directors of the tenant company continue to trade as if nothing has happened, and later apply to restore the company to the register. This may prejudice the landlord, who may well lose the right to end the lease, but who can challenge the restoration of the company to the register.[244]

4. Forfeiture

[27.47] Landlords are best advised to control dealings, to vet prospective tenants for financial solvency, and to obtain guarantees. Commercial leases usually provide that on insolvency or incipient insolvency, the landlord shall have the right to terminate the lease by forfeiture, leaving the landlord free to relet the property. However, if the lease is valuable the trustee in bankruptcy or liquidator can generally obtain relief from the forfeiture and sell the property within one year.[245]

Subtenants are usually offered relief via the grant of a new lease[246] with liability to the extent of an assignee. Lenders will also be entitled to claim relief after forfeiture by proceedings or by peaceable re-entry.[247]

5. Disclaimer

[27.48] Running of rent can be prevented for the future by disclaiming the lease on corporate liquidation or personal bankruptcy.[248] It is possible even after the liquidator or trustee in bankruptcy has entered into possession, endeavoured to sell, or carried out other acts of ownership.[249] Any onerous property[250] can be disclaimed by notice,[251] including any unprofitable contract,[252] any property which is unsaleable,

---

[242] *Re Lomax Leisure* [1999] 2 EGLR 37, Neuberger J.
[243] *Cromwell Developments* v. *Godfrey* [1998] 2 EGLR 62, CA.
[244] *Re Blenheim Leisure (Restaurants)* [2000] BCC 554, CA.
[245] LPA 1925 s 146(4).
[246] *Beegas Nominees* v. *BHP Petroleum* [1998] 2 EGLR 57, CA.
[247] *Barclays Bank* v. *Prudential Assurance Co* [1998] 1 EGLR 44, Ch D.
[248] IA 1986 ss 178–182 (companies), 315–321 (bankruptcy).
[249] IA 1986 ss 178(1), 315(1); *Re Lister* [1926] Ch 149.
[250] *Re Celtic Extraction* [2001] Ch 475, CA (waste management licence); *City of London Corp* v. *Bown* (1990) 60 P & CR 42, CA (not short-term or statutory residential tenancy).
[251] IA 1986 s 178(1), 315(1); SI 1986/1925 rr 4.187–4.189.
[252] *Re Gough* (1927) 96 LJ Ch 233 (contract for sub-sale).

and any which may give rise to any liability.[253] Leases may be onerous because of high rents or large repairing obligations.[254]

Disclaimer ends the leasehold estate future liability on the covenants, and all benefits.[255] Sub-tenancies and other derivative interests end[256] unless the holder exercises his statutory right to claim protection. Notice must be served on all people with known interests and in the case of a dwelling also on all occupiers.[257] On an application for relief the court has power to make whatever order is just.[258] A subtenant[259] must accept liability at least to the extent of a buyer of the lease.[260] Even forfeiture by peaceable re-entry after the disclaimer will not remove a lender's right to relief.[261] The landlord suffers loss from a disclaimer, but can prove in the insolvency,[262] has 14 days to object to the disclaimer,[263] and can force the liquidator or trustee in bankruptcy to decide whether or not he will disclaim.[264] The landlord can enforce substitute liability in this situation.[265]

Similar provisions operate where a company is struck off the company register and dissolved, usually for failure to file company returns. Any property will vest in the Crown, and may be sold if valuable, or disclaimed if onerous.[266] However, the landlord can apply for an order to restore the company to the register, enabling it to review the rent[267] or sue any sureties for rent.[268]

I. SUBSTITUTES

[27.49] Landlords usually seek guarantees that the current tenant will pay the rent. Pre-1996 tenants remained liable on privity of contract, but privity of contract is abolished for new leases to be replaced by authorised guarantee agreements. Almost all commercial tenants are required to provide sureties.

---

[253] IA 1986 ss 178(3), 315(2).

[254] *Eyre* v. *Hall* [1986] 2 EGLR 95, CA; *MEPC* v. *Scottish Amicable Life Assurance Society* [1993] 2 EGLR 93, CA.

[255] *Re Bastable* [1901] 2 KB 518; *Re Hyams* (1923) 93 LJ Ch 184, CA; *Re Wadsley* (1925) 94 LJ Ch 215.

[256] *Sterling Estates* v. *Pickard UK* [1997] 2 EGLR 33; *Re Cock ex p Shilston* (1887) 20 QBD 343. For local land charges see *Hackney LBC* v. *Crown Estate Commissioners* (1996) 72 P & CR 233.

[257] IA 1986 ss 179(1), 317–318.

[258] IA 1986 ss 181, 320. A lender may be required to pay surplus proceeds to the tenant's trustee in bankruptcy: *Lee* v. *Lee* [1998] 1 FLR 1018.

[259] IA 1986 s 320; *Re Vedmay* (1995) 69 P & CR 247; *Beegas Nominees* v. *BHP Petroleum* [1998] 2 EGLR 57, CA.

[260] IA 1986 ss 182, 321. ie not with privity of contract, only privity of estate liability.

[261] *Barclays Bank* v. *Prudential Assurance* [1998] 1 EGLR 44.

[262] IA 1986 ss 178(6), 315(5); *Re Park Air Services* [2000] 2 AC 172, HL (the landlord must allow discount to reflect the fact that he receives rent early).

[263] IA 1986 ss 179, 317.

[264] Ss 178(5), 316; A Waltham & P Cane [1992] 25 *EG* 19.

[265] IA 1986 ss 178(4), 315(5); see below **[27.59]**.

[266] Companies Act 1985 s 656. Sureties are released unless the company is later restored: *Re Yarmarine* [1992] BCLC 276.

[267] *Re Priceland* [1996] EGCS 188, Ch D.

[268] *Allied Dunbar Assurance* v. *Fowle* [1994] 1 EGLR 122, Garland J; *Stanhope Pensions T* v. *Registrar of Companies* (1995) 69 P & CR 238, CA; A Belcher [1995] *Conv* 199.

1.   Privity of contract: pre-1996 leases

(1) Original parties

[27.50] English landlords traditionally enjoyed two alternative remedies for rent, one founded on privity of estate and the other on privity of contract, this last casting a net for the original tenant or his estate. During the recession of the early 1990s many land-lords sought to enforce this liability.[269]

After the Grantees of Reversions Act 1540 allowed the burden of covenants to pass, *Walker's case* (1587)[270] settled that the original tenant remained liable on privity of contract after the assignment of the lease. This point is clear under modern statute law.[271] Hence the original tenant (or landlord) remains liable on the covenants throughout the term of the lease. Kenyon CJ once explained that having chosen his original tenant the landlord should not be deprived of this action by assignment to an untrustworthy tenant.[272] Lord Templeman added in *City of London Corporation* v. *Fell* that:[273]

> "The common law did not release the original tenant from liability for breaches of covenant committed after an assignment. . . . [T]he fortunate English landlord has two remedies after an assignment, namely his remedy against an assignee and his remedy against the original tenant."

The landlord's choice lay between the original tenant (T0)[274] and the current tenant (TC). Contractual liability could be excluded[275] or qualified, for example by making the tenant responsible only for his own personal acts.[276]

An original contracting party remains liable[277] for the duration of the term of the (pre-1996) lease for which he contracted, but no longer. Continuing power to ensure compliance with the covenant is not necessary. An extension of the term of the lease agreed in advance is usually included.[278] However, the original tenant is exonerated once the original term ends[279] and the current tenant holds over. In *City of London Corporation* v. *Fell* a suite of offices in the City was taken by Wilde Sapte – a promi-nent firm of City solicitors – under a ten year lease. They sold the lease to Grovebell Group and those tenants (TC) remained in occupation when the lease expired in 1986,

---

[269] *City of London Corp* v. *Fell* [1993] QB 589, 603H, 604D, Nourse LJ.
[270] (1587) 3 Co Rep 22a, 76 ER 676; *Baynton* v. *Morgan* (1888) 22 QBD 74, 82, Lopes LJ.
[271] LPA 1925 ss 141(1), 142(2); *Re King* [1963] Ch 459, 481, Lord Denning MR; *Friends' Provident Life Office* v. *British Railways Board* [1996] 1 All ER 336, 351a, Sir Christopher Slade.
[272] *Auriol* v. *Mills* (1790) 4 Term Rep 94, 99, 100 ER 912.
[273] [1994] 1 AC 458, 465F.
[274] *Moule* v. *Garrett* [1872] LR 7 Exch 101; *Johnsey Estates* v. *Lewis & Manley (Engineering)* [1987] 2 EGLR 69, CA.
[275] *Eccles* v. *Mills* [1898] AC 360, PC.
[276] Eg not to suffer or permit: *Bryant* v. *Hancock & Co* [1898] 1 QB 716; *Wilson* v. *Twamley* [1904] 2 KB 99, CA; *Villiers* v. *Oldcorn* [1903] 20 TLR 11.
[277] LPA 1925 s 79. On liquor see: *Mumford* v. *Walker* (1901) 71 LJKB 19; *Holloway Bros* v. *Hill* [1902] 2 Ch 612; *Palethorpe* v. *Home Brewery Co* [1906] 2 KB 5. Also *Thames Manufacturing Co* v. *Perrotts (Nichol & Peyton)* (1985) 50 P & CR 1, 6, Scott J.
[278] *Baker* v. *Merckel* [1960] 1 QB 656, CA.
[279] Eg by surrender: *Matthews* v. *Sawell* (1818) 8 Taunt 270, 129 ER 387; but survives forfeiture: *Weaver* v. *Mogford* [1988] 2 EGLR 48, CA.

holding over under the business tenancies legislation.[280] By the time the tenant vacated, the company was in arrears with the rent and was insolvent. The landlord pursued the original tenants, Wilde Sapte, for the unpaid rent, but they lost in each court right through to the Lords.[281] Contractual liability was limited to the 10 year term of the lease, and was not extended by the business tenancies legislation.[282] Contractual liability could be extended by clear wording.[283]

(2) Privity of contract after a sale of the reversion

[27.51] Until a dealing with the reversion, it is obvious that the original landlord (L0) can enforce the contract in the lease. After a sale, privity of contract exists between the current landlord (LC[284] not L0[285]) provided that the covenant touches and concerns and so passes with the reversion.[286] *Arlesford Trading Co* v. *Servansingh*[287] concerned three simple transactions in a common sequence. A lease by L0 to T0, was followed in sequence by an assignment of the lease to TC, and a sale of the landlord's reversion to LC. Although there was never any moment at which T0 was directly a tenant of LC, nevertheless an action lay between them in contract. T0 remained liable on his contract throughout the term to whoever was the current holder of the reversion.

(3) Intermediate tenants not privy

[27.52] An intermediate tenant was not liable once he had sold the lease. However landlords commonly sought to reinforce their position by insisting that a tenant who wished to divest himself of the lease should enter into the licence for assignment[288] in order to provide a guarantee for the whole remaining term.[289] This is additional to any indemnity covenant.[290]

---

[280] LTA 1954 part II.

[281] [1994] 1 AC 458, HL; M Haley [1993] *JBL* 473; PF Smith [1993] *Conv* 164; S Bridge [1994] *CLJ* 28; M Haley [1994] *Conv* 247.

[282] Similarly for sureties: *GMS Syndicate* v. *Gary Elliott* [1982] Ch 1; *Junction Estates* v. *Cope* (1974) 27 P & CR 482; *A Plesser & Co* v. *Davis* [1983] 2 EGLR 70.

[283] *Herbert Duncan* v. *Cluttons* [1993] QB 589, 605–608.

[284] *Thursby* v. *Plant* (1669) 1 Lev 259, 83 ER 359 (L1 could sue T0 in contract as well as covenant). The rules for landlords are a mirror image of those for tenants: LPA 1925 s 142(2); *Stuart* v. *Joy* [1904] 1 KB 362, 367; *Bath* v. *Bowles* (1905) 93 LT 801; *Celsteel* v. *Alton House Holdings (No 2)* [1986] 1 WLR 666, 672–673, Scott J; affirmed [1987] 1 WLR 291, 296D–E, Fox LJ; D Gordon [1987] *Conv* 103.

[285] *Walker's case* (1587) 3 Co Rep 22a, 76 ER 676.

[286] Unless the covenant does not touch and concern: *Bickford* v. *Parson* (1848) 5 CB 920, 136 ER 1141; *Allcock* v. *Moorhouse* (1882) 9 QBD 366, CA; *Eccles* v. *Mills* [1898] AC 360, PC (TC can sue L0).

[287] [1971] 1 WLR 1080, CA (some relevant authorities not cited); D Gordon [1987] *Conv* 103.

[288] If an assignment must be registered with the landlord, liability on the covenants cannot be avoided by failing to register it: *Cerium Investments* v. *Evans* [1991] 1 EGLR 80, CA.

[289] *Friends' Provident Life Office* v. *British Railways Board* [1996] 1 All ER 336, CA; *Estates Gazette* v. *Benjamin Restaurants* [1994] 1 WLR 1528, CA.

[290] *Becton Dickinson UK* v. *Zwebner* [1989] QB 208; P Mc Loughlin [1989] *Conv* 292; *Re a Debtor (No 21 of 1995)* [1996] CLYB 3750.

2. Post-1995 leases

(1) Abolition of privity of contract

[27.53] Privity of contract liability represented an unwarranted trap for tenants, who might be caught many years after selling the lease, especially if there was a recession, and for very large amounts after rents had been reviewed. Law Commission research revealed widespread public ignorance of the potential liability.[291] Abolition was carried out by the Landlord and Tenant (Covenants) Act 1995, though only for "new tenancies". The mechanism, already studied, is that a former tenant obtains a release when he sells on the lease.[292] Any agreement excluding directly or indirectly the right to a release is void.[293] In the short term this may be a small comfort, for the immediate previous tenant will usually be required to enter into an authorised guarantee agreement, but a full release will occur after a second sale.

(2) Authorised guarantee agreement (AGA)

[27.54] Where a tenant assigns a post-1995 lease and is granted a release from liability on a covenant, he may enter into an authorised guarantee agreement.[294] This will not be offered voluntarily,[295] so a landlord will only be able to insist upon it by restricting assignment of the lease so that entry into an AGA is stated in advance as a condition of giving consent.[296] The previous tenant (TC – 1) guarantees the obligations of the current tenant (TC) as a principal debtor, and probably also agrees to take a new lease on a default by the current tenant.[297] Since the current tenant is released when he sells, the AGA is also released.[298] However, an "excluded assignment" – either a transmission or a sale in breach of covenant – offers no release, so the AGA remains in place until the next correct sale.[299]

3. Sureties – all leases (new and old)

[27.55] It is very common for the landlord to demand a surety whose function is to guarantee[300] the performance of the tenant's obligations, either on the grant of a new lease or on an assignment. A guarantee is formed by any promise to accept liability for the failure of another to perform legal obligations.[301] It creates a primary or ultimate obligation (in TC) and a secondary or substitute liability on the surety *for the same*

---

[291] Law Com 174 (1988), [3.15]; R Thornton (1991) 11 *LS* 47, 61.

[292] LT (Covenants) A 1995 s 5; see above [27.22].

[293] S 25.

[294] S 16; MCE Wright [1997] *LT Rev* 52.

[295] *Wallis Fashion Group* v. *CGU Life Assurance* [2000] 2 EGLR 49, Neuberger J; B Dear [2000] 42 *EG* 167; M Haley [2000] *Conv* 566; *London & Argylle* v. *Mount Cook Land* [2002] 50 EG 111 (CS).

[296] LTA 1927 s 19(1A); see above [27.15].

[297] LT (Covenants) A 1995 s 16(7).

[298] S 16(4), (8).

[299] S 16(6).

[300] Although the terms are interchangeable, "surety" is usually restricted to a liability accepted under a deed.

[301] *Moschi* v. *Lep Air Services* [1973] AC 331, 347H, Lord Diplock.

obligation. The surety is a substitute or twelfth man for the tenant's team, who is subject to the same rules and regulations as the player he replaces.[302]

The scope is determined contractually, usually limited to the original contractual term, and extinguished by a holding over,[303] though express wording could extend the duration.[304] If the landlord sells the reversion, the benefit of surety covenants passes to the new landlord at common law,[305] and LC should be the only possible claimant.[306]

Equity protects a surety with the rule that liability is discharged by any prejudicial variation in the primary contract.[307] Insolvency of the tenant also discharges any surety, but sureties are commonly required to accept a new lease themselves if the original lease is disclaimed after insolvency.[308]

J. SUBSTITUTES LIABILITY

[27.56] Landlords have at least two potential defendants in an action for rent,[309] and can choose the plumpest target.[310] Satisfaction of any given debt can only be obtained once,[311] but multiple actions are allowed.[312] Sureties have various protections.

1.   Arrears notice (new and old leases)

[27.57] Substitutes often complain that landlords had no incentive to chase the current tenant. This problem is addressed by sections of the 1995 Act, which apply both to old and new leases and to all forms of substitute liability. Restrictions apply to financial claims, that is for rent, service charge, and liquidated sums payable on a default.[313] A default notice[314] must be served within six months of the sum becoming due, a rule which prevents large arrears being built up without the knowledge of a surety. However, a landlord is not obliged to enforce his rights immediately, since he has the normal limitation period in which to sue and can add accumulating arrears. In

---

[302] *P & A Swift Investments* v. *Combined English Stores Group* [1989] AC 632, 638, Lord Templeman.

[303] *GMS Syndicate* v. *Gary Elliott* [1982] Ch 1, Nourse J; *Junction Estates* v. *Cope* (1974) 27 P & CR 482, MacKenna J; *Plesser* below; all three approved in *Fell* [1993] QB 589, 605D, Nourse LJ, CA, and presumably in HL

[304] *A Plesser & Co* v. *Davis* [1983] 2 EGLR 70, French J.

[305] *Swift*, HL

[306] R Thornton (1991) 11 *LS* 47, 55.

[307] See below **[27.58]**.

[308] *Coronation Street Industrial Properties* v. *Ingall Industries* [1989] 1 WLR 304, HL (the reversion was assigned).

[309] *Allied London Investments* v. *Hambro Life Assurance* (1985) 50 P & CR 207, 210, Ackner LJ.

[310] *Norwich Union Life Insurance Society* v. *Low Profile Fashions* [1992] 1 EGLR 86, CA; S Bridge [1992] *CLJ* 425.

[311] *March* v. *Brace* (1614) 2 Bulst 151, 153, 80 ER 1025 (T1 paid rent; L0 could not sue T0); *Orgill* v. *Kemshead* (1812) 4 Taunt 642, 128 ER 407; *Sturgess* v. *Farrington* (1812) 4 Taunt 614, 128 ER 471.

[312] *House Property & Investment Co* v. *Bernardout* [1948] 1 KB 314.

[313] LT (Covenants) A 1995 s 17; *Commercial Union Life Assurance Co* v. *Moustafa* [1999] 2 EGLR 44, Smedley J; HW Wilkinson [2001] *NLJ* 275.

[314] Prescribed form: SI 1995/2964; PH Kenny [1996] *Conv* 324. However, failure to serve notice is not a defence for other parties: *Cheverell Estates* v. *Harris* [1998] 1 EGLR 27.

Commercial Union Life Assurance Co v. *Moustafa*[315] it was held that a default notice that misstated the amount of the arrears was valid to the extent that it did include genuine arrears.

2. Prejudicial variation of leases

[27.58] The current parties are free to vary the terms of the lease so as to relax the terms or to operate neutrally on sureties.[316] What they cannot do is impose greater burdens on former tenants, since a prejudicial variation will normally destroy the guarantee.[317] In *Holme* v. *Brunskill* a surrender of one field on a hill farm discharged the surety,[318] and so do landlord's improvements[319] and agreed changes of use.[320] Discharge can be prevented by a contractual provision, for example making a substitute liable for the reviewed rent.[321] A release of the current tenant also allows all substitutes to escape.[322]

The Landlord and Tenant (Covenants) Act 1995 protects substitutes against any (immaterial) variation to which the landlord has the right to refuse his agreement.[323]

3. Disclaimer

[27.59] Substitute liability survives disclaimer of the lease[324] – whether under privity of contract in a pre-1996 lease, as a surety, as a later assignee, his surety, or the surety of the current tenant. Similar principles apply under a voluntary arrangement or where a company that has been struck off the register for failing to file returns is later restored to the register or on forfeiture.

4. Overriding leases

[27.60] Commercial leases commonly ensure that if the lease is disclaimed the surety may be compelled to accept a new lease from the original or future landlords.[325]

---

[315] [1999] 2 EGLR 44, Smedley J.

[316] *Friends Provident Life Office* v. *British Railways Board* [1996] 1 All ER 336, CA; *Metropolitan Properties (Regis)* v. *Bartholomew* [1996] 1 EGLR 82, CA; HW Wilkinson [1995] *NLJ* 1141; JE Adams [1995] *Conv* 289; *Beegas Nominees* v. *BHP Petroleum* [1998] 2 EGLR 57, CA.

[317] *Friends' Provident* 342e–345b, Beldam LJ, 350d–h, Sir Christopher Slade; M Davey (1996) 59 *MLR* 78, 82. Normal contractual principles of interpretation apply: *BCCI* v. *Ali* [2001] UKHL 8, [2002] AC 251, HL.

[318] (1877) 3 QBD 495, 505, Cotton LJ. Surely Brett LJ's dissent was correct to suggest that the contractual variation which could only benefit the surety was immaterial.

[319] *West Horndon Industrial Park* v. *Phoenix Timber Group* [1995] 1 EGLR 77, Ch D; HW Wilkinson [1995] *NLJ* 1141; JE Adams [1995] *Conv* 289.

[320] *Howard de Walden Estates* v. *Pasta Place* [1995] 1 EGLR 79, Morland J (test potential prejudice); *Jaskel* v. *Sophie Nursery Products* [1993] EGCS 42, CA; *Averbrian* v. *Willmalight* [1994] CLYB 2799.

[321] *Selous Street Properties* v. *Oronel Fabrics* [1984] 1 EGLR 50, Hutchison J; *Herbert Duncan* v. *Cluttons* [1993] QB 589, 605–608, Nourse LJ; *Friends Provident* [1996] 1 All ER 336, 351c.

[322] *Re EWA* [1901] 2 KB 642, CA; *Deanplan* v. *Mahmoud* [1993] Ch 151; HW Wilkinson [1993] *NLJ* 28; *Friends Provident* at 348h–349, Beldam LJ; *Mytre Investments* v. *Reynolds* [1995] 3 All ER 588; *Morris* v. *Wentworth-Stanley* [1999] QB 1004, CA (discharge of one debtor discharges another unless there is a reservation of the right).

[323] LT (Covenants) A 1995 s 18. This applies to new and old leases.

[324] *Hindcastle* v. *Barbara Attenborough Associates* [1997] AC 70, HL; S Bridge [1995] *CLJ* 253; J Tayleur [1997] *Conv* 24. For the related case law see P Sparkes *NLT*, 786–787.

[325] *Coronation Street Industrial Properties* v. *Ingall Industries* [1989] 1 WLR 304, HL; *Xey* v. *Abbey Life Assurance Co* [1994] EGCS 190 (landlord's refusal would discharge the surety); *Re Spirit Motorsport* [1996] 1 BCLC 684, Laddie J (no right).

Conversely a substitute compelled to make payments under a relevant lease (new or old) can insist on taking an overriding lease[326] which sits between the lease guaranteed and the landlord.

K. REIMBURSEMENT AND INDEMNITY

[27.61] If a substitute is targeted by the landlord, he is entitled to reimbursement from the person with ultimate liability,[327] that is the current tenant.

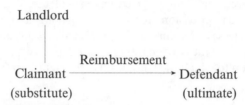

Figure 27-2 A claim to reimbursement

1. Restitutionary claims for reimbursement

[27.62] Where there is no direct contractual relationship between plaintiff and defendant[328] there is a "quasi-contractual" indemnity, better described today as a free-standing obligation in restitution. The current tenant is unjustly enriched at the expense of the surety and is obliged to reimburse him. The factor which makes the enrichment unjust is legal compulsion.[329] As Cockburn CJ stated in *Moule* v. *Garrett*:

> "where one person is compelled to pay damages to the legal default of another, he is entitled to recover from the person by whose default the damage was occasioned for the sum so paid."[330]

So an original tenant required to pay damages for disrepair was entitled to obtain an indemnity direct from the current tenant, despite intermediate assignments.

The payment must discharge a common liability[331] for example an original tenant caught by privity of contract,[332] between tenants of parts,[333] against an intermediate

---

[326] LT (Covenants) A 1995 ss 19–20; SI 1995/3154.

[327] P Sparkes "Reimbursement of Tenant Substitutes" ch 16 in Jackson and Wilde; *Re Downer Enterprises* [1974] 1 WLR 1460, 1470D, Pennycuick V-C; *Kumar* v. *Dunning* [1989] QB 193, 201, Browne-Wilkinson V-C; *Becton Dickinson UK* v. *Zwebner* [1989] QB 208, McNeill J.

[328] So exclusion of a contractual indemnity is irrelevant: *Re Healing Research Trustee Co* [1992] 2 All ER 481, Harman J.

[329] The plaintiff must not officiously expose himself to liability, but this is scarcely likely of a surety.

[330] (1872) LR 7 Exch 101, affirming (1870) LR 5 Exch 132; *Exall* v. *Partridge* (1799) 8 Term Rep 308, 101 ER 1405; *Bonner* v. *Tottenham & Edmonton PIBS* [1899] 1 QB 161, 172–173, Vaughan Williams LJ.

[331] *Duncan Fox & Co* v. *N & S Wales Bank* (1860) 6 App Cas 1, 10, Selborne LC; *Re Downer Enterprises* [1974] 1 WLR 1460, 1468, Pennycuick J; Civil Liability (Contribution) Act 1978; *Royal Brompton Hospital NHS Trust* v. *Hammond (No 3)* [2002] UKHL 14, [2002] 1 WLR 1397 (requirement for shared or common liability).

[332] *Moule* v. *Garrett* (1872) LR 7 Ex 101; *Humble* v. *Langston* (1841) 7 M & W 517, 151 ER 871.

[333] *Whitham* v. *Bullock* [1939] 2 KB 81, CA.

tenant for a breach occurring while he was tenant,[334] and against an equitable assignee.[335] A sub-tenant is not normally liable on the same obligation as the head-tenant.[336] In *Selous Street Properties* v. *Oronel Fabrics*[337] action was also allowed (by both T0 and S0) against an intermediate assignee (T2), and against the surety of the current tenant (SC). These actions where the defendant does not have the ultimate liability are more contentious.

2. Contractual indemnity

[27.63] This is redundant for new leases since liability of a previous tenant cannot survive sale of a post-1995 lease and indemnity covenants are never required.[338] Under pre-1996 leases, statute implied an indemnity covenant into every assignment for valuable consideration.[339] Express indemnity covenants are essential in gifts of old leases and following transmissions on death.[340]

Contractual indemnity relies on a chain of indemnity. A whole sequence of actions is required, or rather one mammoth cause of action into which all parties are drawn by third party notices.[341] The chain may break down because of insolvency or death. It is justice of a sort to require the tenant who sells to the one who becomes insolvent to carry the largest burden.[342]

A great improvement is made by the transitional provisions of the new legislation[343] where the transfer of a pre-1996 lease occurs after the 2002 Act commencement: covenants are implied for indemnity if the whole is transferred and to pay apportioned parts after a division, and they are now implied whether or not the transfer is for value. This is a major improvement.[344]

---

[334] *Burnett* v. *Lynch* (1826) 5 B & C 589, 108 ER 220; *Walker* v. *Bartlee* (1856) 18 CB 845, 139 ER 1004.

[335] *Close* v. *Wilberforce* (1838) 1 Beav 112, 48 ER 881; query whether this is logical.

[336] *Bonner* v. *Tottenham & Edmonton PIBS* [1899] 1 QB 161, CA. Contrast *Electricity Supply Nominees* v. *Thorn EMI Retail* [1991] 2 EGLR 46, CA.

[337] [1984] 1 EGLR 50, 61–62, Hutchison J; C Whippman & C Green [1984] *JBL* 419; P McLoughlin [1984] *Conv* 443; *Cale* v. *Assuidoman KPS (Harrow)* [1996] BPIR 245; P Sparkes, "Reimbursement of Tenant Substitutes" ch 16 in Jackson and Wilde.

[338] LT (Covenants) A 1995 s 14; SI 1995/3153.

[339] LPA 1925 s 77(1)(c) (unregistered); LRA 1925 s 24(1)(b) (registered). This is true whether or not the covenant touches and concerns the land.

[340] *Johnsey Estates* v. *Lewis & Manley (Engineering)* (1987) 284 EG 1240, CA (consideration of £1 is value); *Re Lawley* [1911] 2 Ch 530.

[341] *Baker* v. *Merckel* [1960] 1 QB 656, CA (L sued T0, who brought in T1, who brought in T2).

[342] *Warnford Investments* v. *Duckworth* [1979] 1 Ch 127, 140–141, Megarry V-C; *RPH* v. *Mirror Group Newspapers* (1992) 65 P & CR 252, Nicholls V-C; A Belcher [1995] *Conv* 199.

[343] LRA 2002 sch 12 para 20; Law Com 271 (2001), EN [819–820].

[344] Despite *Current Law Statutes 2002*, 9–111.

28

MORTGAGES AND MONEY CHARGES

Mortgages of registered land: legal; equitable. Mortgages of unregistered land: legal, equitable; protection by deposit of title deeds; land charges. Company charges. Statutory charges. Charging orders. Bankruptcy.

[28.01] No student requires any introduction to the concept of debt. What is borrowed has to be repaid with interest. A mortgage[1] adds an extra refinement to this instrument of torture since what is owed is charged[2] on the borrower's land as security for repayment. Everybody knows that:

"a mortgage . . . is a personal contract for a debt secured by an estate".[3]

The lender is protected on the borrower's bankruptcy or the liquidation of a corporate borrower. A borrower who creates the mortgage of the land is, in old-fashioned technical language, the mortgagor, whereas the lender *to whom* the grant of the land is made as security is called the mortgagee.[4]

Land is immovable, a quality which enables a lender to leave the borrower in possession until repayment.[5] If a borrower makes any default in repayment, a legal lender has the right to take possession and a statutory power of sale.[6] Sale ensures that the first lender is able to vindicate his first claim to the value of the land out of the proceeds of sale, with successive lenders standing in a queue behind. What is left after all lenders are satisfied is called the equity, that is more properly the borrower's equity of redemption.

Example. B's house is worth £100,000. He borrowers £90,000 from L secured by a first mortgage. The residual value after repayment of the loan secured on the house is currently £10,000, but this "equity" will vary as interest accrues and repayments are made. If the house increases in value to £200,000 his equity is worth £110,000. Conversely if prices fall, he may owe more than the house is worth, the trap called negative equity.

[1] Chapelle's *LL* (5th ed) ch 11; Cheshire & Burn (16th ed) ch 22; Dixon's *Principles* (3rd ed) ch 10; Goo's *Sourcebook* (3rd ed) ch 17; Gravells, *LL – Text* (2nd ed) ch 9; Grays' *Elements* (3rd ed) ch 12, 539–554, 598–604; Maudsley & Burn *LL – Cases* (7th ed) ch 11; Megarry & Wade (6th ed) ch 19; L Smith, "Security" ch 5 in Birks' *Private Law*; Smith's *Property* Law (4th ed) ch 22; Thompson's *Modern LL* ch 12.
[2] A charge is any mortgage, charge or lien which secures the payment of money on land: LRA 2002 s 132.
[3] *Quarrell* v. *Beckford* (1816) 1 Madd 269, 278, 56 ER 100, Plumer V-C.
[4] Parties: (1) borrower = mortgagor, chargor (charge) or debtor (existing debt); (2) lender = mortgagee, chargee (charge) or creditor (existing debt). According to *Tristram Shandy* it should be Jester and Jestee since "one raises a sum and other a laugh at your expense".
[5] Personal chattels have to be pledged, that is handed over to the lender.
[6] See below [28].

Mortgages are redeemable: the borrower must be able to recover his land free of the mortgage by repaying what is owing.

"In equity, the estate is no more than a pledge or security for the debt."[7]

There is the English mortgage in a nutshell. What more can there possibly be to say?

A. LEGAL MORTGAGES OF REGISTERED LAND

[28.02] A mortgage of registered land[8] is made using a legal charge and is followed by substantive registration in the charges register of the title forming the security. Legal rights pass when the title is registered, after which the mortgage is described as a registered charge.[9]

1. Who can mortgage?

[28.03] Owners powers include the power to charge registered land at law with the payment of money. Legal mortgages of registered land can only be created by registered proprietors, or those entitled to be registered under a transfer, or the owner before first registration.[10]

2. Form of a legal charge

[28.04] A variety of means are available for mortgaging unregistered land,[11] but the only permissible means of creating a legal mortgage of registered land is the charge by deed by way of legal mortgage.[12] This, the legal charge, was an invention of Lord Birkenhead's legislation.[13] It blends the elegance and simplicity of the charge with the strong protective security of the legal mortgage. Solicitors took decades to warm to it, but it has now gained universal acceptance,[14] and for registered land there is no room left for eccentricity since it is the only way to effect a legal mortgage.[15] A deed is essential, at least until mortgages have to be created electronically.[16] A true mortgage created a security against land by transferring an estate (that is an ownership right) in the land to the lender for the duration of the loan,[17] but a legal charge achieves the same

---

[7] *Quarrell* v. *Beckford* (1816) 1 Madd 269, 278, 56 ER 100, Plumer V-C.

[8] LRA 2002 ss 48–57; Law Com 271 (2001), [7.28ff]; DLRR 2003 rr 102–115; DLRR CD ch 7. The old law is reviewed at Law Com 271 (2001), [7.2].

[9] LRA 2002 s 132(1).

[10] LRA 2002 s 24; rules may extend these categories; see also above at [8].

[11] The unregistered definition of mortgage is adopted: LRA 2002 s 132.

[12] LRA 2002 s 23(1).

[13] LPA 1925 ss 1(2)(c), 87; Law Com 271 (2001), [7.2]. Precursors were (1) registered charges under Land Transfer Act 1875; C Sweet (1912) 28 *LQR* 6, 15–17; A Underhill (1911) 27 *LQR* 173, 175–176; (2) statutory mortgages: Conveyancing Act 1881 s 26; LPA 1925 ss 117–120.

[14] G Battersby (1966) 110 *SJ* 818; WA Green (1974) 118 *SJ* 589, 590.

[15] LRA 2002 s 23; Law Com 271 (2001), [4.1–4.31].

[16] There will be power to require mortgages to be created electronically: LRA 2002 ss 91–93; Law Com 271 (2001), [7.6]; see above at [8].

[17] Benefitting rights are also transferred eg the right to make up an access road: *Nationwide BS* v. *James Beauchamp* [2001] EWCA Civ 275, [2001] 3 EGLR 6.

result by earmarking the land as a security for a loan without passing any estate. A form is now prescribed[18] for the skeleton of the charge, which the parties are free to adapt and flesh out.

Title number XYZ 123
[Property]
LEGAL CHARGE
Date: January 1st 2004.
Parties: (1) Borrower and (2) Lender
1. Borrower charges by way of legal mortgage the property with payment to Lender of the money secured by this charge.
2. [Payment covenants].
3. [Provision for interest].
4. [Repayment by the Borrower on a fixed date or by instalments].
Execution as a deed by [Borrower] in the presence of [Witness].

Figure 28-1 A legal charge

This will not impact, therefore, on the practice of institutional lenders to adopt a bald form of charge with financial details set out in a lengthy supplementary document incorporating standard lending conditions. These standard form charges should be lodged at the land registry.[19]

A legal charge is superior to a mortgage in the clarity of its meaning,[20] in the ease with which successive mortgages can be created and in facilitating a single mortgage of freehold and leasehold land. Legal charges of leasehold land may be possible when an old-style mortgage would be a breach of a covenant against assignment.[21]

Unfortunately the rights of lenders are defined in a backward looking manner, a legal charge giving "the same protection, powers and remedies" as a traditional mortgage by demise.[22] A purposive interpretation has held sway,[23] so that the charge substitutes in all respects for the traditional mortgage by demise,[24] giving the same remedies,[25] an identical right to relief from forfeiture of a lease,[26] and the same rights against occupiers and recipients of rents.[27] Roll on the Law Commission, which pro-

---

[18] LRA 2002 s 25; DLRR 2003 r 58, sch 1; DLRR CD ch 7, [24–26]; LR Form CH1.
[19] No doubt the practice in LRR 1925 r 139 will continue.
[20] P Butt [1993] *Conv* 256 (one traditional mortgage had a mammoth sentence of 1299 words).
[21] G Battersby (1966) 110 *SJ* 818; Law Com 271 (2001), [7.2].
[22] LPA 1925 s 87(1).
[23] *Cumberland Court (Brighton)* v. *Taylor* [1964] Ch 29, 36; *Weg Motors* v. *Hales* [1962] Ch 49, 73, Evershed MR.
[24] *Regent Oil Co* v. *Gregory (Hatch End)* [1966] Ch 402, 431, Harman LJ, 435, Salmon LJ (so covenants run); *Esso Petroleum* v. *Harpers (Stourport) Garage* [1968] AC 269, 325G, Lord Pearce.
[25] Eg appointment of a receiver: *Rhodes* v. *Allied Dunbar Pension Services* [1989] 1 WLR 800, CA.
[26] *Chelsea Estates Investment Trust Co* v. *Marche* [1955] Ch 328; *Church Commissioners for England* v. *Ve-Ri-Best Manufacturing Co* [1957] 1 QB 238, Goddard CJ; *Belgravia Insurance Co* v. *Meah* [1964] 1 QB 436, CA; *Hammersmith LBC* v. *Topshop Centres* [1990] Ch 237.
[27] *Grand Junction Co* v. *Bates* [1954] 2 QB 160, Upjohn J obiter; LA Sheridan (1955) 18 *MLR* 301.

poses to remove all thought of nineteenth century law and to produce a uniform legal charge for land and all other forms of property.[28]

3. The mortgage until registration

[28.05] A mortgage generally comes into effect as soon as the document of charge is executed.[29] It will not be uncommon for the mortgage document to be executed at a moment when the borrower is not the owner of the estate being mortgaged (for example because he is buying land the purchase of which is not yet completed). A valid mortgage is created as between the parties to it by a borrower who does not own the land, and this acquires full legal status against the land if he later acquires title. In *First National Bank* v. *Thompson*[30] the mortgage was held to operate by estoppel on its execution between borrower and lender, and to bind the legal estate when the borrower received it, so as to be registrable. The borrower represented that he had legal capacity to mortgage, an estoppel prevented him from denying this, and that estoppel was fed on acquisition of the estate without any recital of title.[31]

4. A registration requirement

[28.06] Substantive registration is required when a registered proprietor grants a mortgage and also when a registered charge is transferred or is itself mortgaged. On the creation of a charge the obligation is to secure registration in the name of the lender as proprietor of the charge.[32] An equitable mortgage arises. Only on completion of the registration against the estate[33] does a mortgage take effect as a legal charge.[34] Legal remedies flow from substantive registration so this is essential to confer full legal remedies, such as the power of sale.[35] Full powers are given subject only to any restriction on the register.[36]

Documents which must be lodged are the mortgage, a copy, and the application form, and these must be accompanied by the fee.[37] Entry in the charges register[38] reveals the existence of the mortgage but not its amount. When the application is completed the lender formerly received a charge certificate, containing the original mortgage deed bound up within the cover of the charge certificate, but these certificates will no longer be issued in the run up to electronic conveyancing.

---

[28] Law Com 204 (1991); at present this is in abeyance because of opposition from the Council of Mortgage Lenders.

[29] An escrow is possible but unlikely: *Allied Irish Bank Group* v. *Hennelley Properties* [2000] CLYB 4665, CA.

[30] [1996] Ch 231, CA.

[31] The borrower acquires land subject to the mortgage and any other interests are deferred in priority to the mortgage: see above [20].

[32] LRA 2002 s 27(2)(f), sch 2 para 8.

[33] S 13(2), 59.

[34] LRA 2002 s 51.

[35] *Grace Rymer Investments* v. *Waite* [1958] Ch 831; *ES Schwab & Co* v. *McCarthy* (1975) 31 P & CR 196. Note, however, that a person entitled to be registered has power to exercise the owner's powers: s 23(2); so the conventional wisdom on the 1925 legislation may no longer hold good.

[36] LRA 2002 s 52.

[37] DLRR 2003 rr 13, 20, 51–55, 58.

[38] DLRR 2003 r 9; *Lever Finance* v. *Needleman's Trustees* [1956] 1 Ch 375, 382, Harman J.

PROPERTY REGISTER
Title number XYZ 123.
All that freehold land known as 23 High Street shown on the filed plan.

PROPRIETORSHIP REGISTER
January 1st 2003.
[Borrower] of 23 High Street.

CHARGES REGISTER
1. CHARGE dated January 1st 2003 to secure the monies therein mentioned.
2. PROPRIETOR Lender.

Figure 28-2 A register showing a mortgage

Registration guarantees the validity of the charge, and any later disposition by the proprietor will take effect subject to it.[39] The borrower is secure against alteration of the register, before default by his occupation[40] and afterwards if the lender has taken possession by the provision deeming the lender's possession to transfer to the borrower.[41] It does not appear that a lender has any protection when out of possession, possibly because monetary entitlement can be adequately compensated by a monetary indemnity.

There are special provisions about how to register a charge of part.[42]

5. Second and later mortgages

(1) Charge without consent

[28.07] The powers of a registered proprietor are free of any limitation unless reflected by an entry in the register. In fact it is common to impose a requirement when taking a first mortgage that the owner will not remortgage the land without the consent of the first lender, however much this practice is deprecated by second lenders. The Act is neutral, leaving it open to the first lender to impose a requirement that its consent be obtained to a second mortgage,[43] but the second lender will only be bound by it if it is protected by a restriction in the register.[44]

(2) Nature of second mortgage

[28.08] Land registration mechanics facilitate the creation of a string of legal mortgages. A borrower who owns a freehold property subject to a first registered mortgage

---

[39] LRA 2002 s 30.
[40] Sch 4 paras 3(2), 6(2).
[41] S 131.
[42] DLRR 2003 r 73.
[43] Law Com 271 (2001), [7.22–7.28].
[44] LRA 2002 s 52.

proves title to a second lender by producing official copies of the register entries, which reveal the first mortgage. Lender 2 applies for registration of his mortgage, leading to entry of the second mortgage on the charges register, an entry of which lender 1 will be informed.[45] The previous practice of issuing a second charge certificate is now discontinued.

(3) Priority

[28.09] Priority is determined by the order of entries on the Charges Register.[46] Lender 1 can sell free of the second mortgage,[47] whereas lender 2's charge is subject to the paramount rights of the first lender. What could be simpler? Registration mechanics are vastly superior to unregistered mechanics, since the registrar sorts the order of mortgages. Priority should be shown in the charges register.[48]

6. Transfers of mortgages

[28.10] A registered charge is always transferable, after which the new lender takes the priority obtained by the original registration.[49] The borrower is bound by the covenants in the mortgage,[50] but he should be joined to gain his agreement to the amount of the debt.[51] Institutional lenders often transfer an entire portfolio to a new lender,[52] though in such cases it is awkward to join all the borrowers affected.

7. Sub-charges

[28.11] A sub-mortgage is a mortgage of the right to receive the loan.[53] This must be in the prescribed form[54] of a sub-charge and it must be registered in the charges register against the charge which is affected by it,[55] after which the registered proprietor of the sub-charge has (by way of extension of the old law) the powers under the charge affected.[56]

---

[45] S 54.

[46] S 48; Law Com 271 (2001), [7.13]; *Mortgage Corp* v. *Nationwide Credit Corp* [1994] Ch 49, 53F, Dillon LJ; *Lloyd* v. *Nationwide Anglia BS* [1996] EGCS 80 (entries on same day). For the priority of applications see above **[8.41]**.

[47] LRA 2002 s 30; see below at **[29.24]**.

[48] S 46; DLRR 2003 r 102.

[49] Registration requirements apply. It must be in the specified form: LRA 2002 s 52; DLRR 2003 r 115; LR Forms TR3, TR4 and AS2; and completed by registration in the name of the new lender: LRA 2002 s 27(3), sch 2 para 10. Registration requirements do not apply to dispositions by operation of law: LRA 2002 s 27(5).

[50] *Regent Oil Co* v. *JA Gregory (Hatch End)* [1966] Ch 402, CA.

[51] Borrowers beware, since this may capitalise interest. Costs of a transfer should not be charged to a borrower, unless in default: *Re Radcliffe* (1856) 22 Beav 201, 52 ER 1085.

[52] LR Form TR4; LR Practice Leaflet 24 (2000)

[53] LRA 2002 s 23(2)(b), 53, 132(1); Law Com 271 (2001), [7.16]; H Woodhouse (1948) 12 *Conv (NS)* 171.

[54] LRA 2002 s 25.

[55] Ss 27(3), 59(3), sch 2 para 11.

[56] S 53; Law Com 271 (2001), [7.11].

B. EQUITABLE MORTGAGES OF REGISTERED LAND

1. Mortgages other than registered charges

[28.12] A mortgage of registered land can be created off the register. The object of doing this is to save the land registry fees inherent in any substantive registration, but the price that has to be paid is that the mortgage will be equitable and the lender will not have full legal remedies. This price might be accepted for a small loan that leaves a large equity – making the need to sell unlikely – or for borrowing that is expected to be short term. Given that registration requirements attach to a mortgage in the form of a registered charge[57] it may be safer to revert to the historical form of equitable mortgage – a contract to create a legal mortgage – in which case it is important to comply with contract formalities; no mortgage is created by deposit of the land certificate.[58]

If enforcement does become necessary, the mortgage must be registered substantively, when, whatever its form, it will take effect as a legal charge.[59]

2. Priority

[28.13] Any mortgage off the register is equitable.[60] Priority as between equitable interests off the register is determined on the principle of "first in time". It follows that a risk inherent in any equitable mortgage is that no priority is secured over earlier mortgages:[61] A has priority over a later mortgage B, even if B is protected on the register and A is not.[62]

3. Protection

[28.14] An equitable mortgage needs protection on the register to prevent its priority being destroyed by the substantive registration of a later legal mortgage.[63] Protection is by way of a notice on the charges register.[64]

---

[57] LRA 1925 ss 25, 27. S 27 makes clear that the penalty for non-registration is loss of legal status, so an equitable mortgage could arise from keeping a legal mortgage off the register, but s 25 suggests that the transaction "only" has effect when in the legal form.

[58] See above **[22.32]**, below **[28.19]**.

[59] LRA 2002 s 51.

[60] Ss 25–27.

[61] This risk was much lower in the past if the lender secured possession of the land certificate. It may be too great a risk today.

[62] LRA 2002 s 28; see above **[20.40]**.

[63] LRA 2002 s 29.

[64] See above **[20.05]**.

C. LEGAL MORTGAGES OF UNREGISTERED LAND

1. Legal mortgages of unregistered land

[28.15] Most mortgages of unregistered land take the form of legal charges. There is no prescribed form, but the crucial thing is to use a deed showing an intention to charge the land.[65]

Protection is required for mortgages, as for any other money charge, either by deposit of the title deeds or by land charges registration.[66]

An occasional diehard may insist on using a true, traditional, mortgage. In contrast to the legal charge the security of the older form of mortgage consists of a transfer of an estate to the lender to hold until he is repaid. From the seventeenth century onwards[67] it was possible to mortgage land leaving the borrower in possession, using the form of a conditional transfer of the legal estate. The lender acquired unwanted ownership of the legal estate during the life of the mortgage, while the borrower was unwontedly stripped of his legal estate. Second mortgages had to be equitable, and there was always the problem of remembering to re-transfer the estate when the first loan was repaid.[68] Lord Birkenhead's legislation solved these problems. It prohibited transfer of a legal estate in land,[69] and instead required a mortgage to be by way of long legal lease of the property, traditionally called a "demise".[70] If *freehold* land was mortgaged after 1925, the length of the term adopted was always 3,000 years, long enough to pass all real value in the land to the lender.[71] "Cesser on redemption" ensures that when the loan is repaid the mortgage demise becomes a "satisfied term" and disappears.[72] Second mortgages require a reversionary lease.[73] *Leasehold* land was sub-demised for a term traditionally ten days shorter than the lease being mortgaged.[74]

All this complexity explains why legal charges have triumphed. It is time to implement the Law Commission report[75] which proposed complete abolition of true mortgages.[76] A free standing definition of the rights of a lender under a legal charge is required, since otherwise it will always remain necessary to refer back to the old law.

---

[65] *Sopher* v. *Mercer* [1967] CLYB 2543 (document omitting words "by way of legal mortgage").

[66] See below **[28.21ff]**, **[28.28ff]**.

[67] From the time of Glanville (died 1190) until the 17th century the lender had to take possession: JL Barton (1967) 83 *LQR* 229.

[68] Which was held on trust for the borrower: *Re King decd* [1962] 1 WLR 632, Buckley J.

[69] Old mortgages were converted: LPA 1925 sch 1 parts VII–VIII; conversion to a legal charge could occur by notice: s 87(2)–(3).

[70] Pre-1926 examples: *Aldridge* v. *Duke* (1679) Rep t Finch 439, 23 ER 239; *Ex p Knott* (1806) 11 Ves 609, 32 ER 1225; *Hurst* v. *Hurst* (1852) 16 Beav 372, 51 ER 822; *Jones* v. *Rhind* (1869) 17 WR 1091; *Re Russell Road Purchase Monies Mortgage* (1871) LR 12 Eq 78.

[71] LPA 1925 s 85 (purported conveyance by transfer).

[72] LPA 1925 ss 5, 116; this replaced the Satisfied Terms Act 1845.

[73] Entitling the first lender to possession against the second lender, but giving a better right than the borrower's freehold estate; *Re Moore & Hulm's C (No 1)* [1912] 2 Ch 105, Joyce J.

[74] LPA 1925 s 86 (attempted mortgage by assignment); *Taylor* v. *London & County Banking Co* [1901] 2 Ch 231, CA.

[75] Law Com 204 (1991), [2.17–2.19].

[76] As in registered land: LRA 2002 s 4(1)(g), (8), 13.

2. First registration

[28.16] First registration with title absolute is made subject to all mortgages and charges existing at the time of first registration.[77] Mortgages of unregistered land should be protected by deposit of deeds or land charges registration, and consideration should also be given to entry of a caution against first registration.[78]

Since 1997, first legal mortgages have themselves attracted compulsory first registration. The current trigger[79] applies where (1) the mortgage is protected by the deposit of the title deeds, (2) it will take effect as a first mortgage in priority to any others and (2) that it affects a registrable estate – a freehold or a leasehold with seven plus years outstanding. The borrower is under a duty to apply for first registration but in practice the lender will take over the registration since the sanction of avoidance of the title after two months[80] threatens his security.

Of course the commonest situation is that unregistered land is sold to a buyer who is obliged to borrow to fund the purchase; in this case the mortgage can be seen as a dealing by a person entitled to apply to be registered.[81]

D. EQUITABLE MORTGAGES OF UNREGISTERED LAND

1. Nature of equitable mortgages

[28.17] Before 1926 any second mortgage had to be equitable. The 1925 legislation swept away the obstacles to the creation of a sequence of legal mortgages. It should have gone further and insisted that any security had to be legal, given that lenders generally want a clear-cut right to possession and sale, but unfortunately the possibility of creating equitable mortgages was left open. It is common to accept the lesser security of an equitable mortgage[82] when the loan is small, the arrangement is short-term, or the need to borrow is urgent.[83] A higher interest rate is usually demanded in return for the offer of a limited security.[84] The invisible burden on the land represented by the money charge must be protected either by deposit of the title deeds or by protective registration.[85]

2. Contractual basis

[28.18] *Walsh* v. *Lonsdale*[86] demonstrates that a contract for a legal X creates an equitable X where X is a lease, and the same is true of any given X. Equitable mortgages

---

[77] LRA 2002 s 11; DLRR 2003 r 32. Many pre-1926 (possessory) titles were useless because they made no mention of existing mortgages: E Harvey (1912) 28 *LQR* 26, 28.

[78] LRA 2002 s 15(1), (8).

[79] LRA 2002 ss 4(1)(g), 6(2); see above **[9.24]**.

[80] LRA 2002 s 7(1), (2)(b); DLRR 2003 r 21, see above **[9.27]**.

[81] DLRR 2003 r 35; see above **[9.36]**.

[82] For mortgages of equitable interests in land (ie beneficial interests under trusts) see above **[16.23]**.

[83] *Keys* v. *Williams* (1838) 3 Y & C 55, 160 ER 612.

[84] *Fitzgerald's Trustee* v. *Mellersh* [1892] 1 Ch 385, 389, Chitty J; *London County & Westminster Bank* v. *Tompkins* [1918] 1 KB 515, 527, CA.

[85] See below **[28.21ff]**, **[28.28ff]**.

[86] (1882) 21 Ch D 9, CA.

generally take the form of a contract to create a legal mortgage[87] or (today) a contract for a legal charge.[88]

An agreement creates an immediate mortgage even if the lender has to make a demand before he can insist on execution of a legal mortgage.[89] If a legal mortgage does follow the two together create a single security.[90] Equitable security arises only after the money is actually advanced,[91] because only then is specific performance available to supplement common law damages and specific performance is the key to the creation of rights in the land itself.

Modern law requires a contract relating to land to be in writing, and signed by both contracting parties, full 1989 Act formalities being applied by *United Bank of Kuwait* v. *Sahib*.[92] Mere deposit of the land certificate created no charge.[93] No security exists in the absence of formalised writing.

3. Former mortgages by deposit

[28.19] Before the 1989 Act an equitable mortgage was created by a simple deposit of the title deeds with the intention of securing a loan on land. This ancient principle was settled firmly as law in *Russel* v. *Russel* (1783).[94] It could be a direction to hold deeds as a security[95] or a declaration of an intention to deposit deeds when they were available.[96] Joint owners must all consent to the deposit.[97] No formality was required[98] – since deposit of the deeds was part performance of the oral agreement – though it was always best to have a written memorandum.[99] This type of mortgage has been abandoned as a result of the changes in 1989.

4. Passive security

[28.20] Active securities such as legal mortgages entitle the lender to sell after a default. Passive securities provide priority and perfectly adequate protection against

[87] *Downsview Nominees* v. *First City Corp* [1993] AC 295, 311C–D, Lord Templeman; *Edge* v. *Worthington* (1786) 1 Cox Eq 211, 29 ER 1133; *Birch* v. *Ellames* (1794) 2 Anst 427, 431, 145 ER 924, Macdonald CB.

[88] It seems that an *equitable* mortgage can still be made by written assignment of the estate being mortgaged: *Eyre* v. *McDowell* (1861) 9 HLC 619, 11 ER 871; this is not barred by LPA 1925 ss 85–86.

[89] *Re Cook ex p Izard* (1874) LR 9 Ch App 271; *Crosbie-Hill* v. *Sayer* [1908] 1 Ch 866, Parker J.

[90] *Orakpo* v. *Manson Investments* [1978] AC 95, 105D, Lord Diplock; *Property Discount* v. *Lyon* [1981] 1 WLR 300, CA.

[91] *Rogers* v. *Challis* (1859) 27 Beav 175, 54 ER 68; *Sichel* v. *Mosenthal* (1862) 30 Beav 371, 54 ER 932.

[92] [1997] Ch 107, CA; M Oldham [1995] *CLJ* 249; M Robinson (1997) 113 *LQR* 533; see above **[22.32]**. Also *Secured Residential Funding* v. *Douglas Goldberg Hendeles* [2000] Times April 26th, CA (advance cheque released before execution of mortgage document).

[93] Law Com 271 (2001), [7.9–7.10].

[94] (1783) 1 Bro CC 269, 28 ER 1121; *Dixon* v. *Muccleston* (1872) LR 8 Ch App 155, 162; *Maddison* v. *Alderson* (1883) 8 App Cas 467; *Re Wallis & Simmonds (Builders)* [1974] 1 WLR 391; *Re Alton Corp* [1985] BCLC 27.

[95] *Fenwick* v. *Potts* (1856) 8 De GM & G 506, 44 ER 485; *Daw* v. *Terrell* (1863) 33 Beav 351, 55 ER 351.

[96] *Ashworth* v. *Mounsey* (1853) 9 Exch 175, 156 ER 75; *Daw* v. *Terrell* (1863) 33 Beav 218, 55 ER 351; *Tebb* v. *Hodge* (1869) LR 5 CP 73; *Bank of India* v. *Mody* [1998] 12 LSG 29.

[97] *Thames Guaranty* v. *Campbell* [1985] QB 210, 233C–D.

[98] LPA 1925 s 40; *Pattle* v. *Anstruther* (1893) 69 LT 175, CA; *Re Beetham* (1887) 18 QBD 766, CA; *Bank of India* v. *Mody* [1998] 12 LSG 229.

[99] *Ex p Combe* (1810) 17 Ves 369, 34 ER 142, Lord Eldon. On the use of title deeds as security for bail: *R(JR) Stevens* v. *Truro Magistrates' Court* [2001] EWHC Admin 558, [2001] 1 WLR 144.

insolvency. An equitable charge is created by any arrangement to earmark some land as a guarantee against the debtor's insolvency, that is simply by designating an asset to be used in discharge of a particular debt[100] and also by an agreement for value to create a charge.[101] No ownership right passes to the creditor,[102] no right to possession,[103] and no right to sell out of court.[104]

A specialised form is a *floating charge*, where the security consists of all the current assets of the company, not just its land[105] and machinery, but its stock and anything else.[106] The charge hovers over the class of assets designated in the debenture deed, allowing the company to continue to trade with its assets. Crystallisation is the process by which the charge "becomes a fixed charge on the assets comprised in the security"[107] – events which cause this including cessation of business, liquidation, and appointment of a receiver.[108]

An *equitable lien* is a passive equitable charge[109] imposed automatically by equity as an incident of a contract. Its most common manifestation is the unpaid seller's lien, imposed after the buyer has taken possession of land until the seller has been paid the full purchase price. It requires protective registration or occupation.[110]

E. MORTGAGES PROTECTED BY DEPOSIT OF TITLE DEEDS

[28.21] This relates primarily to mortgages of unregistered land in existence before the recent legislation which has caused first mortgages to trigger compulsory first registration.[111]

1. Protection

[28.22] A money charge appropriates specific land to payment of a particular sum of money. Most are mortgages securing a loan, so as to be redeemable when the debt is repaid, but it could be the cost of making up a road or an obligation to repay legal aid contributions from property recovered by publicly funded litigation. No visible sign marks the fact that the land is acting as a security, so any mortgage requires protection. One method is to require the borrower to deposit his title deeds with the lender,

---

[100] *Palmer* v. *Carey* [1926] AC 703, HL; *Swiss Bank Corp* v. *Lloyds Bank* [1982] AC 584, HL; *Carreras Rothmans* v. *Freeman Mathers Treasure* [1985] Ch 203.

[101] *Re Earl Lucan* (1890) 45 Ch D 470 (not a volunteer); *Re Kelcey* [1899] 2 Ch 530.

[102] *Bland* v. *Ingram's Estates* [2001] EWCA Civ 1088, [2002] All ER 264, [18], Nouse LJ, [82], Hale LJ.

[103] See below **[29.15ff]**.

[104] *Orakpo* v. *Manson Investments* [1978] AC 95, HL; *Coptic* v. *Bailey* [1972] Ch 446, Whitford J; see below **[29.26]**, **[29.29]**.

[105] Lenders do not gain priority over preferential debts (back taxes: IA 1986 s 386) unless they also take a fixed charge over land.

[106] RH Pennington (1960) 23 *MLR* 630; *Smith* v. *Bridgend BC* [2002] UKHL 58, [2002] 1 AC 336, HL esp at [41], Lord Hoffmann.

[107] *Downsview Nominees* v. *First City Corp* [1993] AC 298, 311D–E, Lord Templeman.

[108] The receiver may well carry the more extensive powers of administrative receivership that is the power to continue to trade in the hope of rescuing an ailing company from liquidation.

[109] *Capital Finance Co* v. *Stokes* [1969] Ch 261, CA.

[110] See above **[20.05]**, **[20.19]**.

[111] See above **[28.16]**.

the absence of the deeds being a red danger signal to any potential buyer.[112] The old law continues for older legal mortgages and new equitable mortgages secured by deposit.

A lender has the right to the title deeds,[113] formerly as an incident of ownership of the estate mortgaged, and now by statutory right.[114] Apparently a lender is not liable for loss of the title deeds so long as the mortgage continues, but on redemption the deeds must be delivered to the borrower, who can take action at that time if the lender has lost them.[115] Deposit of the title deeds takes a mortgage outside the requirement of registration,[116] but what counts as a deposit is not at all clear: safety requires a lender to take all deeds or at least enough to prevent the borrower deducing title without them.[117]

2. Loss of protection by deposit

(1) Fraud and estoppel

[28.23] Priority is lost if a lender holding the deeds defrauds a later lender[118] or entrusts the deeds to a fraudulent agent.[119] Estoppel works to remove priority from a lender[120] who was honest but whose conduct misled a later lender into believing that his loan no longer existed, for example by failing to disclose his first mortgage when asked[121] or by executing a receipt.[122]

(2) Failure to obtain or retain the title deeds

[28.24] Mortgages of unregistered land are registrable as land charges unless protected by a deposit of documents relating to the legal estate affected. The absence of case-law since 1925 suggests that mortgages are registered in cases of doubt – where some of the relevant deeds are unavailable or where a lender protected by deposit later parts with the deeds.

If a mortgage was protected under the old law, it remains protected today, for the Law of Property Act 1925 does not prejudicially affect

"any question arising out of or consequent upon any omission to obtain or any other absence of possession by any person of any documents relating to a legal estate in land."[123]

---

[112] *Re White Rose Cottage* [1964] Ch 483, 491, Wilberforce J.
[113] Including previous land charges searches: *Clayton* v. *Clayton* [1930] 2 Ch 12, 21, Maugham J.
[114] LPA 1925 ss 85, 86, 96 (right to copies); *Jenner* v. *Morris* (1866) LR 1 Ch App 603; *Leathes* v. *Leathes* (1877) 5 Ch D 221.
[115] *Lewis* v. *Plunket* [1937] Ch 306; *Browning* v. *Handiland Group* (1976) 35 P & CR 345.
[116] LCA 1972 s 4(2); see above [28.21ff].
[117] *Roberts* v. *Croft* (1857) 2 De G & J 1, 44 ER 887, Cranworth LC.
[118] *Heath* v. *Crealock* (1873) LR 18 Eq 215; *Battison* v. *Hobson* [1896] 2 Ch 403.
[119] *Perry Herrick* v. *Attwood* (1857) 2 De G & J 21, 44 ER 895; *Brocklesby* v. *Temperance PBS* [1895] AC 173, HL; *Rimmer* v. *Webster* [1902] 2 Ch 163.
[120] Estoppel may bind later lenders: *Fung Ping Shan* v. *Thong Shun* [1918] AC 403, HL.
[121] *Mangels* v. *Dixon* (1852) 3 HLC 702, 10 ER 278.
[122] *Hunter* v. *Walters* (1871) LR 7 Ch App 75.
[123] LPA 1925 s 13 qualifies s 199 (no notice) but not LCA 1972 s 4 (effect of non-registration).

Section 13 was surely intended to preserve pre-1926 law for pre-1926 mortgages. Megarry & Wade postulate[124] that the old law is also preserved for new mortgages, but it was so inadequate that it seems wrong to strive officiously to keep it alive.

(3) Redundant protection where deeds not obtained

[28.25] Before 1926 the only means of protection was to take the title deeds. A lender who asked diligently for the deeds[125] and was met by a reasonable excuse[126] for non-production took free of any earlier mortgage.[127] Perhaps more was required of an equitable mortgage lender and the later Victorian period saw a toughening of attitude,[128] but "surprisingly frail excuses" continued to be accepted.[129] It may have been more logical to allow excuses when deposit was the only possible protection but quite unfair today when any lender can easily make a protective registration. There should be, and is, a duty of diligence to obtain the deeds.[130]

(4) Redundant protection where title deeds not retained

[28.26] A sensible lender clings tight to the documents of title, or registers if he must part with them. Before 1926 priority was lost by gross negligence but mere carelessness was overlooked. The first lender secured on the *Thatched House*[131] brought the deeds to the house, and released them to the borrower. He took them to another room for an hour, and executed a second mortgage, before returning the deeds to the first lender. Priority of the first lender was retained despite his idiocy, though of course the second lender was also pretty stupid not to insist on keeping and holding the deeds. Absurdity followed in *Northern Counties of England Fire Insurance Co* v. *Whipp*.[132] After a company had taken a legal mortgage over its manager's house, the deeds were deposited in the company safe. Using his duplicate keys, the manager removed the deeds and deposited them with Whipp. The company retained priority, since it was not obliged to guard deeds as if they were fierce dogs.[133] Breathtaking in its unfairness, it is difficult to believe that this decision would now be followed. Registration is so easy that there should now be a duty of care in retention of the deeds.

---

[124] (6th ed), [19.094] n 64.

[125] Priority is lost if no inquiry is made: *Clarke* v. *Palmer* (1882) 21 Ch D 124; *Lloyds Banking Co* v. *Jones* (1885) 29 Ch D 221; *Berwick & Co* v. *Price* [1905] Ch 632.

[126] Inadequate excuses: *Hiern* v. *Mill* (1806) 13 Ves 114, 33 ER 237, Erskine LC; *Oliver* v. *Hinton* [1899] 2 Ch 264, CA.

[127] *Hewitt* v. *Loosemoor* (1851) 9 Hare 449, 68 ER 380; *Espin* v. *Pemberton* (1859) 3 De G & J 547, 44 ER 1380, Chelmsford LC; *Agra Bank* v. *Barry* (1874) LR 7 HL 135; *Whipp's* case (1884) 26 Ch D 482, 491–492, Fry LJ.

[128] *Taylor* v. *Russell* [1892] AC 244, 262, Lord Macnaghten.

[129] Megarry & Wade (6th ed), [19.206].

[130] *Walker* v. *Linom* [1907] 2 Ch 104, Parker J.

[131] *Peter* v. *Russell* (1716) 1 Eq Cas Abr 321, 21 ER 1075; *Thorpe* v. *Holdsworth* (1868) LR 7 Eq 139; *Garside* v. *Liverpool Railway PBBS* (1897) 13 TLR 189, CA.

[132] (1884) 26 Ch D 482, CA; *Taylor* v. *Russell* [1891] 1 Ch 5, Kay J; *Taylor* v. *London & County Banking Co* [1901] 2 Ch 231, 260, Stirling LJ.

[133] At 493, Fry LJ.

3. Registered titles

[28.27] Between 1925 and 2003 the unregistered scheme of deposit was replicated for legal mortgages of registered land by depositing the land certificate at the registry and issuing a charge certificate to the lender. Charge certificates will no longer be issued.[134]

F. MORTGAGES PROTECTED AS LAND CHARGES

[28.28] Land charges are the matters requiring registration against the name of an estate owner who creates them while title remains unregistered.

1. Mortgages

[28.29] Registration is an obvious means of giving tangible protection to an invisible mortgage, and one which has been required since 1928 for all mortgages of unregistered land not protected by deposit of the deeds.[135]

A puisne[136] mortgage of class C(i)[137] is a legal mortgage which is not protected by a deposit of documents relating to the legal estate affected.[138] Usually a first lender retains the title deeds, so second mortgages will have to be registered. It is convenient to restrict class C(i) to legal mortgages since this enables a person investigating title to tell whether a mortgage is legal or equitable. An equitable mortgage is registrable in class C(iii)[139] as a general equitable charge if it charges a loan[140] on specific property and binds the legal estate.[141] Equitable mortgages usually come second to a legal mortgage secured by deposit,[142] and so are registrable.

Equitable mortgages take the form of a contract to create a legal mortgage. However, if a mortgage creates an immediate equitable charge on land it is registrable as an general equitable charge – class C(iii).[143] If the *only* security is a right to request the creation of a legal mortgage in the future, class C(iv) registration is required as an estate contract by *Williams* v. *Burlington Investments*[144] and C(iii) registration is ineffective. Safety first: equitable mortgages may be best entered under both classes.

---

[134] See above **[8.36]**. This is a retrograde step.

[135] LCA 1972 s 2; *Ministry of Housing & Local Government* v. *Sharp* [1970] 2 QB 223, 280, Cross LJ.

[136] Pronounced "puny".

[137] CLR *Report 1995–1996* showed less than 30,000 C(i) registration and 1,500 in class C(iii); the volume must now be reduced almost to zero by changes to the first registration triggers.

[138] LCA 1972 s 2(4)(i); local land charges are not registrable under the central system.

[139] Law Com 18 (1969), [63].

[140] Not an agreement to divide the proceeds of sale: *Thomas* v. *Rose* [1968] 1 WLR 1797, 1807, Megarry J. Charges for indemnity are excluded.

[141] As to mortgages of equitable interests, see above **[16.23]**.

[142] LCA 1972 s 2(4)(iii).

[143] *Property Discount Corp* v. *Lyon Group* [1981] 1 WLR 300, CA.

[144] (1977) 121 SJ 424, HL.

2. Other money charges as land charges

[28.30] A lien is a money charge that arises automatically by operation of law,[145] and if title is unregistered it requires protection in class C(iii). The most common example – the unpaid seller's lien – arises on a sale when some of the price[146] is left outstanding at the time of sale, giving the seller a charge on the land to secure the payment of the remainder of the price, unless he takes a formal mortgage.[147] In *Chattey* v. *Farndale Holdings*[148] 400 flats were to be constructed near the West London Air Terminal and two potential purchasers of individual flats each paid 20% deposits. Even though the contracts were conditional on planning permission being obtained, it was held that the purchasers had a lien for the return of their deposits which had proprietary force against a purchaser of the whole development.[149]

G. COMPANY CHARGES

1. Registrable charges

[28.31] The companies legislation[150] requires registration of charges on a company's[151] property. The duty to register is imposed on the company,[152] but the penalty primarily affects the lender and it is up to the lender to make sure that he is covered by ensuring that his formality is observed. Particulars of any charge must be sent to the Companies' House within a strict time-limit of 21 days from the creation of the charge,[153] after which priority may be lost.

Registration is required of any security interest, either when the company creates a charge itself or when it acquires property subject to an existing charge.[154] The object of the legislation is to get at money charges, that is mortgages, so burdens affecting land itself (such as easements) are outside the net. Fixed charges include legal mortgages,[155] attempted mortgages by assignment,[156] and equitable mortgages,[157] mortgages of land outside the jurisdiction, mortgages of any interest in land, and charges

---

[145] *UCB Bank* v. *Beasley* [1996] CLYB 4951, CA (loss by non-disclosure on inquiry); MP Thompson [1996] *Conv* 44.

[146] *Uziell-Hamilton* v. *Keen* (1971) 22 P & CR 655; *Woolf Project Management* v. *Woodtrek* [1988] 1 EGLR 179 (not contract to pay additional sums if extra land developed); *Barclays Bank* v. *Estates & Commercial* [1997] 1 WLR 415, CA (arrangement to share profits on development was registrable).

[147] *Nationwide Anglia BS* v. *Ahmed* (1995) 70 P & CR 381, CA.

[148] (1998) 75 P & CR 298, CA.

[149] One was binding and the other void for non-registration at the time of first registration of the new developer's title.

[150] Companies Act 1985 part XII ss 395–409; G McCormack [1994] *JBL* 587; J de Lacy [2001] *Conv* 122. Reforms enacted by Companies Act 1989 s 93 have not been implemented.

[151] It also applies to charges created under the Limited Liability Partnerships Act 2000 s 15; SIs 2001/927, 2002/913.

[152] S 399; the company itself must also maintain a register.

[153] S 395(1); *Re CL Nye* [1971] Ch 442 (registrar's certificate conclusive as to date). Electronic delivery is allowed by SI 2000/3373.

[154] S 400; *Capital Finance Co* v. *Stokes* [1969] 1 Ch 261, CA (21 days from acquisition).

[155] S 396(4).

[156] *Re Kent & Sussex Sawmills* [1947] Ch 177.

[157] *Re Wallis & Simmonds (Builders)* [1974] 1 WLR 391; *Re Molton Finance* [1968] Ch 325, CA.

on future interests. Floating charges affect some part of the company's property, but only turn into a fixed charge on specific land when the charge crystallises, for example because the company fails to pay a debt.[158] Enforcement procedures must be registered within seven days.[159] Excluded are mortgages of rents and rentcharges,[160] future charges over present property,[161] and liens which arise automatically.[162]

2. Non-registration

[28.32] The charge remains fully effective against the company and contractual liability is unaffected,[163] though in *Smith* v. *Bridgend CBC*[164] the House of Lords held invalidity of the charge also prevented enforcement of rights conferred by the change, such as the right to plant on the land. The converse decision of the Court of Appeal was startling and unorthodox.[165]

Three major penalties are imposed for missing the deadline for registration. Officers of the company may be liable to criminal sanctions. Court application is essential before the mortgage can be admitted for late registration,[166] and this requires proof of a ground for late admission, such as inadvertence, and a reason for exercising the discretion to permit late registration.[167] Finally, priority is lost since the mortgage is void before the court order,[168] and registration will be allowed only subject to a *Joplin* proviso – that is the recognition of existing rights to priority.[169]

3. Registration of company charges affecting unregistered land

[28.33] The object of Companies Act registration is to tell people dealing with the company the financial position of the company, whereas land charges registration aims to tell the buyer of a particular piece of land what mortgages affect it, so the two registration systems have completely different aims.[170] After 1970,[171] land charges

---

[158] Companies Act 1985 s 396(1)(f); *Smith* v. *Bridgend CBC* [2001] UKHL 58, [2002] 1 AC 336; LS Sealey [1998] *CLJ* 22.

[159] Companies Act 1985 s 405.

[160] S 396(1)(a) as substituted.

[161] *Williams* v. *Burlington Investments* (1971) 121 SJ 424, HL; *Re Gregory Love & Co* [1916] 1 Ch 203; *Re Jackson & Bassford* [1906] 2 Ch 467.

[162] *London & Cheshire Insurance Co* v. *Laplagrene Property Co* [1971] Ch 499; *Re Overseas Aviation Engineering (GB)* [1963] Ch 24, CA; *Re Wallis & Simmonds (Builders)* [1974] 1 WLR 391. If an express charge is void, no lien arises: *Capital Finance Co* v. *Stokes* [1969] 1 Ch 261, CA; *Burston Finance* v. *Speirway* [1974] 1 WLR 1648.

[163] Companies Act 1985 s 404(1)–(2).

[164] [2001] UKHL 58, [2002] 1 AC 336.

[165] At [19], Lord Hoffmann.

[166] Companies Act 1985 s 404; *R* v. *Registrar of Companies ex p Central Bank of India* [1986] QB 1114, CA; G McCormack [1986] *JBL* 282; *Re Chantry House Developments* [1990] BCLC 813, Scott J (interlocutory application on motion is permitted).

[167] Companies Act 1985 s 404(1) (five grounds); *Victoria Housing Estates* v. *Ashpurton Estates* [1983] Ch 110, CA.

[168] *Re Monolithic Building Co* [1915] 1 Ch 643, CA; *Re Telomatic* [1994] 1 BCLC 90, 97. Contrast a case where removal is ordered after an initially valid registration: *Exeter Trust* v. *Screenways* [1991] BCLC 888.

[169] Companies Act 1985 s 404(1)–(2); *Watson* v. *Duff Morgan Vermont (Holdings)* [1974] 1 All ER 794; *Re Chantry House Developments* [1990] BCLC 813, Scott J; *Re Telomatic* [1994] 1 BCLC 90.

[170] DM Hare & T Flanagan [1982] *Conv* 43.

[171] LPA 1969 s 26; LCA 1972 s 3(7).

affecting unregistered land must be registered and companies registration is not sufficient. Floating charges (which affect all property held from time to time rather than
specific land) do not require land charges registration, whenever created. Before 1970
Companies Act registration was all that was required.[172] This reduced the burden of
searching, but was really illogical; in fact little time was saved since a search was
still required for other burdens.[173] The exception has now been removed[174] and dual
registration is required. All purchasers must carry out a land charges search, or land
registration search as appropriate. Charges can only be cancelled on production of a
memorandum of satisfaction accompanied by a statutory declaration.[175]

4.   Mortgages by companies affecting registered land

[28.34] Before a charge by a UK company is sent to the land registry it must first be
subjected to companies registration, and the certificate of companies registration will
be needed to enable title to the charge to be registered.[176] If this has not been done
the register must contain a note that the charge is subject to invalidity under the
companies provisions.

H. STATUTORY CHARGES

1.   Registration of local land charges

[28.35] Local land charges are public burdens recorded by the district councils,
including for example liability to contribute to the cost of making up a road, and road
building agreements.[177] Some are burdens affecting the use of land, but others are
pure money charges. A common example is frontagers' charges when a road is made
up by the highway authority. Registers of local land charges are kept by district councils, operating off the land register.[178] However, when a local land charge consists of
a money charge on a particular piece of registered land and it becomes necessary to
realise it, the necessary first step is substantive registration of the charge at the land
registry. The public authority which has imposed the charge on the land can then
enforce it as a registered charge, that is by sale out of court.[179]

---

[172] *Property Discount Corp* v. *Lyon Group* [1981] 1 WLR 300, 312C–H, Brightman LJ.
[173] *Williams* v. *Burlington Investments* (1977) 121 SJ 424, HL; *Property Discount Corp* v. *Lyon Group*
[1981] 1 WLR 300, CA.
[174] LCA 1972 s 3(7).
[175] Companies Act 1985 s 403.
[176] LRA 2002 s 121; DLRR 2003 r 110. See also the rejection policy, above at **[8.39]**.
[177] *Overseas Investment Services* v. *Simcobuild Construction* (1995) 70 P & CR 322, CA. They bind the
estate and are lost on escheat (unless preserved by the vesting order): *Hackney LBC* v. *Crown Estates
Commissioners* (1996) 72 P & CR 233, Knox J.
[178] LRA 2002 sch 3 para 6; Law Com 271 (2001), [5.80–5.83]; they are no longer overriding interests,
though the effect is the same.
[179] LRA 2002 s 55; DLRR 2003 rr 78, 104–105; DLRR CD ch 7, [23–26]; LR Form SC plus application
form.

2. Statutory charges unregistered land

[28.36] Statutory charges are imposed by an Act of Parliament with the object of enabling a person who has been forced to spend money on land to recoup it from the land owner, the cost being charged on the land, so that the person who has spent money may register the charge and then act as if it had been mortgaged.[180]

Statutory charges against unregistered titles fall into two classes of land charge. Class A dating from 1888 applies to rare cases of charges created by personal application, whereas Class B charges arise automatically, the most numerous being the legal aid charge imposed on property recovered as a result of a successful publicly funded action.[181] Against a registered title, protection for the charge is given by a land registry notice.[182] However, if realisation becomes necessary the charge must be registered substantively and when it is, whatever its form, it will take effect as a legal charge.[183]

3. Inland Revenue Charges for Inheritance Tax

[28.37] The Inland Revenue can impose a charge on land to secure unpaid inheritance tax. If title is unregistered, this needs to be protected as a land charge of Class D(i).[184] Corresponding protection is provided against a registered title by entry of a land registry notice. Until it is protected normal priority rules are suspended and only an honest purchaser is allowed to defeat the unprotected interest.[185]

I. CHARGING ORDERS

1. Nature

[28.38] Any unsecured debt can be charged on land owned by the debtor by a charging order. This is an ancient remedy to enforce a court judgment for debt, much used, and provided with a modern streamlined procedure by the Charging Orders Act 1979[186] and the Woolf reforms.[187]

---

[180] LCA 1972 ss 2(2)–(3), 4(1)–(3), sch 2; *R* v. *Land Registry* (1889) 24 QBD 178. CLR *Report 1995–1996* showed no class A entries and less than 5,000 in class B.

[181] Legal Aid Act 1974 s 9; SI 1989/339 reg. 95; S Shute (1993) 109 *LQR* 636.

[182] LRA 2002 s 50; Law Com 271 (2001), [7.37–7.42]; DLRR 2003 rr 104–105; DLRR CD ch 7, [23–26]; LR Form SC plus application form.

[183] LRA 2002 s 51.

[184] LCA 1972 s 2(5)(i); *Lord Advocate* v. *Countess of Moray* [1905] AC 531, HL; *Bristol Corp* v. *Virgin* [1978] 2 KB 622, 627–628. CLR *Report 1995–1996* noted only 400 or so Inland Revenue Charges a year.

[185] Inheritance Tax Act 1984 s 237, as amended by TLATA 1996; Law Com 271 (2001), [5.22ff]; LRA 2002 s 31; DLRR 2003 rr 104–105.

[186] Law Com 74 (1976).

[187] CPR 73; PD 73; *Towards Effective Enforcement* (LCD, 2001).

2.   The charge

[28.39] The basis is that an unsecured judgment debt is charged on land but only after the court has made a charging order. It is available to creditors who do not hold an existing mortgage or security, though a charging order may be allowed if a creditor has a security but its validity is in doubt.[188]

The first step is a personal action against the debtor and is not registrable. After obtaining judgment for a fixed sum of money[189] plus costs[190] the creditor can then apply for a charging order if no other means of enforcement is in operation.[191] Application is usually made to the court whose judgment is being enforced.[192] When the order is made it imposes a proprietary charge[193] on "such property of the debtor as may be specified in the order".[194] Land is a particularly appropriate target for the enforcement of a debt since it is immoveable and easily saleable. Charging orders are also used to collect council tax,[195] child support,[196] and to confiscate the profits of crime.[197]

3.   Procedure

[28.40] Charging order procedure involves two stages.[198]

Application is made for an interim charging order on a claim form.[199] At this stage the procedure is unilateral: the creditor applies and the debtor is not yet able to dispute it. A single claim can be used to seek several charging orders against separate assets.[200] Evidence must establish the judgment debt, target specific property owned by the debtor and identify others who are potential objectors. The interim order is an almost automatic response to application documents which are in order and acts to impose a temporary charge on the target land.[201]

A court hearing is required before it is decided to make a final charging order. All those interested must be given time (at least 21 days) to decide whether to participate in the court hearing at which the judicial discretion is exercised. The debtor is entitled to object, but so too is anyone else who has a proprietary interest or something analogous.[202] The application for the interim order must include the names of all known

---

[188] *Gillespie* v. *Riddell* [1909] AC 130, HL; *First National Securities* v. *Hegerty* ([1985] QB 850, CA; J Price [1989] *Conv* 133.

[189] COA 1979 s 1(1).

[190] *Holder* v. *APC Supperstone* [2000] 1 All ER 473, Evans-Lombe J.

[191] *Mercantile Credit Co* v. *Ellis* [1987] CLYB 2917 (instalment order).

[192] COA 1979 s 1(2); CPR 73.3(2).

[193] COA 1979 s 1(1)–(3).

[194] S 1(1).

[195] SI 1992/613, regs 32–36, 50–57, sch 2.

[196] Child Support Act 1991 ss 36, 40.

[197] Proceeds of Crime Act 2002.

[198] The final order can be set aside if made without leave: *Clarke* v. *Coutts & Co* [2002] EWCA Civ 943, [2002] 26 EG 140 (CS).

[199] CPR 73; Claim form N379.

[200] PD 73.1.3.

[201] *Clark* v. *Chief Land Registrar* [1994] Ch 370, CA; *Haly* v. *Barry* (1868) LR 3 Ch App 452; *Brereton* v. *Edwards* (1888) 21 QBD 488, CA.

[202] *Banque National de Paris* v. *Montman* [2000] 1 BCLC 576, Ch D.

creditors,[203] and the court may order that other parties should also be served. Unsecured creditors do not have standing to object. The court weighs all circumstances supported by the evidence before it,[204] including the personal circumstances of the debtor and possible prejudice to other secured creditors.[205] Conditions may be imposed and the interim order may be varied.[206] If there is an order allowing a debt to be paid by instalments, this is a factor to be considered when deciding whether or not to confirm a charging order but is not decisive either way.[207] A charging order favours the judgment creditor (previously unsecured) over other unsecured creditors on a subsequent insolvency. So the court has a full discretion either to make a final order or to refuse it.[208] In practice some positive reason is required to place the judgment creditor at an advantage.[209] A final order must be obtained before bankruptcy or the commencement of a winding up,[210] but even a threat of insolvency is a reason to refuse a charging order.[211]

4.   Charging legal estates

[28.41] The interest charged is "any property of the debtor . . . specified in the order",[212] but the primary focus of this book is land within the jurisdiction.[213] If the judgment debtor is sole legal and beneficial owner the charge binds the legal estate. Any genuine dispute about ownership must be resolved by a full trial,[214] but a debtor cannot wriggle out of a charging order by alleging an unproved interest in an outsider.[215]

Enforcement against the legal estate is also allowed where there is "unity of debt",[216] that is a single debt shared by all beneficial co-owners of the land,[217] whether beneficial joint tenants or tenants in common. In *Clark* v. *Chief Land Registrar*[218] Mr and Mrs Jarvis's home Spinners Cottage was charged with a debt of £215,000. Although the legal estate was held on the co-ownership trusts, the non-trust

---

[203] PD 73.1.2(5).

[204] An objector must file and serve written evidence not less than 7 days before hearing; CPR 73.8(1); the court may transfer the hearing to the home court of opposing debtor PD 73.3.

[205] COA 1979 s 1(5); *Rainbow* v. *Moorgate Properties* [1975] 2 All ER 821, CA (old law); Law Com 74 (1976), [43–44].

[206] COA 1979 s 3(1), (5)–(7); *Perotti* v. *Watson* [2000] 1 CLYB 378, CA.

[207] *Ropaigealach* v. *Allied Irish Bank* [2001] EWCA Civ 1790, [2002] 03 EG 130.

[208] CPR 73.8(2).

[209] *Roberts Petroleum* v. *Bernard Kenny* [1982] 1 WLR 301, 307E–H, Lord Brightman approved on this point [1983] 2 AC 192, HL.

[210] IA 1986 ss 183, 346.

[211] *Roberts Petroleum* v. *Bernard Kenny* [1983] 2 AC 192, HL; approving [1982] 1 WLR 301, 307E–H, Lord Brightman in CA; *Rainbow* v. *Moorgate Properties* [1975] 2 All ER 821, CA; *Harman* v. *Glencross* [1986] Fam 81, 93, Balcombe LJ; *Jelle Zwemstra* v. *Walton* [1997] 2 CLYB 3002.

[212] COA 1979 s 1(1).

[213] COA 1979 s 8(3); *Interpool* v. *Galani* [1988] QB 738, 741–742, Balcombe LJ.

[214] *Rosseel* v. *Oriental Commercial & Shipping (UK)* [1990] 1 WLR 1387, CA.

[215] *Barclays Bank* v. *Forrester* [1987] CLYB 2537; *First National Securities* v. *Hegerty* [1985] QB 850, 855E, Bingham J.

[216] The phrase apparently derives from the notes to the old *Supreme Court Practice*.

[217] COA 1979 s 2(1)(b); confirming *National Westminster Bank* v. *Allen* [1971] 2 QB 718.

[218] [1994] Ch 371, CA.

procedure was followed, but the order actually made[219] was adequate to effect a charge of the legal estate in the Jarvis' home.[220]

A legal estate held by *trustees* can be charged in three cases.[221] If judgment is obtained against the trustees as trustees, the legal estate can be charged. If T holds land under a bare trust on trust for B (the debtor) absolutely the legal estate held by T can be charged with B's debt.[222] If T1 and T2 hold on trust for B1 and B2 as beneficial co-owners, the legal estate can be charged with the debts of B1 and B2.

5. Protection

[28.42] A proprietary claim is established at the time that application is made for a charging order, and this should be registered as a pending action relating to the land.[223] An order (interim or final) can be registered as a writ or order affecting land.[224] Protective registration is essential if the charge affects a legal title.[225] A land registry notice is needed against a registered title.[226] Even though a purchaser will be bound by any registration, the court retains a power to discharge the order at the instance of a buyer. This was done in *Howell* v. *Montey*[227] but it was surely wrong to help a buyer who had allowed his search to lapse.

A charging order creates an equitable charge over the property, the proprietary character of the interest being shown by the rule that the creditor with the benefit of charging order has sufficient status to seek relief from forfeiture of a leasehold title.[228]

6. Enforcement

[28.43] Enforcement requires a court order for sale.[229] Enforcement by sale of the legal estate should be by application to the court on a Part 8 claim form.[230] At this stage discretionary factors such as the interests of children should not be considered.[231]

---

[219] At 380–381, Nourse LJ; [1993] Ch 294, 305–308, Ferris J.

[220] Two separate charging orders did not prevent unity of debt, reversing *Irani Finance* v. *Singh* [1971] Ch 59, CA.

[221] COA 1979 s 2(1)(b).

[222] S 2(1)(a)(ii); *Stevens* v. *Hince* (1914) 110 LT 935 (old law).

[223] LCA 1972 s 5; a caution if title is registered.

[224] COA 1979 s 3(2); LCA 1972 s 6. Companies registration is not required: Companies Act 1985 s 395(1); *Re Overseas Aviation Engineering (GB)* [1963] Ch 24, CA, on earlier legislation.

[225] LCA 1972 ss 5(7), 6(4); LRA 1925 s 59(6) (good faith).

[226] LRA 2002 s 87; formerly a caution. Sch 13 repeals COA 1979 ss 3(3), 7(4).

[227] (1990) 61 P & CR 18, CA.

[228] *Croydon (Unique)* v. *Wright* [2001] Ch 318, CA.

[229] COA 1979 s 3(4); CPR 73.10; *Tennant* v. *Trenchard* (1869) LR 4 Ch App 537. Appointment of a receiver is no longer required.

[230] CPR 73.10(3); PD 73; an estimate of the likely sale price is required.

[231] *Wells* v. *Pickering* [2002] 2 FLR 798, Ch D.

J.   CHARGING ORDERS ON BENEFICIAL INTERESTS

1.   Charging orders

[28.44] Under a trust of land, the debt of a beneficiary can be charged on the equitable interest under the trust of land[232] though not on the legal estate.[233] The trustees and all beneficiaries are brought into court.[234] The legal estate cannot be charged. The judgment creditor does not have direct access to the legal estate, unless there is no unity of debt.[235] A charge of the equitable interest can only be enforced by an application for sale as a beneficial co-owner.

A spouse is severely prejudiced by a charging order against the other beneficial interest in the family home, both because of the threat of sale and the reduction in assets for adjustment on divorce. Capacity to challenge a charging order is given to "any person interested in the property to which the order relates."[236] This does not include a wife as such[237] nor a cohabitee, but does include a beneficial co-owner and a spouse who has commenced divorce proceedings.[238]

How property adjustment interrelates with the power to confirm a charging order was considered by Balcombe LJ in *First National Securities* v. *Hegerty*.[239] A charging order made before a divorce application must be made absolute, leaving the spouse to challenge the later decision to order sale.[240] This is likely to be little comfort, since the wife is likely to lose under the general rule favouring creditors over family members.[241] If an application has been made for property adjustment on divorce at the time of a *later* application for a charging order nisi, the court has a full discretion. Creditors prevail over family members unless there is a very clear reason to reverse the normal position. One exceptional case was *Harman* v. *Glencross*[242] where there was unanimous support for postponing the charging order to the wife's application for ancillary relief. This is best explained as a case where the creditor put in no evidence, leaving the court to focus on the wife's desire to preserve her family home.[243]

2.   Charges of beneficial interest not registrable

[28.45] If a beneficial interest under a trust of land can be overreached, then so too can a mortgage or charging order affecting it. It follows that to allow registration of

---

[232] A beneficial interest under a trust for sale could be charged despite conversion theory: COA 1979 s 2(1)(a)(ii); Law Com 74 (1976), [59–66]; this reversed the older law.

[233] TLATA 1996 s 3.

[234] *Harman* v. *Glencross* [1986] Fam 81, 89E, Balcombe LJ. Procedural irregularities may be overlooked: *Clark* v. *Chief Land Registrar* [1994] Ch 370, CA.

[235] See above **[28.41]**.

[236] COA 1979 s 3(5); *Harman* v. *Glencross* [1986] Fam 81, 89C–E.

[237] *Whittingham* v. *Whittingham* [1979] Fam 9, 21H, Balcombe LJ.

[238] *Harman* v. *Glencross* [1986] Fam 81, 89–91, Balcombe LJ, 100–101, Fox LJ.

[239] [1985] QB 850, 99–100. First National had an equitable mortgage anyway.

[240] *Austin-Fell* v. *Austin-Fell* [1990] Fam 172, Waite J.

[241] *Barclays Bank* v. *Hendricks* [1996] 1 FLR 258; NS Price [1997] *Conv* 464. Query the decision in *Austin-Fell* to postpone sale until the younger child attained 18.

[242] [1986] Fam 81, CA doubting *First National Securities* v. *Hegerty* [1985] QB 850, 856, Stephenson LJ.

[243] At 104C.

such a charging order[244] would "cut right across the system of conveyancing." Priorities are based on first in time.

K. BANKRUPTCY

1. Loss of all beneficial property

[28.46] Creditors who are not secured, that is who have no property earmarked for the payment of their debt, have to rely on a claim against the general assets of the bankrupt along with everyone else who is owed money. If a bankrupt has debts of £100,000, but his unmortgaged property[245] is worth £50,000, each creditor will receive only half what he is owed. All the bankrupt's property is taken from him to meet these liabilities, and passes for the benefit of his creditors.[246] A trustee in bankruptcy is appointed to look after the interests of creditors.[247] All property will be vested in the trustee, that is all beneficial or valuable assets of the bankrupt including his land, all freehold and leasehold[248] land, other interests in land, future interests, contracts, powers, and beneficial interests under trusts.[249] Property previously given away by the bankrupt may also be recovered for the benefit of the estate.[250] Onerous property can be disclaimed by the trustee in bankruptcy, an act which may cause the bankrupt's interest in the property to end and hence an escheat.[251] It is possible to create a "protective" trust which gives a life interest determinable on bankruptcy, and protects a beneficiary from the consequences of his own profligacy.[252] Legal estates held by trustees do not pass, though bankruptcy is an event which is likely to lead to removal from office as a trustee.

2. Statutory demand

[28.47] Insolvency arises from the inability of the bankrupt to pay his debts, proved when a demand is made for payment of a debt which he is unable to pay in time. A creditor instigates the procedure by serving a statutory demand on the debtor,[253] in a prescribed form. Three weeks are allowed from the time of service on the debtor for payment to be made. This demand cannot be protected by registration. No blot appears on the title at this first stage of bankruptcy procedure and statutory demands cannot be protected by registration.

---

[244] *Perry* v. *Phoenix Assurance* [1988] 1 WLR 940, 945B, Browne-Wilkinson V-C; JE Martin [1988] *Conv* 286; TLATA 1996 sch 3 para 12.

[245] Secured creditors are largely unaffected by the borrower's bankruptcy, since they can enforce their mortgage by sale; the trustee in bankruptcy takes subject to existing security interests.

[246] *Wright* v. *Fairfield* (1831) 2 B & Ad 727, 732, 109 ER 307, Lord Tenterden.

[247] Contrast the administration or liquidation of a company when title remains in the company though the directors can no longer act, a land registry restriction is required, and the administrator or liquidator has a power of sale: IA 1986 s 163; DLRR 2003 r 184.

[248] See above **[27.03]**.

[249] *St Thomas' Hospital* v. *Richardson* [1910] 1 KB 271; but see *Re Solicitor* [1952] Ch 328.

[250] See above **[24.22]**.

[251] See above **[3.45]**.

[252] TA 1925 s 33; there are many cases.

[253] IA 1986 s 268(1)(a).

3. Bankruptcy petition

[28.48] It is usually a creditor who makes a bankruptcy petition to the bankruptcy court, the usual ground being that the debtor appears to be unable to pay his debts.[254] This marks the onset of bankruptcy, since a bankruptcy is no longer related back to the act of bankruptcy which preceded it,[255] and removes the bankrupt's powers to dispose of his property.[256] The blot on the title needs to be brought to the attention of potential purchasers. At least 14 days must elapse after service of the petition on the debtor before it is considered by the court.

4. Bankruptcy orders

[28.49] Petitions are dismissed if the debt has been paid or if it would be unfair to make an order, but in the normal course the court will make a bankruptcy order. [257] The bankrupt loses title to his assets and can no longer dispose of them. Control passes first to the Official Receiver and afterwards to a trustee in bankruptcy. The creditors need to alert purchasers to the fact that the debtor has lost control of his property, as described below.

5. Protection where title is unregistered

[28.50] A petition should be registered as a pending land action. When this is followed by a bankruptcy order, a fresh registration is required as a writ or order affecting land, whether or not the bankrupt's estate is known to include land.[258] The consequences of failure to register are considered elsewhere.[259] There is a separate register of deeds of arrangement.[260]

6. Bankruptcy of a proprietor of registered land

[28.51] A new simpler scheme is introduced.[261] A petition in bankruptcy should first be entered as a land charge. As soon as practicable afterwards the registrar should enter a notice against any registered title that appears to be affected.[262] This stage of the process is fraught with error: it is all too likely that some land owned by the bankrupt will be missed or that innocent landowners will find themselves wrongly recorded as being in debt. The notice will continue in force until superseded by a restriction or the registration of the trustee in bankruptcy as proprietor.[263] It will prevent the debtor

---

[254] Ss 267–268.
[255] Bankruptcy Act 1914 s 37(1).
[256] IA 1986 s 278, subject to court approval of dealings: ss 283–291.
[257] S 282.
[258] LCA 1972 s 6(1), (5), (6).
[259] See above **[21.33ff]**.
[260] S 7; Deeds of Arrangement Act 1914; voluntary arrangements under IA 1986 ss 252–263 often appear in class C(iii); SI 1999/359; IA 2000 ss 1–3, schs 1–3.
[261] LRA 2002 s 86; Law Com 271 (2001) [6.61]; Law Com 271 (2001) EN [376ff]; DLRR 2003 rr 166–174.
[262] LRA 2002 s 86(2); DLRR 2003 r 166 (enter in proprietorship register if it affects the proprietor of an estate as opposed to a mortgage); notice must be given to the proprietor affected.
[263] LRA 2002 s 86(3). Formerly a creditor's notice.

disposing of his land while the court decides whether or not to make him bankrupt, thus preserving the value of the land for his creditors.

If the decision is to make a bankruptcy order, this should first be registered as a pending action in the land charges register. As soon as practicable afterwards the registrar must find any registered titles affected and enter a restriction reflecting the limitation on the powers of the proprietor. Any attempt at disposition is void unless it has the consent of the trustee in bankruptcy or is ratified by the court.[264] Registration is backdated to the date of the disposition.[265] This blanket ban used to be imposed by an inhibition,[266] but the same result is now achieved by a particularly stringent form of restriction. If a restriction is not entered on the register, the title of the trustee in bankruptcy will be void as against a protected purchaser claiming under a registered disposition for value, but the purchaser must act in good faith and cannot alone rely on the register.[267] Honesty is confined to this narrow situation and is, of course, contrary to the general rule of the registration scheme.

A purchaser of registered land is not required to make a land charges search.[268]

7.   Bankruptcy only land charges searches

[28.52] The unregistered system of protection against names is far more efficient at picking up bankruptcy entries than the registered system in which it is common for errors of matching to occur, that is for an innocent proprietor to have a bankruptcy recorded against him or for the land of a genuine bankrupt not to have a bankruptcy entry made against it.[269] A monetary indemnity is available where mismatching occurs. However, despite the irrelevance of a land charges search once title is registered, many lenders do insist on a "bankruptcy only" search in order to ascertain whether the borrower is, or ever has been, bankrupt before committing themselves to lending money against a registered title. The proper means of protection are described below.

8.   Registration of and sale by trustee in bankruptcy

[28.53] The Official Receiver takes temporary control of the bankrupt's estate, until he calls a first meeting of creditors, which appoints a trustee in bankruptcy.[270] Title of a trustee in bankruptcy derives from the insolvency legislation without conveyancing formalities.[271] However the register should be corrected to show the trustee in bankruptcy as proprietor on production of evidence of the appointment.[272]

---

[264] LRA 2002 s 86(4); IA 1986 s 284; DLRR 2003 r 167; notice must be given to the proprietor.

[265] LRA 2002 s 86(6).

[266] LRA 1925 s 61(3)–(4); Law Com 271 (2001), [11.41].

[267] LRA 2002 s 86(5).

[268] LRA 2002 s 86(7).

[269] In practice it is very common to make a bankruptcy only search. LR *Annual Report 2001–2002*, 49, reveals 1 m land charges searches and 4 m bankruptcy only searches; also: PH Kenny [1999] *Conv* 279; SI 1999/359.

[270] IA 1986 ss 287(1), 292, 293–300.

[271] S 306.

[272] DLRR 2003 r 169. Evidence required is an office copy of the bankruptcy order or a certificate from a conveyancer that he has it. R 171 provides for the insertion in the register of a reference to the fact that

Sale is the inevitable end of successful bankruptcy proceedings, since all assets of the bankrupt will need to be applied towards his debts. The trustee in bankruptcy has the basic function of getting in, realising and distributing the bankrupt's estate. His powers include sale,[273] barring an entail,[274] making contracts, executing deeds, and giving receipts. Creditors have little control and purchasers are protected against procedural defects. Special problems arise with leasehold property.[275]

9. End of bankruptcy

[28.54] A bankruptcy may end before sale of all the assets where a petition or order is cancelled or annulled, usually because all debts have been paid. A bankrupt can apply for a discharge by making a statement of affairs to the bankruptcy court. Any registration must be cancelled or vacated[276] to free the land from the bankruptcy.

10. Special cases

[28.55] Regulations deal with insolvent estates[277] and partnerships.[278]

the proprietor is a trustee in bankruptcy and the name of the bankrupt. R 170 applies when a trustee in bankruptcy vacates office.

[273] IA 1986 s 314.
[274] Sch 5 part II para 14.
[275] See above [27.07].
[276] LRA 1925 s 61(9); DLRR 2003 r 168.
[277] SI 1986/1999; DLRR 2003 r 169.
[278] SI 1994/2421.

29

MORTGAGE DEBT AND DEFAULT

Debt: principal, interest and costs. Overdraft mortgages. Terms fettering redemption. Commercial repossession. Sale: express powers; judicial sale; proceeds and shortfall. Defective sale. Redemption: discharge, disputed redemption.

A. PRINCIPAL, INTEREST AND COSTS

1. Principal

[29.01] Mortgages provide for repayment on a fixed day called the contractual redemption date. Convention dictates that it is six months after the date of the mortgage, and neither lender[1] nor borrower[2] can insist on earlier repayment. The lender should ensure that interest is payable during the mortgage's initial phase.[3] Repayment is not really anticipated on the stated day, the main function of which is to determine when sale may occur.[4]

Common lawyers were literalists, a trait which led their common law courts to mete out very harsh treatment to borrowers. If the borrower missed the day set for repayment the lender became absolutely entitled to the mortgaged property since the mortgage was in those circumstances no longer redeemable. Shakespeare railed against this attitude in *The Merchant of Venice*. Antonio waits in vain for his ships to arrive bringing their cargoes and the means to repay his borrowings; once the contractual opportunity to redeem has gone, Shylock enforces his bond and demands his rights under the letter of his contract, that is his "pound of flesh". Borrowers suffered this same literal interpretation at common law. If a legal charge provides for payment of the debt on one fixed day, and it is read literally, there is no means of discharging that burden at any later time.[5]

As is unconscionable for a lender to enforce his strict legal rights, equity righted the balance. Lord Eldon LC said in *Seton* v. *Slade*[6] that:

---

[1] *Bolton* v. *Buckenham* [1891] 1 QB 278, CA.
[2] *Brown* v. *Cole* (1845) 14 Sim 427, 60 ER 424; unless the lender enforces: *Bovill* v. *Endle* [1896] 1 Ch 684; *Ex p Wickens* [1898] 1 QB 543, CA.
[3] *Re King* (1881) 17 Ch D 191; *Mellersh* v. *Brown* (1890) 45 Ch D 225.
[4] *Smith* v. *Smith* [1891] 3 Ch 550.
[5] Legal charges are better drafted to set a date on which the debt is due (and hence when sale is possible), but so as to allow discharge of the charge at any future date. After 1925 the demise in a true mortgage is removed by cesser on redemption if repayment occurs on the one fixed day, but otherwise a freehold lender is entitled to an apparently irredeemable 3000 year term and relies on equitable protection.
[6] (1802) 7 Ves 265, 32 ER 108.

"The contract is in [Chancery] considered a mere loan of money, secured by a pledge of the estate. . . . [T]his court acts against what is the prima facie import of the terms of the agreement itself . . . [O]nce a mortgage always a mortgage."

So late repayment was forced on the lender who was sufficiently compensated for any delay by payments of interest. This equitable counterbalance of the harshness of the common law ensures that mortgages operate a fair balance.

The *equity of redemption* is the borrower's interest in the land subject to the mortgage. Early forms transferred legal title to the lender, a problem corrected by the ancient invention[7] of an equitable interest in the borrower. In substance a modern legal charge is the same, but since it leaves legal title in the borrower, the "equity" of redemption now includes the legal estate mortgaged,[8] though its most valuable component remains the equitable right to redeem the loan and so free the land of its burden. The borrower is owner of the property subject to the charge,[9] and can dispose of his interest subject to it.[10]

Most domestic mortgages provide for payment by instalments.[11]

2. Interest

[29.02] Mortgages invariably require regular payments of interest,[12] on whatever balance is outstanding. Interest is a percentage of the capital sum calculated over a set period of time, weekly, monthly, or yearly.[13] Although the right is implied[14] it is invariably also expressed, since the rate set by equity is well below commercial levels. Interest rates fluctuate over time guided by the Monetary Policy Committee of the Bank of England.[15] Building societies, banks, and local authorities[16] commonly reserve the right to vary the rate of interest by notice, a practice which is unobjectionable provided that interest is certain at the moment that payment is due.[17] A term may be implied to prevent variation of interest rates for an improper purpose, or to prevent a variation that is dishonest, capricious, arbitrary, beyond what any reasonable lender would have wanted.[18] Fixed rate mortgages provide a measure of protection since the

---

[7] Elizabethan (ie 1558–1603)?; *Pawlett* v. *Att-Gen* (1667) Hardres 465, 469, 145 ER 550, Hale CB; Statute 7 Geo 2 c 20 (1734) required common law courts to give effect to it; *G & C Kreglinger* v. *New Patagonia Meat & Cold Storage Co* [1914] AC 25, 50 (Nottingham LC had used the analogy of legal estates).

[8] In the case of a mortgage by demise, it is the freehold estate subject to the mortgage demise (or leasehold estate subject to the mortgage sub-demise). Equitable mortgages are modelled on legal ones: *Tarn* v. *Turner* (1888) 39 Ch D 456; *Kreglinger* [1914] AC 25, 52, Lord Parker.

[9] *Heath* v. *Pugh* (1881) 6 QBD 345, 359, Selborne LC; *English Sewing Cotton Co* v. *IRC* [1947] 1 All ER 679, 680, Greene MR.

[10] *Tarn* v. *Turner* (1888) 39 Ch D 456, 460, Kekewich J; *Re Webb* [1933] Ch 29, 46, 52; *Chelsea & Waltham Green BS* v. *Armstrong* [1951] Ch 853 (liability of buyer on covenant to lender).

[11] See below [30.14ff].

[12] Separate debt: *Dickenson* v. *Harrison* (1817) 4 Price 282, 146 ER 456. As to statute-barred interest, see above [10.33ff].

[13] Comparison is aided by taking an annual percentage rate (APR).

[14] *Re King ex p Furber* (1881) 17 Ch D 191, 196, Bacon V-C; *Re Drax* [1903] 1 Ch 781; *Stoker* v. *Elwell* [1942] Ch 243 (charging orders); *Al-Wazir* v. *Islamic Press Agency* [2001] EWCA Civ 1276, [2002] 2 P & CR 12 at 157.

[15] Current rates can be found in the financial pages of the newspapers or monthly in the *LSG*.

[16] HA 1985 ss 435–459, sch 16.

[17] *First National Bank* v. *Syed* [1991] 2 All ER 250, 252, Dillon LJ.

[18] *Paragon Finance* v. *Nash* [2001] EWCA Civ 1466, [2002] 1 WLR 685.

interest rate is fixed for a period, of say two or five years, giving a known monthly budget.[19]

Late payment of commercial debt is an increasing problem.[20] Many mortgages provide for an increase in the interest rate after a default has occurred.[21] This may be a penalty if applied retrospectively[22] so it is safer to offer a lower interest rate on prompt payment.[23] Equity is no longer hostile[24] to interest on arrears of interest (otherwise called compound interest or the capitalisation of arrears). After (say) 21 days, arrears of interest will be added to capital, so that the arrears are then subjected to interest. This leads to an enormous increase in the burden of the arrears,[25] and places a strong weapon in the hands of the lender, though care is needed to preserve the power of sale.[26] Nevertheless the provision for interest on interest is not an unfair term.[27]

Christian objections to lending on interest have evaporated, but Muslim mortgages do not provide directly for interest.

3. Costs

[29.03] A mortgage invariably requires the borrower to pay all the lender's expenses, both as a debt and as an addition to the security. Examples are costs of a completed[28] mortgage, money spent in preserving the property,[29] insurance premiums, management expenses, repairs, redemption costs, and interest on prior mortgages.[30] Litigation costs include those relating to the security, its enforcement, or defence of title to the property,[31] but not the costs of asserting the validity of the mortgage itself against an outside party.[32]

Contractual entitlement to costs can only be curtailed by conduct amounting to a violation or culpable neglect of the lender's duty under the contract.[33] Nevertheless

---

[19] Usually there is a penalty against redemption within the fixed period, so the fix may be disadvantageous if interest rates drop.

[20] Late Payment of Commercial Debts (Interest) Act 1998 (8% above base rate).

[21] *Lordsvale Finance* v. *Bank of Zambia* [1996] QB 752, Colman J (valid if increase modest); *Burton* v. *Slattery* (1725) 5 Bro PC 233, 2 ER 648, HL; *Herbert* v. *Salisbury & Yeovil Rly Co* (1866) LR 2 Eq 221; *General Credit & Discount Co* v. *Glegg* (1883) 22 Ch D 549.

[22] *Seton* v. *Slade* (1802) 7 Ves 265, 273, 32 ER 108; *Dunlop Pneumatic Tyre Co* v. *New Garage Motor Co* [1915] AC 79, 87, Lord Dunedin; AC Meredith (1916) 32 *LQR* 420.

[23] *Wallingford* v. *Mutual Society* (1880) 5 App Cas 685, 702, Lord Hatherley. This right is lost (1) by a single default: *Maclaine* v. *Gatty* [1921] 1 AC 376, HL; (2) on taking possession without any default: *Bright* v. *Campbell* (1889) 41 Ch D 388, Kay J; *Wrigley* v. *Gill* [1906] 1 Ch 165, CA.

[24] *Ex p Bevan* (1803) 9 Ves 223, 32 ER 588; *The Maira* [1990] 1 AC 637, HL; *Westdeutsche Landesbank Girozentrale* v. *Islington LBC* [1996] AC 669, 684G, Lord Goff; *Whitbread* v. *UCB Corporate Services* [2000] 3 EGLR 60, CA.

[25] *First National Bank* v. *Syed* [1991] 2 All ER 250, 253g, Dillon LJ.

[26] *Davy* v. *Turner* (1970) 21 P & CR 967, Brightman J.

[27] *Director General of Fair Trading* v. *First National Bank* [2001] UKHL 52, [2002] 1 AC 481; see below [30.07].

[28] Costs of proposed mortgages require a specific agreement, a solicitor's undertaking, or payment of fees up front.

[29] *Sinfield* v. *Sweet* [1967] 1 WLR 1489 (express term).

[30] *Hollis* v. *Wingfield* [1940] Ch 336, CA.

[31] *Re Leighton's Conveyance* [1937] Ch 149, CA; *Halsall* v. *Egbunike* (1963) 187 EG 101; *Saunders* v. *Anglia BS* [1971] AC 1004, HL.

[32] *Parker-Tweedale (No 2)* v. *Dunbar Bank* [1991] Ch 26, CA.

[33] *Cotterell* v. *Stratton* (1872) LR 8 Ch App 295, 302, Selborne LC.

there is power for a taxing master to limit what is proper and reasonable,[34] and the court can control litigation costs – having power for example to deprive a lender of his costs after he has refused a proper tender.[35]

B. OVERDRAFT MORTGAGES AND TACKING

1. Nature

[29.04] Mark Twain defined a banker as "the person who lends you his umbrella when the sun is shining and who wants it back the minute it rains." That encapsulates an overdraft facility. The overdraft may initially be zero,[36] but as money is drawn on the account, the bank is lending money to the customer. Add to that a charge on the land to secure the running balance[37] and you have an overdraft mortgage. The mortgage deed is usually brief, setting a limit to which the customer is allowed to borrow,[38] but securing any amount lent even if greater than the preset limit; this is the so-called "all monies charge".[39]

Usually the amount owing is payable on demand[40] or, what is the same thing, on request.[41] The overdraft conditions may require a demand in writing, which is then a precondition to enforcement. A facility which provides for payment on a fixed day unless called in earlier, requires a reasonable and substantial period of notice giving time to ensure that the money is to hand.[42] If the money is payable on demand the lender has to find the borrower to demand payment: the borrower must keep funds ready, but is allowed time to procure the money and to check the authority of the person making the demand.[43] Time need not be allowed to negotiate a deal to find the money to pay,[44] nor if the debtor company makes clear that it cannot pay.[45]

2. Tacking

[29.05] Tacking enables a loan to gain a higher priority than normal, because the lender is allowed to amalgamate his later advance with the debt secured by an earlier

---

[34] CPR 48; PD 48; *Parker-Tweedale* v. *Dunbar Bank (No 2)* [1991] Ch 26, CA; *Gomba Holdings (UK)* v. *Minories Finance (No 2)* [1993] Ch 171, CA.

[35] Supreme Court Act 1981 s 51(1); *Barrett* v. *Gough-Thomas* [1951] 2 All ER 48, 50, and many earlier cases; *Gomba* at 190H–198F, Scott LJ.

[36] It may still overreach: *State Bank of India* v. *Sood* [1997] Ch 276, CA.

[37] Also an independent debt: *Barclays Bank* v. *Beck* [1952] 2 QB 47, 54, Denning LJ.

[38] The bank could not unilaterally vary the amount guaranteed: *Lloyds TSB* v. *Shorney* [2001] EWCA Civ 1161, [2001] 1 FLR 81. If it does so any surety is discharged.

[39] *White* v. *City of London Brewery Co* (1889) 42 Ch D 237, CA; *Burnes* v. *Trade Credits* [1981] 1 WLR 805, PC.

[40] It is not tortious to call in the money: *Edwin Hill* v. *First National Finance* [1988] CLYB 3417, CA.

[41] *Re Brown's Estate* [1893] 2 Ch 504; *Bradford Old Bank* v. *Sutcliffe* [1918] 2 KB 833, 840, Pickford LJ; *Lloyds Bank* v. *Margolis* [1954] 1 WLR 644.

[42] *Brighty* v. *Norton* (1862) 3 B & S 305, 312, 122 ER 116.

[43] *Toms* v. *Wilson* (1862) 4 B & S 442, 454, 122 ER 524.

[44] *RA Cripps & Son* v. *Wickenden* [1973] 1 WLR 944, 955A.

[45] *Sheppard & Cooper* v. *TSB Bank* [1997] 2 BCLC 222, CA.

mortgage. Further advances rank in priority to subsequent mortgages[46] of the same property[47] thus:

(1) B borrows £X from L1;
(2) B borrows £Y from L2;
(3) B borrows £Z from L1.

If tacking is permitted the first lender may claim priority for the combined loan, thus: L1 (£X+£Z); L2 (£Y); borrower.

3. Priority of a registered overdraft

[29.06] Tacking of overdrafts secured on registered land is put on a new, simpler, basis by the Land Registration Act 2002,[48] the scheme having being copied from the banking practice of other EU states. When tacking is allowed, priority is secured for the principal, interest, and costs due under the mortgage, but not the costs of enforcement. It can now occur in four circumstances:

(R1) A further advance agreed by later lenders;[49]

(R2) Normal overdrafts provide for further loans at the discretion of the lender. The overdraft can be increased until the registrar serves notice on the lender that a second mortgage has occurred; after that time further advances will no longer obtain priority. A further advance may be made by the proprietor of a registered charge at that a time that he has not received from a subsequent lender notice of creation of subsequent charge.[50] Notice is deemed to have been received at the time it ought to have been under the rules.[51] The innovation under this heading is that notice is now given by the second lender and not as previously[52] by the land registry.

(R3) Where there is an obligation to make a further advance, which binds any later lender if the obligation is entered in the register.[53] It is up to the lender who wants to tack to identify the existence of the obligation to the registrar, a separate application now being required.[54]

(R4) Further advances up to a maximum amount,[55] a new head. It is permissible for an overdraft mortgage to state a maximum amount secured, say £100,000, so that when only £80,000 has been advanced any later lender knows that

---

[46] LPA 1925 s 94(1).

[47] Consolidation involves mortgages of different properties; see below **[29.50ff]**.

[48] LRA 2002 s 49; Law Com 271 (2001), [7.18–7.36], EN [225–234]; DLRR 2003 r 106; LPA 1925 s 94(4) is amended by LRA 2002 sch 11.

[49] Priorities can always be varied by agreement: LRA 2002 s 49(6).

[50] S 49(1).

[51] S 49(2). DLRR 2003 r 106 gives the date that notices served by various methods are deemed to be received.

[52] LRA 1925 s 30; LPA 1925 s 94.

[53] LRA 2002 s 49(3). A registered charge is no longer necessary: Law Com 271 (2001), [7.22–7.28]; compare: LRA 1925 s 30(3); *Lloyd* v. *Nationwide Anglia BS* [1996] EGCS 80.

[54] DLRR 2003 r 107.

[55] LRA 2002 s 49(4); DLRR 2003 r 108; LR Forms CH4–CH6.

another £20,000 may be borrowed. The maximum amount must be entered on the register.[56]

4. Priority of unregistered overdraft

[29.07] Section 94 of the Law of Property Act 1925 allows tacking in unregistered land,[57] in four cases:

(U1) If an arrangement to allow tacking has been made with the intervening lender.[58] Lenders are always free to re-order their priorities by mutual agreement.[59]

(U2A) Where a mortgage is made expressly for securing a current account or other further advances, tacking is permitted until the earlier lender receives notice of another mortgage.

Notice may be actual, constructive, or imputed, *but* not through land charges registration:[60] a bank manager is not required to carry out full conveyancing searches before increasing the overdraft limit. Later lenders should give written notice of their security to stop tacking by an earlier lender.

(U2B) Even if further advances are not contemplated by the mortgage, tacking is permitted[61] until the prior lender receives notice[62] of a subsequent mortgage.[63]

(U3) Further advances are obligatory.[64] If a mortgage obliges the lender to lend £100,000 at the time of the mortgage and £50,000 one year later, the mortgage gives priority to a loan of £150,000 and any later lender can discover this. Tacking occurs even if there is notice of a subsequent mortgage.

5. Summary of tacking

[29.08]	Registered	Unregistered
By agreement	(R1)	(U1)
Until notice	(R2)	(U2) (A and B) .
Obligation	(R3)	(U3)
To fixed limit	(R4)	–

---

[56] LRA 2002 s 49(4)–(5); Law Com 271 (2001), [7.32–7.36].

[57] LPA 1925 s 94(4); Megarry & Wade (6th ed), [19.263–19.262].

[58] LPA 1925 s 94(1)(a).

[59] *Cheah* v. *Equiticorp Finance Group* [1991] 4 All ER 989, PC.

[60] S 94(2) excluding s 198. Pre-1926 see: *London & County Banking Co* v. *Ratcliffe* (1881) 6 App Cas 722, HL; *Deeley* v. *Lloyds Bank* [1912] AC 756, HL.

[61] *Marsh* v. *Lee* (1869) 2 Vent 337, 86 ER 473; *Hopkinson* v. *Rolt* (1861) 9 HLC 514, 541, 11 ER 829, Lord Cranworth; *Young* v. *Young* (1867) LR 3 Eq 801, 805, Malins V-C.

[62] Pre-1926 cases: *Hopkinson* v. *Rolt* (1861) 9 HLC 514, 11 ER 829; *London & County Banking Co* v. *Ratcliffe* (1881) 6 App Cas 722, HL; *Bradford Banking Co* v. *Henry Briggs Son & Co* (1886) 12 App Cas 29, HL; *Union Bank of Scotland* v. *National Bank of Scotland* (1886) 12 App Cas 53, HL; *Hughes* v. *Birmingham PBBS* [1906] 2 Ch 607, Kekewich J; *Deely* v. *Lloyds Bank* [1912] AC 756, HL.

[63] LPA 1925 s 94(1)(c).

[64] S 94(1)(c).

C. TERMS FETTERING REDEMPTION

[29.09] Equity intervened to protect borrowers because redemption actions came to Chancery. After 1540 usury laws fixed the maximum interest rate permissible and prohibited extra or disguised profits, but the last statute was repealed in 1854. *G & C Kreglinger* v. *New Patagonia Meat & Cold Storage Co*[65] finally freed the law from this legacy in 1914 and *Knightsbridge Estates* v. *Byrne*[66] disentangled commercial mortgages from the old law of oppression. Thus a commercial mortgage is usually valid in all its terms and fully enforceable. A residual power exists to invalidate terms of mortgage transactions because of technical inconsistency between the clause and the borrower's equity of redemption, though these vestigial traces of the old doctrine against clogs and fetters now operate in a capricious and unjust fashion. So much so that the Master of the Rolls has recently described the doctrine of clogs on the equity of redemption as an appendix to the law which serves no useful purpose and should be excised.[67]

1. Equity will not allow an irredeemable mortgage

[29.10] A transaction which is in substance[68] a loan may be redeemed by repayment. "Once a mortgage always a mortgage."[69] Three tests[70] are entitlement to get back the property by repayments, a duty to account for any surplus on sale, and liability for any shortfall. Problems of differentiation were inevitable in the past when a mortgage took the form of a conveyance of the estate to the lender,[71] but accidental confusion is much less likely after 1925 and the form of the deed is usually conclusive.[72] If a loan is deliberately dressed up as a sale, an old-style mortgage by demise is created.[73]

2. Options to purchase

[29.11] *Samuel* v. *Jarrah Timber Wood Paving Corporation*[74] held to be void an option in a mortgage of debenture stock enabling the lender to buy the mortgaged

---

[65] [1914] AC 25, HL, 47, Lord Parker.

[66] [1939] Ch 441, 454, Sir Wilfrid Greene MR.

[67] *Jones* v. *Morgan* [2001] EWCA Civ 779, [2002] 1 EGLR 125, [86], Phillips MR; MP Thompson [2001] *Conv* 502.

[68] *Baker* v. *Wind* (1748) 1 Ves Sen 160, 27 ER 956.

[69] *Seton* v. *Slade* (1807) 7 Ves 265, 32 ER 108; *Santley* v. *Wilde* [1899] 2 Ch 474, 475, Lindley MR; *Noakes* v. *Rice* [1902] AC 24, 28, Lord Halsbury

[70] *Re George Inglefield* [1933] Ch 1, 27, Romer LJ; *Stoneleigh Finance* v. *Phillips* [1965] 2 QB 537, CA.

[71] *Bowen* v. *Edwards* (1661) 1 Rep Ch 221, 21 ER 555; *Barnhart* v. *Greenshields* (1853) 9 Moo PCC 18, 14 ER 204.

[72] *Barton* v. *Bank of New South Wales* (1890) 15 App Cas 379, PC.

[73] LPA 1925 ss 85(2), 86(2); *Grangeside Properties* v. *Collingwoods Securities* [1964] 1 WLR 139, CA.

[74] [1904] AC 323, HL; F Pollock (1903) 19 *LQR* 359; N Bamforth (1996) 49 *CLP* 207.

property.[75] An option to purchase given on the creation or transfer of a mortgage[76] is void, but one given *afterwards*[77] is valid, as is a right of pre-emption.[78]

This is because an option would put the borrower too much in the power of the lender,[79] and some later cases also rest on the degree to which the borrower becomes vulnerable to pressure. However, *Jarrah Timber* invalidated an option which was entered into freely and at a fair price[80] and oppression is no longer relevant in normal commercial transactions.[81] So, the real ground must be technical inconsistency between the right to redeem and an option granted by the mortgage.[82] There is no legitimate reason to distinguish transactions at the time of the mortgage and subsequent dealings. It would be better to allow any option which is fairly obtained.

Thus in *Jones* v. *Morgan*[83] an agreement to avoid repossession of a nursing home provided for part to be sold and for another part to be transferred to the lender. That agreement reached after and independent of the mortgage was unaffected by the doctrine of clogs and was perfectly valid.

3. Postponement of contractual redemption

[29.12] Equity allows redemption of a mortgage after the contractual redemption date, by tradition six months after the date of the mortgage. Postponement of this date pushes back the chance for the borrower to redeem the mortgage, a perfectly legitimate adjunct to a fixed rate mortgage. No postponement was permitted before the latter part of the nineteenth century,[84] but then the movement towards sanctity of contract created a torrent of cases,[85] raging on into the twentieth century[86] which finally reversed the law on this point. Modern equity permits a postponement of contractual redemption unless the right to redeem is rendered illusory or it is actually oppressive. In *Knightsbridge Estates Trust* v. *Byrne*,[87] a freehold estate was mortgaged to secure a loan of £310,000, payable by half-yearly instalments over 40 years. The borrowers wished to redeem after only six years,[88] but the postponement was held to

---

[75] Including the freehold reversion in a mortgage of a lease: *Nelson* v. *Hannam* [1943] Ch 59, CA; but not an option over other items such as the sheep skins in *Kreglinger* (below).

[76] *Lewis* v. *Frank Love* [1961] 1 WLR 261, Plowman J; EH Scammell (1961) 24 *MLR* 385; PV Baker (1961) 77 *LQR* 163; *Jones* v. *Morgan* [2001] EWCA Civ 779, [2002] 1 EGLR 125.

[77] *Reeve* v. *Lisle* [1902] AC 461, HL. Even one day may suffice: [1904] AC 323, 325, Halsbury LC.

[78] *Re Petrol Filling Station, Vauxhall Bridge Road* (1969) 20 P & CR 1; *Orby* v. *Trigg* (1722) 9 Mod 2, 88 ER 276. Is there a solid distinction?

[79] *Toomes* v. *Conset* (1745) 3 Atk 261, 26 ER 952.

[80] [1904] AC 323, 325, Lord Halsbury (distaste for rule).

[81] Unless perhaps at a very low price or fixed in price over a long period.

[82] [1904] AC 323, 328, Lord Lindley (but see at 326, Lord Macnaghten); *Lewis* v. *Frank Love* [1961] 1 WLR 261, Plowman J.

[83] [2001] EWCA Civ 779, [2002] 1 EGLR 125; MP Thompson [2001] *Conv* 502; *Lewis* v. *Frank Love* applied.

[84] *Jason* v. *Eyres* (1681) Freem Ch 69, 22 ER 1064; *Cowdry* v. *Day* (1859) 1 Giff 316, 65 ER 936.

[85] *Teevan* v. *Smith* (1882) 20, Ch D 724, CA; *Biggs* v. *Hoddinott* [1898] 2 Ch 307, CA; *Bradley* v. *Carritt* [1903] AC 253, 259, Lord Macnaghten; *Williams* v. *Morgan* [1906] 1 Ch 804; *Morgan* v. *Jeffreys* [1910] 1 Ch 620 (28 years); *Davis* v. *Symons* [1934] Ch 442.

[86] *Esso Petroleum* v. *Harper's Garage (Stourport)* [1968] AC 269, 341; *Marden* v. *Multiservice Bookbinding* [1979] Ch 84; *Twentieth Century Banking Corp* v. *Wilkinson* [1977] Ch 99.

[87] [1939] Ch 441, CA; HKM (1939) 7 *CLJ* 146; RE Megarry (1940) 56 *LQR* 504.

[88] Interest rates having fallen, they wished to borrow more cheaply elsewhere.

be valid. Oppression was wholly absent from this commercial arrangement between legally advised parties. Gradual repayment of such a large loan was perfectly natural and anyway, corporate borrowers can issue irredeemable debentures.[89]

Contractual postponements of redemption may not render the right to redeem illusory. The last rule caught the mortgage in *Fairclough* v. *Swan Brewery*.[90] A lease of an hotel with 17 years left to run was mortgaged to a brewery, the hotelier tying himself to Swan's beer. Repayments were to end only six weeks before the expiry of the lease, but the tenant was able to break this arrangement and redeem after only two years. Technical malformation is irrelevant where the postponement has a legitimate commercial object to secure some future obligation. In *Santley* v. *Wilde*[91] a postponement until the last six weeks of a 10 year lease was intended to secure to the lender a one third share of profits accruing in the tenth year. The tenant could not redeem early to deny the lender his profits in later years.[92]

4. Collateral advantages

[29.13] These are rights enjoyed by the lender apart from the return of his loan with interest and costs. Examples are tied house clauses tying a pub to the beer of a particular brewer and corresponding ties to a brand of petrol (solus agreements).

Mortgage transactions were regulated by the usury laws between 1545 and 1854.[93] The overall return was regulated, so equity invalidated any secret profit masquerading as a collateral advantage.[94] Repeal of the usury laws[95] and the shift to sanctity of contract[96] called for a deep-rooted rethink. Collateral advantages are generally valid in modern law, even if limited to continue after redemption unless, that is, the right to redeem is rendered illusory or (very rarely) the advantage is secured by oppression.

The turning of the tide was marked by *G & C Kreglinger* v. *New Patagonia Meat & Cold Storage Co*.[97] A meat preserving company which intended to secure additional funding had a plentiful supply of animal skins. Wool brokers had £10,000 available and wished to secure a supply of sheepskins. A loan was negotiated secured by a floating charge over the assets of the meat preserving company;[98] by a separate document the wool brokers were given a pre-emption for five years over all the borrower's sheepskins at the market price. When the loan was paid off after two years, the right of pre-emption continued in full force for the agreed period.[99] The House of Lords faced a number of binding decisions that collateral advantages were destroyed by redemp-

---

[89] Companies Act 1985 s 193; *Knightsbridge* [1940] AC 613, HL (on 1929 Act).

[90] [1912] AC 565, PC; explained in *Knightsbridge* at [1939] Ch 411, 456–457, Greene MR.

[91] [1899] 2 Ch 474, CA; *Re Cuban Land & Development Co (1911)* [1921] 2 Ch 147.

[92] Later history: (1) disapproved in *Noakes & Co* v. *Rice* [1902] AC 24, 32–33, 34; *Bradley* v. *Carritt* [1903] AC 253, 255–258; (2) approved with reservations in *Bradley* [1903] AC 253, 278, Lord Lindley; (3) approved in *Kreglinger* [1914] AC 25, 43, 56; (4) ignored in *Knightsbridge*, CA.

[93] *Mainland* v. *Upjohn* (1889) 41 Ch D 126; *Noakes* [1902] AC 24, 33; *Bradley* [1903] AC 253, 255; *Krelinger* [1914] AC 25, 37, 54; ECC Firth (1895) 11 *LQR* 144.

[94] *Spurgeon* v. *Collier* (1758) 1 Eden 55, 28 ER 605; *Seton* v. *Slade* (1802) 7 Ves 265, 32 ER 108; *Treevan* v. *Smith* (1882) 20 Ch D 724.

[95] *Barrett* v. *Hartley* (1866) LR 2 Eq 789; *Biggs* v. *Hoddinott* [1898] 2 Ch 307, CA.

[96] *Salt* v. *Marquess of Northampton* [1892] AC 1, 19, Lord Bramwell.

[97] [1914] AC 25, 37, Lord Haldane, 56, Lord Parker.

[98] Ie it charged any asset owned by the company for the time being.

[99] *Biggs* v. *Hoddinott* [1898] 2 Ch 307, CA (tied house clause).

tion, so the technical ratio may be restricted to collateral arrangements reached in a separate (albeit contemporaneous) transaction.[100] However, now that the House of Lords is free to depart from earlier decisions, a wider interpretation of the ratio is likely.

Collateral advantages which create a permanent fetter remain invalid. A borrower cannot restrict his land for ever. *Noakes* v. *Rice*[101] concerned a leasehold pub with 26 years of the term outstanding; a tied house clause throughout the remaining 26 years was invalid from the time of redemption of the loan. Similarly in *Bradley* v. *Carritt*[102] a provision securing to the lender the position of broker to a tea company in a mortgage of shares in the company was void, since the shares were permanently devalued.

5.   Unlawful restraints of trade

[29.14] Any interference with a freedom of action in trading is a restraint, liable to be struck down in English law as contrary to public policy,[103] or by European rules.[104] Restraints of trade survive only if reasonable in the private interests of the parties[105] and also in the public interest.[106] Mortgage terms are open to challenge as shown by *Esso Petroleum Co* v. *Harper's Garage (Stourport)*[107] in the House of Lords. Esso lent £7,000 to Harper's Garage in return for a "solus" agreement preventing the sale of competitors' brands of petrol. The tie on the Corner Garage at Stourport for 21 years was held to be an unreasonable restriction of free competition.[108] A shorter tie for five years affecting a garage at Kidderminster was acceptable.[109] The doctrine is arbitrary since it bites only if a trader loses some existing freedom to trade,[110] but not where he uses a mortgage to fund the initial acquisition of premises from which he never enjoyed uncontrolled trading rights[111] nor where the mortgage and tie are in separate documents.[112]

---

[100]   *Vauxhall* (1969) 20 P & CR 1, 6–9, Ungoed-Thomas J; Glanvill Williams (1944) 60 *LQR* 190.

[101]   [1902] AC 24, 35, Lord Davey.

[102]   [1903] AC 253, HL; approved in *Kreglinger* [1914] AC 25, HL.

[103]   *Nordenfelt* v. *Maxim Nordenfelt Guns & Ammunition Co* [1894] AC 535, 565, Lord Macnaghten.

[104]   *Delimitis* v. *Henniger Brain* [1991] ECR I–935; *Star Rider* v. *Inntrepreneur Pub Co* [1998] 1 EGLR 53, Blackburne J; N Hopkins (1998) 49 *NILQ* 202; *Inntrepreneur Pub Co (CPC)* v. *Price* [1999] EGCS 185, Ch D; *Gibbs Mew* v. *Gemmell* [1999] 1 EGLR 43, CA; *Passmore* v. *Morland* [1999] 3 All ER 1005, CA.

[105]   The relaxed view in *Kreglinger* applies: *Hill* v. *Regent Oil Co* [1962] EGD 452; *Esso* [1968] AC 269, 341G, Lord Wilberforce; *Alec Lobb (Garages)* v. *Total Oil GB* [1985] 1 WLR 173.

[106]   *Nordenfelt* [1894] AC 535, 573–574, Lord Macnaghten.

[107]   [1968] AC 269, HL; PG Whiteman (1966) 29 *MLR* 77; PV Baker (1966) 82 *LQR* 307; PV Baker (1967) 83 *LQR* 478; T Heyden (1969) 85 *LQR* 229, 232 (lease and lease back).

[108]   At 321G, Lord Morris.

[109]   Also: *Texaco* v. *Mulberry Filling Station* [1972] 1 WLR 814 (five years); *Alec Lobb (Garages)* v. *Total Oil GB* [1985] 1 WLR 173 (break clause after 7 and 14 years).

[110]   *Esso* at 298B–E, Lord Reid, 309B–F, Lord Morris, 325C–E, Lord Pearce; *Cleveland Petroleum Co* v. *Dartstone* [1969] 1 WLR 116, CA.

[111]   *Alec Lobb* [1985] 1 WLR 173.

[112]   *Re Petrol Filling Station, Vauxhall Bridge Road* (1969) 20 P & CR 1.

D. COMMERCIAL REPOSSESSION

1. Right to possession

[29.15] Possession is a right of a mortgage-lender whose security is legal.[113] Why? Because a lender with a legal charge has the same rights as a lender by demise, who is entitled as a tenant of the property.[114] This preserves the pre-1926 rights of lenders derived from ownership of the estate mortgaged. A lender with an equitable mortgage does not hold a legal estate, and requires a court order before taking possession[115] or collecting rent.[116] However, it is arguable today that the rights under a *Walsh* v. *Lonsdale* equity[117] should correspond to those under a legal mortgage, given the prospective effect of specific performance. An equitable charge gives no right to possession.[118]

Domestic borrowers are protected against minor defaults by the Administration of Justice Acts 1970–1973.[119] In the commercial sector, possession is not dependent upon default. That the right pre-dates the contractual redemption date is demonstrated by Harman J's remark in *Four-Maids* v. *Dudley Marshall (Properties)*[120] that the lender "may go into possession before the ink is dry on the mortgage." Possession is needed after a default to facilitate a sale and at any other time when the value of his security is threatened, but the lender may take possession even if he cannot demonstrate any reason to go in. Equity never intervened to prevent a common law possession action,[121] a theoretical inequity but one which has proved of little account since equity did compel the lender to account by paying an occupation rent after taking possession for his own purposes.[122] The common law right to repossession was examined in exhaustive detail by the Court of Appeal in *Ropaigealach* v. *Barclays Bank*.[123]

When the Chancery Division assumed exclusive jurisdiction over mortgage repossession in 1936, the only power was to stay proceedings for a short time to enable the mortgage to be redeemed in full, and this remains the only protection for commercial borrowers.[124] Apart, that is, for the contractual provisions, which are generally

---

[113] Sufficiently proved by official copies: CPR 33.

[114] LPA 1925 ss 87, 95(4); *Spector* v. *Applefield Properties* (1968) 206 EG 537 (includes successors). First lenders before later ones if there is a competition: Practice Direction [1968] 1 WLR 422; *Cassell Arenz & Co* v. *Taylor* (1968) 209 EG 357.

[115] *Barclays Bank* v. *Bird* [1954] Ch 274, Harman J; *Ex p Bignold* (1832) 2 Deac & Ch 398, Eldon LC; *Spencer* v. *Mason* (1931) 75 SJ 295.

[116] *Cox* v. *Bishop* (1857) 8 De GM & G 815, 44 ER 604; *Finck* v. *Tranter* [1905] 1 KB 427; *Vacuum Oil Co* v. *Ellis* [1914] 1 KB 693, CA.

[117] RE Megarry (1954) 70 *LQR* 161; HWR Wade (1955) 71 *LQR* 204; see above **[24.05]**.

[118] *Bland* v. *Ingram's Estate (No 2)* [2001] EWCA Civ 1088, [2002] 1 All ER 264, [19].

[119] See below **[30.18ff]**.

[120] [1957] Ch 317, 320.

[121] But see below **[30.34]**.

[122] See below **[29.17]**.

[123] [2000] QB 263, 271–276, Chadwick LJ; *Remon* v. *City of London Real Property Co* [1921] 1 KB 49, CA; *Cruise* v. *Tewell* [1922] 1 KB 644, CA; *Lavender* v. *Betts* [1942] 2 All ER 72.

[124] *Birmingham PBS* v. *Caunt* [1962] Ch 883, 894, Russell J; RE Megarry (1962) 78 *LQR* 171; *Mobil Oil Co* v. *Rawlinson* (1982) 43 P & CR 221, Nourse J; *Ropaigealach* at 272F, Chadwick LJ.

included in commercial mortgages, for example, limiting the right to possession[125] so that it accrues only on default.[126]

2. Position of borrower

[29.16] Borrowers are usually left in possession. They have been viewed successively as tenants at sufferance,[127] and contractual licensees,[128] but are now better seen as exercising ownership until the lender asserts his superior rights. Thus, for example, the borrower may collect rent[129] suing in his own name.[130]

3. Occupation rent where lender takes possession

[29.17] Read literally, mortgages allow the lender at one and the same time both possession of the land *and* interest under the borrower's personal covenant to pay it, but first the usury laws (now repealed) and later equity intervened to prevent this double profit.[131] A lender who takes personal occupation is required to pay an occupation rent,[132] and if he collects rent under an existing lease[133] it must be applied to payment of interest, with surpluses going to reduce the capital debt.[134] Rent and interest were balanced annually if there was no reason to take possession – that is if there was no default and the rents exceeded the interest[135] – but otherwise over the whole period of possession.[136]

The account extends beyond actual receipts to include what the lender ought to have received[137] on the basis of wilful default. Where a purchaser was allowed rent-free occupation for four months before completion of the purchase, a master was left to determine whether wilful default had occurred.[138] Property must be let if possible[139] at a market rent.[140] *White* v. *City of London Brewery Co*[141] bought to book a brewery company which had taken possession of a pub and then let it as a house tied

[125] *Four Maids* [1957] Ch 317, 320, Harman J; *Braithwaite* v. *Winwood* [1960] 1 WLR 1257.
[126] *Birmingham PBS* v. Caunt [1962] Ch 883, 912, Russell J; RJ Smith [1979] *Conv* 266; H Wallace (1986) 37 *NILQ* 336. Some peg is required on which to hang this implication: *Esso Petroleum Co* v. *Alstonbridge Properties* [1975] 3 All ER 358, 367–368, Walton J (default is a once and for all trigger); *Western Bank* v. *Schindler* [1977] Ch 1, CA; (1976) 92 *LQR* 482; *TSB Bank* v. *Ladsky (No 2)* (1997) 74 P & CR 372, CA.
[127] *Thunder d Weaver* v. *Belcher* (1803) 3 East 449, 102 ER 669.
[128] *Rhodes* v. *Allied Dunbar Pension Services* [1989] 1 WLR 800, 807, Nicholls LJ; EC Ryder (1969) 22 *CLP* 129, 142–143.
[129] LPA 1925 s 141(2); LT (Covenants) Act 1995 s 15(1)(b).
[130] LPA 1925 s 98. Defects in Judicature Act 1873 s 25(2) were remedied in 1881: *Turner* v. *Walsh* [1909] 2 KB 484, 496, Farwell LJ.
[131] *Bright* v. *Campbell* (1885) 54 LJ Ch 1077, CA.
[132] *Trulock* v. *Robey* (1847) 2 Ph 395, 41 ER 995; *Marriott* v. *Anchor Reversionary Co* (1861) 3 De GF & J 177, 193, 45 ER 846, Turner LJ.
[133] Possession of rents is taken by giving notice: *Turner* v. *Walsh* [1909] 2 KB 484, 494, Farwell LJ; *Moss* v. *Gallimore* (1779) 1 Doug KB 279, 99 ER 182; *Pope* v. *Biggs* (1829) 9 B & C 245, 109 ER 91.
[134] *Gaskell* v. *Gosling* [1896] 1 QB 669, 691, Rigby LJ dissenting; on appeal [1897] AC 595, HL.
[135] *Wrigley* v. *Gill* [1906] 1 Ch 165, CA. A break in the accounts = a rest.
[136] *Nelson* v. *Booth* (1858) 3 De G & J 119, 122, 44 ER 1214.
[137] *Parkinson* v. *Hanbury* (1867) LR 2 HL 1, 15, Lord Westbury.
[138] *Shepard* v. *Jones* (1882) 21 Ch D 469; *Bright* v. *Campbell* (1885) 54 LJ Ch 1077.
[139] *Brandon* v. *Brandon* (1862) 10 WR 287; *Noyes* v. *Pollock* (1886) 32 Ch D 53.
[140] *Sherwin* v. *Shakespear* (1854) 5 De GM & G 517, 537, 43 ER 970.
[141] (1889) 42 Ch D 237, CA.

to its own beer: the lender was liable to account for the higher rent which could have been obtained as a free house.[142] Although "it is not a pleasant thing to be a mortgagee in possession"[143] the inconvenience of these rules can be overstated. Notice to the borrower of a proposed letting will usually preclude any future complaint.[144]

4. Appointment of a receiver

[29.18] A lender,[145] even one in possession,[146] who wishes to collect rent is best advised to appoint a Law of Property Act receiver,[147] securing the practical benefits of possession without the onerous liability to account. The receiver is an agent of the borrower,[148] but the agency is irrevocable[149] and the receiver acts for the benefit of the lender.[150] Powers include recovery of rent by action, distress, renewal,[151] and giving receipts for rent,[152] and insuring by direction of the lender, as well as delegated powers of leasing and accepting surrenders.[153] Sale requires an express power.[154]

A receiver's basic function is to collect rents. Out of the money collected must be paid prior costs and taxes,[155] the commission of the receiver,[156] insurance premiums, and costs of repairs. The net sum left is applied to the interest due under the mortgage. Any surplus must be used to reduce the principal if the lender so directs, but otherwise it should be handed back to the borrower.[157] A disadvantage is that superior landlords may divert the rents by a statutory notice:[158] *Rhodes* v. *Allied Dunbar Pension Services*[159] decides that the head landlord's rent diversion notice prevailed against the receiver, who was an agent of the borrower. Had the *lender* taken possession of the

---

[142] At 245.

[143] Maitland's *Equity*, 187.

[144] *Hughes* v. *Williams* (1806) 12 Ves 493, 33 ER 187.

[145] A first lender has priority in making an appointment: *Underhay* v. *Read* (1887) 20 QBD 209, CA. However, multiple receivers are a possibility: *Gwembe Valley Development Co* v. *Kosky* [2000] Times February 8th, Rimer J.

[146] *Refuge Assurance Co* v. *Pearlberg* [1938] Ch 687.

[147] LPA 1925 s 101(1)(iii); PJ Millett (1977) 41 *Conv (NS)* 83 (effect of bankruptcy); J White (1993) 8 *Ins L & P* 173. Contrast (1) an administrative receivership under the insolvency legislation; (2) a receiver appointed under a floating charge who may take control of an entire business to run it with a view to its rescue.

[148] *Jefferys* v. *Dickson* (1866) LR 1 Ch App 183, 190, Cranworth LC; *Lever Finance* v. *Needleman's Trustee* [1956] Ch 375; *Solomons* v. *R Gertzenstein* [1954] 2 QB 243, CA.

[149] *Gaskell* v. *Gosling* [1896] 1 QB 669, 692, Rigby LJ, dissenting but approved at [1897] AC 575, HL.

[150] *Re B Johnson & Co (Builders)* [1955] Ch 634, 644, Evershed MR; *Chatsworth Properties* v. *Effiom* [1971] 1 WLR 144.

[151] *Marsh* v. *Mouskos* [1964] 2 QB 23, CA.

[152] He may be liable for negligence eg in failing to serve rent review trigger notices: *Knight* v. *Lawrence* [1991] 1 EGLR 143.

[153] LPA 1925 ss 99, 100(13).

[154] *Phoenix Properties* v. *Wimpole St Nominees* [1992] BCLC 737, 742–743, Mummery J. The duty of a receiver is the same as a lender: *Silver Properties* v. *Royal Bank of Scotland* [2002] EWHC 1976 (Ch), [2002] 41 EG 176 (CS).

[155] *John Willment (Ashford)* [1979] 2 All ER 615; *Ratford* v. *Northavon DC* [1987] QB 357; *Re Kentish Homes* [1993] BCLC 1375, Nicholls V-C; *Powdrill & Lyle* v. *Tower Hamlets LBC* [1993] BCC 212; *Re Sobam* [1996] 1 BCLC 646.

[156] 5% unless otherwise specified: *Marshall* v. *Cottingham* [1981] Ch 82.

[157] *White* v. *Metcalfe* [1903] 2 Ch 567, 570, Kekewich J.

[158] Law of Distress Amendment Act 1908.

[159] [1989] 1 WLR 800, CA.

rent the result would have been reversed, for the rents would no longer have belonged to the borrower company and would not have been vulnerable to diversion.

5. Power to grant leases

[29.19] A lender in possession of the mortgaged property has the power of granting leases binding the borrower and later lenders under statutory powers.[160] Agricultural and occupation leases are authorised to a maximum of 50 years and building leases to a maximum term of 999 years,[161] subject to formal requirements.[162] A lender in possession may also accept a surrender of a lease for the purposes of granting an immediate replacement.[163]

E. SALE UNDER EXPRESS POWERS

1. Sale out of court

[29.20] The usual method of enforcement is by sale. Statutory powers date from 1860[164] but the version now appearing in the Law of Property Act 1925[165] has been refined to the stage at which it is perfectly adequate for all legal lenders, though it is open to amendment.[166] Sale is by the lender alone without reference to the borrower.[167] The power of sale extends to growing crops,[168] fixtures and chattels.[169]

2. Default justifying sale

(1) The power arising

[29.21] This is the purely notional default which is the only check required of a *buyer* in order to guarantee his title. Firstly the buyer must ensure that the mortgage is by deed. Secondly, probably, he must check that it is legal. Thirdly, the statutory power of sale must not be excluded or restricted.[170] A final check is that the mortgage money

---

[160] LPA 1925 s 99 (dating from 1881); Building Societies Act 1986 sch 8 (power to provide any "services relating to land"). Leases also bind later lenders: s 99(2).

[161] Pre-1926, 21 years and 99 years respectively; *Brown* v. *Peto* [1900] 2 QB 653.

[162] Defective leases act as contracts: LPA 1925 s 99(12); they are often validated by ss 99(4), 152; *Iron Trades Employers Assoc* v. *Union Land & House Investors* [1937] Ch 313.

[163] LPA 1925 s 100, introduced in 1911 to reverse *Robbins* v. *Whyte* [1906] 1 KB 125. The power is narrow and best extended.

[164] Trustees and Mortgages Act 1860 (Lord Cranworth's Act) s 11.

[165] LPA 1925 s 101(1)(i); also Building Societies Act 1986 sch 4 para 1; HA 1985 s 17 (local authorities); Megarry & Wade (6th ed), [19.056–19.066].

[166] LPA 1925 s 101(4). This power cannot be used to sell part of a commonhold unit: Commonhold & L Ref A 2002 sch 15. Where there are two powers: LPA 1925 s 104(3); *Phoenix Properties* v. *Wimpole Street Nominees* [1992] BCLC 737, 743e–h.

[167] If the landlord's consent is required this must not be refused unreasonably: LPA 1925 s 89(1).

[168] *Boydell* v. *McMichael* (1834) 1 Cr M & R 177, 149 ER 1043; *Longstaff* v. *Meagoe* (1834) 2 Ad & El 167, 111 ER 65; *Southport* v. *Thompson* (1887) 37 Ch D 64; EC Firth (1899) 15 *LQR* 165; *Monti* v. *Barnes* [1901] 1 KB 205, CA.

[169] LPA 1925 ss 88(4), 89(4); *Botham* v. *TSB Bank* (1997) 73 P & CR D1, CA; see above **[2.25]**.

[170] *Western Bank* v. *Schindler* [1977] Ch 1, CA; *Braithwaite* v. *Winwood* [1960] 1 WLR 1257. Conversely it is possible to exclude the requirement for the mortgage money to be due: *Banque Worms* v. *The Maule* [1997] 1 WLR 528, PC.

is due, meaning that the contractual redemption date has passed (a date convention-
ally six months after the loan), thus creating a debt at law. All are easily verified from
the copy of the mortgage deed recorded on the register or supplied by seller to buyer.
A person who buys before the power of sale has arisen takes a transfer of the lender's
rights but will not defeat the rights of the borrower.[171]

The only problem is with an *instalment mortgage* since the time that the mortgage
money becomes due depends upon the exact phrasing of the mortgage. A pure mortgage providing for instalments but without further express provision was considered
in *Payne* v. *Cardiff RDC*.[172] Lord Hanworth MR decided that the power of sale arose
"when any instalment of the mortgage money has become due in the manner provided
by the mortgage deed". This convenient decision is difficult to justify from the wording of section 101, and in any event, a buyer is left to investigate the repayment schedule to ensure that an instalment is in arrears – a precaution rarely taken in practice.
Uncertainty is avoided by including a default clause making the whole debt repayable
in the event of failure to pay any one instalment. The right to sell is undisputed,
though title remains dependent upon proof that the default clause has operated.
Where repayment is postponed for a fixed period (such as 10 years) a default clause is
absolutely essential to ensure that money may become "due" on a default before the
end of the 10 years.[173]

(2) Exercise

[29.22] The power of sale becomes *exercisable* on the conditions specified in section
103 of the Law of Property Act 1925[174] as modified. Sale before a sufficient default
would lead to a successful objection by the borrower, who could obtain an injunction
to prevent an irregular sale,[175] or recover damages after completion.[176] After the
power has become exercisable the lender can proceed in safety. The grounds are:

(1) default in complying with a notice to repay any of the mortgage money for
three months;[177]
(2) interest remaining unpaid for two months after becoming due[178] – the most
common ground; or
(3) breach of some other condition of the mortgage.[179]

---

[171] LPA 1925 s 104(2)(a); *Frost* v. *Ralph* (1981) 115 DLR (3d) 612.

[172] [1932] 1 KB 241 (charge for street works with the council having statutory powers as if mortgage
lenders); (1932) 48 *LQR* 158; *Walsh* v. *Derrick* (1903) 19 TLR 209, CA.

[173] *Twentieth Century Banking* v. *Wilkinson* [1977] Ch 99, Templeman J (judicial sale ordered).

[174] LPA 1925 s 101(3); *Alliance BS* v. *Shave* [1952] Ch 581 (total exclusion).

[175] *Price Brothers (Somerford)* v. *Kelly Homes* [1975] 1 WLR 1512.

[176] LPA 1925 s 104(2); *Fletcher & Campbell* v. *City Marine Finance* [1968] 2 Lloyds Rep 520.

[177] *Barker* v. *Illingworth* [1908] 2 Ch 20 (time runs from service).

[178] Beware a capitalisation clause which converts interest to capital: *Davy* v. *Turner* (1970) 21 P & CR
967.

[179] *Ladsky* v. *TSB Bank* (1997) 74 P & CR 372, CA (disrepair). If bankruptcy is a ground, leave of the
bankruptcy court is required: LPA 1925 ss 104(2)(c), 110.

(3) Protection of a buyer against non-exercisability

[29.23] Once the power of sale has arisen, the buyer's title is secure even if there is no default to make it exercisable.[180] Buyers need not check the state of accounts between borrower and lender, that notice was given or whether the power was "otherwise improperly or irregularly exercised".[181] Protection certainly attaches to an honest purchaser. There is no duty to make inquiries and it is wise not to ask.[182]

What if the buyer knows that the power is not exercisable, but goes ahead regardless? Read literally, the statutory wording appears to make his title safe,[183] from the time of his contract.[184] However, cases on express prophylactic clauses had not protected a buyer if he actually knew of an abuse, for example that sale occurred after the lender had refused a proper tender of the whole redemption monies.[185] If the defects could be waived, the buyer might be entitled to assume that there had indeed been a waiver,[186] but a majority view was that he had a duty to inquire.[187]

Buyers of registered land may rely on the register and are bound only by matters reflecting a register entry.[188]

3. The buyer's title to unregistered land

[29.24] Sales by lenders are based on a power of sale over an estate which they do not hold. Ordinary conveyancing made the journey from power-based to estate-based transfer in 1925 at the precise moment that sales by mortgage lenders made the reverse trip, so that sale by a lender of registered[189] or unregistered land[190] is based on a statutory power.

Theoretically any lender can sell the land independently of any other lender, but in practice there is little point in a second lender selling unless he secures the first lender's consent by agreeing to redeem him. A sale by a lender overreaches[191] and removes *later* mortgages and the borrower's equity of redemption and shifts them to the proceeds of sale.

A lender sells subject to burdens existing and protected at the time of the mortgage, since the lender cannot pass a better title than that mortgaged to him.[192] However, he

---

[180] LPA 1925 s 113; *Beddoes* v. *Shaw* [1937] Ch 81, Bennett J (limited effect).

[181] LPA 1925 s 104(2).

[182] *Dicker* v. *Angerstein* (1876) 3 Ch D 600; *Kirkwood* v. *Thompson* (1865) 2 H & M 392, 403, 71 ER 515; *Bailey* v. *Barnes* [1894] 1 Ch 25, CA.

[183] LPA 1925 s 104(2); HW Wilkinson [1988] *Conv* 317; *Price Bros (Somerford)* v. *Kelly* [1975] 1 WLR 1512, CA; *Northern Developments (Holdings)* v. *UDT Securities* [1976] 1 WLR 1230, Megarry J; S Robinson [1989] *Conv* 412.

[184] *Waring* v. *London & Manchester Assurance Co* [1935] Ch 310, Crossman J.

[185] *Jenkins* v. *Jones* (1860) 2 Giff 99, 109, 66 ER 43; *Parkinson* v. *Hanbury* (1860) 1 Drew & Sm 143, 62 ER 332, on appeal (1865) 2 De GJ & Sm 450, 46 ER 419; *Selwyn* v. *Garfit* (1888) 38 Ch D 273, CA.

[186] *Selwyn* at 285, Bowen LJ.

[187] At 283, Cotton LJ, 284, Lindley LJ; *Anchor Trust Co* v. *Bell* [1926] Ch 805, 820, Lawrence J.

[188] LRA 2002 s 26; Law Com 271 (2001), [7.8].

[189] LRA 2002 s 23(2)(a); LR Form TR2.

[190] LPA 1925 ss 88, 89, 101(6), 104(1); *Rust* v. *Goodale* [1957] Ch 33, 47, Harman J.

[191] LPA 1925 s 2(1)(iii).

[192] LPA 1925 ss 88(6), 89(6), 104(1). The seller guarantees only that he had not encumbered the land, that is he gives a limited guarantee of title; see above **[11.63]**.

can sell free of burdens subsequently created by the borrower without his consent. Thus in *Lyus* v. *Prowsa Developments*[193] a lender was able to transfer a registered title free of a caution entered on the register to protect a contract made by the borrower. Entries on the charges register of burdens with inferior priority are cancelled after completion of a lender's sale of registered land.[194]

Sale prevents the borrower redeeming the mortgage. This is obvious once sale is completed, but the bar dates from the time of the contract to sell.[195] *Duke* v. *Robson*[196] resolved a contest between two contracting purchasers, in favour of the one buying from the lender and against the one buying from the borrower.

4. Form for sale of registered land

[29.25] Sale uses a form which is much the same as for any other transfer, except that it is modified to make clear that sale occurs "in exercise of the power of sale conferred by the charge."[197] Sale defeats interests entered in the charges register after the mortgage under which sale takes place.[198]

5. Sale under an equitable mortgage

[29.26] Remedies available to an equitable lender are foreclosure[199] and judicial sale.[200] Is sale out of court a further option? Clearly this is only possible if the equitable mortgage is made by deed.[201] Before 1926, legal title was passed to the first legal lender, and since the borrower had no title it was obvious that a later equitable lender could not sell the legal estate.[202]

The 1925 legislation ought to improve the position of the equitable lender since the legal estate remains in the borrower and there is no reason why an equitable lender should not transfer an estate vested in the borrower in the same way as a legal lender, since the estate which an equitable lender "is authorised to sell" includes "such estate and interest as . . . may be subject to the mortgage".[203] Lord Denning MR's support for this view in *Re White Rose Cottage*[204] is often thought to be technically loose, but for once he was correct in law as well as in reason. However, the doubters are sufficiently forceful to prevent buyers accepting title made in this way.

---

[193] [1982] 1 WLR 1044 (obiter).
[194] *Re Winter* (1873) LR 15 Eq 156; *Re Richardson* (1871) LR 12 Eq 398.
[195] *Waring* v. *London & Manchester Assurance Co* [1935] Ch 310; H Potter (1935) 51 *LQR* 434; *Property & Bloodstock* v. *Emerton* [1968] Ch 94, 117G, Danckwerts LJ, 125F, Sellers LJ, 122–123, Sachs LJ (doubtful).
[196] [1973] 1 WLR 267, CA.
[197] DLRR 2003 sch 1; LR Form TR2.
[198] LRA 2002 s 30.
[199] *James* v. *James* (1873) LR 16 Eq 153; *Edge* v. *Worthington* (1786) 1 Cox Eq 211, 29 ER 1133; *Parker* v. *Housefield* (1834) 2 My & K 419, 39 ER 1004; *Carter* v. *Wake* (1877) 4 Ch D 685; *Heath* v. *Pugh* (1881) 6 QBD 345, 359, Selborne LC.
[200] LPA 1925 s 91; *Oldham* v. *Stringer* (1884) 51 LT 895 (1881 Act).
[201] LPA 1925 s 101.
[202] *Re Hodson & Howe's Contract* (1881) 35 Ch D 668, CA.
[203] LPA 1925 s 104(1). Sale under a legal or equitable mortgage is power-based and it seems to make no difference whether the power is legal or equitable.
[204] [1965] Ch 940, 951A–D.

In practice title is stiffened by the use of a conveyancing device:[205] an equitable mortgage generally includes a power of attorney by which the borrower authorises the lender to sell the mortgaged land, a power which is irrevocable while the loan is outstanding,[206] but which suffers from the defect that the transfer of the borrower's interest is subject to any equitable interests created by the borrower.[207]

If title is registered, only a registered proprietor of a charge is entitled to sell, so the power of sale is clearly restricted to a legal lender.[208]

6. Enforcement reform

[29.27] Law Commission reform of mortgage law is proposed,[209] though the Government has requested further work on the present report. Sale would be limited to formal legal mortgages, with the only right for an equitable lender to have the mortgage perfected. Existing powers of possession and sale would be retained. The requirement for a power of sale to arise would be abolished

F. JUDICIAL SALE

[29.28] Section 91 of the Law of Property Act 1925 authorises the court to order a sale.[210] In its current form it dates back to 1881. Application can be made by the lender or any other person interested in the mortgaged property,[211] but the claim must bring all other interested parties before the court.

1. Lenders unable to sell out of court

[29.29] Examples are equitable lenders,[212] and legal lenders whose repayment is postponed without a default clause.[213] Lenders may apply if they have a present right to foreclose the borrower – for example for failure to pay interest – and arguably even if they cannot foreclose immediately.[214] Section 91 may also overcome a borrower who threatens to crab a lender's sale.[215]

---

[205] *London County and Westminster Bank v. Tompkins* [1918] 1 KB 515.

[206] Powers of Attorney Act 1971 s 4 (dating from 1882).

[207] *Re White Rose Cottage* [1965] Ch 940, CA; Lord Denning MR and Russell LJ were agreed on this point.

[208] LRA 2002 s 23(1).

[209] Law Com 204 (1991) part VII; P Jackson (1978) 94 *LQR* 571; AL Diamond (1989) 42 *CLP* 231; GH Griffiths [1987] *Conv* 191; HW Wilkinson [1992] *Conv* 69; GH Griffiths [1992] *JBL* 423; G Frost (1992) 136 *SJ* 267, 292.

[210] *Union Bank of London v. Ingram* (1882) 20 Ch D 463, 464, Jessel MR.

[211] LPA 1925 s 91(2); *Green v. Biggs* (1885) 52 LT 680; *Jones v. Harris* (1885) 55 LT 884.

[212] LPA 1925 s 91(7); *Oldham v. Stringer* (1884) 51 LT 895; see above **[29.26]**.

[213] *Twentieth Century Banking Corp v. Wilkinson* [1977] Ch 99, Templeman J.

[214] But LPA 1925 s 91(1) extended existing rights and subs (2) should be limited to sale in lieu of some other order that is in lieu of an existing right to foreclosure.

[215] *Arab Bank v. Mercantile Holdings* [1994] Ch 71, Millett J.

2. Borrowers seeking sale rather than foreclosure

[29.30] If a lender attempts to foreclose, the borrower or anyone else interested in the equity of redemption may[216] apply for sale to be ordered instead of foreclosure.[217] The benefit of sale is that the equity is salvaged for the borrower, so a request for sale is inevitable whenever there is a surplus. Lenders benefit by avoiding the delays inherent in foreclosure,[218] or conversely in a borrower's redemption action.[219]

3. Borrowers wishing to force lenders to sell

[29.31] The remarkably broad terms[220] of section 91(2) provide that the court may:

"on the request of the mortgagee, or of any person interested either in the mortgage money or in the right of redemption . . . direct a sale of the mortgaged property."

Sale can be ordered against the wishes of the lender.[221] *Palk* v. *Mortgage Services Funding*[222] concerned a thatched property in Sussex subject to a large mortgage with an outstanding debt of £350,000.[223] Sale was likely to raise about £283,000, making the case one of "negative equity", in which the borrowers were not in a position to redeem the entire mortgage. They wanted to curtail the addition of interest at the rate of £43,000 each year, whereas the lenders wished to let the property at £13,000 a year, leaving an income gap, speculating that the property market would eventually rise sufficiently for them to recoup their entire loan.[224] Sale was ordered. Deferral by the lenders should be at their own risk. A lender's objection can be overruled when it is unfair to the borrower, for example where the Palks faced financial haemorrhage for an indefinite period.[225] Through sale, the Palks were able to reduce their debt from £300,000 to a more manageable £75,000.

The lenders' conduct in *Palk* was extreme and exceptional, and unlike any previous reported case.[226] An attempt to generalise the principle of the case to any borrower with negative equity[227] was rejected in the appellate courts.[228] A lender intending to sell and taking active steps to enforce its security is entitled to control the sale process,

---

[216] Sale is discretionary: *Silsby* v. *Holliman* [1955] Ch 552.

[217] Foreclosure is now virtually unheard of: *Palk* [1993] Ch 330, 326E.

[218] LPA 1925 s 91(2); *Palk* [1993] Ch 330, 335, 341; *Jones* v. *Harris* (1885) 55 LT 884; *Woolley* v. *Colman* (1882) 21 Ch D 169.

[219] LPA 1925 s 91(4).

[220] *Palk* [1993] Ch 330, 341D, Sir Michael Kerr.

[221] LPA 1925 s 91(2)(a); dating from 1881: *Woolley* v. *Colman* (1882) 21 Ch D 169; *Brewer* v. *Square* [1892] 2 Ch 111, 114.

[222] [1993] Ch 330, CA; JE Martin [1993] *Conv* 59; HW Wilkinson [1993] *NLJ* 448; A Samuels (1994) 138 *SJ* 1070; R Cottrell (1992) 136 *SJ* 1066; *Polonski* v. *Lloyds Bank* [1998] 1 FLR 896.

[223] High earners are most at risk of repossession.

[224] For the converse case see *Merchant Banking Co of London* v. *London & Hanseatic Bank* (1886) 55 LJ Ch 479; *Provident Clerks' Association* v. *Lewis* (1892) 62 LJ Ch 89, North J.

[225] *Palk* [1993] Ch 330, 344H.

[226] At 344C.

[227] *Barrett* v. *Halifax BS* (1995) 28 HLR 634.

[228] *Cheltenham & Gloucester* v. *Krausz* [1997] 1 WLR 1558, CA; A Kenny [1998] *Conv* 223; *Pearn* v. *Mortgage Business* [1998] 05 LSG 30, Rimer J.

deciding whether a sale price is too low. In a contest about control of sale the lender would win,[229] but *Palk* was a rare case in which the lender did not wish to sell.

4. Terms of sale

[29.32] Conduct of the sale can be given to any party, and perhaps ought to be given to the borrower if there is an equity, since he has the strongest incentive to secure the best price.[230] Some evidence of prospects of a successful sale is required.[231] The court can impose whatever terms it thinks fit for example requiring security for costs,[232] fixing a reserve price or setting a deadline for completion.[233]

G. PROCEEDS OF SALE AND SHORTFALL

1. Accounting for sale proceeds

[29.33] Purchase money must be paid to the mortgage lender, whose written receipt is a sufficient discharge for the buyer.[234]

The lender receives the proceeds on trust. These are applied first in payment of costs, charges, and expenses properly incurred by the lender in sale, attempts to sell, or otherwise. Sale does not effect any change in rights so the lender can deduct from the proceeds all money that was formerly charged on the house.[235] On a sale by a second lender, either sale is subject to the first mortgage or it is necessary to discharge the prior mortgage out of the proceeds. The net balance is applied in discharge of the mortgage under which sale occurs[236] – including the mortgage money, interest,[237] costs and other money due under the mortgage.

Any surplus is held on a trust[238] which, despite the statutory wording, is limited to the surplus.[239] This must be paid "to the person entitled to the mortgaged property."[240] The literal meaning – the buyer (!) – is clearly a slip, and section 105 is intended to refer to the person entitled to the equity of redemption following sale.[241] Any surplus should be paid over to the next secured lender in priority, who deducts

---

[229] *Krausz* at 1562, Phillips LJ.

[230] LPA 1925 s 91(3); *Woolley* v. *Colman* (1882) 21 Ch D 169, 174, Fry J; *Davies* v. *Wright* (1886) 32 Ch D 220; *Christy* v. *Van Tromp* [1886] WN 111 (no general rule); *Brewer* v. *Square* [1892] 2 Ch 111; *Norman* v. *Beaumont* [1893] WN 45 (later lender).

[231] *Provident Clerks'* as above.

[232] LPA 1925 s 91(2)–(3).

[233] Usually three months: *Green* v. *Biggs* (1885) 52 LT 680; *Oldham* v. *Stringer* (1884) 51 LT 895.

[234] LPA 1925 s 107(1). If the price is left outstanding on mortgage, the lender must account to the original borrower as if he has received cash: *Belton* v. *Bass Ratcliffe & Gretton* [1922] 2 Ch 449.

[235] *Barclays Bank* v. *Burgess* [2002] EWCA Civ 291, [2002] 12 EG 135 (CS).

[236] Non registration of the mortgage does not remove the lender's rights against the borrower and unsecured creditors: *Barclays Bank* v. *Buhr* [2001] EWCA Civ 1223, [2001] 31 EG 103 (CS).

[237] *West* v. *Diprose* [1900] 1 Ch 337 (no interest in lieu of notice).

[238] If part is sold see: *Wrigley* v. *Gill* [1905] 1 Ch 241, approved [1906] 1 Ch 165, CA; *Ainsworth* v. *Wilding* [1905] 1 Ch 435.

[239] *Banner* v. *Berridge* (1881) 18 Ch D 254, 269, Kay J; *Locking* v. *Parker* (1872) LR 8 Ch App 30.

[240] LPA 1925 s 105; alternatively to the person "authorised to give receipts for the proceeds of the sale thereof"; *Re Moat House Farm, Thurlby* [1948] Ch 191.

[241] *Re Walhampton Estate* (1884) 26 Ch D 391, Kay J.

what it is owed under his mortgage[242] and pays any balance on to the next entitled,[243] so that after all mortgages have been discharged, a surplus is left to which the borrower[244] is entitled. He may insist on his right to the surplus even if the loan was obtained by the borrower's fraud.[245] Since the borrower recovers his equity, sale is much more favourable to him than foreclosure.

Payment of proceeds to the wrong person may lead to an injunction,[246] or damages[247] or a penalty in costs.[248] Building societies are required to account promptly.[249]

Before distributing proceeds the lender must search the register of title[250] or make a land charges search if title is unregistered.[251]

2. Mortgage indemnity guarantee

[29.34] Proper lending practice leaves a margin between the amount advanced and the value of the security, to allow for falls in the property market. Building societies must take additional protection[252] and this is usual for all lenders. An insurance company provides a mortgage indemnity guarantee (MIG) to cover the lender's risk that a shortfall may arise on sale, on discovery of a forgery,[253] and possibly if the borrower walks away. It protects the lender rather than the borrower, even though the borrower pays the premium.[254] *Woolwich BS* v. *Brown*[255] rejected the argument that the borrower's personal liability should be limited to the loss above that covered by the insurance policy. The mortgage insurance guarantee was for the sole benefit of the lender, whatever borrowers generally believed. Once the insurance company has paid out on the policy, it can pursue a claim against the borrower by subrogation[256] – that is the company stands in the shoes of the lender it has paid.[257]

---

[242] Not: (1) personal claims: *Samuel Keller (Holdings)* v. *Martins Bank* [1971] 1 WLR 43, CA; and many earlier cases; (2) statute-barred debts: *Re Moat House Farm, Thurlby* [1948] Ch 191; *C & M Matthews* v. *Marsden BS* [1951] Ch 258; and many earlier cases; see above **[10.34ff]**.

[243] *Crompton & Evans' Union Bank* v. *Burton* [1895] 2 Ch 711; *Lane* v. *Harlock* (1856) 5 HLC 580, 10 ER 1028.

[244] Special cases: (1) trustees: *Re Bell* [1896] 1 Ch 1, CA; *Hockey* v. *Western* [1898] 1 Ch 350; (2) co-owners: *Re Cook's Mortgage* [1896] 1 Ch 923.

[245] *Halifax BS* v. *Thomas* [1996] Ch 217, CA.

[246] *Thornton* v. *Finch* (1865) 4 Giff 575, 66 ER 810.

[247] *West London Commercial Bank* v. *Reliance PBS* (1885) 29 Ch D 954, 962, Cotton LJ.

[248] *Charles* v. *Jones* (1887) 35 Ch D 544, Kay J.

[249] Building Societies Act 1986 sch 4; SI 1986/2216.

[250] LRA 2002 s 54; Law Com 271 (2001), [7.43].

[251] LPA 1925 s 198 (registration of land charge is actual notice).

[252] Building Societies Act 1986 s 10(2) (75% of value).

[253] *Metropolitan Mortgage Corp* v. *Eagle Star Insurance Co* [1994] CLYB 3287.

[254] Premiums are roughly 7% of the loan above 75%.

[255] [1996] CLC 625, Waller J.

[256] *Ghana Commercial Bank* v. *Chandiran* [1960] AC 732, 745; *Boscawen* v. *Bajwa* [1996] 1 WLR 328, CA; *Faircharm Investments* v. *Citibank International* [1998] Lloyd's Rep Bank 127, CA; *Halifax Mortgage Services* v. *Muirhead* (1998) 76 P & CR 418, CA; *Banque Financière de la Cité* v. *Parc (Battersea)* [1999] 1 AC 221, HL (personal); *Halifax* v. *Omar* [2002] EWCA Civ 121, [2002] 2 P & CR 26 at 377 (proprietary).

[257] Additional to claim against solicitor who acted for lender: *Bristol & West BS* v. *May May & Merrimans (No 2)* [1998] 1 WLR 336, Chadwick J.

3. Shortfall

[29.35] A mortgage involves both a security realised by sale and a debt enforceable (after the contractual redemption date) by personal action for a money judgment within 12 years.[258] The two aspects are independent.[259] Commercial sector lenders are uninhibited in pursuing the personal action and obtaining summary judgment.[260] However, action for debt is only common after the security has been sold, with the money action used to pursue any shortfall. After making allowance for the receipt of the sale proceeds, the borrower continues to owe the balance with interest. The borrower may have a defence of unconscionability[261] or be able to put forward a counterclaim.[262]

H. DEFECTIVE SALE

1. Malicious enforcement

[29.36] Whether and when to sell are decisions to be made solely by the lender. As Kay J said:

> "[T]he mortgagee . . . has a power for his own benefit to enable him better to realize his debt. If he exercises it bona fide for that purpose without corruption or collusion with the purchaser, the court will not interfere . . .".[263]

A lender is not a trustee of the power of sale,[264] not even if the particular mortgage took the form of a trust for sale![265] Lenders may consult their own convenience about the timing of sale, sitting back indefinitely to wait for the market to improve,[266] or the appointment of a receiver.[267] As the Privy Council stated in *China & South Sea Bank v. Tan Soon Gin* the lender is under no duty to sell "at any particular time or at all",[268]

---

[258] Limitation Act 1980 s 20; *Bristol & West* v. *Bartlett* [2002] EWCA Civ 1181, [2002] Times September 9th. Reform is proposed, see above **[10.24]**.

[259] *Northcott* v. *Underhill* (1698) 1 Ld Raym 388, 91 ER 1157 (deed informal; debt valid); *Bank of Ceylon* v. *Kandar* [1962] AC 314, PC (bond not pleaded); *Re BCCI (No 8)* [1997] 4 All ER 568, HL (lender can prove in borrower's insolvency rather than rely on security); R Calman (1998) 114 *LQR* 174; R Goode (1998) 114 *LQR* 178; C Rotherham [1998] *CLJ* 260.

[260] *Newnham* v. *Brown* [1966] 1 WLR 875; *National Westminster Bank* v. *Kitch* [1996] 1 WLR 1316, CA (leave not required). For domestic sector protection, see below **[30.30ff]**.

[261] *Miller* v. *Cook* (1870) LR 10 Eq 641 (interest charged on larger sum than advance).

[262] *Platts* v. *TSB Bank* [1998] 2 BCLC 1, CA.

[263] *Warner* v. *Jacob* (1882) 20 Ch D 220, 224; *Kennedy* v. *De Trafford* [1897] AC 180, 185, Lord Macnaughten.

[264] *Farrar* v. *Farrars* (1888) 40 Ch D 395, CA; *Colson* v. *Williams* (1889) 61 LT 71, Kekewich J; *Re Webb* [1933] Ch 29, 46, Hanworth MR.

[265] *Re Alison* (1879) 11 Ch D 284, CA.

[266] *Cuckmere Brick Co* v. *Mutual Finance* [1971] Ch 949, 965, Salmon LJ; *Palk* v. *Mortgage Funding Services* [1993] Ch 330, 337G, Nicholls V-C.

[267] *Shamji* v. *Johnson Matthey Bankers* [1991] BCLC 36, CA; *Re Potters Oils (No 2)* [1986] 1 WLR 201, Hoffman J.

[268] [1990] 1 AC 536, 545C–G, Lord Templeman; L Bentley [1990] *Conv* 431; *York Buildings* v. *Mackenzie* (1795) 3 Cr S & P 378.

even if there is ample equity.[269] Guaranteed rights of sale on default is precisely what makes mortgages attractive to the lender.[270]

Liability attaches only to a lender who sets out to harm the borrower[271] or acts "with the object of cheating",[272] since an obligation to act in good faith has always been recognised.[273] In *Downsview Nominees* v. *First City Corporation*,[274] the first lender appointed a receiver in order to disrupt a receivership of a Fiat franchise in New Zealand instigated by the second lender and proceeded to reject offers to redeem the first mortgage with such persistence that a court order was eventually required. This particular lender had broken its duties to the borrower and to subsequent lenders.

2. Proper price

[29.37] Since subsequent lenders and the borrower are entitled to any surplus, and are liable for any shortfall, it is they who stand to lose heavily from negligent sales by prior lenders.[275] Wise lenders protect themselves by getting the consent of later lenders and of the borrower to the terms of sale.[276]

Equity has long been in flux, swaying between unacceptable extremes without quite reaching a satisfactory equilibrium. When express powers of sale began to appear during the early 1800s,[277] Chancery treated the lender as a trustee.[278] Lenders were liberated from these onerous duties in the late nineteenth century[279] leaving dishonesty or collusion[280] as the only grounds for attack. Statute has long imposed greater duties on building societies,[281] but a recognition of a generalised duty to obtain a proper price had to wait for a landmark case in 1971. This left law with an uneven weft.[282] A lender must not sell in a cavalier fashion at a knockdown price.[283]

---

[269] Despite: *Hodson* v. *Deans* [1903] 2 Ch 647, 652, Joyce J; *Quennell* v. *Maltby* [1979] 1 WLR 318, CA.

[270] *Kennedy* v. *De Trafford* [1896] 1 Ch 762, 773, Lindley LJ.

[271] Or a judgment creditor: *SS for Environment FRA* v. *Feakins* [2002] BPIR 281, Penry Davey J.

[272] *Bishop* v. *Bonham* [1988] 1 WLR 742, 753, Slade LJ.

[273] *Warner* v. *Jacobs* (1882) 20 Ch D 220, 223, Kay J; *Farrar* v. *Farrars* (1888) 40 Ch D 395, CA; *Tomlin* v. *Luce* (1888) 41 Ch D 573, 575, Kekewich J at first instance; *Shamji* v. *Johnson Matthey Bankers Co* [1991] BCLC 36, CA; *Albany Home Loans* v. *Massey* [1997] 2 All ER 609, 612–613, Schiemann LJ.

[274] [1993] AC 295, PC; R Grantham [1993] *Conv* 401; AGJ Berg [1993] *JBL* 213; *Medforth* v. *Blake* [2000] Ch 86; S Frisby (2000) 63 *MLR* 413; A Kenny [1999] *Conv* 434 (missed discounts on pig feed).

[275] *American Express International Banking Corp* v. *Hurley* [1985] 3 All ER 564.

[276] *Mercantile Credit Co* v. *Clarke* (1996) 71 P & CR D18, CA; *Morgan* v. *Lloyds Bank* [1998] Lloyds Rep 73, CA.

[277] *Croft* v. *Powel* (1738) Comyn's Rep 603, 92 ER 1230; *R* v. *Parish of Edington* (1801) 1 East 288, 102 ER 112; *Downes* v. *Grazebrook* (1817) 3 Mer 200, 36 ER 77.

[278] *Re Bloye* (1849) 1 Mac & G 488, 41 ER 1354; *Robertson* v. *Norris* (1858) 1 Giff 421, 65 ER 983; *Jenkins* v. *Jones* (1860) 2 Giff 99, 108, 66 ER 43; *Marriott* v. *Anchor Reversionary Co* (1860) 2 Giff 457, 66 ER 191; *Wolff* v. *Vanderzee* (1869) 20 LT 353; *Mayer* v. *Murray* (1878) 8 Ch D 424.

[279] *Warner* v. *Jacob* (1882) 20 Ch D 220, 224, Kay J; *Farrar* v. *Farrars* (1888) 40 Ch D 395, CA; *Martinson* v. *Clowes* (1880) 52 LT 706, CA; *Colson* v. *Williams* (1889) 62 LT 71, Kekewich J.

[280] *Hodson* v. *Deans* [1903] 2 Ch 647, 652, Joyce J; *Tomlin* v. *Luce* (1888) 41 Ch D 573, 43 Ch D 191; *Farrar* at 410, Lindley LJ.

[281] Building Societies Act 1986 sch 4 para 1, re-enacting earlier provisions; *Reliance* v. *Harwood-Stamper* [1944] Ch 362, Vaisey J.

[282] P Devonshire (1995) 46 *NILQ* 182.

[283] *Palk* v. *Mortgage Services Funding* [1993] Ch 330, 338F, Nicholls V-C.

Cuckmere Brick Co v. *Mutual Finance*[284] concerned a mortgage of a development site which had the benefit of two planning permissions, one for 35 houses and one for 100 flats. Advertisements for the auction sale referred only to the less valuable houses permission. Land allegedly worth £65,000 was knocked down for £44,000. Assuming the pleaded facts were true, this was careless,[285] even reckless. Salmon LJ preferred the line of cases[286] imposing equitable obligations with respect to price over House of Lords authority[287] and statute.[288] When he described lender and borrower as "neighbours", he was speaking the language of common law negligence,[289] but *Parker-Tweedale* v. *Dunbar Bank (No 1)* decided instead that the duty rested in equity.[290] If the legal estate in the mortgaged property is vested in a wife, her husband is not able to take action as sole beneficiary.[291] The decision appears faulty. Every other person interested in the equity of redemption is protected, including a second lender,[292] so why not a beneficiary?

Quantification of damages is based on the diminution of market value attributable to the negligence of the lender,[293] assessed at the time of trial.[294] Exceptionally large divergences may speak for themselves.[295] Lenders should employ appropriate professional agents,[296] advertise properly,[297] and expose the property to the market. In *Predeth* v. *Castle Phillips Finance Co*[298] a bungalow in poor condition was subjected to a "crash sale" at £6,000, but was resold shortly afterwards for £10,000, and the evidence was that exposure to the market for three months would have yielded at least £8,500. The lenders were liable. Sales commonly occur at auction,[299] but this is not necessarily sufficient.[300] It is not wrong to tell the buyer that the property is repossessed,[301] even though this may reduce offers. The lender has a considerable discretion

---

[284] [1971] Ch 949, CA; (1971) 87 *LQR* 303; *Palmer* v. *Barclays Bank* (1972) 23 P & CR 30 (planning permission unknown to lender, no duty).

[285] At 966B, Salmon LJ, 972G–H, Cross LJ, 977C–978A, Cairns LJ.

[286] *Tomlin* v. *Luce* (1889) 41 Ch D 573, CA; *McHugh* v. *Union Bank of Canada* [1913] AC 299, PC.

[287] *Kennedy* v. *De Trafford* [1887] AC 180, HL; *Johnson* v. *Ribbins* (1975) 235 EG 757, Walton J; *Medforth* v. *Blake* [2000] Ch 86, 92E.

[288] LPA 1925 s 101, 106; *Bishop* v. *Bonham* [1988] 1 WLR 742, 754, Slade LJ.

[289] *Cuckmere Brick* [1971] Ch 949, 966D.

[290] [1991] Ch 18, CA; *China and South Sea Bank* v. *Tan* [1990] 1 AC 536, 543H–544A, Lord Templeman; *Medforth* v. *Blake* [2000] Ch 86, 102E, Scott V-C. One consequence is that the limitation period is six years: *Raja* v. *Lloyds TSB Bank* [2001] 2 EGLR 78, Ch D; L McMurty [2001] *Conv* 423.

[291] Action via the wife as trustee was barred by a pre-suit compromise.

[292] *Downsview Nominees* v. *First City Corp* [1993] 1 AC 295, 311F–312C, Lord Templeman; *Freeguard* v. *Royal Bank of Scotland (No 2)* [2002] Times April 25th, Simon Berry QC.

[293] *Tomlin* v. *Luce* (1889) 41 Ch D 573, CA. No damages accrue if sale is at the correct price reached by the wrong means: *Mount Banking Corp* v. *Brian Cooper & Co* [1992] 2 EGLR 142.

[294] *Adamson* v. *Halifax* [2002] EWCA Civ 1134, [2002] 1 WLR 60.

[295] *European Partners in Capital (EPIC) Holdings* v. *Goddard & Smith* [1992] 2 EGLR 158, CA.

[296] *Tse Kwang Lam* v. *Wong Chit Sen* [1983] 1 WLR 1349, 1356–1357, Lord Templeman.

[297] *Cuckmere Brick* [1971] Ch 949, CA; *Wolff* v. *Vanderzee* (1869) 20 LT 353; *Palmer* v. *Barclays Bank* (1971) 23 P & CR 30; *Skipton BS* v. *Stott* [2001] QB 261, CA; *Struggles* v. *Lloyds TSB Bank* [2000] EGCS 17, QBD.

[298] [1986] 2 EGLR 144, CA; MP Thompson [1986] *Conv* 442; *Routestone* v. *Minories Finance* [1997] 1 EGLR 123, Jacob J; *Meftah* v. *Lloyds TSB Bank* [2001] EGCS 44, Lawrence Collins J; *Cohen* v. *TSB Bank* [2002] BPIR 243, Etherton J.

[299] LPA 1925 s 101(1)(i); *Brouard* v. *Dumaresque* (1841) 3 Moo PC 457, 13 ER 186 (express power).

[300] *Tse* [1983] 1 WLR 1349, 1357H, Lord Templeman; *Davey* v. *Durrant* (1851) 1 De G & J 535, 44 ER 830; *Hodson* v. *Deans* [1903] 2 Ch 647, 653, Joyce J; *Johnson* v. *Ribbins* (1975) 235 EG 757, Walton J.

[301] *Bank of Cyprus* v. *Gill* [1980] 2 Lloyds Rep 51, CA; HW Wilkinson (1982) 132 *NLJ* 883.

about whether to sell as a whole or in parts, and to sell a farm with or without its milk quota.[302]

3. Identity of the buyer

[29.38] Given the obvious conflict of interest,[303] the lender may not buy the mortgaged property[304] – either alone, with others,[305] or through a nominee or fiduciary.[306] In *Williams* v. *Wellingborough Borough Council*[307] a public-sector home was sold to the sitting tenant subject to a mortgage back to the council. As lenders the council later purported to sell the property back to itself so that the house could be taken back into the stock of public housing, but this sale was invalid. A problem also arises where an employee of a building society arranged for a relative to buy a repossessed house at an undervalue.[308]

Too great a leniency is shown towards companies formed by the lender. In *Farrar* v. *Farrars*[309] a company was floated specifically to purchase the mortgaged property, but the sale was allowed to stand. However, equity's blindness to the separate corporate personality is only partial, because the lender has the burden of proving that the sale was at the best price reasonably obtainable, a task which proved beyond the lender in *Tse Kwang Lam* v. *Wong Chit Sen*.[310] His wife had bid at auction on behalf of a company, whose shareholders included the lender (her husband) and other family members. This particular auction had not produced a true price. Although the sale is voidable, there is no point in upsetting the sale unless it was too cheap.[311] The right to rescind (as opposed to the claim for damages) might be lost by delay, acquiescence,[312] or ratification after full and frank explanation of the terms.[313]

4. Reform of duties of lenders

[29.39] Law Commission reform of mortgage law is proposed,[314] though the Government has requested further work on the present report. Exercise for non-financial default would only be possible if there was a substantial threat to the

---

[302] *Huish* v. *Ellis* [1995] BCC 462; *AIB Finance* v. *Alsop* [1998] 2 All ER 929, CA (post office shut by borrower; no duty on lender to sell as a going concern); C Davies [1998] *JHL* 56.

[303] *Re Bloy's Trust* (1849) 1 Mac & G 488, 495, 41 ER 1354.

[304] A second lender may buy from the first: *Kirkwood* v. *Thompson* (1865) 2 H & M 392, 71 ER 515.

[305] *Downes* v. *Grazebrook* (1817) 3 Mer 200, 36 ER 77; *Robertson* v. *Norris* (1858) 1 Giff 421, 65 ER 983.

[306] *Nutt* v. *Easton* [1900] 1 Ch 29, CA (solicitor); *Hodson* v. *Deans* [1903] 2 Ch 647 (solicitor); *Nugent* v. *Nugent* [1908] 1 Ch 546, CA (receiver); *Martinson* v. *Clowes* (1882) 52 LT 706, CA (secretary of building society); *Whitcomb* v. *Minchin* cited at (1888) 40 Ch D 395, 409, Lindley LJ.

[307] [1975] 1 WLR 1327, CA.

[308] *Corbett* v. *Halifax BS* [2002] EWCA Civ 849, [2003] 01 EG 68 (CS).

[309] (1888) 40 Ch D 395, CA.

[310] [1983] 1 WLR 1349, PC; P Jackson [1984] *Conv* 143.

[311] The lender can solve the problem by re-sale: *Henderson* v. *Astwood* [1894] AC 150, PC.

[312] *Tse Kwang Lam* [1983] 1 WLR 1349, PC; *Nutt* v. *Easton* [1900] 1 Ch 29, CA (9 years).

[313] *Re Bloye's T* (1849) 1 Mac & G 488, 41 ER 1354.

[314] Law Com 204 (1991) part VII; P Jackson (1978) 94 *LQR* 571; AL Diamond (1989) 42 *CLP* 231; GH Griffiths [1987] *Conv* 191; HW Wilkinson [1992] *Conv* 69; GH Griffiths [1992] *JBL* 423; G Frost (1992) 136 *SJ* 267, 292.

security. Duties of lenders when selling would be tightened: all remedies should be limited to lenders acting in good faith and for the purposes of protecting or enforcing the security, a duty that would become statutory. There would also be a duty to sell as soon as is consistent with the lender's duty to obtain the best price realisable.

I. REDEMPTION AND DISCHARGE

[29.40] Redemption[315] by the borrower will operate to remove the burden of the mortgage from the land, leaving it as an empty shell, signifying nothing. Formal proof is required on the title.

1. Procedure where redemption occurs on sale

[29.41] Most mortgages are redeemed on sale of the mortgaged house using the proceeds of sale. Theoretically the lender could insist upon completion at the offices of its solicitors,[316] but this would be impossibly cumbersome. Instead, the borrower's solicitor is appointed to act for the lender, and is sent the charge certificate or title deeds in advance of completion. An undertaking will be required that the borrower's solicitor will not part with title documents[317] until he has received the redemption monies by banker's draft (a form of cheque which cannot be stopped). Following completion the discharge form is sent to the lender with the redemption money.[318] The buyer's title is completed by the discharge,[319] forwarded first to the seller's solicitor and then on to the buyer's solicitor. Until then the buyer has to rely on an undertaking by the seller's solicitor to carry out the redemption.[320] This should be carefully worded so as to relate only to events within the control of the borrower's solicitor – that is to forward the discharge on its receipt from the lender, rather than within any specific period.[321]

2. Registered charges

[29.42] Substantive registration of a legal charge has to be cancelled after an appropriate form of discharge and application to the land registry.[322]

---

[315] Megarry & Wade (6th ed), [19.125–19.154].

[316] *Graham* v. *Seal* (1918) 88 LJ Ch 31, 36, Swinfen Eady MR.

[317] *Crickmore* v. *Freeston* (1870) 40 LJ Ch 137; *Rourke* v. *Robinson* [1911] 1 Ch 480, Warrington J; *Walker* v. *Jones* (1866) LR 1 PC 50.

[318] LR Form DS1 or a vacating receipt endorsed on an unregistered land mortgage deed.

[319] As a result the existence of a legal charge is not a defect in the seller's title: *Herkanaidu* v. *Lambeth LBC* [2000] Times February 28th, Ch D.

[320] JE Adams (1973) 70 *LSG* 1346.

[321] Sloppy undertakings are a major cause of claims on the solicitors' indemnity fund: HW Wilkinson [1993] *NLJ* 1344.

[322] LRA 2002 s 56 (a simplified version of LRA 1925 s 32); DLRR 2003 rr 112–114; DLRR CD ch 7, [3]; LR Form DS1 (whole) or DS3 (part) accompanied by an application in AP1. LPA 1925 s 115(10) is amended by LRA 2002 sch 11.

> The lender acknowledges that the property is no longer charged as security
> for payment of sums due under the charge.

Figure 29-1 Discharge of a registered charge

This must be executed as a deed by the registered proprietor of the mortgage, the survivor of joint lenders or the personal representative of the last survivor. Lenders who
are individuals need only to sign the receipt[323] but corporate lenders, who are far more
numerous, must execute formally as a deed. Special arrangements are often made with
the land registry by large corporate lenders.[324] The registrar may act on the basis of
any other sufficient evidence that a loan is repaid.

Tentative steps are being taken towards the development of a system for electronic
discharges, which will be treated the same as a paper discharge.[325]

3. Unregistered land

[29.43] A discharge of a mortgage over an unregistered title is in the form of a vacating receipt. Careful scrutiny is needed to ensure that it is indeed a discharge and not a
transfer of the mortgage debt.[326] Discharge occurs on repayment by the person entitled to the ultimate equity of redemption – usually the original borrower, but possibly
someone to whom he has transferred the land subject to the mortgage. The mortgage
is removed completely and other charges move up.

> Suppose B borrows £50,000 from L1 and £25,000 from L2 on the security of a
> house worth £60,000. B discharges the first loan. L2 will hold the only charge on the
> property for £25,000 and is now fully secured.

When the last mortgage is discharged, the borrower regains the property free from
incumbrances.

Redemption is evidenced by execution of a receipt acknowledging that the money
due under the mortgage has been paid.[327] The receipt can be given by "the person in
whom the mortgaged property is vested", an inapt term obviously intended to point to
the current lender.[328] The receipt is "endorsed on, written at the foot of, or annexed to"
the original mortgage deed.[329] Printed mortgages often have a blank form ready
printed. The statutory form is equally appropriate for legal charges and true mortgages,
can be varied, or adapted,[330] and is modified for use with equitable mortgages.[331]

---

[323] LPA 1925 s 52(1)(e).
[324] Proved by a certified copy of the LR facility letter.
[325] DLRR 2003 rr 113–114; LR Form END.
[326] A confusion made impossible by the distinctive LR forms.
[327] JE Adams (1971) 68 *LSG* 175.
[328] LPA 1925 s 115(1); ie the person in whom the *mortgage* is vested. After a change of lender or corporate identity, proof of the right to give the receipt is essential: *Edwards* v. *Marshall-Lee* [1975] 2 EGLR 149.
[329] LPA 1925 s 115(1).
[330] S 115(5)–(8), sch 3.
[331] S 115(11). It is general practice to accept a letter of release from an equitable charge: RG Rowley
(1962) 26 *Conv (NS)* 445.

> I, [lender] hereby acknowledge that I have this [date] received the sum of £[xxx] representing the principal money secured by the within written mortgage together with all interest and costs, the payment having been made by [the borrower]. As witness [signature of lender].

Figure 29-2 A vacating receipt

It must be signed, though a deed will act as a receipt anyway without statutory support.[332]

The burden on the title is discharged by the receipt without any reconveyance, surrender or release.[333] The pre-1926 rigmarole of dealing with bare legal estates, retransferring them to the borrower or passing them on to second lenders is redundant.

4. Building society receipts

[29.44] Building society receipts do not name the person making the redemption payment,[334] so the mortgage is always discharged.

5. Vacating receipts acting as a transfer

[29.45] The problem considered here relates specifically to unregistered titles. Vacating receipts may either discharge the mortgage or transfer it, making a difference to the priority of later lenders.[335] Payment by the borrower or a nominee[336] effects a *discharge* of the debt. Where it is a person who has bought the land subject to the mortgage,[337] there probably ought to be a discharge, though the possibility of a transfer remains open in the Lords.[338]

Any other person interested in the equity of redemption may redeem,[339] and takes a transfer by doing so. This includes an original borrower who is sued for debt,[340] later lenders,[341] equitable lenders,[342] tenants,[343] a beneficiary entitled in remainder,[344]

---

[332] *Firth & Sons* v. *CIR* [1904] 2 KB 205; *Simpson* v. *Geoghegan* [1934] WN 232, Clauson J; *Erewash BC* v. *Taylor* [1979] CLYB 1831.

[333] Any person may insist on these means: LPA 1925 s 115(4). A mortgage by demise becomes a satisfied term: ss 5, 116; if part of the land is freed from the mortgage, a new term is created affecting that part: s 5(3).

[334] Building Societies Act 1986 s 6C, sch 2A, inserted by Building Societies Act 1997 s 7, sch 2; SI 1997/2869 (prescribed forms); receipts operate under LPA 1925 s 115(1)–(8) but s 115(9) does not apply.

[335] *Cotterell* v. *Price* [1960] 1 WLR 1097, 1102.

[336] LPA 1925 s 115(3).

[337] *Toulmin* v. *Steere* (1817) 3 Mer 210, 36 ER 81, Grant MR.

[338] *Liquidation Estates Purchase Co* v. *Willoughby* [1898] AC 321, HL; *Manks* v. *Whiteley* [1912] 1 Ch 735, 755–756, Fletcher Moulton LJ dissenting; *Whiteley* v. *Delaney* [1914] AC 132, HL; LPA 1925 s 95(1).

[339] LPA 1925 s 116.

[340] *Kinnard* v. *Trollope* (1888) 39 Ch D 636.

[341] *Halifax Mortgage Services* v. *Muirhead* (1997) 76 P & CR 418, 428, Evans LJ.

[342] *Mason* v. *Rhodes* (1885) 53 LT 322. If they pay off a first legal mortgage they will be subrogated to the rights under that first mortgage: *Eagle Star Insurance* v. *Karasiewicz* [2002] EWCA Civ 940.

[343] *Hunter* v. *Macklew* (1846) 5 Hare 238, 67 ER 902; *Tarn* v. *Turner* (1888) 39 Ch D 456, CA.

[344] *Re Chesters* [1935] Ch 77, Bennett J; (1935) 51 *LQR* 433.

a spouse in relation to the matrimonial home,[345] and a judgment creditor with a charging order,[346] or a person without an interest in the land who is allowed to redeem.[347] All these categories avoid repossession, but preserve their right to reimbursement from the current borrower.

The test of a *discharge* is that the person named as making payment in the receipt must be entitled to the estate subject to the mortgage.[348] It will act as a *transfer* if stated to be such,[349] but also if the person named as making payment is not the ultimate estate owner. There is a danger of an accidental transfer if a seller is named in a receipt dated a few days after completion of a sale – since the buyer has then become entitled to the equity of redemption, but this unfortunate accident is avoided by an estoppel if the conveyance recites that sale is free from incumbrances.[350]

J. DISPUTED REDEMPTION

1. Redemption by agreement

[29.46] Redemption will almost always occur by agreement after the borrower has given notice that he intends to pay off the loan. There is no right to redeem a part of a mortgage.[351] A borrower who wishes to redeem after the contractual redemption date must give notice – either six months[352] or some other period stated in the mortgage – or pay interest in lieu of notice.[353] Long ago this was to give the lender time to find an alternative investment for his money,[354] reasoning that scarcely seems appropriate today. The borrower will call for a redemption statement from the lender, stating the principal together with interest and costs that have accrued, but set against repayments and receipts of rent. Interest accumulates on the balance until actual repayment. Redemption by agreement only binds other lenders if they are not parties to the agreement.[355]

2. Tender to preclude dispute about redemption

[29.47] If the quoted redemption figure is disputed, the simplest approach for the borrower is to tender what he believes to be owing. Interest is stopped if the tender is

---

[345] FLA 1996 s 30(3); *Hastings & Thanet BS* v. *Goddard* [1970] 1 WLR 1544, CA.

[346] *Irani Finance* v. *Singh* [1971] Ch 59, CA.

[347] Eg a statute barred lender: *Pearce* v. *Morris* (1869) LR 5 Ch App 227; *Cotterrell* v. *Price* [1960] 1 WLR 1097, 1102, Buckley J.

[348] A discharge may arise in a transfer type case if the receipt expressly provides for it: *Pyke* v. *Peters* [1943] 1 KB 242; also if money is paid from a fund properly applicable to discharge of the mortgage.

[349] *Simpson* v. *Geoghegan* [1894] WN 232.

[350] *Cumberland Court (Brighton)* v. *Taylor* [1964] Ch 29, Ungoed-Thomas J; JE Adams [1985] *Conv* 10.

[351] *Carroll* v. *Manek* (2000) 79 P & CR 173, Ch D.

[352] *Cromwell Property Investment Co* v. *Western & Toovey* [1934] Ch 322; *Centrax Trustees* v. *Ross* [1979] 2 All ER 952, Goulding J.

[353] *Smith* v. *Smith* [1981] 3 Ch 550, Romer J (not if the lender calls in the loan); *Bovill* v. *Endle* [1896] 1 Ch 648, Kekewich J (possession).

[354] *Browne* v. *Lockhart* (1840) 10 Sim 420, 59 ER 678.

[355] The amount of the loan becomes an issue if the mortgage is transferred; see below **[29.48]**.

correct and the necessary money is set aside.[356] What is owed should be paid into court after which the borrower may seek an order for execution of a vacating receipt.[357] Improper refusals will be penalised in costs[358] and possibly by loss of interest.[359] A tender made and rejected is not equal to actual payment – the charge is removed from the land only on payment.[360]

3. Disputed redemption

[29.48] Court action is rarely necessary to settle the terms of a redemption. Disputed redemptions used to involve settling accounts between all parties potentially affected; it was necessary to "redeem up, foreclose down".[361] This is because the value attached to a single mortgage affects the equity available to all later lenders. However, this inconvenient rule is reversed by section 95 of the Law of Property Act 1925, consolidating earlier legislation but still much misunderstood. In 1881[362] a borrower was given the right to find an outside person (X) to pay off his debt, in which case the lender was bound to accept redemption from X and to transfer the mortgage to him. *Teevan* v. *Smith*[363] held that later lenders had to consent – which there were unlikely to do – but that perverse decision was immediately reversed by legislation.[364] Under the current legislation, the right to require transfer belongs to each lender and to the ultimate borrower irrespective of the existence of intermediate mortgages.

All other people affected can be embroiled by seeking an account,[365] and "redeem up, foreclose down" also continues to apply after the lender has taken possession.[366] All intermediate mortgages must be redeemed and (if redemption is used as a defence to foreclosure) all subsequent mortgages foreclosed.[367]

4. Foreclosure

[29.49] Foreclosure is a judicial remedy requiring an order of the Chancery Division,[368] but sale out of court is simpler, quicker and cheaper.[369] Foreclosure

---

[356] *Edmondson* v. *Copland* [1911] 2 Ch 301, Joyce J; *Barratt* v. *Gough-Thomas* [1951] 2 All ER 48, Danckwerts J.

[357] *Bank of New South Wales* v. *O'Connor* (1889) 14 App Cas 273, PC; *Re Uplands* [1948] WN 165, Vaisey J (lender disappeared).

[358] *Smith* v. *Green* (1844) 1 Coll CC 555, 63 ER 541; *Chilton* v. *Carrington* (1855) 16 CB 206, 139 ER 735.

[359] *Cliff* v. *Wadworth* (1843) 2 Y & C Ch 598, 63 ER 268; *Hughes* v. *Williams* (1853) Kay App iv, 69 ER 313.

[360] *Bank of New South Wales* v. *O'Connor* (1889) 14 App Cas 273, PC; query the result in *Graham* v. *Seal* (1918) 88 LJ Ch 31, 39, Duke LJ.

[361] *Pearce* v. *Morris* (1869) 5 Ch App 227, 229, Lord Hatherley.

[362] Conveyancing Act 1881 s 15.

[363] (1882) 20 Ch D 724, CA.

[364] Conveyancing Act 1882 s 12. Incorrect decisions are: *Alderson* v. *Elgey* (1884) 26 Ch D 567; *Smithett* v. *Hesketh* (1890) 44 Ch D 161, 166; *Corbett* v. *National Provident Institution* (1900) 17 TLR 5; *Re Magneta Time Co* (1915) 113 LT 986.

[365] *Watts* v. *Driscoll* [1901] 1 Ch 294, CA; *Mainland* v. *Upjohn* (1889) 41 Ch D 126; *Bentley* v. *Bates* (1840) 4 Y & C Ex 182, 160 ER 971.

[366] LPA 1925 s 95(3); *Hall* v. *Heward* (1886) 32 Ch D 430, 436; *Re Pytheck* (1889) 42 Ch D 590.

[367] *Johnson* v. *Holdsworth* (1845) 1 Sim NS 106, 61 ER 41; *Moore* v. *Martin* (1886) WN 196.

[368] Megarry & Wade (6th ed), [19.048–19.055].

[369] *Palk* v. *Mortgage Services Funding* [1993] Ch 330, 336E, Nicholls V-C; HE Markson (1979) 129 *NLJ* 33.

originated as a counter-balance for the lender to the equitable right of a borrower to a late redemption. Termination of the borrower's interest in the property by a successful foreclosure was a potent threat against a borrower in default or slow to repay his loan. Since 1925, lenders have an adverse charge on the legal estate, so a foreclosure order absolute now transfers the borrower's legal estate to the lender.[370] If, say, a house is worth £100,000 and the borrower owes £15,000, the lender's undeserved bonus is a serious prejudice to the borrower and to all later lenders.[371] An intricate procedure was evolved to give the borrower[372] and all others affected ample time to redeem the mortgage instead. Accounts were taken after a foreclosure order nisi, and at least six months was allowed for the borrower or any lender to redeem before the order could be made absolute,[373] a period during which there is invariably a defence request for sale.[374]

5. Consolidation – unregistered land

[29.50] Mortgages of different properties create distinct contracts with distinct equities of redemption.[375] They are redeemable separately, but "only if and so far as a contrary intention is not expressed in the mortgage deeds or one of them."[376] Hence it is possible for a lender to consolidate two mortgages[377] by reserving the right to do so in either of them. A lender holding two separate mortgages on estates of the same borrower may refuse to accept redemption of one estate without the other.[378] Its greatest practical significance is where the value of one piece of land is deficient as a security, a shortfall that can be made good out of a surplus on the other property.[379]

Consolidation operates fairly and without difficulty *by the original lender against the original borrower*.[380] The essential requirements are:

(1) reservation of the right;[381]

(2) debts secured by mortgages, possibly by deed;[382] and

(3) both contractual redemption dates having passed, since consolidation is an equitable principle.[383]

---

[370] If title is registered the charge is cancelled, as are all interests over which the charge had priority, and the foreclosing lender will be entered as proprietor: DLRR 2003 r 111.

[371] Guarantors gain a discharge: *Lloyds & Scottish Trust* v. *Britten* (1982) 44 P & CR 249.

[372] *Mexborough Urban DC* v. *Harrison* [1964] 1 WLR 733.

[373] LPA 1925 s 95; the borrower must give 7 days notice: Practice Direction [1955] 1 WLR 36.

[374] See above [29.30].

[375] *Willie* v. *Lugg* (1761) 2 Eden 78, 80, 28 ER 825, Northington LC.

[376] LPA 1925 s 93(1).

[377] Cases involving three or more mortgages must be analysed in pairs: LPA 1925 s 93(1); *Re Salmon* [1903] 1 KB 147; *Pledge* v. *White* [1896] AC 187, 191, Lord Davey.

[378] *Jennings* v. *Jordan* (1881) 6 App Cas 698, 700, Selborne LC; *Griffith* v. *Pound* (1890) 45 Ch D 553, 561, Stirling J; *Pledge* v. *White* [1896] AC 187, 191, Lord Davey.

[379] *Barrow* v. *Manning* [1880] WN 108; *Jennings* v. *Jordan* (1881) 6 App Cas 698, 703, Lord Selborne.

[380] *Baker* v. *Gray* (1875) 1 Ch D 491, 494, Hall V-C; *Jennings* at 700, Selborne LC; *Harris* v. *Tubb* (1889) 60 LT 699, Kekewich J.

[381] LPA 1925 s 93(1) (mortgages made after 1881); *Hughes* v. *Britannia PBBS* [1906] 2 Ch 607, 611, Kekewich J.

[382] LPA 1925 s 93(1); *Crickmore* v. *Freeston* (1870) 40 LJ Ch 137.

[383] *Windham* v. *Jennings* (1683) 2 Rep Ch 247, 21 ER 669; *Cummins* v. *Fletcher* (1880) 14 Ch D 699, CA; *Jennings* v. *Jordan* (1881) 6 App Cas 698, 700; *Pledge* v. *White* [1896] AC 187, 191, Lord Davey.

Where consolidation occurs against a *single current borrower* (who is not the original borrower) easily intelligible limits also apply. They are:

(1) the mortgages all made by the same original borrower;[384] and
(2) a single lender seeking to consolidate.[385]

The greatest problem arises where the *borrower's interests have separated*, that is where two different borrowers are now involved. Considerable controversy was provoked right up until the Conveyancing Act 1881 which marked the end of litigation about the right to consolidate. The law was settled by two House of Lords decisions[386] but some of the results are monstrous.[387] Consolidation is not possible where the borrower sells his interest in the first property before the second mortgage is created, since new burdens cannot attach after sale.[388] Nor is there any consolidation if the borrower sells one property before the same lender holds both the mortgages. There must be a *simultaneous union* of mortgages and equities.[389] However, if there was once a simultaneous union, the right to consolidation survives a later split in ownership. B1 appears to own an independent property subject to a mortgage, but he can only repay the mortgage by paying off another mortgage on a different property now owned by B2. There was some moment when a borrower held both pieces of land and a lender held both loans. When one piece of land was sold subject to its mortgage,[390] the purchaser bought subject to that mortgage and also subject to consolidation of the other mortgage against his land.[391] Consolidation has virtually killed the trade in mortgaged land.

6. Consolidation – registered land

[29.51] The proprietor may apply for entry of a notice on the register that the mortgages have been consolidated.[392] The entry is made against each individual register affected.

---

[384] *Sharp* v. *Rickards* [1909] 1 Ch 109 (A and bare trustee for A); *Cummins* v. *Fletcher* (1880) 14 Ch D 699, CA.

[385] *Beevor* v. *Luck* (1867) LR 4 Eq 537; *Riley* v. *Hall* (1898) 79 LT 244; *Jennings* v. *Jordan* at 707.

[386] *Jennings* v. *Jordan* (1881) 6 App Cas 698, HL; *Pledge* v. *White* [1896] AC 187, HL; Megarry & Wade (6th ed), [19.096–19.110].

[387] *Chesworth* v. *Hunt* (1881) 5 CPD 266, 271, Lindley J.

[388] *Jennings* v. *Jordan* (1881) 6 App Cas 698, HL; *Harter* v. *Colman* (1882) 19 Ch D 630, Fry J; *Andrews* v. *City Permanent Benefit BS* (1881) 44 LT 641 (obiter).

[389] *Fosbrooke* v. *Walker* (1832) 2 LJ Ch 161; *Minter* v. *Carr* [1894] 3 Ch 498, CA; *Re Walhampton Estate* (1884) 26 Ch D 391; *Pledge* v. *White* [1896] AC 187, 195–196, Lord Davey.

[390] After 1925, it is believed, a person who buys property subject to a mortgage which does not itself reserve a right to consolidate may be a protected purchaser of a legal estate.

[391] *Vint* v. *Padget* (1858) 1 Giff 446, 65 ER 994; *Pledge* v. *White* [1896] AC 187, 198; *Minter* v. *Carr* [1894] 3 Ch 498, 501, 502.

[392] LRA 2002 s 57; Law Com 271 (2001), [7.44]; DLRR 2003 r 109; LR Form CC; LPA 1925 s 97 is amended by LRA 2002 sch 11.

30

PROTECTION OF DOMESTIC BORROWERS

---

*Domestic sector lenders. Unfair terms. Good lending practice. Instalment
mortgages. Domestic repossession. Consumer credit agreements. Tenants.
Oppression. Equitable misconduct: undue influence etc: infection; avoiding
infection; legal advice; remedies. Nullity.*

[30.01] Domestic borrowers are inevitably at a disadvantage against a commercial
lender. This chapter explores lending controls, protection against repossession,
oppression of borrowers, and undue influence and other forms of misconduct applied
by borrowers to guarantors.

A. DOMESTIC SECTOR LENDERS

[30.02] From one point of view, domestic borrowers are simply consumers,[1] though
peculiarly vulnerable ones. Statutory control of lenders is provided by the consumer
credit and building societies legislation – a patchwork which has not yet coalesced into
an adequate protective shield.

1. Lenders

[30.03] Mutual building societies are regulated by statute.[2] Most of their business
should take the form of loans secured on land, that is a legal estate in a home made
after adequate valuation.[3] Insurance and other activities must be ring-fenced to
prevent borrowers being pressured into buying associated products.[4]

Building societies, local authorities, many insurance companies and friendly societies, and charities are exempt from the control of the Consumer Credit Act 1974.[5]
Banks are controlled, along with the fringe lenders of the second mortgage market, all

---

[1] L Whitehouse "The Home-Owner: Citizen or Consumer?" ch 7 in Bright & Dewar; Grays' *Elements*
(3rd ed) ch 12.
[2] Building Societies Act 1986, as amended by LRA 2002 sch 11; HW Wilkinson [1985] *Conv* 1;
A Samuels [1987] *Conv* 36; GA Morgan [1995] *Conv* 467.
[3] Building Societies Act 1997 part I, amending Building Societies Act 1986 part III.
[4] Building Societies Act 1986 ss 34–35; SI 2001/1826.
[5] Consumer Credit Act 1974 s 16; SI 1989/869 art 2, and regular amendments; there are minor exemptions.

of which require a licence from the Director General of Fair Trading.[6] Ombudsmen provide administrative redress for investors[7] and building society borrowers,[8] even against in-house valuations.[9] There has been a deluge of complaints.

2. Advertising mortgages

[30.04] Consumer credit rules apply to all lenders (exempt or non-exempt) providing any level of credit to individuals. Advertisements must warn that:

> "Your home is at risk if you do not keep up repayments on a mortgage or other loan secured on it."[10]

Interest rates must be calculated in APR format which allows a comparison between different products, however imperfect. Other rules affect "hidden extras" such as endowment schemes, and the method of calculating the cost of borrowing.[11] In *National Westminster Bank* v. *Devon CC*[12] a mortgage provided for the interest rate to be fixed at a low rate for two years; the interest rate was advertised (legitimately) on the assumption that at the end of the fixed rate period the interest rate would remain the same for the rest of the term, even though an increase was inevitable in practice.

3. Mortgage Code

[30.05] A voluntary scheme to secure honesty, transparency, clarity and fairness in the advertisement of business is to be superseded in 2004 by much tougher controls under the Mortgage Code of the Financial Services Authority.[13]

4. Regulated consumer credit agreements

[30.06] Consumer credit agreements are used for buying fridges and cars, but some land mortgages may also fall within the statutory code,[14] which does not mesh well with traditional mortgage law. This applies whenever "credit" is provided to an individual "debtor" – including individuals, couples, sole traders and business partners, but excluding companies. Regulated consumer credit agreements are those by

---

[6] Ss 21–41.

[7] *R* v. *Investors Compensation Scheme ex p Bowden* [1996] AC 261, HL. Building Societies Act 1997 s 32 provides for future amalgamation of various schemes.

[8] Financial Services and Markets Act 2000 ss 225–234, sch 17; A Samuels [1987] *Conv* 36; C Bell & JW Vaughan (1988) 132 *SJ* 1478; SE Edell [1989] *Conv* 253; R James & M Seneviratne [1992] *CJQ* 157; (1994) 23 *Anglo-American* 214.

[9] *Halifax BS* v. *Edell* [1992] Ch 436, Morritt J.

[10] Consumer Credit Act 1974 ss 43–54; numerous SIs state exemptions; *Davies* v. *Directloans* [1986] 1 WLR 823; *First National Bank* v. *SS for Trade* (1990) 154 JP 571, CA.

[11] SI 1989/596; *Lombard Tricity Finance* v. *Paton* [1989] 1 All ER 918, CA (variable rate acceptable); *Scarborough BS* v. *Humberside TSD* [1997] CLYB 965.

[12] [1993] CCLR 69.

[13] Financial Services Authority document CP 146 (2002); see FSA website.

[14] JE Adams (1975) 39 *Conv NS* 94; A Rogerson (1975) 38 *MLR* 435; KE Lindgren (1977) 40 *MLR* 159; R Goode [1975] *CLJ* 79.

non-exempt lenders where the loan does not exceed £25,000.[15] The target is second loans to pay, for example, for home improvements, double glazing and holidays.[16]

Formalities are required for regulated consumer credit agreements, including an opportunity for withdrawal[17] though this is not a requirement when a "restricted use credit agreement" is used to finance (or bridge) the purchase of a house. Regulated mortgages must follow a prescribed form, stating the total amount and rate of the charge for credit, and must be signed by both parties. Enforcement of a deformed mortgage was prohibited out of court and was discretionary in court[18] – but it has been held that the lender's human rights are infringed by this provision and a declaration of incompatibility has been made.[19]

B. UNFAIR TERMS

[30.07] The Unfair Contract Terms Act 1977 has no application to mortgages of land,[20] but a wider scope is allowed to the European-inspired Unfair Terms in Consumer Contracts Regulations 1999.[21] This finer mesh has forced lenders to review and revise standard mortgage conditions to ensure compliance with the new regulations. Terms are potentially vulnerable if not individually negotiated,[22] including pre-formulated standard contracts and terms over which the consumer has no substantial influence.[23]

Core terms about the adequacy of the price[24] are not subject to the test of fairness, the only requirement being that such terms must be in plain intelligible language.[25] An unfair term is any one which causes a significant imbalance in the parties' rights and obligations to the detriment of the consumer (that is the borrower) contrary to requirement of good faith.[26] The nature of the loan and the circumstances attending its completion must be considered. Factors are the relative bargaining positions of the

---

[15] SI 1998/996 (from May 1998); previously £15,000 (from mid 1985) and £5,000 (earlier). Some provisions do not apply to small agreements: SI 1983/1878.

[16] Either by a lender to a borrower (a debtor-creditor agreement) or involving a third party such as a double glazing supplier (a debtor-creditor-supplier agreement).

[17] Consumer Credit Act 1974 ss 58, 67–73; SI 1983/1557.

[18] SI 1983/1553; *R* v. *Modupe* [1991] Times February 27th, CA.

[19] *Wilson* v. *First County Trust (No 2)* [2001] EWCA Civ 633, [2001] QB 74; *McGinn* v. *Grangewood Securities* [2002] EWCA Civ 522, [2002] Times May 30th; *Watchtower Investments* v. *Payne* [2001] EWCA Civ 1159, [2001] Times August 22nd.

[20] Sch 1 para 1(b); *Electricity Supply Nominees* v. *IAF Group* [1993] 1 WLR 1059; *Havenridge* v. *Boston Dyers* [1994] 2 EGLR 73, CA; *Star Rider* v. *Inntrepreneur Pub Co* [1998] 1 EGLR 53; *Paragon Finance* v. *Nash* [2001] EWCA Civ 1466, [2002] 1 WLR 685.

[21] SI 1999/2083, as amended; S Bright & C Bright (1995) 111 *LQR* 655; JE Adams [1995] *Conv* 10. Excluded are eg contracts relating to succession or family arrangements. Consultation is taking place on a reform: Law Com CP 166 (2002).

[22] SI 1999/2083 reg 3(1).

[23] Regs 3(4)(3)–(4).

[24] *Director General of Fair Trading* v. *First National Bank* [2001] UKHL 52, [2002] 1 AC 481, held that a provision for charging interest on interest was not a core term, meaning that the fairness provisions applied, though the particular term was not unfair. See E Macdonald (2002) 65 *MLR* 763; M Dean (2002) 65 *MLR* 773.

[25] Reg 3(2). Law Com CP 166 (2002) proposes a clearer link between what is a central term and the consumer's expectation.

[26] SI 1999/2083 reg 4(1).

parties, inducements offered to accept particular terms, any adaption of the loan to a particular borrower, and the general course of dealings by the lender.[27] Indicative examples of unfair terms are inappropriate exclusion of the lender's liability, disproportionately high sums charged for breaches, terms with which the borrower had no opportunity to become acquainted, and terms allowing providing for unilateral alterations,[28] as well as any term not in plain and intelligible language.[29] The remainder of the loan contract will continue in force if, as is usual, the mortgage makes sense without it.[30]

C. PROPER LENDING PRACTICE

[30.08] Domestic borrowers are consumers who are entitled to expect lenders to act prudently, both for their own protection and to avoid leading borrowers into a debt trap. Administrative controls are tightening.[31]

1. Valuation of property

[30.09] Lenders should appoint a surveyor to report on the value of the property, which necessarily depends on the condition of the property. Proper lending practice allows a margin of at least 10% to cope with falls in property prices or a build up of arrears of interest. The value must be maintained by timely repair and by insurance against fire and other accidents.

A mortgage valuation is not a full structural survey of the property,[32] but rather a check on value. Although the surveyor's contractual duty of care is owed to the lender,[33] some 85% of *borrowers* rely on the mortgage valuation when agreeing to buy. *Smith* v. *Eric S Bush*[34] is the leading decision of the House of Lords. A surveyor, who had been appointed by a building society noticed that two chimney breasts had been removed, but did not check whether they were adequately supported. Had he done so he might have predicted the subsequent collapse of the chimney. The surveyor's firm was held liable to the house buyer in tort since it was foreseeable that he would on the valuation. Liability for negligence was disclaimed by Eric S Bush, but since Smith was a domestic borrower protected against unfair terms[35] and it was held that reliance on the exclusion clause was not reasonable. It would not be fair to exclude liability given the major commitment to a house purchase riding on a careless valuation.

---

[27] Sch 2; *Falco Finance* v. *Michael Gough* [1999] CLYB 2516 (charging interest on the whole loan under a reducing balance loan contravened the regulations; so too did a 5% increase in interest rate after a single default); S Bright (1999) 115 *LQR* 360.

[28] SI 1999/2083 sch 3 (taking only those apparently relevant to mortgages).

[29] Reg 6.

[30] Reg 8.

[31] This will be an important aspect of the FSA *Mortgage Code*; see above **[30.05]**.

[32] Even that is not a guarantee: *Watts* v. *Morrow* [1991] 1 WLR 1421, CA; E Macdonald [1992] *NLJ* 632.

[33] Care is needed where an employee of the lender carries out a valuation: *Halifax BS* v. *Edell* [1992] Ch 436.

[34] [1990] 1 AC 831, HL; there are many later cases.

[35] Unfair Contracts Terms Act 1977 s 2 subjects a disclaimer of liability for negligence to a test of reasonableness.

Losses arising from a negligent valuation are limited to the difference between the valuation figure and the true market value at that time. Valuers cannot be held responsible for unforeseeable falls in the property market.[36]

2.   Creditworthiness of borrower

[30.10] Modern domestic practice always involves some credit checks, though "over gearing" of commercial concerns is just as great a problem. Domestic borrowers usually borrow against their future income, which must be sufficient to service the repayments. A multiplier of 2.5 or 3[37] is applied to the gross annual salary, permitting a borrower earning £20,000 a year to borrow up to £60,000. After the sharp recession in the early 1990s more cautious lending guidelines have returned. Expensive precautions are insurance against illness or redundancy, and life cover to discharge the loan in the event of the death of one of the joint borrowers.

Domestic sector lenders ought to be required to behave professionally when lending, but there is little sign yet of a comprehensive liability in English law for reckless lending.

3.   Guarding against mortgage fraud

[30.11] Mortgage fraud is all too prevalent. The criminal aspects are not considered here. The primary concern of the conveyancer is to carry out preventative checks to reduce the enormous scale of frauds.[38] Many frauds involve misstatement of the identity of the applicant. Loan applications inaccurately stated the borrowers' names, employment and income, their intended use of the property, and the purchase prices of the various properties used in the frauds. Often such frauds prevent a lender getting a valid security for the amount of his loan, but if he does and is able to recover his loan from sale of the security, the borrower is entitled to any surplus.[39] Conveyancers can prevent many frauds by ensuring that they meet unknown clients and checking the stated identities. A receipt clause will not be decisive against a victim of a fraud.[40]

Other frauds involve the property. Sometimes non-existent land is mortgaged, a problem which will self-disclose when the lender tries to repossess it. Rollovers are the commonest fraud, by which land is sold at progressively higher prices using false valuations.[41]

---

[36] *South Australia Asset Management Corporation* v. *York Montague* [1997] AC 191, HL.

[37] Couples: 3 × main income + 1 × smaller income, or 2.5 × joint income. Otherwise additional security may be required. The rapid rise in house prices in the early years of the 2000s combined with low interest rates has led to many lenders stretching this to 5 or even 7 times salary.

[38] M Clarke, *Mortgage Fraud* (Chapman & Hall, 1991); HW Wilkinson [1993] *Conv* 181.

[39] *Halifax BS* v. *Thomas* [1996] Ch 217, CA; AC Spiers [1996] *Conv* 387; *Portman BS* v. *Hamlyn Taylor Neck* [1998] 4 All ER 202, CA.

[40] *Scotlife Home Loans (No 2)* v. *Melinek* (1999) 78 P & CR 389, CA.

[41] *Target Holdings* v. *Redferns* [1996] 1 AC 421, HL; *Paragon Finance* v. *DB Thakerar* [1999] 1 All ER 400, CA (limitation). There are many other cases.

4. Dual representation

[30.12] It is general practice for one solicitor to represent both borrower when acquiring the house and lender when advancing money to complete the acquisition.[42] Dual representation was permitted in 1972[43] to avoid wasteful duplication.

5. Mortgage instructions

[30.13] Mortgage instructions are provided by lenders which determine the functions of a conveyancer when acting for the lender. The solicitor must obtain a valid mortgage. Land offered as security for a loan must be saleable, and easily saleable, so it is vital to investigate title before any money is advanced. After completion the solicitor must ensure that the mortgage is adequately protected by registration and must give notice of the mortgage to the holders of superior titles.[44]

Lenders must ensure that superior titles are kept on foot, with money spent for this purpose being added to the security. This includes interest on prior mortgages,[45] rent under superior leases,[46] and similar outgoings.

D. INSTALMENT MORTGAGES

[30.14] "Your home is at risk if you do not keep up payments on a mortgage or other loan secured on it."[47] This very necessary warning encapsulates two truths. Any debt carries with it the inherent risk of enforcement procedures, including ultimately loss of the property securing the debt. But this should only occur after a default – the key concept of modern mortgage law – with protection for domestic borrowers based on a loose distinction between minor remediable defaults and major arrears justifying immediate sale.[48]

1. Repayment mortgages

[30.15] Most mortgages provide for repayment of what is borrowed by instalments. A person who has borrowed to buy a home obviously cannot repay the money immediately, and needs to be allowed a period of years, common durations being 15, 20 or 25 years.[49]

---

[42] Procedure in a simple mortgage transaction was explained *R* v. *Preddy* [1996] AC 815, 828–829, Lord Goff. The borrower pays all fees.

[43] Solicitors Practice Rules 1988 r 6, as amended in 1998: [1998] 40 *LSG* 42; HW Wilkinson [1998] *NLJ* 1882.

[44] Council of Mortgage Lender *Lender's Handbook* (2002 edition), available on the CML website.

[45] *Re Leslie* (1883) 23 Ch D 552 (add to security); *Sinfield* v. *Sweet* [1967] 1 WLR 1489 (no personal action).

[46] *Brandon* v. *Brandon* (1862) 10 WR 287.

[47] SI 1989/1125.

[48] J Houghton & L Livesey "Mortgage Conditions: Old Law for a New Century?" ch 10 in E Cooke (ed) *Modern Studies in Property Law 1 – Property 2000* (Hart, 2001).

[49] There may be a trend towards flexible mortgages allowing repayments to be varied and additional borrowing: J Morgan "Mortgages and the Flexible Workforce" ch 11 in Jackson and Wilde. Also, apparently, the growth of "100 year inter generational mortgages".

Instalments are calculated so that the balance of the debt (allowing for interest and capital repayments) will be reduced to zero at the end of the term of the loan. In the early years little capital is repaid but as inroads are made into the debt, the balance falls with increasing speed, rising to a gallop in the last few years.[50]

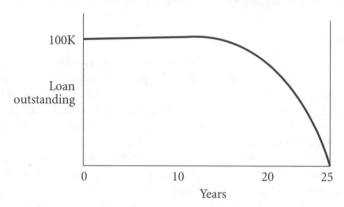

Figure 30-1 A repayment mortgage

Interest rates are usually variable, in which case monthly payments will also vary.

2. Interest-only mortgages

[30.16] Some mortgages provide for an advance over a fixed period of time, perhaps 25 years, with an agreement to leave the capital outstanding for the whole of that time. Interest is payable monthly but so long as the borrower keeps up to date with that, capital is deferred until the end of the fixed term of the mortgage.[51] If B borrows £100,000 in the year 2000, he will owe £100,000 in the year 2025. Repayment may be funded by a prospective inheritance, but usually there is an associated investment vehicle designed to build up a lump sum sufficient to redeem the loan.

Endowment mortgages are linked to an insurance policy. A monthly premium is paid to an insurance company, which invests the accumulating premiums so as to build up a sum large enough to discharge the borrowing.[52] Innocents abroad assume that any surplus belongs automatically to the owner of the house mortgaged, but ownership of the house and of the policy money may easily diverge.[53] In a low interest rates environment, the fund manager may struggle to obtain a sufficient yield of investment income to pay off the mortgage loan, especially if the stock exchange falls, and half a million borrowers or more have been left with shortfalls, some very serious.[54] However, if all goes well a surplus is generated, as illustrated below:

---

[50] A Samuels (1967) 31 *Conv (NS)* 343, 344; *Falco Finance* v. *Michael Gough* [1999] CLYB 2516.

[51] A default clause is essential in case interest payments lapse.

[52] The insurance policy is mortgaged to the lender, ensuring that it has first call on the money invested. This is by assignment (ie like a pre-1926 mortgage of land), notice of which must be given to the insurance company.

[53] *Powell* v. *Osbourne* [1993] 1 FLR 101; better is *Smith* v. *Clerical Medical & General Life Assurance Society* [1993] 1 FLR 47, CA; MC Hemsworth [1998] *CLJ* 15.

[54] *Endowment Mortgages* (FSA, PN/062, 2002).

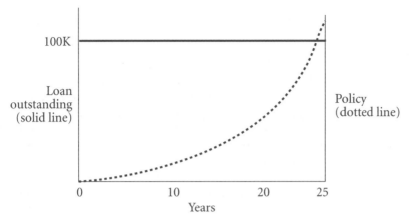

100K

Loan
outstanding
(solid line)

Policy
(dotted line)

0   10   20   25
Years

Figure 30-2 An endowment mortgage

Endowment mortgages have diminished in popularity because of tax changes and inflexibility; borrowers lose if the policy does not remain on foot for the whole 25 year expected life of a mortgage. A variety of other investment vehicles can be used to build up the lump sum to repay the loan – including pension lumps sums and personal equity plans.

3. Default clauses

[30.17] While agreed instalments are paid, there is no action for debt and no possibility of sale, so that security in his home is guaranteed to a punctilious borrower.[55] Lenders need to ensure that their remedies are restored once arrears build up via a default clause which makes the whole loan payable if any instalment is in arrears for a stated period, commonly 14 or 21 days.[56] Acceptance of a late instalment may waive a default[57] but otherwise the courts have tended to take a tough line after there has been any default.[58] Even without a default clause enforcement of the mortgage is usually allowed after any instalment is late,[59] but there is a risk that either party will have the right to insist on earlier repayment.[60]

[55] *De Borman* v. *Makkofaides* (1971) 220 EG 805 (instalments but no interest!); *Curteis* v. *Fenning* (1872) 41 LJ Ch 791, Hatherley LC.

[56] *Keene* v. *Biscoe* (1878) 8 Ch D 201, Fry J (3 days); *Leeds & Hanley Theatre of Varieties* v. *Broadbent* [1898] 1 Ch 343, CA (9 days); NL Macassey (1992) 122 *NLJ* 815. This is not a penalty: *Wallingford* v. *Mutual Society* (1880) 5 App Cas 685, 702, Lord Hatherley; *Walsh* v. *Derrick* (1903) 19 TLR 209, CA; *Congresbury Motors* v. *Anglo-Belge Finance Co* [1969] 3 All ER 545, 553–554, Plowman J.

[57] *Seal* v. *Gimson* (1914) 110 LT 583.

[58] *Maclaine* v. *Gatty* [1921] 1 AC 376, HL; *Coutts & Co* v. *Doutroon Investment Corp* [1958] 1 WLR 116.

[59] *Stanhope* v. *Manners* (1763) 2 Eden 197, 28 ER 873; *Edwards* v. *Martin* (1856) 25 LJ Ch 284, (1858) 28 LJ Ch 49; *Kidderminster MBBS* v. *Haddock* [1936] WN 158; *Payne* v. *Cardiff RDC* [1932] 1 KB 241.

[60] *Williams* v. *Morgan* [1906] 1 Ch 804, Swinfen Eady J.

E. DOMESTIC REPOSSESSION

1. Protected domestic mortgages

[30.18] Although sale is the real remedy, protection for domestic borrowers is provided at the stage of repossession, and a lender who is able to recover possession will be entitled to sell the property.[61] Protection derives either from the Administration of Justice Act 1970[62] or the consumer credit legislation.[63] The domestic sector marked out by the 1970 Act consists of mortgages secured on any dwelling-house, which must be a building and one used as a dwelling. Mixed use was discussed in *Royal Bank of Scotland* v. *Miller*[64] in the context of Afrika's nightclub with a caretaker's three bedroom flat above which, it was decided, fell within the domestic protection. Possession cannot be deferred in relation to part only.[65] The date on which to determine this question is when a claim is made for possession.[66]

The Law Commission proposes[67] to formalise the distinction between commercial and domestic mortgages, drawn either according to the purpose of the loan or the use of the mortgaged property,[68] with much more rigorous patrolling of domestic mortgages, including standardisation of terms,[69] and the abolition of interest penalties and interest in lieu of notice to redeem. An enforcement notice would be required before any action could be taken, the need for enforcement proceedings would be clarified, and the existing powers to suspend possession would be refined.

2. Contractual exclusion of the right to possession

[30.19] Harman J's judgment in *Four Maids* recognised that the lender could contract to restrict the normal right to possession.[70] Older mortgages often contained an attornment clause, by which the borrower declared that he was a tenant at will or periodic tenant of the lender to take advantage of a superior repossession procedure, but this is no longer advantageous.[71] Modern mortgages usually give an express right to possession so long as the borrower pays instalments promptly.

---

[61] *Cheltenham & Gloucester* v. *Booker* [1997] 1 EGLR 142, CA.

[62] S 36, as amended by Administration of Justice Act 1973 s 8; B Rudden (1961) 25 *Conv (NS)* 278; C Glasser (1971) 34 *MLR* 61; H Wallace (1986) 37 *NILQ* 336; HW Wilkinson [1990] *NLJ* 823; updaters by D McConnell in *Legal Action*; L Whitehouse "The Home Owner: Citizen or Consumer?" ch 19 in Bright & Dewar; Megarry & Wade (6th ed), [19.067–19.083].

[63] See below **[30.32]**.

[64] [2001] EWCA Civ 344, [2002] QB 255; RJ Smith [1979] *Conv* 266, 270–271.

[65] *Barclays Bank* v. *Alcorn* [2002] March 11th, Hart J; L McMurty [2002] *Conv* 594.

[66] *Royal Bank of Scotland* v. *Miller* at [25], Dyson LJ.

[67] Law Com 204 (1991); GH Griffiths [1987] *Conv* 191; HW Wilkinson [1992] *Conv* 69; GH Griffiths [1992] *JBL* 423; G Frost (1992) 136 *SJ* 267, 292.

[68] Probably, any mortgage involving a dwelling-house unless the borrower is a body corporate and enforcement would not affect any residential occupier.

[69] Including obliging the lender to keep the deeds safe, giving a borrower the right to possession unless the lender takes it, requiring repair, limiting sale to arrears of instalments or other major breach, and preventing the borrower granting leases without the consent of the lender.

[70] *Four Maids* v. *Dudley Marshall* [1957] Ch 317, 320; see above **[29.15]**.

[71] *Peckham Mutual BS* v. *Registe* (1982) 42 P & CR 186, Vinelott J; *Alliance BS* v. *Pinwill* [1958] Ch 788; and many other cases.

3. Judicial power to defer possession

[30.20] Legislative protection for domestic borrowers was introduced in two stages, the parent provision being section 36 of the Administration of Justice Act 1970. Possession proceedings brought by a mortgage-lender[72] may be suspended where it appears that the borrower is likely to be able to pay any sums due within a reasonable period or to remedy any other default. It follows that the first task is to determine precisely what default has occurred.[73] Minor arrears no longer gave a right to immediate possession. Although the intended target was arrears, the statute failed to land a clean hit when it referred to "any sums due under the mortgage". Unfortunately in the case of an instalment mortgage containing a default clause this could, on a literal reading,[74] means the entire capital balance, though a purposive reading limiting the sum to be paid off to the arrears was obviously intended.[75]

Section 8 of the Administration of Justice Act 1973[76] solves this problem where the borrower is entitled to pay by instalments or where he is entitled or permitted to defer payment. The court applies its discretion to the amount of the arrears ignoring the impact of any default clause. "Sums due" are what the borrower expected to be required to pay, ignoring any provision for earlier payment. Arrears must be cleared within a reasonable time along with current instalments as they fall due, but not the whole capital balance.

4. Other cases of deferral

[30.21] Permanent investment mortgages leave the loan outstanding after the contractual redemption date, until it is made repayable by serving a calling in notice. Under the 1970 Act (viewed in isolation) the court should order possession unless the borrower is able to repay all "sums due under the mortgage" – that is the whole redemption money – by the end of the notice calling in the capital, and could also foreclose.[77] Section 8(1) of the 1973 Act, however, allows the court to ignore any sum of which the borrower is permitted "to defer payment" "otherwise" meaning as a matter of grace.[78] In *Centrax Trustees* v. *Ross*[79] the court ignored a calling in notice, meaning that the borrower was only required to keep up to date with interest, though this was certainly not intended.[80]

---

[72] A "mortgagee", which includes the lender under a charge, and any successor: s 39.

[73] *Halifax Mortgage Services* v. *Muirhead* (1997) 76 P & CR 418, 428, Evans LJ; *Ladjadj* v. *Bank of Scotland* [2000] 2 All ER (Comm) 583, CA.

[74] *Halifax Building Society* v. *Clark* [1973] Ch 307, Pennycuick V-C (arrears £1,000, redemption figure £1,400); PV Baker (1973) 89 *LQR* 171; P Jackson (1973) 36 *MLR* 550; EH Scammell (1973) 37 *Conv (NS)* 133, 213; *Bank of Scotland* v. *Grimes* [1985] QB 1179, 1190, Griffiths LJ.

[75] *First Middlesborough Trading and Mortgage Co* v. *Cunningham* (1974) 28 P & CR 69, 74, Scarman LJ; *Cheltenham & Gloucester BS* v. *Norgan* [1996] 1 WLR 343, 345D–348A, Waite LJ; *Cheltenham & Gloucester* v. *Krausz* [1997] 1 WLR 1558, CA.

[76] (1973) 123 *NLJ* 475; S Tromans [1984] *Conv* 91.

[77] S 36(1) does not apply; *Cheltenham & Gloucester BS* v. *Grattidge* (1993) 25 HLR 454, CA; *Habib Bank* v. *Tailor* [1982] 1 WLR 1218, 1222A–B, Oliver LJ.

[78] RJ Smith [1979] *Conv* 266, 274. Forfeiture is similarly restricted.

[79] [1979] 2 All ER 952, Goulding J.

[80] *Habib Bank* v. *Tailor* [1982] 1 WLR 1218, 1224E, Oliver LJ.

A borrower with an overdraft mortgage is not protected by section 8 of the 1973 Act because the borrower is not entitled or otherwise permitted to defer payment,[81] so it must be possible to clear the overdraft completely.

F. JUDICIAL DEFERRAL OF REPOSSESSION

1. Major arrears

[30.22] Once major arrears have built up, which it is impracticable for the borrower to clear within a short period of time, the tightly defined power of deferment has ended,[82] and the lender is left with an outright entitlement to possession,[83] though the borrower should be allowed 28 days to arrange alternative accommodation. For example, possession was ordered against *Mr* Boland when arrears of £26,000 had mounted up after his business failure.[84] Possession will almost certainly be followed by sale, since the power becomes exercisable when any interest is in arrears for two months.[85]

2. Minor arrears

[30.23] The common law right to possession[86] is replaced by statutory protection for a domestic borrower who demonstrates the ability to clear the arrears and keep up with instalments as they fall due.[87] Usually an order is made for possession, but suspended on terms that the borrower makes monthly payments towards the arrears,[88] those payments clearing what is due within a reasonable period. The Payne Committee considered six months to be a reasonable time,[89] a period taken as a guide to the exercise of the judicial discretion, though one which is flexible. The property slump and negative equity of the early 1990s led to a general extension of this period, certainly to two years with up to four years allowed where there were sound reasons to do so.

Cheltenham & Gloucester BS v. *Norgan*[90] suggested the possibility of extending this time to achieve almost unlimited postponement. The Norgans lived in a period farm-

---

[81] *Habib* at 1225C, Oliver LJ; PH Kenny [1983] *Conv* 80; PH Kenny (1982) 79 *LSG* 1271; HW Wilkinson (1983) 133 *NLJ* 247; S Tromans [1984] *Conv* 91. See also *Marples* v. *Holmes* (1976) 31 P & CR 94, Plowman V-C (all monies charge).

[82] *Cheltenham & Gloucester* v. *Krausz* [1997] 1 WLR 1558, 1567C, Phillips LJ.

[83] Ie as at common law: LPA 1925 s 95(4); *Four-Maids* [1957] Ch 317, Harman J; see above **[29.15]**.

[84] *Williams & Glyn's Bank* v. *Boland* [1981] AC 487, HL.

[85] LPA 1925 s 103(ii); see above **[29.22]**; beware capitalisation clauses which convert interest to capital: *Davy* v. *Turner* (1970) 21 P & CR 967.

[86] *Birmingham PBS* v. *Caunt* [1962] Ch 883, 894, Russell J; *Cheltenham & Gloucester BS* v. *Norgan* [1996] 1 WLR 343, 345–348, Waite LJ.

[87] In 1998 there were roughly 35,000 repossession actions leading to 28,000 orders for possession, of which 17,000 were suspended.

[88] *Citibank T* v. *Ayivor* [1987] 1 WLR 1157, 1163B–D.

[89] Cmnd 3909 (1969), [1383].

[90] [1996] 1 WLR 343, CA; J Morgan (1996) 112 *LQR* 553; MP Thompson [1996] *Conv* 118; HW Wilkinson [1996] *NLJ* 252; M Haley (1997) 17 *LS* 483; M Dixon (1998) 18 *LS* 279; *Household Mortgage Corp* v. *Pringle* (1998) 30 HLR 251, 259, Evans LJ.

house in Wiltshire bought with the aid of an endowment mortgage[91] on terms that the £90,000 loan would be left outstanding for 22 years. Cheltenham & Gloucester took over the mortgage when arrears of interest had reached £7,000, a default which had doubled in size by the time of the hearing. The Court of Appeal allowed the whole remaining term of the mortgage – that is 13 years – to clear the arrears. Waite LJ based his decision on two dicta[92] from another context,[93] deliberately flouting existing county court practice whilst Evans LJ enumerated the factors to be considered.[94] They achieved the rare feat of making one feel sorry for a lender and opened an objectionable chasm between repayment and endowment mortgages. Surely deferral of repayment should be conditional on regular payments of interest?

Borrowers are usually allowed to clear arrears from future income, provided they can also cover future instalments as they fall due.[95] Following job loss, a borrower may have to rely on social security benefits to cover the interest element of mortgage repayments. Rules were tightened after the claim in *Julien* for interest on a loan of £630,000.[96] Benefits have therefore been limited to interest on smallish loans, and income support is restricted for the first six months, so that new borrowers are responsible for insuring themselves against the risk of temporary unemployment.[97]

3. Capital redemption

[30.24] A short fixed period of suspension should be granted if there is a good prospect of complete redemption. Suitable grounds may be a contract to sell, or possibly the grant of planning permission creating firm prospects of a successful sale.[98] In *National and Provincial BS* v. *Lloyd*,[99] the reasonable period was fixed at nine months, but in other circumstances it might vary from say six months up to a year. A mere expression of hope is not enough. In *Bristol & West BS* v. *Ellis*[100] the borrower sought deferral for three to four years until her sons had finished at university, but the court ordered possession. A *Norgan* suspension over the whole remaining term of the mortgage is not available to a person proposing a capital redemption.

If possession is ordered, conduct of the sale will then be given to the lender.[101] Borrowers may get 10% more by avoiding repossession and taking control of a sale.

---

[91] Protection for endowment mortgages was established by *Bank of Scotland* v. *Grimes* [1985] QB 1179, 1189, Griffiths LJ.

[92] *First Middlesborough Trading and Mortgage Co* v. *Cunningham* (1974) 28 P & CR 69, 75, Scarman LJ; *Western Bank* v. *Schindler* [1977] Ch 1, 14, Buckley LJ.

[93] *Norgan* [1996] 1 WLR 343, 353F.

[94] At 357H–358B.

[95] Administration of Justice Act 1973 s 8.

[96] *Town & Country BS* v. *Julien* (1991) 24 HLR 312, CA (large arrears had built up before the application for income support; repossession ordered); *Bristol & West BS* v. *Ellis* (1997) 29 HLR 282, CA.

[97] HW Wilkinson [1996] *NLJ* 252. Payments may be made direct to qualifying lenders: Social Security (Mortgage Interest Payments) Act 1992.

[98] *Target Home Loans* v. *Clothier* [1994] 1 All ER 439, CA; JE Martin [1993] *Conv* 62; JE Adams [1994] *Conv* 11; *Royal Trust Co of Canada* v. *Markham* [1975] 1 WLR 1416, Pennycuick V-C.

[99] [1996] 1 All ER 630, CA; *Polonski* v. *Lloyds Bank Mortgages* [1998] 1 FLR 896; MP Thompson [1998] *Conv* 125.

[100] (1997) 29 HLR 282, CA. Not simply by appointing a conveyancer: *Mortgage Services Funding* v. *Steele* (1996) 72 P & CR D40, CA.

[101] *Cheltenham & Gloucester* v. *Booker* [1997] 1 EGLR 142, CA; A Kenny [1998] *Conv* 223.

But a lender who chooses to exercise his powers can insist on control of a sale of a property suffering from negative equity.[102]

A borrower may say that he expects to be able to redeem the loan by pursuing an action against the lender on a cross-claim. This is not usually a defence with commercial property,[103] nor even with domestic borrowers.[104] Potential litigation successes stand alongside such other hypotheticals as legacies and pools wins.[105] However consideration must be given to hard evidence of reasonable prospects of successful action[106] and there are cases where stays have been ordered.[107] A challenge to the very existence of the mortgage security must be determined before possession can be ordered.[108] Proceedings should not be stayed simply because it is argued that a fair trial has not been provided and the borrower wishes to take that argument to Strasbourg.[109]

4. Non-financial breaches

[30.25] A lender is quite entitled to possession to protect the security, for example to avoid vandalism to the property, or to ensure that premiums under an associated endowment policy are paid.[110]

5. No arrears

[30.26] The court only has power to defer possession if it appears to the court that sums due can be cleared within a reasonable time. Literally this gives no powers where payments are bang up to date. In *Western Bank* v. *Schindler*[111] a mortgage which provided for payment of capital to be deferred for 10 years also – most extraordinarily – deferred interest for the same period. When interest payments ceased there was no default. A majority[112] preferred to read the section[113] with the addition of the words *"but if there is default only* if" it is a serious default, allowing the court to protect a borrower whose nose is clean. This is surely better than relying on the liability of a

---

[102] LPA 1925 s 91; *Cheltenham & Gloucester* v. *Krausz* [1997] 1 WLR 1558, 1562H, Phillips LJ; A Kenny [1998] *Conv* 223.

[103] *Spector* v. *Applefeld Properties* (1968) 206 EG 537; *Mobil Oil* v. *Rawlinson* (1982) 43 P & CR 221; *Samuel Keller (Holdings)* v. *Martins Bank* [1971] 1 WLR 43.

[104] *Citibank T* v. *Aviyor* [1987] 1 WLR 1157; *Abbey National BS* v. *Bernard* [1995] CLYB 3597 (NHBC negotiations).

[105] *Hastings & Thanet BS* v. *Goddard* [1970] 1 WLR 1544, 1548B.

[106] Eg *Boland* [1981] AC 487, 509; approving (1979) 36 P & CR 448, Templeman J; but reversing [1979] Ch 312, 333B, 343F–344A.

[107] *Ashley Guarantee* v. *Zacaria* [1993] 1 WLR 62 (commercial); *National Westminster Bank* v. *Skelton* [1993] 1 WLR 72, CA (reckless lending); *Halifax BS* v. *Stansfield* [1993] EGCS 147, CA; *Albany Home Loans* v. *Massey* [1997] 2 All ER 609, CA; *Household Mortgage Corp* v. *Pringle* (1998) 30 HLR 250, CA.

[108] *Bradford & Bingley BS* v. *Chandock* (1996) 72 P & CR D28, CA (undue influence); *Household Mortgage Corp* v. *Pringle* (1998) 30 HLR 251, CA.

[109] *Locabail* v. *Waldorf Investment Corp (No 4)* [2000] Times June 13th, Ch D.

[110] *Western Bank* v. *Schindler* [1977] Ch 1, 23D, Goff LJ; (1976) 92 *LQR* 482.

[111] [1977] Ch 1, CA.

[112] At 12–15, Buckley LJ, 16–17, Scarman LJ; *Royal Trust Co of Canada* v. *Markham* [1975] 1 WLR 1416, 1420, Sir John Pennycuick; *Cheltenham & Gloucester* v. *Krausz* [1997] 1 WLR 1558, 1567D, Phillips LJ.

[113] Administration of Justice Act 1970 s 36(2)(a).

lender in possession.[114] Still better is to read the "sums due" to include not only arrears, but also future instalments as they fall due, and capital when it has to be repaid.[115] If instalments are up to date at the time of the hearing, the court will be satisfied that the sums due (meaning future instalments as they fall due) will be paid within a reasonable time, and will adjourn proceedings indefinitely. Why else is there an adjournment power?

G. PROCEDURAL PROTECTION OF DOMESTIC BORROWERS

1. No proceedings

[30.27] Borrowers are best protected by ensuring that a court considers all relevant circumstances before ordering repossession. Proceedings are essential if the borrower is in occupation and objecting to repossession.[116] However the lender can simply retake a house given up by the borrower or left vacant. In such a case the suspensive powers of the court do not bite, unless the lender "brings an action" for possession.[117] Alison Clarke argued[118] that the lender's right to possession had been impliedly removed by the Administration of Justice Acts as Parliament presumably intended.[119] In *Ropaigealach* v. *Barclays Bank*[120] the current state of the law was severely criticised by the Court of Appeal, but it refused to imply a rule that Parliament had omitted.[121] Peaceable possession can be taken of a property vacated by the borrower, section 36 never being in play. The result is at once unfortunate and technically correct.

Can the lender simply sell with the borrower still in possession, or would this attract liability for failure to obtain the open market price.[122]

2. Repossession procedure

[30.28] Procedure follows Part 55.[123] The claim form[124] is prescribed, as are the contents of the particulars of claim[125] which must:

identify the land;
state whether it is residential;
give full details of the mortgage;[126]

---

[114] C Harpum (1977) 40 *MLR* 356; echoing *Western Bank* at 26C, Goff LJ.

[115] This 1970 scheme was not appreciated by those drafting the 1973 amendment.

[116] Criminal Law Act 1977 s 6; Protection from Eviction Act 1977 (during contractual postponement of the right to possession).

[117] Administration of Justice Act 1970 s 36(1).

[118] [1983] *Conv* 293; *Ropaigealach* v. *Barclays Bank* [2000] QB 263, 274C–D, Clarke LJ.

[119] *Western Bank* v. *Schindler* [1977] Ch 1, CA.

[120] [2000] QB 263, CA; M Dixon [1999] *CLJ* 281; E Paton [1999] *NLJ* 614; JE Adams [1999] *Conv* 73.

[121] At 283C–D, Clarke LJ, 288A, Henry LJ.

[122] *Silsby* v. *Holliman* [1955] Ch 552; *Holohan* v. *Friend's Provident & Century Life Office* [1966] IR 1 (duty to get vacant possession against unlawful tenants).

[123] CPR 55.1(b); whether legal or equitable and whether by mortgage or charge: CPR 55.1(c), 55.2. Cases will usually be brought in a county court: CPR 55.3; PD 55.3, [1.6].

[124] CPR 55.3(5); PD 1.5; claim form N11M. A money claim can be joined: PD 55.3, [1.7].

[125] CPR 55.4; PD 55.4, [2.1].

[126] S Tromans [1984] *Conv* 91, 95–96; *Bank of Scotland* v. *Grimes* [1985] QB 1179, CA.

list all people known to be in possession

give prescribed details of the state of the mortgage account[127] – the amount of the advance, agreed periodic payments, the redemption figure or credit outstanding, rates of interest throughout the mortgage and a statement of payments and arrears;[128]

include a statement (where appropriate) that the mortgage is a regulated consumer credit agreement;[129]

give relevant information about the defendant's circumstances;

detail any tenancy; and

give details of previous steps to recover the money or property.

Where a matrimonial home right is registered,[130] the proceedings have to be served on the spouse who has registered, and more generally proceedings must also be served on any other occupiers of residential mortgaged property, not less than 14 days before the hearing.[131]

The court will fix a hearing date at least 28 days distant when it issues the claim form, with service required not less than 21 days before hand.[132] An official copy of a charge will be admissible in evidence.[133] Facts may be proved by written evidence in a witness statement, verified by statement of truth, filed at least two days before the hearing, though if the evidence is disputed oral evidence will be required.[134]

Fixed costs apply to possession claims.[135]

3.   Defended actions

[30.29] Defendants to an action for possession of land do not need to serve an acknowledgement of service and, although they should serve a defence to avoid the penalty in costs which may otherwise attach,[136] there is a right to participate in the hearing in any event. If the court is unable to decide the case at the fixed date hearing because of a genuine dispute,[137] the court should give case management directions and track the case according to the amount of arrears and the importance of possession to each party.[138]

---

[127] PD 55.4, [2.5].

[128] If possible arrears should be stated up to the date of the hearing. Evidence must show the amount of social security payments outstanding: PD 55.8, [5].

[129] If so, whether or not it is within Consumer Credit Act 1974 s 141. A Consumer Credit Act defence may be by way of defence or by application notice in the proceedings: PD 55, [7.1].

[130] FLA 1996 s 56(3); DLRR 2003 rr 159–160; PD 55.4, [2.5]; see above **[8.21]**.

[131] CPR 55.10.

[132] CPR 55.5; PD 55.5 [3.1].

[133] CPR 33; LR (No 2) R 2000, SI 2000/2214.

[134] PD 55.8 [5]. *Royal Trust Co of Canada* v. *Markham* [1975] 1 WLR 1416, 1422B; *Cheltenham & Gloucester BS* v. *Grant* (1994) 26 HLR 703, CA.

[135] CPR 38.

[136] CPR 55.7.

[137] CPR 55.8.

[138] CPR 55.9; CPR 26.8.

4. Court powers

[30.30] Discretionary powers permit complete adjournment in the absence of arrears.[139] The lender is entitled to a possession order where there are arrears, though its execution is often stayed or suspended for a fixed period[140] to give the borrower time to remedy the default[141] with a formal condition that arrears are paid by specified instalments.[142] The court's powers end when the warrant for possession is executed.[143] A protected purchaser takes free.[144] A possession order against the borrower is an order for vacant possession to be given, so that the borrower can be ordered to remove furniture, cars and other effects.[145]

5. Money judgment

[30.31] Some lenders apply to the county court[146] for a money judgment at the same time as a possession order, especially if there will be a shortfall after sale of the land, since the lender can enforce its judgment for the shortfall immediately. The right to these cumulative remedies was established in *Cheltenham & Gloucester BS* v. *Grattidge*,[147] but the money order should be suspended on the same terms as the possession order. Borrowers used to experience serious problems caused by entry of such prospective orders in the register of county court judgments, but judgments are now only registrable once enforcement has begun.[148] Contractual entitlement to interest ends to be replaced by a lower rate of interest payable on a judgment debt.[149]

H. REPOSSESSION UNDER CONSUMER CREDIT AGREEMENTS

[30.32] The Consumer Credit Act 1974[150] regulates enforcement of consumer credit agreements, that is where the borrower is an individual, the loan is for £25,000 or less,[151] and the lender is non-exempt.[152] Particulars of claim must state that the

---

[139] Administration of Justice Act 1970 s 36(2).

[140] *Royal Trust Co of Canada* v. *Markham* [1975] 1 WLR 1416, 1421H–1422A.

[141] Administration of Justice Act 1970 s 36(2)(b).

[142] S 36(3); conditions can be varied or revoked: subs (4).

[143] *Cheltenham & Gloucester BS* v. *Obi* (1996) 28 HLR 22, CA; *National Westminster Bank* v. *Powney* [1991] Ch 339 (requires renewal after 12 months); *Mortgage Agency Services No 2* v. *Bal* [1998] 28 LSG 32, CA.

[144] *National Provincial BS* v. *Ahmed* [1995] 2 EGLR 127, CA.

[145] *Norwich Union Life Insurance Society* v. *Preston* [1957] 1 WLR 813; *Minah* v. *Bank of Ireland* [1995] EGCS 144.

[146] *Yorkshire Bank* v. *Hall* [1999] 1 WLR 1713.

[147] (1993) 25 HLR 454, CA; K Manley [1993] *NLJ* 145; *Cheltenham & Gloucester BS* v. *Grant* (1994) 26 HLR 703, CA; MP Thompson [1995] *Conv* 51; *Cheltenham & Gloucester BS* v. *Johnson* (1996) 28 HLR 885, CA; *Cheltenham & Gloucester BS* v. *Fisher* [1993] NLJ 986 (leave is not required).

[148] SI 1993/2173 (after October 1993).

[149] SI 1991/1184 as amended; K Manley [1993] *NLJ* 1451. On issue estoppel: *Lloyds Bank* v. *Hawkins* [1998] 3 EGLR 109, CA; *UCB* v. *Chandler* (2000) 79 P & CR 270, CA.

[150] S 127; Administration of Justice Act 1970 s 38A; A Rogerson (1975) 38 *MLR* 435; KE Lindgren (1977) 40 *MLR* 159; R Goode [1975] *CLJ* 79.

[151] SI 1998/996 from May 1st 1998; previously £15,000 (SI 1983/1878) or £5,000 (before mid-1985).

[152] Consumer Credit Act 1974 s 16; SI 1989/869 art 2 as amended.

mortgage is a regulated credit agreement, so directing procedure into the correct channel.[153] Enforcement can only occur after a default has occurred, and a default notice has been served on the debtor stating what is wrong and allowing a reasonable period for it to be corrected.[154] Judicial proceedings are essential.[155]

Before ordering possession,[156] the court must consider whether to make a time order,[157] which allows the borrower to make repayment "by such instalments as the court considers reasonable". Time orders are actually very similar to suspended possession orders for ordinary domestic mortgages, a congruence illustrated in *First National Bank* v. *Syed*[158] when an order made at first instance under the Administration of Justice Acts was confirmed on appeal as a time order under the consumer credit legislation. A time order must provide for repayment of the entire debt with proper interest.[159] If the borrower will never be able to clear all arrears immediate enforcement should be allowed.[160] *Southern & District Finance* v. *Barnes*[161] considered three successful applications to reschedule indebtedness as a result of temporary difficulty,[162] by extending the time allowed for repayment. Flexibility can be shown towards interest rates,[163] and an extortionate interest rate can certainly be cut – possibly to nothing.[164]

I. TENANTS

1. Leases granted before the mortgage

[30.33] The lender will almost inevitably take subject to any existing leases subsisting at the time of creation of the mortgage, unless he gets priority over a lease which is equitable.

Leases granted before the borrower's acquisition of the mortgaged property create a tenancy by estoppel. If B (who does not own the land) grants a lease to T, this cannot be legal when B has no title, but it does create an estoppel between the two of them.[165] If the estate owner now transfers title to B, legal title to the lease passes to T, the estoppel being fed by the arrival of the legal estate in the landlord.

Where the land acquired is mortgaged, it used to be thought that three stages arose in order: acquisition of the estate, feeding the estoppel, and the mortgage. An instant

---

[153] CPR 55.

[154] Consumer Credit Act 1974 ss 87–89; SI 1983/1561, modelled on LPA 1925 s 146.

[155] Consumer Credit Act 1974 ss 92, 126.

[156] *Southern & District Finance* v. *Barnes* (1995) 27 HLR 691, 695, Legatt LJ.

[157] Consumer Credit Act 1974 s 129(2); R Goode [1975] *CLJ* 79, 112–117; N Hickman (1994) 110 *LQR* 221.

[158] [1991] 2 All ER 250, CA; HW Wilkinson [1991] *NLJ* 793.

[159] *Barnes* (1995) 27 HLR 691, 698, Leggatt LJ.

[160] [1991] 2 All ER 250, 255g–256d, Dillon LJ.

[161] (1995) 27 HLR 691, CA; N Hickman, D McConnell & M Ramsden [1995] 16 *LSG* 17; A Dunn [1996] *Conv* 209.

[162] *Barnes* (1995) 27 HLR 691, 698, Leggatt LJ.

[163] At 698, Leggatt LJ; *Ewart*, at 700.

[164] *Lewis*, at 701, where the terms were bordering on the extortionate: £4,000 borrowed; £15,000 repayable over 15 years; repayment ordered over 18 years without interest.

[165] *Bell* v. *General Accident Fire & Life Assurance Corp* [1998] 1 EGLR 69, CA; this ceases on eviction: *Sadiq* v. *Hussain* [1997] CLYB 4247, CA.

of time[166] between steps (1) and (3) was long enough to create a legal lease in T with priority over the mortgage.[167] This doctrine is now known to be wrong, since *Abbey National BS* v. *Cann*[168] ruled that the land was acquired subject to the mortgage, and there was no moment of time to allow priority to a resulting trust interest. The same applies to leases.[169] Similarly if a defective mortgage is corrected by a second charge executed to vary the first, they form a single transaction with no moment of time between them.[170]

2. Borrower bound by security of tenure he creates

[30.34] In *Quennell* v. *Maltby*,[171] a landlord owned a house worth about £40,000. He mortgaged it to the bank to secure a small overdraft. He granted a Rent Act protected tenancy to nine students of Sussex University without the bank's consent, contrary to the terms of the mortgage. A possession action as *landlord* was blocked by the students' security of tenure. Their landlord tried to circumvent this restriction by arranging for his wife to pay off the overdraft, thereby becoming transferee of the rights under the mortgage, and arranging for her to seek possession as *lender*. Possession was refused. A majority of the Court of Appeal[172] took the view that the wife was acting as agent of the landlord and so was bound by the Rent Act restriction on possession.

Lord Denning MR asserted a more general right to regulate a lender's possession action to ensure that possession was only obtained under as a prelude to a genuine enforcement of the mortgage:[173]

> "A mortgagee will be restrained from getting possession except when it is sought bona fide and reasonably for the purpose of enforcing the security and then only subject to such conditions as the court thinks fit to impose."

But, in fact, Chancery did not interfere with common law ejectment proceedings before the Judicature Act 1873, however strange that denial of equity may be, so that there was and is no equity to prevent a lender taking possession.[174]

3. Leases granted by the borrower after the mortgage

[30.35] Most mortgages exclude the statutory leasing power enjoyed by a borrower[175] as a matter of course,[176] an exclusion that should be noted against a registered title.[177] The lender is not bound by a lease granted by the borrower in defiance of this exclusion.

---

166 A *scintilla temporis*; *Pomfret* v. *Windsor* (1752) 2 Ves Sen 472, 28 ER 302 (estate of Judge Jeffries).

167 *Church of England BS* v. *Piskor* [1954] Ch 553, etc.

168 [1991] 1 AC 56, HL.

169 *First National Bank* v. *Thompson* [1996] Ch 231, CA.

170 *Walthamstow BS* v. *Davies* (1990) 22 HLR 60, CA; JE Adams [1991] *Conv* 12.

171 [1979] 1 WLR 318, CA; JS Fisher (1979) 123 *SJ* 775; RA Pearce [1979] *CLJ* 257.

172 Templeman and Bridge LJJ.

173 At 571 (query whether Bridge LJ agreed with Lord Denning *on this point*); *Albany Home Loans* v. *Massey* [1997] 2 All ER 609, 612–613, Schiemann LJ; MP Thompson [1998] *Conv* 391.

174 *Cholmondeley* v. *Clinton* (1817) 2 Mer 177, 35 ER 359, Grant MR; on appeal (1820) 2 Jac & W 183, 37 ER 527, Eldon LC; *Braithwaite* v. *Winwood* [1960] 1 WLR 1257, 1263.

175 LPA 1925 s 99.

176 LPA 1925 s 99(13); *Public Trustee* v. *Lawrence* [1912] 1 Ch 789.

177 Under the old law LRR 1925 r 141; M Robinson (1997) 113 *LQR* 390; M Robinson (1998) 114 *LQR* 354. Now LRA 2002 s 26(2).

The lease operates as it would have done at common law, binding by estoppel between borrower and tenant, but not affecting the lender.[178] His right is to damages for trespass (mesne profits) rather than rent.[179]

Proceedings are required[180] but the lender has no further concern with security of tenure. It makes no difference whether the tenant claims a contractual tenancy[181] or as a statutory tenant after notice to quit.[182] Since the tenant holds no legitimate estate in the mortgaged land, he has no right to apply for suspension of a possession order.[183]

Acceptance of the illegal tenant by the lender prevents his later removal. The lender may conduct himself in such a way as to confirm the tenancy[184] by giving notice to collect the rent,[185] leading the tenant to believe that the lease has been renewed,[186] or causing the tenant to spend money on repairs,[187] but not through mere knowledge or inaction.[188] A lease granted in breach of covenant may be binding if the lender is estopped from denying its validity.[189]

4. Leasing powers of lender

[30.36] Lenders in possession may let the mortgaged land,[190] and have power to grant a shorthold tenancy. A simple mortgage rescue package may take the form of a lease by a lender in possession back to the borrower, possibly under a sale and lease-back arrangement, though there have been relatively few suitable cases even during the great housing disaster of the early 1990s.

J.   OPPRESSION

[30.37] From Henry VIII's reign until the nineteenth century, usury laws regulated the overall profit a lender could extract from his loan. Repeal of these laws brought back into the foreground even older equitable jurisdictions over oppressive bargains and advantages exacted under grievous necessity.[191] These now apply primarily to

---

[178] *Thunder d Weaver* v. *Belcher* (1803) 3 East 449, 102 ER 669, Ellenbororugh CJ; *Brown* v. *Peto* [1900] 1 QB 346, 355, Bigham J at first instance; *Iron Trades Employers Insurance Association* v. *Union Land & House Investors* [1937] Ch 313, Farwell J; *Rust* v. *Goodale* [1957] Ch 33; *Bolton BS* v. *Cobb* [1966] 1 WLR 1.

[179] *Kitchen's Trustees* v. *Madders* [1950] Ch 134.

[180] Protection from Eviction Act 1977 s 1(1); DG Barnsley [1991] *JSWL* 220.

[181] *Dudley & District Benefit BS* v. *Emerson* [1949] Ch 707, CA.

[182] *Britannia BS* v. *Earl* [1990] 1 WLR 422, CA; S Bridge [1990] *Conv* 450; HW Wilkinson [1990] *NLJ* 823.

[183] *Britannia BS* v. *Earl*; but query whether this follows.

[184] *Parker* v. *Braithwaite* [1952] 2 All ER 837; *Stroud BS* v. *Delamont* [1960] 1 WLR 431; *Chatsworth Properties* v. *Effiom* [1971] 1 WLR 144, CA.

[185] The lender should appoint a receiver; see above **[29.18]**.

[186] *Chatsworth Properties* v. *Effiom* [1971] 1 WLR 144, CA.

[187] *Doe d Parry* v. *Hughes* (1847) Jur 698; *Barclay* v. *Kiley* [1961] 1 WLR 1050 (not sufficient on the facts).

[188] *Parker* v. *Braithwaite* [1952] 2 All ER 837 (8 months); *Taylor* v. *Ellis* [1960] Ch 368, Cross J (20 years).

[189] *Lever Finance* v. *Needleman's Trustee* [1956] Ch 375; A Walker (1978) 128 *NLJ* 773; *Mann* v. *Nijar* (2000) 32 HLR 223, CA.

[190] LPA 1925 s 99; *Berkshire Capital Funding* v. *Street* [1999] 2 EGLR 92, CA (first lender could grant lease binding second lender).

[191] *Barrett* v. *Hartley* (1866) LR 2 Eq 789, 794, Stuart V-C.

domestic mortgages. Equity is only concerned with terms that are oppressive or unconscionable, as opposed to ones that are merely unreasonable.[192]

1. Technical malformation

[30.38] Equity intervenes in mortgage transactions on the technical ground that a transaction renders the right to redeem the mortgage illusory. Examples are options to purchase the mortgaged property and long postponements of contractual redemption of a leasehold estate, the principle applying to commercial mortgages[193] overlapping with the possibility of oppression.

A loan transaction must take the form of a mortgage.[194] Equity insists on a clear demarcation between a sale and a mortgage,[195] allowing redemption of any loan, rewriting any mortgage drafted to take the form of a sale, and invalidating options to purchase and other terms which impede the right of redemption.[196] This is an abstract technical doctrine based on the need for equity to ensure that any loan is redeemable. Postponement of redemption is common in domestic mortgages for a fixed period, during which redemption is prohibited or heavily penalised. If the interest rate is fixed for five years, the lender may insist that the borrower remains committed to the mortgage for that term, but the mortgage must not preclude the borrower from redeeming altogether.[197]

2. Oppression

[30.39] This is a feature of some domestic lending. The most significant indicator is a high interest rate, often exacerbated by postponement of contractual redemption so that the oppressive rate continues over a substantial period of time or by reserving collateral advantages.[198] The whole mortgage must be assessed as a single package. Equitable reform seeks to achieve fair terms by reworking the mortgage, cutting interest rates to a market level, striking out improper collateral advantages, or conducting more radical surgery. Older cases prevented students squandering an inheritance: one Oxford undergraduate with an irregular and extravagant life agreed to act as surety for others' debts under a promissory note providing for interest at 60%, but he was allowed to redeem on repayment of his capital with interest at 5%.[199]

Unreasonableness is not enough. Equitable intervention will only occur if a mortgage contains oppressive terms. Indicators are a borrower in an inferior bargaining position, and a lender taking unfair advantage of that weakness. Professional legal advice will almost certainly save the lender, though it may expose the solicitor to

---

[192] *Knightsbridge Estates Trust* v. *Byrne* [1939] Ch 441, 457, Lord Greene MR.
[193] See above **[29.12]**.
[194] *Quarrel* v. *Beckford* (1816) 1 Madd 269, 56 ER 100, Plumer V-C.
[195] As to instalment sales, see below **[25.87]**.
[196] *Baker* v. *Wind* (1748) 1 Ves Sen 160, 27 ER 956 ("strongest case ever"); *Purcell* v. *McNamara* (1806) 14 Ves 91, 33 ER 455; *Denton* v. *Donner* (1856) 23 Beav 285, 53 ER 112; *Longmate* v. *Ledger* (1860) 2 Giff 157, 66 ER 671.
[197] *Teevan* v. *Smith* (1882) 20 Ch D 724, 729, Jessel MR; see above **[29.10]**.
[198] *James* v. *Kerr* (1889) 40 Ch D 449.
[199] *Croft* v. *Graham* (1863) 2 De GJ & Sm 155, 46 ER 334.

action. An informal distinction emerges between domestic borrowers and commercial borrowers who are left to fend for themselves. These are not rigid analytical categories. After all, a person running a small business will be more vulnerable than a high earning professional employee.

At one end of the spectrum is *Cityland & Property* v. *Dabrah*.[200] A sitting tenant whose lease had expired faced the prospect of eviction from his home. Instead he arranged to buy the freehold of the house from his landlord. He provided £600 cash and borrowed the rest from the landlord. No harsh dealing was alleged beyond the terms of the mortgage.[201] On a loan of £2,900, the borrower agreed to repay £4,500[202] by monthly instalments over six years. The whole sum became repayable if any one instalment was not paid. Over the full six years the interest rate was equivalent to 19% a year, but if he missed the first instalment he would have to pay a 57% capital premium, and in fact his default occurred early on.[203] The prevailing annual interest rate was 6%, so Goff J reconstructed the mortgage to require payments at 7%.[204] The mortgage had terms that were harsh in themselves and the borrower was short of funds. Other indicative facts might be a threat of losing one's home, inability to borrow elsewhere, limited intelligence, lack of advice, and hasty commitment. Oppression consists of taking advantage of a young, inexperienced or ignorant person to impose a term which no sensible well advised person would accept.

Multiservice Bookbinding v. *Marden*[205] concerned a commercial arrangement between a company that wished to borrow £36,000 and a private lender who wished to invest a nest egg he had saved until his retirement due ten years later. The lender's concern was to protect the purchasing power of his investment at a time when sterling was depreciating on the foreign exchanges and there was high inflation at home. A fixed term loan over ten years was index-linked to the Swiss franc. Massive devaluation of the pound sterling led to large uplifts of the capital – a £36,000 advance became a repayable debt of £87,000 – and interest was similarly increased. Public policy did not prevent index-linking. Even if the terms were unreasonable, as the lenders argued,[206] it was not unconscionable. Inequality of bargaining power could not arise where borrowers were represented by reputable City solicitors. Accordingly the mortgage was upheld exactly as drawn. *Knightsbridge Estates Trust* v. *Byrne*[207] was another case involving two competent parties acting under expert advance and presumed to know their own business best.[208] Viscount Maugham emphasised that oppression is particularly unlikely where the borrower is a limited company.[209]

---

[200] [1968] Ch 166; BA Bicknell (1967) 117 *NLJ* 1131.

[201] At 172G, Goff J.

[202] The courts will allow a non-oppressive bonus: *Potter* v. *Edwards* (1857) 26 LJ Ch 468 (£700 advance treated as loan of £1,000); *Tyler* v. *Yates* (1870) LR 11 Eq 265; *General Credit & Discount* v. *Glegg* (1883) 22 Ch D 549; *Mainland* v. *Upjohn* (1889) 41 Ch D 126; *Davies* v. *Chamberlain* (1909) 26 TLR 138, CA.

[203] Interest was equivalent to 38%.

[204] *Wyatt* v. *Cook* (1868) 18 LT 12; *Re Slater's Trusts* (1879) 11 Ch D 227.

[205] [1979] Ch 84; HW Wilkinson [1978] *Conv* 346; WD Bishop & BV Hindley (1979) 42 *MLR* 338; DW Williams [1978] *Conv* 432. Compare *Nationwide BS* v. *Registrar of Friendly Societies* [1983] 1 WLR 1226; HW Wilkinson [1978] *Conv* 346.

[206] At 503c, Browne-Wilkinson J.

[207] [1939] Ch 441, 457.

[208] At 454.

[209] [1940] AC 613, 623.

3. Extortionate credit bargains

[30.40] Consumer credit agreements which provide credit of whatever amount to an individual[210] may be reformed if extortionate.[211] The test is whether the debtor is required to make payments[212] which are grossly exorbitant, taking into account the entire package. Factors are: (1) prevailing interest rates; (2) the debtor's age, experience, business capacity, state of health, and financial circumstances; (3) the creditor, the degree of risk he accepts, his relationship to the debtor, and any cash price quoted; (4) the usefulness of any linked transactions; and (5) any other relevant consideration.

Exorbitance may come to the court by direct application by the borrower, as a defence to enforcement proceedings, or as a side-issue in other proceedings. After reopening a credit agreement, the court seeks to do justice between the parties,[213] typically reducing an interest rate to what is fairly due and reasonable. Transactions can be set aside in whole or in part, repayment limited to part, or any term altered. The limitation period is 12 years from the date of the loan.[214]

Reported cases provide little comfort for borrowers, since the test is gross contravention of principles of fair trading.[215] In *A Ketley* v. *Scott*[216] a bridging loan to cover the cost of buying a freehold reversion on the borrower's home carried interest at 48% a year,[217] but this was not extortionate. A high degree of risk in an open-ended bridging loan carried out at high speed justified the high charge. In *Davies* v. *Directloans*[218] the borrower had been warned by his solicitor about the terms, and interest of over 25% a year over 10 years was justified by the risk taken by the lender. The Act has also proved a defective protection for guarantors.[219]

K. TERMS FETTERING REDEMPTION

[30.41] Equity intervened to protect borrowers because redemption actions came to Chancery. After 1540 usury laws fixed the maximum interest rate permissible and prohibited extra or disguised profits, but the last statute was repealed in 1854. *G & C Kreglinger* v. *New Patagonia Meat & Cold Storage Co*[220] finally freed the law from this

---

[210] Corporate borrowers are outside the Act: Consumer Credit Act 1974 s 8(1); business partners are included by s 189(1).

[211] Consumer Credit Act 1974 s 137; Megarry & Wade (6th ed), [19.158].

[212] Considering also contingent liabilities and payments by relatives.

[213] Consumer Credit Act 1974 ss 138–140. The lender may suffer even if the extortionate advantage is enjoyed eg by a supplier of central heating.

[214] *Rahman* v. *Sterling Credit* [2001] 1 WLR 496, CA.

[215] *Wills* v. *Wood* [1984] CLYB 2039, CA. Only 4 of the first 23 reported cases were successful; HW Wilkinson [1992] *NLJ* 98. One that did succeed was *Falco Finance* v. *Michael Gough* [1999] CLYB 2516; S Bright (1999) 115 *LQR* 360.

[216] [1981] ICR 241, Foster J. The borrower had misrepresented his position and would not have obtained relief anyway.

[217] On the earlier Moneylenders Acts only interest rates exceeding 40% were extortionate(!): Halsbury's *Laws* (4th ed, reissue) vol 32, [420].

[218] [1986] 1 WLR 823.

[219] *Coldunell* v. *Gallon* [1986] QB 1184, 1201, 1210.

[220] [1914] AC 25, HL, 47, Lord Parker; see above **[29.13]**.

legacy in 1914. *Knightsbridge Estates* v. *Byrne*[221] disentangled commercial mortgage law from the old law of oppression. Thus all terms of commercial mortgages are usually valid and enforceable. A residual power exists to invalidate terms of mortgage transactions because of technical inconsistency between the clause and the borrower's equity of redemption, though these vestigial traces of the old doctrine against clogs and fetters now operate in a capricious and unjust fashion, and it should be removed.[222]

L. UNDUE INFLUENCE AND OTHER EQUITABLE MISCONDUCT

[30.42] A careful balance needs to be struck between the need to enable loans to be made to oil the wheels of small business and the need to protect the family of those in business against their homes.[223] *Barclays Bank* v. *O'Brien*[224] achieves a surprisingly good balance.

1. Misrepresentation

[30.43] Mrs O'Brien, the defendant, escaped from the consequences of a mortgage which she had executed over the matrimonial home to guarantee her husband's business debts. He had lied to her about the effect of the mortgage and the bank was held to have constructive notice of this misrepresentation. It had been used as a ground for invalidation in a few pre-*O'Brien* cases[225] and in a flood of later cases,[226] no doubt because this form of misconduct is easier to prove than undue influence.

Mrs O'Brien shared a comfortable life in Slough with her husband and adult children until, that is, she was induced to join in a mortgage of the matrimonial home to provide collateral security for the overdraft of her husband's company. The business failed and the bank tried to recover the debt through sale of the home. Her husband had mis-stated to her the effect of the mortgage, leading her to believe that it was short term and limited in amount to £60,000. In fact, it was indefinite in time and unlimited in amount,[227] and the bank eventually claimed £154,000. Not only was the mortgage

---

[221] [1939] Ch 441, 454, Sir Wilfrid Greene MR.

[222] *Jones* v. *Morgan* [2001] EWCA Civ 779, [2002] 1 EGLR 125, [86], Phillips MR; MP Thompson [2001] *Conv* 502; see above **[29.09]**.

[223] *Royal Bank of Scotland* v. *Etridge (No 2)* [2001] UKHL 44, [2001] 4 All ER 449 (hereafter *Etridge (No 2)"*), see at [2], Lord Bingham.

[224] [1994] 1 AC 180, HL (hereafter "*O'Brien*"). See: SM Cretney [1994] 2 *RLR* 3; JRF Lehane (194) 110 *LQR* 167; B Fehlberg (1994) 57 *MLR* 467; HW Wilkinson [1994] *Conv* 349; SH Goo (1995) 15 *OJLS* 119; MP Thompson [1994] *Conv* 140; A Lawson [1995] *CLJ* 280; B Fehlberg (1996) 59 *MLR* 675; R Bigwood (1996) 16 *OJLS* 503; M Haley [1998] *JBL* 355.

[225] *Kings North Trust* v. *Bell* [1986] 1 WLR 119, CA; *Coldunell* v. *Gallon* [1986] QB 1184, CA.

[226] *Massey* v. *Midland Bank* [1995] 1 All ER 929, CA; *TSB Bank* v. *Camfield* [1995] 1 WLR 430, CA; *Halifax Mortgage Service* v. *Stepsky* [1996] Ch 207, CA; *National Westminster Bank* v. *Gill*, reported with *Etridge (No 2)*, at [276], Lord Scott.

[227] Unlimited guarantees are outlawed by the Council of Mortgage Lender's Code of Lending Practice 1997 [1997] 4 CL 82. See: *Credit Lyonnais Bank Nederland* v. *Burch* [1997] 1 All ER 144, CA; A Pugh-Thomas [1997] *NLJ* 726, 767.

invalid between *Mr and Mrs O'Brien*, but also, it was held, the *bank* was infected by notice of the husband's misconduct[228] and so unable to enforce the mortgage.

Assent to a guarantee transaction is not genuine in the absence of any explanation or after a false explanation,[229] even if a degree of hyperbole is to be expected when a man in business explains his plans to his wife.[230] It must be shown that a particular misrepresentation was an operative factor which induced entry into the transaction. If so, it does not appear to matter much what form of misrepresentation occurs. A fraudulent misrepresentation is a statement made knowing it to be untrue or reckless as to its truth. *O'Brien* clearly applies both to a fraudulent misrepresentation and also, since the consequences are the same, to one that is negligent: that is where the person making the statement has no reasonable grounds for believing it to be true.[231] *TSB Bank* v. *Camfield*[232] held that *O'Brien* constructive notice doctrine also applied to a misrepresentation made innocently, a much less clear example of equitable fraud.

The effect of setting aside a mortgage for misrepresentation was left open in *O'Brien*.[233] Mrs O'Brien knew that she would be liable at least to £60,000 and, so it is generally believed, was required to pay that sum into court as a condition of pursuing her appeal.[234] Subsequent cases have held (wrongly) that a misrepresentation operates to effect a total invalidation of the mortgage,[235] giving rise to restitutionary remedies.[236]

2. Undue influence

[30.44] Equity does not protect people from their own folly, lack of understanding, or hastiness.[237] The task of the law is to set permissible limits to the influence present in almost any transaction.[238] Influence becomes undue in civil law[239] when it arises from a moral ascendancy of which the person in the ascendant takes undue advantage,[240] leading to victimisation.[241] After all:

"He that complies against his will is of his own opinion still".[242]

---

[228] See below **[30.57ff]**.

[229] *Turnbull & Co* v. *Duvall* [1902] AC 429, PC; *Kings North Trust* v. *Bell* [1986] 1 WLR 119, CA; *BCCI* v. *Aboody* [1990] 1 QB 923, CA.

[230] *Etridge (No 2)* at [32], Lord Nicholls.

[231] Misrepresentation Act 1967 s 2; *Royscott Trust* v. *Rogerson* [1991] 2 QB 297, CA.

[232] [1995] 1 WLR 430, CA.

[233] [1994] 1 AC 180, HL.

[234] Where rescission was impossible see: *Cheese* v. *Thomas* [1994] 1 WLR 129, CA; JE Martin [1994] *NLJ* 264; SM Cretney [1994] 2 *RLR* 3; M Chen-Wishart (1994) 110 *LQR* 173; M Dixon [1994] *CLJ* 232; *Mahoney* v. *Purnell* [1996] 3 All ER 61.

[235] *TSB Bank* v. *Camfield* [1995] 1 WLR 430, CA; *Castle Phillips Finance Co* v. *Piddington* (1995) 70 P & CR 592, CA; *Usher* v. *Pavlo* [1995] EGCS 154; *Bank Melli Iran* v. *Samadi-Rad* [1995] 2 FLR 367, CA; *Dunbar Bank* v. *Nadeem* [1998] 3 All ER 877, CA.

[236] *Goss* v. *Chilcott* [1996] AC 788, PC.

[237] *Etridge (No 2)* at [281], Lord Scott.

[238] At [6], Lord Nicholls.

[239] The criminal law will intervene to prevent a person appropriating large gifts from a person of low intelligence: *R* v. *Hinks* [2001] 2 AC 241, HL.

[240] *Etridge (No 2)* at [8], Lord Nicholls; *Bainbrigge* v. *Browne* (1881) 18 Ch D 188.

[241] *Allcard* v. *Skinner* (1887) 36 Ch D 145, 182–183; *National Westminster Bank* v. *Morgan* [1985] AC 686, 705A, Lord Scarman.

[242] S Butler *Hudibras* (1678), II, iii.

Royal Bank of Scotland v. *Etridge (No 2)*[243] redefines the threefold categorisation of the earlier cases, each group involving different matters needing to be proved, though overlapping,[244] and now much looser than before.[245]

3.   Actual undue influence

(1) Proof of misconduct

[30.45] Actual undue influence involves the proof of real pressure applied by the oppressor on his victim.[246] Influence of one mind over another may be very subtle. Clearly unfair influence is more likely against people who are vulnerable by hearing and speech impairment, illness, a weak mental condition, embarrassed circumstances, alcoholism, youth or inexperience. It arises where a victim is forced, tricked or misled, or suffers spiritual tyranny,[247] so that unconscientious advantage is taken of the weaker position of a borrower.[248] In *Williams* v. *Bayley*[249] a son forged his father's signature to obtain money from his bankers who insisted that the father should execute an equitable mortgage to cover the money which his son had stolen. When he did so there was no direct threat of prosecution, but it was a fact in his mind and so his consent was not free and voluntary. Actual undue influence was also the ground of decision in *CIBC Mortgages* v. *Pitt*.[250] Husband and wife jointly mortgaged the family home with the object of buying shares to gamble on the stock exchange. The wife was told by her husband that the shares would be kept for capital appreciation, whereas in fact the husband remortgaged the shares as collateral to find further share purchases, a course which greatly increased the risk. A large loss resulted from the unsuccessful gamble when the stock exchange fell. There was no physical violence but plenty of bitter arguments, escalating to the extent that the windows had to kept closed in summer to prevent neighbours from overhearing, and extended periods of sulking if Mrs Pitt refused to cooperate with her husband's business plans. The mortgage was voidable between them.[251] A person who cannot read or write English may also have an arguable case.[252]

(2) Transactions affected

[30.46] Transactions will only in practice be called into question if they turn out to be disadvantageous.[253] But this is not a requirement. When actual undue influence is used to secure property, the transaction can be set aside if it was, at the time it was

---

[243] *Etridge (No 2)* at [92], Lord Clyde, [107], Lord Hobhouse, [161], Lord Scott.
[244] *Allcard* v. *Skinner* (1887) 36 Ch D 145, 181, Lindley LJ.
[245] *BCCI* v. *Aboody* [1990] 1 QB 923, 953, Slade LJ.
[246] *Goldsworthy* v. *Brickell* [1987] Ch 378, 401A, Nourse LJ.
[247] *Allcard* v. *Skinner* (1887) 36 Ch D 145, 183, Lindley LJ.
[248] *Boustany* v. *Pigott* (1995) 69 P & CR 298, 303, Lord Templeman; J Cartwright (1993) 109 *LQR* 530.
[249] (1866) LR 1 HL 200. Other cases of actual undue influence are: *BCCI* v. *Aboody* [1990] 1 QB 923, CA; *Avon Finance* v. *Bridger* [1985] 2 All ER 281, CA; but the claim failed in *Etridge (No 2)*, HL.
[250] [1994] 1 AC 200, HL; *Bank of Scotland* v. *Bennett* [1997] 1 FLR 801, 827D–G (moral blackmail).
[251] But not on this occasion, against the lender, see below **[30.61]**.
[252] *National Westminster Bank* v. *Amin* [2002] UKHL 9, [2002] 1 FLR 735; M Haley [2002] *Conv* 499.
[253] *Etridge (No 2)* at [12], Lord Nicholls.

entered into, disadvantageous to the victim, but also when it was evenly balanced at that time. *Pitt*[254] concerned a joint loan to husband and wife (from which the wife benefited) which was upset as between the two of them at the wife's request. It is not necessary to show that the transaction would not have been entered into without the undue influence.[255]

4. Abuse of a fiduciary position

[30.47] Undue influence may be presumed,[256] irrebuttably,[257] from a relationship of trust and confidence[258] which suggests that a transaction has arisen from unfair pressure. Some examples are religious superior to inferior, parent to child,[259] solicitor to client,[260] doctor to patient, and employer to employee: in *Credit Lyonnais Bank Nederland* v. *Burch*[261] a tour operator put up her flat up as collateral for her employer's business overdraft – don't!

As with actual undue influence, any transaction can be upset when the challenge arises from an abuse of a fiduciary relationship, whether it is balanced or is disadvantageous to the victim. Thus a client may avoid a sale of his house to his solicitor even if the price was fair at the moment of sale[262] – the client may reap the benefit of any later increase in value.

5. Undue influence arising in a relationship of financial trust

[30.48] It was once thought[263] that a presumption of undue influence could arise within relationships of the type where trust is reposed by one party in the other, in relation to any suspicious transaction that called for explanation. However, the House of Lords were unanimous in *Etridge (No 2)*[264] in their opinion that this was a misleading way of stating the law. The aim is to determine whether unfair advantage was in fact taken. The initial onus is on the surety to show grounds why the charge that she has executed should be treated as invalid, and many cases will fail at this initial stage because the surety fails to raise any case that is arguable. If a sufficient case is raised there may be a shift in the burden of proof, so that the responsibility then falls on the bank to explain why a transaction was entered into when it was one-sided. Many cases will be arguable,[265] so it is difficult to reject cases at an interlocutory

---

254 [1994] 1 AC 200, 209A, 209E–H, Lord Browne-Wilkinson; *Earl of Chesterfield* v. *Janssen* (1751) 2 Ves Sen 125, 28 ER 82; *Allcard* v. *Skinner* (1887) 36 Ch D 145, 181, 185, Lindley LJ; A Phang [1995] *JBL* 552.

255 *UCB Corporate Services* v. *Williams* [2002] EWCA Civ 555, [2002] Times May 27th.

256 This is class 2A of *BCCI* v. *Aboody* [1990] 1 QB 923, 953, Slade LJ.

257 *Etridge (No 2)* at [18], Lord Nicholls.

258 *Goldsworthy* v. *Brickell* [1987] Ch 378, 400H–401H.

259 *Padgham* v. *Rochelle* [2002] WTLR 1483; *Etridge (No 2)* at [18], Lord Nicholls.

260 *Denton* v. *Donner* (1856) 23 Beav 285, 53 ER 112.

261 [1997] 1 All ER 144, CA; M Chen-Wishart [1997] *CLJ* 60; H Tjio (1997) 113 *LQR* 10; *Etridge (No 2)* at [83], Lord Nicholls; *Steeples* v. *Lea* [1998] 1 FLR 138, CA.

262 *Longmate* v. *Ledger* (1860) 2 Giff 157, 66 ER 67, Stuart V-C (fair sale but of feeble intellect; reformed as a mortgage).

263 *BCCI* v. *Aboody* [1990] 1 QB 923, 953, Slade LJ (class 2B).

264 At [15–16], Lord Nicholls, [92], Lord Clyde, [103–107], Lord Hobhouse, [157–161], Lord Scott.

265 *Barclays Bank* v. *Harris*, reported with *Etridge (No 2)*, at [244], Lord Scott.

stage,[266] but once a case is argued out at trial the judge has to decide whether or not influence was applied, the matter no longer being one of presumption, but rather what the evidence has established.[267]

(1) Relationships creating a presumption

[30.49] The mysteries of the old formal classes are now disapproved. Rather the law looks at all the evidence to see whether there was a relationship of trust and confidence,[268] from which it may be possible to infer abuse of that trust or exploitation from the fact that a dubious transaction has been entered into. If a confidential relationship exists the evidential burden shifts, so that it is then up to the party who is in a position to exert influence to show that the transaction is fair.[269] Distressing cases arise where an adult child has induced his elderly parents to mortgage their home to support his business venture.[270]

Most cases arise between husband and wife, but undue influence is not presumed simply because a wife gave a guarantee of her husband's debts.[271] This rule was settled early in the twentieth century[272] and confirmed by *O'Brien*. Rather, a presumption may arise within a particular marriage if one party (invariably in the reported cases the wife[273]) is so totally under the control of the other (her husband) that she is incapable of forming an independent judgement.[274] One 82 year old widow gave away all her property immediately after remarrying,[275] a proceeding that obviously calls for explanation. Clearest of all were the Colemans, since Mrs Coleman was a Hasidic Jew brought up to expect to be subservient to her husband's wishes,[276] where one could expect therefore that as between the couple at least transactions would be entered into not on their merits but at the behest of the husband. There are many successful[277] or unsuccessful[278] invocations of this principle by spouses.

These same principles apply to any other emotional relationship between the parties, for example between unmarried cohabitants, fiancés,[279] a couple who are not

---

[266] *Harris, Wallace,* and *Moore* in *Etridge (No 2)*; also *National Westminster Bank* v. *Kostopoulos* [2000] 1 FLR 815, CA.

[267] Hence the rejection of the cases that had already been tried in *Etridge (No 2)*, including *Etridge* itself, *Gill, Coleman,* and *Bennett.*

[268] *Etridge (No 2)* at [158], Lord Scott.

[269] At [16], Lord Nicholls.

[270] *Coldunell* v. *Gallon* [1986] QB 1184, CA; *Avon Finance* v. *Bridger* [1985] 2 All ER 281, CA; *Cheese* v. *Thomas* [1994] 1 WLR 129, CA; SM Cretney [1994] 2 *RLR* 3; M Chen-Wishart (1994) 110 *LQR* 173; M Dixon [1994] *CLJ* 232.

[271] *Turnbull & Co* v. *Duval* [1902] AC 429, PC; *Chaplin & Co* v. *Brammall* [1908] 1 KB 233; *Howes* v. *Bishop* [1909] 2 KB 390; *Shears & Sons* v. *Jones* [1922] 2 Ch 802.

[272] *Etridge (No 2)* at [19], [34], Lord Nicholls.

[273] Except for *Britannia BS* v. *Rivett* (1997) 29 HLR 893, CA.

[274] *Bank of Montreal* v. *Stuart* [1911] AC 120, PC; *O'Brien* [1994] 1 AC 180, 190H, Lord Browne-Wilkinson.

[275] *Simpson* v. *Simpson* [1992] 1 FLR 601; B Dale [1989] *Conv* 63.

[276] *Barclays Bank* v. *Coleman,* reported with *Etridge (No 2)*, at [283–292], Lord Scott.

[277] *Goode Durant Administration* v. *Biddulph* (1994) 26 HLR 625; *Banco Exterior Internacional* v. *Mann* [1995] 1 All ER 936, 945h; *Bank of Baroda* v. *Rayarel* [1995] 2 FLR 376.

[278] Eg *Morgan, O'Brien, Etridge (No 2)*.

[279] *Zamet* v. *Hyman* [1961] 1 WLR 1442 (couple aged 79 and 71); RE Megarry (1962) 78 *LQR* 24.

cohabiting,[280] a 95 year old man and his mistress,[281] or homosexual partners. Trust and confidence may well be required in asexual relationships,[282] with no formal cut off point,[283] but as a relationship becomes more ephemeral so it will become more difficult to establish that undue influence has arisen.

If the lender is to be bound, it will be important to show knowledge of the existence of the relationship,[284] and it may be very unlikely that a bank will discover a relationship between a couple who are not cohabiting.

(2) Transactions calling for explanation

[30.50] Undue influence can only be presumed where a transaction is one that calls for explanation.[285] It is sensible to assume that pressure led to a gift,[286] or the surrender of a valuable tenancy,[287] but a sale at full market value does not raise any suspicion. *National Westminster Bank* v. *Morgan*[288] held that a presumption only arose in relation to a transaction which was manifestly disadvantageous to the victim. The principle is now confirmed[289] though the utility of the label "manifest disadvantage" is doubtful[290] – it is better to talk of a "transaction calling for explanation". Pressure is much more probable if the transaction is imbalanced,[291] and it would be daft if every Christmas present by a child to his parent was open to challenge.[292] No disadvantage is to be found in a loan used to pay off existing debt to ward of repossession proceedings,[293] nor in a joint loan since each borrower enjoys the use of the money borrowed.[294]

Disadvantage must be clear and obvious, viewed objectively at the date of the charge, but it need not be large provided it exceeds the minimal. *Gifts* and undervalued sales[295] are obviously improvident, whether made in the giver's lifetime[296] or by

---

[280] *Massey* v. *Midland Bank* [1995] 1 All ER 929, CA (parents objected to woman aged 42 living with the father of her two children!); *Allied Irish Bank* v. *Byrne* [1995] 2 FLR 325, Ferris J.

[281] *Clarke* v. *Prus* [1995] CLYB 2196.

[282] *Etridge (No 2)* at [82], Lord Nicholls.

[283] At [82–87], Lord Nicholls.

[284] *O'Brien* [1994] 1 AC 180, 191A, Lord Browne-Wilkinson; *Pitt* [1994] 1 AC 180, 190E, Leolin Price QC (an "invalidating tendency"); see below **[30.61]**.

[285] *Etridge (No 2)* at [14], Lord Nicholls.

[286] *Allcard* v. *Skinner* (1887) 36 Ch D 145, CA; *Hammond* v. *Osborn* [2002] EWCA Civ 885, [2002] WTLR 1125; *Etridge (No 2)* at [21], Lord Nicholls.

[287] *Padgham* v. *Rochelle* [2002] WTLR 1483.

[288] [1985] AC 686, HL; (1985) 101 *LQR* 305; JL Barton and P Rank [1985] *Conv* 387; D Tiplady (1985) 43 *MLR* 579; JE Martin [1986] *Conv* 212; N Andrews [1983] *CLJ* 192.

[289] A question mark put against *Morgan* in *Pitt* [1994] 1 AC 200, 209, is removed by *Etridge (No 2)* at [26], Lord Nicholls; G Andrews [2002] *Conv* 456.

[290] *Etridge (No 2)* at [26–29], Lord Nicholls.

[291] *Dunbar Bank* v. *Nadeem* [1998] 3 All ER 877, CA.

[292] *Etridge (No 2)* at [23–24], Lord Nicholls.

[293] *National Westminster Bank* v. *Leggatt* [2001] 1 FLR 563, CA.

[294] *CIBC Mortgages* v. *Pitt* [1994] 1 AC 200, 209, Lord Browne-Wilkinson; *Dunbar Bank* v. *Nadeem* [1998] 3 All ER 877, CA; PA Chandler (1999) 115 *LQR* 213.

[295] *Cresswell* v. *Potter* [1978] 1 WLR 254n, Megarry J; *Goldsworthy* v. *Brickell* [1987] Ch 378, CA; *Mahoney* v. *Purnell* [1996] 3 All ER 61 (sale of hotel for £64,000, resale at £3.275m); PBH Birks (1997) 5 *RLR* 72; JD Heydon (1997) 113 *LQR* 8; *Claughton* v. *Price* [1997] EGCS 51, CA.

[296] *Allcard* v. *Skinner* (1887) 36 Ch D 145 (defence available); *Simpson* v. *Simpson* [1992] 1 FLR 601; B Dale [1989] *Conv* 63; *Langton* v. *Langton* [1995] 2 FLR 890; D Capper [1996] *Conv* 308.

will.[297] If an inexperienced, religiously minded, young woman is induced by spiritual pressure from her religious adviser to hand over her inheritance to the church, invalidation of the gift restores what she has given away.[298] Possibly dubious are waivers[299] and some guarantees, where the guarantor undertakes the burden of repaying money lent to the borrower without any corresponding benefit.[300] Thus a recently widowed woman suffers a detriment when she mortgages her house to prop up her son-in-law's company.[301] More typically a wife mortgages the family home to secure her husband's business debts,[302] which is especially risky if any future transaction is secured.[303] The old adage was that

"He that will thrive must first ask his wife."

Surely, as this ancient saw suggests, a marriage is a joint venture in which the financial fortunes of the couple are bound up together? So a guarantee does not automatically call for explanation,[304] but it may do so when the terms of the transaction are considered in the light of their relationship. Support by a wife for a business in which she is an active manager does not call for any discussion, since it is more or less a joint loan, but in *Barclays Bank* v. *Harris* it was considered that a presumption could arise in favour of a wife who owned half the shares but took no part in the running of the company.[305]

6. Misconduct by lenders

[30.51] Most borrowers are under financial pressure, but the inequality of bargaining power inherent in a mortgage does not by itself lead to invalidity. Lenders are not presumed to exert undue influence on a borrower,[306] and there is no duty to show that a mortgage is fair,[307] however desirable it would be to develop a principle of unconscionability.[308]

Of course it is possible for a bank to apply actual undue influence.[309] It might also be possible to presume that pressure has been applied where the lender has adopted the role of financial adviser to the borrower, but special facts are required. In *National Westminster Bank* v. *Morgan* the bank manager called at the house to obtain the

[297] *Re Craig* [1971] Ch 95; (1970) 86 *LQR* 447; *Crawden* v. *Aldridge* [1993] 1 WLR 437; R Martyn [1994] *Conv* 446.

[298] *Allcard* v. *Skinner* (1887) 36 Ch D 145, CA (valid on facts).

[299] *Cheese* v. *Thomas* [1994] 1 WLR 129, CA. Personal arrangement such as membership of Lloyd's cannot be rescinded by the court: *Society of Lloyd's* v. *Khan* [1998] 3 FCR 93.

[300] *Etridge (No 2)* at [29], Lord Nicholls.

[301] *Wright* v. *Cherry Tree Finance* [2001] EWCA Civ 449, [2001] 2 All ER (Comm) 877.

[302] *Kings North Trust* v. *Bell* [1986] 1 WLR 119, CA.

[303] *Barclays Bank* v. *Coleman*, reported with *Etridge (No 2)*.

[304] *Etridge (No 2)* at [28], Lord Nicholls.

[305] Reported with *Etridge (No 2)*, at [231], Lord Scott. See also: *BCCI* v. *Aboody* [1990] 1 QB 923, 964H–967A, Slade LJ; *Goode Durant Administration* v. *Biddulph* (1994) 26 HLR 625; *Bank of Baroda* v. *Rayarel* (1995) 27 HLR 327 at first instance; M Richardson (1996) 16 *LS* 368; *Bank of Scotland* v. *Bennett* [1997] 1 FLR 801; *Bank of Cyprus (London)* v. *Markan* [1999] 2 All ER 707, Ch D.

[306] *National Westminster Bank* v. *Morgan* [1985] AC 686, 701–702, Lord Scarman.

[307] *O'Brien* [1994] 1 AC 180, 193B, Lord Browne-Wilkinson.

[308] A Phang [1995] *JBL* 352; M Halliwell (1994) 14 *LS* 15; D Capper (1998) 114 *LQR* 479.

[309] *Williams* v. *Bayley* (1866) LR 1 HL 200; *Lloyds Bank* v. *Ludner* reported with *Etridge* [1998] 4 All ER 705, CA.

wife's signature, and in doing so explained the mortgage to her, but no special duty of confidentiality arose since this particular manager had not gone beyond a banker-customer relationship. Negligent advice would give rise only to damages.[310]

A banker customer relationship may be transmuted into one in which the banker acquires a dominating influence, so that undue influence can be presumed.[311] The majority (apart, that is, from Lord Denning) decided *Lloyds Bank* v. *Bundy*[312] on orthodox undue influence principles. That banker had crossed the line into culpability by indicating the wisdom of the transaction,[313] and, having assumed the status of financial guru to an elderly illiterate farmer, he had used undue influence to secure a mortgage of the father's farmhouse designed to guarantee his son's business debts.

7. Disclosure

[30.52] A security executed by a surety may be invalidated on ordinary principles of the law of guarantees if the lender fails in his duty of disclosure to a surety.[314]

M. INFECTION GEOMETRY

1. Sale

[30.53] Infection principles are clear on sale. After a victim has been induced to transfer his land, his oppressor holds it subject to an equitable obligation to retransfer it.

(1) Unregistered land

[30.54] A protected purchaser takes free. The victim's right to recover the land is a mere equity,[315] so the interest bought to defeat it may be either a legal estate or an equitable interest. He must also buy for value, and display honesty and diligence. Liability is imposed on volunteers irrespective of notice,[316] and on those with notice irrespective of value.[317] Escape from liability involves both value and innocence of notice. Most cases hinge on the requirement of diligence. Occupation by a victim of oppression will call for inquiry[318] but notice of the oppression follows from the occupation only if some reasonable enquiry would have disclosed it.[319]

---

[310] *Lloyds Bank* v. *Egremont* [1990] 2 FLR 351; *Midland Bank* v. *Perry* [1988] 1 FLR 161; E Dumbill [1990] *Conv* 226.

[311] At 707D, Lord Scarman.

[312] [1975] QB 326, CA; LS Sealey [1975] *CLJ* 21; C Carr (1975) 38 *MLR* 463.

[313] Probably an erroneous decision: *Morgan* [1985] AC 686, 707F, Lord Scarman.

[314] *Levett* v. *Barclays Bank* [1995] 1 WLR 1260, Ch D; *Etridge (No 2)* at [183–190], Lord Scott. A successful case was *Bank of Scotland* v. *Bennett* at [345–351], Lord Scott; see also *Kenyon-Brown* v. *Desmond Banks* at [373], Lord Scott (non disclosure of ranking agreement).

[315] *Phillips* v. *Phillips* (1862) 4 De GF & J 208, 217, 45 ER 1164, Lord Westbury LC.

[316] *Bridgman* v. *Green* (1755) 2 Ves Sen 627, 28 ER 399, Hardwicke LC; *Huguenin* v. *Baseley* (1807) 14 Ves 273, 33 ER 526, Eldon LC; *Barron* v. *Willis* [1900] 2 Ch 121, 131, Lindley MR; *Bullock* v. *Lloyds Bank* [1955] Ch 317.

[317] *Addis* v. *Campbell* (1841) 4 Beav 401, 49 ER 394.

[318] *Hunt* v. *Luck* [1902] 1 Ch 428, CA; [1901] 1 Ch 415, Farwell J.

[319] *Smith* v. *Jones* [1954] 1 WLR 1089 (tenant's occupation did not give notice of a right to rectify the lease).

(2) Registered land

[30.55] A purchaser of a registered title is both better and worse placed, because even actual knowledge of an unprotected interest will not make it bind the purchaser.[320] But actual occupation by a victim of oppression will make his equity to set it aside an overriding interest, at least if it is discoverable.[321]

2. Infection of lender by borrower's oppression

[30.56] *Barclays Bank* v. *O'Brien*[322] was not a classic priority struggle between a person claiming an earlier equity against a person who has acquired an estate by transfer. Mrs O'Brien signed a legal mortgage in favour of Barclays Bank and successfully argued that the mortgage should be upset because of a lie by her husband. The case was tripartite.[323] Lord Browne-Wilkinson[324] held that the bank would be bound if the bank had notice (actual or constructive) of the husband's oppression. He would, apparently,[325] have been first to recognise that this was not a traditional application of notice doctrine.[326] It is not a case where notice is given of a pre-existing interest to someone acquiring a legal estate and since its geometry is atypical, notice applies even though the title is registered.[327] Indeed the formal structure of the transaction is irrelevant,[328] so it matters not one whit whether there is a joint loan,[329] a secured guarantee,[330] a contractual guarantee, or a waiver.[331] Notice doctrine works well in practice but it would probably have been more consonant with other areas of equity to establish a fault-based principle based on knowledge.[332]

N. INFECTION BY NOTICE

[30.57] Infection is the term that Oliver LJ used to describe how a lender becomes legally responsible for misconduct between the borrower and the guarantor.[333]

---

[320] See above **[20.45]**.

[321] LRA 2002 sch 3 para 2; *Hodgson* v. *Marks* [1971] Ch 892, at first instance; *Blacklocks* v. *JB Developments (Godalming)* [1982] Ch 183; *Barclays Bank* v. *Khaira* [1993] 1 FLR 343, CA; *Halifax BS* v. *Brown* [1996] 1 FLR 103, CA; *Nurdin & Peacock* v. *DB Ramsden & Co* [1999] 1 WLR 1249, Ch D; see above **[20.16ff]**.

[322] [1994] 1 AC 180, HL.

[323] *Etridge (No 2)* at [40], Lord Nicholls.

[324] [1994] 1 AC 180, 195E–F, 195H–196A.

[325] *Etridge (No 2)* at [39], Lord Nicholls, [146], Lord Scott; *Barclays Bank* v. *Boulter* [1999] 4 All ER 513, 518d–g; K Barker [1999] 7 *RLR* 75.

[326] MP Thompson [1994] *Conv* 140; P Sparkes [1995] *Conv* 250; J Mee [1995] *CLJ* 536, (1995) 46 *NILQ* 147; E O'Dell [1997] *CLJ* 71.

[327] P Sparkes [1995] *Conv* 250; *Barclays Bank* v. *Boulter* [1997] 2 All ER 1002, 1010e–g, Mummery LJ. The decision in *Pitt* could be justified on the basis of LRA 1925 s 114 (fraudulent disposition void in same circumstances as if title unregistered), but there is no corresponding provision in LRA 2002.

[328] M Dixon and C Harpum [1994] *Conv* 421; G Battersby (1995) 15 *LS* 235; A Lawson [1995] *NLJ* 286.

[329] *Pitt* [1994] 1 AC 200; *Talbot* v. *Von Boris* [1911] 1 KB 854, CA.

[330] *O'Brien* [1994] 1 AC 180, HL.

[331] *King's North Trust* v. *Bell* [1986] 1 WLR 119, CA.

[332] *Kempson* v. *Ashbee* (1874) LR 10 Ch App 15, 21, James LJ. In Scotland see: *Mumford* v. *Bank of Scotland* [1996] 1 FLR 344; *Smith* v. *Bank of Scotland* [1997] 2 FLR 862, HL.

[333] *Coldunell* v. *Gallon* [1986] QB 1184, 1196C.

O'Brien suggested that the basic infection principle is notice, earlier cases based on agency theory being expanded to provide better protection.[334]

1,   Actual knowledge

[30.58] Actual knowledge of the undue influence will clearly lead to infection.[335]

2.   Constructive notice

[30.59] Undue influence type notice is like true notice in that the burden of pleading that the bank had constructive notice rests with the surety (the wife) who seeks to avoid the mortgage against bank,[336] and again all is left to particular facts.[337] Little is needed to shift the onus off the wife and on to the bank since the threshold is low:[338] even a weak case may have to go to trial. Two facts combined together[339] give notice of the risk of misconduct, and put on the bank the obligation of showing that they transaction was the free choice of the surety.

(1) Relationship

[30.60] A bank is put on enquiry when it knows of a substantial risk of an equitable wrong done in procuring the wife to act as surety. It may, for example, know that its customer (the husband) is cohabiting with the surety (the wife) or knows of a sexual relationship. But this is not necessary,[340] and the vital point is knowledge by the outside party of the relationship which gives rise to the possibility of pressure.[341] Barclays Bank knew that Mrs O'Brien[342] would derive no personal benefit from the guarantee and they were fixed with notice of a lie made by Mr O'Brien to his wife about the terms of the transaction, even though they were unaware of the statement.

(2) Transaction

[30.61] The second thing which should alert the bank is the fact that the transaction being entered into is not on its face to the financial advantage of the wife. Imbalance is essential because a lender is not put on inquiry about a transaction which appears to be fair:[343] Barclays Bank knew that Mrs O'Brien[344] would derive no personal benefit from the guarantee.

---

[334] [1994] 1 AC 180, 194–195, Lord Browne-Wilkinson.

[335] *Kempson* v. *Ashbee* (1874) LR 10 Ch App 15; *Bainbrigge* v. *Browne* (1881) 18 Ch D 188; *BCCI* v. *Aboody* [1990] 1 QB 923, 973B, Slade LJ.

[336] *Barclays Bank* v. *Boulter* [1999] 1 WLR 1919, HL (the issue was costs). *Bainbrigge* v. *Brown* (1881) 18 Ch D 188, 197, Fry J; *Re Nisbett & Potts C* [1906] 1 Ch 386, CA.

[337] *Etridge (No 2)* at [13], Lord Nicholls.

[338] At [44], Lord Nicholls, [108], Lord Hobhouse.

[339] Constructive notice could arise in other ways, *Etridge (No 2)* at [46], Lord Nicholls.

[340] *Etridge (No 2)* at [47], Lord Nicholls; *Massey* v. *Midland Bank* [1995] 1 All ER 929, 933, Steyn LJ.

[341] Not eg in *Barclays Bank* v. *Coleman* reported with *Etridge (No 2)* at [292], Lord Scott (Hasidic Jew).

[342] [1994] 1 AC 180, HL.

[343] *Pitt* [1994] 1 AC 200, HL (joint loan).

[344] *O'Brien* [1994] 1 AC 180, HL.

The disadvantage must be apparent on the face of the transaction. A bank would only have cause to suspect undue influence if the imbalance to one party is "manifest", the element which is crucial to infection of an ·outside observer such as a bank. In *CIBC Mortgages* v. *Pitt* [345] a disadvantage to the wife arose from the fact that the husband proposed to use the money borrowed to gamble on the stock exchange, making the mortgage voidable between husband and wife (disadvantage) but the lender thought that there was a joint loan to husband and wife so that disadvantage which in fact existed was not manifest to the bank. Constructive notice of misconduct will not arise in such circumstances.

3. Imputed notice

[30.62] In normal cases a solicitor employed to advise a wife will generally be acting as her solicitor, giving no reason to impute knowledge across from solicitor to bank.[346] If, however, it can be found that the solicitor is acting for the bank throughout, because the wife has not agreed to be represented by the solicitor, anything discovered by the solicitor can be imputed across to the bank.[347]

4. Agency

[30.63] A lender is bound by any act of its agent, including a borrower if the lender chooses to appoint him as its agent in a guarantee transaction. Strict agency is necessarily rare, but an "equitable agency"[348] may be established where the lender leaves it to the borrower to obtain execution of a guarantee. In *Kings North Trust* v. *Bell*[349] a waiver form was sent by the lenders to the husband's solicitors who in turn entrusted it to the husband. The lenders were bound when the husband exerted pressure on his wife. Similarly in *Avon Finance* v. *Bridger*[350] the lenders appointed the borrower to procure his parent's execution of the security.[351] However, in *Coldunell* v. *Gallon*,[352] when the lenders communicated with the borrower's elderly parents direct, and did not know that the son intercepted the letters and pressured his parents,[353] so the lender was allowed to enforce the mortgage.

---

[345] [1994] 1 AC 200, HL; *Scotlife (No 2)* v. *Hedworth* (1999) 78 P & CR 389, CA; *Britannia BS* v. *Pugh* (1997) 29 HLR 423, CA.

[346] *Etridge (No 2)* at [176–179], Lord Scott.

[347] See below **[30.74]**.

[348] *Turnbull & Co* v. *Duval* [1902] AC 429, PC; *BCCI* v. *Aboody* [1990] 1 QB 923, CA; *O'Brien* [1993] QB 109, 119G, Scott LJ.

[349] [1986] 1 WLR 119, CA. The question under current law is whether the solicitor has begun to act for the wife.

[350] [1985] 2 All ER 281, CA.

[351] *Barclays Bank* v. *Kennedy* [1989] 1 FLR 356, CA; *Midland Bank* v. *Shepard* [1988] 3 All ER 17, CA; B Dale [1989] *Conv* 63 (obiter).

[352] [1986] QB 1184, CA; *Chaplin & Co* v. *Brammall* [1908] 1 KB 233; *Talbot* v. *Van Boris* [1911] 1 KB 854 (duress not known to lender); *Midland Bank* v. *Perry* [1988] 1 FLR 161, CA; *Lloyds Bank* v. *Egremont* [1990] 2 FLR 351.

[353] *O'Brien* [1993] QB 109, 130–131, Scott LJ.

O. AVOIDING INFECTION: A FACE TO FACE INTERVIEW

[30.64] The bank may follow the practice enunciated in *Barclays Bank* v. *O'Brien*[354] to ensure that before a wife enters into a disadvantageous guarantee that she receives adequate advice. Written warnings are often not read and are sometimes intercepted,[355] so the bank should insist that the wife attend a private meeting without the presence of the husband. There she should be told of the extent of her liability,[356] warned of the risk she is running, and urged to take independent advice. Further steps will be necessary if the lender knows of additional facts which make the presence of undue influence probable[357] – where the wife shows signs of unease at the interview,[358] or the transaction is exceptionally one-sided.[359] Banks are not generally prepared to accept the risks inherent in this procedure.[360]

P. AVOIDING INFECTION: LEGAL ADVICE

[30.65] Independent legal advice may, and usually will, have an emancipating effect, freeing the lender of any liability for misconduct between borrower and surety.[361]

1. Avoiding the risk of misconduct

[30.66] Mrs O'Brien[362] had received no advice whatever, an inadequate procedure which destroyed the bank's security. Undue influence is rebutted by the full, free and informed consent of the supposed "victim".[363] A borrower must know the value of the property, appreciate the risk, and act deliberately.[364] Consenting adults are free to inflict financial pain on themselves. Lenders must be reasonably prudent, no more,[365] and should not provide advice.[366] Unlike conventional notice doctrine, *O'Brien* states what action must be taken to avoid liability.[367]

---

[354] [1994] 1 AC 180, 198, Lord Browne-Wilkinson.

[355] At 198B; *Coldunell* v. *Gallon* [1986] QB 1184, CA.

[356] Eg onerous contribution terms: *Levett* v. *Barclays Bank* [1995] 1 WLR 1260.

[357] [1994] 1 AC 180, 197A–B.

[358] *BCCI* v. *Aboody* [1990] 1 QB 923, CA (unease known to solicitor); *Cooke* v. *National Westminster Bank* [1998] 2 FLR 783, CA (known to bank).

[359] *Credit Lyonnais Bank Nederland* v. *Burch* [1997] 1 All ER 144, CA; *Steeples* v. *Lea* [1998] 1 FLR 138, CA.

[360] *Etridge (No 2)* at [51], Lord Nicholls.

[361] *Etridge (No 2)* at [20], Lord Nicholls.

[362] *O'Brien* [1994] 1 AC 180, HL.

[363] *Allcard* v. *Skinner* (1887) 36 Ch D 145; *Zamet* v. *Hyman* [1961] 1 WLR 1442, Evershed MR; *Goldsworthy* v. *Brickell* [1987] Ch 378, 407, Nourse LJ.

[364] *Merediths* v. *Saunders* (1814) 2 Dow 514, 3 ER 950, HL.

[365] *Etridge (No 2)* at [172], Lord Scott; *Woolwich* v. *Gomm* (2000) 79 P & CR 61, [28], Clarke LJ.

[366] *Banco Exterior Internacional* v. *Mann* [1995] 1 All ER 936; *Bank of Baroda* v. *Rayarel* [1995] 2 FLR 376.

[367] *Etridge (No 2)* at [41], Lord Nicholls.

It is extraordinary that *O'Brien* did not make clear that independent legal advice had a purifying effect.[368] It has always been sufficient to ensure that the decision to enter into a transaction[369] or refinancing[370] is the free choice of the person executing it. Advice may be given by a solicitor or legal executive.[371] Lack of clear guidance and a proliferation of conflicting decisions led to a definitive restatement of the law in *Royal Bank of Scotland* v. *Etridge (No 2)*. There are two fundamental issues. On independence of the solicitor the Lords[372] were even more pro-bank than the pro-bankers of the Court of Appeal.[373] However, on the quality of the advice required the Lords were alarmed by the perfunctory nature of the advice in some of the cases before it, which made the giving of advice a charade,[374] and on this issue they stiffened the law considerably, especially for the future. So bankers thus have safe procedures by which they can advance money,[375] even if the emancipating effect of outside advice remains in each case a question of fact.[376]

2.   When is a solicitor independent?

(1) Solicitors generally independent

[30.67] Independent advice is provided by a solicitor even if he is also advising other parties to the same transaction. The solicitor acts for the wife, even if he also represents the husband,[377] the professional responsibility of the solicitor is a sufficient guarantee against conflicts of interest.[378] Thus a solicitor who is retained by the husband may provide advice to the wife that is independent.[379] No protection is provided if advice is given by a solicitor acting for the wife who is also the company secretary actively involved in raising finance.[380]

Even more extraordinary is the rule that the bank is protected if it arranges for the bank's own solicitor to advise its own sureties – the bank escapes come what may however unwise it is for a solicitor to accept instructions to act.[381] Knowledge acquired by the solicitor from the wife is not imputed to the lenders, since they are not

---

[368] *Shears & Sons* v. *Jones* [1922] 2 Ch 802; *Kempson* v. *Ashbee* (1874) LR 10 Ch App 15; *Bullock* v. *Lloyds Bank* [1955] Ch 317; *Errington* v. *Martell-Wilson* [1980] NLJ 545; HW Wilkinson [1995] *NLJ* 792.

[369] *Barclays Bank* v. *Caplan* [1998] 1 FLR 532, CA.

[370] *Locabail (UK)* v. *Bayfield Properties* [2000] QB 451, CA

[371] *Barclays Bank* v. *Coleman* reported with *Etridge (No 2)*, at [292], Lord Scott.

[372] R Bigwood (2002) 65 *MLR* 435; D O'Sullivan (2002) 118 *LQR* 337; M Pawlowski & S Greer [2001] *Conv* 219; PH Kenny [2002] *Conv* 91; MP Thompson [2002] *Conv* 174; S Wong [2002] *JBL* 439; R Auchmuchty (2002) 11 *Social & Legal Studies* 257; M Pawlowski [2002] 95 *PLJ* 5; J Phillips [2002] *OUCLJ* 47; J Robson [2002] 5 *JHL* 19.

[373] [1998] 4 All ER 705, CA; MP Thompson [1999] *Conv* 126; S Bridge [1999] *CLJ* 28; MJ Draper [1999] *Conv* 176.

[374] *Etridge (No 2)* at [52], [68], Lord Nicholls.

[375] At [2], Lord Bingham, [69], Lord Nicholls.

[376] At [20], Lord Nicholls.

[377] At [75–79], Lord Nicholls.

[378] At [77], Lord Nicholls.

[379] *Banco Exterior Internacional* v. *Mann* [1995] 1 All ER 936, CA; the dissent of Hobhouse LJ is much more convincing; *Barclays Bank* v. *Thompson* [1997] 4 All ER 816, CA.

[380] *National Westminster Bank* v. *Breeds* [2001] Lloyds Rep Bank 98, Lawrence Collins J.

[381] *Etridge (No 2)* at [75–79], Lord Nicholls; [1998] 4 All ER 705, [24], Stuart Smith LJ.

acting in the course of a single transaction.[382] Mrs Etridge herself fell foul of this rule since when she mortgaged her home, Laverstoke Rectory,[383] since her decision to deal with the bank's solicitors led to them becoming her advisers as well. *Etridge* sets the bar too low, since independence from the lender is a crucial aspect of reducing the risk of improvident and unwise guarantees.[384] The rectory is one or two miles down the road from Lord Denning's old home in Hampshire: what would he have made of it all?

(2) Steps to ensure the independence of the solicitor

[30.68] *Etridge (No 2)* does raise the bar in relation to the quality of the advice, so it is vital to the bank's protection that it can show that, as things appear to the bank from the facts known to it,[385] the solicitor has indeed become the adviser of the surety. If this is not clear a case will be allowed to proceed to trial.[386] Best practice is to get a written certificate from a solicitor confirming that he has provided independent advice, in the face of which a finding of undue influence would be unthinkable.[387]

(3) Independence: post-Etridge transactions

[30.69] In order to be safe, post-*Etridge*, the bank should:[388]

(1) communicate with wife directly explaining to her that she is required to consult a solicitor;
(2) ask her to nominate a solicitor and make clear that it may be different from the husband's; and
(3) obtain her written confirmation that she wants that solicitor to act.

The substance of the advice to be given is considered below.[389]

3. The advice

(1) The test

[30.70] A bank need do no more than satisfy itself that the wife has had brought home to her in a meaningful way the practical implications of the proposed transaction, so that she enters into the transaction with her eyes open.[390] It is not for a solicitor to

---

[382] LPA 1925 s 199(1)(ii)(b); *Halifax Mortgages* v. *Stepsky* [1996] Ch 207, 215F–216C, Morritt LJ; *National Westminster Bank* v. *Beaton* (1998) 30 HLR 99, CA; *Etridge (No 2)* at [122], Lord Hobhouse, [173], [178], Lord Scott.

[383] *Etridge (No 2)* at [226–227], Lord Scott.

[384] *Banco Exterior Internacional* v. *Thomas* [1997] 1 WLR 221.

[385] *Barclays Bank* v. *Coleman* decided with *Etridge (No 2)* at [292], Lord Scott.

[386] *UCB* v. *Moore* decided with *Etridge (No 2)*, see at [307], Lord Scott.

[387] *National Westminster Bank* v. *Gill* reported with *Etridge (No 2)* at [79], Lord Nicholls, [277], Lord Scott; *Bank of Scotland* v. *Hill* [2002] EWCA Civ 1081, [2002] 29 EG 152 (CS).

[388] *Etridge (No 2)* at [65], Lord Nicholls, [116–120], Lord Hobhouse; also at [163–165], Lord Scott, approving [1998] 4 All ER 705, [44], Stuart Smith LJ.

[389] See at **[30.72]**.

[390] *Etridge (No 2)* at [50], [54], Lord Nicholls.

veto a transaction,[391] and irrelevant whether a competent solicitor would advise the wife to enter into the transaction.[392] The issue is whether she has given her free assent.

(2) Pre-Etridge transactions

[30.71] The interview should be conducted face to face in the absence of the husband, a novelty attributable to *O'Brien*.[393] *Etridge (No 2)* ups the standard of advice required as a response to the many past cases in which the advice given was perfunctory.[394] Deficiencies in the advice given are generally a matter between the party advised (the wife) and the solicitor acting for her.[395] Falling short of the ideal may or may not[396] expose the solicitor to liability for damage, but even gross errors have not invalidated the mortgage.[397] Examples from earlier cases are omission to advise on the total amount of the loan,[398] difficulty by the person advised in understanding English,[399] advice of a wife in the presence of her husband,[400] delivery of advice by telephone,[401] and variant advice from different solicitors.[402] Some of these cases may no longer hold good but it has never been enough merely to witness the wife's signature.[403]

(3) Advice to be given in post-Etridge transactions

[30.72] What has to be explained to the wife?[404] The solicitor's private interview with the surety should cover:

(1) the purpose of the document;
(2) the purpose of advice from the solicitor is to protect the bank;
(3) confirmation that she wants solicitor to act;
(4) the nature of the documents and the consequences for the home of non-payment or the husband's bankruptcy;
(5) the seriousness of the risk;
(6) the proposed facility and its amount, liability under guarantee and any provision to increase it;

---

[391] *Boustany* v. *Pigott* (1995) 69 P & CR 298, PC; *Etridge (No 2)* at [61], Lord Nicholls.

[392] *Etridge (No 2)* at [63], Lord Nicholls.

[393] *Etridge (No 2)* at [66–69], Lord Nicholls.

[394] At [52], [698], Lord Nicholls.

[395] At [72–78], Lord Nicholls.

[396] *Kenyon Brown* v. *Desmond Banks & Co* at [372–373], Lord Scott.

[397] *National Westminster Bank* v. *Gill*, reported with *Etridge (No 2)* at [279–281], Lord Scott.

[398] *Lloyds Bank* v. *Egremont* [1990] 2 FLR 351; P O'Hagan [1996] *NILQ* 74; *Barclays Bank* v. *Thompson* [1997] 4 All ER 816, CA; *National Bank of Abu Dhabi* v. *Mohamed* (1998) 30 HLR 383, CA.

[399] *Bank of Baroda*. v. *Rayarel* [1995] 2 FLR 376, CA.

[400] *TSB Bank* v. *Camfield* [1995] 1 WLR 430, CA; *Banco Exterior Internacional* v. *Mann* [1995] 1 All ER 936, CA.

[401] *Midland Bank* v. *Serter* [1995] 1 FLR 1034, CA.

[402] *Banco Exterior Internacional* v. *Thomas* [1997] 1 WLR 221.

[403] *Coldunell* v. *Gallon* [1986] QB 1184, CA; *Bradford & Bingley BS* v. *Chandock* (1996) 72 P & CR D28, CA; *Lloyds TSB Bank* v. *Holdgate* [2002] EWCA Civ 1543, [2002] 43 EG 203 (CS) (case allowed to proceed despite certificate, because one had to check that the quality of advice was adequate). See also *Scottish Equitable Life* v. *Virdee* [1999] 1 FLR 863, CA; *Abbey National* v. *Tufts* [1999] 2 FLR 399, CA.

[404] *Etridge (No 2)* at [64–65], Lord Nicholls, [170–175] Lord Scott.

(7) the wife's financial means and any other assets available for repayment;[405] and

(8) confirmation that despite the fact that she has a choice that she wishes nevertheless to proceed.

The bank should obtain written confirmation from the solicitor that he has advised the wife.[406]

4. Cases where bank might be liable despite intervention of solicitor

[30.73] The bank may be liable in the cases that follow.

(1) Solicitor is not acting for wife

[30.74] Deficiencies of advice matter if the solicitors act as agents for the bank. The solicitor had never begun to act for the wife in *Midland Bank* v. *Wallace*.[407] She met a solicitor, instructed by the bank and on its panel, for three minutes at most and received no explanation of any kind. In essence the solicitor merely witnessed the signature and the lack of explanation was the bank's failure.[408]

(2) Doubt about consent

[30.75] The bank may be liable where material known to it casts doubt on the consent of the surety,[409] that is if it is glaringly obvious that a wife is being grievously wronged so that a solicitor should not act.[410]

(3) Defective advice

[30.76] The bank will not escape if facts known to it show that the wife was not advised or was not given appropriate advice.[411] In *National Westminster Bank* v. *Amin*[412] two Urdu speaking parents signed a charge of their home to help finance the business of their English speaking son. Execution took place in the presence of a solicitor, but **he did not speak Urdu** and offered no advice at all. Since the bank knew that the sureties could not speak English, special steps were required and the case was allowed to proceed to trial.

---

[405] This requires information from the bank: at [67], Lord Nicholls.

[406] *Etridge (No 2)* at [116–120], Lord Hobhouse.

[407] Reported with *Etridge (No 2)* at [190], Lord Nicholls, [253], Lord Scott.

[408] Notice was imputed under LPA 1925 s 199(1)(ii)(b).

[409] *Etridge (No 2)* at [79], Lord Nicholls; *BCCI* v. *Aboody* [1990] 1 QB 923, CA (husband burst into interview room and applied pressure to both wife and solicitor); *Credit Lyonnais Bank Nederland* v. *Burch* [1997] 1 All ER 144, CA.

[410] *Etridge (No 2)* at [62]; *Powell* v. *Powell* [1900] 1 Ch 243, 247, Farwell J; *Wright* v. *Carter* [1903] 1 Ch 27, 57–58, Stirling LJ.

[411] *Etridge (No 2)* at [175], Lord Scott.

[412] [2002] UKHL 9, [2002] 1 FLR 735; M Haley [2002] *Conv* 499.

Q. REMEDIES FOR UNDUE INFLUENCE

[30.77] The claim for undue influence against the bank is parasitic on the claim against the husband. Wives will not be allowed to pursue cases on mutually inconsistent grounds, for example defending a claim for possession on the basis that the security is invalid and at the same time claiming ancillary relief.[413] In an extreme case such as *Barclays Bank* v. *Harris*[414] if the wife dies the husband as her personal representative may end up using his own misconduct as a defence against the bank! An irony is that the husband's occupation of the house is protected as well, since there is no point in ordering protection against one of them in isolation.[415] Another is that both parties remain vulnerable because the bank may treat the mortgage as a charge on the husband's beneficial interest and then seek sale as a co-owner. Or the lender can sue the husband on his personal debt, bankrupt him, and leave the trustee in bankruptcy to force a sale against the wife.[416]

R. NULLITY

[30.78] A person who executes a document cannot be allowed to disavow its contents.[417] Business confidence requires that reliance can be placed on signed documents.[418] Nullity is rare, but when it arises the transaction is void, and any later mortgage suffers from derivative invalidity.

1. Forgery

[30.79] A mortgage only validly charges the land if it is executed by the person who owns the land as his deed. A forgery has no effect and the land is not mortgaged.[419]

2. Not his doing

[30.80] *Non est factum* is the plea that "I did not do it". The defence is only available to a person with a defective understanding of the document, perhaps as a result of blindness. The test is whether he would be able to detect a fundamental difference in the nature of the document. An elderly woman with defective eyesight avoided a document which she was unable to read because she had broken her glasses.[420] The

---

[413] *First National Bank* v. *Walker* [2001] 1 FLR 505, CA.
[414] Reported with *Etridge (No 2)* at [247], Lord Scott.
[415] *Albany Home Loans* v. *Massey* [1997] 2 All ER 609, CA.
[416] *Zanfarid* v. *BCCI* [1996] 1 WLR 1420; *Alliance & Leicester* v. *Slayford* (2001) 33 HLR 66, CA; MP Thompson [2002] *Conv* 53.
[417] *Gallie* v. *Lee* [1969] 2 Ch 17, 37, Lord Denning MR; on appeal *Saunders* v. *Anglia BS* [1971] AC 1004, 1033, Lord Pearson.
[418] At 1015G, Lord Reid.
[419] *Saunders* [1971] AC 1004, 1015G, Lord Reid; *Norwich & Peterborough BS* v. *Steed (No 2)* [1993] Ch 116, 125D, Scott LJ; *Halifax Mortgage Services* v. *Muirhead* (1998) 76 P & CR 418, CA (mortgage altered by solicitor after execution by borrower); see above **[24.26ff]**.
[420] *Saunders* [1971] AC 1004, 1034F, Lord Pearson.

defence has been widened beyond blindness,[421] to cover permanent or temporary causes, such as illiteracy,[422] defective education, illness or innate incapacity.[423]

Few lay clients read or understand legal documents in depth, so that the invalidity arises only if the document is radically different[424] from what was believed,[425] either in character[426] or substance.[427] An all-monies charge is radically different from a charge limited to the value of land acquired with the loan.[428] *Saunders* v. *Anglia BS* failed even this more liberal test.[429] A 78 year old widow (Gallie)[430] signed a document which had been represented to her by Lee as a deed of gift of land in Dagenham to her nephew. In fact she signed an assignment to Lee, the nephew's business partner, a distinction which she did not detect because she had broken her glasses. Her attempt to upset the transaction failed. Her intention was to provide the value of her home as security for the business debts of her nephew, and in substance this was what she achieved.[431]

Care in execution is required.[432] A blind or illiterate person should ensure that the document is read over before signing. It may be invalid if read over fraudulently,[433] or after dishonest replies to enquiries about it.[434] Successful pleas often rely on a trick, but this is neither sufficient[435] nor essential. Many cases have revealed carelessness. A person who signed a promissory note through holes cut in blotting paper, thinking that he was witnessing family documents, was obviously careless.[436] *Norwich & Peterborough BS* v. *Steed (No 2)*[437] considered a mortgage executed by an attorney. If the mother was incapable of understanding the transaction, she should not have been appointed as an attorney, and anyway the evidence stated that she had failed to take ordinary precautions.[438]

---

[421] *Foster* v. *Mackinnon* (1869) LR 4 CP 704, 711–712; [1971] AC 1004, 1019H–1020B, Lord Hodson.

[422] *Lloyd's Bank* v. *Waterhouse* [1993] 2 FLR 97, CA (better decided on misrepresentation).

[423] *Saunders* at 1016A Lord Reid; *Shulter's* case (1611) 12 Co Rep 90, 77 ER 1366 (man aged 115).

[424] Test variously stated: *Saunders* [1971] AC 1004, 1017A–C, 1021B, 1026, 1039B.

[425] Test subjective: [1971] AC 1004, 1035H–1036A, Lord Pearson.

[426] *Thoroughgood's case* (1584) 2 Co Rep 9a, 76 ER 408; *Howatson* v. *Webb* [1908] 1 Ch 1, CA.

[427] *Saunders* v. *Anglia BS* [1971] AC 1004, 1018C–1019, 1021G–1022H, 1024G–1025C.

[428] *Lloyds Bank* v. *Waterhouse* [1993] Ch 116, CA; *Lewis* v. *Clay* (1897) 77 LT 653.

[429] [1971] AC 1004, HL; AL Guest (1971) 87 *LQR* 145; J Stone (1972) 88 *LQR* 190; JH Baker (1970) 23 *CLP* 53; RJ Bragg (1971) 35 *Conv (NS)* 231.

[430] After her death the action was continued by Saunders her executor.

[431] It was voidable for misrepresentation by Lee; but not against the building society who had lent in good faith.

[432] *Foster* v. *Mackinnon* (1869) LR 4 CP 704; *Saunders* [1971] AC 1004, 1016E, 1019E, 1023A–1023E, 1026, 1036H–1038H. *Carlisle & Cumberland Banking Co* v. *Bragg* [1911] 1 KB 489 was disapproved.

[433] *Thoroughgood's case* (1584) 2 Co Rep 9a, 76 ER 408.

[434] *Lloyds Bank* v. *Waterhouse* [1993] 2 FLR 97, CA.

[435] A trick is not enough standing alone: *Hunter* v. *Walters* (1871) LR 7 Ch App 75; *National Provincial Bank of England* v. *Jackson* (1886) 33 Ch D 1; *King* v. *Smith* [1900] 2 Ch 425; *Saunders* [1971] AC 1004, HL.

[436] *Lewis* v. *Clay* (1897) 77 LT 653.

[437] [1993] Ch 116, CA.

[438] At 125D–G, Scott LJ; *Hambros Bank* v. *British Historic Buildings Trust* [1996] 2 CLYB 4987, Ch D.

31

PARTS

Parts. Fixing boundaries. Presumed boundaries. Horizontal divisions.

A. PARTS

1. Search of part

[31.01] Searches of part are required where a person buys a plot on a large estate. One method is to lodge a search with a plan showing the part against which a search occurs.[1] On a large building estate, the buyer would be distracted by unnecessary details. This difficulty is smoothed over by the procedure for the developer to secure approval for an estate layout plan after which it is only necessary to cite a plot number in order to effect a search.[2] The result is a certificate of inspection of the title plan, which confirms that the plot searched is part of the developer's title and reveals details of any entries affecting that plot, but eschewing details of plot sales elsewhere on the title.

2. Transfer of part

[31.02] A significant number of dealings involve transfers of part – in the most recent year there were 182,000 as against 3.4 million dealings with whole titles.[3] Many of these were sales by developers of individual houses on new estates or of individual flats in new blocks. Transfers of part are sufficiently different from sales of the whole to require a distinctive form (Form TP1).[4] The form used under the Land Registration Act 2002 is broadly that introduced when all the forms were reviewed in 1999,[5] when a large numerical identifier (supposedly mnemonic) was introduced as standard in the top left hand corner. This contains three main elements outlined below.

---

[1] DLRR 2003 r 148; LR Form OSP.
[2] The application is for a certificate of inspection of the title plan: DLRR 2003 r 143; LR Practice Leaflet 7 (1999) and 5 supplements. Hi tech methods are available as for normal searches, see above **[8.17]**, **[9.12ff]**.
[3] LR *Annual Report 2001–2002*, 83.
[4] LR Form TP1; also TP2 (transfer of part by a lender), AS3 (assent of part).
[5] DLRR 2003 sch 1; previously LRR 1999, SI 1999/128; PH Kenny [1998] *Conv* 433; C West [1999] 24 *LSG* 42.

(1) The transfer

[31.03] In this aspect the form for a sale of part is exactly the same as for a transfer of a whole title. The form provides for stamp duty particulars, identification of the title affected, the date, the consideration, and any title guarantee. *New Land Lawyers* will describe the parties as seller and buyer, the operative words being that "The Seller transfers the property to the Buyer." Or, in the usual case of joint proprietors, to "the Buyers", in which case a declaration of trust will be required to indicate whether the parties are to take as beneficial joint tenants, equal tenants in common or tenants in common in unequal shares. The form requires execution in the usual way.[6]

(2) Identification of the part sold

[31.04] Transfers of part require precise identification of the part sold, first in the contract and then in the transfer giving effect to the contract, using a plan[7] which must be descriptive and not merely identificatory.

(3) Rights and duties to neighbours

[31.05] Any sale of part creates two new neighbours, so the transfer needs to spell out a framework of rights to govern their future relationship, including rights granted to the buyer of part and rights reserved to the person retaining the other part.[8] The main rights are easements and restrictive covenants.[9] The form contains space for any agreement or declaration defining the precise line of the agreed boundary. It is possible to add personal covenants or other non-standard elements.[10]

Electronic forms are coming, with flexibility to adapt to changed circumstances automatically and so to remove unnecessary certificates.

3. Registration of parts

[31.06] The standard form of application for registration covers dealings with parts as well as the whole.[11] Normally a transfer of part will result in a new register being opened for the part sold and the title from which it is sold being marked to indicate the removal of that part. Each register will need to record the easements and covenants created.

Where the buyer already owns land in the vicinity, this may well lead to an untidy situation in which an owner's title is divided between several individual registers.[12] Provided that each title refers to the same estate and has the same proprietor the

---

[6] DLRR 2003 sch 8; see above **[7.06]**.
[7] DLRR 2003 r 210; Around 1/8th of plans had serious defects: (1969) 32 *MLR* 127; LR leaflet Practice Advice Leaflet 8 (1995).
[8] See below **[35.02]**.
[9] See below **[32]**.
[10] C West [1999] 24 *LSG* 42; see below **[32.52]**.
[11] LR Form AP1. There are around 180,000 transfers of part a year as against 3.4 million dealings with the whole: LR *Annual Report 2000–2001*, 83.
[12] DLRR 2003 r 2(2).

registrar can amalgamate titles, and conversely he can separate titles where there is, for example, a mortgage of a part, either of his own volition or on the application of the proprietor.[13]

B. FIXING BOUNDARIES

[31.07] A boundary is only the imaginary line which divides two contiguous properties.[14] Robert Frost rightly observed that *"Good fences make good neighbours"*, the unstated corollary being that indistinct ones provoke disputes and litigation and, all too often, "some unreasonable and extravagant display of unneighbourly behaviour which profits no one but the lawyers."[15] The bitterness with which disputes are pursued is often quite disproportionate to the value of the land in issue.

1. Agreed boundaries

[31.08] Boundaries are best fixed by formal declaration in a transfer or conveyance. Division of land is the vital moment, because when two holdings are made out of one it becomes necessary to provide a precise definition of the boundary separating the two plots. Registered and unregistered practice is very similar. Almost all titles derive from a time when the site was part of a larger plot,[16] and the conveyance of part remains for all time a vital document of title. A plan is essential on a sale of part.[17] Sale by reference to pegging out on the land is unsatisfactory, since the pegs soon vanish.[18] Statement of the area of land sold is also dangerous because estimates are often unreliable.[19]

2. Other evidence of agreed boundaries

[31.09] Reliance can be placed on any agreement used to settle a genuine dispute which is seen as an agreement to settle potential litigation rather than a transfer of tiny strips of land.[20] Repair and other acts of ownership may be of some evidential value, the modern tendency being to look at all the evidence.[21] Once an agreed boundary is acted on by repair an estoppel may arise.[22] Limitation has a vital role both in altering

---

[13] R 3.

[14] A Pottage (1994) 57 *MLR* 361; A Sydenham [1998] 31 *EG* 90.

[15] *Alan Wibberley Building* v. *Insley* [1998] 1 WLR 881, 882D, Ward LJ; the case involved a worthless strip 87' x 6' which cost £250,000 to litigate to the CA, not counting the appeal on to the HL.

[16] Eg an enclosure award dividing land into fields or a sale by a developer of an individual plot on an estate.

[17] *Scarfe* v. *Adams* [1981] 1 All ER 843, CA (scale 1:2500 inadequate).

[18] *Willson* v. *Greene* [1971] 1 WLR 635; JT Farrand [1983] *Conv* 338.

[19] The danger is much reduced by stating a particular area, such as 84 acres 3 roods and 4 perches, but adding "or thereabouts": *Eastwood* v. *Ashton* [1915] AC 900, HL.

[20] *Neilson* v. *Poole* (1969) 20 P & CR 909, 918–919, Megarry J; *Burns* v. *Morton* [2000] 1 WLR 347, 351–352, Swinton Thomas LJ.

[21] *Clarke* v. *O'Keefe* (2000) 80 P & CR 126, CA.

[22] *Hopgood* v. *Brown* [1955] 1 WLR 213, CA.

boundaries and in confirming the physical boundaries laid out on the ground, whether title is unregistered or registered.[23]

3. Registered boundaries

[31.10] The casual approach of the conveyancing process to identification of the extent of land being transferred amazes non-lawyers. Registration provides little improvement over the unregistered system, except that the extent of all registered titles is made public by means of the index, which can be searched.[24] The property register usually gives little more than the postal address,[25] delineation being achieved by an extract from the ordnance survey map.[26] Small scale plans are used for agricultural land and building estates,[27] but at least they show the current extent of the title after successive deletions or additions.[28] However, the small scale adopted for suburban development restricts its function to locating the land and makes it useless for fixing precise boundaries. It would be desirable to aim in the direction of larger scale more precise plans over the next century or two.[29]

Lines shown on a filed plan represent general boundaries.[30] Ownership of hedges, ditches, roads or streams[31] is not stated conclusively. In *Lee* v. *Barrey*[32] the true line on the transfer plan diverged from the land registry filed plan by ten feet, so great a discrepancy that a house was built on land registered in the name of the neighbour. This is by no means unique. Plans are vulnerable to rectification,[33] after adverse possession or if the register conflicts with a transfer or the pre-registration title deeds. If two adjoining titles include the same land one or other must be corrected, the gainer usually being the party with possession, and the loser being recompensed with an indemnity if innocent.

4. Exact boundaries

[31.11] Users surely expect that the register will identify precise boundary lines and that the precise boundary should carry a land registry guarantee and indemnity rights.

---

[23] LRA 2002 sch 6 para 5(4); see above [11.25].

[24] See above [8.17].

[25] DLRR 2003 r 5(1)(a).

[26] H Potter, *The Principles of Land Law under the Land Registration Act 1925* (Sweet & Maxwell, 1941), 12; A Pottage (1994) 57 *MLR* 361.

[27] Scales used are: 1/1250 (fully developed; at this scale 1 millimetre = 4 feet); 1/2500 (little or no development); 1/10,000 (moors etc). Linear measurements must be metric: SI 1994/2866.

[28] A new edition is usually prepared after a change: DLRR 2003 r 3. Colouring conventions are: (1) red edging: the extent of the land; (2) green edging: land removed from the title; (3) green tinting: islands excluded from the title.

[29] *AJ Dunning & Sons (Shopfitters)* v. *Sykes & Sons (Poole)* [1987] Ch 287, 303F, Donaldson MR.

[30] LRA 2002 s 60; Law Com 271 (2001), [9.4–9.5], EN [260]; DLRR 2003 r 119; *Alan Wibberley Building* v. *Insley* [1999] 1 WLR 894, 896C–897B, Lord Hoffmann; *Clarke* v. *O'Keefe* (2000) 80 P & CR 126, 133, Peter Gibson LJ.

[31] *Hesketh* v. *Willis Cruisers* (1968) 19 P & CR 573, CA.

[32] [1957] 1 Ch 251. A dotted line indicated greater than usual uncertainty and the register noted that boundaries were subject to revision.

[33] That is an alteration which will prejudice the title of a neighbour: LRA 2002 s 65, sch 4; see above [11.44ff].

That this rarely happens is, primarily because it is necessary to involve all neighbours affected and either secure their agreement or determine the precise legal position.

The 1925 Rules laid down a procedure by which exact boundaries could be fixed at the request of a registered proprietor, but it was used on only nine occasions in 35 years.[34] The procedure has now been updated and made less rigorous in order to speed up the process and to encourage applications.[35] End points will be determined to within a one cm square, as will points where the lines change direction, this being done by co-ordinates and by verbal description, though the fix only affects the part of the boundary determined.[36] This may be done if a transfer of part contains sufficient information for the line to be fixed to that degree of precision.[37]

Otherwise exact lines will only be fixed after an application is made by the registered proprietor[38] and then only after the neighbours have been involved and given a chance to object.[39] If no objection is received, the register can be amended to record the fix, but any dispute must be resolved first.[40] A fix will also be required before a claim to move a boundary by adverse possession is determined.[41] When a fix has occurred that fact and the details of the boundary will be recorded in the property register.[42]

5. Unregistered parcels

[31.12] Unregistered conveyances use a parcels clause to define the land.[43] On a sale of the whole, verbal description is normal and proper.[44] The parcels clause simply passes on the land transferred by the previous conveyance.[45] Descriptions inevitably fall out of date,[46] since conveyancers tend to repeat the description given in earlier deeds to prevent accidental changes to the extent of the land sold. Where a person is selling all his land, it will be presumed that all land is included in the conveyance. In *Alan Wibberley Building* v. *Insley*[47] the House of Lords rejected in its entirety the following:

> "10.39 acres or thereabouts particularly delineated for the purposes of identification only on the plan hereto and more particularly described as OS Parcel No 6751."

The hedge and ditch presumption was applied to avoid the literal result that the seller (Beard) retained a useless and isolated strip of hedge and ditch.

---

[34] LRR 1925 r 278; Law Com WP 45 (1972), [34].

[35] LRA 2002 s 60; Law Com 271 (2001), [9.4–9.5], EN [260]; DLRR 2003 rr 116–122; DLRR CD ch 8, [2–10].

[36] DLRR 2003 r 119.

[37] R 121; also if there is some other written agreement fixing the precise line: r 117.

[38] R 116; LR Form DB.

[39] DLRR 2003 r 117 allows 30 days unless extended.

[40] R 117.

[41] R 120.

[42] R 118.

[43] If this does not reflect what is contracted to be sold there is a problem of misdescription, for which see standard conveyancing texts.

[44] No right to insist on a plan: *Re Sharman's Conveyance* [1936] Ch 755; AE Randall (1910) 26 *LQR* 268.

[45] Deleting any land lost by adverse possession: *Eastwood* v. *Ashton* [1915] AC 900, HL. Problems can be reduced by describing the land as that "now in the occupation of the seller".

[46] *Hopgood* v. *Brown* [1955] 1 WLR 213, CA; JT Farrand [1983] *Conv* 335.

[47] [1999] 1 WLR 894, HL.

Serious problems of description arise where land is divided and the extent of the land sold is described in multiple ways that conflict. Any manifestly inaccurate description is rejected in favour of one which is accurate.[48] *Eastwood* v. *Ashton*[49] involved four modes of description – the name of the farm, the extent of the land occupied by named tenants, the area, and a plan[50] – all conflicting, of which the last predominated on the facts. Conflicts should be resolved in advance by stating whether the verbal description or plan is to prevail,[51] using one of two traditional phrases:

> a plan *for identification purposes only* allows the verbal description to prevail[52] whereas land *more particularly delineated* in the plan enables the plan to prevail over the parcels clause.[53]

The objective opinion of a reasonable observer is more important that the subjective views of the parties.[54]

C. PRESUMED BOUNDARIES

1. Open land and gardens

[31.13] A fence is deemed to belong to the person on whose side the rails and posts are sited to avoid the tiny slivers of land between the posts becoming unusable.[55]

Where land is divided by a man made ditch and bank (or one that is woman made), *Alan Wibberley Building* v. *Insley*[56] decided that it was important to know when the ditch was dug in relation to the time that the boundary was fixed. If the ditch predates the division of the land, there is no artificial presumption and all depends upon the correct interpretation of the conveyance which effects the division.[57] However, if the land was divided first and the ditch is dug afterwards, the law assumes that the fullest possible use is made of land: it is presumed that the ditch is dug out at the extremity of the land and the soil thrown back onto the land to form the bank, so that the boundary lies at the far extremity of the ditch.[58] This is a presumption which can be rebutted by a careful plan.[59]

Boundaries usually run through the centre line of a hedge.[60]

[48] *Falsa demonstratio non nocet* (= a false description does not invalidate a deed) *cum de corpore constat* (= if it is clear what is intended).

[49] [1915] AC 900, HL.

[50] A plan physically attached to a conveyance may be used even if not directly mentioned: *Leachman* v. *L & K Richardson* [1969] 1 WLR 1129; PV Baker (1969) 85 *LQR* 461; *Freeguard* v. *Rogers* [1999] 1 WLR 375, CA.

[51] Use of both in *Neilson* v. *Poole* (1969) 20 P & CR 909, 916, Megarry J, was "mutually stultifying".

[52] *Hopgood* v. *Brown* [1955] 1 WLR 213; unless the verbal description is inadequate: *Wigginton & Milner* v. *Winster Engineering* [1978] 1 WLR 1462, CA; *Targett* v. *Ferguson* (1996) 72 P & CR 106, CA; *Woolls* v. *Powling* [1999] Times March 9th, CA; *Smith* v. *Royce Properties* [2001] EWCA Civ 949, [2002] 2 P & CR 5 at 67.

[53] *Eastwood* v. *Ashton* [1915] AC 900, HL.

[54] *Targett* v. *Ferguson* (1996) 72 P & CR 106, 114; *Toplis* v. *Green* [1992] EGCS 20, Butler Sloss LJ.

[55] JE Adams (1971) 68 *LSG* 275, 375.

[56] [1999] 1 WLR 894, HL.

[57] *Fisher* v. *Winch* [1939] 1 KB 666.

[58] *Vowles* v. *Miller* (1810) 3 Taunt 137, 138, 128 ER 54, Lawrence J; *Weston* v. *Lawrence Weaver* [1961] 1 QB 402; *Davey* v. *Harrow Corp* [1958] 1 QB 60, CA.

[59] *Alan Wibberley Building* v. *Insley* [1999] 1 WLR 894, HL (presumption applied despite plan).

[60] *Davey* v. *Harrow Corp* [1958] 1 QB 60, CA.

2. Highways

[31.14] A highway is a way dedicated to the public for the purpose of passage. The surface of a highway maintainable at the public expense is vested in the highway authority[61] and control can be exerted over the air space above.[62] The authority acquires a determinable fee simple so long as the highway remains, which confers the legal estate.[63]

The soil remains vested in the neighbouring landowner, and his rights become absolute if the highway is shut or abandoned. Ownership of the adjoining soil confers all rights except rights of passage,[64] so public toilets cannot be constructed beneath the highway.[65] Occupiers liability attaches to the highway authority, so the neighbouring owner has no responsibility to those passing.[66] The boundary of two plots is assumed to be in the middle of the highway.[67] The middle line rule can be excluded by any contrary indication,[68] and it is now common to exclude the roads when selling plots on a building estate.[69] Land registry plans usually exclude public roads, but this does not remove the ownership of the soil.[70]

3. Foreshore

[31.15] The foreshore lies between the high and low water mark of ordinary tides alternately covered and left dry by the flux and reflux of the tide.[71] As sea level changes so does the geographical extent of the foreshore, so this is a title to a moveable piece of land. Foreshore may shift and eventually move to a completely different site.[72] But the assumption that foreshore is moveable was rebutted in *Baxendale* v. *Instow PC*[73] where the title plan "more particularly delineated and described the land", and thus fixed the high-water mark boundary.

Rules are complex and in need of demystification.[74] Much of the foreshore belongs to the Crown or the Royal Duchies though private ownership is possible by Crown

---

[61] Highways Act 1980 s 263; *Coverdale* v. *Charlton* (1878) 4 QBD 104 (including pasturage rights on the verge); *Att-Gen* v. *Beynan* [1970] 1 Ch 1.

[62] *Schweder* v. *Worthing Gas Light & Coke Co (No 2)* [1913] 1 Ch 118, 124, Eve J; *Att-Gen* v. *Brotherton* [1992] 1 AC 425, 436A, Lord Oliver.

[63] LPA 1925 s 7; *Tithe Redemption Board* v. *Runcorn Urban DC* [1954] Ch 383, CA.

[64] *Vestry of St Mary Newington* v. *Jacobs* (1871) LR 7 QB 47; *River Lee Navigation* v. *Button* (1881) 6 App Cas 685, HL.

[65] *Tunbridge Wells Corp* v. *Baird* [1896] AC 434 (Pantiles).

[66] *McGeown* v. *Northern Ireland Housing Executive* [1995] 1 AC 233, HL.

[67] *Goodtitle d Chester* v. *Alker* (1757) 1 Burr 134, 97 ER 231; *Minting* v. *Ramage* [1991] EGCS 12, CA (including verges); *Pardoe* v. *Pennington* (1998) P & CR 264, CA (bridleway).

[68] *Commissioners for Land Tax* v. *Central London Rly Co* [1913] AC 364, 379, Lord Shaw; *Collett* v. *Culpin* [1996] 2 CLYB 5020, CA; *Pardoe* v. *Pennington* (1998) 75 P & CR 264, CA (cess pit); *Hale* v. *Norfolk CC* [2001] Ch 717 CA.

[69] *Leigh* v. *Jack* (1879) 5 Ex D 264, CA; *Giles* v. *County Building Constructors (Hertford)* (1971) 22 P & CR 978, 981.

[70] *Russell* v. *Barnet LBC* [1984] 2 EGLR 44.

[71] *Adair* v. *National Trust* [1997] Times December 19th, Girvan J; *Government of S Penang* v. *Oon* [1972] AC 425, 435–436, Lord Cross; LRA 2002 sch 6 para 13; Law Com 271 (2001), [3.5].

[72] *Scratton* v. *Brown* (1825) 4 B & C 485, 107 ER 1140; *Mellor* v. *Walmesley* [1905] 2 Ch 164.

[73] [1982] Ch 14, Megarry V-C; RE Annand [1982] *Conv* 208, 208 (diagram of facts); *Theosophy* [1982] AC 706, 718F–G, Lord Wilberforce.

[74] BS Flushman *Demystifying Land Boundaries Adjacent to Tidal or Navigable Water* (Wiley, 2002).

grant or adverse possession.[75] In either case the public[76] have rights of navigation and fishing, and to take lugworms, winkles and whelks, but not rights of passage, bathing, taking recreation, or preaching.[77] Similar rules apply to tidal rivers: the bed belongs to the Crown,[78] subject to public rights of fishing and navigation,[79] but only so far as the point at which the river ceases to ebb and flow.

There is a new power to extend the registration of title to the seabed outside the current administrative areas out to the submarine base line.[80] This would protect Crown rights in the sea bed against adverse possession, but is unlikely to be implemented because of the expense of mapping.[81]

4. Land fronting water

[31.16] Non-tidal rivers are usually in private ownership, the presumption being that the bed of the river belongs to the riparian owners (ie the owners of the banks) with the boundary half way across.[82] Fishing lines may nevertheless be cast beyond the midpoint of the river.[83] The right to fish passes with the river, unless the fishing rights are severed from the freehold.[84] Conversely, ownership of an exclusive fishery implies ownership of the river itself.[85]

Landowners have no property in the water, whether it flows in a river or percolates under the land,[86] but riparian owners have a natural right to take water from a river. This right may be removed by statute, grant or prescription and is now controlled in that abstraction of water requires a licence from the Water Authority,[87] except where it is for household use or agricultural purposes.[88] The riparian owner can also grant the right to take water to another as an easement, so long as the abstraction does not materially affect the river's flow.

---

[75] *Fowley Marine (Emsworth)* v. *Gafford* [1968] 2 QB 618, CA.

[76] *Att-Gen for British Columbia* v. *Att-Gen for Canada* [1914] AC 153; *LLandudno Urban DC* v. *Woods* [1899] 2 Ch 705.

[77] *Adair* v. *National Trust* [1997] Times December 19th, Girvan J.

[78] Territorial Waters Jurisdiction Act 1878; *R* v. *Keyn* (1876) 2 Ex D 63, 199.

[79] *Blundell* v. *Catterall* (1821) 5 B & Ald 267, 294, 106 ER 1190, 1199; *Micklethwait* v. *Newland* (1886) 33 Ch D 133. The Crown has not been able to remove public fishing rights since Magna Carta: *Gann* v. *Whitstable Free Fisheries* (1865) 11 HLC 192, 11 ER 1305.

[80] Convention on Territorial Sea 1958 art 4.

[81] Law Com 271 (2001), [3.5].

[82] *Tilbury* v. *Silva* (1890) 45 Ch D 98, 109, Kay J; *Land Tax Commissioners* v. *Central London Rly Co* [1913] AC 364, 379, Lord Shaw. Presumption not applied: *Micklethwait* v. *Newland* (1886) 33 Ch D 133 (rebutted on facts); *Chamber Colliery* v. *Rochdale Canal Co* [1895] AC 564, 576, Lord Herschell (canal); *Swan Hill Developments* v. *British Waterways Board* [1997] EGCS 33, CA (private bridge over site of canal: depended on Canal Act).

[83] *Fotheringham* v. *Kerr* (1984) 48 P & CR 173, 186–187, Lord Fraser.

[84] *Att-Gen for British Columbia* v. *Att-Gen for Canada* [1914] AC 153, 168, Lord Haldane.

[85] *Hesketh* v. *Willis Cruisers* (1968) 19 P & CR 573, CA.

[86] *Ballard* v. *Tomkinson* (1885) 29 Ch D 115, 120, 126.

[87] Water Resources Act 1991 s 24; Megarry & Wade (6th ed), [3.055–3.059].

[88] Spray irrigation does require a licence.

5.   Moving boundaries (accretion and diluvion)

[31.17] Registration of title depends upon pinning down an abstract estate to a fixed area on an Ordnance Survey plan. Earthquakes apart,[89] land is generally immovable, but this is not necessarily the case: land fronting water, such as coasts and river banks, can be eroded or increased.[90] *Southern Centre for Theosophy* v. *South Australia*[91] concerned an inland lake in Australia, reduced in extent by 20 acres by sand deposits over a period of 60 years. The Crown owned the lake, but lost title to this part. By the doctrine of accretion, the new area of land was added to the title of the person who owned the lakeside. Accretion applies where the addition of material is gradual and imperceptible, a condition just satisfied in the *Theosophy* case.[92] The doctrine works well, both for registered[93] and unregistered titles, since most disputes can be settled out of court.[94]

Any agreement about how accretion or diluvion is to affect a registered title may be noted on the register.[95]

Some titles cannot be analysed on geographical principles. Lot meadows were an old form of communal farming where each farmer had the right to a certain number of strips in a large field allocated by ballot.[96] In the same way, accretion also creates a freehold estate in a movable piece of land.[97]

D. HORIZONTAL DIVISION

[31.18] Land can often be thought of as flat, that is in two dimensional terms, because the important boundaries are those laid out flat on the surface of the earth which separate one parcel of the earth's surface from its neighbour. More properly that surface line drawn on a plan is a vertical plane cutting though the surface and so enclosing a solid shape, including part of the surface, a block of subterranean land, and also, above, a block of high rise building or airspace. This third dimension[98] may be important when, for example, deciding whether a person is entitled to paraglide over your land, whether the owner of a top floor flat can extend build upwards through the existing ceiling, or if a council wishes to construct an underground toilet. Landowners are free to divided their land into strata titles, though this can only be done by agreement

---

[89] *Cricklewood Property & Investment Trust* v. *Leighton's Investment Trust* [1945] AC 221, 229, Viscount Simon LC; *National Carriers* v. *Panalpina (Northern)* [1981] AC 675, 691, Hailsham LC; PBH Birks "Before We Begin: Five Keys to Land Law" ch 18 in Bright & Dewar, 462.

[90] *Mercer* v. *Denne* [1904] 2 Ch 534, Farwell J.

[91] [1982] AC 706, PC; P Jackson (1983) 99 *LQR* 412; W Howarth [1986] *Conv* 247.

[92] At 722. It was found as a fact that change was imperceptible.

[93] LRA 2002 s 61; Law Com 271 (2001), [9.14–9.15], EN [266–269].

[94] (1982) 132 *NLJ* 1164.

[95] DLRR 2003 r 122.

[96] *Welden* v. *Bridgewater* (1595) Cro Eliz 421, 78 ER 462; S Farrar (1936) 1 *Conv (NS)* 53; (1978) 122 *SJ* 723. The surviving field system at Laxton, Notts, has fixed strips.

[97] The fee simple is not determinable and was never subject to the Settled Land Act; contrast RE Annand [1982] *Conv* 208, 211.

[98] Grays' *Elements* (3rd ed), 16.

and not by compulsory purchase,[99] though as soon as they do so support and repairing obligations and the defective common law.

1. Mines

[31.19] John Paul Getty wisecracked that:

"The meek shall inherit the earth, but not the mineral rights."

He knew just how valuable mineral rights can be.[100] Gold and silver falls to the Crown under its prerogative,[101] whereas statutory rights create Crown title in oil and natural gas.[102] Coal was nationalised[103] (most recently being vested in British Coal) but remaining coal mines have been reprivatised.[104] Other minerals may be owned privately. Very often mineral rights over large areas are owned separately from the surface, so that ownership of the soil excepts the mineral rights beneath and the seams needed to work them.[105]

Rights of support for the surface are of fundamental importance to maintaining the value of the surface land.[106] The owner of the surface is entitled to protection against his land slipping into the workings.[107] However, some grants of mineral rights also confer the right to let down the surface of the land,[108] usually subject to compensation[109] Licensed operators of coal mines may withdraw support[110] but must take remedial action and provide compensation.[111] If the surface can be let down without payment[112] land above the mine will be almost valueless.

Rights to extract sand, gravel, ice, or turf[113] usually take the form of profits.

Land that can be registered includes mines and minerals.[114] So rules about transfers and first registration apply with some modifications;[115] in particular the compulsion

---

[99] *English Property Corp* v. *Kingston upon Thames RLBC* (1999) 77 P & CR 1, 6, Morritt LJ.

[100] Megarry & Wade (6th ed), [3.052].

[101] *Case of Mines* (1586) 1 Plowd 310, 336, 75 ER 472; Royal Mines Acts 1688, 1693; *Att-Gen* v. *Morgan* [1891] 1 Ch 432.

[102] Petroleum (Production) Act 1934 s 1(1); *Earl of Lonsdale* v. *Att-Gen for Duchy of Lancaster* [1982] 1 WLR 887, 947E. Slade J decided, at 908–924, that minerals are essentially *solid* substances dug out of the earth by means of a mine, thus excluding oil and natural gas.

[103] Coal Act 1938 s 3 (unworked coal); Coal Industry Nationalisation Act 1946 s 5 (mines and all colliery businesses).

[104] Coal Industry Act 1994.

[105] *Dyson* v. *Forster* [1909] AC 98, HL; *Eardley* v. *Granville* (1876) 3 Ch D 826.

[106] The existence of coal working can be discovered by a mining search: PH Kenny [1998] *Conv* 245; also now from a NILS search.

[107] *Butterknowle Colliery Co* v. *Bishop Aukland Industrial Co-operative* [1906] AC 305.

[108] *Hext* v. *Gill* (1872) LR 7 Ch App 699; *Sitwell* v. *Earl of Londesborough* [1905] 1 Ch 460. Lord Byron's home, Newstead Abbey, is held on these terms.

[109] *Love* v. *Bell* (1884) 9 App Cas 286; *New Sharlston Collieries Co* v. *Westmorland* (1900) [1904] 2 Ch 443n, CA.

[110] Coal Industry Act 1994 s 39.

[111] Coal Mining Subsidence Act 1991 part II; there are many cases.

[112] *Rowbotham* v. *Wilson* (1860) 8 HLC 348, 11 ER 483; *Duke of Buccleuch* v. *Wakefield* (1869) LR 4 HL 377; *Buchanan* v. *Andrew* (1873) LR 2 HL Sc 286.

[113] *Lowe* v. *JW Ashmore* [1971] Ch 545; it is possible, though rare, to sever the ownership of growing turf: LPA 1925 s 205(1)(ix); *Lowe* at 555, Megarry J.

[114] LRA 2002 s 132(1).

[115] DLRR 2003 rr 24 (first registration of mines), 30 (first registration of land excluding mines).

does not apply to mineral rights held apart from the surface.[116] Mineral rights generally override the register,[117] unless the position regarding mines and minerals has been noted on the register.[118]

2.   Subterranean rooms

[31.20] A freehold or leasehold estate can be created in an underground room, a cavern or a railway tunnel,[119] but it needs to be made clear that ownership is detached from the land above. As Brightman J remarked in *Grigsby* v. *Melville* "a purchaser does not expect to find the vendor continuing to live, mole-like, beneath his drawing room floor".[120]

3.   Flats

[31.21] A flat is an artificial division of the space above the surface, requiring precise definition.[121] A flat will be presumed to include the whole of external walls[122] but only a portion of those which are internal. The upper boundary is somewhere in the floor joists to which the ceiling is fixed,[123] a rule which also fixes the lower limit of the flat above.[124] The airspace above the building's roof is usually excluded from individual flats.[125] These rules are subject to variation.[126] The landlord is obliged to keep in repair the exterior and structure of a block of flats let on short residential leases.[127]

Most estates are firmly rooted in the soil, but it is not necessarily so. A freehold estate can be created in a cubic or polyhedric space not anchored to the earth.[128] Flying freeholds exist by statute in Lincoln's Inn,[129] and why not a hanging garden? Although some pre-war flats were sold freehold,[130] lenders remain reluctant to accept freehold flats as security for a mortgage,[131] since the repairing obligations are uncertain.

These obstacles are overcome at present by selling flats leasehold, and for the future by commonhold schemes.[132]

---

[116] LRA 2002 s 4(9).
[117] LRA 2002 schs 1/3 paras 7–9; Law Com 271 (2001), [5.95–5.98].
[118] DLRR 2003 rr 71–72; PH Kenny [2002] *Conv* 305.
[119] *Metropolitan Rly* v. *Fowler* [1893] AC 416, 420.
[120] [1972] 1 WLR 1355, 1360G; DLRR 2003 r 25; Grays' *Elements* (3rd ed), 21–22; Megarry & Wade (6th ed), [3.045–3.046].
[121] DLRR 2003 r 25.
[122] *Sturge* v. *Hackett* [1962] 1 WLR 1257, 1266.
[123] At 1266.
[124] *Phelps* v. *City of London Corporation* [1916] 2 Ch 255.
[125] *Davies* v. *Yadegar* [1990] 1 EGLR 70, CA; *Haines* v. *Florensa* [1990] 1 EGLR 73, CA; *Ibrahim* v. *Dovecorn Reversions* [2001] 2 EGLR 46, (2001) 82 P & CR 28 at 302, Rimer J; *Hallisey* v. *Petmoor Developments* [2000] Times November 1st, Patten J; N Roberts [2001] *Conv* 387; JE Adams [2001] *Conv* 373.
[126] *Hatfield* v. *Moss* [1988] 2 EGLR 58 (roof included).
[127] *Campden Hill Towers* v. *Gardner* [1977] QB 823, reversed by LTA 1985 s 11(1A).
[128] K Gray [1991] *CLJ* 252; *Wright* v. *Macadam* [1949] 2 KB 744, 747, Jenkins LJ.
[129] Lincoln's Inn Act 1860; M Vitoria (1977) 41 *Conv (NS)* 11.
[130] SM Tolson (1950) 14 *Conv (NS)* 350.
[131] *CML Handbook for Solicitors* (Council of Mortgage Lenders, 2002), [5.5].
[132] See above **[4.12ff]**, **[4.16ff]**.

4. Tort actions

[31.22] Ownership in the lower airspace can be asserted though an action in trespass or nuisance. Trespass is a better way of asserting pure ownership because it requires no proof of damage. Any invasion suffices, for example when a horse pokes its head through a boundary fence. An injunction can be obtained to order removal of an intrusion or to restrain a threatened intrusion without showing that the landowner is actually inconvenienced.[133] Lateral invasions which occur without the licence of the landowner are actionable in whatever form: when building eaves overhang the neighbouring land,[134] advertising signs protrude over the neighbouring airspace;[135] or cranes are erected so that the jibs swing over neighbouring land.[136] The owner of the soil could cut down a wire placed above his land without licence.[137]

Invasion by overhanging tree branches is treated as nuisance,[138] which can be abated by lopping them off, and which gives rise to an action for damages for any injury caused.[139] In defiance of the general rule mentioned above, an injunction can be obtained for the removal of branches without proof of damage.[140]

5. Airspace

[31.23] Common law ownership extended up to the sky and down to the centre of the earth.[141] That "sweeping, unscientific and unpractical" doctrine[142] could not survive the development of balloons and aircraft.[143] In the lower region close to the ground, the owner of the soil has virtually complete control,[144] and he retains control to a height "necessary for ordinary use and enjoyment of the land."[145] A Croydon man who put a fibreglass spitfire on his roof challenged planning controls but raised no property issue.[146] Professor Gray has speculatively placed the division at a height of

---

[133] *Kelsen* v. *Imperial Tobacco Co (of GB and Ireland)* [1957] 2 QB 334, McNair J; *John Trenberth* v. *National Westminster Bank* (1979) 39 P & CR 104, 106.

[134] *Baten's case* (1610) 9 Co Rep 53b, 54a–b, 77 ER 810; *Fay* v. *Prentice* (1845) 1 CB 828, 838, 135 ER 769; *Ward* v. *Gold* (1969) 211 EG 155, 159; *Tollemache & Cobbold* v. *Reynolds* (1983) 268 EG 52.

[135] *Kelsen* [1957] 2 QB 334 (projection of 8 inches).

[136] *John Trenberth* (1979) 39 P & CR 104, 107–108; E McKendrick (1988) 138 *NLJ* 23.

[137] *Wandsworth Board of Works* v. *United Telephone Co* (1884) 13 QBD 904, 919, Bowen LJ.

[138] *Pickering* v. *Rudd* (1815) 4 Camp 219, 221, 171 ER 78; *Lonsdale* v. *Nelson* (1823) 2 B & C 302, 311, 107 ER 396; *Lemmon* v. *Webb* [1895] AC 1, HL (branches); *Mills* v. *Brooker* [1919] 1 KB 585 (cannot take fruit); *Morgan* v. *Khyatt* [1964] 1 WLR 475, PC.

[139] *Davey* v. *Harrow Corp* [1958] 1 QB 60, CA; *Smith* v. *Giddy* [1904] 2 KB 448; *Butler* v. *Standard Telephones & Cables* [1940] 1 KB 399; *Solloway* v. *Hampshire CC* (1981) 79 LGR 449; *Russell* v. *Barnet LBC* [1984] 2 EGLR 44; *Hampshire CC* v. *Milburn* [1991] 1 AC 325, HL.

[140] *McCombe* v. *Read* [1955] 2 QB 429; *King* v. *Taylor* [1976] 1 EGLR 132, Eveleigh J.

[141] Latin: *Cujus est solum, ejus est usque, ad coelem et ad inferos.*

[142] *Commissioners for Railways* v. *Valuer-General* [1974] AC 328, 351, Lord Wilberforce.

[143] PBH Birks "Before We Begin: Five Keys to Land Law" ch 18 in Bright & Dewar, 462; K Gray [1991] *CLJ* 252, 305; Grays' *Elements* (3rd ed), 16–21, 30–41; Megarry & Wade (6th ed), [3.051]; Panesar's *General Principles*, 163–167.

[144] Air is not land: *Great Western Rly Co* v. *Swindon & Cheltenham Extension Rly Co* (1884) 9 App Cas 787, HL.

[145] *Bernstein* v. *Skyviews & General* [1978] QB 479, 486F, Griffiths J.

[146] *Croydon LBC* v. *Gladden* [1994] EGCS 24, CA.

200m.[147] A flat field grazed by sheep might require very little protection of airspace, so that drifting close to the surface of a field in a balloon would not be a trespass.[148] Build if a skyscraper is built on the field the position must change, so that trespass would protect the walls of the building from being hit by a balloon or aircraft.

Little control exists over the higher airspace, despite the medieval assertion that ownership extends indefinitely upwards. Overflight by aircraft or satellites does not involve even a technical trespass. The claimant in *Bernstein* v. *Skyviews & General*[149] was offered an aerial photograph of his country house, but even if the plane had flown directly over land that he owned no trespass had been committed.[150]

---

[147] K Gray [1991] *CLJ* 252, 254; K Gray & SF Gray, "Property in Things" ch 1 in Bright & Dewar; PBH Birks, "Before We Begin: Five Keys to Land Law" ch 18 in Bright & Dewar, 467–470.

[148] *Pickering* v. *Rudd* (1815) 4 Comp 219, 220, 171 ER 70; *Saunders* v. *Smith* (1838) 2 Jur 491.

[149] [1978] QB 479.

[150] Anyway there was a defence under Civil Aviation Act 1949 s 40(1) (now the 1982 Act s 76(1)); at 488G–489H, Griffiths J (passage and aerial photography permitted, but not acrobatic display).

32

NEIGHBOUR OBLIGATIONS

Neighbours. Easements: rights of way; services; boundary structures; miscellaneous affirmative rights. Easement-like character and novel rights. Licences. Restrictions. Rights to light. Novel restrictive easements. Non-derogation. Restrictive covenants. Positive obligations between freeholders. Means of enforcing positive obligations.

A. NEIGHBOURS

1. Unsatisfactory state of the law

[32.01] No land is an island. Even land surrounded by water has boundaries beneath the water. However extensive his domain, the landowner has neighbours – a necessary adjunct of the division of land – and whether he likes it or not, to have neighbours is to have a relationship with them, at least at a legal level. Division implies the need to delineate boundaries, and the need for rights over the adjacent land.

Easements developed earlier than restrictive covenants, the one being recognised at common law whereas the other is a construct of equity leaving historical anomalies to permeate the law. These two basic categories interlock with a series of other rights – rights to sue in tort, the natural rights of all landowners, public rights, commons, profits and so on – along with shadowy principles such as non-derogation from grant and benefit and burden (in two flavours pure and impure). Finally there is an astounding defect in our law which does not permit the imposition by one freeholder of a positive obligation affecting a neighbour's freehold land so as to bind his successors. Positive obligations are non proprietary. Many neighbours do want to make binding commitments of just this kind, and it is simply not possible to operate a block of flats without a scheme of considerable ingenuity and complexity designed to circumvent this defect in the common law.[1]

Although property law has not yet developed it, there is a category of rights needed to regulate the legal relationship of neighbours.[2] They have a minus – in the shape of land burdened by the obligation – counterbalanced by a plus, that is land benefitted.[3] This disparate category is yet to fuse into a coherent whole.

---

[1] See above **[4.22ff]**.

[2] The Law Commission proposal to create a category of land obligations replacing restrictive covenants without assimilating easements was too limited: Law Com 127 (1984); more work is to be done on this proposal.

[3] The neighbour principle; see below **[33]**.

At present two expositions are required in parallel, one (this chapter) describing the rights which may be needed between adjacent owners and the other (the three succeeding chapters) outlining the main methods of creation – expressly, by division of the land and by long use (by prescription).

2. Types of neighbour obligations

[32.02] Neighbour obligations fall into three main categories

(1) Affirmative rights: rights to make use of neighbouring land:
affirmative (positive) easements such as rights of way; also public rights, profits and commons.
(2)   Restrictions: rights to restrict the use of a neighbour's land:
restrictive easements such as rights to light and support; rights created by non-derogation from grant; also restrictive covenants.
(3) Positive obligations: rights to have a neighbour spend money for the benefit of adjacent land:
freehold covenants are not proprietary but there are several means of evasion such as leasehold schemes, estate rentcharges, conditional benefits, and now commonholds.

B. RIGHTS OF WAY

1.   Private rights of way

[32.03] Access to a house is obviously essential. A right of way to particular land over neighbouring land is the archetype of an easement.[4] It is a private right enjoyed by one particular landowner as an adjunct to his ownership, but shared with the owner of the land.[5]

Most commonly rights of way are granted for general purposes, including use by any form of vehicle.[6] Under *White* v. *Grand Hotel, Eastbourne*[7] the way is not restricted to the use or requirements existing at the time of the grant.[8] The scope of any restriction is determined from the wording of the deed of grant. Use may be limited to foot traffic, or with various classes of animal, or it may be vehicular. Permitted

---

[4] Gale on *Easements* (Sweet & Maxwell, 16th ed by J Gaunt & P Morgan, 1997); also Chappelle *Land Law* (5th ed) ch 12; Cheshire & Burn (16th ed) ch 18; Dixon's *Principles* (3rd ed) ch 7; Goo's *Sourcebook* (3rd ed) ch 16; Gravells, *LL – Text* (2nd ed) ch 7; Grays' *Elements* (3rd ed), 450–514, 591–597; Maudsley & Burn *LL – Cases* (7th ed) ch 10; Megarry & Wade (6th ed), [18.040–18.078]; Smith's *Property Law* (4th ed) ch 20; Swadling "Property" ch 4 in Birks' *English Private Law*, [4.149–4.153]; Thompson's *Modern LL* ch 13.

[5] *Thorpe* v. *Brumfitt* (1873) LR 8 Ch App 650; *Jelbert* v. *Davis* [1968] 1 WLR 589, CA.

[6] *Kain* v. *Norfolk* [1949] Ch 163, Jenkins J; *Jelbert* v. *Davis* [1968] 1 WLR 589, CA; *Robinson* v. *Bailey* [1948] 2 All ER 791, CA (building materials); *Rosling* v. *Pinnegar* (1987) 54 P & CR 124 (public visits to stately home); *Jalnarne* v. *Ridewood* (1989) 61 P & CR 143; *McKay* v. *Surrey CC* [1998] EGCS 180, Ch D.

[7] (1912) 106 LT 785, CA.

[8] *Finch* v. *Great Western Rly* (1879) 5 Ex D 254; *Coopind (UK)* v. *Walton Commercial Group* [1989] 1 EGLR 241, Hoffmann J; HW Wilkinson [1989] *NLJ* 1384; *Jalnarne* v. *Ridewood* (1989) 61 P & CR 143; *Fairview New Homes* v. *Government Row Residents Ass* [1998] EGCS 92, Scott V-C.

purposes can also be limited. A right of way to carry materials to repair a cottage does not authorise the carrying of construction materials.[9] Access for agricultural purposes does not permit access for a caravan park.[10] Limited access can be granted for repair of the gable wall of a cottage,[11] or to drive a land rover on to down land to fill water troughs.[12]

The width of the way is of vital importance. Ownership of a driveway carries with it the right to build right up to its boundary,[13] and trivial interferences or alterations to the burdened land have to be tolerated,[14] but action can be taken against any substantial interference with the right granted.[15] Examples are narrowing the way,[16] restricting the height of a right of way,[17] making access to a garage more difficult,[18] removing footpaths on either side of a carriageway,[19] or parking cars of other tenants.[20] Alterations may be allowed by reserving a right of variation.[21] There is no right to deviate from the line of a right of way[22]

A right of way may or may not include a claim to park whilst loading and unloading.[23]

2. Ransom strips

[32.04] Gaps between land and the adjacent public highway are called ransom strips. Rights of way are not necessarily implied and it is quite possible for a house to be landlocked, a fact which will greatly reduce its value.[24]

The owner of the strip is entitled to charge for its use, holding the landlocked owner to ransom or indeed to refuse all use of it. Neighbours cannot be compelled to grant easements. Whatever the moral position, there is nothing legally improper about exploiting a ransom strip and the onus is on a person buying land to ensure that he has all necessary rights over neighbouring plots.

---

[9] *Wimbledon & Putney Commons Conservators* v. *Dixon* (1875) 1 Ch D 362, CA.

[10] *RPC Holdings* v. *Rogers* [1953] 1 All ER 1029; *Johnson* v. *Record* (1998) 75 P & CR 375, CA.

[11] *Ward* v. *Kirkland* [1967] Ch 194; *Williams* v. *Usherwood* (1983) 45 P & CR 235, CA.

[12] *White* v. *Taylor (No 2)* [1969] 1 Ch 160.

[13] *Minor* v. *Groves* (2000) 80 P & CR 136, CA; *Soper* v. *Leeman-Hawley* [1993] CLYB 1622; *West* v. *Sharp* (2000) 79 P & CR 327, CA (right not limited to hardcore track).

[14] *Dawes* v. *Adela Estates* (1970) 216 EG 1405 (automatic lock on external door of block did not interfere with the access to the flats).

[15] *Petty* v. *Parsons* [1914] 2 Ch 653.

[16] *B & Q* v. *Liverpool & Lancashire Properties* [2001] 1 EGLR 92, Blackburne J.

[17] *VT Engineering* v. *Richard Barland & Co* (1968) 19 P & CR 890, Megarry J.

[18] *Celsteel* v. *Alton House Holdings* [1985] 1 WLR 204, Scott J; on appeal [1986] 1 WLR 512, CA.

[19] *Scott* v. *Martin* [1987] 1 WLR 841, CA.

[20] *Hilton* v. *James Smith & Sons (Norwood)* [1979] 2 EGLR 44, CA.

[21] *Overcom Properties* v. *Stockleigh Hall Resident Management* [1989] 1 EGLR 75, CA. Complete removal of a promised right may be a derogation from grant: *Saeed* v. *Plustrade* [2001] EWCA Civ 2011, [2002] 2 EGLR 19.

[22] *Bullard* v. *Harrison* (1815) 4 M & S 387, 105 ER 877; *Selby* v. *Nettlefold* (1873) LR 9 Ch App 111.

[23] Affirmative answer in *VT Engineering* v. *Richard Barland & Co* (1968) 19 P & CR 890, Megarry J; negative in *London & Suburban Land & Building Co (Holdings)* v. *Carey* (1991) 62 P & CR 480, Millett J.

[24] *J Murphy & Sons* v. *Railtrack* [2002] EWCA Civ 679, [2002] 31 EG 99; see below **[34]**.

3. Public highways

[32.05] Public rights exist over ways called highways. These are available to all members of the public, without any requirement for landownership and no easement is required.[25] Access may be controlled for example by planning rules.

4. Private street works

[32.06] John Betjeman's subaltern fantasised about being driven by "roads 'not adopted', by woodlanded ways" to dance with Miss Joan Hunter Dunn.[26] The poet encapsulated the status value of living on a private street, but it can be a costly privilege. The highway authority may choose to execute works on an unsatisfactory private street, apportioning the cost between the owners fronting the street (frontagers).[27] New buildings fronting a private street will not be permitted until the builder has paid over to the highway authority the cost of any works required to the street.[28] On a new building estate, the builder constructs the roads, but invariably enters into an agreement with the local highway authority to ensure that the estate roads will be adopted as highways maintainable at public expense on an agreed date.[29] The cost of making the road up to the proper standard falls on the builder. A person buying a house on a new building estate must ensure that there is an adequate provision for adoption of the estate roads and for maintenance in the interim period.[30]

C. RIGHTS TO SERVICES

[32.07] Le Corbusier said that a house is a machine for living in. Services are needed to keep that machine running.

1. Pipes and cables

[32.08] Access is needed for pipes and wires – for water, electricity, telephone wires, rainwater, and foul water waste and hi-tech cables for electricity and computers.[31] These must be secured independently of and in addition to any right of way.[32] Pipes may be shared with the owner, but drains[33] and cables are more likely to be exclusive, in which case they may fall into the next category.

---

[25] *Dovaston* v. *Payne* (1795) 2 Hy Bl 527, 531, 126 ER 684, Heath J; *Rangeley* v. *Midland Rly Co* (1868) LR 3 Ch App 306, 311, Cairns LC.

[26] *A Subaltern's Love-Song*, l 29.

[27] Highways Act 1980 s 205 (private street works code).

[28] S 219 (advance payments code); a buyer must check on compliance.

[29] S 38(3).

[30] This is achieved by a bond ie a deposit of money with a bank to cover the developer's commitments.

[31] *Trailfinders* v. *Razuki* [1988] 2 EGLR 46, Ch D

[32] *Penn* v. *Wilkins* [1975] 2 EGLR 113, Megarry J.

[33] *Simmons* v. *Midford* [1969] 2 Ch 415; *Lee* v. *Stevenson* (1858) EB & E 512, 120 ER 600.

2. Corporeal parts

[32.09] A corporeal thing has a tangible existence (animal, vegetable or mineral) so that it can be touched, as for example with houses, trees, and gardens.[34] Exclusive or unrestricted use of a thing passes the property or ownership in it as land, as opposed to giving an easement to use it.[35] Examples are tunnels,[36] gateways,[37] coal shoots,[38] overhanging eaves of a house,[39] and the name plate.[40] These pass automatically on sale, and on a division of ownership the thing attaches to the part with which it is naturally enjoyed, whether it is the part sold or the part retained.[41]

3. Wayleaves for utilities

[32.10] Many easements are created by statute or under statutory powers,[42] for example wayleaves for telephone wires or electricity cables, usually subject to the payment of compensation.[43] Statutory rights may[44] operate within the framework of easement law, but they do not need to do so.[45] Services provided by public undertakers include mains water and sewerage,[46] electricity,[47] gas,[48] and telecommunications.[49] Undertakers generally have a duty to provide a supply to an existing infrastructure,[50] and a power to install new infrastructure paid for by the consumer,[51] with necessary powers to construct new infrastructure under public roads and streets,[52] and compulsory purchase powers.[53] Properties abutting the public street will be able to secure direct access to mains services but if private land has to

---

[34] As with land itself, ownership of a "corporeal hereditament" consists of an abstract right to the physical thing.

[35] *Crown Estate Commissioners* v. *City of London* (1994) 158 LGR 681, CA.

[36] *Metropolitan Rly Co* v. *Fowler* [1893] AC 416, HL; C Sweet (1916) 32 *LQR* 70, 427.

[37] *Reilly* v. *Booth* (1890) 44 Ch D 12, CA.

[38] *Hinchliff* v. *Kinnoul* (1838) 5 Bing NC 1, 132 ER 1004.

[39] *Simmons* v. *Midford* [1969] 2 Ch 415, Buckley J. Eavesdrop is an associated easement giving the right to drain rainwater on to the neighbouring garden off the eaves of a thatched house, though not in a spout: *Reynolds* v. *Clarke* (1725) 2 Ld Raym 1399, 92 ER 410.

[40] *Francis* v. *Hayward* (1882) 22 Ch D 177, CA.

[41] *Wheeldon* v. *Burrows* (1879) 12 Ch D 31, 60–61, James LJ; *Union Lighterage Co* v. *London Graving Dock Co* [1902] 2 Ch 557.

[42] JF Garner (1956) 20 *Conv (NS)* 208.

[43] *Mercury Communications* v. *London & India Dock Investments* (1995) 69 P & CR 135.

[44] *Mason* v. *Shrewsbury & Hereford Rly* (1871) LR 6 QB 578.

[45] *Great Western Rly Co* v. *Swindon & Cheltenham Extension Rly Co* (1884) 9 App Cas 787, 792, Lord Fitzgerald; *Taff Vale Rly Co* v. *Cardiff Rly Co* [1917] 1 Ch 299, 316, CA (statutory right could be exclusive).

[46] Both under the Water Industry Act 1991.

[47] Electricity Act 1989; Utilities Act 2000.

[48] Gas Act 1986; Utilities Act 2000.

[49] Telecommunications Act 1984; Cable and Broadcasting Act 1984; Broadcasting Act 1990.

[50] Water Industry Act 1991 s 106–109; Gas Act 1986 ss 7–8; etc.

[51] Gas Act 1986 ss 7–8; Electricity Act 1989 s 19; Water Industry Act 1991 s 98–99; s 219(1); *Thames Water Utilities* v. *Hampstead Homes (London)* [2002] EWCA Civ 1487, [2002] 43 EG 202 (CS) (office conversion to flats).

[52] Telecommunications Act 1984 sch 2 para 9; Electricity Act 1989 sch 4; Gas Act 1986 sch 4. Traffic managers are to co-ordinate work.

[53] Telecommunications Act 1984 ss 34–41; Gas Act 1986 sch 3; Electricity Act 1989 sch 3.

be crossed a private easement is required ("a wayleave") unless undertakers have the right to cross private land.[54]

Private sewers can be adopted by agreement or by declaration by the sewage undertaker.[55] On a new housing estate the developer will construct the sewers and enter into a sewerage agreement to ensure that they are taken over by the undertaker.

4. Perpetuity

[32.11] Easements to use existing services may continue indefinitely, but an easement to use a feature to be constructed in the future must be confined within a perpetuity period. An easement to use "sewers hereafter to pass" was void since it gave a right to use future easements without limit of time.[56] The decision attracted considerable opprobrium.[57] Under modern law it would be possible to wait and see, and it is usual to adopt the statutory perpetuity period of 80 years, thus validating an easement to use a feature actually constructed within that period.[58] It is now proposed to remove easements from the scope of the rule completely, a most welcome development.[59]

D. BOUNDARY STRUCTURES

1. Party walls

[32.12] A boundary dividing the land of two neighbours may be in the sole ownership of one or other of them.[60] Practice has sanctioned the use of a T mark on plans, the head of the T pointing into the land carrying ownership of the fence.[61] Alternatively two neighbours may be joint tenants[62] of the boundary, in which case neither can deal with it without the consent of the other. More common still is a party arrangement, particularly where a wall separates two terraced or semi-detached houses. Each owns half to a vertical line down the middle of the wall,[63] but removal of that half is prevented by an obligation on owner A to support B's half of the wall, that obligation being either expressed or created by prescription after 20 years.[64] *Prudential*

---

[54] Telecommunications Act 1984 sch 2 para 10 (3 m above ground and 2 m clear of buildings); Electricity Act 1989 sch 4 para 6; *British Waterways Board* v. *London Power Networks* [2002] EWHC 2417, [2003] 1 All ER 187; Water Industry Act 1991 ss 46, 159; etc.

[55] Water Industry Act 1991 ss 102–104; there is an appeal mechanism.

[56] *Dunn* v. *Blackdown Properties* [1961] 2 All ER 62, Cross J; RH Maudsley (1961) 25 *Conv (NS)* 415, 416–418; *South Eastern Rly Co* v. *Associated Portland Cement Manufacturers (1900)* [1910] 1 Ch 12, CA (equivocal); *Newnham* v. *Lawson* (1971) 22 P & CR 852; *Nickerson* v. *Barraclough* [1981] Ch 426, 434G, Brightman LJ.

[57] G Battersby (1961) 25 *Conv (NS)* 415; JT Farrand (1962) 106 *SJ* 123, 147; L Elphinstone (1963) 107 *SJ* 2; K Scott [1961] *CLJ* 175.

[58] Perpetuities and Accumulations Act 1964 ss 1, 3; J Tiley (1966) 110 *SJ* 694, 720.

[59] Law Com 251 (1998), [7.41]; P Sparkes (1998) 12 *TLI* 148, 156.

[60] *Jones* v. *Stones* [1999] 1 WLR 1739, CA (flowerpots on wall were trespass).

[61] They have been included on LR filed plans since 1962 if: (1) referred to in the documentary title; or (2) contained without explanation on pre-registration plans.

[62] LPA 1925 s 34. An attempt to create a legal tenancy in common in a boundary structure operates to create a party wall: s 38(1).

[63] Disputes: s 38(2); A Samuels (1993) 137 *SJ* 331.

[64] *Jones* v. *Pritchard* [1908] 1 Ch 630; *Sack* v. *Jones* [1925] Ch 235.

Assurance Co v. *Waterloo Real Estate*[65] shows that it is possible to take adverse possession of the other half of a party wall of it by repairing the whole and by including the whole in a lease.

2. Support

[32.13] There is no right to insist that the neighbour's land is kept in its natural condition, but there is a right to insist that he will provide support if he digs it out.[66] This is a *natural* right of support for *land* as an incident of ownership. Lateral support is required where the ground is dug away, for example to form a gravel pit, to extract clay,[67] or to prepare foundations for building work or where cliffs collapse into the sea.[68]

Buildings require an *easement* of support. The leading case, *Dalton* v. *Henry Angus & Co*[69] concerns support by one building for another, but exactly the same principle applies to a terrace of buildings,[70] within a block of flats,[71] where a building is supported by neighbouring land, or timber structures are supported.[72] A right of support is sometimes described as a restrictive (or negative) easement, since the main obligation is not to withdraw support,[73] and is usually enforced by an injunction.[74] However, a majority of the House of Lords regarded it as affirmative (or positive), since use is made of the neighbouring building by the pressure exerted upon it.[75] The right is almost always created by prescription.

3. Work to party walls

[32.14] The Party Wall etc Act 1996[76] applies when work is proposed on a boundary after June 1997.[77] Existing rules governing Inner London[78] are clarified and extended to the whole country.[79] A building owner[80] must serve a notice on the adjoining owner

---

[65] [1999] 2 EGLR 85, CA.

[66] *Dalton* v. *Henry Angus & Co* (1881) 6 App Cas 740, 791, Selborne LC, 808, Lord Blackburn; *Grays' Elements* (3rd ed), 11.

[67] *Morris* v. *Redland Bricks* [1967] 1 WLR 967, CA.

[68] *Holbeck Hall Hotel* v. *Scarborough BC* [2000] QB 836, CA.

[69] (1881) 6 App Cas 740, HL; JF Garner (1948) 12 *Conv (NS)* 280; EH Bodkin (1962) 26 *Conv (NS)* 210; TH Wu [2002] *Conv* 237.

[70] *Solomon* v. *Vintner's Co* (1859) 5 H & N 585, 157 ER 970; *Dalton* at 826.

[71] Impressively early is *Pomfret* v. *Ricroft* (1669) 1 Wms Saund 321, 85 ER 454, note (b).

[72] *Woodhouse* v. *Consolidated Property Corp* (1993) 66 P & CR 234, 243, Glidewell LJ.

[73] *Dalton* v. *Henry Angus & Co* (1881) 6 App Cas 740, 763, Lindley J, 776, Fry J; *Byard* v. *Co-operative Permanent BS* (1970) 21 P & CR 807. There is no duty to repair: *Southwark & Vauxhall Water Co* v. *Wandsworth Board of Works* [1898] 2 Ch 603, CA.

[74] *Morris* v. *Redland Brick* [1967] 1 WLR 967, CA.

[75] *Dalton* at 792, Selborne LC, 797, Lord Watson, also Pollock B, Lindley and Bowen LJJ; *Great Northern Railway Co* v. *IRC* [1901] 1 KB 416, 429, Stirling LJ; *Phipps* v. *Pears* [1965] 1 QB 76, 82C, Lord Denning MR (hybrid).

[76] JE Adams [1996] *Conv* 326; G Powell (1998) 142 *SJ* 772.

[77] SI 1997/670.

[78] London Building Acts (Amendment) Act 1939 ss 45–59, as amended; D Wright (1955) 18 *Conv (NS)* 347.

[79] Except the Inner Temple and certain Crown interests: ss 18–19.

[80] S 20. An "owner" includes a person in receipt of rent and a purchaser under an agreement; excluded are lenders, yearly tenants, those with lesser terms, and statutory tenants: *Frances Holland School* v. *Wassef* [2001] 2 EGLR 88, Ct Ct.

before commencing work, as otherwise the work is a nuisance.[81] Work covered falls into three categories:[82] (1) New boundaries which are to be party structures require the neighbour's consent, but notice must also be given of any new wall in sole owner-ship. (2) Work to existing party structures requires notice, whether a repair or a tying in. (3) Excavation within six metres of a boundary. In each case notice and counter notice procedures are laid down, with disputes resolved by an agreed surveyor.[83] Work must respect the neighbour's existing rights to light, other easements, and other property rights.[84]

4. Hedges

[32.15] It is estimated that there are 17,000 problem hedges in England and Wales, almost all *Leylandii*, a vigorous cypress growing at up to two metres a year and poten-tially reaching 130 feet. The High Hedges Bill 2002[85] aims to give councils discretion to act against evergreen trees exceeding two metres in height. A hedge is a barrier formed by two or more evergreens.[86] The basis for complaint would be that the hedge was unreasonably restricting light to domestic property of residential occupiers, such as a house or garden.[87] A protocol will require two written requests to the owner followed by an official notice procedure and appeal process which will bind future owners.[88]

E. MISCELLANEOUS AFFIRMATIVE RIGHTS

1. Storage rights

[32.16] Easements may not give exclusive rights over another's land,[89] but they may confer limited rights of storage or parking. The distinction turns on the degree of interference with the use of the burdened land by its owner. An easement to use a gar-den leaves the soil and its produce unaffected.[90] The right to use a toilet discussed in *Miller* v. *Emcer Products*[91] was clearly exclusive during actual use, but overall this exclusion was trivial.

Storage highlights this problem of allocation. Exclusion occurs while items are stored, but according to the degree it may exclude the burdened owner from his land

---

[81] *Louis* v. *Sadiq* [1997] 1 EGLR 136, CA; *Sims* v. *Estates Co* (1866) 14 LT 55 (injunction); *Lehmann* v. *Herman* [1993] 1 EGLR 172 (all joint tenants).

[82] Respectively Party Wall etc Act 1996 ss 1, 2, 6.

[83] Grounds must be stated in the award: *Frances Holland School* v. *Wassef* [2001] 2 EGLR 88, Ct Ct; it is not registrable: *Observatory Hill* v. *Camtel Investments* [1997] 1 EGLR 140, Ch D.

[84] S 9; *Crofts* v. *Haldane* (1867) LR 2 QB 194; *Burlington Property Co* v. *Odeon Theatres* [1939] 1 KB 633, CA (conversion of window to door refused).

[85] HL Bill 4; HW Wilkinson [2002] *NLJ* 10.

[86] Cl 2.

[87] Cl 3.

[88] Cls 4–9.

[89] See below **[32.24]**.

[90] *Re Ellenborough Park* [1956] Ch 131, 176; *Mulvaney* v. *Gough* [2002] EWCA Civ 1078, [2002] 44 EG 175.

[91] [1956] Ch 304, CA.

or it may exclude him from a defined part of a larger whole. Suitably limited, the right can be an easement.[92] A burial right is one, rather final, illustration.[93] *Wright* v. *Macadam*[94] accepted a right to store coal in a coal cellar, following an earlier case on storage of goods awaiting shipment on a foreshore,[95] but not an unlimited right of storage in a confined space.[96] Leniency is appropriate since the doctrinal issue is not whether to create a proprietary burden but merely how to classify a known burden.

2. Parking

[32.17] Parking merits separate treatment only because the common law has moved so slowly to reflect the general use of cars. In *Copeland* v. *Greenhalf*[97] a garage owner failed in a prescriptive claim to have a right to use a strip of land adjoining the lane leading to his garage to store vehicles which were waiting to be repaired. Unlimited parking[98] and exclusive use of a private garage would fail for the same reason. No easement can exist if the true owner is excluded from his land or his ownership has become illusory.[99]

However, a limited parking right can be an easement, even if easement-like status is not finally settled at appellate level.[100] Indeed, few rights would be more important to the owner of a flat in a city centre than the right to park his car on nearby land. So, in *Handel* v. *St Stephens Close*[101] rights to park on the access roads to a block of flats were recognised as an easement attached to the flats in the development, and the developer was prevented from interfering by marking out parking bays. Another case recognises the right to load or unload a lorry.[102] Shared use of a visitors' parking space on a flat development should occur by easement.[103] More borderline is a claim by long term parking on one particular spot on a larger servient tenement – does this exclude the owner from that particular space or is it a non-exclusive use of the larger servient plot?

Parking rights that are precarious cannot create easements but a more limited protection may be available in the principle of non-derogation from grant.[104]

---

[92] *Mast* v. *Goodson* (1772) 2 Wm Bl 848, 96 ER 500; *Wood* v. *Hewett* (1846) 8 QB 913, 115 ER 1118.

[93] *Bryan* v. *Whistler* (1828) 8 B & C 288, 108 ER 1050; P Sparkes [1991] *Ecclesiastical LJ* 133.

[94] [1949] 2 KB 744.

[95] *Att-Gen for Southern Nigeria* v. *John Holt & Co (Liverpool)* [1915] AC 599, PC; *Smith* v. *Gates* [1952] Ch 814.

[96] *Grigsby* v. *Melville* [1974] 1 WLR 455, CA; JR Spencer [1974] *CLJ* 51.

[97] [1952] Ch 488, Upjohn J; P Luther (1996) 16 *LS* 51.

[98] A claim to adverse possession might just have succeeded if the case had been pleaded differently; only 12 years possession is required.

[99] *Batchelor* v. *Marlow* [2001] 1 EGLR 119, CA; *(No 2)* [2001] EWCA Civ 1051, (2001) 82 P & CR 36.

[100] *Saeed* v. *Plustrade* [2001] EWCA Civ 2011, [2002] 2 EGLR 19, [222], Sir Christopher Slade; *P & S Platt* v. *Crouch* [2002] EWHC 2195 (Ch), [2002] 45 EG 153 (right to moor).

[101] [1994] 1 EGLR 70; HW Wilkinson [1994] *NLJ* 579; *Penn* v. *Wilkins* [1975] 2 EGLR 113, Megarry J; *London & Blenheim Estates* v. *Retail Parks* [1994] 1 WLR 31, CA.

[102] *Thorpe* v. *Brumfitt* (1873) LR 8 Ch App 650.

[103] *Patel* v. *WH Smith (Eziot)* [1987] 1 WLR 853, CA (conceded).

[104] *Hair* v. *Gillman* [2000] 3 EGLR 74, CA; *Saeed* v. *Plustrade* [2001] EWCA Civ 2011, [2002] 2 EGLR 19.

3.   Other miscellaneous rights

[32.18] Rights may be needed to overhang or fix to a neighbour's land. A wall may need support from a tree,[105] or a wharf from the bed of the Thames,[106] and it may be necessary to hang washing over a neighbour's yard[107] or fix advertisements on his wall.[108] On a grander scale, drainage and sea defences are fruitful sources of easements. Cases recognise the right to protection of a house from the sea,[109] a right to enter land to open a sluice,[110] and a right to have a dock kept open.[111]

F.   EASEMENT-LIKE CHARACTER

[32.19] Cheshire set out the classical statement of the requirements for the existence of an easement, which are:[112]

(1) Dominant and servient tenements (that is land benefitted and land burdened);
(2) Accommodation of (that is benefit to) the dominant tenement;
(3) Separate ownership or occupation of the two tenements; and
(4) A right capable of forming the subject matter of a deed of grant.

Cheshire's first and third points make clear that easements must comply with the neighbour principle, so that rights unattached to land are not easements,[113] the principle discussed in the next chapter. Here attention is focused on the quality of the rights which are easement-like, but Cheshire's grouping has become imbalanced because more and more sub-heads cluster around rule 4, whereas rule 2 has little substance. This book seeks a pattern which more nearly reflects the emphasis of the modern law listing a series of factors which negate a claim to the status of an easement.

1.   Non-accommodation (non-relation to land)

[32.20] An easement is an right incident to and annexed to property for its more beneficial and profitable enjoyment.[114] This appears as Cheshire's requirement for it to be "accommodated".[115] Excluded are rights which merely benefit the landowner

---

[105] *Hawkings* v. *Wallis* (1763) 2 Wils KB 173, 95 ER 750; *Simpson* v. *Weber* (1925) 133 LT 46 (creeper).
[106] *Lancaster* v. *Eve* (1859) 5 CB (NS) 717, 141 ER 288.
[107] *Drewell* v. *Towler* (1832) 3 B & Ad 735, 110 ER 268.
[108] *Hoare* v. *Metropolitan Board of Works* (1874) LR 9 QB 296; *Moody* v. *Steggles* (1879) 12 Ch D 261; *Francis* v. *Hayward* (1882) 22 Ch D 177 (house name plate).
[109] *Philpot* v. *Bath* (1905) 21 TLR 634.
[110] *Simpson* v. *Godmanchester Corp* [1897] AC 696, HL.
[111] *Morton* v. *Snow* (1873) 29 LT 591, PC.
[112] Cheshire & Burn (16th ed), 570–574; *Re Ellenborough Park* [1956] Ch 131, 163, Evershed MR; *Ward* v. *Kirkland* [1967] Ch 194, 222, Ungoed-Thomas J.
[113] See below **[33]**.
[114] *Mounsey* v. *Ismay* (1865) 3 H & C 486, 499, 159 ER 621, Martin B.
[115] *Keppell* v. *Bailey* (1834) 2 My & K 517, 537, 39 ER 1042, Brougham LC; *Re Ellenborough Park* [1956] Ch 131, 169, Evershed MR.

personally.[116] Increase in value of the land is indicative of a benefit to the land, but is not alone sufficient. A right of free entry to Lords Cricket Ground might enhance the value of a house in south London but could not be easement. In *Re Ellenborough Park*,[117] a mid-Victorian development in Weston-super-Mare was laid out around a central railed garden, shared in common by the owners of all the houses round the park. Enjoyment of this communal garden was annexed to neighbouring houses,[118] pleasure being incidental,[119] though rights cannot be easements if they are "mere rights of recreation, possessing no quality of utility or benefit".

Hill v. *Tupper*[120] concerned a rural idyll in the unlikely setting (to modern eyes) of the Basingstoke Canal. The tenant of a piece of land adjoining the canal had the exclusive right of letting pleasure boats for hire on the canal. He sued a publican who had placed his own boats on the canal, but failed. No doubt the *canal company* would have succeeded, and they may have been liable for allowing the publican to infringe the exclusive contract they had given. Direct action by the grantee of this right against the intruder depended on the existence of an easement. Only an estate in the site of the canal could bind someone outside the contractual relationship.[121] The plaintiff failed, according to Evershed MR's later rationalisation,[122] because he:

> "was trying to . . . set up, under the guise of an easement, a monopoly which had no normal connexion with the ordinary use of his land, but which was merely an independent business enterprise."

Businesses can of course make use of recognised easements. In *Moody* v. *Steggles*,[123] a long established pub successfully claimed the right to fix a pub sign on the adjoining house. Accommodation only becomes an issue with marginal rights. Loss of the benefit should end the easement.[124]

2. Precariousness

[32.21] An easement must create a right, and so use of a feature that is dependent on the whim of the burdened owner cannot be an easement.[125] A right of way fails if it is only available when gates are open and when the way is not required for the landlord's business,[126] as does a claim to take water if and when available[127] or to parking at the landlord's discretion.[128]

---

[116] Benefit to other land is no problem: *Bailey* v. *Stephens* (1862) 12 CB (NS) 91, 142 ER 1077; *Simpson* v. *Godmanchester Corp* [1897] AC 696, HL.

[117] [1956] Ch 131, CA; RE Megarry (1956) 72 *LQR* 16; RN Gooderson [1956] *CLJ* 24.

[118] At 175, Evershed MR; *Mulvaney* v. *Gough* [2002] EWCA Civ 1078, [2002] 44 EG 175.

[119] At 164, 172, 178–179; *Mounsey* v. *Ismay* (1865) 3 H & C 486, 159 ER 621 (horse racing).

[120] (1863) 2 H & C 121, 159 ER 51; *Ackroyd* v. *Smith* (1850) 10 CB 164, 138 ER 68.

[121] At 128, Martin B.

[122] *Re Ellenborough Park* [1956] Ch 131, 175.

[123] (1879) 12 Ch D 261, Fry J; *Copeland* v. *Greenhalf* [1952] Ch 488, Upjohn J.

[124] *Huckvale* v. *Aegean Hotels* (1989) 58 P & CR 163, CA; G Kodilinye [1990] *Conv* 292.

[125] *Arkwright* v. *Gell* (1839) 5 M & W 203, 151 ER 87; *Brett* v. *Clowser* (1880) 5 CPD 376, 383, Denman J.

[126] *Green* v. *Ashco Horticulturalist* [1966] 1 WLR 889, Cross J; S Roberts (1966) 29 *MLR* 574.

[127] *Burrows* v. *Lang* [1901] 2 Ch 502; *International Tea Stores* v. *Hobbs* [1903] 2 Ch 165, 171–172, Farwell J; *Schwann* v. *Cotton* [1916] 2 Ch 120; *Wright* v. *Macadam* [1949] 2 KB 744, 750, Jenkins LJ; *Goldberg* v. *Edwards* [1950] Ch 247, 255–256, Evershed MR.

[128] *Saeed* v. *Plustrade* [2001] EWCA Civ 2011, [2002] 2 EGLR 19.

3. Uncertainty

[32.22] Any easement must be precisely defined, so that the parties can tell whether or not it has been infringed. Limiting the width of possible rights ensures that ownership of land cannot be completely negated by the grant of an easement,[129] reasoning which applies with equal force to documentary and to prescriptive easements. Case-law examples give a feel for the test. A right to wander at pleasure is accepted if confined to a specific garden,[130] but not over a much wider area such as a park or golf course. A right to light on a whole building is not accepted, but to a particular window it is.[131]

Uncertain rights have a different jizz.[132] No wonder that a right to an unlimited current of air has been rejected, however important it was for the paper drying industry,[133] when contrasted with the well recognised easement of drawing air through a precisely defined ventilation shaft.[134] Rejected for vagueness are rights to privacy, to a view, and to protection from the weather by an adjoining house. Lord Denning MR has said such an easement would unduly restrict a neighbour in his enjoyment of his own land and hamper legitimate development,[135] though curiously the same restriction could be imposed as a covenant.[136]

4. Positivity

[32.23] Expense incurred by the burdened owner is a bar to the recognition of a putative right since easements of all kinds (with the sole exception of fencing) must be negative in nature.[137]

5. Exclusivity

[32.24] This rule is concerned with the allocation of burdens between different legal categories. Exclusive possession may be conferred by a freehold estate, a lease or a licence.[138] Easements operate as a burden on other ownership rather than as an ownership right in the land used. The distinction turns on the degree of interference with the use of the burdened land by its owner. An easement to use a garden leaves the soil and its produce unaffected.[139] The right to use a toilet discussed in *Miller* v. *Emcer Products*[140] was clearly exclusive during actual use, but this was a trivial exclusion

---

[129] *Copeland* v. *Greenhalf* [1952] Ch 488, Upjohn J; *Dyce* v. *Hay* (1852) 1 Macq 305, 312, Lord St Leonards LC; *Re Webb's Lease* [1951] Ch 808, 815, Evershed MR.

[130] *Re Ellenborough Park* [1956] Ch 131, 177–187, Evershed MR. Earlier authorities on the *jus spatiendi* were mixed: *Duncan* v. *Louch* (1845) 6 QB 904, 115 ER 341; *Keith* v. *20th Century Club* (1904) 20 TLR 462; *International Tea Stores Co* v. *Hobbs* [1903] 2 Ch 165; *Att-Gen* v. *Antrobus* [1905] 2 Ch 188, Farwell J.

[131] See below **[32.28]**.

[132] A term applied to birds which, without any overt distinguishing characteristics, seem different to an observer.

[133] *Webb* v. *Bird* (1862) 13 CB (NS) 841, 143 ER 332; *Chastey* v. *Ackland* [1897] AC 155, HL.

[134] *Bass* v. *Gregory* (1890) 25 QBD 481; *Wong* v. *Beaumont* [1965] 1 QB 173, CA.

[135] *Phipps* v. *Pears* [1965] 1 QB 76, 83E.

[136] At 83D; *Webb* v. *Bird* as above; EH Bodkin (1971) 35 *Conv (NS)* 324.

[137] See below **[32.49]**, **[36.27]**.

[138] Statutory rights can be proprietary: *Taff Vale Rly Co* v. *Cardiff Rly Co* [1917] 1 Ch 299, 316, CA.

[139] *Re Ellenborough Park* [1956] Ch 131, 176.

[140] [1956] Ch 304, CA.

overall. Storage and parking provide most of the case law illustrations of these principles.[141]

G. NOVEL AFFIRMATIVE RIGHTS

[32.25] Easements were once thought to form a closed category.[142] Novel burdens might reduce the market value of land or render it completely unsaleable or, as Pollock CB put the same argument in *Hill* v. *Tupper*:[143]

> "New rights or incidents of property cannot be created at the pleasure of the owners. . . . [T]he owner of an estate must be content to take it with the rights and incidents known to and allowed by the law."

Land must not be carved up into infinite number of tiny use rights.

This principle remains accepted law for restrictive (negative) easements[144] but a more relaxed view is now taken of claims to new affirmative (positive) easements.[145] Novel rights were once considered by analogy to existing ones. A wayleave for telephone wires is similar to the old easement to run a washing line across a yard and recognised on that analogy, but this inherently conservative principle was a hit or miss way of dealing with new technological developments. Lord Evershed MR broke the mould in *Re Ellenborough Park* by deciding in favour of the new easement (to use a private garden) without establishing the analogy of the *jus spatiandi* (a right for perambulators to wander about), or similarity to any other existing right. Once a new easement right passes the hurdles set out above for easement-like character, the presumption shifts in favour of recognising it. Technological innovation is so rapid that the courts must be able to adapt property law to cope. Railways, canals, telegraphs and telephones have all required new rights. The challenges have moved on to helicopters, hi-tech cables and parking, and there are new ones as yet undreamt of to come.[146]

H. LICENCES

[32.26] Other easement-like rights may create licences, because of informality,[147] charitable instinct,[148] lack of some essential characteristic of an easement,[149] or lack

---

[141] See above **[32.16ff]**.

[142] *Keppell* v. *Bailey* (1834) 2 My & K 577, 39 ER 1055; *Ackroyd* v. *Smith* (1850) 10 CB 164, 138 ER 68.

[143] (1863) 2 H & C 121, 127, 159 ER 51.

[144] *Phipps* v. *Pears* [1965] 1 QB 76, CA; see below **[32.33]**.

[145] [1956] Ch 131, 140, Dankwerts J.

[146] *Dyce* v. *Hay* (1852) 1 Macq 305, 315, St Leonards LC.

[147] *Fentiman* v. *Smith* (1803) 4 East 102, 102 ER 770; *Hyde* v. *Graham* (1862) 1 H & C 593, 158 ER 1020; *Winter* v. *Brockwell* (1807) 8 East 308, 103 ER 359; *Tayler* v. *Waters* (1816) 7 Taunt 374, 129 ER 150; *Duke of Devonshire* v. *Eglin* (1851) 14 Beav 530, 51 ER 389.

[148] *Wallis* v. *Harrison* (1838) 4 M & W 538, 150 ER 1543.

[149] Use of the word "licence" is not decisive: *IDC Group* v. *Clark* [1992] 2 EGLR 184, CA; HW Wilkinson (1993) 143 *NLJ* 1544.

of authority to grant an easement.[150] The licence may be revocable at will,[151] contractual, or have proprietary force with the support of an estoppel.[152] After sale of the burdened land, a licence will not do and it is necessary to discover a proprietary right.[153]

I. RESTRICTIONS

[32.27] Restrictions affecting a neighbour's land might be:

rights to light (but there is no wider category of restrictive easements);
rights created to prevent a derogation from grant; or
restrictive covenants.

These require treatment in turn.

J. RIGHTS TO LIGHT

1. Light requires acquisition as an easement

[32.28] A landowner does not have a right to receive light on to his garden or open land,[154] but light can be acquired as an adjunct to an adjoining *building*,[155] or more precisely under *Colls* v. *Home & Colonial Stores*[156] for the benefit of a particular window.[157] When a new window is made, the neighbour may build to block light getting to it,[158] but his right to block it is lost after the 20 year prescription period.[159]

2. Measure of light

[32.29] Should the owner of a window be entitled to continue to enjoy the light previous enjoyed by his window? This is the maximum possible quantum of light for

---

[150] *Evans* v. *Cynon Valley BC* [1992] EGCS 3, CA.

[151] LPA 1925 s 54(1); *Liggins* v. *Inge* (1831) 7 Bing 682, 131 ER 263.

[152] *R* v. *Horndon on the Hill* (1816) 4 M & S 562, 105 ER 942; *Armstrong* v. *Sheppard & Short* [1959] 2 QB 384, CA; *Ward* v. *Kirkland* [1967] Ch 194; *ER Ives (Investments)* v. *High* [1967] 2 QB 379, CA; *Crabb* v. *Arun DC* [1976] Ch 179, CA; *Dance* v. *Triplow* [1992] 1 EGLR 190, CA; JE Martin [1992] *Conv* 197; *Handel* v. *St Stephens Close* [1994] 1 EGLR 70 (parking, passive inducement).

[153] *Re Ellenborough Park* [1956] Ch 131, 159, Evershed MR; *Wong* v. *Beaumont* [1965] 1 Ch 173, CA.

[154] *Potts* v. *Smith* (1868) LR 6 Eq 311.

[155] Statutory prescription is linked to a "dwelling house, workshop or other building"; *Att-Gen* v. *Queen Anne Garden & Mansions Co* (1899) 60 LT 759, Kekewich J; *Hyman* v. *Van den Bergh* [1908] 1 Ch 167, CA (cowshed); *Clifford* v. *Holt* [1899] 1 Ch 698 (church); *Allen* v. *Greenwood* [1980] Ch 119, 125 (greenhouse).

[156] [1904] AC 179, HL.

[157] *Tapling* v. *Jones* (1865) 11 HLC 290, 305, 11 ER 1344, Westbury LC; *Dalton* v. *Henry Angus & Co* (1881) 6 App Cas 740, 794, Selborne LC, 824, Lord Blackburn; *Levet* v. *Gas Light & Coke Co* [1919] 1 Ch 24 (not doors); *Easton* v. *Isted* [1903] 1 Ch 405 (conservatory); *Allen* v. *Greenwood* [1980] Ch 119 (panels in greenhouse). It may benefit other rooms: *Colls* at 204, Lord Davey; *Carr Saunders* v. *Dick McNeil* [1980] 1 WLR 922; S Bridge [1987] *CLJ* 26.

[158] Subject to planning and building controls; conversely Building Acts permitting party walls do not justify darkening light: *Wells* v. *Ody* (1836) 1 M & W 452, 150 ER 512

[159] *Colls* [1904] AC 179, 186, Lord Macnaghten.

prescriptive claims and for those created impliedly on division of the land,[160] and usually also for express grants.[161] However, in *Colls* v. *Home & Colonial Stores* the House of Lords rejected the argument that there was an entitlement to this maximum.[162] Instead they adopted a rule, less logical but more practical, which ensures that building work is possible and towns can continue to grow:[163] an interference with light is actionable only if it creates a nuisance.[164] The test is not what light was previously received, but rather whether enough light is left from all sources for comfortable use of premises.[165] This standard varies with the locality and may increase as general living conditions improve,[166] but ignore subjective factors affecting an individual occupier.[167] Partial blockage gives no cause of action,[168] unless the light is reduced to a level at which the premises cannot be used with ordinary comfort.[169] Despite improvements in scientific technique[170] there is no precise test.

Colls has been applied to an express easement[171] though it fits more comfortably with prescriptive rights.

Different levels of light can be demanded for a dwelling, an office, a factory,[172] and a church.[173] In *Allen* v. *Greenwood*[174] a domestic greenhouse had been in use for 20 years before the neighbour erected a fence, leaving insufficient light for growing plants which is the ordinary use of a greenhouse. The owner obtained an injunction for the removal of the fence to avert that ultimate middle class nightmare, the inability to ripen his tomatoes. A point which remains open is whether a specially high level of light[175] can be prescribed for by special use of a building. Can a *house* which is used for 20 years[176] to *grow plants* acquire the level of light appropriate to a *greenhouse*? Both Goff and Buckley LJJ felt that this was allowed if the extraordinary use was

---

[160] *Leech* v. *Schweder* (1874) LR 9 Ch App 463; *Corbett* v. *Jonas* [1892] 3 Ch 137.

[161] Eg *Newnham* v. *Lawson* (1971) 22 P & CR 852, though an express deed could define its own level of light.

[162] [1904] AC 179, 182, Lord Halsbury, 195, Lord Davey; *Kine* v. *Jolly (No 1)* [1905] 1 Ch 480, 489.

[163] [1904] AC 179, 182, Lord Halsbury.

[164] *Att-Gen* v. *Nichol* (1809) 16 Ves 338, 33 ER 1012, Eldon LC.

[165] [1904] AC 179, 204, Lord Davey; *Higgins* v. *Betts* [1905] 2 Ch 210, 215–216, Farwell J. In *Jolly* v. *Kine* [1907] AC 1 the House of Lords divided 2:2 on similar facts, but the CA decision thus confirmed is surely wrong. Also *Paul* v. *Robson* (1914) 30 TLR 533, 534, Lord Moulton; *Gamble* v. *Doyle* (1971) 219 EG 310, Ungoed-Thomas J.

[166] *Jolly* v. *Kine* [1907] AC 1, HL; *Fishenden* v. *Higgs & Hill* (1935) 153 LT 128; *Ough* v. *King* [1967] 1 WLR 1547, 1552G, Lord Denning MR.

[167] *Colls* [1904] AC 179, 209, Lord Lindley.

[168] *Fishmongers' Co* v. *East India Co* (1752) 1 Dick 163, 21 ER 232; *Charles Semon & Co* v. *Bradford Corp* [1922] 2 Ch 737.

[169] *Martin* v. *Headon* (1866) LR 2 Eq 424.

[170] *Ecclesiastical Commissioners for England* v. *Kino* (1880) 14 Ch D 213, CA (45 degree rule); AH Hudson (1960) 24 *Conv (NS)* 424; *Ough* v. *King* [1967] 1 WLR 1547, CA (Waldram method); *Gamble* v. *Doyle* (1971) 219 EG 310 (sky visibility and grumble line tests); *Deakins* v. *Hookings* [1994] 1 EGLR 190, Ct Ct; HW Wilkinson [1994] *NLJ* 875.

[171] *Frogmore Developments* v. *Shirayama Shokusa* [2000] 1 EGLR 121, Ch D.

[172] *Colls* [1904] AC 179, 202, Lord Davey; *Allen* v. *Greenwood* [1980] Ch 111, 130, Goff LJ, 135, Buckley LJ.

[173] *Newham* v. *Lawson* (1971) 22 P & CR 852.

[174] [1980] Ch 119; FR Crane [1979] *Conv* 298.

[175] On poor light see: EH Bodkin (1974) 38 *Conv (NS)* 4; AH Hudson [1984] *Conv* 408.

[176] *Lanfranchi* v. *Mackenzie* (1867) LR 4 Eq 421; *Ecclesiastical Commissioners for England* v. *Kino* (1880) 14 Ch D 213; *Warren* v. *Brown* [1900] 2 QB 722.

known to the servient owner.[177] Prescription should be allowed of a right to solar
heating as well as for illumination.[178]

3. Acquisition of light

[32.30] Although rights to light may be created expressly this is unusual, and the
usual methods of creation are by implied grant on physical division[179] and by
prescriptive long use.[180]

K. NOVEL RESTRICTIVE EASEMENTS

1. Restrictive easements

[32.31] In *Phipps* v. *Pears*, Lord Denning MR drew a distinction between the class of
affirmative easements such as rights of way, which give the owner of land *a right himself to do something* on or to his neighbour's land and another class:

> "negative easements, such as a right of light, which gives him *a right to stop his neighbour
> doing something* on his (the neighbour's) own land."[181]

In this book this second category are called restrictive easements, to highlight their
analogy to restrictive covenants. Like all easements they must be negative in nature,
imposing no duty to expend money.[182]

2. No easement of weatherproofing

[32.32] New restrictions would prevent desirable development and stunt the growth
of towns.[183] In *Phipps* v. *Pears*[184] two buildings in Market Street, Warwick, were built
so as to touch but with the two walls not bonded together. The ownerships were separated in 1931 and in 1962 the council ordered the demolition of No 14, leaving the
flank wall of No 16 exposed to the weather. Damp penetrated, the water froze, and
this caused cracking. An action for damages failed, since protection from the weather
was not a right known to law, though the However, since an express covenant is
valid[185] it can be seen that the real objective is to limit the kinds of restriction which

---

[177] *Allen* v. *Greenwood* [1980] Ch 119, 131B, 136C; *Colls* [1904] AC 179, 203, Lord Davey (hostile);
Ambler v. *Gordon* [1905] 1 KB 417, Bray J; *Warren* v. *Brown* [1900] 2 QB 722, 733 (approved in *Colls*);
Newham v. *Lawson* (1971) 22 P & CR 852, 859, Plowman J.
[178] *Allen* v. *Greenwood* [1980] Ch 119, 134D, Goff LJ.
[179] See below **[35.26]**.
[180] See below **[36.28ff]**.
[181] [1965] QB 76, 83E.
[182] See above **[32.23]**.
[183] *Att-Gen* v. *Doughty* (1752) 2 Ves Sen 453, 28 ER 290, Hardwicke LC.
[184] [1965] 1 QB 76, CA; RE Megarry (1964) 80 *LQR* 318; MA Peel (1963) 28 *Conv (NS)* 450; K Scott
[1964] *CLJ* 203; HW Wilkinson (1964) 27 *MLR* 614; *Bond* v. *Nottingham Corp* [1940] Ch 429; *Marchant* v.
Capital & Counties Property Co [1982] 2 EGLR 156, CA.
[185] *Phipps* v. *Pears* [1965] 1 QB 76, 83, Lord Denning MR; *Webb* v. *Bird* (1862) 13 CB NS 841, 143 ER
332.

can be created by prescription.[186] The decision itself is largely superseded by the decision in *Rees* v. *Skerrett*[187] which recognises a common law duty to weatherproof a neighbour's wall in the ordinary law of tort, without any need for acquisition of a right as an easement. One property in a terrace was demolished leaving a neighbour's end wall exposed to damage, and it was held that the common law would recognise a duty to do what was reasonable in the circumstances to minimise damage to neighbouring property, and there is also a limited duty of care to prevent loss of support by natural causes where a defect is patent.

All of these cases concern adjoining freeholds, but this line of authority has been extended in *Abbahall* v. *Smee*[188] to flying freeholds, so as to compel the owner of the upper floor to repair the roof so as to avoid damage to the ground floor flat. An occupier must do what it is reasonable to expect of him[189] though the test is objective and does not depend upon the parties' means.[190]

3. Policy against novel restrictions

[32.33] Negative easements are anomalous.[191] What is in theory a class actually consists of rights to light, with the arguable addition of rights of support.[192] Such easements remain a closed category,[193] so pure restrictions must be created by covenant[194] or by non-derogation. Recognition of new restrictions would substantially hinder future development and might reduce the market value of land or render it completely unsaleable.

Numerous cases show that it a person is entitled to build on his own land subject to planning requirements. Interference with his neighbour is irrelevant, even one seriously detrimental to the amenity of his land.[195] Cases have rejected claims to a right to a view,[196] since light is a necessity whereas a prospect is a delight.[197] Similar rejection faced claims to receive a flow of air,[198] (unless in a defined ventilation shaft[199]) or to

---

[186] *Phipps* at 84A, Lord Denning MR.

[187] [2001] EWCA Civ 760, [2001] 1 WLR 1541; *Goldman* v. *Hargrave* [1967] 1 AC 645; *Holbeck Hall Hotel* v. *Scarborough BC* [2000] QB 836, CA; *(No 2)* [2000] Times March 2nd, CA. The claim failed on the facts.

[188] [2002] EWCA Civ 1831, [2002] Times December 28th.

[189] At [13], Munby J.

[190] At [56], Munby J.

[191] *Hunter* v. *Canary Wharf* [1997] AC 665, 726F–H, Lord Hope.

[192] *Colls* [1904] AC 179, 186, Lord Macnaghten; *Phipps* v. *Pears* [1965] 1 QB 76, 82E, Lord Denning MR.

[193] *Keppell* v. *Bailey* (1834) 2 My & K 577, 39 ER 1055; *Ackroyd* v. *Smith* (1850) 10 CB 164, 138 ER 68; *Hill* v. *Tupper* (1863) 2 H & C 121, 159 ER 51.

[194] *Woodhouse & Co* v. *Kirkland (Derby)* [1970] 1 WLR 1185, Plowman J.

[195] *Hunter* v. *Canary Wharf* [1997] AC 665, 685D–F, Lord Goff, 709B, Lord Hoffmann, 724D–F, Lord Hope. Planning permission is not itself a defence: *Wheeler* v. *JJ Saunders* [1996] Ch 19.

[196] *Richardson* v. *Taylor* (1694) Comb 242, 90 ER 454; *Att-Gen* v. *Doughty* (1752) 2 Ves Sen 453, 28 ER 290; *Fishmongers' Co* v. *East India Co* (1752) 1 Dick 164, 21 ER 232; *Butt* v. *Imperial Gas Co* (1866) LR 2 Ch App 158; *Smith* v. *Owen* (1860) 35 LJ Ch 317; P Polden [1984] *Conv* 429.

[197] *Dalton* v. *Henry Angus & Co* (1881) 6 App Cas 740, 823–824, Lord Blackburn, 794, Selborne LC.

[198] *Bland* v. *Mosely* (1587) 9 Co Rep 58a, 77 ER 817; *Webb* v. *Bird* (1862) 13 CB NS 841, 143 ER 332; *Bryant* v. *Lefever* (1879) 4 CPD 172; *Chastey* v. *Ackland* [1897] AC 155, HL; *Hunter* v. *Canary Wharf* [1997] AC 665, 709B, Lord Hoffmann.

[199] *Bass* v. *Gregory* (1890) 25 QBD 481; *Wong* v. *Beaumont* [1965] 1 QB 173, CA.

privacy.[200] The same applies to light falling outside the scope of an easement to a particular window,[201] such as general rights to all light falling on a garden are not allowed. Most of the claims just discussed fail for uncertainty,[202] but there are more fundamental reasons for rejecting them. Allowing new restrictions would impede residential and commercial development. So residents on the Isle of Dogs have no right to complain if the Canary Wharf tower blocks their radio reception.[203] The parties must know what right has been granted and whether or not it has been infringed and the extent of the burden imposed on land must be controlled.[204]

4. Limits to prescription

[32.34] Lord Denning MR has said such an easement would unduly restrict a neighbour in his enjoyment of his own land and hamper legitimate development.[205] However, the same restriction could be imposed as a covenant,[206] and it can therefore be seen that the real objective is not to limit the types of restriction recognised by the law, but rather to limit the kinds of restriction capable of being created by prescription.[207] The fact that a neighbour has allowed his land to continue in its existing state is in no way a recognition that it will remain so.

L. NON-DEROGATION

[32.35] Restrictions can be created when land is divided into two parts by the principle of "non-derogation from grant".[208]

M. RESTRICTIVE COVENANTS

[32.36] *Tulk* v. *Moxhay*[209] gives its name to the doctrine that a restrictive covenant[210] creates a burden binding the land affected by it. Later purchasers are bound (accord-

---

[200] *Aldred's case* (1610) 9 Co Rep 57b, 77 ER 816; *Knowles* v. *Richardson* (1670) Holt KB 55, 86 ER 727; *Arnold* v. *Jefferson* (1679) Holt KB 498, 90 ER 1174; *Chandler* v. *Thompson* (1811) 3 Camp 80, 170 ER 1312; *Tapling* v. *Jones* (1865) 20 CB NS 166, 177, 191, 144 ER 1067.

[201] *Bury* v. *Pope* (1587) Cro Eliz 118, 78 ER 375.

[202] See above **[32.22]**.

[203] *Hunter* v. *Canary Wharf* [1997] AC 655, HL; I Dawson and A Dunn (1998) 18 *LS* 510.

[204] *Copeland* v. *Greenhalf* [1952] Ch 488, 496, Upjohn J; *Hill* v. *Tupper* (1863) 2 W & C 121, 128, 159 ER 51, Martin B; *Dyce* v. *Hay* (1852) 1 Macq 305, 312, Lord St Leonards; *Re Webb's Lease* [1951] Ch 808, 815, Evershed MR.

[205] *Phipps* v. *Pears* [1965] 1 QB 76, 83E.

[206] At 83D; *Webb* v. *Bird* (1862) 13 CB (NS) 841, 143 ER 332; EH Bodkin (1971) 35 *Conv (NS)* 324.

[207] *Phipps* at 84A, Lord Denning MR.

[208] See below **[35.27]**.

[209] (1848) 2 Ph 774, 41 ER 1143, Cottenham LC.

[210] The leading text is Preston & Newsom, *Restrictive Covenants Affecting Freehold Land* (Sweet & Maxwell, 9th ed, 1998). Also: Chapelle's *LL* (5th ed) ch 15; Cheshire & Burn (16th ed) ch 20; Dixon's *Principles* (3rd ed) ch 8; Goo's *Sourcebook* (3rd ed) ch 15; Gravells' *LL – Text* (2nd ed) ch 8; Grays' *Elements* (3rd ed) ch 10; Maudsley & Burn *LL – Cases* (7th ed) ch 12; Megarry & Wade (6th ed), [18.014–18.039]; Smith's *Property* Law (4th ed) ch 21; Swadling "Property" ch 4 in Birks' *English Private Law*, [4.156–4.162]; Thompson's *Modern LL* ch 14.

ing to the date of creation of the covenant) either by notice or registration. Burdens are potentially perpetual and may devalue the land substantially.[211]

1. *Tulk* v. *Moxhay* itself

[32.37] In 1808 Tulk sold land which formed the centre of Leicester Square in London – then a pleasure ground with an equestrian statue surrounded by iron railings – retaining several houses around the square. Elms paid £200, a high sum at that date for a sterile piece of ground. As buyer, he covenanted for himself and his heirs and assigns[212] to maintain the garden as a pleasure ground, to keep it in an ornamental order and in an open state uncovered with buildings, and to allow the inhabitants to have a key on paying a reasonable rent. The garden was sold several times, before it passed in 1848 to Moxhay who had notice of the 1808 covenant. When Moxhay began to cut down shrubs preparatory to building, an injunction was issued to restrain any use other than as a garden.[213] Lord Cottenham LC continued an interim[214] injunction granted by the Master of the Rolls. The right to enforce the covenant against the original contracting party (Elms) was undoubted. Since the price he paid valued the land subject to the covenant, it would be inequitable for Elms to resell it at a greater price to a purchaser free of the burden. The buyer was bound because of his notice of the covenant when he bought. *Tulk* v. *Moxhay* ensures that a landowner can sell part of his land secure in the knowledge that what he retains cannot be made worthless.

2. A clean break?

[32.38] It is a matter of some nicety to know whether *Tulk* v. *Moxhay* followed existing precedent. Most probably Lord Cottenham invented a new equitable interest, deliberately extending leasehold covenants enforceable at law to a new category of covenants between neighbouring freeholders enforceable in equity, but also drawing an analogy with the easement of light. Judicial recognition lagged far behind development practice. Covenants were imposed in 1675 to regulate building in Bloomsbury (then on the outskirts of London) but these were not litigated until 1822,[215] around the time that layout covenants affecting Georgian Bath and Cheltenham began to reach the courts.[216]

Restrictive covenants were enforced in equity at first instance in *Duke of Bedford* v. *Trustees of British Museum*,[217] but Eldon LC's appellate judgment equated covenants enforceable at law and in equity,[218] an equation confirmed by Lord Brougham LC in

---

[211] *Carter* v. *TG Baynes & Sons* [1998] EGCS 109 (£218,000 damages).

[212] Heirs = successors entitled to freehold land on death intestate before 1926; assigns = purchasers.

[213] *R* v. *Westminster CC ex p Leicester Square Coventry Street Association* (1989) 59 P & CR 51, Simon Brown J (local government legislation overrode the covenant); *Tulk* v. *The Metropolitan Board of Works* (1867) LR 3 QB 94; London Squares Preservation Act 1931.

[214] (1848) 18 LJ Ch 83, 87, Langdale MR; query the history in R Griffith [1983] *Conv* 29; Shadwell V-C had generated the original injunction.

[215] *Duke of Bedford* v. *Trustees of British Museum* (1822) 2 My & K 552, 39 ER 1055.

[216] *Schreiber* v. *Creed* (1839) 10 Sim 9, 59 ER 515 (Pittville, 1827).

[217] Sugden on *Vendors* (Sweets, 10th ed, 1846) app, 57, Leach V-C.

[218] (1822) 2 My & K 552, 39 ER 1055 (injunction refused because of change in character of estate).

Keppell v. *Bailey*.[219] Neighbourhood covenants are not enforceable at law.[220] Soon afterwards Lord Cottenham LC referred to "cases before the Vice Chancellor of England" in which restrictive covenant doctrine had been put beyond dispute,[221] meaning presumably *Whatman* v. *Gibson*[222] and *Mann* v. *Stephens*.[223] Full recognition of restrictive covenants between freehold neighbours rests on *Tulk* v. *Moxhay* itself and thus on a shaky doctrinal base. The Master of the Rolls treated *Keppell* v. *Bailey* as obiter[224] whereas the Lord Chancellor stated it as authority for the opposite of what it decided. In truth *Tulk* v. *Moxhay* was a clean break with the past,[225] and, like so many seminal cases, one based on a convenient misunderstanding of existing law.[226]

3.   Parties affected

[32.39] Three forms of action must be distinguished. (1) Both positive and negative covenants were enforceable against Elms the original covenanting party.[227] The legal contractual action for damages is supported by equity's ancillary jurisdiction which makes an injunction available. (2) Leasehold covenants run between current landlord and current tenant at common law.[228] (3) Restrictive covenants are enforceable against a purchaser of the burdened freehold land. When the site of Leicester Square had passed "by divers mesne conveyances" into the hands of the defendant Moxhay bought with notice of the covenant.

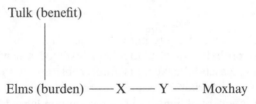

Figure 32-1 The parties in *Tulk* v *Moxhay*

Lord Cottenham confirmed the injunction against Moxhay, which shows that the covenant had created an equitable burden on the site of the square.[229] Endurability requires a restrictive covenant meeting the rules set out in this chapter and is today

---

[219] (1834) 2 My & K 517, 39 ER 1042.
[220] *Haywood* v. *Brunswick PBS* (1881) 8 QBD 403, CA; *Austerberry* v. *Oldham Corp* (1885) 29 Ch D 752, CA; *Hall* v. *Ewin* (1887) 37 Ch D 74, 79; *E & GC* v. *Bate* (1935) 79 LJ News 203, Macnaghten J.
[221] *Tulk* v. *Moxhay* (1848) 2 Ph 774, 777, 41 ER 1143; CD Bell [1981] *Conv* 55.
[222] (1838) 9 Sim 196, 59 ER 333.
[223] (1846) 15 Sim 377, 60 ER 665.
[224] (1848) 18 LJ Ch 83, 84.
[225] It is now followed: *Coles* v. *Sims* (1853) Kay 56, 69 ER 25, Page Wood V-C; *Keates* v. *Lyon* (1869) LR 4 Ch App 218, 222–223, Selwyn LJ; *Renals* v. *Cowlishaw* (1878) 9 Ch D 125, 129, Hall V-C.
[226] Modern rationalisation is explained in *Rhone* v. *Stephens* [1994] 2 AC 310, 317E–318C, Lord Templeman.
[227] *Federated Homes* v. *Mill Lodge Properties* [1980] 1 WLR 594, CA.
[228] *Spencer's case* (1583) 5 Co Rep 16a, 77 ER 72; now LT (Covenants) A 1995; see above **[27.18ff]**.
[229] At 778.

dependent on registration of the burden.[230] A similar principle applies to ship charterparties.[231]

4. Covenant must be restrictive

[32.40] The essential requirement for the operation of the modern doctrine of *Tulk* v. *Moxhay* is that the covenant should be restrictive in character. The case itself involved a covenant by the purchaser of Leicester Square and his successors

> "[to] keep and maintain the said piece of ground and square garden and the iron railing round the same in its then form and in sufficient and proper repair as a square garden and pleasure ground, *in an open state, uncovered with any buildings*, in neat and ornamental order . . .".

The italicised words are negative in a sea of the positive. An injunction was granted to stop building and to restrain the owner of the square from altering its character.[232] Lord Cottenham's judgment referred to any covenant of which a purchaser had notice,[233] suggesting that notice of a positive covenant might create a proprietary burden,[234] but after some doubt[235] positive covenants were excluded by *Haywood* v. *Brunswick Permanent BS* (1881).[236]

Restrictive character can be tested by the rule that the burdened owner must not be required to expend money,[237] though this is not decisive. Certainly positive are to fence, to clean a cesspool, to pay water rates, to contribute to the cost of a road, or to repair.[238] The test is substantive, rather than being based on the grammatical form of the covenant. Elms covenant in *Tulk* v. *Moxhay* to "keep and maintain the said piece of ground . . . in an open state, uncovered with any buildings" was a restriction on building. Good and bad parts of the covenant are separated out,[239] unless they are inextricably intertwined.[240]

Only a small number of covenants are in common use. Archetypal examples are against building, including use as agricultural land or as a small holding. Many covenants are designed to preserve an estate layout on a residential development-*Federated Homes* v. *Mill Lodge* itself involved a covenant about building density. A major function of restrictive covenants is to restrict the use of neighbouring land. A covenant to use as a house is broken by conversion of a single house into two flats[241]

---

[230] See below **[33.07]**.
[231] *Law Debenture Trust Corp* v. *Ural Caspian Oil Corp* [1993] 1 WLR 138, Hoffmann J; [1995] Ch 152, CA.
[232] Query the dicta at (1848) 18 LJ Ch 83, 86–87, Lord Langdale MR.
[233] *Cox* v. *Bishop* (1857) 8 De GM & G 815, 821; *Leech* v. *Schweder* (1874) LR 9 Ch App 463, 475; *Luker* v. *Denis* (1877) 7 Ch D 227.
[234] C Bell [1981] *Conv* 55; R Griffith [1983] *Conv* 29.
[235] *Cooke* v. *Chilcott* (1876) 3 Ch D 694; *Morland* v. *Cook* (1868) LR 6 Eq 252 (explicable as a rentcharge).
[236] (1881) 8 QBD 403, CA.
[237] *Hall* v. *Ewin* (1887) 37 Ch D 74, 79, Cotton LJ.
[238] See below **[32.44ff]**.
[239] *Shepherd Homes* v. *Sandham (No 2)* [1971] 1 WLR 1062, 1066H–1067F, Megarry J; *Clegg* v. *Hands* (1890) 44 Ch D 503, CA.
[240] At 1067E.
[241] *Ilford Park Estates* v. *Jacobs* [1903] 2 Ch 522; *Sunderland & S Shields Water Co* v. *Hilton* (1928) 97 LJ KB 516. The court has power to authorise such a conversion under HA 1985 s 610.

or by erection of a block of flats,[242] or by use for holiday lettings,[243] but it does not control the highly undesirable activity of letting a house to a group of four students.[244] A covenant to preserve residential use is broken by conversion to multiple residences or by institutional use.[245] Many covenants prevent use for trades or the sale of alcohol. A common covenant in a sale of a pub is a clause creating a tied house and preventing the sale of guest beers; this clause is a valid restrictive covenant,[246] since the grant of an exclusive right is held to be equivalent to a negative covenant.[247]

Leach V-C recognised in *Duke of Bedford* v. *Trustees of British Museum*[248] the use of covenants to preserve the pleasure or profit of land.[249] The basic object is to seek conformity across a development.[250] Restrictive covenants can prevent obstruction of a view, keep a garden unbuilt on, protect a landscape,[251] or regulate car parking.[252] No doubt a covenant to preserve privacy would be too uncertain, but this may be the indirect effect of restrictive covenant[253] and loss of privacy is relevant when determining a remedy.[254]

Clear wording is required since restrictions are construed against the person imposing them.[255]

5. Neighbour principle

[32.41] It is necessary for a restrictive covenant to comply with the neighbour principle – it must burden the land of one landowner and must benefit the land of a neighbour.[256]

---

[242] *Rogers* v. *Hosegood* [1900] 2 Ch 388, CA. Use as *a* private dwelling does not necessarily mean a single one: *Briggs* v. *McCusker* [1996] 2 EGLR 197, Ch D

[243] *Caradon DC* v. *Paton* [2000] 3 EGLR 57, CA.

[244] *Roberts* v. *Howlett* [2002] 1 P & CR 18 at 230, CA.

[245] Statute allows hostels for former mental patients under the "care in the community" scheme: National Health Service and Community Care Act 1990 sch 2 para 6; L Ref HUDA 1993 s 89; C & G *Homes* v. *SS for Health* [1991] Ch 365, CA; *National Schizophrenia Fellowship* v. *Ribble Estates* (1993) 25 HLR 476; *Cadogan* v. *Royal Brompton Hospital NHS Trust* [1996] 2 EGLR 115; *Brown* v. *Heathlands Mental Health NHS Trust* [1996] 1 All ER 133.

[246] *Wilson* v. *Hart* (1866) LR 1 Ch App 463; *Catt* v. *Tourle* (1869) LR 4 Ch App 654; *Clegg* v. *Hands* (1890) 44 Ch D 503, CA; *Morrells of Oxford* v. *Oxford United FC* [2001] Ch 459, CA. Many such covenants may infringe EU or domestic competition law.

[247] *Holmes* v. *Eastern Counties Rly* (1857) 3 K & J 675, 69 ER 1280.

[248] Sugden on *Vendors* (Sweets, 10th ed, 1846) app, 57; on appeal (1822) 2 My & K 552, 39 ER 1055.

[249] A covenant to use for recreation is broken by a lease to professional football club: *Thames Water Utilities* v. *Oxford CC* [1999] 1 EGLR 167.

[250] *Oceanic Village* v. *United Attractions* [2000] Ch 234, 252E, Neuberger J.

[251] *Crawley* v. *Wolff* (1888) 4 TLR 434, CA; *Tulk* v. *Moxhay* (1848) 2 Ph 774, 41 ER 1143; *Western* v. *Macdermott* (1866) LR 2 Ch App 72; *Re Freeman-Thomas' Indenture* [1957] 1 All ER 532 (park); *Gee* v. *National Trust* [1966] 1 WLR 170, CA.

[252] *Mount Cook Land* v. *Spring House (Freehold)* [2001] EWCA Civ 1833, [2002] 2 All ER 822.

[253] *Manners (Lord)* v. *Johnson* (1875) 1 Ch D 673.

[254] *Sharp* v. *Harrison* [1922] 1 Ch 502, Astbury J.

[255] *German* v. *Chapman* (1877) 7 Ch D 271, 276–277, James LJ; *Elliott* v. *Safeway Stores* [1995] 1 WLR 1396.

[256] See below **[34.11ff]**.

6. Proprietary covenants

[32.42] It is possible to word a covenant so that it binds only the original owner or so as to extend to any future owner. Endurability against a buyer depends upon the contractual wording showing that the latter is intended. To use the old phrase, there must be "an intention to bind the servient land". Thus in *Rogers* v. *Hosegood* a covenant entered into "with the intent that it might so far as possible bind the premises thereby conveyed and every part into whosesoever hands the same might come" created a valid restrictive covenant.[257] Before 1926, a covenant was presumed to be personal only,[258] so it was necessary to include a reference to "assigns" (that is buyers).[259] The 1925 legislation reversed the presumption,[260] so that if a particular covenant relates to land owned by the covenanting party,[261] it is presumed to be proprietary unless it is stated that it is intended to be personal.[262]

N. POSITIVE OBLIGATIONS BETWEEN FREEHOLDERS

[32.43] Neighbours often wish to create three kinds of positive burdens on land: to carry out work, provide services, or make payments.[263] Our law remains defective, for as it stands there is no mechanism by which these burdens can be imposed on future neighbours. The basic rule will be considered before the means of avoidance – estate rentcharges, leasehold schemes and commonholds.[264]

1. Burden does not pass

[32.34] In *Rhone* v. *Stephens*[265] the House of Lords reconfirmed the old established rule that the burden of a positive covenant cannot pass.[266] When Walford House was split in 1960, the owner of the main house covenanted with the purchaser of the cottage (which formed one wing of it) to maintain the roof. Both parts changed hands several times. The Rhones, current owners of the cottage, were held not to be entitled to enforce the covenant against Mrs Stephens, the current owner of the house.

---

[257] [1900] 2 Ch 388, CA.

[258] *Re Fawcett & Holmes' C* (1889) 42 Ch D 150, CA; *Groves* v. *Loomes* (1885) 55 LJ Ch 52.

[259] *Powell* v. *Hemsley* [1909] 2 Ch 252. Pre-1926 "heirs" related to freehold land, whereas "executors and administrators" took leaseholds.

[260] LPA 1925 s 79(3) (new in 1924); *Shepherd Homes* v. *Sandham (No 2)* [1971] 1 WLR 1062, 1066, Megarry J.

[261] *Tophams* v. *Sefton* [1967] 1 AC 50, 73; Lord Upjohn (no land benefitted); LPA 1925 s 79(2) (true restrictive covenants).

[262] S 79 operates subject to any contrary intention *expressed* or (despite its wording) deduced from the words of the conveyance: *Re Royal Victoria Pavilion, Ramsgate* [1961] Ch 581, Pennycuick J; *Lynnthorpe Estates* v. *Sidney Smith (Chelsea)* [1990] 1 EGLR 148, 152, Warner J; on appeal [1990] 2 EGLR 131, CA; *Morrells of Oxford* v. *Oxford United FC* [2001] Ch 459, CA ("vendors not to permit" – personal).

[263] Law Com 127 (1984), [6.6–6.10].

[264] See below **[32.53ff]**.

[265] [1994] 2 AC 310, HL; SH Goo [1993] *Conv* 234; NP Gravells (1994) 110 *LQR* 346; M Codd (1993) 137 *SJ* 970; J Snape [1994] *Conv* 477; L Tee [1994] *CLJ* 446; S Gardner [1995] *CLJ* 60, 63–68.

[266] Except by statute: *Fortescue* v. *Lostwithiel & Fowey Rly Co* [1894] 3 Ch 621.

Passage of the *benefit* presented no difficulty,[267] but a successful action was precluded by the fact that the *burdened* land had been sold. Ownership of land could be negated if it was possible to impose expensive duties on it.

The law remains firmly settled. Entry on a charges register does not make a positive covenant bind later proprietors.[268] The burden of a covenant to maintain a hedge cannot run so as to bind successors in title even if the obligation is created in a statutory inclosure award.[269] Neither does an obligation to contribute to cost of maintenance of common parts on a housing estate.[270] Other examples of positive covenants involving expenditure of money[271] are fencing, cleaning a cesspool, paying water rates, contributing to the cost of a road,[272] and repairing.[273]

2.   Limitation of *Tulk* v. *Moxhay*

[32.35] *Tulk* v. *Moxhay*[274] enabled covenants to pass to buyers with notice. Since the remedy granted was a negative injunction,[275] it only acted to stop building and prevent alteration in the character of the square. Lord Langdale MR indicated that Moxhay could to some extent be compelled to maintain the square as a garden,[276] but on appeal Lord Cottenham LC did not refer to the precise terms of the injunction. Thus the report of the case poses this question: was the doctrine inherently and immediately limited to negative covenants?[277] One or two cases did permit the enforcement of positive covenants,[278] but in 1881 *Haywood* v. *Brunswick PBS* laid down that a positive repairing covenant was outside the scope of the equitable doctrine.[279]

3.   Positive burdens can be disclaimed after insolvency

[32.46] The value of land can be eaten up by imposing onerous covenants or indemnity obligations. On insolvency land subject to positive covenants can be disclaimed by the trustee in bankruptcy or liquidator.[280] When the land passes to the Crown as

---

[267] See below **[32.51]**.

[268] *Cator* v. *Newton* [1940] 1 KB 415, CA.

[269] *Marlton* v. *Turner* [1998] 3 EGLR 185 CA.

[270] *Thamesmead* v. *Allotey* [1998] 3 EGLR 97, CA.

[271] *Hall* v. *Ewin* (1887) 37 Ch D 74, 79, Cotton LJ.

[272] *Austerberry* v. *Oldham Corp* (1885) 29 Ch D 752; *E & GC* v. *Bate* (1935) 79 LJ News 203; *Cator* v. *Newton* [1940] 1 KB 415, CA.

[273] *Haywood* v. *Brunswick PBS* (1881) 8 QBD 403, CA; *Re Fitzherbert-Brockhole's Agreement* [1940] Ch 51; *Rhone* v. *Stephens* [1994] 2 AC 310, HL

[274] (1848) 2 Ph 774, 41 ER 1143.

[275] *Law Debenture Trust Corp* v. *Ural Caspian Oil Corp* [1993] 1 WLR 138, Hoffmann J; reversed on another point [1995] Ch 152, CA.

[276] (1848) 18 LJ Ch 83, 86–87.

[277] C Bell [1981] *Conv* 55; R Griffith [1983] *Conv* 29.

[278] *Morland* v. *Cook* (1868) LR 6 Eq 252 (rentcharge); *Cooke* v. *Chilcott* (1876) 3 Ch D 694, Malins V-C (supply of water); on appeal (at 703) the case was decided on the admission of liability.

[279] (1881) 8 QBD 403, CA; *London & SW Rly* v. *Gomm* (1882) 20 Ch D 562, CA (covenant to retransfer); *Clegg* v. *Hands* (1889) 44 Ch D 503, 506, Bristowe V-C; *Powell* v. *Hemsley* [1909] 2 Ch 252; *Simpson* v. *Att-Gen* [1904] AC 476, HL (no duty to maintain locks); *London CC* v. *Allen* [1914] 3 KB 642, 653, 663–664; *Smith* v. *Colbourne* [1914] 2 Ch 533, CA (block up windows).

[280] Old law: *Re Blackburn & District Benefit BS ex p Graham* (1889) 42 Ch D 343, CA; *British General Insurance Co* v. *Att-Gen* [1945] LJ NCCR 113; RE Megarry (1946) 62 *LQR* 223; *Re Nottingham General Cemetery Co* [1955] Ch 683 (cemetery full to capacity and with onerous maintenance obligations).

bona vacantia, it is still burdened by the repair obligations.[281] Since the Crown will not want it on those terms, the Treasury Solicitor may serve a notice to disclaim it,[282] causing an escheat. When land returns to the Crown it is shorn, this time, of the onerous burdens attached to the former estate. Others interested in the land may apply to the court for a vesting order if they are prepared to accept the burden.[283]

4. Reform

[32.47] There have been numerous complaints about the state of the law, ranging from academic opinion,[284] through the Wilberforce Committee,[285] to early Law Commission reports.[286] However, attention must now focus on the Law Commission Report on *The Law of Positive and Restrictive Covenants* published in 1984,[287] which continues the campaign against the restrictive/positive divide and proposes the creation of a uniform statutory scheme of land obligations. Further work is to be undertaken on this important proposal, though it needs to be broadened out to include easements.

5. Positivity generally a bar to easement status

(1) General bar

[32.48] If a right throws an expense on to the burdened owner, this prevents recognition as an easement, since easements must be negative in nature. They must not entail the servient owner in spending money.[288] This applies primarily to affirmative easements though it is equally true of easements creating restrictions. One can have a right to light but not, sadly, a right to have one's windows cleaned.

A right to a supply of water claimed in *Rance* v. *Elvin* would have required the servient owner to pay the charges of the water company. The negative aspect of the right – to have whatever water came into the pipe pass through it – was allowed on appeal,[289] but the duty to supply water was not. Problems were overcome by allowing a restitutionary claim for reimbursement of money spent on water charges. Similarly an easement cannot impose an obligation to repair on the servient owner,[290] so a canal owner is not obliged to carry on repairing the locks long after the canal has lost its

---

[281] Companies Act 1985 s 654.

[282] Ss 656–658, 686; DW Elliott (1954) 70 *LQR* 25 (Eastville Cemetery, Bristol).

[283] IA 1986 ss 178–182 (companies), 315–321 (individuals); *Hackney LBC* v. *Crown Estates Commissioners* (1996) 72 P & CR 233, Knox J.

[284] EH Scammell (1954) 18 *Conv (NS)* 546.

[285] *Report of Committee on Positive Covenants* (1965) Cmnd 2719; JF Garner (1966) 110 *SJ* 860.

[286] Law Com 11 (1967); HW Wilkinson (1967) 30 *MLR* 681; Law Com WP 36 (1971); HWR Wade [1972B] *CLJ* 157; A Prichard (1973) 37 *Conv (NS)* 194.

[287] Law Com 127 (1984); P Polden (1984) 47 *MLR* 566; HW Wilkinson (1984) 270 *EG* 1154; SB Edell [1984] *JPL* 222, 317, 401, 485; HW Wilkinson (1984) 134 *NLJ* 459, 481; HW Wilkinson [1988] *Conv* 157.

[288] Cheshire's categorisation (as an aspect of the need for an easement to be capable of forming the subject matter of a grant) is suspect since a deed could grant positive and negative rights but only the negative part is an easement: Cheshire & Burn (16th ed), 577.

[289] (1985) 50 P & CR 9, CA; *Duffy* v. *Lamb* (1998) 75 P & CR 364, CA (electricity).

[290] *Austerberry* v. *Oldham Corp* (1885) 29 Ch D 752 (road); *Jones* v. *Pritchard* [1908] 1 Ch 630, 637 (chimney flue, bridge obiter); *Crow* v. *Wood* [1971] 1 QB 77, 84, Lord Denning MR.

viability.[291] There is no duty on the burdened owner to repair the land which he owns to make it suitable or convenient for use by the benefitting neighbour,[292] and he is not an occupier so he does not attract tort liability.[293] If the servient owner does repair, the work must be done properly.[294] A benefitted owner may enter and do work to enable him to exercise the right granted,[295] for example by making up a road[296] or repairing it.[297] This right is often an express addition to the terms of the easement.

(2) Fencing

[32.49] By way of exception, positive rights to fencing can be created by prescription.[298]

6. Positive covenants – original parties

[32.50] There is nothing to stop the current owner of land contracting that *he* will carry out positive work. It is also possible that he agrees to create an extended liability by agreeing that he will accept liability if a future owner of the burdened land, who is not himself liable,[299] commits a breach. Continuing liability exists under post-1925 covenants if they relate to any land of a covenantor,[300] but it is generally better to curtail this continuing liability – expressly or by implication[301] – so as to make the covenant bite only during land ownership.

7. Positive covenants – benefit

[32.51] The benefit of a positive covenant may pass at law. In *Packenham's case*[302] P sued in 1369 for breach of a covenant by a prior to say divine service weekly which had

---

[291] *Simpson* v. *Att-Gen* [1904] AC 476, 483, Lord Macnaghten.

[292] *Pomfret* v. *Ricroft* (1669) 1 Wms Saund 321, 85 ER 454; *Taylor* v. *Whitehead* as above; *Colbeck* v. *Girdler's Co* (1876) 1 QBD 234; *Duke of Westminster* v. *Guild* [1985] QB 688, CA; P Jackson [1985] *Conv* 66; *Stokes* v. *Mixconcrete (Holdings)* (1978) 38 P & CR 488, CA (make up road).

[293] *Holden* v. *White* [1982] QB 679, CA; K Stanton (1982) 98 *LQR* 541; R Griffith [1983] *Conv* 58; *Greenhalgh* v. *British Railways Board* [1969] 2 QB 286, CA; *McGeown* v. *Northern Ireland Housing Executive* [1995] 1 AC 233, HL (public rights).

[294] *Saint* v. *Jenner* [1973] Ch 275, CA.

[295] *Miller* v. *Hancock* [1893] 2 QB 177, 182, Kay J.

[296] *Newcomen* v. *Coulson* (1817) 5 Ch D 133, CA; *Jones* v. *Pritchard* [1908] 1 Ch 630, 638; *Taylor* v. *Whitehead* (1781) 2 Doug 745, 749, 99 ER 475, Mansfield CJ; query the decision in *Redland Bricks* v. *Morris* [1970] AC 652, 665E, Lord Upjohn.

[297] *Mills* v. *Silver* [1991] Ch 271, CA. But pouring 700 tons of stone onto a right of way goes far beyond what is a repair: at 286F–287F, Dillon LJ.

[298] See below **[36.27]**.

[299] *Tophams* v. *Earl of Sefton* [1967] 1 AC 50, 78, Lord Upjohn, 81, Lord Wilberforce; PB Fairest [1966] *CLJ* 169; *Federated Homes* v. *Mill Lodge* [1980] 1 WLR 594, 606B, Brightman LJ; *Rhone* v. *Stephens* [1994] 2 AC 310, 322D.

[300] LPA 1925 s 79 (dating from 1924); there is now no difference between things in existence and those not.

[301] *Re Royal Victoria Pavilion, Ramsgate* [1961] Ch 581, Pennycuick J. Before 1926 this was done by omitting the reference to "assigns": *Groves* v. *Loomes* 53 LT 592, Bacon V-C; *Re Fawcett & Holmes' C* (1889) 42 Ch D 150, CA.

[302] YB 42 Edw III (1369) hil pl 14, f 3 (*Prior's case*); *Spencer's case* (1583) 5 Co Rep 16a, 17b, 77 ER 72; OW Holmes *The Common Law* (Boston, 1881), 395–398; Holdsworth's *History* vol III, 157–166; AWB Simpson *History of the Land Law* (Clarendon Press, 2nd ed , 1986), 140–141.

been made with his great grandfather and which was now enforced by P as purchaser of the *manor*.[303] More recently, in *Smith & Snipe's Hall Farm* v. *River Douglas Catchment Board*,[304] the Board covenanted with the owner of land adjoining the Eller Brook to maintain a wall to stop the brook flooding. The farm was sold to John Smith with the benefit of this agreement and the Board was liable to him. Covenants only pass with land benefitted by the obligation,[305] so that without the land no benefit can pass. Covenants may be attached to land because the covenant benefits certain land,[306] or otherwise because it affects the nature, quality, value, or mode of using the land.[307] Examples are protection of low-lying farm land from flooding, and a guarantee of the structural integrity of a new house.[308]

At least since 1925, the effect is much like annexation of a restrictive covenant though without any special wording at the time of creation.[309] Passage is automatic on sale,[310] and for post-1925 covenants follows any division, lease or sublease, and also passes to an occupier.[311]

8. Chains of indemnity

[32.52] Original covenanting parties should take an indemnity from the person buying the land,[312] because they will remain liable for breaches caused by future owners.[313] It is usually express. Enforceability of positive obligations may be secured over long periods, but only so long as each person in the chain remains alive, solvent, and traceable. Positive and indemnity covenants can be referred to on the proprietorship register of the title affected, but entries must be removed if the burdened title is sold and the covenant ceases to bind the current owner – the entry being a warning of the need to obtain an indemnity covenant on sale.[314]

---

[303] Apparently the covenant did not mention assigns.

[304] [1949] 2 KB 500, CA; EH Scammell (1954) 18 *Conv (NS)* 546, 553–556; *Amsprop Trading* v. *Harris Distribution* [1997] 1 WLR 1025.

[305] *Congleton* v. *Pattison* (1808) 10 East 130, 103 ER 725 (covenant to hire workers only within the Parish; no benefit to the land).

[306] *Smith* at 516, Denning LJ.

[307] *Dyson* v. *Forster* [1909] AC 98, 102, Lord Macnaghten (covenant not to let down surface did enhance the value of the surface).

[308] *Marchant* v. *Casewell & Redgrave* [1976] JPL 752.

[309] LPA 1925 s 78; *Rogers* v. *Hosegood* [1900] 2 Ch 388, 394, Farwell J at first instance (express wording required before 1926; can be excluded); *Shayler* v. *Woolf* [1946] Ch 320, CA (covenant to supply bungalow with water; passed without mention of assigns); on annexation see below **[34.25ff]**.

[310] *Griffith* v. *Pelton* [1958] Ch 205.

[311] *Smith & Snipe's Hall* [1949] 2 KB 500, CA (farming by wholly owned company); *Williams* v. *Unit Construction Co* (1955) 19 Conv (NS) 262, CA (sub-tenant). The old law only allowed covenants to pass with the identical legal estate.

[312] *TRW Steering Systems* v. *North Cape Properties* (1995) 69 P & CR 265, CA; *Radford* v. *De Froberville* [1977] 1 WLR 1262, Oliver J.

[313] *Re Poole & Clarke's C* [1904] 2 Ch 173, CA.

[314] DLRR 2003 rr 65–66.

O. MEANS OF ENFORCING POSITIVE OBLIGATIONS

1. Estate rentcharges

[32.53] The Rentcharges Act 1977 prevents the creation of new rentcharges as a source of profit,[315] but it allows "estate rentcharges". These are imposed in three forms to secure the enforcement of positive covenants[316] – widely used and the best method currently available for freehold housing estates.

(1) Nominal rentcharges designed to secure enforceability of covenants

[32.54] Estate rentcharges of purely nominal value can be used as a vehicle "for the purpose of making covenants to be performed by the owner of land affected by the rentcharge enforceable by the rent owner against the owner for the time being of the land".[317] Covenants could not be made to run with a rentcharge as such,[318] so it is arguable that the Act only removes perpetuity problems from rights of entry.[319] However, the point of re-entering is not to secure a money profit but because the underlying positive obligation has been broken, so the rentcharge itself is a sufficient peg on which to hang a scheme of positive covenants, and to render the covenants annexed to a nominal rentcharge inherently proprietary.

(2) Variable rentcharges to reflect the cost of work

[32.55] Repairing obligations can be made to bind successive owners by reserving the cost as a rentcharge. Pre-Act validity[320] is preserved. The legislation refers to reasonable amounts for "meeting or contributing towards the cost of performance by a rent owner of covenants for the provision of services, carrying out of maintenance or repairs, effecting of insurance or the making of any benefit of land affected by the rentcharge of the benefit of that and other land."[321] Provided the rentcharge commences immediately, subsequent fluctuations in amount under an agreed formula create no perpetuity problems. A covenant to pay 10% of the gross rateable value as a contribution to the cost of maintenance of roads is valid indefinitely.[322] Adoption of the roads raises no perpetuity issue. Also within the Act is a covenant to pay rates.[323] Benefit must be commensurate with the price to ensure that the obligation is a true estate rentcharge.[324]

---

[315] See above **[3.29ff]**.
[316] Rentcharges Act 1977 s 2(3)(c), (4); S Bright [1988] *Conv* 99.
[317] S 2(4)(a).
[318] *Haywood* v. *Brunswick PBS* (1881) 8 QBD 403, CA; *Torbay Hotel* v. *Jenkins* [1927] 2 Ch 225, 239; W Strachan (1921) 40 *LQR* 344.
[319] S Bright [1988] *Conv* 99, 103–104.
[320] *Beachway Management* v. *Wisewell* [1971] Ch 610, Plowman J; *Morland* v. *Cook* (1868) LR 6 Eq 252.
[321] Rentcharges Act 1977 s 2(4)–(5).
[322] *Beachway Management* v. *Wisewell* [1971] Ch 610, Plowman J; *Re Cassel* [1926] Ch 358, Russell J; Rentcharges Act 1977 s 2.
[323] *Orchard Trading Estate Management* v. *Johnson Security* [2002] EWCA Civ 406, [2002] 18 EG 155; S Bright [2002] *Conv* 507.
[324] At [29], Peter Gibson LJ.

(3) Statutory charges

[32.56] Also exempted from the creation and extinguishment provision of the Rentcharges Act 1977 are statutory charges to pay for work, or commuting obligations to pay for work, and rentcharges created under court orders.[325]

(4) Remedies to secure payment of rentcharges

[32.57] Rentcharges must be enforced within the limitation period.[326] The major remedy is re-entry[327] which is usually an express right. If lenders jib at lending on a terminable freehold estate the right of re-entry can be excluded,[328] but such a concern is illogical, since lenders happily accept forfeiture provisions in leasehold schemes, and lenders can obtain relief against unreasonable forfeitures.[329] Less important remedies are distress[330] and taking possession.[331] A contractual action in debt is available against the "terre tenant",[332] but not by[333] or against future owners.

(5) Sale

[32.58] Transfer of a registered title subject to a rentcharge is complicated by the need to deal with the covenants for payment.[334]

(6) Ending estate rentcharges

[32.59] Redemption procedures do not apply to estate rentcharges, which in their nature are designed to be perpetual burdens,[335] and indeed there is no procedure to modify positive covenants which have become obsolete.[336] Termination depends upon release[337] or merger.[338]

---

[325] Rentcharges Act 1977 s 2(2)(d)–(e).

[326] Now 12 years from the last acknowledgement of title: *Owen* v. *De Beavoir* (1847) 16 M & W 547, 153 ER 1307; *Shaw* v. *Crompton* [1910] 2 KB 370 (personal and real remedies both extinguished).

[327] Perpetuity is not an issue: LPA 1925 s 121(6), as amended by Perpetuities and Accumulations Act 1964 s 11(2); this was so even before 1964: SM Tolson (1950) 14 *Conv (NS)* 350, 354–357.

[328] N Dyer [1994] 27 *LSG* 16; J Snape (1994) 33 *LSG* 15.

[329] *Shiloh Spinners* v. *Harding* [1973] AC 691, 722A–725F, Lord Wilberforce.

[330] LPA 1925 s 121, dating from 1730, as amended in 1881 and 1911. A rent without a power of distress is a "rent seck": *Re Lord Gerard & Beecham's C* [1894] 3 Ch 295.

[331] LPA 1925 s 121(3)–(4).

[332] *Thomas* v. *Sylvester* (1873) LR 8 QB 368; *Christie* v. *Barker* (1884) 53 LJ QB 537; *Searle* v. *Cooke* (1890) 43 Ch D 519, CA; *Pertwee* v. *Townsend* [1896] 2 QB 129; *Re Herbage Rents* [1896] 2 Ch 811, Stirling J; T Cyprian Williams (1897) 13 *LQR* 288; *Cundiff* v. *Fitzsimmons* [1911] 1 KB 513 (lender in pre-1926 form liable).

[333] *Grant* v. *Edmondson* [1931] 1 Ch 1, CA; W Strachan (1931) 47 *LQR* 380 (critical).

[334] DLRR 2003 r 70.

[335] Rentcharges Act 1977 s 8(4).

[336] Contrast restrictive covenants; see below **[34.37ff]**.

[337] *Booth* v. *Smith* (1884) 14 QBD 318, CA.

[338] Now depends on intention: W Strachan (1911) 27 *LQR* 341, 344.

2. Free-standing rights of entry

[32.60] A right of entry may be reserved to take back property if a breach of covenant occurs, even if the covenant it supports is unenforceable.[339] In *Shiloh Spinners* v. *Harding*[340] a right of forfeiture was created on the sale of part of a leasehold mill to conserve the seller's right to support of the buildings he retained. This was enforceable when a subsequent buyer removed support, and without needing registration.[341] There is power to relieve against loss of the land – but forfeiture will be allowed after flagrant breaches. However, there is little point in adopting this dubious technique when estate rentcharges are so convenient.

3. Conditional benefits

(1) Benefit and burden

[32.61] In its pure form the doctrine of benefit and burden asserted that "anyone who takes the benefit of a deed must accept its burden",[342] but there is in fact no such rule.[343] *Rhone* v. *Stephens* shows that a right to support for a roof may be enjoyed by Walford Cottage, independent of the obligation on the owner of the House to repair the roof.[344]

(2) Doctrine of conditional benefits

[32.62] There is, however, a conditional benefits principle, first described by Lord Coke, that a person who takes the benefit of a deed is bound by a condition affecting it.[345] When exercising any right, one must observe any condition imposed at the time of its creation. Pre-eminent among the case-law illustrations[346] is *Halsall* v. *Brizzell*.[347] Cressington Park was developed in 1851 as a building estate with 174 plots on the basis that each owner agreed by deed to pay a fair proportion of the overall expenses incurred by the builders in repairing the sea wall, estate roads and sewers. The interest of the case lies in Upjohn J's obiter discussion of the basis on which the 1851 covenants were binding. If the owner of a house wished to use the roads and the

---

[339] However, perpetuity is an issue: Perpetuities and Accumulations Act 1964 s 12; *Re Trustees of Hollis' Hospital & Hague's C* [1899] 2 Ch 540; *Re Da Costa* [1912] 1 Ch 337.

[340] [1973] AC 691, HL; SM Tolson (1950) 14 *Conv (NS)* 354; PB Fairest [1971] *CLJ* 263. Free standing rights must be limited to a perpetuity period.

[341] At 717F, Lord Wilberforce; *Doe d Freeman* v. *Bateman* (1818) 2 B & Ald 168, 106 ER 328; *Hyde* v. *Warden* (1877) 3 Ex D 72, 84, CA.

[342] *Tito* v. *Waddell (No 2)* [1977] Ch 106, 289–310, Megarry V-C.

[343] *Rhone* v. *Stephens* [1994] 2 AC 310, 322E, Lord Templeman; *Law Debenture Trust Corp* v. *Ural Caspian Oil Corp* [1993] 1 WLR 138, 146E–147G, Hoffmann J; on appeal [1995] Ch 152, CA.

[344] *Rhone* may cast doubt on *ER Ives (Investment)* v. *High* [1967] 2 QB 379, CA.

[345] Coke on *Littleton*, [230b]; *Elliston* v. *Reacher* [1908] 2 Ch 665, 669, Cozens-Hardy MR; *Rhone* [1994] 2 AC 310, 322F–323A.

[346] *R* v. *Houghton-le-Spring* (1819) 2 B & Ald 375, 106 ER 403; *Chamber Colliery Co* v. *Twyerould* [1915] 1 Ch 268n, HL; *Kidner* v. *Stimpson* (1918) 35 TLR 63, CA; *Westhoughton Urban DC* v. *Wigan Coal & Iron Co* [1919] 1 Ch 159; *Naas* v. *Westminster* [1940] AC 366, 373, Viscount Maugham (settlement); *Montague* v. *Long* (1972) 24 P & CR 240, Graham J; *Tito* v. *Waddell (No 2)* [1977] Ch 106, 289–310; FR Crane (1977) 41 *Conv (NS)* 432; EP Aughterson [1985] *Conv* 12.

[347] [1957] Ch 169, Upjohn J; HWR Wade [1957] *CLJ* 35; RE Megarry (1957) 73 *LQR* 154.

sewers, he was obliged to meet the condition of contributing to the overall expenses of the estate, though he had the option of ceasing to use those advantages.[348]

The principle is decidedly limited. Owners must be free to choose. Since the defendant in *Rhone* v. *Stephens* was not free the principle did not apply, and anyway only reciprocal benefits were within the principle.[349] *Thamesmead Town* v. *Allotey*[350] illustrates the other problem that if the owners are free they may indeed choose not to make use of the rights and so avoid liability to pay for them, in that case communal open space and footpaths on a London County Council overspill estate.

4. Leasehold flat schemes

[32.63] The difficulty of securing the running of positive covenants under freehold schemes has led many developers to use leasehold estate schemes, especially for blocks of flats.[351] Covenants in leases are generally enforceable by and against future owners. This is invariable practice for flats. Housing estates may be sold leasehold, but the scheme can be disrupted by enfranchisement of individual leasehold titles, and to avoid this the ground landlord had to opt to set up an estate management scheme.[352] It may also be possible to create binding freehold covenants in those rare cases where leases are open to unilateral extension to freeholds.[353]

5. Commonhold

[32.64] Commonholds are a new method of combining freehold ownership of a part of a building (a unit, that is a flat) with secure communal management of the block and common parts by a commonhold association.[354]

The commonhold community statement will lay down the mutual scheme of regulation between the unit-holders, making provision for the rights and duties of a commonhold association and the unit-holders.[355] The form and many of the contents will be prescribed. The revolutionary feature of commonholds will be the facility with which reciprocal positive covenants may be imposed and passed on.[356] Unit holders will have duties to pay for works.[357] The commonhold association will prepare a commonhold assessment[358] taking into account the global sums spent on repairs and these will be allocated to individual units in accordance with a scheme contained in the commonhold community statement. Forfeiture of units will not be allowed, but arrears could be charged on individual units.[359] There will be an ombudsman scheme for dispute resolution.[360]

---

[348] *Parkinson* v. *Reid* (1966) 56 DLR (2d) 315.
[349] [1994] 2 AC 310, 322E–323A, Lord Templeman; CJ Davis [1998] *CLJ* 522.
[350] [1998] 3 EGLR 97, CA.
[351] DN Clarke "Occupying 'Cheek by Jowl': Property Issues Arising from Communal Housing" ch 22 in Bright & Dewar; see above [4.13ff].
[352] L Ref A 1967 s 19A, as amended.
[353] LPA 1925 s 153 (lease for 300 years with no rent); TPD Taylor (1958) 22 *Conv (NS)* 101.
[354] Chold and L ref A 2002; see above [4.16ff].
[355] Ss 31–33.
[356] S 16.
[357] S 31(3)–(5).
[358] S 38.   [359] S 31(8).
[360] S 42.

33

NEIGHBOUR BURDENS

Unregistered land: legal burdens; land charge. Registered land: neighbour burdens on the register; overriding interests.

[33.01] Property rights are needed to regulate the relationship between neighbouring land owners but from the point of view of the land affected it is simply a burden just like a mortgage or a lease – and there is the usual concern to ensure that a person buying the land becomes aware of the burden and values the land he is buying taking its burden into account. The subject of this chapter is that minus. It considers first unregistered land where the rules are relatively simple and then registered – where the categories are more confused but the practical operation is much simpler.

A. LEGAL BURDENS ON UNREGISTERED LAND

1. Legal easements

[33.02] Whilst title is unregistered burdens are either legal or equitable. Legal rights bind the world. So it is a matter of no interest whether a buyer knows of a right. All that matters is that a legal right is first created. Legal easements are automatic burdens, though generally there will be a deed of grant or conveyance of part with the title deeds.[1] Possible rights are severely limited. In terms of legal easements, the interest must be for a term matching one of the legal estates – either in fee simple or for a term of years absolute[2] though there is no need for strict words of limitation.[3]

2. Non documentary easements

[33.03] Easements can be implied when land is divided,[4] the grant or reservation being non-documentary and based on the demonstration of a necessity or use at the time of division. If title is unregistered, the conveyance effecting the division remains part of the title and one can identify readily enough the potential for an implied grant (or more rarely for an implied reservation). Grants or reservations implied at the time

---

[1] LPA 1925 s 52(1); *Wood* v. *Leadbitter* (1845) 13 M & W 838, 842, 153 ER 351, Alderson B; *Dodd* v. *Burchall* (1862) 1 H & C 113, 120, 158 ER 822, Pollock CB; *McManus* v. *Cooke* (1887) 35 Ch D 681, 686–689, Kay J.

[2] LPA 1925 s 1(2)(a); JF Garner (1948) 12 *Conv (NS)* 202; see above **[21.04]**.

[3] A Underhill (1908) 24 *LQR* 199; TC Williams (1908) 24 *LQR* 244.

[4] See below **[35]**.

of a legal conveyance are themselves legal easements, automatic in their effect against later owners. Prescriptive burdens are created by long use,[5] and these informal rights necessarily operate off the documentary title. The easement created by prescription is a legal interest, binding all comers with or without notice.[6]

3. Other legal interests

[33.04] Rentcharges and some old rents can also exist at law.[7]

B. LAND CHARGES (EQUITABLE BURDENS ON UNREGISTERED LAND)

[33.05] Land charges are the matters requiring registration against the name of the unregistered estate owner who creates them. Registration binds all later owners.[8]

1. Easements

[33.06] Many easements are legal, but others are equitable. Registration was not retrospective, and pre-1926 land obligations may continue to affect the land indefinitely, equitable rights binding according to the doctrine of notice.[9] Registration applied from 1925 onwards.

Registration under class D(iii) applies to any post-1925 equitable easement, and also to easement-like rights and privileges affecting land.[10] A true easement must benefit the land of a neighbouring owner. In *London & Blenheim Estates* v. *Ladbroke Retail Parks*[11] a right to park could be extended to benefit further land by a notice, but in advance of an extension notice this potential right was not registrable.

Class D(iii) is vague and uncertain of definition.[12] Clearly within it fall easements for life or other periods which cannot be legal.[13] Lord Denning MR narrowed the class in *ER Ives Investment* v. *High*[14] to this type alone, and hence excluded any equitable easement created by use of contractual formalities.[15] This drastic constriction is inconsistent with the plain wording of the definition of class D(iii), but the solution is just since the formality of registration is inappropriate for informally created rights.[16]

---

[5] See below [36].

[6] LPA 1925 s 12.

[7] See above [21.05ff].

[8] LPA 1925 s 198; *Newman* v. *Real Estate Debenture Corp* [1940] 1 All ER 131; *Marten* v. *Flight Refuelling* [1962] Ch 115, 140, Wilberforce J; *Wrotham Park Estate Co* v. *Parkside Homes* [1974] 1 WLR 798, 809, Brightman J; see above [21.26].

[9] Class D charges are never registrable if created before 1925: LCA 1972 s 4(7).

[10] *Lewisham BC* v. *Maloney* [1948] 1 KB 50, CA (requisition not an equitable easement).

[11] [1994] 1 WLR 31, CA.

[12] Law Com 18 (1969) nevertheless recommended no change; S Cretney (1969) 32 *MLR* 477, 487.

[13] LPA 1925 s 1(2)(a).

[14] [1967] 2 QB 379, 395, CA; *Poster* v. *Slough Estates* [1969] 1 Ch 495, Cross J; AG Guest & J Lever (1963) 27 *Conv (NS)* 30, 33. Contrast registered land below at [33.21].

[15] CV Davidge (1937) 53 *LQR* 259; HWR Wade [1956] *CLJ* 216, 225–226.

[16] [1967] 2 QB 379, 395; Roxburgh Committee (Cmnd 9826, 1956), [16]; HWR Wade [1956] *CLJ* 216; Law Com 18 (1969), [63]; S Cretney (1969) 32 *MLR* 477, 487; G Battersby (1995) 58 *MLR* 637, 645–648.

A better way to achieve the same contraction is to exclude from Class D(iii) any interest created by estoppel,[17] a tenant's right to remove fixtures at the expiration of the
lease[18] and equitable rights of re-entry.[19]

2. Restrictive covenants

[33.07] Restrictive covenants are usually created by a deed of covenant, though *Tulk*
v. *Moxhay*[20] shows that formality is not essential. The burden is proprietary if (1) the
covenant is restrictive, (2) the wording is proprietary, and (3) the neighbour principle
is complied with – there must be land to be benefitted and actual benefit of it. If these
requirements are met, there is a restrictive covenant which is an equitable interest
in the land, and so one which is protectible and if unprotected is vulnerable to a
protected purchaser.

Class D(ii)[21] requires registration of any "covenant or agreement restrictive of the
user of land" against the name of the landowner burdened by it. Unfortunately this
name has often slipped off a modern unregistered title making the registrations almost
undiscoverable.[22] Restrictive covenants entered into with local authorities require
entry as local land charges instead.

3. Pre-1926 restrictive covenants affecting unregistered land

[33.08] Registration was not retrospective, and notice continues to apply to pre-1926
restrictive covenants.[23] Many towns were developed in the Victorian or Edwardian
periods, and those restrictive covenants will not appear on the register. Notice doctrine to pass the burden of restrictive covenants so as to bind later owners[24] of unregistered titles developed by analogy with equitable easements.[25] "No one purchasing
with notice of the equity can stand in a different situation from the party from whom
he purchased."[26] Buyers usually get notice because a memorandum of the covenants
is endorsed on the conveyance creating a division,[27] because sellers disclose them,[28]
and because covenants are always repeated in later sales of the burden land.[29]

---

[17] *ER Ives* at 405C–F, Winn LJ; see above **[23.41]**.

[18] *Poster* v. *Slough Estates* [1969] 1 Ch 495, Cross J.

[19] *Shiloh Spinners* v. *Harding* [1973] AC 691, HL; D Yates (1974) 37 *MLR* 87; PB Fairest [1971] *CLJ* 258,
[1973] *CLJ* 218.

[20] (1848) 2 Ph 774, 778, 41 ER 1143; *Brooker* v. *Drysdale* (1877) 3 CPD 52, 57–58; *Westacott* v. *Hahn*
[1918] 1 KB 495, 504, Pitchford LJ.

[21] LCA 1972 s 2(1)(ii); RG Rowley (1956) 20 *Conv (NS)* 370.

[22] See above **[21.32]**.

[23] In operation a purchaser with actual knowledge of a restrictive covenant is often unfairly to defeat it
for non-registration.

[24] *Tulk* v. *Moxhay* (1848) 2 Ph 774, 41 ER 1143, Cottenham LC; *Mann* v. *Stephens* (1846) 15 Sim 377, 60
ER 665; *Jay* v. *Richardson* (1862) 30 Beav 563, 54 ER 1008.

[25] S Gardner (1982) 98 *LQR* 279; W Strachan (1930) 46 *LQR* 159; JF Garner (1962) 26 *Conv (NS)* 298;
DJ Hayton (1971) 87 *LQR* 539; S Robinson (1974) 38 *Conv (NS)* 90; JDA Brooke-Taylor [1978] *Conv* 24.

[26] *Tulk* at 778, Cottenham LC; *McLean* v. *McKay* (1873) LR 5 PC 327, 336; *Haywood* v. *Brunswick PBS*
(1881) 8 QBD 403, 409, CA; *Rogers* v. *Hosegood* [1900] 2 Ch 388, 401; *Re Nisbett & Pott's C* [1906] 1 Ch
386, CA; *Wilkes* v. *Spooner* [1911] 2 KB 473; *London CC* v. *Allen* [1914] 3 KB 642, 665.

[27] Conveyancing Act 1911 s 11 (now superseded by registration).

[28] *Faruqi* v. *English Real Estate* [1979] 1 WLR 963, Walton J (registered land).

[29] *Rogers* v. *Hosegood* [1900] 2 Ch 388, 394, Farwell J.

4. Landlord and tenant

[33.09] Covenants entered into between landlord and tenant are not registrable as restrictive covenants, since they run as leasehold covenants and anyway a person buying the lease will read the lease and obtain notice in that way.[30] This is so even if the benefit of the covenant attaches to *neighbouring* land of the landlord,[31] though this kind of covenant is much more like a true restrictive covenant and should surely be treated as such.[32]

C. NEIGHBOUR BURDENS ON THE REGISTER

[33.10] If title is registered, any burden should be protected on the register by a mutual or unilateral notice.[33]

1. Legal easements

[33.11] The benefit of a legal easement is recorded and guaranteed on one register and the corresponding burden is recorded by notice on another. Other easements are recorded as burdens without any guarantee of the benefit; examples are "legal" easements created against unregistered owners or where only the burdened title is registered, equitable easements created by a contract for an easement,[34] and other equitable easements.[35]

2. Rentcharges, franchises and profits

[33.12] These interests are substantively registrable, but the burden appears by notice against the title bound.[36] Examples are rentcharges (until extinguished in 2038),[37] franchises, profits, and any other interest or charge which benefits or burdens an interest with a registered title.

Profits are rights to use another's land for activities such as grazing or fishing; if they are used in common they are registrable under the Commons Registration Act 1965, but individual profits will be registrable for the first time. Rights may exist in gross, that is without specific land to benefit and such profits as fishing rights may

---

[30] LCA 1972 s 2; *Newman* v. *Real Estate Debenture Corp* [1940] 1 All ER 131; DW Logan (1940) 56 *LQR* 361, (1940) 4 *MLR* 51; AK Kiralfy (1949) 13 *Conv (NS)* 173; *Langevad* v. *Chiswick Quay Freeholds* [1999] 1 EGLR 61, 62L–M, Buxton LJ; *Oceanic Villages* v. *United Attractions* [2000] Ch 234, Neuberger J (void for non-registration).

[31] *Dartstone* v. *Cleveland Petroleum Co* [1969] 1 WLR 1807, Pennycuick J.

[32] Compare registered land, see LRA 2002 s 33(c).

[33] See above **[20.01ff]**.

[34] *East India Co* v. *Vincent* (1740) 2 Atk 83, 26 ER 451; *McManus* v. *Cooke* (1887) 35 Ch D 681, Kay J; *Cory* v. *Davies* [1923] 2 Ch 95, PO Lawrence J; *Mason* v. *Clarke* [1955] AC 778, HL; HWR Wade [1955] *CLJ* 161; G Williams (1955) 18 *MLR* 408; G Williams (1961) 25 *Conv (NS)* 497.

[35] CV Davidge (1937) 53 *LQR* 259; P Jackson (1968) 32 *Conv (NS)* 135.

[36] See above **[20.04]**.

[37] Rentcharges Act 1977 s 3.

have considerable economic value. Franchises are things like grants of market rights or toll bridges; this provision is new.

3. Restrictive covenants

[33.13] Covenants are proprietary if (1) the covenant is restrictive, (2) the wording is proprietary, and (3) the neighbour principle is complied with – there must be land to be benefitted and actual benefit of it.[38] An equitable interest is created in the burdened land, which is protectible by notice.

4. First registration of unregistered titles

[33.14] On first registration of title adverse interests apparent from the title from searches or from disclosure to the registrar should be transferred to the register and protected by notice.[39] Entry of a notice on the register does not create a building scheme.[40] Restrictive covenants are often not disclosed at the time of first registration, and if so there is a problem about whether to alter the register to include them.[41] Positive covenants do not create burdens,[42] and the covenant may only be recorded against the individual proprietor affected and not as a burden on the charges register.[43]

5. Removal of entries

[33.15] Entries are discharged on production of adequate evidence that the right has ended,[44] whether by formal release, informal release by contract, or circumstances that amount to abandonment of the right.

D. OVERRIDING INTERESTS

1. Interests overriding first registration

[33.16] First registration takes effect subject to any legal easement or profit a prendre.[45] On first registration this is not limited in any way – easements will override whether the easement is formal or created by informal grant or by prescription. However, unregistered rights should be disclosed on first registration when a notice will be entered, and it is vitally important as will appear below to get easements on to the register if at all possible. If easements are omitted from the first register, this can be altered later to bring on the rights omitted.[46]

---

[38] See above **[32.40ff]**.
[39] DLRR 2003 rr 32–34; *Hodges* v. *Jones* [1935] 1 Ch 657; see above [9.32].
[40] *Willé* v. *St John* [1910] 1 Ch 84; on appeal [1910] 1 Ch 325, CA.
[41] See above **[11.44ff]**.
[42] *Cator* v. *Newton* [1940] 1 KB 415, CA; *Barnes* v. *Cadogan Developments* [1930] 1 Ch 479.
[43] See above **[32.52]**.
[44] See above **[20.12]**.
[45] LRA 2002 sch 1 para 3; Law Com 271 (2001), [8.23–8.25], EN [584–586].
[46] See above **[11.40]**.

2. Formal easements

(1) Created before the 2002 Act commencement

[33.17] The wide scope of the definition of the overriding interest under the old legislation was astounding. Strictly it is unnecessary to enter any legal easement on the register of the burdened land,[47] since it would take effect anyway as an overriding interest. Express easements created before the 2002 Act could continue to be overriding.

(2) Express easements and profits granted out of registered titles

[33.18] Overriding status can no longer be claimed for an easement or profit created out of a registered title after the 2002 Act commencement; only legal rights override and legal status is dependent upon completion of the registration requirements.[48] Indeed in future no right will exist unless electronic formality has been followed by automatic registration.[49] Overall therefore there has been a profound and welcome change of emphasis from the days when interests were removed from the register if they would in any event be overriding interests.[50]

3. Easements created on division or by prescription

[33.19] After first registration it is not easy to tell from the title the sequence of divisions and hence whether there has been a case for implied grants or implied reservation, and if so with which neighbours. Any easement that is implied will override, despite being detectable only from their use.[51] Information about the history of a title can now be obtained from the registry.[52]

Prescriptive burdens create rights which operate off the documentary title. The legal rights created against an unregistered title are matched by an interest that overrides a registered title.[53]

4. Undiscoverable easements excluded

[33.20] Easements will not be able to override a transfer if they are undiscoverable. Overriding status is withdrawn from an easement[54] if it is:

registered under Commons Registration Act 1965;
within the actual knowledge of the purchaser;
one that would have been obvious on a reasonably careful inspection of the land; or
one that has been exercised within the year before the transfer.

---

[47] An easement appurtenant to an interest that overrides will itself continue to override.
[48] LRA 2002 s 27(1), sch 2 para 7.
[49] Law Com 271 (2001), [8.2], [8.53].
[50] *Willies-Williams* v. *National Trust* (1993) 65 P & CR 359, 362, Hoffmann LJ.
[51] LRR 1925 r 258; M Davey [1986] *Conv* 296.
[52] LRA 2002 s 69; Law Com 271 (2001), [9.58–9.60], EN [306–309]; DLRR 2003 rr 144–145; C Hood [2002] 28 *EG* 124; see above **[8.16]**.
[53] LRA 2002 schs 1/3 para 2; [2002] 09 *LSG* 42.
[54] LRA 2002 sch 3 para 2; Law Com 271 (2001), [8.68–8.72], EN [623–625]; C Hood [2002] 28 *EG* 124.

5. Transitional protection for equitable interests

[33.21] The overriding status of equitable easements is preserved transitionally.[55] The statutory wording of the 1925 Act[56] excluded equitable rights but these were brought back into overriding status by n incautiously worded rule.[57] Equitable easement now need registration, as they would if title was unregistered,[58] but overriding status is preserved for three years to allow time for registration to occur.[59]

6. Others

[33.22] Overriding interests considered above include customary and public rights and a miscellaneous category preserved for a transitional 10 year period.[60]

---

[55] Law Com 271 (2001), [8.73], EN [608].
[56] LRA 1925 s 70(1)(a).
[57] LRR 1925 r 258; *Celsteel* v. *Alton House Holdings* [1985] 1 WLR 204, Scott J; on appeal [1986] 1 WLR 512, CA; MP Thompson [1986] *Conv* 31; PH Kenny (1985) 82 *LSG* 339; AM Prichard, [1987] *Conv* 328; M Davey [1986] *Conv* 296; *Leeman* v. *Mohammed* (2001) 82 P & CR 14 at 159, CA.
[58] See above **[33.06]**.
[59] See above **[20.29]**.
[60] See above **[20.30]**, **[20.33]**.

34

NEIGHBOUR BENEFITS

Easements: neighbour principle; loss of benefit. Restrictive covenants:
neighbour principle; schemes of development; neighbour obligations;
annexation; failure of benefit; remedies; modification.

A. EASEMENTS: NEIGHBOUR PRINCIPLE

1. Requirement for benefitted land

[34.01] The minus, in the shape of land burdened by the obligation,[1] must be balanced by a plus. Land benefitted by an easement is traditionally called a dominant tenement.[2] If there is no land to benefit, the right is said to exist in gross, but in truth this is just another way of saying that it is not an easement.[3] A right of way can exist as an easement to get to a house or other land, but not as a benefit to a non-landowner.[4] Hence, a right to put deckchairs on the seashore is not an easement.[5] Nor is it possible to separate an easement from the land benefitted.[6]

What degree of proximity is required? The need for an actual benefit has always ensured that there has been a fairly close proximity between the land benefitted and that burdened. Touching has never been necessary.[7] The right to use a pleasure park in *Re Ellenborough Park*[8] extended beyond the houses fronting on to the garden to embrace other houses in the immediate locality. But the connection may be meta-physical as well as physical.[9] Technological innovations make it possible to conceive of situations in which the two pieces of land may be separated by a considerable distance. Could a right to use a helicopter landing pad on the Cornish mainland be an easement benefitting land in the Isles of Scilly?[10] Or a storage facility in Kent benefit a

---

[1] Exercise of a right creates no corresponding right in the burdened owner to its continuance: *Mason* v. *Shrewsbury & Hereford Rly* (1871) LR 6 QB 578, 586.

[2] Coke on *Littleton*, [121b], says no; but the modern law is that it could benefit a fishing right or other intangible right: *Hanbury* v. *Jenkins* [1901] 2 Ch 401.

[3] MF Sturley (1980) 96 *LQR* 557; S Gardner (1982) 98 *LQR* 305; P Brett (1950) 14 *Conv (NS)* 264. Contrast profits, below **[36.34]**.

[4] *Smetebee* v. *Holt* YB 21 Edw 3 (1347) fo 2 pl 5; *Thorpe* v. *Brumfitt* (1873) LR 8 Ch App 650; *Hamble PC* v. *Haggard* [1992] 1 WLR 122, Millett J.

[5] *Ramsgate Corp* v. *Debling* (1906) 22 TLR 369; *Rangeley* v. *Midland Rly Co* (1868) LR 3 Ch App 306, 310–311; *London & Blenheim Estates* v. *Ladbroke Retail Parks* [1994] 1 WLR 31, 36, Peter Gibson LJ.

[6] *Ackroyd* v. *Smith* (1850) 10 CB 164, 188, 138 ER 68, Cresswell J.

[7] *Todrick* v. *Western National Omnibus Co* [1934] Ch 190, Farwell J; approved [1934] Ch 561, CA; *Pugh* v. *Savage* [1970] 2 QB 373, CA; *Voice* v. *Bell* (1995) 68 P & CR 441, CA.

[8] [1956] Ch 131, 167, Evershed MR; *Mulvaney* v. *Gough* [2002] EWCA Civ 1078, [2002] 44 EG 175.

[9] *Moody* v. *Steggles* (1879) 12 Ch D 261, 266, Fry J.

[10] MF Sturley (1980) 96 *LQR* 557, 565, 567–568.

haulier's business in Calais? An artificial connection could be created between two plots of land many miles apart by a pipeline running between them,[11] but easements are not an appropriate way to give effect to such ephemeral connections.

2. Separate owners

[34.02] An easement is a right exercised over someone else's land, so the existence of the right necessarily suggests the existence of two different owners. After all, a person exercising rights over his own land acts as owner. It is sometimes said that he exercises a "quasi-easement", but this has no significance until a physical division, when some quasi-easements in use at that moment can be converted to full easements.[12] A landlord's reversion is a sufficient estate in the land to form either benefitted or burdened land,[13] especially where the lease affects part only of his land, but where a landlord grants access rights to his tenant or vice versa, it is better to see such rights as leasehold obligations.[14]

Any easement is destroyed by *unity of ownership*,[15] that is common ownership of the entire legal and equitable interests in both properties.[16] Already old in 1694,[17] this rule applied to express grants, implied grants,[18] and by prescription.[19] New easements will have to be created if the two old tenements, having once been united, are once again divided.[20] If occupation is shared while the ownership remains separate[21] any easement is suspended, but such that it can spring back to life if the occupation once again separates.[22]

3. Extent of the benefitted land

[34.03] Initial identification of the two tenements should occur in the deed granting the easement.[23] If this is overlooked extrinsic evidence may be used,[24] and this is inevitable when rights are acquired by use.

Unilateral extension of the land benefitted at the instance of its owner is not allowed. Otherwise he might start with one field and buy another, and another,

---

[11] *Stockport Waterworks Co* v. *Potter* (1864) 3 H & C 300, 327, 159 ER 545.

[12] See below [34].

[13] *Thorpe* v. *Brumfitt* (1873) LR 8 Ch App 650.

[14] See above [27.40ff].

[15] Except possibly an easement of necessity: *Sury* v. *Pigott* (1676) Pop 166, 79 ER 1263; *Buckby* v. *Coles* (1814) 5 Taunt 311, 128 ER 709.

[16] *Hinchliff* v. *Kinnoul* (1838) 5 Bing NC 1, 132 ER 1004 (lease).

[17] *Peers* v. *Lucy* (1694) 4 Mod Rep 362, 87 ER 444; *Tyrringham's case* (1584) 4 Co Rep 36b, 38a, 77 ER 973; *Gateward's case* (1607) 6 Co Rep 59b, 77 ER 344.

[18] *Morris* v. *Edginton* (1810) 3 Taunt 24, 128 ER 10; *Barlow* v. *Rhodes* (1833) 1 Cr & M 439, 149 ER 471; *Ward* v. *Kirkland* [1967] Ch 194.

[19] JDA Brooke-Taylor (1977) 41 *Conv (NS)* 107; *White* v. *Taylor (No 2)* [1969] 1 Ch 160.

[20] *Barlow* v. *Rhodes* (1833) 1 Cr & M 439, 149 ER 471 (express); *James* v. *Plant* (1836) 4 Ad & El 749, 111 ER 967 (implied).

[21] Eg A owns plot X and holds plot Y as tenant.

[22] *R* v. *Inhabitants of Hermitage* (1692) Carth 239, 241, 90 ER 743; *Thomas* v. *Thomas* (1835) 2 Cr M & R 34, 40, 150 ER 15, Abinger CB; *Simper* v. *Foley* (1862) 2 John & H 555, 563, 564, 70 ER 1179; *Richardson* v. *Graham* [1908] 1 KB 39.

[23] *McKay* v. *Surrey CC* [1998] EGCS 180, Ch D.

[24] *Johnstone* v. *Holdway* [1963] 1 QB 601, CA.

increasing the burden to a great extent.[25] Use of a way attached to field A as a means of gaining access to field B is an excess of the right.[26] Similarly if the owner of No 3 in a private cul-de-sac buys an adjoining building plot, he needs a separate right of way to the building plot.[27] Intentions are irrelevant.[28] However a right of way to Figsbury Rings could be used as an access to a visitor's car park sited just off the Rings since this was reasonably incidental,[29] there being no objection to an accidental benefit to other land.[30] Prescriptive easements are limited in the same way.[31] In *Massey* v. *Burden*[32] a vehicular access across a common could be acquired so as to benefit not only School Cottage East, but also the two adjoining parish rooms which were incorporated into the house in 1977; access to those additional rooms was purely ancillary.

Attempts to reserve a right to benefit later acquisitions have foundered in several recent cases. *Voice* v. *Bell*[33] restates the rule that future undefined land cannot form a dominant tenement. Further refinement occurred in *London & Blenheim Estates* v. *Ladbroke Retail Parks*[34] On a sale of part of its land to London & Blenheim in 1987, Leicester Co-op granted the right to park on its retained land and this was extended (by clause 11) to any other land bought by London & Blenheim within five years once notice had been given to include it. Additional land was bought in December 1987 but, before notice could be given, the Co-op sold the burdened land. It was held that no easement existed in relation to the additional land against its new owners (Ladbrokes).

Alterations to the dominant tenement have created problems, both in the context of the right to light[35] and other easements.[36]

4. Passage of easements on sale of the land benefitted

[34.04] It is general practice when selling unregistered land to sell "together with" the benefit of specific existing express easements.[37] Legal easements benefitting registered titles are guaranteed and entered as pluses on the property register, and pass

---

[25] *Lawton* v. *Ward* (1696) 1 Ld Raym 75, 91 ER 946.

[26] *Skull* v. *Glenister* (1864) 16 CB NS 81, 143 ER 1055.

[27] *Bracewell* v. *Appleby* [1975] Ch 408, Graham J; *Das* v. *Linden* [2002] EWCA Civ 590, [2002] 2 EGLR 76.

[28] *Nickerson* v. *Barraclough* [1980] Ch 325, Megarry V-C; on appeal [1981] Ch 426, 436–437, Brightman LJ; *Harris* v. *Flower* (1904) 74 LJ Ch 127.

[29] *National Trust* v. *White* [1987] 1 WLR 907, Warner J; JE Martin [1987] *Conv* 365; *Graham* v. *Philcox* [1984] QB 747, CA.

[30] *Simpson* v. *Godmanchester Corp* [1897] AC 696, HL; *Britel Developments (Thatcham)* v. *Nightfreight (GB)* [1998] 4 All ER 432, Ch D.

[31] *Howell* v. *King* (1674) 1 Mod Rep 190, 86 ER 821.

[32] [2002] EWCA Civ 1634, [2003] 06 EG 147.

[33] (1993) 68 P & CR 441, CA.

[34] [1994] 1 WLR 31, CA.

[35] *Ecclesiastical Commissioners* v. *Kino* (1880) 14 Ch D 213, CA; *Scott* v. *Pape* (1886) 31 Ch D 554; *Andrews* v. *Waite* [1907] 2 Ch 500 (no window); *Ankerson* v. *Connelly* [1900] 2 Ch 544, on appeal [1907] 1 Ch 678, CA.

[36] *Liggins* v. *Inge* (1831) 7 Bing 682, 131 ER 263; *National Guaranteed Manure Co* v. *Donald* (1859) 4 H & N 8, 157 ER 737; *Carr* v. *Lambert* (1866) LR 1 Ex 168 (pasture); *Ray* v. *Fairway Motors (Barnstaple)* (1968) 20 P & CR 261 (support); S Cretney (1969) 119 *NLJ* 852.

[37] *Roswell* v. *Prior* (1701) Holt KB 500, 90 ER 1175.

automatically.[38] Even more basically, easements are enjoyed "by the owner of one estate, whoever he may be, over the other estate, into whose hands soever it may come."[39] Transfer on sale of the benefitted land is automatic, and the benefit is split on a sale of part[40] or the grant of a lease.[41]

5. Related rights not requiring a dominant tenement

[34.05] Some rights can be enforced by a person who does not own neighbouring land, that is they may exist in gross. Examples are profits, customs, public rights, true incorporeal hereditaments and statutory rights.[42]

B. EASEMENTS: BENEFITTING RIGHTS

[34.06] Unregistered title deeds should show by inclusion what rights are conveyed "together with" the land, that is what rights are appurtenant to the land. Legal rights appurtenant to registered titles may be noted in the register.[43]

C. EASEMENTS: LOSS OF BENEFIT

1. Release

[34.07] Termination of an easement at law requires the formality of a deed, and (where title is registered) application for removal of the entries on benefitted and burdened land.[44] A contract to release is effective in equity. The person who releases must be fully informed of his rights.[45] An estoppel might end an easement after proof of expenditure.[46]

2. Abandonment

[34.08] There is no statutory procedure for terminating private easements.[47] So if an easement becomes out of date it is necessary to prove an intention to abandon the

---

[38] In any event, general words pass existing easements: LPA 1925 s 62. The specific words for registered land in LRR 1925 r 251 have not been replaced.

[39] *Keppell* v. *Bailey* (1834) 2 My & K 517, 528, 39 ER 1042, Brougham LC; *Beddington* v. *Atlee* (1887) 35 Ch D 317, 326, Chitty J.

[40] *Newcomen* v. *Coulson* (1877) 5 Ch D 133, CA.

[41] *Skull* v. *Glenister* (1864) 16 CB NS 81, 143 ER 1055.

[42] See above **[32.24]**.

[43] DLRR 2003 rr 31, 74–75.

[44] See above **[20.12]**, **[33.15]**.

[45] *Obadia* v. *Morris* (1974) 232 EG 333.

[46] *Tehidy Minerals* v. *Norman* [1971] 2 QB 528, CA.

[47] De facto variation occurs if notice is given of a proposed realignment of a right of way, and no objection is taken: *Greenwich Healthcare NHS Trust* v. *London & Quadrant HT* [1998] 1 WLR 1749, Lightman J.

easement.[48] This is not presumed[49] since lack of practical use is not the same as abandonment.[50] No abandonment was shown by non-use over 175 years since 1818[51] or by non-use while obstructed by an Air Ministry requisition.[52] However, where a right is blocked and use is impracticable – perhaps because a factory has been built over a right of way,[53] or because concrete blocks have prevented parking over many years without objection,[54] the right to equitable remedies may be lost

Again, register entries should be removed when adequate evidence is produced.[55]

3. Excessive use – as a breach

[34.09] Use of the land made by the benefitted owner must fall within the terms of the easement. Trivial variations will not matter,[56] but the burden must not be substantially increased.[57] The test is whether there is a significantly greater burden thrown onto the servient tenement. For example in *Todrick* v. *Western National Omnibus Co* the use was heavier than the road could bear.[58] Having conferred a limited right over his land there is no reason why the burdened owner should be compelled to grant a greater right.

4. Excessive use – as a ground to terminate the right

[34.10] Does excessive use terminate an easement for the future? This question has divided the judiciary. Some judges say that the right is removed where the mode of use is altered so substantially as to prejudice the enjoyment of the servient tenement by its owner.[59] But in *Graham* v. *Philcox*[60] May LJ doubted (obiter) whether excessive use of a right of way could ever extinguish or suspend it. Reversion to a lawful use would render any excessive use irrelevant.

An application to establish termination of right of way needs protection on the register.[61]

---

[48] Onus on the person alleging it: *Ray* v. *Fairway Motors (Barnstaple)* (1980) 20 P & CR 261, 272, Russell LJ.

[49] *Snell & Prideaux* v. *Dutton Mirrors* [1995] 1 EGLR 259, CA (blocked by protest; damages only); C Davies [1995] *Conv* 291.

[50] *Swan* v. *Sinclair* [1924] 1 Ch 254, CA; *Gotobed* v. *Pridmore* (1971) 217 EG 759, CA; *Obadia* v. *Morris* (1974) 232 EG 333; *Williams* v. *Usherwood* (1983) 45 P & CR 235, CA; *Bosomworth* v. *Faber* (1992) 69 P & CR 288, CA.

[51] *Benn* v. *Hardinge* (1992) 66 P & CR 246, CA; *Wyld* v. *Silver* [1963] Ch 243, CA. (1875); *New Windsor Corp* v. *Mellor* [1975] Ch 380, CA.

[52] *Mann* v. *RC Earys* (1973) 231 EG 843.

[53] *Snell & Prideaux* v. *Dutton Mirrors* [1994] EGCS 78, CA.

[54] *West* v. *Sharp* (2000) 79 P & CR 327, CA.

[55] See above **[20.12]**.

[56] *Harvey* v. *Walters* (1873) LR 8 CP 162; *Attwood* v. *Bovis Homes* [2001] Ch 379, Neuberger J; HW Wilkinson [2001] *NLJ* 1207.

[57] *Wong* v. *Beaumont* [1965] 1 QB 173, CA; *Skull* v. *Glenister* (1864) 16 CB NS 81, 143 ER 1055, Williams J; *White* v. *Richards* (1995) 68 P & CR 105, CA; *Jelbert* v. *Davis* [1968] 1 WLR 589, CA (caravans); *Fairview New Homes* v. *Government Row Residents Assoc* [1998] EGCS 92, Scott V-C.

[58] [1934] Ch 190, Farwell J; approved [1934] Ch 561, CA.

[59] *Ray* v. *Fairway Motors (Barnstaple)* (1980) 20 P & CR 261 (support increased).

[60] [1984] QB 747.

[61] *Willies-Williams* v. *National Trust* (1993) 65 P & CR 359.

D. RESTRICTIVE COVENANTS: NEIGHBOUR PRINCIPLE

1. Application to restrictive covenants

[34.11] A restrictive covenant creates a relationship between two pieces of land, one subject to the burden of the covenant and the other carrying the benefit of it. In this way covenants reflect the restrictive easements on which they are modelled.[62] Common ancestry is most apparent in the neighbourhood principle, that is the rule that both easements and restrictive covenants require benefitted land.[63] In *Tulk* v. *Moxhay* itself, Tulk owned several houses in Leicester Square which were benefitted by the restriction on building. Lord Cottenham LC[64] allowed enforcement of the restrictions because otherwise it would be impossible for a landowner to protect his retained land against devaluation by the use made of it by the buyer of a neighbouring part.[65]

An absolute requirement for benefitted land was settled by a series of Court of Appeal decisions around 1900[66] leading to a definitive statement in *London County Council* v. *Allen*.[67] Mr Allen covenanted with the Council (which owned no nearby land) not to build over the site of a proposed road. He conveyed the site to Mrs Allen, who took with notice of the covenant, but who proceeded to ignore the covenant. No doubt Allen's breach of contract was actionable in damages, but that was a marginal consolation to the council which failed to protect the line set aside for the road. A covenant lacking land to benefit did not create an endurable burden even against a purchaser with notice.

Planning authorities,[68] housing authorities[69] and local authorities[70] can now enforce covenants as such without benefitted land, a concession also extended to the National Trust[71] and some environmental agencies.[72]

2. Identification of the benefited land

[34.12] Land benefitted by a covenant must be ascertainable.[73] Precise delineation in the covenant itself is best, but it may suffice to use an ambiguous phrase such as

---

[62] *London & SW Rly* v. *Gomm* (1882) 20 Ch D 562, 583, Jessel MR; *London CC* v. *Allen* [1914] 3 KB 642, 655, Buckley LJ; *Rogers* v. *Hosegood* [1900] 2 Ch 388, 394, Farwell J (more doubtful).

[63] The "dominant tenement" of an easement (a common law phrase) is replaced in the law of covenants by "dominant land" to reflect the equitable origin of restrictive covenants. Indeed a legal estate is unnecessary: *Rogers* v. *Hosegood* [1900] 2 Ch 388, CA.

[64] (1848) 2 Ph 774, 777, 41 ER 1143; see above **[32.37]**.

[65] *London CC* v. *Allen* [1914] 3 KB 642, 654, Buckley LJ, 665, Scrutton LJ; CD Bell [1981] *Conv* 55.

[66] *London & SW Rly* v. *Gomm* (1882) 20 Ch D 562, CA; *Formby* v. *Barker* [1903] 2 Ch 539, CA.

[67] [1914] 3 KB 642, CA; *Tophams* v. *Sefton* [1967] 1 AC 50, HL (covenant failed because of absence of benefitted land).

[68] Town and Country Planning Act 1990 s 106.

[69] Housing Act 1985 s 609.

[70] Local Government (MP) Act 1982 s 33.

[71] National Trust Act 1937 s 8; *National Trust* v. *Midland EB* [1952] Ch 380 (Malvern Hills); *Gee* v. *National Trust* [1966] 1 WLR 170, 174E; *Re Whiting's Applic* (1989) 58 P & CR 321 L Tr.

[72] R Castle & I Hodge [1994] *Conv* 122.

[73] *Formby* v. *Barker* [1903] 2 Ch 539, 554, Romer LJ; *Re Rutherford's Conveyance* [1938] Ch 396, Simonds J.

"adjoining land"[74] or rely on its identity being implicit in the purpose of the sale.[75] In *Marten* v. *Flight Refuelling*[76] a purchaser covenanted "with the vendor and its successors in title" to use land only for agriculture, but it was possible for the parties to agree a map of the Crichel Estate owned by the vendor which benefitted. Where title is registered. Identification takes place at the date of the transfer rather than the later date of registration.[77]

3. Actual benefit

[34.13] Actual benefit is a requirement for restrictive covenants as it is for easements. Like pre-1996 leasehold covenants, the test is: does the covenant touch and concern the land? It may do so because it affects the mode of occupation or because it inherently affects the value.[78] Covenants accepted include to erect only one house on a residential plot, to use only as a dwelling, or not to build. Novel covenants not yet considered in the courts inevitably give more pause for thought but the subjective view of the neighbour who imposes the covenant may be decisive.[79]

Very frequently an attempt is made to benefit a wide area. Case-law shows that wide areas can be within the potential benefit of a covenant, especially covenants to protect agricultural land. In *Marten* v. *Flight Refuelling*[80] a covenant affecting a 200 acre airfield was held to be capable of benefitting the whole of the Crichel Estate, spreading over 7,500 acres of east Dorset.[81]

4. Unity of ownership

[34.14] A restrictive covenant ends if the benefitted and burdened land pass into the same hands at any time after the creation of the covenant. So-called "unity of seisin" extinguishes the burden, and the possibility of assignment of the benefit.[82] However, restrictions under building schemes survive despite shared ownership of plots.[83]

---

[74] (1) "Neighbouring land": *Re Selwyn's Conveyance* [1967] Ch 674; JW Harris (1968) 31 *MLR* 459; (2) "adjacent land" need not be touching: *Re Ecclesiastical Commissioners for England's Conveyance* [1936] Ch 430; (3) "adjoining land" does generally touch: *Harrison* v. *Good* (1871) LR 11 Eq 338; *Caldy Manor Estate* v. *Farrell* [1974] 1 WLR 1303.

[75] *McLean* v. *McKay* (1873) LR 5 PC 327, 335; *Sheppard* v. *Gilmore* (1887) 57 LT 614; *Newton Abbot Co-operative Society* v. *Williamson & Treadgold* [1952] Ch 286, Upjohn J; *Re Hextall's Applic* (2000) 79 P & CR 382, L Tr (agricultural covenant clearly benefitted houses sold under the public sector right to buy).

[76] [1962] Ch 115, Wilberforce J; L Elphinstone (1952) 68 *LQR* 353; *Leicester* v. *Wells-next-the-Sea UDC* [1973] Ch 110, 124–125, Plowman J; *Shepherd Homes* v. *Sandham (No 2)* [1971] 1 WLR 1062, 1070.

[77] *Mellon* v. *Sinclair* [1997] 2 CLYB 4258, CA.

[78] *Rogers* v. *Hosegood* [1900] 2 Ch 388, 395, Farwell J at first instance; see above **[27.39]**.

[79] *Wrotham Park Estate Co* v. *Parkside Homes* [1974] 1 WLR 798; CT Emery [1974] *CLJ* 214; *Northborne* v. *Johnston & Son* [1922] 2 Ch 309.

[80] [1962] Ch 115, 136, Wilberforce J; PV Baker (1968) 84 *LQR* 22; *Leicester* v. *Wells-next-the-Sea UDC* [1973] Ch 110, Plowman J (18 acres burdened, 32,000 acre Holkham Estate benefitted); RJ Smith [1973] *CLJ* 28.

[81] At 138; JAG Griffith (1955) 18 *MLR* 557 (political ramifications).

[82] *Keates* v. *Lyon* (1869) LR 4 Ch App 218; *Re Tiltwood, Sussex* [1978] Ch 269, Foster J.

[83] See below **[34.15ff]**.

E. RESTRICTIVE COVENANTS: SCHEMES OF DEVELOPMENT

[34.15] Schemes of development allow mutuality in the enforcement of covenants which are restrictive but not under present law of positive obligations.[84]

1. Requirements

[34.16] There are three essentials. (1) A scheme must be planned in advance,[85] since common restrictions must be imposed on an area of land divided into plots.[86] The building scheme for a residential estate is the most common species within the wider genus,[87] with each plot representing one house. The same principle has been applied to a scheme of commercial business leases within a single development.[88] Continuing restrictions maintain the tone of the estate, preventing further division, imposing building lines, or regulating fences and roads. Schemes of development might also govern the division of an existing block of flats,[89] an existing housing estate,[90] or (in theory) an industrial estate. (2) The geographical scope of the development must be defined since a local law is created for a particular area which must be ring fenced[91] on an estate plan. There are substantial difficulties with sub-schemes.[92] (3) Mutuality is required. Two early cases pre-date *Tulk* v. *Moxhay* (1848),[93] but the law was authoritatively restated by Lord Macnaghten in *Spicer* v. *Martin*:[94] "Community of interest necessarily . . . requires and imports reciprocity of obligation."[95] It is usual for purchasers to enter into a deed of covenant[96] but mutuality is often inferred, as must now be explained.

---

[84] *Baxter* v. *Four Oak Properties* [1965] Ch 816, 826, Cross J.
[85] *Re Wembley Park Estate Co's Transfer* [1968] Ch 491, Goff J; *Emile Elias & Co* v. *Pine Groves* (1993) 66 P & CR 1, PC.
[86] *Re Nottingham Patent Brick & Tile Co* v. *Butler* (1886) 16 QBD 778, 785, Esher MR.
[87] *Elliston* v. *Reacher* [1908] 2 Ch 665, CA; *Re Dolphin's Conveyance* [1970] Ch 654 (near Birmingham University campus); *Brunner* v. *Greenslade* [1971] Ch 993, 999F, Megarry J.
[88] *Williams* v. *Kiley* [2002] EWCA Civ 1645, [2003] 06 EG 147; Chitty on *Contracts* (Sweet & Maxwell, 27th ed, 1984), [40–058].
[89] *Torbay Hotel* v. *Jenkins* [1927] 2 Ch 225.
[90] *Re Pinewood Estate, Farnborough* [1958] Ch 280 (surely wrong); PV Baker (1970) 86 *LQR* 445; HWR Wade [1957] *CLJ* 146; DG Valentine (1957) 20 *MLR* 646.
[91] *Kelly* v. *Barrett* [1924] 2 Ch 379, 413–414, Sargant LJ; *Osborne* v. *Bradley* [1903] 2 Ch 446; *Reid* v. *Bickerstaff* [1909] 2 Ch 305, 319, Cozens-Hardy MR; *Torbay Hotel* v. *Jenkins* [1927] 2 Ch 225; *Lawrence* v. *South County Freeholds* [1939] Ch 656, 673, Simonds J; *Whitgift Homes* v. *Stocks* [2001] EWCA Civ 1732, [2001] 48 EG 130 (CS).
[92] *Spicer* v. *Martin* (1888) 14 App Cas 12, HL (sub-purchaser against purchaser); *Renals* v. *Cowlishaw* (1878) 9 Ch D 125 (no head-scheme); *Brunner* v. *Greenslade* [1971] Ch 993, 1006, Megarry J (sub-scheme ended head scheme).
[93] *Whatman* v. *Gibson* (1834) 9 Sim 196, 59 ER 333; *Schreiber* v. *Creed* (1839) 10 Sim 9, 59 ER 515.
[94] (1888) 14 App Cas 12, 25; *Western* v. *Macdermott* (1866) LR 1 Eq 499, 507, Romilly MR at first instance; *Keates* v. *Lyon* (1869) LR 4 Ch App 218, Selwyn LJ; *Renals* at 129; *Re Dolphin's Conveyance* [1970] Ch 654, 663E, Stamp J; *Ridley* v. *Lee* [1935] Ch 591; *Lawrence* at 675, Simonds J.
[95] The burden may survive surrender of a lease: *Pigott* v. *Smith* (1859) 1 De GF & J 33, 45 ER 271; LRR 1925 r 205 (noting on register).
[96] *Baxter* v. *Four Oaks Properties* [1965] Ch 816; *Elliston* v. *Reacher* [1908] 2 Ch 665, 674, Farwell LJ (covenant to observe earlier deed).

2. Mutuality inferred from common restrictive covenants

[34.17] Mutual enforceability may rise from a decision to sell lots at auction or by gradual sales of plots on an estate. Four requirements were crystallised from the earlier case-law by *Elliston* v. *Reacher*,[97] and fairly strict adherence to Parker J's four requirements is still required.[98] (1) Both parties must derive title from a common seller.[99] (2) The estate must be lotted[100] (usually according to an estate plan[101]) subject to common restrictions. This commonality may be demonstrated by a successful auction sale[102] or by private sales over a period of time with identical[103] restrictions.[104] (3) A scheme requires an independent right for individual purchasers to enforce the estate rules without needing the support of the developer.[105] This is implicit in estates where the developer promises to take similar covenants from all buyers[106] or estate lacking any duty of enforcement by the builder.[107] (4) Reciprocity arises from purchase knowing of, and buying on the basis of, mutual enforceability.[108]

3. A private law

[34.18] Mutuality creates a private law for the defined area of the scheme, overcoming privity of contract,[109] lack of annexation, absent assignments, failure to include earlier purchasers,[110] and the problem of lack of benefitted land after the last plot is sold.[111] There is no difficulty about covenanting with oneself after 1925,[112] and problems of sub-lotting are removed by a scheme.[113] Registration is still, apparently, required for restrictive covenants.

[97] [1908] 2 Ch 374; approved at 685, CA.
[98] *Page* v. *King's Parade Properties* (1967) 20 P & CR 710, 716, Goff J; *Re Wembley Park Estate Co's Transfer* [1968] Ch 491, 499C, Goff J; *Lund* v. *Taylor* (1975) 31 P & CR 167, 177, Stamp LJ.
[99] Work may be split: *Re Dolphin's Conveyance* [1970] Ch 654.
[100] *Kelly* v. *Barrett* [1924] 2 Ch 379, 401, 406.
[101] *Peacock* v. *Penson* (1848) 11 Beav 355, 50 ER 854; *Sheppard* v. *Gilmore* (1887) 57 LT 614; *Rowell* v. *Satchell* [1903] 2 Ch 212; *Lawrence* v. *South County Freeholds* [1939] Ch 656, 673.
[102] *Spicer* v. *Martin* (1888) 14 App Cas 12, 25, Lord Macnaghten; *Re Birmingham & District Land Co & Allday* [1893] 1 Ch 342; *Osborne* v. *Bradley* [1903] 2 Ch 446, 454, Farwell J; *Page* (unsuccessful sale).
[103] *Rowell* v. *Satchell* [1903] 2 Ch 212; *Reid* v. *Bickerstaff* [1909] 2 Ch 305, 320; *Lund* v. *Taylor* (1975) 31 P & CR 167, 174; *Kingsbury* v. *LW Anderson* (1979) 40 P & CR 136, 142.
[104] *Eagling* v. *Gardner* [1970] 2 All ER 838 (15 out of 16); *Torbay Hotel* v. *Jenkins* [1927] 2 Ch 225; *Emile Elias & Co* v. *Pine Groves* (1993) 66 P & CR 1, PC (no scheme).
[105] *White* v. *Bijou Mansions* [1937] Ch 610, CA; *Page* v. *King's Parade Properties* (1967) 20 P & CR 710, Goff J; *Re Dolphin's Conveyance* [1970] Ch 654.
[106] *Re Dolphin's Conveyance* [1970] Ch 654, 662, Stamp J; *Texaco Antilles* v. *Kernochan* [1973] AC 609, PC.
[107] *Elliston* v. *Reacher* [1908] 2 Ch 374; *Dolphin* at 663; *Eagling* v. *Gardner* [1970] 2 All ER 838, Ungoed-Thomas J; *Texaco* at 624H, Lord Cross.
[108] *Spicer* v. *Martin* (1888) 14 App Cas 12, HL; *Elliston* v. *Reacher* [1908] 2 Ch 374, 385; *Reid* v. *Bickerstaff* [1909] 2 Ch 305, CA; *Lund* v. *Taylor* (1975) 31 P & CR 167, CA; *Kingsbury* v. *LW Anderson* (1979) 40 P & CR 136.
[109] Eg where one is dead: *Elliston* v. *Reacher* [1908] 2 Ch 374, 385, Parker J; *Baxter* v. *Four Oaks Properties* [1965] Ch 816, 826C, Cross J; *Re Dolphin's Conveyance* [1970] Ch 654, 663C-D, Stamp J.
[110] *Brown* v. *Inskip* (1884) 1 Cab & El 231.
[111] *Eagling* v. *Gardner* [1970] 2 All ER 838.
[112] LPA 1925 s 82. This reverses the old law: *Ridley* v. *Lee* [1935] Ch 591; *Re Pinewood Estate, Farnborough* [1958] Ch 280.
[113] *Brunner* v. *Greenslade* [1971] Ch 993, Megarry J; *Texaco Antilles* v. *Kernochan* [1973] AC 609, PC; *Kingsbury* v. *LW Anderson* (1979) 40 P & CR 186.

4. The developer

[34.19] A fully mutual scheme binds the developer just as much as individual plot purchasers[114] because he is not allowed to derogate from his own grants. This inflexibility may lock a builder into a development plan that proves to be uneconomic. Proper practice is to reserve an express[115] right for the builder to alter the details of the scheme,[116] whilst leaving individual purchasers mutually bound.[117]

F. RESTRICTIVE COVENANTS: NEIGHBOUR OBLIGATIONS

[34.20] Neighbour obligations are those imposed by covenanting with specific neighbours. A claimant seeking to enforce the restriction must show that he was the person originally benefitted (the covenantee) or that the benefit has passed to him from such a person.

1. Original benefits

[34.21] A covenant is a promise by deed, which can be enforced as a contract against the original covenantor.[118] An original party can obtain damages or an injunction so long as he retains land which is benefitted. After he has sold it all, no injunction will be granted because he has no interest in actual performance, and his contractual damages will be nominal.[119] The covenant can be enforced by[120] or against[121] personal representatives or a trustee in bankruptcy.[122]

2. Original benefit: existing neighbours – land registry transfers

[34.22] If a builder sells plot 2 on a building estate, the builder takes the benefit for plots 3 onwards, but it is also necessary to benefit the existing purchaser of plot 1. A deed poll is a deed made by one party which is viewed a quasi-public statement, and which have always been allowed to confer benefits on people who are non-parties.

---

[114] *Spicer* v. *Martin* (1888) 14 App Cas 12, HL; and many other cases.

[115] This may be implied: *Re Birmingham & District Land Co* v. *Allday* [1893] 1 Ch 342.

[116] *Elliston* v. *Reacher* [1908] 2 Ch 665, CA; *Re Beechwood Homes's Applic* [1994] 2 EGLR 178, CA; and many other cases.

[117] *Re Wembley Park Estate Co's Transfer* [1968] Ch 491, Goff J; *Re Elm Avenue (Nos 6–12), New Milton ex p New Forest DC* [1984] 1 WLR 1398, Scott J.

[118] Assignable: (1) at law if notice is given: LPA 1925 s 136; or (2) in equity without notice: *Tailby* v. *Official Receiver* (1888) 13 App Cas 523, 546.

[119] *Stokes* v. *Russell* (1790) 3 Term Rep 678, 100 ER 799; *London CC* v. *Allen* [1914] 3 KB 642, 660.

[120] *Formby* v. *Baker* [1903] 2 Ch 539, 554, Romer LJ, 556–557, Stirling LJ; *South Eastern Rly* v. *Associated Portland Cement Manufacturers (1900)* [1910] 1 Ch 12; Law Reform (MP) Act 1934 s 1(1); *Beswick* v. *Beswick* [1968] AC 58, HL.

[121] *Youngmin* v. *Heath* [1974] 1 WLR 135. Liability is attracted by entry under a lease, unless avoiding action is taken.

[122] *Beckham* v. *Drake* (1849) 2 HLC 579, 627; *Jennings Trustees* v. *King* [1952] Ch 899; see above **[27.19ff]**.

Land registry transfers are a form of deed poll, so benefits can be given to those outside the transfer.[123]

3. Original benefit: existing neighbours – conveyances of unregistered land

[34.23] An unregistered conveyance is an indenture, that is a private arrangement between two parties. Outsiders had to be joined as parties at common law,[124] but this archaic rule was amended in 1845,[125] and again by section 56 of the Law of Property Act 1925. An immediate benefit is now allowed to a person who is not a party to the deed.[126] People named take as original covenantees.[127] If a husband conveys the matrimonial home to his wife on terms that she covenants with the mortgage lender to pay mortgage instalments, the lender is able to enforce that covenant without being joined in the conveyance.[128] A buyer of plot 2 can covenant with the existing buyer of plot 1.[129]

Non-parties are included only if an attempt is made to covenant with them.[130] In *Beswick* v. *Beswick*, a covenant between nephew and uncle did not purport to confer a pension directly on the plaintiff widow, so she was not able to enforce the promise in a personal capacity.[131] In *Lyus* v. *Prowsa Developments*[132] a sale of a building estate subject to an contract to sell one plot to Lyus gave him no rights against the buyer of the whole development. *Wiles* v. *Banks*[133] was a successful case in which sale of land subject to a new access for the owner or occupier of the vicarage did confer a right of way on the vicar.

People to benefit may be identified by being named individually, by reference to the owners of particular land,[134] or by defining a class, such as "existing plot owners".[135]

Rights granted under the modern wording include options,[136] contracts,[137] easements[138] and future rights. Restrictive covenants have been in since 1845,[139] but the

---

[123] *Chelsea & Waltham Green BS* v. *Armstrong* [1951] Ch 853, Vaisey J.

[124] *Beswick* v. *Beswick* [1968] AC 56, 102–103, Lord Upjohn; G Treitel (1967) 30 *MLR* 687, 688.

[125] Real Property Act 1845 s 5; G Treitel (1967) 30 *MLR* 687, 690.

[126] *White* v. *Bijou Mansions* [1937] Ch 610, 623, Simonds J; on appeal [1938] Ch 351, CA. Not other documents despite the last word; *Beswick* v. *Beswick* [1968] AC 56, 106G, 107A; JA Andrews (1959) 23 *Conv (NS)* 179; G Treitel (1967) 30 *MLR* 687, 690 (not ratio?).

[127] DW Elliott (1956) 20 *Conv (NS)* 43, 114 (excellent review of the land cases before *Beswick*).

[128] *Re Windle* [1975] 1 WLR 1628, Goff J.

[129] *Re Selwyn's Conveyance* [1967] Ch 674, Goff J.

[130] *White* v. *Bijou Mansions* [1937] Ch 610, 624, Simonds J; on appeal [1938] Ch 351, 365, Lord Greene MR; *Smith & Snipes Hall Farm* v. *River Douglas Catchment Board* [1949] 2 KB 500, 517, Denning LJ; *Amsprop Trading* v. *Harris Distribution* [1997] 1 WLR 1025, Neuberger J.

[131] [1968] AC 56, HL; G Treitel (1967) 30 *MLR* 687, 690.

[132] [1982] 1 WLR 1044, Dillon J.

[133] (1985) 50 P & CR 80, Megarry V-C at first instance; *Beswick* [1968] AC 56, 75D, Lord Reid.

[134] *Kelsey* v. *Dodd* (1881) 52 LJ Ch 34, 39, Jessel MR; *Westhoughton UDC* v. *Wigan Coal & Iron Co* [1919] 1 Ch 159; *Pinemain* v. *Welbeck International* [1984] 2 EGLR 91.

[135] *Dyson* v. *Forster* [1909] AC 98, HL; *Re Ecclesiastical Commissioners for England's Conveyance* [1936] Ch 430; DW Elliott (1956) 20 *Conv (NS)* 43, 48–49; *Re Shaw's Applic* (1995) 68 P & CR 591, L Tr.

[136] *White* v. *Bijou Mansions* [1937] Ch 610, 624, Simonds J; *Stromdale & Ball* v. *Burden* [1952] Ch 223, Danckwerts J.

[137] *Lyus* as above.

[138] *Wiles* v. *Banks* as above.

[139] *Re Ecclesiastical Commissioners for England's Conveyance* [1936] Ch 430; LPA 1925 s 56(1): *Re Selwyn's Conveyance* [1967] Ch 674, Goff J.

1925 wording extends to covenants not touching and concerning the land.[140] The 1845 Act covered freehold land[141] but was extended in 1925 to include leases.[142] However, *Beswick* v. *Beswick* decided[143] that the historical context requires restriction to land, excluding for example ordinary contracts and insurance policies.[144] In these contexts the Contracts (Rights of Third Parties) Act 1999 now permits the assignment of benefits but in relation to land it does not add much to section 56.

G. RESTRICTIVE COVENANTS: ANNEXATION

[34.24] Annexation is a process undertaken at the time of creation of the covenant to affix its benefit to particular land.[145] Once done:

> "[T]he benefit will pass automatically on a conveyance of the land, without express mention, because it is annexed to the land and runs with it."[146]

This treasure may lie hidden, awaiting discovery in the hour of need.[147]

1. Post-1925 statutory annexation

[34.25] Section 78 of the Law of Property Act 1925 effects annexation for any restrictive covenant made after 1925 unless its effect is excluded. Brightman LJ's judgment in *Federated Homes* v. *Mill Lodge Properties*[148] settled this point, at least as far as the Court of Appeal.[149] Section 78(1) of the Law of Property Act 1925 provides for a restrictive[150] covenant relating to any land of the covenantee to include:

(1) the covenantee;
(2) his successors in title;[151]

---

[140] *Beswick* v. *Beswick* [1968] AC 58, 79C, Lord Hodson; G Treitel (1967) 30 *MLR* 687, 689–690; Wolstenholme & Cherry, *Conveyancing Statutes* (13th ed), 133; *Re Ecclesiastical Commissioners for England's Conveyance* [1936] Ch 430, 438, Luxmoore LJ. Old law: *Grant* v. *Edmondson* [1931] 1 Ch 1, CA; *Foster* v. *Elvet Colliery Co* [1908] 1 KB 629, CA; despite [1909] AC 98, 102, Lord Macnaghten.

[141] Real Property Act 1845 s 5.

[142] *Stromdale & Ball* v. *Burden* [1952] Ch 223, Danckwerts J.

[143] [1968] AC 58, 77C, 79H–80A, 85D–E; but see to the contrary at 94, 106–107.

[144] *Re Sinclair's LP* [1938] 3 All ER 124; *Re Foster* [1938] 3 All ER 357; *Re Distributors and Warehousing* [1986] 1 EGLR 90, 94.

[145] *Rogers* v. *Hosegood* [1900] 2 Ch 388, 407, Collins LJ; *Formby* v. *Barker* [1903] 2 Ch 539, 551, Vaughan Williams LJ; *Re Heywood's Conv* [1938] 2 All ER 236.

[146] *Federated Homes* v. *Mill Lodge Property* [1980] 1 WLR 594, 603C, Brightman LJ; *Miles* v. *Easter* [1933] Ch 611, 628, Romer LJ.

[147] *Lawrence* v. *South Counties Freeholds* [1939] Ch 656, 680; *R* v. *Westminster CC ex p Leicester Square Coventry Street Association* (1989) 59 P & CR 51, 57, Simon Brown J; *Rogers* v. *Hosegood* [1900] 2 Ch 388, 408, Collins LJ; *Reid* v. *Bickerstaff* [1909] 2 Ch 305, 320, Cozens-Hardy MR.

[148] [1980] 1 WLR 594, CA; DJ Hayton (1980) 43 *MLR* 445; A Sydenham [1980] *Conv* 216; *Smith & Snipes Hall Farm* v. *River Douglas River Catchment Board* [1949] 2 KB 500, CA; *Williams* v. *Unit Construction Co* (1951) 19 Conv (NS) 262.

[149] [1980] 1 WLR 594, 603C Brightman LJ (obiter); *Roake* v. *Chadha* [1984] 1 WLR 40, 45A–E (ratio); *Shropshire CC* v. *Edwards* (1982) 46 P & CR 270; *J Sainsbury* v. *Enfield LBC* [1989] 1 WLR 590; *Robins* v. *Berkeley Homes (Kent)* [1996] EGCS 75; *Whitgift Homes* v. *Stocks* [2001] EWCA Civ 1732, [2001] 48 EG 130 (CS).

[150] Category (3) does not apply to positive covenants.

[151] Ie those who take on his death.

(3) the owners or occupiers for the time being of the land of the covenantee intended to be benefitted; and

(4) persons deriving title under the earlier categories.[152]

Category (3) implies by statute the *Drake* v. *Gray*[153] formula for express annexation – "and the owners and occupiers for the time being". Professor Radcliffe[154] first suggested that statutory annexation must follow. Despite the numerous cases which had ignored the section,[155] Radcliffe's argument was finally accepted (many years late) in *Federated Homes*. Action was taken against the original covenanting party (Mill Lodge)[156] to enforce a covenant not to build more than 300 houses on its blue land, Mill Lodge obtained planning permission for a further 32 houses which, if built, would have reduced the density permitted on the land protected by the covenant. The red part was sold several times, on the last occasion by a registered transfer to Federated Homes which omitted any direct mention of the covenant. There was neither words of annexation nor a complete chain of assignments, but the covenant had passed to Federated Homes by statutory annexation.[157]

A minimum requirement for statutory annexation is that the benefitted land should be described in the conveyance[158] or indicated by necessary implication:[159] a bald covenant by "A with B" would not effect annexation.

2. Pre-1926 covenants

[34.26] Express annexation is required if the covenant was created before 1926.[160] The Conveyancing Act 1881 applied to covenants entered into between 1882 and 1925 but it refers to specific persons[161] rather than to successive owners of the benefitted land. This is "insufficient without more" to effect annexation."[162]

Classic *Rogers* v. *Hosegood*[163] formulae for express annexation were:

(1) a covenant with the covenantee "and the owners for the time being of the benefitted land"[164]; or

---

[152] LPA 1925 s 79 is similar for burdens but they are not annexed without registration: *Tophams* v. *Earl of Sefton* [1967] 1 AC 50, HL (Aintree racecourse); PB Fairest [1966] *CLJ* 169; *Federated Homes*, at 606B, Brightman LJ (s 79 involves "quite different considerations").

[153] [1936] Ch 451, CA; *Rogers* v. *Hosegood* [1900] 2 Ch 388, CA; *Kelly* v. *Barrett* [1924] 2 Ch 379, 403, Pollock MR; *Miles* v. *Easter* [1933] Ch 611, CA; see below **[34.26]**.

[154] GRY Radcliffe (1941) 57 *LQR* 203, 204–207; HWR Wade [1972B] *CLJ* 157; PV Baker (1968) 84 *LQR* 22; DJ Hayton (1971) 87 *LQR* 339.

[155] Eg *Zetland* v. *Driver* [1939] Ch 1, CA; *Re Jeff's Transfer* [1966] 1 WLR 841.

[156] Ie enforcement was contractual rather than proprietary.

[157] At 607C, Brightman LJ.

[158] *Federated Homes* at 604.

[159] *Bridges* v. *Harrow LBC* [1981] 1 EGLR 143, 146H–147A, Stuart-Smith J; F Webb [1984] *Conv* 313; *Re Hextall's Application* (2000) 79 P & CR 382, L Tr.

[160] *Newton Abbot Co-operative Society* v. *Williamson & Treadgold* [1952] Ch 286, Upjohn J; L Elphinstone (1952) 68 *LQR* 353.

[161] Conveyancing Act 1881 s 58 – basically the covenanting party and his successors on death.

[162] *J Sainsbury* v. *Enfield LBC* [1989] 1 WLR 590, 601E, Morritt J; see: *Renals* v. *Cowlishaw* (1878) 9 Ch D 125; *Reid* v. *Bickerstaff* [1909] 2 Ch 305; *Ives* v. *Brown* [1919] 2 Ch 314; *Miles* v. *Easter* [1933] Ch 611; *Shropshire CC* v. *Edwards* (1982) 46 P & CR 270.

[163] [1900] 2 Ch 388, CA (home of Sir John Everett Millais).

[164] See above **[34.25]**.

(2) a covenant "for the benefit of the benefitted land"[165]; or

(3) equivalent phrases identifying the land.[166]

Annexation may be implied where there is no express formula[167] but an intention to annex can be collected from the surrounding circumstances.[168] Such a case was *Shropshire County Council* v. *Edwards*.[169] The site of Nobold House was sold in 1908 with a covenant that the seller was to use his remaining land only for agriculture. Since the intention was to secure a supply of water and to protect Nobold House from building, the benefit was clearly intended to pass to successive land owners.[170] The current owners could prevent the County Council from turning the land into a site for gypsy caravans. It is questionable whether implied annexation will survive scrutiny at appellate level.

3. Annexation to parts

[34.27] A covenant is attached to each part of the benefitted land by annexation, whether the process if express[171] or statutory,[172] and a covenant also passes to a lease-holder.[173] Hence a covenant does not fail in its entirety merely because the benefit is defined to include land incapable of benefit.[174] Specific wording may limit this effect, for example limiting the benefit to the purchaser of the entire development site as opposed to the buyers of individual plots.[175]

4. Assignable covenants

[34.28] Statutory annexation is not in fact "Automatic Annexation",[176] since it can be excluded,[177] for example by indicating that the benefit requires express assignment.[178]

[165] *Russell* v. *Archdale* [1964] Ch 38; *Re Jeff's Transfer* [1966] 1 WLR 841; *Stilwell* v. *Blackman* [1968] Ch 508; *Wrotham Park Estate Co* v. *Parkside Homes* [1974] 1 WLR 798.

[166] [1900] 2 Ch 388, 406, Collins MR; *Renals* v. *Cowlishaw* (1879) 11 Ch D 866, 868; *Reid* v. *Bickerstaff* [1909] 2 Ch 305, 321, 325; *Ives* v. *Brown* [1919] 2 Ch 314; *Re Sunnyfield* [1932] 1 Ch 79; *Miles* v. *Easter* [1933] Ch 611, 634–636.

[167] At 638A, Harman LJ.

[168] *McLean* v. *McKay* (1873) LR 5 PC 327; *Rogers* v. *Hosegood* [1900] 2 Ch 388, 408, Collins LJ; *Westhoughton UDC* v. *Wigan Coal & Iron Co* [1919] 1 Ch 159, Swinfen Eady MR; *Marten* v. *Flight Refuelling* [1962] Ch 115; EC Ryder (1972) 36 *Conv (NS)* 20; *Re Hextall's Applic* (2000) 79 P & CR 382, L Tr.

[169] (1983) 46 P & CR 270.

[170] Contrast *J Sainsbury* v. *Enfield LBC* [1989] 1 WLR 590; S Goulding [1989] *Conv* 52; JE Martin [1989] *Conv* 358; *Re Jeff's Transfer (No 2)* [1966] 1 WLR 841, Stamp J.

[171] *Drake* v. *Gray* [1936] Ch 451, 465, Romer LJ; *Zetland* v. *Driver* [1939] Ch 1, CA. There are a number of contrary dicta.

[172] *Federated Homes* [1980] 1 WLR 594, 606G–607D, Brightman LJ, 607H–608D, Megaw LJ; *Williams* v. *Unit Construction Co* (1961) 19 Conv (NS) 262.

[173] *Taite* v. *Gosling* (1879) 11 Ch D 273; *Holoway* v. *Hill* [1902] 2 Ch 612; *Westhoughton UDC* v. *Wigan Coal & Iron Co* [1919] 1 Ch 159; *Long* v. *Gray* (1913) 58 SJ 46, CA.

[174] *Re Ballard's Conveyance* [1937] Ch 473, Clauson J; but see *Zetland* v. *Driver* [1939] Ch 1, CA.

[175] *Miles* v. *Easter* [1933] Ch 611, 628, Romer LJ; *Drake* v. *Gray* [1936] Ch 451, 459–461, Slesser LJ; *Re Selwyn's Conveyance* [1967] Ch 674, 686–689, Goff J; *Re Jeff's Transfer (No 2)* [1966] 1 WLR 841, Stamp J; *Wrotham Park Estate Co* v. *Parkside Estate* [1974] 1 WLR 798; *Everett* v. *Remington* [1892] 3 Ch 148; *Robins* v. *Berkeley Homes (Kent)* [1996] EGCS 75.

[176] Despite GH Newsom's counterblast, (1981) 97 *LQR* 32, against the monstrous regiment of annexers.

[177] At 46; *Federated Homes* [1980] 1 WLR 594, 606, Brightman LJ; L Elphinstone, *Covenants Affecting Land* (Solicitors' Law Stationery Society, 1946), 17; contrast s 79 on burdens.

[178] *Roake* v. *Chadha* [1984] 1 WLR 40, Ch D; PN Todd [1984] *Conv* 68; PN Todd [1985] *Conv* 177.

Assignable covenants were created before 1926 by (1) including reference to "assigns"[179] but (2) omitting any reference to future landowners.[180] This achieved assignability without annexation. [181]

A restrictive covenant cannot be assigned in isolation from the land, so that the seller must own land before the sale[182] and the buyer afterwards.[183] Unregistered land is usually sold "together with" the benefit of existing covenants "so far as the same are still subsisting".[184] The chain of assignments must be complete.[185] In *Federated Homes* v. *Mill Lodge* the *green* land was sold by Mackenzie Hill to Brandts to Federated Homes with a complete series of express assignments,[186] but the chain broke in relation to the *red* land after compulsory registration of title and a transfer that did not refer to the covenant.

5. Personal covenants

[34.29] It is of course possible to go further and to make clear that the covenant is personal between the original landowners[187] but since 1881[188] assignability is assumed and explicit words have been required to exclude it.[189]

H. RESTRICTIVE COVENANTS: FAILURE OF BENEFIT

[34.30] The court has power to declare whether or not a restrictive covenant applies in any given event[190] on the application of any person interested.[191] Restrictive covenants are declared to be moribund once there is no person in existence able to enforce them. Successful applicants must prove (1) the absence of original covenantees, (2) the failure of annexation, assignment and building schemes and (3) sale of the benefitted land by the original covenantees precluding the possibility of future

---

[179] Between 1882 and 1925 "assigns" were included by statute: Conveyancing Act 1881 s 56; *Ives* v. *Brown* [1919] 2 Ch 314; *Miles* v. *Easter* [1933] Ch 611; *Forster* v. *Elvet Colliery Co* [1908] 1 KB 629, CA; *Re Pinewood Estate, Farnborough* [1958] Ch 280; *J Sainsbury* v. *Enfield LBC* [1989] 1 WLR 590, Morritt J.

[180] *Kelsey* v. *Dodd* (1881) 52 LJ Ch 34, Jessel MR; *Renals* v. *Cowlishaw* (1879) 11 Ch D 866, CA; *Reid* v. *Bickerstaff* [1909] 2 Ch 305, CA.

[181] *Newton Abbot Co-operative Society* v. *Williamson & Treadgold* [1952] Ch 286, Upjohn J (covenant made in 1925); L Elphinstone (1952) 68 *LQR* 353; *Marten* v. *Flight Refuelling* [1962] Ch 115, 130, Wilberforce J.

[182] *Chambers* v. *Randall* [1923] 1 Ch 149, Sargant J; *Miles* v. *Easter* [1933] Ch 611, 636, Romer LJ; *Re Sunnyfield* [1932] 1 Ch 79.

[183] *Formby* v. *Barker* [1903] 2 Ch 539, 554, Romer LJ.

[184] *Stilwell* v. *Blackman* [1968] Ch 508, Ungoed-Thomas J.

[185] Some cases suggest the possibility of delayed annexation ie that occurring on a first (or later?) assignment: *Rogers* v. *Hosegood* [1900] 2 Ch 388, 408, Collins LJ; *Stilwell* v. *Blackman* [1968] Ch 508, 522–523; *Federated Homes* [1980] 1 WLR 594, 603–604, Brightman LJ. This is surely dubious.

[186] [1980] 1 WLR 594, 603B.

[187] *Osborne* v. *Bradley* [1903] 2 Ch 446, 450, Farwell J.

[188] Conveyancing Act 1881 s 56; *Stilwell* at 525; LPA 1925 s 78; *Caerns Motor Services* v. *Texaco* [1994] 1 WLR 1249.

[189] *Federated Homes* at 601E–603A.

[190] LPA 1925 s 84(2); *Re MCA (East)* [2002] EWHC 1684 (Ch); modification is left to the L Tr under ss (1); *Griffiths* v. *Band* (1974) 29 P & CR 243, Goulding J.

[191] Costs are payable while potential objectors consider their position: *Re Jeff's Transfer* [1965] 1 WLR 972; *(No 2)* [1966] 1 All ER 937; *Re Wembley Park Estate Co's Transfer* [1968] 1 All ER 457, Goff J.

assignment.[192] Many cases fall short,[193] but in a successful case the court will declare that the covenant is unenforceable,[194] binding the land, extinguishing the covenant, and leading to cancellation of protective entries.[195]

I.   RESTRICTIVE COVENANTS: REMEDIES

1.   Remedies for breach of an easement

[34.31] There are two remedies for infringement of an easement. Abatement is physical obstruction or removal of an offending item Thus if a right of way is blocked up or a locked gate erected, it can be torn down. It is closely controlled: force used must be reasonable with no injury to others or the public, and no breach of the peace. Service of a notice is wise but not essential.[196] An action may seek damages – recoverable in trespass without proof of actual damage – but other appropriate remedies include an injunction to prevent future interference, a mandatory injunction to require removal of an obstruction, or a declaration. There is power to refuse an injunction, as in a parking case where the dominant tenement had been extended, and award damages in lieu.[197]

2.   Injunctions for breach of a covenant

[34.32] Equity usually enforces restrictions. A full injunction follows as of course after proof of any deliberate violation[198] since *Doherty* v. *Allman* removes any general discretion to balance the convenience of the parties.[199] Seriousness of the injury suffered is only relevant, when deciding whether to substitute an award of damages.[200] *Mandatory* injunctions are issued more sparingly,[201] and it will probably be too late to obtain an injunction if demolition is required.[202]

---

[192] Or that the benefitted attached to a whole estate which no longer exists: *Re Freeman-Thomas Indenture* [1957] 1 All ER 532.

[193] *Shropshire CC* v. *Edwards* (1983) 46 P & CR 270 (implied annexation); *Re 6–12 Elm Avenue, New Milton ex p New Forest DC* [1984] 1 WLR 1398, Scott J.

[194] *Re Sunnyfield* [1932] 1 Ch 79; *Re Pinewood Estate, Farnborough* [1958] Ch 280; *Re Wembley Park Estate Co's T* [1968] 1 All ER 457.

[195] *Re Sunnyfield* [1932] 1 Ch 79. For land registry mechanics see above at **[20.12]**.

[196] *Lane* v. *Capsey* [1891] 3 Ch 411, Chitty J (pulling down house); *Hill* v. *Cock* (1872) 26 LT 185 (limited to least act needed); *Roberts* v. *Rose* (1865) LR 1 Ex 82 (block watercourse); *Davies* v. *Williams* (1851) 16 QB 546, 117 ER 988; *Perry* v. *Fitzhow* (1846) 8 QB 757, 115 ER 1057 (cannot pull down house in occupation); *Lagan Navigation Co* v. *Lambeg Bleaching etc Co* [1927] AC 226, 244, Lord Atkinson (liable without notice).

[197] *Das* v. *Linden* [2002] EWCA Civ 590, [2002] 2 EGLR 76.

[198] *Mann* v. *Stephens* (1846) 15 Sim 377, 60 ER 665.

[199] (1878) 3 App Cas 709, 720, Lord Cairns; *Osborne* v. *Bradley* [1903] 2 Ch 446, 450–451, Farwell J; *Re Lancaster Gate (No 108)* [1933] Ch 419.

[200] *Western* v. *Macdermott* (1866) LR 2 Ch App 72; *Leech* v. *Schweder* (1874) LR 9 Ch App 463; *Manners* v. *Johnson* (1875) 1 Ch D 673; *Richards* v. *Revitt* (1877) 7 Ch D 224.

[201] *Morris* v. *Redland Bricks* [1970] AC 652, 665.

[202] JE Martin [1996] *Conv* 329, 330–335.

Interlocutory injunctions are also obtainable as of right.[203] Megarry J refused an interim injunction in *Shepherd Homes* v. *Sandham*[204] which would have required the removal of fencing on an open-plan estate at Caerphilly, despite repeated incursions by Welsh mountain sheep. Enforceability of the covenant was left for consideration at full trial.

3. Damages in lieu of injunction

[34.33] Lord Cairns' Act 1858[205] created the power to award "equitable damages" when there is power to grant an injunction, but damages would be more appropriate.[206] In *Wrotham Park Estate Co* v. *Parkside Homes*[207] a mandatory injunction to knock down houses was refused, but the case was tailor-made for the award of damages in place of an equitable remedy. If all benefitted land has been sold, the covenant is no longer enforceable in equity and this removes the power to award equitable damages.[208] Damages are a particularly appropriate remedy where the covenanting party has been lulled into a false sense of security.[209]

Quantification is governed by *Shelfer* v. *City of London Electric Lighting Co.*[210] The injury must be small, translatable to money, and capable of compensation by a small payment. Compensation for a past one-off breach is identical at law and in equity, and may possibly be zero.[211] If covenants are enforced against buyers, who are not liable at law, new compensation rights are created. Awards of damages give a forced licence for the future wrong, so the neighbour must be compensated for the continuing loss,[212] and the neighbour necessarily receives more than common law damages as in *Wrotham Park Estate Co* v. *Parkside Homes*[213] and *Jaggard* v. *Sawyer*.[214] The measure is what the sum reasonable parties would reach by negotiation.[215] Further development of the concept of restitutionary damages[216] may result in a developer being required to account for the profit he makes from breaking his contract: traditional damages compensate for loss, but there is also a role for punishment of a flagrant breach of covenant for commercial reasons.[217]

---

[203] *Hampstead & Suburban Properties* v. *Diomedous* [1969] 1 Ch 248; *Shepherd Homes* v. *Sandham* [1971] Ch 340, Megarry J; JE Martin [1996] *Conv* 329, 332–334.

[204] [1971] Ch 340, Megarry J.

[205] Chancery Amendment Act 1858 s 2; the jurisdiction survives repeal of the Act.

[206] *Jaggard* v. *Sawyer* [1995] 1 WLR 269, CA; *Gafford* v. *Graham* (1999) 77 P & CR 73, CA.

[207] [1974] 1 WLR 798, 811D–816C, Brightman J.

[208] *Surrey CC* v. *Bredero Homes* [1993] 1 WLR 1361, CA.

[209] *Shaw* v. *Applegate* [1977] 1 WLR 970, CA; *Gafford* v. *Graham* (1999) 77 P & CR 73, CA.

[210] [1895] 1 Ch 287, 322–323, AL Smith LJ; *Ketley* v. *Gooden* (1997) 73 P & CR 305, CA; P Jolowictz [1975] *CLJ* 224.

[211] *Johnson* v. *Agnew* [1980] AC 367, 400C, Lord Wilberforce.

[212] *Jaggard* v. *Sawyer* [1995] 1 WLR 269, 285G–H, Millett LJ; *Leeds Industrial Co-Operative Society* v. *Slack* [1921] AC 851, HL; *Amec Developments* v. *Jury's Hotel Management (UK)* [2001] 1 EGLR 81, Ch D.

[213] [1974] 1 WLR 798, Brightman J; *Baxter* v. *Four Oaks Property* [1965] Ch 816; *Surrey CC* v. *Bredero Homes* [1993] 1 WLR 1361, 1369F, Steyn LJ. (contrary to Dillon LJ at 1366–1367); T Ingram [1994] *Conv* 110; P McDermott (1991) 107 *LQR* 652.

[214] [1995] 1 WLR 269, CA; JE Martin [1996] *Conv* 329, 339.

[215] *Amec Developments* v. *Jury's Hotel Management (UK)* [2001] 1 EGLR 81, Ch D.

[216] PBH Birks (1993) 109 *LQR* 518; *Att-Gen* v. *Blake* [1998] Ch 439, 455–459, Lord Woolf MR; on appeal [2001] 1 AC 268, HL; M Chen-Wishart (1998) 114 *LQR* 363.

[217] *Wrotham Park SE* v. *Hertsmere BC* (1993) 33 RVR 56, CA; *Jaggard* v. *Sawyer* [1995] 1 WLR 269, 281, Bingham MR, 291D, Millett LJ.

4.   Defences – where unconscionable to enforce

[34.34] A court of equity is bound to enforce the covenant unless the plaintiff has become disentitled to sue, either by his own acts or those of his predecessors.[218] A contractual release is a defence.[219] However in most cases the issue is whether there has been an equitable release on one of two grounds:

(1) Acquiescence or delay

[34.35] What is required[220] is conduct by the claimant or his predecessors constituting an estoppel, so that it is now inequitable to allow him to take action, though it is not necessary to find all the probanda of passive inducement.[221] Acquiescence in minor breaches does not affect the right of action on a more serious breach[222] or one which is different in character.[223] One claimant[224] failed in his attempt to close down an off-licence from which he himself had bought beer.

Acquiescence slips seamlessly into delay. A building obviously should not be demolished after it has been allowed to remain for five years.[225] Five months was suf-ficient to bar one old claim,[226] but more recent cases have allowed enforcement after significant delays.[227] Interim or mandatory remedies may be lost after very short periods,[228] for example in *Shaw* v. *Applegate*[229] where an amusement arcade was allowed to run in breach of covenant between 1971 and 1976 before an action was instituted. Where it is unconscionable to enforce the covenant, damages may be awarded in lieu.

(2) Change in neighbourhood

[34.36] A covenant may become obsolete because of changes in the character of the neighbourhood it protects. *Bedford* v. *British Museum Trustees*[230] concerned a covenant imposed in 1675 restricting development round Montagu House, now a con-stituent part of the British Museum. A proposal to build additional space to house the Elgin marbles infringed the wording of the 1675 covenant, but the covenants were no longer binding. Bloomsbury had been engulfed by urban London, to such an extent that earlier restrictions had ceased to have any relevance. This same change of local-

---

[218] *Osborne* v. *Bradley* [1903] 2 Ch 443, 450–451.

[219] *Elliston* v. *Reacher* [1908] 2 Ch 374, Parker J; *Re Pinewood Estate, Farnborough* [1958] Ch 280.

[220] *German* v. *Chapman* (1877) 7 Ch D 271, CA; *Knight* v. *Simmonds* [1896] 2 Ch 294, 298, Lindley LJ.

[221] *Osborne* v. *Bradley* [1903] 2 Ch 443, Farwell J; *Shaw* v. *Applegate* [1977] 1 WLR 970, Goff LJ.

[222] *Western* v. *MacDermott* (1866) LR 2 Ch App 72; *Meredith* v. *Wilson* (1893) 69 LT 336.

[223] *Chatsworth Estates Co* v. *Fewell* [1931] 1 Ch 224.

[224] *Sayers* v. *Collyer* (1884) 28 Ch D 103; *Goddard* v. *Midland Rly Co* (1891) 8 TLR 126 (plaintiff also in breach).

[225] *Gaskin* v. *Balls* (1879) 13 Ch D 324 (5 years); *Gafford* v. *Graham* (1998) 77 P & CR 73, CA.

[226] *Roper* v. *Williams* (1822) Turn & R 18, 22, 37 ER 999, Eldon LC.

[227] *Northumberland* v. *Bowman* (1887) 56 LT 773 (14 months); *Elliston* v. *Reacher* [1908] 2 Ch 374, Parker J.

[228] *Shepherd Homes* v. *Sandham* [1971] Ch 340.

[229] [1978] 1 All ER 123, CA.

[230] (1822) 2 My & K 552, 39 ER 1055.

ity defence has succeeded in a few later cases,[231] but there are many more that have failed.[232] The defence applies where the change in the neighbourhood is attributable to the claimant, his predecessors,[233] or (probably) anyone else.[234]

J. RESTRICTIVE COVENANTS: MODIFICATION

1. Application to modify to Lands Tribunal

[34.37] The Lands Tribunal[235] has jurisdiction to discharge or modify restrictions[236] on the application of any person interested in the land affected. Application to the Lands Tribunal can be used as a temporary defence,[237] justifying a stay of enforcement proceedings until the Tribunal ruling,[238] though a cross-undertaking is required for damages.[239] The status quo is maintained pending a hearing.[240]

2. Covenants affected

[34.38] Most applications are to vary freehold restrictions, whether or not in the form of covenants, whether pre-1926 or post-1925 in origin, and whether or not title is registered.[241] Different schemes apply to covenants imposed on the enfranchisement of long residential leases and in the public sector,[242] but positive covenants are beyond the reach of the Tribunal.[243] An alternative power is to discharge or modify restrictive covenants in long leases – meaning a term over 40 years[244] – after 25 years of the lease have run.[245] Estate management schemes created on the enfranchisement of long

---

[231] *Peek* v. *Matthews* (1867) LR 3 Eq 515 (same if defendant buys after breaches); *Kelsey* v. *Dodd* (1881) 52 LJ Ch 34; *Sobey* v. *Sainsbury* [1913] 2 Ch 513 (Boscombe Manor Estate of the Shelley family); *Att-Gen for Hong Kong* v. *Fairfax* [1997] 1 WLR 149, PC ("clearest possible case").

[232] Eg *Tulk* v. *Moxhay* at first instance (1848) 18 LJ Ch 83; *Elliston* v. *Reacher* [1908] 2 Ch 374, Parker J (no appeal on this point); *Robins* v. *Berkeley Homes (Kent)* [1996] EGCS 75.

[233] *Bedford* v. *British Museum*; *Sayers* v. *Collyer* (1884) 28 Ch D 103, CA; *Osborne* v. *Bradley* [1903] 2 Ch 443; *Pulleyne* v. *France (No 1)* (1912) 57 SJ 173, CA.

[234] *German* v. *Chapman* (1877) 7 Ch D 271, 279, James LJ; *Knight* v. *Simonds* [1896] 2 Ch 294, CA; *Sobey* v. *Sainsbury* [1913] 2 Ch 513, Sargant J; *Chatsworth Estates Co* v. *Fewell* [1931] 1 Ch 224.

[235] LPA 1969 s 28(1).

[236] LPA 1925 s 84(1); P Polden (1986) 49 *MLR* 195.

[237] Forfeiture proceedings (leasehold land) will not be stayed: *Iveagh* v. *Harris* [1929] 2 Ch 142, Eve J; query whether this is logical.

[238] LPA 1925 s 84(9); *Fielden* v. *Byrne* [1926] Ch 620; *Richardson* v. *Jackson* [1954] 1 WLR 447 (not if the application will clearly fail); *Shepherd Homes* v. *Sandham* [1971] Ch 341, 352F, Megarry J.

[239] *Hanning* v. *Gable-Jeffreys Properties* [1965] 1 WLR 1390; *Shepherd Homes* at 353.

[240] *Holdom* v. *Kidd* [1991] 1 EGLR 57, CA (agricultural purposes; gypsy site).

[241] LPA 1925 s 84(7)–(8); the wording is varied by LRA 2002 sch 11; *Langevad* v. *Chiswick Quay Freeholds* [1999] 1 EGLR 61, CA.

[242] L Ref A 1967 s 19 as amended; TCPA 1990 s 106A (inserted in 1991); *Re Milius' Applic* (1995) 70 P & CR 427; *Re Willis' Applic* [1997] 2 EGLR 185.

[243] *Westminster CC* v. *Duke of Westminster* (1992) 24 HLR 572, CA (covenant to use for the working classes); *Re Bedwell Park Quarry Co* v. *Hertfordshire CC* [1993] JPL 349, CA (infilling).

[244] LPA 1925 s 84 (as amended; originally 50 years); *Ridley* v. *Taylor* [1965] 1 WLR 611, CA; *Re St Mary Magdalene, Stoke Bishop* (1969) 20 P & CR 508, L Tr (1000 year leases).

[245] LPA 1925 s 84(12); mining leases are excluded; *Ridley* v. *Taylor* [1965] 1 WLR 611, CA (25 years from latest modification); *Cadogan* v. *Guinness* [1936] Ch 515, Clauson J (reckon from the date of grant of lease).

leases can be modified.[246] Minor exclusions affect public purposes, some Royal property, and military and aviation land.[247]

A buyer of the land may apply straight after his purchase,[248] and the original covenanting party may also apply.[249] Variation is discretionary, and the courts are naturally slow to allow any change to a recent covenant.[250] It is quite different if there is a change of circumstances, for example the intrusion of Welsh mountain sheep into an open plan estate.[251]

3. Grounds for variation of covenants

[34.39] The Lands Tribunal[252] has jurisdiction to discharge or modify[253] restrictions under section 84 on the following grounds:

(a)   the restriction is obsolete;
(aa) the restriction impedes reasonable use of the land and secures no substantial benefit;
(b)   those benefitted consent; or
(c)   no injury would result.

Any case must first be brought within one of the statutory paragraphs[254] after which the Tribunal must decide as a matter of discretion whether it should exercise its powers.[255]

4. Objectors

[34.40] Potential applicants are all those interested in any land affected by any restriction.[256] Claims are advertised to alert potential objectors,[257] who must be drawn into the proceedings, that is any neighbour entitled to the benefit of the restrictive covenant[258]

---

[246] *Re Calthorpe Estate* (1973) 26 P & CR 120; D Marcus [1995] 11 *EG* 132.

[247] LPA 1925 s 84(7), (11); *Westminster CC v. Duke of Westminster* [1991] 4 All ER 136.

[248] *Re Wickin's Application* (1962) 183 EG 541, Denning LJ; *Jones v. Rhys-Jones* (1974) 30 P & CR 451, CA.

[249] *Ridley v. Taylor* [1965] 1 WLR 611, 618, Harman LJ; *Shepherd Homes v. Sandham* [1971] Ch 341, 352.

[250] *Cresswell v. Proctor* [1968] 1 WLR 906, 913, Russell LJ; *Ridley v. Taylor* [1965] 1 WLR 611, CA; *Gilbert v. Spoor* [1983] Ch 27, 32, Eveleigh LJ; PH Kenny [1982] *Conv* 452.

[251] *Shepherd Homes v. Sandham* [1971] Ch 341; *(No 2)* [1971] 1 WLR 1062; contrast *Jones v. Rhys-Jones* (1974) 30 P & CR 451, CA (10 years).

[252] LPA 1925 s 84(2); SI 1996/1022, rr 13–20; *Re Purkiss' Application* [1962] 1 WLR 902, Upjohn LJ; *Shepherd Homes v. Sandham (No 2)* [1971] 1 WLR 1062, 1064–1066; *Re Girl's Day School Trust (1872)'s Applic* [2001] EWCA Civ 380, [2002] 20 EG 227; *Purfleet Farms v. SS for Transport LG&R* [2002] EWCA Civ 1430, [2003] 02 EG 105.

[253] LPA 1925 s 84(1C) added in 1969.

[254] Appeal lies on point of law.

[255] Reviewable for public law unreasonableness: *Gee v. National Trust* [1966] 1 WLR 170, CA (must act on relevant evidence).

[256] LPA 1925 s 84(1).

[257] LPA 1925 s 84(3); SI 1996/1042 r 14. *Re O'Reilly's Applic* (1993) 66 P & CR 485 (1100 circulars raised not one objection).

[258] All actual objectors must be joined; they are not liable for costs in the Tribunal but become liable if they defend subsequent court proceedings: *Re Jeff's Transfer (No 1)* [1965] 1 WLR 972, Buckley J; *(No 2)* [1966] 1 WLR 841, Stamp J; *Re Girls Day School Trust (1872)'s Applic* [2001] EWCA Civ 380, [2002] 20 EG 227 (permission to appear if points of law which might succeed).

according to property law rules of transmission.[259] If there is no qualified objector, modification may occur without a hearing,[260] though the Tribunal would still need to consider whether there had been sufficient advertisement.[261] Orders are proprietary and bind those who have not objected.[262]

5. No injury – Ground (c)

[34.41] Variation may occur if the proposed discharge or modification will not injure the persons entitled to the benefit.[263] A landowner is usually entitled to judge his own interests.[264] However, in *Gee* v. *National Trust*,[265] the National Trust were overruled since the Tribunal decided that a proposed new house was fully screened and created no visual detriment to the Fal estuary. Even if there is no injury, variation still remains discretionary.

6. Restriction obsolete – Ground (a)

[34.42] Some restrictions become obsolete because of fundamental changes to the character of the neighbourhood,[266] meaning that an injunction can no longer be obtained and the Lands Tribunal has a parallel jurisdiction to modify the covenant.[267] The Tribunal also has wider power to deem a covenant obsolete because of less fundamental changes in the neighbourhood or other material circumstances.[268] On demolition of a large mansion covenants taken to protect it become obsolete.[269] Other examples are residential estate covenants once the area changes beyond all recognition[270] or where the company granting approvals is dissolved.[271] A covenant may even be obsolete immediately.[272]

Most covenants are upheld, especially if protecting the residential character of a development. Those benefitted are entitled to object to proposals which represent the thin end of a wedge.[273] Restrictions created in 1865 at Wimbledon Common remained

---

[259] LPA 1925 s 84(3A); no appeal: *Re Lancaster Gate (No 108)* [1933] Ch 419.

[260] SI 1996/102 r 17. Ground (c) applies anyway.

[261] *Re University of Westminster's Applic* [1998] 3 All ER 1014, CA.

[262] LPA 1925 s 84(5); *Shepherd Homes* v. *Sandham* [1971] Ch 341, 353, Megarry J; *Re Ghey & Galton's Applic* [1957] 2 QB 650.

[263] LPA 1925 s 84(1)(c); not if money could be demanded for a release: *Ridley* v. *Taylor* [1965] 1 WLR 611.

[264] *Re Ghey & Galton's Applic* [1957] 2 QB 650.

[265] [1966] 1 WLR 170, CA; *Re Whiting's Applic* (1989) 58 P & CR 321, L Tr.

[266] *Knight* v. *Simmonds* [1896] 2 Ch 294; *Sobey* v. *Sainsbury* [1913] 2 Ch 513; *Chatsworth Estates Co* v. *Fewell* [1931] 1 Ch 224; *Re Lancaster Gate (No 108)* [1933] Ch 419.

[267] LPA 1925 s 84(1).

[268] Para (a); *Re Truman Hanbury Buxton & Co's Applic* [1955] 3 All ER 559, 564A, Romer LJ.

[269] *Re Freeman-Thomas Indenture* [1957] 1 All ER 532; contrast *Re Sheehy's Applic* (1992) 63 P & CR 95.

[270] *Re Kennet Properties's Applic* (1996) 72 P & CR 353, L Tr; *Wards Construction (Medway)'s Applic* (1994) 67 P & CR 379, L Tr; *Re Lloyd's Applic* (1993) 66 P & CR 112; *Re Marcello Development's Applic* [2002] RVR 146, L Tr.

[271] *Crest Nicholson Residential (S)* v. *McAllister* [2002] EWHC 2443 (Ch), [2002] 48 EG 140 (CS).

[272] *Re Quaffer's Applic* (1988) 56 P & CR 142, L Tr.

[273] *McMorris* v. *Brown* [1999] 1 AC 142, PC.

of use in 1940.[274] Covenants survive minor changes to the area.[275] Prevention or back-land or cul-de-sac development may survive as a purpose over a long period.[276]

7. Restriction impedes reasonable use – Ground (aa)

[34.43] This ground was remodelled in 1969, when it was separated from the obsoles-cence ground and significantly widened.[277] Paragraph (aa) applies where the contin-ued existence of the restriction would impede some reasonable use of the land for private or public purposes,[278] for example, perhaps, building a bungalow on vacant land on Wentworth estate,[279] or erecting fences to keep sheep out of gardens.[280]

Variation can occur only if no substantial benefits accrue.[281] This filter cuts out some cases within the wording of paragraph (aa) because someone retains a substan-tial benefit,[282] such as a resplendent view over the Tyne valley.[283]

Next step is for the Tribunal to balance the respective interests of the applicant and the objecting neighbours. Factors to be considered include the development plan, any pattern of grant or refusal of planning permission, the period at which and the context in which the restriction was created, and any other material circumstances.[284] Grant of planning permission is not decisive,[285] but considerable weight is attached to pub-lic interests including employment prospects.[286] There is a presumption in favour of continuing covenants in a building scheme,[287] or any estate scheme which is regularly enforced.[288] Modification is likely if the covenant has already been waived in other respects.[289]

Compensation[290] is possible where an obsolete restrictive covenant is varied, but it is most often awarded after modification of a restriction which retains some value.[291] The Tribunal can award such sum as it thinks just. The basis of assessment is either (a) sums needed to make up loss or disadvantage suffered; or (b) a sum to make up for the reduced price paid when the restriction was imposed.[292] Compensation is only

---

[274] *Re Henderson's Conveyance* [1940] Ch 835; *Re North's Applic* (1998) 75 P & CR 117, L Tr; *Re Diggen's Applic (No 2)* [2001] 3 EGLR 163, L Tr; *Re Azfar's* Applic [2002] 1 P & CR 18 at 215, L Tr; and many others.

[275] *Driscoll* v. *Church Commissioners for England* [1957] 1 QB 330, Denning LJ.

[276] *Re Beechwod Homes's Applic* (1992) 64 P & CR 535, L Tr.

[277] LPA 1969 s 28; Law Com 11 (1967).

[278] A less used ground is that the restriction is contrary to the public interest.

[279] *Re Kalsi's Applic* (1993) 66 P & CR 313, L Tr.

[280] *Shepherd Homes* v. *Sandham* [1971] Ch 341.

[281] LPA 1925 s 84(1A); LPA 1969 s 28, sch 3; *Re Hydeshire's Applic* (1993) 67 P & CR 93, L Tr.

[282] *Re Snaith & Dolding's Applic* (1996) 71 P & CR 104, L Tr; *Re Milius' Applic* (1995) 70 P & CR 427, L Tr.

[283] *Gilbert* v. *Spoor* [1983] Ch 27, CA; *Re Bushell's Applic* (1987) 54 P & CR 386, L Tr.

[284] LPA 1925 s 84(1B) introduced in 1969; eg the conduct of estate managers.

[285] *Re Martin's Applic* [1989] 1 EGLR 193, CA; *Re Hopcraft's Applic* (1993) 66 P & CR 475, L Tr.

[286] *Re Hounslow & Ealing LBC's Applic* (1996) 71 P & CR 100, L Tr.

[287] *Re Bromor Properties' Applic* (1995) 70 P & CR 569; *Re Lee's Applic* (1996) 72 P & CR 439.

[288] *Re Purnell's Applic* (1988) 55 P & CR 133, L Tr; and many later cases.

[289] *Re Bradley Clare Estate's Applic* (1988) 55 P & CR 126, L Tr.

[290] LPA 1925 s 84(1); *Re Kennet Properties' Applic* (1996) 72 P & CR 353; *Re Jillas' Applic* [2000] 2 EGLR 99, L Tr; HW Wilkinson [2000] *NLJ* 1523, 1623.

[291] *Re Spencer Flats* [1937] Ch 86 (award £200 each upheld); *Re Davies' Applic* [2001] 1 EGLR 111, L Tr; *Re Hextall's Applic* (2000) 79 P & CR 382, L Tr.

[292] LPA 1925 s 84(1); head (a) or (b) but not both.

required for a proved loss.[293] Expropriation is not intended[294] but the changes in 1969[295] do effectively compel one person to accept payment for relaxing a restriction.[296]

8. Reform

[34.44] In 1991 the Law Commission proposed reform of the law of *Obsolete Restrictive Covenants*.[297] If enacted, the automatic lifespan of freehold[298] covenants would be limited to 80 years. However any person benefitted could apply to the Lands Tribunal for a prolongation. These proposals may prove controversial, for they will mark a significant shift of power away from residents and towards developers, but something needs to be done.

---

[293] *Moody* v. *Vercan* [1991] 2 EGLR 288, CA; *Re Kennet Properties's Applic* (1996) 72 P & CR 353 (objectors themselves in breach of covenant); *Re Bennett & Tarmarlin's Applic* (1987) 54 P & CR 378 (waivers for payment).

[294] *Re Henderson's Conveyance* [1940] Ch 835, 846, Farwell J; *Scott* v. *UK* [1984] 41 D & R 226; N Dawson [1986] *Conv* 124.

[295] LPA 1969 s 28, in force January 1st, 1970.

[296] *Stockport MBC* v. *Alwiyah Developments* (1983) 52 P & CR 278, CA; *Abbey Homesteads (Developments)* v. *Northampton CC* [1992] 2 EGLR 18, CA. (valuation); many L Tr cases.

[297] Law Com 201 (1991); HW Wilkinson [1992] *Conv* 2.

[298] Leasehold covenants and planning agreements would be unaffected.

35

DIVISION

Grants and reservations. Use-based grants. Access to repair. Necessity. Implied reservations. Light acquired on division. Non-derogation from grant.

[35.01] Land is divided into physical parts when the owner of a whole title sells a part of it to a buyer. The buyer may acquire some rights associated with the land, called grants, but it also possible that the act of division will create rights kept back in favour of the seller, called reservations. Naturally enough the rights granted are more extensive than those reserved. Division is the occasion on which most express easements and covenants are created, but the subject of this chapter is the creation of rights through the act of division itself.[1] Three main groups of rights are considered; affirmative easements, rights to light, and rights created by the principle of non-derogation from grant.

A. GRANTS AND RESERVATIONS

1. Effect of division

[35.02] Division creates two new neighbours, and this is the vital moment to crystallise the rights and obligations that will regulate the relationship between the landowners for the future. Easements, restrictions and positive covenants may all be required, and should be set out expressly and in detail in the deed causing division, but other rights may be implied.

2. Reservations

[35.03] Rights conferred on a buyer of part are called grants. They may be express[2] or implied.[3] Reservation occurs where a landowner divides his land and keeps rights over the part sold for the benefit of the land retained,[4] of where a landlord reserves rights

---

[1] Hopkins *Informal Acquisition*, 185–250; Megarry & Wade (6th ed), [18.079–18.120].

[2] It is not necessary to use the word "grant": *Rowbotham* v. *Wilson* (1860) 8 HLC 348, 362, 11 ER 463, Lord Wensleydale; *Mobil Oil Co* v. *Birmingham CC* [2001] EWCA Civ 1608, [2002] 2 P & CR 14 at 186.

[3] See below **[35.06ff]**.

[4] *Morris* v. *Edgington* (1810) 3 Taunt 34, 36, 128 ER 10; *Dynevor* v. *Tennant* (1888) 13 App Cas 279, HL (easement).

when granting a lease.[5] Most reservations are express, because the grounds for implied reservation are extremely restricted.[6]

Grants and reservations are distinguished simply by the sequence of the transactions. One example among many is *Bridle* v. *Ruby*.[7] A company developing an estate transferred plot 12 to X (who later sold it to the defendant) and subsequently sold plot 13 to Y (who sold it on to the claimants). The division occurred on the first mentioned sale to X, who acquired grants for the benefit of No 12, leaving the company with reservations for No 13. Later sale of this plot (No 13) did not effect any further division, but merely passed any reservations created by the initial division of the two plots.

Since 1925,[8] the seller passes the land to the buyer, keeping back out of the sale the right reserved.[9] Hence it is possible to reserve a legal right even if the buyer does not execute the conveyance, and even if the right comes back to someone other than the seller.[10] Nonetheless a reservation is treated as a regrant by the buyer, so as to be it is construed against the buyer and more favourably to the seller,[11] according to *St Edmundsbury & Ipswich Diocesan Board of Finance* v. *Clark (No 2)*.[12]

3. Simultaneous conveyance

[35.04] Simultaneous conveyances create grants in favour of each part.[13]

4. Proprietary character of implied grant

[35.05] Rights implied on a legal division of unregistered land are themselves legal, and they will override a transfer of part of a registered title.[14]

B. USE-BASED GRANTS

[35.06] The rules discussed here apply only to grant, as explained below,[15] and are not available to create reservations.

---

[5] A Samuels (1963) 27 *Conv (NS)* 187.

[6] See below **[35.25]**.

[7] [1989] QB 169, CA; *Peckham* v. *Ellison* (2000) 79 P & CR 276, CA..

[8] LPA 1925 s 65. A partial reform occurred in 1881: *Cordell* v. *Second Clanfield Properties* [1969] 2 Ch 9, 14, Megarry J.

[9] Old law distinguished *exceptions* of things in existence (trees and minerals) from *reservations* of services (leasehold rent, easements, "sporting" rights and other profits) which had to be by regrant: *Mason* v. *Clarke* [1954] 1 QB 460, 466–467, Denning LJ. But *Hill* v. *Booth* [1930] 1 KB 381, 387, Scrutton LJ, permits reservations of both sorts.

[10] LPA 1925 s 65(1); *Johnstone* v. *Holdway* [1963] 1 QB 601, CA; RE Megarry (1963) 79 *LQR* 182.

[11] Reversing pre-1926 law: *South Eastern Rly Co* v. *Associated Portland Cement Manufacturers (1900)* [1910] 1 Ch 12, CA.

[12] [1975] 1 WLR 468, CA; PB Fairest [1974] *CLJ* 52; F Glover [1974] *NLJ* 184; *White* v. *Richards* (1994) 68 P & CR 105, CA; *Wellbarn Shoot* v. *Shackleton* [2002] 18 EG 151 (CS).

[13] *Selby DC* v. *Samuel Smith Old Brewery (Tadcaster)* [2001] 1 EGLR 71, CA.

[14] See above **[33.19]**. They will only continue to override if used each year or if discoverable at the time of a subsequent transfer of the burdened land, see above **[33.20]**.

[15] See below **[35.25]**.

1.   General words passing rights in use

[35.07] General words are included in every conveyance or transfer of land by section 62 of the Law of Property Act 1925.[16] Contractual conditions usually include similar terms.[17]

Pre-existing easements are transferred, but the general words have the more radical effect of creating new easements from informal rights in use at the time of the division, as a short extract shows:

"A conveyance of land shall . . . operate to convey with the land all . . . liberties, privileges, easements, rights and advantages whatsoever appertaining . . . to the land, or at the time of the conveyance, demised, occupied, or enjoyed with, or reputed or known as part or parcel of or appurtenant to the land . . .".

The dynamic effect arises from the fact that this wording extends beyond easements to "liberties, privileges, easements, rights and advantages"[18] and the fact that it embraces not only true appurtenances but also things "demised, occupied, or enjoyed with" the land.

Creation is based on *use* before the time of division, the fact of use being more significant than how it came about.[19] Permissive use of a coal shed by a tenant converts into an easement on renewal of the lease,[20] friendly short cuts are promoted into rights of way,[21] and licences to park become full easements.[22] Repair of a gable wall carried out by permission of the neighbour becomes a right to do so when the ownership is divided.[23] Other cases have involved permissive parking,[24] light,[25] rights of way,[26] the use of a private garden,[27] fencing,[28] and profits.[29]

Although section 62 includes "all privileges . . . enjoyed with the land", it only allows the creation of rights which are easement-like: it replaces words put into conveyances by the parties themselves and does not allow landowners to break property

---

[16] The section operates on conveyances executed after 1881; *Simmons* v. *Dobson* [1991] 1 WLR 720, CA (division on September 7th 1925); *Borman* v. *Griffith* [1930] 1 Ch 493. LRR 1925 r 251 provided a tailor made form of words in registered conveyancing but DLRR 2003 has no provision, leaving matters to s 62.

[17] Standard Conditions of Sale (3rd ed), [3.4]; *Selby DC* v. *Samuel Smith Old Brewery (Tadcaster)* [2001] 1 EGLR 71, CA; (Law Society's Conditions); on express words: *Pitt* v. *Buxton* (1970) 21 P & CR 127, CA; *Pallister* v. *Clark* (1975) 30 P & CR 84, CA.

[18] *Roswell* v. *Prior* (1701) Holt KB 500, 90 ER 1175; *Kay* v. *Oxley* (1875) LR 10 QB 360; *Barkshire* v. *Grubb* (1881) 18 Ch D 616; *Roe* v. *Siddons* (1888) 22 QBD 224, CA; P Jackson (1966) 30 *Conv (NS)* 340, 340–346.

[19] *May* v. *Belleville* [1905] 2 Ch 605.

[20] *Wright* v. *Macadam* [1949] 2 KB 744, CA; RE Megarry (1950) 66 *LQR* 302; L Tee [1998] *Conv* 115.

[21] *International Tea Stores* v. *Hobbs* [1903] 2 Ch 165; *Roe* v. *Siddons* (1888) 22 QBD 224, CA.

[22] *Hair* v. *Gillman* [2000] 3 EGLR 74, CA.

[23] *Ward* v. *Kirkland* [1967] Ch 194; *Graham* v. *Philcox* [1984] QB 747; P Todd [1985] *Conv* 60.

[24] *Handel* v. *St Stephens Close* [1995] 1 EGLR 70, Aldous J; HW Wilkinson [1994] *NLJ* 579; *P & S Platt* v. *Crouch* [2002] EWHC 2195 (Ch), [2002] 45 EG 153 (mooring).

[25] *Lyme Valley Squash Club* v. *Newcastle-under-Lyme BC* [1985] 2 All ER 405.

[26] *Graham* v. *Philcox* [1984] QB 747, CA; *Pitt* v. *Buxton* (1970) 21 P & CR 127, CA; *Nickerson* v. *Barraclough* [1981] Ch 426, CA.

[27] *Mulvaney* v. *Gough* [2002] EWCA Civ 1078, [2002] 44 EG 175.

[28] *Crow* v. *Wood* [1970] 1 QB 77, CA.

[29] *National Trust* v. *White* [1987] 1 WLR 907, 1028 (commons).

law rules.[30] Excluded from its scope are personal rights not related to the land,[31] public rights,[32] access enjoyed when convenient,[33] and non-easements such as protection from the weather.[34]

2.   Continuous and apparent easements under *Wheeldon* v. *Burrows*

[35.08] A person selling land is not permitted to grant the land with one hand and withhold the rights necessary for enjoyment of the land with the other. That moral principle was applied to easements by Thesiger LJ in a lengthy *obiter* discussion in *Wheeldon* v. *Burrows*.[35] He confirmed that the implication of easements is limited by restrictive conditions, summarised by Bowen LJ in *Ford* v. *Metropolitan and Metropolitan District Rly Cos*[36] in this way:

> "A grant of a part of a tenement will pass to the grantee all those *continuous and apparent* easements over the other part of the tenement which are *necessary to the enjoyment* of the part granted and have been hitherto used therewith."

These conditions are cumulative.[37]

(1) Continuous and apparent

[35.09] The need for an easement to be *continuous* was laid down in connection with light,[38] the continuity of which is not affected by the odd moonless night.[39] Rights of way and other affirmative rights are not continuous in any literal sense, but the condition has been diluted so severely as to become unidentifiable. Thus a right to use a wire permanently laid in the ground is continuous, even when the electricity is switched off.[40] Rights of way are also now[41] admitted, if used when appropriate and with some degree of continuity.[42] Projection of bowsprits of ships undergoing repair over an adjoining dry dock is non-continuous.[43]

More limiting is the need for an easement to be *apparent*. Some permanent physical adaption of the burdened land is required which demonstrates the existence of the

---

[30] *Burrows* v. *Lang* [1901] 2 Ch 502.

[31] *Goldberg* v. *Edwards* [1950] 2 Ch 247, CA (access for customers; a tough decision?)

[32] *Le Strange* v. *Pettefor* (1839) 161 LT 300.

[33] *Green* v. *Ashco Horticulturalist* [1966] 1 WLR 889; *Bartlett* v. *Tottenham* [1932] 1 Ch 114.

[34] *Phipps* v. *Pears* [1965] 1 QB 76, 84, Lord Denning MR.

[35] (1879) 12 Ch D 31, 49, 58–59; *Russell* v. *Watts* (1885) 10 App Cas 590, 596, Earl of Selborne (light); *Dalton* v. *Henry Angus & Co* (1881) 6 App Cas 740, 820–821, 826, Lord Blackburn; *Sovmots Investments* v. *SS for Environment* [1979] AC 144, 168D–169C, Lord Wilberforce, 175A–176E, Lord Edmund-Davies.

[36] (1886) 17 QBD 12, 27.

[37] *Millman* v. *Ellis* (1996) 71 P & CR 158, 162, Bingham MR.

[38] *Palmer* v. *Fletcher* (1663) 1 Lev 122, 83 ER 329; *Allen* v. *Taylor* (1880) 16 Ch D 355; *Phillips* v. *Low* [1892] 2 Ch 47.

[39] *Compton* v. *Richards* (1814) 1 Price 27, 145 ER 1320; *Wheeldon* v. *Burrows* (1879) 12 Ch D 31, 60, Thesiger LJ.

[40] *Harvey* v. *Walters* (1873) LR 8 CP 162, 164, Grove J (eavesdrop).

[41] Initially excluded: *Watts* v. *Kelson* (1871) LR 6 Ch App 166. But later admitted: *Thomas* v. *Owen* (1877) 20 QBD 225; *Schwann* v. *Cotton* [1916] 2 Ch 120, Astbury J.

[42] *Aldridge* v. *Wright* [1929] 2 KB 117, 124, CA; *Hall* v. *Lund* (1863) 1 H & C 676, 158 ER 1055 (discharge of pollution 7 times a fortnight held continuous); *Borman* v. *Griffith* [1930] 1 Ch 493, 499.

[43] *Suffield* v. *Brown* (1864) 4 De GJ & S 185, 46 ER 888.

right to a knowledgeable observer making a careful inspection.[44] Light is apparent since it must pass through a window.[45] Drains can pass,[46] but not a claim to enter the neighbour's yard to repair the end wall of a cottage which has no feature specific to its maintenance.[47]

A right of way is not apparent if there is no gate or opening to it.[48] But it can pass if there is visible evidence of the way,[49] examples being a back lane leading to a terrace of houses,[50] an access through a hall,[51] a formed way leading to gates in a wall,[52] a made way,[53] and an undefined way between two defined gates.[54] Use of a lay by may be apparent from the fact that it shares a single tarmac coating with the access drive.[55]

(2) Necessary for reasonable enjoyment of land sold

[35.10] Use-based easements need not be necessary in the literal and physical sense, since the test is what is needed for reasonable enjoyment.[56] Light is needed before a house can be occupied.[57] Factors affecting rights of way include the layout of the property, the convenience of alternative accesses, and the cost of provision of an alternative access.[58] In *Borman* v. *Griffith*[59] a right of way over the main driveway through a park was reasonably necessary, since the alternative rear access was an unmetalled track which was muddy and potholed and unsuitable for the tenant's poultry dealing. On the other hand in *Goldberg* v. *Edwards*[60] a business tenant failed to obtain access through the hall of an office building to a rear annexe since a previous tenant had managed without it. In *Millman* v. *Ellis*,[61] an express easement permitted access to a main road but only by way of a sharp and dangerous turn onto the main road, but a much safer sweeping turn on to the main road making use of the seller's lay-by was "necessary" when the increased safety was considered.[62]

---

[44] *Pyer* v. *Carter* (1857) 1 H & N 916, 156 ER 1472, Watson B (this point remains sound); *Ward* v. *Kirkland* [1967] Ch 194, 225, Upjohn J.

[45] *Compton* v. *Richards* (1814) 1 Price 27, 145 ER 1320; *Wheeldon* v. *Burrows* (1879) 12 Ch D 31, 60.

[46] *Simpson* v. *Weber* (1925) 133 LT 46.

[47] *Ward* v. *Kirkland* [1967] Ch 194.

[48] *Roe* v. *Siddons* (1888) 22 QBD 224, CA; *Titchmarsh* v. *Royston Water Co* (1899) 81 LT 673.

[49] *Glave* v. *Harding* (1858) 27 LJ Ex 286, 292, Bramwell B; *Schwann* v. *Cotton* [1916] 2 Ch 120, Astbury J.

[50] *Hansford* v. *Jago* [1921] 1 Ch 322.

[51] *Ford* v. *Metropolitan & Metropolitan District Rly Cos* (1886) 17 Ch D 12, CA.

[52] *Brown* v. *Alabaster* (1887) 37 Ch D 490, Kay J.

[53] *Watts* v. *Kelson* (1871) LR 6 Ch App 166; *Kay* v. *Oxley* (1875) LR 10 QB 360; *Barkshire* v. *Grubb* (1881) 18 Ch D 616; *Bayley* v. *Great Western Rly* (1884) 26 Ch D 434, CA.

[54] *Aldridge* v. *Wright* [1929] 2 KB 117, CA.

[55] *Millman* v. *Ellis* (1996) 71 P & CR 158, CA; J West [1995] *Conv* 346.

[56] *Wheeldon* v. *Burrows* (1879) 12 Ch D 31, 49, Thesiger LJ; *Union Lighterage Co* v. *London Graving Dock Co* [1902] 2 Ch 557, 573, Stirling LJ.

[57] *Palmer* v. *Fletcher* (1663) 1 Lev 122, 83 ER 329; *Wheeldon* v. *Burrows* (1879) 12 Ch D 31, 58, Thesiger LJ; *Ray* v. *Hazeldine* [1904] 2 Ch 17.

[58] *Pyer* v. *Carter* (1857) 1 H & N 916, 156 ER 1472; *Watts* v. *Kelsen* (1871) LR 6 Ch App 166, 174 (tank to water cattle).

[59] [1930] 1 Ch 493; H Potter (1930) 46 *LQR* 271; *Brown* v. *Alabaster* (1887) 37 Ch D 490 (back way to garden). Compare *Wheeler* v. *JJ Saunders* [1996] Ch 19, 25F, Staughton LJ; MP Thompson [1995] *Conv* 239.

[60] [1950] Ch 247, CA; RE Megarry (1950) 66 *LQR* 302.

[61] (1996) 71 P & CR 158, CA; J West [1995] *Conv* 346.

[62] At 163–164, Bingham MR.

(3) Satisfactory conditions?

[35.11] Gale's book was responsible for importing the *Wheeldon* v. *Burrows* conditions into England from the *Code Napoléon*.[63] Although at first sight illogical, they achieve a pragmatic and workable synthesis. It is sensible to allow non-documentary rights, but also to confine them to important rights (those reasonably necessary) which are discoverable by a potential buyer (apparent).

3. Use

[35.12] An easement which has never been exercised cannot be granted impliedly as a use-based right.[64] *Sovmots Investments* v. *Secretary of State for the Environment*[65] concerned Centre Point, the familiar landmark on the corner of Tottenham Court Road and New Oxford Street. The developer had left it empty for many years, until the council eventually resolved on compulsory purchase of a block of flats forming part of the rear of the site. Access was required through the remainder of the development including lifts and staircases. No right could be implied under either section 62 or *Wheeldon* v. *Burrows*, since no access had ever been obtained.[66] Section 62 is limited to things which exist at the time of the conveyance,[67] so that light will not pass when a new house is sold by the builder.[68]

Use *at the time of the grant* mentioned in *Wheeldon* v. *Burrows*[69] is more satisfactorily formulated as "hitherto used therewith."[70] A use that ceased many years before division could not be revived on sale,[71] but a use-based grant should be allowed despite a temporary suspension at the time of division – perhaps because both properties were empty awaiting sale.[72] Quantification follows from the actual use of the property made before the division[73]: thus in *Nickerson* v. *Barraclough*[74] an agricultural right of way was implied from agricultural use, but not an access for so as to allow building.

---

[63] French law could imply *reservations* as well as grants; ECC Firth (1894) 10 *LQR* 323; AWB Simpson (1967) 83 *LQR* 240.

[64] *Compton* v. *Richards* (1814) 1 Price 27, 145 ER 1320 (light to a proposed building).

[65] [1979] AC 144, 168D–169C, 175A–176E, 179B, 183C–G; P Smith (1978) 42 *Conv (NS)* 449; C Harpum (1977) 41 *Conv (NS)* 415; *Suffield* v. *Brown* (1864) 4 De GJ & S 185, 194, 46 ER 888, Lord Westbury LC; *Titchmarsh* v. *Royston Water Co* (1899) 81 LT 673.

[66] The compulsory purchase legislation did not (at the time) contain the necessary power to secure easements but Compulsory Purchase Act 1965 sch 3 is now amended to allow this.

[67] *Roe* v. *Siddons* (1888) 22 QB 224, 235; *Ward* v. *Kirkland* [1967] Ch 194, 229G.

[68] *Birmingham Dudley & District Banking Co* v. *Ross* (1888) 38 Ch D 295, CA. (on 1881 Act); *Broomfield* v. *Williams* [1897] 1 Ch 602, CA; *Godwin* v. *Schweppes* [1902] 1 Ch 926, Joyce J; *Frederick Betts* v. *Pickfords* [1906] 2 Ch 87, Kekewich J; *Lyme Valley Squash Club* v. *Newcastle under Lyme BC* [1985] 2 All ER 405.

[69] (1879) 12 Ch D 31, 49, Thesiger LJ; *Sovmots* [1979] AC 144, 169A, Lord Wilberforce.

[70] *Ford* v. *Metropolitan and Metropolitan District Rly Cos* (1886) 17 QBD 12, 27, Bowen LJ.

[71] *Re Broxhead Common* (1977) 33 P & CR 451 (non-exercise 1926–1948); *Payne* v. *Inwood* (1997) 74 P & CR 42, CA (non-exercise 1969–1979); MP Thompson [1997] *Conv* 453.

[72] *Simmons* v. *Dobson* [1991] 1 WLR 720, CA; *Costagliou* v. *English* (1969) 210 EG 1425, 1429 (lane not used for 10 months); *Pretoria Warehousing Co* v. *Skelton* [1993] EGCS 120; A Dowling [1994] *Conv* 238.

[73] Similar to an express grant of a way "as hitherto used and enjoyed": *Nicklin* v. *Pierson* (1971) 220 EG 649, CA; *Miller* v. *TG Dobson & Co* (1971) 220 EG 1595.

[74] [1980] Ch 325, 336E, Megarry V-C; on appeal [1981] Ch 426, 442H–445C, Brightman LJ.

4.   Use-based rights restricted to grants

[35.13] Use-based rights pass only to buyers under grants. When land is divided by a voluntary act[75] a grant occurs in favour of a person who receives a part, whether as buyer, or donee or under a gift by will.[76] Simultaneous sales – usually at auction[77] – have only buyers, and implied grant operates in favour of all. Use is not a basis for implied reservation.[78] Sellers can only continue uses that have been expressly reserved. Ever since 1894 some people have thought that the order of sales should be irrelevant,[79] but this has become more pressing with the growth of registered titles because one cannot tell from a register the order of sale of two adjoining plots of land.

5.   Who exercises use-based grants?

[35.14] There are two fundamental situations, but four permutations created from the two heads of use-based grants.

(1) Owner occupier dividing his land

[35.15] During unity of ownership, the landowner exercises rights of ownership[80] possibly including easement-like rights called quasi-easements. These are not true easements because a person does not need rights over parts of his own land. On physical division, *Wheeldon* v. *Burrows* converts quasi-easements to full easements, provided of course that they are continuous and apparent and reasonably necessary. However, section 62 of the Law of Property Act 1925 will not imply easements in this case when it is most often needed,[81] because the section only applies to the division of ownership of land already in separate occupations. Emphatic dicta in *Sovmots Investments* v. *Secretary of State for the Environment*[82] limited section 62. Compulsory purchase of part of an empty development passed no rights since during common ownership there were only acts of ownership. Express general words overcome this limitation if they refer to quasi-easements.[83]

---

[75] Not on compulsory purchase: *Serff* v. *Acton Local Board* (1886) 31 Ch D 679; *Sovmots Investments* v. *SS for Environment* [1979] AC 144, HL; *Proctor* v. *Hodgson* (1855) 10 Exch 824, 156 ER 674 (escheat).

[76] *Phillips* v. *Low* [1892] 1 Ch 47; *Pearson* v. *Spencer* (1863) 3 B & S 761, 122 ER 285; *Milner's Safe Co* v. *Great Northern & City Rly Co* [1907] 1 Ch 208. After 1925 legal division occurs by assent.

[77] Irrespective of the order of completions: *Swansborough* v. *Coventry* (1832) 9 Bing 305, 131 ER 629; *Russell* v. *Watts* (1885) 10 App Cas 590, 612, Lord Russell; *Hansford* v. *Jago* [1921] 1 Ch 322; *Allen* v. *Taylor* (1880) 16 Ch D 355; *Long* v. *Gowlett* [1923] 2 Ch 177.

[78] See below [35.25].

[79] E Firth (1894) 10 *LQR* 323, 329.

[80] *Greathead* v. *Morley* (1841) 3 M & G 139, 133 ER 1090; *Martyn* v. *Williams* (1857) 1 H & N 817, 830, 156 ER 1430, Martin B.

[81] *Long* v. *Gowlett* [1923] 2 Ch 177; C Harpum (1979) 43 *Conv (NS)* 113; *Bolton* v. *Bolton* (1879) 11 Ch D 968; P Jackson (1966) 30 *Conv (NS)* 340, 346–348.

[82] [1979] AC 144, HL; but for light see below [35.26].

[83] *Simmons* v. *Dobson* [1991] 1 WLR 720, CA; P Sparkes [1992] *Conv* 167, 177–178.

(2) Separate occupiers

[35.16] If there is common *ownership* of benefitted and burdened land but the *occupation* is divided,[84] both forms of use-based rules are in play. Personal exercise by the grantor is not required[85] and use by a tenant suffices.[86] General words also operate[87] even where the right is exercised for the benefit of more land than that included in the conveyance.[88]

6. Contract and conveyance

[35.17] *Wheeldon* v. *Burrows* applies to transactions operating either at law or in equity, including a freehold conveyance and the grant of a legal lease,[89] but also a contract for sale or equitable lease[90] – even if the formal conveyance is never executed. By way of contrast, section 62 applies only to a "conveyance", a term defined[91] to include a transfer of part of a registered title, a conveyance of unregistered land, a legal lease by deed, and informal short legal lease[92]; but if the interpretation is liberal, benevolence is exhausted at the point of contracts and equitable leases which fall outside section 62.[93] These rules are complex and unsatisfactory. Contractual rights are superseded once a conveyance is executed, but it is often possible to rectify the deed to make it correspond to contractual rights provided that no third party is injured in the process.[94] Under an open contract section 62 rights may be excluded from the conveyance.[95] Problems arise if the sequence of contracts and transfers is distorted.[96]

7. Exclusion

[35.18] All implied grants are based on the presumed intention of the parties, and can be excluded,[97] since there would be no justice in continuing existing uses against the

---

[84] *MRA Engineering* v. *Trimster Co* (1988) 56 P & CR 1, CA.

[85] Despite *Wheeldon* v. *Burrows* (1879) 12 Ch D 31, 49, Thesiger LJ.

[86] *Ford* v. *Metropolitan District Rly Cos* (1886) 17 QBD 12, 28–29, Bowen LJ; *Borman* v. *Griffith* [1930] 1 Ch 493; *Goldberg* v. *Edwards* [1950] Ch 247; *Ward* v. *Kirkland* [1967] Ch 194; DA Stroud (1940) 56 *LQR* 93; P Sparkes [1992] *Conv* 167.

[87] *International Tea Stores* v. *Hobbs* [1903] 2 Ch 165; *May* v. *Belleville* [1905] 2 Ch 605; *Crow* v. *Wood* [1971] 1 QB 77, CA (previous tenant).

[88] *Graham* v. *Philcox* [1984] QB 747; P Todd [1985] *Conv* 60; S Tromans [1983] *CLJ* 15. But not so as to benefit land excluded from the conveyance: *Nickerson* v. *Barraclough* [1981] Ch 426, 442–445, Brightman LJ (plot 78A).

[89] Easements implied into a lease are limited to the duration of the leasehold estate: *White* v. *Bass* (1862) 7 H & N 722, 158 ER 660 (merger); *Warner* v. *McBryde* (1871) 36 LT 360; *Westwood* v. *Heywood* [1921] 2 Ch 130.

[90] *Borman* v. *Griffith* [1930] 1 Ch 493, Maugham J; H Potter (1930) 46 *LQR* 271.

[91] LPA 1925 s 205(1)(ii).

[92] S 54(2); *Wright* v. *Macadam* [1949] 2 KB 744, CA.

[93] *Borman* v. *Griffith* [1930] 1 Ch 493.

[94] *Clark* v. *Barnes* [1929] 2 Ch 368; *Bolton* v. *Bolton* (1879) 11 Ch D 968; *Peck & London School Board's C* [1893] 2 Ch 315, 321, Chitty J; *Lyme Valley Squash Club* v. *Newcastle-under-Lyme BC* [1985] 2 All ER 405; *Holow (470)* v. *Stockton Estates* (2001) 81 P & CR 404, Ch D.

[95] *Re Walmsley & Shaw's C* [1917] 1 Ch 93; *Re Lyne-Stephens & Scott-Miller's C* [1920] 1 Ch 472.

[96] *Beddington* v. *Atlee* (1887) 35 Ch D 317 (claimant with the second contract obtained the fist conveyance; plot 2 received no light over plot 1); *White* v. *Taylor (No 2)* [1969] 1 Ch 160, 183–184, Buckley J; also *Booth* v. *Alcock* (1873) LR 8 Ch App 663; *Quicke* v. *Chapman* [1903] 1 Ch 659.

[97] Eg if a faculty is required from a Church court: *Re St Clements* [1988] 1 WLR 720.

wishes of the parties. Exclusion of the rule in *Wheeldon* v. *Burrows*[98] may be express, implicit in the grant of inconsistent rights,[99] or implied.[100] *Birmingham Dudley & District Banking Co* v. *Ross*[101] shows that no right to light arises if the right to build is clearly reserved. Section 62 applies in the same way: it applies only to the extent that no contrary intention is expressed in the conveyance,[102] for example by reservation of the seller's right to build.[103] However, an express easement is granted, section 62 may nevertheless operate to confer wider rights than those conferred by an express grant,[104] or a more limited form of general words[105] unless the drafting is clear to exclude this, and separate exclusion of *Wheeldon* v. *Burrows* is required.[106]

C. ACCESS TO REPAIR

[35.19] Access to repair has not been viewed as a "necessity" for a householder in modern cases such as *Kwiatkowski* v. *Cox*.[107] A house was built so as to be flush to the plot boundary creating a self-evident need to gain access for repair, but not, Goff J held, any implied right of access. Parliamentary intervention became necessary. The proximate cause of the legislation was a dispute about the side wall of a bungalow on the outskirts of Poole to which access was refused, apparently after a disagreement about the pruning of an apple tree.[108]

Sterilisation of land is avoided by the Access to Neighbouring Land Act 1992[109] which gives a right to seek an access order.[110] Orders are discretionary with much reliance on what is "reasonable".[111] An access order can be obtained by any person[112] who wishes to enter neighbouring land for the purpose of carrying out works to his land and who cannot obtain the necessary permission to do so.[113] *Dean* v. *Walker*[114] decided that the Act included work on a party wall (which counts as "land") but left open whether the Act could apply to work on the *neighbour's* land. An order can be

---

[98] *Borman* v. *Griffith* [1930] 1 Ch 493, 499, Maugham J.

[99] *Millman* v. *Ellis* (1996) 71 P & CR 158, 164–165, Bingham MR; J West [1995] *Conv* 346; *Mobil Oil* v. *Birmingham CC* [2001] EWCA Civ 1608, [2002] 2 P & CR 14 at 186.

[100] *Wheeler* v. *JJ Saunders* [1996] Ch 19, 31B, Peter Gibson LJ (covenant to erect fence excluded right of way); MP Thompson [1995] *Conv* 239.

[101] (1888) 38 Ch D 295, CA; *Broomfield* v. *Williams* [1897] 1 Ch 602, CA; *Godwin* v. *Schweppes* [1902] 1 Ch 926, Joyce J; *Frederick Betts* v. *Pickfords* [1906] 2 Ch 87, Kekewich J; *Paragon Finance* v. *City of London Real Property Co* [2002] 1 P & CR 470, Ch D.

[102] *Jelbert* v. *Davis* [1968] 1 WLR 589, 593H, Lord Denning MR; *Hansford* v. *Jago* [1921] 1 Ch 322; *Lyme Valley Squash Club* v. *Newcastle under Lyme BC* [1985] 2 All ER 405; *Selby DC* v. *Samuel Smith Old Brewery (Tadcaster)* [2001] 1 EGLR 71, CA.

[103] *Quicke* v. *Chapman* [1903] 1 Ch 659; *Green* v. *Ashco Horticulturalist* [1966] 1 WLR 889.

[104] *Gregg* v. *Richards* [1926] Ch 521; *Hapgood* v. *JH Martin & Son* (1934) 152 LT 72.

[105] *Hansford* v. *Jago* [1921] 1 Ch 322.

[106] *Re Peck & London Schools Board's C* [1893] 2 Ch 315.

[107] (1969) 213 EG 34; contrast *Williams* v. *Usherwood* (1981) 45 P & CR 235, 254, Cumming Bruce LJ.

[108] *Hansard*, HL vol 531 (1991), cols 166–168.

[109] Law Com 151 (1985); RT Oerton (1992) 136 *SJ* 466; JE Adams [1992] 26 *EG* 136; G Sheriff [1992] 27 *LSG* 23.

[110] HW Wilkinson [1992] *Conv* 225.

[111] *Hansard*, HL vol 533 (1991), col 824, Lord Wilberforce; R Hudson [1992] *NLJ* 316.

[112] Widely defined to include owners, licensees, and service providers.

[113] S 1(1).

[114] (1996) 73 P & CR 366, CA.

made if access is strictly necessary or if the alternative would be substantially greater difficulty unless an order will create an unreasonable interference.[115] The right to an order cannot be excluded, a fact which will encourage negotiation.[116] Work should be allowed if it is reasonably necessary for the preservation of the land, a concept tightly defined to include maintenance, repair, and renewal of the fabric of the land, similar works to drains and other services, the treatment of hedges, trees, and shrubs, and filling in a ditch. Orders may also cover alterations and improvements to the land or demolition of the whole or part of a building.[117]

Homes remain castles while turrets are repointed and fenestration is checked![118] Precise works must be specified as must the area affected, and the date and duration of access.[119] Applications require careful drafting, though orders can be varied as work proceeds.[120] Terms and conditions can be imposed to minimise the damage to the burdened land and the inconvenience and loss of privacy.[121] Payment cannot be required for a licence to enter residential land, but it will be commonplace for work in the commercial sector.[122]

Access arrangements need to be registered so as to bind purchasers of the land – as a pending land action at the application stage and as a writ or order when a final order is obtained. Neither is overriding.[123] Although the benefit does not pass directly on sale, new owners can be authorised to exercise the rights.[124]

D. NECESSITY

[35.20] Necessary easements are implied by the law on the division of land, but necessity excludes rights which would be no more than convenient or helpful. Justice requires a grant in favour of the buyer to enable him to profit from the seller's grant.[125] Reservations to the seller are also allowed:[126] the justice may be less obvious, but the right of a seller to get access to land he himself causes to be landlocked is well settled.[127]

1. Ways of necessity

[35.21] If the division of land leaves a part of it landlocked, a way of necessity will be implied to enable the part owner to reach his land.[128] Victorian case law suggests that

---

[115] Access to Neighbouring Land Act 1992 s 1(3); R Hudson [1996] *NLJ* 316.
[116] Access to Neighbouring Land Act 1992 s 4(4); G Sheriff [1992] 27 *LSG* 23.
[117] Access to Neighbouring Land Act 1992 s 1(2)–(5).
[118] HW Wilkinson [1992] *Conv* 225, 231.
[119] Access to Neighbouring Land Act 1992 s 2(1).
[120] S 6.
[121] S 2(2)–(4).
[122] S 2(5)–(6).
[123] S 5, as amended by LRA 2002 sch 11.
[124] Access to Neighbouring Land Act 1992 s 4(2).
[125] *Clarke* v. *Cogge* (1608) Cro Jac 170, 79 ER 149.
[126] *Crossley & Sons* v. *Lightowler* (1867) LR 2 Ch 478, 486, Chelmsford LC.
[127] *Wheeldon* v. *Burrows* (1878) 12 Ch D 31, 57–58, Thesiger LJ; *London Corp* v. *Riggs* (1880) 13 Ch D 798, 808, Jessel MR.
[128] JF Garner (1960) 24 *Conv (NS)* 205; P Jackson (1981) 34 *CLP* 133.

it was not unusual to buy land without any guaranteed access! Land is landlocked if completely surrounded by the seller's land (or partly his and partly a stranger's),[129] judged at the time of the division.[130] In *Nickerson* v. *Barraclough*[131] Aylward acquired ownership of plot 78A in 1906 but no way of necessity was implied, because at that moment he owned five adjoining plots which gave him the access he needed. Necessity is limited to the purpose for which the land is used at the time of division, perhaps for example for agriculture.[132]

The alternative access[133] might be over a private right of way,[134] or a public footpath[135] or by water.[136] Legal rights of access remove any necessity even if a cutting 20 feet deep has to be dug to reach it.[137] Many potential accesses are prevented by highway or planning considerations and the law needs to be recast to take account of that problem. Termination of the necessity extinguishes the implied easement.[138] A way of necessity usually follows the route of the access used before the sale,[139] but if there was no particular path, it is left to the seller to nominate the route.[140]

Very old cases recognised the necessity for water, support, flues,[141] or even light.[142] Most such cases now fit better into other heads of implied creation,[143] and appeals to necessity are rarely successful.[144]

2. Easements necessary to complete an express easement

[35.22] If an easement is only partially expressed, it can be completed by implication of associated rights provided they are strictly "necessary".[145] Parking rights in a garage imply the need for access to reach the garage. A right to draw water from a spring is nugatory unless it implies the right to reach it.[146]

---

[129] *Titchmarsh* v. *Royston Water Co* (1899) 81 LT 673; *Barry* v. *Hasseldine* [1952] 2 All ER 317, Danckwerts J.

[130] *Bolton* v. *Bolton* (1879) 11 Ch D 968, Fry J. Not by the act of an outside person: *Penn* v. *Wilkins* [1975] 2 EGLR 113, Megarry J.

[131] [1981] Ch 246, CA; P Jackson (1982) 98 *LQR* 11; HW Wilkinson (1982) 132 *NLJ* 224; L Crabb [1981] *Conv* 442; reversing: [1980] Ch 325, Megarry V-C; P Jackson (1980) 96 *LQR* 187; JT Farrand [1980] *Conv* 95. See also *Dodd* v. *Burchell* (1862) 1 H & C 113, 158 ER 822; *Thomas* v. *Waterlow* (1868) LR 6 Eq 36.

[132] *London Corp* v. *Riggs* (1880) 13 Ch D 798.

[133] Necessity exists where access is permissive: *Barry* v. *Hasseldine* [1952] Ch 835, Danckwerts J.

[134] *Staple* v. *Heydon* (1703) 6 Mod 1, 87 ER 768.

[135] *MRA Engineering* v. *Trimster Co* (1988) 56 P & CR 1, CA.

[136] *Manjang* v. *Drammeh* (1990) 61 P & CR 194, PC; C Harpum [1992] *CLJ* 220.

[137] *Titchmarsh* v. *Royston Water Co* (1899) 81 LT 673.

[138] *Pomfret* v. *Ricroft* (1670) 1 Wms Saund 321, 85 ER 454; and many later cases.

[139] *Pinnington* v. *Galland* (1853) 9 Exch 1, 156 ER 1.

[140] *Bolton* v. *Bolton* (1879) 11 Ch D 968, Fry J; *Brown* v. *Alabaster* (1887) 37 Ch D 490, 500, Kay J; *Deacon* v. *South Eastern Rly* (1889) 61 LT 377; *Wellbarn Shoot* v. *Shackleton* [2002] 18 EG 151 (CS).

[141] *Nicholas* v. *Chamberlain* (1607) Cro Jac 121, 79 ER 105 (flue); *Wheeldon* v. *Burrows* (1879) 12 Ch D 31, 50–51, 54, Thesiger LJ; *Greg* v. *Planque* [1936] 1 KB 669, CA.

[142] *Ray* v. *Hazeldine* [1904] 2 Ch 17, Kekewich J obiter.

[143] *White* v. *Bass* (1862) 7 H & N 722, 158 ER 660, Wilde B.

[144] *Union Lighterage Co* v. *London Graving Dock Co* [1902] 2 Ch 557, 573, Stirling LJ; *Milner's Safe Co* v. *Great Northern Rly Co* [1907] 1 Ch 208.

[145] *London & Suburban Land and Building Co (Holdings)* v. *Carey* (1991) 62 P & CR 480, Millett J (unloading); *Handel* v. *St Stephens Close* [1994] 1 EGLR 70 (parking, triable issue).

[146] *Pwllbach Colliery Co* v. *Woodman* [1915] AC 634, 646, Lord Parker; *Hinchcliff* v. *Kinnoul* (1835) 5 Bing NC 1, 24, 132 ER 1004; *Duke of Westminster* v. *Guild* [1985] QB 688, CA; P Jackson [1985] *Conv* 66; *Lomax* v. *Wood* [2001] EWCA Civ 1099, [2001] June 11th, CA (right to construct gate).

3. Easements necessary to achieve an intended purpose

[35.23] Necessity may spring from the purpose for which land is sold rather than its physical layout. As Lord Parker stated in *Pwllbach Colliery Co* v. *Woodman*:[147]

> "The law will readily imply the grant or reservation of such easements as may be necessary to give effect to the common intention of the parties to a grant of real property, with reference to the manner or purposes in and for which the land granted or some land retained by the grantor is to be used."[148]

Purpose-based implication is based on necessity as opposed to mere convenience.[149]

In *Wong* v. *Beaumont*,[150] a basement in Exeter, just along from the Law Faculty building of the author's time as a student, was let for use as a Chinese restaurant. It was so badly ventilated that a duct had to be fixed to the landlord's property above to take away cooking smells. Public health regulations prohibited use of the basement for the purpose intended by the lease without this additional ventilation, though this legal necessity was unknown to either party at the time of the lease. A successor landlord was bound by the declaration granted to the tenant.

Necessity arises from future intended purposes and is not constrained by the earlier use.[151] A sale of building land may require the implication of a whole range of easements to facilitate the building.[152] Where the intended layout of the houses and estate roads is indicated, rights of way might be implied over intended future roads,[153] a wide potentiality recently confirmed in *Stafford* v. *Lee*.[154] This is also used to create reservations. In *Peckham* v. *Ellison*[155] the right included was use of a track at the back of a house acquired under the right to buy scheme. It was a necessary inference that the common intention both parties was that the seller was to have use of track. Reservation will not occur where the facts do not establish a common intention or suggestion imprecision.[156] This was one of several unsuccessful attempts to push the door further ajar.[157]

---

[147] [1915] AC 634, 646; *Jones* v. *Pritchard* [1908] 1 Ch 630, 636.

[148] No rights should be implied on compulsory purchase since the owner whose land is taken has no intention: *Sovmots Investments* v. *SS for Environment* [1979] AC 144, 175–176, Lord Edmund-Davies.

[149] *White* v. *Taylor (No 2)* [1969] 1 Ch 160, 196G–197F, Buckley J (well); *Kwiatkowski* v. *Cox* (1969) 213 EG 34 (repair of gable wall).

[150] [1965] 1 QB 173, CA; RE Megarry (1964) 80 *LQR* 322; HW Wilkinson (1964) 27 *MLR* 720.

[151] Query *Nickerson* v. *Barraclough* [1981] Ch 426, CA (access to land sold as building plots restricted to agriculture); the more extensive rights implied at first instance are more satisfying.

[152] *Rigby* v. *Bennett* (1882) 21 Ch D 559, CA (support).

[153] *Dann* v. *Spurrier* (1802) 7 Ves 231, 32 ER 94; *Davies* v. *Sear* (1869) LR 7 Eq 427, Lord Romilly MR (access through arch); *Wheeldon* v. *Burrows* (1879) 12 Ch D 31, 58.

[154] (1992) 65 P & CR 172, CA; HW Wilkinson (1993) 143 *NLJ* 1544.

[155] (2000) 79 P & CR 276, CA; HW Wilkinson [2000] *NLJ* 1015.

[156] *Chaffe* v. *Kingsley* [2000] 1 EGLR 104, CA (no right over road extension marked on plan); HW Wilkinson [2000] *NLJ* 1015.

[157] *Holow (470)* v. *Stockton Estates* (2001) 81 P & CR 404, Ch D; *Mobil Oil* v. *Birmingham CC* [2001] EWCA Civ 1608, [2002] 2 P & CR 14 at 186.

4.   Exclusion of easements of necessity

[35.24] Liberal rules for implying grants and particularly reservations were once ascribed to the public policy of ensuring that land was capable of cultivation.[158] Access may be needed to prevent sterilisation of land. Megarry V-C adopted this reasoning at first instance in *Nickerson* v. *Barraclough*.[159] A 1906 conveyance of plot 78A on a building estate stated that no rights of way were to be granted over the estate roads until they were made up. After reviewing Commonwealth authorities,[160] English dicta,[161] and academic opinion,[162] Megarry V-C enunciated a public policy that no transaction should be effective to deprive land of a suitable means of access[163] without good reason. The Court of Appeal[164] reversed this decision, reasoning that implication is contractual in character, revealing the presumed intention of the parties. Since land could be left without access by compulsory purchase[165] or adverse possession, or escheat,[166] or for the purpose of rent review,[167] and therefore an easement necessary to give effect to the common intention of the parties could be (and had been) excluded. Land can be landlocked by express agreement.

E.   IMPLIED RESERVATIONS

[35.25] Use-based grants are founded on non-derogation from grant, a rule of common honesty.[168] A person is not allowed to sell land on the one hand and withhold the rights needed to enjoy it on the other, but this reasoning does not require reservations to be kept back for the seller. The general words state that a "conveyance of land shall . . . operate to convey with the land",[169] wording which does not reserve any rights to the seller. Non-derogation was restricted to grants by *Suffield* v. *Brown*,[170] a rule restated and set in concrete by Thesiger LJ in *Wheeldon* v. *Burrows*.[171] Knowledge that the seller used a particular right makes no difference.[172]

---

[158] *Dutton* v. *Tayler* (1700) Lutw 1487, 125 ER 819; *Wheeldon* v. *Burrows* (1878) 12 Ch D 31, 58, Thesiger LJ.
[159] [1980] Ch 325; on appeal [1981] Ch 426, CA.
[160] *North Sydney Printing Pty* v. *Sabemo Investment Corp Pty* [1971] 2 NSWLR 150.
[161] *Packer* v. *Wellstead* (1658) 2 Sid 111, 112, 82 ER 1284; *Brown* v. *Burdett* (1882) 21 Ch D 667.
[162] EH Bodkin (1973) 89 *LQR* 87.
[163] [1980] Ch 325, 333.
[164] [1981] Ch 246, CA.
[165] *Sovmots Investments* v. *SS for Environment* [1979] AC 144, HL.
[166] *Proctor* v. *Hodgson* (1855) 10 Exch 824, 156 ER 674.
[167] *J Murphy & Sons* v. *Railtrack* [2002] EWCA Civ 679, [2002] 31 EG 99.
[168] *Harmer* v. *Jumbil (Nigeria) Tin Areas* [1921] 1 Ch 200, 225; *Sovmots Investments* v. *SS for Environment* [1979] AC 144, 175, Lord Edmund-Davies; *Wheeldon* v. *Burrows* (1882) 12 Ch D 31, 49, Thesiger LJ.
[169] LPA 1925 s 62(1).
[170] (1864) 4 De GJ & S 185, 46 ER 888, Lord Westbury LC.
[171] (1878) 12 Ch D 31, 49–57 (light); *Union Lighterage Co* v. *London Graving Dock Co* [1902] 2 Ch 557, CA.
[172] Necessary easements can be reserved: *Re Webb's Lease* [1951] Ch 808, CA; *Peckham* v. *Ellison* (2000) 79 P & CR 276, CA.

Implied reservation is allowed in cases of physical necessity,[173] or of necessary implication. Other cases are conceivable.[174] Easements arise from a necessary dependence in construction,[175] for example if a house is built against the boundary and no express right to repair is given.[176] Reciprocal easements might be reserved where the rights are needed on both plots irrespective of the order of sales,[177] for example where houses require mutual support, or a mutual drainage system.[178]

F. LIGHT ACQUIRED ON DIVISION

[35.26] *Colls* v. *Home & Colonial Stores* (1904)[179] established the nature of the right to light for the benefit of a particular window. Such rights are frequently implied on the division of land. *Wheeldon* v. *Burrows* itself exemplifies the rule that if the owner of a house sells it he is not at liberty to build on land which he retains so as to block the windows of the house which he sold.[180] Section 62 of the Law of Property Act 1925 also operates to pass light – in this exceptional case even where land in a single occupation is divided.[181] Light is commonly excluded by reservation of the right to build on the retained land.[182] The seller's windows are not be protected, since there is no implied power of reservation, that being the precise point of decision in *Wheeldon* v. *Burrows*.[183]

G. NON-DEROGATION FROM GRANT

1. The principle

[35.27] Light apart, restrictions on neighbouring land cannot generally be created by implication, since restrictive covenants required express creation, but a possibility of imposing restrictions arises under the principle of non-derogation from grant. When a person sells part of his land he accepts the obligation not to use his retained land so as to defeat the purpose of the sale.

---

[173] *Crossley & Sons* v. *Lightowler* (1867) LR 2 Ch 478, 486, Chelmsford LC; *Liddiard* v. *Waldron* [1934] 1 KB 435.

[174] *Wheeldon* (1878) 12 Ch D 31, 49, Thesiger LJ.

[175] *Pearson* v. *Spencer* 1863) 3 B & S 761, 122 ER 285; *Ford* v. *Metropolitan and Metropolitan District Rly Cos* (1886) 17 QBD 12, 27, Bowen LJ.

[176] *Ward* v. *Kirkland* [1967] Ch 194, Ungoed-Thomas J (non-derogation from grant); *Williams* v. *Usherwood* (1981) 45 P & CR 235, 254 (was necessary).

[177] *Russell* v. *Watts* (1885) 10 App Cas 590, HL; *Cory* v. *Davies* [1923] 2 Ch 95, PO Lawrence J.

[178] *Pyer* v. *Carter* (1859) 1 H & N 916, 156 ER 1472; *Re Webb's Lease* [1951] Ch 808, 827, Jenkins LJ; *Union Lighterage Co* v. *London Graving Dock Co* [1902] 2 Ch 557, 565, 570.

[179] [1904] AC 179, HL; see above **[32.29]**.

[180] *Palmer* v. *Fletcher* (1663) 1 Lev 122, 83 ER 329; *Russell* v. *Watts* (1885) 10 App Cas 590, 596, Earl of Selborne; *Phillips* v. *Low* [1892] 1 Ch 47, 53; *Newnham* v. *Willison* (1988) 56 P & CR 8.

[181] *Broomfield* v. *Williams* [1897] 1 Ch 602; *Sovmots Investments* v. *SS for Environment* [1977] AC 144, 176C, Lord Edmund Davies.

[182] See above **[35.18]**.

[183] (1882) 12 Ch D 31, CA; *White* v. *Bass* (1862) 7 H & N 722, 158 ER 660. Reservation depends upon a necessity.

"Derogation from grant" is a rule of common honesty.[184] A person who sells a part of his land for a particular purpose is not allowed to withhold the rights necessary to enjoyment it for that purpose. When a landlord lets part of his land, there is some overlap with the covenant for quiet enjoyment,[185] but non-derogation can also apply to freehold division. The *buyer* is not restricted in his use of his land, so the seller must create express covenants.[186]

2. The purpose derogated from

[35.28] In a successful case the width of the purpose determines the corresponding width of the restriction, but it is difficult to win. In *Browne* v. *Flower*[187] an iron staircase was erected outside the window of the plaintiff's flat, severely impairing his privacy. No derogation occurred. Interference with the plaintiff's comfort did not derogate from his ability to reside in the flat. In *Port* v. *Griffith*[188] a landlord let one shop for the sale of wool followed by a second, nearby, for the same purpose. The first tenant suffered a loss of profit, but her shop was no less fit for use as wool shop so she had no action. Although a doctrine of law,[189] the sting can be drawn by a contractual exclusion limiting the purpose.[190]

3. Forms of right created

[35.29] The rules for affirmative easements have already been considered.[191] Restrictive easements can undoubtedly be created on non-derogation principles. Thus in *Johnston & Sons* v. *Holland*[192] an action in derogation succeeded in preserving the right to use the flank wall of a building let for displaying advertisements, being a restriction on building to block the advert.[193] Light[194] and support[195] could be acquired in the same way.

Wider restrictions can be imposed. Use of land next to an explosives magazine is restricted by statute in the interests of public safety. When the landlord involved in *Harmer* v. *Jumbil (Nigeria) Tin Areas*[196] let part of his land for this dangerous use the terms of his licence prevented public access within 134 yards, building within 355 yards, and any Royal palace within 4¾ miles! As a result the landlord was restrained

---

[184] *Harmer* v. *Jumbil (Nigeria) Tin Areas* [1921] 1 Ch 200, 225; *Sovmots Investments* v. *SS for Environment* [1979] AC 144, 175, Lord Edmund-Davies; *Johnston & Sons* v. *Holland* [1988] 1 EGLR 264, 267J, Nicholls LJ.

[185] P Sparkes *NLT*, 716–718.

[186] *Suffield* v. *Brown* (1864) 4 De J & S 185, 46 ER 888, Lord Westbury LC; *Wheeldon* v. *Burrows* (1878) 12 Ch D 31, 49–57, Thesiger LJ; *Union Lighterage Co* v. *London Graving Dock Co* [1902] 2 Ch 557, CA; see above **[35.25]**.

[187] [1911] 1 Ch 219, 227, Parker J.

[188] [1938] 1 All ER 295.

[189] *Molton Builders* v. *Westminster LBC* (1975) 30 P & CR 182, CA.

[190] *Re Beechwood Homes' Applic* [1994] 2 EGLR 178, CA (right to vary layout of building scheme).

[191] See above **[35.08]**.

[192] [1988] 1 EGLR 264, CA.

[193] *Frederick Betts* v. *Pickfords* [1906] 2 Ch 87, Kekewich J.

[194] *Master* v. *Hansard* (1876) 4 Ch D 718, CA (unsuccessful on facts).

[195] *Popplewell* v. *Hodkinson* (1869) LR 4 Exch 248.

[196] [1921] 1 Ch 200, CA.

from building on his adjoining land, since that would have led to the revocation of the tenant's licence to keep explosives. So non-derogation fostered a novel restriction,[197] and did not stop short with easements.[198] Nicholls LJ concluded in *Johnston & Sons v. Holland*,[199] that non-derogation could impose any form of restriction on the activities of the grantor on his retained land and it could also prevent the revocation of an informal right.[200] So, in *Chartered Trust v. Davies*[201] the landlord of a mall in Bognor Regis High Street was found to have derogated from the use of one shop for the sale of executive toys by letting another unit as a pawnbrokers and allowing long queues to form outside.

4. Proprietary character

[35.30] Rights created in favour of buyers are proprietary: they bind subsequent owners of the retained land.[202] So it was, in *Harmer v. Jumbil (Nigeria) Tin Areas*,[203] that an injunction was granted against the tenant under the mining lease, who derived title from the common landlord bound by the initial obligation. The right implied into a legal lease is itself legal, and so binds the world, a limitless and almost undiscoverable incumbrance in a non-documentary way.[204]

---

[197] DW Elliott (1964) 80 *LQR* 244; compare MA Peel (1965) 81 *LQR* 28 (erroneous extension).

[198] At 225–226, Parker J; *Herz v. Union Bank of London* (1854) 2 Giff 686, 66 ER 287 (unusual lights); *Williamson v. Sunderland Corp* (1892) 9 TLR 143; *Aldin v. Latimer Clark Muirhead & Co* [1894] 2 Ch 437, 447, Stirling J (air to timber merchant); *Grosvenor Hotel Co v. Hamilton* [1894] 2 QB 836 (freedom from vibration); *Cable v. Bryant* [1908] 1 Ch 259, 264–265, Neville J (access of air to ventilators in stable); *Kelly v. Battershell* [1949] 2 All ER 830, 836–837, Cohen LJ; RE Megarry (1950) 66 *LQR* 23 (change of use of remainder of house to hotel).

[199] [1988] 1 EGLR 264, CA.

[200] *Saeed v. Plustrade* [2001] EWCA Civ 2011, [2002] 2 EGLR 19, [34–36], Sir Christopher Slade.

[201] (1998) 76 P & CR 396, 401–404, Henry LJ.

[202] *Allen v. Taylor* (1880) 16 Ch D 355, 357, Jessel MR; *Miller v. Jackson* [1977] QB 966, CA.

[203] [1921] 1 Ch 200, CA.

[204] Despite LPA 1925 ss 1(1)–(2), 4; *Johnston & Sons v. Holland* [1988] 1 EGLR 264, 268H–K, Nicholls LJ.

36

PRESCRIPTION

Role of prescription. Lost modern grant. Use as of right. Tortious and illegal use. Statutory prescription. Freehold prescription. Affirmative easements. Ancient lights. Several profits. Commons and public rights.

A. ROLE OF PRESCRIPTION

1. Policy considerations

[36.01] Prescription is a means of creating rights by long use.[1] "Antiquity of time justifies all titles and supposes the best beginning the law can give."[2] Courts should try so far as they can to clothe the fact with the right.[3] As Lord Herschell put it[4]:

> "The Courts will presume that those acts were done and those circumstances existed which were necessary to the creation of a valid title."

Regular use of a right over a neighbour's land may therefore create an easement. Two essentials are use that is prescriptive and use over a prescriptive time.[5] Prescriptive *use* entails the assertion of a right by use of neighbouring land.[6] No length of time will ever create the right from an act for which the burdened owner has given permission. Prescriptive *time* is in rough terms 20 years, but the precise rules are different for each of the four variants – common law, lost modern grant (now almost universal), the 20 year Prescription Act 1832 period and the 40 year statutory period. It suffers from one major defect which calls for urgent reform,[7] since lost modern grant is not dependent upon recent use, so it is possible for land to be subject to the trap of legal rights created many years in the past.[8] Any change would need to be balanced by significant improvements in the drafting of the 1832 Act.

---

[1] Grays' *Elements* (3rd ed), 514–526; Megarry & Wade (6th ed), [18.121–18.170]; Smith's *Property Law* (4th ed), 513–521.
[2] *Johnson* v. *Barnes* (1872) LR 7 CP 592, Willes J at first instance.
[3] *Moody* v. *Steggles* (1879) 12 Ch D 261, 265, Fry J.
[4] *Philipps* v. *Halliday* [1891] AC 228, 231.
[5] *Dalton* v. *Henry Angus & Co* (1881) 6 App Cas 740, 809; Coke on *Littleton*, [113b–114a].
[6] Older texts tend to talk of "user"; in this book "use" refers to the exercise of a right and "user" to the person who exercises it.
[7] Law Reform Committee 14th Report (1966) Cmnd 3100; HW Wilkinson (1967) 30 *MLR* 189; Law Com 36 (1971).
[8] This problem is partly solved for registered land; LRA 2002 sch 3 para 3; see above **[33.20]**.

2. Proprietary burdens

[36.02] Prescriptive burdens create rights which operate off the documentary title. If title is unregistered, the easement or whatever created by prescription is a legal interest, binding all comers with or without notice,[9] and prescriptive rights will override a registered title[10] and operates off the register as interests that override the register. The benefit may be entered as a plus on the property register of the title.[11]

B. LOST MODERN GRANT

1. The doctrine

[36.03] Lost modern grant evolved as a judicial response to the inadequacy of common law prescription. That required use to have started before 1189, so that it was a defence to show that prescriptive use was impossible at any intervening date. By way of contrast, lost modern grant is based on the fiction that use of an easement for twenty years was initially permitted by an express deed (a grant) which has disappeared (that is it has been lost).[12] Since the presumed grant is modern, this technique overcomes the difficulty that most rights cannot have existed continuously since 1189.

After use as of right[13] for a full 20 years, lost modern grant operates automatically, but no period short of that suffices.[14] The period may have been taken by analogy from the old statutes of limitation.[15] In *Tehidy Minerals* v. *Norman* a successful claim to common rights was made after grazing for 21 years and 8 months.[16] A clear advantage to a person acquiring a right is that the 20 year period may have run at any time in the past. Thus in *Mills* v. *Silver*[17] proof of use between 1922 and 1981 established lost modern grant, but the effective non use of the drive between 1981 and the time of the claim in 1986 knocked out any possibility of statutory prescription.[18] This poses a serious disadvantage to a buyer, since no matter how long it can be proved that the land has been free from the exercise of adverse rights, it is still possible for it to be subject to an unknown burden.[19]

Lost grant is admittedly artificial, a "revolting fiction".[20] Its origin lay in a true presumption, an invitation to juries to assume that an easement had been granted by deed

[9] LPA 1925 s 12; see above **[33.03]**.
[10] LRA 2002 schs 1/3 para 3; see above **[33.19]**.
[11] DLRR 2003 r 74.
[12] *Bryant* v. *Foot* (1867) LR 2 QB 161, Cockburn CJ; *Dalton* v. *Henry Angus & Co* (1881) 6 App Cas 740, HL; *Russell* v. *Watts* (1885) 10 App Cas 590, 611, Lord Blackburn.
[13] Eg not permissive etc; see below **[36.05ff]**.
[14] A Prescription Act claim may be possible after 19 years; see below **[36.18]**.
[15] *Lewis* v. *Price* (1761), Wilmot J, see at 2 Wms Saund 172, 175, 85 ER 926.
[16] [1971] 2 QB 528, CA (Llanhydrock estate). A claim to a profit under the Prescription Act 1832 requires 30 years' use; see below **[36.37]**.
[17] [1991] Ch 271, CA.
[18] See below **[36.18]**.
[19] Where title is registered see above **[33.20]**.
[20] *Henry Angus & Co* v. *Dalton* (1877) 3 QBD 85, 94, Lush J; *Bryant* v. *Foot* (1867) LR 2 QB 161, 181, Cockburn CJ; *Duke of Norfolk* v. *Arbuthnot* (1886) 5 CPD 290; *Wheaton* v. *Maple & Co* [1893] 3 Ch 48, 63, Lindley LJ.

in cases where there was indeed some factual evidence to support such a case. Later it was applied when the thing to be presumed had probably not taken place,[21] and, finally, to cases where it could be proved that no grant had actually been made. This is the basis of the leading House of Lords decision in *Dalton* v. *Henry Angus & Co*[22] and is settled in modern law by *Tehidy Minerals* v. *Norman*.[23] It remains a defence to show that the grant as pleaded[24] would not have created an easement.[25] Lost grant has become a purely technical device for validating long established use[26] which, from the point of view of a person acquiring a right, is almost always a superior alternative to Prescription Act prescription.[27] For example lost modern grant can step in to vindicate a claim to the use of a track in Savernake Forest which has not been used for over a year.[28]

2. Quantification

[36.04] The right created reflects the use made of the servient tenement during the prescriptive period[29]: a right of way prescribed for agricultural use does not allow use for a caravan park,[30] nor does a right of way to carry repair materials to a cottage permit the carriage of materials for building a new house.[31] What degree of generality[32] is appropriate was considered in *Cargill* v. *Gotts*.[33] Cattle had been watered from 1928 onwards, but a tenfold increase in use occurred during the 1950s for spray irrigation. This fluctuation in use did not destroy or alter the right. Gallonages were irrelevant, and provided that water was always used for farming no new right was being asserted.[34]

---

[21] *Bright* v. *Walker* (1834) 1 Cr M & R 211, 217, 149 ER 1054, Parke B.

[22] (1881) 6 App Cas 740, 800, Selborne LC, 812, Lord Blackburn.

[23] [1971] 2 QB 528, CA; *Bridle* v. *Ruby* [1989] QB 169, CA.

[24] The only requirement is to place the deed before or after a certain date: *Palmer* v. *Guadagni* [1906] 2 Ch 494; *Gabriel Wade & English* v. *Dixon & Cardus* [1937] 3 All ER 900; *Tremayne* v. *English Clays Lovering Pochin & Co* [1972] 1 WLR 657.

[25] *Cowlishaw* v. *Cheslyn* (1830) 1 Cr & J 48, 148 ER 1330.

[26] *Bass* v. *Gregory* (1890) 25 QBD 481, 484, Pollock B.

[27] *Bright* v. *Walker* (1834) 1 Cr M & R 211, 217, 149 ER 1054, Parke B; *Simpson* v. *Godmanchester Corp* [1897] AC 696, HL; *Gardner* v. *Hodgson's Kingston Breweries Co* [1903] AC 229, HL; *Dalton* v. *Henry Angus & Co* (1881) 6 App Cas 740, HL; *Aynsley* v. *Glover* (1875) LR 10 Ch App 283, 285, Mellish LJ.

[28] *Smith* v. *Brudenell-Bruce* [2002] 2 P & CR 4 at 51, Pumphrey J.

[29] *Metropolitan Board of Works* v. *London & NW Rly* (1881) 17 Ch D 246; *Att-Gen* v. *Acton Local Board* (1882) 22 Ch D 221, Fry J.

[30] *RPC Holdings* v. *Rogers* [1953] 1 All ER 1029; *Williams* v. *James* (1867) LR 2 CP 577.

[31] *Wimbledon & Putney Commons Conservators* v. *Dixon* (1875) 1 Ch D 362, CA.

[32] *Dare* v. *Heathcote* (1856) 25 LJ Ex 245.

[33] [1981] 1 WLR 441, CA.

[34] *British Railways Board* v. *Glass* [1965] Ch 538 (increase in number of caravans no breach); RE Megarry (1965) 81 *LQR* 17; P Jackson (1965) 28 *MLR* 216; HW Wilkinson (1967) 117 *NLJ* 562; *Woodhouse & Co* v. *Kirkland (Derby)* [1970] 1 WLR 1185 (agricultural right could not be extended for mineral working); *Millington* v. *Griffiths* (1874) 30 LT 65; *Bradburn* v. *Morris* (1896) 3 Ch D 812.

C. USE AS OF RIGHT

[36.05] Use of any affirmative easement must assert a right to secure prescription under any of the four possible methods.[35] Different rules apply to light.[36] As in the group of fans who hate Manchester United, so too with use as of right the concept can only be defined negatively by three "nots", that is *nec vim, nec clam et nec precario* – without force, stealth or permission.[37]

1. Peaceable use

[36.06] Prescriptive use must be peaceful. No recently reported case has involved physical force, but many involve exercise of a right against a backdrop of continuous protest, which ensures that use is not as of right.[38] In *Newnham* v. *Willison*[39] a drive in the shape of a "swept" curve which could be negotiated with a horse box had been used for 23 years running up to 1983, but all along the owner of the drive maintained that there was only a right to use a sharp-angled drive unsuitable for a horse box. Use in the face of this protest was use by "force" which was not prescriptive.

2. Open use

(1) Requirement for open use

[36.07] Concealed use of neighbouring land is not prescriptive. A claim to fix the side of a dock to the soil of the wharf by underground rods which went undetected for 20 years did not create a right,[40] and nor did the discharge of pollutants into a public sewer by night.[41]

When advising the House of Lords in *Dalton* v. *Henry Angus & Co*,[42] Fry J stated the basis on which acquiescence by the burdened owner arose as follows:

"1, knowledge of the acts done;
 2, power in him to stop the acts or to sue in respect of them[43]; and
 3, abstinence on his part from the exercise of such power."

Cheshire[44] and other derivative sources treat this as the basis of modern prescription, but Fry J himself did not adopt it! All 18 judges who decided the case agreed that support is acquired if one building leans against another for 20 years,[45] but, according to

---

[35] Prescription Act 1832 s 2; *Tickle* v. *Brown* (1836) 4 Ad & El 369, 111 ER 826; *City of London Brewery Co* v. *Tennant* (1873) LR 9 Ch App 212.
[36] See below **[36.29]**.
[37] A maxim borrowed by Bracton from Roman law.
[38] *Eaton* v. *Swansea Waterworks Co* (1851) 17 QB 267, 117 ER 1282.
[39] (1988) 56 P & CR 8, CA; *Lyell* v. *Hothfeld* [1914] 3 KB 911.
[40] *Union Lighterage Co* v. *London Graving Dock Co* [1902] 2 Ch 557, CA.
[41] *Barney* v. *BP Truckshops* [1995] CLYB 1854.
[42] (1881) 6 App Cas 740, 773–774; S Anderson (1975) 38 *MLR* 641.
[43] *Murgatroyd* v. *Robinson* (1857) 7 E & B 391, 119 ER 1292, Coleridge J.
[44] Cheshire & Burn (16th ed), 595.
[45] (1881) 6 App Cas 740, HL; *Tehidy Minerals* v. *Norman* [1971] 2 QB 528, 547–549, Buckley LJ.

the opinion which won out,[46] the only requirement was discoverability – it was decided that knowledge was irrelevant.[47] Misadoption of Fry J's advice as a basis for acquiescence dates from *Union Lighterage Co* v. *London Graving Dock Co*,[48] where subterranean support rods had visible nuts, but their presence was not acquiesced in by the burdened owner. It seemed to follow that absence of the servient owner should be a defence to prescription, as held in *Diment* v. *NH Foot*,[49] but the correct question in all these cases was whether the use was continuous and open.

(2) Continuity of use

[36.08] Some easements are literally continuous, such as a window receiving light or a drainage pipe set in the ground. Rights of way are exercised at intervals, and in such cases the use should be continual, as appropriate.[50] The exact degree varies according to the right claimed,[51] but use must be sufficiently continuous to show that a right is being claimed[52] and interruptions might well cast doubt on the *right* to make use of the neighbour's land.[53] Discontinuous periods cannot be added together to make up a twenty year prescription period.[54]

Enjoyment in alternate weeks was not sufficient.[55] Locking an access generally prevents a right of way,[56] though locking a gate at night might be consistent with the acquisition of a right of way during office hours.[57] In *Hollins* v. *Verney* a way to remove timber cut from a wood was exercised only three times, at intervals of 12 years, and was clearly not prescriptive.[58] Lindley LJ pointed out that the burdened owner must have an opportunity to resist the right.[59] One harsh application was the rejection of a claim to a right of way over a drive where its use was limited by petrol rationing.[60] Prescription can be continued through a period of non-exercise by continuous assertion of the right.[61]

[46] Pollock B, Field, Manisty and Fry JJ; Lords Coleridge, Selborne LC, Blackburn, Watson, and Penzance; Brett LJ in CA; *Gray* v. *Bond* (1821) 2 Brad & Bing 667, 129 ER 1123.

[47] The view of Lindley, Lopes, & Bowen JJ (HL) as well as Cotton and Thesiger LJJ (CA). Fry J (at 779) favoured this view in logic but considered himself bound by authority to the reverse. Continuing knowledge is not required: *Schwann* v. *Cotton* [1916] 2 Ch 120.

[48] [1902] 2 Ch 557, 568, Vaughan Williams LJ; *Lloyds Bank* v. *Dalton* [1942] 2 Ch 466; *Oakley* v. *Boston* [1976] QB 270, 285B, Goulding J in CA.

[49] [1974] 1 WLR 1427, Pennycuick V-C; *Davies* v. *Du Paver* [1953] 1 QB 184; *Bright* v. *Walker* (1834) 1 Cr M & R 211, 149 ER 1054.

[50] *Hollins* v. *Verney* (1884) 13 QBD 304, 307–308, Lindley LJ.

[51] *Dare* v. *Heathcote* (1856) 25 LJ Ex 245.

[52] *Miles* v. *Silver* [1991] Ch 271, CA.

[53] *Eaton* v. *Swansea Waterworks Co* (1851) 17 QB 267, 117 ER 1282.

[54] *Onley* v. *Gardiner* (1838) 4 M & W 496, 156 ER 1525; *White* v. *Taylor (No 2)* [1969] 1 Ch 150, 194B, Buckley J (requisition).

[55] *Monmouth Canal Co* v. *Harford* (1834) 1 Cr M & R 614, 631, 149 ER 126, Parke B.

[56] *Att-Gen* v. *Antrobus* [1905] 2 Ch 188, 201.

[57] *Woodhouse & Co* v. *Kirkland (Derby)* [1970] 1 WLR 1185.

[58] (1884) 13 QBD 304, CA. Prescription Act 1832 s 4 which refers to a continuous period of 20 years may require use at least once each year.

[59] At 308, 315.

[60] *Healey* v. *Hawkins* [1968] 1 WLR 1967, Goff J.

[61] *Ward* v. *Kirkland* [1967] Ch 194.

3.   Permission

[36.09] Permissive use is clearly not prescriptive,[62] but the exact operation of that principle depends upon the form of permission and the head of prescriptive acquisition being employed.

(1) Documentary rights

[36.10] Exercise of a documentary right is not prescriptive,[63] even after the longer (40 year) statutory period. Express grants cannot be modified by prescription,[64] unless a use falls so far outside the framework of the existing right so as to create a new one.[65]

(2) Mistaken belief of legal right

[36.11] Users often mistake the basis on which they enjoy rights over the neighbouring land. A person who thinks that he already has an easement can create that same easement by prescription.[66] In *Bridle* v. *Ruby*,[67] the initial draft of a conveyance included a reservation of a right of way over the driveway of one of the properties, but this was deleted before the conveyance was executed. After use of the drive for 22 years in the mistaken belief that the right had been reserved, and the seller successfully claimed it to be prescriptive.[68] Indeed, people who assert rights are often mistaken about the law.[69]

(3) Effect of permission

[36.12] Leave from time to time is a total bar to prescription under all heads. In *Gardner* v. *Hodgson's Kingston Breweries Co*[70] a way to a house did not become an easement after use for 40 years because 15 shillings (75p in new money) had been paid each year for use of the way. Nor is payment the only way of showing that use is permissive.[71]

Prior permission continues during the use, preventing prescription.[72] It cannot ripen into an easement under *lost modern grant* at any time in the future, especially if

---

[62] *R(JR) Beresford* v. *Sunderland CC* [2002] QB 874, Dyson LJ.

[63] So too with a statute: *Thomas W Ward* v. *Alexander Bruce (Grays)* [1958] 2 Lloyds Rep 412, Vaisey J; or custom: *Wynstanley* v. *Lee* (1818) 2 Swans 338, 36 ER 643. An old charter or statute may simply confirm an established prescription: *Simpson* v. *Godmanchester Corp* [1897] AC 696, HL.

[64] *Labrador Co* v. *Reg* [1893] AC 104, PC; *Gardner* v. *Hodgson's Kingston Breweries Co* [1903] AC 229, 239, Lord Lindley; *Chamber Colliery Co* v. *Hopwood* (1886) 32 Ch D 549, CA.

[65] *Hapgood* v. *JH Martin & Son* (1934) 152 LT 72.

[66] *Campbell* v. *Wilson* (1803) 3 East 294, 300–301, 102 ER 610, Ellenborough CJ.

[67] [1989] QB 169, CA; G Kodilinye [1989] *Conv* 261; AH Hudson (1989) 40 *NILQ* 64.

[68] At 177E, Parker LJ.

[69] At 178G, Ralph Gibson LJ.

[70] [1903] AC 229, HL; *Monmouth Canal Co* v. *Harford* (1834) 1 Cr M & R 614, 149 ER 1226, Lord Lyndhurst CB; *Tickle* v. *Brown* (1836) 4 Ad & El 369, 111 ER 826; *Healey* v. *Hawkins* [1968] 1 WLR 1967, Goff J.

[71] *Bosomworth* v. *Faber* (1995) 69 P & CR 288, CA.

[72] *Rafique* v. *Walton Estate Trustees* (1992) 65 P & CR 356, Walton J; H Wallace [1994] *Conv* 196.

there is a tacit understanding that the permission continues to be effective.[73] Permission may be expressly revoked or impliedly revoked by changed circumstances.[74] Where prescription is claimed under the *statutory 20 year period*, permission before use began is a continuing defence, since claims may be defeated "in any other way by which the same is now" (ie at common law) "liable to be defeated." This includes any type of permission – oral or written, with or without payment. An advantage of the *statutory 40 year period* is that the right is deemed "absolute and indefeasible" unless it was enjoyed by some express consent or agreement "made for that purpose by *deed or writing*." Hence a prior oral permission is overridden after 40 years. Permission from time to time during the prescription period remains fatal in almost all cases.

(4) Tolerance by burdened owner is not permission

[36.13] Permission must be contrasted with tolerance by the neighbour, which may certainly be a defence to a claim to a public or customary right,[75] but, one aberrant decision apart,[76] does not affect the acquisition of private law easements. Tolerance was discussed and largely dismissed as a defence in *Mills* v. *Silver*.[77] Without toleration use could never last long enough to become prescriptive, because pushing a privilege into a right necessarily leads to opposition.[78]

(5) Temporary features

[36.14] A further dubious rule is the one which presumes permissive use of temporary features, such as a mill race or a drain in a mine,[79] because of the possibility of suspension.[80] This reasoning is not entirely convincing.

D. TORTIOUS AND ILLEGAL USE

1. Tortious use

[36.15] Prescription for rights other than light[81] should only arise from a use which can be prevented, usually by an action in tort. In *Sturges* v. *Bridgman*[82] noise coming from a chemist's pestle and mortar was not loud enough to constitute a nuisance and,

[73] *Jones* v. *Price* (1992) 64 P & CR 404, CA.
[74] *Healey* v. *Hawkins* [1968] 1 WLR 1967, Goff J.
[75] *R(JR) Sunningwell PC* v. *Oxfordshire CC,* [2000] 1 AC 335, 353B; see below **[36.41]**.
[76] *Patel* v. *WH Smith (Eziot)* [1987] 1 WLR 853, CA.
[77] [1991] Ch 271, CA; C Harpum [1991] *CLJ* 220. But, on village greens, see *Ministry of Defence* v. *Wiltshire CC* [1995] 4 All ER 931, Harman J; *R(JR) Sunningwell PC* v. *Oxfordshire CC* [2000] 1 AC 335, HL.
[78] *Alfred F Beckett* v. *Lyons* [1967] Ch 449, 470, Harman LJ.
[79] *Burrows* v. *Lang* [1901] 2 Ch 502; *Whitmores (Edenbridge)* v. *Stanford* [1909] 1 Ch 427; *Arkwright* v. *Gell* (1839) 5 M & W 203, 151 ER 87.
[80] *National Guaranteed Manure Co* v. *Donald* (1859) 4 H & N 8, 157 ER 737; *Bartlett* v. *Tottenham* [1932] 1 Ch 114.
[81] See below **[36.29]**.
[82] (1879) 11 Ch D 852, CA; *Webb* v. *Bird* (1862) 13 CB NS 841, 143 ER 332.

no prescriptive right arose from this unstoppable use. Support for buildings follows this rule because it is always a nuisance to take support from an adjoining building without an easement, and so *Dalton* v. *Henry Angus & Co* permitted prescription.[83] Admittedly the burdened owner could only effect a physical interruption by knocking down his own building – an extreme solution[84] – but the point is legal interruptibility.

2. Illegal use

[36.16] Prescription is a means of legitimising a continuing trespass,[85] but it cannot be created by serious illegality, for example use that offends the criminal law or a statute. In modern law[86] why look beyond *Cargill* v. *Gotts*?[87] From 1928 water had been drawn from a pond[88] to water cattle, and after 1957 the amount taken increased greatly to allow spraying of crops. An easement had been acquired by 20 years lawful use up to 1965. From June 1965 abstraction of water became illegal without a licence,[89] and so unlicensed use could no longer create any right.

The same principle has been applied in *Hanning* v. *Top Deck Travel Group* to deny a prescriptive right to a person who drove across a strip of common to get access to this house.[90] Statute has tried to prevent encroachments on common land by regulating the access of motor vehicles and making driving an offence to drive over any part of a common[91] – any open land, to a track over a village green, and to a footpath[92] – other than a road open to the public.[93] This extreme application of the illegality defence is obnoxious, for the utility of prescription in quieting titles is severely diminished. It is also wrong. The landowner could have granted an express right of way in which case driving over the common would not have been a crime, and lost modern grant should therefore act to presume that the landowner has indeed given this licence. This is quite different from unlicensed water abstraction which is inherently criminal and the need for a licence cannot be waived by the landowner. *Hanning* should be overruled in the Lords[94] or if not let us hope that a public law challenge will succeed.[95]

---

[83] (1881) 6 App Cas 740, HL.

[84] At 796–797, Selborne LC, 816, Lord Blackburn; *Liverpool Corp* v. *H Coghill & Sons* [1918] 1 Ch 307, Eve J; *Hulley* v. *Silversprings Bleaching & Dyeing Co* [1922] 2 Ch 268. It may be possible to obtain a declaration or sue to recover the space into which a building leans: *Solomon* v. *Vintner's Co* (1859) 5 H & N 585, 157 ER 970.

[85] *Hanning* v. *Top Deck Travel Group* (1994) 68 P & CR 14, 23, Kennedy LJ.

[86] Earlier authorities include: *Rochdale Canal Co* v. *Radcliffe* (1852) 18 QB 287, 312, 118 ER 108, Campbell CJ; *Neaverson* v. *Peterborough RDC* [1902] 1 Ch 557, CA (grazing contrary to Inclosure Act); *Hulley* v. *Silversprings Bleaching & Dyeing Co* [1912] 2 Ch 268 (pollution); *Selby* v. *Whitbread & Co* [1917] 1 KB 736 (Building Act support).

[87] [1981] 1 WLR 441, CA; P Jackson (1981) 97 *LQR* 382; FG Glover (1981) 131 *NLJ* 920.

[88] If a person abstracting water does not own the source (eg a well) or own land adjoining a river (so-called riparian land), he must have an easement permitting extraction.

[89] Now Water Resources Act 1991 s 24.

[90] (1994) 68 P & CR 14, CA.

[91] LPA 1925 s 193; Road Traffic Act 1930.

[92] *R* v. *SS for Environment ex p Stevens* [1998] Times February 20th (bridleway).

[93] *Massey* v. *Boulden* [2002] EWCA Civ 1645, [2003] 06 EG 147.

[94] *Bakewell Management* v. *Brandwood* [2003] Times February 5th, CA.

[95] *R(JR) Barron* v. *Surrey CC* [2002] 20 EG 225 (CS).

Regulations[96] made under statute[97] ameliorate the position of that numerous group of people suddenly landlocked in their country homes. Where the only objection to the creation of a prescriptive right is that use of a way across land constituted an offence under an enactment, a right of way may be created by notice to the landowner. This must be made while the use is continuing or within a year of an interruption in use. There is a notice procedure by which the servient owner may object, with disputes referred to the Tribunal. The solution is partial because payment will be required: it is intended to cap charges at 2% of the value of the house built after 1930.[98] The legislation prevents people being landlocked by the lord of the manor but at an iniquitous price. An unfortunate and inappropriate legislative imprimatur is apparently conferred on the dubious decision in *Hanning*.

3. Lack of power to grant

[36.17] The owner of the burdened land is presumed to have created an easement by deed after long use. So it is a defence to prescription to show that he had no power to grant the alleged easement.[99] The defence can often be sidestepped, because the law can also presume the lost grant of any permission needed from outside bodies, such as a faculty from the ecclesiastical authorities for the use of a pew in a church[100] or to wheel supermarket trollies across a churchyard.[101] It is also possible to presume a surrender,[102] a consent to military acquisition of a drill hall,[103] or the grant of a franchise ferry.[104]

E. STATUTORY PRESCRIPTION

[36.18] Lost modern grant has destroyed much of the potency of statutory prescription. After twenty years have gone by the doctrines usually operate in tandem, but any obstruction lasting for a full year ends statutory prescription, leaving lost modern grant to soldier on alone. Statutory[105] prescription is advantageous in three cases:

---

[96] Vehicular Access Across Common and Other Land (England) Regs 2002, SI 2002/1711; A Samuels [2002] Conv 434; Massey v. *Boulden* [2002] EWCA Civ 1645, [2003] 06 EG 147 (problem of extension of the benefitted land).

[97] Countryside and Rights of Way Act 2000 s 68; G Laurence [2001] 06 *RWLR* 39.

[98] Reduced to 0.25% if the house was in existence at the end of 1905 or 0.5% for those built before November 30th 1930.

[99] *Preston Corp* v. *Fullwood Local Board* (1885) 53 LT 718 (corporation surveyor); *Hulley* v. *Silversprings Bleaching & Dyeing Co* [1922] 2 Ch 268 (former incapacity of married woman); *Rochdale Canal Co* v. *Radcliffe* (1852) 18 QB 287, 118 ER 108 (canal company limited by statute).

[100] *Philipps* v. *Halliday* [1891] AC 228, HL; *Oakley* v. *Boston* [1976] QB 270, CA (knowledge of Ecclesiastical Commissioners should not have been relevant); TG (1976) 120 *SJ* 279; M Vitoria (1976) 125 *NLJ* 1226.

[101] *Re St Martin le Grand, York* [1989] 2 All ER 711, 731j, Coningsby Ch.

[102] *Att-Gen* v. *Simpson* [1901] 2 Ch 671.

[103] *Re Edis* [1972] 1 WLR 1135.

[104] *Att-Gen* v. *Wright* [1897] 2 QB 318.

[105] Despite its wording, the Act is not restricted to way and water: *Bass* v. *Gregory* (1890) 25 QBD 481; *Dalton* v. *Henry Angus & Co* (1881) 6 App Cas 740, 798, Lord Selborne V-C; *Simpson* v. *Godmanchester Corp* [1897] AC 696, 709, Lord Davey.

(1) Where use can be shown for 19 years but less than 20 years – the main advantage of statutory prescription;

(2) The 40 year period overcomes prior oral permission;[106] and

(3) For light – the period is 20 years.[107]

A fundamental principle of the 1832 Act is that use must be for the twenty years "next before some suit or action wherein the claim . . . shall . . . be brought into question".[108] Until action is taken, there is an inchoate claim to an easement,[109] its validity being coextensive with the success of litigation to assert it, but evaporating a year after use ceases.[110] A right of way started in 1922, used for 60 years, and blocked in 1981 cannot not be asserted in litigation begun in 1986.[111] This is because prescriptive use under the statute must be "without interruption".[112] A five year gap between 1981–1986 was a bar,[113] but a person blocked has a reasonable time to take advice. Section 4 lays down the rule to be followed:

> "[N]o act or other matter shall be deemed to be an interruption . . . unless the same . . . shall be submitted to or acquiesced in for one year after the party interrupted shall have had . . . notice thereof . . .".

Thus if A uses a way for 20 years before B erects a gate to block it, A has one year in which to sue. A sufficiently clear objection lodged by the user may also preserve the prescriptive claim.[114]

If A uses for 19 years and 10 days before B blocks the way, A has ten days in which to sue, the litigation window opening after 20 years have passed[115] but closing after 20 years and 10 days. The absolute minimum for a Prescription Act claim is use for 19 years and one day.[116]

F. THE FREEHOLD PRESCRIPTION RULE

1. Freehold theory of common law prescription

[36.19] Prescription is the acquisition of a right by the freehold owner of a dominant tenement against the freehold owner of a servient tenement.[117] Lord Coke in 1612

---

[106] See above [36.12].

[107] See below [36.29].

[108] Prescription Act 1832 s 4.

[109] *Wright* v. *Williams* (1836) 1 M & W 77, 150 ER 353; *Richards* v. *Fry* (1838) 7 Ad & El 698 112 ER 632; *Cooper* v. *Hubbuck* (1862) 12 CB (NS) 456, 142 ER 1220; *Hyman* v. *Van den Bergh* [1908] 1 Ch 167, 171–172, Cozens-Hardy MR.

[110] *Smith* v. *Brudenell-Bruce* [2002] 2 P & CR 4 at 51, Pumphrey J.

[111] *Mills* v. *Silver* [1991] Ch 271, CA. This makes it much easier to discover statutory rights.

[112] Partial blockage is irrelevant: *Rolle* v. *Whyte* (1868) LR 3 QB 286, 302. For light, see below [36.29].

[113] *Mills* v. *Silver* [1991] Ch 271, CA.

[114] *Carr* v. *Foster* (1842) 11 LJ QB 284; *Bennison* v. *Cartwright* (1864) 5 B & S 1, 122 ER 733; *Glover* v. *Coleman* (1874) LR 10 CP 108. The onus shifts: *Dance* v. *Triplow* (1991) 63 P & CR 1, CA (extension built November 1980; complaint August 1984; light blocked); *Presland* v. *Bingham* (1889) 41 Ch D 268.

[115] *Flight* v. *Thomas* (1840) 10 LJ Ex 529; *Bridewell Hospital* v. *Ward Lock Bawden* (1892) 62 LJ Ch 270; *Battersea* v. *London City Sewers Commissioners* [1895] 2 Ch 708; *Reilly* v. *Orange* [1955] 2 QB 112, CA.

[116] *Hollins* v. *Verney* (1884) 13 QBD 304, 307, Lindley LJ; *Newnham* v. *Willison* (1988) 56 P & CR 8, 11, Kerr LJ.

[117] *Kilgour* v. *Gaddes* [1904] 1 KB 457, 467, Matthews LJ.

treated this as an established and essential hallmark of prescription.[118] It was logical while claims arose at common law. The old common law stuck at the accession in 1189 of Richard I (he of the Lionheart),[119] as a basis both for limitation of actions and claims to easements. When a fixed period of years was adopted for the limitation rule in the reign of Henry VIII, the rule for prescription was left unchanged.[120] Use in 1189 cannot be proved[121] but the impossibility of use at such an early date often can be proved, for example by showing the inevitability of an interruption since that date. Almost every feature of the land is recent by this test – even a burial chapel built under Richard II around 1380[122] – and almost all buildings, railways, canals, and roads.

Common law prescription retains its significance only for the rule deduced from it, that prescription operates against a freehold estate and in favour of a freehold owner. The freehold owner of burdened land is not bound while it is let. As a limiting factor on statutory claims and lost modern grant this is both illogical and inconvenient.

2. Prescription by and against tenants

[36.20] A tenant cannot prescribe against his landlord. Use between 1836 and 1881 failed to secure an easement, since the prescriber had been a yearly tenant of the person against who he was prescribing until 1867 and to allow such a claim would be "subversive of all reason and justice".[123] By extension, tenants of a common landlord cannot prescribe one against the other, since a landlord cannot acquire easements over his own land.[124] *Simmons* v. *Dobson*[125] neatly illustrates these two fundamental restrictions. Two houses in Leigh were let by a single lease in 1891, but the leasehold title was divided in 1925. By 1990, the plaintiff owned No 153 (the part sold in 1925) and the defendant owned No 151 (retained in 1925). A claim to a right of way along a passage on number 151 failed despite use since 1925, as the two parties were tenants of a single landlord.

A tenant may prescribe against a freehold neighbour, but only to acquire an easement which is freehold, rather than one limited to his own term of years.[126] In other words, the tenant prescribes on behalf of his landlord.[127]

Prescription is most limited when the burdened land is tenanted. The right created must bind all titles in the land. If prescription starts against a freeholder entitled in possession, it continues after a lease of the land burdened.[128] A freeholder exempt from prescription (in old law for example the Bishop of Worcester) secures an exemp-

---

[118] *Rowles* v. *Mason* (1612) 2 Brown 192, 198, 123 ER 892, Coke CJ.

[119] *R(JR) Sunningwell PC* v. *Oxfordshire CC* [2000] 1 AC 335, 349H–350A, Lord Hoffmann.

[120] *Bryant* v. *Foot* (1867) LR 2 QB 161, 180, Cockburn CJ; A Wharam (1972) 1 *Anglo-American* 262.

[121] At 177, Blackburn J.

[122] *Duke of Norfolk* v. *Arbuthnot* (1880) 5 CPD 390, CA; *Philipps* v. *Halliday* [1891] AC 228, HL.

[123] *Outram* v. *Maude* (1881) 17 Ch D 391, 406, Bacon V-C.

[124] *Winship* v. *Hudspeth* (1854) 10 Ex 5, 156 ER 332; *Derry* v. *Saunders* [1919] 1 KB 223, 237 (copyhold land); *Harris* v. *De Pinna* (1886) 33 Ch D 238, CA (light); *Kilgour* v. *Gaddes* [1904] 1 KB 457 (affirmative easement, 40 years use); *Davis* v. *Whitby* [1973] 1 WLR 629.

[125] [1991] 1 WLR 720, CA; C Harpum [1992] *CLJ* 220; P Sparkes [1992] *Conv* 167.

[126] An express grant is valid: *Fear* v. *Morgan* [1906] 2 Ch 406, 418, Vaughan-Williams LJ.

[127] *Pugh* v. *Savage* [1970] 2 QB 373, 380G, Cross LJ.

[128] *Cross* v. *Lewis* (1824) 2 B. & C 686, 107 ER 538. Use must be open: *Diment* v. *NH Foot* [1974] 1 WLR 1427.

tion for all his tenants.[129] Use starting against a tenant[130] normally binds the tenant, but cannot bind the freeholder[131] even if he knows about it.[132]

If "lands are let for 99 years or even 999 years, no right of way can be acquired between two tenements where they have the same owner in fee simple."[133] A long leaseholder is restricted to rights granted by the lease. *Simmons* v. *Dobson* refused a claim between two leasehold neighbours, and so illustrated the need for a rule validating rights actually exercised over a long period of time between leaseholders.

3. Modern forms of prescription

[36.21] *Simmons* v. *Dobson* establishes that the freehold rule must be applied to lost modern grant, which is merely a form of common law prescription.[134] This is illogical, since this method should allow the creation of any right which could be created expressly.[135] The rule is different for rights to light,[136] was possibly new in 1832,[137] and is much criticised by academics.[138] The freehold prescription rule also applies to the statutory periods, including the 40 year period, even though an easement is said to become "absolute and indefeasible".[139] The landlord can exclude the duration of any lease from the forty year period, provided he resists the right within three years of the end of the lease.[140]

4. Equitable interests

[36.22] Many problems caused by the divisible freehold[141] were removed in 1925. Perpetual freehold ownership under Lord Birkenhead's reforms ensures that prescription occurs between two adult freehold estate owners capable of asserting and challenging the right prescribed for. Excluded from the 20 year period is any period during which the burdened owner was a minor, mentally incapable, or tenant for life challenged by the person holding a "reversion".[142] However, the legal estate should now always be vested in a capable trustee.

---

[129] *Bright* v. *Walker* (1834) 1 Cr M & R 211, 149 ER 1054.

[130] *Pugh* v. *Savage* [1970] 2 QB 373, CA (use against freehold from 1932 for 8 years, allowed during subsequent lease).

[131] *Davies* v. *Du Paver* [1953] 1 QB 184; RE Megarry (1956) 72 *LQR* 32.

[132] *Daniel* v. *North* (1809) 11 East 372, 103 ER 1047; *Roberts & Lovell* v. *James* (1903) 89 LT 282, CA. Contrast *Davies* v. *Stephens* (1836) 7 C & P 570, 173 ER 251 (knowledge presumed after long period).

[133] *Derry* v. *Saunders* [1919] 1 KB 223, 237 (copyhold); *Simmons* v. *Dobson* [1991] 1 WLR 720, 724D, Fox LJ.

[134] [1991] 1 WLR 720, 725B, Fox LJ; *Wheaton* v. *Maple & Co* [1893] 3 Ch 48, 63, Lindley LJ; *Kilgour* v. *Gaddes* [1904] 1 KB 457; *Derry* v. *Saunders* [1919] 1 KB 223.

[135] *Fear* v. *Morgan* [1906] 2 Ch 406, Vaughan-Williams LJ.

[136] *Frewen* v. *Phillips* (1861) 11 CB NS 449; approved in *Morgan* v. *Fear* [1907] AC 425, HL.

[137] *Bright* v. *Walker* (1834) 1 CM & R 211, 221, 149 ER 1054, Parke B; *East Stonehouse Urban DC* v. *Willoughby Brothers* [1902] 2 KB 318, 332, Channell J.

[138] AK Kiralfy (1948) 13 *Conv NS* 104, 105–106; VTH Delaney (1958) 74 *LQR* 82; P Sparkes [1992] *Conv* 167.

[139] *Bright* v. *Walker* as above; *Damper* v. *Bassett* [1901] 2 Ch 350; *Kilgour* v. *Gaddes* [1904] 1 KB 457, 464–465, Collins MR.

[140] Prescription Act 1832 s 8; *Bright* v. *Walker* at 220, Parke B.

[141] *Roberts & Lovell* v. *James* (1903) 89 LT 282, CA.

[142] Prescription Act 1832 s 7. This may include a remainder: *Symons* v. *Leaker* (1885) 15 QBD 629;

G. AFFIRMATIVE EASEMENTS

1. Prescriptive rights must be easement-like

[36.23] Since creation is based on what an express deed could do, prescription can operate only for rights which are easement-like; there must be two tenements,[143] two owners, and actual benefit to the dominant tenement. Many of the sub-heads of the rule that an easement should be capable of forming the subject matter of a grant are directly concerned to limit possible prescriptive claims, excluding rights which are uncertain,[144] wide, or exercised by members of the public.[145] Natural rights do not need prescriptive acquisition.[146] On the other hand it is possible to acquire a right to commit a nuisance.[147]

2. Exclusivity – prescription and adverse possession contrasted

[36.24] Prescription is closely linked to adverse possession, both doctrines being concerned with quieting title to land through long enjoyment. At the extremes the choice is clear, since adverse possession is concerned with an exclusive claim to ownership whereas prescription secures a limited right as a burden over the land of a neighbouring owner. Non-exclusivity is the key to easement status. Thus in *Copeland* v. *Greenhalf*[148] a claim to park vehicles awaiting repair on land, framed as a prescriptive claim to an easement, was rejected because the claim was too extensive. It probably also failed as a claim to adverse possession, because there were times when the burdened owner was not excluded.[149] Exclusive rights in footings, drainpipes,[150] tunnels,[151] coal, and other minerals,[152] must be claimed by limitation. Parking might fall into either camp.[153]

3. Unity of ownership and occupation

[36.25] It is a defence to a claim for prescription to show that unity of ownership occurred at any time during the prescription period.[154] Common law prescription is

Wright v. *Williams* (1836) 1 M & W 77, 150 ER 353; or exclude a remainder: *Laird* v. *Briggs* (1881) 16 Ch D 440, 447, Fry J; the CA left the point open: (1881) 19 Ch D 22, 34, Jessel MR, 36, Brett LJ, 38, Cotton LJ.

[143] Profits can arise in gross.
[144] *Chastey* v. *Ackland* [1895] 2 Ch 389, CA.
[145] *Att-Gen* v. *Antrobus* [1905] 2 Ch 188, Farwell J.
[146] *Palmer* v. *Bowman* [2000] 1 WLR 842, CA (drainage of natural water from higher to lower land).
[147] I Dawson & A Dunn "Acquiring a Prescriptive Right to Commit a Nuisance" ch 12 in Jackson & Wilde.
[148] [1952] Ch 488.
[149] *Lyell* v. *Hothfeld* [1914] 3 KB 911 (claim to feed sheep amounting to ownership not profit).
[150] *Williams* v. *Usherwood* (1981) 45 P & CR 235, CA; M Dockray [1983] *Conv* 398; HW Wilkinson (1984) 134 *NLJ* 144; MP Thompson (1984) 128 *SJ* 44.
[151] *Bevan* v. *London Portland Cement Co* (1892) 67 LT 615, Romer J.
[152] *Wilkinson* v. *Proud* (1843) 11 M & W 33, 152 ER 704.
[153] MJ Goodman (1968) 32 *Conv (NS)* 270; *Lord Advocate* v. *Lord Lovat* (1880) 5 App Cas 273, HL; *Paveledes* v. *Ryebridge Properties* (1989) 58 P & CR 459, Knox J.
[154] *Crow* v. *Wood* [1970] 1 QB 77, CA; *Outram* v. *Maude* (1881) 17 Ch D 391, 404. The principle is old: *Robins* v. *Barnes* (1615) Hob 131, 80 ER 280; *Peers* v. *Lucy* (1694) 4 Mod Rep 362, 87 ER 444.

prevented by unity of ownership at any time since 1189,[155] though sharing possession is not fatal.[156] The same principle applies during the shorter periods for lost modern grant[157] or statutory prescription.[158]

4. Prescription of positive burdens

[36.26] Positive burdens can be created after long exercise. If a rentcharge has been paid for over 100 years to charity trustees for land occupied by a turnpike road, it may be presumed that the rent was created by an old deed.[159] Similarly claims to the payment of fees may be prescriptive, though in practice common law claims are usually invalidated by changes in the value of money.[160] In the last resort it is possible to presume a lost statute, so that any right is a possibility. However, in practice the implication of positive obligations is limited by the very tight restrictions imposed on the recognition of easements with a positive character. Fencing is well-established, but others require express creation as a covenant.

5. Prescription of fencing

[36.27] Fencing obligations cannot create proprietary covenants[161] or easements.[162] However, the right of fencing against cattle[163] was recognised as a valid easement by the medieval common law before the modern rules for easements were fixed,[164] and this is left today as a spurious anomaly.[165] Simple repair raises no entitlement,[166] but only if fencing is carried out over a prolonged period at the request of the benefitted owner.[167] Twenty years repair should raise a lost modern grant.[168] However, if repair has been carried out by one owner consistently over a very long period, a customary right may be presumed.[169] Statute requires certain types of occupier to fence their land.[170]

---

[155] *Hulbert v. Dale* [1909] 2 Ch 570; *White v. Taylor (No 2)* [1969] 1 Ch 150, 194, Buckley J.

[156] *Aynsley v. Glover* (1875) LR 10 Ch App 283.

[157] *Hulbert v. Dale* [1909] 2 Ch 570.

[158] *Winship v. Hudspeth* (1854) 10 Ex 5, 156 ER 332; *Onley v. Gardiner* (1838) 4 M & W 496, 150 ER 1525; *Damper v. Bassett* [1901] 2 Ch 350, Joyce J (40 year period).

[159] *Foley's Charity Trustees v. Dudley Corp* [1910] 1 KB 317, CA.

[160] *Bryant v. Foot* (1867) LR 3 QB 497; but see *Shephard v. Payne* (1864) 16 CB NS 132, 143 ER 1075 (reasonable fee allowed).

[161] *Potter v. Perry* (1859) 23 JP 644.

[162] *Rance v. Elvin* (1985) 50 P & CR 9, CA; reversing (1985) 49 P & CR 65, Nicholls J.

[163] The duty is to erect such a fence that a pig "not of a peculiarly wandering disposition, nor under any excessive temptation will not get through it.": *Child v. Hearn* (1874) LR 9 Exch 176; *Coaker v. Willcocks* [1911] 1 KB 649, 654, Darling J (Scottish sheep).

[164] *R v. Byron* (1622) 5 Bridg 23, 123 ER 1173.

[165] *Crow v. Wood* [1971] 1 QB 77, 84F–85A, Lord Denning MR; PV Baker (1971) 87 *LQR* 13; RJ Smith [1971] *CLJ* 27; HW Wilkinson (1971) 34 *MLR* 223; HW Wilkinson (1970) 120 *NLJ* 917.

[166] *Jones v. Price* [1965] 2 QB 618, CA; K Scott [1966] *CLJ* 38; *Cordingley v. Great Western Rly* (1948) 98 LT 35; *Crow v. Wood* [1971] 1 QB 77, CA.

[167] *Hilton v. Ankesson* (1827) 27 LT 519, Kelly CB; *Boyle v. Tamlyn* (1827) 6 B & C 329, 108 ER 473, Bayley J; *Lawrence v. Jenkins* (1873) LR 8 QB 274, Archibald J (40 years; 19 years on notice); *Jones v. Price* [1965] 2 QB 618, 634A–63E, Willmer LJ, 639E–640B, Diplock LJ; G Williams (1938) 54 *LQR* 405.

[168] *Lawrence v. Jenkins* (1873) LR 8 QB 274 (19 years repair on notice proved).

[169] *Egerton v. Harding* [1975] QB 62, CA; CF Colbert [1975] *CLJ* 34; FT Poole [1974] *JPL* 587; *London & NW Rly v. Fobbing Levels Sewerage Commissioners* (1896) 66 LT QB 127 (duty accepted since 1818).

[170] Highways, railways, burial grounds, etc.

H. PRESCRIPTIVE RIGHTS TO LIGHT

1. Nature of right

[36.28] It has already been shown that the right of access of light to a particular window can be an easement, and is one that restricts the neighbouring owner in his use of the land.[171]

2. Statutory prescription

[36.29] "Ancient lights" was the common law term for easements of light acquired by use since 1189 but given that most buildings have been put up since then, the term has now been appropriated to cover more recent windows with Prescription Act 1832 rights.[172] The nature of the right is unchanged,[173] but the method of acquisition has altered fundamentally.[174]

After the access of light to a building has "been actually enjoyed therewith for the full period of 20 years without interruption" the right to it is deemed to be "absolute and indefeasible."[175] Prescription Act prescription depends on the period being the next before action,[176] with light remaining inchoate until legal action is taken.[177] Nevertheless a building which is reconstructed with new windows takes over the rights enjoyed with the earlier building.[178]

Although section 3 refers to *use* of light, it is unnecessary to look out of the window,[179] or to occupy the building at all.[180] Nightfall or closing the shutters of a shop all weekend does not interrupt the continuity of prescription.[181] Two features of section 3 make it particularly efficacious. Twenty years enjoyment of light makes the right to light "absolute and indefeasible", thus corresponding to the 40 years needed for affirmative easements. Even stronger is the omission of the words "claiming right

---

[171] See above **[32.28]**.

[172] *Colls* v. *Home & Colonial Stores* [1904] AC 179, 204, Lord Davey.

[173] *City of London Brewery Co* v. *Tennant* (1873) LR 9 Ch App 212, Selborne LC; *Kelk* v. *Pearson* (1879) LR 6 Ch App 809.

[174] *Scott* v. *Pape* (1886) 31 Ch D 554, 571, Bowen LJ; (but see *Colls* [1904] AC 179, 199, Lord Davey); *Sturges* v. *Bridgeman* (1899) 11 Ch D 852, 863, Thesiger LJ; *Perry* v. *Eames* [1891] 1 Ch 658 (s 2 does not apply); Megarry & Wade (6th ed), [18.201–18.207].

[175] Prescription Act 1832 s 3. A temporary extension by the Rights to Light Act 1959 (to 27 years for actions begun before 1963) prevented widescale acquisition of rights to light over bombsites in London.

[176] Prescription Act 1832 s 4; *Flight* v. *Thomas* (1841) 8 Cl & Fin 231, 8 ER 91, HL. There are no deductions for incapacity or during a lease. Unity of possession will prevent prescription: *Harbridge* v. *Warwick* (1849) 3 Exch 552, 154 ER 964.

[177] *Colls* [1904] AC 179, 188, Lord Macnaghten; *Hyman* v. *Van den Bergh* [1908] 1 Ch 167, 171–172, Cozens-Hardy MR. An unfortunate application is *Greenhalgh* v. *Brindley* [1901] 2 Ch 324.

[178] *Tapling* v. *Jones* (1865) 11 HLC 290, 11 ER 1344; also numerous other cases.

[179] *Glover* v. *Coleman* (1874) LR 10 CP 108; *Smith* v. *Baxter* [1900] 2 Ch 138, 143; *Colls* [1904] AC 179, 205, 206, Lord Lindley.

[180] *Coutauld* v. *Legh* (1869) LR 4 Exch 126; *Collis* v. *Laugher* [1894] 3 Ch 659; *Allen* v. *Greenwood* [1980] 1 Ch 119, 136, Buckley LJ.

[181] *Cooper* v. *Straker* (1888) 40 Ch D 21; *Smith* v. *Baxter* [1900] 2 Ch 138. Contrast boarding over a window.

thereto",[182] removing as defences protest, oral consent, and non-continuity. The most difficult easement to acquire has become the easiest.[183] After 20 years, the only defences left are (1) written consent of the benefitted owner, or (2) interruption.[184]

The freehold prescription rule does not apply to light,[185] and prescription can occur by[186] and against leaseholders, and also between tenants of common landlords.[187] Prescription is obviously suspended if both properties are both owned *and* occupied together.[188]

3. Preventing prescription

(1) Written permission

[36.30] After a window has been in place for 20 years, it acquires a right to light even if it was originally put there by permission, and even if oral permission has been repeated during the 20 years,[189] or payments have been made.[190] The burdened owner only escapes if light is "enjoyed by some consent or agreement expressly made or given for the purpose by deed or writing."[191] When land is divided the seller very commonly reserves the right to build on the land retained to prevent the part sold acquiring rights to light.[192]

(2) Interruption

[36.31] Twenty years run until an interruption occurs and is acquiesced in for more than one year.[193] An intention to oppose a blockage must be communicated to the neighbour[194] but, at least in the short term, it is not necessary to take legal action.[195]

---

[182] *Flight* v. *Thomas* (1840) 11 Ad & El 688, 113 ER 575, Maule B at first instance; *Colls* [1904] AC 179, 205, Lord Lindley. This was surely a slip in drafting.

[183] Megarry & Wade (5th ed), 889.

[184] *Hyman* v. *Van den Bergh* [1908] 1 Ch 167, 176, Farwell LJ; *Colls* [1904] AC 179, 190, Lord Macnaghten.

[185] *Broomfield* v. *Williams* [1897] 1 Ch 602; *Sovmots Investments* v. *SS for Environment* [1979] AC 144, 176C, Lord Edmund Davies.

[186] *Truscott* v. *Merchant Tailor's Co* (1856) 11 Exch 805, 866, 156 ER 1079, Williams J; *Allen* v. *Greenwood* [1980] 1 Ch 119, 125, Goff LJ.

[187] *Frewen* v. *Philipps* (1861) 11 CB NS 449, 455, 142 ER 871; *Wheaton* v. *Maple & Co* [1893] 3 Ch 48; *Fear* v. *Morgan* [1906] 2 Ch 406, 422, Vaughan Williams LJ; on appeal *Morgan* v. *Fear* [1907] AC 425, HL.

[188] Not by unity of ownership alone: *Simper* v. *Foley* (1862) 2 John & H 555, 70 ER 1179; *Richardson* v. *Graham* [1908] 1 KB 39, CA.

[189] *London Corp* v. *Pewterers' Co* (1842) 2 Moo & R 409, 174 ER 333; *Ruscoe* v. *Grounsell* (1903) 89 LT 426, CA (stone tablet in wall); *Mallam* v. *Rose* [1915] 2 Ch 222.

[190] *Plasterers' Co* v. *Parish Clerks' Co* (1851) 6 Exch 630, 155 ER 696.

[191] Prescription Act 1832 s 3; *Smith* v. *Colborne* [1914] 2 Ch 533, CA; *Paragon Finance* v. *City Land Real Property Co* [2002] 1 P & CR 36 at 470, Ch D.

[192] *Haynes* v. *King* [1893] 3 Ch 439; *Foster* v. *Lyons & Co* [1927] 1 Ch 219; *Willoughby* v. *Eckstein (No 2)* [1937] Ch 167; *Blake & Lyons* v. *Lewis Berger & Sons* [1951] 2 TLR 605. A tenant can bar his landlord by signing a waiver: *Bewley* v. *Atkinson* (1879) 13 Ch D 283, CA; *Hyman* v. *Van den Bergh* [1908] 1 Ch 167, CA; tenants usually covenant not to do so.

[193] Prescription Act 1832 s 4.

[194] *Dance* v. *Triplow* [1992] 1 EGLR 190, CA.

[195] *Glover* v. *Coleman* (1874) LR 10 CP 108.

Blocking light requires an obstruction[196] in place for a full year. It was usual in the past to erect a brick wall or hoarding,[197] but physical barriers require planning permission, and it is often impossible to build high enough to blot out a block of flats. The Rights to Light Act 1959 removed the need for any tangible obstacle.[198] Instead, registration of a light obstruction notice[199] as a local land charge creates a notional wall of stated dimensions and location – the effect is to interrupt the light reaching the building for one year.[200] A certification procedure involving the Lands Tribunal gives the owner of the window a chance to object.[201] The whole procedure needs to be repeated before another 20 years have elapsed.

4.   Older forms of prescription to light

[36.32] The Prescription Act claim to light in practice supersedes older methods of prescription,[202] provided action against a blockage is taken within a year. Otherwise prescription might be available at common law after use as of right to a window dating from 1189.[203] Lost modern grant is more likely,[204] and helps with claims against the Crown,[205] and where the benefitted structure is not a "dwelling house, workshop or other building".[206]

I.   SEVERAL PROFITS (GRAZING, FISHING AND "SPORTING")

1.   Several profits and commons

[36.33] A profit is the right to take a part of the land or the natural produce of land,[207] limiting the ownership of the land but not excluding it.[208] Hence its full name, the profit à prendre – the right to take. An easement is a right to use land – which includes a right to take water – whereas a profit is a right to take part of the land or its produce

---

[196] *Mayor of Paddington* v. *Att-Gen* [1906] AC 1, HL.
[197] *Tapling* v. *Jones* (1865) 11 HLC 290, 11 ER 1344.
[198] HWR Wade [1959] *CLJ* 182.
[199] (1968) 118 *NLJ* 355.
[200] *Bowring Services* v. *Scottish Widows' Fund & Life Assurance Society* [1995] 1 EGLR 158 (temporary notice on August 12th 1991 for 4 months; writ October 1992; sufficient obstruction).
[201] *Hawker* v. *Tomalin* (1966) 20 P & CR 550, CA (discretion to vary).
[202] *Tapling* v. *Jones* (1865) 11 HLC 290, 318, 11 ER 1344, Cranworth LC; *Hyman* v. *Van den Bergh* [1908] 1 Ch 167, 178, Farwell LJ; *Colls* [1904] AC 179, 182, Lord Halsbury.
[203] *Aldred's case* (1610) 9 Co Rep 57b, 58a, 77 ER 816; *Aynsley* v. *Glover* (1874) LR 10 Ch App 283, Mellish LJ; *Duke of Norfolk* v. *Arbuthnot* (1880) 5 CPD 390, CA (Fitzalan Chapel).
[204] *Duke of Norfolk* v. *Arbuthnot* (1880) 5 CPD 390; *Wheaton* v. *Maple & Co* [1893] 3 Ch 48; *Smith* v. *Baxter* [1900] 2 Ch 138; *Bowring Services* v. *Scottish Widows' Fund & Life Assurance Society* [1995] 1 EGLR 158 (custom in London to rebuild).
[205] *Kilgour* v. *Gaddes* [1904] 1 KB 457, CA; *Perry* v. *Eames* [1891] 1 Ch 658, Chitty J; DA Stroud (1941) 58 *LQR* 495.
[206] *Harris* v. *De Pinna* (1886) 33 Ch D 238 (timber store).
[207] A right to use land is an easement (illogically including a right of water abstraction).
[208] *Lowe* v. *JW Ashmore* [1971] Ch 545, 556, Megarry J; *Lyell* v. *Hothfeld* [1914] 3 KB 911.

– including fish or game.[209] Whatever is taken under a profit must be susceptible of ownership.[210] Profits can be enforced in trespass or nuisance.[211]

Those exercised to the exclusion of all others, including the landowner, are said to be several.[212] Profits which are shared – either with the land owner[213] or with other users – are rights of common.[214]

2. Profits in gross

[36.34] A profit may exist *in gross*, that is without land to be benefitted. Thus in *Nicholls* v. *Ely Beet Sugar Factory*[215] a person who owned no land in the neighbour-hood had an exclusive right to take fish in a defined piece of the River Ouse.[216] The point was decided definitively by *Bettison* v. *Langton*.[217] Prescriptive grazing rights attached to Sina Farm on the edge of Bodmin Moor was sold in 1987 by the owner of farm sold grazing rights to Bettisons. The farm was repossessed and when the lenders sold the farm, they did not pass the grazing rights; they had already been detached in 1987. That a profit could exist in gross was clear from a deluge of authoritative dicta[218] and textbooks, though no direct decision had been made on the point before 2001.

3. Profits of grazing

[36.35] One archetype of a profit is a grazing rights, allowing animals to be fed on grass, acorns or other produce of the burdened land.[219] Profits can be acquired in the same way as easements, though it is not necessary that the person with the benefit is a neighbouring landowner, prescription being most common.

4. "Sporting" rights

[36.36] Sporting rights are profits to take fish, deer[220] or game birds.[221] When killed and reduced into possession, ownership passes to the landowner, unless someone else

---

[209] *Mason* v. *Clarke* [1955] AC 778, HL.

[210] *Lowe* v. *JW Ashmore* [1971] Ch 545, 557D, Megarry J; *Alfred F Beckett* v. *Lyons* [1967] Ch 449, 474, Harman LJ, 482–483, Winn LJ.

[211] *Nicholls* v. *Ely Beet Sugar Factory* [1936] Ch 343; proof of damage is unnecessary in trespass.

[212] The word "several" need not appear in the grant: *Hanbury* v. *Jenkins* [1901] 2 Ch 401.

[213] Assumed for rights other than fishing: *Dunsany* v. *Bedworth* (1979) 38 P & CR 546, Browne-Wilkinson J.

[214] See below **[36.39ff]**.

[215] [1936] Ch 343; *Lovett* v. *Fairclough* (1990) 61 P & CR 385, Mummery J.

[216] Presumed to constitute an ownership of the river rather than a profit to take fish: *Hanbury* v. *Jenkins* [1901] 2 Ch 401, Buckley J.

[217] [2001] UKHL 24, [2002] AC 27.

[218] At [35–47], Lord Scott.

[219] For minerals see above **[31.19]**.

[220] *Inglewood Investment Co* v. *Forestry Commission* [1988] 1 WLR 1278, CA (deer are not game).

[221] *Mason* v. *Clarke* [1955] AC 778, HL; HWR Wade [1955] *CLJ* 161; G Williams (1955) 18 *MLR* 408; (1961) 25 *Conv (NS)* 497; *Pole* v. *Peake* [1998] EGCS 125, CA (owner of profit not liable to owner of land for damage caused by breeding or feeding of pheasants).

has a profit to take them away.[222] The natural assumption is that fishing rights and other sporting rights are exclusive.[223]

5. Prescription of several profits

[36.37] Profits can be acquired in the same way as easements, though prescription is most common, particularly claims based on lost modern grant after use for 20 years.[224] Statutory periods are 30 and 60 years.[225]

Profits are usually enjoyed by a neighbour as an appurtenance to his land, in which case the right will be limited according to the needs of that land, to prevent the land being exhausted. Unlimited prescriptive rights ("without stint") cannot be recognised.[226] For the same reason, a profit cannot be claimed by a fluctuating body because exercise by an unlimited group of people would exhaust the burdened land.[227]

J. COMMONS

[36.38] Most profits are shared, either with the land owner[228] or with other users. Both types are called rights of common.

1. Registration of common rights

[36.39] Since the medieval period, commons have nearly always been created by prescription. Rights existing in 1970[229] have been recorded under the Commons Registration Act 1965,[230] and rights existing then but not registered have been extinguished. New rights may still be created off the register.

Commons may be appurtenant, appendant, or in gross.[231] Appurtenant rights benefit particular land but must be limited to prevent exhaustion of the burdened land.[232] They are generally created by prescriptive use, which must be as of right.[233] Alternatively, but rarely, it could be a right in gross,[234] that is one enjoyed by someone who is not a neighbouring landowner. Such a right usually arose from severance, where a common right was sold detached from the land which it originally benefitted. Even rarer is a common appendant which arose when a lord of a manor granted some

---

[222] A profit à prendre, in contradistinction to a profit à rendre where the creature caught has to be handed over.

[223] *Dunsany* v. *Bedworth* (1979) 38 P & CR 546, Browne-Wilkinson J.

[224] *Tehidy Minerals* v. *Norman* [1971] 2 QB 528, CA.

[225] Prescription Act 1832 s 1; *Papendick* v. *Bridgwater* (1855) 5 El & Bl 166, 119 ER 443.

[226] *Lord Chesterfield* v. *Harris* [1908] 2 Ch 397, CA; [1911] AC 623, HL.

[227] *Goodman* v. *Saltash Corp* (1882) 7 App Cas 633, HL.

[228] This is assumed for rights other than fishing: *Dunsany* v. *Bedworth* (1979) 38 P & CR 546, Browne-Wilkinson J.

[229] SIs 1966/1470, 1970/383.

[230] A Samuels (1963) 28 *Conv (NS)* 385, [1985] *Conv* 24; Megarry & Wade (6th ed), [18.176–18.184].

[231] *Godley* v. *Frith* (1609) Yelv 159, 80 ER 106.

[232] *Anderson* v. *Bostock* [1976] Ch 312; *White* v. *Williams* [1922] 1 KB 727; *Staffordshire & Worcestershire Canal Navigation* v. *Bradley* [1912] 1 Ch 91 Eve J.

[233] *R(JR) Sunningwell PC* v. *Oxfordshire CC* [2000] 1 AC 335, HL.

[234] Eg *White* v. *Taylor (No 2)* [1969] 1 Ch 160, 189E–190E, Buckley J; GD Gadsden [1983] *JPL* 219.

of the manor's arable land to be held of him by a freehold tenant before 1290[235] along with grazing rights over the waste land. Prescriptive acquisition was not required, but in any event such rights are now validated and quantified by registration. Common rights may be mutual so as to allow animals to stray across unfenced commons from one manor to the next.[236]

2. Waste land of manors

[36.40] A manor[237] was formed by a grant by a feudal lord so as to create a new tier in the feudal pyramid before the Statute *Quia Emptores* 1290. One created from out of the lord's holding since 1290 is called a reputed manor, though the effect is the same in modern law.

A manor usually corresponded in size to the modern parish.[238] In the medieval period this was the primary unit of government and judicial control, but over the centuries lords of the manor have lost all administrative status. The common agricultural system was broken up during the inclosure movement of the 17th to 19th centuries during which time the open fields and much of the waste were inclosed and allotted to the lord and individual tenants. Lordship of the manor is left as an empty title without real rights or responsibilities, but which is marketable as a piece of property. However, title to a manor as such can no longer be registered.[239] Theoretically, sale of the lordship could carry with it[240] any demesne lands still retained by the lord (that is the principal house and park) and any waste land (subject to all registered common rights) but in practice physical land is usually sold separately.

In human terms a medieval manor consisted of a lord of the manor and his tenants, free and unfree, as well as the parish priest. The demesne of the lord of the manor was the manor house, the park and agricultural land belonging to the lord. A manor also consisted of the land of free tenants, the copyholders' land, open fields cultivated in common by the tenants, and waste of the manor. Watson B stated that waste land is the land in a manor which is open, uncultivated and unoccupied;[241] it was the uncultivated land used to support cattle and so forth. Here lay the genesis of the modern common rights. Lowland England was inclosed by the creation of separate fields, but any land left was the waste, including moorland,[242] woodland, foreshore,[243]

---

[235] Ie before *Quia Emptores*; since then sale has been by alienation out of the manor: *Davies* v. *Davies* [1975] 1 QB 172, 176–177, Lord Denning MR.

[236] A right *pur cause de vicinage*: *Norman* v. *Bennett* [1981] QB 726 (New Forest cows); AA Preece [1981] *Conv* 315.

[237] C Jessel, *Law of the Manor* (Barry Rose, 1998); PH Kenny [1998] *Conv* 344.

[238] *Hampshire CC* v. *Milburn* [1991] 1 AC 325, 338, Lord Templeman.

[239] Manors are omitted from LRA 2002 s 2(a); the last substantive speech on the Bill was on manorial registration: *Hansard* HC 1916 (2002) February 1st, cols 41–43. There is power to deregister manors: LRA 2002 s 119.

[240] LPA 1925 s 62(2).

[241] *Att-Gen* v. *Hanmer* (1858) 27 LJ Ch 837, 840; TE Scrutton (1887) 3 *LQR* 373; *Re Britford Common* [1977] 1 WLR 39; *Hampshire CC* v. *Milburn* [1991] 1 AC 325, 338G–339B, Lord Templeman.

[242] *Lewis* v. *Mid Glamorgan CC* [1995] 1 WLR 313; M Welstead [1995] *Conv* 500.

[243] *Att-Gen* v. *Hanmer* (1858) 27 LJ Ch 837; *Baxendale* v. *Instow PC* [1982] Ch 14 (conveyance of manorial waste excluded accretion to foreshore).

commons, odd scraps of vacant land, and roadside verges. These last have become a goldmine as a result of charges for vehicular access to houses.[244]

Any land belonging to a manor with no common rights is waste,[245] and this is conclusively presumed if land is registered under the Commons Registration Act 1965 without the burden of any common rights.[246] There is at present no regulatory framework.[247] Waste land is registrable if it had formed part of a manor at any time in the past. It is not true,[248] as once thought,[249] that land ceases to be waste if it was sold from the manor. So waste land continues to be registrable for all time if it is now part of a manor, or was formerly part of one, or had a manorial origin, and common land is preserved for the future.[250]

3. Town or village greens

[36.41] Three variant forms of town or village green are registrable.[251] One is a statutory allotment for the exercise or recreation of inhabitants of any locality.[252] The second is land over which there is a customary right to indulge in lawful sports or pastimes,[253] for example after proof of use for 300 years until 1875 with no abandonment.[254] The third is land used for recreation for not less than 20 years[255] provided that the use has been as of right.[256] In the leading case, *R(JR) Sunningwell PC* v. *Oxfordshire CC*,[257] 10 acres of glebe land near the village church were preserved from building because the land had been used for recreation; the Lords held that a subjective belief by the users that they had the right to use it was not required. The relevant issue was the view of the landowner. Rights are to use the land and not for occupation.[258] Rights exercisable before 1970 have been extinguished if not registered; but this does not affect the creation of new rights by use for 20 years after August 1970 (if no attempt was ever made to register the land) or the later date of final rejection of a claim for registration.[259]

---

[244] See above [36.16].

[245] Commons Registration Act 1965 s 22(1)(b).

[246] *Corpus Christi College, Oxford* v. *Gloucester CC* [1983] QB 360.

[247] *R* v. *Mid Sussex DC ex p Ridd* [1993] EGCS 183.

[248] *Hampshire CC* v. *Milburn* [1991] 1 AC 325, HL.

[249] *Re Box Hill Common* [1980] Ch 109, CA (land severed from manor in 1878). This unfortunate decision led to the deregistration of much waste land.

[250] At 343H, Lord Templeman.

[251] Commons Registration Act 1965 s 22(1).

[252] Ie under an Inclosure Act but not a local private Act: *Re The Rye* [1977] 1 WLR 1316.

[253] *Fitch* v. *Rawling* (1795) 2 Hy Bl 393, 126 ER 614; *Hammerton* v. *Honey* (1876) 24 WR 603; *Abbot* v. *Weekley* (1665) 1 Lev 176, 83 ER 357; *Hall* v. *Nottingham* (1875) 1 Ex D 1 (maypole); *Bowle* v. *Davis* (1889) 44 Ch D 110.

[254] *New Windsor Corp* v. *Mellor* [1975] Ch 380, CA.

[255] Also *New Windsor Corp*; Countryside and Rights of Way Act 2000 s 98, amending Commons Registration Act 1965 s 22.

[256] Not by licence: *R(JR) Beresford* v. *Sunderland CC* [2001] EWCA Civ 1218, [2002] QB 874, [27–33], Dyson LJ (maintenance of sports arena in Washington).

[257] [2000] 1 AC 335, HL.

[258] *Epsom BC* v. *Nicholls* (1999) 78 P & CR 348, Ebsworth J.

[259] A Samuels [1992] *Conv* 434; HW Wilkinson [1995] *Conv* 286; A Samuels (1995) 139 *SJ* 948. An application is valid even if it includes non-common land: *R(JR) McAlpine Homes* v. *Staffordshire CC* [2002] All ER (D) 96, Sullivan J.

4. The register

[36.42] The Commons Registration Act 1965[260] requires county councils in England and Wales[261] to maintain registers of individual parcels of common land. Each unit consists of: (1) the land section showing what land is burdened; (2) the rights section, including the rights established which are quantified,[262] the people entitled to exercise them, and any property to which the rights are appurtenant;[263] and (3) the ownership section, which shows the owner of the common[264] until title is registered at the land registry.[265] All disputed claims are now finalised, and registration is conclusive evidence of the matters registered.[266] Unregistered rights have ceased to be exercisable and are extinguished.[267] Final registration implicitly confirms the validity of rights registered,[268] so that title is no longer based on inclosure, prescription, or express grants.

Commons registers are public and can be searched.[269] This is a vital part of the conveyancing process for any land likely to be affected by a commons registration, especially where access to a property is acquired over a verge.[270] Any open land may require a search. In *G & K Ladenbau (UK)* v. *Crawley*[271] solicitors instructed to acquire some vacant development land adjoining the River Usk and the M4 near Newport omitted this search (not unreasonably given the locality) but unfortunately for them an erroneous application had been made to register. The solicitors were held liable for the delay caused in resale of the land. It might be safe to omit a search if the site is fully developed or there has never been any public access.[272]

Amendments[273] to the register may be required to delete rights lost by abandonment,[274] surrender or compulsory purchase. New rights might be created by express grants, but also by prescriptive use starting since the register closed[275] – if more than 20 years have elapsed a lost modern grant[276] might be presumed.

---

[260] Following the *Royal Commission on Common Land* (1958) Cmnd 426.

[261] S 2; or London borough councils. Registers exclude the New Forest, Epping Forest, the Forest of Dean, and other prescribed areas.

[262] *Bettison* v. *Langton* [2001] UKHL 24, [2002] AC 27, [60] Lord Scott.

[263] Notes may refer to easements, exclusive profits, franchises, rights other than ownership of the lord of the manor, severed minerals, mining leases, and rights of statutory undertakers.

[264] Unclaimed town or village greens have been vested in the local authority; Parliament will decide how to deal with unclaimed common land.

[265] Commons Registration Act 1965 s 12.

[266] S 10.

[267] S 1(2); *Central Electricity Generating Board* v. *Clywd CC* [1976] 1 WLR 151, Goff J; *Howse* v. *Newbury DC* (1999) 77 P & CR 231, CA.

[268] *New Windsor Corp* v. *Mellor* [1975] Ch 380, 392F, Lord Denning MR.

[269] SI 1966/1471, as amended by SI 1989/2167.

[270] See above **[36.16]**.

[271] [1978] 1 WLR 266, Mocatta J.

[272] At 278–281.

[273] Commons Registration Act 1965 ss 13–14; *Howse* v. *Newbury DC* (1999) 77 P & CR 231, CA.

[274] *Re Yateley Common, Hampshire* [1977] 1 WLR 840 (not during use as an airfield).

[275] *Dynevor* v. *Richardson* [1995] Ch 173, Knox J (refusal of application to register in 1983 prevented lost modern grant in 1992).

[276] *Tehidy Minerals* v. *Norman* [1971] 2 QB 528, CA; the Prescription Act 1832 requires 30 or 60 years but Commons Registration Act 1965 s 16 excludes: (a) any period of requisition; and (b) periods during which animal health regulations prevented grazing.

5. Erroneous registration of houses and gardens

[36.43] The Commons Registration Act 1965 was too conclusive, since there was no procedure to remove land which was clearly registered by mistake after the end of the inquiry procedure.[277] An Act in 1989[278] created a one-off chance (now long since expired) to secure the removal of some erroneous registrations of dwellings.[279]

6. Inclosure

[36.44] In modern life land left open for cattle to roam freely provides open spaces for public enjoyment, such as the New Forest and Dartmoor. The need to preserve open land was recognised by the Commons Act 1876 which prevented further inclosure unless it benefitted the neighbourhood and no application for inclosure has been made since 1914. Fencing or building on any land subject to rights of common is unlawful without the consent of the minister of agriculture.[280]

7. Regulation of common land

[36.45] No doubt increased public use can create a substantial nuisance.[281] Problems unresolved according to Lord Templeman were illegal encroachment, the disappearance of commoners, the disappearance of lords of the manor, and the nuisance caused by members of the public. Existing controls apply to metropolitan commons,[282] animals,[283] and land of unknown ownership,[284] plus any under local byelaws.[285] Rural commons remain largely uncontrolled,[286] until such time as the Royal Commission proposals for a general scheme of regulation are implemented.

8. Public rights over common land

[36.46] The general public had no rights over common land[287] but the decline of the commoner's way of life has shifted the emphasis to public use of common land for

---

[277] *R* v. *Norfolk CC ex p Perry* (1997) 74 P & CR 1, Dyson J. Unless by fraud: s 14.

[278] Common Land (Rectification of the Register) Act 1989; A Samuels [1989] *Conv* 384; A Favell (1992) 24 *LSG* 18; SI 1990/311; HW Wilkinson [1990] *Conv* 463.

[279] *Re White Row Cottages, Bewerley* [1991] Ch 441; *Land at Freshfields* (1993) 66 P & CR 9; *Storey* v. *Commons Commissioner* (1993) 66 P & CR 206; *Cresstock Investments* v. *Commons Commissioners* [1993] 1 All ER 213.

[280] LPA 1925 s 194; *National Trust* v. *Ashbrook* [1997] 4 All ER 76 (fencing of A39 in Quantocks permitted by National Trust legislation).

[281] *Hampshire CC* v. *Milburn* [1991] 1 AC 325, 340B, Lord Templeman.

[282] Metropolitan Commons Act 1866–1898 (prevents inclosure); Commons Act 1899 (extends some powers to rural commons).

[283] Commons Act 1908

[284] Commons Registration Act 1965 s 9

[285] Subject to ultra vires: *DPP* v. *Hutchinson* [1990] 2 AC 783, HL (convictions at Greenham); *Howse* v. *Newbury DC* (1999) 77 P & CR 231, CA.

[286] Local Government Act 1972 s 120 (benefit, improvement or development of area); *R* v. *Teignbridge DC ex p Street* (1989) 154 LGR 659; *R* v. *Mid Sussex DC ex p Ridd* [1993] EGCS 183; *R* v. *Somerset CC ex p Fewings* [1995] 1 WLR 1037, CA (banning hunting).

[287] *Hampshire CC* v. *Milburn* [1991] 1 AC 325, 338H–339A, Lord Templeman.

leisure. Most common land is open and public access to the land is general. If the common was situated in a borough or urban district in 1925, a right of access for air and exercise was granted.[288] The report of the Royal Commission on Common Land (1955–1958)[289] recommended the grant of legal rights of access as a logical conclusion of the long process

> "of widening and establishing more firmly free access over common land which the public has enjoyed in fact . . . for a much longer period."

The wisdom of this was recognised in *Hampshire County Council* v. *Milburn*.[290]

9. Right to roam

[36.47] Part I of the Countryside and Rights of Way Act 2000[291] enacts the long held dream of a public right to roam. Any person has the right to enter and remain[292] on access land, observing the restrictions.[293] It will apply to access land shown on definitive maps drawn up (in England) by the Countryside Agency.[294] Land to which access should be given includes open country, mountain, moor, heath, down, registered common land, land over an altitude of 600 metres, and land dedicated for public access. Land within 20 metres of a dwelling is excluded, and other exclusions relate to fire risk, nature conservation, defence, and the preservation of natural scenery.[295] Owners will be subject to a specially limited regime of occupier's liability,[296] and will have rights to shut up the land for up to 28 days a year by notice to the authority. The authority will be responsible for securing means of access.[297]

K. PUBLIC RIGHTS

1. Customs analogous to easements

[36.48] These are similar to easements or profits used by particular landowners. The difference is that they are exercised by all the inhabitants of a defined locality, called in the case-law a fluctuating body.[298] A geographical area such as a town or village must be defined with precision[299] and within it the custom must have some degree of

---

[288] LPA 1925 s 193; *R* v. *SS Environment ex p Billson* [1999] QB 374.
[289] Cmnd 462 (1958).
[290] [1991] 1 AC 325, HL; PH Kenny [1998] *Conv* 345 (right to roam).
[291] Ss 1–46.
[292] S 2.
[293] S 17, sch 2.
[294] Ss 4–11; SI 2001/3301.
[295] Sch 1.
[296] Ss 12–13.
[297] Ss 34–39.
[298] *Foxall* v. *Venables* (1590) Cro Eliz 1880, 78 ER 436; *Lockwood* v. *Wood* (1844) 6 QB 50, 67, 115 ER 19, Tindal CJ; *Wolstanton* v. *Newcastle-under-Lyme Corp* [1940] AC 860, 876, Viscount Maugham; *Egerton* v. *Harding* [1975] QB 62, 68, Scarman LJ.
[299] *Alfred F Beckett* v. *Lyons* [1967] Ch 449, CA (not inhabitants of Durham); *New Windsor Corp* v. *Mellor* [1975] Ch 380, Foster J.

generality.[300] Successful cases allow drying of fishing nets,[301] fairs,[302] perambulation of parish boundaries,[303] and horse racing.[304] Many customs are recreational, and others regulate drainage, water supply, and fencing.[305]

Customs are presumed from use. A presumption of immemorial origin is raised by testimony going back as far as living memory can go,[306] unless there is evidence that the custom originated after 1189 which destroys its validity as a legal custom. Customary use must be as of right[307] and continuous – though minor changes, perhaps in the manner of drying fishing nets, makes no difference.[308] They must be certain,[309] based on lawful use,[310] and reasonable.[311] Customary fees are claimed as whatever fee is reasonable, a formulation which avoids the problem of monetary inflation.[312]

2. Customs analogous to profits

[36.49] A claim to a profit by custom is not allowed. The produce of land would soon be exhausted if any inhabitant could take it.[313] The rule was applied arbitrarily in *Alfred F Beckett* v. *Lyons*[314] to prevent coastal villagers collecting coal washed up on the shore, even though exhaustion of this bounty from the sea was irrelevant. In any event a means of circumventing the logic of exhaustion was discovered in *Goodman* v. *Saltash Corporation*. Inhabitants of the borough successfully claimed a customary right to an exclusive oyster fishery. A grant to the corporation was presumed[315] subject to a condition or trust in favour of the inhabitants. A charitable trust could in theory be presumed in the absence of any body with corporate status though claims have tended to fail on the facts,[316] or because the title deeds have proved that there was no trust.[317]

---

[300] *Fowley Marine (Emsworth)* v. *Gafford* [1968] 2 QB 612, CA (moorings); *Egerton* v. *Harding* [1975] QB 62, CA (fencing throughout manor).

[301] *Mercer* v. *Denne* [1905] 2 Ch 538, CA.

[302] *Lockwood* v. *Wood* (1844) 6 QB 50, 115 ER 19.

[303] *Chesterfield (Lord)* v. *Harris* [1911] AC 623, HL. Parishioners have a right to get to the parish church: *Brocklebank* v. *Thompson* [1903] 2 Ch 344.

[304] *Mounsey* v. *Ismay* (1865) 3 H & C 486, 159 ER 621.

[305] *Egerton* v. *Harding* [1975] Ch 62, CA.

[306] *Wolstanton* v. *Newcastle-under-Lyme Corp* [1940] AC 860, HL.

[307] *Att-Gen* v. *Antrobus* [1905] 2 Ch 188, Farwell J.

[308] *Mercer* v. *Denne* [1905] 2 Ch 538, CA.

[309] *Smith* v. *Archibald* (1880) 5 App Cas 489, 512, 513; *Fowley Marine (Emsworth)* v. *Gafford* [1967] 2 QB 808, 839–840, Megaw J.

[310] Not if in conflict with a statute: *Fowley Marine* [1967] 2 QB 808, CA (harbour by-laws).

[311] Excluding eg a right to mine without compensating for subsidence: *Wolstanton* as above.

[312] *Bryant* v. *Foot* (1867) LR 2 QB 161 (13 shilling fee for marriage); *Robinson* v. *Smith* (1908) 24 TLR 573.

[313] *Gateward's* case (1607) 6 Co Rep 59b, 77 ER 344.

[314] [1967] Ch 449, CA.

[315] (1882) 7 App Cas 633, HL; *Rivers (Lord)* v. *Adams* (1878) 3 Ex D 361; *Beckett* [1967] Ch 449, 466–468, Harman LJ; *Peggs* v. *Lamb* [1994] Ch 172, Morritt J.

[316] *Beckett* as above.

[317] *Att-Gen* v. *Antrobus* [1905] 2 Ch 188; query whether this should be a defence given modern developments in lost modern grant.

3. Public highways

[36.50] A highway is a way open to the public.[318] Most roads are maintainable at the public expense, and these can be identified from a list kept by the highway authority. Other public ways can be identified from the definitive map[319] and fall into three categories.[320] Out of roughly 105,000 miles of rights of way in England, 80% are *footpaths*. A second category consists of *bridleways* open to riders on horseback and cyclists[321] as well as walkers. The final category is *bye-ways open to all traffic*, consisting of unmetalled tracks, including many "green lanes" previously classed as *roads used as a public path*.[322] Four wheel drive vehicles may be barred.[323] The Rights of Way Act 1990[324] protects the interests of the walker and rider by making it an offence to disturb the surface of the path, or make exercise of the public right of way inconvenient. Most public ways were originally prescriptive.

4. Creation of public highways by use

[36.51] Highways were created by dedication of the route of the highway to the use of the public,[325] a matter often presumed from public use, though the grounds for prescription of public rights are rather more liberal than for private rights.[326]

---

[318] *R* v. *Saintiff* (1704) 6 Mod Rep. 255, 87 ER 1002; *Ex p Hood* [1975] 1 QB 891, 897, Lord Denning MR; *Att-Gen* v. *Brotherton* [1992] 1 AC 425, 432H, Lord Oliver.

[319] National Parks and Access to the Countryside Act 1949 ss 27–38; Countryside Act 1968 sch 3; now Wildlife and Countryside Act 1981 ss 53–58. Unrecorded ways are being extinguished: Countryside and Rights of Way Act 2000 s 56.

[320] *Suffolk CC* v. *Mason* [1979] AC 705, 710A, Lord Diplock.

[321] Countryside Act 1968 s 30; Countryside and Rights of Way Act 2000 s 53.

[322] National Parks and Access to the Countryside Act 1949 s 27(6); Countryside Act 1968 s 30; Wildlife and Countryside Act 1981 s 54; Countryside and Rights of Way Act 2000 ss 47–50 (reclassification as restricted by-ways).

[323] Countryside and Rights of Way Act 2000 s 67.

[324] Highways Act 1980 ss 131A, 134, 137A, sch 12A; M Harwood [1991] *NLJ* 15.

[325] *Att-Gen* v. *Brotherton* [1992] 1 AC 425, 435H, Lord Oliver.

[326] *NLL* (1st ed), 676–677.

INDEX